A HISTORY OF
THE CANADIAN WEST
TO 1870–71

A HISTORY OF
The Canadian West
TO 1870-71

BEING

A HISTORY OF RUPERT'S LAND
(THE HUDSON'S BAY COMPANY'S TERRITORY)
AND OF THE NORTH-WEST TERRITORY
(INCLUDING THE PACIFIC SLOPE)

BY

ARTHUR S. MORTON

M.A.(EDIN.), F.R.S.C.

Head of the Department of History of the University of Saskatchewan

SECOND EDITION
EDITED BY LEWIS G. THOMAS

PUBLISHED IN CO-OPERATION WITH
UNIVERSITY OF SASKATCHEWAN
BY
UNIVERSITY OF TORONTO PRESS

Second edition
© University of Toronto Press 1973
Toronto and Buffalo
Printed in Canada

ISBN 0-8020-4033-0
Microfiche ISBN 0-8020-0253-6

The first edition of this work appeared in 1939.

The quotations from documents in the Archives of the
Hudson's Bay Company which appear in this work are by the kind
permission of the Governor and Committee of the Company.

CONTENTS

CHAPTER V

A Chapter of Approaches—Rupert's Land and the North-West
approached by the Pedlars—The Pacific North-West
approached by the Russians, Spaniards, English, and
Americans, 1763–93 256

SKETCH-MAPS
(envelope inside back cover)

PREFACE TO THE SECOND EDITION

Arthur Silver Morton's *A History of the Canadian West to 1870–71* was published in 1939 without footnotes but with an appendix composed of bibliographical notes arranged by chapters. In his Preface (p.xix) he explains that it was his aim "to suggest to the reader the source from which the information is drawn—this without plaguing him with the bibliographical footnotes." He adds that "the bibliography is so extensive it would make this work, large enough as it is, too cumbersome for any but a scholar." His apology did not prevent Professor Chester Martin from expressing in the *Canadian Historical Review* his regret at "the absence of footnotes or documentation of any kind." Many other readers have agreed that a more conventional approach to the bibliographical problem would have enhanced the *History*'s value.

Morton himself seems to have been satisfied that the bibliographical appendix would be an adequate guide to the reader interested in his sources. He often includes in the text dates and titles that would ordinarily be relegated to footnotes and he is most liberal in quotation. So consistent is his practice that it seems on the whole unlikely that this was a matter of revision carried out to accommodate a publisher's decision to eliminate conventional footnotes in the interest of economy. It is extremely difficult to believe that a scholar of Morton's integrity would have accepted the publication of his major work, the fruit of the labours of more than twenty years, in a form which he did not approve.

Whatever the author's feelings about the original publication he did provide a partial annotation in the proof copy, on the outside paper of which appears the following note, with his signature: "A number of footnotes which might have been put into the book had there been space, will be entered in this page-proof form." These notes form the basis of the appendix I have prepared for the new printing by the University of Toronto Press. Page and line numbers of the text are given in the appendix, together with the last word in the sentence to which Morton's marginal note appears to apply. There are occasional departures from this practice when it seemed to make the application of the note clearer.

I am sure that the author did not regard his annotation as in any way complete and I can only hope that my guesses at his intention are not too often wide of the mark. Time has taken its toll of the pencilled notes, but, so precise was the author's hand and so sharp his pencils, none proved indecipherable. There is however a great variation in their frequency. For chapter III, with 72 pages, there were some 203 notes, for chapter IV, with 131 pages, there were 332, for the last three chapters there were only 12. For chapter XI, indeed, there was only one note, "Hunt up Hansard," conclusive evidence that Morton did not regard his annotation as complete.

At first I hoped it might be possible to make a distinction, perhaps by varying the type, between Morton's notes and any I might add, but it soon became evident that this would be, if not impossible, hopelessly clumsy. I have tried, however, to make apparent to the reader without resort to such a mechanical device any departure from or addition to the original notes. Most of his references have been verified and, in the case of reference to the Hudson's Bay Company Archives, the present classification has been added. It was Morton's use of Company sources that more than anything else gave his *History* its unique value. Therefore it seemed particularly important to ensure that the reader could if he wished find the original document in the microfilm available in Ottawa. Morton himself worked in the London repository before the present classification was in use and the references he gave in the notes in the proof copy are not always easily traced.

The form in which he gave his references to materials in the Public Archives of Canada, the Public Record Office in London, and the Archives nationales in Paris should present no difficulty and generally speaking his listing has not been changed even when there have been changes in the method of classification. In the case of materials in the Public Record Office, for example, Morton sometimes seems to have made his own transcripts, though he may also have worked from transcripts available in Ottawa. Today much of this material is on microfilm and the student will probably prefer to consult that rather than the transcripts upon which Morton had to depend.

I have not presumed to suggest sources for passages Morton himself did not document in either the text or the notes he made in the proof. The great value of the notes he pencilled into proof is the way in which they serve to reveal the man and to give some insight into the mind of the scholar at work. Although it did not seem practicable to distinguish mechanically between Morton's notes and my amendments or additions, I have tried not to destroy the peculiar flavour of the original. Like many scholars he put a good deal of himself into what some profess to regard as the dullest part of any book. Some direct quotations have been more exactly located and where material that he used in manuscript is now available in print I have supplied a reference. These additions will not, I trust, obtrude themselves between the reader and the workings of a profoundly scholarly mind.

The lapse of time since the *History* was published makes it seem desirable at least to mention some of the more recent major publications in the field it covers. These are listed at the beginning of the notes for each chapter and are intended to supplement the "Brief Bibliographical Notes" of the original printing. Occasionally I have inserted elsewhere a reference to a book or article published since 1939 that has a direct relevance to Morton's text. Generally speaking there is no attempt in the notes to compare Morton's views with those put forward by later writers, though occasionally this has been done, especially when later research has proved Morton clearly wrong on matters of detail. It also seemed proper to call attention to obvious misprints and such errors as the identification of Queen Anne as James II's sister. Some of these were covered in the *errata* slip inserted in the original printing and others the author himself points out in the proof copy.

I have not been able to find and verify all the references. Where I have failed, an indication has been given. Occasionally the annotation consisted only of a question mark in the margin and it was not always possible to decide precisely to what part of the adjacent sentence or paragraph the query pointed. In a few of these extreme cases it has not seemed worth while to insert a note at all. Others yielded quite readily to the consultation of an obvious source. For verification of the notes on the sections on the far west I am deeply indebted to the staff of the Legislative Library and the Archives of British Columbia.

It is a pleasure to express my appreciation of the assistance so generously rendered by institutions and individuals alike. I am particularly indebted to Mrs. Arthur S. Morton and the late Professor George W.

Brown for their unfailing interest and their willingness to share their unique reminiscences. Dr. W. Kaye Lamb and the staff of the Public Archives of Canada and the Hudson's Bay Company and its Archivist, Miss A.M. Johnson, not only gave me the opportunity to use the microfilm of the Hudson's Bay Company Archives and the rich resources of their respective collections but were also the source of much wise advice. I am also most grateful to the staff of the Archives of the Province of Saskatchewan, particularly to Mr. Douglas H. Bocking and Miss Evelyn Eager, to Mr. Willard E. Ireland and the staff of the Archives of British Columbia, and to the Libraries of the Universities of Saskatchewan and Alberta. Mr. Frits Pannekoek gave generously of his time to verify and correct citations to materials in the Public Archives of Canada. Among those who have drawn my attention to particular points in the *History* are Mr. William Douglas of Winnipeg, Mr. John M. Gray of Toronto, Miss D. Isabel Loggie of Fairview, and Mr. George E. Thorman of St. Thomas. The trustees of the John S. Ewart Memorial Fund and the University of Alberta have generously rendered financial assistance. My students have made stimulating contributions to our protracted discussions of Morton as an historian and my colleagues in the Department of History at the University of Alberta have placed me under a similar obligation. The latter will also appreciate my special gratitude to Mrs. R. Whamond, our departmental secretary. Among those who contributed interesting recollections of Professor Morton are Professor George Simpson, the late Professor Morden H. Long, Professor Hilda Neatby, Miss Norah Story, and Professor Lewis H. Thomas. Lastly I must thank the University of Toronto Press and especially its former Managing Editor, Dr. Francess G. Halpenny, and its Executive Editor, Miss M. Jean Houston: the Press for making the reprinting possible and Dr. Halpenny and Miss Houston for their patience and their counsel.

In the first edition the assistance of the Carnegie Corporation in making possible the publication of this *History* was acknowledged. Its republication has been assisted by a grant from the Social Science Research Council of Canada, using funds provided by the Canada Council, and by a grant from the University of Saskatchewan.

The rarity of the first edition necessitated a search to discover a copy that could be used for reproduction. Grateful acknowledgment goes to Professor Ralph F. Shaner of Edmonton, who donated his copy of the book for the purpose.

LEWIS G. THOMAS,
University of Alberta.

PREFACE TO THE FIRST EDITION

This work is devoted to the history before Confederation of that part of. Canada which lay north of Lower Canada that was, and north and west of Upper Canada. An attempt is made to treat the region as essentially a unit. True, the exploration of, say, Hudson Bay might not seem to be connected in the remotest degree with that of the Pacific coast, but, after all, the one and the other issued in a traffic in furs, and in time the fur trade of the continent from Labrador to the Columbia and the Pacific sea was brought under one controlling "concern," the North West Company, and from 1821 the Hudson's Bay Company, by which the North West Company was absorbed. Slowly the history of the east and of the west grows into one story, and during the first half of the nineteenth century it is of one texture. Nor is its unity wholly destroyed when the movement of settlement westward introduces a new theme. The fur trade still remains the centre of the narrative—a fur trade slowly yielding ground to agricultural colonization. The first retreat was in the Oregon, and brought with it the establishment of the colony of Vancouver's Island, especially devised and consciously organized to stay the progress of the American migrants into British territory and into the precincts of the fur company. To prevent American colonization from passing north of the International Boundary as settled by the Treaty of Oregon, an agricultural colony of the English kind was established under the ægis of the great fur-trading Company in what was the most difficult part of the British Empire to reach. The rush of seekers after gold in British Columbia led to the formation of another colony and to the dethronement of the fur trade in the Pacific Slope. The fear of the American migrants "rushing" the fertile prairie West and the desire of the people of the Canada of that day to have a western sphere of expansion of their own, comparable to that of the Americans, led to the course of events whose issue was the surrender of its Charter by the Hudson's Bay Company, the transfer of Rupert's Land to the Queen, and by her to the Dominion of Canada, and the establishment of agricultural settlements where once the fur trade was supreme. Looked at in the broad it is all one story. It is believed that when so treated, the history of the Canadian West is seen in a fresh perspective. In many a minor matter this is so. Vancouver's delineation of the Pacific coast is not the concern solely of British Columbia; it is connected with the illusion, that persisted in the face of hard facts, that somewhere there was a passage through milder climes from Hudson Bay to the Western Sea. Vancouver was instructed to follow every inlet to its head in the hope that the long-sought water-way might be found—this though Samuel Hearne had placed the Polar shore approximately where we know it to be.

The proper effects are not perceived if the history of the country is written simply as a prologue to this or that Province; nor if the journeys of the fur-traders as they moved westward are wrested from their setting and treated as explorations pure and simple. The Alexander Mackenzie who turned every stone to bring the fur trade of the continent under the control of a great British fur-trading company with a Charter is a much greater man than he was simply as the explorer of a couple of summers to the Arctic and to the Pacific. His explorations take their proper setting in the light of his aims as an exponent of a scheme of continental organization. Similarly a fresh perspective is gained by placing Lord Selkirk's colony on the Red River in its setting. The interest in this experiment in colonization, great as it is in itself, is enhanced by the knowledge of the part it was devised to play in the reorganization of the Hudson's Bay Company of 1810 and the following years. The agricultural settlement in the midst of the Company's domain was to provide cheap provisions and a reservoir of cheap and efficient labour to enable the English Company to keep on its feet in the life and death struggle with the North West Company. Moreover, the Hudson's Bay Company knew that it could not hope to prosecute the Canadians in the courts of Britain for breaches of its monopoly, but it was advised by its lawyers that its right to the soil under the Charter was indisputable. The Grant to Lord Selkirk and the establishment of a colony within the Company's domain would give outward demonstration that the soil was theirs and would prepare for some favourable moment when the Canadian traders could be warned off the land.

It would be little short of inhuman to leave the reader of a work like this dealing with a strange land—strange even to the Canadians—without the assistance of maps. The attempt has been made not simply to assist him, but to enable him to become familiar with the country through which he is travelling. It must be understood that the sketch-maps are not accurate to the last degree. In placing the flags representing the posts on the map it is not always sure on what side of the river or lake they should stand, nor whether the English or the Canadian post stood farther upstream. Apart from this the maps may be regarded as in the main reliable.

It has been the aim to base the history entirely on the primary sources, and to suggest to the reader the source from which the information is drawn—this without plaguing him with the bibliographical footnotes. Indeed, the bibliography is so extensive it would make this work, large enough as it is, too cumbersome for any but a scholar.

The author's principal obligations are to the various Archivists who have afforded him every facility and guided him to the material under their charge. The kindness and assistance of Mr. H.M. Healy of the Archives of the Province of Manitoba, and of my lamented friend the late Mr. John Hosie, at the time Archivist of the Province of British Columbia, and of Dr. Biggar of the office of the Public Archives of Canada in London, remain pleasant memories, and have also left their mark on many a page in this book.

Special mention must be made of the late Sir Arthur Doughty, whose genius for collecting made the Public Archives of Canada in Ottawa a place of resort for scholars from many parts. Through long years he not only made the material in the Archives available to me, but enriched the library of the University of Saskatchewan with material needed by me between whiles. Nor must I omit mention of the late Mr. William Smith, Deputy-Archivist, a prince among friends; the many carbon copies of material gathered by him, which he presented to the library of my university, will keep his memory fresh for coming generations of students. They have left their mark at many points in this book.

The author lies under very special obligations to Governor Ashley Cooper of the Hudson's Bay Company and his Board for access to the rich Archives of the Company, granted without restrictions of any kind. Without the privileges so generously accorded this work had been but a torso. Many a phase of our history hitherto unknown has been brought into the clear light of day by the documents of the Company, and the perspective given by the Canadian documents, which as a whole is due to the North West Company's propaganda, has been adjusted to the truth by the daily entries of the Journals and by the correspondence of the forts with the Governor and Committee in London. In certain cases the questions raised by the Company and the replies given by their lawyers under their signatures have given the key to the course of events in the Company's territory overseas. I should fall short of my duty were I to fail to mention my obligation to the officers of the Company, to Mr. R.G. Leveson Gower the Archivist, to Mr. F.A. Stacpole of Beaver House, and to Mr. J. Chadwick Brooks the Secretary. Their friendship and co-operation made my year and more in London one long happiness. The generosity of Mr. Leveson Gower in placing before me biographical and other collections made by him has not only relieved the burden of my work; it has contributed materially to the accuracy and the range of vision of this book.

Finally, the author is greatly indebted to Professor H.A. Innis of the University of Toronto, to Mr. John W. Dafoe of the *Winnipeg Free Press*, and to President J.S. Thomson of the University of Saskatchewan, for their interest in bringing this volume to the light of day; and to James Richardson, Esq., Winnipeg, for his generous support.

ARTHUR S. MORTON,
The University of Saskatchewan,
Saskatoon, Saskatchewan.

INTRODUCTION

When Arthur Silver Morton died in 1945, the Fellows of the Royal Society of Canada spoke of him in an obituary note as one of the giants of Canadian history. The passage of a generation has a way of making giants look smaller but Morton's stature has not noticeably diminished. His most important work, *A History of the Canadian West to 1870–71*, appeared in 1939 under the grim handicaps of depression publishing. Thomas Nelson and Sons' original edition has long been exhausted but demand for the *History* has continued and indeed increased. It remains a standard work in the history of western Canada and is still indispensable to the student in that field. The present reprinting provides an opportunity to make available the notes that the author added to his proof copy. These notes not only add considerably to the documentation provided in the text and bibliographical appendix of the original printing but have a considerable intrinsic interest for the light they shed on the scholarly methods of a distinguished Canadian historian.

Arthur Silver Morton, born in Nova Scotia in 1870, was the son of a Presbyterian minister of Scottish origin. His father took his family to Trinidad where he had founded the Canadian mission work among the Hindu labourers on the sugar plantations and the young Morton was educated in West Indian schools. Thence he went to Edinburgh to take his Master of Arts in the humanities as well as his Bachelor of Divinity. One summer he spent in France, two later summers he studied at Berlin under Harnack. In 1896 he returned to Canada. He was ordained to the Presbyterian ministry, and after serving parishes in New Brunswick he lectured at Pine Hill, the Presbyterian theological seminary in Halifax. From 1907 to 1912 he devoted himself to research at the British Museum in the historical geography of the Roman Empire, the Middle Ages, and the Reformation. Then he lectured in church history at Knox College, Toronto, until in 1914 he went, as Professor of History and Librarian, to the youthful University of Saskatchewan, summoned there by his Edinburgh contemporary, Walter Charles Murray.

At Saskatoon at the age of forty-four he began a new career in an institution which, although by no means inhospitable to religion, was avowedly secular in tone. At this point the threads of influence that determined Morton's outlook on history can be knotted together—his Nova Scotian, West Indian, and Scottish background, his rigorous training in church history and historical geography, his full exposure to the winds of secularism and modernism that, in the decades before and after the turn of the nineteenth century, blew through the Presbyterian seminaries and, even more briskly, through the new universities of western Canada.

Almost immediately upon his arrival at Saskatoon the War of 1914–18 began. Too old for active service, Morton remained at the University while younger men went forth to the wars. Morton was now cut off from the sources of his research and this, as well as his sense of his duty to his adopted province, turned his attention from mediaeval church history to the history of the Canadian West. In the thirty years that followed he was to establish himself as the premier figure in the latter field. In 1932 he was elected a Fellow of the Royal Society of Canada and in 1941 he was awarded the Tyrrell Medal.

His achievements in western Canadian history went beyond his writings for an academic audience. He was not without talent as a popularizer and his work for extension in a university that saw itself as dedicated to the needs of the people of a predominantly agricultural province was a major factor in giving Saskatchewan a consciousness of its history, one deeper perhaps than that of any other western province. He explored the historic sites of the region, he gave public lectures, he wrote for the newspapers, he arranged historical exhibits, he wrote and produced historical pageants. From his arrival in 1914 he built up the University library's excellent historical collection. In 1937 he was appointed Keeper of the Provincial Records, and the establishment of an archives procedure and organization that is the envy of other Canadian provinces was largely his accomplishment. Perhaps the most remarkable of the distinctions that came to Arthur Silver Morton was an address presented in 1943 by the government and people of Saskatchewan expressing their appreciation of his work for the province.

Historians are judged, however, not by their popular successes, but by the quality of their writings. Almost all Morton's published work, and all his work after 1916, was on western Canadian themes. His training in mediaeval history drove him to the documents and he spent the generous summer recesses of a Canadian professor in the various archives that held collections in his chosen subject. He was a familiar figure in the provincial archives at Victoria and Winnipeg and summer after summer he was one of the closely knit band of scholars who worked in the Public Archives of Canada at Ottawa. Even more important was the sabbatical year and three subsequent summers that he spent in the Hudson's Bay Company Archives in London. That vast collection had in the early thirties been little used by scholars and Morton's thorough investigation of its riches is a milestone in the development not only of Canadian but of American and Commonwealth studies.

His pattern of publication may seem somewhat old-fashioned in these times. The results of his studies appeared in a series of papers, articles, and reviews, some in learned journals, some in newspapers. His edition of the Journal of Duncan M'Gillivray appeared in 1929 but it was not until 1938 that he published his *History of Prairie Settlement* as part of a volume in the Canadian Frontiers of Settlement series. This work was far overshadowed by his *History of the Canadian West to 1870–71*, which appeared in 1939. In 1944 he published a biography of Sir George Simpson.

In his *History of the Canadian West* Morton distilled the essence of twenty-five years' study of the subject to which he had turned after his arrival in Saskatoon. It is by this work that his quality as an historian may most fairly be judged. The *History of Prairie Settlement* was a commissioned work and Morton was the obvious person to commission, but his enthusiasm lay in the earlier period, his vitality must have been drained by the writing of the work he published the next year, and not nearly enough basic work had been done on the history of prairie settlement to permit the generalization that a book of this kind seems to demand. The life of Simpson was published when he was 74; it falls between the scholarly and the popular. Morton's admiration of Simpson is apparent and he leaves himself open to the charge that, in deference to the great Company to which he was under such substantial obligation, he has left the less praiseworthy side of Simpson's character unexplored. From the point of view of the student the biography does not go much beyond the history, and as a popular work it is less successful than *Under Western Skies*, in which in 1937 Morton gathered together for the general public some of the lively and provocative re-assessments of western history that had earlier appeared in the Saskatoon *Star-Phoenix* and which were given further substance in the *History*.

The *History* itself is not without its faults. It is sometimes unendurably tedious, and only the most concerned reader will not flag as he makes his way through the discussions of the location of fur-trading posts and those movements of the MacTavishes, M'Gillivrays, Macdonalds, and Macdonnells that confused even the indexer. There are passages that are far from clear, for example the discussion of the proposed reorganiza-tion of the Hudson's Bay Company in 1810 (p.531) when the scheme for the division of the profits of the trade appears to leave nothing at all for the shareholders. There are errors in fact, for example the dating of the journeys of Simon Fraser (p.471–4). He refers to Queen Anne (p.95) as the *sister* of James II and his confusion over Judge Jeffreys confirms the impression that he had an uncertain grasp of the later Stuart period.

Morton also had his prejudices. He did not greatly admire the French, he had his doubts about Americans, he regarded the Indian as an inferior, and he appears to have disapproved of the traders' practice of taking Indian wives. It would be wrong to attach undue significance to such attitudes. Illiberal as they may seem to a later generation, they are not surprising in one whose mind was formed in the late nineteenth-century environments that Morton knew as a young man. In matters of theology and church polity he was by no means a conservative, for his first published work, *The Way to Union* (Toronto, 1912), expressed views consistent with an advanced position on what was then a major issue in Canadian Protestant circles. Indeed one suspects that his radical views made the atmosphere of a secular institution more congenial than that of either a theological college or a parish. It must be admitted, how-ever, that he held stiffly to his own opinions and was reluctant to change them even in the face of what might appear incontrovertible evidence. To this rigidity his controversy with Tyrrell over the respective roles of David Thompson and Duncan M'Gillivray in the crossing of the Rockies adequately attests.

A rather more serious charge is that of a bias in favour of the Hudson's Bay Company. Certainly the Company appears from his pages usually to have been in the right. Morton mentions in the Preface of 1939 (p.ix) his "very special obligations" to the Company. Anyone who

studies the history of the Canadian West must be sensible of an obligation to the corporation which has preserved and made available such
invaluable source materials. If Morton displays less than complete ob-
jectivity in relation to the Company, his bias springs not from a wholly
proper appreciation of the assistance afforded him but from the fact
that he worked so largely from Company documents. It is understand-
able he should come insensibly to adopt the viewpoint and attitudes
reflected in the sources with which he achieved such a remarkable
familiarity. It does seem that he was inclined to accept as irrefutable
evidence for the behaviour of the Company's servants in the field the
intentions of the Company's management revealed in the directives
issuing from London. "From this time on [c. 1834, p.742] the English
Company had no difficulty in keeping the American traders practically
out of the country. It has often been said that they succeeded in this by
instigating the Indians against them. This is incorrect. It would have
been in the teeth of the instructions of the Company." Certainly Morton
did not confine his researches solely to Company sources but their sheer
physical weight had its effect.

His command of the sources is extraordinary, especially in view of
the difficulties of access to them that confronted him when research
grants were rare and the possibilities of microfilm unexploited. Had
some of the facilities of a later generation been available to him he might
have made use of the voluminous writings of the missionaries active in
the west from early in the nineteenth century. Such sources would have
afforded him access to an outlook divergent from that of an organization
of which the missionaries did not always take an entirely kindly view.

Morton was indeed working in a field in which the established doctrine was highly unfavourable to the Hudson's Bay Company, for Canadian historians had tended to identify themselves with the interests of
the rivals who had their headquarters in Montreal. They had been
prone, for the period after the union of the companies and the eclipse
of the Canadian interest, to see the English company as a major obstacle
to Canadian expansion westward. Morton had no disposition to view
Canadian history as past politics. The preoccupation with the development of Canadian autonomy that obsessed many of his colleagues was
to Morton a matter of indifference. Though he could scold David
Thompson for what he saw as his share in the loss of the Oregon country
to the British Crown, he did not necessarily exult when British Columbia
entered the Canadian federation. Nothing perhaps better illustrates

Morton's detachment from the main stream of Canadian historiography. His Nova Scotian origin, his West Indian experience, his British education, his western domicile, explain an attitude that is less than ardently Canadian nationalist.

Morton indeed never seems to have thought of himself as a historian of Canada in the accepted sense. His range of teaching was exceedingly broad, including ancient and mediaeval history and a course in biblical literature. He preferred to leave the survey of Canadian history to his colleagues, though his specialized courses on the Canadian West appear for the first time in the calendar of the University of Saskatchewan for 1926–7. Professor Chester Martin's criticism of the *History* for failure to deal adequately with "factors from Canada, Britain and the United States" may go too far but it does suggest the impression Morton's work made on Canadian historians with different preoccupations.

This detachment had its advantages for it enabled him to reassess in the light of his researches several legendary figures. Certainly his views on the relationship between Radisson and Groseilliers and of Le Vérendrye's conception of his mission in the west are remote from more romantic conceptions advanced by earlier writers. His view of Alexander Mackenzie as an imperial planner is by no means fully developed but has in it something of the same demythologizing spirit. Perhaps the freshness of his approach to the heroic figures of the western past is most clearly illustrated by his highly unflattering treatment of David Thompson. This provoked heated rejoinders, not all as closely reasoned as Tyrrell's, but his interpretation has to a large extent been supported by the most authoritative later students of the career of a man evidently more complex than has been supposed by some of his fervent admirers.

The detachment that enabled Morton to discern new directions in which the interpretation of western Canadian history might move does not make it easier to determine the nature of his philosophy of history. Some of his readers have wondered whether he had indeed such a philosophy. Certainly he is not an easy man to label. One may call him a regionalist if one likes, for he confined his writing to western Canada. One may, however, doubt whether the label means very much, for the region expanded and contracted as he told its story and political boundaries cut sharply across the physiographical. He never really succeeded in fitting the mountain and Pacific regions neatly into his pattern although he recognized, as indeed must be recognized, that the history of the fur trade, his dominant theme, would be meaningless if due attention is denied its activities west of the mountains. He is by no means the only Canadian historian to find Canada's physiographic divisions unwieldy, but for Morton the far west proved peculiarly intractable.

Morton avowed himself an environmentalist in his opening page, but as the *History* proceeds it is apparent that he was not entirely convinced that physical environment inevitably or exclusively moulds historical events. He believed that an intimate knowledge of the geography of a region was essential to the delineation of its history. This belief prompted him to make the substantial collection of papers now in the possession of the University of Saskatchewan. To use his own words, "It represents the knowledge which I had to acquire in the matter of geography to write my *History of the Canadian West.*" Geographical knowledge he recognized as vitally important to the historian. To this extent he was an environmentalist but his readers may well feel that such a description is incomplete.

Certainly he was no adherent of the "great man" view of history. Even his major figures, Mackenzie, Selkirk, Simpson, and the rest, are developed not biographically but only so far as to speed the progress of his narrative. Flashes of insight may illuminate them but Morton does not pause to develop his view of a particular personality. Nor does he seem to see them as held in the relentless grip of forces beyond their control or as bending history in their own strong hands. His heroes rise to meet their opportunities, they do not create them. Morton was not uninterested in the individual but it would never have occurred to him to suggest that there was no history, only biographies.

His closest colleague observed in the *Canadian Historical Review* (XXVI, June, 1945, 225) that Morton "viewed Western Canadian history as part of the story of the great frontier of the British Empire." The operative word here is "empire," not "frontier." Morton was no Turnerian. In 1940, when the Canadian Historical Association officially discussed the frontier hypothesis, he made no contribution. Indeed, readers of the history may wonder whether he was at all conscious of the existence of the writings of Frederick Jackson Turner, though he does speak (p.758) of the gentleman farmers of Vancouver Island as "not in keeping with the genius of the new land." His sharpest insights, his appreciation, for example, of the impact on the west of the intellectual movements of eighteenth- and early nineteenth-century England, indicate an attitude of mind remote from that of the apostle of the frontier.

Morton indeed does not in his writings suggest that he had any more interest in theories of history than he had in the developing nationalism that attracted his Canadian contemporaries. He seems, like H.A.L. Fisher, to have detected in history "no plot, no rhythm, no predetermined pattern." He was content simply to find out what had happened. Quite late in life he settled on a field that, more or less by chance, offered him an opportunity to use his admirable training and his considerable talents. Scholarly work had been and was being done by others on the history of the Canadian West but no one had tackled the formidable task of organization, of providing the chronological and topical structure that forms the necessary skeleton of historical writing. To create such a structure required a familiarity with the sources that might have daunted a man past middle age, a man who, by his training, had a lively conception of what he was undertaking. He was not content, as other and eminent Canadian historians had been, to work from documents collected by deputy. "At the very first," he observes in a note among his papers at the University of Saskatchewan, "I attacked the major masses of original sources." The collections through which he worked so doggedly were not all as manageable as they are today. The Hudson's Bay Company, for example, was still in the process of arranging its enormous weight of papers; they were not, when Morton was granted access to them, conveniently available in Ottawa on microfilm. His industry and devotion were to give a weight of scholarship to the *History* not matched by many works in the same field.

The sharp-edged tools Morton had learned to use in the tangled thickets of mediaeval history served him well as he hacked a trail through the undergrowth of the history of the Canadian West. There are few who have since worked in that field who have not followed gratefully in his footsteps. Not only is the debt acknowledged in formal bibliographies; it is evident in the very structure of much subsequent writing. There is little evidence that Morton cared much about the why of history and no one would claim him as a master interpreter of the past; it was not for him to illuminate the whole glade of history. But he opened his chosen preserve to the light of day and occasionally he shed a searching beam down some obscure or even unsuspected byway.

LEWIS G. THOMAS

CHAPTER I

THE THREE NORTH-WESTS AND THEIR ABORIGINAL TRIBES *

SINCE Confederation the term " The Canadian North-West " has pictured to our minds spacious prairies rapidly passing into the greatest wheat-field of our time. In the previous century " The North-West " called up a vision of the vast forest belt to the north, broken on every side by lake, and marsh, and stream—the greatest fur region of the world. In truth these are two North-Wests. Still farther north, beyond the height of land which faces the Polar Sea and Hudson Bay, there is yet a third, with a character all its own —" The Barren Grounds," a wilderness of stony hummocks and frozen mossy bogs stretching to a horizon that seems limitless. Beyond these North-Wests there is the Pacific West. Here range succeeds range of forest-clad, snow-capped mountains. Between, and sometimes through these, flow turbulent rivers—silver threads on which elongated lakes are strung like so many sparkling beads. Finally, by the shore of the Western Sea there are many deep estuaries and a thousand islands, really the peaks of a range of sunken mountains rising above the surface of the ocean. Together, these last make a tangle of inner seas and water-ways beside the broad Pacific.

The varying aspect of the three North-Wests and the Farthest West explains much in the story of the several regions. Their plant and animal life have fixed the conditions under which man has lived, and have determined his settlements and his institutions, as well as the nature of the trade which he has been able to carry on.

The prairie North-West is a triangle with the Rocky Mountains and the International Boundary westward from the Lake of the Woods for its two sides, and for its base the wooded belt running north-westward from near the Lake of the Woods to the Rocky Mountains. It does not differ greatly in its climate from the forest region to the north except in its rainfall, particularly in the distribution of its moisture throughout the year ; its winds are more persistent and violent. These differences, slight as they seem, make it no land of trees, but a happy home for the grasses. Trees spread their roots deep and wide in the subsoil and thus resist drought,

* Illustrated by Sketch-map No. 1 at p. 2.

but the moisture which they draw from the ground " transpires " through their leafage into the air. On the prairies the summer sun is so strong, the air is so dry, and the winds are so persistent, that the transpiration is very great—often too great for the moisture which a tree can draw from the soil. The annual rainfall in some parts south of the South Saskatchewan falls as low as ten inches; from the Red River eastward it rises to more than twenty inches, while the average for the valley of the Saskatchewan is about fifteen. This comparatively low precipitation would be less harmful to tree life if evenly distributed through the year, but most of the rain falls in June and July, and is preceded and succeeded by more or less prolonged droughts, which are made doubly trying by the restlessness of the winds. When rains do break the drought, they often come as scattered showers; but at times they burst like a deluge across the plains, the flood pouring off the surface into the gulleys and rivers. In either case the moisture does not penetrate down to the deeper soil tapped by the roots of the trees unless the land has been cultivated. Hence the spacious upland levels which stretch from the International Boundary to the upper edge of the valleys of the rivers Assiniboine and Saskatchewan are not in their natural state a happy home for trees, at least not for such as have a large leafage. In favourable spots trees with small leaves and scanty foliage, like the poplar, the aspen, and the birch, preserve their slender existence. In contrast, the grasses are well able to face the struggle for existence. They do not tower into the air, but are close to the soil and more or less protected from the transpiration due to the winds. They get the moisture of the melting snow in the period of their germination and first growth. They spread their roots through the upper mould, and are thus able to take advantage of the summer showers and downpours. Their leafage is subject to comparatively little transpiration, and their period of rest synchronizes with the drought. The prairie region, then, is the natural home of the grasses. It appeared to the fur-trader, as he looked across from the bank of the North Saskatchewan, like a great ocean of grass whose farther limits were scarcely known.

The next North-West is an extensive forest running north of the Laurentians and from Lake Superior and the Lake of the Woods north-westward along the upper edge of the valley of the Assiniboine to Mackenzie River and the Rockies. Its ground formation is mostly rocky. Its precipitation, rather higher than that of the prairies, averages twenty inches and more. What really counts is that it is more evenly distributed throughout the year. In particular its snowfall is heavier, and its winds less persistent. It is a happy home for trees whose leaves and foliage are such as to reduce the transpiration of moisture to a minimum. Consequently, the aspen, the poplar, and the birch of the deciduous family flourish, as well as the conifers, spruce, pine, and larch. The trees tend to retain the moisture in the soil. The late spring and heavier snowfall work in the same direction. Thus the forest belt becomes a maze of swamps and streams and lakes.

The third North-West is gifted with the dreary name of the Barren Grounds. Because it is so far north, the soil thaws to too little depth, and the summer warmth is too short to make the growth of trees happy or even possible. It is a weary land of rocks and moss. However, the surface thaws enough in summer to make it a region decorated with flowers, grasses, and herbs. In winter it is covered with a blanket of snow and ice, which only ends at Hudson Bay and the Arctic Ocean.

The forest belt fixes the northern limits of the prairies and the southern bounds of the Barren Grounds, but its edges are not easy to define. On the prairie side the forest was once farther south than it is to-day, but prairie fires have eaten into it and claimed the land for the grasses. The map at page 2 indicates the northern limit of the true prairie and the southern edge of the true forest as Palliser conceived them (1857–59). The area between these two limits was probably park grasslands gradually receding before prairie fires. When Anthony Henday passed westward in 1754, on a course slightly north of Humboldt, crossing the South Saskatchewan not very far north of Saskatoon, and running through the Eagle Hills and south of the valley of the Battle River, very near the limit of the true prairie, fresh moose—that elusive forest game—was brought to his camp from time to time. This suggests that the " strong woods " then reached out, probably as a park area, into the plain. The stretch between the Qu'Appelle River and the Saskatchewan below its forks must have become prairie soon after, for Alexander Henry the elder says that at his date (1776) the prairie crossed the Saskatchewan a little above Fort des Prairies, near the present La Corne, and he entered the plains not far south of the fort. On the north the limit of the forest areas is even harder to define. Beyond the watershed of the Churchill and Mackenzie rivers the woods become gradually less truly forest, the trees growing smaller and more stunted, until at its outer limit we have " the land of little sticks " of the Indians ; first the hilltops grow bare, then the hillsides, and finally the river banks. Beyond is a forlorn panorama of rocky mounds and basins, and ridge-encircled streams and lakes, far as the eye can see.

The climate, then, and in particular the moisture of these three North-Wests, determines the plant life in the respective areas. The plant life in turn limits the animal life, and all of these together define the possibilities of human existence. On the Barren Grounds the heat of a short summer is sufficient to thaw only the surface of the soil. Moisture is assured from the melting of the ice beneath. Grasses and diminutive shrubs leaf out and flower. Almost in a day the wilderness blossoms as the rose. Soon the shrubs bear fruit in the form of berries. Samuel Hearne, the second European *

* The first European to cross the Barren Grounds was William Stewart, servant of the Hudson's Bay Company at York Fort, in 1715. See at p. 133.

to cross the region, mentions gooseberries, cranberries (which are said to reach their greatest perfection near the northern border of the forest), heathberries, dewaterberries, currants (red and black), juniper berries, strawberries, blueberries, and apparently the hips of rose bushes. The grasses and berries are the food of vast flocks of birds, swans, geese, and ducks of many varieties which visit these northern latitudes during the spring and pass on northward to their breeding-ground.

The moss and grasses of the open north and the belt of dwindling forest to the south explain also the movements of the caribou of the Barren Grounds, to which Richardson applied the epithet " arctic." This species is considerably smaller than its relative whose perennial abode is the forest, and it is likewise more gregarious. Franklin says that a full-grown animal weighed from 90 to 130 pounds. Its slender leg and large concave cloven hoof with sharp knife-like rims, spreading as it presses on the ground, give it great facility in travelling over swamps, through deep snow, and on ice. Males and females winter in the dwindling forest, the bucks deeper in the woods. In the early spring the does escape from the flies by wandering north-eastward to the sea coast, grazing on the dried grass of the previous year and on the mosses. Near the coast they drop their young, and about September return to meet the males, which have moved outward in a more leisurely manner. Throughout the year the herds are large ; the autumn migration is sometimes enormous almost beyond belief.

The birds, and for the most part the caribou, are only summer visitors on the Barren Grounds. The animal population of the winter is very sparse. It is confined to stragglers from the herds of caribou, to two types of partridge (ptarmigans), to ground squirrels and mice, and to the arctic fox and the musk-ox. All these, scattered as they are over an immense area, constitute a food supply too small and too precarious for human beings.

Accordingly the movements of man in this region, his habits, and his institutions, were dictated by the migratory food supply. He too was but a summer visitor on the Barren Grounds. The Eskimo, who found his winter food on and under the ice of the Arctic Sea and Hudson Bay, wandered inland for his summer hunt of musk-ox and caribou, which not only afforded him food, but material for his robes and tents. The Indian made the shelter of the forest his winter home. Here he had the caribou to provide him with meat. Here too he could fish through the ice of the lakes. In spring he followed the geese and duck out to the Barren Grounds. Then came the caribou, the chief source of his summer food supply and of the skins from which he made his clothing and tents. From the " land of little sticks " his women carried the poles for his tipi and the canoe in which he crossed the rivers. As autumn deepened the Indians followed the caribou back into the woods to a comparatively assured winter fare. Consequently the Barren Grounds in winter were a dispeopled land. When in 1688 Henry Kelsey landed somewhere to the north of Fort Churchill, then being first built, to seek out the Indians and bring them to the fort to trade, he travelled two hundred miles without meeting a soul. He returned to the fort defeated by the emptiness of the land.

It is not easy to say what was the former range of the tribes of these parts. In Jérémie's day (1694–1714) the Dogribs frequented the mouth of Churchill River, but they had ceased to do so in Hearne's time (1771). In more recent times the tribes living on the edge of the forest, with the Barren Grounds for their summer resort, have been the Chipewyans in two groups—an easterly one north of the Churchill River and a westerly group on Lake Athabaska ; the Caribou-eaters on Great Slave Lake and eastward ; the Yellow-knives, or Copper Indians, so called from their copper implements, on the same lake and ranging from Yellowknife River north-east-ward beyond the waters of Coppermine River ; the Dogribs on the east shore of Great Bear Lake and wandering into the valley of the Coppermine ; and the Hares, so called from their chief food and skin supply in the far north, on the northern shore of Great Bear Lake and on Mackenzie River.

These tribes are known as Déné (Tinneh), a large group of the far-flung Athapaskan stock. Their hard struggle with nature and their unsettled mode of living placed them in the lowest scale of North American Indian culture. The tribe which we shall meet oftenest is the one which ranged from Reindeer (Caribou) Lake to the mouth of the Churchill River, and which was known to the traders at Fort Churchill as the " Northern Indians." They received the name Chipewyan, " Pointed Skin," from the Crees, because their robes ran to a tail-like point at the front and back. Among the Dénés they were " the people of the Rising Sun," *i.e.* of the east. Their mode of life may be taken as typical of the Indians of the Barren Grounds. Though conscious of the individuality of their tribe, they were innocent of anything like tribal government and even of association in bands such as we find among the Indians of the prairies. Large camps were impossible where the food supply was so precarious. Considerable assemblages might be found on rare occasions, when the caribou hunt or war brought numbers together for a brief association. The vital organism was the family gathered around some more or less successful hunter. The man occupied himself simply with the finding and killing. The more successful he was in his hunting, the more his need of women to handle the carcasses, to prepare food, make pounded meat, dress the skins, and make tents and clothing, and finally to carry his baggage on to the next camping-place. Accordingly he multiplied his wives in proportion to his success in killing for food. In the same ratio the women came to him as wives. Hearne says of Matonabbee, his guide to Coppermine River :

He has now no less than seven [wives], most of whom would for size have made good grenadiers. He prided himself much in the height and strength of his wives, and would frequently say few women would carry or haul heavier loads ; and though they had, in general, a very masculine appearance, yet he preferred them to those of a more delicate form and moderate stature. In a country like this, where a partner in excessive hard labour is the chief motive for the union, and the softer endearments of a conjugal life are only considered as a secondary object, there seems to be a great propriety in such a choice. . . . Ask a Northern Indian, what is beauty ? he will answer, a broad flat face, small eyes, high cheek-bones, three or four broad black lines across each cheek, a low forehead, a large broad chin, a clumsy hook-nose, a tawny hide, and breasts hanging down to the belt. Those beauties are greatly heightened, or at least rendered valuable, when the possessor is capable of dressing all kinds of skins, converting them into different parts of their clothing, and able to carry eight or ten stone in Summer, or haul a much greater weight in Winter. These, and other similar accomplishments, are all that are sought after, or expected, of a Northern Indian woman. (A Journey from Prince of Wales Fort . . . to the Northern Ocean, pp. 88–90.)

If a good hunter and a strong man needed an additional wife of this kind, he took her from any weaker fellow upon whom he might stumble. If his act were contested, it was not in a bloody fray, but in a strenuous wrestling match, for which all weapons were laid aside.

The way in which they tear the women and other property from one another, though it has the appearance of the greatest brutality, can scarcely be called fighting. I never knew any of them receive the least hurt in these rencontres ; the whole business consists in hauling each other about by the hair of the head ; they seldom know either to strike or kick one another. It is not uncommon for one of them to cut off his hair and to grease his ears immediately before the contest begins. This, however, is done privately ; and it is sometimes truly laughable to see one of the parties strutting about with an air of great importance and calling out, " Where is he ? Why does he not come out ? " when the other will bolt out with a clean shorned head and greased ears, rush on his antagonist, seize him by the hair, and though perhaps a much weaker man, soon drag him to the ground, while the stronger is not able to lay hold on him. It is very frequent on those occasions for each party to have spies, to watch the other's motions, which puts them more on a footing of equality. For want of hair to pull, they seize each other about the waist, with legs wide extended, and try their strength by endeavouring to vie who can throw the other down.

On these wrestling occasions the standers-by never attempt to interfere in the contest ; even one brother offers not to assist another, unless it be with advice, which, as it is always delivered openly on the field during the contest, may, in fact, be said to be equally favourable to both parties. It sometimes happens that one of the wrestlers is superior in strength to the other ; and if a woman be the cause of the contest, the weaker is frequently unwilling to yield, notwithstanding he is greatly overpowered. When this happens to be the case, the relations and friends, or other bye-standers, will sometimes join to persuade the weaker combatant to give up the contest, lest, by continuing it, he should get bruised and hurt, without the least probability of being able to protect what he is contending for. I observed that very few of those people were dissatisfied with the wives which had fallen to their lot, for whenever any considerable number of them were in company, scarcely a day passed without some overtures being made for contests of this kind ; and it was often very unpleasant to me to see the object of the contest sitting in pensive silence watching her fate, while her husband and his rival were contending for the prize. (Ibid., pp. 105–6.)

This picturesque contest reveals the main characteristic of the Chipewyan. Physically he was a coward, cringed before his mortal enemy the Cree, and shrank from bodily injury at the hand of his fellow-tribesman. Consequently his manners were mild except, on occasion, to his women. He rarely went to war, and he never shed the blood of his kith and kin. At the same time, physical strength and skill at the hunt gave men their rank in society on the Barren Grounds.

To return to the hunter—the easiest way for him to provide for his dependents was by the " pound," especially if several families were in the neighbourhood to assist, which would usually be in the winter and in the timber area. Lines of brush were placed on either side and at an angle to some frequented caribou track to form a bay into which the prey were driven. At the bottom of the bay an opening was left of the size of a gate. Beyond this a series of hedges with openings formed something like a maze, in every opening of which a snare was set in the form of a noose made with thongs of skin tied to poles. When the caribou were caught in these they dragged the poles after them until their progress was arrested, when they were speared by the hunters. Many beasts were dazed by the maze and rushed about in confusion only to meet a like fate. Out on the Barren Grounds the hunting must have been a much more arduous affair both for men and women. Poles for the tents had to be taken from the edge of the forest, wood for sleds, birch bark, and, if not the canoe itself, the parts for the frame of the canoe with which to cross the rivers. All this, with the tent skins and utensils, were carried by the women and girls. The men and boys, as became their higher status, carried but the implements of the hunt, full-sized or diminutive. To approach the caribou in the open ground was no easy task, but, fortunately, the herds wandering out or in would be shepherded here and there by hills, lakes, and rivers, into a customary trail to some well-known crossing where the Indians would await them. If the prey came, there was abundance, feasting, and merry-making, and in August and September, when the skins were prime, much preparation of skins for clothing. If the deer failed to come, there were lean days tempered by such supply of fish as could be procured from river and lake.

It was from the parties out on the Barren Grounds that in after times Fort Churchill drew to itself bands of visiting Indians. They were such as had traded English wares with the Indian trappers of the forest belt about Lake Athabaska and Great Slave Lake for beaver, otter, and marten skins, and had taken these with them to the summer's hunt out on the Barrens. There they would leave their families at some point where food could be secured, possibly in the form of fish, while they made a swift excursion, not without danger of starvation, to trade with the Englishmen by the shore of the Bay. At suitable spots they would cache pounded meat for the return voyage.

The Indian of the forest belt was more sheltered, but his livelihood was hardly less precarious than that of his fellow of the Barren Grounds. True, big game—moose, caribou of the woods, bear, as well as smaller game such as beaver—was all around him, but it was not easy to catch, and though plentiful to-day, might be hard to come by to-morrow. Moose was the staple food of the Indian of the woods. The name is the Indian *Mooswa*, said to mean " twig-eater," for the creature lives largely on the tender branches of the aspen and willows, of which there is abundance in its forest home.

What the buffalo was to the Plains . . . and the caribou to the Barrens, the Moose is to this great northern belt of swamp and timber land. It is the creature that enables the natives to live. Assisted in warm weather by various fish, it bears practically the burden of their support. Its delicious steaks are their staple food, but its nose or muffle is a delicacy. Its hide furnishes the best clothing and moccasin leather, or provides snow-shoes that enable the hunter to kill more Moose. Its back sinew is the sewing thread of the country, its horns and bones make tools ; its hoofs can be converted into rattles, and its coarse bristly mane, six inches long, and white except the tips, furnish raw material for embroidery. When dyed with native dyes and skilfully worked into leather and birch-bark, these bristles are as effective as Porcupine quills—are indeed often mistaken for them by the uninitiated. (E. T. Seton : *Life Histories of Northern Animals*, vol. i. p. 181.)

A medium-sized moose would weigh 500 pounds and more ; a large one near 1,000 pounds ; so that a single catch would bring temporary abundance to an Indian family, but this abundance is really deceptive. With no vegetables and no bread, and with the keen frost of a northern winter, a pound of flesh goes but a little way. At any rate the voracious appetite of the Indians of the forest has always been a marvel to the white man. Charles Mair breaks the narrative of his journey, *Through the Mackenzie Basin* (1899), to record his astonishment at it.

Mr. Young, of our party, an old Hudson's Bay officer, knew of sixteen trackers who, in a few days, consumed eight bears, two moose, two bags of pemmican, two sacks of flour, and three sacks of potatoes. Bishop Grouard vouched for four men eating a reindeer (caribou) at a sitting. Our friend, Mr. d'Eschambault, once gave Oskinequ, " The Young Man," six pounds of pemmican, who ate it all at a meal, washing it down with a gallon of tea, and then complained that he had not enough. . . . Our old friend, Chief Factor Belanger, once served out to thirteen men a sack of pemmican weighing ninety pounds. It was enough for three days ; but there and then they sat down and consumed it all at a single meal. . . . When it is remembered that in the old buffalo days, the daily ration per head at the Company's prairie posts was eight pounds of fresh meat, which was all eaten, its equivalent being two pounds of pemmican, the enormity of this Gargantuan feast may be imagined. In fact, we were always hungry. So I do not reproduce the foregoing facts as a reproach, but rather as a meagre tribute to the prowess of the great of old—the men of unbounded stomach. (Pp. 100–101.)

With the demands of the body, or at least of the appetite, so great, a single moose would not go far, and David Thompson tells us that moose were " not numerous in proportion to the extent of the country but may even be said to be scarce." Then, too, it was game hard to catch.

It is of a most watchful nature ; it's long, large, capacious ears enables it to catch and discriminate every sound ; his sagacity for self-preservation is almost incredible ; it feeds in wide circles, one within the other, and then lies down to ruminate near the centre ; so that in tracking of it, the unwary, or unskilful, hunter is sure to come to windward of, and start it ; when, in about two hours, by its long trot, he is at the distance of thirty or forty miles from where it started ; when chased it can trot (it's favorite pace) about twenty-five to thirty miles an hour. (*Narrative*, ed. by Tyrrell, pp. 95–96.)

Manifestly moose constituted a hard earned and at best a precarious food supply—all the more as it is the least gregarious of the deer kind.

After the moose came the woodland caribou (*caribou rangifer*). There is a very large caribou in the Mackenzie River basin near the Rocky Mountains, but the denizen of the main forest belt is of a medium size, standing about four feet high, while the moose approaches six feet. The meat which the woodland caribou provided would be proportioned to its height, but this would be compensated for by the fact that it is much more gregarious than the moose, and is found in winter in small bands of from five to twenty. On the other hand, as the Latin name suggests, it is greatly given to wandering, so that the Indian family dependent upon it for food might be in abundance to-day and starving to-morrow.

After moose and caribou, and we may add the bears, the Indian of the forest had the beaver, the French *castor*, the Cree *ah-misk*. It is a very large rodent of aquatic habits, about three and a half feet long. Its tail, remarkable for its flatness, is sixteen inches long and four and a half inches broad. A thirty-pound beaver is considered of fair size, but some have been weighed at sixty pounds and more. The beaver's home is some more or less sluggish stream or small lake, in either case with banks of clay. The water must be deep enough not to freeze to the bottom. If there is any fear of its freezing, the beaver makes a dam to back the water up and to give the requisite depth. It lays down twigs and branches, fastening them to the bottom and to one another with stones and mud and sod. Something of a curve facing the onset of the stream is given to the dam. It is sedulously patched and improved during the winter, night after night, and season after season, until it appears to be a solid barrage of earth across the creek. The beaver makes its home in a lodge of sticks and mud in the pond, with refuges under the bank of the stream, the entrances in either case being beneath the surface of the water. The water-way leading in may be as much as ten or twelve feet long ; the den itself may be as large as six feet in diameter ; its mud walls are patted firm ; at some point its roof is brought near enough to the surface to admit air. Besides ensuring a deep pool of still water, the dam often backs the water up into side channels, which the beavers skilfully improve, sometimes by subsidiary dams, into a system of runs to bring their food to their home. The favourite fare is the roots of reeds in streams and lakes and marshes, and the bark and wood of the willow, alder, aspen, poplar, and birch, which they cut and store for the winter at the entrance to their den. They will not touch the resinous woods. Thus the great forest belt of the North-West with its many muddy streams and creeks bordered by alder, willow, aspen, and poplar (the spruce and the pine being mostly away from the water and on the hillsides) is *par excellence* the home of the beaver, although the range of the species extends as far south as Virginia. In the days when beaver was the most prized of furs the northern forest was the Eldorado of the fur-trader.

Beavers live in colonies, five to seven in each lodge—the parents, for it is a monogamous animal, and their young of two seasons. Gestation lasts three months and the birth-time is May. Mating comes at two years, and death of old age at twelve to fifteen years. Thus the rate of increase is rapid. Accordingly, the beaver offered a stable food supply of its kind and raw material for clothing to the Indians of the woods—all the more as it does not travel far from its lodge. Its beautiful coat of fur—a thick growth of fine wool near the skin with longer and coarser hairs protruding beyond—offered ample protection from the winter's blast.

As a food supply the beaver takes a prominent place. The flesh is good and the tail is considered a delicacy. . . . In a vast proportion of the Mackenzie Valley the beaver serves the Indians as the buffalo did those of the plains. It is their staff of life ; it feeds and clothes them, as well as supplies the necessary peltry to barter with traders for other things desired.

But the beaver did not offer an abundant supply of food such as the buffalo gave and, especially in winter, it was hard work catching him, as the fur-traders' term " working beaver " suggests. The hunter had to break the frozen dam to drain the pool, and had to dig through much ice and hard soil to reach the den. The total meat gained was not large as measured by the effort put out, or by the Indians' appetite for flesh.

Finally, there were the fish in the rivers and lakes. These were plentiful and easily caught in the autumn and spring. Some lakes, however, only gave a fishery in the autumn. As the winter wore on the fish retired into the depth of the lakes, so that even with the more efficient appliances of the white traders the catch dwindled to one or two a day—meagre fare when the allowance per head was eight pounds *per diem*. The varieties most used were white fish and pike. Trout, which often attained to the weight of twenty pounds, frequented the deep lakes ; and sturgeon weighing from ten to fifty pounds were found in muddy lakes. Small carp were caught about the rapids, but some were so bony that the head and shoulders only were eaten, Thompson tells us.

Although there was thus a considerable number of different types of food to be had in the timber region, the total supply was not great. This, and above all the uncertainty of it, constituted the controlling influence on human life. It put an inexorable limit to the possible total of population—a total which is astonishingly small when we consider the wide area involved.

A French estimate of the year 1737 placed the people described as " Les gens des terres " (*Têtes de Boule*) in the region between Three Rivers and the upper Ottawa—an area of about 200 square miles—and counted that they could muster only 400 warriors. If we multiply this by four we have the probable population. In the stretch of about 400 miles from Lake Abitibi to the Nipigon River there were, according to the estimate, but 470 warriors— Abitibis at the extreme east and Monsonis at the extreme west. It was believed that the manhood of the valley of the Kaministikwia, which must measure nearly 100 miles, was but 60 warriors. The Monsonis about Rainy Lake were counted at 100, the Crees at the Lake of the Woods at 200, with an additional 60 hunting north of Lake Nipigon. The Assiniboins west of Lake of the Woods were thought to number 150 only. All this, the French knew, was in sharp contrast with the Indians of the plains, for they believed the Sioux could muster 2,000 warriors. Finally, the estimate put the Saulteurs, probably so called from an Indian name " People of the Sault or rapid," otherwise known as Ojibway, or Chippewas, at 200 warriors. They were scattered from the Sault Ste. Marie along the south shore of Lake Superior, a distance of little less than 400 miles.

The population in the timber area north of Lake Winnipeg and of the River Saskatchewan would not exceed the average of this French estimate. David Thompson was of opinion that there were but 92 families in the region which he called the Muskrat Country, having 248 square miles of hunting ground for each family. In 1789 William M'Gillivray expected 50 beaver hunters in the Reed Lake area, but there were only 10, with a few adherents of the Hudson's Bay Company. In 1809 William McKay, a partner of the North West Company, travelled from Cross Lake to and beyond Lake Sipiwisk, probably a distance of 60 miles, before he found any Indians. Even then he came upon " but two lodges, say 13 men," assembled waiting for the Hudson's Bay Company's boats. Few as they were, by the end of January these Indians were starving. The Northwester had to send fish from his post, near a fishery, and sleighs, to bring out those who were so feeble they could not walk.

The various groups of Indians mentioned above, with the exception of the Sioux and their kinsmen the Assiniboins, were branches of two more comprehensive Algonkin tribes, the Saulteurs (including the Monsonis) and the Crees, inhabiting the timber region as far as Lake Winnipeg. The Wood Assiniboins were in the forest west of the lake.

Beyond to the north-west lay a succession of tribes of the Northern Dénés. Their alignment before the White Man came is not easy to discover. Probably the Chipewyans were south of the Churchill, with the Slaves, as the Crees called them, to the west, on Athabaska River and Lesser Slave Lake, and south of what they called the Beaver River, our Peace River.

A great displacement took place at the beginning of the eighteenth century, when the Crees, who had been bringing down their furs to the White Men's forts, had become the happy possessors of guns. Armed with these, they drove the defenceless Dénés out of the great beaver region to the north-west.   The Journals of the Governors Knight and Kelsey at York Factory show that the Hudson's Bay Company's officers put out every effort to secure a peace which would protect the northern tribes and permit them to trade at the fort, but all in vain.   The Crees drove the Chipewyans north of the Churchill and occupied their territory.   Probably these Chipewyans, later armed in turn with guns from Fort Churchill, drove their own kinsmen before them, and caused a general northward movement of the tribes ranging through the Barren Grounds and the forests on their edge.

At any rate, the Dogribs, who according to Jérémie frequented the mouth of the Churchill in the first decade of the eighteenth century, were found by Samuel Hearne (1771) in the secluded north, and were kept away from Fort Prince of Wales on that river by the eastern Chipewyans, who guarded most jealously the position which they had won as middlemen between the distant tribes and the fort.

There was a similar displacement farther west.   The Slaves (Beaver Indians) were driven from their position about Athabaska River and Lesser Slave Lake north to the river and the great lake which the fur-traders named after them.   Even there they were pursued by their enemies, as we know from Samuel Hearne and from Sir Alexander Mackenzie.   This group appears in the time of the fur-traders under the names of Beaver, Strong Bow, and Strong Wood Indians, in the region west of Mackenzie River and as far as the River Liard.   A kindred Beaver group maintained itself on the north bank of the Beaver (Peace) River.   When the force of the Crees was spent, doubtless after they had been decimated by small-pox in 1781, this Déné tribe, now to some extent armed with guns, wrested a peace from them at a great council on the banks of the river at the traditional Peace Point.   The French servants of the Montreal fur-traders knew the river thereafter as La Rivière de la Paix, our Peace River.

Alexander Mackenzie ascribes to the Crees of his time the country south of the Churchill and Peace rivers as far as the source of our Beaver River, which flows into Lake Île-à-la-Crosse.   The Crees, but more probably the Beaver Indians, armed with guns, drove the tribe to their west, the Sekanais, across the Rockies, on whose rugged slopes they found their livelihood extremely precarious.

In contrast the movement of the Sarsi, a group kindred to the Sekanais, southward into association with the Blackfoot tribes of the plains, whose manner of living they adopted, was due to a blood feud.

The tribe north of the Liard was the Nahanais, who were pressed up against the Rockies at the headwaters of that river.   Wentzell puts them on the Nahanni River with the " Dahedinnes," Dahedénés, " Men of the Rocks," to the north. He says a wide tract of unoccupied country lay between the two tribes. The northern limit of the Dahedénés was in the latitude of the Fort Good Hope of that day, 1821.

Last of all, facing the Eskimos on both sides of the Mackenzie towards its delta, were the Squint Eyes (Loucheux, the Quarrellers of Alexander Mackenzie), trading afterwards at Fort Good Hope. Groups kindred to these stretched westward beyond the Rockies and along River Yukon into Alaska.

Of all these tribes of various stocks the Cree may be taken as the typical people of the forest belt. Their name *Kenistenoag* was made Kristinaux by the French and shortened into Cris. Sir John Richardson says that they were called " Opimmitish Iniwuc," " Men of the Woods," and the term Wood Crees has persisted to this day to distinguish them from their kinsmen of the plains. They also called themselves Nahathaway, and so David Thompson knows them. Their original territory extended from the Moose River to the swampy region north of Lake Winnipeg, the country of the Maskegons or Swamp Crees. They were much more warlike than the Chipewyans, which may explain their somewhat stronger sense of tribal unity, but their hard life in the forests meant that they rarely came together in crowds ; rather they lived in groups of a few families, which did not wander outside their recognized region. They also differed from the Chipewyans in the use of the canoe as a means of transportation. This made the lot of their women much lighter than that of the women of the Northern Indians, for mostly the family moved from place to place on the water. Though capable of deeds of violence they were a mild, affable, and hospitable people, and scrupulously honest. One marvels at the sense of security of the solitary fur-trader camped in their midst in the forest.

In their primitive state the tribes of the forest made their implements and utensils out of the materials to hand. Fish bones made their hooks ; the fibrous roots of the spruce made the twine (*watap*) for sewing their bark canoes and for their nets. All that they had for delving after the beaver in his den was a sharpened stick. In tracing the tracks of the moose and caribou through the woods they showed an extraordinary alertness—born, doubtless, from the fact that starvation stared them so often in the face. Their bows and arrows, however, were feeble weapons against such big game. Accordingly, when the White Man came with his gun and iron tools, he came as the friend of the people of the woods, for his implements made it easier to secure the means of existence. Hence those happy relations between the Crees and the Whites which have meant that but little mention is made of these interesting Indians in the pages of those who have written books and journals.

At an early date Crees wandered over into the prairies and adopted the very different manner of living which characterized the buffalo country. These are distinguished as the Plain Crees.

Conditions of animal and of human life on the prairies presented a vivid contrast to those of the timber region. The spacious plains, though their grass was far from deep or thick per square yard, in the sum afforded a food supply which was very abundant—a paradise for many species of the graminivora. The one drawback was that the enemy, wolf or man, could sight his prey from afar. Consequently those species survived which were fleetest of foot like the red deer and the buffalo, but added to their fleetness the security of numbers. The gregariousness of these animals, if it preserved the species in the face of danger, afforded an easy abundance of food to men.

Of the various animals on the prairies providing food and the necessaries of life to the Indians the buffalo was without rival. True, the herds wandered far across the plains, but their course was fairly well defined. H. Y. Hind tells us that there were two principal herds in our North-West. One wintered in the brushwood of the Côteau de Missouri from Pembina River westward, and in spring drifted northward to the open prairie ; it crossed the valley of the Qu'Appelle, east of the present Regina, grazing eastward to the Assiniboine and southward to Red River, and so to its winter home. The other made the region between the two Saskatchewans its winter haunt, and moved southward with spring. It grazed across the plains about Regina and wandered westward towards the Rockies, and so back to its wintering ground. During the summer the herds broke up into bands scattered over a wide area. Indeed, the bands kept within their own definite range of about four hundred miles of their wintering ground. When the herd was together its numbers blackened the plains. We are told that it grazed so securely that a way had often to be made through it for the Red River carts. Thus, though the buffalo wandered far, the Red Man knew their course and could trace them from a great distance. If they got out of range, scouts were sent out, who would find the prey and signal its presence by setting the prairie on fire.

Buffalo were stalked and were brought down by arrows long after guns were introduced, for firearms stampeded the herd ; but the favourite way was to drive them into pounds. The pounds upon the plains were even more deadly than those on the edge of the Barren Grounds, for the prey was driven into a bay of brushwood, and was terrified by the howling of Indians sheltered behind the brush, and rushed madly through the gap at its bottom over some precipice or steep incline into a hollow from which they could not escape. Here the bellowing beasts were shot down to the last hoof, when silence fell on the bloody scene. As the bulls averaged about 1,800 and the cows 1,200 pounds, the sum of meat from the slaughter would be very great. What flesh was not needed was cut into strips, dried and pounded into something like flaked meat, which could be stored indefinitely if kept dry. The fat on the back, the *dépouilles*, "back-fat," of the fur-traders, was melted down, and this "grease" poured upon the pounded meat, and possibly flavoured with berries such as the saskatoon, made "pemmican"—a preserved meat calculated to tide the people over any period of scarcity, or to sustain them while on a long march to war.

Not only did the buffalo afford an ample food supply for the Indians of the plains, it offered almost all the necessaries of their primitive life, and made their lot very happy compared with that of the " Men of the Woods."

The wild ox alone supplies them with everything which they are accustomed to want. The hide of this animal, when dressed, furnishes soft clothing for the women ; and, dressed with hair on, it clothes the men. The flesh feeds them ; the sinews afford them bow-strings ; and even the paunch provides them with that important utensil, the kettle. The amazing numbers of these animals prevent all fear of want ; a fear which is incessantly present to the Indians of the north. (Alexander Henry : *Travels and Adventures*, ed. by Bain, pp. 317–18.)

The prairies were also frequented by large herds of red deer. Moreover, in summer moose were driven by the mosquitoes out of the woods, and could be caught in the park grasslands on the edge of the forest. Their hides made excellent garments.

The abundance of food found upon the plains made the life of their peoples a picturesque contrast to that of the timber region and of the Barren Grounds. Great camps were often formed, in which the happy people feasted, and drummed, and danced, over a considerable portion of the year. No solitary families here. Whole bands under chiefs lived in temporary villages during peace, and when on the war-path against distant tribes travelled in large parties under chosen war chiefs. In the camp of peace among the Piegans there was something like a civil chief, who presided at councils and maintained order among his people. One of his functions was that of village orator, passing through the camp in the evening haranguing his subjects, giving them the news, and reporting where the herds of buffalo were feeding, and the direction which they were taking. War gave the chiefs great authority, and inculcated discipline in the ranks. Among the Blackfoot tribes the sense of tribal unity was so far developed that each group, Blackfoot, Blood, and Piegan, acknowledged the leadership of a single chief.

The woman of the plains, like her sister of the north, was wife, servant, and beast of burden to her lord, but conditions of life made her lot easier. There was abundance in her larder. She had not so incessantly to move her tipi. When the camp moved on, dogs carried much of the burden on *travois*, that is, a frame of poles crossing one another at the end laid on the animal's back, and kept spread out at the other by crossbars, on which the bundles were tied. The dogs dragged these along with one end on the ground. The Indians of the prairies did not use canoes.

The alignment of the tribes of the plains before the Whites came can be sketched with tolerable accuracy. From the narrative of La France, printed in the report of the Committee of the House of Commons inquiring to the Hudson's Bay Company, 1749, we know that the Crees were on the east side of Lake Winnipeg and the Assiniboins on the plains to the west and south. Wood Assiniboins were north of their kinsmen of the plains, and bordered on the Crees in the neighbourhood of the lower Saskatchewan. In 1691 Henry Kelsey was with Assiniboins on the prairies between the Red Deer River and the Touchwood Hills. At this early date there were Crees on the plains. Indeed, the tradition is that this people welcomed the Assiniboins to the prairies, when they broke away from their parent tribe the Sioux. The new-comers would occupy first the valleys of the Red River and the Assiniboine, where La Vérendrye found them in 1738. The Assiniboin name signifies " He cooks with stones." Hence the frequent appellation, Stoneys.

To the west of the Assiniboins were the *Beaux Hommes* of La France, the Naywatamee Poets of Henry Kelsey. These are almost certainly the *Gros Ventres*, " Big Bellies," so called, not because they were corpulent, but because in the sign language the tribe was indicated by a gesture over the stomach, signifying " always hungry," " beggars." The Blackfoot name for them was Atsena, " Gut people." They also appear under the name of Fall or Rapid Indians. David Thompson attributes these last names to the fact that they lived at the rapids a hundred miles west of Cumberland House ; that would be near the present Nipawi Rapids. Before the White Men came their country must have been south of the main Saskatchewan and east of the South Saskatchewan.

According to the story of the old Piegan chief Saukamappee, " Young man," communicated by David Thompson in his own *Narrative* (p. 328ff), the Piegans were formerly on the plains about the North Saskatchewan and the Eagle Hills, and no doubt the other Blackfoot tribes, the Bloods and the Blackfeet proper, near them. They were being hard pressed by the Snakes, who were on the " Stag River " or Red Deer River, which was the name of the South Saskatchewan as well as of our present Red Deer River, its tributary. This would be when the Kutenais were east of the Rockies and pushing northward into the valley of the Belly River. Such was the alignment of the Indians of the plains before the White Man came. In these times, before the horse was known and when war-parties marched on foot to attack their enemies, the various tribes may well have been tolerably secure within their extensive prairie homes, and their several positions fairly stable.

The influence of the Europeans was felt long before they appeared in person in these regions. Their horses, their guns, and their small-pox came before them and wrought drastic changes on the plains. The story of Thompson's old Piegan chief Saukamappee, told in 1788 when he was seventy-five or eighty years old, enables us to see the combined effect of these three deadly weapons of revolution upon the Indians of the valley of the Saskatchewan, and likewise to date their first appearance in the region.

Saukamappee was by birth a Cree. His people were living hard by Assiniboins on the plains. When he was about sixteen years of age, which would be about 1728, Crees, including his father and himself, were sent for by the Piegans to help them against the Snakes on the " Stag River," the reason manifestly being that they had some European weapons, viz., " a few guns " with " very little ammunition," lances pointed with iron, and arrows with iron points. The father carried his knife on his breast and his axe in his belt. The son had a knife of which he was very proud. The clash came on the plain of the Eagle Hill, probably our Eagle Hills, south-east of Battleford. When Saukamappee became a man and married (Thompson tells us that the Piegans married at twenty-two years or more, so this would be about 1734) the Snakes were bearing hard on the Piegans, for they now had " a few horses . . . on which they rode, swift as the Deer, on which they dashed at the Peeagans, and with their stone Pukamoggan [tomahawks] knocked them on the head, and they [the Piegans] had lost several of their best men." In a word, Piegan infantry could not withstand the charge of the Snake cavalry. Accordingly, Crees to the number of three, Saukamappee among them, and Assiniboins to the number of seven, armed with ten guns and each with thirty balls, were requisitioned to save the day. In the battle, which was fought on a wide plain, the Snakes engaged had no horses. They lay on the ground behind a wall of shields, three feet wide and touching one another, and they would rise to let fly their arrows. At this favourable moment the gunners fired with deadly aim. The firing which began at noon must have been as deliberate as the Red Man's speech, for it was still going on and their few balls were not exhausted when the sun was not yet half down. Now the Snakes began to crawl away from their shields and take to flight. At this point the Piegan warchief, stepping to the front, gave the signal for a charge of the whole line. There was a wild cry and a rush upon the enemy. Many scalps were taken. Alas, the gunners took none, and could not return in triumph to their families bearing those coveted tokens of victory.

At the commemoration of the victory next day, those who had killed a foe came with their faces blackened and with red streaks, but the war-chief told the gunners to paint their foreheads and eyes black, and the rest of the face dark red ochre. The scalps were now displayed—so many souls of the enemy given to " our relations which are in the other world to be their slaves." A long theological discussion took place as to whether those who had taken scalps from the dead enemies, that is, from those who had been shot by the gunners, possessed their souls and could present them to relatives beyond the grave. The matter was decided in the negative, the scalps and the souls represented by them being awarded to the gunners. Thus the men with the guns were able to satisfy the shades of their departed friends and return in triumph to their homes. The terror of that battle and of the guns put an end to general engagements. War took the form of ambuscades and surprises of small camps.

Saukamappee's story runs on :

We thus continued to advance through the fine plains to the Stag River when death came over us all, and swept away more than half of us by Small pox of which we knew nothing until it brought death among us. We caught it from the Snake Indians. Our Scouts were out for our security, when some returned and informed us of a considerable camp which was too large to attack and something very suspicious about it ; from a high knowl they had a good view of the camp, but saw none of the men hunting, or going about ; there were a few Horses, but no one came to them, and a herd of Bisons was feeding close to the camp with other herds near. This somewhat alarmed us as a strategem of War. . . . Our Scouts had been going too much about their camp and were seen ; they [the Snakes] expected what would follow, and all those that could walk, as soon as night came on, went away. Next morning at dawn of day, we attacked the Tents, and with our sharp flat daggers and knives, cut through the tents and entered for the fight ; but our war whoop instantly stopt, our eyes were appalled with terror ; there was no one to fight with us but the dead and dying, each a mass of corruption. We did not touch them, but left the tents, and held a council on what was to be done. We all thought the Bad Spirit had made himself master of the camp and destroyed them. It was agreed to take some of the best of the tents, and any other plunder that was clean and good, which we did, and also took away the few Horses they had and returned to our camp.

The second day (*sic*) after, this dreadful disease broke out in our camp, and spread from one tent to another as if the Bad Spirit carried it. We had no belief that one Man could give it to another, any more than those that were near the river, into which they rushed and died. We had only a little brook, and about one third of us died, but in some of the other camps there were tents in which every one died. When at length it left us, and we moved about to find our people, it was no longer with the song and the dance ; but with tears, shrieks, and howlings of despair for those who would never return to us. War was no longer thought of, and we had enough to do to hunt and make provision for our families, for in our sickness we had consumed all our dried provisions , . . we believed the Good Spirit had forsaken us, and allowed the Bad Spirit to become our Master. What little we could spare we offered to the Bad Spirit to let us alone and go to our enemies. To the Good Spirit we offered feathers, branches of trees, and sweet smelling grass. Our hearts were low and dejected, and we shall never be again the same people . . , we thought of War no more, and perhaps would have made peace with [the Snakes] for they had suffered dreadfully as well as us, and had left all this fine country of the Bow River [the South Saskatchewan] to us. (Pp. 336–37.)

There was a great epidemic of small-pox among the Iroquois and among the French at Montreal in 1732. This passed westward to the Miamis and Potawotamis about Lake Michigan, and may have been given to the Sioux and by them to the Assiniboins and Snakes, as was the case with the scourge of 1781. At any rate, there was small-pox on the Winnipeg River in 1737, as La Vérendrye reports, though he says that it came from the English at Hudson Bay. Whatever its origin, the dire scourge and the guns, together, wrought a change in the territories held by the Indians of the valley of the Saskatchewan.

Thompson says of the Piegans and the other Blackfoot tribes, that their old men always pointed to the north-east as the region from which they came. Thus they moved from the neighbourhood of the North Saskatchewan south-westward to occupy the upper waters of the South Saskatchewan, driving the Snakes back on the upper Missouri and the Kutenais across the Rocky Mountains. The

Piegans took possession of the present Bow River and a long stretch along the Rockies. The Bloods came to the present Red Deer River and the Blackfeet proper to the upper waters of the Battle south of the present Edmonton. Their allies, the Déné tribe passing under the name of Sarsi, migrants from the upper Peace River, were north of these last two tribes and on the left bank of the North Saskatchewan. Into the vacancy left by the Blackfeet came the Rapid Indians (Gros Ventres or Big Bellies), driven before the Crees and the Assiniboins, armed with guns. They occupied the open plains to the south, while the Assiniboins took possession of the North Saskatchewan, the Eagle Hills, and the lower Battle River. The Crees possessed themselves of the north bank of the Saskatchewan and the wooded country north of it. This was the alignment of historic times, that is, when Europeans first penetrated into the country.

The first White Man to see the Blackfeet (the Bloods) in their own land was Anthony Henday of the Hudson's Bay Company— the first European to set eyes on the northern Rockies (1754). He met the Archithinues, " The Enemy " as the Crees called them, west of the Red Deer River.

I took a view of the camp. Their tents were pitched close to one another in two regular lines, which formed a broad street open at both ends. Their horses are turned out to grass, their legs being fettered ; and when wanted are fastened to lines cut of Buffalo skin, that stretches along & is fastened to stakes drove in the ground. They have hair halters, Buffalo skin pads and stirrups of the same. The horses were fine tractable Animals. The Natives are good Horsemen, and kill the Buffalo on them. These Natives are drest much the same as the others, but were clean and sprightly. They think nothing of my tobacco, & I set as little value on their's, which is dryed Horse-dung. They appear to be under proper discipline & obedient to thier Leader, who orders a party of Horsemen Evening and morning to reconoitre & proper parties to bring in provisions. . . . Saw many fine girls who were Captives ; and a great many dried Scalps on poles on and before the Leaders tent. They follow the Buffalo from place to place ; and that they should not be surprized by the enemy, encamp in open plains. Their fewel is turf & Horse-dung dryed ; their cloathing are finely painted with red paint, like unto English Ochre : but they do not mark nor paint their bodies.

The camp, Henday says, numbered three hundred and twenty-two tents.

Another displacement of tribes due to the White Man's terrible gun was seen to the south. The Saulteurs, on the south shore of Lake Superior west of Sault Ste. Marie, armed by the French, drove the Sioux south-westward upon the Missouri, out of the wooded area which is the present South Minnesota, and in particular from Mille Lacs where they were in Radisson's day. The Saulteurs now came into contact with the Mandans " on the southern branches of the Red River," as David Thompson tells us in his *Narrative* (p. 230f).

As Manoah was a Native with them I enquired if they had any traditions of ancient times ; he said, he knew of none beyond the days of their great

great grandfathers,* who formerly possessed all the Streams of the Red River, and head of the Mississippe, where the Wild Rice, and the Deer were plenty, but then the Bison and the Horse were not known to them ; on all these streams they had Villages and cultivated the ground as now ; they lived many years this way how many they do not know, at length the Indians of the Woods armed with guns which killed and frightened them, and iron weapons, frequently attacked them, and against these they had no defence ; but were obliged to quit their Villages, and remove from place to place, until they came to the Mississourie River, where our fathers made Villages, and the Indians of the Woods no longer attacked us. . . . Beyond this tradition, such as it is, I could learn nothing.

Thompson thus elaborates Manoah's narrative :

South eastward of [the Mandans] were the Sieux Indians, although numerous, their stone headed arrows could do little injury ; on the north east were the Chippeways [Saulteurs] in possession of the Forests ; but equally weak until armed with Guns, iron headed arrows and spears ; the Chippeways silently collected in the Forests ; and made war on the nearest Village, destroying it with fire, when the greater part of the Men were hunting at some distance, or attacking the Men when hunting ; and thus harassing them when ever they thought proper. The mischief done, they retreated into the forests, where it was too dangerous to search for them. The Chippeways had the policy to harass and destroy the Villages nearest to them, leaving the others in security. The people of this Village removed westward from them, and from stream to stream, the Villages in succession, until they gained the banks of the Mississourie, where they have built their Villages and remain in peace from the Chippeways, the open Plains being their defence. (P. 225f.)

Thompson places the lower Mandan village of his time in lat. 47° 17′ 22″ and long. 101° 14′ 24″, which, Tyrrell says, would be between Stanton and Hancock on the Northern Pacific Railway in North Dakota and below the Big Knife River.

A different tradition was given to Lewis and Clark, the first Americans to cross the continent by land. They wintered about four miles below the lower Mandan fort of their time and about half-way between the Big Knife River and the sweep of the Missouri towards the south. Their fort was in lat. 47° 21′ 47″ ; it was built in the autumn of 1804, seven years after Thompson's visit. They were told that forty years before the Mandans occupied the nine villages whose ruins they had seen below on either side of the Missouri, and above the Heart River; that, devastated by small-pox and pressed by the Sioux, they had come north to join the Ricara nation at a middle position. Here they were in three villages, one on the left bank of the river. Finding themselves still insecure, they removed to the position below the Big Knife River. " In this situation they were found by those who visited them in 1796."

It is probable that both traditions contain truth. Thompson's information carries us further back. It indicates a retreat of the Mandans before the Saulteurs on a wide front to the Missouri. The later tradition tells of a further retiral, about 1760, now before the Sioux, to the neighbourhood of friendly tribes to the north. Thomp-

* As Thompson was here in 1797 this would be about a century earlier.

son's account is unaware of this later movement, but implies a retreat in direct line from the Red River to the region then held. Moreover, it is dated as in the time of " our fathers," *i.e.* beyond the memory of those then alive, which would be something like eighty years before 1798. All this is consonant with the Journals of the La Vérendryes, who visited the Mandans in 1738 and immediately subsequent years. The Mandan fort on a small stream in the open prairie * some distance from the river may have been the rearguard of the retreat to the Missouri from Red River. Here La Vérendrye himself remained, but sent his son, the Chevalier, to the fort on the river to see if it promised a course to the Western Sea. The report rendered ran : " According to the compass the river appeared to run south-west by south ; and by the signs which [the Mandans] had made it may flow into the sea in a direction south-west by west." This would be where the Missouri turns definitely to the south below the village visited by Thompson.

We shall meet the Mandans in connection with the La Vérendryes and with excursions to them by traders of the North West Company. In great contrast with all the Indians who are of immediate interest for the history of the North-West, they were a sedentary people raising abundance of food in their gardens—corn (maize), pumpkins, beans, and the like. These they supplemented with meat from the plains. With such a food supply they could live in villages, one close to the other. Thompson describes the many villages of Fall Indians and Mandans on the Missouri within about a dozen miles below the Big Knife River as "so many hives clustered together." He estimates the Mandan population at 1,520 souls. We find nothing like this in the Canadian North-West. On the other hand, this people had little to offer the fur-traders but the spectacle of a most interesting and altogether lascivious society.

The Saulteurs, before whom the Mandans retired, were the Indians with whom Alexander Henry the younger was trading on the Red River at the International Boundary and southward in 1800 and after. When the Assiniboins about the Forks of the Red and the Assiniboine rivers were ravaged by small-pox in 1781 they passed down the dispeopled valley. We shall find them treating with Lord Selkirk for the surrender of the ground for his Red River Colony.

While attention has been centred hitherto on the North-West, it should be noted that the forest belt, as described, extends westward from the Atlantic on the coast of Labrador. It skirts the southernmost shore of James Bay, and is never very far from the south coast of Hudson Bay. It runs along north of the valley of the St. Lawrence and of the Basin of the Great Lakes. Thence it sweeps northwestward to the Rocky Mountains. Naturally, it was the eastern section—the northern forest—that was first approached by Europeans.

* See at p. 193ff.

CHAPTER II

THE EUROPEAN APPROACH TO THE FUR
FOREST OF THE NORTH AND WEST *

THE first fishermen from Europe to frequent the Gulf of St. Lawrence
were hunting for riches in the depths of the sea. They little dreamed
of the wealth which lay behind the dark coasts off which they plied
their trade. Behind the height of land of Labrador, that tangle of
lake and stream skirted by a wide forest of poplar, aspen, and
willow—the natural home of the beaver—stretched westward to the
Rocky Mountains. On the southern shore of the gulf beaver were
also to be found, though not in the same abundance. The fishermen
who dried their fish on shore were the first to make this discovery.
They found the Indians robed in beaver. The offer of a few toys and
trinkets, knives or implements, was enough to induce the savages
—men, women, and children—to disrobe themselves and give over
their furs. This is the Canadian fur trade at its source.

The value of an article as merchandise, however, lies less in itself
than in the need and demand for it on the part of the purchaser.
At the outset there was no special demand for beaver in Europe, not
until the hat-makers realized its value for their craft. The fur of
this amphibious creature is made up of two types of hair—the long
and coarser hairs which made its outer surface, and the fine wool
within near the skin. In the process of preparing the skins for use
the Indians scraped their inner side, and thereby injured the roots
of the long hairs, so that they fell out with the wearing, leaving only
the fine wool. Moreover, they wiped their greasy hands on the robe
and gave it something of a gloss. In this form the fur was called
castor gras, fat (really greasy) beaver, by the French, and coat beaver
by the English. The attention of the hatters in France and England
was probably first arrested by beaver of this class. The fine hairs
of the wool are spicated and are thus easily made to adhere to the
felt to give a fluffy surface. Beaver hats became the rage, and the
value of beaver fur was enhanced accordingly. The traffic in fur
now began in earnest. Its development was greatly facilitated by the
fact that the home of the beaver was a land of lake and stream, for
these became the water-ways by which the fur could be carried with

* Illustrated by Sketch-map No. 2 at p. 26, and for the more distant West by Sketch-map
No. 1. at p. 2.

ease down to the sea. Then, too, the birch-bark canoe was ready to
hand, a swift means of carriage, light enough to be taken overland
past falls or rapids, or from stream to stream, and withal easily
repaired with fresh bark and gum, the product of the land.

The great forest belt north of the Laurentians—the happy home
of the beaver—and the region south of it were so amply watered
that the trade had a wide choice of water-ways, some running north
into Hudson Bay, others south to the St. Lawrence, and so to the
Atlantic. The furs of its eastern section might be taken northward
by the Rupert River, the outflow of Lake Mistassini, or by the
Nottaway, which drains Lake Mattagami into Rupert Bay, the
southernmost arm of Hudson Bay, or they might be brought down
southward by the Ashwapmuchuan River and the Saguenay to the
St. Lawrence at Tadoussac, or by the St. Maurice to Three Rivers.
The peltries of the upper waters of the Moose River and its tributaries
which drain the wide region between Lake Abitibi and the height of
land north-east of Lake Superior might move northward downstream
to James Bay, or southward by the Abitibi River, the Ottawa,
Lake Timiskaming, and again the Ottawa to the St. Lawrence, or
they might debouch on Lake Superior at Michipicoton from the
Missinaibi and Moose rivers, and pass by the Sault Ste. Marie to
Lake Huron and Georgian Bay, and thence up the French River to
Lake Nipissing and down the Mattawa to the Ottawa River and
Montreal. The furs north and north-west of Lake Superior might
be taken down the River Albany, again to James Bay, or southward by the Ogoki and Ombabika rivers and Lake Nipigon, or by
the Kaministikwia and the waters west of it to our Fort William
or to Grand Portage, and thence by the water-way of the Great Lakes
whose far end was the Ottawa and St. Lawrence, as above. Consider the trade of the wide basin of Lake Winnipeg. The Saskatchewan debouching into that lake, the Red Deer and the Swan
rivers flowing into Lake Winnipegosis, the smaller streams crossing
through lakes Dauphin and Manitoba, and finally the Assiniboine,
formerly called the Upper Red River—all draining into Lake
Winnipeg—form a wonderful series of water-ways leading from the
southern parts of the forest belt as far as the Rockies themselves.
The streams of fur coming down all these water-routes might pass
northward by the Hayes or Nelson down to the Bay ; or they might
be diverted by the Winnipeg River, Lake of the Woods, Rainy
River and Lake and the waters along which the International
Boundary runs to Lake Superior and the trade route to Montreal.
Even the furs of distant Athabaska, and of the Peace and Mackenzie
rivers, might be directed into this route by the Churchill, Portage du
Traite, the Sturgeon Weir and Saskatchewan rivers, instead of going
across the Barren Grounds or down the Churchill to the Bay. A
rival route to this trunk water-way to Montreal ran from Winnipeg
River up to its tributary the English River and Lac Seul over the
height of land to Lake St. Joseph, and by the Albany River to Albany
Fort in James Bay.

The abundance of beaver in the forest belt of the north, the extraordinary ease of transportation in birch-bark canoes by these numerous water-ways, the great value of the beaver wool in the eyes of the fashionable hat-makers of Europe—these all were factors in the development of the fur trade and went to making the history of the North-West. The choice of routes northward to Hudson Bay, or southward and eastward to the St. Lawrence, brought about a struggle between the English Adventurers trading into Hudson Bay and the French, and after them the English, fur-traders on the St. Lawrence. It is a conflict of interests which runs all through our history, and whose counterpart is with us even in this age of railways. The easy route from Lake Ontario by Oswego, and from the St. Lawrence below Montreal by the River Richelieu and Lake Champlain, to the River Hudson at Albany, gave two outlets on the Atlantic to the continental fur trade, and brought the French, and later the English, on the St. Lawrence into a struggle with the Dutch, and after them the English, on the Hudson—a struggle which greatly affected the history of the fur trade, though it is only occasionally a matter of concern to the story of the Canadian North-West.

After the discovery of beaver robes and other furs by the fishermen, a regular trade began with the Indians in which profits from the fisheries were enhanced by dealings in peltry. The savages would take their own furs and such others as they had traded with more distant tribes down the St. Lawrence to the fishermen. The next stage was for the Europeans to push on up the arms of the sea to gain closer contact with their savage customers. This approach to the forest belt was greatly advanced by the search for the route to Cathay, a country of teeming population, which was supposed to be on the north-eastern coast of Asia, and much farther east than the continent which we know. To the successors of Christopher Columbus America was a barrier in the ocean route to this market whose supposed wealth attracted all the explorers. In 1513 Balboa crossed the isthmus of Darien and found the Pacific but a short distance from the Atlantic. In 1530 Magellan worked his way through the straits which bear his name to the much sought for " Southern Sea." Might not any opening in the coast of America reveal an easy passage to that sea and to the markets of Asia ? It may be uncertain whether Verazzano ever made such an extensive voyage as that which he claims to have done for Francis I. of France in 1524. At least his letter reveals the ideas of explorers westward in his time. " My intention was to reach Cathay, on the extreme coast of Asia, expecting, however, to find in the newly discovered land some such obstacle as it has proved to be, yet did not doubt that I should penetrate by some passage to the eastern ocean." The openings at what is now New York on the River Hudson, the Gulf of St. Lawrence, and Hudson Strait, known as early as 1540, if we may rely on the charts, lured the venturesome to explore them. In 1535 Jacques Cartier penetrated up the St. Lawrence only to prove that there was no sea-way there. How near to the westward of his Hochelaga, our Montreal, the Pacific Ocean might be remained to be proved. The substantial result of his voyage was that the first approach to the great fur region was made on the south, and by Frenchmen. Our information as to the extent to which the fishermen availed themselves of the discovery to prosecute their trade in peltries is of the most meagre. A monument should be erected by Canadian historians to the whale which upset a boat laden with furs on the St. Lawrence in 1558, thus causing the fur trade to be put on record in the documents of the day.

Apparently in 1581 the trade in peltries was breaking away from the fishing business. In that year merchants from St. Malo sent a vessel of thirty tons up the St. Lawrence for furs. The profits of the venture were so great that a ship of eighty tons was equipped in the following year, and as many as three ships the year after. By 1608 the fur trade was so great and competition so ruinous that De Monts was able to secure the monopoly of the trade of the river, and Champlain as his officer founded Quebec. The great founder of La Nouvelle France did not find any striking abundance of furs in the river valley itself. Its forests were of hardwood, and its population comparatively large. Beaver were probably never plentiful and the people had already done much to exterminate them in the region. Champlain did, however, find that what might be called a continental trade had been inaugurated. The furs of the north and west were passing from tribe to tribe southward and eastward, and were being brought to the traders by middlemen. The Montagnais about Lake St. John came down the Saguenay to Tadoussac with the peltries of the north. The furs farther west were brought by Hurons of the Georgian Bay and by Algonkins of the Ottawa Valley, as middlemen, down the Ottawa to the St. Lawrence, at Lachine hard by Montreal. To protect these customers of the French traders from their enemies the Iroquois, whose home was on the upper waters of our River Hudson, Champlain penetrated up the River Richelieu to beyond Lake Champlain (1609). Thus he was the first to explore the route by which in later times the furs passed down, in the eyes of the French all too easily, to the Dutch, and later to the English traders at Albany (Fort Orange) on the River Hudson. Champlain defeated the Iroquois, and afforded protection to his Huron middlemen, at least for the time. As will be seen, Henry Hudson two months later explored the river now bearing his name and opened what was to be a fresh outlet to the sea for the furs of the north. In 1613 Champlain received from a lad previously sent up country to live with the Algonkins on Lac des Alumettes, an expansion of the Ottawa, a report which, if it was not fabricated, was a strangely garbled rumour of the expedition of Henry Hudson to Hudson Bay in 1610-11. Champlain also knew of Captain Thomas Button's expedition to the Bay of 1612. To make contact with the Algonkins of the upper Ottawa, and to reach the North Sea (Hudson Bay), he penetrated up the Ottawa, but had to turn at Lac des Alumettes. In 1615 he took up the unfinished task, passed from Lac des Alumettes up the rivers Ottawa and Mattawa and from Lake Nipissing down what came to be known as the French River to Georgian Bay of Lake Huron. He visited the Hurons between Penetanguishene Bay and Lake Simcoe, and led them across Lake Ontario to war with the Iroquois. Champlain opened to European eyes the great trade-route from the St. Lawrence by the Ottawa to Lake Huron. While he made this voyage in the course of his duty towards the fur-trading company of which he was an officer, he never lost the hope of finding the Western Sea.

The search for Cathay and its rich markets led also to an approach to the forest belt of the North-West by way of Hudson Strait. The English had shown themselves deeply interested in possible routes by the far north. In 1553 the merchant adventurers known as the Muscovy Company tried the Polar Sea of Europe and Asia. In 1576 Martin Frobisher dared the icy seas north of America ; he found our Frobisher Bay, which he took to be a strait, but the Company of Cathay, which was thereafter formed, devoted its attention to a vain search for gold. The explorations of John Davis (1585–87) kept interest in this route alive, though they did no more than increase men's knowledge of the Arctic north and Davis Strait in particular. According to an account published in *Purchas his Pilgrimes*, 1625, one Juan de Fuca, a Greek pilot in the service of the Spaniards, in 1592 entered " a broad Inlet of the sea on the Pacific coast of America between 47 and 48 degrees of Latitude " and sailed on a general north-easterly course to the " North Sea." De Fuca is reported as offering his services to England and as declaring that he would perform the journey through the strait in thirty days. The story is generally taken to be the fabrication of a seaman seeking employment with the English. Preserved among Purchas's narratives of explorations, it was believed to be true, and was never forgotten. It influenced explorers and geographers through the centuries until Vancouver's delineation of the Pacific coast proved it false. Even so, the discovery of an inlet of the Western Sea south of Vancouver Island near the proper latitude, and named therefore after the old pilot Juan de Fuca Strait, leaves room to wonder whether there may not have been some little truth and much speculation at the back of the old salt's story.

There is no evidence that this fabrication was known to Henry Hudson, but it was communicated in 1596 to Lord Cecil, to Sir Walter Raleigh, and to Richard Hakluyt, "that famous Cosmographer," and it may have been current in circles interested in the search for a way to Cathay.

In those days the English merchants most intent on finding the way to China were the Muscovy Company doing business with Russia by the White Sea. Their dream was to find a north-easterly passage along the Polar Sea of Asia. Their navigator, Henry Hudson, made two vain attempts in that direction. He seems to have fallen out with his employers. Certainly his third attempt was in the service of the Dutch East India Company. That he had an alternative plan in his mind is suggested by the strict injunction of his new masters to return home directly should he fail. The hardship of the journey brought about a mutiny in the ship, the *Half Moon*, which Hudson used as the occasion for turning back. He had information from Captain John Smith of Virginia fame, in the form of charts and letters, to the effect that he would find a course to the Western Sea in latitude 40° north on the American coast. This was probably Smith's interpretation of some Indian report of a route by the River Hudson to the Great Lakes. Hudson, in spite of his instructions, agreed with his mutinous crew to try this route, and thus came to his exploration of the river known since by his name (1609). He thus gave his Dutch employers their approach to the fur region. In 1615 Fort Orange was established at Albany, where the Indian track from Lake Ontario converges with that from the St. Lawrence up the River Richelieu and across Lake Champlain. The English fell heir to this outlet of the forest belt of the north by their capture of New York in 1664, and by the peace of 1674. Hudson's search for the Western Sea, like Cartier's, did no more than lead the traders towards the fur fields of the north.

When the *Half Moon* entered the English port of Dartmouth, Hudson came within the reach of the English Government, who forbade him to sail for foreign and rival merchants. Accordingly, his next expedition was made under the auspices of English Adventurers. He had proved that the way to the East did not lie through the gap in the American coast where New York now stands. Cartier had shown that it was not to be found by the St. Lawrence. Hudson now hoped to find it by the next opening, that to the north in latitude 60°, and through the Bay whose existence, if not already known, was at least surmised. Individual members of the Muscovy Company, Sir Dudley Digges, Sir Thomas Smith, and Master John Wolstenholme, equipped the ship *Discovery* for him, and he sailed from Gravesend on April 17, 1610. On the outward voyage he hugged the southern shore of Hudson Strait and Bay as far as might be, apparently seeking the most southerly route possible. His course is marked by names which are with us yet—on the north shore of the Strait, The Isles of God's Mercy, where he narrowly escaped shipwreck, Salisbury Cape (Island), Digges Cape (Islands), and Wolstenholme Cape, "where great store of fowle breed," at the exit of the Strait. As the instructions to Captain Thomas Button in 1612 seem to show, Hudson may have at some time or other sighted the west coast of the Bay about 58° of latitude.* He finally penetrated into James Bay, and wintered somewhere in Rupert Bay, its extremity, probably opposite the mouth of Rupert River.† Here he was within easy reach of the forest belt which

---

* Hudson's " card " or chart, published by Hessel Gerritz in 1612, contains the configuration of the western shore of Hudson Bay—put in imaginatively, surely. This would explain Button's instructions.

† This is the traditional view, based on Prickett's apparent statement that the wintering place was reached on a south-westerly course. But Prickett says that Hudson went off in a boat in the spring to find the Indians, sailing in south-westerly and southerly directions,

subsequently proved a world of wealth to the fur-traders. As the shore of the Bay was the summer hunting-ground of the natives rather than their winter home, Hudson made no real contact with them. Indeed, he saw but one Indian. From him he traded deer skins and two beaver skins, and exacted the promise to return with meat. Had the voyage had a happier issue this might have been the beginning of a fur trade through the Bay, but the expedition ended in grim tragedy.

Seamen in those days were a turbulent race. Hudson had convicted Robert Juet, his mate, of insubordination long before the hardships began, in fact when the ship had got no farther than Iceland. Juet and many of the men had sailed in the northern seas, and seem to have questioned Hudson's policy of searching out every opening in the southern coast. The spirit of disaffection had gone so far in September that Hudson displaced Juet from office and took Robert Bylot for mate. To allay the discontent inevitable with these changes " the Master promised, if the offenders yet behaved themselves henceforth honestly, he would be a means for their good, and that he would forget injuries." The hardships of the winter only increased the disaffection. Even a ne'er-do-well named Henry Greene, whom Hudson had befriended, turned against him. It is true, a good " store of fowl " and some fish were procured in the autumn and spring, but by June 18, 1611, when the Bay was freed of ice so that they could sail, only a remnant of the original provision was in hand to take them back to England. These " the Master " divided among his men. Habbakuk Prickett, one of the crew, whose account survives, admits : " He wept when he gave it to them." Caught three days later in a field of ice, doubtless in James Bay, the crew lost its last trace of discipline. A command to search the men's lockers for food brought the final outbreak. Hudson and his son John and six men, of whom some were sick, were seized, and along with the carpenter who refused to leave his master, were placed in the shallop or dinghy ; they were given " a peece [gun], powder and shot and some pikes, an iron pot, with some meale and other things." The mutineers managed to get the ship clear of the ice, the shallop in tow. As the wind filled the sails, and the ship bounded forward, they cut the shallop loose and left her hapless crew to their fate. Soon they hove to and gave themselves up to plunder. Hudson, doubtless hoping against hope that the angel of mercy was hovering at the last moment over his ship and

and the course on which the ship sailed away was north-westerly. This indicates the east shore of Rupert Bay. Somewhat definite information seems to be conveyed in a map prepared by the Hudson's Bay Company in 1709 (see Sketch-map No. 4 at p. 66), on which Canuse River, north of Rupert River, is given the alternative name of Hudson's River. As there is no trace of a servant of the Company bearing that name, it may be taken that the tradition of the service, doubtless derived from the Indians, was that Hudson had wintered in its mouth, which would afford the requisite shelter. Its approximate latitude is 52° 25'. Radisson's statement in an affidavit copied in the Company's *Memorial Book* that Charles Fort on the Rupert was built on the ruins of Hudson's house may be taken as one of his characteristic, shall we say, inexactitudes. True, Rupert River is clearly indicated on Hudson's chart, and is in latitude 52°, but it is not easy to see how Hudson could sail in his boat south-west and south from it.

its pitiless crew, made full sail to come up to them. Prickett's narrative continues : " Now it was said that the shallop was come in sight, they let fall the mainsayle and out with their topsayles, and fly as from an enemy." * The mutineers had acted throughout as though they could manage the expedition better than the master, but in truth they fumbled their way northward. They ran upon a rock and thought themselves lost. However, they got some food— thirty-six gulls. In due course they made Digges Islands, where the fowl bred. Here they fell in with Eskimos, who appeared very friendly and helped them to secure a bag of game, but foolishly going on shore two days later, unarmed, they were attacked and fell victims to the savages' poisoned arrows. Henry Greene died of his wounds on the way to the ship, and was cast into the sea from the boat. Most of the other wounded died on the ship, " William Wilson [who had bound Hudson's arms behind him] swearing and cursing in most frightful manner." So perished " the only lustie men in all the ship." On the broad Atlantic Juet himself died of starvation. With food got in Ireland the sorry remnant of the crew reached Plymouth, and finally Gravesend in the Thames. With the exception of Robert Bylot and Habbakuk Prickett and two others, they were cast into prison. The survivors naturally threw the responsibility for abandoning their master upon his own conduct in the first place, and in the second, upon the dead Greene and Juet. Bylot and Prickett were so far exonerated as to be sent with Captain Thomas Button next year, in part to search for Hudson, but really to complete the discovery of the North-West Passage, for Hudson's exploration seemed to leave it beyond doubt that by sailing south-westward the Pacific would be reached. A company of adventurers, including, beside Hudson's supporters, many of the great men of the day, applied for and soon got a charter under the title of " The Governor and Company of Merchants of London, Discoverers of the North-West Passage." Henry, Prince of Wales, was " Supreme Protector of the said Discovery and Company." Captain Button, " his servant," was instructed to pass through Hudson Strait, whence, " remembering that your end is the West, we would have you stand over to the opposite Main, in the latitude of 58°, where, riding at some Headland, observe well the flood ; if it come in SOUTH-WEST, then you may be sure the passage is that waie ; yf from the NORTH or NORTHWEST, your course will be upp into it."

Button's expedition sailed from Gravesend on April 15, 1612, in the *Resolution* and, Hudson's craft, the *Discovery*. † After

* In 1632 Captain Thomas James, who had wintered on Charlton Island, saw on Danby Island, about two-thirds of a mile south-east from the south-easterly point of Charlton Island, " some stakes . . . droven into the ground about a foote and a halfe, and fire-brands where a fire had been made by them. I puld up the stakes, which were about the bignesse of my arme, and they had been cut sharpe at the ends with a hatchet, or some other good Iron toole and driven in, as it were with the head of it." James argued that this was the work of Europeans. Did Hudson's party, cast away on the sea, reach this spot in safety ? If so, what followed ?

† The plan was that, as soon as Button should become assured that he had entered the strait leading to the Pacific, he should dispatch the *Discovery* homeward to report, while he proceeded to Cathay in the *Resolution*.

visiting Digges Islands, and possibly searching there for Hudson, it passed across the Bay by Coates Island, naming its southerly cape Cary's Swan Nest. It reached the west shore at 60° 41' north latitude. The feelings on board the ship are registered in the name given to the spot—Hopes Checked. Coasting southward in search of a passage, Button entered the estuary of the River Nelson, which he named Port Nelson, after the master of the *Resolution*, who died and was buried there. He planted the King's arms and took possession of the country in the name of England. The party wintered by a creek on the north shore, where the river was not a mile wide, and had the good fortune to kill 1,800 dozen partridges and other birds for their table. Yet a number of the men died of sickness. The river was not completely frozen till 16th February. Its ice began to break up on 5th April, but the ships were not able to sail for another two months. During all that winter Button's party did not see any Indians, for they would be inland in the forest. No vision of a possible fur trade could have come to the Englishmen, though they were so near the fur region. Scurvy had wrought such havoc with the crew, it was deemed advisable to abandon the *Resolution* and prosecute the discovery in the *Discovery*. " The Summer following [Button] found about the latitude of 60 degrees a strong race of tide, running sometimes Eastward, sometimes Westward ; whereupon Josias Hubbard in his plat [chart], called that place Hubbarts Hope." So Purchas was informed. The only part of the coast which runs east and west is at Cape Churchill, a degree farther south than that given. Henry Brigges's map, published by Purchas, has a wide opening in the coast north of Port Nelson without any suggestion of the river. On the way home Button entered Roe's Welcome, the strait between Southampton Island and the mainland, naming it Ne Ultra ; it was later named after Sir Thomas Roe by Luke Foxe. He named Mansel Island on his course to Hudson Strait.

The failure of this expedition to find the North-West Passage did not discourage its supporters. In 1615 they equipped another expedition with Robert Bylot for master, and with William Baffin for pilot, in Hudson's serviceable ship, the *Discovery*. The expedition ran along the north shore of Southampton Island, gave Cape Comfort its name, and penetrated to the neighbourhood of our Frozen Strait. In 1821 Captain William Parry commemorated its presence in this region with the names of Cape Bylot and Baffin Island. In 1616 Bylot and Baffin were exploring in Davis Strait and on the coast of Baffinland.

It seems strange that Bylot should have been so trusted after the shameful abandonment of Henry Hudson as to be sent on these expeditions by the very supporters of Hudson. Meanwhile the other mutineers were languishing in prison, doubtless till it could be reasonably certain that Hudson was dead. In October 1611 five of them made their depositions before the authorities of Trinity House, who opined that they " deserved to be hanged." In 1617 a True Bill was found against most of them, this time Bylot included, with a view to a trial in Oyer and Terminer. Before the Trinity House authorities the mutineers had put in their plea. "They all charge the master with wasting [*i.e.* filching] the victuals by a scuttle made out of his cabin into the hold, and it appears that he fed his favorites, as the surgeon, etc. and kept others at ordinary allowance. All say that, to save some from starving, they were content to put away [abandon] so many." Edward Wilson, the surgeon, testified : " The reason why the Master should soe favour to give meat to some of the companie and not the rest [was because] it was necessary that some of them should be kepte upp," that is, to navigate the ship. Bylot made no charge before the Admiralty Court, but simply said that " the discontent [was] by occasion of the want of victualls." On July 24, 1618, the High Court of Admiralty discharged four of the prisoners as being not guilty. Whoever the guilty may have been, they cast a foul blot on the annals of Arctic exploration, written for the most part in golden deeds.

Between 1576 and 1630–32 seventeen voyages were made in search of a North-West Passage to the Western Sea. All of these save one were planned in England and commanded by Englishmen. The exception was the Danish expedition of 1619–20. The Danes had long been noted for their overseas enterprises. Naturally their interest was centred on the North Atlantic and the Polar Seas, on Iceland and Greenland, and on the northern whale fisheries. Under their energetic King Christian IV. their ventures were sketched on a national scale. They must have watched the English search for the North-West Passage with peculiar interest, and when it appeared that Henry Hudson and Thomas Button had all but found the way to the Western Sea, they bestirred themselves to complete the discovery and stake out a claim. Under royal management, the *Unicorn* and the *Lamprey* were equipped, and that lavishly, with all that was thought necessary for success. Unfortunately two mistakes were made. As Hudson Strait was nearly in the latitude of the extreme north of Denmark, and the expedition was to sail southward in Hudson Bay, it was assumed that no warmer clothing was needed than was worn in the Scandinavian countries kissed by the warm waters of the Gulf Stream. The men were sent off without furs. Then, too, the dried meat used by the Scandinavians would have warded off scurvy, but the ships were provisioned with salted meat in ample store. The expedition was put in charge of the most experienced Danish navigator of the Polar Sea of the day, Jens Munck. With him were two Englishmen, William Gourdon (Gordon), an acquaintance of Baffin's if not formerly of his crew, and one Watson ; both secured, doubtless, for their knowledge of the achievements of the English, perhaps for their actual experience of the waters to be visited. Munck's instructions have not been found, but his Journal has survived, one of the treasures of the Royal Library at Copenhagen. It was edited by the explorer himself and published in 1624 under the title

Navigatio Septentrionalis. It is manifest that he was to explore
the whole of the western coast of the Bay. When he entered Hudson
Bay at Digges Islands he sent his sloop, the *Lamprey*, in a westerly
direction to search " the northern land where an open passage was
supposed to exist, but there was none." This was probably to
explore the region above and below the 60th degree of north latitude
named Hubbard's Hope by Button after one of his crew, because
its racing tide—sometimes eastward and sometimes westward—
seemed to indicate a strait in those parts. Meanwhile Munck in
the *Unicorn* sailed across the Bay on a south-westerly course past
Mansel Island to the rendezvous, which proved by chance to be at
the mouth of the River Churchill. There he was rejoined by the
sloop.

The Churchill River itself rushes into a tidal lagoon five miles
long and four broad, and there pursues its course to the sea between
stony flats, which may be seen at low water.* As it enters the sea
it is hemmed in by two rocky ledges, which form a landlocked
harbour. After sending his boats to explore the coast for a better
port north or south, Munck decided to winter here. To escape from
floating ice he beached his ship at high tide four and a half miles from
the harbour mouth (which would be one and a half miles within
the lagoon) and on the western shore. The spot was close to the
Hudson's Bay Company's first post of later times, and was named
Munck's Cove by the Englishmen, because they found one of his
cannon there. Small houses were erected for the stores, but the crew
wintered in the large vessel. A party went out in search of the
natives, but found a dispeopled land. The Indians must have
been in the interior in their winter home in the forest. This was
unfortunate, for they might have helped to keep the expedition in
fresh meat and free from scurvy. As it was, ptarmigans and hares
were shot during the autumn, but thereafter resort was had to the
salted meat. Wood was cut on the shores of the lagoon. On
30th October the river was frozen solid. On 21st November the
sea outside was still open. With the New Year scurvy became
prevalent. One by one the crew succumbed. At first the survivors
honoured the dead with a proper burial. Munck's Journal keeps
count of the deaths—Feb. 20th " 21 corpses " ; 25th " 22 corpses " ;
June 4th " 61 dead." By 12th May it was too great an effort
to bury the dead ; they were thrown overboard or left to rot on
the deck. By 28th May only seven were alive, waiting, doubtless
with attenuated hope, for the return of open water and the green
spring. On 4th June but three remained of the sixty-four men
who had sailed a twelvemonth before with high hopes of reaching
the mild climate of spice islands and the wealth of far-famed Cathay.
All expectation of being able to return had passed away, even from
the breast of the indomitable Munck. The entry of his Journal for
that day ends : " Inasmuch as I have now no more hope of life in
this world, I request, for the sake of God, if any Christian men should

* See Sketch-map No. 3 at p. 34.

happen to come here, that they will bury in the earth my poor body, together with the others which are found here, expecting their reward from God in Heaven : and, furthermore, that this my journal may be forwarded to my most gracious Lord and King (for every word that is found herein is altogether truthful) in order that my poor wife and children may obtain some benefit from my great distress and miserable death. Herewith, good-night to all the world ; and my soul in the hand of God.—Jens Munck.''

With the return of spring and a diet of fresh fish the health and strength of the three men revived. With vast labour they unloaded the *Lamprey*, and got her afloat upon a high tide. At last they had her reloaded, and they sailed her safely back to the homeland— surely a marvellous feat of navigation. King Christian planned a second expedition, but the Thirty Years' War, like a dark cloud on the horizon, bade him rather trim the sails of the Ship of State for the storm soon to burst over it. In that war Munck rendered distinguished service to his country. He died on active service in 1628, one of the leading commanders of the Danish navy. The sequel of the expedition to the Churchill River as gleaned from the Indians is reported by M. Nicolas Jérémie, who was stationed at the French Fort Bourbon on the Hayes River from 1694 to 1714 :

Next summer, when the natives reached the place, they were much astonished to see so many dead bodies, the more so as they had never seen men of that kind before. Terror-stricken, at first they ran away, not knowing what to make of such a sight. Then, when fear had given way to curiosity, they went back thinking they would secure the richest spoils that had ever been obtained. Unfortunately there was powder, and knowing nothing of its properties or its power, they foolishly set fire to it, with the result that they were all killed, and the house and everything in it were burnt up. So the others who came later got nothing except the nails and pieces of iron, which they gathered up from the ashes of the conflagration.

It was not to be expected that these early searchers for the way to Cathay should explore the possibilities of the lands discovered. Their interest was wholly centred on the sea-ways reaching westward. Moreover, the call of the hatmakers for beaver did not reach the ears of these seamen. In any case, no contact had been made with the peoples of the lands touched other than the Eskimo, and nothing intimate with them. Hudson alone had seen so much as one Indian and two beaver skins. The existence of the forest belt was not even surmised, nor the possibilities of a trade in beaver so much as guessed at. The same is true of the voyages of Luke Foxe and Thomas James. In 1631 Luke Foxe, supported among others by Sir Thomas Roe of the East India Company, crossed the Bay to the west of our Southampton Island, to which he gave the name of Sir Thomas Roe's Welcome. He followed the coast to Port Nelson, where he replaced the King's arms erected by Thomas Button, and added an inscription of his own. He then sailed eastward past our Cape Tatnam, and at Cape Henrietta Maria came upon Captain James. Returning northward from the neighbourhood of the Cape, he entered Foxe Channel. Queen and Weston capes named by him mark his progress. He turned at " Foxe his farthest " in 66° 47′ north latitude, where the land trended to the south-east, *i.e.* at the entrance to Foxe Basin.

In the same year rival merchants in Bristol fitted out Captain Thomas James. He reached the west shore of the Bay somewhat north of Churchill River, and followed the coast southward, naming Cape Henrietta Maria after his Queen. Amid unspeakable hardships the party wintered on Charlton Island (which he named after the King) in James Bay (called after him), without so much as seeing a soul. Next spring he retraced his course along the west coast, and made a brave attempt on Foxe Channel, following its western shore. He turned homeward in the neighbourhood of Baffin Island.

Thus by 1631, three years before the death of Champlain, the northern forest belt had been approached almost to its border at Rupert Bay and at Port Nelson by the English, and again at the mouth of the Churchill by the Danes. This from the north by way of Hudson Strait and Bay. On the south, the French had come within easy reach of it from the St. Lawrence. It was not, however, to be seen by European eyes, either French or English, till a whole chapter of changes were brought about in the valley of the St. Lawrence.

I.—GROSEILLIERS AND RADISSON CROSS THE FUR FOREST

Groseilliers and Radisson, both men of marked personality and distinguished achievements, stand at epoch-making turns in the history of New France and of the Canadian North-West. Until they stepped upon the stage, the French on the St. Lawrence had been content to be simple receivers of the furs which came down to them, from the north to Tadoussac and Three Rivers, and from the west by the River Ottawa to Montreal and again Three Rivers. These furs were not brought in by the tribes which trapped them, but rather by those which traded them from " nations " which had no direct, certainly no intimate, contact with the Europeans up to this point. The "nations" in the forest region to the north hunted the beaver and otter by the lakes and streams which constituted their wandering ground, and trafficked them with their neighbours to the south for such articles got from the French as they were willing to part with. Thus the furs drifted into the valley of the St. Lawrence. The most important of the tribes which played the part of middlemen to the French was the Hurons.

Much in the same way the Dutch on the River Hudson were the receivers of such furs as wandered down to them in the hands of their middlemen, the tribes of the Iroquois confederation. In such a system there was little real rivalry between the Europeans, French and Dutch, for they played a comparatively passive part, one comparable to that of the Adventurers of England trading into Hudson's

Bay in later times. The trade rivalry really lay between the middlemen on either side, the Hurons and the Iroquois. It was just such a rivalry as has in times past brought Christian nations to seek its end by the arbitrament of the sword. How much more so with warlike savages who nursed immemorial blood-feuds one against the other? In all such wars the final issue is ordained by superiority in organization and discipline, by strategic position, and above all by superiority of arms. In this case almost every factor was in favour of the Iroquois. Their abundant food supply from the cornfields sown by the women left them free for distant campaigns. Their constitution could bring the full manhood of the Five Nations into a wide field of action. With a spirit of discipline to be found nowhere else among Indian tribes, with a geographic position which enabled them to strike suddenly by the water-ways which led out of their territories —north-east by the St. Lawrence; north-west by the River Ottawa; west by the Niagara; and south-west by the Ohio—above all, armed with the White Man's gun, the Iroquois were to show themselves the masterful people of the American continent. The Hurons in their villages between Lake Simcoe and Lake Huron slumbered peacefully, as the storm gathered on the southern horizon. They had a substantial food supply, for they traded their corn with the tribes to the north; they had a strategic position within reach of lakes Huron and Ontario, but they lacked unity and foresight, and were comparatively unarmed. They lay all unconscious of their perilous position. Nor did the French perceive the coming storm. The priests in the Huron Mission, the " black robes " as the Indians called them, praying for the souls of their heathen flock, sought to ward off the customs and ways of the European and to keep the savages within the shelter of their own primitive social system. The result was disastrous, for when the storm came in 1650 it broke upon a helpless people and beat them down before it. Seventeen Huron settlements between Lake Simcoe and Georgian Bay were destroyed. The Algonkin country about the River Ottawa was dispeopled. The Ottawas on Manitoulin Island fled in panic, and the surviving remnant of the Indians from the south-east shores of Lake Huron followed in their wake. A wreckage of humanity was swept through strait and river into lakes Michigan and Superior to be washed up on their distant shores. When all was over the machinery of the French fur trade lay shattered. The middlemen had fled. The River Ottawa, the water-way to Montreal and Three Rivers, had become the hunting-ground of the enemy. Ships were sent back empty to the homeland. The whole economic structure of the colony collapsed. The *Jesuit Relation* for 1652–53 reveals the sad state of affairs.

Before the devastation of the Hurons, a hundred canoes used to come to trade, all laden with Beaver-skins; the Algonquins brought them from all directions; and each year we had two or three hundred thousand livres' worth. That was a fine revenue with which to satisfy all people, and defray the heavy expenses of the country. The Iroquois dried up all these springs.

The Beaver are left in peace and in their place of repose ; the Huron fleets no longer come down to trade ; the Algonquins are depopulated ; and the more distant Nations are withdrawing still farther, fearing the fire of the Iroquois. For a year the warehouse of Montreal has not bought a single skin from the Savages. At Three Rivers the little revenue that has accrued has been used to fortify the place, the enemy being expected there. In the Quebec warehouse there is nothing but poverty ; and so every one has cause to be dissatisfied, there being no means to supply payment to those to whom it is due, or even to defray a part of the most necessary expenses of the country.

It made for the fame of Groseilliers and Radisson—particularly Groseilliers—that they stepped on the stage of history at this tragic juncture. First of all they were to play their part in rehabilitating the machinery of the French fur trade by bringing down the demoralized middlemen, Hurons and Ottawas, from what was now in very truth " les pays d'en haut," the Upper Country, to renew their trade. They were then to get behind these middlemen and penetrate into the northern forest home of the beaver in the endeavour to tap the stream of furs at its very source. Their early experience had schooled them for just such a task.

Médard Chouart, called also des Groseilliers, though why is not exactly apparent, was born in France at Brie near Meaux on the Marne. He is said to have come to Quebec in 1642 when about seventeen years old. He must have been a somewhat devout Catholic, for he entered the service of the Jesuits as a *donné*, that is, not as a servant but as a lay helper, *given up* to labour for the order without remuneration other than his keep. His place was in what we would call the transportation service between Quebec and the Huron Mission south of Penetanguishene Bay, on Georgian Bay. On the Ottawa route to the Jesuit Mission he became an expert in all that had to do with travelling in the Indian canoe, not only in shooting rapids, but in securing a precarious food supply by the way, and above all in the knowledge of the Huron tongue and in the subtle art of managing Indians.

In the autumn of 1647 he was in Quebec marrying Helène, the daughter of Abraham Martin, owner of what has become famous in Canadian history as the Plains of Abraham. His son Médard was born in 1651 in the capital. Thus Quebec must have been headquarters for the father. In 1653 Groseilliers returned from a trip to Acadia and (his wife being dead since 1651) married Marguerite, the widowed stepsister of Radisson, whose home was in Three Rivers.* Thus he was bound to Radisson by a family tie, which finds expression in the phrase " my brother " recurring throughout Radisson's *Narratives*.

Pierre-Esprit Radisson, the fit mate to Groseilliers in his adventurous career, was at this time having his own painful schooling in the art of living like an Indian. Born in 1636 in the Papal territory

* The eldest child of this marriage was Jean-Baptiste, born at Three Rivers in July 1654. He will figure in the struggle between the French and the English at Port Nelson in 1682 and subsequently.

of Avignon,* on the River Rhone, which was not at this time in the possession of France, he probably spent his boyhood days in Paris. He came to New France in 1651 and went to Three Rivers to his sister Marguerite. At fifteen years of age he enjoyed sport to the full, learned the art of canoeing, and picked up something of the Huron and Algonkin tongues from the Indians about the place. In June of the next year he was shooting in the outskirts of the settlement along with two companions. Fear of the Iroquois bade them return, but Radisson rallied his fellows on their cowardice and went on hunting. As he came back, he fell into the hands of the enemy, who had killed his shooting companions. Because they had witnessed his daring, or it may have been because of the manliness of the lad, the Iroquois spared his life and carried him captive up the Richelieu to their village not very far from the Dutch Fort Orange at Albany of to-day. The whole story of his capture, his adoption by Iroquois parents in the place of a son killed in the wars, his first attempt at escape, his recapture at Lac St. Pierre within sight of his home, the ghastly tortures inflicted on him in revenge, his rescue by his adopted parents and sisters, who had learned to love him, his subsequent happy relations with the Iroquois around him, his campaigns as one of their warriors, and his final escape to Orange and return to Three Rivers by way of New York and Holland is told in his first *Narrative*.

A considerable portion of Radisson's career may be gathered from *Narratives* of six voyages and a few stray documents coming from his own pen. The last *Narrative*, that of 1684–85, is in French; the others are in English of a sort, and must have been written in England to give his English associates some idea of the wonderful man that Radisson was. Four of these last were once the property of Mr. Pepys, Secretary of the Admiralty during the reigns of Charles II. and James II., but known rather for his inimitable diaries. These English *Narratives* do not make easy reading. The sentences are frequently obscure, as is natural in one writing in a foreign tongue. Yet the man shines out through the obscurities. His love of the woods and their wild life appears in many a picturesque touch. " Ending the lake we came into a beautiful sweet river." Again, the Iroquois are like " the owl that sees better in the night than the day." At an impending attack from the Iroquois " all those beasts [the Hurons] gathers together againe frighted. Seeing no way to escape, gott themselves all in a heape like unto ducks that sees the eagle come to them." Similarly, his fondness for the Indians and their life, not excluding its bloodshed and cruelty, is writ on many

---

* Radisson's mother was Madeleine Hénault, who married Sébastien Hayet of St. Malo. As a widow she married Pierre Radisson at Paris. In representations made to the English Government the Hudson's Bay Company asserted that Radisson was an Italian (Public Record Office, *Board of Trade, Hudson's Bay*, vol. i. p. 21) ; and more specifically that he came from Avignon, probably the birthplace of his father : " The [French] cannot alledge, that Raddisson as a ffrenchman Acted any thing for the Advantages of ffrance. 1st, Because he is from Avignon, and was consequently a Subject of the Popes till made a Denison of England by the Commands of King Charles the second of blessed Memory " (*Ibid*, vol. i. p. 167).

a page. When among the Iroquois he had accompanied the braves of his village on a long war-path. " After 10 dayes' march [we completed our journey] through a country covered with water and where also are mountains and great plaines. In those plaines we killed stagges, and a great many Tourquies. Thence we came to a great river of a mile wch made us stay there 10 or 12 dayes making skiffs of ye rind of walnut trees. We made good cheere and wished to stay there longer." In that war they took many scalps, massacred the people, and brought women home for slaves. At the triumphant return home " my [Iroquois] brother and I had a man and woman with 4 heads to our share." Radisson must have distinguished himself in the bloody scene, as is shown by his description of his return, this time not as twice before a prisoner, but as an Iroquois brave.

All the way the people made much of me, till we came to the village, and especially my 2 sisters, that in all they shewed their respects, giveing me meate every time we rested ourselves, or painting my face or greasing my haire or combing my head. Att night they took the paines to pull off my stokins & when I supped they made me lay downe by them and cover me wth their coats, as if ye weather had been cold. . . . My mother comes to meet mee, leaping & singing. I was accompanied wth both my sisters. Shee takes the woman slave yt I had, and would not that any should medle with her. But my brother's prisoner, as ye rest of ye captives, weare soundly beaten. My mother accepted of my brother's 2 heads. My brother's prisoner was burned ye same day, and ye day following I received the sallery of my booty, wch was of porcelaine necklaces, Tourns of beads, pendants, and girdles. There was but banqueting for a while. The greatest part of both young men & women came to see me & ye women [brought] ye choicest meats, and a most dainty and cordiall bit. . . . After I stayed awhile in theis village wth all joy & mirth, for feasts, dances and playes out of mere gladness for our small victorious company's retourne."

Looking back on his days among the Iroquois, in spite of his early tortures and hardships, Radisson says : " Friends, I must confesse I loved those poore people entirely well." This love of the Indians and Indian life is the key to the achievements of the man. Escaped from the Iroquois by way of Orange, Radisson was in Holland in January 1654. He returned to Three Rivers in 1657, the year after the Jesuit Mission was started among the Onondagas, to find his sister married to Groseilliers. Meanwhile he must have been in France or Acadia, for he says that his friends had thought that he was dead long since. That summer he went with an expedition to the Jesuit Mission among the Onondagas. In his *Narrative* of this his second voyage he tells of the alarms of the winter, of his part in the subtle strategy by which the Frenchmen escaped, and of their safe arrival in Montreal. In April 1658 he was once more in Three Rivers.

Radisson was now twenty-two years of age and had acquired an experience of Indian ways unmatched in his time. His days of schooling in Indian life over, he is prepared to begin the spectacular career which left its mark on the history of New France and of the Canadian North-West.

The years following the devastation of the villages of the middle-men of their fur trade by the Iroquois were, as has been seen, lean years for the French. They brought dire suffering to the Hurons and Ottawas in their distant adopted countries. These had prospered by being the medium of trade between the French and the distant tribes which trapped beaver, mostly in the forests of the north. Moreover, they had grown accustomed to the French goods and implements and could not well do without them, but the water-way to the St. Lawrence lay in the hands of the enemy. According to La Potherie, three Ottawas took the first step to reopen trade relations. To avoid the Iroquois on the Ottawa they passed from Lake Superior, presumably at Michipicoton, from river to river and by portage after portage, to the headwaters of the St. Maurice and so to Three Rivers. At the same time three canoes of Hurons dared the Ottawa route. The united parties ventured this route on their return without mishap. Encouraged by their success, next year (1654) a band of 120 Hurons and Ottawas came down from the Upper Lakes with a fine body of furs. With the permission or by the arrangement of Jean de Lauzon, the Governor, two Frenchmen went with these Indians to the Upper Country to set up again the machin-ery of the trade and to bring the Indians and their furs down in a steady stream. It has been assumed that these two men were Groseilliers and Radisson, but as Radisson only came back from the Iroquois to his friends in 1657, his name must be eliminated. More-over, his *Narrative* of his third journey, his first to the Upper Country, 1658, shows that he had not been in that region before. Indeed he refers to the two Frenchmen as though he was not of them. As for Groseilliers, we do not know his whereabouts during these years. The presumption is that one who was as well acquainted with the way to Lake Huron as he would be chosen for such a mission. More definite evidence is to be found in Radisson's *Narrative* of his own first journey to the Upper Country, taken in company with Groseil-liers. Referring to his visit to the Ottawas on the south shore of Lake Superior, Radisson says: " We know those people well. We went to them almost yearly, and the company that came up wth us weare of ye said nation." This is demonstrably untrue of Radisson himself, but would be accurate of Groseilliers if he was up in 1654–56, 1656–57, and finally with Radisson in 1658. Thus the task of restoring the machinery of the French fur trade was commenced by Groseilliers with a companion. It was accomplished with supreme success. Nothing could show more definitely the joy felt at the happy result than the exemption granted the men from the duty of 25 per cent. due to the company of merchants who held the monopoly of the fur trade of the colony. The ships which were about to re-turn to France without a cargo soon left bearing a precious freight. Above all, the achievement of Groseilliers brought the dawn of prosperity to the colony after a dark and hopeless night. A spirit of exuberance runs through the account of it given in the *Jesuit Relation*.

. . . The two Pilgrims fully expected to return in the Spring of 1655, but those People did not conduct them home until towards the end of August of this year, 1656. Their arrival caused the Country universal joy, for they were accompanied by fifty canoes, laden with goods which the French come to this end of the world to procure. The fleet rode in state and in fine order along our mighty river, propelled by five hundred arms, and guided by as many eyes, most of which had never seen the great wooden canoes of the French—that is to say, their ships.

Having landed, amid the stunning noise of cannon, and having quickly built their temporary dwellings, the Captains [Chiefs] ascended to Fort St. Louis [Quebec] to salute Monsieur our Governor, bearing their speeches in their hands.

Some thirty Frenchmen and two Jesuit Fathers were for accompanying these savages on their return. The *Jesuit Relation* of 1655–56 makes the French turn back at Three Rivers. The priests and three Frenchmen went on, only to find the Iroquois in possession of a portage at the Long Sault on Ottawa River. The Hurons got away after a fight by giving presents and by a ruse in which their swiftness with the canoes played a part. The small French party, however, was in a desperate plight, one of the Jesuit priests, Father Gareau, having been mortally wounded. They returned to Montreal.

Radisson embroiders his narrative of the journey of 1658 with this incident, and says that he and Groseilliers got through to the Upper Country. As he had not yet returned from his Iroquois experiences to Three Rivers, it might be taken that Groseilliers was one of the two Frenchmen who got through, and that Radisson was adding to his glory by letting the reader infer that he was the second Frenchman. This inference is supported by Radisson's assertion that Groseilliers was in the Upper Country the year before the voyage of 1658, that is, in 1656–57. Difficulties in the way of this conclusion are that Groseilliers was present at a trial in Three Rivers on July 18, 1657, and that his daughter Marie-Anne was born and baptized there on 7th August following. From this last fact it has been assumed that he was at Three Rivers with his wife nine months before. The only escape from this conclusion is to take it that he had his wife with him on his voyage, but while this is possible, it is far from probable. It would have been possible for them to arrive at Three Rivers by 18th July, if an early start were made from the Upper Country. This is not the only occasion in which Radisson's statements put the historian on the horns of a dilemma.

The year 1657 was marked by a real gain for the French towards Hudson Bay. On the 20th April eight Frenchmen left Three Rivers with twenty canoes of Algonkins. They went northward by the River Batiscan below the St. Maurice, passed seventy-four rapids or portages to reach their objective point on 28th May. By 15th July they were back laden with beaver skins. They saw Poissons Blancs, probably towards Lake St. John, and heard of Crees " near the northern sea." The French were getting a clearer knowledge of the route northward towards the Bay, and knew of water-ways to it from Tadoussac by Lake St. John, and from Three Rivers, as well as from the Ottawa River and from the north of Lake Huron.

The certainty that the Iroquois would beset them on the River Ottawa and carry off their furs to the Dutch on the River Hudson prevented the Hurons and Ottawas from coming down with their precious cargo during the two years 1657–58. Once more La Nouvelle France stood face to face with disaster. It was to save the colony that Groseilliers took the route to the middlemen on the Great Lakes in 1658. Radisson, who had returned from the expedition to the Onodagas, tells us that Groseilliers invited him to go with him on the ground that his (Radisson's) previous voyages had made him " fitter and more faithful for the discovery that he was to make." The *Narrative* of this, Radisson's third voyage, presents serious difficulties to the historian. The party was away but two years, yet the account indicates three winters spent in the Upper Country. Radisson indicates that it was his first voyage to that region, yet he says in connection with his visit to the Ottawas: " We know these people well. We went to them almost yearly." Moreover, the *Narrative* begins with a brush with the Iroquois at the Long Sault on the Ottawa, in which a priest was killed and a party of twenty-nine Frenchmen turned back, evidently the incident of 1656, for there is no record of the like in 1658. Groseilliers and Radisson, we are told, slipped through with the Indians and in their canoes. Probably Radisson, writing for an English audience which could not check his account, embroidered it with the dramatic struggle with the Iroquois of the two years before. It has been argued above that it is not wholly impossible, in spite of the birth of his child at Three Rivers in August 1657, that Groseilliers was one of the Frenchmen that slipped through in 1656, for Radisson says that Groseilliers had been in the Upper Country the year before, 1656–57.

It is probable that Groseilliers's experience and conclusions of this and a still earlier year, viz. 1654, are woven by Radisson into his *Narrative* ; the great fur-trader was a great story-teller, a not very subtle adept in the art of self-glorification.

That the two " brothers " were conscious of the nature of the task to which they had set themselves is evident in the first pages of the *Narrative.* Some of the Savages from the West (the reference is probably to 1656) visited the Governor " who together with the Fathers thought fitt to send a company of French to bring backe, if possible, those wild men the next yeare, or others, being that it [the fur trade] is the best manna of the country by which the inhabitants doe subsist, and makes the French vessells to come there and goe back loaden with merchandises for the traffique of furriers [Indians] who comes from the remotest parts of the north of America." It is not necessary here to disentangle the story of the movements of the voyageurs or to determine the country visited. They spent their second winter among the Sioux west of Fond du Lac, and came down in the spring with three hundred Indians and a great wealth of furs, not without a severe struggle with the Iroquois

on the River Ottawa. The furs were valued at 300,000 livres.
Radisson says proudly :

> We came to Quebec, where we are saluted with the thundering of guns
> & batteryes of the fort, and of the 3 ships that weare then att anchor, which
> had gone back to France without castors [beavers] if we had not come.
> We were well traited [treated] for 5 dayes. The Governor made guifts
> & sent 2 Brigantins to bring us to the 3 rivers where we arrived the 2nd day
> of [blank] & the 4th day they went away.

By the voyage of 1658–60 Groseilliers and Radisson made a
substantial contribution towards reconstituting the fur trade of
the St. Lawrence ; but they were not the men to be satisfied with
the good when the better came into view. Groseilliers had opened
up an entirely new vista for the fur trade by his voyages, for he had
gained an insight into the true source of the streams of fur which
were passing down to the St. Lawrence. He noted that the Indians
with whom he travelled, the middlemen of the trade, made " the
barre of the Christinos [Crees] from whence they have the Castors
that they bring to the french." He found out that these Crees
spent the summer on the shores of the " salt water, and in the land
in the winter-time." Radisson states that when he and Groseilliers
were at the Sault Ste. Marie " We by all means would know the
Christinos," that the Indians of the Sault went to trade with that
people :

> As for those towards the north, they are the most expert in hunting
> & live uppon nothing else the most part of the yeare. We were long there
> [on the west end of Lake Superior] before we gott acquaintance with those
> that we desired so much, and they in like manner had a fervent desire to
> know us, as we them. Heer comes a company of Christinos from the Bay
> of the North sea, to live more at ease in the middle of woods & forests, by
> reason they might trade with those of the Sault & have the conveniency to
> kill more beasts. . . . At last we declared our mind to those at the Sault,
> encouraging those of the North that we are their brethren & that we would
> come back & force their enemy [the Sioux] to peace or that we would help
> against them.

The knowledge thus gained and the determination based upon
it opened up a new chapter in the careers of Groseilliers and Radisson.
Hitherto they had been fain to build anew the scheme by which
the Hurons and Ottawas played the part of middlemen bringing the
furs down to the French on the St. Lawrence. Now they would
get behind this business machine and in their own persons deal with
the trappers in the very home of the beaver. They took pains to
keep this their purpose a secret. However, their intentions leaked
out, Radisson suggests through Groseilliers's wife and the priests.
When the Jesuits tried to retain him to open up a way for the beaver
of the Bay of the North to be brought down to the Saguenay, he
believed that they were trying to separate him from his " brother,"
and to forestall his plans and make themselves " masters of the
trade." In spite of his refusal, the Jesuit father Gabriel Druillettes
and the Sieur de la Vallière with a party started, and penetrated

to the height of land near Lake Mistassini with great difficulty. There they were stayed by word of the destruction of the next people to the north by the Iroquois. They contented themselves with taking possession of the Baie du Nord (Hudson Bay) from that distance in the name of the King of France (1662) and beating a hasty retreat.

The plan which the Governor of the colony devised when he surmised the purposes of the " two brothers " was less subtle than that of the Jesuits, but equally selfish. When they applied for a licence to go to the Upper Country he consented, but on condition that two of his servants should go with them and take half of the profit. Groseilliers and Radisson scorned the suggestion that inexperienced men should come in and share their returns. They believed that they had rejuvenated the fur trade and saved the country, and they were not now to be fleeced in the interest of the Governor and his underlings.

That the governor should compare 2 of his servants to us, that have ventured our lives so many years and maintained the country with our generosity in the presence of all ; neither was there one that had the courage to undertake what wee have done. We made the governor a slight answer, and tould him for our part we knewed what we weare, Discoverers before Governors. . . . We should be glad to have the honour of his company, but not that of his servants.

The issue was that they were forbidden to go without a licence ; but they went. The Governor of Three Rivers, under whom Groseilliers held office as Captain of the Guard, also refused his leave. Even this did not hold them back, for they were conscious that their voyages were for the good of the colony.

We tould him that the offense was pardonable because it was every one's interest ; nevertheless we knewed what we weare to doe, and that he should not be blamed for us. . . . We made ready in the morning, so that we went, 3 of us about midnight. Being come opposit to the fort they aske who is there. My brother tells his name. Every one knows what good services we had done to the countrey, and loved us, the inhabitants as well as the souldiers. The sentry answers him, " God give you a good voyage."

Thus, in the summer of 1661 they left with a small party of Saulteurs, who had come down from the Sault Ste. Marie by devious ways and finally by the River St. Maurice to Three Rivers. They joined another small band of savages who had ventured the Ottawa route to Montreal. The party counted fourteen canoes all told.

The course of these daring men is definite enough during the first twelve months. They got the better of a small band of Iroquois on the Ottawa, and finally passed through the Sault Ste. Marie into Lake Superior. They then followed the south shore, portaged across Keweena Point, and built a fort on Oak Point, looking on Chagouamegon Bay. They went on, however, to winter with the Sioux. In the spring they returned to their fort on Chagouamegon Bay to a cache. In sharp contrast with the definiteness of the story, so far, is the vagueness and sketchiness of the narrative of the journeyings during the summer *; so much so, that many have claimed that " the brothers " got no farther than the Lake of the Woods or Lake Winnipeg, while others assert that they reached James Bay. An explanation may be found in the fact that Radisson did not wish to advertise his course, but tried to keep the venture a secret. He was therefore careful not to give his itinerary. Accordingly the question of the course of his journeys must rest on somewhat general considerations, on a few of the statements of the narrative, but above all on the subsequent deeds of the men. The traverse of fifteen leagues from the fort on Chagouamegon Bay brought them to the Crees, the people of the forest belt, near Grand Portage. In a single line Radisson's *Narrative* brings us to the " great river " and the " sea-side," to " an old house all demolished and battered with boullets," where the Indians gave them " particularities of the Europeans." This suggests some part of Hudson Bay, in fact Rupert Bay, where Hudson had wintered fifty years before. The probability becomes a certainty in view of the fact that it was this region to which the Frenchmen brought the English a few years later, for they had promised the Crees to come back to those parts " with such ships as we invented." Dr. George Bryce argues that they were near the prairies, say at Lake of the Woods, because they passed from isle to isle through the summer, and the region had " a great store of cowes," which he interprets as buffaloes. But Radisson used the term of female deer killed in the valley of the Ottawa, where it would refer to female caribou. Miss Agnes Laut argues for Lake Winnipeg. Two facts make this impossible. Radisson did not meet the Assiniboins, as he would have done in the region of Lake Winnipeg; he only sent messengers to them. Secondly, he came back from the sea to Lake Superior by a different river. The only second water-way back from Lake Winnipeg would be by the Red River through the heart of the Assiniboin country. From the neighbourhood of the Pigeon River the " brothers " probably skirted the shore of Lake Superior and passed down to James Bay and Rupert Bay by the Michipicoton, Missinaibi, and Moose rivers, and returned by the Albany, whence Indians going westward would take his message to the Assiniboins. The Frenchmen would reach Lake Superior by Lake Nipigon. Radisson has an obscure sentence to the effect that they passed the summer at a place where was a river that " comes from the lake and empties itself in the river Sagnes [Saguenay] called Tadoussac, which is a hundred leagues in the grand rive

---

* We are accepting Radisson's *Narrative*, but a real difficulty lies in the statement of Father Jerome Lalemant in the *Jesuit Relation* under the date of May 1662 : " I left Quebec on the 3rd for 3 rivers. On the way I met des Grosillers, who was going to the North Sea. He passed before Quebec during the night with ten men, and, having arrived at Cap Tourmente, he wrote to the Governor." This argues that Groseilliers was on the St. Lawrence about the time at which Radisson says he was leaving Lake Superior to explore to Hudson Bay. An even greater difficulty lies in the indication that the route taken was by the Saguenay and the Rupert rivers, for Father Lalement met Groseilliers above Quebec and had word that he passed Quebec by night, and that he wrote to the Governor from Cap Tourmente (about thirty miles farther down the St. Lawrence).

of Canada, as where we weare in the Bay of the North." The confusion probably arises through the words indicating the actual streams, when Radisson really meant the water-way, portages, and all. The route up the Rupert River leads to Lake Mistassini and by portage to the Achwapmuchuan River, to Lake St. John and the Saguenay, at whose mouth Tadoussac stands. The Frenchmen spent the summer among the islands off the mouth of Rupert River, the very region to which Groseilliers brought the Englishmen in 1668.

Groseilliers and Radisson were the first Europeans to penetrate into and cross the forest belt of the north, the secluded haunt of the beaver; the first, too, to secure intimate relations with the Crees, *par excellence* the hunters of beaver. Of these Crees Radisson says: " They are the best huntsmen of all America, and scorns to catch a castor in a trappe. . . . They kill not the young castors, but leave them in the water, being that they are sure they will take them againe, which no other nation doth."

After spending the winter of 1662–63 at Chaguamegon Bay the two Frenchmen passed out of Lake Superior by the Sault Ste. Marie and reached Montreal. What they had really done was to ignore the official trading Company and its monopoly, snap their fingers at the Governor, pass by the Indian middlemen, and gather the furs at their source from the Cree hunters themselves. For all this they had to pay the penalty. They were fined " 4,000 pounds," the same to go to the fortification of Three Rivers and " 6,000 pounds " for the general treasury. Radisson says the Governor " did grease his choppes with it." They were forced by the monopoly to pay 24,000 pounds in dues to the Company. They were thus left with but 22,000 pounds, probably as many dollars of our money, out of which the expenses of their trading over two years had to come. Notwithstanding these considerable profits they were stung with a sense of the injustice of the treatment meted out to them, for they were deeply conscious of the value of their operations for the colony, and, because of the excellence of its peltries, of the worth of the new fur area tapped. Radisson says the factors at the fur Company's stores said to him :

" In which country have you been ? From whence doe you come ? For wee never saw the like. From whence did come such excellent castors ? Since your arrivall is come into our magazin very near 600,000 pounds Tournois of that filthy merchandize, which will be prized like gold in France, and them were the very words they said to me."

Indignant at the wrong done him, Groseilliers, manifestly the important personage in the partnership, resorted to measures to secure redress. He went to France to appeal to the authorities, but was met with fair words and promises, and no remedy. It may be presumed that he tried to organize a venture direct from the mother-country to Hudson Bay, but failed. His next scheme was just such an expedition financed by the French colony at Cadiz in Spain, which would not be held so firmly in the meshes of the monopoly granted to the merchants trading to Quebec. In this he appeared to have succeeded, for a vessel was to meet him with the necessary goods at Isle Percée, south of Gaspé Basin, in the spring. He hastened to New France to bring Radisson and seven other men, doubtless skilled voyageurs, to complete his party. When he reached Isle Percée in a small ship from the St. Lawrence, ships had just arrived from France, but not the expected bark. A Jesuit priest, newly arrived, informed him that his plans were known, that their object was to destroy the colony on the St. Lawrence and wrong its people, that is by diverting the fur trade through Hudson Strait to the mother-country, and that he had secured an order which would put an end to their scheme.

It is interesting to speculate on what would have been the course of our history had Groseilliers's insight been appreciated at the French court and had his plan been allowed to come to its natural fruition. Would the French have secured a practical monopoly of the fur trade of North America for the homeland, with all the wealth which that involved ? With the furs of the forest belt passing to Europe by way of Hudson Strait, would the colony on the St. Lawrence, while not losing all its fur traffic, have had to settle down to agriculture like the English settlements on the Atlantic coast ? Under such conditions would a tide of settlers have flowed into the lower valley of the St. Lawrence, and perhaps have brought about a different decision when the great struggle with the English for the mastery of the continent came to its crisis ? Had Canada remained in the hands of the French, would the English colonies have remained within the British Empire ? It is enough for us that the rejection of Groseilliers's scheme was to give to the English an entrance to the great fur region of the North, and to be decisive for the history of the Canadian North-West.

2.—THE FIRST ADVENTURERS OF ENGLAND
TRADING INTO HUDSON BAY

Groseilliers and Radisson were nonplussed at the position of their affairs and wandered on in their little ship of Quebec to try to do business at St. Pierre in Cape Breton and at Canso with what goods they had with them ; but they were " threatened to be burned by the French." Groseilliers, who was really the master mind shaping events, now divulged to Radisson a plan which had been maturing in his fertile brain. It was to have recourse to New England. The " brothers " sailed on to Port Royal at the present Annapolis in Nova Scotia, then an English fort, and were invited by some English shipmasters on to Boston. There the sharp Yankees saw at once the significance of their plans. An expedition was arranged for the approaching spring. It reached Hudson Strait, but its navigator, who was accustomed to fetch sugar from Barbados, took fright at the icebergs, though, as Radisson remarks facetiously, they really looked like sugar-candy. He insisted that the ship was not fitted out to endure a winter in the Arctic, and turned her homeward. A contract involving two ships was now arranged for the coming year, but the loss of one of them on Sable Island prevented it from being implemented.

It was an era of expansion for England, and a group was gathered around the throne of Charles II., intent on developing the colonies in the interest of the trade of the mother-country. In 1664 plans were laid to conquer the Dutch colony of New Netherland, the prospective conquest being granted as a colony to the Duke of York, the King's brother. A commission with an extensive mission was sent out with the warships, and took part in the capture of New Amsterdam, whose name was changed to New York, August 27, 1664. One member of the commission, Colonel George Cartwright, was sent up the Hudson River ; he seized Fort Orange, and incidentally sealed a friendship between the English and the Iroquois which later proved of great value in the rivalry of the Englishmen with the French on the St. Lawrence. A part of the commission's duty was to settle boundary disputes between the English colonies and to report on the colonial governments of New England. From February till May 1665 it sat in Boston, and George Cartwright came to know of Groseilliers's plan to open a trade by Hudson Strait with the fur region south of the Bay. He induced the Frenchmen to proceed to England, and there he put them into relation with the powerful group of expansionists which surrounded the throne.

Among these was Sir George Carteret. He belonged to a family whose seat was in Jersey. During the civil war he had been Lieutenant-Governor of the island, and made it a base for naval operations against the party of Parliament. He had entertained Prince Charles when he fled from England, and at the Restoration he was placed in high offices. He was at this time a member of the Privy Council and Treasurer of the Navy. When the Duke of York received the proprietorship of the colony of New York, in anticipation of the capture of New Netherland, he granted the region between the Hudson and the Delaware to Sir George, whose connection with Jersey accounts for the name New Jersey given to the colony. A kinsman, Sir Philip Carteret, was sent out as Governor.

It was an ill time for new ventures, what with the Dutch war and the plague. The King, Charles II., was in Oxford to escape from the scourge raging in London. There Sir George Carteret, whose offices in the State and in the royal household gave him direct access to the throne, laid Groseilliers's scheme before His Majesty, and presented the two Frenchmen to the King. Charles II. was much more interested in the economic welfare of England than has been suspected of that idle monarch. Groseilliers and Radisson were well received, and in the meantime were quartered at the King's expense at Oxford, and later at Windsor, with an allowance of forty shillings a week. Sir Peter Colleton, afterwards a stockholder in the Hudson's

Bay Company, was given charge of the plan for an expedition, but the Dutch blockade of the Thames and the attack on Chatham (1667) made it futile to attempt anything. Meanwhile there seems to have been an attempt made by a Frenchman named La Tourette to win Groseilliers away from the English. An inquiry was held. La Tourette insisted that he had no connection with the Dutch Government, which the English thought was in the plot, nor with the French ambassador in Holland. Groseilliers was able to free himself of all suspicion of complicity. This was in the autumn of 1666. Peace came with the treaty of Breda, signed on July 10, 1667, but it was too late to allow of a voyage that year. It was not till the Frenchmen's third year in England that any definite steps could be taken.

The expedition took on the aspect of a national enterprise. The chief ship, the *Eaglet*, was transferred from the Royal Navy under instructions from the King. The order for the transfer shows that the Englishmen, allured by the representations of the two Frenchmen, not only envisaged a fur trade, but thought they were in sight of the discovery of a passage to the Western Sea, or as it was also called, the Southern Sea. "Whereas [Our] Dear Cousin Pr. Rupert, George Duke of Albemarle, William Earle of Craven & others, having been informed by two Frenchmen who have lived long in Canada & have been up in ye great lakes that lye in the midst of that part of America. That there is great hope of finding some passage through those Lakes into the South Sea . . . & have accordingly resolved to set out ships for a further discovery thereof ; and the better to enable them in that their undertaking they have humbley besought Us to Lend them one of Our small Vessells for the first expedicion only . . ." orders shall be given for the *Eaglet*, ketch, to be delivered to them. The Englishmen of that day were blissfully ignorant of the geography of the Great Lakes ; they therefore fell an easy prey to the designs of the Frenchmen and to their picture of the coveted English water-way to the profitable commerce of the Far East. But Groseilliers and Radisson knew the country. Radisson had probably reached the Mississippi by way of Lake Michigan and Green Bay (Stinking Lake), and probably believed that that great river flowed into the Western Sea, but both he and Groseilliers had crossed the forest belt from Lake Superior to James Bay ; they knew the dreary distance and the turbulent streams. Their assertion, with a view to establishing a company trading to Hudson Bay, that a water-way might be found through that region to the Pacific, writes them down as company promoters of the most artful sort. It should, however, be remembered in their favour that their representations as to the abundance of the furs in the forest and their superior quality were true, and that the plan of establishing a trade in furs by way of Hudson Strait was thoroughly sound.

The Adventurers (to use a term common in the business world of that day) found the money to refit the *Eaglet*, Captain William Stannard in command, and to equip the *Nonsuch*, ketch, whose captain was Zachary Guillam, a New Englander.   Under the direction of the Frenchmen they gathered an assortment of goods for the trade in furs, which was to bring them, as they believed, a substantial profit and, as they hoped, would incidentally cover the expense of finding the water-way through the continent to the Pacific Ocean, and lead to the larger profits of a trade with the Far East.   Their instructions, signed by Prince Rupert, the King's cousin; by the Duke of Albemarle, better known as George Monck, who had effected the Restoration and placed Charles on the throne; by the Earl of Craven, one of the King's most trusted ministers; by Sir George Carteret, Privy Councillor, Commissioner of the Board of Trade and Vice-Chamberlain to the King's Household; by James Hayes, Prince Rupert's secretary; and by Sir Philip Colleton, show to what an extent the great of the land were behind the enterprise. They also show clearly the plans and the hopes entertained.   The ships were to sail " to such place as Mr. Gooseberry [the translation of the French Groseilliers] and Mr. Raddison shall direct . . . in ordr to trade with the Indyans there."   On the advice of the Frenchmen, the goods were to be delivered by the ships' captains cautiously in small parcels of no more than fifty pounds out of each ship at a time.   The wampum (shells used by the Indians of the St. Lawrence as currency), bought by the Adventurers from the Frenchmen, was to be delivered by the ships' captains " by small quantityes with like Caution as the other goods."   On arrival at their destination the ships' crews were to build a fortification on shore, with quarters for men and goods.   As soon as commodities of considerable value were got together, they were to be put on the *Nonsuch*, and Captain Stannard was to take over her command, placing Guillam in charge of the *Eaglet*, and to sail home, that very summer, with Groseilliers. Stannard was urged to bring home samples of copper or any other mineral that might be found.   Captain Guillam and Radisson were to winter in the country along with Thomas Gorst, the accountant of the expedition, and to trade with the Indians.   A ship was to be sent out to them in the following summer.

Explicit instructions were given in the matter of the North-West Passage :

" You are to have in yor thoughts the discovery of the Passage into the South sea and to attempt it as occasion shall offer with the advice and direction of Mr. Gooseberry and Mr. Raddison, or one of them, they having told us that it is but 7 daies padling or sailing from the River where they intend to trade and Harbour unto the stinking Lake [Green Bay, Lake Michigan] and not above 7 daies more to the streight wch leads into that sea they call the South sea and thence but forty or fifty leagues to the sea it selfe, in all wch streight it Ebbs and flowes by meanes whereof the passage up and downe will be quicke, and if it be possible you are to gett so much light in this matter before the returne of the *Nonsuch* Ketch as may encourage us the next spring to send a vessell on purpose for that discovery."

Should it happen that the place and trade indicated by the Frenchmen could not be found, the ships were to sail for Newfoundland, and to dispose of any goods possible to the people there ; the remainder was to be taken to New Jersey (Sir George Carteret's colony), where Philip Carteret, Sir George's kinsman, the Governor, would give advice as to whether the better market would be New Jersey or New York. It was the custom of those times for any one to give goods as a " venture " to captains sailing to foreign markets. The instructions directed that such goods should not be sold otherwise than the wares of those undertaking the expedition, that is, through Groseilliers and Radisson, who were to play the part of traders and interpreters. The English character of the expedition was preserved by placing Stannard and Guillam in command, but the Instructions show plainly the important part to be played by the Frenchmen. " Lastly, we desire and require you to use the said Mr. Gooseberry and Mr. Raddison wth all manner of civility and courtesy and to take care that all your company soe beare a perticuler respect unto them, they being the persons upon whose credit wee have undertaken this expedition, which we beseech Almighty God to prosper."

The ships sailed from Gravesend in the Thames on June 3, 1668. They were struck by a storm four hundred leagues from the north of Ireland. As the *Eaglet* was of low board, she suffered most, and her masts had to be cut to save her. Captain Stannard returned to England, bringing Radisson with him—a much disappointed man, surely. Captain Guillam brought the *Nonsuch*, with Groseilliers, his passenger, through the gale and reached Resolution Island at the entry of Hudson Strait on the 4th of August. On the 19th he entered Hudson Bay at Digges Islands. On the 31st he cast anchor at an island in 57° 49' north latitude, which would be south of The Sleepers, and he reached the East Main on the 4th of September in 55° 30', therefore north of Great Whale River. Thereafter he must have followed the coast, searching for the part in which Groseilliers had summered five years before. He was in our Rupert Bay on the 25th of the month, and on the 29th cast anchor in the Nemiskau River of the Indians, naming it Rupert's River after the Prince. There, Charles Fort was built, so called after the reigning sovereign, who had done so much for the expedition.

Little is known of the doings at the fort during the winter 1668–69. Certainly Groseilliers would be the directing mind. He knew the language of the natives, and doubtless had met many of them during his previous visit ; indeed, he had led them to expect his return in a great ship. The welcome given to the Englishmen would be largely the welcome accorded to him, as a former acquaintance. It would be his part to show the natives how to cure the skins, and all the trading would be done by him. It may be regarded as the contribution of the Englishmen that a treaty was made with the Indians securing them, in return for presents given as purchase money, the right to trade and the possession of the region. This, with the proclamation of the land as belonging to the King of England and the planting of the King's arms, would complete the taking possession of the country. But even here the Frenchman would figure as the interpreter and go-between, speaking for both parties and drawing up the terms of the first of a long line of Indian treaties giving room to the White Man, while recognizing the rights of the Red. Even in building the post to afford some degree of comfort in the Arctic winter Groseilliers would be the controlling force.

In thus placing Groseilliers, and not Radisson, in dominance at Charles Fort Fate was just, for while Radisson's *Narratives* place their writer in the front of the stage, they do not conceal the decisive part played by the elder man. He had already been up to the Great Lakes when he invited Radisson to join him in another voyage. The journey across the fur forest to James Bay must have arisen out of his greater intimacy with the trading Indians of those parts. When the French Governor inflicted resentful penalties on the pair for scorning his prohibitions and going without a licence, it was Groseilliers that crossed to France to seek redress. There he attempted to form a French company trading directly with Hudson Bay, and failing in that, he tried to form a company of Frenchmen living in Cadiz and somewhat beyond the influence of the prohibitions of the French court. The plan of going to New England, which led the pair to England, was his. When the documents of the Hudson's Bay Company bracket the two names, Groseilliers's always comes first. A silent man of decision, he has fallen into the background with the passage of centuries and left Radisson, his publicity agent, in the limelight. It is the reward of one who writes about himself that subsequent generations take him at his own estimate.

Such definite information of this the pioneer expedition to Hudson Bay as is existent is in a letter dated at Deal, October 11, 1669, and written by one Richard Watts to the Secretary of State. " Last Satterday night came in the *Nonsuch* Ketch from the North-west passage. Since I have endeavoured to find the proceedes of their voyage, only understand they were environed with ice about 6 monethes, first haleing theire ketch on shore, and building them a house. They carryed provisions on shore and brewed Ale and beere and provided against the cold which was their work : They report the natives to bee civill and say Beaver is very plenty." Leaving Charles Fort in the warmth of June, the ketch arrived in the Downs on 9th October.

Meanwhile the Adventurers had not been inactive. They transferred the *Eaglet* back to the Navy, as being of too low board for the rough seas of the north Atlantic, and asked for the *Hadarine*, a pink, in her stead, " shee being a Vessell of less worth to his Majesty and much more fit [than] the other for the said expedition." James, Duke of York, for the Admiralty, reported that the *Hadarine* was on active service and not available. King Charles then ordered some other ship to be provided, and the *Wivenhoe* was placed at the service of the Adventurers. Captain Stannard was put in command, with Robert Newland for mate. Presumably the same Adventurers who had stocked the ships of 1668 with goods entered this new venture. The captain was provided with a map of the Bay made by one Norwood according to Captain Thomas James's description. The ship sailed in May 1669, Radisson on board, and went to Rupert River. Thereafter she followed the coast westward, doubtless in search for the Frenchmen's great river leading to the Great Lakes! She must have entered the Albany and Severn rivers. She is definitely reported as entering the estuary of the Nelson, Port Nelson as it was called. There the land was taken possession of in the name of the King, and the royal arms placed in a suitable position. This would be in the presence of Radisson, who, as will be seen, later chose to ignore the fact. The *Wivenhoe* arrived in England towards the end of the year.

Many ships have plied to and from Hudson Bay in the last two hundred and sixty years and more. Some brought the first settlers to the Red River ; all brought the means of subsistence to many men, White and Red, but none was more epoch-making than the little ketch, the *Nonsuch*, and after it the *Wivenhoe*, for they effected the first direct and vital contact of the North-West with hoary Europe—a contact which brought about a trade and a connection which, however changed in aspect, are with us to this day.

Chapter III

ENGLISH AND FRENCH STRUGGLE FOR THE POSSESSION OF HUDSON BAY, 1670–1713

THE wealth in furs of the great northern forest of America was now known, and the several approaches to it were not only explored, but held as possessions. The French rejoiced in the magnificent waterway afforded by the St. Lawrence and its tributaries, down which trading Indians brought the furs to them. The English enjoyed a much nearer approach to the fur forest through Hudson Bay; Charles Fort was on the very border of the woods. Of especial importance was the English claim to the estuary of the Nelson, for it became the outlet for the furs of the wide stretch of forest from Lake Winnipeg to the Rocky Mountains, at that time far beyond the reach of the French. At James Bay the English could claim the country by right of the discoveries of Henry Hudson and Thomas James, and in virtue of a settlement effected on the Rupert, and of the purchase by treaty with the Indians of the region and of the right to trade. Yet, though the French, at least none other than Groseilliers and Radisson, had not explored the territory, French trade had penetrated to some parts of it, notably to the valley of the Moose and the Nottaway rivers, and to the upper Rupert. Indian tribes there passed their furs southward to their neighbours, who delivered them to the middlemen, traders with the French at Montreal, at Three Rivers, and at Tadoussac at the confluence of the Saguenay and the St. Lawrence. Consequently the establishment of English posts on James Bay, the Bottom of the Bay, as it was called, appeared to the French in the light of an encroachment.

For nearly a century the traders of the two nations, indeed the Governments of France and England themselves, strove to win control and possession of the wealth-producing region which lay between their several water-ways. The French aimed at drawing the Indians southward by lake and stream to that great trunk water-route, the St. Lawrence. The English persuaded the natives to pass with their furs downstream northward to the Bay. For forty-three years the centre of the struggle was in Hudson Bay itself, and for the short route through Hudson Strait. In the subsequent half-century the forest belt itself was the scene of the rivalry. As the French trade and claims were pushed by the highly centralized Government of New France, the English trade and rights could only have been protected and made good by a powerful corporation actively supported by the Government of England. That corporation was the Company of Adventurers of England trading into Hudson's Bay, in short, the Hudson's Bay Company. As the Englishmen, and indeed the English King, hoped to find a way through the continent to the Pacific Ocean and the marts of the East, a Charter was issued under the Great Seal, not only incorporating the Company, but envisaging the establishment of a colony which should consolidate the claim of England to the region. The colony was called Rupert's Land.

I.—" ONE OF OUR PLANTATIONS OR COLONIES IN AMERICA, RUPERT'S LAND "

The Hudson's Bay Company's Charter, May 2, 1670

The *Nonsuch* arrived in the Downs on October 9, 1669, and shortly thereafter reached the Thames with a rich cargo of furs. Captain Guillam's report on the North-West Passage is not on record. It must have brought disappointment—a disappointment tempered by the success of the trade in furs. Those who had undertaken the venture hastened to stake out an exclusive claim to this trade, and to a land through which a water-way might yet be found to the Pacific. On 21st October a royal Grant was made to Sir Edward Hungerford, Sir John Robinson, and four others, of all the seas, straits, bays, rivers, lakes, and creeks within Hudson Strait, with all the lands, lakes, rivers, and the like not now occupied by the subjects of any other Christian Prince, with the sole commerce to the said places, and all mines and minerals and royal and other fishing, the same to be held as of the manor of East Greenwich, on the rent of two elks and two black beaver yearly. This document is really the first draft of the Hudson's Bay Company's Charter. It was probably drawn hastily in the name of a few men to anticipate a rush into the trade of Hudson Bay, and to preserve the rights of the first Adventurers till a mature scheme could be prepared. That scheme received royal sanction on May 2, 1670, a little more than six months later, and the Hudson's Bay Company came into being.

By a piece of good fortune it is possible to judge how far the men in the first ventures were also Charter members of the Hudson's Bay Company. Certain goods were left on the hands of the Adventurers from the miscarriage of the *Eaglet*, and after the two ships, the *Nonsuch* and the *Wivenhoe*, returned. These were thrown into the first venture of the Chartered Company and entered on the credit side of the Company's Ledger Book No. 1. All but two became members of the Hudson's Bay Company, allowances being made for the following changes. The Duke of Albemarle, better known as George Monck, who had been the means of effecting the Restoration and putting Charles II. on the throne, died three months before the

Charter was issued. His son Christopher held his interest when the Chartered Company was formed.* Sir George Carteret, whose contribution towards the first ventures was of the first moment, was not a Charter member; his son Sir Philip Carteret held his stock and was a Charter member of the Company. On Sir Philip's death in 1672 the stock reverted to the father. Sir George was for a time Deputy-Governor of the Company.

Inasmuch as all overseas enterprise on the major scale among such nations as the English, the Dutch, and the French was at that time carried on by companies with the royal or some governmental sanction, it was natural for the Adventurers to seek a charter from the sovereign. On the second day of May 1670, King Charles II., of his royal prerogative and, as was the practice in Stuart times, without consulting Parliament, granted incorporation to "The Merchant Adventurers of England trading into Hudson's Bay." The patent, issued under the Great Seal, gave two privileges to the Company—the monopoly of the trade through Hudson Strait, and exclusive possession of any territory to be reached through the Strait, which they might discover and occupy and settle with a view to that trade. The territory was to be one of His Majesty's colonies or plantations, and was to bear the name Rupert's Land. As has been said, it was hoped a strait or succession of rivers would be discovered leading south-westward to the mild climate of the Pacific, and so to the envied marts of the East. Therefore the territory on either side of the water-route, in whatever latitude it might be, would be included in the Company's colony of Rupert's Land, provided it were not already conceded to another English colony and were not already the territory of some Christian prince. The approach to the region must, of course, be through Hudson Strait. In the light of subsequent history the rights conceded to the Company and the territory granted were great indeed.

Modern views of monopolies and of the prerogatives of the King apart from Parliament must not be allowed to put the Charter in an unhistorical setting. To begin with, colonies created out of the royal domain were for long constituted by an act of the Crown. It was not till well on in the nineteenth century that the feeling that they should be established by Act of Parliament arose. Then, too, that memorable document, the Charter of the Hudson's Bay Company, is but one of a hoary line of patents granted to English merchant adventurers from the day of Edward III. onward. At the beginning the charters envisaged, not companies in England, but

* The £82, 5s. 3d., the value of goods, " the remains of a former cargo," mentioned in the ledger, must have stood to the credit of George Monck, the first Duke of Albemarle, who figures in the King's order for the transfer of the *Eaglet* (see at p. 48. The son Christopher was at that time but sixteen years of age.) When the ledger was written up about 1675 this sum was credited to Christopher (the second), Duke of Albemarle, who personally contributed £217, 14s. 9d. to the first outfit of the Chartered Company, thus holding the £300 credited to him. The participation of Sir George Carteret is not capable of the same proof, but it is more than probable that the payment credited to his son of £20 in 1667, and the three payments of £30, £100, and £50 towards the outfit of 1668 were really the father's, but placed by him to the credit of his son at the formation of the Company.

Englishmen abroad trading at some centre. The patent granted to the merchant adventurers at Bruges in Flanders, or at Hamburg, was devised to bring all English merchants trading in the particular city under a general control. It gave them a system of government and provided law courts for all English traders making the city their resort. When such merchants came to operate in common in England a charter gave them a governing body, but no law courts. When Europe entered the age of overseas enterprise, whether of trade or settlement, the English, Dutch, and French Governments avoided the responsibility of establishing, and the difficulties of administering, distant colonies by granting the territory involved to a company, with the obligation of founding and managing the colony and its trade, both of which were expected, not only to enrich the company, but to prove beneficial to the motherland. In England, the Crown, in virtue of the royal prerogative, granted to the great colonizing companies, as, for example, the Virginia Company, the possession of the land and natural resources, and prescribed systems of government for the company both at home and abroad. The Hudson's Bay Company's Charter was no exception to this practice.

The royal Patent granted wide privileges to the Company, but it imposed upon it the obligation of establishing a trade and the settlements incident to it—these last to be " reputed as one of our plantations or colonies in America, called Rupert's Land." Connection with the Crown was to be visibly preserved by the practice of " yielding and paying yearly to us and our successors, for the same, two elks and two black beavers whensoever, and as often as we, our heirs and successors, shall happen to enter into the said countries, territories and regions, hereby granted " ; and by the stipulation that the laws of the colony were not to be repugnant to the laws of England.

The Charter incorporated certain men named to be one body corporate and politic under the title of "The Governor and Company of Adventurers of England trading into Hudson's Bay." It provided for a Government at home which should control both the Company in England and its colony or colonies overseas. The stockholders were to assemble in a " General Court " for the transaction of the business of the Company, and in particular to elect its officers. On November 17, 1673, a General Court ordained that every one hundred pounds of stock should have one vote, members being allowed to vote by proxy, while none should be chosen of the Committee who had not at least two hundred pounds of stock. According to the Charter, one of the Company was to be elected Governor, Prince Rupert, the King's cousin, being named such for the meantime. The Governor and Company assembled in a " General Court " were to elect a Committee of seven which, together with the Governor, should have the management of all business, subject of course to the conditions laid down in the Charter. To get the Company under way the first Committee was named in the Patent, to wit, Sir John Robinson, Sir Richard Vyner, Sir Peter Colleton,

James Hayes, John Kirke, Francis Millington, and John Portman. (Sir John Robinson was made Deputy-Governor by the Committee.) Power was given by the Charter to draw up oaths to be administered to the officers on coming into their several offices, as well as to members of the Company.

In the charters granted to the great overseas colonization companies, and even those granted to individual proprietors such as William Penn, who founded Pennsylvania, the lands, mines, minerals, fisheries, and other natural resources, were given outright to be held in " free and common soccage as of our manor of East Greenwich," or Windsor, as the case might be. In the Hudson's Bay Company's Charter it is East Greenwich. The granting of such wide territory and such rich resources was no mere favouritism. It carried with it the obligation first of all to put out the private capital to make the natural resources available, and then to use these to establish settlements and to govern the colony. In this connection it should be noted that the group of men to whom this Charter was granted had already risked large sums of money, and had thereby laid the foundation of a trade which promised, and indeed which proved, to be of great value to the mother-country ; and they were prepared to finance a colony out of the profits.

In the case of the Atlantic colonies the ownership and control of the soil and of the natural resources under these conditions was never regarded as illegal, and it seemed perfectly natural, when the Crown displaced the companies and proprietors, that the resources of the individual colony should continue to be used for its administration and development. In the case of the Hudson's Bay Company, would-be rivals and dispossessors, such as the North West Company and later the Government of Canada, questioned the validity of the Charter and the extensive privileges conferred by it, but these were never held in doubt by the law officers of the Crown in England. It was always the quiet assumption of the English Government that the Company must develop the trade of the country granted, and effect such settlements as the climate and the conditions of the land would permit.

As to the government of the colony of Rupert's Land, it was in the first place entrusted to the Governor and the Company, duly assembled in a General Court, " to make, ordain and constitute such and so many reasonable laws, constitutions, orders and ordinances as to them or the greater part of them . . . shall seem necessary and convenient for the good government of the said Company, and of all governors of colonies, forts, plantations, factors, masters, mariners and other officers to be employed in any of the territories." They could impose penalties and fines, the same to be at the service of the Company, but the laws, constitutions, orders, and ordinances must be " reasonable and not contrary or repugnant, but as near as may be agreeable to the laws, statutes or customs of this our realm." So far only the control of the employees of the Company is envisaged, but the concession included sovereign control of much more. " All

lands, islands, territories, plantations, forts, fortifications, factories
or colonies . . . shall be immediately under the power and command of the said Company . . . saving the faith and allegiance due
to be performed " to the sovereign. In this sphere, much wider
than the Company and its employees, " The Governor and Company
shall have liberty, full power and authority to appoint and establish
Governors and all other officers to govern them." Further, a
sketch is given of the system under which plantations and colonies
shall be administered. A Governor with a Council is to be constituted, and they " may have power to judge all persons belonging
to the said Governor and Company or that shall live under them,
in all cases, whether civil or criminal, according to the laws of this
kingdom, and to execute justice accordingly." Power is given to
Chief Factors, where there may be no judicature, to transmit cases
to a plantation where such judicial machinery may exist. To
defend the colony, the Company may make peace or war with any
people whatsoever that are not Christians, or upon any nation whatever, whether Christian or not, that may " interrupt, wrong or
injure them in their said trade." They may build forts and colonies
" as they in their discretion shall think fit and requisite." In the
interest of internal order they may inflict punishments for misde-
meanours or impose fines for the breach of their orders.

In the feudal system the power to make laws, administer justice,
and make war were, and they are still counted *regalia*, sovereign or
royal rights. To these in modern times has been added the possession of all natural resources. All these were conceded to the
Hudson's Bay Company. By their patent the sovereign rights
passed out of the hand of the King into those of the Company, as
they passed also to the chartered companies which built up the
Atlantic colonies. The sphere in which these rights were to be
exercised was necessarily vaguely indicated. In the other charters
the territorial concessions usually involved a definite and known
part of the Atlantic coast, described as being between such and such
parallels of latitude, while the western limit might be fixed at so
many miles inland. The limits of the Hudson's Bay Company's
territory were much more vaguely stated, as was natural, since the
area concerned was but surmised. What is definite is that the
Company's colony and trade were to be established through Hudson
Strait.

> We have given, granted and confirmed . . . the sole trade and commerce
> of all those seas, straits, bays, rivers, lakes, creeks, and sounds in whatsoever
> latitude they be, that lie within the entrance of the straits, commonly called
> Hudson's Straits, together with all the lands and territories upon the countries,
> coasts, confines of the seas, bays, lakes, rivers, creeks and sounds aforesaid,
> that are not already possessed by or granted to any of our subjects, or pos-
> sessed by the subjects of any other Christian Prince.

In view of the prospect held out by Groseilliers and Radisson that
a large river would lead to the Great Lakes, and another to a strait

leading to the South Sea, it must be concluded that the phrase " seas, straits, bays, rivers, lakes . . . in whatsoever latitude found," was drafted to give to the Company the land on the whole of the water-way to the Pacific, should it be discovered. The northern limits of the colony-to-be were partially known under the names of Hudson Strait and Bay. All the other limits were unknown and were to be written in by history. From this point of view the Charter partook of the nature of a blank cheque, the sum of the area conceded to be written in when trade and discovery through Hudson Strait should reach their natural limits. Accordingly we must examine the limits of the trade monopoly granted. It included the entire trade which should be developed through Hudson Strait "to the territory and places aforesaid," but also the whole and entire trade and traffic to and from :

all havens, bays, creeks, rivers, lakes and seas into which they [the Company] shall find entrance or passage by water or land out of the territories, limits or places aforesaid ; and to and with all other nations inhabiting any the coasts adjacent to the said territories, limits and places which are not already possessed as aforesaid [that is by other English subjects or another Christian Prince]."

This means that the Company could penetrate by water and land as far as it pleased, always provided that its trade was through Hudson Strait. Had they found a way by water to Alaska, or by land to the British Columbia of to-day, and thence to China, they would have enjoyed the monopoly of that trade, and by inference, if they had planted colonies on the Pacific coast for the prosecution of the trade, these would probably have been counted within the limits of Rupert's Land. As it proved, the Company's dream of an easy route by land or water to the Pacific was insubstantial. There was no passage to a mild climate where a prosperous colony could be established. The vision of settlements on a large scale, along with the route to China, faded as the Company found itself confined to the inhospitable climate of the Bay. Only posts manned by its servants existed until the second decade of the eighteenth century, when Lord Selkirk, that embodiment of idealism and shrewd business, planned the Red River Settlement. In the meantime Rupert's Land was a series of fur posts whose trade expanded from decade to decade ever farther into the interior. The form of government sketched by the Charter was so far followed that the heads of the " plantations " on James Bay and at Port Nelson were " governors," each summoning his " council " when the business of the region required it, and especially when he needed support in dealing with delinquencies and crimes.

A sketch of the early organization of the Company is essential to the understanding of the part played by it in the history of the North-West. The Charter ordained that the Company should be administered by a Governor, a Deputy-Governor, and a Committee of seven. It named Prince Rupert, the King's cousin, Governor for the meantime. That dashing cavalry officer of the army of Charles I. was now a veteran fifty-one years of age, stalking grimly through the scenes of gaiety in the Whitehall of his cousin King Charles the Second. He moved among the young set that surrounded the throne, but was not of it. In the eye of men about the court " he was tall and his manners were ungracious ; he had a dry hard-favoured visage, and a stern look, even when he wished to please ; but when he was out of humour, he was the true picture of reproof." His chief recreation was found in his private laboratory carrying on experiments in science and working out mathematical problems. Though he took no part in politics, he was deeply interested in the welfare of England. He appears to have given himself heart and soul to the Company and to Rupert's Land, England's latest colony overseas. Of the thirteen General Courts of his time of which we have record, eleven appear to have been held in his lodgings in Spring Gardens, Whitehall, and he was the only Governor of the Company for many years to sign all the commissions of the officers overseas and all the letters of instructions to them and to the captains of the ships. He died on November 29, 1682, still Governor of the Company.

As head of the Company Prince Rupert presided at the general meetings of the stockholders, who, according to the Charter, were to " hold court for the Company " (hence the name General Court) and control its policies. For a few years General Courts were held frequently. As was natural in the early stages when the machinery for carrying on business was being framed, their influence was steady and decisive. For example, a General Court held " at Sr. Robert Vyner's " on October 24, 1671, " ordered that upon the first Tuesday in December next about three thousands pounds weight of beaver bee putt to sale by the Candle [that is, by auction, bids being received till a lighted candle, an inch in length, went out] & the like quantity to be putt to Sale about the 12th of March next following ; and public notice to be given that no more shall bee sould before March nor that any second Sale shall be without publicke Notice first be given thereof." Thus was inaugurated the system of two annual sales. The sale here contemplated for December was held at " Mr. Garway's Coffee house " on January 24, 1672. A meal with wine was usually provided at the Company's expense to members and purchasers. There was much wisdom in limiting the sales to two, and especially in guaranteeing that there would be no furs sold between whiles. It stabilized the trade. More important still, so long as the Company had a satisfactory control of the fur market, it tended to give the purchasing furriers a practical monopoly in the months between sale and sale, and so moderated hostility to the more far-reaching monopoly of the Company.

The particularities of the preparation for the above-mentioned sale were arranged by the Committee, whose Chairman in these early years was the Deputy-Governor. They decided on the place of the sale and appointed a small committee to see to the sorting and packing of the furs. Mr. Bayly, Governor returned from the Bay, Mr. Radisson and Mr. Groseilliers as experts, were to advise and assist. Sorting furs in a dingy warehouse in London, the two Frenchmen, who had gloried in the wild life of adventure on the streams and in the forests of the North-West, must surely have chafed at the cage within which circumstances had placed them.

At a General Court held on November 21, 1671, in the Tower of London, of which Sir John Robinson, Deputy-Governor of the Company, was " Lieutenant," arrangements were made to borrow money from Mr. Portman, a member of the Company, to pay the wages of the ship *Wivenhoe*. Many such items in the Minutes bring out the methods of financing employed by the Company. After the manner of the early adventurers each expedition was treated as a separate venture, the dividend being declared after the furs were sold. Liquid money was got by borrowing at 6 per cent. from the members themselves. It must have been for simplicity's sake that the Company had recourse later to financial firms like Stephen Evance & Company. Its credit was so good that loans were freely arranged, but in the precarious days of French aggression the Company had to fall back to the old practice of borrowing from its own membership.

At the beginning the Company owned its ships. Accordingly the Committee appointed Captain Guillam to care for them, and the General Court of 21st November required him to dispose of the old provisions, and make an estimate of the ships and supplies necessary for the next venture. After Captain Guillam, an official called the " husband " was appointed to this task. It was, however, an object of concern between whiles, that is, during the winter, how to use the ships to profit. Accordingly, the Company began to hire vessels, paying for the freight and passengers, but it had to revert to owning its ships when the French aggressions made the risks of the voyage great and ran up the rates of freight.

The General Court of November 30, 1671, was concerned about the safe-keeping of its precious Charter. By resolution it was put into the hand of Prince Rupert himself. Later we find it in the care of Sir Robert Cleyton, Lord Mayor of London and treasurer of the Company. Finally an iron chest was secured, and the keys of its great lock and of its two smaller ones were assigned to the keeping of the Deputy-Governor and two members of the Committee. On the occasion of a petition to His Majesty to issue a proclamation devised to protect the monopoly of the Company from interlopers, the Patent was ordered by resolution of the Committee to be taken out and entrusted to an official to display to the Lord Keeper of the Privy Seal, to assure him of the validity of the monopoly claimed by the Company, as the proclamation passed through his hands. Similarly, in the case of the prosecution of interlopers for infringing upon the privileges of the Company, the cherished Charter would be taken out to be produced in court. In the course of time many other prized documents were added, notably those tending to prove

the rights of the English to Hudson Bay as against the French.
Thus the priceless archives of the Hudson's Bay Company came into
being.

Within a very short time the General Court, in truth a very
clumsy governing instrument, ceased to care for the commonplace
needs of the Company and became a simple annual meeting whose
chief business was the election of officers. (General Courts would
be specially called in some crisis, for example, to petition His
Majesty for protection and for redress of wrongs perpetrated by the
French.) This policy was accentuated after the death of the first
Governor, Prince Rupert, in 1682. The new Governor, the Duke of
York, soon to be King under the title of James II., kept somewhat
aloof from the daily affairs of the Company. So too, though to a less
degree, did the third Governor, Lord Churchill, afterwards the Duke
of Marlborough. Though often consulted and often proffering
advice, he found his other duties too insistent to allow of close
attendance on the business of his Company. Thus the Committee
became the real governing machine, and it has continued so to be
ever since. It met oftenest during the busy season from the time of
the expected arrival of the ships about October till the accounts
were settled after the ships departed, usually in the first week in
June.

The Committee carried out punctiliously the policy of requiring
all servants to take an oath of fidelity on their appointment. Its
doings were, of course, recorded in its Minutes, but its orders entered
there were handed in writing to the members or servants affected.
Every officer commissioned by it received his instructions in writing
(the secretary keeping a " faire coppye ") and was required to
report on paper how far he had carried them out. Under Prince
Rupert the commissions and instructions were unfailingly taken to
the Governor to receive his signature in addition to the seal of the
Company, but under the Duke of York they were signed in the
Governor's name by the secretary. Copies of bills of lading, of
inventories of goods in the factories, daily journals of captains and
factors, all contracts and oaths of fidelity were kept by the secretary,
and from early in the eighteenth century went to swell the archives
of the Company. The journals and reports of commissioned servants
were laid before the Committee, later before a sub-committee, when
the secretary would be ordered to make précis for the next meeting.
These précis were carefully studied, and any servant affected by a
report would be summoned before the Committee if he were at
home. Any charges would ultimately be handed to him in writing,
and he would be required to give his answer on paper. After the
Committee had considered these, the servant would be summoned
to appear in his defence, and any necessary witnesses would be called.
After this very formal and elaborate procedure the final decision
would be reached. It was a highly centralized system. Its danger
lay in that it tended to suppress the initiative of the officers, but
it kept the Committee, composed as it was of able business men,

entirely conversant with the course of their affairs. It should, however, be mentioned that the system as carried out gave considerable latitude to trusted servants, always provided they reported themselves to the Committee. Moreover, officers who did remarkably well were from time to time granted bonuses in addition to their salaries. The system seems to have been regarded as cramping to the genius by such Frenchmen as Groseilliers and Radisson, while in the opinion of the English merchants of Montreal, who created the North West Company, no sufficient hope of advancement was offered to attract young men of conspicuous enterprise to the service. Rigid as the system might seem to some, it has carried the Company through more than two centuries and a half of successful business.

It was a matter of incessant concern to the Committee to maintain their monopoly of the trade unimpaired. The seamen on the ships and the servants in the factories could become possessors of precious furs traded with the Indians at no more expense than that of a few beads, toys, jack-knives, or in fact any truck which might take the savage fancy ; but if they had been allowed to do so it would have become an increasing embarrassment to the Company. Moreover, there were technical and legal reasons for making no exceptions, but asserting the monopoly against one and all. At first the servants made a somewhat free use of their opportunities. Captain Guillam, Groseilliers, and Radisson all came home with their private store of furs. The Company met this situation with various devices. Every servant was required to take his oath of fidelity, in which a clause was inserted promising not to engage in private trade. As soon as the ships arrived, even if they were anchored out in the Downs, " waiters " or watchmen were put on board to prevent the secret landing of private stores of furs. When the ships came into the Thames, members of the Committee went out to them to search the lockers, beds, and clothing of one and all. Under certain circumstances concessions had to be made. There were occasions when the factory had traded all its blankets and goods, yet the Indians must not be sent away dissatisfied after their long journey from up country. Seamen were allowed to trade their private possessions, but the pelts had to be placed in the Company's warehouse at home, due compensation being made in cash. Apart from beaver and the more valuable furs, the Company was not against its servants trading, but all such traffic must be with the knowledge of the Factor and pass through the Company's warehouse, to be released only on an order from the Committee.

A much more difficult problem was the interloper, that is the outsider who fitted out an expedition to the Bay. There was a remedy against him in the Charter, if he were English, even if he were of the colonies. Once, when an English firm was fitting out a ship, recourse was had to the law courts and the interloper was required to enter into bonds not to sail into Hudson Bay. To meet the case of English subjects in the American colonies a proclamation was obtained from James II., and orders to the governors in New

England to stop all interloping expeditions. The Company watched Britain and the colonies with anxious eye to maintain its monopoly, and with entire success. It was, however, a problem of an entirely different complexion to control the French, for they did not recognize the Charter, but considered the English trade on the Bay as interloping on a major scale and a menace to the fur trade of the St. Lawrence.

" The Adventurers of England trading into Hudson's Bay " included many of the most distinguished men of the day. Prince Rupert, their Governor, was the King's cousin. He had won fame during the Civil War by the gallant if reckless charges of his body of cavalry. The Earl of Craven was a gallant soldier, a faithful official in the court of Charles's aunt, Elizabeth, Queen of Bohemia, mother of Prince Rupert, and had been sworn of the Privy Council but four years before the Company was formed. Lords Arlington and Ashley were at the time members of that inner cabinet of five of the King's Ministers known as " The Cabal " from the initials of their names. Ashley was " much the ablest of the group." The other adventurers, though many of them titled men, were in the business world of the day. Sir John Robinson, baronet and Deputy-Governor, had been Lord Mayor of London in 1662–63. He was a Member of Parliament from 1660 till his death in 1679–80, and during the same period he was Lieutenant of the Tower. He also held office in the East India Company. Sir Robert Vyner, a baronet, was soon to be Lord Mayor of London. Sir Peter Colleton, another baronet, was one of the most prominent planters of Barbados, already an English colony. He had been a leading figure in the settlement of Carolina (1663), and he was one of the Lords Commissioners for Trade and the Plantations, a committee of the Privy Council which played the part of our Colonial Office. Also of this committee was Sir George Carteret, who had brought Groseilliers and Radisson to the presence of the King. All these stockholders, men in high station, were engrossed in politics and in vast colonial enterprises. They thought they saw much more in the Hudson's Bay Company than a good speculation in trade. They wished to play their part in establishing a great colony on what it was hoped would prove a direct route to the rich marts of Asia, and one which was to be retained in the exclusive hand of England.

When, however, the inhospitable climate of Hudson Bay and the insoluble problem of transportation into the interior of the continent confined the operations of the Company to a series of factories on the shore of the Bay, the management of the trade and the shaping of the destiny of the Company fell to the hands of the lesser men whose talents had been developed in the business of the city and whose minds were centred on trade. Of these the most outstanding was James, from June 1670 Sir James, Hayes, Knight, whose devotion to the affairs of the Company, and whose keen insight and swift decision not only established the prosperity of the " concern," but did much to make good the English claims to the Bay.

Mention may be made of John Kirke of Boston, whose family was associated with the capture of Quebec by the English in Champlain's day (1629), and who became Radisson's father-in-law; and of John Portman, citizen and goldsmith and moneylender.

Since it included at its inception some of the most outstanding men of the day in politics, colonial establishments, and business, the Hudson's Bay Company partook of the nature of a national enterprise. As such it was to assert and maintain the claims and rights of England in the northern seas of America against the French. The English title had hitherto rested on the shadowy ground of discovery and proclamation, as when Captain Thomas Button took possession of Port Nelson by planting the King's arms, and when Captain Thomas James repeated the ceremony at Charlton Island. The Charter, followed by immediate settlements and what passed in the phraseology of the time as "plantations" and colonies, made England's claims substantial.

The Hudson's Bay Company chose as its first Governor overseas one Charles Bayly, a prisoner in the Tower of London; like the Company itself, Bayly came from the immediate entourage of Charles II. Two letters written by him to the King show that he was on speaking terms with him, and references to fatherly admonitions of Charles I. to his son suggest that Bayly may have been an attendant of some sort upon the young Prince and present on the occasions referred to. If so, Bayly did not manage to cast off his sense of responsibility for the morals and welfare of his former charge, though now grown to manhood and seated on the throne. Added to this was a profound religious emotion, which drove him to warn His Majesty to flee from the wrath of God to come. First definite news of Bayly is derived from a letter written to the King on September 4, 1663. The writer had had a vision of the whirlwind of the Lord sweeping down on the kingdom. Those who surrounded the throne were feeding as for the slaughter. When last he, Bayly, had spoken to His Majesty he had promised to warn him of anything which might work his harm. He therefore urged him to avoid rioting and excess, chambering and wantonness. Bayly, for the King's sake, would not like to see his subjects injured, and pleaded that the oppression for which the land mourned should cease. He reproached the King with the blood of good men who had died or were dying in nasty holes and dungeons, and urged His Majesty to repent. The letter ended by stating that he, Bayly, was a prisoner in Newgate jail in Bristol. There he was known as a Quaker. The grounds on which he was incarcerated may be readily surmised.

A few months later Bayly appears above the horizon in the clutches of the Mayor of St. Albans, a borough about twenty-one miles north of London. The necessary warrants were issued and he was imprisoned in the Tower. But years of incarceration did not dampen his regard for the King nor his sense of responsibility for the kingdom. In 1667 he wrote His Majesty again, this time as the bearer of a message from the King of Heaven to the King of England.

" The bearer of this message loves His Majesty, and would not that any harm should befall him, and therefore wishes him to help the innocent, to remember his promises made in secret to the Lord, and in public to his people, and restore liberty of conscience ; then there would be no plot nor conspiracy against him, as it would remove the very ground of evil surmisings, and the nation would be the happiest under heaven." Here he reminded Charles of the counsel given him by his late father.

Bayly was held in prison for " seditious practices," but contrary to the custom of the time by which prisoners saw to their own keep, he fared at the expense of the King. He was never brought to examination, possibly because it might be beyond the lawyers to bring his regard for the King and his sense of responsibility for the kingdom under the head of sedition. In truth he was no more than a nuisance, and the Tower was the easiest way of getting rid of him. In July 1669 he was released on a bail bond to allow him to visit France, but he re-entered the Tower, as the bond required him to do, on his return. He must have won the respect of Sir John Robinson, the Lieutenant of the Tower, and one of the prime movers in the ventures to Hudson Bay. To Robinson must be attributed the subtle scheme at one and the same time to relieve the King of a needless annoyance, to release a good man from prison, and to secure an honest Governor overseas for the Hudson's Bay Company. In December 1669 Bayly petitioned His Majesty for freedom, urging his nigh six years of imprisonment and that he had " demeaned him- selfe during the time of his enlargement in no waies prejudiciall to His Majesty's Government or Dignity and would to the utmost promote the one and quietly live under the other, were his Majesty pleased to grant him his Liberty." Charles was not one to nurse ill-will. In Privy Council " It was Ordered, his Majestie present in Councill, that in case the said Charles Bailly will betake himselfe to the Navigation of Hudsons Bay, and the Places lately Discovered and to be Discovered in those parts, which Sir John Robinson, Lieutenant of the Tower, hath undertaken that he shall doe, Provided the Adventurers in the said Navigation will assure unto him the said Charles Bayly such conditions and allowances as may be agreeable to reason and the nature of his Employment, the Petitioner is there- upon to be sett at Liberty."

Thus the gates of the Tower opened for Charles Bayly, and the prisoner of six years passed out the Governor-to-be of the latest of His Majesty's colonies. In May he left for his command on the King's ship the *Wivenhoe*, under Captain Newland, escorted by the *Nonsuch*, under Captain Guillam. His secretary and accountant, Thomas Gorst, and his interpreters and mouthpieces, Groseilliers and Radisson (probably one in each ship) may be regarded as his staff. The *Nonsuch* sailed to Rupert River, and the *Wivenhoe* to the estuary of the Nelson. There the former prisoner in the Tower, now the representative of the King and the Company on Hudson Bay, performed his first official act ; he planted the King's arms and formally laid claim in the name of His Majesty to what was to prove an almost continental domain. Truly that was an age of transformation scenes.

The intention of the Company was to occupy its concession on a wide front. Bayly was to effect a settlement on the Nelson, while Guillam held Charles Fort on James Bay.* Doubtless there was a Frenchman with each party to act as interpreter. Whichever one, Groseilliers or Radisson, was with Bayly would be witness of the taking possession of the country, in which he later played a strange part. It is probable that Bayly saw few, if any, Indians. At any rate, when a storm forced the *Wivenhoe* out of the river, and adverse winds prevented her return, he sailed away to Charles Fort. Meanwhile Captain Guillam would have arrived in the Rupert. His first act would be to place in position the guns from the Royal Arsenal put at the disposal of the Company by King Charles. Bayly's first concern on his arrival was to renew the league with the Indians by which they surrendered their rights to the region. In connection with this he formally took possession of the country. Thus the title of the English rested on discovery, on formal annexation, on the surrender of the land by the Indians, and finally on actual occupation. In this way the Company sought to make good the rights granted to it in the Charter. But while the land had been in no wise occupied by the French, the people of Canada looked upon it as theirs ; it was surely part and parcel of the valley of the St. Lawrence, with maps and royal Patents to show it ; moreover, their trade had penetrated into the north. While no French had actually been in the country, French goods passed from Indian tribe to Indian tribe, from the valley of the Ottawa into that of the Moose, and from Tadoussac and the Saguenay into the region of Rupert River. In the course of time the conflicting interests of the English and the French must reveal themselves.

Bayly's relations with the Indians proved good. Attash, the chief of the region, called by the Englishmen "The Prince," and two other conspicuous natives, "The Chancellor" and "Peter," visited the fort in a friendly spirit. (Peter's region was the river bank north of Charles Fort.) There was no need to be concerned about the savages. The real cause of anxiety was the daily welfare of the occupants of the post. There was an ample supply of salted provisions, but fresh meat was necessary to ward off scurvy. For that Bayly would rely on his Indian friends, but what with the migratory habits of the caribou, and to a less extent the moose, the Indians of the forest were often face to face with starvation. So it proved this winter. So far from supplying the fort, Prince Attash, the Chancellor, and Peter, and their families, came in almost starved and had to be fed. Finally, Bayly sent them off to seek for game and fish for themselves, and himself ascended the river in a canoe to hunt for his men. He brought down two moose, and the Prince brought in a young deer, while the Chancellor and his squaw appeared with fish and moose.

* For map of James Bay see Sketch-map No. 4 at p. 66.

When the autumn season for geese came there was plenty. The partridge season, which followed, proved a poor one. Parties sent out to the north to Peter's region, to the south to Frenchman's River (the Nottaway), and up and down the Rupert, had the same ill-luck. By December and January the cold was so severe the Englishmen, who appear to have not yet learned how to dress for the climate, could not stay out. Their inactivity and their diet of salted meat left them easy victims to scurvy. On 25th January some relief came when Indians brought in some beaver and moose flesh, but by February the men were down with the fell disease. By the middle of March the situation must have been desperate. Governor Bayly, accompanied by John Abraham, travelled on the ice across Rupert Bay to Point Comfort, the peninsula which forms the western shore of that bay, to procure of the Indians there what fresh or dried meat he could. In his absence a chief, Cuscudidah, arrived with his following. He had probably come down towards the shore for the goose season, but a full guard was placed over the fort. At last the Governor returned with a small supply of moose meat. Fortunately the spring goose season came early and proved exceedingly good. Some of the men must, however, have succumbed to the scurvy. At any rate Captain Newland of the *Wivenhoe* died on this voyage.

To all appearance Governor Bayly played his part with ability, but in one matter he fell short of his instructions. The Company had provided him with a Book of Common Prayer and the Book of Homilies, and had ordered that prayers should be read daily in the fort. This proved too much for the Quaker Governor. Because of his religious scruples Charles Fort went without prayers all through the years of his command.

With spring came the trading season. Bayly now became aware of the existence of a traffic between the Indians and the French. The chief Cuscudidah's people had arrived almost without furs ; they had sent their pelts off to the French. Even so, Cuscudidah's gesture of friendship on coming to the fort seems to have exposed him to the hostility of the Nottaways, the people of the river of that name to the west of the Rupert, who probably played the part of middlemen to the Indians who took the furs down to the French. None the less good returns must have been secured, for three thousand pounds of beaver were offered at the first sale of the Company, that at Garraway's Inn on January 24, 1672, and an equal weight at the spring sale.

The trading over, Charles Fort was closed and all sailed for home. Bayly, Groseilliers, and Radisson next figure in London preparing the furs for the sale. The two Frenchmen's account with the Company shows that they received, from the month before their departure in 1670 to their departure in 1672, £354, 10s. Governor Bayly's salary was £50 a year, so that in what was probably a comparable period he received but £100. The Frenchmen were not being treated illiberally.

During the eighteen years after the granting of the Charter to the

Hudson's Bay Company Stuart sovereigns sat upon the English throne. The Stuart kings had the misfortune to be theorists in a land in which political theorists have always been suspect. The theory in this case, the Divine Right of Kings, was in truth a menace to the liberties of England. It could not be made good in English governance without civil strife. By persistently pressing the issue Charles I. brought himself to the scaffold. Under Charles II. and James II. the situation was essentially the same. It was, however, masked by the reaction against the Puritans and the determination of the people to maintain the monarchy. If they were ever to achieve the triumph of their theory, these kings must have the support of France, the model autocracy of the day, for England herself would be divided. Moreover, they were both drawn to France by personal ties. Their mother Henrietta Maria was a French princess. Their youth had been spent in her country, and their leanings were to Roman Catholicism, for the one was to die a Catholic and the other was openly living as such. Thus they were brought by their political, their intellectual, and their personal needs into sympathy and dependence upon their distant cousin Louis XIV., the model autocrat among the sovereigns of Europe. It was their misfortune, however, that Louis was aiming at the dominance of France upon the Continent and in the world, and that therefore the political, the commercial, and the Protestant interests of England ran counter to the views of the men who sat on the English throne. These national interests of the English people were to lead to the banishment of James, to the enthronement of William of Orange and Mary, with the triumph of constitutional government, and to the great wars which maintained the balance of power in Europe, checked the dominance of France, and closed the reign of " Le Roi Soleil " in gloom. Meanwhile, however, the crowns of England and France were still bound by close ties of friendship and interest. Nor was this appreciated only on the Stuart side. Louis XIV. could only master Europe if England were with him, or at least were kept out of the game. Accordingly he had his reasons for fostering intimate co-operation with his English cousins.

It was on this stage and with this scenery in the background that the drama of the struggle for the trade of Hudson Bay was to be enacted in the years up to 1688. The interests of the French on the St. Lawrence and the English on Hudson Bay were diametrically opposed. Neither people could sit still and let the other possess the Bay. Consequently there was to be a sharp struggle, but one carried on so as not to break up the friendship of the sovereigns or involve the two nations in war. Clashes there will be, but the remedy for these will be sought not in war, but in that more refined struggle which passes under the name of diplomacy.

To the French on the St. Lawrence the entry of the English into Hudson Bay was an act of aggression. The Intendant Talon knew of it on November 10, 1670 (N.S.). He had heard through Algonkins of two European vessels visiting the Bay. He argued that they were

English, brought thither by Groseilliers. He reports the news to Jean-Baptiste Colbert, Marquis de Seignelay, Louis XIV.'s minister, and adds that he will send in adventurers overland to persuade the Crees, who have handed over their furs to the Ottawas as intermediaries, henceforth to bring them down and themselves play the part of middlemen to the savages in their region. In this way the French would be dealing directly with them and would not have to pay the cost of bringing the furs down through Lake Superior—a wide detour of 300 or 400 leagues.* Talon began by sending Father Charles Albanel, a Jesuit, and the Sieur de St. Simon, " a gentleman of Canada recently honoured by the King with a title," north to reconnoitre and to see how far it might be possible for ships to winter in the Bay, with a view to forming an entrepôt on its shores, and with the additional hope of finding a way to the Southern Sea—a hope with which all such ventures at this time were gilded.

According to first intention this expedition, which might be taken by the English for a counter-offensive, was to be informal and private, and might be disowned by the French King should any trouble arise. Father Albanel's presence gave it the aspect of a missionary enterprise. It is true, however, that the good Father had been a missionary at Tadoussac as well as on the south bank of the St. Lawrence for wellnigh twenty years without being led to the Bay by his evangelic zeal. The way was hard ; the portages many, rough, and long ; the people, scattered and restless nomads, were few, no field ripe unto the harvest ; but when the English came, the call was loud to take the Sacraments to the benighted north. The expedition, true to its design of being informal, started without letters from the Government. Father Albanel left Quebec on August 6, 1761 (N.S.). His narrative of the journey, embodied in the *Jesuit Relation* of 1671–72, tells of his difficulties in persuading the Indian intermediaries between the northern savages and the French at Tadoussac to take the party through to their customers towards the Bay, and of his meeting Attimegues and Mistassinis at Lake St. John, who reported ships on the Bay of the North and showed him a hatchet and tobacco which they had traded with the English. All tried to strike him with terror by tales of fighting to the north and of danger to his own life. The result was that the good Father decided to winter on the spot and to send to Quebec for passports. Letters from the Bishop of Quebec and passports from Monsieur de Courcelle, the Governor, and Monsieur Talon, the Intendant, arrived with formal instructions to take possession of the land. On June 1, 1672 (N.S.), the journey was resumed under the guidance of Mistassinis. By dint of many presents and much emphasis on the part played by the French as the saviours of the Indians of the north from the Iroquois, Father Albanel overcame the opposition of the Indian middlemen. His arguments were a curious mixture of religion and trade :

* The reference is to the trade of the region of Missinaibi River, a tributary of the Moose. Its furs were tapped by way of Michipicoton on Lake Superior.

" I love God," says the Frenchman to you. " I will have no allies or kinsfolk that acknowledge the Demon for their master and have recourse to him in their needs. My friendship, alliance and kinship are not to be merely on earth and in this world ; I desire them to be continued in the other, after death and to be maintained in Heaven. And to this end, abandon the plan of carrying on commerce with the Europeans who are trading toward the North Sea, among whom prayer is not offered to God ; and resume your old route to Lake St. John, where you will always find some black gown to instruct and baptize."

This was surely a gospel to the mind of the shrewd Intendant Talon.

On the 10th of June the party was at the height of land : " a small tongue of land," strictly a ridge, bounded by two lakes from each of which a river flowed—from the one, Lake Mistassini, to the Bay of the North, and from the other to the Saguenay. On the 18th it was on Lake Mistassini. On the 28th it came upon an hoy of ten or twelve tons carrying the English flag and a lateen sail. As has been seen, the English fort had been left by Bayly closed ; the ships for the coming trade-season had not yet arrived. A musket-shot beyond the hoy the Frenchmen " entered two deserted houses " ; Father Albanel says nothing of tearing down the arms of the King of England erected at the spot. The party continued down to the Bay, to a point six leagues farther on, where they amused themselves watching the sea which they had so long sought, " that famous Hutson's Bay," and returned to the Englishmen's houses, in one of which Father Albanel says he slept. They again descended to the Bay, to a promontory—doubtless Point Comfort, the north-west extremity of Rupert Bay—ten leagues beyond the English post. The narrative now lays stress on Father Albanel's spiritual dealings with the savages and on his baptizings : " It was a cause of very keen regret to me to find myself, on the fifth, obliged to leave so fair a Mission-field, especially after tasting these first delights."

The Frenchmen began their return journey on the 6th of July, thus their evangelizing efforts on the Bay lasted but seven days. On the 9th they planted the French King's standard on the point of the island intersecting Lake Nemiskau. On their farther way up the Rupert River they met many Indians, doubtless going down to trade with the Englishmen. " I had the consolation to see the glory of Jesus Christ, and his flock, increased by thirty-three little inno-cents upon whom I conferred Baptism before my departure," wrote Father Albanel. The Sieur de St. Simon doubtless had his consola-tion in the form of furs. The party reached Lake St. John on the 23rd and Chicoutimi on the 29th. The journey was estimated at 800 leagues, and involved 200 waterfalls with the necessary portages, and 400 rapids in which long poles must be used to surmount them. Two hundred children and adults were baptized. (The furs gathered pass without mention.) No wonder the good Father was happy at the success of his mission, but after all he and his Frenchmen and Indians had done little more than make an incursion of a few days into a region occupied at its rim by the English ; they had staked a counter-claim for France and done something to persuade the

Indians to trade with the French overland, and not with the English by the Bay.

Meanwhile under the inspiration of Talon the French were taking possession of the Upper Country upon a major scale. The Governor sent the Sieur de St. Lusson up to the Great Lakes. Nicolas Perrot, his interpreter, went off to round up the various tribes. The formal act of annexation was performed at the Sault Ste. Marie on June 14, 1671 (N.S.), at the season when the Indians gathered after their winter hunt to trade and to fish. There were present sixteen Frenchmen and the chiefs of some fourteen tribes, mostly from the south-west but Crees, called in one document Nipissings, and Monsonis of the immediate north were among them. After a sham battle and a game of lacrosse, St. Lusson led the motley crowd to the top of the hill overlooking the falls. The Jesuits present were Claude Dablon, Superior of the Missions of the Lakes, Gabriel Druillette, Claude Allouez, and Louis André. A large wooden cross was blessed and solemnly raised by Father Dablon. As it was being planted in the ground the Frenchmen sang the *Vexilla regis*. Beside it St. Lusson erected a post with a metal plate engraved with the King's arms, the Frenchmen the while singing the *Exaudiat*. St. Lusson now stepped to the front, his sword in one hand, in the other a sod of earth, and made proclamation of the title of the French to the land. His defining of the territory as bounded by the Seas of the North (Hudson Bay and Strait) and South (the Pacific), discovered and undiscovered, would appear to give the French a claim to the whole of the North-West as far as the Pacific Ocean. At that time such a claim could exist only on paper. Indeed, the metal plate was torn down by the Indians for fear of some magic spell. Much more important were the voyages and the Missions established in the subsequent years. Louis Joliet and Père Marquette penetrated south-westward down the valley of the Mississippi to the Arkansas River in 1673, and La Salle was to follow after them. The easiness of the route, the abundance of the food supply, the villages of more or less sedentary Indians offering a fairer field to the missionaries than the scattered nomads of the north, and finally the hope of reaching the Western Sea and China all tended to lure the Frenchmen in the westerly and south-westerly direction. The shaggy North could be left unexplored so long as furs drifted southward to the valley of the St. Lawrence. It was the presence of the Englishmen on Hudson Bay that taught the Frenchmen the value of the North and roused them to those activities which made for actual possession as contrasted with empty claims.

The Company's ships did not get away from Gravesend in 1672 till about 22nd June. Captain Guillam sailed in the *Nonsuch*. As the King had withdrawn the *Wivenhoe*, her place was taken by the *Dogger*, commanded by Captain Morris. A sloop, the *Imploy*, under Captain Samuel Cole, was sent out to remain in the country for general service and for exploration. Radisson had married, or, as one document puts it, "deluded and secretly married," one of the daughters of Sir John Kirke a member of the Committee ; he stayed on in England, but Groseilliers embarked, and with him another Frenchman, Peter Romulus (Romeu), entertained as surgeon for Charles Fort. Governor Bayly returned at the head of the diminutive fleet. His instructions ran, that he was to build a post on Moose River. The late date of sailing made it impossible for the ships to return that summer, with the result that no ship was sent out in the following spring.

During the summer of 1673 Bayly carried out his instructions and built a small house at Moose River for occasional occupation. The site was on the main channel of the river at Hayes (Factory) Island, about a mile from its westerly end. According to Oldmixon, the Governor felt the competition of the French (that is, the French Indians) more here than at Rupert, and was forced to reduce his prices. None the less the trade at Moose proved more considerable than that at Rupert River. The region was formally taken possession of, and a treaty with the Indians gave the English the right to trade and to the possession of the soil.

In June Bayly sent Captain Cole in the *Imploy*, with Groseilliers as interpreter and trader, to test the possibilities of trade at the River Nelson once more. Sir Thomas Button's wintering place was visited. Fifteen days were spent in the river, during which Groseilliers must have at least noted the existence of the Hayes River, whose estuary is really that of the Nelson. As no Indians were seen, presents of goods were left in a conspicuous place in the hope that the Indians would expect the traders to return in the following summer, as was planned.

When the *Nonsuch* and the *Dogger* reached England in the autumn of this year, war with the Dutch was on. Their course had been along the west coast of Ireland and into the English Channel. For safety they ran into Portsmouth and Plymouth respectively. The two captains, Guillam and Morris, took advantage of the absence of supervision to carry on a surreptitious trade in furs. This became the occasion of the drawing up of the oath authorized by the Charter, which all members of the Company and its service were required thereafter to take. It included a solemn promise not to engage in an illicit trade in furs.

The ships had taken two years for their voyage. The Committee chafed at having their capital locked up and at paying interest on it during that length of time. They instructed Captains Guillam and Morris to draw up a scheme by which the ships could return in the summer of sailing.

Next year, 1674, Governor Bayly felt the results of Father Albanel's incursions. No upland Indians came down to trade. They were attracted southward by a French post which was being built at Lake Mistassini.

An Indian of Chief Cuscudidah's band discovered his squaw within Charles Fort, and in a fit of jealousy gave her a desperate though not a fatal wound on the head with a hatchet. Intent on preventing such incidents and on keeping good relations with the natives, Governor Bayly posted orders that only the chief and his councillors should be admitted to the fort. Subsequently the Committee made it law that Indian women should not be allowed within the gates; and to prevent illicit trade on the part of the servants, Bayly's orders, that only the principal Indians on a visit to the Governor in his quarters should be admitted within the fort, became the rule of the Hudson's Bay Company.

Though Cuscudidah's band brought few furs, its friendship was fostered. It staged a great feast at the fort, the Governor providing the tobacco for the occasion. Oldmixon, who had the fort Journal before him, describes the banquet.

They all sat down together, and one Man, a Kinsman of the King's, broke the Meat and Fat in small Pieces, according to the Number of Men there. After a short Speech made by the King, the Substance of which was, for them to take Courage against their Enemies, and other Stories. The Company shouted, and then the Man who broke, distributed the Meat about to them, they crying, *Oh! Ho!* as much as to say, *I thank you.* 'Tis incredible, to tell the Abundance of fat Beaver, Moose Flesh, and Fat, they eat together with the Broath, and Fat as black as Ink, which they drink. Then every Man had a small Piece of Tobacco distributed to him, and they all fell to Smoaking. Some afterwards danc'd; some sung, and a Man beat a Drum, which was a Skin put over a Kettle, lac'd a-thwart. They continue this commonly all Night, and when they go home, carry what Meat is left to the Sqwaws, it being very rare for them to admit the Women to their feasts.

On the 22d of May, the Indians at their Wigwams, near the Fort, had a *Powwow*, or sort of Conjuring; which is thus, There's a small Tower built, with *Wyth* Sticks, about 8 Foot high, the Top being open; but the rest cover'd very close with Skins, that none may see into it. In the Night, the Man that *Powwows* goes into the Tower; the rest sit nigh it, and in their Places ask him several Questions, which in a manner they know already; as, When any Strangers will be here? The *Powwower* guesses at the time, and answers accordingly. The *Maneto*, or their God, told them, the *Nodways* would come down upon them e're long, and advis'd them to be upon their Guard, as also against the *Mistigooses*, or English.

The hostility of the Nottaways to Cuscudidah's band and to the English was due to their position as middlemen passing the furs southward to the French. Bayly and a body of armed English and Indians went to the Bottom of the Bay (James Bay) and to the Frenchmen's River (the Nottaway) to meet the hostile tribe, but came on none.

That summer the question of making Moose the principal factory was raised. At a council Groseilliers was in favour of simply sending a ship there during the trading season. Bayly stood for making Moose the principal fort. From the point of view of economy, Groseilliers may have been wise, but in the matter of taking possession of the Company's territory Bayly's judgment was the more correct. Moreover, the approach to the factory at Moose was much safer for the ships, and the valley drained by the river and its many tributaries was very wide and much richer in furs. The Company accepted Bayly's judgment, and Moose soon became the principal factory on the Bottom of the Bay. Charles Fort was not abandoned;

it was held as a necessary buffer against the French. Groseilliers and Gorst, the accountant, were sent in the *Imploy* to trade at Moose. The returns were few, for the Abitibi Indians had been won to the French by presents. Groseilliers got no more than 250 skins. Oldmixon charges him with being too hard on the Indians ; they would not come to trade with him. When Governor Bayly arrived the scales were turned in his favour by the appearance of Indians from the Shechettawam (Albany) River. He got 1,500 skins. By 24th June the trading was over and the Indians away to their hunting-grounds.

The Governor employed the rest of the summer exploring the Company's domain. He left Mr. Gorst in charge of Charles Fort and embarked in the *Imploy*, doubtless with Groseilliers as his interpreter and trader. His first visit was to the Albany River " where no Englishman had been before." The Indians had no furs to trade, for they had already traded them at Moose. Governor Bayly made the usual treaty with the chief of those parts and promised to return in the following summer. On their part, the Indians engaged themselves to have a store of beaver and to bring the upland natives down to trade.

From the Albany Governor Bayly sailed northward past Akimiski (his Vyner's) Island. At Cape Henrietta Maria he entered the broad inland sea which the Company always called Hudson Bay in distinction from the Bottom of the Bay. On a general westerly course he came to the New Severn River, whose Indian name, Washahoe, is associated with the band living on its banks. It was his intention to go on to the Nelson River, where presents had been left the summer before to induce the Indians to expect and await them, but provisions were now short. Moreover, the *Imploy* had already narrowly escaped disaster in the ice of the Bay, and the Indians reported great sheets of ice to the west. The voyage to Port Nelson was therefore abandoned. On the return course the sloop was driven eastward on to Charlton Island, and Bayly lay there in distress for three days. The extensive exploration of this summer gave the Company a clear view of its territory and led to the determination to take possession of it by establishing a post at the mouth of each of its great rivers. Even Charlton Island was brought into its scheme for the organization of the trade. The former prisoner of the Tower was proving a good Governor.

After Governor Bayly's return to Charles Fort on August 30, 1674 (O.S.), Father Albanel arrived in a canoe accompanied by an Indian of Cuscudidah's band. On 13th November (N.S.) of the previous year Louis de Buade, Comte de Frontenac, Governor-General of La Nouvelle France, had word that Groseilliers's presents were winning the Indians to trade at the Bay, and that even the Ottawas, who brought the furs of the more distant tribes down to Montreal, were being enticed with gifts. He wrote his Minister, Colbert, that he had availed himself of the zeal of Father Albanel to send him on a mission to those parts. The *Jesuit Relation* tells of the priest's departure from Quebec for the North " to minister to many Christians whom he baptized there and to increase their number," but it is hard to avoid the inference that his evangelic mission was gilded with the hope of winning Groseilliers and Radisson back to the service of the French. The party wintered 100 leagues from Quebec, no doubt building a post on Lake Mistassini. It is reported to have endured great suffering from want of provisions, indeed, to have been broken up, the laymen returning to Canada and the Indians scattering to hunt. Father Albanel, however, proceeded alone, doubtless with a few presents with which to win the support of the savages. For long Quebec had no news of the adventuresome priest. Rumours floated in that he had been killed, and finally that he had been taken by the English and sent to England. Our English sources tell us of his arrival at Fort Charles with a friendly letter from Frontenac asking Governor Bayly in the name of the friendship between the two Crowns to treat the priest well and to help him in his work, and promising like treatment to any Englishman who should come to Quebec. Any pleasant feelings which this cordial letter may have created in the breast of the Company's principal servant must have vanished when he discovered that a letter had been brought to Groseilliers also.

In spite of charges made to the contrary, the Jesuit Father was treated leniently. The dire necessities of the post must have weighed more heavily on the mind of Governor Bayly than anything else, for the stock of provisions was low and winter was at hand, yet the ships had not arrived from England. It was decided that, if relief did not come by 11th September, the party should risk the return across the Atlantic in the little coasting sloop, the *Imploy*. " All the Flower and Bread they had left, did not make above 300 Pound. They had but two Barrels of good Pease and 30 Geese in Pickle, to victual their Bark with for the voyage; and having but a very little Powder in the Store-house, they despaired of killing much more game."

Such was the deplorable situation when Father Albanel, Groseilliers, and " another Frenchman," no doubt the surgeon Peter Romulus, for Radisson was at this time in London, went down to the seaside to perform their devotions. Across the water there came the dull but distinct boom of seven guns. The Frenchmen returned breathless with the news. Powder was taken from the precious remnant in store, the three great guns charged and an answering salute given. A night and a whole day passed in anxious expectancy, rapidly declining to despair when the coasting sloop which had been away at Comfort Point sailed up the river bringing five Englishmen with the news that the *Prince Rupert*, Zachary Guillam in command, had arrived with the new Governor, William Lydall, on board. The next day Bayly and his clerk, Mr. Gorst, sailed for the Point, to find that the *Shaftesbury*, under Captain Shepherd, had also arrived. Governor Lydall displayed his Commission and Instructions and formally took over the post. As it was too late to unload and reload for England, it was decided that all should winter on the Bay. Houses were built, including a brewhouse and bakehouse, to accommodate the increased garrison. Relieved as all must have been, the situation was far from cheerful, for the provisions brought out were scarcely sufficient to meet the needs of the crowded fort. However, the winter was tided over, and Governor Lydall sailed for England next summer, Groseilliers and Father Albanel with him. The Jesuit priest does not seem to have been treated as a prisoner, though he must have been closely watched, must even have been under some sort of arrest. In England the relations between the two Crowns forbade extreme measures. When Father Albanel consented to promise to refrain from all action prejudicial to the Company he was set free and given money to take him to France. For all that, he kept up his communications with Groseilliers and Radisson, and was the means of winning them back to the French cause. Thus, in spite of many adverse circumstances, the Father achieved the object of his evangelic mission to the north.

The position of Groseilliers and Radisson in the service of the English Company was necessarily uneasy. As Frenchmen they could not be given high position in an English enterprise in keen rivalry with the French; they were, however, well paid. Apart from the question whether they could be trusted, it was in the nature of things that the English should take care that their colony on the Bay should appear the work of their own hands. The Frenchmen would naturally chafe at being kept in the place of underlings when, in fact, the great Company owed its existence to them. Moreover, Radisson tells us that there were differences as to policy. His advice " was rejected with contempt." This must mean that the Frenchmen wished, as of old, to penetrate into the interior to the heart of the beaver forest, while the English, possibly distrusting them, persisted in keeping to the coast, and relied upon persuading the Indians to bring their furs down to them. However this may have been, the offer of a large reward and a conspicuous position in the French fur trade, held out by Louis XIV.'s Minister Colbert through Father Albanel, ultimately prevailed, even though Radisson was married to the daughter of Sir John Kirke. They drew their salaries on 29th November and fled to France. Radisson says : " We resisted for a long time . . . but seeing our affairs going from bad to worse in the Company, apparently with no reason to expect good treatment, we at last accepted the terms offered to us of 400 gold louis in cash, all our debts to be discharged, and to be given employment. We went to France on these conditions agreed upon in the month of December 1674 [1675]." The Adventurers trading into Hudson Bay took immediate action in keeping with the situation. Their Governor stood by the steps of the throne, and could win the King's quick attention. The King was in close friendship with the French monarch. Accordingly they sent in a petition to King Charles to the effect that Father Albanel had torn down the King's arms at Charles

Fort and had been therefore arrested and brought to England, that he had been released on condition of doing nothing to the damage of the Company, yet he had insidiously won Groseilliers over to the French. They prayed His Majesty to make representations to the Marquis of Ruvigny, envoy of France, urging that Louis should take action both in France and Canada to prevent operations being initiated against " their Colony and Trade " on the Bay.

Whatever may have been the effect of the memorandum presented by the Secretary of State to the Marquis de Ruvigny, it is certain that the way of the two Frenchmen in France proved far from easy. Radisson was told that he could not be employed, for confidence could not be placed in him so long as his wife, the daughter of a stockholder in the English Company, was in England. He and his brother-in-law were, however, directed to Frontenac, Governor of Canada. They crossed the Atlantic, but the merchants of the colony looked askance at their proposed expedition to Hudson Bay by sea, no doubt because it might injure the fur trade of the St. Lawrence, even though in French hands. Returning to France, Radisson entered the French navy and served under Maréchal Jean d'Estrées in expeditions to Guinea in West Africa and to Tobago (1678) in the West Indies. Presented with a gratification of 100 louis, and enjoined to show all diligence in bringing over his wife, Radisson visited London, but as Sir John Kirke would not allow his daughter to cross the Channel, he returned in October 1679, only to be told again that under the circumstances he could not be trusted. Fortunately for him, Radisson now came into relations with M. de la Chesnaye, the most potent merchant doing business with Canada, who recommended him to visit London once more, ostensibly to bring over his wife but really to find out the plans of the English Company. He then went to Canada, where Groseilliers had come to terms with De la Chesnaye for an expedition to Hudson Bay from Quebec by sea.

In the spring of 1674 the Committee had recalled Governor Bayly and had sent out William Lydall to take his place. Lydall was a captain who had made many voyages to Russia and had lived several years in that country. His experience should have made him a good Governor, but, fifty years of age, he proved unwilling to submit to the occasional hardships incident to life in Rupert's Land. His first problem was that of carrying the servants in the country and the crews of the two ships happily through the winter. Ex-Governor Bayly, the thrifty Quaker, occupied Moose Fort ; he seems to have had no difficulties, but Governor Lydall at Charles Fort, when Gorst the accountant began to ration the provisions, ordered the full allowance to continue, saying : " If we starve, we'll starve altogether." The result was that the fort was reduced to great straits. When spring came the new Governor retired from his command in disgust, putting Bayly back into full charge of the Company's concerns. When he sailed away he left Charles Fort manned by but four men. This marks the eclipse of that post and the rise of Moose to the position of headquarters and residence of the Governor.

In 1675 Bayly sent home Prince Attash, the chief from whom the Company secured its rights to the Rupert River region, on a princely visit to England. He was accompanied by another prominent Indian, but this man died on the voyage, so that the Prince arrived in London without his staff. An account in the Ledger shows that the Company treated its guest liberally. He stayed with Captain Tatnam, a servant of the Company, whose name had been given to the cape east of Port Nelson. An attendant was provided for His Highness. The total cost of the visit was £86, 18s. 11d.

An interesting fact is revealed by the Journals of the Company, that is, its daily cash books, which begin in 1676. In 1677 Bayly sent home two Frenchmen, Thomas Leclerc and Eustache Prevost, by the *Shaftesbury*. These must have been men of some importance, for they were guests of the Committee on several occasions, and payments were made to them between November and January amounting to £280, 15s. 8d. They were probably *coureurs-des-bois* from the French fort on Lake Mistassini. They had probably encountered difficulties over the disposal of their furs in Quebec, for these would be got within the area of Tadoussac, whose monopoly was in other hands. They must have been testing the possibility of disposing of their furs and securing the goods for their trade through the Hudson's Bay Company's fort on the Rupert. However, no arrangement was effected. In 1679 another Frenchman, Jolliet, penetrated down the Rupert to Charles Fort. He made a map to accompany his report ; on this a French fort is placed at Lake Mistassini, at or near the mouth of the river flowing into it from Lake Albanel.

Bayly continued to explore as heretofore. He entered a river to the north where he discovered isinglass, also known as slude * ; hence the former name of the stream, our Eastmain River. He likewise reported deposits of another material called by the same name on Moose River. The Company ordered the deposit to be worked, and gave James Knight, one of its first servants then at home, the task of selecting and buying the tools. The eagerness of the Committee in this matter may be partly explained by the necessity of finding ballast for their ships, for the furs, though very valuable, were of light weight and by no means made a cargo. Some commodity like slude, which would serve as ballast, and could be sold at a profit in London, was altogether to be desired. However, nothing came of the scheme.

It was in Bayly's time that trade on the Albany was begun.

* Isinglass, German *hausenblase*, literally " sturgeon's bladder," is a " firm whitish semi-transparent substance (being a comparatively pure form of gelatin) obtained from the sounds or air-bladders of some freshwater fishes, especially the sturgeon ; used in cooking for making jellies, etc., also for clarifying liquors, in the manufacture of glue, and for other purposes " (*Oxford Dictionary*). This sort was found by Bayly floating in the river which passed under the name Isinglass and alternatively Slude, later Eastmain River. The word was applied to " mica, from its resembling in appearance some kinds of isinglass." The Russian word *slyuda*, " mica in transparent plates," was anglicized as " slude."

He must have kept his promise to the Indians and visited the river in the spring of 1675. Probably he began with a small house to accommodate the trading party when there. At any rate, when he retired in 1679, the Committee wrote : " Wee are well pleased that there is a house of some strength built at Chichiwewen, Mr. Baily having assured us that the quantity of Beaver from thence will be very extraordinary, And we desire you [Governor Nixon] to let Mr. John Bridgar who is chief Factor there and all those employed with him there know, wee have great expectations from their care & industry in that place." The fort was on a large island bearing Bayly's name, on the north side of the main channel, and near the lower end of the island. Bayly's activities on the East Main were put on record by giving his name to another island off the mouth of Slude (Eastmain) River. The Governor must have made it a base for his visits to the East Main. Certainly, this Bayly's Island served that purpose in the early part of the eighteenth century.

The Company did not drop its plan for the ships to accomplish the round trip and be back in the autumn. On Bayly's advice Charlton Island out in James Bay was chosen for a depot to which the ships could come with ease and run no risk of being caught in the ice if they were there late in the autumn. Sloops could take the goods from the depot to the several forts and bring the furs out in time for the ships. Here again the beginnings may have been in a small way. In May 1680 the Committee wrote to Governor Nixon, Bayly's successor : " Wee do judge by the situation of Charlton Island, that no place is so convenient for the Rendez-vous from our severall Factories, to attend the arrivall of our Ships from home, and wee hope before this comes to you a good large dry substantiall Warehouse will be there erected to receive the Cargo wee send you, as it was agreed to be, before Mr. Baily left you, and that all the goods [furs] you have . . . will be ready packed up to be put on board the *Prudent Mary*, that she may be dispatched as soon as may be, wch will import us much." Thus, when Governor Bayly left his command, the organization of the Company's trade at the Bottom of the Bay was practically complete.

Bayly was recalled in the spring of 1679 ; the indications are that this was with a view to sending him as Governor to Hudson Bay, to inaugurate the Company's trade at Port Nelson and on the River Severn. The Committee felt, however, that there was somewhat in connection with his administration which should be inquired into, and an order was given, as usual in such cases, that charges should be put in writing. This was on 17th December, but no accusations were brought forward at the meeting of the Committee of the 23rd. Bayly died on 6th January following. The charges against him may have had to do with presents of furs received from the Indians, as he bade them farewell. They could not have seriously affected his honour, for he died at the home of Mr. William Walker, a prominent member of the Company, on the Strand, where he must have been staying as guest. The Committee met on the day of his

death and took upon itself the cost of the funeral, voting twenty
pounds (a much larger sum then than it is to-day) for that purpose.
In the gloom of night, by torchlight, the procession, which included
members of the Committee and stockholders in the Company, and
the officers of His Majesty's ship, the *John and Alexander*, by which
Bayly had come home, passed from the Strand to St. Paul's, Covent
Garden, and there, by the grave within the church itself, paid honour
to the former prisoner of the Tower, the first Governor of Rupert's
Land. By the next ship the Company sent out an escutcheon to be
set up at Moose Fort " for the observation of the Indians, that they
may understand that he is dead, and yt the Compny used him
kindly."

John Nixon was sent out in 1679 as Governor in the place of
Charles Bayly. As the Company's Letter Books begin in 1680,
a clearer view can now be obtained of its policy and spirit. The first
Instructions extant are the renewed instructions to Nixon. They
begin :

> 1st—In the first place Wee do strictly enjoyn you to have public prayers
> and reading of the Scriptures or some other religious Books wheresoever you
> shall be resident, at least on the Lord's days. As also to order the severall
> chiefs in each Factory under your command to do the same, That wee who
> profess to be Christians may not appear more barbarous than the poor
> Heathens themselves who have not been instructed in the knowledge of the
> true God, This is what we have formerly directed, and have sent over the
> proper books for the use of the Factory, to wit, the Common prayer Book,
> the Bible and the Book of Homilies wch contains choice & well approved
> Sermons for Instruction. But wee understand there hath been little or no
> use of them heretofore, wch neglect wee desire you will reform for the future,
> that wee may more reasonably expect the blessing of God to attend your
> endeavours and to prosper ye interest of ye Company.

Nixon is being amply supplied with goods ; he is to take care
that (those hard bargainers) the Indians do not encroach upon him
in the trade ; Moose Fort on Hayes Island is to be the chief factory,
" to prevent the encroachment of the French too far upon the West
Main, where we caution you to be always more than ordinary vigilant
and never so remiss in your guard as to tempt either them or the
Natives to affront or injure us " ; he is to prosecute the discovery
of isinglass on the Slude River, and Charles Fort is not to be abandoned, but to be kept up as " being a kind of bulwark to prevent any
inroad of the French upon that part of the East Main, from whence
that commodity is principally expected." In view of subsequent
events, Nixon's instructions to care for " the settling of Factories
at Port Nelson and New Severn " are of special interest. " We judge
it to be of great moment to our security, that it be suddenly put in
execution, for we understand there are designs already on foot of
interloping " ; Captain Draper of the *Albemarle* is instructed and
equipped to visit New Severn on his way to Charlton Island, and,
if possible, to make a settlement there. (He entered the Nelson, but
made no establishment there, nor at Severn.) Nixon is to labour
to make treaties with the native chiefs for the proprietorship of those

rivers. Defective goods are to be sent home, and directions given as to the goods suitable for the trade. Garden seeds are being sent out; swine can be propagated on Hayes Island (on which Moose Fort stood). The London Letter of the following year indicates the provision made to implement this last instruction : " We have sent 1 he Goate & 2 she Goates, 1 sow with Pigg which we have done in hopes thay will increase in ye Country & be of use & comfort to our people which is a thing that deserves your utmost care as well for the Good of the Factory as for the ease of the Compa. in the business of Provisions."

The London Letter of 1682 conveyed a caution to Nixon not to be morose towards the natives, as the Committee had heard he had been. The Committee had also heard that Indian women were debauching its servants, and consuming the provisions of the post ; no women were to be allowed within the factory. Nixon was to send men up into the interior to invite the Indians down, " which indeed is a thing Wee wonder you have not in all this time put in practice, Govr Baily haveing often told us it was a matter of greater moment, therefore we doe earnestly recomend it to yor carefull pformance, for all stratagems ought to be used for advancement of the Compas Interest, whose Expences are constantly great and no profit hitherto."

John Nixon was a disappointment as Governor. He was morose with the Indians and with his officers. In particular, he refused to listen to reasonable suggestions made by his subordinates in connection with the wreck of the *Prudent Mary* on Tetherly Island as she was returning home from Charlton Island in the autumn of 1680, thereby increasing the loss of furs incurred. Moreover, he reduced prices arbitrarily without consulting the Committee. He was recalled in 1683, and Henry Sergeant appointed in his place. Sergeant's Instructions were to a large extent Nixon's repeated. He was to abolish the entertaining of Indian women in the factories ; to send proper servants into the country to invite the Indians down ; to cultivate the land, seeds being sent out for that purpose, and " to try the utmost if you can grow anything in that country " ; he was to treat the Indians with justice and humanity. " Finally, we recommend unto you the care of the service and honour of God, yt you punish & discourage all dissolute and prophane persons & we doe hereby require & command yt the Common Prayer be daily read in all our Factories & yt the Lds Day be Duely observed." It became the tradition at the forts not to trade with the Indians on Sunday. A mess of oatmeal and pease would be given to them to keep them quiet and patient till Monday. Instructions directed to the situation as it was at Sergeant's appointment were that Albany was to become the chief factory and that he was to guard against the Company's enemies, the French and interlopers.

The documents are so few for the early years it is not possible to say what the Company may or may not have done towards installing the complete form of government overseas prescribed

by the Charter. Governors there were, but what about Councils ?
The first definite information comes from the Instructions to Sergeant.

And to the end that all matters of moment & greatest importance to
ourselves may be Debated & throughly considered and your orders therein
may be made wth as much care and solemnity as may be, we do thinke fitt
that your Depty Governour, the Chiefes of our respective Factories, and the
Commanders of our respective Shipps for the time being, shall by virtue of
their Offices be your Councell with whom or wth such of yem as shall be on
the place wth you, you shall consult & advise in all weighty matters and you
may also make such other person of your Councell that you may judge
qualified for it though they are not emploied in any of the aforesaid Offices
unto all which the Following Oath is to be administered by you.

It is to be noted that what is here envisaged is a Governor of the
whole region, the Bottom of the Bay, with a Council drawn from all
parts of his sphere of administration. As the factors of the several
factories took their furs to Charlton Island in the late summer to
meet the ships from England, Council would meet there, and usually
only at that time of the year. In the eighteenth century, when there
was no such rendezvous and the posts were self-dependent, Councils
were erected at each of the forts, and there existed no Council of the
whole region. Further, the members of the Council were appointed
by the Governor and Committee at this time, not by special warrants,
but in virtue of the Instructions issued to them individually and to
the Governors. The members sat on the Council *ex officio* as factors
or captains. If a factor died, his successor for the time being,
appointed by the Governor, would be of the Council. Finally,
because the powers of the Company were delegated to the Governor,
he could appoint suitable men to the Council—always subject to the
approval of the Governor and Committee in London.

The Instructions of 1680 to Nixon show that the Committee
was concerned to take possession and effect settlements on the
Severn River and Port Nelson, and to make good its ownership of
the soil by treaties with the Indians surrendering to it the proprietorship of the region. This would be a safeguard against attempts
by the French and by interlopers to take possession of these rivers.
The immediate danger was that Groseilliers and Radisson would
bring the French to a region which they had visited as servants of
the Company. Whatever may be made of Radisson's account of his
movements as given above, it is clear from a dispatch of Frontenac
of November 1681 that Radisson was in Quebec some time previous,
possibly during the autumn before, as the Governor-General apprehended, returning from his service in the West Indies under Maréchal
d'Estrées. He had already the backing of the Sieur Aubrey de la
Chesnaye, and appealed to Frontenac for permission to effect
establishments at the mouth of the St. Lawrence and on Hudson
Bay. Frontenac gave two reasons for not acceding to the request ;
these posts would divert the furs from the King's Post at Tadoussac,
and at Hudson Bay the English might be met with and difficulties
follow—claim and counter-claim. Radisson must have had the

establishment of a French post on James Bay in his mind at this time. Frontenac referred the matter to his minister, M. de Seignelay (Colbert), adding that Radisson was on his way to England to see his wife. That he did visit London is evidenced by a statement in the letter of June 1681 from the Committee to Governor Nixon ; they had been informed by Radisson that the French had settled a factory a day's journey up the river from Charles Fort. This would appear to fix the date of the establishment of the French fort on Lake Nemiskau. As the official documents point to 1685 as the date of that post, Radisson may have been treating what he knew was being planned as actual fact. It is entirely likely that, when in England, he came to know of the purpose of the Hudson's Bay Company to build a post on the Nelson River, whose shores he had visited of old. He swiftly readjusted his scheme. He would avoid all competition with the King's Post at Tadoussac, and at the same time keep clear of the English by taking an expedition to Port Nelson, if possible, before the English got there. He could take possession of the country in the name of the French King and, if the English appeared on the scene, treat them as aggressors. This plan avoided all the objections raised by Frontenac. Indeed, the prospect of taking possession of what was believed to be and what proved to be a most valuable fur region, so far to the west as not to interfere with the fur trade of Canada, was alluring. The consequence would be that the English would be confined to the Bottom of the Bay, close enough to Canada for the French to seriously limit their traffic and, in case of war, to drive them out.

De la Chesnaye and his associates, conspicuous merchants in the trade of the St. Lawrence, took up Radisson's scheme and, as " The Company of Hudson's Bay," received the necessary sanction for it from M. de la Barre, Frontenac's successor. Thus the Hudson's Bay Company was to suffer seriously from the inaction of Governor Nixon and Captain Draper. Another planting of the King's arms, a log hut, and a treaty with the Indians was all that was necessary for a definite establishment of the English claim to a region taken possession of on paper as early as the visit of Thomas Button (1612). Failing these, the French claim that the region was unoccupied bore at least the appearance of truth.

The centre of interest now passes from the Bottom of the Bay to Hudson Bay proper.

2.—WAR ON THE BAY IN A TIME OF PEACE, 1682–89

In the summer of 1682 three several expeditions were pushing through the ice of Hudson Strait with Port Nelson the goal of their hopes.* Benjamin Guillam in the *Bachelor's Delight* left Boston on 21st June, with a licence from the Governor of Massachusetts, and

* For map of Port Nelson see Sketch-map No. 5 at p. 90, based on Robson's Draught of 1752.

arrived in the Nelson on the 18th or 19th August (O.S.). He passed
up the estuary to an island, which still bears his name, and began
to build. In his wake came two French ships, the *St. Pierre* and the
Ste. Anne, equipped at Quebec by M. de la Chesnaye and his
associates and bearing Groseilliers and Radisson with a letter of
commission from the Governor of Canada, De la Barre, but, as the
English pointed out later, with no royal Patent. On the 2nd of September (N.S.), which would be the 24th of August according to the
English calendar, they entered the Hayes River, the Ste. Thérèse
as they named it, and passed fifteen miles up to a creek near some
islands. The spot can be recognized on Robson's map as the " place
of retreat " of the French of a later date. Radisson left his brother-
in-law to build two houses while he passed on upstream in a canoe
with his nephew, Jean-Baptiste Chouart, Groseilliers's son, in search
of the Indians. In eight days he travelled forty leagues, say a
hundred miles, probably up to the confluence of the Hayes and the
Fox rivers, where he came upon them. The savages were alarmed,
but Radisson won their friendship with consummate skill, and
brought them down to the ships to trade.

The Hudson's Bay Company's ships were delayed in the Thames
by the negligence of Captain Zachary Guillam, Benjamin's father,
who had returned to the service for the voyage to Port Nelson. He
absented himself persistently from his ship, and allowed the goods
to be heaped up on the deck, so that the provisions had to be taken
out and loaded on the right vessels. On 27th May the Committee
served notice on him that if he were not ready to sail on the following
Monday he would be dismissed. On the 31st five ships were sent
off from Gravesend, three for the Bottom of the Bay, one, the
Albemarle, for Port Nelson to winter there and to proceed to Charlton
Island in the spring, while the fifth, the *Prince Rupert*, under Captain
Guillam, was to assist in building the fort at Port Nelson and to
proceed to Charlton Island to winter. John Bridgar, recently Chief
Factor at Albany, was commissioned Governor of the new post,
Hayes Fort, to be built on the banks of the Nelson. The two
ships bound for the port arrived on 17th September (N.S.), which
would be 7th September of the English calendar, a fortnight after
Groseilliers.

Apart from trading in furs, the intention of the French expedition
was to stake out a claim to Port Nelson for France before the English
could arrive, and on their arrival to treat them as aggressors. While
Groseilliers and Radisson were outwardly private adventurers, they
had the Governor of Canada and even the French King behind them.
Accordingly, they were supported diplomatically. On November 11,
1682 (N.S.), the Canadian Governor, M. de la Barre, made representations to the French Court that the English Company had for
twenty years taken possession of Hudson Bay and built forts there ;
there was no reason to disturb their trade by sea but, " if they
[pushed] forward their vilainous forts into the territory of the King
to debauch the Indians ; he would cause them to be driven out " ;

he recommended that his Britannic Majesty should be informed of this his view and that he did not wish to do anything unpleasant unless forced. (In view of this statement of policy, Radisson must have gone to Port Nelson with the assurance that any violence committed by him would be condoned by the Government.) A memorandum in this sense, enclosing the pertinent part of De la Barre's dispatch, was presented in London by the French ambassador and passed on by King Charles to the Hudson's Bay Company, with the request that they give an account of their title to the Bay and its territories. In reply they referred to their first expedition, their Charter granted by His Majesty himself, to Frontenac's friendly letter, delivered by Father Albanel, which made no suggestion that the English were encroaching upon French territory. All their forts had been built after " solemn compacts and agreements with the Natives for their rivers and Territories." They prayed for His Majesty's protection. The substance of this reply was transmitted to the French Government. As no answer was received, the Company took it that the validity of their claim was recognized.

The course of events at Port Nelson in the trading year 1682-83 is given in Radisson's highly coloured account of his doings, but it may also be traced in a series of affidavits made by those who suffered at his hands, notably one by Benjamin Guillam. The French were on the Hayes River. Across the tongue of land dividing the Hayes from the Nelson, on Guillam (Gillam) Island close to the north bank of the Nelson, lay Benjamin Guillam's party. (Farther down the river and on the north bank the English Company's fort was soon built.) The sound of cannon, said to have been discharged at the funeral of one of young Guillam's men, betrayed the presence of the New Englanders to the Frenchmen. Radisson forthwith visited Guillam, whom he knew personally, and they " mutually caressed each other." He declared that he was settled in the country before the party from New England, which was not the fact, and that he had force enough to overpower them. He gave them leave to build, but not to fortify themselves. The two parted well satisfied. So far Radisson's *Narrative*. Guillam's affidavit shows that the New Englander's satisfaction was really due to a bargain which he had made to supply the Frenchman with provisions and goods, receiving beaver in the spring as payment. Certain provisions were advanced in the meantime. Disarmed by the apparent friendliness of this arrangement, Guillam later visited the French post, but after a stay of two weeks he was seized by Groseilliers and kept in the closest confinement. Radisson then proceeded to master his captive's post. He left a number of his men in ambush in the woods on the south bank of the Nelson and asked the men in the fort to go out to meet their commander, who, he said, was following on but was exhausted. Taking brandy with them, several of the men in the fort went out and were caught by the ambush. The rest came out to await their master. The Frenchmen rushed on them and captured the fort and ship. The flag of France was run up on the staff. Of this

Boston party some at least were kept in close confinement in Radisson's post with scarcely enough to eat, while the French revelled in their new-found plenty. Some were treated as slaves and set to work cutting and hauling wood for their captor's fort. In the spring they were left to starve on an island opposite Radisson's post on the Hayes, so the affidavits run, and Indians who desired to bring them food were driven away. Guillam with some of his men was brought to Quebec, a prisoner in the hold of his own ship, on the verge of starvation all the way. On October 1st (N.S.) he presented a humble petition to the Governor, De la Barre, narrating these facts and pleading for justice on the ground of " the good peace " existing between the Crowns of England and France. Because of the " union of the two Crowns " De la Barre restored his ship to him and his goods on condition that he should sail immediately and without taking any furs. Such was the sorry close of the interloper's enterprise ; but the end was not really here.

In June 1682 the Hudson's Bay Company knew that Benjamin Guillam's interloping expedition had intended to sail from Boston in the spring. They forthwith petitioned the King, setting forth their monopoly and asking for an Order-in-Council protecting them against interlopers, after the manner of a recent Proclamation in favour of the East India Company. The matter was referred to the Lords of Trade and Plantations and by them sent to the law officers of the Crown " to Report whether the same may be granted by Law." At the proper time the Company's Charter was taken from the iron chest and laid before the Lord Keeper of the Privy Seal, to testify to the privileges granted to the Company. Finally, an Order-in-Council was issued on August 12, 1683, to the Governor and Council of the colony of Massachusetts in New England, stating that divers ill-disposed persons intended to destroy or make of no effect " Our Charter granted to the sayd Company, without whose license or Consent no persons ought to Trade in those parts " ; and that on information given of any ship presuming to trade to and from Hudson Bay without the Company's licence, it was to be seized, ship, crew, and all, and a prosecution entered according to the law.

Not content with the assertion of their legal right thus enforced, the Committee of the Company took active steps towards prosecuting Benjamin Guillam ; Sir James Hayes, the indefatigable Deputy-Governor, interviewed the agents of New England, and induced them to write to the Governors of their colonies. On 1st August it was ordered by the Governor and Committee that Edward Randolph, Esq., Collector of His Majesty's Customs at Boston, should be given power of attorney to seize all interlopers who should arrive at that port. On 10th August—two days before the Order-in-Council was issued—Randolph received his power of attorney duly sealed with the Company's seal. On 18th August the King's letter also was in his hand on the way across the Atlantic. Subsequently a silver tankard of the value of £10 was forwarded to him in appreciation of his activities on behalf of the Company. On July 5, 1684, Sir James

Hayes laid before the Committee a letter from the Governor of Massachusetts stating that Benjamin Guillam had been arrested on his arrival at Boston. Doubtless his ship was likewise seized. Truly the way of interlopers was made hard unto them ; but the greatest of Guillam's sufferings came, not from the Company's action, but from the hand of Groseilliers and Radisson. In this light the Frenchmen, so far from harming the Company, were doing them the benefit of helping to clear interlopers out of the Bay.

Interlopers from England also met a hard fate. In 1680 the *Prudent Mary*, as has been seen, was wrecked on Tetherley's (Tidderly's) Island, north of Charlton. Her mate Richard Lucas had assisted in rescuing and storing the furs. In 1682 he secured a ship, the *Expectation*, and sailed to the Bottom of the Bay to gather the rich booty at little cost. The Company ordered the commanders of its ships to arrest the interloper and seize his vessel. In 1683 Captain Nehemiah Walker of the ship *Diligence* intercepted the *Expectation* and brought her crew home in his ship. He was instructed by the Committee to let the men go. Some entered actions against the captain for the illegal detention of their property and for false imprisonment, and had him in turn arrested. Daniel Lane, who was most responsible for the expedition, was kept in prison and an action was brought against him by the Company for £3,000 damages. He ended by offering to tell the whole story of the interloping enterprise, was released and, along with Richard Lucas and others, was taken into the Company's employ. Some of the London merchants who supported the expedition persisted in their suits, only to drop them in the end. One case, that of Mr. Charles Boone, came to trial in the Court of Admiralty and was decided in favour of the Company. Another, brought before the King's Bench, was drawn out for five years, when the Company thought it wise to compromise with a payment of £200. This disposed of the problem of protecting the Company's monopoly against interlopers for many years. The Frenchmen had led the main assault against them ; the Company came after, mopping up. From this point of view the operations of the Frenchmen on the Nelson worked out great gain for the Englishmen.

According to Radisson's own *Narrative*, his chicanery was supremely successful in his dealings with John Bridgar, the Governor of the Hudson's Bay Company's post. As he came down the river from his first visit to Benjamin Guillam he saw two English ships (the *Prince Rupert* commanded by Guillam, the father, and the *Albemarle*) entering the port. He immediately landed on the south shore. The spot was scarce three leagues (seven and a half miles) downstream from Gillam Island, and opposite the creek near which the English were to build their post called Hayes Fort. This would be the first creek below Flamborough Head, as on Robson's map (p. 90). Radisson made a smoke to attract attention. The English came to anchor opposite him, but remained on board all night. Next morning a boat with Governor Bridgar drew near. Radisson re-

vealed himself. Some one asked : " What is your business ? We
are English." He replied : " I am French and order you to retire,"
adding that they had come too late, for he had taken possession of
the place in the name of the King of France. The English Governor
maintained his right, asking if it was not there that an English ship
commanded by Sir Thomas Button had formerly wintered. Radisson,
who knew the spot from his early visit with the English, replied :
" Yes," and pointed to the place to the north, probably to the point
indicated on Robson's map as " foot of the high bank." Their
several claims asserted, the two got on friendly terms and went on
board the *Prince Rupert*. Radisson repeated to Bridgar a story with
which he had deceived young Guillam, that he had two ships with
him, and another expected. " I was right to conceal from him and
do what I did ; Not having men enough to come to an open struggle,
it was necessary to make use of stratagem." The Frenchman left,
promising to return in a fortnight. The English were busy in the
meanwhile building their post.

Radisson came back after a little more than eight days. It was
low tide and the English ship lay in the mud about a mile off the
fort, " for the creek in which it was to be berthed was frozen," as
Radisson, who probably did not know of the order of the Committee
that the *Prince Rupert* should winter at Charlton Island, inferred.
As to the house which was being built, it offered little chance to resist
an assault, he thought. He continued his deception by passing off
one of his men as the captain of the expected ship. The English
were in no way on their guard ; apparently they assumed that
both parties would trade peaceably in the region. Radisson says
that he warned Captain Guillam of the danger to his ship, lying in
the open, but without effect. On 21st October (N.S.), the 11th (O.S.),
a great storm, which must have driven the gathering ice out of the
estuary, carried her from her moorings out to sea. As there were
but five men on board, eighteen of the crew being on shore, it must
have been impossible to manage the ship, and she was lost. The
Hudson's Bay Company must have had reason to believe that the
French contributed to the disaster, say by partly cutting the cable
(which in those days was always of hemp), for they afterwards
claimed damages of them for the loss of the ship.

Radisson's chief concern was to keep the two parties of Englishmen, the New Englanders and the Company's servants, from uniting
against the French. This led him to capture the fort and ship of young
Guillam in February. He represents Governor Bridgar as in grave
necessity through lack of provisions and ammunition, and pretends
to have played the part of benefactor to the suffering Englishmen.
This may have been so, if all had been lost on the *Prince Rupert*,
but she had been long enough in port to have unloaded her cargo.
And what of the *Albemarle*, which was to have wintered in Port
Nelson ? There is evidence that Bridgar may have come through
the winter in tolerable comfort. Radisson goes on to tell how
Bridgar tried to capture the interloper's ship, of whose existence he

had come to know, not realizing that the French had seized her shortly before, his object being to secure some gunpowder. Subsequently Radisson entered Bridgar's house with twelve men simply to intimidate him. He put out all his effort to prevent the Englishmen from trading and to force them to leave in the spring. Finally, on Bridgar's visiting Radisson in Guillam's fort, he was held temporarily, storming all the while. When the Governor later visited Radisson's fort on the Hayes, he was treated well and allowed to return. Radisson represents the Governor as bullying his men, and pictures himself as stepping in to protect them.

All the while Jean-Baptiste Chouart, Groseilliers's son, was up country to bring down the Indians in the spring to trade. When they came they were ready to stand by the French, even anxious to attack the English. Radisson claims to have restrained them. At the flood of the river the French had the mortification to see their ships, berthed in a creek, crushed by an ice jam. They had perforce to build a ship, taking the bottom of the *Ste. Anne* and building the upper part out of the wreckage of the *St. Pierre*. Preparations were now being made for sailing. It was decided to seize the English Governor and his fort. His goods would stock the French post for the summer and until the arrival of the next ship from Quebec. Bridgar was invited to Guillam's fort and there seized. Radisson then went down to Hayes Fort, to all appearance on a friendly visit, but his men suddenly made themselves masters of the place. Radisson says that he offered the Englishmen the choice of going to Quebec or remaining where they were, and that all but two chose to go to Quebec. The interloper's ship, the *Bachelor's Delight*, was brought down and the Company's effects, duly inventoried, loaded on her, presumably to be taken to the French fort on the Hayes. The forts of the two English parties were burned down. Some of the English were placed on an island opposite the fort on the Hayes, others on the north shore near the mouth of the river. Their affidavits complain that they were given scant fare, while the French had abundance. On 27th July (N.S.) all save Jean-Baptiste Chouart and some seven men, who were left to hold the post, sailed on Guillam's ship and the reconditioned *Ste. Anne*. They were caught in the ice of the Bay, and the frail *Ste. Anne* was split open. Her cargo was unloaded on to the ice, and she was careened and repaired. At this point Bridgar offered to buy the ship to sail to the Bottom of the Bay. This was agreed to, and the Governor gave Radisson a receipt for her. The English were sent off in the crazy craft, but in spite of the bargain Bridgar was held, for Radisson thought that he intended to sail back to the Nelson and to capture the few Frenchmen left in the fort on the Hayes. Accordingly, Bridgar was taken to Quebec, where he arrived about the end of October. So far, Radisson's *Narrative*.

The documents in the archives of the Hudson's Bay Company suggest that Radisson, writing in French for the French, has suppressed many facts in his story and drawn an exaggerated picture of himself lording it over the Englishmen. According to the orders of the Committee, the *Albemarle* was to winter in Port Nelson, and almost certainly did so. Radisson himself saw her arrive. Then, too, about eighteen men of the *Prince Rupert* were on shore and not lost with the ship. Hayes Fort was amply garrisoned. This would naturally make it necessary for Bridgar to be careful of his provisions, but the *Albemarle* would be stocked with food for a year. Bridgar's men would not be in great need, save for fresh meat against the scurvy. Zachary Guillam's ship, the *Prince Rupert*, was to assist in building the fort and then sail to Charlton Island. This would explain her position in the river on 11th October. Hayes Fort, manned by the usual complement, with the crew of the *Albemarle* and the men from the *Prince Rupert*, must have been too strong for the Frenchmen through the winter. In the spring the *Albemarle* would sail probably in the early half of June for Charlton Island, taking the men of the *Prince Rupert* and possibly such furs as Bridgar may have gathered with her. Only after she sailed would Bridgar's garrison be so small that Radisson could effect its capture. This was done, according to Bridgar's statement to Governor De la Barre, on 6th July (N.S.), which would be 26th June of the English calendar. The English affidavits put it in June.

The loss at Port Nelson was only an incident in the Hudson's Bay Company's operations of the year. The ships from the Bottom of the Bay returned with rich freights, and the Company paid a dividend of 50 per cent. on the paid-up capital.* None the less its position was made very difficult by the Frenchmen's raid, for the French persistently presented it in the light of an intruder into their territory.

If Radisson had had it much his own way in the winter of 1682–83 at Port Nelson, the English were masters of the situation a month after he left, for on 27th August the *Albemarle* was back in the river along with the ketch *George*, dispatched under Captain John Abraham from the Thames at the unprecedentedly early date of 27th April. Jean-Baptiste Chouart told Radisson, when he returned in 1684 in the English service, that something like warfare was waged between his men and the English newcomers, and that his Indians had killed some Englishmen. If so, this did not hinder the rebuilding of

---

* This large dividend has been taken by writers as normal for the early years of the Company's existence. It is thus made to appear that the Company was amassing great wealth. But the perspective is altered by the fact that no dividends were paid in the first thirteen years. Writing to Governor Nixon on May 22, 1682, the Governor and Committee said : " All stratagems ought to be used for advancement of the Compas. Interest, whose expenses are constantly great and no profit hitherto." The Company appears to have earned profits, but these had to be used in expanding the business. Thus, though the original paid-up capital was £10,500, the actual capital put out was greater. The dividend of 50 per cent. was paid, however, on the original capital. It would have stood at a more modest figure if calculated on the actual capital invested. In the main the Company continued to put its profits into the business, for it paid further dividends only in 1688 (50 per cent.) and in 1689 (25 per cent.). In 1690—that is at the end of twenty years, during which the only dividends paid were the three above—the actual capital in the business was considered to be the treble of the original capital. Accordingly, the General Court felt free to treble the stock in the hands of the stockholders. See at p. 113f. A dividend of 25 per cent. was paid on the trebled stock. As will be seen, there followed a period of no less than twenty-eight years during which no dividend was paid. This was followed by a second trebling of the stock. See at p. 141f.

Hayes Fort and a considerable traffic with the Indians. Chouart was short of guns and some other articles in demand among the natives, who appear to have come down in considerable numbers too late to meet Radisson. They resorted to the Englishmen freely, and the ketch *George* sailed away with a sufficient quantity of furs to have the parchment beaver from Port Nelson a separate feature at the autumn sale, and the coat beaver at the spring auction. For security, Chouart abandoned Groseilliers's post on the Hayes and built a stronghold on Pakwaik, or Frenchman's Island, now Rainbow Island, five miles above the tidal water of the Hayes and above the first rapid on that river. There he was in a position to intercept the Indians coming down, and could trade with them as far as his shortage of goods would allow. He expected to be supported by a ship from Quebec, but none arrived in the summer of 1683.

The Hudson's Bay Company was made aware of the destruction of their fort and the capture of their Governor when the *George* arrived in the Thames towards the end of October. Such violent deeds would in our time have led to war, but in those days colonial rivalries came to ill deeds without breaking the peace between the mother-countries. The nations involved would regard the forward actions of the colonials as " an affair of merchants." Accordingly, the Hudson's Bay Company sought redress by diplomacy rather than by arms. Its appeal was to the King to bring pressure to bear on the French Court to recognize their title and to make good their losses. It was in a favourable position for such an appeal. Prince Rupert had died in 1682, but on January 3, 1683, the General Court had elected the King's brother and presumptive successor, James, Duke of York, to the vacant office of Governor. The head of the Company, therefore, continued to stand beside the throne. A deputation consisting of Sir James Hayes, the Deputy Governor; Sir Christopher Wren, the builder of St. Paul's Cathedral and a member of the Committee; and Mr. William Walker, at whose home Bayly had died, was appointed to wait upon His Royal Highness to announce his election. It was introduced by the Earl of Craven, still a member of the Company. The Duke accepted the office, having the necessary stock through a free gift to him of £300, presented as early as 1672. Thus the Company's appeal to the King for redress of their wrongs would find a ready hearing.

On November 14, 1683, a petition was presented by the Company to the King praying to be taken under the royal protection, and that measures be adopted to induce the King of France "to speed his effectual commands to the Governor [of La Nouvelle France] to make reparation for the loss sustained," and failing this, that the Company be given authority " to repair themselves and to defend the Rights of your Crown and their just Properties." In December a memorial was presented to the ambassador of France in London by Sir Leolin Jenkins, Secretary of State. Representations were also made directly to the French King by Lord Preston, Ambassador Extraordinary at the French Court. His lordship did not let matters lie, but presented several memorials, always getting the answer that a reply from the Governor of Canada was being awaited. The Company again approached the throne with the prayer that Lord Preston be urged to press the French King to issue orders that his subjects who had taken possession of Port Nelson by violence withdraw from that region and that no such injuries should be perpetrated in the future.

Meanwhile Radisson was having his own troubles with the authorities at Quebec, for M. de Meulles, the Intendant, insisted on the furs from Hudson Bay paying the usual toll exacted on the peltry of the St. Lawrence. Moreover, as has been seen, the Governor felt called upon to maintain the friendship between the two Crowns, and gave his ship back to Benjamin Guillam, sending Governor Bridgar with him to Boston. As the remains of the two French ships had gone to rebuild the *Ste. Anne,* and she had been sent to the Bottom of the Bay with the English prisoners, the Frenchmen found themselves without any ship at all. Governor De la Barre was not in favour of making De la Chesnaye and Radisson pay toll for furs gathered in a region as far from Quebec as was the coast of France. He therefore sent Radisson overseas to lay his case before the Minister M. de Seignelay (Colbert). Radisson arrived at La Rochelle on December 18, 1683 (N.S.), and Groseilliers soon after him. By 5th January (N.S.) the Hudson's Bay Company had news of his arrival, and Sir James Hayes was writing to the Secretary of the Duke of York to get the King's diplomatic machine into motion to call on the French monarch " to cause exemplary justice to be done on Radisson." On 26th January (O.S.) Lord Preston, Ambassador Extraordinary to France, called the attention of the French King to the man's presence in Paris, and prayed that action should be taken to punish one guilty of such violent deeds as his. In reply the French claimed that the English were the real aggressors, for the country was part of Canada. However, if we may trust an affidavit sworn to by Radisson before the notorious Judge Jeffreys in August 1687, the Company's resort to diplomacy was not in vain. M. de la Callières, by the direction of M. de Seignelay, the Minister, called Radisson to him and had him, in his presence, write directions to the effect that, to terminate the differences between the two nations, he was to go to Hudson Bay, with a passport from the English Company, and bring away the furs which the French had left at Port Nelson and all their property, the indemnity demanded by the English to be made up from the furs and goods, or their equivalent in value. As this affidavit was sworn to for evidence to be laid before a commission of which M. de la Callières was a member, it may be taken as embodying the truth. The document, written by Radisson, remained in the hand of Lord Preston, who produced it later for the inquiry by the commission.

Sir James Hayes's version of this strange incident runs :

. . . two Gentlemen very well known to [Lord Preston] brought him a proposition in writeing (which they also assured his Lordship wold be made good) importing that one De Grosiliers and his brother Radisson, who had conducted that action at Port Nellson, should under the Passports of the Hudson's Bay Compa returne to Port Nellson and fetch from thence the french they had left behind them, and a certain time was also therein proposed wherein the Compa should receive satisfaction for ye Damage by them sustained, which proposition was communicated by the Lord Preston to the Earle of Sunderland, and soone after, when the Companies shipps were ready to sayle for the Bay, Radisson came to London, and tendered his service to the Compa to go over upon their ships & without further trouble to bring away all those of his Nation that he had left behinde, whereupon he was presented to His Majesty & his Royall Highness & having done every thinge whereby he might conciliate credit and confidence, he was last spring sent upon a ship belonging to ye Compa to effect what he had undertaken, that being judged the most gentle way of putting an end to that business without engaging ye Crownes any further therein.

Radisson's reward for returning to the Company's service was a gratuity of £25, a salary of £50, and the benefit, without the actual ownership, of £200 of stock in the Company.   Groseilliers, impervious to all inducements, remained in France, and finally returned to live and die at Three Rivers on the St. Lawrence.   The Company showed its gratitude to Lord Preston for his services by banqueting him on his return to England, and by presenting him with a fur coverlet for his bed.   Radisson took the oath of fidelity once more, and on 17th May was on his way to Port Nelson in a ship not inappropriately named the *Happy Return*.

When Radisson reached Port Nelson he found Hayes Fort on the Nelson doing a thriving business.   His nephew Chouart was lodged in his fastness on Rainbow Island anxiously awaiting a ship from Quebec to relieve him.   Indians brought him down to meet his uncle, and Radisson's terms, that he was to be taken home by way of England and was to surrender his goods, were readily accepted.   As many as 239 packages of beaver, containing 12,000 skins, were put into the hands of George Geyer, the Hudson's Bay Company's Governor.   Merchandise to the value of 7,000 to 8,000 beaver was also given up, doubtless much of it the goods seized during Radisson's raids.

It was the policy of the Company to safeguard its title to Port Nelson by keeping a post on both of its rivers.   Governor Geyer built this autumn a post on the Hayes a mile and a half from its mouth and on the left bank.   This is York Fort, the oldest permanent settlement in the present Province of Manitoba.

A disagreement arose between Governor Geyer and Radisson over the treatment of the Frenchmen who had given themselves up. Chouart and others were willing to stay on in the Company's service, and Radisson wished them to be sent into the country to bring the Indians down.   Geyer insisted that the original arrangement should be adhered to.   As will be seen, this was wise, for the position would have been very awkward when a French expedition appeared in the river a few weeks later.   Chouart's furs were brought down to York Fort, which was a-building, and loaded on the *Happy Return*, and on 4th September Radisson and his fellow-countrymen sailed for

England. Chouart arrived in London in October, and agreed to enter the Company's service. He was given £100 to fit himself out with and £100 a year during his engagement of four years. Four other Frenchmen, one Elie Grimard among them, were retained for four years at a salary rising with the years from £30 to £45. Yet four others, whose services were not wanted, were given £25 each and let go. The gratitude of the Committee towards Radisson was evidenced by their taking him to be presented to the King and the Duke of York, the Governor, and by a gratuity of 100 guineas voted to him.

On April 2, 1685, the Company's Governor became King as James II. A General Court elected John Lord Churchill to fill his place. When but fifteen years of age he had been page of honour to the Duke. He continued in great favour with him when King, and with his sister, afterwards Queen Anne. This was the reason for the choice.

In 1684 the French Court, without repudiating its claim to Port Nelson asserted by Groseilliers and Radisson, had sacrificed the interests of the Canadian company which they represented by agreeing to Radisson's return to the English and by compensating the Hudson's Bay Company for its losses. This action, if not the result of a Court intrigue, would be due to the European policy of Louis XIV., who had begun his advance to the Rhine marked by the seizure of Strasbourg. Spain had declared war on France ; some sacrifice must be made to keep England friendly and out of the war. At the same time there was no intention to abandon Hudson Bay to the English. On the contrary, the feeling that the English were the enemy in America grew intenser, especially in Canada. It was felt that definite action must be taken to oust the intruders from the Bay of the North. Accordingly, Monsieur de la Barre, relying on a dispatch from the King dated August 5, 1683, issued an order on March 18, 1684, looking to the continued assertion of the rights of the French at Port Nelson. " We, on the part of and in the name of His Majesty, order the sieurs Pachot and Lazeur, directors [of the company which had established the post on the River Sainte-Thérèse (Hayes)] to send promptly a ship of forty to fifty tons to succour the post of the Nelson River with men, munitions of war, and the goods necessary for the maintenance and preservation of it . . . until the King has made known his intentions . . . and we assure them in our own and private name that we will be responsible for the costs." The company responded by sending out two ships, commanded by Claude de Bermen, Sieur de la Martinière, a member of the Council of Quebec, and Pierre Allemand, a young but skilful " pilot." The scribe of the expedition was the Jesuit Father, Antoine Silvy, whose Journal is a lively account of the proceedings of the year. A similar order issued by De la Barre the following day to Zachary Jolliet, to proceed to Rupert River to take steps looking to the expulsion of the English, will be referred to in a different connection.

On September 4, 1684, the Hudson's Bay Company's ship, the

Happy Return, sailed away from Port Nelson bearing Radisson, and with him Chouart and the remnant of De la Chesnaye's expedition of 1682, furs and all, along with the peltry traded during the current season. Eight days later the two ships equipped in Quebec by the enterprising De la Chesnaye and his associates entered the mouth of the Hayes River to find a fort standing on its north bank and the English flag floating on the breeze. The Hudson's Bay Company's Governor, John Abraham, sent out a Frenchman in the service to know their object. The result was an altercation to the following effect : " This is French territory." " No, it is English." " But the French under Radisson arrived first." " They did not, the English were on the ground first." A second messenger was sent out with the proposal in writing, that, as there was no war between the two countries, they should live in amity as two families ; let the newcomers meet the Governor to make an arrangement. Monsieur de la Martinière refused to recognize the Governor, but agreed to a meeting. At this it was concluded that the Frenchmen might build where they chose, but neither party should fortify its post. Père Silvy, however, asserts that the English put their cannon in place. A messenger was sent to demand that they be dismounted, but was told by Governor Abraham that they had been in position for long, and that the French could trust his word as a gentleman. La Martinière sent two men in a canoe upstream to seek a site for their house, but they returned reporting that they had been fired on with ball as they were passing the English fort. The English claimed afterward that they were not aware of the presence of the Frenchmen, which was probably true, for the men's story was that they were concealed in the bush and could have shot down a number of Englishmen, who were walking carelessly on the beach a few yards from them. That night La Martinière tried an assault on York Fort, on the ground that the English had broken the truce by firing on his men. The assault failed, for the men felt that they were out on a trading expedition, and were not called on to sacrifice themselves for a victory whose gains would go to their masters. Père Silvy reports a number of movements made by the English during the autumn and in the spring, which came to naught because they were cowards. It is more than likely that the English servants took the same view as the French as to the extent of their obligations to their employers, and that they were doing no more than watching the movements of their opponents.

Had the French taken their ships above York Fort, they and their furs might have been bottled up by the English when the time for sailing came. They therefore berthed them in a small stream, the Gargouse, the " Frenchmen's Creek " of Robson's map (at p. 90), flowing into the Hayes from the east a little below that fort. On the seaward side of the creek they built a fort with palisades enclosing three houses. A detachment sent up the river found Groseilliers's two houses standing, and an even more commodious house ten miles farther up, Chouart's place of refuge. It was the intention to occupy these, but after a hostile demonstration on the part of the English, which was, however, not pressed home, it was decided for the sake of strength to keep the party together at the fort beside the ships, at least during the winter. The English forthwith burned the French houses up the river to prevent them from being occupied in the spring, and the Indians from being intercepted on the way to York Fort. None the less the French opened a store at an advantageous point ten miles above their creek and sent men up to meet the Indians in trade. Assiniboins brought down a beautiful body of furs in ninety-one canoes. The French were not interfered with as they brought the peltry past York Fort. On 5th July (O.S.) La Martinière burned down his fort and left for Quebec, apparently well satisfied with the season's returns. La Potherie, however, says that he did a very mediocre business with the Indians.

On his way across the Bay La Martinière must have passed an English frigate unseen, outward bound with Radisson on board. However, he came upon a smaller vessel, the *Perpetuana Merchant*, pink. He summoned its captain, Edward Hume, on board by firing across his bow, and demanded his Commission. Hume showed his sailing orders signed by the Committee of the Hudson's Bay Company. Let Père Silvy continue the story :

We asked him if this Company was the same as that of the year before and when he told us that it was, M. de la Martinière and M. l'Allemand asked me my opinion as to what they should do, and if they should capture this ship, although there was no war between the two nations. I told them that there was no reason to hesitate, that since they had robbed the Company of Canada [of Chouart's furs] . . . they could and should capture it by virtue of natural justice which is not dependent on any one at all. We told the English captain then that he was taken prisoner, and we sent at the same time to take possession of the ship. He said that the ship belonged to him, and not to the Company, which owned only the cargo. We replied that he had nothing to fear, that the Company of England was too just to let him lose anything without compensating him.

Thus early the great Company had won a reputation for fairness it would seem.

Coming on a second small vessel, a ketch, La Martinière summoned its captain in vain. He then attacked the ship, but without success. On withdrawing from the combat he was pursued by a large English frigate bound for the Bay. The small French ships found a refuge in a rocky cove which the large vessel could not enter. Thus they escaped and arrived safely in Quebec. The " war of merchants " was ending in deeds of violence and rapidly drifting towards a conflict of arms between the two nations.

The determination of the French to win the ground on the Bay lost to the English was being manifested in various ways. *Coureurs-des-bois* were allowed—it may be said encouraged—to cross the height of land into the territory claimed by the Hudson's Bay Company, to divert the furs to the St. Lawrence. The English Company complained of this in a petition to the King, and the correspondence with its Governors overseas shows that its trade with the Bottom of the Bay was diminishing. Port Nelson was too far west to be affected. In 1684 De la Barre expressed his satisfaction at the post established by Du Lhut on Lake Nipigon. It stood on the north-east shore of the lake at the mouth of the Ombabika (La Maune) River, and was called La Maune, and alternatively La Tourette. It would be the point of departure for outrunners into the valley of the Albany by way of its tributary the Ogoki, or by the Little Current and Kenogami rivers. It was by one of these routes that Monsieur Péré and two Frenchmen reached Albany Fort in the middle of July that year. They professed to be on the way to Port Nelson, and begged for a little pease, for powder and shot. These were given. They returned in the absence of Governor Sergeant at the rendezvous at Charlton Island, but were sent away. When they returned a third time the English concluded, not without reason, that they were spies and seized them. The two men were sent to Charlton Island, where they could be allowed freedom to hunt, but Monsieur Péré was kept at Albany Fort under arrest. In connection with this incursion the French built a small outpost, Fort des Français, at the confluence of the Albany and the Kenogami, to bar the way of the Indians to Albany Fort, 1685. Farther west an attempt was made to reach out to the Indians who went down to trade at Port Nelson. In 1688 Monsieur de Noyon built a post, probably where La Vérendrye's Fort Pierre stood later, on Rainy River at its outflow from the lake of that name.

On March 20, 1684, the day after he issued the Commission to La Martinière for his expedition to Port Nelson, De la Barre signed a similar order to Zachary Jolliet. "Having received orders by His Majesty's despatch of August 5th last to trouble the English on Hudson's Bay as much as possible and to hinder the establishment with all his might," he decided to cut the Indians off from going down to the Bay and to compel them to trade with the French. To this end he ordered Jolliet, who was well acquainted with the tribes of those parts, to go with thirty or forty suitable men and the necessary goods, to build a fort and to plant the arms of the King and tell the English that they were enemies of the French. Jolliet spent the first year at the fort on Lake Mistassini, which he called Nemisko, for Hugh Verner the Factor at Charles Fort wrote that a French post was three hundred miles up the Rupert River. In June 1685 the Frenchman wrote to Hugh Verner to say that in keeping with the King's order of August 5, 1683, he had been commissioned by De la Barre to carry out the Instructions of which he enclosed a copy. He accordingly took the liberty to write a few lines to warn an old friend to retire from the region as soon as possible, especially as he had received a letter from the Governor that he was sending more men to his support ; he would be sorry, after having been entertained by Governor Bayly, dined and slept with him, and having been given the freedom of the fort, and after having been for so long neighbour to Mr. Verner, to fight him to capture the post. It would be his " last regret " so to do ; would Mr. Verner have the kindness to drop him a line to tell him what he proposed to do in the circumstances ; he must not be surprised if he (Jolliet) carried his orders out to the letter, but he assured him that he personally would do all that he could to have things go smoothly. He signed himself Mr. Verner's " humble and affectionate servant."

A similar letter, presumably in less affectionate terms as he was a stranger, was addressed to Governor Sergeant at Albany Fort. The packet reached Charles Fort in September and was forwarded to Albany as soon as the ice made travel easy. Unfortunately for him, Sergeant took the communication for no more than a trick of the French. Verner had asked his chief for directions as to fortifying Charles Fort, but got no more than Sergeant's frivolous interpretation of the communication of Jolliet. On his own initiative he began strengthening the defences of his post, and was still at the task in June 1686. This may explain why a ladder stood outside, leaning against one of the bastions, on a fateful evening in that month. Sergeant afterwards claimed that he had given orders and plans to all the forts for their fortification, but he was charged with being negligent in the matter even at his own post, Albany. Evidently both at Albany and Moose Jolliet's communication was taken as a joke.

Meanwhile the storm was gathering to the south. De la Barre was replaced by Jacques René de Brisaye, Marquis de Denonville, in August 1685. From the actions of the new Governor, who came directly from the French Court, his instructions can be readily gathered. Along with him came five hundred soldiers for a campaign against the Iroquois, and Pierre, Chevalier de Troyes, an experienced officer, ostensibly with the same end in view. But in the spring following De Troyes was placed at the head of a flying column, composed of thirty regulars and seventy Canadian volunteers, as Denonville's Instructions ran, to establish a trading post on Hudson's Bay. Never before nor since has a force of such size and composition been employed for the simple task of opening a fur post. Under De Troyes there served as second in command Jacques le Moyne, Sieur de Sainte-Hélène, Charles de Longueil's son, who had been in the army for now twenty-seven years. Sainte-Hélène's brother Pierre, Sieur d'Iberville, a trained naval officer, served as second lieutenant. Another brother, Paul, Sieur de Maricourt, who now began his military career, served as major. Pierre Allemand, newly returned from his expedition to Port Nelson, was placed over the commissariat, while Father Silvy played the part of chaplain. The astonishing journey of this large body of men from Montreal to James Bay is a subject of just pride to the people of Quebec. The journey up the Ottawa amid the melting snow of spring and the course over the height of land to Lake Abitibi and down the Abitibi and Moose rivers are a testimony to the endurance of the Frenchmen of the St. Lawrence and their power to adapt rude means to great ends. De Troyes and the officers handled the men admirably, so that they reached the broadening estuary of the Moose a comparatively disciplined force. In the English forts, the objective of the expedition, there lay small bodies of civilians, mostly labourers picked up in the London market, all unconscious of the storm about to burst upon them.

De Troyes's Journal is written in the grand military style, showing all the precautions taken and his disposition of the troops. A ram was prepared, and some sort of a movable shield to protect the men operating it. On 10th June (O.S.), under cover of night, the force landed on Hayes Island, half a league from Moose Fort. Detachments of eighteen men each, under Sainte-Hélène and Iberville, were placed to attack the flanks of the post, three men with axes being told off to cut down the palisades. A false attack on the rear was provided for. The main attack was to be on the front gate. De Troyes passed from one detachment to another encouraging his men. The assault began in the gloom of the early dawn of the 21st with a general fusillade on every side. Sainte-Hélène and Iberville clambered over the palisades and advanced, sword in hand. The main attack found the back gate not so much as locked and the English guns unloaded. The French now fired into the inner building through its windows. The ram forced its door. At this point the English called for quarter, and De Troyes summoned them to surrender. As an Englishman showed fight by directing a cannon in place on one of the bastions upon the French below, he was shot down and the assault was continued. Iberville pushed through a door, sword in hand, and was momentarily isolated when the inmates closed it upon him. De Troyes brought up the ram, forced open the door, and came to the relief of the daring young man. The English again called for quarter and surrendered. In half an hour the fort was taken and the French flag run up on the staff. So far De Troyes's grandiloquent Journal. The fort was occupied under the name St. Louis.

The Hudson Bay documents show that, in spite of the grand military style of De Troyes, there really was no fight. So little was danger suspected at Moose, the day before the attack Chief Factor John Bridgar left on the sloop *Craven* for a jaunt to Charles Fort, taking with him all his officers—Bronson, Garland, Norbury, Miners, and Oake. He left an underling in charge. No watch was kept, and all were asleep when the fusillade began. There was no one in the fort capable of leading, and no concerted defence was offered. Seventeen Englishmen in their night-shirts surrendered to an armed force of a hundred men. During the attack the *Craven* with Bridgar and his officers lay at anchor at Willow Island, four or five miles down the river, and out of hearing. French canoes went down to her that night and found her without watch, an easy prey. They allowed her to go to Charles Fort, to be captured there.

De Troyes's force reached the Rupert River and Charles Fort on 23rd June. Scouts reported the *Craven* as anchored in the stream over against the fort, and a ladder outside the palisade leaning against a bastion, as they thought to serve as a fire-escape. De

Troyes ordered a simultaneous attack on ship and fort in the dusk of early dawn. He sent Iberville to deal with the *Craven*. Access to the fort was gained by the ladder leaning on the bastion. A general fusillade awoke the sleeping inmates. From the roof a soldier threw a grenade down a stove-pipe. It shattered the stove and wounded Mrs. Verner, who was probably the first English woman to see the Rupert River. Verner, the Factor, kept up a defence from within the house for half an hour, and only surrendered when the building was undermined and ready to be blown up. The French occupied the fort under the name St. Jacques.

Meanwhile Iberville's party reached the sloop in their silent canoes and jumped on board. The watchman lay asleep in his blanket and a number of men in the berths below. The Frenchman stamped on the deck to arouse the sleepers. The watchman immediately assumed an attitude of defence. He was shot down. The men below came rushing up towards the deck. Iberville struck the leader on the head with his sword. When the man showed fight and called to his companions for support, Iberville ran his sword through his body. The Frenchmen hacked a hole into the sleeping quarters and shot at the Englishmen caught like so many rats in a hole. Some were wounded, and all surrendered forthwith. Had such deeds been perpetrated in open warfare, the French would be justified in their pride at them. Perpetrated in a time of profound peace, they dishonour the race.

De Troyes set fire to Charles Fort after loading the *Craven* with the furs and goods. At Moose Fort he took on the great guns of its battery and sailed for Albany Fort. Some of his canoes arrived before the sloop, and his scouts were able to report on the defences of the post. Governor Sergeant only became aware of the impending attack two hours before the enemy arrived. It was Friday the 9th of July. De Troyes spent Sunday and Monday making his plans. On this last day he sent a drummer to the fort to summon it to surrender. The answer was that the demand was very surprising, all the more as there was no rupture between the Crowns ; the fort would be defended as long as possible. De Troyes now brought his force of some sixty men across the river and erected a battery at a point at which only two of the guns of the fort could be directed upon it. Most of the French troops were kept under the bank of the river, but guns of the fort cost two men their lives. All Wednesday the French were quiet, and on Thursday Governor Sergeant sent out two men to report on the enemy's dispositions. These stated that the battery consisted of the great guns from Moose, and was finished, and that they would probably hear from them in a few hours. Five guns were fired that evening and three in the fort replied. On Friday the French kept up a bombardment from eight o'clock in the morning until seven in the evening—173 shots in all. They then began, as the men in the fort thought, to erect another battery on the other side of the fort. This brought difficulties within the post to a head. Sergeant declared afterwards to the Committee that his men now refused to carry on, and insisted that, if he would not go out to surrender, they would, for if they lost limbs in the fight there was no assurance that the Company would pension them, as the King did the men in the army. Sergeant now sent his minister, apparently the first chaplain in these parts, to arrange a conference, and finally surrendered the fort on terms. The French occupied the fort under the name Ste. Anne.

The Articles of Surrender included clauses binding the French to take the Company's servants to Charlton Island to meet the ship from England, and to provide provisions for them while on their hands and for their journey. It is not known whether the prisoners were taken to Charlton ; in any case, the ship *Happy Return* was crushed in the ice of Hudson Strait on the way out to the Bay, and no return was possible that way. Governor Sergeant and as many as could be put on the *Craven* were sent to Port Nelson. The large number suddenly quartered on York Fort led to difficulties. The Committee charged Sergeant with being the centre of something like a mutiny during the winter. At home he was charged with surrendering Albany Fort out of cowardice, and dismissed the service. Some twenty-two men had been left on the hands of the French at Moose Fort. They were given meagre quantities of powder and shot from time to time, and were left to shift for themselves as best they could. Some were taken by the Indians, as the French suggested, and spent the winter with them. Those who found no such refuge endured terrible sufferings, four dying of starvation. In the following summer they were made to work their way with the canoes to Canada, shipped to La Rochelle, and there cast adrift. They finally worked their passages on English ships to England.

Some time after his capture at Charles Fort, Hugh Verner, the Factor that was, had an illuminating conversation with the Sieur d'Iberville. In answer to a question, Iberville assured him that had he done what he had done without a Commission from the King of France "he could expect nothing but hanging, pointing to his throat when he spoak." Asked " how they Could answere the affront they had done the King of England in burneing and wasteing his Country with fire and Sword and in killing and famishing his Subjects. De Bervill's answer was that the King of England would not Quarrell with his Brother the King of France for such a trifle." This conversation reflects the actual situation. Louis XIV. was above all responsible for the capture of the English forts at the Bottom of the Bay, and his officers were no more than carrying out his desires. The seizure of the forts was but one part of a game, of which the other part was played by negotiations which bore the outward appearance of the utmost friendliness. James II. was beguiled into a " Treaty of Peace, good Correspondence and Neutrality in America," which ostensibly put an end to all the difficulties between the colonies of the two nations. Neither nation was to fit out ships or soldiers against any colony of the other. The fourth clause ran : " It's

agreed, That both Kings shall have and retain to themselves all
the Dominions, Rights and Preeminences, in the American Seas,
Roads and other Waters whatsoever, in as full and ample manner
as of Right belongs to them, and in such manner as they now possess
the same." At the time King James was all unconscious that De
Troyes had seized the Bottom of the Bay. Not so Louis XIV. The
signing of the treaty gave the English forts to the French, for they
were then in possession, and it prevented the English from taking
any action to recover them. Diplomacy has conquests to its credit
no less than war.

In January 1687 the Hudson's Bay Company got its first news of
the loss of its forts on James Bay. The Committee decided that the
gravity of the situation called for a meeting of the General Court.
On 14th February Lord Churchill, Governor of the Company, laid the
whole matter, including the letters conveying the news, before the
General Court. A petition was agreed to, and it was arranged that
not only the Governor and the Committee, but members of the Court,
should wait upon the King to present it. On 17th February Lord
Churchill and an assemblage of the stockholders presented the
petition "showeing the great Insults and damages done to this
Company by the French at the Bottome of the Bay." The Minute
of the Committee runs on : " His Matie received the same and was
gratiously pleased to Answer in these words: Gentlemen, I understand yor buisinesse ; my honour and yor money are concerned ;
I assure you I will take a particular Care in it and see you righted."
These were brave words, but the King's hands were tied by the
Treaty of Peace, good Correspondence and Neutrality, not to speak
of the misunderstandings between him and the people of England.
As Iberville had said, it was impossible for him to quarrel with
Louis XIV.

All that came out of the representations made by the King's
Ministers to the Court of France was an agreement to refer the
question of the titles of the two nations to Hudson's Bay to a Commission. The papers laid before the Commissioners show the course
of the diplomatic struggle. The English claimed title in virtue of
a succession of discoveries by Henry Hudson, Sir Thomas Button,
Luke Foxe, and Thomas James, some of whom had taken possession
in the name of the King of England and planted his arms ; and
finally on the firm ground of continuous possession from " 1667 "
(it should be 1668) ; and from 1670 by the Hudson's Bay Company
with a royal Charter ; and on a succession of treaties with the
natives. The French rebuttal was based on the contiguity of the
Hudson Bay region with Canada ; it was all one country, and when
they settled Canada they became possessed of Hudson Bay ; they
put forward a series of explorations : Champlain's in the valley of
the Ottawa and Lake Huron, and Jean Bourdon's to Labrador
(which would be pertinent if the principal of contiguity were accepted) ;
they laid special stress on proclamations of possession, as for example,
those by Father Albanel and the Sieur de St. Lusson ; and, as against

the Hudson's Bay Company's Charter of the late date of 1670, on the Letters Patent given by Henry IV. to Jacques Cartier and those of Louis XIII. to the Company of the One Hundred Associates, which gave them from Florida to the Bay of the North, that is, Hudson Bay. In reply the English laid stress on continuous settlement as giving a valid title; that in spite of the Letters Patent granted by Louis XIII., the Atlantic coast north of Florida had become English in virtue of the colonies actually settled in a part of the region granted. A serious point made by the French was that the Treaty of St. Germain-en-Laye, by which the English returned Canada to the French after its capture in Champlain's time, was interpreted at the time by all parties in their sense as including Hudson Bay. Agreement on the ground of title was found to be impossible.

In August the French Commissioners proposed a division of the area in dispute, the French to give up the Bottom of the Bay to the English, and the English to surrender the Port Nelson region to the French. The substance of this proposal was determined by a discussion which had taken place the autumn before. The Governor of Canada, Denonville, had received a dispatch stating that it was considered that King James would agree to the two nations holding Port Nelson in common. Writing on 10th November, he replied at great length on the situation on the Bay. He had ordered De Troyes simply " to go and choose some forts at the Bottom of the Bay to hinder the English trade and to recall the Sieur Péré and two other Frenchmen, whom he knew the English kept in chains. . . . The success of the journey lay in that De Troyes and the Canadians had found the secret of making themselves masters of three forts. . . . He did not command the English forts to be taken, only that Radisson,* who he knew was in the fort there, should be carried off." As to the agreement that the River Bourbon [Nelson] should be common to the two nations, that would not do, for the English goods were so cheap that even the French *coureurs-des-bois* would take their furs to them. It would be of great advantage to surrender the posts at the Bottom of the Bay to the English, and for the French to keep the River Bourbon, because from Lake Nipigon they could hinder the savages from going to Albany and easily cut across the trade of the English, while at Port Nelson a vast number of tribes as yet unknown could be reached and their furs got ; moreover it was possible that there the way to the Western Sea would be found. The reply of the Hudson's Bay Company to the proposal that it should exchange York Fort for the posts at the Bottom of the Bay was that, so far from being a compromise, it meant that they should give some of their own territory in exchange for their own.

In November the English Commissioners reported to the King : " It plainly appears that your Majesty has a Right to the whole Bay and Streights of Hudson," and that the French Commissioners

* Radisson had not been in James Bay since 1674.

were " ready to do all that is necessary for the regulation of Limits between the Dominions of both Crowns." In this they were out of keeping with the facts, for, strange to say, the final agreement drawn up on December 11, 1687, omitted all reference to the right of possession of either country and recommended a delimitation of frontiers by a future Commission. It contented itself with announcing that until " their most serene majestys shall send any new and Express orders in writeing concerning this matter, It shall not be lawfull for any Governor or Commander in chief of the Colonies . . . in America to commit an act of hostility against or Invade the subjects of the other King." After all this negotiation, then, not only were the French left in possession of the Bottom of the Bay, but the English Company was forbidden to take any steps to recover its lost posts. This was in truth a conquest in time of peace made valid by diplomacy. The weakness of the position of James II. in his own country explains his surrender. He could not allow the difficulties of a few fur-traders to embroil him with his cousin, of whose support he might be in need.

Before this decision, so unfortunate for the Hudson's Bay Company, was made known, the Committee had sent out two ships to York Fort, leaving it to the discretion of the Council there to decide on the course to be pursued. The decision at York Fort was not to attempt to recover the captured posts. When the Committee heard later that there were only fifteen Frenchmen left at the Bottom of the Bay it deplored this inaction. The failure to assume the aggressive appeared all the more deplorable when, on 22nd January following, Lord Sunderland wrote to Lord Churchill, the Governor of the Company, conveying to him His Majesty's letter forbidding all hostility between the English and French in America, and enclosing a copy of the treaty. On 8th February the Committee decided to observe the letter of the treaty, but to keep alive the Company's title to the Bottom of the Bay by sending an expedition " to make a Settlement without annoying the French and to stay there the next winter."

Meanwhile the Company was continuing its normal course, developing the area on Hudson Bay within its control, and taking possession of the mouths of its rivers, lest the French or the equally dreaded interlopers should stake out a first claim. In 1685 the Severn was settled, and Churchill Fort, the first post so called after the Governor, was built there.

On 25th June of the following year Captain Michael Grimington, with Captain John Abraham and four others, was sent from York Fort to explore the possibilities of the great river in which Jens Munck had wintered. On account of besetting ice the outward voyage took no less than twenty days. The river was reported to afford excellent accommodation for ships, being twenty-two fathoms deep at the mouth, and as much as four fathoms at the falls about three leagues up. The land on the south bank was full of trees and underwood, but the reckless explorers started a fire which burned for eight days. Abundant signs of Indians gave promise of a good trade, while deer and partridges would afford a satisfactory food supply. On the voyage "many thousands of white whales were seen." In the autumn the Committee received the glowing report of its expedition, and forthwith ordered the river, to which they gave the name Churchill after the Governor, to be settled. They were urgent in their commands, because John Abraham had been so struck with its possibilities as to prepare, in conjunction with John Outlaw, his fellow-captain in the Company's service, an interloping expedition to occupy the ground first. The Committee planned a summer settlement for whale fishing, Thomas Savage to be chief ; the sloop *Colleton* was attached to the post and a harpooner was employed. The party organized in 1688 devoted itself to whale-fishing and sent home sixty tons of blubber. At the same time there was to be a trade in furs, and Henry Kelsey was sent out on a vain search for Indians. The whole scheme received a setback when the house which was being built was destroyed by fire. As the Company had established a first claim, and was deeply and disastrously engaged elsewhere, it sisted proceedings on the Churchill River.

That summer the Company's great expedition to the Albany River was on its way out. As it was passing through Hudson Strait it came upon Captain Abraham's interloping expedition, bound for Churchill River, its ship crushed in the ice and ready to sink. All the crestfallen interlopers were rescued and taken to York Fort, and finally home to England. The Company had taken care to secure a royal proclamation against interloping. Doubtless Abraham's first attention on board the Company's ship was directed to this. In the issue the savage ice of Hudson Strait was, in all probability, as great a bar to interlopers as royal proclamations.

The Company's ships broke company in Hudson Bay. Two went on to York Fort. Three kept in consort till the Bottom of the Bay was reached. There the *Churchill*, frigate, under the command of Captains John Marsh and Andrew Hamilton, with Captain William Bond for navigator, and the newly built frigate *Yonge*, Captain John Simpson in command, sailed for Albany, while the *Huband*, frigate, under Captain Richard Smithsend, with Hugh Verner, late Factor at Charles Fort, continued on to the Rupert River. As has been stated, the Committee found its hands tied by the prohibition of all hostile incursions by English and French against one another. Yet it was determined to keep alive its claim to the Bottom of the Bay by active settlements. The Instructions to the several officers were carefully drawn in this sense. Forts were to be built and commerce with the Indians re-established. The chief officers were to be " jealous of the French," and to guard against them by fortifying the posts, but they were to keep on friendly terms with them, for they were told to arrange a trade with them for the small furs, which were much in demand at the time and very profitable. Copies of the Treaty of Neutrality between the two Crowns were placed in the hands of the principal officers with instructions that it should be observed. If the French should be the first to break it, they must use force against force. Important decisions were to be taken only in a council of the responsible officers.

Everything had been done to ensure success in the delicate task prescribed. Lord Churchill himself had chosen Captain John Marsh, an experienced military man, to be the new Governor of the Bottom of the Bay and commander of the expedition. His Deputy was Captain Andrew Hamilton, another soldier. Captain Bond of the *Churchill* had long been in the Company's service. To heighten the courage of the seamen and its servants the Company promised pensions at least equivalent to those given in the army to any who should be wounded. The ships were provided with cannon.

About the 8th of September the *Churchill* and *Yonge* reached the Albany River. They passed the old English fort at the eastern extremity of Bayly's Island, now under the French flag, Iberville in command, without hostile demonstration on either side. Governor Marsh landed twenty men beyond on the island, and raised a barricade for their defence. The next morning French sharp-shooters shot one of the men. A fortnight later a fort was begun on an island opposite the western extremity of Bayly's Island and on the other side of the river. While the building was going on three men were shot by the French. The truce was thus broken. Governor Marsh now had grounds for using his superior force against the enemy. His failure to do so when his strength was at its greatest proved disastrous to the expedition. In December the French captured Captain Bond and his first mate while out hunting. The English now fell victims to scurvy, and Governor Marsh himself died. His Deputy, Captain Hamilton, availed himself of a clause in his Instructions to make an arrangement with Iberville to supply him (Iberville) with goods in exchange for furs. The two nations were to keep on friendly terms. There was considerable come and go between the forts. But when the English garrison was crippled with scurvy, Iberville decided to tear up the agreement, on the flimsy ground that an Irish Catholic in the English fort had told him that the English intended to capture the French post in the spring. Without giving any notification that the friendly agreement was at an end, he treacherously sent an armed party to ambush unarmed Englishmen out with their sleds getting wood. Twenty were brought in. Iberville's opportunity had now come, for many of the remaining English were sick. He demanded the unconditional surrender of their fort, but was met with a sharp refusal. He thereupon began a siege. The enfeebled garrison held out for several days against his bombardment, and even made attempts at sallies. When at last there were only eight " sound men " left they surrendered. Probably because the fort was much more substantial than the old one built ten years before, Iberville moved into it. In the spring he turned its guns to his use and laid siege to the ships. They were in an isolated position, and he forced them to surrender. Thus the great effort of the

Company to maintain its title to the Albany River or, alternatively, to recapture its post brought nothing but disaster. The loss was put at £15,000.

The expedition to the Rupert River was no less unfortunate. When summer came Iberville sailed up the river and captured the *Huband*, frigate. All unknown to this buccaneer and his victims, war against France had been declared on 17th May by William III. and Mary, now sovereigns of England. Thus the capture of the *Huband* was the first seizure by the French for which the justification of war might be pleaded. For eight years they had carried on a war in a time of peace. That phase was at an end. It was now open war on the Bay.

3.—OPEN WAR ON THE BAY, 1689-1713—HENRY KELSEY

When the Prince of Orange ascended the throne of England as William III. the country had a king who identified himself closely with the economic and political interests of the nation. Moreover, William was head and front of the opposition to the dominance of France under Louis XIV. On May 17, 1689, he declared war against that monarch, and England fell into line with Holland and the other European Powers in the Grand Alliance. Among the reasons for this course given in the declaration of war was the action of the French King on Hudson Bay, " seizing our forts, burning our subjects' houses and enriching his people with the Spoil of their Goods and Merchandizes," and killing the people when " at that very time he was negotiating here in England by his Ministers a Treaty of Neutrality and good Correspondence in America." The war with France was what men of that time might well have called a world war. It lasted for a quarter of a century, with one interlude of peace. The battle front was in Europe, but the extreme westerly wing was on Hudson Bay. When the French chose, they had their way on the Bay. Not so in Europe. After a long period of stalemate Britain and her allies, finally led by that great military genius John Churchill, Duke of Marlborough, sometime Governor of the Hudson's Bay Company, brought France to her knees. When at last peace was made England was able to impose her will upon France on the Bay as well as in Europe, and the long struggle for Rupert's Land, at least so far as its sea coast was concerned, came to an end.

Lord Churchill, for us Governor of the Hudson's Bay Company, but to England of that day an outstanding political power and prop of the throne of James II., assured the success of the Revolution by deserting his master and bringing Princess Anne, afterwards Queen, over to William's side. He was rewarded with the title of Earl of Marlborough. The Hudson's Bay Company had many reasons for being wholly with him, nor could he have been altogether oblivious of its interests, for in April 1690 the Committee presented him with a gold plate " for his great care and troubles in their concernes." After the triumph of constitutional government, the Company must have felt that the Charter, granted to them by Charles II. in virtue of the royal prerogative, was open to attack, that they would be wise to come to terms with the new epoch of parliamentary rule. They hastened, therefore, to secure the sanction of Parliament for their monopoly. At a General Court on April 3, 1690, they adopted a petition asking for an Act of Parliament confirming their Charter, and ordered that several members of the Company be prepared to meet the House of Commons or committees of Parliament. Four days later leave was given in the House to present a Bill, and the Company's case was distributed to members. Apparently no great opposition was expected, but the furriers of London appeared against the Bill, and some of the Atlantic colonies made representations against it, doubtless through their agents in England. On the Bill coming to its third reading, a rider was proposed to limit the grant of the monopoly to ten years. The House of Lords amended this to read seven years, and this was accepted by the Commons. It was afterwards claimed by the North West Company and by Canadian writers that the Charter became invalid when this Act was not renewed at the expiry of the time limit, but it will be seen that this was not the view taken by the English Government, nor even by Parliament, for Acts were passed in nearly every subsequent reign which, in one way and another, assumed the validity of the Charter granted by Charles II. For example, the " Act for the encouragement of the Trade to America," 1707, had a limiting clause 23 : " Provided always that nothing in this Act shall any ways extend or be construed to take away or prejudice any of the estates, rights or privileges of or belonging to the Governor and Company of Adventurers of England trading in Hudson's Bay." Again, when the French in keeping with the Treaty of Utrecht surrendered their posts to England, Governor James Knight and his Deputy Henry Kelsey of the Hudson's Bay Company's overseas service were given a commission by Queen Anne to receive possession of Fort Bourbon from the French, and all parties accepted it that the Company was simply coming back into its own.

The Company had suffered great loss of property when the French seized their forts at the Bottom of the Bay. They put the claim of damages at £100,000. The loss in their annual trade was by no means comparable. Their practice was not to gather the largest possible bulk of peltries and throw them on the market, but rather to restrict the quantity to the demands of the London market so as not to lower the prices. As Port Nelson, with its wide beaver region inland, was proving the most productive of the areas so far tapped and one which admitted of expansion, it was in a measure possible to procure the furs required in spite of the loss of the posts on James Bay. Accordingly, the Committee put out every effort to increase production in the area remaining in their possession. The instrument of this policy was Henry Kelsey, one of the three outstanding personalities of this generation of Englishmen on the

Bay, John Fullertine and James Knight being the others. Long an obscure character, and even thought by some to be mythical, Kelsey has come to his own in our time, through the discovery of his original Journals and their publication jointly by the Public Archives of Canada and the Public Record Office of Northern Ireland (1929), and through the painstaking researches of Dr. Kenney of the Canadian Archives. As a mere boy he entered the service of the Company on April 14, 1684. He went out to Port Nelson in the year of Radisson's happy return to their employ. In his first summer he saw the Frenchman's successful *coup* in bringing over his nephew Chouart and the French furs to his English masters. In the following years he served side by side with Radisson and Chouart. The spirit of the great prototype of the *coureurs-des-bois* descended upon him. He consorted much with the Indians, learning their language, certainly the Cree and possibly the Assiniboin. He loved the ways of the savages, and a sentence written in Cree in one of his Journals shows that he liked their women. He is our first example of that comparatively rare species, the Indianized Englishman. He must have seen the cogency of Radisson's view that the traders should go inland to meet the Indians, induce them to " work beaver," show them how to put up the skins, and persuade them to bring them down to the fort by the sea. Certainly he saw from the battlements of York Fort the success of the method as practised by La Martinière in 1684–85. Kelsey's first recorded service was in 1688. " After 3 Indians being employed for great rewards to carry letters from Hayes river to New Severn, they returned without performing the business although paid ; then I was sent with an Indian boy and in a month returned with answers." At that time the policy of expansion was in full swing. Governor Abraham, having discovered, or more strictly rediscovered, three years before " a faire River " fifty leagues to the north of Port Nelson, a post was ordered to be built upon it under the name of the Churchill River. This post on the edge of the Barrens had, of course, to make contact with the Indians. To this end instructions were sent out " that the boy Kelsey be sent to Churchill with Thomas Savage, because we are informed he is a very active lad, delighting much in Indians' company, being never better pleased than when he is travelling amongst them : nevertheless would not have him too soon trusted amongst those unknown natives, without a pledge from the Indians." Accordingly Kelsey was taken in a shallop northward from the post a-building, and, when the coast proved too shoaly to keep close inshore, was landed with his Indian companion of that spring. He penetrated some two hundred miles north of Churchill, but seems never to have been very far from the sea. He returned without meeting a soul, defeated by the emptiness of the land. The fort on the Churchill, as has been seen, was burned down before it was finished and, possibly because of Kelsey's failure to meet Indians as well as the troubles of subsequent years, was not rebuilt till 1717.

The desire of the Deputy-Governor and Committee, following

Radisson's principle, was that some of their servants should penetrate inland to bring the Indians down in greater numbers to trade
at York Fort, but their officers on the ground, who had not the
Frenchmen's art of adapting themselves to Indian life, had reported
to the contrary. It was too often the weakness of the Company's
system that passive resistance on the part of the men could defeat
the Committee's plans. Messrs. James Knight (who was to prove
afterwards a most enterprising officer) and Richard Stanton had
reported in 1686 : " There is no possibility of sending Englishmen
up to the Heads of the Rivers but the way to Improve our Trade
& to destroy that of the French is to Imploy the Indian Capts
[" leaders "] who leye up at a Great Distance to persuade & Invite
the Indians to come to the English Factories."   In this instance,
however, the Committee persisted. In 1690 Jean-Baptiste Chouart
and Elie Grimard, Frenchmen whom we have seen in their service,
were sent inland, but Kelsey says that they did not go so much as
two hundred miles. That autumn renewed instructions from the
Committee arrived, and Governor George Geyer was able to report
by return ship that he had sent up Henry Kelsey " to the country
of the Assinae Poets [Assiniboins] to invite the remoter Indians to
a trade with us."

Kelsey left York Fort on June 12, 1690. Like Anthony Henday
after him in 1754 and Matthew Cocking in 1772, he went with Indians
who had come to the fort to trade, and were returning by their
customary route. The number of portages and lakes passed leaves
it certain that he followed the route taken by his successors—up the
Hayes to its confluence with our Fox River and up the south branch
of the Fox and over into Cross Lake, an expansion of the River
Nelson. Crossing the current of the Nelson flowing through the
lake, he would pass through the western extension of the lake and
come to the Minago River. This he would ascend. From its source
he would cross over to Moose Lake, and by its outflow reach the
Saskatchewan. At some spot on the Saskatchewan, where the river
took a sharp curve and made what was called a " point," Kelsey
made something like a base camp, " Dering's Point," as he called
it, after the Deputy-Governor of the Company of the time. Its
position may be gathered from the course followed by Matthew
Cocking and his Indians. To avoid the long northward sweep of the
Saskatchewan, the " Swift Current " as it was deservedly called,
they passed by the Birch River into the still waters of Saskeram
Lake, and from its upper stream portaged back into the Saskatchewan,
somewhere below the present Cumberland House. So did Kelsey
and his Indians in 1691. As the point at which they left the Saskatchewan was eighteen miles above Dering's Point, it follows that
the Point was the sharp bend of the river about twelve miles below
the present The Pas.

Henry Kelsey's doings during his first twelvemonth inland
are vaguely referred to in his Journal of the following trade season.
He was on the upper Red Deer River, for the Indians there welcomed

his return the year after; and in all probability he was on the prairies farther south, for he refers to a plain forty-six miles wide. On his return to Dering's Point in the spring he sent the report of his proceedings to Governor Geyer by the Indians going down with their furs. It ran that the savages were continually at war ; that the Indians trading at the Bay and armed there with guns were preying upon the defenceless tribes beyond them ; that he had promises that these last would get beaver, and come down the following year. Governor Geyer replied by the returning canoes with an order to continue his efforts.

On July 5, 1691, Kelsey passed upstream from Dering's Point. Eighteen miles up he entered a creek (Birch River) and passed through a succession of ponds, probably the marshy Saskeram Lake. Finally he portaged over half a mile and " came back at the river-side again," forty miles or more, by the course taken, above the point at which he had left it. He was now no great distance below our Cumberland House. His intention was to continue up the river (as Matthew Cocking did some eighty years later), but finding the current too swift he made a cache, that is a concealed storage, to await his return (presumably down the river). The party now took to foot and cut across into the valley of the Carrot River. They travelled eighty-three miles with "heavy mossy going" before reaching " good going." Kelsey was invited to meet Indians on the " Waskashreeseebee," Waskasew-sipi, the Red Deer River. These he reached on 30th July. " They were very glad that I was returned according to my promise." The next band he met was the " Eagle brich," possibly the Eagle Hills Creek Indians from the Elbow of the North Saskatchewan wandered across to trade. He was very anxious to meet with the " Naywatame poets," but he got word that the " Nayhaythaways," the Crees, had attacked them and put them to flight. On 6th August he was on the Red Deer where it (the course upstream is meant) trends to the south. The river, he heard, flowed from a lake (our Nut Lake), and from that same lake was fed the " Mith . . ." (The word is illegible, but it is probably Mithcou, Red River, the early name of our Assiniboine. This river is not actually fed by the lake, but rises not very far to the east.) Here again the route is probably indicated rather than the actual course of the stream. Forty miles farther on Kelsey reached the park grasslands, the clumps being of birch and poplar. He was probably now crossing where the present Canadian National Railway from Kamsack to Humboldt runs. Some fifty more miles brought him to the open prairies and the buffalo. He would now be on the plain forty-six miles wide of his first journey. Forty miles out on the prairies he came to the Mountain Poets, the Hill Stoneys, i.e. Assiniboins, probably of the Touchwood Hills. Forty-six miles brought him to the woods, probably the wooded Touchwood Hills.

So far Kelsey was travelling with and among Assiniboins. He now turned his attention to the Naywatame Poets and travelled north to find them. According to such knowledge as we have of the alignment of the Indians in the days before the White Men came, these should be the Gros Ventres, the Fall or Rapid Indians who, David Thompson says, got their name because they lived at the falls a hundred miles west of Cumberland House, that is, the Nipawi rapids some fifty miles below La Corne.* The name which Kelsey gives this people has puzzled all writers. " Poets " is his version of the Chippawa (Saulteur) *bwan*, the Cree *pwat*, the name given to the Sioux. His " Mountain Poets " above are the Assiniboins of the Hill, the Assiniboins being a branch of the Sioux. His Naywatame Poets might be the Assiniboins or Sioux living on a cape or point of the river, *nayow*, at the bottom of the hill, *netamutin*, which would be a possible description of the " point " of the Saskatchewan at the Nipawi falls. On the other hand, the Fall Indians were not of Siouan extraction. Kelsey's own narrative shows that this mysterious people were not of Siouan stock, for he and his Assiniboins had to have an interpreter in dealing with them. Travelling from the region of the Touchwood Hills for 127 miles more or less northward, that is in the direction of Nipawi, Kelsey with his Assiniboins met the Naywatame Poets. In a council he presented their chief with a coat and sash, a cup and one of his guns, with a small quantity of powder, and with knives, awls, and tobacco. He promised to prevent the Crees from killing them. The chief, on his part, agreed to forget the murder of his kindred, and promised to meet him at Dering's Point in the spring with furs, and to go down to the fort on the Bay. It was, however, beyond the Englishman to restrain the Crees in their triumphant march westward with their guns. The Naywatame chief sent word to him in the spring that his people had again been attacked and that he was afraid to come down.

From the place of meeting Kelsey must have turned to spend the winter on the prairies north-east of Saskatoon, hunting buffalo to procure pemmican for the return journey, and trapping furs with his Assiniboins. He would visit his cache as he moved homeward, probably down the Saskatchewan, in the spring, and would wait at Dering's Point for the canoes to assemble for the journey to the Bay. Finally he arrived at York Fort with " a good fleet of Indians." His Journal closes with a description of the ways of the Indians of the plains as the first European eyes saw them.

It is a surprise that the position of the Hudson's Bay Company after their loss of the posts on James Bay was far from uncomfortable. In 1690 they had in their warehouse furs and goods equal in value to the total capital represented by the stock of the Company, namely £10,500. The value of the cargoes sent out that year was reckoned at the same amount, without considering the profits to accrue. There was an increasing trade at their posts on Port Nelson and New Severn, estimated for the year at £20,000 ; and they entertained hopes that the war would end with England victorious, and that the French would be made to honour their claim of £100,000 for damages suffered in the past. Then, too, there was a desire in these troublous

---

* See at p. 16.

times to " make the stock of the Company as diffusive amongst their Majesties' subjects as possible and more and more a national interest for justifying their proceedings," so that the nation would the more readily stand behind them. It was accordingly decided on September 3, 1690, to treble the stock, valuing it at £31,500. On this trebled stock a dividend of 25 per cent. was paid that year. As it proved, the Company was enjoying but a burst of sunshine before the storm.

At the outset of the war the French concentrated all their naval power in the English Channel in the hope of winning the command of the sea and of invading England. The effects of this policy were felt at once by the Hudson's Bay Company. In 1689 they equipped two ships, promising the crews pensions in case of disablement in a fight. Off the Scilly Isles one, the *North West Fox*, under Captain Ford, was captured by French privateers. The other, the *Royal Hudson's Bay*, frigate, under captains Edgecombe and Grimington, put up a grim fight, and was finally able to draw off to Plymouth. It took so long to refit her, and so many seamen deserted, it proved impossible to get her off for the Bay within the sailing season, to the great distress of York Fort that winter. Hard on the heels of this misfortune came the news of the disastrous end of the expedition to the Albany River, involving the loss of the three ships at the Bottom of the Bay and their goods.

The French on Hudson Bay also felt the effects of the policy of concentrating all the naval force of France in the Channel. At Fort Ste. Anne, as Albany Fort had been renamed, Iberville was left to his own resources. In 1690 he sailed northward with the two ships of the French company (the Compagnie du Nord), the *Ste. Anne* and the *Armes de la Compagnie*, intent on capturing York Fort. He cast anchor near the Hayes and landed with ten men in the hope of surprising some Englishmen, from whom he could learn the situation at the fort. He was perceived by the look-out and the alarm was raised. The Hudson's Bay Company's ship was in the river and was sent in pursuit, but the fall of the tide prevented her from getting out, and Iberville sailed away. On his homeward journey he entered the Severn to seize Churchill Fort, but Indians reported his appearance in time for John Walsh, the Factor there, to get his goods into the woods and blow up the fort. The French claimed to have captured the furs. The small body of men at this outpost made their way in safety overland to York Fort.

The French hopes of commanding the home seas were dashed to the ground when their great fleet was destroyed at La Hogue. This made joyful news for the Committee's letter to York Fort of May 1692.

It is with great difficulty that we have been able to sett out soe chargeable an Expedition, both in respect of the Shipps it required & for the procuring of Seamen at this Juncture, when our Navy Royall was not only put to Sea but also ready to engage the Enemy, which God be praised they have already done with that magnanimity & success that we have obtained the most compleat & remarkable Victory over the French Fleet that Ever was gott at Sea ; We burnt & tooke 23 or 24 of their best & Capitall shipps & when ye Admirall of France fairely run away & gott into a Creek amongst Rocks and shelves & Mounsr Turville [Tourville] the Admirall himselfe was gott on shore, Our undaunted Seamen went in with Boates & fire works & burnt ye Royal Sunne (She was the Admirall called) & the Vice Admirall of France & 4 or 5 great shipps more, in the sight of Mounsr Tourville, who had ye pleasure to stand upon the shore & see his Shipps burne, which was one of the bravest actions done by the true English seamen that perhaps was ever known in any age.

The difficulties in getting seamen, to which the Committee referred, were overcome, and James Knight was sent out at the head of a flotilla of three ships to recover the posts at the Bottom of the Bay.   Knight went first to York Fort, but he wintered on Gilpin's Island,* off the Eastmain River, where he secured an abundance of geese and fish, with which he brought his men through free from scurvy.   In the early summer he sailed southward.   At Cape Hope he gave his men their last drill.   These elaborate precautions proved unnecessary;   there were but three men in Fort Ste. Anne, La Potherie asserts.   After a brush in which these Frenchmen shot three Englishmen, they abandoned the post and made their way overland to Canada.   The fort captured was not the original Albany Fort, but the one built by Captain Marsh in 1688 and occupied by Iberville.   It was on a creek between two islands, and not easily reached by ships, in fact, in a very defensible position.   It was held by the English all through the wars of King William and Queen Anne.   Four days after Knight captured the post, the vessel of the Compagnie du Nord, the *Ste. Anne*, arrived off the river with the annual supplies and the summer's garrison for it.   An English vessel was sent after her, but she made her escape.

Governor James Knight also entered the Moose and Rupert rivers and burned down the forts there, without, however, attempting a reoccupation.

In 1693 the English were triumphant on the Bay ; the French held only the inland post on Lake Nemiskau, about a hundred miles up the Rupert River, and a post on Lake Abitibi immediately north of the height of land of the Ottawa River.   The Hudson's Bay Company recognized its indebtedness to Governor Knight by a gratuity of £500—a very large sum in those days.   As they had not the hard money to give, the payment took the form of an interest-bearing bond.   Knight was thus accumulating the wealth which enabled him to reach the financial standing in the Company necessary for his election, which took place in 1700, to serve on the Committee.

After the battle of La Hogue the French avoided concentrated fleets and ranged battles in the home seas, and resorted to harassing British commerce in more distant waters, and to attacking outlying and somewhat defenceless parts of the Empire.   From the beginning of the war Frontenac, once more Governor of La Nouvelle

* For this island see Sketch-map No. 4 at p. 66.

France, was intent on capturing York Fort. Efforts were made to secure an adequate force and strong ships for Iberville, but without success. But in 1694 he was given the *Poli* and the *Salamandre* to seize on the coveted post. On 14th September (24th N.S.) the ships anchored in the Nelson River. An attempt was made to effect a surprise, but the English were alert. Iberville now went about his task in a systematic way. The *Poli*, the larger ship, was kept in the Nelson to winter there, the *Salamandre* was brought up the Hayes and berthed half a league above York Fort. " We harassed them " says Nicolas Jérémie, who was with Iberville, " from September 25th [15th O.S.] . . . until 14th [4th O.S.] October." During a feint on the fort, devised to keep the English from taking advantage of the difficulties in which the French found themselves, Iberville's brother, M. de Chateauguay, was wounded and afterwards died. Steadily, if slowly, batteries were built, and the fort completely invested. On 4th October, before launching the bombardment and assault, Iberville summoned Governor John Walsh to surrender. A Mr. Matthew, the clergyman of York Fort, and Henry Kelsey were sent out with a flag of truce and with Walsh's terms, but Iberville was in a position to impose his own will. Stipulations agreed upon were : "As to the garrison's provisions, they shall have it as the French. . . . As to their treatment, they may be assured that no injury shall be offered to any of the garrison." The English afterwards claimed that they were worked as slaves and on the meanest fare, while the French were well provided for. If this is so, it was sheer cruelty, as well as a breach of the terms of surrender, for each party had been well provided for. Fifty-three men surrendered, among them Henry Kelsey.

Iberville renamed the captured post Fort Bourbon. Jérémie thus describes it :

The fort had four bastions, forming a square of thirty feet, in which was a large warehouse of two storeys. The trading store was in one of these bastions ; another served as a supply store, and the other two were used as guard houses to hold the garrison. The whole was built of wood. In line with the first palisade were two other bastions, in one of which the officers lodged, the other serving as a kitchen and forge for the garrison. Between these two bastions was a kind of half-moon space in which were eight cannon, throwing an eight pound ball, which commanded the river side. Below this half-moon space was a platform, at the level of the water, which held six pieces of heavy cannon. No cannon was mounted on the side of the woods [that is, the rear], all the cannon and swivel guns were on the bastions. There were altogether in the fort, which had only two palisades of upright logs, thirty-two cannon, and fourteen swivel guns.

In 1695 the Hudson's Bay Company was not aware of the loss of York Fort. As they believed their posts to be safe and as the war was having a disastrous effect upon the market for furs, they felt it unwise to send any ships to the Bay. They wrote in the following spring : " It may be reasonable for us to let you know ye Cause why wee Sent noe ships the last yeare, our warehouses were full of goods,

& the marketts in London soe dull we could sell none & the Comittee were of opinion you wanted nothing & thats the reason wee kept our ships at home the last yeare, which proves verry happy, for had they gone to port Nelson in all probability wee should have lost them both, there being 2 french men of Warr there at that time."

In 1696 the Company secured assistance from the Government in their attempt to recover York Fort. Two men-of-war, the *Bonaventure*, commanded by Captain Allen, and the *Seaforth*, under Captain Grainge, were sent out with the Company's ship, the *Hudson's Bay*, frigate, by which Henry Kelsey was a passenger. Allen's Instructions, drawn up by the Committee, were to capture the fort and hand it over with all its equipment and goods to the Company's Governor. All through the struggle on the Bay it proved the case that no garrison of fur-traders was either willing or able to hold out against a trained military or naval force. The French commander Gabriel Testard, Sieur de la Forest, had of necessity to surrender (30th August). Captain Allen's stipulations left him in possession of his furs. When the ships returned to England the Company claimed the peltry on the ground that Captain Allen had acted beyond his Instructions in granting possession of it to De la Forest, and alternatively, that the furs had been secured with the Company's goods captured by the French at York Fort. An appeal to the King was answered by a royal warrant requiring the Customs to deliver the furs to the Company. La Forest entered an appeal with the Privy Council and remained in England to prosecute his cause, but died in August 1697. As will be seen, the Treaty of Ryswick required payment to be made for the furs.

The year 1697 saw the French counter-stroke. Iberville returned with four ships of war. He himself commanded the *Pelican*, De Serigny the *Palmier*, Dugué the *Profond*, and Chatrie the *Vespe*. The Company and the Admiralty were prepared for this contingency. The warship *Hampshire* was placed at the service of the Company to act as convoy for the *Hudson's Bay*, frigate, and the *Dering*, frigate. A second warship, however, would have brought this little fleet more on an equality with Iberville's squadron. The English ships passed through Hudson Strait in the wake of the French. At the entry to the Bay, when the fog suddenly lifted, the *Hudson's Bay* and the *Dering* came on the *Profond* (on which were all the munitions and provisions for Port Nelson). They gave chase, and to save himself Dugué ran his ship into a sheet of ice, which barred approach to the enemy. A strange combat ensued. The position of the *Profond* in the ice allowed the use of no more than her two stern guns. All through the day (25th August, N.S.) the two English ships kept firing intermittently on her. When the *Hampshire* came up in the evening the three ships gave her their broadsides and sailed away believing that she must inevitably sink. Iberville's ship, the *Pelican*, had not been seen. When she got free from the ice she sailed for the Nelson, expecting to meet her consorts there, but they had gone to the Churchill River, no doubt, for repairs to the *Profond*.

On his arrival in Port Nelson Iberville was surprised not to find his three other ships there. When three sail came up next day, he signalled to them, taking them to be his own. On receiving no reply, he realized that he was facing an overpowering force of the enemy. It is in such a situation that a commander's genius shines. To retreat into the Nelson was to be bottled up and forced to surrender. Iberville knew that in such a situation the attack is the best form of defence. Though twenty-two of his men had already been sent ashore, he went out to meet the foe. The three English ships came on in a line, led by the *Hampshire*. Iberville, who at this time had the wind in his favour, sailed so close up to the warship that her commander, Captain Fletcher, thought he intended to grapple and board. He therefore veered off. Iberville was thus enabled to sail on and pour broadsides into the *Hudson's Bay* and *Dering*. The *Pelican* had now lost its favourable position, and the *Hampshire* and the two other English ships, now to the windward, were able to fire from time to time upon her. For two and a half hours she was getting the worst of it. Worse still, she was dangerously near a shoal. To bring the battle to a decision Fletcher sailed down on the *Pelican*, apparently to get her to the leeward and towards the shoal. A great storm had blown up, and had he succeeded probably victory would have been in his hands. Iberville, very cleverly, got the *Pelican* to the windward, with the *Hampshire* between him and the shoal, and gave her a broadside at close quarters, so that she sank, as the French documents tell us.

In connection with the matter of a pension for Captain Fletcher's widow, an affidavit was laid before the British Admiralty, sworn to by Thomas Morris, " master's mate " of the *Hampshire*, who had been placed on board the *Dering*, and Samuel Clarke, master's mate of the *Hudson's Bay* :

" On the 26th of August 1697 about six a clock in the morning they saw a ship to the windward, which proved to be a ffrench man of Warr called the Pellican Monsr D'Brevile Comander, And some times bearing down towards them, and afterwards keeping her Wind, the said ship Hampshire with the Merchant men turned to the Windward to get up with her, And betwixt eight and nine a clock there were some Gunns ffired on both sides, as they continued at a distance till about eleven ; And then the Hampshire Tackt, and got to Windward of him, bore down upon him, and gave him two broad sides, Yard Arm and Yard Arm (as near as these Deponts. could diserne) : And after the Hampshire had given the Second broad Side filling her head Sayles to Wear, she sunck ; At which time there happened a fflaw of Wind, but whether that or the damage she might have received from the Enemy, was the occasion of her sincking these Deponts. cannot say ; And further the said Samuel Clarke Saith That he being taken by the ffrench ; Dureing the time he continued on Board the ffrench Man of Warr wch the said Monsr. D'Brevile had the Comand of in his returne home ; Hee the said Samuel Clarke having some Discourse with the said ffrench Captaines brother, who spoke English ; He told the said Depo^{nt}. That Capt. fflettcher (who Comanded the Hampshire) was a brave man, and just before he gave his last broad side, called to the said Monsr. D'Brevile, bidding him Strike, which he refuseing to do, Capt. ffletcher took a Glass and drank to him, telling him, he should dine with him immediately ; Upon which the said ffrench Capt. Pledged him in another Glass. And thereupon his Men ffired a Volley of Small Shott upon the Hampshire which was returned with a like Volley to the ffrench man; And after that the said Capt. ffletcher was not seen; So that it was supposed the said Capt. ffletcher was then killed, as the said ffrench Cap^{ts}. brother informed the said Depon^t. Samuel Clarke.

It would appear that there may be some truth in the tradition passed on by Joseph Robson, that the *Hampshire* was " overset," as she would be on a shoal with sails set, in a squall or flaw of wind. The fact remains that Fletcher's strategy failed, while Iberville's was supremely successful. With the loss of the *Hampshire*, the *Hudson's Bay* surrendered, and the *Dering* took to flight. The sea was too wild to save the men of the *Hampshire*. In the only battle on the Bay with trained forces on either side, Iberville, though out-numbered, showed the skill that turns defeat to victory.

The battle was fought in a gathering storm and among shoals. It was no sooner over than Iberville had to face the worst. Both his ship and her prize were lost, though the crews were saved. What had been his misfortune now proved his salvation. His other ships, which he must have longed for on the day of the battle, came up after the storm blew over and gave the force with which to capture York Fort. After due preparations Iberville began the bombard-ment of the Factory. For a fur-trading post it put up a real fight and took considerable punishment. The end was inevitable. On 3rd September the fort surrendered, Henry Kelsey being again the go-between.

Peace came a week after York Fort was captured and became once more Fort Bourbon. The eighth clause of the Treaty of Ryswick, signed on 10th September (O.S.), dealt with the conflicting claims to Hudson Bay. Under an earlier clause requiring the restitution of conquests on both sides, York Fort would be restored to the English. The eighth clause secured to the French " those places which were taken by the French during the peace that preceded this present war and were retaken by the English during this war." As the English had contented themselves with burning down the forts on Rupert and Moose rivers without occupying them, and as the French had returned to those rivers, all that the English had to actually sur-render was Albany Fort. The clause went on to deal with the claim of the French company to the furs secured to them by the agreement at their surrender of Fort Bourbon (York Fort). " The capitulation made by the English on the fifth of September 1696 shall be observed according to its form and tenor," the value of the furs to be deter-mined by Commissioners. There remained the question of the boundaries between the possessions of the two nations on the Bay. This was relegated to the Commissioners with full powers to make arrangements, which were to be as binding " as if they were inserted word for word in the present treaty." The Commissioners were to meet within three months, and to conclude their labours within six months after meeting.

The Commissioners met in London in the spring of 1698. A

multitude of documents passed from one side to the other. In connection with the estimate of the amount due for the furs taken at Fort Bourbon, the Hudson's Bay Company raised issues which were really beyond the terms of the treaty, but which arose out of their sense that their claim to the Bay was good and that the furs were theirs. They claimed that the title to the furs depended upon the title to Port Nelson where they were got, and they proceeded to show their title to that region, and finally, that the furs were traded from the Indians with the Company's goods, which the French had captured. In the end they were required to pay £7,000—no easy task, for the Company had been making no profits since 1690.

The question of the boundaries was a thorny one, chiefly because, though the English Commissioners brought considerable pressure to bear upon the Company, it was reluctant to compromise. On 10th July a General Court agreed to submit it to the English Commissioners, that the north boundaries of the French should be the Albany and the Rupert rivers. Further pressure from the Commissioners got no greater concession from the Company than that the French boundary in the East Main should be the Canuse, a diminutive stream north of Rupert River. Meanwhile neither England nor France took any steps looking to the exchange of Albany Fort for Fort Bourbon, nor did the Hudson's Bay Company make payment for the furs as assessed. The result was that the question of the rights of the several nations on the Bay remained open when war broke out again on May 4, 1702. From the point of view of the English it was an advantage, due, it should be said, to the Hudson's Bay Company's stiff assertion of its title. The English claims to the Bay had been kept active, while the French must have been satisfied to be in possession of the rich fur region whose outlet was Fort Bourbon, conceding to the English Albany Fort, exposed as it was to competition and attack from Canada. Indeed, this was put forward by the French Commissioners on April 29, 1700, as the solution of the question preferable to them.

During the war of the Spanish Succession the position of affairs on the Bay remained stable. Both nations were exerting their full strength in Europe. Albany Fort, however, was so exposed to attack from Canada as to appear to offer an easy prize. In 1709 a force of one hundred men from Canada aspired to repeat the feat of the Chevalier de Troyes of 1686. There was one great difference in the occasions. Then the Company's forts slumbered in a time of peace. Now war was on, and they were alert. The Canadian force passed down the Moose River from the Ottawa, as De Troyes had done. From their post St. Louis, on the Moose, they skirted the coast in canoes, hoping to take Albany Fort by surprise. They landed seven miles from the fort and made their way through the woods under cover of darkness. As they approached the post they were marching concealed by the river bank. They were, however, perceived before the attack was launched. The alarm bell of the fort was rung by the men on watch, and the drum beat the defenders to their quarters. Governor Fullertine had trained his men and had them completely in hand. The French retired with a loss of sixteen men, and no one wounded in the Factory. They came on two of the Company's servants returning to the fort in a boat close inshore. From an ambush in the brush on the bank they fired a volley on them and killed them. They returned as they came by way of the Moose River and the Abitibi.

During the periods when the French occupied Fort Bourbon Monsieur Nicolas Jérémie was of the staff there, as second and finally as first in command. He employed his ample leisure in inquiries about the interior, and wrote a description of the region and a brief account of the history of the forts on the Bay. He speaks with authority only about the scenes in which he took part, namely, the capture of York Fort by Iberville in 1694, its recapture by the English in 1696, when he was taken prisoner, and finally its recovery by Iberville in 1697. The main interest of his narrative lies in the knowledge of the country which he gathered. He is the first to tell of the Barren Grounds. The country is " very barren, without beaver." The people live on fish and caribou. From his pen comes the earliest description of the musk-ox, which was then to be found as far south as between the " Danish River " (the Churchill) and the Seal River, " so called from the number of seals at its mouth." The Crees, armed with guns from Fort Bourbon, were driving the defenceless Dogribs, who lay behind the Seal River, before them in flight. Jérémie is the first to mention the copper mine which was said to exist in the Dogribs' country. " I have seen this copper very often, as our natives [Crees] always bring some back when they go to war in those parts." The Dogribs had no iron save what they had gathered from the Danish ships at Churchill.

Farther south, Jérémie knew that one could go up the Churchill River and pass into the Deer River, Rivière du Cerf, that is the Saskatchewan, the Assiniboin name for which was " Opah," Red Deer. The reference may be to the water-way by the Portage du Traite, or the route by the Kississing River and Lake. He describes the Deer River as "a river of such length that our natives have never yet been able to reach its source." This information Jérémie may have got from Kelsey, whom he does not mention, but who was with him in the fort as a prisoner in the winter of 1694-95. Lakes Winnipeg and Winnipegosis, which Kelsey had not seen, are described but vaguely. " Assiniboils, Crees and Saulteurs occupy the regions " around the latter. Another lake is mentioned under the name Tacamamiouen, the Indian name of Rainy Lake. Jérémie has confused this with Cedar Lake, for his Deer River, the Saskatchewan, which is so long that its sources are unknown, flowed into it. He applied the name "Saskatchewan" to the Nelson, the Bourbon River of the French. The route followed by the Indians to the fort was down the Bourbon, through Landing Lake to Split Lake, " the Lake of the Forts," that is, by which they went to the forts. Thence they would travel by our Fox River to the Hayes and Fort Bourbon.

These were years of great difficulty for the fur-traders on the Bay, both French and English. The French had a fine array of forts, it is true, and could gather large supplies of furs, but it must have been no easy matter to get them into France, or to bring out goods, with the English fleet upon the seas. Losses may have been heavy. At least we know that there was a dearth of beaver in Paris during the war, and that substitutes were in use ; and that *coureurs-des-bois* resorted to smuggling furs across to the English at Albany Fort. When James Knight, as Governor, took over Fort Bourbon from Jérémie in 1714 for the Hudson's Bay Company, he found the post altogether dilapidated : " Never set my eyes on such a confused place in my life before. Not a dry place to put one's head into and all their huts or houses ready to fall."

These were lean years also for the English Company. From 1690 it paid no dividends. The decline in the price of its £100 stock is eloquent of its troubles. In 1692 it stood at £260. After a decline there was a recovery in June 1695 to £230. When the loss of York Fort became known that autumn it fell to £130. In June 1696 it was £98, and later fell even lower. After the Peace of Ryswick it fluctuated between £100 and £110.

The difficulties of the Company may also be traced in its dealings with Radisson. The turn of the tide of the Frenchman's fortunes came in the late 'eighties. His reward for returning to the Company in 1684 had been an annuity of £50 and the benefit of £200 of the Company's stock (without actual ownership) as long as he should live. His dividends from this in 1688 and 1689 amounted to £150. After his success in bringing over Chouart and his furs to the Company in 1684, he received a gratuity of £100. In 1685 Radisson was made " Superintendant and Chiefe Director of the Trade at Port Nelson." This may be taken as the culmination of his career. With an appropriate salary, his annuity of £50, and the dividends on his stock, he was in a comfortable position. The turn of his fortunes came in 1687. He laid serious charges against George Geyer of York Fort, the best Governor the Company had had since the day of Charles Bayly. On his return to England, Radisson was called on to make good his charges before the Committee, but failed to convince his rulers. Then, too, as Superintendent he was expected to go inland and bring the Indians down to trade. This he had not done, thereby putting himself in the position of a fifth wheel on the coach. The Committee gave much needed unity to the service at York Fort by withdrawing Radisson, but sought to make amends to him by the promise of Lord Churchill to secure him a place in the King's service. Till the promise should be made good it raised his annual allowance from £50 to £100. That there was no hostility in the Committee to Radisson is shown by their trebling his stock along with that of all the others, so that he received a dividend of £150 in 1690. Over against this, at the end of that year, when the disastrous issue of the attempt to continue trading at the Albany brought the Committee into difficulties, they reduced the annual allowance to the original

£50. This would not have borne so hardly upon the man had the Company continued to pay dividends, but it was his misfortune that his eggs were in the same basket as the Company's.   In 1692 his position was desperate, partly from the debts which he had contracted and partly because he had married a second time, and had a small family of four on his hands and a fifth expected.   His friends made a special effort to bring the Committee to his relief.   The Earl of Marlborough wrote in his behalf, and Mr. William Yonge, who had been instrumental in bringing him back to the Company, laid a long document in his favour before the Committee, but it stood by its previous decisions.   In 1694 Radisson entered a suit in Chancery against the Company to have his annuity calculated on the basis of the £100 from which it had been reduced, and won a favourable verdict.   The financial difficulties against which the Committee was struggling are revealed by the fact that it was only able to pay the arrears due to the Frenchman by instalments.   In 1697 there was a financial crash in London, and 70,000 coat beaver lay in the Company's warehouse unsaleable.   Orders were sent out to the Bay to burn coat beaver before the eyes of the Indians to convince them that the Company wanted no more.

Up to the end of his life Radisson drew a quarterly payment from the Company of £12, 10s., and his annuity of £50, making an income of £100 a year, though he was not in the Company's employ.   The last payment on record was ordered on March 29, 1710.   Shortly thereafter Radisson died, seventy-four years of age.   In 1729, nineteen years later, the Committee voted £10 to his widow as charity, " She being ill and in great want."

When Radisson died the tide had turned and was running fast in favour of the English, and by inference in favour of the Hudson's Bay Company, and a triumphant peace was within sight.   The great victories of Marlborough—Blenheim, 1704, Ramilies, 1706, Oudenarde, 1708, Lille, 1709, and in the same year Malplaquet, at which La Vérendrye fought and was wounded—had restored the Balance of Power in Europe.   By the Treaty of Utrecht, 1713, England imposed her will on France, and her will was that her claim to Hudson Bay should be recognized.   The tenth clause of the Treaty ran : " The said most Christian King shall restore to the Kingdom and Queen of Great Britain, to be possessed in full right for ever, the bay and streights of Hudson, together with all lands, seas, sea-coasts, rivers and places situate in the said bay and streights, and which belong thereunto, no tracts of land or of sea being excepted, which are at present possessed by the subjects of France. . . ."   On Saturday the 11th of September, 1714, Fort Bourbon was surrendered according to the form prescribed by the treaty to England (and to the Hudson's Bay Company) in the persons of the Queen's Commissioners and the Company's Governor and Deputy-Governor, James Knight and Henry Kelsey, and the curtain was rung down on the long struggle of the two nations for the Bay.

To this issue, so happy for itself, the Company had contributed much. It had maintained its trade on the Bay amid a succession of disasters. During twenty-three years never a dividend was paid, but the claim of England and of the Company to the Bay had not been allowed to lapse. It was kept active, not only beyond the sea, but in the embassies of the two nations. At the end the Company got no more than its reward. A picturesque feature of this happy consummation was that it was largely brought about by victories won by Lord Churchill, sometime Governor of the Hudson's Bay Company, now Duke of Marlborough.

CHAPTER IV

ENGLISH AND FRENCH STRUGGLE FOR THE GREAT
FUR FOREST IN THE HINTERLAND OF THE BAY,
1714–63.*

THE cession of Hudson Bay by the French to the English was a
triumph for the Hudson's Bay Company, but a triumph accompanied
by anxieties. The wealth of the Company came, not from the Bay
nor from its inhospitable shores, but from the forest rich in furs,
which was the main feature of the hinterland. North of the Lauren-
tian Mountains, which marked the height of land of the Bay, ran
the belt of poplar and aspen woods westward, no one knew how far,
from which the posts on the Bay drew their trade, and the Treaty
of Utrecht left its possession undetermined. The tenth clause, it is
true, arranged that a commission should fix the boundaries between
the possessions of England, that is, the Hudson's Bay Company's
colony of Rupert's Land, and those of France, but this led to nothing
more than a prolonged assertion and denial of the claims on either
side. Their greater knowledge of the country at this time enabled
the English Company to give a definite interpretation to the terms
of the Charter, so far, at least, as their territory towards the valley
of the St. Lawrence was concerned. Resting on the tenth clause of
the Treaty of Utrecht, which, like the Charter, gave them not only
the Strait and Bay, but their lands and rivers, they claimed the
valleys of all the streams flowing into Hudson Strait and Bay, and
drew a line from Grimmington Island on the Strait along the height
of land of Labrador to Lake Mistassini and thence along the watershed of the Bay and the St. Lawrence into the distant and unknown
west. In their mind this was no more than claiming the area through
which their trade had penetrated, for the Indians at the sources of
the rivers Rupert, Moose, and Albany, and even, as we know from
French sources, from lakes Nipigon and Superior, brought their furs
to the forts on the Bay.

The French stoutly refused this boundary, insisting that the
territory conceded to the English was no more than the strip along
the Bay in which the Company's forts stood. This claim was
weakened by the fact that at the time they had no posts in the region
in dispute, for they had abandoned their posts on the Albany and

* Illustrated by Sketch-map No. 6 at p. 130.

on Rainy Lake when they got possession of forts on the Bay; that is, they had ceased the attempt to bring the furs by the costly route through the Great Lakes to Montreal, and had adopted the English Company's policy of persuading the Indians to bear the cost of transportation to the shores of the Bay, whence the peltries could be taken overseas in ships cheaply. The French claim was accordingly based on what were put forward as binding documents. Had not the English in returning La Nouvelle France to the French by the Treaty of St. Germain-en-Laye, 1632, held the view accepted by all at that time that the sixtieth parallel of north latitude was the northern limit of the colony? This boundary, the claim ran, still held good; the Treaty of Utrecht modified it only by conceding to the English the strip of territory along the coast in which their posts stood. During half a century these claims and counter-claims jostled one another in the Foreign Offices of the two nations. Not even a possibility of agreement was reached; the commission required by the treaty never met. The issue, like that of the possession of the Bay itself, was settled on distant battlefields and by international treaty. The English victory on the Plains of Abraham and the surrender of La Nouvelle France to Britain by the Treaty of Paris, 1763, made good the Hudson's Bay Company's claims to their full extent. Indirect though it was, it constituted a second triumph for the Company.

But, while the diplomats of Britain and France were seeking possession of the coveted forest belt by a war of documents, other methods of gaining the prize were open. As the fur fields of the South-West became depleted, the French turned their attention to the north, and the commercial rivalry grew in intensity. Finally, in 1731 the policy of occupying the great fur belt of the North-West was inaugurated by the French Governor Beauharnois and by La Vérendrye. A line of forts was established through the forest north-west of Lake Superior, which diverted the peltries, in some measure, to the St. Lawrence, and gave the French a very definite claim to the area concerned. This struggle in the domain of commerce, like the war of documents, was ended adversely for the French by the Treaty of Paris and the surrender of Canada to Britain, and the history of Rupert's Land entered an entirely new phase.

I.—THE HUDSON'S BAY COMPANY, 1714–31—GOVERNORS JAMES KNIGHT AND HENRY KELSEY

On the eve of the Treaty of Utrecht the Hudson's Bay Company had but one post on the Bay, Albany Fort, but a sloop was equipped for coastal trade in the autumn, wintered on Bayly's Island off the Slude (Eastmain) River, and in the spring traded with the Indians of the eastern shore of the Bay, a wide region passing under the name East Main. The Treaty brought the Company back to the Hayes River, the French Fort Bourbon becoming York Fort once more. The two English posts were separated by a thousand miles of coast, and were more easily managed from London than from any one point in the country. Accordingly there had been, and there will be, two self-dependent governors, the one " in the Bottom of the Bay," as the curious phrase ran, namely, James Bay, and the other at Port Nelson, really York Fort, on the west bank of the Hayes, a mile and a half from its mouth. For the time being, however, James Knight and, after him, Henry Kelsey were given the more pretentious title of Governor-in-Chief of the Territory of the Company of Adventurers of England trading into Hudson's Bay.

The commercial hinterland of Albany Fort, which included the valleys of the Rupert, of the Moose with its many tributaries, and of the Albany, ran along the rugged height of land and up the valley of the last river to the lower basin of Lake Winnipeg, and to lakes Manitoba and Winnipegosis, where it coincided with the upper country of York Fort. The Indians of these last two lakes, according to their whim, went into Lake Winnipeg by the Little Saskatchewan, our Dauphin River, ascended Winnipeg River and its tributary the English River to Lac Seul, and crossed the height of land to Lake St. Joseph and the Albany, and so to Albany Fort ; or they passed through Lake Winnipegosis and Cedar Lake, down the Saskatchewan to Lake Winnipeg, and down the branch of the Nelson known as East River to Cross Lake, whence they reached the Hayes River and York Fort by the Leaf River, the south branch of the Fox. In view of the competition with the French for the trade of the forest belt, the hinterland of Albany Fort was seriously exposed to danger, for " the enemy," as the French are called in the Company's Journals, hemmed its trade area in and lay on its flank all the way from Lake Nipigon, north of Lake Superior, to Lake Mistassini on or near the head waters of the Rupert and the Saguenay. In contrast, the hinterland of York Fort was not only free from the menace of the French, but was known vaguely to be of vast extent and to produce pelts of a superior quality. It was simple wisdom on the part of Governor Knight to press on the commercial penetration of this sheltered area, whose easiest outlet was at York Fort and, as was proved later, at the mouth of the Churchill River.

Governor Knight arrived in the Hayes River on September 5, 1714. The Upland Indians, as they were vaguely called, would not be down till the following summer. In the meantime his attention was concentrated on taking possession of Fort Bourbon and re-establishing the English régime in it under the old name of York Fort. The French commissioner, Monsieur J. B. Cullerer, had come out with him in the ship *Union* to surrender Fort Bourbon according to the terms of the treaty. The day after their arrival at the mouth of the river M. Jérémie, governor of the fort, came on board, and the following day, in a wild storm, the ship was brought to anchor over against the fort. Knight managed to land at four in the afternoon. As the storm prevented him from returning, he spent the night in the fort, utterly disgusted with its state. His Journal runs : " [I never sett my foot into such a confused place in my life before, not a Dry Place to put my head into and all there hutts or Houses Ready to fall." The dilapidated state of the fort may, perhaps, be explained by its comparative isolation during the war, perhaps also by the lack of labourers due to the murder of a number of the Frenchmen by irate husbands for meddling with their squaws. The next day was spent making an inventory of the Frenchmen's goods. According to the arrangement, these were to be sent home, but it was so late in the season, Knight was afraid lest the packing and loading of them would end in the ship having to winter in the country. After some haggling he bought the goods where they lay for £277, 3s. 11d. On Saturday the 11th all hands were assembled before the warehouse and " in the gallery," that is, on the walk built a few feet below the top of the palisade for purposes of defence —an excellent grandstand for the spectacle. Down below by the flagstaff the French Governor read publicly his orders for the surrender of the post, and struck the French flag by the halyard at one end of the cross arm. Simultaneously with this last move, Governor Knight stepped to the halyard at the other side of the staff and hoisted the flag of England. He then read publicly his own Commission. Her Majesty's health was drunk, such guns as were available fired off, and a cask of strong beer broached, that all might make merry. By the 30th the Frenchmen and their furs were on board, the draft for their goods passed over, and the necessary receipts given. Three days later the ship managed to work her way out of the river, and the Frenchmen saw their last of Port Nelson. They had had their troubles with the Indians, yet true to their race they had made themselves loved by them. After Governor Knight had run the Jack up on the flagstaff, one of the natives came to him and said that he did not love to see it so ; he loved to see the white one. Knight wrote to the Governor of the Company : " So there, Many of the Indians has Great Friendship for the French here."

Before the French were out of the place, indeed on the next day after the formal transfer of the fort, Knight was faced with one of the main tasks of his administration. The Indians came to him to hold a council. " The great Deal of ceremony " to which he refers, would follow the usual Indian ritual. " The present of Beaver, Moose Skins, Deers flesh, tongues and some salt " would be laid on the ground before the Governor. Upon a beaver skin of superior quality the calumettes—pipes with long stems decorated with colours and feathers and, by common acceptance, the symbols of peace—would be laid. A prolonged silence. At last the leading chief would rise and present his particular pipe to the Governor, who would light it, a young Indian holding the unwieldy article all the while, for some were four, five, and even six feet long. Taking the calumette by its middle, the Governor would point the stem to the rising sun, to the height of midday, to the setting sun, and then to the ground, and would finally twirl it round and present it to its owner, the chief. Thereupon the whole council would cry : *Ho !*

Ho! Ho! crescendo, thus signifying their thanks.   The chief would now take the number of whiffs which were traditional for his part of the country, and pass the calumette round the circle, each member of the council taking the prescribed number of puffs. Last of all the Governor would receive it, puff the requisite number of puffs, and solemnly place it on the beaver skin, when the sky would ring with cries of *Ecco*, significant again of thanks.   All this would be no more than the beginning.   The ritual would be repeated with every pipe lying upon the beaver skin.   Knight wrote in the Fort Journal : " My taking so many whiffs out of every pipe at the end of Each Ceremony . . . has brought me to be an Absolute Smoker."   The long silence which followed the smoking would be broken by the leading chief's invocation of the presence of the Great Manitou (Spirit), by the assertion that his tongue was not double, but his words straightforward and true.   Then expressions of friendship, betokened by the presents ; lamentations at the misery of his people ; and a plea for generosity ; finally, assurances of gratitude and loyalty.   Native orator after native orator in the same strain. At last the Governor's turn would come, and, if one may judge from his entries in the Fort Journal, his speech would match those of the chiefs, not only in picturesqueness but in length—both a source of great satisfaction to the council.   Governor Knight struck the keynote of the Company's policy towards the natives—encouragement to trap furs, with the promise of " fair Dealing."   He ended with the Company's presents in return for theirs.   The council lasted for three hours, and was followed by a similar scene on the following Wednesday.   In the fact that councils of this kind were regarded by the Company's servants as no mere outward ceremony, but as issuing in solemn pacts with the natives, lies the secret of the marvellous security of their persons in a barbarous land, and of the sway which they gained over a fretful race.

Three days after the ship disappeared below the horizon Governor Knight addressed himself to the task of establishing discipline among the officers and men within the palisades.   He posted his orders for the behaviour of the servants in the factory.

1. That all Persons give there attendance to come to prayers without any Pretentions and Excuses.
2. You are Commanded to Live Lovingly one with Another, not to Swear or Quarrel but to live Peaceable, without Drunkenness or Prophaneness.
3. Yt no Man do Meddle or make with the Indians nor trade directly or Indirectly nor affront any Person of them but above all to be Carefull not to Concern themselves any ways with there Women wch was the Occasion of So many French Men being Cutt [off] by there Jealousy ; now he that shall go Contrary to wt is here forewarned Shall be made a Public Example for the rest to take Warning by, & that before the Indians as they shall abuse or give Cause of Jealousy too.
4. That no Man presume to go abroad Hunting or Elsewhere without Leave first ask'd & obtain'd.

Other items dealt with stealing ; with avoiding the risk of fire, which, of course, in the depth of the winter of those parts would be a terrible calamity ; with maintaining the watch ; and with cheerfulness and willingness while at work. Finally, the men are told that such furs as they might personally trap would be registered and sent home in their name, and that they would be given half of the proceeds, the Company taking the other half " as finding you Victuals, Drink & Wages." While the enforcement of these rules would depend much upon the character and personal life of the individual governor and head of a post, the establishment of the code showed the consciousness of the Company and of Governor Knight that discipline within the fort was essential to happy relations with the natives, and was necessary for success in the trade.

Knight was shocked at the state of the fort in which he and his men were to face the fierce winter of the North. To Captain Merry of the Committee he wrote : " The Place I have to live in this Winter is not half so good as our Cow house was in ye Bottom of ye Bay & I have never been Able to see my hand in it, since I have been here, without a Candle ; it is so black & Dark, Cold & Whett, withal nothing to make it better but heaping up Earth abt it to make it Warm." The warehouse had to be patched up to prevent the goods from being damaged by the rain. With characteristic swiftness Knight decided to abandon the place in the spring. He had the new site chosen before the ship sailed for England. He wrote : " I find a Place about ½ a Mile below this House, a very convenient Place for it is upon a Growing point where the land comes up Gradually from the Water Side Riseing without a Caveing Bank to ware away & on a point yt Commands ye River much better than ever this did & the Ships must Come very near to it that comes in ; neither can [it] be attacked by any Enemy but [on] one Side & yt with Great Difficulty." During the winter wood was cut many miles upstream for the new buildings. It was none too soon, for the ice of the spring flood, which had carried away the bank up to the base of the front palisade, this year went far towards demolishing the post. The south-west bastion was brought to the ground, along with the palisade and the river gate. The south-east bastion in which Knight lived was " broke all to pieces." It was necessary to patch the place up to give security during the trading season, when the Indians would be assembling in considerable numbers. In June the foundation of the new fort was laid, and in the autumn the place was occupied.

In the summer, when band after band of Indians came down the Hayes, or round from the Nelson, with their furs to trade, Governor Knight held a series of councils with them to inaugurate his policy of expansion. As he saw it, the great obstacle in his path was the incessant warfare among the tribes ; peace was a necessity if the natives were to busy themselves " working beaver," and especially if new nations were to be persuaded to bring their furs past their enemies down to the fort. The situation was none other than that of a quarter of a century before, when Henry Kelsey was inland—bands armed with guns preying upon their defenceless neighbours and carrying off their furs to trade them at the post for more guns and ammunition. Knight, with Kelsey at his side as Deputy, saw it so. He used all his persuasion to win the Red Men before him to a policy of peace.

During the winter events had drawn attention especially to the " Northern," the Chipewyan, Indians, who had been, as we know, driven by the Crees out of the wooded valley of the Churchill River on to the dismal Barren Grounds, with only the adjacent woods for shelter from the blasts of winter. Even there they were not safe. Knight had found at the fort a " Slave" woman carried off in the previous winter during a cruel raid. She died in the fort on 22nd November, but not without telling him enough of her people to satisfy him that trade with them would be of great profit to the Company. As fortune would have it, two days later another " Slave woman " was brought in by one of the servants. She was a victim of the same raid as the deceased. She and a third unfortunate had been held as slaves by their captors, but the two had escaped and had tried to reach their own countrymen across the Barrens. It was too late in the year to meet them and, rather than starve to death on the pitiless plains of the north, they had turned back on their track and had wandered towards the Nelson River with York Fort as their objective. The woman brought in reported that her companion had died of starvation on the way (Knight rather thought that she had been killed by her desperate starving fellow), and that she herself had happily fallen upon the track of the Company's servants and had followed it to their hunting cabin. This squaw, who knew enough Cree to make herself understood, proved a remarkable character. Treated with kindness at the fort, she overcame the reticence of her race and spoke freely of her people. She drew aside for the Englishmen the veil which concealed the Barren Grounds and the land of great lakes beyond—lakes which the Englishmen inferred were the Pacific Ocean. Knight understood her to say that on a great river flowing into the sea the tide ebbed and flowed, and that the stream scarcely froze in the winter. At the outset he was attracted most by her report of the many nations who lived beyond her people. Here was the field for expansion which he sought. But there could be no relations with these northern tribes so long as the Crees about York Fort and on the Churchill River kept preying on them. The Governor, therefore, took practical measures to bring about peace. On 11th June he called the Home Indians to a council, and by the promise of " Large presents of Powder, Shott & tobacco with other Necessarys " enlisted a band of twelve, willing to go with an Englishman and the " Slave woman " to the Northern Indians to arrange a treaty. Lured by the offer of further generous rewards on their return, the party grew to twenty-five Indians, travelling as customary with their families. William Stewart, the servant chosen for the enterprise, and the "Slave woman" were given generous gifts for the strange people. On the 18th the Governor gave a lavish feast, at which he instructed the ambassadors how to conduct themselves.

During the next week more Indians came in. More councils, presents, and pledges. On the 27th the peacemakers set off. By firmness and generosity the Governor had imposed his will on the rabble. The French had allowed them to bring the booty of their raids in blood-stained hands to the fort. He would tolerate no such thing. They could take their ill-gotten gains away. But let them make peace with the defenceless and their reward, he promised, would be great.

But what likelihood was there that a rabble of Crees armed with guns would meet those who had been hitherto their victims in a council of peace ? Fortunately some returned before going far. The band was still too large to hold together passing over the foodless Barrens. Faced with starvation, it broke up into parties seeking game along the several lines of march. The party which first came into contact with the Northern Indians, in self-defence, as they alleged, fired on them and killed nine. Women and children were taken captive. However, a squaw and a boy were sent to the main body to say that they had not come to war but to make peace ! When the party with Stewart and the "Slave woman" came up and saw the bodies of the slain it was swept by a sudden panic : the enemy knew of their presence and would be upon them to avenge the dead. The panic was allayed, however, by the masterful will of the "Slave woman." She won the Crees to remain where they were for ten days, promising to bring her people to a peace council within that time. She then followed the track of the fugitives and found the tribe assembled for the counter-offensive. In the long councils which followed, she urged her people to look beyond the tragedy of the moment and meet their foes in a council of peace. "The woman made herself so hoarse with her perpetual talking to her Country Men in persuading them to come with her that [when she returned] she could hardly speak." She brought the tribe with her prepared for war. The main body, 400 strong, was left in the rear, ready for action. A party of one hundred and sixty, willing to enter into a conference, remained within hailing distance of the Cree camp, which had in the meantime been rudely fortified. The masterful advocate of peace and two of her race came in within the limit of the ten days, when the Crees were actually preparing to decamp. All appearing well, she called her countrymen to the council. Under Stewart's direction the Cree chief explained that his party had had no part in the death of the nine.

So he pulled out his pipe and Stemm and made a long harangue of the Sacredness of that thing & that it was not to be touched without they were resolved to be true and perform what it was brought there for . . . he Lighted it and handed it about and after every one had taken so many whiffs as was agreed on and all had [accepted] it, none refusing it, he told them they were now to be perpetual friends ; with that they all gave thanks and a [shout] and Rised up and stroke them all on the head ; they spent the best part of 2 Days together & made severall presents of Goods as they had traded with us ; they received their Hostage[s] by adopting some of the Young Men for their own sons and so parted very good friends.

On 7th May Stewart, the "Slave woman," and their band of Crees reached York Fort—six weeks less than a year after their departure—and brought ten Northern youths with them. The "Slave woman" had explained the trade to her countrymen, what furs to get, and how to stretch and cure them. These ten were to learn the Cree tongue and become interpreters with a view to trade. The spadework necessary for a peaceful traffic had been well done. As Knight says : " The Slave woman was the chief Instrument in finishing of it."

It is not possible to say definitely how far Stewart had penetrated into the country. He reported that he had gone " N NWt about 400 miles, then they went N Wt to Cross that Baren Desarts and when they had cross'd them, they went W N Wt and came into a very Plentiful Country for Beasts." This can hardly mean anything but that they had crossed the Barren Grounds diagonally, and had come into the wooded country east of Slave River and south of Great Slave Lake—the wintering ground of the caribou and of the Indians. Confirmatory evidence lies in the statement that they had crossed seventeen rivers beyond the Churchill, that after the third river they found no woods, but came to them again at the thirteenth stream " and [at] all the other 4 Rivers the woods begin to grow bigger, and thicker and the 17th River [*i.e.* its trees] is bigger than any of the rest." Stewart asserted that they had travelled 1,000 miles returning, and done it in sixty days, counting those on which they did not travel. Knight, who was anxious to minimize the length of the journey to his coveted customers, argued for a less distance ; that twenty miles a day was too much for the Indians with their families. Stewart probably covered something less than seven hundred miles, that being the distance to the eastern extremity of Great Slave Lake. It should be borne in mind that the journey was, for the most part, on snow-shoes, and would be swift and, over lakes and swamps, more direct than in summer travel. As early as 1716, near half a century before Canada became British, English eyes, in the person of William Stewart, saw the Barrens and a portion of the wooded valley of the Slave River, and Governor Knight knew, however vaguely, of a great river (the Slave), of a great sea (Great Slave Lake), and of yet another river flowing by a mountain of copper (the Coppermine). Moreover, a quarter of a century earlier Henry Kelsey had visited the prairies east of the South Saskatchewan. Yet our books keep suggesting that the Hudson's Bay Company, to use Robson's biting phrase, slept by the frozen sea.

Governor Knight's attention was far from being centred upon the Northern Indians alone, though they appeared the most promising sphere for expansion before him. " I am endeavouring," he wrote in the Fort Journal for the eye of the Committee in London, " to make a peace in the whole Country Round from N to S Wt for a 1000 Miles." All the savages were to be drawn beneath the Company's shield of peace. When those miscreants, the Crees, who had driven the Chipewyans out of the valley of the Churchill, came to the fort in June 1715, the Governor met them in council. They told of another sea (Lake Athabaska) beyond the head of Churchill River and of a river (Athabaska River) which ran down into it ; they showed him salt and brimstone from the region. The Governor discoursed to them on the necessity of peace, and they showed themselves " Inclinable to it," " as likewise all Indians that hath been here that borders anywhere about the Country." One Indian chief, The Swan, undertook to be an ambassador of peace to the people beyond the head-waters of the Churchill. He did not return from his distant mission for two years. His report ran that after the first alarm of his presence was over, a number of the natives, doubtless Beaver Indians, then of the valley of the Athabaska, came to him. " They feasted, sung Danced & Smoked the Friendly Pipe with Great Rejoicing "—as well they might, for the White Man's goods, especially his guns and ammunition, promised more easily procured provisions and greater security from the attack of foes. A great peace gathering had been arranged for him on his return. In June 1719, after a second absence of two years, The Swan returned and reported to Henry Kelsey, now Governor, that he had wintered peacefully in the country beyond the Churchill, on a river which the natives said ran no great distance to the sea (Lake Athabaska). He brought a sample of " that Gum or pitch that flows out of the Banks of that River," doubtless from the " bituminous fountains " which Sir Alexander Mackenzie saw on the bank of the Athabaska River. The Déné tribe of that river never came to York Fort. Rather, for the time being, men like The Swan became the middlemen, overleaping the tribal passions in the prosecution of the fur trade. (Later, the Crees drove the Beaver Indians out of the Athabaska region to the far side of the Peace River.)

Governor Knight was much more successful in bringing the Indians of the South-West to trade. His pressure upon the native traders secured peace between band and band along the water-way to the fort, and his gifts, sent through leading Indians, brought down the people of the Askee country, the dry land Indians who wandered over the region south of the united Saskatchewan River. Beyond them would be the Muscuty Indians, the men from the buffalo plains who are reported as visiting the fort. Drawn by the offer of presents broadcasted inland, a mysterious people, the Mountain Indians, appeared upon the scene. Knight says " They came the farthest and bordered on the worst sort of Indians in the country. They had not been this way for fifteen or sixteen years." Cross-examined concerning their country, they told of mountains so high that their tops could not be seen, and, as Knight took it, of a great sea not far to the west of their land. It would be midwinter before they would reach their homes, and they did not know but that most of their families would be cut off by the enemy before they returned. There was little beaver in their country, but plenty of buffalo, red deer, and the smaller fur-bearing animals. They lived on plums and hazel-nuts, and grew corn. It is far from probable that Indians from as far west as the Rocky Mountains visited York Fort as early as this. The Piegans and Blackfeet, people unaccustomed to canoes, were then in the neighbourhood of the Eagle Hills and the Battle River. Indians to the west of them would hardly get through, and in any case did not grow corn. The nearest people who gardened were the Mandans, at this time on the upper waters of the Red River.* Their story of mountains penetrating into the sky beyond the sight, and of the sea to the west, may be no more than embroidery made from the report of peoples to the west, and to the south, towards the Rockies and the Gulf of Mexico. Knight's name for them, Mountain Indians, must be an anglicized version of their name, as given in Kelsey's Journal of May 26, 1721, the Mai-tain-ai-thi-nish. The conjecture may be hazarded that these were that horticultural and keenly commercial people, the Mandans, who, according to David Thompson, were driven from the Red River to the Missouri. Allured by Knight's offer of presents, and perhaps hoping to procure guns with which to cope with the Saulteurs, armed with guns from the French posts on the Great Lakes and pressing hard upon them, this mysterious people may have paddled down the Red River and all the way to Hudson Bay. They waited long for the ship, but it did not come, as will be seen. It was later reported that winter overtook them, and that they never reached their homes. Parties visited the fort every second year till 1721. In that year they arrived on 26th May. Their home could not therefore have been much farther away than the Red River. Their name does not occur thereafter in the Journals. Even more mysterious are the Crow Indians who came to the fort in 1716 and never returned.

Governor Knight may be looked upon as the rule of the Hudson's Bay Company personified. With the support of no body of police pervading the land, at present without any posts in the interior, it inaugurated a reign of comparative peace, under the shelter of which its trade ran far afield. The instruments of this policy were the "Indian Leaders." The Company traded its goods with these Leaders. But a small proportion of the native fur-trappers ever came down to the Bay. They traded their furs with the Leaders, who gathered around themselves bands of young men, trappers at times, traders on occasion ; and these came with them bringing the furs of their region to the fort on the Bay. The Leaders were treated with distinction on their arrival, were received within the palisades and in the Governor's quarters, and were loaded with the "customary presents." The goods which they traded and the presents thus given, placed them in a position all their own when they returned to their country. The more the savages grew accustomed to English goods, to the use of "iron works" in catching beaver and of guns at the chase and in war, the more they cherished the presence of the Leader and his band in their midst. The Leading Indians thus grew into a sphere of power very different from that of the more or less hereditary chief of a band. He was dominated by tribal passions, carried on the ancient feuds, and was all too ready to lead his

* See at p. 19ff.

warriors out to war. The Leaders saw the value of peace for their trade and for the extension of their influence. They became the willing instruments of the policy of peace, and in the interests of business made inter-tribal connections. Tribal wars continued, and often drew the natives away from trapping, but the Leaders passed through the war zones unafraid and, most probably, exerted their influence in favour of peace, without which the harvest of furs would be but scant.

In the autumn of 1715 the policy of expansion by means of peace suffered a series of rude shocks. By 10th September Governor Knight was in despair at the failure of the ship to arrive with the goods and supplies for the following year. Hope revived when Indians heard reports of great guns out on the foggy sea, and when the doctor, out in the marshes by the shore shooting geese, saw a sail off the estuary of the Nelson. But the ship, like a phantom, vanished into the vast mists of the Bay. When the Governor heard a year later that she had actually been anchored in the estuary in six fathoms, yet had sailed away to England, he poured out his rage in the pages of the fort Journal at that " harebrained crazy fellow " the captain, who had come so near his port and had sailed away panic-stricken at its shoals. He even asserted that, if the captain had allowed the ship to drift with the tide, he would have found himself in front of the fort. The disastrous result was that the many Indians that came down to trade in 1716, in response to his offer of generous treatment, arrived only to find the warehouse well-nigh empty. To be just to all, the Governor rationed out his goods— one gun to every five canoes, and, at the last, one to every ten canoes. So angry were the savages (some of whom had been travelling for months towards the fort) that there was danger of their carrying the place by storm. Every Englishman stood at his station, in case of an attempt at surprise. The rage of the Indians was certainly natural, for they needed ammunition to hunt by the way as they returned. Those who came down the following summer reported that one-third of their people had died of starvation on the way home. The Askee or Land Indians from the Saskatchewan were particularly unfortunate, for they had waited till late in the autumn for the ship. Most of the Mountain Indians were starved to death.

The plight of the Governor and his people during that winter was terrible. The flood in the spring had damaged a part of the provisions ; the wild geese on their autumn flight to the south had stayed but eight days ; the supply of powder for the Indians was scanty, and little shooting was done. But a small store was laid up for the winter. On 25th January all the flour was expended and two-thirds of the pease, and the winter but half gone. In February, Knight, who was well up in years, for he had entered the Company's service more than forty years before, was afflicted with fainting spells. It says much for his command of his men that the crisis was faced without unpleasant incidents. Rather, out of the misfortune came great good. The Englishmen had been too dependent upon supplies from

England. With these forthcoming, they had not learned to live on the country. This winter taught them a great lesson. They began to depend on the resources to hand for food. It may be surmised that the Deputy-Governor, Henry Kelsey, who had been with the Indians inland for two winters living from hand to mouth on the chase, made his contribution. Henceforth much more dependence will be laid on the supplies of meat to be had from the land around, caribou at the time of their migrations, geese on their flight northward and southward, in the dead of winter partridges and rabbits. In winter meat could be preserved frozen, but in the course of time the killing and salting of geese and venison became a prominent part of the activity of the fort. The Englishmen were now in the way of adapting themselves to the life of the land in which they traded. Great anxiety prevailed at the fort when September of the following year came without any sign of the ship. The rejoicing was proportionately great when the *Hudson's Bay*, frigate, Richard Ward in command, sailed into the river on the fourth day of the month, with abundant provisions and an ample supply of goods for the trade.

Meanwhile Knight's scheme of extending the trade to the Northern Indians had met with blow upon blow. In spite of the pipe of peace, the Home Indians assumed a threatening attitude to the Northern men whom they had brought in to the fort. So much so, that the Governor, after loading his prized guests with presents and repeating his instructions about curing the beaver skins, felt constrained, for security's sake, to send them off by boat as far as the Nelson (May 30, 1716). Two months later word came in that the party had been massacred by the Eskimos as it was crossing the Churchill River. Then, too, the Crees began again to make raids into the northern country. Knight had all along been planning to build a post at the mouth of the Churchill, where a whale fishery might bring valuable returns in oil. The persistent hostility of the Crees towards the Northern Indians led him to broaden out this plan. The post on the Churchill would be built to be the resort of the northern tribes ; they could reach it with tolerable safety across the Barrens. A first necessity was the means of communicating with tribes of a strange language—interpreters. Two Northern lads were sent out to winter with Home Indians to learn the Cree tongue, but they were treated so cruelly they fled back to the fort. In the autumn Knight had intended to send the "Slave woman," whose influence had proved so beneficial, to bring her people down to the new factory, but he was restrained by the fear that she would be killed on the way by the Crees. She made great progress with English, as also a Northern lad. But life at the fort undermined their health, and both died after lingering illnesses. Not only had the Governor lost the means of communication with the strangers, but likewise the one messenger who could be relied on to rally them to the new post. Two months later, however, he secured a substitute. He wrote on 16th May: " Yesterday the Indian as came in brought a Northern slave woman which I bought this day, having a great deal of difficulty to get her ;

and paid dearly for her, for she cost me above 60 skins value in goods ; but have her I must, let it cost me what will, for here is no one else as can speak one word of that country language and this." The woman was destined to be the first interpreter at Churchill Fort.

Meanwhile Knight had made other necessary dispositions. During the short time that the *Hudson's Bay* had lain in the river, the ship's carpenter had been commandeered to begin the construction of a sloop. He had the frame raised and part of the planking done, when he sailed away. On June 8, 1717, the completed hoy was launched and christened the *Good Success*. An advance party was sent in a small boat or " shallop " to make the first preparations for building. William Stewart, whose journey to the neighbourhood of the Great Slave Lake had issued in first contact with the Northern Indians, was the logical man for the command. He took with him the surgeon, John Caruthers, in case of any accident during the building. An Indian was sent overland to provide for the party by hunting. On 10th July Knight placed York Fort in the charge of his Deputy, Henry Kelsey, and sailed in the *Good Success*, accompanied by the *Prosperous*, a hoy brought from Albany for the purpose. On the fifth day the sloops lay in the Churchill River.

It proved scarcely less difficult to establish a post by the desolate estuary of the Churchill than for a tree to strike root in its rock-bound shore. Knight dropped anchor within the river two miles from Eskimo Point, the northern promontory at its mouth, only to receive a none too happy report of the situation from the surgeon, Mr. Caruthers. Search had revealed no more suitable spot for the post than the bare rocky point at which Munck had wintered ; water was not to be had within a quarter of a mile ; wood was scarce and would have to be carried three-quarters of a mile to the river through mud half-way up the men's legs ; ships could not come in to the shore for the ledge of mud and rock laid bare when the tide receded. Not content, Knight made his own survey from his next anchorage, off Munck's Point, five miles from the entrance. He condemned Eskimo Point, so called from being the resort of that savage race, for it was so exposed to the Arctic blast as to be " Impossible for any European to live at." The position of the fort commenced in 1689 some distance west of Munck's Point was unfit ; the men in the fort could be " pickt off " by an enemy on the rocky height behind, and the snow would slide down the steep upon the house. Open as Munck's Point was to all the winds of heaven and without enough soil to bank up the sides of the houses, it was yet easily defensible, a most important feature, for Knight had been alarmed at the presence of Eskimos. He had never seen such a miserable place in all his life, and the site hardly contained so much compass of ground as the Royal Exchange stood upon, yet he saw no other possibility. There, over the bones of the Danish dead, and looking down on Munck's brass cannon in the tidal mud-flat, Knight built Fort Churchill, or as it soon came to be called, Prince of Wales's Fort. In view of the danger of attack by the Eskimos, the construction of the houses was postponed. The palisades were erected with four flankers or bastions commanding them, the men to be quartered within three of these, while the Governor was to occupy the fourth and to have the goods there, immediately under his eye. The wood was brought some thirteen miles down stream, and had most of the time to be dragged over the mud-flat to the fort. Some sawed lumber, however, had been brought from York Fort in the sloops.

Mosquitoes, horse-flies, and sand-flies descended on the men, and at times halted them at their work. Knight remarks : " Certainly these be ye flyes that was Sent to ye Egyptians as caused a Darkness over the Land and brought such blotches and boiles as broke out all over them into Sores." These were trifling worries, which the cold weather would end. An overmastering anxiety lay in the scarcity of provisions. It was not the time of year for the caribou ; it was too early for geese ; assiduous attention to the fishing nets brought meagre results. " So here is neither fish, fowl, nor Venison to be gott," wrote Knight thrice in his Journal. The tense situation was relieved by the early arrival, on 14th August, of the ship from England with abundant supplies. " Ye Ship came in a very Good time, wee haveing nothing but a little Oatmeal & Cheese left, besides Flower," wrote the relieved Governor.

The task of unloading the vessel was no light one. She lay out in the channel of the river beyond the mud-flat, more than a mile away, and the boats could only come in at high tide ; stormy days there were when even this proved impossible. The stores landed, and three of Munck's brass cannon put on board, the ship sailed away leaving the post well supplied, " haveing flower & Pease enough for 2 year."

After the return of the peace party from the Northern Indians, Governor Knight began to have visions of wealth pouring into the coffers of the Company, not from the animal but from the mineral resources of their lands. The men from the north confirmed the " Slave woman's " reports of copper and, more alluring still, of a people living farther to the west and by the sea, whose ornaments were yellow but of a different metal.

All the Knives, awls, hand-cuffs, Rings, bands as goes about their [the Northern Indians'] headgear [are] of Pure Virgin Copper as they take up out of a River from among the Sands in the Stream ; one of them told me as he has got a great deal of it in his time and this was his way of getting it ; they go into the River ; the water is up to [their] knees ; they Put down there hands and take up handfulls of Sand and amongst that Sand bitts of Copper, some bigg, some Small as you will see by [Severall] things as I have sent home. . . . But that is not still what I am Endeavouring to gett or Endeavour to discover ; there is a Parcell of Indians as lyes upon the west Seas as has a Yellow Mettle as they make Use of, as these do Copper. . . . They told me there is a very Great River that comes out of the West Sea [doubtless meaning the Mackenzie out of Great Slave Lake] and is in the bottom of a very great Bay where there lyes 3 Islands in the mouth of the Bay allmost out of sight of the Land where them Indians [that] Inhabit there brings a Yellow Mettle from thence and wares it as they and the Copper Indians doth for hoops for there heads, hand-cuffs and Rings, made after the same form of them Copper ones as I have sent home ; but for the Copper they tell me it is found in a River that runs by the side of a Great Mountain that is on one side of it of that Mettle and all the bottom of that River is full of bitts of it, that the Grounds looks red with it.

This vision of copper in the foreground and the gleam of gold in the background took increasing possession of Governor Knight. It became an obsession. The lust for gold, which no more than a generation ago led hundreds of Canadian youths to face the mad journey overland a thousand miles from Edmonton to the Yukon, swept the old man of sixty and more off his feet. He dared not face the voyage across the terrible Barren Grounds. Could he reach the land of his dreams by sea by a North-West Passage and, entering the copper and the gold rivers, return with a fortune of incalculable greatness for himself and his Company ? He cross-examined his Indian informants with the utmost care. Was there a sea or some strait that could bring him to those rivers ? All agreed that there was none. Yet Knight fashioned an argument to meet his desires. They had told him that after the Barrens were crossed, the trees by the rivers grew larger and yet larger, as one went north-westwards. This surely was due to the increasing proximity of the sea and its milder climate. The way by water was open to him, he argued, shutting his eyes to the great lacunæ in his geographical scheme. Accordingly, when his more immediate objective, the establishment of Churchill Fort and a trade with the Northern Indians was accomplished, the aged Governor decided on action, concealing his design from his colleagues with all the care of a hunter for gold. At the expiry of his contract with the Company he embarked for England, leaving Henry Kelsey duly appointed Governor of York Fort, and Richard Staunton in charge of Prince of Wales's Fort.

Knight was welcomed by the Governor and Committee in London on 18th November. He may well have laid his scheme before them at that time, but the Minutes of the Committee show no trace of it till March 20, 1719. As the Minute Book is often referred to as the " Order Book," this need create no surprise, for no decisions were taken and no orders given until the spring, and therefore none entered in the Minutes. This silence might lend colour to Joseph Robson's statement that the Committee was opposed to the scheme, and only adopted it when Knight threatened to carry it out in spite of them with the support of outsiders, but there is very definite evidence that the Committee, and indeed the whole Company, were as much carried away by the dream of copper and gold as their overseas Governor. In the summer of 1720 they made financial provision on a most ample scale " for Enlargeing & Extending ye Comps Trade in Hudson's Bay and Buss Island." Their plans had two ends in view, to bring their stock in line with the actual capital, and to avail themselves of the goodwill of the stockholders resulting from that action, to raise a large capital sum with which to extend their business.

The stock of the Company had been trebled in 1690, and had since stood at £31,500. From that year no dividends had been paid until 1718. During the wars the Company had met with serious losses, but after the return of their territory to them by the French profits had been large ; they had, however, not been paid out as dividends, but had been put into equipment for their greatly extended trade. York Fort had returned to them, and its large trade had to be provided for ; in 1717 Churchill Fort had been built ; a considerable sum had been put into new sloops and ships, including the two sent out on Knight's expedition ; the money in the goods and furs of their extended trade was great. The Committee estimated that the capital put into all these amounted to £94,500, "at a moderate valuation." It was deemed by the Committee and the General Court only just that the stock should be raised to the actual value represented by the Company's equipment and goods ; indeed, in view of the long years—twenty-eight in all—without dividends, it was so. The stock was accordingly raised to £94,500, in fact trebled. As it was not placed on the market, and was represented by capital actually invested, it stands in sharp contrast with the speculative stock sold to a gullible public by the South Sea Company.

The second part of the Committee's plans, namely, raising money for the extension of their trade in Hudson Bay, can have no other reference than to the expansion expected to result from Knight's expedition to the copper mines, for which very large capital would be necessary; £283,500 was the estimate. The stock of the Company was to be further raised to £378,000, the additional £283,500 to be in no sense nominal, but to be paid for by the stockholders by instalments of 10 per cent., payable every three months until the whole was raised. But the financial difficulties due to the bursting of the South Sea Bubble made it impossible for the members of the Company to pay even the first instalment. The scheme was therefore modified in November to read that additional stock would be issued only to the value of the money paid in. On 23rd December this amounted to no more than £2,419, 12s. To all appearance the Company itself was finding it difficult to get credit with which to carry on. Moreover, no returns had come in from Knight's expedition, into which £8,000 had been put, and the *Hudson's Bay*, frigate, had been lost in Port Nelson. At any rate, the General Court of 23rd December made the offer to the stockholders, that all who should pay in the 10 per cent., that is £10 per £100 share, would receive stock for £30. It is indicative of the difficulties of the time that only £750 additional was raised, making, with the £2,419 already paid in, £3,150 of new capital for which £9,450 of stock was given. The addition of this to the £94,500 to which the stock had been raised by the trebling, made the total stock £103,950. It stood at this figure till after the union of 1821. These financial arrangements are intelligible only when read in the light of Knight's expedition to open up copper and, it might be, gold mines for exploitation by the Company. As Knight's expedition proved a failure they were not revived, but they show that the Company was wholeheartedly behind it.

On March 20, 1719, a letter from James Knight embodying his proposals was before the Governor and Committee. It was referred, not to the standing Sub-committee, whose minutes survive, but to a special group of four whose proceedings are not on record, unfortunately. On 1st May the Agreement was signed and sealed. Orders now went through in quick succession—for goods to trade with the Indians; for the materials for winter quarters, brick and lime, coal, and the like; for servants to be engaged, for example, a gun-smith for each ship. At the end of the month Sailing Orders for the officers, Captain George Berley of the *Albany*, frigate, and Captain David Vaughan of the *Discovery*, sloop, were signed and sealed. The Committee showed its complete confidence in Knight by placing these commanders under his orders in all matters save the actual sailing of their ships, and by drawing his own Instructions to read that the expedition was committed to his unfettered guidance. On the 3rd and 4th of June the Governor and Committee, in keeping with the practice from the beginning, were at Gravesend to send their ships off, paying the sailors of their four ships, for two were going to the forts; tipping the officers and men of the *Albany* a guinea for drink; those of the *Discovery* half a guinea; ordering gratuities of fresh provisions for the captains. The letters for the posts, constituting what was called the packet, were signed and delivered to the proper ships, and their Sailing Orders placed in the hands of the captains. The Instructions to Knight, and Instructions to be followed in case of his death, were handed to that brave, ardent, but deluded old man. He was to "find out the Streight of Anian [which geographers of those days placed between America and Asia] in order to discover gold, and other valuable commodities to the northward." The Minutes close with the Governor, Deputy-Governor, and Committee wishing all a prosperous journey and safe return, " as Likewise of Captain James Knight who is gone with the *Albany* . . . in order to A Discovery of a Passage beyond Sir Thos Buttons, which is supposed to Lye to the northwards of 64 degrees, in order to Enlarge & Improve ye Comps trade with A Discovery [of] Severll mines according to ye Information of Indians to our Govr in the Country & allso to Establish A Whale fishery (who will saile Early Tomorrow morning)."

With the disappearance of his ships into Hudson Bay the painful story of their end begins. Neither Knight nor a single man on board ever returned. The account of the tragic fate of the expedition has been told by Samuel Hearne who, with other seamen, saw the wrecks of the ships near half a century later. It has been accepted hitherto as all that will ever be known.

Notwithstanding a sloop was annually sent to the Northward on discovery, and to trade with the Esquimaux, it was the Summer of one thousand seven hundred and sixty-seven, before we had positive proofs that poor Mr. Knight and Captain Barlow had been lost in Hudson's Bay.

The Company were now carrying on a black whale fishery, and Marble Island was made the place of rendezvous, not only on account of the commodiousness of the harbour, but because it had been observed that the whales were more plentiful about that island than on any part of the coast. This being the case, the boats, when on the look-out for fish, had frequent occasion to row close to the island, by which means they discovered a new harbour near the East end of it, at the head of which they found guns, anchors, cables, bricks, a smith's anvil, and many other articles, which the hand of time had not defaced, and which being of no use to the natives, or too heavy to be removed by them, had not been taken from the place in which they were originally laid. The remains of the house, though pulled to pieces by the Esquimaux for the wood and iron, are yet very plain to be seen, as also the hulls, or more properly speaking, the bottoms of the ship and sloop, which lie sunk in about five fathoms of water, toward the head of the harbour. The figurehead of the ship, and also the guns, &c. were sent home to the Company, and are certain proofs that Messrs. Knight and Barlow had been lost on that inhospitable island, where [neither] stick nor stump was to be seen, and which lies near sixteen miles from the main land. Indeed the main is little better, being a jumble of barren hills and rocks, destitute of every kind of herbage except moss and grass ; and at that part, the woods are several hundreds of miles from the sea-side.

In the Summer of one thousand seven hundred and sixty-nine, while we were prosecuting the fishery, we saw several Esquimaux at this new harbour ; and perceiving that one or two of them were greatly advanced in years, our curiosity was excited to ask them some questions concerning the above ship and sloop, which we were enabled to do by the assistance of an Esquimaux, who was then in the Company's service as a linguist, and annually sailed in one of their vessels in that character. The account which we received from them was full, clear, and unreserved, and the sum of it was to the following purport.

When the vessels arrived at this place (Marble Island) it was very late in the Fall, and in getting them into the harbour, the largest received much damage ; but on being fairly in, the English began to build the house, their number at that time seeming to be about fifty. As soon as the ice permitted, in the following Summer, (one thousand seven hundred and twenty,) the Esquimaux paid them another visit, by which time the number of the English was greatly reduced, and those that were living seemed very unhealthy. According to the account given by the Esquimaux they were then very busily employed, but about what they could not easily describe, probably in lengthening the long-boat ; for at a little distance from the house there is now lying a great quantity of oak chips, which have been most assuredly made by carpenters.

Sickness and famine occasioned such havock among the English, that by the setting in of the second Winter their number was reduced to twenty. That Winter (one thousand seven hundred and twenty) some of the Esquimaux took up their abode on the opposite side of the harbour to that on which the English had built their houses and frequently supplied them with such provisions as they had, which chiefly consisted of whale's blubber and seal's flesh and train oil. When the Spring advanced, the Esquimaux went to the continent, and on their visiting Marble Island again, in the Summer of one thousand seven hundred and twenty-one, they only found five of the English alive, and those were in such distress for provisions that they eagerly eat the seal's flesh and whale's blubber quite raw, as they purchased it from the natives. This disordered them so much, that three of them died in a few days, and the other two, though very weak, made a shift to bury them. Those two survived many days after the rest, and frequently went to the top of an adjacent rock, and earnestly looked to the South and East, as if in expectation of some vessels coming to their relief. After continuing there a considerable time together, and nothing appearing in sight, they sat down close together, and wept bitterly. At length one of the two died, and the other's strength was so far exhausted, that he fell down and died also, in attempting to dig a grave for his companion. The sculls and other large bones of those two men are now lying above-ground close to the house. The longest liver was, according to the Esquimaux account, always employed in working of iron into implements for them ; probably he was the armourer, or smith.

Hearne's aged Eskimo informants may be excused for picturing their fierce countrymen in the part of benefactors to the unfortunate Englishmen. Much can now be added to their moving account, explaining it and modifying it. To begin with, the Company envisaged the possibility of Knight getting round the North-West promontory of Hudson Bay, visiting the Coppermine River and the river of the gold country in turn, finding the climate milder as he ran south-westward, and finally entering the Western Sea by the Strait of Anian. Not to hear from the expedition might mean success fully as much as disaster. No note of alarm was sounded in the Committee's letter of 1720 to York Fort, and even in that of 1721 there was no more than an expression of wonder at getting no news, meaning, doubtless, through the medium of the Northern Indians. If there were chances that Knight was sailing homeward on the balmy Western Sea, why send out a relief expedition to nobody could just say where ? At any rate, in sending out the *Whalebone*, sloop, Captain George Scroggs, commander, as the Company did in 1721, their first thought was not the search for Captain Knight. The *Hudson's Bay*, which had sailed from the Thames along with Captain Knight's ships, had been wrecked as she sailed into Port Nelson. The sloop *Whalebone* was sent out in the first instance to take the place of any ship which might meet with a like disaster, and to bring home the packet and at least a portion of the furs. Till such emergency occurred, she was to sail northward on discovery well into the region where Knight expected to find his strait, and she was to trade as she went. It fell to the Governor, Henry Kelsey, to issue Sailing Orders to Captain Scroggs for the northward voyage of the summer of 1722. They followed the Company's Instructions closely. Scroggs was to lose no time surveying the near coast, but to proceed to Sir Thomas Roe's Welcome and up to 66° 30′ north latitude ; precautions were prescribed for trading with the Eskimos, with emphasis on " civility." Scroggs was to turn homeward on 15th August. So far the Company's Instructions. But Kelsey was concerned for the fate of Knight. He himself had been in the waters of Marble Island in the weeks of 1719, when Knight was entering Hudson Bay. In the following year Captain John Hancock had been in charge of the northern expedition, and had reported that " the gold-finders wintered where we [*i.e.* Kelsey and he] had been last summer, and had traded with those Indians and spoiled our trade," but he had been prevented by adverse winds from sailing as far north. In 1721 Kelsey himself had sailed in the sloop northward, with an Indian to show him copper. Contrary winds had driven him southward to Churchill. Now, without diverting Scroggs's expedition from its original objects of exploration and trade, possibly concluding wisely that the way to discover Knight was to trade with the Eskimos and make inquiries, he inserted directions to the Captain to make such discoveries as he could westward and southward towards Carey's Swan Nest, and especially to the back of that land " where we are informed the Copper Mines are ; when you are upon that coast you are to fire a Great Gun Morng, Noon and Night." In a postscript he added : " Capt Knight wintered in about 62° 30m odd." There can be but little doubt that Scroggs, while keeping to the object of his expedition, was to find Knight. He sailed into Roe's Welcome and named Cape Fullerton, turning back somewhere north of it in what he made 64° 30' north latitude, though it has been suggested that his quadrant was defective and that he did not reach Wager Inlet. Going or returning he entered the harbour in which Knight had wintered, and he saw the wrecks of the ships. Unfortunately his log is lost, but when windbound on the coast north of Churchill as he returned, he reported himself by letter overland to Richard Staunton, who made entry in the Churchill Journal of July 25, 1722 : " He had been where the *Albany* and *Discovery*, sloop, both ship-wracked, and he doth affirm that Every man was killed by the Eskemos." The logs of the whaling-sloops whose commanders visited the spot in 1767 contribute, along with Hearne's picturesque account, to the complete reconstruction of the story of the fate of the gold-finders.

Knight, according to the Eskimos, did not enter the harbour till late in the autumn. He must have spent August, at least, feeling his way for a passage westward to his copper and gold rivers. Baffled by an unbroken coast, he returned southward to winter. Marble Island, sixteen miles from the West Main and from the principal habitations of the Eskimos, would be chosen for safety's sake. The harbour selected is of the snuggest within, but there is no entry except at high tide because of a rocky bar across its mouth. As the ships were found at the head of the haven, three anchors on shore above the tide, the hawsers worn, as the observers concluded, by chafing on the ice, they must have got in without injury. The materials for building, the coals for warmth, and other necessaries, were unloaded, and a house forty-seven feet by twenty-nine was built. The graves at the site surely tell the tale of deaths by scurvy, for, while there were caribou on the island, they are reported as few and wild, so that little fresh meat would be procurable. Scroggs's statement that all perished at the hands of the Eskimos must therefore be modified. Probably in the spring of 1720, before the party could sail and when it was depleted by death and undermined by sickness, the Eskimos, feeling it now safe to attack, overmastered it. A few, like the carpenter and the blacksmith, may have been spared for the time, to make implements of wood and iron for the victors, but only to be finally abandoned to their fate. The ships were wrecked by the savages for the wood and iron, so precious in the eyes of the Eskimos. As Hearne's account indicates, only the bottoms were left to sink.

A succession of incidents shows that the first impulse of the Eskimos, on contact with Europeans with their wealth of wood and iron equipment, has been to plunder.   But here, too, the servants of the Company, by treating the savages with " civility," yet with firmness, won them to peaceful trading.   In 1720 Governor Kelsey dismissed Captain Hancock from the York Council " for firing his gun at the Eskimos," and for going to knock a savage down with a handspike.   Captains of the trading-schooners took warning and learned to control their fierce customers without show of violence. Forty-five years later Moses Norton, Chief at Churchill, whose father had been with Scroggs as mate at the discovery of the wreck of Knight's ships, made this proud entry in his Journal in reference to the massacre of the Englishmen :

" I don't doubt but what some of the said vessels' crews might be destroyed by the Esquemays, as they was at that time not in the least Civilized, but I have the vanity to think that if any accident was to happen to an English vessel now, as did to Knight and Borlow (which God forbid) I have reason to believe that the Natives as far north as Marble Island would rather assist a man in distress than to do otherwise by him."

This remarkable change was wrought by the " civility " to the natives which was law through the service of the Hudson's Bay Company.

In 1718 Henry Kelsey was appointed Governor-in-Chief in Hudson Bay in succession to Governor Knight.   He held office in virtue of a commission under the common seal of the Company.   Like Knight, he held also a commission from the Crown (George I.) issued under the Great Seal, constituting him Governor and Commander-in-Chief of all the Forts and Territories within Hudson Strait and Bay—one of a long line of recognitions of the rule of the Company by the British Government.   Kelsey had already made his contribution to the success of the Company.   As a boy he had adapted himself to the ways of the Indians.   He had learned the language of the Crees, and in 1710 the Company had printed his " dictionary," and sent out copies to him at Albany, that " he might the better instruct the young lads about him in the Indian language."   His adaptation of himself to Indian life was such that he may be regarded as the first Indianized Englishman in Rupert's Land.   As has been seen, while still but a lad, he had been sent inland to bring the natives down to York Fort to trade, a special feature of his mission being to secure peace between tribe and tribe.   In 1714, as Deputy to Governor Knight, he had been commissioned, along with his chief, to receive the Hudson Bay Territory surrendered by the French according to the Treaty of Utrecht.   His activities as Deputy are obscured by the dominant personality of Knight, but it may be safely assumed that he contributed greatly to the happy relations which subsisted between the fort and the savages as well as to the success of the policy of making peace among the natives.   He appears in Knight's Journal at humbler tasks, such as hunting deer and shooting geese for the tables of the fort ; seeking for the wood for the new factory ; laying the buoys annually to guide the ship into the river ; and as piloting it to its anchorage. As Governor his first duty was to work towards the objectives set before the Company by his predecessor, but at the outset he had to meet charges made against him by his late chief. These seem to have arisen through disapproval of his intimate relations with the Indians. According to the custom of the Company, the charges were put in writing and sent to him for a written answer. That the reply was not unsatisfactory to the Committee is proved by his being retained as Governor till the autumn of 1722.

In 1719 the annual ship, the *Hudson's Bay*, was driven ashore to the east of Hayes River. Kelsey called a Council, which decided to send the packet, and as much of the furs as might be, home by the hoy *Prosperous*. She was speedily fitted for the voyage and sailed on 17th September, but when the crew faced the dangers of the Bay in their frail craft, their courage failed them. They returned to port next day. By vigorous action Kelsey was able to save all the goods for the year's trade from the wreck, but the provisions were damaged beyond use. By calling on the Indians to hunt for the fort he was able to minimize the hardship involved. " Had it not been for them," Kelsey wrote to Richard Staunton at Churchill Fort, " it would have been very hard for us this winter." On another issue the new Governor had trouble with his men. On Christmas Eve they fell to fighting among themselves and refused to obey the Deputy's order to stop. Kelsey got out of bed to quiet them, but they continued their " audacious and insolent manners," even to him. Two days later he brought the offenders to judgment. " I had Henry Veal and John Burry stripped to their waist and gave the former 11 lashes and the latter 24 lashes with the cat-of-nine-tails, for being ringleaders of a riot on Thursday." In May fifteen lashes were administered to one man for stealing, and twenty to another for trading the Company's furs. These punishments were no more severe than those in vogue in the navy of the time. They stand out in the Journals of the forts as resorted to only in extreme cases.

Though on the most friendly terms with the natives, Kelsey could be stern with them also. A few weeks before his commission as Governor arrived, Crees came in with furs gathered in a murderous raid on the Northern Indians. Kelsey's dealing with them is recorded in the York Journal of August 1, 1718 : " After having discoursed those Indians I told them we would not trade with them and they might go see if they could find any of our goods in that country where they destroyed the natives and that we did not bring guns, powder and other necessaries to destroy mankind but to kill food for them and their families. So they promised to desist."

Partly to expand the trade, but not without the hope of falling in with the coveted copper mine, Kelsey began a series of expeditions in the sloop up the west coast of Hudson Bay into the Eskimo region. As has been seen, he was about Marble Island in 1719, in the region in which Knight's party afterwards met its tragic end. Unable to go in person next year, he sent Captain John Hancock, who reported Knight as wintering " where he had been last year but he (Hancock) could not reach that place." Hancock, it will be remembered, was put off the Council at York Fort by Kelsey for his violent ways with the Eskimos. In 1721 Kelsey sailed north in the sloop, *Success*, taking Richard Norton and an Indian, who professed to be able to show him copper. In 1722 came the voyage of Captain John Scroggs. These expeditions established friendly relations with the Eskimos and began what proved in time a valuable trade to the Company, but until the natives learned what was wanted of them the returns were small and the cost great. In the autumn of that year Kelsey was recalled on the general ground that he had been four years Deputy-Governor and four Governor-in-Chief, but most probably because the returns of his administration were impaired by its great expenditures. That year the financial diffi- culties of London were still great after the bursting of the South Sea Bubble; the Company was suffering from the loss of between £7,000 and £8,000 through Knight's expedition, and its dividend was but 5 per cent.

In 1724 Kelsey applied to the Company for employment as captain of the *Hannah* in the room of Captain Gofton deceased, but this ship was not sent out that year. This is the last footprint traceable of a character as interesting as it is illusive. Between January 1729 and February 20, 1733, Kelsey's widow, Elizabeth, was hard pressed launching her sons into careers. That the Company had no ill-will towards her husband is proved by their gratuities of ten guineas towards placing young William Kelsey as an apprentice to one Thomas Fanner, a cordwainer, and of six guineas for clothing for his brother John, the widow " being wholly incapable to do it herself."

Kelsey was succeeeded at York Fort by Thomas Macklish, who had worked his way up in the service from carpenter to captain of the East Main sloop, and to Governor at Albany Fort. With him the Company abandoned the expensive and cumbersome procedure involved in the issue of a commission by the King. It fell back on the constitution sketched in the Charter, and issued a commission under its own common seal. At the same time the office of Governor- in-Chief was abolished. Henceforth " Hudson's Bay " and " the Bottom of the Bay " were two self-dependent commands. York Fort was now in the full stride of its trade.

At all the forts the trading year was reckoned from the arrival of the ship from England. At the proper time the Hayes River was buoyed. A beacon indicated the shoal at the entrance to Five Fathom Hole—the outer anchorage where the ship was often dis- charged of heavy goods, to make her passage to the fort safer. Buoys were set as guides into Three Fathom Hole, and over a stony bar above. At the factory there was a wharf to facilitate unloading, and farther up a slip for repairing and building sloops and boats. When out in Port Nelson the ship fired the number of guns required by a secret code, and the fort replied with the number prescribed for it. The fort stood a short distance from the bank in a clear space surrounded by woods. A battery a little way below guarded the approach. The area between the battery and slip was called " the plantation." On this the Indians pitched their tents when they arrived to trade. There was generally a tent or two of old and infirm men and women who picked up a living at the fort, presumably by making moccasins and stringing snow-shoes. The plantation was separated from the fort by two rows of high fences, between which were store-houses, the cookery, and workshops. Within the inner fence were plots of turnips, collard, lettuce, and the like, belonging to the Governor and the officers. The factory itself was a square fort having four bastions, each two storeys in height, with platforms on the top and parapets. Here the heavy guns were placed. Palisades ran from bastion to bastion. In the centre of these were buildings with projections from the second storey, from which defenders could command the palisades and gates. Following a wooden walk from the river bank, one passed through the gate into an open space dominated by the bastions. In the upper storey of the south-easterly bastion was the Governor's apartment, four rooms, with a fire-place in the largest. In the lower storey were the quarters of the Deputy-Governor and of those who formed the Governor's mess. In the large mess-room stood a brick stove, by means of which both storeys were warmed. Doors opened into diminutive bedrooms. In the lower storey of the north-eastern bastion similar apartments accommodated the steward's mess. The two other bastions and the other buildings were used for magazine, trading-room, and stores.

York Fort, as indeed every fort on the Bay, must be thought of as housing a little community of Englishmen living, as far as might be, the life of England under strange skies. The " regulations " required divine service, according to the forms of the Church of England, to be read every Sunday and at other appropriate times, such as Christmas Day. Some of the factors read sermons, such as Boyle's and Tillotson's, as well. If any of these proved too long for the patience of the men, or too much for the wind of the factor, he stopped in the middle, and read the rest on the following Sunday. St. George's Day, Christmas, and Guy Fawkes's Day were observed, with the special allowance of liquor which the celebration called for. The regular toasts on Guy Fawkes's Day were to the King and the royal family, confusion to the enemies of the Established Church, and success to the Honourable Company of Adventurers trading into Hudson Bay and to its trade. War was never declared in England, or peace proclaimed, without printed copies of the Proclamation— forwarded by the Secretary of State to the Company, and by the Company to the several factors overseas—being publicly read and posted in the fort. The accession of the successive sovereigns was proclaimed as solemnly at York Fort to less than two score men as it was at Mansion House to the mass of Londoners. George I. was proclaimed in England on August 1, 1714 ; Governor Knight proclaimed him with due ceremony at York Fort on September 6, 1716, more than two years later. The delay, due to the failure of the ship of 1715 to arrive, does not seem to have staled the ardour with which the new king's health was drunk.

The garrison of the fort lived under regulations issued by the Governor in accordance with instructions from the Committee in London. When occasion called for it, these were publicly read and were posted in the fort. The Governor, in whose charge lay their enforcement, paced up and down within the palisades with the sense of authority and of responsibility of a captain upon his ship. Disregard of the rules touching fires and lamps, or slackness on the part of the summer watch, when Indians were encamped about the post, might in this desolate region lead not only to disaster to the fort, but to the loss of the lives of the garrison. The correspondence between the Committee and the factors shows that the Company was concerned to maintain the sobriety of the service within the limits signified by the term in those days. The prudent factor was not less anxious, for most of his troubles arose from the occasional excesses in which individuals found relief from the monotony and drabness of life under sub-arctic conditions. He had, of course, control of the amount of brandy which a servant could purchase. He watched carefully lest his men procure secret quantities from the crew of the annual ship. When outbreaks came, few factors showed the severity of Henry Kelsey. The drunken and riotous might be placed in irons till sober, but the usual form of punishment was the public reprimand duly recorded in the Journal of the fort, and so placed before the Committee in London. At times the factor asked for the recall of servants—lazy, insolent, or turbulent. At others, they fell back on the constitution prescribed by the Charter and called a Council. The decision was usually to send the offender home.

At this stage the Council was constituted somewhat informally. In 1714 the Governor and Committee referred it to Governor Knight to choose "discreet persons" to be of his Council, and expressly conferred on him the power to remove any member from that body. They recommended frequent meetings, and strictly required a book of the proceedings to be kept and sent to them by the annual ship for their supervision. It has been seen that Governor Kelsey removed Captain Hancock from the Council as a reprimand for his violent ways with the Eskimos. In keeping with the earliest regulations, it was the practice for the Governor to call to his Council his second in command, the surgeon, and the captain of any ship or sloop which lay in port at the time. Council met when there was special call for discipline, and to sign the report of the year going home by ship. In the ordinary, it decided who should be sent or be allowed to go to England, and who should remain ; in case of a discussion about wages, it made temporary agreements subject to the decision of the Governor and Committee in London, as indeed were all its findings. At the death of a factor it named his successor for the time being, and awaited the appointment which should be made by the Committee. Its duty was to strengthen the hands of the Governor in every emergency, as when, in Kelsey's time, it supported him in the decision that, the annual ship being lost, the hoy *Prosperous* was fit and should be sent to England with packet and furs. While strengthening the hand of the factor, the Council was a check on his arbitrariness, for out of prudence he would avoid actions in which his fellow officers would not uphold him. Its power to send offenders home acted as a restraint on the men, who frequently sought and were granted pardon on the promise of better conduct. Outbreaks there were at rare intervals; their recurrence was guarded against and general discipline maintained by purging the personnel when the annual ship came in.

Control of the factor and the fort was exercised by the Governor and Committee in London through its system of business. The annual ship brought out " the packet," which included the " general letter " to the factor and his Council commenting on their administration, raising issues, and suggesting or commanding action, as also private letters to individuals as the need might arise. The information on which these letters were based was drawn from the annual letter of the factor and his Council, and from the Fort Journal, in which the factor, or his accountant for him, entered the happenings at the fort from day to day. Moreover, each factor was required to send home a copy of such letters as passed between him and his colleagues in the other forts or any other person—all for the information of the Committee. The correspondence between the Committee and the factors, the Journals of the forts, and the inter-fort letters, form a large and valuable part of the Archives at Hudson's Bay House, London. In general they are complete from 1714, and especially from 1730. The " London Book," in which the outgoing letters were copied, is complete almost from the establishment of the Company.

The correspondence between the factors and the Governor and Committee shows a remarkable frankness on either side. The factors were no obsequious flunkeys, nor did the Committee show the arbitrariness of men ruling from their office chairs. This is well illustrated by the discussions which took place about the trading-goods sent out. It was not our age of machine-made goods of even quality and standardized. Everything was being made by hand, and it was all too easy to have a percentage of a consignment below standard. Factors freely and frankly protested against any poor articles sent out, for if the goods traded were defective—for example, if the "ears" of the kettles were too weak to stand the rough usage of Indian life—the natives would not come all the way to the Bay to trade furs for them. This was especially true in areas and at times when the forts were subject to competition with the French. The complaints of the factors were loud when the goods fell short in quality. The Governor and Committee at the other end do not appear to have resented this.   They established the rule that defective samples, indeed samples of most of the goods and of the provisions, should be sent home to them, doubtless that they might deal with the merchants in England.   Thus gradually standards for goods were established, and quality became the cornerstone of the trade.   As is natural, this is more noticeable at Albany Fort, where competition with the French was most keenly felt.

A post required to be well manned during the summer when the Indians came down to trade in considerable numbers, but the men could not be left idle during the long winter months without great loss to the Company.   At a later time, and in the interior, superfluous hands were sent out, as the French voyageurs were, to winter with the Indians and to gather provisions and furs at little or no expense to the fort.   This could not be done on the Bay, where both provisions and furs were scarce.   The solution of the problem was simple enough in the age before the Industrial Revolution, an age in which everything was made by hand.   Labourers could be kept busy during the winter manufacturing articles for the summer's trade.   Thus the factory, which was strictly a store overseas at which a factor or agent traded for his company, became a factory in the more modern sense of a place where goods were manufactured.   There was a tailor at each factory, making caps, coats, and what not, for the servants and for the Indian trade.   A blacksmith made the nails, hinges, locks, and the like for the factory ;   and ice chisels, hatchets, and " bayonets " or spear heads, for traffic with the Indians.   The armourer repaired the guns, making any parts that were needed.   The guns of the Indians were repaired at the fort without charge.   The cooper made wooden buckets, and casks for salting geese and venison and for the furs to be shipped to England.   Other servants were the bricklayer, who made the stoves and ovens, plastered the walls of the apartments, and built the platforms of the batteries which protected the forts ; and the carpenter, who on occasions mended and even built boats and sloops.   Oats were sent out whole and oatmeal made as required. Kilns were erected for making lime.   From time to time two men were kept busy brewing beer, including spruce beer, which acted as an antiscorbutic.   Scurvy was rare in the service.   During the proper seasons men were out hunting and shooting geese, or cutting lumber for building or wood for the fires.   Lumber was cut to measure, to stow the cases and casks of fur securely for the journey across the Atlantic, and was sold in London.   Servants were often allowed to go out trapping and were given 50 per cent. of the proceeds of their peltries.   The busy seasons were at the arrival of the ship and at the coming of the Indians, when the servants were engaged loading and unloading, or were on guard to prevent petty thefts or surprise by the savages.

The Governor and Committee were much concerned to keep the servants from too intimate relations with the Indians.   They might encourage the choice few to learn the language, but not the general run of servants.   This was, in the first place, to prevent an illicit trade in furs. There was real danger that the armourer or the tailor might trade goods made of the Company's material and send the furs home secretly by a confederate on the ship. None but the factor and his " assistance " had to do with the natives, and no savage was allowed in the warehouse or in the apartments of the men. The prohibition of intercourse with the natives was also intended to debar the men from relations with the Indian women, because the savages were easily stirred by jealousy to deeds of violence. Such contact as the servants had with the natives was illicit, by scaling the palisades at night, or when they were out hunting or on lumbering expeditions. Naturally, the observance of the regulations varied with the character of the chief factor, but the general result was that no swarm of half-breeds was found at the forts, depending on the Company for maintenance.

As soon as the rivers were clear of ice, usually towards the end of April, the Indians began to arrive to trade. First came the Home Indians, then the Half Home Indians. These were, for the most part, the trappers themselves, coming in small bands with their harvest. Towards the end of May or in June the Uplanders, often referred to as the " trading Indians," came down two or three men in a canoe, usually in large bands of from twenty to sixty canoes, under a number of " Leaders." These brought the results of their trading in the interior as well as of their own trapping. They gathered at certain points from which the bands made their way individually to the next rendezvous, and finally they reassembled under a conspicuous and usually aged Leader, and arrived at the fort in imposing numbers. There they pitched their tipis or tents, each band under its Leader. The head of all the bands was now waited on by an officer of the fort with an invitation to meet with the Governor. Within the fort he was presented " with a great many fine things & Drest as he imagin's Like a fine man." Then came the interview with the Governor. The two sat and smoked in silence for half an hour. At last moved to speech, the aged Leader reported the number of his following, told of the conditions affecting the season's hunt, and gave the news of the interior. The interview over, he was given the presents for his gang—two inches of tobacco and a pipe for each individual, and, after the French custom came in, some brandy. The next morning the aged Leader sent one of his men round to collect what was practically a tax—a beaver skin or its value in other furs from each tipi—to be a present for the Governor. A formal request for admission to the fort led to the ceremonial procession of the younger Leaders led by the aged chief, conspicuous features being the calumettes or pipes of peace and the gifts of furs. A specially fine pelt was laid on the Governor's table, and the calumettes placed upon it. The aged Leader was then given a chair beside the Governor, while the others sat on nature's seat in a circle round the room. The ceremony of smoking has already been described in connection with Governor Knight. It was followed by a long silence. When at last the spirit moved the aged Leader to speak and present their requests, the Governor signified his satisfaction or agreement by appropriate gestures and in the Indian phrase for " very well." As the value of the speech was considered to lie largely in its length, there were many repetitions. A typical speech is reported in James Isham's *Observations on Hudson's Bay*, written in 1743, when French competition was being felt at York Factory. The words were uttered slowly, with long pauses between the sentences.

" You told me last year to bring many Indians ; you See I have not lyd ; here is a great many young men Come with me ; use them Kindly ! use them Kindly, I say ! give them good goods ; give them good goods, I say ! we Livd hard Last winter and in want, the powder being short measure and bad, I say ! tell your Servants to fill the measure and not to put their fingers within the Brim ; take pity of us ; take pity of us, I say ! we Come a Long way to See you ; the French sends for us but we will not here [hear] ; we Love the English ; give us good [brazil] tobacco, black tobacco, moist & hard twisted ; Let us see itt before op'n'd ; the Guns are bad ; Let us trade Light guns small in the hand, and well shap'd, with Locks that will not freese in the winter, and Red gun Cases (for if a gun is bad, a fine Case oftn puts it of, being great admirers of Differt Colours). Let the young men have Roll tobacco Cheap, Kettles thick high for the shape and size, strong Ears, and the Baile to Lap Just upon the side. Give us Good measure in Cloth. Let us see the old measures. Do you mind me ? "

The aged chief's speech was followed by a long silence. Who was to speak after him was revealed by a gathering storm of emotion culminating in a succession of forced sighs. His speech was of like tenor with the first, but led up to a reference to the gaps made in the band by death and the mention of the dead by name. At this the whole council would howl with a tearless grief for a minute or more. Finally came an appeal to the younger men to trade quietly and, as Isham has it, "not be obstrobilious." Trade now commenced in earnest. Isham describes the closing scenes. The aged Leader entered his tipi for an hour of meditation, after which he stood at the entrance and addressed the gang in a loud voice : " Do not Quarrell or Leave one another. Let the youngmen hunt as they go, till they come to Such a place ; their stay till all Comes. I will make a feast." When the feast was over, he once more addressed the gang : " I shall be the following year at the same English settlement, having Been well us'd ; meet me at such a place in the following Spring and Bring ye Rest of your Countrymen with you, in order to approach to the said Settlement."

A surprising feature is the orderliness of the trade in the first third of the eighteenth century. The natives were trading " the necessaries "—guns, ammunition, iron implements such as bayonets for hunting venison or spearing sturgeon, ice chisels for cutting out the beaver from their frozen pools, kettles, blankets, and the like. When occasion called for the entertainment of the savage visitors, they were given " burgoe," a thick oatmeal porridge served to ships' crews, or a mess of pease. At times these were flavoured with brandy. Small bands frequently left on the day of their arrival,

large bands often as soon as the next day.   Taken all in all, this was
the ideal age of the fur trade.   The vices of the European had not
taken root among the savages, and the whole situation dictated
happy relations between the two parties trading.   The Indians came
voluntarily all the way down to the posts on the Bay.   Any undue
severity or malpractice on the part of the factor and his assistants
would diminish the numbers coming.   The White Men learned to
treat the natives with mingled kindness and firmness, and they
reaped their respect and trust in return.   Of course, this was good
business.   During the first seventy years of the trade of the Hudson's
Bay Company—the most dangerous period of all, when the savages
were being trained in the way of peace—not a single Englishman was
struck down by the hand of an Indian, and not a single outrage is
recorded as perpetrated by an English hand upon a native.   The
traditions created in this the formative period of the Company's
trade cast their influence over subsequent generations of the services
and stood them in good stead in the days of the violent struggle with
the Canadians.   They proved a steadying influence in stormy times.

Certain functions of the forts which partook of the nature of
philanthropy, but which were really prudent business, call for mention.   As has been shown in the early part of this work, the Indians of
the North were subject, on account of the uncertain migrations of the
animals which constituted their food, to alternate periods of abundance and of dire distress.   In their day of utter despair the forts were
their last hope of life.   From the Company's point of view, it would
not do to allow its hunters to be swept away by famine.   In " hard
winters," and especially towards spring, starving Indians gathered
about the posts.   There they would be served with emergency
provisions—salted geese, burgoo, and pease—until the geese came in
the spring, when they would be provided with powder and shot to
enable them to forage for themselves.   If occasion called for it,
supplies would be sent far afield and assistance to bring the distressed
in.   The Journal of York Fort describes the winter of 1731 as hard.
On 23rd March, twenty-two Indians came in "for Relief, so that here
is 68 Indians young and old."   Provisions were given to all.   On
1st April messengers came to report their families as starving on the
way to the fort ;   "victuals" were sent out, and six days later the
band, twenty-five in all, joined the relief camp.   Soon the geese
descended on the marshes, and all were happy, not least the economical Thomas Macklish, Governor of York Fort.   On April 1, 1726,
Macklish sent a man forty miles with " victuals " for starving families.
In December 1730 Joseph Adams, in charge of Albany Fort, sent
men out to the rescue of starving Indians to the north.   The distressed were brought in, old men being so far gone as to have to be
drawn on sleds.

At the main forts the Company kept a surgeon to care for its
servants.   It is probable that the Indians regarded his skill as greatly
inferior to that of their own medicine men.   In extreme necessity,
however, they turned to him as a last resort.   Health restored

became a bond between the Red Man and the White. The feelings of his people towards York Fort once found eccentric expression on the lips of an aged native dying " on the plantation." He asked to be buried within the palisades. This strange request was honoured at his death.

At the close of the period under review the trade of Prince of Wales's Fort was drawn from the valley of the Churchill and from the wooded region east of the Slave River by way of the Barren Grounds. The trade of York Fort extended to the head-waters of the Churchill River, whence the Crees brought down their furs, some gathered in the valley of the Athabaska River. Crees and Sinnepoets (Assiniboins) came in from the Rat Country west of the Nelson. From the Saskatchewan, the Sturgeon Indians on the river of that name west of Cumberland Lake, and Uplanders probably from as far west as the neighbourhood of Prince Albert and the Thickwood Hills, visited the post almost annually. Assiniboins and Crees from the Askee or dry region and the Muscuty plains south of the united Saskatchewan, and from the Red Deer River ; Susanews from the Swan River and lakes Winnipegosis and Manitoba ; and Bungees or Swampy Crees from Lake Winnipeg ; and Crees from the valley of the Severn completed the list of trading Indians. The returns of an average year were between 30,000 and 40,000 made beaver, that is, peltry of the value of so many beaver.

In the region of the lakes the commercial hinterland of York Fort ran into that of Fort Albany. " In the Bottom of the Bay" Albany played the part of York Fort in Hudson Bay. All through this period a sloop went north-eastward to trade along the East Main, as the Churchill or York sloop traded northward along the West Main. For long it wintered on Bayly's Island, off the East-main River, and visited that stream in the spring, but in 1723-24 a post, called East Main and at times the Slude Fort, was built by Joseph Myatt on the continental coast at its mouth. The Indians from the Rupert River came overland to trade, for Fort Charles in their midst was not rebuilt when the French gave up the territory. Albany Fort stood on the east bank of the river of that name, not on the main stream but on the " back creek " formed by a row of four islands. It was approached by the " Fishing Creek," which ran between the two most westerly of the islands. The site was most inconvenient, for not even the sloop could come to the fort. Built during the struggle with the French, it may have been placed where no direct attack could be made upon it by water. In 1721 the post was removed to Bayly's Island (not to be confused with the island off Eastmain River), which lay off the opposite shore. The new site was on the main stream about a mile above the position of Governor Bayly's post, which was near the lower end of the island. The sloop could now unload at the fort. On account of the treacherous shoals in the river, the ships from England lay at its very mouth, in " Albany Roads." The East Main sloop always arrived in time to act with the craft of the fort as tender to the ship.

As has been said, the flank of the hinterland of Albany Fort was exposed to the French all the way from Canada to Lake Superior. Consequently it bore the brunt of the attack of the Canadians upon the English fur trade. The tributaries of the Moose and Albany afforded " the enemy " convenient water-ways into the English trade area. French traders came up the Ottawa to their post on its expansion, Lake Timiscaming. Their method of trade gave them a great advantage over the English, for the voyageurs, who would otherwise be idle all winter at the expense of their master, were sent out in bands to support themselves and to trap and trade with the Indians. They usually built " huts," as the English called them, at vantage points for trade with the band of the region. The Indians found guns, ammunition, clothing, and, most alluring of all, brandy at their door, took credit, and had, of course, to bring their furs in payment. Such furs as the French had no market for were brought down to the English on the Bay. The advantage of the English lay in the cheapness and in the quality of their goods, but above all, in Brazil tobacco, which outstripped the French article by far in the minds of the Indians. From Lake Timiscaming the *coureurs-des-bois* or " wood-runners " ascended the Ottawa, portaged over the height of land to Lake Abitibi within the country claimed by the English, and at times descended the river of that name towards the Moose River and the Bay ; in fact, followed the route taken by De Troyes and Iberville when they captured Moose Fort in 1686. Probably they built a mere outpost on Lake Abitibi at a very early date. During most of the period under review, Paul Guillet enjoyed the *congé*, or licence to trade, of this region. Sieur Gamelin, later associated with La Vérendrye, supplied him with goods. To judge by the *congés* published by the Quebec Archives, Guillet was doing a very modest business in 1720, with one canoe and three men. In 1722 and 1723 it took two canoes and six men to bring up his goods ; in 1724, four canoes and sixteen men.

One of the tricks of the French was to announce that they were about to attack the Company's post in great force. The Indians would take care to keep away from the scene of hostilities. On June 4, 1729, Thomas Macklish at Albany heard of an impending attack by ten canoes of French and fifty canoes of French Indians, but that very day two young men came forward to inform him that they had been at the French post " at a lake beyond Tibitiby," and seen the French going off with their furs to Canada. In 1724 Joseph Myatt, the new chief at Albany, had word that the Abitibis were trading with the enemy, and promising themselves gain by bringing an ample supply of goods to trade with their neighbours near Moose Fort, that was. From 1724 visits of these Indians were rare at the English post, Albany Fort.

The French had access to the valley of the Moose, also from Lake Superior. In 1717 a new command, Les Postes du Nord, was created on the north shore of that lake ; it included forts at Kaministikwia where Fort William now stands, and at the mouth of Nipigon River, with an outpost at Michipicoton. From this last their outrunners could ascend Michipicoton River, cross to Lake Missinaibi, and descend the river of that name to the Moose. Thus the Indians of the tributaries of the Moose were drawn away from Albany in two directions—all the more easily as the passage from the Moose, whether overland or along the dangerous shore of the Bay, was a definite obstacle in the way of their trade. By 1730 Moose Indians in any numbers had become rare at Albany. Moose Fort was therefore built to win back the trade of the valley. It stood on the same island as the post of Bayly's time, about a mile farther upstream, near its westerly end.

The passage for the French into the valley of the Albany, from their post on Nipigon River, lay up the Ombabika River and down the Ogoki, or alternatively, down the Little Current and Kenogami rivers. Their "wood-runners" built temporary shacks at points at which they could intercept the trading Indians on their way from the sources of the river and from the valley of Lake Winnipeg down to Albany Fort. As early as July 1716 Governor Macklish informed his Company of a settlement effected that winter " 7 Days Paddling up this river." Negotiations were on foot in 1719 to settle the boundary between Rupert's Land and Canada. The Company, therefore, mentioning this encroachment, urged His Majesty's Government to secure a definite boundary, so as to exclude the French from coming northward into what they claimed was their territory. The diplomatic discussions proved futile. In 1722 Macklish reported Canadians never so numerous among the natives.

La Vérendrye was in command of the Postes du Nord in 1729, with his quarters at Kaministikwia, and with the Sieur de Verchères, commandant at Nipigon. One or other, or both of these officers, resorted to new and somewhat reprehensible methods of aggression. The rumour was circulated that the French were bringing the Mohawks down on Albany Fort. Men appeared about the palisades at unseasonable hours, and guns were fired from the bush on servants out at work—all, as Governor Myatt inferred, to prevent the Indians from coming down to trade. The watch was doubled, and one night an aggressor was fired upon. Next year Indians reported that there had indeed been Mohawks about the post, that the man fired at had been killed, and that his intention had been to set the fort on fire; that the Mohawks now were coming in a body to avenge his death. The rumour did not require to be true to affect the trade of the English fort.

Under the strain of this competition, which increased with the years, the English Company's system of trade was threatened with collapse. Its principle was dependence upon the Leaders and their bands of young men to bring the furs down to the Bay. Many of these came as of old but brought few furs, and those such as the French had rejected or for which they had no goods to trade. When taxed with this, and with frequenting the French posts, they replied that they could not control their young men. In truth, the bands of trading Indians were breaking up. Their former customers, the trappers, no longer traded with them, but dealt directly with the *coureurs-des-bois* quartered near at hand, often in their very midst. The young men of the band did the same. One Leader reported at Albany that all his men had forsaken him. However, the effects of French competition must not be exaggerated. The fort had complete command of a considerable trade from its own area. The quantity of goods taken in by the French was limited by the difficulties of transportation. This was especially true of the heavy articles. They depended much on brandy for their profits. There thus remained a considerable demand for the wares at the English post. Moreover, the quality and the cheapness of these were recognized, and drew the Indians down to the Bay, at least from time to time. Governor Macklish wrote to the Committee on July 16, 1716 : " They all in Generall told me that the French trades hard with them & that I give them twice the value in Beaver and all other furrs, Cats excepted." Above all, the excellence of the Brazil tobacco, which the savages greatly preferred to the article at the French posts, kept a large proportion of the bands to their annual pilgrimage to the Bay. The policy of continuing the " customary presents " to the Leaders, and even enlarging them, though the furs brought down were disappointing, tended to maintain the trade even when it did not check the decline altogether.

The introduction of brandy as an article of trade was the greatest menace to the English Company's system. From early days in Canada the evils of this traffic had been deplored by the Jesuits and in a measure by the administration. Indeed, the use of brandy in trading with Indians had been prohibited, but the *coureurs-des-bois* had proved beyond control. The system of licences conveying to the traders the monopoly of the trade in a region was intended to bring this traffic under control. Only a modest quantity for the use of the post was permitted, but the authorities shut their eyes to the amount being carried, lest the fur trade by which the colony was financed should decline. Thus the evils of the traffic reappeared. Brandy lured the savages to the French posts, and gave the out-runners a subtle means of getting furs. Gifts of the liquor gave them a lien on the savages' peltries, and justified violence in taking them. The English factors and the Leaders were helpless in the face of the desire for intoxicants created in the Indians. Hitherto brandy had not been an article of barter with the Hudson's Bay Company. In the Journals it figures only as an occasional gift to Home Indians for fresh meat sent in to the fort and as an incentive to the hunters, as when Henry Kelsey in a time of need gave them a feast of burgoo and a present of brandy to induce them to hunt for the factory. As late as 1745 that hostile critic of the Company, Henry Ellis, who spent the winter on the Hayes with the *Dobbs Galley*, testified that the Uplanders did not drink brandy. Hence the orderliness of the traffic at the factory. In the face of the lavish use of brandy by the French as gifts and in the trade,

Governor Macklish at Albany began to trade brandy for the small furs, but not for beaver. On July 16, 1716, he wrote to the Committee : " Brandy is a rare commodittee for I can have more done towards promoting the Trade In small furrs for 2 Gall. of Brandy than for 40 Beaver in any other sortt of goods. In the Factory It is become a Liquor amongst all the Indians Especially amongst those that Trades with the French." On May 17, 1724, Governor Staunton wrote of two visiting bands : " Got all their furs in spite of their saying they would go to the French where they could have brandy and everything they wanted. . . . As for brandy I did not know yt all the Indians did so love it for when I was here there were none but ye home Indians that Did love it, but now all Doe." In 1738 the Committee inquired of all the forts the extent to which the brandy was being watered. The answer was generally three of brandy to one of water. The more detailed answer from Moose Fort shows what had become the general practice by that time. " What watter we Mix with the Brandy is very Uncertain for when we Mix it for our hunters the Usual Quantity is 1/3 because it is become a Custom he that Shoots five pounds of Powder must have a Bottle of Brandy, or else no Indian Hunters, which I think is an Evil Custom now brought up, and when I am sure that an Indian comes from the french I sometimes let them have it Neat, but at other times for Martins or small furrs not above 1/4 Water."

Another blow to the English system of trade struck by the French was their countenance and even encouragement of the Indians to resort to war on the trading Indians going to the English posts, as the easiest means of procuring furs. Here the trade of York Fort was involved as well as that of Albany, for the hinterlands of these posts met in the south basin of Lake Winnipeg and on Lake Manitoba. It would be from this region that the Indians estimated as travelling eight hundred miles to Albany would come. During the period under study the region covered by the trade of York Fort was too distant to be affected by competition with the French. Yet the Governor of the distant post by the Bay received information of the doings of "the enemy," which cannot be found in the French documents. In 1717 the Sieur de La Noue established a post on the Kaministikwia, where Fort William is to-day, and it was proposed to build also on Rainy Lake. French sources give no hint that this was done fourteen years before La Vérendrye entered the country. But on June 11, 1719, Henry Kelsey was informed that French " wood-runners " were quartered there and that their chief was called " Moosooh " (Monsieur). These must have visited or been visited by the Assiniboins who were on the Red River and on the Assiniboine in La Vérendrye's time. On May 17, 1718, Upland Indians informed Governor Macklish at Albany that " a Nation called Poets (Assiniboins) had destroyed a great number of their countrymen, that frequented this place, the said poets being Encouraged by the French to Destroy the said Indians," and, of course, get their furs. The attack provoked a war of reprisal, which was

no less deplored by the English than the first aggression, for it drew
the Indians away from trapping furs. Assiniboins made a similar
raid on the trading Indians of York Fort. Henry Kelsey was informed on June 3, 1722, that the attack was instigated by the
French.

The York Journals make no further reference to the French
until the year after La Vérendrye was appointed to the Postes du
Nord (Kaministikwia, etc.), when the attack was renewed. On
August 8, 1728, Macklish, now Governor at York, wrote the
Committee : " It is much to be wished for, that your Honours
could prevent the French from encouraging [the Assiniboins].
Nay several of the French goes yearly with the Poits to warr with
most of our Indians here." At this early date Frenchmen must
have been in the valley of Lake Winnipeg trading, and encouraging
a trade war. Only so can Macklish's further statement be explained.
" Here came at least 40 Canoes of Indians this summer most of them
Cloathed in french Cloathing that they traded with the french last
summer. They likewise brought several strong French Kettles &
some french powder in their Horns, which they upbraided us with
Comparing with ours." Macklish went on to put in this plea with
the Company : " I affirm that man is not to be Entrusted with the
Company's Interest here, or in any of their factories that does not
make rather more profit to the Company in a good commodity than
in a bad, for now is the time to obliege the Natives before the french
draw them to their Settlement, which is not above four Days
paddling from the Great Lake [Winnipeg]." * The wood-runners
would be from La Vérendrye's post on the Kaministikwia. Five
days before Macklish wrote, the trading Indians returning from
York Fort were attacked by Assiniboins led by eight French wood-
runners and suffered a severe defeat.

In 1730, when the trading Indians of those parts were away at
York Fort, the Assiniboins came on another raid, which, the natives
informed Macklish, was instigated by the French, and they " destroyed 30 men, women and children, so that most of our Indians
are resolved to go to Ware wth the said Poets to revenge the Death
of their Relations, which we are sorry for, by reason it will lessen
our next years trade." This instigation of the Indians to go on the

---

* The sites of such outposts as the " wood-runners " from Kaministikwia built are indicated thus vaguely in the documents of the Hudson's Bay Company. The " very old French
fort " noted on the right bank of the Winnipeg River, seven miles above the English River
by which the Indians turned eastward to go to Albany, by David Thompson as he returned
from Grand Portage in 1797 may be the post here referred to. The freighted canoes of the
North-West Company took five days to pass downstream from this point to Lake Winnipeg.
A post on Ball lake, an expansion of the English River, is probably also of the years immediately before La Vérendrye's entry into this region. The Journal of the Hudson's Bay
Company's Escabitchewan House on this lake, at December 10, 1792, contains this from the
pen of James Sutherland : " Self took a walk along Shoar and had the good luck to find the
ancient remains of an old French House, The Indians told me in the fall of one being here
but it is out of their memory, except Nacanaps mother, a woman apparently about four
score years of age who remember'd a House here when she was a young woman." At April 7,
1793, of the Journal the house is attributed to one Burdino or Burdigno, " who died at Grand
Portage in 1780 a very aged man ; it is about Sixty years since he wintered here." It
was in 1732 that La Vérendrye built Fort St. Charles on the Lake of the Woods. Burdino's post was probably occupied in the years immediately before that.

war-path to plunder the furs of the English natives places the
French in a sorry light in contrast with the Englishmen's persistent
policy of making peace.   In his letter of the following year to the
Committee, Macklish informed them that the French had a settlement " at the Southernmost end of the Great Lake [Lake Winnipeg]
that feeds this River [the Hayes] Likewise Port Nelson River ;
whereas here came but 16 Canoes, the Rest went to the French the
first of this Summer, not for their being more kindly used by the
French but out of Fear.   For last September 3 Cannoes of the
French Wood Runners after their return from Canady went into
the great Lake to the most Noted Places where the Indians Resorts
. . . threatening to Proclaim Warr against them Provided they
Came to trade here."   It would appear then that La Vérendrye and
his family were far from being the first Frenchmen on Lake Winnipeg,
and that the thrust against the English which must be associated
with their name was begun by outrunners from Kaministikwia when
he was commandant there.

2.—THE FRENCH SEARCH FOR THE WESTERN SEA, 1717–31 *

From the generation after Christopher Columbus the nations of
Europe engaged in overseas commerce knew that whole continents lay
between them and the prized markets of the Indies.   The Portuguese
made the tedious route round Africa their own, while the Spaniards
claimed the dangerous course round South America, or they might
transport their goods across the narrow isthmus of Darien for shipment to the East.   The English sought a way for themselves by icy
waters round North America, but finally gave the enterprise up as
vain.   A century later England and France alike would fain have
found an easy route to Cathay by sea and land through Rupert's
Land and La Nouvelle France respectively.   When the Hudson's
Bay Company found no strait or water-way passing through their
territory, and when La Salle passed down the broad stream of the
Mississippi only to learn that it was the main drainage of the continental watershed and that it flowed into the Gulf of Mexico, the hope of
a practicable commercial route through the continent to the Far
East passed away.   But intellectual interest in the Search for the
Western Sea remained, especially with the French, who felt that the
course of circumstances had imposed it on them as something of a
duty.
    It was now known that the Vermilion Sea—the South Sea, the
Sea of the West, as it was in turn called, our Pacific Ocean—lay
beyond the Rockies, west of the Mississippi.   A succession of explorations, not without their political and commercial aims, showed that
the route to Cathay by way of the lower tributaries of that " river
of many waters " was barred by the towering mountain mass.   Ac-

* See Sketch-map No. 7 at p. 162 illustrating ideas of the west coast of America prevailing
in the first half of the eighteenth century, after De L'Isle's map of 1752.

cordingly interest was deflected northward to the Missouri and the upper Mississippi, and finally to the water-way leading westward from Lake Superior. Speculation about routes by the North was greatly stimulated by the report, said to be based on Spanish explorations, that there was a large gulf running eastward from the Pacific at Capo Blanco, near the forty-ninth parallel of north latitude, and that this gulf cut deep into the continent and, as its currents seemed to suggest, was entered by large rivers. Reference to the map at page 162 will show what was in men's minds in the early half of the eighteenth century.

The argument of Father Bobé (1718 and 1722) may be taken as typical of the speculations of the decade immediately before La Vérendrye. It is known that there are vast prairies beyond the sources of the Mississippi and the Missouri. It cannot be that this spacious area is without a great river ; that would be contrary to all experience. The Sioux and other Indians report a lake (manifestly our Lake Winnipeg) from which a large stream flows westward (evidently meaning our River Nelson, which, however, flows northward). This must lead more or less directly into the gulf whose mouth is at Cap Blanc, and whose strong currents, as reported by Spanish explorers, show that several great rivers must flow into it. Father Bobé's argument concludes with the enumeration of six possible routes. It dismisses those which lie between the Missouri and the Gulf of Mexico as impracticable. It regards as most feasible those up to the headwaters of the Mississippi and the Missouri, beyond whose height of land the River of the West must flow. The method should be to build a fort on the river chosen, to be a base for the enterprise. The argument concludes with the water-way leading westward through Rainy Lake (Lac Tacamamiouen) from Lake Superior at Kaministikwia, where Fort William now stands, and where La Vérendrye was subsequently in command. This is the most convenient, the surest, and possibly the shortest route to the Sea of the West. It is true that the constant wars between the Sioux and the Assiniboins make it a perilous route, but the remedy is to build simultaneously a fort at the western extremity of Lake Superior to win the Sioux to peace, and another at Kaministikwia to control the Crees and the Assiniboins. When finally the explorer has penetrated to the Assiniboin country he will be sure to find several rivers flowing towards the setting sun and into the Western Sea. Down these the voyage will be easy. Not to omit any possible route, Father Bobé says that it would be possible even to cross to the Western Sea by land over the prairies, but this would not be practicable for the French at present (presumably because no horses would be available), feasible though it be for the Indians.

The first stages of the way from Lake Superior to the Sea of the West, as has been already seen, were traversed by the French in the person of Jacques de Noyon as early as 1688. The route was not forgotten, for in a joint memoir drawn up on November 12, 1716, by M. de Vaudreuil, Governor, and M. Bégon, Intendant, its rivers, lakes, and even its portages are indicated as far as the issues of the Rainy River from Rainy Lake (Lac des Cristinaux, Lake of the Crees), where De Noyon had built his post, and even thence to the Lake of the Woods (Lac des Isles, Lake of the Islands, called also Lake of the Assiniboiles). " From the end of this lake there is yet another river [our Winnipeg River] which flows into the Sea of the West [our Lake Winnipeg], according to the report of the Indians." The French mistranslated the Indian name " Winnipe," dirty water, as nasty, salt water, and therefore the sea. Lake Winnipeg continued to be called La Mer de l'Ouest, the Western Sea, throughout their régime. In the light of the speculations about the Sea of the West this could not but be misleading, all the more as the report ran that there was an ebb and flow on the lake, as indeed there is at the mouth of the Red River with a strong wind from the north.

Vaudreuil's memoir stated that papers captured at Fort Bourbon, York Fort that was, by Iberville showed that the English had twice attempted to reach the Western Sea by ship, but the vessels had been lost. In a joint letter from Vaudreuil and Bégon covering the memoir, the proposal was made to build posts at Kaministikwia, at Rainy Lake, and at Lake of the Woods, with a view to the discovery of the Western Sea. That this plan was far from emanating from a simple geographical curiosity is shown by the key-note struck in the first sentence of the letter : " Messieurs de Vaudreuil and Bégon believe that one of the ways which may be taken be extend the commerce of the colony and to make it profitable to France would be to carry out the discovery of the Western Sea [apparently meaning Lake Winnipeg], which is the only part which no one has yet tried to penetrate." The establishment of forts at Kaministikwia, Rainy Lake, and Lake of the Woods, it was argued, would prevent the Indians from taking their furs to the English, for they would prefer trading with the French at their very doors ; after the posts were firmly established a small expedition could be sent to the Western Sea [apparently still meaning Lake Winnipeg] with Indians whose wont is to resort thither ; its report will give the information for the discovery of the whole country and for building establishments in it. Fifty men should be sent in, and the total cost would be 50,000 francs. The memoir and letter were considered in the King's Council, le Conseil de la Marine, on February 3, 1717. The decision of the King, noted in the margin of the letter, was, that the three posts should be built, that the cost must be kept as low as possible, and that further details should be secured. By 17th December the King had agreed that a separate fund should be established for the purpose, and that this be kept down to the lowest figure possible. A memorandum from the King dated June 26, 1718, sent by the Minister of Marine and the Colonies, finally conveyed the royal will to De Vaudreuil and Bégon. It pointed out that the trade in furs could bear the cost of the three forts, but that the exploration beyond, involving as it must the abandonment of trade for the time, would be unremunerative ; the expense must be borne by the King :

" As for discovery it is absolutely necessary that the King should undertake the expense, because those who will be engaged in it will be obliged to forego trading, because they will necessarily be travelling and that over a long distance "—a decision which the reader should bear in mind when he comes to judge the treatment meted out to La Vérendrye.

In keeping with De Vaudreuil's scheme, Zacharie Robutel de la Noue built a post on the Kaministikwia in 1717. The next step was to secure peace between the Sioux and the Indians of the forest region by erecting forts simultaneously, among the former on the river St. Croix, and among the latter on Rainy lake. The reasons for this proposal given by an officer named Pachot, who was sent in to win the Sioux to the plan, again have little to do with the Search for the Western Sea. They are: the large quantity of beaver to be secured, and that beavers, which form the chief trade of the colony, are beginning to be exterminated at all the other posts. The advantage of the new posts will lie in keeping the warlike tribes about them at peace, in diverting the furs from the English on Hudson Bay to the French on the St. Lawrence, and finally, in offering the prospect of recapturing the posts on the Bay with the aid of the Indians. The scheme was so far carried out, as the Indians informed Governor Kelsey at York Fort, that French *coureurs-des-bois* were settled, apparently in a temporary outpost, on Rainy Lake (1718), and, in 1722, these instigated the Assiniboins to attack the Indians trading at York Fort. Thanks to the confusion of Lake Winnipeg with the Sea of the West, a confusion which may have had an element of deliberateness in it, the aggressive against the English fur trade, which had been growing more and more intense on the Albany front, was extended on the left flank into the hinterland of York Fort, under the thin veil of the Search for the Western Sea.

The keen interest in western exploration prevailing in the Court in France led the Regent, the Duke of Orleans, to send Father Charlevoix to Canada to inquire into the best course to be followed in the Search for the Western Sea in the sense of the Pacific Ocean. The distinguished priest and writer arrived in Quebec in September 1720, and spent the winter in interviews and inquiries. With summer he proceeded up to the Great Lakes by way of Niagara. More interviews and inquiries. De la Noue of Kaministikwia was questioned. From Michilimackinac Charlevoix passed through Lake Michigan to the River St. Joseph and down the Mississippi to its mouth, whence he returned to France by sea. His report was rendered in 1723. It placed the much-sought-for sea west or southwest of the Lake of the Assiniboins (Lake of the Woods), as far as could be judged, in the fiftieth degree of north latitude—a near guess at the position of Lake Winnipeg, which is about sixty miles north of the present city of Winnipeg, which is very close to the fiftieth parallel. It urged that exploration should be pushed up to the sources of the Mississippi or of the Missouri, which certainly would be not far from the sea, as Indians with one voice testified. (The route followed in later times to Lake Winnipeg was up the Mississippi to the headwaters of the Red River and down that stream to the lake.) An alternative would be to establish a mission among the Sioux, where the missionaries would soon get all the information necessary for further efforts.   The King's decision on the report was to send missionaries to the Sioux, but to discontinue the Search for the Western Sea, in the hope that such knowledge would be procured as would make the enterprise an assured success or lead to its final abandonment.   Accordingly, Fort Beauharnois was established among the Sioux of the River, as distinguished from those of the Prairies.   It stood on that broadening of the Mississippi known as Lake Pepin.   Its commandant was M. Boucher de la Perrière, the missionaries being Fathers Guignas and Gonor, Jesuits.

Fort Beauharnois proved difficult to hold, for the route to it ran through the territory of the Foxes (Renards), whose attitude was definitely hostile.   For years they harassed the French and their allies, carrying off voyageurs and surprising detachments.   Open hostilities broke out in 1730 and forced the abandonment of the post.   Yet, as it proved, it had not been occupied in vain, for in the war, which led to the almost complete extermination of the Foxes, the Sioux ranged themselves on the side of the French.   After the danger was passed Fort Beauharnois was re-established (1731) for the benefit brought by its trade, as well as to secure peace between the Sioux and the Assiniboins.   The Governor of the time, Charles, Marquis de Beauharnois, after whom the fort had been named, wrote that the re-establishment of the fort "was needed for the success of the undertaking of the Sieur de la Véranderie, inasmuch as it is absolutely necessary that that nation should be in our interest, to allow of our trading with the Assiniboils and the Cristinaux, through whose country one must pass to the discovery of the Western Sea."

It may be said of the Search of the Western Sea that it was the special interest of the Jesuits, who were ever looking for new fields for their missionary zeal, and also of men about the Court in France, whose desire for fresh geographical knowledge was an adornment to their characters and an honour to their time.   Official Canada had its own point of view.   The Search for the Western Sea, ever receding from the reach of the explorers, never failed to minister to the expansion of the colony and to bring about a recovery of its fur trade when the beaver areas were depleted.   It was the steady policy of the local administration to encourage interest in the Sea of the West, but always on the assumption that forts for trade would be established and the exploration as such relegated to some more convenient season.   If such convenient season should never arise no great harm would be done, for French arms would have been carried far afield and the stream of French furs would continue to flow between full banks.   This was the view of official Canada before La Vérendrye's day, and it explains both the plan of his enterprise and the unfailing support which he received from the wise Governor Beauharnois and the efficient Intendant, Giles Hocquart.

There were special reasons at this time for opening up new beaver regions. The old hunting-grounds were being depleted. The constant restlessness of the Foxes and their allies kept their neighbours from applying themselves to the hunt, all the more because it was growing more arduous as the fur-bearing animals diminished. English traders from New York, Pennsylvania, and Virginia, through their intermediaries, the Iroquois and allied tribes, were enlarging under-ground channels by which a serious leakage in the stream of furs going down the St. Lawrence was threatened. This was all the more a matter of concern, because the system by which the French carried on their beaver trade was vicious. Accordingly, the old bad way of granting a monopoly of much of the trade of the colony to some company, which took its toll upon certain goods coming in and going out, was abolished. The new company of the West devoted itself more exclusively to the fur trade and offered more reasonable prices, but French brandy and French cloth goods remained dearer than " English " rum from the West Indies and cloth from the looms of England. In these circumstances no administrative supervision could be devised to prevent the Indians, or even the French *coureurs-des-bois*, from taking their furs to the Iroquois, and so to the English market at Albany (Orange). To foster the illicit trade the English opened a post at Chouengen, now Oswego, on the south shore of Lake Ontario (1726). Against this, official Canada protested both to the Governor of New York and to the French Minister, but as it was the corner-stone of French foreign policy at the moment to foster friendship with England, nothing was done. Such being the situation, official Canada would naturally support La Vérendrye's proposal to open up that rich fur field, the land of forest, lake, and stream, stretching north-westward from Lake Superior. It was an added inducement, and one calculated to win the support of the Court in France and the Jesuits, that it offered some promise, how-ever distant, of an easy route by canoe to the long-dreamed-of Sea of the West, wherever that might be.

3.—THE FRENCH OCCUPATION OF THE FOREST BELT BETWEEN LAKES SUPERIOR AND WINNIPEG, 1731–34—LA VÉRENDRYE

The occupation of the forest belt between Lakes Superior and Winnipeg by the French from 1731 onwards was initiated by Pierre Gaultier de Varennes, Sieur de la Vérendrye. He was born in 1683 at Three Rivers, the fourth son of the then Governor of the settlement, which ranked after Quebec and Montreal as an administrative centre in La Nouvelle France. As a young man he set his heart on a military career, and served in campaigns on the New England frontier and in Newfoundland. In 1709 he was seeking fame on the battlefields of Europe, and received nine wounds in the bloody battle of Malplaquet. It may be inferred that the impending peace of Utrecht, 1713, and the consequent reduction of the army, would leave little chance of promotion for a colonial officer of limited means and influence. At any rate La Vérendrye returned to Canada, where he married in 1712 and begat four sons, who grew up to share in their father's career. In 1715, probably to meet the needs of his growing family, he established a fur-trading post at La Gabelle, his ancestral estate. It was at a portage on the River St. Maurice above Three Rivers and was well calculated to catch the traffic with the Indians before it reached the town. The merchants of the place lodged a protest with the Governor to the effect that the post was destroying their trade, but the son was left in peace, on the ground that his father had occupied the post in 1673. This is the first evidence of La Vérendrye's interest in the fur trade, and has nothing to do with the Search for the Western Sea. In 1725 the future explorer of the West was still looking to France for advancement. Along with three other officers he asked leave to pass overseas, but was told through the Governor that, unless indispensable private business was the reason for his request, he had better avoid the expense of his journey, for it would not bring him any advancement other than what was open to him in his native land. It was probably this push for promotion that brought him his appointment as commandant of the " Postes du Nord " on the northern shore of Lake Superior, namely Kaministik-wia and Nipigon, with an outpost at Michipicoton, 1727. These posts were the bases from which the French had been seeking to win the trade of the valleys of the Moose and the Albany. From Michipi-coton the wood-runners had penetrated the forest belt northward down the Missinaibi River towards the main stream, the Moose. From Nipigon River and Lake they had reached the Albany by the Omba-bika, flowing southward, and the Ogoki, running northward into that stream. From Kaministikwia their course was westward to Rainy Lake and through the Lake of the Woods to the Winnipeg River and Lake.

That great efforts were put out by La Vérendrye and his colleague the Sieur de Verchères, to divert the fur trade of the north to the St. Lawrence is shown by the *congés*, or licences, issued. From 1724 to 1726 inclusive, but one canoe with five men supplied the Postes du Nord annually. No *congés* have been published for 1727, the year in which La Vérendrye went to the Upper Country, but in 1726 Madame de Varennes (de la Vérendrye) sent up three canoes and sixteen men with provisions and goods to the support of her husband, and in 1729 La Vérendrye and the Sieur de Verchères had four canoes with twenty-two men bring up their supplies.

As has been seen, the English traders at Albany and York Fort were aware of a fresh aggressive on the part of the French during the years which are marked by La Vérendrye's command in the Postes du Nord, 1727–30. In 1728 Governor Macklish reported that the French with the Assiniboins went yearly to war with most of the Indians frequenting Albany Fort, and that they had a settlement four days' paddling from the Great Sea (Lake Winnipeg). The reference must be to outrunners from La Vérendrye's post at Kaministikwia. Five days before Macklish wrote, trading Indians on their way to York Fort were attacked by Assiniboins led by eight French wood-runners and were severely defeated. This must have been at the north end of Lake Winnipeg or on Lake Winnipegosis, on the trade route to the factory. In 1730 a similar attack was made on the Indians of the hinterland of Albany by the Assiniboins, said to be instigated by the French. Frenchmen, therefore, knew the way to Lake Winnipeg and to the trade route skirting its north shore, and must have been aware that the lake was drained by the Nelson into Hudson Bay.

That La Vérendrye's conduct in his command did not meet with an unqualified approval on the part of the authorities is shown in the general report on the State of the Colony in 1730. This report affirmed that the profits of the Postes du Nord exceeded 32,000 livres, that the " officers in these posts only served their own interests," and that the King should reserve the trade for the Treasury. Whether the Sieur de Noyan, who made the report, disapproved of La Vérendrye swelling the volume of his furs by raids on the English Indians calculated to create friction between England and France, then in close friendship, or whether there had been a more reckless use of brandy in the trade than the authorities and the Jesuits in particular could tolerate, or whether the zealous official was no more than concerned to swell the receipts of the royal treasury by reserving the trade for the King, is not indicated. The significant fact is that the report was prepared for the home government, and would come under the eye of the Minister of Marine and the Colonies, Jean Frédéric Phélypeaux, comte de Maurepas. It may well have contributed to that Minister's obsession that La Vérendrye was nothing but a fur-trader seeking to amass a fortune.

In 1728 the Search for the Western Sea came up in a new aspect through the inspiration of La Vérendrye. As has been seen, it had been thought that the line of advance to the coveted ocean would be revealed either at Fort Beauharnois on the Mississippi, or at Kaministikwia on Lake Superior. Father Gonor, who had been sent to the former post almost to play the part of the man on the watch-tower, had now given up all hope of progress north from the Mississippi, because of the confirmed hostility of the Sioux of the Plains. In 1728 he met La Vérendrye at Michilimackinac and lent a ready ear to a proposal put forward by him to push to the western shore of the continent from Lake Superior and through Rainy Lake. Unfortunately the memoir sent down to the Governor Beauharnois in Father Gonor's hand does not exist, but its purport may be gathered from a second memoir presented by La Vérendrye himself. It runs to the effect that La Vérendrye has been making careful inquiries of several reliable Indian chiefs concerning the way to the Sea of the West, and has definite information of the River of the West and of the Lake of the River of the West (manifestly

Winnipeg River and Lake), and of the extension of the River of the West flowing out of the lake towards the setting sun, it is presumed to the Western Sea. (It is to be noted Sea of the West is now conceded as being beyond Lake Winnipeg.) He expects Indians, who have been very far down this river, to come to his post in the spring, and these will be able to supply a map of the water-way they have followed. He has chosen an Indian named Auchagah, a savage of his post, for guide. As to the route, there are three rivers leading westward to Rainy Lake, one at Fond du Lac (the St. Louis), another the Pigeon at Grand Portage, and the third the Kaministikwia. Preference is expressed for the route by the Pigeon River. An Indian map was forwarded illustrating the memoir. It showed the lakes to be crossed, and in great detail the portages on the rivers. Lake Winnipeg is made to run east and west and not north and south, and a river flows out of it towards the west, and is named the River of the West.

The remarkable feature of this memoir is its silence about the previous and contemporary penetrations westward by Frenchmen. The information gained by Jacques de Noyon as early as 1688, and embodied by De Vaudreuil and Bégon in their memoir of 1716; La Noue's post of 1718 on Rainy Lake; the more recent outposts occupied by outrunners from La Vérendrye's own post at Kaministikwia and their penetration to the trade route leading down to York Fort, the information they could have given, and almost certainly did give, that Lake Winnipeg ran north and south and is drained into Hudson Bay—all is suppressed. What is given is a picturesque description of the western country and the probable route to the Sea of the West now at last revealed by the Indians, and La Vérendrye stands to the front ready to penetrate into the unknown country.

That La Vérendrye's proposal was put in this form was probably due to the known antagonism of the Court to the dispersal of the small French population of the colony over a vast area. Only two years before, Maurepas had laid it down in a dispatch to Hocquart and duplicated to Beauharnois, that no one should be given occasion to infer " that the French wish to make new establishments. The genius of the people in New England is to labour to bring the soil into cultivation and expand slowly. The people of New France think otherwise, and wish always to press forward, with the result that the English colonies are more populous and more firmly established than ours." In the face of this, a request to be allowed to occupy the forest belt west of Lake Superior would meet with a refusal. But Maurepas was greatly interested in geographical exploration,*

* "Maurepas . . . rendered real service to the Navy : he conceived the idea of making it minister to the progress of the sciences and reciprocally of making the sciences minister to the efficiency of the Navy. He attached geometricians and astronomers to his Department ; he sent scientific expeditions to the equator and towards the North Pole to determine simultaneously two degrees of the meridian. La Condamine, Maupertuis, Clairaut, Lemonnier, Bouguer, Godin, are the names of some of the scientists to whom he gave the opportunity to make themselves known. At the same time he visited all the ports of the realm, and determined to reform the methods of naval construction by the application of science to them. He established a school at Paris, ordered new maps and had the coasts of France explored."—La Nouvelle Biographie Générale, Article Maurepas, in tome 34.

and the Jesuits were deeply committed to the expansion of their missions and consequently eager for the Search for the Western Sea. The occupation of new territory as a step to the discovery of the Sea of the West would meet with favourable consideration. Hence the form and contents of La Vérendrye's memoir.

The memoir came to a somewhat tame conclusion with the statement that, to settle the question of the outflow of the Lake of the Sea of the West a post must be established on the lake, and that this must be done at once for " the English have every interest in getting ahead of us." Finally, independently of the discovery of the Western Sea, the colony will receive a new benefit from the quantity of furs which will be secured. The two memoirs were forwarded to the Minister of the Colonies, Maurepas, and were supported by letters from the Governor and the Intendant. The second, above the signatures of both Beauharnois and Hocquart, defines La Vérendrye's proposal :

> To go and establish a post on the shores of Lake Winnipeg. . . . He adds to this proposition an undertaking to find voyageurs to conduct him to that place, and to take with him men to the number of sixty, without obligation on His Majesty's part to incur any expense for the expedition, save for a few presents to be made to the savage tribes through whose territories he will pass, which will not amount to any great sum. . . . We have decided to let him go up to that place next spring, on the understanding that after he has established that post he shall be guided by the views the Court may appear to entertain respecting the prosecution of the discovery in question.

The third letter indicates the nature of the post to be established:

> The sieur de la Veranderie is to leave next spring to go to establish a post for trade on Lake Winnipeg west of Lake Superior. I shall await news concerning the discovery of the Sea of the West to have the honour of imparting them to you, and if there is any prospect of success, I shall take steps to engage merchants to send goods to the new establishment to conciliate all the savages of those parts and to divert the Nations from going to the English, which will be easy, for it will bring to their door what they are obliged to go far to procure.

Clearly the country as far as Lake Winnipeg was to be occupied and the fur trade won from the English. No more than further news is promised concerning the Western Sea. The second letter, however, left it to the Minister to issue instructions in the matter of its discovery.

Maurepas submitted the memoirs to Father Charlevoix, who, as has been seen, had been commissioned some ten years before to report to the Government on the best route to the Western Sea. Charlevoix reported, with great insight as the sequel proved, that the establishment of which La Vérendrye spoke would be of little value for exploration, would be an expense, and " might degenerate into a mere business of fur trading," and that " the discovery of the Western Sea was a matter which should be carried through continuously without a stop." Any post formed should be no more than an encampment for the winter and for collecting information. Maurepas forwarded a copy of this report to Beauharnois, and in a letter to the Governor and the Intendant, dated April 10, 1731, said : " I have considered with pleasure the enterprise of Sr. de la Vérendrye for the discovery of the Western Sea and I have approved of his being charged with it, without His Majesty entering into any other cost than presents for the Indian tribes through which he must pass. . . . I shall await with much impatience news from you of the success of this enterprise." The Minister assented to the establishment of the post on Lake Winnipeg and, by inference, to the occupation of the country, but expressly made the Search for the Western Sea the immediate object of the mission. To this Beauharnois replied that La Vérendrye never " meant to speak of anything but an entrepôt where he might find shelter " and make acquaintance with the Assiniboins and other savages. There was no ground, therefore, for the post degenerating into a market for peltries. It was not possible for La Vérendrye to undertake an exploration without carrying on a trade, " the King not having thought proper to provide for the expenses which that officer had assumed." Beauharnois was manifestly trying to put the best face possible on things.

By his decision Maurepas had upset the apple-cart for La Vérendrye and Beauharnois. These men were acting from the Canadian point of view, that the Search for the Western Sea should serve to expand the colony and rehabilitate the fur trade which was, as it were, its life's blood. They aimed at the occupation of the west to this end, and only envisaged exploration as to be carried on at some convenient time and at the King's expense. It had been the practice all along for commandants to enjoy the monopoly of their posts as offering no more than a normal reward for their labours. Indeed, the King's Council had laid this down as a definite principle in 1717, as has been seen, and that exploration, in as much as it precluded all trading, must be carried on at the King's expense. But Maurepas now required La Vérendrye to press on to the Search, and that at his own cost. In very truth that officer was being required to make bricks without straw. All unconscious of this, La Vérendrye was on his way to the Upper Country, intent on building a series of posts through the forest belt as far as Lake Winnipeg, knowing that in so doing he would be carrying the King's arms far afield, enlarging the colony, and extending its commerce.

La Vérendrye's aims come clearly to view in a letter which he addressed to the Minister, Maurepas, at Michilimakinac on August 1, 1731. It seems to imply that he had just heard that there was no commandant at his recent station, the Posts of the North, but it is altogether probable that Beauharnois had given him leave to station himself there if he found it advisable.

In consequence of the memoirs which I have had the honour to present to the Marquis of Beauharnois . . . he has done me the honour to detach me to go and establish a post at Lake Winnipeg with fifty men and one missionary. Next year I shall have that of informing him very exactly respecting all the particularities of my journey ; and if he considers it advisable to send me to penetrate into the heart of the west, I shall be ready at once to start with my nephew La Jemeraye who is my second in command, and my three children whom I have with me. I have taken the liberty of representing to your Highness that in my present enterprise I am only seeking to carry the name and arms of His Majesty into a vast stretch of countries hitherto unknown, to enlarge the colony and increase its commerce. I therefore humbly beg you to grant me for the period of five years, without counting this one, the North, that is Kaministikwia and the Nipigon with exemption from *congé* for the said period, so that I may avail myself of them as entrepôts for the enterprise I have in hand and leave men there with provisions and canoes. The expenses I have incurred, with a few persons who are accompanying me, are very considerable. I should not take the liberty of troubling your Highness were I able to dispense with the North as an entrepôt.

Some idea of the arrangements made by La Vérendrye with merchants supporting him may be got from an original contract preserved in the Public Archives of Canada. By this agreement the commandant's son, Jean-Baptiste Gauthier, Sieur de la Veranderie, enters into a partnership for three years with Nicolas Sarasins and Eustache Gamelin. His father, "Commandant of the King at Winipegon," is to grant a licence for one canoe, gratis ; the licence of a second is to be purchased from him for 100 livres, the payment being made by Gamelin. In return the partnership is to convey 200 pounds' weight of goods for the Commandant to his post in the north free of charge, and 100 pounds on the return trip. The participants in the agreement are to convey their own goods in their canoes and to be allowed to trade with them. They are to be fed at their own expense as a partnership. Sarasins is to ply his trade as blacksmith at the post, the Commandant paying half the cost of equipment, the partners the other half. Fifty per cent. of the profit or loss is to be placed to the account of the partnership, the other fifty to that of the Commandant. It is not known under what conditions the goods in La Vérendrye's other canoes were procured ; presumably part at least on credit with the promise to make payment at the end of the trading season, possibly in furs.

The route fixed upon ran west from Lake Superior along the water-way which now forms the boundary between the United States and Canada. As the lower course of the Pigeon River and its outflow into the lake were impracticable, a bay south of the present International Boundary and sheltered by an island was used as affording a secure landing-place. This necessitated a long portage of nine miles (hence the name Grand Portage) to the quieter reaches of the river. Here there could have been little more than an Indian track to begin with. A convenient path for carrying goods had to be cut. The name Grand Portage was subsequently conferred upon the landing-place.

According to Beauharnois's report of the first trading season's operations, La Vérendrye reached Grand Portage with fifty men in six canoes, but the voyageurs mutinied at the length of the carrying-place. Moreover, the season was too far on for advance far inland. La Vérendrye had to content himself with sending his nephew, La

Jemeraye, and, according to a memoir of his of 1744, his own son, into the interior with but three medium-sized canoes. He himself was forced to winter at Kaministikwia with the rest of his men. There can be no surprise at the caustic comment on these proceedings conveyed by Maurepas in a letter to Beauharnois, dated March 24, 1733 : " With regard to the enterprise of the discovery of the Western Sea with which Laveranderie is charged, the stopping of this officer at Kamanastigoya would appear susceptible of the suspicion of self interest ; we know beaver is plentiful in these quarters and attraction of that peltry may well have been the principal reason for his wintering there." Out of fairness it should be mentioned that La Vérendrye refers to the difficulty with his men as the first of a long line of hindrances to his Search : " It injured me considerably both for the payment of employees and the merchandise with which I was charged without any hope of having any return for this expense, which was considerable." Whatever may be the truth, Beauharnois, one of the wisest governors the French ever had in Canada, was whole-heartedly behind his officer's plan as sketched in his letter to Maurepas—to carry the name and arms of His Majesty into a vast stretch of countries hitherto unknown, to enlarge the colony and increase its commerce—and he allowed him to hold Kaministikwia for a number of years as his base on Lake Superior.

The country which La Vérendrye was about to enter to claim it for New France was hilly and broken, intercepted by rapid rivers and widespread lakes. Its interest to the Frenchman lay, not in its geological formation, but in its streams and lakes as means of transportation, and in its woods and rivers as the home of the marten, the lynx, the otter, and the beaver, and finally in its savage peoples, the Monsonis and Crees, *par excellence* the trappers of those days. The region was entered by La Jemeraye in August 1731. From Grand Portage he followed the water-way which is now the International Boundary and built a post near Rainy Lake. Though he was a young man of about twenty-two years, Christopher Dufrost, Sieur de la Jemeraye, had proved his mettle in so dangerous a post as Fort Beauharnois on the Mississippi among the Sioux. When there had been a call for a Frenchman to go with a band of Foxes and Puants of doubtful intentions to the fort at St. Joseph's River, he had stepped out, and, though at one time in a very precarious position with the savages, he so far won their favour as to be taken safely through. This daring and experienced young officer chose an entirely suitable spot for his fort " St. Pierre." He placed it on the right bank of Rainy River near its outflow from the lake of the same name. The site is said to have been identified at a spot two miles east of the present Fort Frances. Below the rapids at which it was built a very abundant fishery was the source of food for the Indians of the region during a large part of the year, while in the marshes of the lake wild rice was plentiful in the autumn. The post was fifty feet long, having two gates opposite one another, the front one, of course, facing the water-way. Two bastions protected these gates. An elevated walk ran round the interior from bastion to bastion to enable the defenders to shoot at the enemy without. There were two main buildings, each with two rooms and a double chimney. The people of the surrounding country were Monsonis. La Jemeraye saw none other, although Crees and Assiniboins of the Lake of the Woods and beyond were invited to the post.

La Jemeraye busied himself through the winter with the fur trade, but he had to face the standing menace not only to that business, but to the French rule through all this region, namely, the incessant warfare between the Indians of the forest region, the Monsonis and the Crees, and the Sioux to the south and south-west and their allies the Saulteurs to the south-east on the shores of Lake Superior. Without peace there would be little or no trapping. It says much for the personality of the young officer that he was able to turn several parties of Monsonis from the war-path to the more profitable ways of peace and hunting, but the Crees and Assiniboins did not come to trade, but went away to war. The result of the winter's trade was disappointingly small. An inconsiderable harvest of peltries was sent out in the spring under the care of La Vérendrye's son, the route taken being a variation of the Kaministikwia water-way, one with but nine portages ; it was doubtless the Dawson Route of 1870 by the chain of lakes including Kashaboy and Sheban-dowan, along which the Canadian National Railway now runs, and it came down the Mattawan River. It was longer than the Grand Portage water-way and the Mattawan was too shallow for freight canoes. Hence its abandonment. The peltries were sent by La Vérendrye, still in his son's charge, from Kaministikwia to Michili-mackinac for Montreal, the canoes bringing back the goods for the coming winter's trade.

La Vérendrye's plans for the trading season 1732–33 were drafted before he heard that Maurepas had made the Search for the Western Sea the main object of his mission. They aimed at the occupation of the country as far as Lake Winnipeg with a chain of posts. According to the report of Beauharnois of October 13, 1732, a fort was to be built beyond Fort St. Pierre at some spot on the Lake of the Woods, and La Jemeraye was to be sent forward to examine the river (Winnipeg) which flows from it to Lake Winnipeg with a view to an establishment on the shores of that lake. The post near Rainy Lake and the fort on the Lake of the Woods are notable departures from the plan sketched in La Vérendrye's early memoir, which only speaks of an establishment on Lake Winnipeg. However, no protest was made by either the Governor or the Minister.

On the 8th of June La Vérendrye, and with him the Jesuit missionary Father Charles-Michel Mesaiger, left Kaministikwia for the interior by the Grand Portage route. After some delay, due to work done to make the portages more passable, they reached Fort St. Pierre near Rainy Lake on the 14th of July. Thence the party was escorted on its way to the Lake of the Woods by fifty canoes of Indians, and was no doubt guided by them to a suitable site for the new post. It may be mentioned that at this early date La Vérendrye showed his love of assembling the savages in crowds around him, but, as it meant great feasts and many presents given in return for their gifts of furs, oftentimes all too small, it must have been on the whole a sad drain on his slender resources.

When the flotilla of canoes entered the Lake of the Woods, it must have taken a northward course, in general along the present International Boundary. It would cross the open lake, passing by (on the left) the bay from which the 49th parallel of latitude runs westward through the prairie country. It would proceed along the western shore of Big Island and cross the open lake, seeking the shelter of a succession of islands, one of which was to be the scene of a terrible tragedy within the short space of four years, the Massacre Island of the Canadian maps of to-day. Still following the general direction of our International Boundary through the islands which run across the lake, it would arrive at the present American Point. Here it entered an inlet which runs into the western shore and which the Boundary Commissioners have defined as " the North-West Angle " of the lake and the northerly limit of American territory. In a cove on its south shore, about two miles from American Point and within the borders of the present State of Minnesota, La Vérendrye landed and built a fort which he named St. Charles, after the patron saint of Governor Beauharnois and of Father Charles-Michel Mesaiger, the chaplain of the expedition. The site was identified in 1905. The post was 60 by 100 feet, with two gates on opposite sides, one, of course, facing the water ; the palisades were a double row of stakes, standing fifteen feet out of the ground ; four bastions and a watch-tower guarded the gates. Within were a house for the missionary, a chapel, a house for the Commandant, four main buildings with chimneys, a powder magazine, and a storehouse—all rough cabins, made of logs and clay and covered with bark, but destined to play the part of the Commandant's capital fort, and to be the scene of solemn councils with Indian tribes from far and near.

There was no need to be concerned about the food supply, for abundance could be procured by fishing and hunting and by gathering wild rice—so much so that La Vérendrye found it possible to save the Indian corn which he had brought with him. Moreover, the soil was good. Fire was set to the woods to clear the ground for next spring's sowing. Thus there was promise of ample provisions and cheap ; there would be no need to bring corn all the way from Michilimakinac.

As there was little knowledge of the means of securing a food supply for a post on Lake Winnipeg and as the Indians discouraged the French from proceeding farther—as was their way with all the traders, for they always wished to be the medium of traffic with the more distant tribes—it was the end of the winter before La Vérendrye sent his eldest son Jean-Baptiste and his nephew towards Lake Winnipeg, not according to the original plan to build a fort immediately, but to invite the savages of the region to come to him at Fort St. Charles for the spring trade. As La Vérendrye's map of 1734 gives only the route by the Winnipeg River, that stream must have been the line of advance. At fifteen or twenty leagues from the lake the party was halted by the state of the ice. Young La Vérendrye remained to prosecute the journey when conditions should permit. La Jemeraye returned to reassure his chief. He was then sent down to Quebec to report progress.

The Commandant's two letters to Beauharnois describing the activities of the year scarcely refer to the Search for the Western Sea. They merely mention that a map is being forwarded, on which the route to be taken to the River of the West is indicated. That illusive river is no longer the outflow from Lake Winnipeg, which is shown as running north and south and emptying into Hudson Bay, but is our Missouri, to be reached only by an overland journey from the River Assiniboine. The letters have much to say about the Indians, Crees and Monsonis, around the fort, of their welcome to the French, and of the furs that can be diverted from the English at Hudson Bay. A paragraph is devoted to the prospect of weaning the Indians from trading with the English.

At a great council with the Crees, the people of the Lake of the Woods, held in the spring, La Vérendrye was presented with a collar for the Governor, to express the joy of the Indians at having a French fort in their midst, and a second collar as a gauge of their fidelity in obeying the Commandant's orders not to make war with the Sioux of the French post on the Mississippi. Already he was able to assert his ascendancy over his dusky subjects and could prevent them from raiding tribes friendly to the French, but with an ominous exception ; he had to permit them to take the war-path against the Sioux of the Plains.

In his reports La Vérendrye skilfully places himself, his sons, and his establishments in the limelight, by inference, in a hitherto unknown country and at the farthest limits explored. He is silent about his outrunners—men sent out from the forts, sometimes far afield, to relieve the pressure for provisions by living and trapping with the Indians, and commissioned, by giving the savages goods and brandy at their very doors, to compel them to bring their furs in to pay their debts at the main establishment. The persuasions of these men were not always of a gentle order. But it is the movements and actions of these " wood-runners " which were reported most exactly at the English posts on the Bay. Then, too, La Vérendrye writes of Fort St. Pierre without reference to the outposts which had preceded it in these parts. To the English Factors this advance of the French was simply the continuation of what had been there for long. On August 17, 1732, while La Vérendrye was building Fort St. Charles, Governor Macklish of York Fort reported to the Committee in London :

I expected at least 60 Cannoes this Summer of those Indians that borders near the French Settlement att the Southernmost of the Great Lake (Winnipeg), . . . whereas here came but 16 Cannoes, the rest went to the French at the first of this Summer, not for their being more kindly Used by the French but intirely out of Fear, for Last September 3 Cannoes of French Wood Runners, after their return from Canady, went into the great Lake to the most noted Places where the Indians Resorts, and what with threatening to proclaim Warr against them Provided they came to trade here, Likewise to Encourage their Common enemys the Poets (Assiniboins) to break the Peace with them made two years ago

induced them to visit the French posts. The distance by which these *coureurs-des-bois* outran the Vérendryes is surprising. The Journal of York Fort of June 16, 1732, shows that (while La Vérendrye had got no farther than Kaministikwia and La Jemeraye than Rainy Lake) wood-runners, doubtless from Fort St. Pierre on Rainy River, were among most of the English Indians and threatened to proclaim war, and that most of the Sturgeon Indians—whose region was the valley of the river of that name west of Cumberland House of later times, and north of the Saskatchewan—steady traders at York Fort, had gone to trade with the French and would not be down that year.

On the Albany and Moose front also the English were aware of an accentuated pressure on the part of the French. In February 1732 a Frenchman, giving his name as Joseph Deslestre, penetrated with his " slave," that is, his purchased squaw, to Moose Fort and to Albany from the post at Lake Timiscaming on the Ottawa route. He reported himself as seeking out Indians indebted to his master, but Joseph Adams, Governor at Albany, was convinced that he was a spy, and was there to draw off the Home Indians. He was treated, after the tradition of the Hudson's Bay Company, civilly, but was watched closely. He reappeared on the scene in the same month of the following winter. In the summer of 1733 Adams got word that several French Canadians had wintered among his Upland Indians and had fortified posts stocked with goods among them—a vague report of the existence of forts St. Pierre and St. Charles. The Canadians had drawn away the most part of the Indians that came down to Albany, and if these were reluctant to trade, they were compelled to do so by force. This must mean that Indians who had taken credit during the winter were compelled to pay their debts. The French naturally did not concern themselves with the debts owed at Albany. Next year Crees, constant traders at Albany, reported that the furs which they were trading had been brought down by stealth. Adams wrote to the Governor and Committee : " Unless some Expedient can be thought on to suppress these French wood-runners, I fear in a little time they will Incroach all ye trade to themselves." Manifestly the *coureurs-des-bois*, the advance guard of the La Vérendrye movement, were much farther afield than the Commandant himself.

In one of his letters to Beauharnois La Vérendrye entered a plea that consideration be given to the great cost of his expedition, and stated that there was reason to hope for a large return of peltries

in the end. In consultation with La Jemeraye, who had brought the
letters with him to Quebec, the Governor and the Intendant got a
clear view of the situation in the Upper Country, and they now knew
that Maurepas regarded exploration as the primary object of La
Vérendrye's mission. In a joint letter they reported to the Minister
that La Jemeraye had reached Lake Winnipeg and that they believed that he could " easily succeed " in the Search for the Western
Sea, but the loss incurred so far had been 43,000 livres ; the voyageurs would go no farther without payment of the wages due them ;
in fact, their contract did not require them to proceed beyond Lake
Winnipeg ; moreover, the merchants would not supply the goods
for further explorations. Permission was sought to pay the wages
of the men to the amount of 30,000 livres out of the King's stores.
In a separate letter Beauharnois sketched the plans for the next
year, 1733–34, in terms calculated to placate the Minister. They
are based on the understanding that the River of the West is no
longer the outflow of Lake Winnipeg but the stream on which the
Mandans lived, viz., our Missouri. La Jemeraye and La Vérendrye's
son, it was asserted, would winter on Lake Winnipeg, and would
proceed during the following spring with Cree guides to the habitat
of that people " where they can get information as to how to get
down to the Western Sea, in which to all appearance that great
river discharges." This notable change of the River of the West from
one easily approached by canoe through Lake Winnipeg to the Missouri, only to be seen after a hard overland voyage, and the fathering
of this new and much more arduous and costly Search for the Western
Sea upon La Vérendrye, and at his own expense, became the source
of much misunderstanding between that officer and Maurepas. The
sequel might have been different if the Minister had given ear to the
plea of Beauharnois and had allowed the grant of the 30,000 livres
towards the wages of the Commandant's men. This he obstinately
and unjustly refused to do. On his part La Vérendrye put out no
great effort to carry out an exploration which would spell financial
ruin to himself. He coolly continued to play his rôle of Commandant
at Fort St. Charles. He had not personally pushed on to the Assiniboins at Lake Winnipeg, though they alone could give definite
information of the region farther west. Rather, he invited them to
come to him at his fort, the main seat of his activities. Wellnigh
eighteen months passed before they appeared.

La Vérendrye's chief concern was to keep the Indians of his region
at peace and to win them to the gentle art of trapping furs. But the
war spirit was supreme, doubtless because the guns and ammunition
brought in by the French afforded the Indians of those forest regions
the hope of turning the fortunes of war, which had hitherto been
against them. Bands of Monsonis and Crees to the numbers of three
and five hundred gathered around the fort asking for powder, balls,
and tobacco. It says much for his hold upon them that La Vérendrye
was able to win from them the promise to refrain from attacking their
ancient foes the Saulteurs and the Sioux of the River Mississippi, the

allies of the French. Yet this he secured only at the cost of liberal gifts of powder, balls, guns, butcher knives, daggers, and sundry other articles. In fact, however, the two bands went off on the war-path and had encounters with both the Saulteurs and Sioux, who apparently were found on the outskirts of their territory.

The summer season of 1733 was so wet, the rivers so swollen, and the marshes so flooded, that it was impossible to fish or to gather rice. Even the Indians were in want, and La Vérendrye had to give them the pease and unripened corn which he had grown. However, in the autumn they brought in meat from their hunt of the larger animals and, along with this, their furs.

At last, on January 1, 1734, Assiniboins from Lake Winnipeg came in with a small present—one package of furs and a hundred pounds of beef fat. La Vérendrye's presents to them included a sack of corn, thirty pounds of powder, forty pounds of balls, twenty axes, sixty knives, large and small, and forty-six yards of tobacco, supplemented next day by more provisions and ammunition. The Assiniboins told of the country beyond them, of its metals, of its people, the Mandans, with whom they traded, their physical form, their ways of living, their " forts," and their rulers. They told of the Mandans' river and its size, but knew nothing of its lower reaches. They conveyed to the Commandant an invitation from the Mandan chief to visit him, but he replied that he could not do so in less than a year, for his men were to go to Montreal for supplies for the Indians of his fort. Finally, he gave them more presents, powder, balls, and the like, and won from them the promise that they would return to Fort St. Charles the next year. The visit was a costly one, surely, but the Commandant's policy was to win all of these tribes to the French, cost what it might.

After this interlude La Vérendrye had again to face the question of peace and war. He went to Fort St. Pierre to bar the road to the Monsonis who were eager to move out against the Saulteurs and Sioux. This he succeeded in doing, but not without the concession that they might march against the Sioux of the Plains. He closed the council by presenting the war chief with a tomahawk and singing the war-song himself. The martial spirit of the Indians was fanned to a flame. In the spring the Crees and Monsonis went so far as to ask to be allowed to adopt the Commandant's eldest son, Jean-Baptiste, and to take him on the war-path with them. The council held at Fort St. Charles on 9th May is eloquent of the methods employed by La Vérendrye. It deserves to be given in all its picturesque details.

The scene is the courtyard of the fort, whose bastions break through the woodlands by the placid waters of the North-West Angle. Six hundred and sixty dark-skinned warriors, Crees and Monsonis, are packed within the palisades ; fourteen chiefs, in full attire, feathers and paint, occupy the spot prepared for them. On the other side La Vérendrye, doubtless in the rich garb of the French officer, has his seat ; near him his eldest son stands. In the centre are the presents, the gifts of the Commandant to his tawny subjects, children of the French King—" one 50 pound barrel of powder, 100 pounds of ball, 400 gunflints, fire-steels, ramrods, awls, butcher knives in proportion, and 30 fathoms of tobacco." The ostensible object of the solemn council is to receive the answer to the request of the warriors that young La Vérendrye go with them to war against the Sioux of the Plains. The real issue is the life-and-death struggle of the Indians of the Woods with their mighty foe. Now at last the tide will turn to victory. As the eyes of the war-scarred chiefs rest on the bastions of the fort, the powder magazine, the great White Man and his son, and most of all on the powder and shot heaped up for the campaign, the gleam of coming triumph may be seen on their countenances. Armed with the guns they have secured from the French, and equipped with this generous gift of munitions, they will drive back the fierce Sioux to their distant plains, and with security from the foe will come the ease and plenty which a fur-trade post can bring. This surely is a momentous day for the hunters of the forest region.

The council opens with more than the usual hush. La Vérendrye beckons his son to take a place at his side and turns to address the chiefs : " My children, see what we have prepared for the war. I make you a present of it and you will distribute it among you all, except the chiefs." To each of these he gives two pounds of powder, four pounds of ball, two fathoms of tobacco, one butcher's knife, two awls, six flints, and one gun-screw. In spite of all this the Commandant is a fur-trader and does not wish the Indians to go to war. Far better that they stay at home to trap and to bring furs to his post. Accordingly, he reminds them that they have been getting the better of their enemies in the last campaigns, and he entreats them in the name of their Father, the French King, to keep the peace. However, as they prove determined on war, he gives these munitions and entrusts his son to them.* Two chiefs, Cree and Monsoni, rise in turn to thank him for the confidence which he is showing in trusting his offspring to them. The son thanks the chiefs for their words. La Vérendrye now rises and presents a tomahawk to the Cree war chief and, in true Indian style, sings the war chant and recommends him to do his duty well ; he tells the savages how they fight in France and shows them the wounds of Malplaquet on his body.

The council now breaks up for the feast provided by the Commandant for the 660 warriors and their women and children, after

* La Vérendrye explains his motives in giving his son to the Indians for the war-path : " Were I to refuse them, there was much reason to fear that they would attribute it to fear and take the French for cowards, with the result of their shaking off the French yoke "— an unconvincing explanation, surely, for risking the life of his child. The Albany Fort Journal for August 8, 1735, the news of the factory being usually a twelvemonth after the event, suggests a more adequate reason. Indians reported that several of the French had been destroyed by the Poets, here probably meaning the Sioux, " Ye French that has escaped with several more of their Nation & all the Indians they can gett by any means are a Going to Warr wth them ye Ensuing Spring, wch makes us much Afraid it will be a Great Determent [detriment] to Yr Honrs Trade throughout ye Country, if it be true what ye Natives Reports."

which they all join in a wild chanting of the war-song. The North-West Angle rings with the loudest war-cry its rocks have ever echoed. The grand council finally closes with a harangue from La Vérendrye, the fur-trader, on the benefits conferred on his hearers by the French trading their furs on the spot ; they must not carry them to the English; the French goods may be a little dearer but they are better, and the French are really friendly. " Men, women, and children, you come into our houses and into our fort whenever you please and are always well received. . . . So now take courage and hunt well." The last scene on this woodland stage is the presentation of a collar to the Commandant by the Indians, with their assurance that they agree to all his requests : " If you go down to Montreal . . . speak for us to our Father, the great chief, as we are of the number of his children."

This barbaric scene reveals the consummate art of the French in winning to themselves the affection and loyalty of the natives of the land. It also shows that to win this loyalty was the supreme object of La Vérendrye as the Commandant of the Posts of the West. Anxious as he was for peace—the peace without which there could be little trading in furs—rather than lose the Indians' support or have them believe that the French were cowards, he armed the savages and gave them his son for the war. But this was, as the history of the fur trade on the Saskatchewan later showed, a very dangerous game. The more distant tribes, who suffered defeat at the hands of foes armed with the White Man's guns, looked on the traders as their enemies and found occasion to break through to them and strike hard. La Vérendrye was to learn this in two years' time by sad experience. Not only was his extravagant policy to bring bankruptcy. It was to bring disaster in its train.

After the council two of La Vérendrye's explorers, one of whom was probably his second son Pierre, returned from Lake Winnipeg, reporting a favourable reception at the hand of the Assiniboins there, and the choice of a suitable site for a fort on the River Maurepas (at this time the Red River). La Vérendrye embarked for Montreal immediately thereafter, leaving his second son, Pierre, in charge of Fort St. Charles, for his eldest was away on the war-path. From Kaministikwia he sent the Sieur Cartier, a merchant supporter, with three canoes and twelve men to build the post on the River Maurepas. At Michilimackinac on 6th July he met La Jemeraye returning from Quebec, and ordered him to relieve Pierre at Fort St. Charles, that he might follow Cartier to assist in the building of the post. This is the first Fort Maurepas. It stood five leagues up the Red River from Lake Winnipeg, on a fine point commanding a distant view, where the marshes of the lake shore end, and the banks of the river rise to some height. The site has not been identified. It must have been near Nettley Creek.

On his arrival in Montreal La Vérendrye proudly reported to the Governor-General that he was in perfect health, with no anxiety for the four posts (Kaministikwia, St. Pierre, St. Charles, and

Maurepas) for which he had provided. His arrival after an absence of three years without personally getting any farther than Lake of the Woods, long since known to the French, was calculated to put him and also Beauharnois in a difficult position with the Court in France, eagerly waiting for news of the River of the West, if not of the Western Sea. In an apologetic report the Governor expressed himself as certain of the zeal of La Vérendrye in the matter of the Search for the Western Sea. He laid great stress on the value of his posts to the colony, and the advantage derived from deflecting the fur trade of those parts from the English to the St. Lawrence. The debts incurred by his officer might well have repelled him from a task which none other would undertake, but he was led on by the hope that the King would have a personal interest in his venture. The report spoke of Fort Maurepas as an established fact, called attention to its being but a hundred and fifty leagues from the Mandans, and assured the Minister that when La Vérendrye left in the spring (1735) he would go to them and the River of the West, taking with him his son, who had a great aptitude for languages, and his nephew, La Jemeraye. It finished : " I venture to assure you that the zeal which he manifests for this enterprise cannot be suspected of any other motive than the well-being of the service and of the Colony and that, up to the present it has been a very costly thing." Omitting any excessive zeal for the Search for the Western Sea, the Governor's judgment of La Vérendrye was just. He was getting large returns in furs, it is true, for six hundred packages came down to the St. Lawrence with or after him, but he was lavishing presents and feasts on the Indians to win them to the Frenchmen. The net result was great gain to the colony, but heavy loss to the Commandant himself. Beauharnois's final word was that the King show some consideration in the matter of the expenses incurred, but Maurepas remained obdurate. No doubt, in view of the River of the West unexplored, he was deciding that his officer was a stark fur-trader in the guise of an explorer.

Had Father Mesaiger found Fort St. Charles a happy mission field, and had he remained with La Vérendrye, he could have given a report of him which would have stood him in good stead with the Jesuits, who were so eager for a Search that would open up the way to new missionary enterprises. But the nomad Indians of the Woods were too transitory visitants at the fort to offer much hope of success to the most ardent missionary. At any rate the good Father had returned to Montreal at the end of a year, in the company of the Sieur de la Jemeraye when he was sent down to report progress.

4.—LA VÉRENDRYE UNDER ORDERS TO EXPLORE—THE MASSACRE
OF THE LAKE OF THE WOODS—1734-37

It has been seen that La Vérendrye was playing the part of Commandant of the Posts of the West, while Maurepas regarded him as charged with the Search for the Western Sea. During the winter of 1734-35 Beauharnois was hard at work disentangling these cross-purposes. La Vérendrye was now fully aware of the orders of Maurepas for the Search. Doubtless at Beauharnois's suggestion, he wrote to the Minister describing his journey as for the discovery of the Sea of the West. He had orders to continue that discovery, and that was " sufficient to secure obedience." He would push the exploration as far as it would be possible to go. At the same time, the Governor warned the Commandant that if he were not diligent in the discovery some one else would have to take his place. To free his officer from his pre-occupation with the fur trade, he arranged to farm out the trade of the command to merchants, the fees of whose licences, no doubt payable in goods and furs, would furnish the Commandant with the wherewithal to carry on. He even found presents from the royal stores for the Indians to be visited. La Vérendrye left for the Upper Country in the spring of 1735, accompanied by Father Aulneau, a Jesuit, and by his youngest son, Louis-Joseph, who had been trained in mathematics and drawing to be able to map the country his father should pass through. But all was in vain. Nothing was done in the way of exploration, for the policy of the first years could not be reversed, and the fateful deeds of the past must bring their doom.

If we may judge by his actions, La Vérendrye had little faith that he could meet his debts and the costly exploration across the prairies without devoting himself ardently to trading for furs. He must have relied on the consequent expansion of the colony and increase of its trade to placate Maurepas and bring him advancement in the royal service. This course naturally led to misunderstandings. The Jesuit priest of Sault St. Louis on the Ottawa route, Father Nau, wrote of having a " pretty long conversation " with him on his way up, and inferred that not much reliance could be placed on what he said concerning " white-bearded Indians," that is, the Mandans. " The Western Sea would have been discovered long ago, if people had wished it. Maurepas was right, the officials in Canada were not looking for the Western Sea, but for the sea of beaver." This unsympathetic but penetrating view grew up out of the dilettante Maurepas's interest in scientific exploration and the Jesuits' genuine zeal for new fields of missionary enterprise. These blinded the one and the others to the real value of La Vérendrye's posts for French influence and French trade. In contrast, official Canada and the Commandant of the Western Posts knew that the new forts were a definite gain to the colony, compared with which exploration was speculative and uncertain.

La Vérendrye's Journal for the winter of 1735–36 is lost, but it is clear that, in spite of his promises, he stood by his capital, Fort St. Charles, up to June 1736, and busied himself with the needs of his command. In his apology of 1744 he attributes this to the fact that, through the bad management of the guide, the canoes of the merchants did not get beyond Lake Superior, that is Kaministikwia, that autumn. Such progress as was being made was under La Jemeraye and La Vérendrye's son, Pierre, on the Red River. A new route from St. Charles westward was opened through the bay from which the International Boundary runs to the prairies from the Lake of the Woods, over the Portage de la Savanne to Reed (Roseau) Lake, and by Roseau River to the Red River near the forty-ninth parallel of latitude, and so to Fort Maurepas near its mouth. Thus the Red River was explored from Lake Winnipeg almost to Pembina River at the International Boundary.

The year June to June 1736-37 was one of disasters—such disasters as might well have stayed the steps of the most eager explorer. The quiet of Fort St. Charles was disturbed on the second of June 1736 by the news of the death of La Jemeraye ; the Commandant's brilliant and experienced chief officer had passed away on 10th May at the forks of the Roseau and Red rivers. The loss was beyond repair. Then, too, Beauharnois's scheme of farming the trade of the Western Posts was working badly ; the canoes with necessary supplies had not reached Fort St. Charles in the autumn, and had not arrived even in the following spring ; the post was without provisions and goods, and particularly without sufficient powder, while the Sioux were known to be on the war-path. A council was held, and it was decided to send light canoes to Kaministikwia and Michilimackinac for relief. La Vérendrye's eldest son, Jean-Baptiste, who had led the Indians of the region on their war-path against the Sioux of the Plains, and was therefore the natural object of their revenge, was put in command. Father Aulneau, like Father Mesaiger, in despair of the success of a mission to the nomads of the forest, decided to accompany the party. With the Sioux in the neighbourhood, the contingent was made strong—twenty-one men all told, armed with powder and ball. They were warned to be on their guard. Surely, they drew away from the post on that summer day, June 5th, not without misgivings in the heart of the Commandant of Fort St. Charles. First news of the party came in on the 12th from three Monsonis, who had met a trader, René Bourassa, and on the 14th in the form of a letter from the trader himself. He had left three days before the emergency expedition, and was met by the Sioux twenty-five miles from the fort. They must have come by the traditional " war road " reaching the lake near the International Boundary, and must have been lurking about the islands which close the lake up, south-east of Fort St. Charles. They accused the French of arming their enemies, and were proceeding to kill Bourassa when his woman, a Sioux by birth, travelling with him, *en façon du nord*, as both servant and wife, intervened with her fellow-tribesmen, pleading that Bourassa had delivered her from slavery and had treated her well. The Sioux, according to one account, now proceeded against Crees in the neighbourhood of the fort ; according to another, they were informed of the emergency expedition by Bourassa's woman, and went in search of it. On the 17th the Sieur le Gras, one of the merchants to whom the trade was farmed out, arrived at the fort from Kaministikwia with two canoes laden with the belated goods. He had seen nothing of the expedition on the way. The suspense at Fort St. Charles must now have been almost unbearable. On the 19th Le Gras left to return to Kaministikwia. A canoe with eight men commanded by a sergeant was sent with him to search for the lost. On the 22nd the sergeant returned with the staggering news of the massacre of the whole party of twenty-one men on a small island about twenty-one miles from the fort. (It has been identified, and is known to-day as Massacre Island.) Most of the bodies were headless, and lay in a circle as though killed during a council, as La Vérendrye thought. The heads were wrapped in beaver robes. Two of the canoes were afterwards found along with twenty Sioux canoes (the Sioux band was from ninety to a hundred strong) in which there was much blood, suggesting that the enemy too had suffered.

It is not necessary to attempt to reconstruct from conflicting accounts the tale of the tragedy on that little isle of the Lake of the Woods. There can be no doubt but that the attack of the Sioux was their reply to La Vérendrye's arming the Indians of the forest, and to Jean-Baptiste's going on the war-path. Had the French been aware of the impending attack, armed as they were, they would not have been massacred to the last man. It must have been a case of surprise. It is possible that, even so, they acquitted themselves like men, as the blood in the canoes would suggest. The scene of the massacre is twenty-one miles, half-a-day's journey, from the fort. If the party left in the morning, they would have landed for a mid-day meal; if at noon, for their evening meal and for the night's encampment. Were they, all the while, being waited for by the Sioux lurking in their canoes under the lea of the isle ? Did the island, far out in the lake, give them a false sense of security, so that the arms were left at the canoes on the shore, or were thrown carelessly aside ? Did the wild war-cry break upon them like a clap from a thunder-cloud, swimming in the blue ? None can answer. What is certain is that no greater blow could have been dealt to La Vérendrye's command or to any exploration than to have snatched away by death what may have been near one-half of its personnel, including the capable son, now second in command—all men who knew the country and who had become familiar with its peoples and their ways of trade, and probably to some extent familiar with their languages. La Vérendrye's lament ran : " In that calamity I lost my son, the Reverend Father, and all my Frenchmen, to my life-long regret." On 17th September the bodies of Jean-Baptiste La Vérendrye and Father Aulneau were taken up and buried in the chapel of the fort, the heads of the others with them. They were discovered *in situ* by a party from St. Boniface College, Manitoba, on July 10, 1908.

In June of the following year, 1737, two several bands of trading Indians from these parts reported the massacre to Governor Adams at Albany Fort. During the long record of more than three-score years of the Hudson's Bay Company the like had never happened to its servants. Writers exalt the Frenchmen as past-masters in the art of handling the Indians, and not without some justification. But in many ways the English managed the savages more wisely than they. There is no record during the sixty-six years of the Company's rule so far of an Englishman raising his hand against an Indian ; nor of a servant of the Company leading one tribe to war against another. Rather, the Governors put out every effort to maintain peace among all tribes alike. The soil of Rupert's Land remained unstained by English blood.

Though the massacre of the Lake of the Woods was partly due to La Vérendrye's policy of arming his Indians against the Sioux, some responsibility must be laid at the door of Governor Beauharnois. His scheme of farming out the fur trade of the command had thrown more difficulties in the way than it was intended to remove. In the early years, when La Vérendrye was fur-trader-in-chief and associates were working with and under him, no difficulties are reported. Under the farm arranged by Beauharnois the traders thought themselves free to follow plans which would bring them the largest profits. They left the Commandant to care for his own interests while they cared for theirs. The payment for their licences was to be made in goods, but they more than once left his forts unprovided. When he returned to the Upper Country in 1735 he reached Fort St. Charles on the 6th of September. Such goods as he had for his exploration he sent forward to his son and La Jemeraye at Fort Maurepas. As has been seen, the traders, "through the mismanagement of their guide," got no farther than Kaministikwia, where doubtless they did a good trade, but they left Fort St. Charles unprovided for. Evidently La Vérendrye expected relief in the spring, but none came. As the post was without goods, and especially without powder, the party had perforce to be organized and dispatched for relief, though, and indeed because, the Sioux were known to be in the neighbourhood. Hence the disaster of 5th June. On 17th June, eleven days too late, the Sieur le Gras arrived with two canoes of goods from Kaministikwia, but he could not recall the past, nor bring back the twenty-one men who lay dead on the Island of the Massacre. The misfortune was in no small measure due to lack of co-ordination.

But this was not the only instance of the kind. On one occasion La Vérendrye asked the traders to send to the Portage de la Savanne for furs en cache ; they refused, with the resulting loss of thirty-six of the packages. Again, the traders who should have spent the winter of 1736–37 at Fort St. Pierre elected to stop at Lake Vermilion, where the route came in from Fond du Lac, because they thought they would do better there. When ordered to come on they replied that it was too late, that the ice had formed. Finally, when La Vérendrye requested certain traders at Fort St. Charles to send two canoes with goods to Fort Maurepas, they declined to go, asserting that they had no orders. As a result the arrangement that La Vérendrye's son should go to the Mandans could not be carried out for lack of goods. La Vérendrye's exclamation in one case can be applied to all : " Voilà les inconvéniens ! " (" Such are our difficulties ! ") What with lack of men and want of goods, exploration was out of the question after the massacre of the Lake of the Woods.

In these harassing months the Commandant had to face not only personal grief and financial ruin, but the certainty of condemnation by his masters for his duty as an explorer left undone. Yet he showed an indomitable spirit in holding on to his fort with a handful of men through that long summer when retreat might well have been excused.

In the winter, when things had quieted down, he penetrated in person for the first time to the then farthest limits of his command, arriving at Fort Maurepas, probably by a direct overland route, on the 25th of February. In his usual fashion he called the Indians, Assiniboins and Crees, to meet him in council, giving them till early in March to assemble. He spent the interval gaining information of the geography and of the possibilities for trade of the basin of Lake Winnipeg " surrounded by wooded mountains extending from the north to the south-west and abounding in martens and lynxes." In his report he made his first definite reference to the River Saskatchewan, *La rivière blanche*, the White River, apparently so called from the foam below the Grand Rapids, one and a half miles up from Lake Winnipeg. When the council assembled, the Indians began by weeping for the dead and symbolically covering their corpses with presents of meat and beaver skins. These La Vérendrye returned, not being able to carry the stuff away. A Cree chief reminded him of a promise to build a fort among his people at " the bottom," that is at the north end of Lake Winnipeg, and asked that La Vérendrye's son be adopted by his people. Similarly, an Assiniboin chief recalled a promise of a fort among his people at the " fork of the Red River," presumably at the site of the present Winnipeg. La Vérendrye accompanied his speech in reply " with very fine presents consisting of blankets, breeches, leggings, axes, knives, powder, balls, lead bullets." In his report he wrote : " My son, who has a great desire to make himself useful to the colony, seemed flattered at the idea of going with them [the Crees] and bringing them back in the spring to Fort St. Charles, and accordingly I let them have him." Manifestly he still felt himself the Commandant whose chief duty it was to extend French influence and commerce, and St. Charles was still his capital fort.

The answer to the Assiniboins was that a fort would be built later among them at the forks of the Red River. When they offered guides to the Mandans on the River of the West, they were put off for the present on the pretext that La Vérendrye wished to explore the River Winnipeg, which, as has been seen, had already been traced by his son and La Jemeraye. They were told, however, to promise the Mandans French friendship and to invite them to meet him at the proposed fort at the forks, and let them come with horses, and Indian corn, and beans, and any of their metals.   With that the Commandant turned his face towards Fort St. Charles.   It is hard to avoid the inference from his action at this council that his duties as Commandant were close to his heart, and that he did not relish the idea of entering upon the arduous journey on foot across the prairies to the River of the West.   Hence the invitation to the Mandans to come to him and to bring horses.

On 3rd June La Vérendrye left Fort St. Charles for Quebec with eleven French and three Indian canoes loaded with peltries, yet not able to take all with him.   Once more in consultation with Beauharnois he wrote to Maurepas to allay the Minister's surprise at his return from the interior without having pushed his discovery any farther than before : " The sad accident [of the massacre] is the principal cause of my having done so, joined to the considerable loss I have suffered in men and effects necessary to enable me to advance further, obliged as I was in the previous autumn and during the winter to provide for the needs and subsistence of the fort, which I found on my arrival destitute of everything through the fault of those at the fort who were responsible."   The Indians had entreated him for supplies.   For these and for the needs of his own exploration he had come down ; he would return again with diligence to carry through his project.

Meanwhile Maurepas had written to Beauharnois on receiving news of the massacre : " All that has come to my knowledge as to the causes of that misadventure confirms the suspicion I have not concealed from you, that the beaver trade had more to do than anything else with the Sieur de la Vérendrye's Western Sea expedition."   Beauharnois, replying to this, repeated in substance La Vérendrye's defence of himself, and insisted that, to his personal knowledge, it was true, adding that, moreover, the connections which he had formed with the Indians could not fail to procure great advantage to the colony.

Once more the Governor warned his officer—more definitely this time—that if he came down again he would not return, and he extracted a promise from him that he would reach the Mandans that very winter.   From the fact that during this next year, 1738–39, the traders followed close on the explorer's footsteps and worked in harmony with him it may be inferred that Beauharnois dealt faithfully and sternly with them also.

5.—THE OCCUPATION OF THE FOREST BELT WEST OF LAKE WINNIPEG BY THE FRENCH — THEIR EXPLORATIONS IN THE VALLEY OF THE MISSOURI, 1738–44

Now that La Vérendrye had been warned for the second time that he would be recalled if he did not press his exploration, and now that he had promised to reach the River of the West that very winter, he began to show the true manner of an explorer. He hastened on to the extreme limits of his command, and beyond, before the ice could stay his progress. He left Michilimackinac on July 20, 1738, with six light canoes manned by twenty-two men and equipped for fast travelling. He remained in the Pays Plat, " the flat country " at the mouth of the Nipigon River on the north shore of Lake Superior, but three hours for a council with the Indians there. He arrived at his Fort Kaministikwia on 5th August and left on the 6th. On the 22nd, at Rainy Lake, another council and he was away. On the 31st he was at Fort St. Charles and held another council. Here he waited, expecting Charles Nolan, Sieur de la Marque, one of the traders, to catch up to him. When he failed to arrive La Vérendrye pressed on, reaching Fort Maurepas on the Red River on the 22nd of September. Still he moved on. The 24th saw him at the forks of the Red and the Assiniboine, where the city of Winnipeg now stands. Two days later he was ascending the tortuous Assiniboine. On 3rd October he was choosing the site for a new post well beyond the former limits of his command, and set his men to work immediately building Fort de la Reine, commonly known as Fort La Reine.

The site of this new post is usually taken to be the present Portage la Prairie, where in the next generations was the south end of the carrying-place from the Assiniboine to Lake Manitoba. But the survey of the river in 1808 by the Hudson's Bay Company's surveyor, Peter Fidler, puts it at what would be on the left bank of the river about two miles south-east of Poplar Point station on the Canadian Pacific main line, and about twenty-one miles east of the present Portage la Prairie. It would be at an equal distance with the subsequent Fort La Reine from Lake Manitoba.* La Vérendrye placed his post with a steady eye to the fur trade, for it was in the region through which the Assiniboins passed to Lake Manitoba on their way to the English York Fort on Hudson Bay, and within easy reach of the beaver country north of the River Assiniboine. For the immediate purpose of reaching the Missouri it was on the edge of the prairies, which constituted an open road to the Mandans.

The Commandant's first act at his new post was to hold a council with the usual presents to the Indians, and to " receive them into the number of the Governor-General's children," with the promise that the French would never abandon them so long as they acted sensibly. On 8th October the Sieur de la Marque with his brother the Sieur Nolan and eight men arrived in two canoes. He had left men at the posts along the water-way to trade. Hastening on breathlessly he reached Fort La Reine but seven days after La Vérendrye himself. The relations of the traders and the Commandant were now of the most cordial, the Sieur de la Marque even offering to share in

---

* What appears to be its remains, seen in 1938, indicate that the site was occupied for but a year. As there are no cellars or chimney heaps, the buildings must have been no more than shacks within the palisades, traces of which can be seen after two hundred years. The post was probably moved up to the neighbourhood of the present Portage la Prairie during the following summer.

the expense of the explorations to the Mandans. Beauharnois had not dealt with him in vain.

It is in place here to ask why, if La Vérendrye's object was to reach the Mandans, did he not follow the short route from Fort St. Charles by the bay of the Lake of the Woods from which the International Boundary runs westward, over the Portage de la Savanne, and down the Roseau River to the Red near Pembina River, and thence into the course which he actually followed a few weeks later to the Missouri. That that route was more exposed to the Sioux would be reason enough, but the Commandant was simply developing his previous plans. He had promised the Assiniboins a fort in their own territory and had provisionally put it at the forks of the Red River. Moreover, the Mandans had been invited to meet him there. The traders did actually open a post there, Fort Rouge, but La Vérendrye pushed on to a site across the path of the Indians to the English and much nearer the rich beaver region north of the Assiniboine, while the road to the Mandans still lay open before him.

On 18th October La Vérendrye left Fort La Reine in charge of one Sanschagrin, " an intelligent, discreet and prudent man," and committed the Indians to kill buffalo for the post. The party for the exploration consisted of the Commandant with his sons François and Louis-Joseph—nicknamed the Chevalier, the astronomer of the expedition—and La Marque with his brother Nolan, together with twenty hired men, ten of them La Vérendrye's and ten the traders'. Indians brought the total up to fifty-two. Each of the men, French and Indian, was given a bag of powder, sixty bullets, and two fathoms of tobacco. La Vérendrye had a slave loaded with his personal effects, while the wife of the guide carried a bag of presents for the Mandans.

The main body left in the morning, the leaders at noon—all on foot, for a journey which proved to be, according to their reckoning, 120 leagues or 300 miles. Their course was " south one point west," that is, south-by-west, 26 leagues (65 miles) to the first mountain. The direction and distance would bring them up the slope known as Pembina Mountain, but which is really the bank of an ancient lake, on to the second prairie level, and probably to Mount Paquewin of Palliser's map near the point at which the Pembina River, flowing south-eastward, crosses the International Boundary, or else to Tête du Bœuf. Thence the course ran "west one point north," that is, west-by-north, 24 leagues (60 miles) to "the second mountain." This indicates that they touched the north-east end of Turtle Mountain. From this point La Vérendrye wished to go direct to the Mandans, but his guides insisted on going out of their way to visit a band of 102 lodges of Assiniboins. Presumably these were about the Souris River north-west of Turtle Mountain. On his arrival La Vérendrye held a council with the band, gave the usual presents, and received them into the number of the Governor-General's children with the ceremony of placing hands upon the heads of them all. The band now insisted on following the French to the Mandans. It must have been a picturesque scene — the Assiniboins marching in three columns, the scouts ahead, wings thrown out on either side and extending to the rearguard. Within these lines the old men, the children, the women with their burdens, trudged along, and, no doubt, the dogs with their loads on *travois*. The French were grouped together, it may be surmised, as far as might be from the noise and confusion of the caravan.

On the morning of the 28th of November this motley crowd reached the point at which Mandans were to meet them. La Vérendrye was surprised to find that this people, whose civilization had been described to him in extravagant terms, were in no way different from the other savages, for they wore but a buffalo robe and a loin cloth. The Mandans did not wish a whole village and more of Assiniboins to visit their fort, because it was their practice to find provisions for visitors. They accordingly raised the alarm that the Sioux were coming. It is one of many indications of the hold the intrepid Commandant gained on the Indians that this alarm only stiffened the determination of the Assiniboin warriors to accompany him as a guard to the Mandan fort. The women were left in a place of security with a number of men to protect them, and some six hundred braves with a few women and children went forward with the explorer's party.

At a league and a half from the Mandan fort a body of Mandans met the Frenchmen with prepared food—cooked grain and flour worked into a paste with pumpkin—and tobacco to refresh the visitors. After a rest of two hours the procession was formed for the ceremonial entry into the fort, which is described as on a small stream in mid-prairie a short distance from a small river. La Vérendrye's son, the Chevalier, carried a flag bearing the coloured arms of the King of France at the head of the procession. Nolan stepped with him to relieve him at times. The French followed in marching order, La Vérendrye being carried in Mandan fashion in their midst. An elevation without the fort and the ramparts within were lined with spectators. At the elevation the pipe of peace was presented and two collars—presents sent by La Vérendrye some three years back—were displayed. A salute was fired by the French to end the ceremony. At four o'clock in the afternoon of 3rd December, after forty-six days' travel, the explorer entered the first Mandan village, the French and Assiniboins marching in good order with their guns.

In spite of the colourful scene and the cordial welcome, misfortune dogged La Vérendrye's footsteps. In the press of the crowd around the chief's tent, where he was being received, the bag of his special presents was stolen. It was never recovered. One wonders whether this was not just a Mandan ruse, devised to prevent the French from going any farther. However, at the council next day La Vérendrye was able to make a presentation of powder and shot. A Mandan chief, speaking in Assiniboin to a Cree interpreter, and he in turn to

La Vérendrye's son, who interpreted to his father, begged to be admitted, and have his people admitted, to the number of the Governor-General's children. This was granted in due form by the Commandant placing his hands on the head of each chief. At the end of six days the Mandans, tired of feeding the voracious Assiniboins, again gave the alarm that Sioux were coming, this time with more success. The terrified Assiniboins hastily decamped. The ruse, however, brought a second misfortune upon La Vérendrye. His Cree interpreter, who had become enamoured of an Assiniboin woman, went off after her. Without presents and without his interpreter La Vérendrye, greatly perplexed, decided that his exploration could not go much farther.

As a last effort he sent his son the Chevalier, with the Sieur Nolan, six Frenchmen, and several Mandans, to visit the nearest of the Mandan forts on the bank of the River of the West. It surely shows a significant incuriosity on the part of the explorer that, though so near, he did not now, nor at any time, see with his own eyes the much talked of River of the West. His heart could scarcely have been given to this exploration.

For lack of an interpreter, all that the son and his party could gather was that men like the French lived at the mouth of the river and that they fabricated stuffs and linens. As to the course of the stream, " according to the compass the river appeared to run south-west by south, and by the signs which they had made it may flow into the sea in a direction south-west by west."

On the return of the party to him, La Vérendrye required his son to take the latitude of the prairie fort. He calculated it to be " forty-eight degrees, twelve minutes." In spite of this definite indication it is not easy to fix the site. Assuming that David Thompson was given a correct account by the Mandans when he visited them in 1797, and that they had retired from the Red River before the attacks of the Saulteurs in the time of their great-great-grandfathers, the forts on the River of the West at this time would be where Thompson found them on the Missouri below the Big Knife River ; the fort visited by the son would thus be at or near Washburn, where the Missouri takes its definite turn to the south. The village visited by the father would be where the parallel of latitude given crossed the Commandant's course from Turtle Mountain to the villages on the Missouri. This may well be at the great bend of the Souris River or on a small tributary flowing into it from the south, which would be the small stream out on the prairie on which the village is said to have stood, a short distance from the River of the West.

This is not the place in which to give a minute description of the Mandans : the fairness of many of their women's hair and complexion, the mild temper of the men, the industry of the people, their fields of corn and pumpkins, their provisions carefully stored in cellars beneath the palisaded forts, the endless feasting and hospitality of the chiefs shown to the French. Without presents and without interpreter, La Vérendrye felt that no more could be done at the moment in the Search for the Western Sea. However, he left two intelligent Frenchmen, one of whom knew how to write, to learn the Mandan language with a view to further and more exact information. The farewell ceremonies show that here, as everywhere, La Vérendrye had won the loyalty and affection of the natives. These heaped up flour for his journey beyond the needs of his party. In return he gave the assembled chiefs a fresh present of powder, and balls, and a few small articles, the principal chief being presented with a flag and a leaden tablet, adorned with ribbons, commemorating the taking possession of the land. It is noteworthy that while he thus claimed the Mandans for the children of the French King, he did not erect a fort and made no provision for trade with them. In truth the Mandans had nothing much to offer, and the voyage overland was too arduous for intimate connections. The Commandant's eyes were not turned in this direction, but looked northward to the forest lands rich in fur. On 8th January, the very eve of his return, La Vérendrye was taken seriously ill, but after five days he recovered sufficiently to struggle back to the Assiniboin band, to his box of medicines which had been lost, but which was now restored. He reached Fort La Reine on 1st March after an absence of less than five months.

The Governor of York Fort received word in June 1739 of the movements of the French during the previous autumn. Trading Indians informed him that there were three French settlements where before there had been but one. (These would be Fort Rouge at the present site of Winnipeg and Fort La Reine, in addition to Fort Maurepas.) The statement that the French were leading the Indians to war against the Poets (doubtless in the sense of the Sioux) was probably an unintelligent interpretation of the expedition to the Mandans. The fort Journal for 1739-40 is wanting. The General Letter of 1740 to the Governor and Committee in London reported the arrival of French Indians at the post to trade who had never been down before. " I do not Doubt but [they] will Continue to Come hereafter, with Civility & good usage showd them." Civility and good usage were the weapons in which the Englishmen put their trust, but they were proving frail against the Frenchmen's settlements in the midst of the Indians. The French Indians brought a letter from " the French Settlement up port Nelson River," which was forwarded to London. They informed Governor Isham that their fort was much like his, but somewhat larger and manned by thirty men. He calculated by the nights passed by the Indians on the way that it was four hundred miles and upward from York Fort. This would suggest the north end of Lake Winnipeg or Cedar Lake, where there may have been a French outpost, but the size of the fort argues that the reference is to La Reine.

In the spring of 1739 La Vérendrye was once more in full activity supervising the fur trade, but the returns were not large ; the three forts were too close to one another for profitable business. (Fort

Maurepas was abandoned in favour of Fort Rouge at the forks of the Red River.) The meagre returns were all the more unfortunate as the voyage to the Mandans brought nothing but expense. The Commandant now turned to tap the wealth of the forest belt to the north. He sent the Chevalier to explore the region about Lake Winnipeg and the rivers flowing into it, in particular *La rivière blanche* (the Saskatchewan) and the outlet of the lake. He wrote to Beauharnois that he would himself make the circuit of the lake in the following autumn to try to prevent the Indians from going down to the English. (There is not so much as a hint that Frenchmen had been in these parts before him.) His next year was probably taken up with these plans.

In spite of the interest of Maurepas in the River of the West, La Vérendrye left further exploration in that direction to his subordinates. The pressure of his creditors goes far towards affording an adequate reason. From 1739 to 1740 the two Frenchmen left with the Mandans were learning the language and gathering information. When the Commandant went down to Quebec in the spring of 1740, he passed the duty of further exploration over to his son Pierre. The plan was for him to meet the tribes of horsemen who were in the habit of visiting the Mandans for trade, and who were said to have dealings with a people taken to be Europeans living on the shore of the Great Sea. In the summer of 1741, when his father was on his way back to the Upper Country, Pierre was carrying out his commission. According to Beauharnois's report to Maurepas, the equestrian tribes failed to appear that spring, and after waiting two months for them he returned, bringing two horses with him. This would be the first appearance of a horse in the valley of the Assiniboine. But in a memoir written after his father's death and setting forth his own claims Pierre ascribes to himself an extensive exploration. " In 1741 he went alone with two Frenchmen to make new discoveries, which he pushed to a point not far from two Spanish forts ; but a well-founded fear that he had of enemies and still more the lack of a guide, obliged him to return sooner than he would have done." It would be this expedition that brought the knowledge that the River of the West was the Missouri and that its waters entered the Gulf of Mexico and not the Western Sea.

In the winter of 1740–41 La Vérendrye was in Quebec, where he once more promised to penetrate to the most distant region possible. Immediately on his return to Fort La Reine he sent his son Pierre, recently back from the Mandans, to establish Fort Dauphin. A memorandum of 1749 gives the course to his new post : " From Fort La Reine there is a portage of three leagues to the north-east to get into the Lake of the Prairies (Lake Manitoba). You follow the south shore of the lake till you come to the mouth of a river coming from the great Prairies, at the lower end of which is Fort Dauphin." Bougainville's memo of 1756 places it on the Minanghenachequeke, " L'Eau qui trouble," identified by Mr. J. B. Tyrrell as our Mossy River flowing out of Lake Dauphin and into Lake Winnipegosis.

In 1889 Mr. Tyrrell found remains of a fort or forts on the east bank, three-quarters of a mile from its mouth.

In the same year, 1741, Fort Bourbon was built. The memorandum of 1749 describes the course to it from Lake Winnipeg as leading " as far as Rivière aux Biches [the Saskatchewan, so called, as we know, from Jérémie's *Narrative*, where the alternative name Rivière du Cerf is used] where Fort Bourbon is, close to a lake of the same name," that is Lac Bourbon, our Cedar Lake. Peter Fidler's map has a " French Ho " on the island facing the inflow of the Saskatchewan into the lake. This is our Duncan's Island, on which there are traces of an ancient post.

In the spring of 1742 La Vérendrye kept his promise to penetrate to the most distant parts possible, not in person, but by sending two of his sons, François and Louis-Joseph, to explore beyond the Mandans. As the Missouri was now known not to be the River of the West, there was no plan of paddling downstream to the Western Sea. Attention was centred on an equestrian tribe to the south-west, the Gens des Chevaux, who came every spring to the Mandans to trade. They had told the two Frenchmen left at the Mandan fort of a White people living on the shore of the sea, the nation of the west, who prayed to the great Master of Life in books, who sang in great houses of prayer, and used the names of Jesus and Mary, and among other things had saddles and stirrups like the French. A chief of the Gens des Chevaux professed to have traded with this nation, and offered to provide the Frenchmen with horses and guides for the journey. The prospect of an easy ride with the Gens des Chevaux to neighbours to their west who lived on the Western Sea prescribed the form which this fresh exploration was to take.

The expedition reached the Mandans on the 19th of May. It waited for the Gens des Chevaux till 23rd July, when it was concluded that they were not coming that year. The La Vérendrye sons then got two Mandan guides to take them to that elusive people. For twenty days they travelled on foot in a west-southwesterly direction, which, says the Chevalier, " did not promise well for our route," presumably because he expected to go more to the west. The party passed several places in which were " earths of different colours, as blue, a kind of crimson, grass-green, shining black, chalk-white, and ochre," which Parkman argues must be the " Bad Lands " of the valley of the Little Missouri. On 11th August they reached the Mountain of the Gens des Chevaux, probably some " butte " not very far from the bend of the Little Missouri River, without meeting a soul. From this vantage point they watched for thirty-four days for the smoke of some passing camp, but saw none till 14th September. The course now taken veered towards the south, and brought them to a camp of Beaux Hommes. Here the last of the Mandan guides left them. After a stay of twenty-one days with this band they moved, Beaux Hommes and all, now on a south-south-westerly course, towards the Gens des Chevaux. On the second day they met a band called Petit Renards (Little Foxes) which joined them in the search for the elusive equestrian tribe. They then came to a Piowa (possibly Kiowa) band whom they asked to take them to some tribe on the road to the Western Sea. After drifting on a general south-south-westerly course for eleven days they reached a village of the Gens des Chevaux on 19th October.

Thus ended the first stage of their journey as planned, but it only brought disappointment. The Chevalier wrote: "I enquired among the Gens des Cheveux whether they were acquainted with the nation living on the coast. They replied that no one of their tribe had ever been there, the road being barred by the Gens des Serpents (the Snakes, perhaps a general term for the enemy); we could see later, by making a great detour, some tribes that traded with the whites on the coast." The Sea of the West must have seemed to the La Vérendryes ever to recede as they advanced towards it. In the hope of getting some more promising word, they moved on towards the Gens de l'Arc (the Bows), the only tribe brave enough not to stand in dread of the Snakes. Moving now south-westward for something like a month, they came to "a very populous village of the Gens de la Belle Rivière" on 18th November. As the Sioux are said to have always called the Cheyenne River the Beautiful River, a name which seems to survive in the Belle Fourche, its northerly branch, the position of the La Vérendryes may be roughly guessed at. Two days later they reached the Bows, of whom the usual inquiry was made: Did they know the Whites on the coast, and could they take them thither? They were told that they only knew them through prisoners taken by the Snakes. Their description indicated the Spanish. Hence the Chevalier's remark: "All that cooled my ardour considerably for a sea already known." Evidently he was now convinced that he was heading for the Gulf of Mexico. Reduced to following the exigencies of the moment, he joined the Bows on the war-path against the Snakes. (The Bows were probably in the Kiowa-Comanche alliance; their range was the Black Hills in South Dakota.) On 1st January they came in sight of the mountains, and near them left the non-combatants and the baggage. On the 12th the war party reached the actual mountains. The Chevalier was greatly vexed because, on account of the war, they could not climb them to see beyond. In spite of the reputed bravery of the Bows, they took panic and fled to their camp and baggage.

The La Vérendrye party now began the course which made the third side of the oblong figure cut by their travels. They drifted with the Bows, at first through two feet of snow, for there had been a blizzard, south-south-eastward till 1st March, when they halted to learn what reception they might meet with from the Gens de la Petite Cerise, a tribe whose haunt was the western bank of the Missouri. The story of the parting with the Bows is the unfailing one that the La Vérendryes had won the affection of the savages. "I communicated our plan to the chief of the Bows who was greatly affected at finding us resolved to leave him. We were not less so at parting from him on account of the kindly treatment we had always received at his hands."

On the 19th of February the party was with the Gens de la Petite Cerise on the banks of the Missouri. At the end of the month, when about to leave for the north, the Chevalier secretly deposited in the ground a tablet of lead with the arms of the King and an inscription, and erected a pyramid of stone over it, which they told the Indians was in memory of their visit. On the 2nd of April they took their way homeward, apparently along the east bank of the Missouri. They arrived among the Mandans on 18th May, forty-seven days later. They reached Fort La Reine on the 2nd of July.

The oblong traced by this expedition helps us to follow it in a vague way. The southerly side of the oblong has been fixed beyond a peradventure by the discovery in 1908 at Fort Pierre, opposite the town of Pierre on the Missouri, of the tablet buried by the Chevalier de la Vérendrye. To this point, the course taken by the party ran south-south-east from a point at the northerly edge of the Black Hills, twenty-one days' journey as an Indian tribe, men, women, and children, would travel under winter conditions, estimated at a hundred and fifty miles at most. Into this course the western side of the oblong ran in a general south-south-westerly direction and no farther west than the valley of the Little Missouri River, probably beginning near the great bend of that stream. The northerly side of the oblong ran west-south-west to the bend from the Mandan village, the starting-point.

The exploration of the area between the Missouri, the Little Missouri, and the Cheyenne River by the two Vérendryes is interesting as a part of the gradual exploration of the continent, but to the explorers themselves it was one long disappointment. From the point of view of the Search for the Western Sea it was nothing but a fiasco. To the Minister Maurepas it was without significance for the discovery of the Western Sea. After looking over the Chevalier's Journal he wrote to Beauharnois: " I have quite failed to find anything satisfactory in it so far as the Search for the Western Sea is concerned, nor anything that tends to justify the views of the Sieur de La Vérendrye in carrying on the enterprise, inasmuch as the Journal clearly shows from the route laid down in it, that neither that officer nor his sons have chosen the one which might lead to the desired discovery." Such a censure foreshadowed the resignation or recall of the Commandant of the Western Posts.

6.—LA VÉRENDRYE, LAST PHASE, 1744-49—THE OCCUPATION
OF THE LOWER SASKATCHEWAN, 1748-49

The dissatisfaction of Maurepas with the course of the exploration for the Western Sea was now finding its expression in a scheme which could scarcely lead to any end but a request from La Vérendrye to be relieved of his command. The plan had been first put forward in 1742 that an officer be placed under the explorer to help him in his explorations, the cost to be met from the Commandant's profits from the fur trade. Beauharnois seems to have protected La Vérendrye by quietly ignoring the suggestion, but Maurepas returned to the charge the following year. In reply the Governor argued that the posts could not bear the cost of the new officer; that forts Dauphin and Maurepas had been abandoned * for lack of provisions; that La Vérendrye was still 50,500 livres in debt, and could not hope to free himself from his obligations till the returns of the year came in ; he had therefore to help the Commandant, remitted the 3,000 livres due from him for the farming of his command ; for the same reasons he had not appointed a second under him. Except in the matter of pressing for the exploration to the Mandans, La Vérendrye had nothing whereof to complain in his chief. The same letter informed Maurepas that La Vérendrye had applied to be relieved in 1744 on account of ill-health. There was time for word of Maurepas's scheme as mooted in 1742 to reach the Commandant before his application was made, and so to be the cause of his resignation, but there is no evidence that it did so.

In March 1744 Maurepas replied to Beauharnois that the grounds given were not sufficient to justify delay in appointing the second in command : " Whether the Sieur de la Vérendrye decides to return or whether he wishes to continue the exploration, that arrangement must be put in force." That autumn the Journal of the exploration of the La Vérendrye sons beyond the Missouri was brought down by their father and was forwarded to the Minister. La Vérendrye added a long defence of himself : " The glory of the King and the advantage of the Colony have been the only motives which have actuated me in this enterprise." The plea ran on that he had ever been eager for the Search for the Western Sea, but had been checked by a succession of hindrances to the number of five—accidents which he could not prevent, and opposition which he could not overcome. He repudiated the charge that he had sought to make his fortune in the fur trade :

Money, Monseigneur, was . . . always a secondary consideration with me, and though I am poorer to-day than I was before I began my explorations, I should consider myself completely compensated if the care and attention I have devoted to the business had merited me the favour of your Highness, as I hope it yet may, if you will grant some reward for nine wounds that I have on my body, thirty-nine years of service in France and in this Colony, and to the difficulties and fatigues that I have endured during the last thirteen years in order to create the establishments which I have made in places where no person before myself had ever penetrated, which will effect a considerable augmentation in the trade of the Colony, even if no one fully succeeds in discovering the Western Sea, and for which I did not involve His Majesty in any expense.

---

* The next Fort Maurepas was built on the right bank of the Winnipeg River about six miles from Lake Winnipeg. It is placed there on maps which depict the country as it was when La Vérendrye retired in 1744. Apart from its fur trade, it was a convenient depot for provisions for the canoes passing in and out. When Saint-Pierre reached the fort on his way to the innermost posts his plans were greatly upset by not finding provisions awaiting him there. The name Maurepas was transferred, like the fort, to the Winnipeg River.

This is the dignified though warm self-defence of a noble nature, based on substantial benefits rendered to his King and his native land, but it was made to a Colonial Minister who, throughout all his correspondence in the matter of the Western Posts, showed not the faintest shadow of interest in the political expansion or commercial welfare of the colony under his charge. However, for once the appeal was not without its influence. Promotion to a captaincy was for some time La Vérendrye's due, but junior officers had been advanced before him. Now at last his merits were so far recognized that he was given the rank of captain in the troops. It was but a small recompense, especially if, as a phrase in a dispatch of La Galissonnière, Beauharnois's successor, suggests, he was recalled and did not retire voluntarily.

La Vérendrye's successor was the Sieur de Noyelles. In appointing him, Beauharnois does not seem to have emphasized his duties as an explorer so much as those of Commandant, for he describes him to Maurepas as " the most suitable person both for negotiating with the savages of the place and getting them to trouble the English. He will not lose sight of the discovery of the Western Sea." Official Canada really never veered from its policy of expansion at the expense of the English fur trade—expansion and, incidentally, exploration. Maurepas, at the same time, never swerved from his aim—the discovery of the Western Sea. However dissatisfied the Minister might be with him, La Vérendrye was a man after Beauharnois's own heart, and already in 1746 the Governor was urging his reappointment upon the home authorities. But this staunch supporter was soon removed from his position. The Court attributed the fall of Louisburg (1745) to the inefficiency of Beauharnois and recalled him. The Marquis de la Jonquière, sent out to succeed him, was captured by the English at sea. The Marquis de la Galissonnière administered the colony in the meantime. In a letter to Maurepas he associated himself with the late Governor in his estimate of La Vérendrye's services. In reply Maurepas adhered to his adverse view. But at this point he too disappeared from the stage. He ventured to protest to the King against Madame de Pompadour's interference with the administration, and he was suspected of being the author of a clever but wicked piece of verse upon the physical ailings of the favourite.

The new Minister, the Comte de Jouy Rouillé, perhaps for the sake of official consistency, gave his adhesion to Maurepas's view, but in fact proved much more favourable to La Vérendrye. On May 4, 1749, he gave his consent to his reappointment and decorated him with the Cross of St. Louis. The fortunes of the La Vérendrye family were once more in the ascendant, for the year before (1748) both the eldest surviving son Pierre and the youngest, the Chevalier, had been given ensigncies in the troops, and had immediately left for the Western Posts, confident that their father would soon be with them taking up once more the task for which the family had made great sacrifices.

It does not appear that misfortune had broken La Vérendrye's will into subordinating the good of the colony to speculative exploration. In a letter of thanks to Rouillé for his reappointment he spoke of himself as under orders " to continue the establishment of posts and the exploration of the West." The order in which he placed his duties is significant. At the same time he renewed his promise to advance to the farthest point within reach.

The plan of exploration as it stood now must have been much more to La Vérendrye's liking than that across the prairies on foot to the Missouri. He was to winter (1750–51) at Fort Bourbon on Cedar Lake, an expansion of the Saskatchewan, and in the spring of 1751 to journey by canoe upstream, with the river itself for his guide and the Cree language, spoken by his children, to carry him all the way to the height of land beyond which lay the descent to the Sea of the West. The Governor-General La Jonquière's sketch of the plan ran :

(The River Paskoyac) is the most convenient route by which to pursue the discovery of the Western Sea from the ease with which you can transfer your effects thither by canoe, get guides there easily and have always the same tribe, Cree, to deal with as far as the height of land, which is not the case by the prairie road. There you encounter different tribes, all enemies, and different languages, causes of hindrance and difficulty which occasioned considerable expense formerly to the Sieur de la Vérendrye. He did not know the Paskoyac river at that time.

La Jonquière ends his memoir with the judgment of his officer to which we have grown accustomed from the pen of Beauharnois and La Galissonnière : " The Sieur de la Vérendrye will neglect nothing that may aid in fulfilling the intentions of the King as he is anxious to dispel from the mind of the Court the unfavourable impressions which some evil-minded persons have unjustly created in regard to him. . . . His one object in his undertaking having been the glory of the King and the advantage of the Colony, an object of which he will never lose sight." But, once more in command of the posts of the West, with the long vista of the Saskatchewan before his eyes, La Vérendrye died in Montreal on the 6th day of December 1749.

The life of the man is not without its enigmas. Was he primarily Commandant, or explorer pure and simple, or fur-trader masquerading as explorer ?

The persistent charge of Maurepas, that he had devoted himself all too much to the fur trade, cannot be lightly set aside. In 1735 six hundred packages of furs were made up at Fort Maurepas alone. That year Beauharnois and Hocquart reported on the fur trade of the colony : " The receipts from beaver skins have been considerable, notwithstanding the troubles and the war expeditions in the Upper Country, because the post among the Sioux and the new posts of the West have secured nearly a hundred thousand good skins. The total receipts amounted to 178,000 livres." In 1737 thirteen canoes left Fort St. Charles loaded and not able to carry all away.

For all his thriving trade in furs La Vérendrye was constantly in financial difficulties. At the end of the first two years the losses amounted to more than 43,000 livres, the voyageurs were refusing to go without their pay, and the merchants declining to furnish goods on credit. In view of this, Beauharnois and Hocquart proposed to pay the wages of the voyageurs for the first three years, at an estimated cost of 30,000 livres. The Minister refused to countenance this expenditure : the exploration must be carried on with the profits of the fur trade.

In 1733 La Vérendrye improved the water-ways, reducing the number of the portages and lightening the labour of carriage over them, and on this ground he reduced the wages of the men, which were probably high at the outset, because they were apprehensive of the dangers of a little known country. Still the expenditure was greater than the returns. In 1734 eleven canoes left for the east with two hundred and seventy-five packages of furs; yet La Vérendrye remained deeply in debt. In 1735, the happy year, six hundred packages were sent out from Fort Maurepas and the posts were beginning to pay, but precisely at this point Beauharnois, with the best intentions in the world, to free La Vérendrye's hands for the exploration to the Mandans, gave the traffic in furs over to traders, leaving to the Commandant but the fees of their licences. There followed the disastrous year of the massacre of the Lake of the Woods. Henceforth it is not easy to calculate the profits of the enterprise, for nothing is known of the returns of the trade to the merchants, nor of their payments to the Commandant, but 1737 must have been a fairly good year, for, as has been seen, La Vérendrye went down with eleven canoes and two hundred and seventy-five packages of his own, and not able to take away all the furs gathered. That this success did not leave him with money to spare is proved by his financial dealings of 1738. He got 6,683 livres in merchandise from François Larie Soumande de Lorme, his nephew-in-law, payable in August 1739 in Montreal, and from Louis d'Ailleboust, Sieur de Coulonges, 2,787 livres, also in goods, payable at Michilimakinac. To the former he made the promise on his honour that he would send down, immediately on his arrival in the Upper Country, 1,000 lb. of beaver, no doubt peltries left at his posts, with a canoe-load of skins that would cover his debt. He did send down the 1,000 lb. of beaver, but with an order to use them in paying certain debts and certain drafts which he would be making on De Lorme. This order the creditor faithfully observed, but he subsequently discovered La Vérendrye's indebtedness to D'Ailleboust, and the promise to pay in peltries delivered at Michilimakinac, contrary to the practice of the trade of the time, which was to bring the furs down and clear up accounts in Montreal. La Vérendrye's promise to D'Ailleboust in effect made him a preferred creditor, and was, Hocquart in trying the case declared, unusual and crooked. The whole suit, which was ultimately settled by an order of the court that the furs must be brought to Montreal, shows the financial straits in which La Vérendrye found himself in 1738–39, the year of his expedition to the

Mandans, a year of considerable extra expense and no large returns. He could only get his goods for the outfit by offering a preferred position to one of his furnishers. De Lorme took the unwise course of protecting himself by sending no goods up to La Vérendrye in 1740. This must have greatly diminished the trade of that season and left La Vérendrye without the means of paying his debts the following year.

La Vérendrye was still involved in 1742, at this time to the Sieur de la Marque, his companion to the Mandans, and to his associate the Sieur Gamelin. These creditors claimed sixty-five packages of beaver as still their due, for equipping him for his discovery of the Western Sea. By a contract dated October 12, 1740, La Vérendrye committed himself to deliver thirty-three packages to them in the spring of 1741 and thirty-two in 1742. The delivery in 1741 amounted to but nine packages, the default being doubtless due to De Lorme sending up no goods. The traders appealed to Maurepas, possibly passing over Beauharnois as being too staunch a friend and supporter of his officer. Maurepas instructed the Governor to see into the matter. Beauharnois accordingly gave the complainants an order to the Commandant at Michilimackinac to see to it that the fifty-six packages due them were taken from La Vérendrye's furs as they came out from the interior. A further claim on goods lying at Kaministikwia and at Fort St. Charles was to be met by payment on the basis of 40 per cent. added to the Montreal price. Should La Vérendrye fail to meet this, the complainants were empowered to seize effects in the forts up to their due. The indebtednesses were satisfactorily paid by the autumn of 1742. In his defence of 1744 La Vérendrye put his debts at 40,000 livres, and the testimony of Beauharnois bears him out. This means that he was never able to make good the losses of his first year's outfit, which were necessarily heavy.

Granting that Maurepas was correct and that La Vérendrye did carry on " a considerable business " at his posts, what was the cause of the financial embarrassment which blighted his career ? First of all Maurepas was to blame, for, as has already been seen, in 1717 the Court laid down the principle in connection with the establishment of forts at Kaministikwia, Rainy Lake, and Lake of the Woods, which La Noue was to build preparatory to the exploration to the Western Sea, that the trade in furs must be assigned to cover the cost of the forts, and that, as the exploration beyond would of necessity be unremunerative, because of the distance of the journey and the impossibility of carrying on a trade while making it, the expense would have to be borne by the King. In the teeth of this, Maurepas insisted that the trade of La Vérendrye's forts must bear the cost of the exploration, pressed for discoveries by him, and, when he appeared to be paying great attention to his command and its trade, accused him of being more interested in beaver than in the Sea of the West. In all fairness, either the King's treasury should have borne the cost of the exploration or La Vérendrye should have been left to carry on the discovery at the time dictated by the exigencies of his command and in the way which he should judge to be best. Some responsibility for La Vérendrye's embarrassments lies with Beauharnois. To free his officer for the exploration impatiently watched for by the Minister, he introduced the traders into his command just at the time when the very rich fur region of the basin of Lake Winnipeg was being tapped and giving promise of ample returns. Worse still, the traders brought disorganization into the command and contributed in no small measure to the disasters of the year of the massacre of the Lake of the Woods.

La Vérendrye's financial distresses must, however, be laid to some extent at his own door. The methods by which he brought the Indians to loyalty to the French were successful, but they were excessively extravagant—council upon council, feast after feast set before hundreds of hungry savages, presents heaped up and heaped up again. It is true that the Indians gave presents in return, but not in proportion to his generosity. Repentigny, who was placed in his command in 1750, found the Indians of Rainy Lake " very impertinent, which can be attributed only to the too great indulgence with which they have been treated." In a word he could not, or would not, maintain the scale of generosity with which La Vérendrye had treated them.

La Vérendrye, then, was no mere fur-trader, greedy of gain, and hoarding his gold unto the day when he could shake from his feet the dust of the Upper Country, and retire to his native Three Rivers to lord it for the rest of his life over the greatest of his home settlement. He sought wealth in the beaver trade only to spend it in making his command a supreme success, in winning a vast stretch of country for France, and in swelling the volume of trade passing down the St. Lawrence. Beauharnois thus bore him witness : " It is none the less true that he gave himself wholly to [his] task and devoted to it the whole proceeds of the new posts which he established with so much trouble and care, and with extreme risk." He loved the life of a commandant. He took delight in solemn councils in the presence of hundreds of dusky warriors. When the chiefs boasted of brave deeds he rose to proclaim his own, to show the wounds on his body, and to tell how they fought in France. When they chanted the war-cry, he chanted with them. The palisades of his forts might be no more than a double row of logs, the Commandant's quarters but log huts with roofs of bark covered with clay ; he made them the scene of pomp and circumstance dear to the heart of the French. He knew that this pomp and circumstance endeared him to the savage host before him and bound them to his country and King, and he spent all that he had to maintain it. But his eyes were not set solely on the forest stage upon which he played his part. He had begun his career as a military man, seeking advance in the King's service upon the battlefields of Europe. When advance in the gilded ranks of that service was perforce denied him, he believed that he could find it in the service of his native colony, as Commandant in a forest fort. As the King's officer in command of the Postes du Nord he had the eye to see the true line of advance for the French, and the way of prosperity for New France. It was to occupy the forest belt that lay to the north-west, rich in the richest furs, to confine the English to a barren and unproductive coast and pre-empt a continent for his country. His initial mistake lay in cloaking this issue by holding out the prospect of an advance to the Western Sea. But amid all the vicissitudes of his career as Commandant of the Posts of the Western Sea, in the face of persistent pressure from those in high places to force him into vague and unproductive explorations, he adhered to his vision of what was the true future for his native colony. When he entered the Upper Country, the English had long won the Indians of a wide river system to their cause and service. Monsonis and Crees at the Lake of the Woods, Assiniboins and Crees in the basin of Lake Winnipegosis and from the Saskatchewan beyond the Forks, frequented the posts on Hudson Bay and found there their necessities for peace and war. When he died a far-flung line of forts had won many of these savage tribes, now the children of the French King, to find their requirements through friendly and intimate intercourse with the French. Forts St. Pierre and St. Charles made Rainy Lake and the Lake of the Woods so many French inland seas. Fort Maurepas, now at the mouth of the River Winnipeg, and Fort La Reine at the portage to Manitoba Lake, turned the stream of Assiniboin furs eastward to the St. Lawrence. Even as he was preparing to return to his life's task his sons were building a new post—Fort Paskoyac, at the Pas, on the Saskatchewan—to divert to New France the furs which passed from that mighty water-way by Moose Lake, the Minago River, and Cross Lake to York Fort, long the Mecca of the "Western Indians."

In spite of their strange neglect, and even of their persistent belittling of La Vérendrye's achievements, officials in France began to see, before his death, the value of his posts in case of war with England, and planned to send his devoted Indians to capture the factories on the Bay. Had France been able in the Seven Years War to fill Canada with troops and to hold it, and had she had the good fortune to see an officer of Iberville's calibre in command of the Western posts, the campaign of these armchair strategists might have changed the course of Western history. As it was, the French lost Canada, and with it the perspective in which to see the real greatness of La Vérendrye. Champlain made the East and La Vérendrye grasped the West for the French. Together, they made the French masters of little short of a continent—of a vast domain which smaller men were to lose. In a land in which too many officials proved greedy and corrupt, La Vérendrye, the peer of Champlain in unselfish devotion, cast himself, the lives of his sons, the profits of the fur trade, even his private fortune, into the scale for his country, and turned the balance definitely in favour of France. The conquest of Canada by the English and the occupation of the West under the ægis of the British Crown have thrown a cloak over the true achievements of the man, and have left only the geographers and circles of intellectuals interested in travels and explorations or in local history to honour his name. They belaud the explorer and miss the sight of the Commandant. It remains true, however, that the development of the command and of its trade took the La Vérendryes farther west than their explorations for the Western Sea, for the policy of establishing posts and cutting off the furs from the English took the Chevalier as far up the River Saskatchewan as the Forks, where the north and south branches meet, and this is considerably more than a degree, probably more than a hundred miles farther west than the Black Hills, the extreme limit reached by the expedition of the two sons in 1742-43 in search of the Western Sea. Had the great Commandant been left un-disturbed to follow out his policy aiming at the expansion of New France and at diverting the wealth of the forest belt into French channels, and had he been allowed to reach towards the Sea of the West only so far as was permitted or dictated by these altogether substantial gains, he might well have brought the French to the Rockies by way of the River Saskatchewan, the only easy route, within his lifetime, and the honour of his country would not have been tarnished by his death in comparative poverty, a misunderstood and even a maligned man.

7.—THE HUDSON'S BAY COMPANY AND THE DOBBS CRISIS, 1731-49

Though the Hudson's Bay Company had confined its forts to the coast of the Bay, it had created a trade machine which went far towards occupying the area claimed in virtue of its Charter. Trading Indians—with the furs of Lake of the Woods, of the valley of the Winnipeg River, and the southern basins of lakes Winnipeg and Winnipegosis—took the water-way up the English River, an easterly tributary of the Winnipeg, into the Albany River and so to Albany Fort. At the great council of 1734, at Fort St. Charles on the Lake of the Woods, La Vérendrye urged the Indians before him not to go to the English at the Bay. French goods might be a little dearer, but they were better and offered at their door, and the French were more friendly. His forts St. Pierre, St. Charles, Maurepas, La Reine, and Dauphin were designed to occupy this hinterland of Albany, and to give the French a more substantial claim than the English Company could assert in virtue of its Charter, or even its trade con-nections. But the French had penetrated also into the hinterland of York Fort. The Indians of Manitoba, Winnipegosis, and Cedar lakes were taking their furs in person to forts Dauphin and Bourbon. The trading Indians might go down to York Fort as of old, but their cargoes were dwindling in value. The rich fur fields of the Saskat-chewan remained so far intact, for Fort Paskoyac was not established till 1750 and Fort La Corne not till 1753, but the French would soon be settled there also. The yearly returns of York Fort had dropped

from more than 30,000 made beaver to little more than 20,000 ; the
returns at Albany Fort were reduced to something like the half.
With the certainty that the Saskatchewan water-way would be
occupied next, the Hudson's Bay Company was faced, as will be
seen, with a difficult situation. But this was a small matter compared
with the crisis, which came on when it was realized in England that
the French had occupied the central plain of America behind the
Company's forts, had confined the English to the barren shores of
the Bay, and were capturing the fur trade. To patriotic Englishmen
and to men interested in British manufactures and overseas trade
this was nothing short of a disaster. It was easy to lay the blame for
it on the inertness of the Hudson's Bay Company and to find the
basal cause of that inertness in the vicious system of monopolies.

The issue did not come up in this direct form, but through the
English Search for the Western Sea by way of the North-West
Passage, a search which was prosecuted, like that of La Vérendrye,
more in the interest of the expansion of British trade than from
scientific curiosity. This revival of English dreams of the North-
West Passage was due primarily to Arthur Dobbs, an Irish gentleman
of means and of an inquiring mind. Dobbs had inherited his father's
property and had added to his wealth by a judicious marriage with
an heiress. From his father came contacts with the governing class.
The father had been high sheriff of the county of Antrim. The son
occupied that position from 1720. From 1721 to 1730 he was a
member of the Irish House of Commons. In this last year he was
introduced by the Archbishop of Armagh to no less a personage
than Sir Robert Walpole as " one of the members of our House of
Commons, where he on all occasions endeavours to promote his
Majesty's service. He . . . has for some time applied his thoughts
to the trade of Great Britain and Ireland, and to the making our
colonies in America of more use than they have hitherto been."
The reference was to Dobbs's *Essay on the Trade and Imports of
Ireland*, the first part of which had been published the year before ;
the second part appeared the year after his introduction to Walpole.
Dobbs was now appointed engineer-in-chief and surveyor-general in
Ireland. Clearly, he was in a position to win the hearing of men in
high places ; by his talent as a writer he was able to gain the ear of a
wider public.

To his concern for the trade of the Empire Dobbs added a lively
interest in certain aspects of science. In 1726 he contributed a paper
on the aurora borealis to the Royal Society, and in the following
years he was poring over the Journals of the explorers of the Polar
Sea. By 1731 he had prepared " an abstract " of all the Journals of
the explorers of Hudson Bay. It was much more. It embodied
his conclusion that an opening on the north-west coast of Hudson
Bay, " no farther north than the Latitude of sixty-five degrees," was
a strait leading to the Western Sea. Arguments were advanced in
support—the flow of the tide from the south-west, and the presence
of black whales on the western and not on the easterly coast of the

Bay. It could be no inlet ; it was a strait, and the tide and the whales came from the Western Sea. In 1733, when on a visit to London, Dobbs gave a copy of his " abstract " to Sir Charles Wager, First Lord of the Admiralty (hence the subsequent name for the supposed strait). Through Sir Charles he met Mr. Samuel Jones, Deputy-Governor of the Hudson's Bay Company, but got no encouragement from him. Through Colonel Bladen of the Admiralty Office Dobbs now procured a reading of the Company's Charter ; he was astonished at the privileges and powers conveyed by it to the Company. Obsessed with his idea about the North-West Passage, he laid special stress on the references in the Charter to the discovery of the Passage, and convinced himself that the Company had secured its privileges on the condition that it should prosecute exploration to that end. He now obtained an interview with Sir Bibye Lake, whom he described as " perpetual Governor," for his has been the longest tenure of the Governor's chair in the history of the Company. Dobbs's plea with Sir Bibye was that it would redound to the honour of the Company, and bring large profits, if the way to the Western Sea and the marts of the East were discovered by it. When Lake mentioned the failure of Knight's expedition and the Company's loss of £7,000 to £8,000, Dobbs urged that the dispatch of two sloops from Churchill Fort to enter the inlet and return as soon as it was ascertained to be a strait would involve no great expense. Sir Bibye Lake agreed, but asserted that it could not be done at the moment when war with France was threatened.

In 1735 orders were sent out by the Governor and Committee to Churchill Fort, looking to a voyage for exploration by the Churchill sloop during the following year. A twelvemonth later the order ran that, as soon as the ship should arrive, which it was estimated would be in July, the sloop *Churchill*, under the command of Captain James Napper with twelve sailors, and the *Musquash*, under Captain Robert Crow with six of a crew, should proceed north to Sir Thomas Roe's Welcome, observing the tides and at times sending parties ashore to take note of the soil and minerals. A suitable harbour for trade with the Indians was to be chosen, and the natives were to be told that the sloops would return the next year. This was intended to be no more than a preliminary voyage. In the following year the sloops were to repair to the base on Sir Thomas Roe's Welcome and await the annual ship from England, with which they were to sail northward to what discoveries they could. As the ship of 1736 did not reach Churchill till 12th August, the sloops could not sail that autumn. On 4th July of the following year they sailed on what was still the preliminary voyage and reached Pistol Bay (Rankin Inlet), which Dobbs later thought was the passage to the Western Sea, and showed as such on a map illustrating one of his pamphlets. The captains met with the natives and arranged a rendezvous at " Eskimaux Point " somewhat to the south. Captain Napper died on 8th August and his ship reached Churchill on the 18th. The *Musquash* arrived on the 22nd. For some reason unknown the larger scheme of exploration northward in the following year was not carried out.

Meanwhile Dobbs was not satisfied to leave matters in the hands of the Governor, but put himself into relation with the servants of the Company to gather further information. He found a ready supporter in the person of Captain Christopher Middleton, probably the most intelligent navigator in the service of the Company at that time. Middleton had taken employment with the Company about 1720, and when at Churchill in 1721 had made observations of the variations of the magnetic needle. He had secured a Hadley's quadrant soon after it had been introduced to a meeting of the Royal Society in 1731, and he claimed that from 1737 he had been able with it to obtain the true time at sea by taking eight or ten different altitudes of the sun or stars when near the prime vertical—a method now in general use at sea. Whether he found the method out for himself or not, he must have been one of the first to practise it. He became a member of the Royal Society, and between 1737 and 1742 made a number of communications to it on the variations of the magnetic needle in the northern seas, based on his experience as navigator in Hudson Bay, where proximity to the magnetic pole, at that time unknown, presented serious problems. Middleton had been at Churchill Fort in 1722 when Captain Scroggs went northward on his voyage of trade and discovery. He regarded Scroggs as too ignorant for such a task, and this may explain why the Captain refused to take him on the voyage, though eager to go. Middleton's view was that the present Wager Inlet in about 63° 30′ north latitude was a strait and would lead westward. Here was a ready associate for Dobbs in his enterprise. The knowledge of the Hudson's Bay Company's territory which Dobbs gained, his reading of the Journals of the Company's officers, including that of Scroggs now lost, and his contact with its servants, must have been largely through Captain Middleton as medium. Thus he became the best-informed subject of the King outside of the Company's service on the whole situation on Hudson Bay. This knowledge of his was, however, distorted by his obsession that the North-West Passage was practicable, and by his eagerness to be the means of its discovery. By 1740 he had convinced himself that the Hudson's Bay Company had played him false, that the voyage of the sloops was a sheer pretence, and that the Company was determinedly opposed to exploration. He turned therefore to his friends at the Admiralty, of whom Sir Charles Wager at least had been convinced by his " abstract " and was prepared to assist.

The Admiralty decided to send out a warship, and Dobbs, by the promise of a permanent post in the Navy, persuaded Captain Middleton to leave the employ of the Company and take command of the expedition. No better appointment could have been made, for the Captain had much experience of Hudson Bay, and his conviction that the inlet in question was a strait leading to the Western Sea gave assurance that the enterprise would be prosecuted with zeal. The Admiralty secured an order from the Governor and Committee of the Company to their several factors to render the expedition "the best assistance in their power." In the spring of 1741 the Captain sailed from the Thames in H.M.S. *Furnace*, a gunboat, accompanied by the sloop *Discovery* commanded by Captain William Moor, like his chief, lately of the Company's service. On 8th August he was off the mouth of the Churchill River, in which he proposed to winter. When the two ships were seen approaching, Robert Pilgrim, then temporarily in charge of the stone fort just built and newly armed, acted swiftly on the general instructions for such a case—instructions really aimed at the French. He called in his men, loaded the guns, and aimed a shot at the ships. In response a white flag was raised and an officer sent to the fort with the Company's orders to assist the expedition.

Captain Middleton, as a former servant of the Company, was on easy terms with James Isham, who soon arrived from York Fort to take command for the winter. He was quartered along with a number of his officers in the stone fort itself. His men repaired the old factory recently abandoned, the Company's bricklayer restoring the stoves there for the comfort of its occupants. Isham sent to York Fort for Indian hunters, for his own Indians were in distant parts of the interior at their winter grounds, but at York Fort also the natives were away. For lack of fresh meat some of Middleton's crew were stricken with scurvy ; eleven died. But with the arrival of the wild geese in the spring, and with them of the Indians to hunt, the situation was saved. When the Company's armourer died, the very skilful workman in Middleton's crew took his place and prepared the guns for the spring trade of the fort. When the Indians came to trade in the spring, Middleton allowed a servant of the Company to be quartered in his ship to prevent the crew from trading in peltries. Thus relations between the fort and the ships were not only correct but happy. Some friction there was, however, before the ships sailed, for five men left the Company's service and engaged themselves to Captain Middleton—welcome substitutes for the dead. The Journal of the fort for June 30 reads : " . . . at ¼ past 9 at Night ye Furnace & Discovery, his Majestys ships & the Churchill sloop sett sail for their voiage, whom God send Safe."

Middleton explored the inlet opposite Marble Island and named it after his mate John Rankin. He called a cape at the entrance to the inlet farther north, which he was sent to explore, Dobbs, and the inlet itself he named Wager after Sir Charles. He satisfied himself that the Wager was no more than an inlet leading to a river. When his progress northward was stayed by ice in Frozen Strait, he returned southward to Wager Inlet and thence sailed for England. In spite of his former belief to the contrary, he reported that there was no strait in those parts leading to the Western Sea. But Dobbs was of that type of mind which clings to a theory long after the facts have exploded it. Moreover, ulterior motives, of which Middleton became aware on his return, began to appear. Dobbs intended to use his Search for the Western Sea to destroy the monopoly of the

Hudson's Bay Company, and to secure a concession for himself and his supporters. He sent a series of " queries " to the Admiralty questioning Middleton's conclusions and suggesting that the Captain had been guilty of dereliction of his duties. Later this took the form of definite charges that he had been bribed by the Company and had falsified his log. Middleton was required by the Admiralty to answer the " queries." By publishing his *Vindication* he began a wearisome war of pamphlets.

Of course, time has justified Middleton. There is no strait on the shore of Hudson Bay in question. Captain Parry, who above all should know, bore this testimony : " The accuracy of Captain Middleton is manifest upon the point most strenuously argued against him, for our subsequent experience has not left the smallest doubt of Repulse Bay and the northern part of the Welcome being filled by a rapid tide flowing into it from the eastward, through Frozen Strait." In a similar strain, John Barrow, son of Sir John the historian of Arctic exploration : " On looking through the correspondence at the Admiralty, it is impossible not to be struck with the straight-forward manliness, candour and honesty of purpose, exemplified by Captain Middleton throughout this trying business. . . . That the Lords of the Admiralty were perfectly satisfied with his conduct, there is every reason to suppose, as in the following year he was placed in command of the *Shark*, sloop." After this commission Middleton was retired on a pension, which he drew till his death in 1770.

In 1744 Dobbs launched his attack on the Hudson's Bay Company in his best known book, *An Account of the countries adjoining to Hudson's Bay . . . containing a description of their lakes and rivers, the nature of the soil and climates, their methods of commerce &c shewing the benefit to be made by settling colonies and opening a trade in these parts ; whereby the French will be deprived in a great measure of their traffic in furs, and the communication between Canada and the Mississippi be cut off : with an abstract of Captain Middleton's Journal and observations upon his behaviour during his voyage and since his return . . . the whole intended to shew the great probability of a North-west Passage, so long desired ; and which (if discovered) would be of the highest advantage to these kingdoms.* This portentous title-page is a summary of the book and of Dobbs's subsequent campaign. Throw the trade open ; settle the country ; create an English colony stretching from James Bay to the Great Lakes and Pennsylvania, and thereby cut the connection of the French colony on the St. Lawrence with Louisiana on the Mississippi ; hem the French in to the shores of the Atlantic ; finally, discover the North-West Passage and secure an English route to the rich commerce of the east—a very simple and easy task, as depicted on the printed page, but the North-West Passage has only been discovered after many voyages and considerable loss of life, and it will never be used as a route to China. As to settling the country between James Bay and the Great Lakes, the region is to this day the most derelict part of Canada—

vast stretches of marsh in the north, in the south a succession of barren hills, studded with granite boulders between which slender trees, mostly spruce and poplar, maintain a precarious growth. But Dobbs asserted that life in this region was dismal only because it was not settled, and it was not settled wholly because of the vicious monopoly of the Hudson's Bay Company.

The Reason why the Manner of living there at present appears to be so dismal to us in Britain, is intirely owing to the Monopoly and Avarice of the Hudson's Bay Company . . . who, to deter others from trading there, or making Settlements, conceal all the Advantages to be made in that Country, and give out that the Climate, and Country, and Passage thither are much worse, than they really are, and vastly worse than might be, if those Seas were more frequented, and proper Settlements and Improvements were made, and proper situations chosen for that Purpose ; this they do that they may engross a beneficial Trade to themselves. . . . They also prevent their Servants from giving any Account of the Climate or Countries adjacent, that might be favourable, and induce others to trade or settle there; nor do they encourage the Servants, or even allow them to make any Improvements without their Factories, unless it be a Turnip Garden. . . . If the Trade was opened, and these Rivers on the Bottom of the Bay were settled farther up in the Country, they would have a very temperate, fine Climate, with all the Necessaries for Life, and even for Luxury. Here are very fine Woods of all Kinds of large Timber for Shipping or Building, where they may have all sorts of Fruit and Grain, tame Cattle and Fowl. . . . But besides the Advantage to be made of these Countries adjoining to the Bay, by opening the Trade, and settling there, a still more considerable one might be made, by opening a Communication with our present Northern Colonies upon that Continent by the Means of the Canada Lakes, by forming a Settlement on the River Condé, which is navigable into the Lake Erie, which is within a small Distance of our Colonies of Pennsylvania and Maryland. . . . We should thence, in a little Time, secure the Navigation of these great and fine Lakes . . . we should cut off the Communication betwixt [the French] Colonies of Canada and Mississippi, and secure the Inland Trade of all that vast Continent.

Dreaming at his desk in Dublin, Dobbs was achieving for the English on paper what La Vérendrye had already gone far towards making a reality for the French—the occupation of the great central plain of America. To the dreamer there was no obstacle on the way but the monopoly of the Hudson's Bay Company. Patriotic Englishmen who hated to think that the French were getting the better of the English, others again, who regarded all monopolies as vicious and obstacles to progress, manufacturers and merchants eager for new markets for their goods, rallied to his support and precipitated a crisis in England for the Company.

In March 1744 Dobbs presented a petition to the King in Council praying " that two proper Vessels be provided for the Discovery of a Passage through Hudson's Bay to the Western American Ocean, which is so near being brought to perfection," or, in case the vessels cannot be spared (for there was war with France), that a sufficient premium be granted to such persons as might be willing to make the discovery at their own expense. Merchants in London petitioned the House of Commons in the same sense in the following January. As a result, an Act of Parliament was passed offering the reward of

£20,000 to such British subject or subjects as should discover the North-West Passage (May 2, 1745). Dobbs and his supporters forthwith organized a copartnership with an executive of nine, generally spoken of as the North-West Committee. Subscribers took shares of £100, subject to an immediate call for £20. Subscriptions were asked for up to £10,000. Two ships were purchased and named the *Dobbs Galley* (180 tons) and the *California* (140 tons). Captain Moor, who had navigated the sloop *Discovery* in Middleton's expedition, and in the controversy had sided with Dobbs against his chief, was placed in command of the *Dobbs Galley*, while a Captain Francis Smith commanded the *California*. These officers were given no letter from the Governor and Committee of the Hudson's Bay Company to the factors requiring them to afford any necessary assistance. No such thing was asked for. Henry Ellis sailed on the *Dobbs Galley* as agent for the North-West Committee, and probably as historian of the expedition. Mr. Drage was on the *California* as clerk. His desire to see all the reports suggests that he too aimed at writing up the discovery, and this may be the explanation of the enmity which grew up between the two men. The ships held commissions from the Admiralty empowering them to act as privateers should occasion call for it, and, as such, giving them the right to call for assistance from all British subjects. They sailed from the Thames in May 1746 and were accompanied part of the way by the Company's ships, Governor Isham on board for York Fort. It is a picturesque feature of their voyage that they were convoyed to safety out into the Atlantic by Captain Middleton in command of H.M.S. *Shark*. On 12th August the expedition was off the south-west coast of Marble Island. The next four days were spent observing the tides.

The question had now to be faced, should the expedition proceed northward for discovery or hasten to winter quarters, and if the latter course were taken, where would they winter. In keeping with instructions, a meeting of the council of officers was called. The obvious plan would be to avoid long preparations for winter by occupying the old fort at Churchill River, to act on the knowledge that that port would be open late in the season, and meanwhile to prosecute the exploration with vigour. But the council decided to winter in the Nelson River, on the grounds that it afforded an ample supply of wood, was more frequented than the Churchill by Indians who could hunt for provisions, and the ice broke up earlier in the spring. It was regarded as a definite advantage to be away from the Company's posts, and to have immediate relations with the Indians. The choice of the Nelson affected the course of the summer's exploration, for allowance had to be made for the return to the Churchill should no safe harbourage be found in the Nelson. The Council decided, therefore, to leave for the south immediately, with the somewhat ridiculous result that the exploration of the first summer was confined to four days' observation of the tides between Marble Island and the West Main.

On 25th August the ships anchored in the open at the mouths

of the Hayes and the Nelson, which are separated from one another only by the tongue of land on which York Fort stands. A day was spent sounding for the channel of the Nelson, and in the early afternoon of the next day the ships unintentionally stumbled into the channel of the Hayes. The *California* cast anchor in Five Fathom Hole, the usual outer anchorage of the Company's ships, but the *Dobbs Galley* ran aground. The British colours were flying over both. Meanwhile Governor Isham, who had arrived by the Company's ship some time before, and had already dispatched it for England, was observing their manœuvres, remembering that there was war with France, and that York Fort had been captured by just such an expedition as he saw in the river. The report of the Indians that there were four ships (they had counted in the boats out sounding) must have tended to increase his caution. The British colours, as he says in his Journal, might be used to effect a surprise. He must have shrewdly suspected that he had really to do with Dobbs's expedition, but no boat had been sent up to the fort with commissions from His Majesty or orders from the Company. He decided to follow his instructions to the letter. He promptly called in his men, loaded his guns, and sent a boat downstream to remove the buoys. When the outer beacon, which marked a shoal and indicated the channel to Five Fathom Hole, was being cut down, a boat was sent from the ships to protest. The only answer possible in the circumstances was given, that the Governor's orders must be obeyed. On the return of his men Isham knew definitely that these were Dobbs's ships. But according to his general instructions he could not admit any ship to the river without authorization from the Company, and that had not been produced. The next day the *Dobbs Galley* was floated and brought safely into Five Fathom Hole. The ships now saluted the fort with seven guns, but no reply was made. When boats left the ships, not to come up to the fort, but to sound, Isham fired off two twelve-pounders which, he says, " Brought Ym too." The shot fell half-way between the fort and the ships. The Governor's next step was to send a boat out with a letter demanding " a proper authority from the Governmnt or the Company " for their entry into the river. A council was called hastily to consider the answer. According to Drage all were non-plussed, for they had no papers, but Captain Smith remembered that there was a clause in the commissions of the ships as privateers giving them the right to assistance at any British port. Two boats were forthwith sent up to the fort with the commissions and with a letter claiming shelter and assistance " Comformable to His Majesty's Commission." After consulting his Council, Isham accepted the papers as proper authority for the ships wintering within his command. The Governor had taken all precautions in case of an attack and had asserted the rights of the Hudson's Bay Company in the face of Dobbs's expedition successfully.

The question was now, Where should the ships be berthed ? Apart from the difficulty of getting them above the fort, Isham was anxious that they should not lie between him and the Indians coming down in the spring to trade. He invited the captains ashore for a conference, and urged the safety of the harbourage of Churchill River. When that failed, he affirmed that the Nelson was much safer from the rush of the ice in the spring flood than was the Hayes, and he induced them to make a more careful survey. A channel was found and a safe berth at " Gillam's Creek," but Captain Moor refused to take his ship through the shoals, although Captain Smith offered to navigate the *California* through first and to return to pilot the *Dobbs Galley*. When it became evident that the determination was to winter in the Hayes, Isham urged that the only berths safe at the going out of the ice were below the fort. After a survey both captains asserted that these were impossible. An exploration up-stream beyond the fort led to the decision to winter in the mouth of Ten Shilling Creek, a narrow branch of the Hayes from a point some thirty miles higher up. Meanwhile Isham had secured an assurance that there were to be no dealings on the part of the intruders with the Indians. He even obtained the promise that all their trading goods should be lodged in the fort. This was not kept in the deed, but the two captains carefully refrained from trade relations with the savages. Here again the Governor was succesful in asserting the rights of the Company.

It was now possible for Isham to give such assistance as would not hamper the summer's trade of the fort. This was all the easier as the expedition was fitted out to be self-sustaining. Guns and heavy stores were put ashore some distance below the fort that the ships might ascend the shallower reaches of the river. More goods were landed from the ships when anchored before the fort. Isham chose a favourable spot on the plantation for the burial of the supply of beer for the summer's exploration, out of reach of the frost. Storage for perishable supplies such as cheese, flour, beer, and the like were provided in the buildings of the fort. When the ships were berthed in Ten Shilling Creek, the crews were put to the task of building. A two-storeyed house—named Montague House from the Duke, an ardent supporter of Dobbs—with a passage-way through the centre accommodated most of the personnel. The officers of the *Dobbs Galley* occupied the top storey at the front, those of the *California* the back across the passage-way. The men of the two ships were similarly quartered below. Small " cabins " were built for kitchens and workshops, and " log tents " were erected at distant points which promised good hunting. Partridges and rabbits proved to be plentiful in the autumn months. When called upon to supply bricks and lime for the stoves to heat the house Isham gave enough to build one stove and loaned his brick-layer for the occasion. The crews were inadequately supplied with clothes for the winter. Isham loaned forty-four coats for the season. The fort blacksmith was placed at the disposal of the captains. In return, the ships' tailors worked at the fort, at first assisting at furbishing up the fur coats, and then at making coats for the Company's trade. At times men were sent down to lodge in the fort and work as ordered by the Governor. Parties arrived at regular intervals to carry up instalments of the provisions stored in the fort. All these dealings are recorded in the objective manner characteristic of the Company's Fort Journals in a special book kept by Isham for the purpose, in which also all the letters which passed to and fro are duly engrossed.

Scurvy appeared among the men in December as the supply of partridges and rabbits dwindled. An appeal was made to Isham for Indians to hunt. As these had dispersed to their distant wintering grounds, as usual, immediately after the Company's ship had sailed, none were available. The arrangement made with Captain Moor was that he should supply the powder and shot, so as not to diminish the supply of the fort, which would no more than meet the needs of the trade. Isham was to give to the captain the fresh meat procured by two of the fort hunters, taking the equivalent in salted beef from the store of the expedition, thus providing against the diminution of the fort's food supply. When there was need in the spring for suitable lumber to build a boat, the sawyers of the fort prepared it. Although the captains were peeved at Isham because he placed his " wooders " near Montague House and later near the ships to cut lumber, it is true, but also to make sure that his Indians had no clandestine dealings with the ships, relations with him, without being cordial, were by no means strained, as the letters of thanks for his assistance show.

Isham's relations with the personnel of the expedition stand in sharp contrast with the attitude of the two captains to one another and of the feelings harboured by the two historians, the one to the other. When Captain Moor kept the first birds—one hundred and thirty-five partridges in all—procured by the Indian hunters and gave none to the crew of the *California*, Captain Smith wrote to Isham pouring out his complaints against his colleague. Isham accepted Captain Moor's statement that his action was due to his understanding the arrangement about the hunters as being simply for his ship, from whose store the powder and shot used had come. He detailed a third hunter to supply the ships and required Captain Smith to provide the necessary powder and shot. Thenceforth he divided the birds to the ships in proportion to the crews. When the feud between the two captains grew intolerable, Smith applied to be boarded at the fort. Isham avoided being drawn into the trouble by inviting both captains to visit him. Moor failed to appear. Smith came with his wife Kitty—the first Englishwoman on record as treading the soil at York Fort. When Smith asked leave to stay on, Isham acted on the assumption that a short separation would bring the captains to happier relations. So it proved. Smith returned to Montague House after two months, and thenceforth the captains resumed speaking terms. It was the historians' turn next. Henry Ellis poured a long story into Isham's ears about Drage plotting to murder him, and Drage sought refuge at York Fort, fleeing from what he took to

be an attempt on his life by the men of the other ship. Isham
refused to be drawn into the feud. Drage was told that he could not
be received at the fort ; if he chose he might occupy the log cabin
at the marsh. There is no record of his accepting an offer which
may be said to have been cold in more senses than one. When,
on June 24, 1747, the ships sailed off for their discovery, Isham did
not, as was usual in the Company's Journals at that time, consign
the seafarers to the protection of the Almighty. The omission is
excusable.

On 2nd July the ships were in latitude 62° 24′ N., between
Marble Island and the mainland. The method of exploration
adopted was to send the boats out with provisions for a month to
trace the successive inlets to their head. They entered the opening
in the coast which had been visited by the sloops in 1737, and which
Middleton in 1741 had named after his mate Rankin. Dobbs had
claimed that it was an arm of the sea leading south-westward to the
Western Sea, and had published a map to show it. It proved to be
no more than an inlet. Chesterfield Inlet was explored for a considerable distance. At the part where it curves south-westward
the water proved to be so fresh at low tide that the mate in charge
argued that it was the estuary of a great river. So it is. But the
circumstance that it was not followed to its head left it open to
Dobbs to claim that here was the long-sought-for strait. Wager
Inlet, to their great mortification, led to a stream issuing from a great
lake. It will remain a mystery why the expedition went to the east
of Cary's Swan Nest to test the tides and did not complete the
exploration of Chesterfield Inlet as they passed by. On 25th August
the decision was made to sail for England. In the two summers
but fifty-eight days were spent in the actual field of inquiry. The
ships arrived in the Thames in the middle of October.

The stage was now set for the attempt by Dobbs and the subscribers to the expedition to attain their ulterior objective. They
petitioned the King in Council to incorporate them and their successors as a company, in recognition of the discoveries which had
been made and the expenses incurred. They prayed that they
should be granted all the lands which they should discover or settle
in America adjoining Hudson Bay and Strait for a period to be
specified, with " the like Priviledges and Royalties " as had been
granted to the Hudson's Bay Company. They asked that, during
the infancy of their Settlements, an exclusive trade should be theirs
" for such a Term of Years as may be granted to discoverers of New
Arts and [trades]." There might be reserved to the present Company
their forts and a reasonable district around each one. On January 5,
1748, this petition was referred to the Committee of the Privy
Council, which in turn referred it to the Attorney-General and the
Solicitor-General. These, the Law Officers of the Crown, held
sessions at which both the petitioners and the Company submitted
their diverse pleas. The Hudson's Bay Company's reply to the
specific statements of the petition ran, that they had made attempts

to discover the North-West Passage, and in one case suffered the
loss of two ships, that the four summers of recent exploration had
got no nearer to success than themselves, that the Company had
really made great discoveries along the coast and inland. So far
from encouraging the encroachments of the French, as alleged,
that nation was their great enemy, and they had put out their
utmost endeavours against them. The formation of a rival English
company, so far from driving the intruders out, would lose the whole
trade, to the misfortune of the English manufacturers. It was
pointed out that the petitioners complained of the Company keeping
strangers out of the country, but they asked for the like exclusive
privileges for themselves. If the petitioners had their way, the
district around each fort to be left to the Company would prove to
be no more than the ground occupied by the house and garden. The
Company expressed the hope that they would preserve their property
in virtue of their Charter long and often recognized by the Government. Affidavits were put in by both parties in support of their
several pleas. Finally counsel was heard.

The report of the Law Officers of the Crown to the Committee
of the Privy Council, dated August 10, 1748, was unfavourable to
Dobbs and his supporters. To the plea that the Hudson's Bay
Company's Charter was invalid, because issued by Royal Prerogative and because of the uncertainty of its extent territorially,
they asserted: "We cannot think it adviseable for his Majesty
to make any express Declaration against the validity of it, till there
has been some judgment of a Court of Justice to warrant it." On
the plea that the Company had forfeited its Charter " by Non-user
or Abuser " in not attempting to discover the North-West Passage
nor extending their settlements through the limits of their Charter,
but had confined their posts to the sea coast, and thereby encouraged
the French, the report ran : " On the Consideration of all the
Evidence laid before us, by many affidavits on both sides . . . we
think these charges are either not sufficiently supported in point of
Fact or in a great measure accounted for from the Nature or Circumstances of the Case." Presumably the reference is to the climate
and soil and the difficulties of transportation. As to the charter
sought for by Dobbs and his friends, the report doubted " whether
it will be proper at present to grant a Charter to the Petitioners,
which must necessarily break in upon the Hudson's Bay Company,
and may occasion great Confusion by interfering Interests of Two
Companies setting up the same Trade against Each other in the
same Parts, and under like exclusive Charters." The only crumb
of satisfaction offered Dobbs by the Law Officers of the Crown was
the affirmation that the Company's Charter did not exclude the
petitioners from the use of the ports in the Bay in the form of
expeditions for exploration. In December the Company's solicitor
applied to the Committee of the Privy Council for a confirmation of
this report. He was informed that all further proceedings were
postponed.

Arthur Dobbs was not prepared to accept defeat at the hands of the Privy Council. He turned to the House of Commons for a favourable decision. To secure this a large public must be won to his support. The press was called in to rouse the people at large, and petitions were circulated to bring the House to the desired action. In 1748 Henry Ellis's *Voyage to Hudson's Bay by the " Dobbs Galley " and " California "* gave a highly-coloured account of the experiences of the expedition in which he acted as agent for the North-West Committee. Governor Isham's order to cut down the beacon and his attempts to persuade the captains to winter elsewhere than above the fort were put in the worst light. His assistance was passed over in silence. " Resolved to distress us, he sent most of the Indians, whose chief employment is to kill Deer, Goose &c into the Country." When scurvy broke out application was made to him for Indians to hunt ; he would not allow it ; the Indians themselves desired to serve ; the Governor intimidated them. The story of the failure to prove that the Wager was a strait had of necessity to be told. The book, however, ended with the assertion that Chester-field Inlet was the strait long sought for, and multiplied arguments were advanced in proof. Mr. Drage, the clerk on the *California*, in his *Account of a voyage for the discovery of the North-West Passage by Hudson's Streights*, gave a like view of Isham's actions at the ships' arrival in the Hayes and in reference to the Indians, but for the rest his tone was objective, and he did not fail to indicate Isham's contribution to the solution of the problems of the winter.

When Parliament met in the early months of 1749 no less than seventeen petitions were laid before the House of Commons by merchants and manufacturers in all parts of the country—London, Bristol, Birmingham, Manchester, Leeds, Liverpool, Carlisle, and many small boroughs. These called for the abolition of the monopoly of the Hudson's Bay Company and for the discovery of the North-West Passage. On 9th March the House ordered an inquiry by a select committee. Lord Strange was appointed chairman and William Pitt, afterwards Lord Chatham, was of the committee. In view of this action the Governor and Committee of the Company busied themselves the day following with their *Case*, for distribution to the Members of Parliament. They emphasized the validity of the Charter, the losses sustained by the Company at the hands of the French during peace and during the subsequent wars of King William and Queen Anne. The surrender of Hudson Bay by the French after the Treaty of Utrecht into the hands of the overseas governor of the Company and his commission for that purpose issued by her Majesty Queen Anne were put to the front. The recognition of the Company by the Act of Parliament " for encouraging Trade to America " (1707) by the clause which expressly enacted that " nothing in that Act should extend to take away or prejudice any of the Rights or Privileges of the Hudson's Bay Company " was urged. The Company had sent out ships to discover the Passage ; its servants had been in many parts where it was said to be, and had inquired diligently of the natives, but found no evidence of it ; the "private adventurers" had sent out their ships in vain. Failing to secure the reward which would have paid their expenses, they hoped to recoup themselves from the trade which was the Company's by law, and had appealed to the Privy Council ; the decision of the Attorney-General and the Solicitor-General had been in the Company's favour. The Company had kept the French out of the Bay, and had carried on the trade to the satisfaction of the furriers. On account of its climate the country could never be settled ; their forts had to be supplied with a large part of their provisions from England.

The Select Committee took evidence. Dobbs placed before it a narrative by Joseph la France, a French-Canadian half-breed who had come to York Fort in 1742 for employment with the Hudson's Bay Company, but had been sent home to England. It described the water-ways, the multitude of Indians and peltries, and the mild climate. Dobbs was carefully cross-examined as to the accuracy with which La France's statements had been taken down. Joseph Robson, mason and surveyor at Churchill and York Fort, said that it would be a great advantage to the Company to grow wheat at York Fort, but many things were not done which would be of great advantage. He had been forty or fifty miles up the Nelson and had " sailed up the falls very easily." The country up that river could be settled ; he did not doubt but he could find three or four hundred British subjects who would willingly go there to live, winter and summer. Richard White, who had served at Albany, told of the French intercepting the Indians coming down ; they travelled into the interior while the English clung to the shores of the Bay. He had himself conversed with the Frenchman Joseph Deslestres, who wintered several years among the Indians. The English could increase their trade, if they would send men into the interior to live in like manner. At Moose Fort he had seen barley in the ear in August. He apprehended that the countries adjoining Hudson's Bay could be settled and improved. John Hayter, house carpenter at Albany, had been as far as Henley House, 150 or 200 miles up the Albany River. He had seen large tracts of land which would bear corn (wheat), if cultivated, the climate being much warmer inland. Matthew Gwynne, surgeon, who had been with Captain Middleton on his discovery in 1741, and with Captain Moor in the *Dobbs Galley*, told of Middleton's sailing north-eastward, when a north-westerly course might have revealed the North-West Passage. Captain Moor repeated Ellis's story of the ill-treatment meted out to his expedition by Governor Isham. He believed that there was a North-West Passage, but farther north than the Wager, where he had been. (He did not mention Chesterfield Inlet, Dobbs's latest strait, which is to the south.)

The only witness favourable to the Company was Henry Spurling, a merchant dealing in furs, and at the time a stockholder in the Company. Asked the reason for the trebling of the stock in 1720, he said he knew nothing about it, but " it could not be to make a Bubble of it, since none of the Stock ever came to the Market." He bought furs of the Company, and sold in Europe. The quality of the Company's furs, due to the northerly position of their settlements, was such that they drew higher prices than those of the French. When the French East India Company was selling beavers in Holland at sixty stivers each, he had sold Hudson's Bay Company's beavers at one hundred. He knew the French market at La Rochelle; very few furs of the quality of the Company's peltries were offered in it. He pointed out that the sale of furs varied with the fashions, and that at times large quantities were left on the hands of the furriers ; that when a great quantity of any species was imported the price fell. The Company understood its interest and dealt in commodities that turned to the best advantage. When asked if the trade could not be doubled or trebled, he replied that he thought not, that the Indians who killed the beasts were too indolent to kill more than would procure them " absolute necessaries." Merchants from London, Bristol, and Liverpool, and the Provost of Glasgow, all spoke in the interest of an " open trade." This they believed would greatly increase the export of British manufactures to a vast region.

The defence of the Hudson's Bay Company was largely embodied in a series of documents placed before the Committee—the Charter, a list of the vessels which had been sent out on exploration (the trade aspect of the voyages was not indicated), the instructions given to their captains, the Journal of Henry Kelsey's penetration to the prairie region, and the like. A number of schedules were submitted indicating the course of the Company's business during the last ten years. These may be tabulated (omitting the shillings) simply as follows, the years being trading seasons and not calendar years.

Year.	Fur Sales (in pounds, omitting shillings and pence).	Ships in Service.	Ships' Tonnage in Service.	Value of Exports (including goods for the service, etc.).
	£	No.	Tonnage.	£
1739	23,328	3	420	4,994
1740	30,279	3	420	5,630
1741	28,877	2	290	5,622
1742	22,957	2	290	4,007
1743	26,804	2	290	4,894
1744	29,705	4	610	6,736
1745	30,147	4	610	5,462
1746	26,350	4	610	5,431
1747	24,849	4	610	4,581
1748	30,160	4	610	5,102

Doubtless these figures were given to show that the French occupation of the interior had not seriously damaged the Company's trade —that the fur sales, the shipping in use, and the manufactures exported, so far from declining, had actually increased in the course of the decade.

Year.	Value of Trading Goods only (exported).	The Charge attending the carrying on of the Company's Trade.
	£	£
1739	3,477	12,245
1740	4,052	13,346
1741	4,028	11,757
1742	3,618	12,084
1743	3,613	12,772
1744	4,152	20,201
1745	3,810	21,702
1746	3,390	19,360
1747	3,143	16,609
1748	3,453	17,352
Total .	36,741	157,431
Grand total, with trading goods (£36,741) . . .		194,174
Yearly average		19,437

The intention in showing these figures must have been to indicate the value of the Company's business to the manufacturer and merchants of England and to the country at large. Dobbs persistently gauged this by the trading goods exported, which he put at £4,000. But the value of the Company's business to the country lay also in the money put into ships and their equipment, and that spent on their various services in wages, clothing, provisions, and the like. The schedules showed that the figure should be £19,437 and not £4,000, as Dobbs had it, per year. The Company went on to show the contribution of their trade to the finances of the realm by presenting a statement of the customs duties paid in the ten years previous, and put the figures beyond question by having them certified by the customs office.

The excess of the duties on imports over those on exports, as shown on opposite page (shillings and pence omitted), may have been included to suggest that the Company's trade showed a balance in favour of England. The substantial character of this defence stands in sharp contrast with the sweeping generalizations put before the Committee as evidence by Dobbs and his supporters.

A crucial point was the trebling of the Company's stock in 1690 and again in 1720. Dobbs had made these transactions appear as a flotation of valueless stock, a " bubble " comparable to the stock of the South Sea Company. Mr. Spurling, however, indicated in his evidence that it could not be so, for the stock of the Company was not sold to the public. The Company placed before the Committee the minutes of their Committee of 1690, and of the Committee and the General Court of 1720 trebling the stock. These would make it clear that the new stock was represented by equipment and goods actually in hand.* From 1714 to 1718, and indeed from 1690 to 1718, no dividends had been paid. The profits, which must have been large after the surrender of the Bay in 1714, had of necessity to be put into new ships and equipment, and into a much larger body of goods for the expanded business. The trebling of the stock in 1720 was, therefore, only distributing to the stockholders stock representing profits which had not been paid out as dividends, but had been put into capital equipment. The minutes affirmed that, on a moderate estimate, the total possessions of the Company were equal in value to the total stock after the trebling.

YEAR.	Custom Duties certified as paid.		
	Exports.	Imports.	Imports exceed the Exports.
	£	£	£
1736	1,519	9,924	8,374
1737	4,124	10,813	6,688
1738	3,879	10,821	6,941
1739	3,984	13,659	9,675
1740	3,837	11,869	8,032
1741	4,203	9,656	5,452
1742	3,028	12,647	9,618
1743	3,644	12,466	8,822
1744	4,871	11,036	6,164
1745	3,795	11,380	7,585
1746	3,320	8,560	5,239
Total.	40,240	122,835	82,595

Lord Strange for the Select Committee reported to the House on 24th April, and the report, that is, the evidence given and the papers submitted, was ordered to be printed. When the report came up for consideration on 1st May, a petition from the Hudson's Bay Company was read. A motion was passed calling for the Commissions issued by Queen Anne in 1714 to James Knight and Henry Kelsey, Governor and Deputy-Governor for the Company in the country, to be laid before the House. Other motions called for a statement of the Company's losses at the hands of the French in time of peace, and a similar statement of their losses during the wars, both of which had been laid before the Government in former times.

On 24th May the House sat as a Committee of the Whole to consider the report. Thomas White and James Isham, both formerly governors of York Fort, and other servants of the Company gave evidence on its behalf. They denied that grain could be grown at

* The trebling of the stock has been treated in its historical setting at p. 114f. and p. 141f.

the Bay, and asserted that but a small percentage of the timber there was serviceable for building ; no self-sustaining settlement could be effected. As to going into the interior, the cost of transportation would eat up the profits. Isham stated that he had fired towards the Dobbs Expedition believing they might be enemies, for they had not sent in any commission authorizing them to enter the river. He had supplied fresh meat to the ships until there was great need for it at the fort itself.

Meanwhile, Dobbs and his supporters were not idle. In rebuttal of the Company's *Case* as circulated to the members of Parliament, and in criticism of the papers submitted to the Select Committee, they distributed a three-page leaflet bearing the title, *A Short view of the Countries and Trade carried on by the Company in Hudson's Bay : showing the Prejudice of that exclusive Trade, and the Benefit which will accrue to Great Britain by opening and extending that Trade, and settling those Countries.* Much stress was laid on the fact that the Company's monopoly was not granted by Act of Parliament and that, when it applied to Parliament for an Act, the enjoyment of the monopoly had been limited to seven years. " As that Act expired in 1698, the Company have had no legal Right to that exclusive Trade from that Time." The Act of 1707 opening the trade of the New England colonies, and expressly excluding the Company's trade from the jurisdiction of the Act, did not make the monopoly legal. Much was made of the trebling of the Company's stock in 1690 and 1720, the additional stock being described as " nominal " and "imaginery." The French, by giving better prices, have been carrying off the lightest and best furs ; the Company gets no more than what the Indians choose to bring down to its forts. Settlement and civilizing of the Indians so that they would desire European goods, with lower prices, would win the trade back for the British manufacturers. No settlements have been made, though barley, oats, and rye ripen at Moose Fort, and wheat survives the winter there. " The most Part of the Countries around the Bay are in temperate Climates, great Part of it proper for Tillage, and Cattle may be bred and kept in all Parts of it. . . . The Countries South and West of the Bay are equally temperate within Land as in the Continent of Europe in the same Latitudes." All the voyages of discovery, Kelsey's, Scroggs's, and that of 1737, referred to in the papers, had been made for trade, save Knight's, and his came to nothing. The recent voyages to discover the North-West Passage had discovered inlets unknown to the Company.

More elaborate pamphlets were thrown into the campaign. *A Short state of the countries and trade of America* was written by Dobbs himself but published anonymously, and probably also *Reasons to shew that there is a great probability of a navigable passage to the American Ocean through Hudson's Streights and Chesterfield Inlet.* But Dobbs's arguments were now falling on deaf ears. The failure of the two expeditions to find the North-West Passage, the application for a charter giving him and his friends exclusive rights such as he denounced in the Hudson's Bay Company, the adverse report of the Law Officers of the Crown, and the documents placed before the Committee by the Company were devastating.   The losses suffered by the Company in time of peace and during the wars, their holding on to the Bay and maintaining Britain's title to the whole region, and their recognition by the Government and by Acts of Parliament were telling in their favour.   In his final pamphlet, *A Short Narrative and Justification of the Proceedings of the (North-West) Committee*, Dobbs says that an application had been made for support for a fresh petition to a Member of Parliament, " a Gentleman of known abilities and extensive knowledge in Trade, whose established Character had been to extend all Trade, and lay open all exclusive illegal Monopolies in Trade," but he (Dobbs) had been surprised and concerned " to find he was in Opinion against it, and under a prepossession in favour of the Hudson's Bay Company, that they had done their utmost in extending the Trade, that it could not be farther extended, that by opening the Trade or others embarking in it, might ruin the Trade and the Whole be lost, and that it would be hard to attack the Company's property."   The views of this gentleman may be taken as the opinion of the House of Commons at large.   Indeed, Dobbs himself took them as such, for he did not go on with the petition.

On 8th May the House once more considered the Report in Committee of the Whole.   Captain George Spurrell, long in the service of the Company, gave evidence in its favour.   Dobbs had made much of the description of the country taken down by him from the French-Canadian half-breed, La France.   Spurrell, questioned concerning the man, said, " I conversed with him often in our passage Home.   He said the reason of his coming from his country was his killing his consort ; I've seen his narrative and don't think a word of it true."   In this sweeping statement Spurrell was unjust. La France's description of the country is straightforward and sober. Cross-examined, Spurrell gave as his ground for his statement that the narrative was not consistent with what La France had told him in conversation.   Continuing, he said : " He was an Ignorant Man, read nothing but a French Prayer Book—knew nothing of figures." After counsel for both sides had been heard by the Committee, a motion was made for an address to His Majesty that he would be pleased to have a proper method taken to try the Right claimed by the Hudson's Bay Company to exercise an Exclusive Trade under the Charter.   The motion was lost, 65 voting nay and but 29 yea.

Dobbs took this vote as decisive.   In the pamphlet already mentioned, *A Short Narrative and Justification*, he published his valedictory :

The Person who had promoted this Discovery, after it had been so long dormant, to which he applied his Thought and Time for eighteen years, in order to improve the Wealth, Trade and Navigation of *Britain*, hopes it won't be taken amiss of him, that after so many Years Trouble and Attendance at a great Expence to his Private Fortune, and Loss to his Family, that he should hereafter retire and leave the Prosecution of the Discovery of the Passage and the Extension of the British Trade to some more happy Adventurer.

In 1754 he was appointed Governor of North Carolina. He died in that colony in 1765.

The decision of the House of Commons left the Company in the full enjoyment of its rights as defined in the Charter. The attempt to deprive it of those rights by a frontal attack in Parliament was never renewed. The Attorney-General had pointed out another line of assault, by an action in the Courts devised to show that the Charter was not valid at law on the grounds of " non-user or abuser." None, not even the Government of Canada in the nineteenth century, with whom the expense of this procedure would not figure, ventured on that uncertain path. Other ways there were of rendering the monopoly null and void. Traders might, like the French, enter the country and trade, and show thereby that the Charter was no more than a piece of parchment. This course was taken after the conquest of Canada by men from Montreal and by the North West Company. Meanwhile the French were invalidating the claims of the Company by the simple process of occupying the territory claimed by it.

8.—THE HUDSON'S BAY COMPANY ADJUSTS ITS TRADE SYSTEM— ANTHONY HENDAY AND INLAND VOYAGES—THE CONQUEST OF CANADA LEAVES THE COMPANY IN POSSESSION OF THE TRADE OF RUPERT'S LAND, 1749–63

During much of the period covered by the Dobbs controversies there was danger that the French might renew their direct attack upon the English settlements on Hudson Bay. In 1731 the cords which had bound Britain and France in a common policy were wearing thin, and the Hudson's Bay Company anticipated war. It took stock of its system of defence and ordered the factors to maintain the utmost vigilance. The guns at the forts were refurbished, and their carriages made to carry. Batteries were repaired and, in some cases, new defences erected. The abiding monument of this activity is the stone fort at Churchill. Up to this time Prince of Wales's Fort had been subordinate to York Factory. Its trade had grown till the average of the returns for the years 1728 to 1730 was 9,612 skins, made beaver. Its factor now became his own master. Because the Churchill River could be easily entered, and afforded a commodious anchorage, and because it offered great facilities for defence, it was decided to build a massive fort on the northern promontory commanding the entrance to the harbour, and to equip it with heavy guns.* The fort was begun in 1731 on plans drawn up by Captain Middleton, the foundation-stone being laid on 3rd June of the following year. The original plan was soon modified as too elaborate and costly. From 1734 the fort was continued after plans drawn by

* See map of Port Churchill at p. 34.

Captain Spurrell. In 1739 the factory house within was begun. It was occupied by Richard Norton, the Governor, in the following year and, as has been seen, Captain Middleton wintered in it in 1741 on his way to the search for the North-West Passage. Thereafter the ramparts were completed. Building went on intermittently till 1771, when the fort was regarded as finished. Mr. J. B. Tyrrell's description of the ruin as he saw it in 1892 runs :

> It is 310 feet long on the north and south sides, and 317 feet long on the east and west sides, measured from corner to corner of the bastions. The walls are from 37 to 42 feet thick, and 16 feet 9 inches high to the top of the parapet, which is 5 feet high and 6 feet 3 inches wide. On the outside the wall was faced with dressed stone, except towards the river, while on the inside undressed stone was used. The interior wall is a rubble of boulders held together by a poor mortar. In the parapet are forty embrasures and forty guns ; from six to twenty-four pounders are lying on the wall near them, now partly hidden by low willows, currant and gooseberry bushes.

The strategical ideas entertained by the Company in building this elaborate fort are not easy to fathom, all the more as it was garrisoned by little more than the usual personnel of a trading post. Clearly, it was to play a larger part than a local defence. The plan must have had to do with the ships taking refuge in the commodious harbour under the shelter of the fortifications. In that case their crews would go to manning the fort. During the war, 1744-48, the ships were required to sail in consort to the latitude of Churchill. In case of meeting the enemy in overpowering numbers they could find safety in the Churchill River, the crews man the fort, and present an impregnable front to the foe.

Joseph Robson was sent out in 1733 as a mason to work at the fort. In his *Account of six years residence in Hudson's Bay* he pours contempt on the manner in which the building was being carried on. At the end of three years he threw the job up as hopeless. In 1744, however, he re-entered the Company's service, and as surveyor made an interesting map of Port Nelson. In the autumn of 1746 he went to Churchill to act as supervisor of buildings. The parapet was still being built. His old quarrel with Governor Norton broke out again. It is probably just another instance of the expert and the administrator failing to pull together. Moreover, Robson was unwilling to submit to the red tape of the routine of the fort, while Norton was bound that he should. At any rate, Robson returned to England in 1748 with a bias against the Company which made any hearsay report picked up in the country absolute truth to him. He was the first witness put up by Dobbs before the Select Committee of the House of Commons, and in 1752 he published his *Account*—a bitter attack on the Company. As the decision of the House of Commons had ended the controversy three years before, there was little room for the volume to play any part. The question of the reliability of its statements is still of some concern. Robson says that he was told that Henry Kelsey had prepared a vocabulary of the Indian language, and that the Company had suppressed it. The fact is that the Company had it printed and sent it out to Kelsey, hoping that it would be used to teach the young men the language. Robson says that when Governor Knight and Captain Barlow laid their scheme for a voyage to the copper mine before the Committee, they found no encouragement. " They told the Company, with a becoming spirit, that *if they did not chuse to equip them for this service, they would apply to those that would do it cheerfully.** Upon this the Company complied." As has been seen, so far from being opposed to Knight's scheme, the Company was carried away by it, and in 1720 arranged to raise new capital to the amount of £283,000 within the Company itself to meet the expected expansion of their trade with the land of copper and gold. The most interesting example of the extent to which his imagination ran away with Robson is his statement that some of the rivers flowing into the Bay were " navigable as far southward as 45 degrees thro' many spacious lakes encompassed by populous nations," when he could not but have known that the Indians were nomads scattered in small bands over a wide area. His navigable rivers to the 45th parallel of latitude, *i.e.* as far south as Minneapolis, are pure inventions. This inability to differentiate between truth and fiction must militate against an unreserved acceptance of statements by Robson which may be true.

War with France came in 1744, but never a French sail was seen on the Bay. The centre of the struggle in America was in the gulf of St. Lawrence, where Louisburg was besieged and captured by the English (1745). Beauharnois had definite plans for attacking the Company's posts overland, with a force like that of De Troyes and Iberville, or with Indians marshalled at the French fur posts. The danger point for the English was Henley House, built in the summer of 1743, only a year before hostilities broke out. It stood 160 miles up the Albany from the factory on the Bay.

In the summer of 1743 three Frenchmen had come into the region and traded the best of the furs, not simply of the Uplanders but even of the Home Indians. These all appeared afterwards at Albany Fort clad in French garments and without furs worth trading. Joseph Isbister, now once more Governor at Albany, made the swift decision to establish an inland outpost, especially as the Frenchmen had told the Indians that they would be returning in the autumn to build. Isbister himself led the party inland. They found the journey upstream almost too great a task, " Considering ye Capacity of our men who are but Covenanted Servants & Commonly old before they Come into this Country & that they are intirely unhandy in Canoes & unfitt for this way of life." They passed the spot which had been occupied by the French and built a small post on the north bank of the Albany, looking up its tributary, the Kenogami. William Isbister was placed in charge. Henley House was not intended to be a fur post so much as a sort of outwork protecting the trade of the main factory, Albany Fort. It gathered a few furs from the neighbourhood, but it acted also as a wayside inn for the Indians on their long

* The italics are Robson's.

and wearisome journey, and sent them off to Albany Fort refreshed and, if necessary, provided with provisions, much of which was brought up from the post below. Its assortment of trading goods was small ; its personnel no more than half a dozen men. Though the French built a temporary post above on the Albany near its confluence with the Ogoki, their water-way from Nipigon, and a little below Martin's Falls, Henley House passed through the war unapproached.

In 1743 orders were received at Albany Fort to explore the whole coast of East Main. In the following summer the East Main sloop and a consort entered all the rivers on its shore up to the 57th parallel of north latitude. In 1749 orders were sent out to Albany to open a new post in those parts. The frame of a house and the lumber were prepared. The post was built by Captain Coates and John Potts on Richmond Gulf, on the south shore of an island near the southern shore of the inlet. It is not possible to say whether the moving factor in building this post was the desire for a refuge for the ships far to the north, near the entrance to the Bay, or the fear of an interloping expedition then being talked of by the supporters of Dobbs, or the knowledge of traces of copper gained by the explorers. Every attempt was made to get a profitable trade. At Little Whale River, to the south, traces of copper were found and worked by miners, but in vain. A small house was built at that river to accommodate the miners, and for men engaged in whaling. The fur trade of the region proved but small. The post was closed in 1759.

Richmond Fort bears the ill-repute of being the one post in Rupert's Land at which the blood of natives was shed. Eskimos, who had never seen Europeans, had been received at the fort and treated with civility. Later, finding only a boy in charge of the house at the Little Whale River, they plundered the place and carried off the boy. Two Eskimos visiting the fort were seized in the hope that the lad would be given up in exchange. They were put in irons. Unfortunately, ignorance of the language made explanations impossible, but, as the men took their seizure composedly, it was thought that they understood. As the boy was not brought in (he had in fact been murdered), an armed party was sent out to search for him. When the Eskimos saw it leaving they grew excited, and seizing guns which stood in the apartment used them as bludgeons to attack some servants. The servants knew the guns to be loaded and, fearing for their lives should they go off, shot the Eskimos down. The lack of the language to make explanations and a decision taken in a panic resulted in an episode which stands by itself in the annals of the region east of the Rocky Mountains.

The plan sketched by Beauharnois at the beginning of the war, to attack the Company's posts, might have come to reality if La Vérendrye and his three sons had been in the Western Posts. Their hold of the Indians was such that they might have led them down against York Fort, and an enterprise of the kind would have been undertaken with ardour. Nicolas-Joseph de Noyelles, Sieur de

Fleurimont, successor to La Vérendrye, was an officer of a different temperament. True, his record as a man and as commandant from time to time at Detroit was faultless, but he had been blamed for his conduct of the war with the Sakis in the valley of the Mississippi, particularly for coming to terms with them when the desertion of his Indians had left him with what he considered an inferior force. His position in his new command during the war must have been far from comfortable. He was a stranger to the savages, and his posts were ill-supplied with men and goods, for the British Navy made the overseas trade of La Nouvelle France precarious. At the end of his second year he asked to be relieved, but was kept at his post for a third year (1744–47). In announcing his appointment to Maurepas, Beauharnois had written that he was the " most suitable person both for negotiating with the savages . . . and for keeping them at peace with the Sioux and getting them to trouble the English," but he remained passive of necessity. Beauharnois added a phrase to placate the Minister : " That officer will not lose sight of the discovery of the Western Sea," but, in truth, Noyelles remained so inactive as to be regarded by the Court as " even more inefficient than the others in pursuing the work of exploration." Nothing could demonstrate more clearly the unreasonableness of Maurepas in the matter of the Search for the Western Sea than his condemnation of Noyelles for slackness in the pursuit of that enterprise during the difficult years of the war and at his own cost, when the returns of the trade were probably slim.

That the French were comparatively inactive during the first two years of Noyelles's command is testified by the correspondence of York Fort, which makes no mention of their encroachments beyond the fact that they had not been able to fit so many pedlars of late. However, in 1746, according to the report of Governor Isham, they arrived with " 6 Large Luckage boats to their nearest fort to us (being 3 forts but a small distance from Each other) and I am informed there will be as many more this fall." The forts would be Bourbon on Cedar Lake (the nearest), Dauphin, and La Reine. Isham added despairingly : " I Doubt itt will be unpossible to Encrease ye trade to any Hight at this place." An Indian reported that an attack on York Fort was being planned for the following year. Noyelles retired in 1747 and was placed temporarily in command at Michilimackinac, where there was trouble with the Indians.

On October 15, 1746, Beauharnois wrote to Maurepas contrasting La Vérendrye's fitness for the Search for the Western Sea with the standstill of Noyelles for two years. The Court seems to have made no definite response. Apparently, relying on the favourable light in which Noyelles's inertness had placed the La Vérendryes, in 1747 he sent Pierre and the Chevalier de la Vérendrye to carry on the trade of the Western Posts, doubtless hoping that the Court would relent, as indeed it did, and reappoint the father. The sons spent the winter at the northerly posts facing the English. In the spring of 1749 the Chevalier ascended the River Saskatchewan (Paskoyac), probably from Fort Bourbon, to the confluence of the north and south branches " where is the rendezvous every spring of the Crees of the Mountains, Prairies and Rivers to deliberate as to what they shall do—go and trade with the French or with the English." That year the French carried off the main part of the trade in small furs at the expense of York Fort. There is no evidence that Fort Paskoyac, at the present The Pas, was built at this time. The Chevalier may well have pointed out the advantage of the site on the waterway of the Indians to York Fort. The post must have been built at the order of Pierre la Vérendrye in the summer of 1750 and have been first occupied by Niverville that autumn.

In the summer of 1749 the Chevalier went down to Montreal with the furs, and was present at his father's death in December. Pierre spent the winter of 1749–50 in the southern part of the command, rebuilding Fort Maurepas on the River Winnipeg, which had been burned by the Indians, and repairing La Reine, which was in a dilapidated state. This does not imply that the northern posts were unoccupied. Indeed François Jérôme, a servant at Fort Bourbon, wrote to York Fort by an Indian saying that he had heard from the bearer that there was an intention of sending an Englishman inland. " You can do it with safety ; have no fear of us." He inquired whether the English would make cash payments for furs ; if so, a little trade could be carried on secretly ; he would have to have a list of the prices. He sent an oboe, the first evidence of the plaintive reed by the shores of a western lake, in the hope that it could be repaired. The instrument was sent back repaired (by the blacksmith ?). John Newton, then in charge, replied haughtily that his employers were too generous with their servants to leave room for any temptation to carry on an illicit trade ; " if Yours are Different, I am sorry for it."

Pierre la Vérendrye took out his furs to Michilimackinac in the spring of 1750. There he heard of the death of his father. He hastened to Quebec to urge his claims to the command of the Western Posts, only to find that the whole administration of the colony had been changed to the disadvantage of his family. At least the new men were oblivious of their achievements. The French Court had blamed Beauharnois for the loss of Louisburg to the English (1745) and recalled him. The Marquis de la Jonquière had been appointed Governor-General in his place, but had been captured on his passage out by Admiral Anson at the battle of Cape Finisterre (1747) and was held in England. The Marquis de la Galissonnière was placed temporarily in charge of the colony. He landed at Quebec in September 1747. He was much impressed with the value of the services of La Vérendrye, and secured his reappointment to the command of the Western Posts, but his short-lived authority came to an end when La Jonquière landed in Canada on August 15, 1749, and assumed the government.

Jacques-Pierre de Taffanel, Marquis de la Jonquière, now about sixty-five years of age, had spent his life in the navy ; his courage was offset by his parsimony. Already rich, he won the reputation of grasping at wealth, though tottering to the grave, and of hoarding his gains to the end of his days. His dealings in the fur trade drew sharp criticisms upon his administration, but it is only fair to add that he claimed that his rigour in suppressing the illicit trade with the English was the secret of the calumnies heaped upon his head. He appears to have governed Canada well, but certainly he was grossly unjust to the La Vérendrye sons. He found them with very definite claims upon the Posts of the West. After all, the great command west of Lake Superior was not the creation of the father alone, but of the whole family. One son, Jean-Baptiste, had come by death in what his father took to be the cause of France. The second son, Pierre, had served in the command for fifteen years at least with fidelity. He had acquired the language of the Crees—a very great asset, surely. Under his father he had made good the French claim to the basin of Lake Winnipeg by building forts Dauphin and Bourbon. He claimed that his exploration of the Missouri in 1741 had brought him to the neighbourhood of two Spanish posts. During the war he had served under M. de Saint-Pierre on a foray from Montreal to Saratoga (1745). In the following year he was in Acadia, and served in a raid against the English, who then held the Fort La Joye, where Charlottetown the captial of Prince Edward Island now stands. In the winter of 1746–47 he was again in Canada, and served with a force under M. de Saint-Pierre shielding Montreal from the Mohawks. His services were so far recognized that he was gazetted ensign in 1748. He had returned to the Posts of the West in 1747 and, as will be seen, the goods lying there were his, and he was under contract to pay the men in the service.

La Vérendrye's third son, François, eludes close observation. As he did no more than earn his epaulettes as a cadet, his services could not have been conspicuous. The youngest son, Louis-Joseph, for some reason dubbed Le Chevalier, appears to have inherited his father's power to win the affection of the savages. Too young to go into the Upper Country when first the La Vérendryes went, he spent the winter of 1734–35 learning mathematics and drawing so as to be able to map the regions being occupied, and in the spring went into the interior with his father. He must have been at Fort St. Charles at the time of the massacre, for what with the dearth of men he was put in charge of the canoes going in the autumn to Fort Maurepas. He was instructed to go to the Mandans, should circumstances permit. Next autumn Crees from this fort, at a council held at Fort St. Charles, asked to have him winter with them as an adopted son. When his father reached Fort Maurepas in the winter, the Chevalier went with his savage relatives north into the lower basin of Lake Winnipeg. He is next heard of as in charge of Fort St. Charles during his father's absence in Canada in 1737–38. During the Mandan expedition he bore the standard of France at the head of the host, acted as Cree interpreter, and took charge of the detachment which went on to visit the forts on the Missouri. It was his compass that indicated the direction of the river as south-west-by-south, and his calculation that registered the latitude of the prairie fort. No sooner was the party back at Fort La Reine than the Chevalier was told off to make the circuit of Lake Winnipeg and choose the sites for Forts Dauphin and Bourbon, where they would hold the Indians from going to the Bay. Again, when the father was in Montreal in 1741–42, Pierre being with the Mandans, the Chevalier was left in charge of the command. In 1742–43 he and his brother François made their fine, if mistaken, attempt to reach the Sea of the West with the assistance of the Gens des Chevaux. In these last years, till the spring of 1749, he had been in the Posts of the West with Pierre. His services were not without recognition, for he was gazetted as ensign of the second class on his return.

Altogether the La Vérendrye family, and particularly the Chevalier, merited some consideration on the part of La Jonquière, more especially as they had goods stored in the posts and Indians indebted to them, but they were summarily set aside in favour of Jacques Repentigny Legardeur de Saint-Pierre, who had been Pierre la Vérendrye's superior officer during the war and who held at the time the important command of Michilimackinac. Saint-Pierre was experienced both in Indian warfare and managing posts, for he had been in charge of Fort Beauharnois at Lake Pepin among the Sioux. Probably he did not know the language of the Crees, and there would be some presumption that the Indians who had grown attached to the La Vérendrye sons would not welcome him greatly. Lack of knowledge of the man and of the circumstances of the appointment make it impossible to assert that it was a bad appointment, but it can be said that the transfer of the Western Posts to him was carried out with a total disregard of generosity, not to say justice, to the great Commandant's sons.

Pierre la Vérendrye forthwith addressed an appeal to the Minister Rouillé in which he rehearsed his own and his family's services to the colony, and added :

Not only have they incurred heavy losses in the establishment of the Posts of the West, but they have in addition been deprived of the enjoyment of an advantage which they regarded as the fruit of their labours, have devoted their youth, expended their means, sold even any property they possessed in Canada to make up what was lacking to perfect a system of establishments so profitable to Canada. After all their outlay they had the grief of seeing a stranger pluck the grapes from the vine which they had had the trouble of planting, the credits which they had given [to the Indians] lost, such of their goods as remained in the forts given away without hope of deriving profit from them, their provisions consumed by outsiders, while in addition to all this, the hired men whom they have to pay are being employed by others. All this will reveal their situation, their father gone, their money gone, without advancement, without fortune, burdened with debts, and with no visible hope of discharging them.

The Chevalier's appeal to the Minister Rouillé for some sort of employment, dated September 30, 1750, shows that the La Vérendrye

sons were allowed to do something towards liquiding their assets in
the Upper Country, but the " envy " and " calumny " which deprived them of the succession to their father followed them even in
their attempts to escape from their calamity with the least possible
loss.

Great as was my grief at the time, I could never have imagined or
foreseen all that I lost in losing my father. Succeeding to his engagements
and responsibilities, I ventured to hope that I should succeed to the same
advantages. I had the honour to write on the subject at once to the Marquis
de la Jonquière, informing him that I had recovered from an indisposition
from which I had been suffering, and which might serve as a pretext to some
one seeking to supplant me. His reply was that he had chosen Monsieur
de Saint-Pierre to go to the Western Sea. I started at once from Montreal
where I was for Quebec ; I represented the situation in which I was left by
my father ; there was more than one post in the direction of the Western
Sea ; I and my brothers would be delighted to be under the orders of Monsieur
de Saint-Pierre ; we would content ourselves, if necessary, with a single
post and the most distant one ; we even limited our request to going in
advance, so that, while pushing the work of exploration we might be able
to derive advantage from my deceased father's latest purchases and from
what remained to us at the posts ; that we should thus have the consolation
of making our utmost efforts to meet the wishes of the Court. The Marquis
de la Jonquière, though feeling the force of my representations, and as it
seemed to me touched by them, told me at last that Monsieur de Saint-Pierre
did not want either me or my brothers. I asked what would become of our
credits, but Monsieur de Saint-Pierre had spoken, and I could not obtain
anything. I returned to Montreal with this consoling information and
offered for sale a small piece of property, all that I had inherited from my
late father, the proceeds of which served to satisfy my most urgent creditors.
Meanwhile the season was advancing ; it was a question of going as usual
to the rendezvous assigned to my hired men so as to save their lives, and
get the returns which without this precaution, would be liable to be pillaged
and abandoned. I obtained permission to do this, in spite of Monsieur de
Saint-Pierre, and only subject to conditions and restrictions such as might
be imposed on the commonest voyageur ; even so, scarcely had I left before
Monsieur de Saint-Pierre complained of my having done so, alleging that
my starting before him injured him to the amount of more than ten thousand
francs ; he also accused me without the slightest ceremony of having loaded
my canoe beyond the permission accorded me. The accusation was examined
and my canoe pursued. . . . He overtook me at Michilimackinac, and if I
can believe what he said, he was in the wrong in acting as he did ; he was
vexed with himself for not having me and my brothers with him. He
expressed much regret to me and paid me many compliments. However
it may be, that is his mode of action ; it is difficult for me to recognize either
good faith or humanity in it. . . . All the same I am ruined ; my returns
for this year only half collected, and then after a thousand difficulties, make
the disaster complete ; with credit stopped in relation both to my father and
myself, I am in debt over twenty thousand francs ; I remain without funds
and without patrimony ; I am a simple ensign of the second grade ; my
elder brother has only the same rank as myself, while my cadet brother is
only a cadet with epaulettes. . . . There are in the hands of Your Highness
resources of compensation and consolation, and I venture to hope for some
benefit from them. To find ourselves thus excluded from the West would
be to find ourselves robbed in the most cruel manner of a species of heritage
of which we should have had all that was bitter and others all that was sweet."

It was in vain. The La Vérendrye sons, for all their experience
and gifts, were excluded from the command, even from the most

subordinate post in the West, and denied the meanest appointment in their native colony. Yet they, with their father, stand out to-day as embodying the finest spirit of the French race. Few countries have the perception to honour their best children in their lifetime. They all raise fulsome monuments to them when their bodies have mouldered in the grave.

We have the story of Saint-Pierre's day of command in the form of a Journal. It may, of course, have come down to us in an imperfect form, but even allowing for that, it shows neither the clearness nor the intelligence, not even the carefulness, much less the vivacity and joy in description of the La Vérendrye Journals. The date at its end is August 1752, when it should be 1753. The direction to a supposed European post on the Western Sea is given as west-by-west! At one point a blank is left for a place name. It might be supposed that some copyist had failed to decipher the name were not similar blanks left for most of the dates. The Journal was written by him after his return, and he had not seen things with sufficient clarity to convey to the reader a distinct view of his doings. The many obscurities brand the author as of a calibre much below that of either La Vérendrye the father or the Chevalier.

Then, too, Saint-Pierre proved unable to manage the Indians as his skilful predecessor had done. At Fort St. Pierre, after a good reception, he found the Monsonis " unsettled and very impertinent." This is attributed to the " too great indulgence with which they have been treated. They are not satisfied whatever presents are given them. They would exhaust the King's stores." Manifestly the new officer had not the open hand of the great Commandant. He complained that there were not enough provisions in Fort St. Charles, and in the fort at the bottom of the River Winnipeg (Fort Maurepas), so much so that his subordinate, the Chevalier de Niverville, had to go on to winter on the Paskoyac (Saskatchewan) River, while he proceeded to Fort La Reine on the Assiniboine. Father Lamorenerie of the Company of Jesus was with him, but, like Father Mesaiger and Father Aulneau, he proved unable to bear the spiritual distress of ministering to casual nomads. He remained for but the short space of one winter. Even in his second year at Fort La Reine Saint-Pierre had not won the loyalty of the Assiniboins—at least not of the whole of that turbulent tribe—for a band invaded the fort for plunder. Nothing but the courage, which the most hostile critic cannot deny to him, saved the day. He stood at the door of the powder magazine, a blazing brand in his hand, and threatened to blow them all up, himself with them. The savage intruders scampered for the open, while Saint-Pierre quietly closed the gates behind them. For all that, four days after the usual departure in the spring with the furs for Grand Portage, the band returned and burned the fort to the ground. Saint-Pierre spent the next winter—his last in the command—on the Red River, doubtless at the Forks, probably rebuilding Fort Rouge.

Saint-Pierre's second in command was Joseph-Claude Boucher,

Chevalier de Niverville. In 1746, during the war, he had led a band of Canadians and Indians on a raid far into New England, and spread desolation as far as Hartford, Connecticut. A similar foray in the spring of 1748, before peace was declared, had been less successful. In the Posts of the West he was placed on the River Saskatchewan. Indians reported next summer at Churchill Fort that the French had arrived in the autumn before, fifty strong and with seven freight canoes. At York Fort the news was that the French had threatened to kill any Indians that came down to trade at the factory. Those who did arrive had been forced to steal by them under cover of darkness. All of which indicated that the French had come in determined on expansion, and had occupied a post on the water-route from the Saskatchewan to York Fort. That post was Fort Paskoyac. The Chevalier de la Vérendrye had explored the river in 1749, and probably pointed out the strategic value of the site of the present The Pas between the Indians of the Saskatchewan and the English fort. As Pierre La Vérendrye does not claim in the memorandum of his services, dated 1750, to have built the post, it could not have been in operation in his time. This is confirmed by the lack of reference to it in the York Fort correspondence. Pierre probably left orders for it to be built when he went out with his furs in the spring of 1750, expecting to bring in a large complement of men along with his father. That it was built by Niverville is not likely, for he came in so late in the autumn that he had to abandon his canoe and part of his goods by the way and travel with sleds on the ice. Whether it was built by the one or the other, Niverville was the first to occupy it. Apart from its place in the fur trade, it was intended as the base for a fort to be built far towards the Western Sea. It was visited by Anthony Henday on his voyage into the interior in 1754-55, and is described by him. " There were a Master & 9 men. . . . The Master [not Louis Chapt, Chevalier de la Corne, Saint-Pierre's successor, for he was away taking out the furs] invited me in to sup with him, and was very kind ; He is very Genteel, but the men wear nothing but thin drawers, & striped cotton shirts ruffled at the hands & breast. This House has been long a place of Trade belonging to the French, & named Basquea. It is 26 feet long ; 12 feet wide ; 9 feet high to the ridge ; having a slopeing roof ; the walls Log on Log ; the top covered with Birch-rind, fastened together with Willows. . . . It is divided into three apartments ; One for Trading goods, one for Furs, and the third they dwell in."

Saint-Pierre's command is distinguished by a fresh push towards the Sea of the West, marked by the building of what was called Fort La Jonquière, in honour of the Governor-General. In furtherance of the plan, what appeared to be a peace among the tribes was brought about, particularly between the Yhatchelini, the Brochets [Pikes, the Kinougeouilini] and the Gros Ventres. The first-mentioned will be met in connection with the journeys of Anthony Henday and Matthew Cocking in 1754 and 1772. There they figure as the Archithinues, " the enemy," " the strangers," a term applied by the Crees to the hostile equestrian tribes on the plains of the Far West, particularly the Blackfoot tribes and the Gros Ventres (Fall Indians).

Saint-Pierre gave orders to Niverville at Fort Paskoyac to establish a fort 300 leagues up the Saskatchewan, the plan being to proceed by and from that river to the sources of the Missouri where, it was believed, streams would be found running westward to the sea.   This argues that the expedition would take the South Saskatchewan rather than the North Branch.   Ten Frenchmen left Fort Paskoyac in two canoes (Niverville being too sick to go with them) in the spring of 1751 and built, it is stated variously, at or near the Rocky Mountains.   The tradition that its site was at Calgary is based on the casual inference of an officer of the North-West Mounted Police concerning the remains of a post of an American fur company of 1833 found there when the police built a post near by, and began what is now a great city.

On 14th November following Saint-Pierre, as he professed, left Fort La Reine to visit the new fort and to reach out to the Western Sea, but he was met with the news

of the treason of the Assinipoels towards the Yhatchelini, who were to be my guides as far as to the Kinougeouilini.   This is the result of the treason. The Assinipoels going to where the French were newly established at the Rocky Mountains, found the Yhatchelini there to the number of forty to forty-five cabins. . . . The Assinipoels, seeing that they were much more numerous than the others, slaughtered them, and no mention is made of a single person saved, except a few women and children whom they carried off as prisoners.   This unfortunate event totally deranged my plans, and compelled me, most unwillingly, to abandon them.

Saint-Pierre wrote his Journal after he had left his command.   He could not remember the dates, and left them blank, and here he has made a fine muddle of his plans, probably by confusing the Indians. The Kinougeouilini, " the fish-eaters," had as their habitat the wooded region of many lakes north of the Saskatchewan.   That he should go to the Blackfeet within reach of the Missouri to be taken to the Kinougeouilini is beyond all reason.   Probably the " Fish-eaters," with whom the French had dealings, were to introduce him to the Gros Ventres beyond the South Saskatchewan, one of the tribes known as Yhatchelini.   For this a natural place would be La Corne.   It is equally beyond reason that Saint-Pierre should leave Fort La Reine, at Portage la Prairie, on 14th November, with the blizzards of winter ready to break upon the treeless plains, to travel on foot across unknown territory and among tribes till recently bitterly hostile to one another, a distance of some five hundred and fifty miles.   Then, too, his narrative shows that, in spite of his mention of the Rockies, the fort could not have been so far west. It is not conceivable that the Assiniboins could assemble in numbers " much more numerous " than the forty-five tents of the Blackfeet in the heart of the Piegan country.   Fort La Jonquière must have been at farthest near the Elbow of the South Saskatchewan on the border of the lands roamed over by the Assiniboins and facing the region of the Gros Ventres—an impossible place for a fur post. Such would be in the fur region of the lower South or of the united Saskatchewan. Saint-Pierre was on his way to meet Niverville, whose quarters were at The Pas. He was therefore making for a point on the Saskatchewan able to support a post of its own. Remains of an unknown post two hundred yards west of La Corne's fort, as below, may be of La Jonquière. Here the Assiniboins in their own land could outnumber the Gros Ventres.*

Saint-Pierre's successor was Louis Chapt, Chevalier de la Corne, an experienced officer of about fifty years of age. Gazetted captain in 1744, he proved himself a brilliant leader during the war. He was second under M. de Ramezay in command of a force of two hundred and fifty Canadians and sixty Indians, which sustained a toilsome march on snow-shoes through the woods, and attacked a force of some six hundred English soldiers quartered in the houses at Grand Pré in Nova Scotia. When Ramezay was wounded at the beginning of the fight La Corne took command, and led the assault, which cost the English one hundred and forty killed and fifty-four made prisoners. In reward for his gallantry La Corne was decorated with the Cross of St. Louis in 1749. He came into the Western Posts in 1753 and built a new post (possibly within two hundred yards of the Fort La Jonquière of 1751) on the Saskatchewan. It stood on the fine alluvial flat on which the Hudson's Bay Company built their Fort à la Corne towards the middle of the nineteenth century. Its remains lie a mile west of the site of the Company's post. It was no more than an outpost of Fort Paskoyac.

Fort St. Louis, as La Corne's post was called, was visited by Anthony Henday on his return from trapping within sight of the Rocky Mountains. Henday's Journal of 23rd May runs : " came to a french House where was 5 french men ; the Govr came with his hatt in his hand, and followed a great deal of Bowing and Scraping, but neither he understood me, nor I him ; he treated me with 2 Glasses Brandy and half a Bisket ; this Evening he gave the Inds 2 Gallons Brandy, for to get them to trade, but he got but very little trade." On the following day, however, the brandy accomplished its purpose. " The Natives received from the Master ten Gallons of Brandy half adulterated with water, and when intoxicated they traded cased cats, Martens & good Parchment Beaver. In short he received from the Natives nothing but what were prime winter Furs." The day after, Henday adds : " I could not get the Natives away to-day. It is surprizing to observe what an influence the

* Mr. J. B. Tyrrell places Fort La Jonquière no farther up the Saskatchewan than at Fort La Corne, which would be about twenty miles below the Forks. He refers to Saint-Pierre's statement : " The order which I gave to the Chevalier de Niverville, to establish a post three hundred leagues above that of Paskoya, was executed on the 29th May, 1751. He sent off ten men in two canoes. . . ." " They might have got thus far [i.e. to La Corne] up the river from The Pas by May 29, but they would not have been able to get within sight of the Rocky Mountains so early in the year " (Journals of Samuel Hearne and Philip Turnor, Champlain Society, Toronto, 1934, pp. 23–24).

French have over the Natives. I am certain he hath got above
1,000 of the richest skins." On the following day Henday managed
to draw his Indians off.

La Corne's establishment completed the long chain of French
posts designed to confine the Hudson's Bay Company to the shores
of the Bay, to divert the furs of the great forest belt of the North-
West to the St. Lawrence, and to make good the French claim to
the country. Their posts now were St. Pierre on Rainy River,
St. Charles of Lake of the Woods, Maurepas " at the bottom of the
River Winnipeg," La Reine at the portage from the Assiniboine to
Lake Manitoba, Fort Dauphin on Mossy River flowing out of Lake
Dauphin into Lake Winnipegosis, Bourbon on Cedar Lake facing the
inflow of the Saskatchewan and on the water-way from Lake
Winnipegosis to York Fort, while Paskoyac and St. Louis farther
up the Saskatchewan barred the way of the Indians of that mighty
river to the Bay. Add to these the outpost on a lake on the Severn
River mentioned in the York Fort correspondence, and it will be
appreciated how effectually the French were cutting the English off
from the great central plain of America.

Hitherto these pages have been filled with the occupation of the
forest belt by the French and with laments at the English posts at
the capture of the furs by the pedlars. It is necessary now to seek
for the true perspective by raising such questions as—How far was
the trade of the English Company in jeopardy? Was the Company,
as Robson puts it, asleep for eighty years by the frozen sea? In view
of the possible complete loss of its trade, was it inert? Should it not
have taken steps to make good its claim under the Charter to the
whole basin of Hudson Bay—its rivers and its great forest belt, the
source of its trade in peltries?

To begin with, Robson's " eighty years " made no allowance for
the years during which the Bay was being occupied, nor for the period
of some twenty-five years of war from Kelsey's sojourn in the
interior till the Company became possessed once more of its rights
by the Treaty of Utrecht (1713), nor, finally, for the following years
necessary for putting its house in order. The French encroachments
became definite about 1720. The period in question is therefore
from that year till the encirclement of the English forts became
complete by the establishment of La Corne's Fort St. Louis. This
occupation of the hinterland by the French and the alarms of the
Chief Factors in their posts by the Bay may well leave a false impression, and make the situation of the English Company appear
more desperate than it was in reality. Such is indeed the case,
as very trustworthy criteria such as the dividends paid and the
volume of peltry flowing through its channels show. Averaging the
two years 1723 and 1724 at 10 per cent., the dividends from 1722
to 1745 stood steadily at that figure, save for the two years, 1737–38,
when they fell to 8 per cent. Dividends fell during the two years of
war, 1746–48, to 8 per cent., for the number of ships sent out was
increased for safety's sake. In 1749 and 1750 but 7 per cent. was

paid; thereafter a steady 8 per cent. In this light the damage done to the Company's trade by the French cannot be said to have been alarming.

The record of the peltries shipped to England bears this out, and helps to put the situation in its true perspective, especially when connected with certain steps taken by the Company to safeguard its business. In the Company's books the peltries are all estimated on the basis of the prime beaver skin as the unit in barter and reported as so many skins " made," that is, calculated on the basis of a prime " beaver." Look first at the trade of James Bay as a whole, where the pressure of the French was first felt, and where it was greatest because Canada, the basis of supplies, was so near and transportation proportionately cheap. The average returns in furs for the period of five years from 1721 to 1725 was 19,594 " made beaver." In the next five years the average fell to 17,508. At this point the Company built Moose Fort to regain the ground lost, with the result that the averages for the next two periods of five years, that is to 1740, rose to 19,840 and 18,524. The establishment of Moose Fort was timely and effective. The Company was not satisfied with this, and Henley House was built 160 miles up the Albany River in 1743 to safeguard the trade of Albany Fort. The returns of the next two years show that the move checked the incipient decline, for in the following period of five years the Company held its own, the average being 18,251. During the last five years of the 'forties the Company was favoured by the scarcity of goods with the French during the war, and the average ran up to 20,950. It was only after the war that the situation became bad ; the average for the years 1750 to 1755 fell to 15,042.

The total of the furs gathered at all the posts tells the same tale. It was as follows :

1721–25 . . . 59,052	1741–45 . . . 68,459
1726–30 . . . 63,816	1746–50 . . . 59,459
1731–35 . . . 68,515	1751–56 . . . 52,568
1736–40 . . . 65,307	

Again the decline is in the 'fifties and after the war. It was only then that the effects of encroachment by the French began to be seriously felt.

Another means of gauging the actual situation is the sales of furs in London. If the Company were not securing the peltry required by the market, and there were a scarcity, prices would rise. It was the custom of the Governor and Committee to put an upset price on the furs offered at the auction sales. From 1723 to 1756 there was but one change in the upset prices fixed for coat beaver and parchment beaver, the staples of the trade, and for martens, the most valued of the small furs; that was in 1746, when the upset price for martens was reduced from 5s. per skin to 4s., indicating a glut in the market for that particular fur. Manifestly the London market was a stable one, and there was no dearth of furs which could be pleaded for increasing the upset prices. The same conclusions follow from the movement of the prices actually realized for the furs. The prices for coat beaver remained stable till 1750, when they rose from an average of about 5s. for the period of fourteen years after 1736, when the Company's record of prices begins, to 6s. 1d. in 1750, 8s. in 1751, 8s. 9d. in 1752, 1753, and 1754, and 10s. 2d. in 1754 and 1755. While parchment beaver did not rise so sharply in the 'fifties, there was a definite trend upwards from an average of about 6s. for 1736 to 1749 to a price fluctuating between 7s. 6d. and 11s. 4d. The fluctuations in the price of martens were less marked. Looking over the whole period, the demand for furs in the London market was steady, and the Company was able to meet it up to 1750 in spite of the encroachments of the French. Only in the 'fifties was a crisis threatened. As will be seen, the Company met that crisis from 1754 by sending servants into the interior to accompany the trading Indians past the French posts, and they were preparing to build forts inland when the Seven Years War broke out, and seemed to make these unnecessary. So far as its trade from year to year goes, up to 1750 the Company was meeting a steady market with a steady supply of furs.

As a matter of fact, however, there was an increasing demand on the part of the Indians for European goods as they grew accustomed to and felt the need of them, and a larger body of furs was gathered to obtain them. This increase went to the French, and was multiplied by the existence of their forts in the midst of the natives, creating new customers. This was particularly true of the Indians' demand for brandy, which was the most important single article of barter at their forts.

On the more far-reaching question—whether the Company was not imperilling its trade of the more distant future and actually allowing its monopoly, and with it the claim of Britain to the interior, to lapse by suffering the French to advance into the area claimed as Rupert's Land, and by not entering into the land and making good their counter-claim—there is room for an adverse judgment. If Arthur Dobbs was wrong in assuming that the volume of furs could be increased many fold to the advantage of the fur-traders and manufacturers, he was justified in his dread of the loss of the whole of the trade, and with it the loss of the country to France. The Company appears to have been actuated by the English instinct to leave well alone and not to face a crisis until it should come. In so far as the Seven Years War rid it of " the enemy," events upheld this policy. But it did not really close the chapter, for the French passed on the trade machine which they had created to the English colonists on the St. Lawrence. These found Frenchmen at their beck and call who knew the country back of the Company's factories and how to carry on a successful trade in those distant parts. After a short interval they made their way in canoes paddled by voyageurs and guided by Frenchmen into the forest belt and precipitated a competition far more damaging than that of the French; they brought long years of lean dividends, and even years of no dividend at all. Not less damaging, from the point of view of the Company, was it that in so doing they were rendering its Charter of no force and were negativing its claim to the soil. This might well have been avoided by a sharp aggressive against the French at the very beginning. There are many signs that the Governor and Committee in London and the factors overseas felt that something should be done. The factors appealed to the Committee to take steps to stay the encroachments of the French ; the Committee urged the factors to safeguard the trade in every possible way, but neither in London nor in the factories was there any clear vision of what could be done. All were wedded to the old trade machine—the trading Indians bringing down the furs to the Bay.

Governments and corporations seldom see beyond the vision afforded them by the several organs of their administration. The vision of the Committee was to a large extent limited to the London market. It was, however, aware that the encroachments of the French threatened the claim of Britain to Rupert's Land and their own monopoly. All the remedy that they could suggest was to have the British Government make good their claim by diplomatic action. This they did at the beginning in 1719, and again when the terms of peace were being drawn up in 1748. The vision of the factors was confined to the horizon of their forts. They did not know the interior, and clothed it with difficulties and even terrors. When they contemplated the inexperience of their labourers and their inefficiency, and when they saw no birch bark fit to make canoes in the woods around them and none who could make canoes like those of the French capable of carrying much freight, their hands fell in helplessness. What was wanted was an officer overseas identified with no fort but watching the interests of the Company at large—one playing the part of Sir George Simpson in the great days after 1821. It is conceivable that he would have made a point of getting an adequate knowledge of the geography of the Company's territory ; that he would have built Henley House at the mouth of the Kenogami twenty years earlier, when the French first became a menace ; that when the next aggressive of the French came about 1728 he would have had enough servants trained in the art of river navigation to go deeper into the country, say, to the mouth of the Ogoki, down which the wood-runners came from Nipigon. When some six years later the great drive of La Vérendrye's came, he would have advanced into the valley of the River Winnipeg. Conscious now that the French were contesting the claim of Britain and the Company to the great fur forest, and with men experienced in the art of travelling into the interior, he would have pointed the way to stay the French advance by a screen of forts. The Company held the Indians in friendship ; it had cheap goods and of desirable quality. It could have screened the hinterland of York Fort off from the French and made their trade to these distant parts too unprofitable for further advance, and it would have been prepared to meet the English fur-traders from Montreal in the days after the conquest of Canada. This is, of course, pure speculation. It may, however, help to explain how it was that the Company had no clear sight of how to meet a crisis of which it was but dimly aware.

In sharp contrast with its inaction in the distant field of French aggression is the Company's swift decision when faced with a clearly seen menace at home. On May 8, 1749, the inquiry of the House of Commons closed with the decision that the Government should not be required to put the validity of the Charter to the test of the law courts. But there was another way of rendering the monopoly of the Company void ; interlopers could go in and assert for themselves the freedom to trade in the chartered area. Word came to the Governor and Committee that a combination of merchants of London, Bristol, and Liverpool intended to send out an expedition to this intent, and that Port Nelson or the Hayes River would be the scene of their aggression. In the light of this plan, the choice of the Hayes or Port Nelson by Dobbs's expedition of 1745–46 for winter quarters suggests that it was as intent on spying out the land as on the discovery of the North-West Passage. On 16th May, eight days after the decisive vote of the House of Commons, the Governor and Committee wrote John Newton, then Governor of York Fort, of the proposed interloping expedition and ordered a post to be immediately built on the south shore of the estuary of the Nelson opposite Flamborough Head—hence its name Flamborough House, though Newton called it Cumberland House, doubtless after the victor at Culloden Moor, 1746. Isham was placed in charge and was ordered to offer the most strenuous opposition to the interlopers. The alarm continued in 1750. The Governor and Committee were determined to turn every stone to defeat the enemy. They ordered a survey of a comprehensive kind, and sent out surveying instruments and a wheel for recording distances. There was to be an exploration of the two water-ways used by the Indians coming down to York Fort to the Forks, the point where they branched off from one another to form what was believed to be an island which was called Hayes Island, bounded on the west by the Nelson and on the east by the Hayes. Instructions ran that if the interlopers appeared on the scene, a post should be built at the Forks in the interior, and that the furs of the Indians should be collected there to prevent them from coming down to the Bay and making connections with the interlopers. Pursuant with this order James Isham, who had succeeded to John Newton, drowned in June 1750, absolved himself from the regulation which required the Governor to be at his fort, much as the captain on his bridge, and travelled on the ice up the Hayes to its confluence with the Fox River. In the following year he repeated his journey and sent a map of the region to the Committee. By this time it was evident that there would be no interloping expedition, and a year passed with no further survey.

Now James Isham had long been of opinion, in spite of his evidence to the contrary given to the House of Commons, that the only way to meet the French competition was to form settlements in the interior. He had expressed this view as early as 1743 incidentally to the Governor and Committee in his *Observations on Hudson's Bay*, an interesting sketch of the climate and of the human and animal population of the region. In the winter of 1752–53 a French outpost, of which nothing further is known, was in operation, as was reported, on a lake on the Severn River a few days' paddle from its mouth. In 1752 Isham, forewarned by the Indians of the French plan, suggested a voyage into the interior to explore the situation, and in 1753 received commendation of the scheme from the Governor and Committee. Anthony Henday (the name Hendry is not to be found in the documents) offered himself for a voyage.

Anthony Henday was an Englishman born in the Isle of Wight. In an age when smuggling was looked on as something short of dishonourable, he found a precarious livelihood by it, but he had the misfortune to fall into the hands of the preventive officers and was outlawed. All unaware of this, the Company took him into its service in 1750 as a labourer, adding a gratuity for his netmaking. He is described by Andrew Graham, who knew him at York Fort, as " a bold and good servant "—a testimony borne out by his Journal.

In February and March 1754 Henday with a party of Indians travelled on the ice, dragging the measuring wheel after him up the Hayes River to the Fox, and up the Fox and by its northerly branch to Split Lake, an expansion of the Nelson River. Thence he followed the Nelson down to the Bay and to York Fort. The success of the voyage encouraged Isham to send him far into the interior. The plan was that he should travel with a trusted band of trading Indians in one of their canoes, in which three men could travel, and that he should live like an Indian. So indeed Henday did. When the band reached their families in the valley of the Carrot River and began to travel overland to the plains, they would pass over their burdens for the squaws to carry along with the rest of the baggage. Probably at this point Henday took unto himself a squaw and was free to march and hunt with the men. Incidentally, on more than one occasion when there was difficulty, this lady, whom Henday describes in his Journal as his bedfellow, contributed to the success of his voyage by keeping him well informed of what the Indians about him were saying and proposing. As connections of the kind were prohibited in the service, Isham eliminated all reference to her in the official copy of Henday's Journal forwarded to the Governor and Committee. The connection is prophetic of changes to be wrought in the service when the Company will form settlements in the interior.

Henday received Instructions from Isham in the formal manner customary with the Company. He was to go with a trusty Indian named Conawapa for his companion, and to proceed with the captain of the band, Attikosish, who had undertaken to conduct him safely to his country and as far as the Earchithinues (Blackfeet), who had not yet come to traffic at the fort. To these (and indeed to all the tribes) he was to give presents to win them to peace with the other tribes, and he was to instruct them how to catch beaver and to cure the skins, and how to paddle canoes, of which they were ignorant, and finally he was to persuade two or three to come to the fort with him, assuring them that they would be treated with civility and generosity. He was to keep a Journal, noting his directions and distances, the character of the water-way and of the country around it. He must be back by 10th August, presumably, of the following year. If he should meet with the French he was " to use them kindly," but he could not be " too Carefull in regard to their fondling and Skeeming Disposition." He was to encourage the natives to trade with the fort, and he could depend on receiving a sufficient reward from the Company. Henday's Journal has survived in the official copy sent by Governor Isham to the Governor and Committee, and in two versions made, both with the original before the copyist. These last date from some fourteen years later, when the intrusion of the Englishmen from Montreal turned the attention of the Committee once more to the policy of building posts in the interior. The three versions are necessary for a full sight of Henday's doings in the Upper Country.

On 26th June Henday left York Fort and was taken by the Indians along one of their customary water-routes to the Saskatchewan. He ascended the Hayes to the Fox River. By its southern branch, our Leaf River, he came to the portage leading to the expansion of the Nelson River known as Cross Lake, his Nelson Pond. At the western end of this he entered the Minago, his Minishco River, and portaged from its upper waters into " Othenum " (the Oo-tea-towen or Mesha, *i.e.* Mooswa Lake of Matthew Cocking), our Moose Lake. Its outlet brought him into the Summerberry branch of the Saskatchewan. This he ascended, reaching the French Fort Paskoyac on 22nd July.

The ways of censors are mysterious. At any rate, Isham judged it necessary not to pass on to the Governor and Committee in its entirety Henday's description of what he saw at " Basquiea."

On my arrival, two french men Came out, when followed a great deal of Bowing and Scraping between us, and then we entered their fort (or more properly a Hogstye) for in short it is no Better ; they have neither victuals nor drink, Except a Little Ruhigan [dried meat] ; they are very lazy, not one stick of wood anigh their house ; they asked me where the Letter was ; I told them I had no Letter, nor did not see any reason for one, but that the Country belonged to us as much as to them ; he made answer it did not, and that he would detain me there, and send me home to france ; I said I knew france as well as he did and was not afraid to go [there], more than himself, which made Monsieur a Little Cooler.

Here follows the description of the building already given. The next day relations were improved by Henday's gift of two feet of Brazil tobacco and the return gift of dried meat, which was very acceptable, for the Englishman had not a morsel to eat.

On the following day Henday's party proceeded six miles up the

Saskatchewan. They then avoided the long sweep of the river to the north with its strong adverse current by entering the Birch River, and so to the still water of Saskeram Lake. Here the Indians must have found signs indicating that their families were up the valley of the Carrot River. Turning back they ascended that stream to its shoals, where they abandoned their canoes. By a quick and hungry march they reached their families. A further forced march, for all were starving, brought them to a land of many berries and of moose and red deer. On 31st July two tents of Assiniboins were met with whom Henday smoked and talked, urging them to go with him to York Fort the following spring. This was the Englishman's constant theme, but in this case the disconcerting reply came : " We are conveniently supplied from the French House." Henday's party continued in a general south-westerly direction, now over hills and through dales, now in light woods and along tall " ledges " of trees, and many a happy hunt there was of red deer and moose.

It was a land of plenty, for the Journal tells of "feasting, smoking, drinking, dancing, and conjuring." It was all to Henday's liking, for he wrote in his Journal, only to have the decorous Governor Isham cut it out of the official copy: " I am not behind, thank God a good stomach, and as I am looked on as a Leader, I have Ladies of different ranks to attend me ; please to observe the men does nothing but hunt, and we Leaders hath a Lady to hold the thogin with water to our heads when we drink."

Henday's happy journey soon brought him to the great prairie. The two lakes passed on 12th August on a south-south-westerly course may be Dead and Gertrude lakes north-west of Humboldt. On the following day they were out on the Muscuty, the buffalo grass plains in a region of salt lakes. On 17th August they appear to have crossed the ridge, Henday's Large Hill, which limits the horizon east of Saskatoon to about six miles. They then turned northward and reached the South Saskatchewan near Clarkboro, where the Canadian National Railway crosses the river, or more probably farther north at Osler Crossing. In Henday's manuscript the name of the river must have been difficult to decipher. Isham's version makes it Wapesekcopet (seepee, river) : the other two have it Wapesue and Wapesew. The original must have been Waskesew or Red Deer, the Assiniboin equivalent being Opah, the name often given to the united Saskatchewan. The two later versions of the Journal have notes at Henday's crossing of our Red Deer River in Alberta, one of the upper tributaries of the South Saskatchewan, one of which runs: " . . . Waskesew is Keiskatchewan River and only goes [i.e. goes only] by this name in the Muscuty [prairie] Country." This is of great importance in determining the several branches of the Waskesew River referred to in the Journal.

One and three-quarters of a century ago English eyes first rested on the beautiful South Saskatchewan. It was then much as it is to-day almost anywhere north of Saskatoon, " large ; the banks are high, on which grow Birch, Poplar, Hazle, Elder, Fir etc." The next day after reaching it Henday's party crossed the stream " in temporary canoes made of willows covered with parchment [cured] Moose skins." From the South Saskatchewan Henday passed over an almost waterless prairie to the Elbow of the north branch of the Saskatchewan. He calls the river here the Sachown River, probably from the Ojibway *seeguong*, spring. It was the river he was to come down by in the spring. It was then much as it appears to-day from the Canadian National Railway bridge at Ceepee : " full of sandy Islands ; . . . the banks high, on which grow Birch and Hazle trees."

Passing over some of the western spurs of the Eagle Hills, Henday's party directed its course along the southern edge of the wooded valley of the Battle River, killing now moose of the woods, now buffalo on the prairie. The three creeks passed in the first week of September must be so many tributaries of the Battle. On September 15th it was in sight of a large lake (Manito Lake) beyond which it reached the Battle River, Henday's Countenack, the river of the Nootinitoowuk, the people who fight one another. This he crossed twice, and on 11th October, on a general south-westerly course came to the Waskesew River, our Red Deer River of Alberta, one of the upper waters of the South Saskatchewan, and then bearing the same name as it did. His Journal indicates that at this point the course of the river was " NWt & SE " and that he crossed it at its south-easterly course. He was, therefore, at the point about three miles west of the present Nevis, where the stream turns from a north-easterly (as Henday should have it) course to run in a south and south-easterly direction into our South Saskatchewan. Continuing south-westward, Henday reached the Earchithinues (here the Bloods) somewhere west of the present Balermo.* The encampment consisted of two hundred tents pitched in two rows. Henday passed up the opening between the rows to the great tent of the chief. After the ritual of the pipe of peace he delivered his message through his guide. " He had been sent by the great Leader who lived down at the great waters, to invite the young men down to see him and to bring with them beaver skins and wolf skins ; they would get in return powder, shot, guns, cloth, beads and the like." The chief made little answer beyond that the distance was great, and the young men could not paddle. At the council of the following day he gave his definite reply. " It was far off, the young men could not live without buffalo flesh. On the prairies they never wanted for food, for they followed the buffalo and killed plenty ; the natives who went down to the Bay were often-times starved while on their journey." Henday adds his own sentiments : " Such remarks I thought exceeding true."

A note at this point in Isham's copy of Henday's Journal runs : " Here was the End of Captn Hendey's Journey which he performed

---

* The term Earchithinues was applied to the four equestrian tribes, the Gros Ventres, and the three Blackfoot groups, the Blackfeet proper, the Bloods, and the Piegans. Here it is used of the Bloods, for Henday was in their country, which was south of the upper waters of the Red Deer River.

with not a little difficulty . . . after this they only pitch'd too & froe to get furrs and provision, till they came to make Canoes to Return to ye Fort in the Spring." In fact, the trading Indians with Henday now began to break up into small bands, going in different directions to their customers and their hunting-grounds. On 24th October Henday's diminished party crossed the Red River once more—at a point where the river flowed eastward—and drifted in a north-westerly direction into the country east of the Clearwater River, near whose confluence with the North Saskatchewan the Rocky Mountain House of the North West Company later stood. Here, within sight of the Rockies, in a bush country with many creeks—a fine country for beaver—the party spent two months gathering furs, though often forced to move out into the open prairie to hunt buffalo for provisions. By referring to different "Leaders" about him Henday advances abundant testimony to the marvellous range of the trade of the Hudson's Bay Company. It covered the country from the Bay along the Nelson and the Saskatchewan to within sight of the Rocky Mountains.

After the return journey was begun on a general eastward course, on 23rd December Henday crossed a branch of the Waskesew River (probably our Blindman River). The next day, from a high knoll he bade farewell to the Rocky Mountains under their Cree name : " I had a fine View of Arsinie Watchie att a farr distance it being the Last Sight that I Ever shall have of it this Year."

Henday's party now drifted, trapping as it went, in a general north-easterly direction towards the North Saskatchewan. The branches of the Waskesew River passed on 22nd January and 20th February were the upper streams of the Battle River. His Ear-chithinue Sokohegan (Blackfoot Lake) of 27th February would be Saunders Lake, ten miles north-west of Wetaskiwin. On 3rd March he reached a " large creek," " another branch of the Waskesew River " ; it was the North Saskatchewan by which he was to journey homeward. He travelled twenty-five of his miles north-east on its ice to the spot at which the canoes were to be made. As he mentions a large creek on the western shore, it was probably at the confluence of the Sturgeon and the Saskatchewan, at the lower end of the present Saskatchewan Settlement. Here St. George's Day was duly celebrated on 23rd April 1755, the first of many observations of the day on the Saskatchewan. " Displayed my flag in Honour of St. George ; the leaders did the same, after acquainting them and explaining the reason. . . . In the Evening we had a grand feast with Dancing, Drumming, Talking [speeches]."

Henday's description of the branch of the Waskesew River by which he descended tallies with the North Saskatchewan below Edmonton : " The River large, with several islands and high banks and tall woods." In any case general considerations indicate that river as his homeward route. When the party put its canoes on the water they made a "brigade" of twenty. When it reached the neighbourhood of the Forks it numbered sixty canoes. As the

Indians of the South Saskatchewan, which runs out into the prairies, were not trappers and were unfamiliar with the use of the canoe, that route is out of the question.   The North Saskatchewan ran along the edge of the forest belt, the home of the Wood Crees and Wood Assiniboins, expert trappers and canoe builders.   Hence the growth of the brigade as it went along.   The trapping Indians with Henday were also trading Indians, middlemen to the Indians of the valley of the Saskatchewan, and of the prairies.   Beyond the Elbow they were met by the Blackfeet (Bloods) whom Henday had seen, and by the Assiniboins of the Eagle Hills, and traded their " Wolves, Bears and Foxes "—all furs of the open plains.

On 23rd May Henday's flotilla reached La Corne's post.   There were but six men in the fort, but they had plenty of brandy.   " The Governor came with his hatt in his hand, and followed a great deal of Bowing and Scraping, but neither he understood me, nor I him, he treated me with 2 Glasses Brandy and half a Bisket ; this Evening he gave the Indians 2 Gallons Brandy, but he got but very little trade."   It would have been well if Henday had been able to draw off his followers immediately, but he was not able to do so. The next day the brandy did its work.   " The Natives received from the Master ten Gallons of Brandy half adulterated with water, and when intoxicated they traded cased cats, Martens & good Parchment Beaver skins, refusing Wolves & dressed Beaver :   In short he received from the Natives nothing but what were prime Winter Furs." Henday remarks :   " It is surprising to observe what an influence the French have over the Natives ; I am certain he hath got above 1000 of the richest skins."   At last, on the fourth day, Henday was able to bring away his brigade.   Similar scenes were enacted when it arrived at Fort Paskoyac.   Henday breakfasted with the Master, who must have been La Corne himself, for this was the chief post of the district, who showed him a " Brave parcel of Cased Cats and parchment Beaver."   Henday adds :   " The French talk several languages to perfection :   They have the advantage of us in every shape, and if they had Brazil tobacco . . . they would entirely cut off our trade."

On the fourth day the Englishman succeeded in drawing off his Indians with such furs as they had been unable to trade with the French.   However, so far from being diminished, his brigade now numbered seventy canoes ; their cargo must have still been of considerable value.   On the 20th of June this flotilla reached York Fort and " were kindly received."   So ended one of the most astonishing journeys in the astonishing history of the fur trade of the North-West.   Alexander Mackenzie and David Thompson not only had a generation of experience to guide them, but were the representatives of a powerful Company entrenched in the midst of the Indians. Moreover they had disciplined crews to carry out their will.   Anthony Henday, relying solely upon the good graces of Indians who habitually visited York Fort, so won them to him as to be able to pass safely with them a thousand miles by stream and prairie to within sight of the Rockies and the thousand miles back, all in one year less six days. There is no feat in all the story of North-Western travel that surpasses this, and no adventurer who more truly deserves the characterization of Andrew Graham, clerk at York Fort : " This person was bold and enterprising."

Anthony Henday's voyage stands in sharp contrast with La Vérendrye's explorations. Henday travelled alone with the Indians and lived like an Indian. La Vérendrye set out from Fort La Reine with a large company—in all three Frenchmen and twenty servants. The one went out to view the country and bring the Indians to trade. The other went as a Commandant with his staff and his bodyguard to annex the land. Consequently the French advance westward was slow, and it was left to English eyes to see the Rocky Mountains of the north before any other European.

From the point of view of the Company's trade Henday's voyage gave the service a new outlook, and issued in methods hitherto regarded as impracticable, indeed as impossible. It led to the determination to send servants into the interior as a practice, the hope being that they would be able to get the Indians past the French posts. In reply to Isham's report of 1754 that Henday had gone on a voyage into the interior, the Governor and Committee wrote in the following May : " We shall be glad that others may be Encouraged to do the same." Then, too, Henday's voyage showed that it might be possible, and that it was desirable to establish posts in the hinterland. The view now held was that it was not necessary to go as far as the French, that the loyalty of the Leaders and the quality of the English goods would draw the Indians past the forts of the enemy to any post of the Company which might be placed within reasonable distance to save them the long journey to the Bay. Accordingly, Isham sent Henday inland in the following year, 1756, with William Groves for companion, with special instructions to examine Moose Lake, recommended by him as a region suitable for a fort. But the plan was frustrated by a sickness which brought Henday back to the fort within a week.

A second party was sent up that year on a similar mission to examine the route from Cross Lake to Lake Winnipeg and Cedar and Winnipegosis lakes. Joseph Smith, with Joseph Waggoner for companion, left York Fort on 23rd August with a band of trusty Indians from the Swan River region. The party followed the usual route to Cross Lake on the Nelson, where they turned upstream with Lake Winnipeg for their immediate objective. They avoided the full force of the current of the Nelson by ascending its branch, the East River, along whose meandering course they could secure abundance of fish and venison. On 21st September they were on Little Playgreen Lake, and next day on Lake Winnipeg. There they were windbound for a fortnight, and only reached the Saskatchewan on the 8th of October. On the 31st they were at Fort Bourbon on Cedar Lake, but the occupants were away at the time. They now were travelling on the ice and overland. When they reached the

Porcupine Hills they began to fall in with Frenchmen out wintering with the Indians. The river with high hills on either side would be the Swan flowing between the Porcupine and the Duck mountains. The river crossed on 30th November must be the Assiniboine. Beyond, they began hunting buffalo on the prairie to make pemmican for the return journey. Out on the plains they met six Frenchmen, one of whom elected to winter with their band. " The Frenchman that was in our Company all winter always told us he would certainly kill us, but the Indians said if they did or offer'd to do any harm to us they would kill them all." At the end of February news came in of the death of two Frenchmen at the hands of the Assiniboins. In March the party drifted back to the Swan River and built their canoes. On 5th May the start was made for York Fort. Smith passed down the river, through Swan Lake and Lake Winnipegosis to Mossy Portage. There the French who had wintered around them overtook him. The Indians helped them across the portage and all went to their house, Fort Bourbon. The trading of brandy began. Smith's relations with the master were cordial enough. " The Master invited us both in to his House ; there was meat and fatt, but for bread none ; there we smoakt and drank brandy all together." The French left for Grand Portage the following day, and Smith and Waggoner proceeded to York Fort. At Little Playgreen Lake, at a sturgeon fishery, the Indians told Smith that Isham had said that he wished to build a fort there. This would be near where Norway House now stands. Smith and Waggoner reached York Fort by the Echimamish River and Oxford and Knee lakes, the first Englishmen to travel over what became the trunk route from the factory on the Bay to the interior.

The plan of building an inland post at Moose Lake or at Little Playgreen Lake was dropped. The war was crippling the French trade, and the Company's servants sent inland were bringing the stream of furs back into the old channel to York Fort. With this the Governor at the factory and the Committee in London were satisfied. It is perhaps asking too much of human nature to expect any Governor of York Fort to push enthusiastically the policy of building inland posts which would have, in a sense, dethroned him and taken from his immediate dealings the bands of Indians who had for so long come down to his post. Isham was ready to do so in the crisis brought on by the French encirclement of his fort. When the crisis began to pass, he fell back on the hitherto very successful scheme of leaving the difficulties of transportation to the Indians and waiting for them at the Bay. But in the light of subsequent events it would have been well for the Company if it had persevered and built an inland post, say on Little Playgreen Lake. By the time the English from Montreal came in, it would have solved the problems of communication with the interior ; it would have had a band of servants trained to river navigation and to building birchbark canoes ; it would have been within reach of an abundant supply of bark. As it was, true to Britain's form, it refused to prepare for the renewal of the crisis, and as a consequence it had to develop its organization, so to say, after the war had broken out, slowly, painfully, and in the meantime with great losses.

However, things did not fall back wholly into the old way. Servants went into the interior from year to year and brought large bands of Indians back with them. For example, Joseph Smith and Joseph Waggoner returned to the interior with their Indian friends a week after their return to York Fort. They passed through Lake Winnipegosis to Manitoba Lake, and through the bush country east of Lake Dauphin to the Assiniboine. They then drifted up the valley of that river, hunting buffalo, and gathering provisions for the journey homeward as they went ; and in the spring they built the canoes for their return on Swan River. They arrived at York Fort at the head of fifty-seven canoes. That same year Isaac Batt with George Potts wintered on the Saskatchewan west of Cumberland Lake. He brought down with him sixty-four canoes of Sturgeon Indians. Batt spent the next season (1759–60) in the same region. That same year the redoubtable travellers Anthony Henday and Joseph Smith wintered in the region of Henday's former journey and returned with sixty-one canoes. After this Bloods, a tribe of the Blackfeet, began to trade at York Fort. In 1760–61 Joseph Waggoner was sent off with " Uplanders," and came home at the head of sixty-five canoes. In 1761 Henry Pressick was sent into the country of the Bloods and the Blackfeet. In all, nine voyages were made into the interior from 1754, when Henday showed the way, till Pressick's return in 1762.

One marvels at the safety with which these Englishmen travelled and wintered among the savage tribes. No hand was lifted against them. In this they present a striking contrast with the French, who, for all their popularity with the natives (a popularity of which their is abundant evidence) were struck down from time to time. One reason for the difference is the recklessness of the French in the matter of the Indian women. The servants of Fort Bourbon on the Hayes, just before Governor Knight took possession, are an example. At an outpost, probably Fort Phélipeaix (Philipshuck of Robson's map), the men carried off a number of young squaws into their house, evidently against their will. The young women found the means of dampening the charges of their captors' guns, and gave the signal to their irate husbands, with the result that when the house was attacked the Frenchmen could not defend themselves and were cut down to the last man. In this matter the English were wiser. Instructions to servants going inland warned them not to forget their duty to God. Pressick, for example, was cautioned not to busy himself with the Indians' wives ; it might be his ruin, and it would be a detriment to the trade. This does not mean that the men who went into the interior did not take squaws unto themselves, for only so could their burdens be carried and they be free to travel along with the hunters. Rather, they must have secured their young women according to the formalities of Indian society, by purchase and with the consent of the parties interested. In such case, so far from involving danger, the connection with the band would make for safety.

Then, too, the French recklessly involved themselves in tribal feuds and wars. This was probably the cause of the murder of the servants of La Vérendrye, which led him to send his son off on the war-path against the Sioux, and certainly the massacre of the French brigade on the Lake of the Woods was the result of the young La Vérendryes supporting the Indians of the forest under arms against their foes.

Another cause of the shedding of French blood by the savages was their imprudence in making brandy one of their principal articles of gift and of trade, whereas in the minds of the English drunken Indians were dangerous men. It was probably in a drunken fracas that one Frenchman was murdered in 1746 and two in 1753. In the spring of 1757, when Joseph Smith and Joseph Waggoner were wintering safely on the upper Assiniboine, two Frenchmen were struck down by the savages.

Similarly there were attacks on the French forts. True, they were in the very nature of things more exposed to attack than the English factories, yet the number of the Frenchmen's forts destroyed shows that their reputation as masters in dealing with the natives must be to some extent discounted. Fort Maurepas and Fort La Reine were both burnt by the savages, and in 1758, as Joseph Smith passed through the land in perfect security, Fort Bourbon was plundered and burnt.

Beside this impressive succession of ruptures of the good relations of the French with the natives must be placed the massacre of the men of the Hudson's Bay Company's Henley House in 1755. There had been a period of relaxed discipline at Albany Fort, in which an Indian woman and her family lorded it over the Governor's mess. When a new Governor, a strict disciplinarian, took charge they were ousted from their position, to their great discontent. Two young squaws of the connection were kept in Henley House against the will of their husbands. Here was, so to say, a powder magazine with train set ready for lighting. French emissaries fanned the anger of the husbands to a flame. The Master of the House was shot within his apartment in the absence of the men at their traps. The servants were dispatched one by one as they returned to the post. The goods were carried off. The three Indians implicated were formally tried by the Council at Albany Fort and were hanged.

The second destruction of Henley House is a very different matter. It was at the height of the Seven Years War. From its very position the post was exposed to the enemy. A body of Canadians and French-Indians from Nipigon, led by one Ménard, hid behind the river bank and when George Clark, the Master of Henley, opened the gates in the morning and walked towards the river, shot him down. The servants in the post sustained the attack through the day and effected their escape under cover of gathering dusk. Possibly it was because Ménard was wounded that the war-party did not go down against Albany Fort.

Apart from this attack on Henley House, the war passed over without any more than a succession of alarms at the English posts. Its most visible effects were seen in the receding tide of French trade. At the beginning, officers like La Corne were called in to join their regiments and defend Quebec. The Frenchmen remaining at the posts were little more than voyageurs and clerks long in the trade. Among them, probably, were Louis Ménard at Nipigon, the illusive François on the Saskatchewan, and perhaps a Blondeau at La Reine. One by one the posts were abandoned, no doubt for lack of goods. La Reine was still open in the winter of 1757–58, when Joseph Smith was on the Assiniboine. In the spring Fort Bourbon was burnt. It was not reoccupied. In 1757 La Corne's Fort St. Louis was closed ; in 1759, Fort Paskoyac. That summer a French-man named Jean-Baptiste Larlee came down from this last post to York Fort to seek employment. He was sent off to England. He reported that the two posts on the Saskatchewan were closed, but that Frenchmen were building where Henday had proposed that the Company should open a post (at Moose Lake). By 1760 all the French posts on the Saskatchewan were closed.

As the numbers of the Frenchmen in the country declined, their reluctance to engage in hostilities would increase, especially as the English Company was bound by many ties to the Indians around them. The Master of Fort Bourbon in 1757 said to Joseph Smith over a pot of brandy : " What if the King of England and the King of France are att warrs together, that is no reason why we should, so Lett us be friends."

The English were not able to make as much as might be expected from the decline of the French trade—at least not for two years—for a disorder passed through the tribes which hampered the business of getting furs. The death-rate was very great, and at one time Governor Isham had fourteen widows and children on his hands at York Fort.

The wider aspect of the Seven Years War is of little import for the history of Rupert's Land, but its origin is not without its interest, and the terms of the treaty with which it closed are of supreme importance. After the French had built a line of posts hemming in the English on the Bay to the coast, they turned to the task of doing the same to the English colonies on the Atlantic. The chain of posts from Rainy Lake to the Saskatchewan had its counter-part in Fort Rouillé (1749), where Toronto now stands, Fort Pres-qu'ile on Lake Erie, and forts le Bœuf (1753) and Venango (1754) reaching towards the River Ohio. Had this movement been allowed to reach its objective the French would have definitely staked out their claim to the central plain of America. The war broke out through the attempt of the English to check the building of Fort Duquesne at the confluence of the Alleghany with the Monongahela to form the Ohio. The attempt of both nations to build at this point, where Pittsburg now stands, brought the clashes which precipitated the war. Inevitably the final issue would be of the utmost importance for the claim of the Hudson's Bay Company and Britain to the basin of Hudson Bay. In the fields of Prussia, on the Plains of Abraham, and upon the high seas the fate of Rupert's Land was being settled. The cession of Canada to Britain assured the hinterland of Hudson Bay to the Hudson's Bay Company if only by implication, as the Treaty of Utrecht gave them the Bay itself. The struggle between the English and the French for Hudson Bay and for the fur forest of the north lasted ninety years. It closed with the claim of Britain made good. A new chapter in the history of Rupert's Land begins.

CHAPTER V

A CHAPTER OF APPROACHES, 1763-93

RUPERT'S LAND AND THE NORTH-WEST APPROACHED BY THE PEDLARS *
—THE PACIFIC NORTH-WEST APPROACHED BY THE RUSSIANS,
SPANIARDS, ENGLISH, AND AMERICANS.†

WHEN Canada was conquered by the British the Hudson's Bay
Company had come to a more definite though still vague conception
of the limits of the area conceded to them by the Charter and named
Rupert's Land ; it was the country drained by the streams flowing into Hudson Strait and Bay. Thus the eastern and southern
boundaries of the territory would be the height of land at the back
of Labrador, wherever that might be, and that to the north and
west of the waters of the St. Lawrence ; farther west it would include the valley of the Red River, much of which is south of the
present International Boundary, and therefore American territory
to-day. The western limit would be the Rocky Mountains, from
which the Saskatchewan pours its waters into Hudson Bay.

But streams flow from the Rockies into the Polar Sea, notably
the Athabaska and Peace rivers, becoming the Slave and Mackenzie
rivers farther north. Other streams flow westward or northward
into the Pacific Ocean—notably the Columbia, the Fraser, and the
Skeena running westward ; and flowing northward, the Yukon. By
the Company's interpretation of the Charter, the area drained by
these two groups of rivers (the existence of all save the Slave was
unknown in 1763) would be beyond Rupert's Land. So also would
be the valley of the Coppermine River, which flows into the Arctic
Ocean, though it was discovered by Samuel Hearne, a servant of the
Company, in 1772, and formally claimed by him for his masters.
By the first quarter of the nineteenth century much of this region was
known. It was distinguished by the vague term North-West Territory. The traders from Montreal, however, used the term " North-
West " of the whole country beyond Lake Superior, and the term
" South-West " of the region beyond Lake Michigan, the point of
departure in either case being Michilimackinac. It makes for clarity
to adhere to the nomenclature which was later stereotyped by Acts

* Illustrated by Sketch-map No. 8 at p. 258.
† Illustrated by Sketch-map No. 9 at p. 362.

of Imperial Parliament and to distinguish Rupert's Land from the North-West Territory.

The history of the Canadian West from 1763 to 1793 forms a chapter of approaches. Rupert's Land and the North-West Territory were approached by the fur-traders of Montreal, the Pacific coast by Russians, Spaniards, English, and Americans. Looked at from the point of view of the several nations, the approaches from the east and from the west and south were in no relation to one another, but inasmuch as they were all reaching towards the great fur field of America, they ultimately met one another. The several threads are woven finally into the fabric of the history of the Canadian West. This chapter carries the narrative on till Alexander Mackenzie crossed the continent to the Pacific Ocean and almost fell in with Vancouver, who was surveying the coast after the evacuation of Nootka Sound by the Spaniards.

The use of the term "Pedlar" in this chapter calls for explanation. It was the name given by the Hudson's Bay Company's servants to the French and English fur-traders from Montreal. It points at a difference in their methods of trading. The English Company waited for the Indians to come down to its forts on the Bay. Even when its servants travelled inland, as they did steadily from 1754, they did not go to trade, but with presents to rally the Indians for the voyage to the factory. In contrast the French, and after them the English from Montreal, went to the natives and established posts among them; they even sent servants out to the Indians' tents with assortments of goods to trade *en derouine*, as it was called. Hence the term "Pedlar." The word is used here as a convenient name for the individual traders from Montreal who came in as rivals of the Hudson's Bay Company, and is confined to the period before the formation of the "General Partnership," known as the North West Company.

I.—THE ORGANIZATION OF CONQUERED CANADA—THE PEDLARS KEPT OUT OF RUPERT'S LAND, 1763-68

The cession of Canada by France to Great Britain, formally sealed by the Treaty of Paris, 1763, was necessarily followed by the organization of the territory involved. Only such phases of this readjustment as may bear more or less directly upon the history of Rupert's Land call for attention here. The first decisions were registered in the Proclamation of October 7, 1763, after careful inquiries and many reports received from America. One of the Governments erected was that of Quebec. Its northern boundary was made to run from the head of the River St. John through Lake St. John to the south end of Lake Nipissing. Thus the claims of La Nouvelle France to all the territory to the north up to a narrow fringe on Hudson Bay occupied by the English Company were definitely set aside. Yet the southern boundary of Rupert's Land was in no ways fixed. Indeed, it was not even mentioned. As the Company claimed to the height of land, and the northern boundary of Quebec was placed well to the south, the Proclamation left a strip of no-man's-land between. This was reserved as hunting-ground for the Red Men within which the White Men were not to settle. The western boundary of Quebec was drawn to run southward from Lake Nipissing, "crossing the River St. Lawrence and the Lake Champlain in 45 Degrees of North Latitude." West of this was again Indian Territory into which Europeans were not to migrate, but the Indians, and by implication the fur trade, were to be supreme. Any claim which Canada had to the North-West in virtue of La Vérendrye's chain of forts ended when the western boundary of Quebec was thus fixed by law. On the other hand, the boundary of Rupert's Land is not so much as mentioned. The very silence of the Proclamation indicates that the rights of the Chartered Company were unaltered.

To discuss the many reasons for creating the great Indian Reservation would take us too far afield. The friendship of the Iroquois had, in certain phases, been a decisive factor in the late war on the side of the British, though their former treatment by the English colonists had all but thrown them into the arms of the French. It was due to the genius of Sir William Johnson, Superintendent of Indian affairs on behalf of the Imperial Government, that their hostility was allayed, so that the British could carry on campaigns through their territory and even gain battles with their help. The promise which won over the warlike Five Nations was that they would enjoy their territory undisturbed, and that no lands were to be taken from them but by formal purchase by His Majesty the King. Thus they would be protected from the dreaded encroachments of colonists. To us who have experienced the peaceful working out of such a policy, from the purchases by the Hudson's Bay Company of the rights to build their forts down to the long succession of Indian treaties which preceded the settlement of the North-West, this policy appears as doing no more than justice to the Indians, quite apart from the treaties which promised it to them—no mere scraps of paper, surely. So far from precluding the manifest destiny of the White Race on this continent, it really provided for an orderly and peaceful expansion. In a pamphlet of the time, believed to embody the ideas of one of the British Ministers, this view is expressed.

It will hereafter appear desirable to pass these boundaries upon many occasions and to make settlements in remote countries, for particular purposes; but this should always be a measure of government, prudently concerted and cautiously executed nor left to the decision of a single governor, but much less to the interested views of any individual or set of individuals. (*Regulations lately made concerning the Colonies and the Taxes imposed upon them, considered,* pp. 20–21).

The colonists, however, had habitually ignored the Red Man, and now persuaded themselves that, with the French driven out, the West had become theirs. Real estate speculators and eager migrants, ignoring the treaties and the right of the Crown to create such an

Indian Reservation, and dominated by an overmastering will to possess, poured across the Alleghanies and even beyond the Ohio. Parkman thus depicts the attitude of the Indians.

Already their best hunting-grounds were invaded, and from the eastern ridges of the Alleghanies they might see, from far and near, the smoke of the settler's clearings, rising in tall columns from the dark-green bosom of the forest. The doom of the race was sealed, and no human power could avert it ; but they, in their ignorance, believed otherwise, and vainly thought that by a desperate effort they might yet uproot and overthrow the growing strength of their destroyers.

This desperate effort was the Pontiac Rebellion.

Our only interest in the rebellion is in that it saw the massacre of the English garrison at Michilimackinac, the point of departure at the time for Rupert's Land, and that the trade-routes became so insecure as to prevent the immediate revival of the Montreal fur trade, which had intruded into the Hudson's Bay Company's territory ; and finally, in so far as it was a justification for the regulation of trade relations between the Europeans and the Indians by the Imperial Government—all of which isolated Rupert's Land and saved the Hudson's Bay Company for the time being from the rivalry of the traders from Montreal following in the footsteps of La Vérendrye. One of the causes of the rebellion was the hostility of the Indians to the English hunters and traders. A rude and coarse race, without the Frenchman's instinctive perception of the Red Man's view or of his love of Indian ceremonial, these Anglo-Saxons bullied and cheated him, as indeed the French had done, but they lacked the Frenchman's subtle flattery of the savage ; they humiliated him and roused his deepest indignation. In the view of the Indian Department in America, and of the Lords of Trade and Plantations in England, this shameful handling of the savage demanded a systematic regulation of the fur trade by officers of the Crown appointed for the purpose. Hence the scheme foreshadowed in the Proclamation of October 7, 1763, and drawn up in July 1764. The first clause threw the Indian trade open to all His Majesty's subjects, with the very important limitation, " so as not to interfere with the Charter of the Hudson's Bay Company." It was a scheme for the trade of the Indian Territory, but not for Rupert's Land. All trading was to be at posts where officials of the Indian Department were to be stationed. Clause 23 ran :

That for the better regulations of the Trade with the said Indians, conformable to their own requests and to prevent those Frauds and Abuses which have been so long and so loudly complained of in the manner of carrying on such Trade, all Trade with the Indians in each District be carried on under the Direction and Inspection of the Agents or Superintendents, and other Officers to be appointed for that purpose. . . .

This meant that the goods must be taken from the point of departure to the post of trading unopened ; it manifestly precluded the long journey into Rupert's Land with its trading for provisions by the way. Similarly, Clause 28, which limited the period of the licences to one year, precluded the voyage to the North-West, which required some seventeen months. The list of Indians envisaged by the plan and attached to it omits all the tribes of Rupert's Land. Finally, the posts actually established at Green Bay and Michilimackinac were too far away for them to visit, and in hostile territory to which they would not go. Manifestly the plan was drawn up for the trade on the borders of the Atlantic colonies and had the effect of safe-guarding the rights of the Chartered Company. The Montreal fur-traders could go up to Michilimackinac and might secure such furs as came down from Lake Superior, but they could not themselves penetrate beyond. Thus the Hudson's Bay Company was protected from a rivalry such as it had experienced at the hands of the French from La Vérendrye's day onward.

The agitation of the Quebec merchants against the Regulations of the Trade will be considered in another connection ; the readjust-ment of the system installed in the Indian Territory must be briefly sketched. The plan of Imperial supervision broke down. The Montreal merchants complained bitterly of the injustice involved in preventing them from going in to meet the Indians of the north, including those beyond Lake Superior. Many traders ignored the Regulations and went off to the unpoliced woods to traffic with the savages in their hunting-grounds. The Imperial servants were at times corrupt, and plundered the goods sent in the name of the King as presents to the Indians, and used them for a private fur trade. The difficulties of the situation were most acutely felt at Michili-mackinac, for during the French régime much of its trade had come in from Rupert's Land. Captain William Howard, the commander of the post, made no scruples at continuing the old French scheme, and granted a monopoly of the trade of Lake Superior to Alexander Henry, with permission to winter among the savages. Henry gives July 1765 as the date. When Captain Robert Rogers, who had made a reputation for himself during the war as commander of Rogers's Rangers, came to the post early in August in the double capacity of commander and Indian agent, with an independence and ambition characteristic of the man and a sweeping vision sullied by debauchery and greed, he set himself to do as he thought wise for his post and his private fortune. To make his schemes legal he petitioned to have his command made independent of Sir William Johnson. Meanwhile he acted as if he were lord of all he surveyed. In spite of the Regula-tions he allowed Henry and his partner Cadotte to winter among the Indians of Lake Superior. He allowed French-Canadians like François le Blanc of Fort la Prairie on the Saskatchewan and one Blondeau of Fort Dauphin and of Fort la Reine on the Assiniboine to come and go with their rich cargoes, for these enhanced the im-portance of his post and won for its commander the applause of the fur-traders of Montreal. Under the cloak of explorations and with Government goods he equipped Jonathan Carver for what was no more than a trading expedition to the Mississippi by way of Lake

Michigan. Under pretext of discovering the route to the Oregon (our Columbia River) and the Western Sea he furnished one Captain James Tute for a voyage inland from Fond du Lac on Lake Superior. When Tute, who was joined by Carver, came out to the lake, and so to Grand Portage, in the following spring, he was to be equipped with goods to winter at Fort la Prairie on the Saskatchewan, but Rogers had become too involved to furnish them. In 1768 Rogers played the lord at a great convocation of Indians at his post at which he lavished presents upon the delighted savages—all got on credit from the Montreal traders. It creates little surprise to read that he drew on Sir William Johnson that summer for something like $25,000.

Rogers's subsequent disgrace is of no concern here. His whole career at Michilimackinac shows the difficulties which the Government faced with its plan of regulating the fur trade. In the final issue it shrank from the financial burden involved. In a circular to the Governors of the colonies, dated April 15, 1768, Lord Hillsborough, then Secretary of State, abandoned all responsibility for the control of the Indian trade :

> Upon mature consideration of the present Regulations, the great expence of the variety of Establishments far exceeding the value of the object ; and the difficulties which have attended the Execution of the Plan in general, for want of a due authority in the Superintendents, his Majesty has thought fitt that it shall be laid aside : that the Regulation of the Trade shall be left to the Colonies, whose Legislatures must be the best Judges of what their several situations and circumstances may require, that the Office of Superintendents shall however be continued for such matters [as] are of immediate Negotiation between his Majesty and the Savages, and cannot therefore be regulated by Provincial Authority ; and that the Boundary Line between the Indians and the Settlement[s] of his Majesty's Subjects (everywhere negotiated upon and in many parts settled and ascertained) shall be finally ratified.

This circular left it open for the Governor of Quebec to permit the fur-traders of Montreal, under their licences allowing trade to Michilimackinac, to penetrate into Lake Superior and far beyond. Thus the Hudson's Bay Company was to be subjected to a competition which was to prove much more damaging than that which they had experienced at the hands of the French, and its Charter and monopoly were seriously challenged.

The boundary line referred to was one being drawn by Sir William Johnson at a succession of councils with the great tribes on the borders of the Atlantic colonies and westward on the Ohio as far as the Mississippi. The Indians surrendered the land south of the Ohio to His Majesty in return for presents received, thus leaving that region open to settlement, and reserving the north as Indian Territory. As the circular allowed the traders from the various colonies to enter Indian Territory—a policy which was sure to end in occasional violence and wrong-doing—it was clear that there should be some authority within the Indian lands responsible, as the Imperial Superintendents had been, for law and order. It was therefore determined by the Quebec Act, 1774, that this responsibility should lie with the Province of Quebec, to which the Indian Territory was now formally annexed. We cannot enter into the question how far the boundary defeated the ambitions of dealers in real estate, conspicuous among whom was George Washington, or how far it contributed to the agitation against the Act and to the final stand taken against the Imperial Government in the War of Independence by men interested in the development of the " old North-West." What is of concern here is that new boundaries were drawn for Quebec, giving it the west—a limited west, however. Even before the Proclamation of October 7, 1763, there were those who proposed to give this region, as far as the Mississippi, to the colony on the St. Lawrence, but they withdrew their advocacy of the plan when the Lords of Trade and Plantations pointed out, among other things, that this might be interpreted to mean that the western region was won from the French when in truth it had been claimed as English all along. Accordingly the boundary of 1763 had been drawn to deny the claims of the French, and ran from Lake Nipissing southward to the St. Lawrence and Lake Champlain. This objection would not hold in 1774, for the limits of a colony could be extended at the will of the Imperial Government. Thus the west was granted to Canada as English territory and not for any claims which the French had upon it. This must be remembered when the Canadians, and even the Canadian Government, after the middle of the nineteenth century, will be seen advancing claims to the North-West as theirs, because the French had first exploited its trade and occupied it with a string of forts. All that came by law to Quebec is specified by the Act. The southern and western boundaries are indicated very specifically. After the line struck the Ohio it was to run " along the bank of the said river westward, to the banks of the Mississippi, and northward to the southern boundary of the territory granted to the Merchants Adventurers of England, trading to Hudson's Bay." In view of the particularity of the delineation of the southern border it is remarkable that the boundaries to the north are not mentioned. Here again the Charter of the great Company is recognized, but the area covered by it remains without delimitation. Once more this was left to the decision of subsequent events. It is definite, however, that the Quebec Act gave Canada no rights west of the line running north from the Mississippi (which would be, roughly, the longitude of the present westerly boundary of Ontario), nor north beyond the boundary of Rupert's Land. As the Company claimed the country to the height of land (a claim which the Imperial Government recognized in the nineteenth century), and as that height of land is here in the United States, the west granted to Canada by the Quebec Act was indeed restricted. The assertion of the North West Company, and later of the Canadian Government, that the west belonged to Canada had no foundation in law.

2.—THE PEDLARS FROM MONTREAL APPROACH RUPERT'S LAND, 1768–71

The French fur trade had long been the envy of the English colonies to the south. Indeed, the English traders at Albany, New York, with the Iroquois for their middlemen and Oswego for their port, had been able to divert, to some extent, the stream of furs to the River Hudson. It was natural, then, that many should enter Canada in the wake of the invading army, hoping to make their fortunes in the conquered land by means of a trade in peltry. Among these were Forrest Oakes, James Stanley Goddard, and William Grant, who, on September 16, 1761, made a contract with one, Ignace Pinsonneau de la Fleur to go as bowsman with a canoe of goods to Michilimackinac. An interesting feature of the agreement, which is in the French form, is that the three Englishmen describe their partnership as the " N. W. Société." The North-West referred to must be the area so called from the point of view of the English colonies, the " old North-West " in fact, for Michilimackinac is west from Montreal.

Of the seekers after fortune in the fur trade Alexander Henry, the elder, may be taken as typical. In his *Travels and Adventures in Canada and in the Indian Territories* he has left us a vivid and vivacious account of his experiences, which are often little short of thrilling. Thus he lives to-day when all the others are, so to say, buried in their graves. Henry was born in New Jersey in 1739. He may have been connected with a William Henry, a fur-trader who was captured by Senecas in 1755, and was kept captive for six years and more. This would explain the lively interest in the fur trade which led him in 1760, when but twenty-one years of age, to follow the British Army under General Gage down the St. Lawrence to Montreal. His immediate object was to make a little money trucking with the soldiers, but his real motive soon appears. He brought a second consignment of goods from Albany, but had to dispose of it to the garrison at Fort Levis on the St. Lawrence because of the lateness of the season. Making his way to Montreal on foot, he came upon a Mr. Leduc, an old fur-trader, who told of the conditions of the trade at Michilimackinac and introduced him to a voyageur. Doubtless these men said that the French winterers were ready to take their old routes into the Upper Country, and to bring their furs to Michilimackinac, that mart of the west, to such merchants as should appear to provide them with goods and to purchase their furs. Henry, who had been planning a trip to Michilimackinac, there and then engaged the voyageur for his guide. He hastened once more to Albany for the necessary goods, engaged an experienced Frenchman, Étienne Campion, at Montreal as his assistant, and began battering at the door of General Gage for a licence to permit him to proceed inland. " His Excellency . . . very reluctantly granted me the permission, at this time requisite, for going to

Michilimackinac," for no treaty of peace had been made with the Indians, and he was apprehensive that both property and life would be in danger. Henry left on August 3, 1761, in the wake of a Mr. Henry Bostwick, who also had secured leave to go to the Upper Country. He soon found, however, that the Commander-in-Chief knew the actual situation, as he did not. After he had passed up the River Ottawa and down the French River, when he was skirting the north shore of Lake Huron he felt it wise to disguise himself as a French voyageur. In this unwonted garb he arrived safely at Michilimackinac, then on the south shore of the strait leading into Lake Michigan.

> Within the stockade are thirty houses, neat in appearance and tolerably commodious ; and a church in which mass is celebrated by a Jesuit missionary. The number of families may be nearly equal to that of the houses ; and their subsistence is derived from the Indian traders, who assemble here, on their voyages to and from Montreal. Michilimackinac is the place of deposit and point of departure between the upper countries and the lower. Here, the outfits are prepared for the countries of Lake Michigan and the Mississippi, Lake Superior, and the north-west ; and here the returns in furs are collected and embarked for Montreal.

It may be noted here that it was from the point of view of this busy fur mart that the Canadian North-West got its name, the region about Lake Michigan and the Mississippi being the South-West.

The Chipeways (Saulteurs) of the neighbourhood immediately levied toll from Henry in goods and " English milk," as they called rum. These were given under the form of a present. On news of this the Ottawas from L'Arbre Croche, about twenty miles farther west, came up to find that the adventurous trader had already engaged " clerks " to take goods to the south-west and north-west. Everything was ready for departure, but the savages brought all the English merchants now in the place—Alexander Henry, Stanley Goddard, and one, Ezekiel Solomon, a Jew—before their council, and made demands for goods which would have left them impoverished. A day was given for compliance. Luckily for the Englishmen, British troops arrived the very next day to garrison the fort. Henry now sent off his canoes unmolested.

During his stay at the post Henry had a strange experience, which showed him endowed with that gift, rare in the English, but which was to be a notable characteristic of the men from Montreal, a gift for friendship with the savages. A Saulteur named Wa-wa-tam came to his house with his whole family and made a large present of skins, maple sugar, and dried meat. He went on to make this curious explanation. In a period of devotion to solitude, to fasting, and to prayer to the Great Spirit for protection, he had dreamed of adopting an Englishman. As soon as he had seen Henry, he had recognized in him the person whom the Great Spirit had been pleased to point out as his brother. The fur-trader accepted the proferred relationship, was adopted into the Indian's family, and frankly assumed the fraternal rôle imposed on him by his strange visitor.

In the spring Henry made his way to the Sault Ste. Marie at the entrance to Lake Superior, where he won the friendship of Jean-Baptiste Cadotte, interpreter to the late French garrison at the fort of the place. Later Cadotte became his partner in ventures on Lake Superior and on the Saskatchewan. He was married to a Saulteur chief's daughter, a woman of uprightness, energy, and force of character, and through her he was able to play the part of *marchant voyageur* for the Indians of the lake. It says much for Henry's genius for friendship, as it was to mean much for his safety, that he won to his person the attachment of this able and influential couple. The pleasant surroundings of their home, the abundant food supply in the form of fish, and the desire to acquire the Indian tongue, the only one used in the Cadotte home, led him to spend the winter of 1762-63 with them. It was a good school for the would-be fur-trader.

In February of 1763, the year of the outbreak of Pontiac's Rebellion, Henry returned to Michilimackinac. Becoming aware of rumours of an impending attack by the Indians on the fort, he cautioned Major George Etherington, in command of the detachment of the 60th Regiment in garrison, to be on his guard. That officer brushed the idea of danger lightly aside, and, for that matter, so did Henry. On 2nd June Wa-wa-tam, the fur-trader's adopted brother, appeared and tried to induce him to return to the Sault, hinting in extravagantly figurative language at the massacre of the garrison. If Henry had the native tongue well enough to know what was said, he was not yet sufficiently intimate with the Indian's mental make-up to perceive the impending danger figured in his " brother's " extravagant metaphors ; he replied that he could not go. Early next day Wa-wa-tam returned, but was sent away unsatisfied, with tears in his eyes. On the following day, 4th June, the King's birthday, the Indians of the various tribes thronged to the fort and finally went out to a game of lacrosse played between two of the tribes. Major Etherington and some of his officers and men were looking on with quiet amusement. Henry was in a house writing letters for immediate dispatch to Montreal. He was disturbed by a wild war-cry, rose and went to the window, only to see the soldiers being massacred. " I saw several of my countrymen fall, and more than one struggling between the knees of an Indian who, holding him in this manner, scalped him, while yet living." Perturbed beyond description, Henry rushed to the house of his next-door neighbour, a M. (Charles) Langlade, a Frenchman, and appealed for protection ; but the French that day, as more than once in the history of British Canada, were neutral ; they would hurt none, but they would help none. It was the Indian maidservant of Langlade who found the fur-trader a refuge in the attic of the house.

It is not necessary to follow Henry through the startling changes of fortune of the next hours and days and months. It was due to his adopted brother, Wa-wa-tam, in the first instances, and to Cadotte's squaw in the last, that some twelve months later he was in safety and on his way to the Cadotte home at the Sault. Henry's parting from Wa-wa-tam, his protector all this while, was as from a loving brother. " All the family accompanied me to the beach ; and the canoe had no sooner put off than Wa-wa-tam commenced an address to Ki'chi'Ma'nito [the Great Spirit] beseeching him to take care of me, his brother, till next we should meet. . . . We had proceeded to too great a distance to allow of our hearing his voice, before Wa-wa-tam had ceased to offer up his prayers."

Of the ninety men in garrison about seventy were killed. The rest ultimately fell into the hands of the Ottawas, who were offended at the Saulteurs for not inviting them to join in the assault and plunder. They were handed over in safety at the peace.

Messengers came to the tribes of the lakes from Sir William Johnson, a name to conjure with even in those distant parts, inviting them to come to Fort Niagara for a great council. Henry went down with the deputation. He was present at this the initial council of peace, as also at the relief of Detroit which marked the beginning of the end of Pontiac's Rebellion. Troops proceeded up the river and across Lake Huron, Henry with them, and once more garrisoned Michilimackinac. Henceforth the trade-routes from Montreal to that fort were secure, and traders began to pass to and fro in the eager quest of wealth. It will be readily perceived that the disturbances prevented the revival of the fur trade in any part of the country, so that during these years the Hudson's Bay Company was carrying on its customary traffic without fear of competition.

In the next phase, and partly as a result of the rebellion, the Imperial Regulations of the fur trade were promulgated and in force. They were drafted, as has been seen, solely for the trade on the outskirts of the Atlantic colonies, of which Quebec was now one, and they safeguarded the trade of Rupert's Land in the interests of the great Company. Traders had to meet the Indians at some recognized post, in this case Michilimackinac, and were not allowed to go beyond or to winter in the forest with the Indians. Moreover their licences were only good for a twelvemonth, and precluded the voyage into Rupert's Land. Had these regulations been strictly enforced at Michilimackinac they would have destroyed a goodly part of the trade of the post, but there is much evidence to suggest that Captain Howard and his successor in the command of the fort, Captain Rogers, played a free hand and did what appeared best for their post, not to say their private fortunes. Howard, following the French practice, gave Alexander Henry the monopoly of the trade of Lake Superior and allowed him to winter with the Indians. Rogers did not disturb this arrangement. In July 1765 Henry entered into partnership with Cadotte and spent several winters on the lake, mostly at Michipicoton. His attention was divided between the fur trade and copper, and thus he failed to be the first Englishman from Montreal to enter Rupert's Land. Others made first connections with Frenchmen who knew the country, and finally themselves went into the interior and reaped the first harvests of wealth.

When the Seven Years War broke out in 1756, and the French officers at the " Posts of the Western Sea " were recalled to defend Canada, some of their servants remained and carried on the trade with Michilimackinac as best they could. The abandonment of Fort Paskoyac in 1759 marks the end of the French fur trade in Rupert's Land. Sir Alexander Mackenzie says : " For some time after the conquest of Canada, this trade was suspended, which must have been very advantageous to the Hudson's Bay Company, as all the inhabitants to the westward of Lake Superior were obliged to go to them for such articles as their habitual use rendered necessary. Some of the Canadians who had long lived with them, and were become attached to a savage life, accompanied them thither annually, till mercantile adventurers appeared from their own country, after an interval of several years." There is no evidence of these annual visits in the Journals of York Fort.. Two Frenchmen, Louis Primo and Jean-Baptiste Larlee, growing tired of life with the savages, went to York Fort in 1765 for employment, and were taken into the service.

In curious contrast, a Mr. Isbester and John Patterson of the Company's service deserted to the interior to live with and like the savages. They must have made their way to Grand Portage with Indians, or with some Frenchmen who had remained in the Upper Country, and there got goods from some French or from some English trader like Henry, for in 1764 Indians reported that they had been coming to the country back of the Company's forts with fifteen canoes and a body of men ; they got drunk and stove their canoes, and were obliged to winter where they found themselves.

Among the Frenchmen who knew the country, and were waiting to return to its trade, would be Maurice Blondeau. The Minutes of the Beaver Club in Montreal indicate that he had been in the Upper Country as early as 1752, though just where is not stated. The fort to which he or his relative Bartholémi Blondeau came was named La Reine, and Jonathan Carver shows that La Reine was occupied in 1766. Another was named François, almost certainly the Mr. Francis, whose surname is given in a Carver manuscript in the British Museum as Le Blonc. The Indians knew him as Sasswe. Doubtless Blondeau's and Le Blanc's canoes were among the one hundred which Alexander Henry says came to Michilimackinac from Grand Portage in 1767. It has been seen that Major Rogers had expected to supply Captain Tute with goods at Grand Portage with which to winter at Fort La Prairie on the Saskatchewan. François was doubtless intended to take the goods to that point, and to guide Tute to the Saskatchewan. When the goods were not forthcoming it was " Mr. Francis " who conveyed the information to Tute at the Portage.

The situation in 1767 comes clearly into view in the licences issued by Major Rogers at Michilimackinac. According to the schedule *Return of Peltries*, Maurice Blondeau sent little short of 1,400 beaver skins, not to mention others, down to Albany, on Hudson River, while the *Account of Canoes gone out Wintering* shows him, or his relative Bartholémi (under the name of Blendeau), going to Fort la Reine and Fort Dauphin with two canoes, one " Spicemaker " (Spiesmacher), an officer of the garrison, and " Blendeau Junr." putting up the security. The *Account*, which exists only as a copy made by an Englishman innocent of French, seems to refer to François le Blanc under the name Blancell, the flourish at the end of the name being taken for the three last letters. He is entered as gone to the North-West to " Fort Daphne " [Dauphin] and " La Pierce " [La Prairie], Mr. Alexander Baxter standing security for him. That François le Blanc was handling business (for himself or for others) in a large way is shown by the value of his cargo—£2,400. Other Frenchmen whose names are on the register as going to the North-West are Louis Ménard and Campion. Ménard, who had Forrest Oakes for his security, and was going with three canoes to the Nipigon country, was probably the man of that name who used to go to Rainy Lake in the French times, and who led the assault on Henley House during the war.

As soon as traffic on the route between Montreal and Michilimackinac became secure, English and French merchants went up in a rush to that rendezvous of the west, and Frenchmen who had already gone into the interior came out with their furs. Thus the machinery of the fur trade between Montreal and Rupert's Land was reconstituted. The schedules of the Indian Commissary at Michilimackinac for the summer of 1767 reveal the relative parts being played by the English traders from Montreal and Albany and the French. Of the men going to winter to the North-West only one was English—Thomas Curry [Corry], gone to Kaministikwia. (As will be seen, he may have really gone on to Lake Winnipeg and wintered on the Assiniboine River.) Isaac Todd was his security. The five other traders to the North-West were all Frenchmen. Most of these French traders were backed by English capitalists, such as Forrest Oakes, Benjamin Frobisher, Isaac Todd, James McGill (the founder of McGill College), Alexander Baxter, and Alexander Henry, while John Christopher Spiesmacher was an officer of the garrison. The *Return of Peltries* indicates that those who sent furs down to Montreal and Albany were largely English, though by no means exclusively so.

From the schedules it might be inferred that the English had not yet penetrated into the interior. Somewhat at variance with this is the statement of Benjamin and Joseph Frobisher in a letter to Governor Haldimand, dated October 4, 1784, that the first adventurer inland went from Michilimackinac in 1765, but his canoes were plundered at Rainy Lake by the Indians, who would not allow them to proceed any farther. His similar attempt in 1766 met a like disaster. He was, however, successful in 1767, and penetrated to beyond Lake Winnipeg. In view of Matthew Cocking's Journal of 1772, which says that James Finlay was in the fort on the Saskatchewan, which he passed on 9th August, five years before, the temptation is to believe that this adventurer was Finlay, but the Hudson's Bay Company's documents make the trade-season of 1768-69 his first on the Saskatchewan. There is presumptive evidence that the venture referred to by the Frobishers was that of Thomas Corry, who secured a licence, as has been seen, in 1767 to go from Michilimackinac to Kaministikwia. When Donald MacKay of the Hudson's Bay Company's service passed up the Assiniboine to establish Brandon House, he entered in his Journal of September 23, 1793 : " Past Mr. Currie's old Fort of 1767." Thomas Corry was, however, preceded by Forrest Oakes, who was guided into the country by his partner Charles Boyer, apparently a trader at Rainy Lake during the French régime. The partnership occupied a post— probably in the immediate neighbourhood of Dynevor, Manitoba, about three miles north of Selkirk—during 1766-68. It built Pine Fort in 1768.* There were then three posts on the Assiniboine—Fort la Reine at upper Portage la Prairie was the most easterly, and Pine Fort, the Fort des Epinettes of the voyageurs, the most westerly, standing on the left bank of the river some six miles south-east from Brandon Junction station on the Canadian National Railway line, and about a mile south-west, as the crow flies, from the mouth of Peter Fidler's Root River. Corry's Fort was the Middle Fort, the mysterious Fort du Milieu of the voyageurs.

It was a great risk of capital on the part of any one to venture into Rupert's Land in spite of the Regulations of the Fur Trade, which were supposed to be still in force. However, the merchants of Montreal were conducting a long and promising campaign against them. The regulations were not wholly unsuited to the conditions prevailing on the borders of the old colonies. They certainly were ill-adapted to promote the trade with the more distant Upper Country on which Canada had prospered under the French régime. On March 30, 1766, the merchants of the St. Lawrence signed a memorial against them. They found Governor Murray wholly on their side. He replied on 5th April, that inasmuch as the period of twelve months prescribed by the licence as the limit of its duration prevented them from going to the distant wintering grounds, he would disregard it. This was, however, no more than the opinion of an individual governor, and, moreover, one soon recalled. Among the signatures to the memorial were those of James Finlay, who figured later on the Saskatchewan. In 1767 the supervisors of the Indian trade showed themselves yielding reluctantly to pressure. Traders were allowed to proceed under a fresh licence from Michilimackinac to winter among the Indians. Hence the schedules kept by the Indian Commissary at that post. This must have still been a precarious basis on which to risk large capital. The agitation against the Regulations continued. On March 27, 1767, Lieut.-Governor Carleton urged upon Sir William Johnson the necessity of releasing

* See the author's " Forrest Oakes, Charles Boyer, Joseph Fulton, and Peter Padgmen," in *Trans. of Royal Soc. of Can.*, 1937, section 2.

the trade from its present restraints, lest it be ruined to the profit of the French residing on the Mississippi. Next day he forwarded to the Lords of Trade and Plantations a memorial dated September 20, 1766, largely signed by the merchants of Montreal, both English and French. It asked for a free trade with the Indians, and bore the signatures of men like Isaac Todd, Edward Chinn, Forrest Oakes, and Richard Dobie, and again of James Finlay—all interested in the Upper Country. The Lords of Trade and Plantations were now carefully considering the policy to be followed in the trade with the Indians, and were reading letters from many quarters, and conferring with London merchants. Memorials continued, however, to be drawn up. One from Detroit, dated November 26, 1767, to Sir William Johnson bears the signature of Peter Pond, who was soon to have a spectacular career in the North-West. In March 1768 the Merchants of Montreal submitted to Governor Carleton a penetrating criticism of the Regulations clause by clause. They admitted that the traffic in liquor with the Indians had led to grave abuses, and suggested that only a limited quantity of rum should be allowed to each canoe. They showed how impossible it was not to break open their packages of goods during the journey to dry them, and for trade to secure necessaries such as provisions by the way. They insisted that it was a breach of the liberty of the British citizen to be obliged to show all his business concerns to a Commissary, who might be partial, and they claimed the Briton's right to trade freely so long as they acted within the law. But the battle was already won. On April 15, 1768, Lord Hillsborough as Secretary of State issued a circular to all the Governors of the colonies directing that the Indian trade be laid open. On 30th July this decision was duly recorded in the Minutes of the Council of Quebec. The cry which ran through the half-breed crowd outside of the Quarterly Court of the Red River Settlement in 1849 may well have been heard now in many a counting-house in Montreal—" La traite est libre ! La traite est libre !!"

Now began the rush of the English into Rupert's Land—a rush which displaced most of the Frenchmen in the trade. Perhaps, true to the genius of their race, the French were content to come home to the sociable life of Quebec with a competence, while the English, greedy of wealth and yet more wealth, pushed on, reducing such French-Canadians as remained to a subordinate place as servants, and admitting a very few as their partners. Yet the early achievements of the English were largely due to the French, who had already been in the country. These introduced them to the routes, taught them to shoot the rapids, to live in a hostile climate, to overcome the terrors of starvation, and to win the friendship of the Indians. In 1769 Forrest Oakes came up with two canoes of his own consigned to Michilimackinac and, doubtless, with the two canoes provisioned by his brother-in-law, Lawrence Ermatinger, and licensed to proceed to " La Mer de l'Ouest." He would meet Charles Boyer at Grand Portage and proceed with him to his Pine Fort on the Assiniboine. A Frenchman, Jean-Baptiste Adhemar, secured a licence for one canoe to "Michilimackinac and beyond" and, doubtless, took its goods to the fort which John Macdonell pointed out in 1795 as Adhemar's Fort, six miles below Portage la Prairie. Maurice Blondeau had a licence for three canoes "to Michilimackinac & la Mer de l'Ouest." The goods were valued at £1,350 and must have gone to the post indicated by John Macdonell as Blondishe's Fort, but named La Reine, whose position appears to have been west of our Baie St. Paul, and not far below La Vérendrye's Fort la Reine at Poplar Point. Five canoes with which the Frobisher name is connected went up to Michilimackinac this year, and three in 1770 to "Michilimackinac and Grand Portage." The letter of Benjamin and Joseph Frobisher to Governor Haldimand, referred to above, ran on : " From this period the Trade of that Country was attempted by other Adventurers with various success, and we were among the number in the year 1769, when we formed a connection with Messrs. Todd and McGill of Montreal, for the purpose of carrying on Business, but the Indians of Lake La Pluye [Rainy Lake], still ungovernable and rapacious, plundered our Canoes, and would not suffer any part of our goods to be sent further. Before we could be acquainted with this misfortune, our Goods for the following year were at Grand Portage and we were then too far engaged to hesitate for one moment. A second attempt was made in which we were more successful. Our Canoes reached Lake Bourbon, and thenceforward we were determined to persevere." On this joint venture with Todd and McGill the Frobishers went to the Red River in 1770 and established " Lake Fort." It was between Nettley Creek and Selkirk, probably at the Dynevor site. It would be a fur fort, but with a view to the needs of the brigade of the partners who later went to Cedar Lake, it would procure or make the pemmican necessary to bring the canoes of the partnership out to Grand Portage. Todd and McGill in the partnership sent Thomas Corry to Cedar Lake apparently in 1771, though Sir Alexander Mackenzie makes the date 1770. As we have seen, he had been backed by Todd in 1667 on a venture to Kaministikwia, though he really penetrated to the Assiniboine. He built his post in the neighbourhood of La Vérendrye's Fort Bourbon, probably on the left bank of the Saskatchewan near its entrance to the lake, and about a mile and a half above the French site. Here Corry, like La Vérendrye, was astride the route of the Indians from Lake Winnipegosis and Cedar River to York Factory, and in the way of gathering an easy and rich harvest of furs. There was an excellent fishery near by from which to provision the post, but meat would be scarce. Hence the reliance, as has been assumed, on Frobisher's fort on the Red River for provisions to bring the furs out. In spite of Sir Alexander's Mackenzie's statement that Thomas Corry was the first trader to venture thus far, James Finlay, in 1768, had passed on up the Saskatchewan and occupied a house at Nipawi.

The entry of the Pedlars into Rupert's Land renewed the competition of the Hudson's Bay Company with the fur-traders from Montreal, as it was to experience, in a more violent form. It meant more. It was a challenge to the validity of the Charter, and it threatened to reduce the monopoly of the English Company to a nullity.

3.—THE PEDLARS IGNORE THE HUDSON'S BAY COMPANY'S CHARTER, 1769-73

It was the wont of the fur-traders from Montreal to proclaim it upon the housetops that they came into an unexplored and un-occupied North-West, and that thereafter the Hudson's Bay Company followed in their footsteps from place to place, and this legend has been the subject of self-glorification to Canada ever since. If the boast is confined to the establishment of trading posts, it is true. It is demonstrably false if it infers that the Company's trade and the Company's servants had not penetrated far into the interior. As has already been seen, when Anthony Henday travelled across the land in 1754 to within sight of the Rocky Mountains, he was simply following the lines of the Company's trade with a party of its "trading Indians." From the year after his return practically never a trading season passed without two or more, sometimes six men of the Company, passing the winter with bands of Indians in different parts of the hinterland. In the period now under considera-tion, from the acquisition of Canada in 1763 to the establishment of Cumberland House, the first post of the Company in the interior, in 1774, no less than forty-four journeys were accomplished by the Company's servants to the wintering grounds of the "Leaders," often on the upper waters of the Saskatchewan and at times of the Churchill River.

As each of the Company's servants travelled with a trusted Leader and his band, the routes followed were the customary water-ways. Familiarity with these routes is necessary for a clear vision of the course of events. With a map before him, the reader would jump to the conclusion that that magnificent stream the Nelson would be the most frequented course from York Fort inland. It was often used by Indians descending to the Bay, for it was easy and swift, but it did not afford the abundance of venison required by the travellers, and the banks were often obstructed with great blocks of ice, making tracking and the crossing of the portages both difficult and dangerous. The River Hayes was the trunk route along which the great majority of the natives travelled from York Fort. From it they entered the Fox River (their Fire-steel) and ascended to the confluence of its two branches. Here a choice of routes lay before them. The more frequented one was up the south branch, the Leaf River, portaging into waters flowing into Cross Lake, an expansion of the River Nelson, for this was the way to the basin of Lake Winnipeg as well as to the Saskatchewan. From Cross Lake the Indians from Winnipeg and the south ascended, not the main Nelson, but its wandering branch known now as the East River, for though winding and long—a matter of no moment to the leisurely natives—it afforded good hunting and fishing. This water-way passed through Little Playgreen Lake, where Norway House now stands, and led to Lake Winnipeg and to the mouth of the Saskatchewan. A mile and a half up this stream the Grand Rapids necessitated a long portage ; thence the course upstream led to Cedar Lake, a good fur region itself. Many bands crossed over Mossy Portage into Winnepegosis Lake, by which they reached their several wintering grounds on the Red Deer and Swan rivers, and, farther south, the Mossy River and Lake Dauphin. Joseph Smith, in 1756 and 1757, was the first European to follow this route.

Returning now to Cross Lake—the Saskatchewan Indians left that lake by the Minago River at its south-westerly end, and passed through the swamps at its water-shed to Moose Lake and the Saskatchewan, which they followed to their wintering grounds, wherever these might be. The first European to use this route was Henry Kelsey in 1690. After him came Anthony Henday in 1754 and many others, practically yearly, thereafter.

Return now to the confluence of the north and south branches of the Fox River. The water-way up the north branch led to Split Lake (the Lake of Straight Wood), another expansion of the Nelson. At this lake the comparatively few Indians from the region south of the Churchill River took the Burntwood River to their hunting grounds, perchance on the Churchill itself. The great majority of Indian travellers, however, ascended the Nelson the short distance to the Grass River, which they followed upwards through Paint, Setting, Wekusko (Sweet Herb), Reed, and the Cranberry lakes, through a fine fur region with excellent hunting and fishing by the way. The Saskatchewan Indians (for this was a through water-way) crossed the Cranberry Portage into the waters flowing into their home river, which they reached by the Athapapuskow Lake and River, the Goose Lake and River (Rat River), the Sturgeon-Weir, and by Sturgeon (Namew) and Cumberland (Pine Island) lakes. The first European known to have followed this route was Joseph Smith on his outward journey in 1763. In 1778 Philip Turnor came up the Nelson with much toil, ascended the Grass River, and reached Cumberland House on his Pine Island Lake, putting his course on record.

There was a " Middle Road " from the north branch of the Fox River to the Grass River. It reached the Nelson south of Split Lake and followed that stream downwards to the present Armstrong River, by which and by Armstrong and other lakes and by portages the Grass River route was reached. Samuel Hearne and his Indians reached the site of Cumberland House, which he built in 1774, by this water-way.

These three water-ways from the Hayes by the Fox River to Cross Lake, to Split Lake, and to the Nelson River, so frequently travelled by the Hudson's Bay Company's servants more than a hundred and sixty years ago, are practically unknown to-day.

A route less frequented by the natives ran from the Hayes at its confluence with the Fox, through Swampy, Knee, and Oxford lakes, and came down into the route from Cross Lake to the basin of Lake Winnipeg by the Echimamish River, which flows into the East River branch of the Nelson. This route was first used by a European when Joseph Smith returned to York Fort in 1757. It became the great trade route from York Fort into the interior after posts had been established inland and large canoes and York boats were in use to carry the heavy freights required by the new situation.

The wintering grounds visited by the Company's servants now claim attention. In the summer of 1763 Joseph Smith was sent into the interior with a band of Indians. His Instructions ran :

You are to take Perticular Care that the way of Liveing of those People you are going with be no Inducement to You to Forget your Duty to God. . . . You are not to appropriate [your outfit] to Private Trade And what Furrs you Trap, Catch or Shoot, or that you have any Claim to Otherwise, you are on Your arrival back to this Factory to Deliver them up the Chief to be Sent Home in Your Name to the Company. [He would be credited with half their selling price.] You are to Encourage the Indians to get all the Furrs they Can, and use your Best Endeavours to prevent their going to Warr. You are to make Inquiry & get what Intelligence you Can of the approaches of the People of Canada, how far they have Penetrated into the Country, and what the Chiefest of the Persons Names are that advances into the Inland Country to Trade. Lastly, We wish you Health and a safe Return with a great Number of Indians and Plenty of Furrs.

The party of Indians with whom Smith travelled from York Fort took the Grass River route to the Saskatchewan and ascended this river to a point not far beyond Nipawi. Abandoning their canoes, they worked their way along the bank of the river, killing beaver. On approaching the prairie region at La Corne, they cut tent-poles for service out on the treeless plains. The winter was spent trapping and securing provisions for the return voyage by hunting buffalo. Canoes were made on the South Saskatchewan, probably north-east of the present Birch Hills station on the Canadian National Railway. The bark for the canoes was got on the Birch Hills to the south-west. In the middle of May the various bands, with which Smith had " smoked " during the winter gathered at the confluence of the North and South Saskatchewan, the usual rendez-vous whence, to prevent congestion, they would pass in separate bands down to an appointed place of assemblage. Thence they would go in grand style as a single body to York Fort. Smith reported that the upper French House (La Corne's) had been burnt down by the Indians.

This year another servant, Isaac Batt, went up with Smith, but near the confluence of the two branches of the Fox River left his company, probably taking the southerly route to the wintering ground of his own Indians in the region of Pasquia (The Pas), for he became the most influential of the Company's servants with the natives of those parts. Batt brought back thirty-nine canoes with him. Smith's band came down seventy-one canoes strong, but without their Englishman. He had died on the return voyage. The Leader faithfully delivered Smith's furs at the fort, and Smith's " canoe and tent mate " brought his personal effects and her child. The Governor, Ferdinand Jacobs, gave the woman the value of the furs in " Necessarys for the Support of her Self and his child."

Jacobs wrote the Governor and Committee in London that he had no news of the people from Quebec being inland this year.

In 1765-66 Isaac Batt wintered inland once more. An interesting addition to the wintering servants of the Company was made in the person of a Frenchman, Louis Primo, as the Journals spell his name. Primo was born in Quebec of an English father and a French mother, and had been a servant at the former French posts in the hinterland of York Fort. When these were closed and the French retired, he elected to live as an Indian with the Indians. Growing tired of their life of alternate feast and famine, he came to York Fort to seek employment. He was sent inland with instructions in the usual form, the Assiniboins being marked out for his special attention. The two men brought down thirty-three and twenty canoes respectively in the following summer.

This year there were Pedlars in the country. Governor Jacobs reported to London : " I am credibly informed that most of those Indians [come down with Louis Primo] traded goods with Englishmen in the winter. They say there were two gangs of men, about 8 in each gang and that . . . Mr. Isbester [the renegade servant of the Company already mentioned] is chief over all." The other Englishman was his mate Patterson. These men either got their goods from Pedlars on the Assiniboine like Blondeau, or brought them in themselves from Grand Portage.

In the following season, 1766-67, no less than six servants of the Company were in the wintering grounds of the Indians. Louis Primo was sent to " the famous . . . Beaver River," which had not yet been seen by European eyes. He must have travelled up the Churchill River, with which he is later reported as being familiar. James Dearing went off with Attikasish, Anthony Henday's leader of 1754. The fur region about the Red Deer River of our Alberta, within sight of the Rocky Mountains, would be his wintering ground. Edward Lutit travelled far up the North Saskatchewan with Assiniboins, " the first of our servants that ever went with these Natives." James Allen went with an imporant trading Indian Ca-pouch (Cabosh) by name, well up the North Saskatchewan. Isaac Batt's wintering ground remains unrecorded ; it was probably on the lower Saskatchewan at Pasquia or on the Sturgeon River, with which he is later reported as being familiar. William Pink was committed to the care of the Leader with whom Joseph Smith had wintered in 1763-64. The band appears to have gone to the same region, but to have hunted buffalo to the west of the South Saskatchewan. At any rate, on 8th February, on an easterly course they came to " a large River Runing to the E.N.E." down which they were to travel towards the fort in the spring. The band made its canoes on the north-west side of the river, and got the birch four days' journey to the southward " whare there is a Larg Hummocke or Ridge of Burch wood," the Birch Hills, in fact. Pink saw the ruins of " an old French house " (La Corne's), which the Indians said had been deserted ten years before." He passed the lower French House (at Pasquia), " where the French has been Gone from about 7 years." On 25th June the four Englishmen who had wintered on the Saskatchewan, William Pink among them, arrived at York Fort at the head of 156 canoes. The returns of the Factory for the year were 31,640, made beaver. The system of sending servants to winter among the Indians was certainly a success—in the absence of opposition in the interior.

There were no Canadians, French or English, on the Saskatchewan that winter. Maurice Blondeau, or his relative Bartholémi, as has been indicated, was on the Assiniboine; certainly Carver says that Fort La Reine was occupied. Governor Jacobs reported to London that he heard nothing of any English trading inland. His Indians did not come from the Red River and Assiniboine. In truth an Englishman, as we have argued, Forrest Oakes, and Frenchmen were in opposition to one another on the Red River, with two or three posts farther west—on the Assiniboine and at Fort Dauphin, where perhaps François le Blanc wintered. The canoes from these posts would be among the hundred which Alexander Henry says passed from Grand Portage to Michilimackinac in 1767.

Of these posts, which were in the hinterland of Severn Fort, Humphrey Marten, Factor there, was made aware in the summer of 1767. He sent in William Tomison, afterwards the most notable servant of the Company in his time, to winter among Indians who frequented Severn Fort. Tomison ascended the Severn to lakes from which it flows, and got across to other lakes on the Berens, but more probably, the Pigeon River, which he descended to its inflow into Lake Winnipeg. It must have been at the mouth of Winnipeg River that he found many Indians awaiting English and French Pedlars from Canada. They reported two houses at the Misquagoma [the Red] River, half a day's paddle across the lake, one held by an Englishman with eight servants and two large canoes of goods, the other by a Frenchman with sixteen servants and four canoes of goods. The Englishman would be Forrest Oakes, as has been argued, the first of his race to come in from Montreal. These pedlars were at their forts in 1766 for they were now away with their furs at Grand Portage, but they returned in the late autumn. Farther west, Tomison was told, there were three houses, probably Blondeau's below Poplar Point, called La Reine, for it was near La Vérendrye's post of that name, while Adhemar's was above Poplar Point. Certainly Blondeau shipped furs from Michilimackinac to Albany on the Hudson River this summer, and he secured a licence there to proceed beyond Lake Superior to Fort Dauphin and La Reine. The third, as already suggested, was probably that of François le Blanc, the Blancell of the schedule of the Indian Commissary at Michilimackinac, who was given a licence to go beyond Lake Superior to Fort Dauphin and La Prairie.

On 2nd October, a trader who can be no other than François, for his name was Saswe, came upon Tomison and his Indians. Tomison offers an interesting description of this illusive character :

> His dress was a ruffed Shirt, a Blanket Jacket, a pair of Long trousers without stockings [leggings] or Shoes, his own hair with a hatt bound about with green beinding, a poor looking Small man about fifty years of age ; he Seemed to have a great Command over the men ; he lay in the Middle of the Canoe with his wife and Son.

Saswe would not converse with Tomison, but one who could speak English told him that his master did not own the goods, but that they belonged to a French merchant in Montreal ; that there were two other traders on the west side of the lake, but none had as many canoes as his Master. After trading four bags of rice to provision the canoes, Saswe hurried on, for 2nd October was late to be so far from his destination, which was given as Pasquia (Paskoyac). Indeed, he did not stop at Pasquia, but went on to winter at Pemmican Point, as will be seen.

Tomison and his Indians wintered in the neighbourhood of Lake Winnipeg. All his persuasions were of no avail in monopolizing the trade of his companions, for whenever they got a few furs they went off with them to the Canadian fort. He remarks despairingly that, were it not for Brazil tobacco, very few would come to Severn Fort. In the spring Tomison paddled westward (to the Red River) and saw two old French houses, doubtless the ruins of the first Maurepas and of Fort Rouge. He would be the first Company's servant to see the site of the present city of Winnipeg.

In the summer in which Tomison went inland, the six men of the season before returned from York Fort to winter in the interior. William Pink's Journal shows where most of them went. Pink himself reached the Saskatchewan by the Fox River–Cross Lake–Minago route. At the site of Paskoyac he met Indians with French goods and utensils, doubtless traded with François at Fort Dauphin. At the ruins of the upper French House his Indians threw away their canoes, and on 7th August began their long journey home overland. They travelled north-westward on the north side of the river and appear to have passed up the valley of the Shell River. The small river running into the main river, the North Saskatchewan, out of a large lake and crossed on 5th September was probably Jack Fish, west of North Battleford, while the large lake, Mis-Ca-nock, from which a small river ran into the Saskatchewan, would be Turtleford Lake. Passing through a region of swamps and ponds, on 16th August Pink crossed a small river flowing northward, probably the Muriel River of the survey map flowing into the Beaver River. Three days later he was on the bank of the "Amisk-o-Cepee," the Beaver River itself, "a noated River for Beaver." On the 27th he crossed Mous-wa-Cheu-Cepee, the river flowing out of Moose Lake, the Lac

d'Orignal of the North West Company of a later day.   On 5th
November he was at the confluence of two branches of the Beaver
River, both called Beaver River by him.   They are now known, the
one by the English name, the other by the Indian equivalent, Amisk.
The one from the west-north-west would be our Beaver River coming
from the direction of Lac la Biche, Alberta.   Crossing this, Pink and
his Indians travelled westward, and on 16th November, somewhere
towards its source, crossed the other Beaver River, our Amisk, on a
southerly course.   They had been trapping in a fine beaver region
north-east of the present Edmonton and had gathered their furs.
They now began to travel eastward and southward.   Passing probably through the region of St. Paul des Métis, Alberta, they reached
the North Saskatchewan after three days' travel and crossed it.   The
Indians now began hunting buffalo to make provision for their
journey to the Bay, and trapping wolves and foxes for the trade.
This over, they crossed back to the north bank of the river and drifted
past Mooswa Creek, which is north of Vermilion station of the Canadian National Railway, in Alberta.   Still trapping, they reached the
North Saskatchewan once more beyond a river flowing south-eastward into it, where they began to build the canoes for the return
voyage.   Here Pink was visited by a large band of Archithinues,
probably Blackfeet.

    The other wintering servants had been as far, or nearly as far, up
the Saskatchewan as Pink.   Edward Lutit and his Assiniboins were
building their canoes above, at Mooswa Creek, while James Allen and
his leader Cabosh were two days' paddle downstream.   Pink embarked for York Factory on 8th May and fell in with James Allen
and James Dearing two days later.   After two days' journey farther
on he came on Archithinues of a different kind, and at war with his
earlier visitors.   These would be the Gros Ventres or Fall Indians.
On the 22nd Pink passed the ruins of the upper French house, and on
the 25th, below Nipawi, he unexpectedly came to a fort being built
by François le Blanc (Saswe).   It stood, as Cocking's log of 1772 and
Fidler's Journal of 1792 indicate, a little above Pemmican Point.
The post was manned by twelve Frenchmen, including one Lewis
" Beesolay " and a " Roseprue," commanding men, who are said to
have been, most of them, on the river about ten years before, which
would be at the end of, or after, La Corne's time.   Pink was told that
they expected two canoes that summer and several Englishmen
(from Montreal) to join them, and that they were going farther upstream to build a proper house.   The Company's men had much
difficulty in getting their Indians to pass on with their furs from this
French-Canadian post.   The Pedlars had goods to offer ; the English
had no more than persuasions and promises.   On the third day
eighty canoes resumed their course downstream.   Eighteen of these
elected to go to Churchill Fort and took the route through Cumberland Lake.   At the site of Fort Paskoyac the party proceeding to
York Fort saw Isaac Batt, who had wintered on the upper waters of
the Assiniboine and was waiting for his Indians to join him.

Pink reached York Fort on 3rd July, after a notable journey. He had been on the upper waters of the Churchill River, almost to the height of land beyond which the river Athabaska flows towards the Polar Sea ; in fact, he had penetrated practically to the limits of the Chartered Territory in those parts. No less remarkable was the area covered by the other servants of the Company. Their several wintering grounds were in western Saskatchewan and in Alberta.

The winterers, including Louis Primo, were able to keep Governor Jacobs well informed, not only of the actual situation, but of the impending incursion of English Pedlars. He, in turn, reported the presence on the Saskatchewan of Saswe, whose surname he makes " Serdaw," and of the impending arrival of the Englishmen, and urged the Governor and Committee in London to face the situation by sending the wintering servants inland in a body to build a house or houses in the most convenient places. This, he thought, would stop the Pedlars from robbing the Company of its trade. He pointed out the necessity of long boats of light draft for the transportation of the goods. When the houses were built notices should be served on the Pedlars warning them off the Company's property.

In 1768–69 the area covered by the wintering servants was scarcely less extensive than that of the season before. Pink took the middle road from the Fox to the Nelson and by Armstrong River and Lake into the Grass River route, and so to Cumberland Lake and the Saskatchewan. He found that François le Blanc had abandoned his house of the autumn before and had built at Nipawi on the right bank of the river (in S.E. ¼, sect. 13, tp. 50, r. 15, W2, immediately north of Codette). Following his course of the year before, he reached Frog Creek, in Alberta, on September 30th and Mooswa Creek on the following day. With his Indians he spent the winter south of the North Saskatchewan somewhere west, say, of Vermilion, Alberta. There he happened on Isaac Batt and his band. While building his canoes at Mooswa Creek he was joined by James Allen and his Indians. Edward Lutit and his group built their craft a day's journey downstream, while James Dearing was not very far below them. When the united bands came to Nipawi, to Saswe's post, they found James Finlay, the first Englishman from Montreal to reach the Saskatchewan, in charge, with twelve Frenchmen. Finlay's account of the visit runs that they were collecting the Indians and driving them like slaves down to York Fort ; and that they had printed sheets with them warning all intruders out of the Company's Territory. Such warning, of course, had the effect in law of maintaining the Company's title, even though the intruders might take no notice of it. Finlay, by way of rejoinder, informed the Company's men that the regulation of the trade had been abolished by the Imperial Government ; he asserted that he and the men from Montreal had liberty to come and go as they chose, as the Charter had to do only with the coast of the Bay. Finlay tried to win some of them over to his service by offers of high wages. It was a week before Pink and his colleagues could draw off the Indians and resume the journey to York Fort.

Finlay's argument calls for some comment. All that had happened to change the situation was that the Imperial Government had left the regulation of the fur trade of the Indian Territory adjacent to the several colonies to the colonial Governors. The Governor of Quebec had allowed the traders to winter among the Indians, and to enable them so to do, had extended to eighteen months the period during which the licence held good. A colonial Governor could not confer legal rights within the area granted to the Hudson's Bay Company by a Charter emanating from the Crown. It was necessary, therefore, to assert that the hinterland of the Company's forts was not within the chartered territory, was in fact Indian Territory. This was done by reviving the old French claim that the Company's Territory was limited to the shore of the Bay. This doctrine, as will be seen, was cherished by the North West Company until its proprietors entered the Hudson's Bay Company, when they suddenly began to assert that the Company enjoyed the monopoly of the trade and title to the soil of the whole area drained by the rivers flowing into Hudson Bay. When the transfer of Rupert's Land to Canada came in view in the middle of the nineteenth century, the Canadian Government reasserted the French claim, only to come by disillusionment when the terms of the transfer were laid down by the Imperial Government.

As Pink and his companions had learned that Finlay had an outpost at Pasquia (it was on the left bank of the Saskatchewan, opposite the mouth of the Carrot River), they avoided it by taking their Indians by the Grass River route down to York Fort. The factory's returns this year were reduced by about one-third to 22,039, made beaver. Governor Jacobs felt constrained to renew his plea that a post be built inland. He suggested the Grand Rapids of the Saskatchewan, on the track of the Pedlars, as a suitable site.

In the season 1769–70 six servants of the Company, including Louis Primo, wintered inland. William Pink took the Minago route to the Saskatchewan, doubtless to see what the Pedlars were doing at Pasquia. He found but one Englishman there, possibly William Bruce, who will be found there in 1773. As the lone Pedlar had received no goods in the autumn, he could have done little business. Higher up Finlay's house was closed. Leaving their canoes in the region of La Corne's post, Pink and his Indians travelled by land to the South Saskatchewan and beyond to the Eagle Hills. They passed along the north shore of Manitou Lake, and spent the winter on the plains beyond. There Pink had to do with Blackfeet, Bloods, and Assiniboins. In the course of the winter, at one point and another, he came upon his fellow servants, James Dearing, James Allen with his "Leader" Cabosh, and Thomas Haddle, who had taken Edward Lutit's place. On the way home Finlay's house at Nipawi was found closed. The lone Englishman at Pasquia was still without goods. While Pink was there, a canoe came to take him away to a post somewhere to the south. The explanation given for the want of goods was the Indians on the route into the country had plundered the Pedlars' canoes. Benjamin and Joseph Frobisher's reference to their losses of the summer of 1669 in this way has already been mentioned. With the failure of the Pedlars to return to the valley of the Saskatchewan, the furs went down the old channel to York Fort. The returns there were 34,002, made beaver, for the season, roughly, a third larger than those of the previous year.

An insight into the situation to the south during this season, 1769–70, is got from the Journal of William Tomison, who once more came inland from Severn Fort. Descending to Lake Winnipeg by the Berens or by the Pigeon River, he crossed the lake and passed up the Little Saskatchewan, our Dauphin River, to Lake Manitoba. This was the Pedlars' track to the Fort Dauphin region. About one hundred tents of Indians were at Meadow Portage, which the Canadians would take to get into Lake Winnipegosis, and so to Mossy River, on which their post stood. Here also the raid of the Indians on the canoes coming in was felt. No Pedlars arrived. Tomison and his Indians paddled down the west shore of Manitoba Lake for some distance. Leaving their canoes, they travelled through the bush country east of Lake Dauphin to the prairies on the River Assiniboine. As Tomison was west of the Pedlars' houses on that river, he had little to report, but he mentioned that a messenger reached his band on 12th December to announce the arrival of the traders at their house with goods.

Tomison's band wandered up the valley of the Assiniboine north-westward, hunting buffalo by the way. Before they turned their face towards the Lake Dauphin region, several Indians went off to the Pedlars' houses with a few skins from each man. They were away more than a month. Probably at Bird Tail Creek above Birtle, Manitoba, the band turned north-eastward and wandered down what appears to be the valley of the Ochre to Lake Dauphin, where they made their canoes for the return to Severn Fort. In May they paddled across the lake and down its outflow, our Mossy River. About twelve miles down this stream, and eight miles from Lake Winnipegosis, which it enters, they came on a hundred tents of Indians awaiting the arrival of the Pedlars, who, perhaps because of the raid of the Indians of the autumn before, had not been able to reach their destination. Word had, however, been received that they were coming " from the Great Lake." The number of expectant tents, according to Tomison, had increased to two hundred when the Pedlar, his book-keeper, and ten servants arrived in two canoes. Tomison says that none spoke English. All the Indians, including Tomison's own band, traded their furs with these men. It was the fifth day before the Englishman could draw his men off. Then, because of a false report that Severn House had been abandoned, he shaped his course for York Fort. Crossing to Lake Manitoba and descending the Little Saskatchewan, he made his way along Lake

Winnipeg to Little Playgreen Lake, and then by East River and Cross Lake to York Fort. His four canoes brought no more than 387 beaver worth of furs, exclusive of his own trapping.

In the trading season of 1770–71, three English servants and Louis Primo were inland. They returned with 131 canoes, and the returns of York Fort were 29,215, made beaver. The Pedlars could not have been on the Saskatchewan in any great force, if at all. Saswe had been expected by the Indians, but it is not likely that he was there.

In 1771–72 but two men, Isaac Batt and the Frenchman Primo, were sent inland. It is possible that Governor Jacobs was losing faith in the scheme. The servants sent inland had fallen into smuggling furs into the fort and to the ship ; the Indians leaders were demanding larger and larger generosity of the Governor, especially in the form of brandy, and assuming a threatening attitude when denied. Within the fort itself there was increasing insubordination. An old officer like Jacobs, who knew the former times, must have sighed for their return.

The Pedlars too suffered from the rough times which they had introduced. They had their troubles both with the Indians and with their servants. In the autumn of 1771, as has been seen, Thomas Corry had come in for the Todd–McGill–Frobisher partnership, and built a post near old Fort Bourbon on Cedar Lake, and across the path of the Indians of the basin of Lake Winnipegosis going down to York Fort. Writing in the following summer to Andrew Graham, temporarily in command of York Fort, he excused himself from writing at greater length : " You must think in what confusion I am with too hundred Drunken villions around me." It was in connection with his troubles with his men that he wrote. He deplored the villanies of one John Cole and a Frenchman " Bove," and asked Graham to take them prisoners and ship them to London.

Isaac Batt and Louis Primo did exceptionally well inland, and came down the Saskatchewan with no less than 160 canoes (1772). But the fleet was waylaid by out-runners from Corry's fort with news that the house on Cedar Lake awaited customers. These forthwith forgot their many promises to the Company's men and ran downstream to the lake, as easy to approach as it was near. Batt and Primo reached York Fort with but thirty-five canoes. The returns of the Fort for the season fell to 21,577, made beaver, more than onethird below normal.

That summer John Cole, Corry's renegade servant, went down to York Fort to seek employment. He was able to give Governor Jacobs, now returned, clear information of the doings of the Pedlars. Corry had captured the services of a noted Indian "Leader" named Wappenassew, who had traded at York Fort for wellnigh twenty years, a man, in the eyes of Governor Jacobs, " of prime Consideration" with the natives and of extensive influence. Corry, though an illiterate Scotsman, was endowed with the art of handling the savage. He treated him with the utmost honour, took him to

live in the house with him, had him dine at his own table, clothed
his family, so to say, with scarlet and gold, and took care never to
refuse any favour asked for. Then, too, Cole revealed the financial
strength of Corry's supporters. Two Frenchmen, Blondeau by name,
were in the " concern." (Their fort by the buffalo plains of the
Assiniboins would provide the pemmican, with which the canoes
from Corry's fort on Cedar Lake, where fish was the main form of
provision, would be provisioned for the long journey from Lake
Winnipeg to Grand Portage on Lake Superior.) Strong firms like
Todd and McBeath (he could have added, and the Frobishers and
McGill) provided the goods for the trade and got them to Grand
Portage, where their canoes received the furs from Cedar Lake for
the return voyage. A very capable trader, John Erskine (Askin),
at Michilimackinac, according to Cole, was in the partnership, and
watched its interests (doubtless in the way of providing the corn to
provision the canoes at Grand Portage). Two servants, François
Boyer and Michel Boyer, were stationed at Rainy Lake to care for
the brigades by provisioning them with rice, and by keeping the
Indians friendly and willing to allow the goods to pass through
without plundering. (The Frobishers arranged with the other
Pedlars to contribute to the support of these two men, policemen on
the water-way ensuring safe passage to one and all.)

Then, too, Thomas Corry was lodged right on the path to York
Fort of the Indians from the basin of Lake Winnipegosis, that is,
from Red Deer River, Swan River, and the Lake Dauphin region.
What with the disruption of the whole system of " trading Indians,"
on which the Hudson's Bay Company had long relied with supreme
success, and the onset of the men from Montreal, something must
be done. Andrew Graham, chief at Severn Fort and acting-chief
at York Fort during the absence of Governor Jacobs in England,
wrote :

It appears to me that the only way of increasing the Fur Trade is to
have an Inland Settlement to supply the Natives with Necessarys ; Ammunition, Tobacco & Brandy . . . the Principal Articles ; without the latter
[which was only allowed by the Company as a gift to the Leaders and in the
trade of small furs] the Indians would not resort to your House, if they
could procure it elsewhere. John Cole declared that he would engage to
conduct large loaded Canoes up to the river Du Paw [Opas, the Saskatchewan]
in forty Days with fine Weather ; the falls and carrying Places are far less
Numerous [than on the Grand Portage route] ; no Natives to pass thro'
but such as annually take Debt at the Facty [factory] & are in friendship
with us ; the Brazile Tobacco would be strong enticement to the Indians and
the largeness of the Company's Standard [meaning the cheapness of their
trading rates] seems likely to deter the Canadians from pursuing a traffick
which must be carried on under disadvantages. . . . I have often reflected
that the Accounts given us by Men sent Inland were incoherent and un-
intelligible. I thought therefore that a sensible Person might Answer the
Purpose much better & make many observations which would be of Utility
& mentioning my Sentiments to Mr. Cocking [the accountant at York Fort]
he readily offered himself for any service to promote your Interest ; I have
therefore sent him Inland with a Leading Indian ; he will give a rational
Account of Things.

Graham's dispatch of Matthew Cocking into the interior to report on the whole situation is one of many examples of the freedom of the Factors to take the initiative.

Graham also engaged John Cole and sent him inland. He sent also the hitherto faithful, if profligate, Louis Primo. The doings of these two are not on record. The experiences of Cocking and his observations are embodied in his Journal. He and his band of Indians left York Fort on June 27, 1772, and reached the Saskatchewan at Pasquia (The Pas) by the Minago route. Proceeding upstream he avoided the swift current and the great northward bend of the river by passing, as Henday and Kelsey had done, into Saskeram Lake. The route up the Birch River led him to a portage by which he crossed into the channel which the Saskatchewan followed at that time. Proceeding upstream about eleven miles he came to the portage leading northward across into Cumberland Lake, by which Indians passed to the north toward the Churchill River, and near which Cumberland House was built two years later. As he passed up the Saskatchewan, he met fifteen canoes which had been trading with the Pedlars. On 7th August he passed " an old Trading house belonging to the French before the conquest of Quebec," really François's house of 1767–68, for there is no reference to any such post in the documents of the French régime. On 9th August he passed another old house (at Nipawi). " One Mr. Finlay from Montreal resided in it five [four] years ago." On the 11th he was at the site of La Corne's fort. " Formerly the French had a house here," he remarks. From this place the Indians, now with their families, drifted across the prairies, hunting, feasting, drumming, and dancing. They did not cross either the Carrot River or Peonan Creek, but passed between them, till they had the South Branch of the Saskatchewan two miles to the west. They were probably about seven miles north-east of the present St. Louis. Next day Cocking passed some hillocks named Birch Hills and the Younger Brothers that bore south, and the day after he reached the South Saskatchewan, either at Gardepuy's Crossing or at St. Laurent le Grandin of modern times ; probably the former. He notes here among the Indians that they had grown accustomed to the Pedlars bringing goods to trade with them : " I find they consider an Englishman's going with them as a person sent to collect furs & not as an encouragement to them to trap furs & come down to the Settlement." The import of this discovery was, of course, that the English Company must come inland or lose its Indian customers.

Across the South Branch of the Saskatchewan, Cocking travelled through a hilly country with " a few small sticks and ponds in places" to the edge of the Barren Grounds, that is, through the present Forestry Reserve to the level prairie north of Duck Lake. He gives his latitude as 52° 37', which would be twenty miles farther south and well out into the plain ; however, he later confesses that his instrument was practically useless. He now made his way across

the prairie to the North Branch of the Saskatchewan, and followed
it upward to The Elbow, where the Canadian National Railway now
crosses the river to run westward to North Battleford. Here he met
a forlorn Frenchman cast off by François seven years before, possibly
when the latter was at Fort Dauphin in 1766. Cocking then crossed
the Little Eagle Hills Creek to the Eagle Hills and turned southward.
On 9th September his band broke up, some leaving to winter, as
Anthony Henday's Indians did, at the Rocky Mountains, some
parting to go to Manitou Lake and those parts, as Pink's band did in
1768. His immediate following trapped beaver up the Eagles Hills
Creek to the neighbourhood of the present Asquith, Saskatchewan.
Thence they drifted south-westward and spent some time trapping
wolves by lakes west of Biggar, and not farther west than Tramping
Lake.

It was Cocking's desire to meet natives who had never traded at
York Fort, to persuade them to trap beaver, and to take them as
new customers in triumph with him down to the Factory. He was
now in the hunting-grounds of the " Powestic-Athinuewuck, *i.e.*
Waterfall Indians," variously called the Fall or Rapid or Gros
Ventres (Big Bellies), the most easterly of the equestrian tribes.
They had been driven westward to this region from the falls or
rapids at Nipawi by the terrible firearms of the Crees. On 1st
December this tribe visited Cocking. It proved very friendly and
hospitable and feasted the Englishman and smoked with him. When
urged to go down with him to the fort, they answered much in the
terms of the Bloods to Henday eighteen years before : the distance
was great ; they did not know canoes ; they would be starved.

After this pleasant interlude, Cocking passed in a north-easterly
direction to the western slope of the Eagle Hills and crossed the
Saskatchewan on the ice. His course from the river would be somewhat east of Denholm, north-eastward to the easterly incline of the
" Sakitakow-wachee," the Thickwood Hills, in the forest area, where
the Indians were trapping beaver. In the spring he and the Indians
that had gathered around him proceeded to the North Saskatchewan
River in the neighbourhood of the later Fort Carlton. There, on the
edge of forest land and prairie, they built their canoes for the journey
down the river and to the Bay, and made up their last store of
provisions.

Cocking kept urging the Indians not to deal with the Pedlars,
whether François or Corry, and to come with him to York Fort,
but was all the while conscious that his plea was falling on dull ears.
Taking to their canoes, Cocking's Indians, now in great numbers,
reached the Forks of the Saskatchewan on May 19, 1773. During
the following day they reached François's " plantation," at Finlay's
fort at Nipawi. Cocking's Journal runs :

The house is a long square ; built log to log ; half of it is appropriated
to the use of a kitchen ; the other half used as a trading room & Bedroom ;
with a loft above, the whole length of the building where He lays his furs ;
also three small log houses, the Men's apartments ; the whole enclosed with

ten feet Stockades, forming a Square about twenty yards. . . . I believe
Francois hath about twenty men, all french Canadians. . . . He is an old
ignorant Frenchman ; I do not think he keeps a proper distance from his
men ; they coming into his apartment & talking with him as one of themselves. But what I am most surprised at, they keep no watch in the night ;
even when the Natives are lying on their plantation.

This is an unperceiving Englishman's criticism, surely. François,
long acquainted with the country, with his French love of Indian
life, and probably with an Indian Chief's daughter for squaw,
was as much at home and safe among the Indians as they were with
him. Cocking continues :

On our arrival the Frenchman introduced the Natives unto his house,
giving about 4 inches of tobacco. Afterwards they made a collection of furs,
by the bulk about 100 Beaver, presenting them to the Pedler, who, in return,
presented to them about 4 Gallons liquor, Rum adulterated : also cloathed
2 Leaders with a Coat & Hat. I endeavoured all in my power to prevent the
Natives giving away their furs, but in vain ; Liquor being above all persuasion
with them.

Cocking, with no goods, no rum, and but little tobacco, a stranger,
with a great gulf—an English gulf—between him and the Indians,
was helpless before this Indianized Frenchman.

At last Cocking persuaded his party to move on. Down the
Saskatchewan he found eight more tents of Indians, who had traded
their furs with the Pedlar, who resided on this side Basquia (opposite
the mouth of the Carrot River). At Basquia the Pedlar, elsewhere
named Bruce by Cocking, was encamped with six tents of Indians.
Two canoes of furs had been sent away already ; a large one was
ready to leave for Grand Portage. Then, too, Corry was down at
Cedar Lake. It was a gloomy view Cocking, as the Great Company's
man, was getting of the country.

Such Indians as had inferior furs, or who arrived after the
Pedlar's goods were expended, went on to the Bay, shepherded by
their crestfallen English leader. They arrived at York Fort with
no more than sixteen canoes. So much for the success of Cocking's
inland voyage. One of the other servants inland did not so much as
return ; Louis Primo was won over to the service of the Pedlars
by the promise of a visit to his beloved Quebec—an enticement
which no true French-Canadian could resist. John Cole returned
and was sent off for a second winter in the Indians' wintering-
ground. The returns of York Fort for the year were 22,790, made
beaver—an increase of 1,215 on the previous year.

The day of the policy of sitting on the shores of the Bay, easy,
comfortable, and profitable, as it had been, was manifestly done.
The Great Company knew it, and before Cocking's report reached
them it decided to go inland to meet its rivals. In thus establishing
posts in the interior it was following in the Pedlars' footsteps, but
in view of the many journeys made by its servants in the previous
twenty years, it cannot be said to have entered an unknown country

in their wake. The boast of the North West Company that they were always the first in the field ignored the picturesque history of a third of a century, and thereby distorted the perspective of the history of the Canadian West for future generations.

It may be said by way of excuse for the Pedlars' boast, that through miscarriages the trading season 1773-74, in which they crowded into Rupert's Land, saw no Hudson's Bay Company's servants in the interior, save Joseph Hansom from Churchill Fort. John Cole, as has been said, was sent inland, but deserted to the Pedlar Joseph Fulton, Peter Pangman's partner, at Fort Dauphin. A party of three men, Isaac Batt, James Allen, and James Batt, was directed to go to Pasquia and to notify the Indians in those parts that the Company would build a post among them in the following year. In view of the lack of suitable craft for transporting goods into the interior, they were to persuade the Indians to build a number of canoes, and bring them down in the following summer. They left on August 23, 1773, but returned a fortnight later, claiming that the streams were so low that they could not get beyond the Hill River, that is the confluence of the Hayes and the Fox. Their failure was a misfortune, for the Company was to find that the problem of providing craft for transporting goods into the interior was far from easy of solution.

The disappearance of the Company's servants from inland for that season coincided with a great invasion of Pedlars. They were reported at York Fort to have come in with forty-five canoes. The Frobisher-Todd-McGill-Blondeau "concern" spread itself over the hinterland. Bartholémi Blondeau left two canoes at the Jack River, that is, in the channel leading from Lake Winnipeg to Little Playgreen Lake, on which Norway House now stands, and on the route of the Indians from the basin of Lake Winnipeg to York Fort. Two canoes were left by him on the Red Deer River about ten miles above Red Deer Lake. He himself built a post eighteen miles below the site of La Corne's post and within reach of the prairies. When Isaac Batt deserted the Company and enlisted with the Pedlars he was employed in this house ; thus it came to be known as Isaac's House to the Englishmen. It stood in N.W.$\frac{1}{4}$, sect. 18, tp. 49, r. 17, W2. on a beautiful level bottom of the river stretching back for nearly two miles. It must have been at one time a great resort of beaver, for not far below the ruins of the house an enormous beaver dam several hundred yards long can still be traced. Joseph and Thomas Frobisher themselves spent the winter in a small log-house on Whitey's Narrows at the east end of Cumberland Lake and on the water-way leading northward to Churchill River. It stood about ten miles north-east of the first Cumberland House, built in the following year. François is said to have brought in eleven canoes. He probably came in with James Finlay. He reached his and Finlay's house at Nipawi with the intention of going farther upstream, but was stayed by ice. As it was too late to build the intended post, he arranged a partnership with Blondeau, that is, a pooling of their

goods and a sharing of the furs and provisions in the spring in proportion to the goods placed in the " common concern." When the
ice on the river admitted of travel, he moved up to Blondeau's
post, Isaac's House. It seems probable that the Todd-McGill-
Frobisher fort on Cedar Lake was occupied this season. Then, too,
the Oakes-Boyer-Pangman-Fulton partnership was in evidence,
Joseph Fulton being at Fort Dauphin. It was beyond the natives
to resist such widespread temptation and to pass the Pedlars' forts
and their rum besetting the routes to York Fort. The returns of
York Factory dropped to 8,037, made beaver, roughly to one-third
of the returns of the previous year, and mostly gathered from the
Home and Half-Home Indians of the Nelson and the Grass River
regions.

The hinterland of Severn and Albany forts were likewise beset
by the Pedlars. Adhemar held his post on the Assiniboine, probably
in the interest of the Blondeau-Frobisher partnership. He would
supply their northern canoes with provisions at the mouth of the
Winnipeg River at what was called Pemmican Point, on their way
to Grand Portage. Probably Forrest Oakes was playing the same
part for Pangman and Fulton.

The Pedlars were not without their problems. The monopoly
of the Hudson's Bay Company was not felt to be an obstacle, for the
Canadians adopted the French view as held before the conquest of
Canada and, in spite of the Proclamation of October 7, 1763, and the
Quebec Act of 1774, claimed the West for Canada and confined the
chartered territory to the shores of Hudson Bay. Their competition
with one another subjected their profits to hazard ; this, however,
was partially discounted by the several traders occupying different
regions. The inescapable problem was the cost of transportation
from and to Montreal. In the summer of 1773 Peter Pangman, who
may have been with his partner Fulton at Fort Dauphin, but may
have been on Cedar Lake in opposition to Thomas Corry (as the
number of sites of former forts on the lake, which must date at this
period, would suggest), ran down to York Fort with a small consignment of furs. His object was to trade with the Hudson's Bay
Company, and thus to get his goods cheap, because of the low cost
of the ocean freightage to the Bay, and because of the short carriage
into the interior. He met, however, with a sharp rebuff. Ferdinand
Jacobs, Governor at the Factory, and his Council were aware that
any arrangement with the Pedlars would proclaim the Charter
invalid. They might have seized him and shipped him to England
for trial as an interloper, but they avoided the uncertain decisions
of law and contented themselves with seizing his furs. Not to inflict
too great a hardship upon the man who had put himself into their
power, they fitted him out " with a sufficient Supply of necessarys
and Provisions to carry him back from whence he came." At the
same time they served notice on him to remove from the Company's
lands, and sent a like notice by him to Joseph Fulton at Fort
Dauphin. By this procedure Jacobs and his Council kept active in

law the claims of the Company to the monopoly of the trade and the title to the soil of Rupert's Land. Next spring the Governor and Committee wrote highly approving of the action of the Council, and commended the seizure of the furs as consistent with the Charter. They thought, however, that the supplies given to the interloper were more generous than there was call for.

Until 1770 Churchill Fort took no part in the voyages into the interior. Its trade was not as exposed to intruders as was that of York Fort and was more varied in character, being drawn from different areas. There was the trade of the sloop with the Eskimos along the West Main, and the attempt in the 'sixties to establish a whale fishery at Marble Island in addition to that at the fort itself. There was the traffic over the Barrens conducted by the Chipewyan trading Indians as middlemen with the tribes in the valley of the Slave River and on the rivers of Great Slake Lake. There was the commerce with the Chipewyans of the basin of Lake Athabaska, the trade route being along the valley of the Churchill River. Finally, trading Indians brought in the furs of the Carrot and Saskatchewan rivers, that is, of the region east of the South Branch. This last was thought to be the only interest of the fort within the reach of the Pedlars, and it was cared for by the servants going inland from York Fort. At times Indians rallied by them elected to go to Churchill Fort rather than to York. In 1770 the attention of Moses Norton, Governor at Churchill, was rather directed northward to the copper mine, as will be seen. In 1773, however, he became nervous lest even the secluded trade of his post would be tapped by the Pedlars. He sent Joseph Hansom inland to observe and report. This servant travelled with Indians by their customary route, if not up the Churchill, by the North River and its head-waters into the Churchill at South Indian Lake and from the Churchill by the Kississing and over the height of land to Athapapuskow Lake. Here he would be on waters falling into the Saskatchewan and get into the Grass River route from York Fort. Descending the Sturgeon-Weir and passing Namew and Cumberland lakes, he entered the Saskatchewan. As he returned he came on Thomas Frobisher's log-house at the east end of Cumberland Lake, on Whitey Narrows. Here he spent the winter. The information which he gathered from the Frobishers indicated nothing short of an invasion by the Pedlars. Joseph Frobisher and François were on the Saskatchewan in the Frobisher-McGill-Blondeau interest. William Bruce, Frobisher's officer, was on the "Bloody" (Red) River "more towards the eastern posts" of the Company, that is, in the hinterland of Severn and Albany. Captain James Tute represented McBeath and Graham on the Red Deer River with six canoes. Blondeau (probably Bartholomew) was on the Saskatchewan with three canoes. An old Canadian, who had been upwards of thirty years among the Indians, had come in with three canoes equipped by one Solomon, a Jew in Montreal.

Frobisher had Louis Primo, formerly in the Hudson's Bay

Company's employ as winterer, as interpreter and guide at his post on Cumberland Lake. After observing the doings at this post, Hansom went off to rally his Indians for the journey to Churchill Fort. When he was returning to the Churchill by the Sturgeon-Weir route and as he crossed Portage du Traite to the Churchill, he was surprised to find Joseph Frobisher there in a " log tent." Louis Primo had rallied the Indians of the region, which he had formerly traversed in the interest of the English Company, to meet the Pedlar, who had lodged himself on the route taken by the natives down to Churchill Fort. Their peltry was for the most part due to the Hudson's Bay Company for " debts," that is, for equipment previously given. The Indians, more innocent of commercial dishonesty than was Frobisher, were reluctant to trade, as Sir Alexander Mackenzie himself admits. " In the spring of 1775 [1774] Mr. Frobisher met the Indians on the way to Churchill Fort at Portage du Traite [so named from the remarkable trade he carried on there], on the banks of the Missinipi or Churchill River. It was indeed with some difficulty that he could induce them to trade with him, but he at length procured as many furs as his canoes could carry." Rejoicing over his booty and doubtless provisioned with dried meat from the prairie fort on the Saskatchewan, Frobisher passed out to the rendezvous at Grand Portage, where his brother Benjamin and the other partners would have a fresh supply of goods, and whence their canoes would take the furs down to Montreal. Joseph Hansom returned to Churchill Fort with a report which must have been something of a shock to Governor Moses Norton.

The effect of Frobisher's raid upon the trade of Churchill Fort must not be exaggerated. The returns there varied greatly. Taken over a number of years, they averaged about 13,000, made beaver. In the season marked by Frobisher's coup they were 15,846. It will be a different story when the Frobishers will have forts on the Churchill, and the Indians will have grown accustomed to resorting to them. It was already evident that the trading system of the Hudson's Bay Company had completely broken down, and that the decision to build posts inland was taken none too soon. Within about a month of Frobisher's feat at Portage du Traite, Samuel Hearne left York Fort (June 23, 1774) to establish an inland post and inaugurate a new epoch in the history of the Company. This difficult task was thrust upon him by the Governor and Committee in recognition of his remarkable feat in penetrating across the Barren Grounds to the copper mine and to the polar shore of the North American continent.

4.—THE DISCOVERY OF THE COPPERMINE RIVER, THE POLAR SHORE,
GREAT SLAVE LAKE, AND SLAVE RIVER BY SAMUEL
HEARNE, 1769–72.*

The success of the servants of the Hudson's Bay Company in travelling as Indians with the Indians from York Factory made it natural, when the occasion for an exploration of the interior arose at Churchill Fort, not only that a servant should be ordered to go, but that one should be found ready for the task. The discovery by the Company's servants, prosecuting the black whale fishery off Marble Island in 1767, of the relics of Governor James Knight's expedition of 1719 sent out to seek for the copper mine, turned the eyes of all once more to the fabulous wealth which might be within their reach. Then, too, in the spring of 1768 Northern Indians brought several pieces of copper to Churchill Fort, said to come from the great river flowing into the north sea. The Governor of the post, Moses Norton, was the half-breed son of the Richard Norton who had sailed north with Kelsey to trade and to discover copper, and who afterwards, as Governor of the post, had never lost his interest in the copper mine, said to be only 400 miles from the Churchill. Stirred by the ambitions of his father, Moses Norton took the ship for England that very summer to induce the Governor and Committee to take up the enterprise once more. It was decided that Samuel Hearne should be sent overland and that he should travel with the Indians trading at the post.

Samuel Hearne was born in 1745. As a boy he had abhorred the conventional education of the schools without being either dull or indolent. He was therefore drafted into the Navy, but after several years he entered the service of the Company as mate of one of its sloops doing service on the Bay out from Churchill Fort. On July 6, 1767, he put himself on record by carving his name on a smooth rock at Sloops Cove, where the ship lay through the winter, and there it can be seen to this day. In the summer of awakened interest in copper, a Mr. William Wales, F.R.S., astronomer and mathematician, was sent to Churchill Fort to observe the transit of Venus of June 3, 1769, Captain Cook being commissioned to take a similar scientific expedition to Tahiti for the same purpose. It is assumed that Hearne increased his knowledge of astronomical science by association with this distinguished visitor during the year of his sojourn at the fort. Be that as it may, Hearne had already marked himself out from among his associates " by his ingenuity, industry and a wish to undertake some arduous enterprise by which mankind might be benefitted."

The plan of the expedition was much like that of Anthony Henday and the travellers inland from York Fort. Hearne with a small party was to accompany Indians trading at the post towards their hunting-ground, and then was to be taken to the coveted goal.

* Illustrated on Sketch-map 1 at p. 2.

Here the similarity ends. Henday had a well-defined trade route to follow ; he could take provisions for many days with him in his canoe, and when he abandoned the water-way he speedily found himself in that happy hunting-ground, the prairie region, with its herds of red deer and buffalo. Moreover, the Indians with him were accustomed to camp life regulated by chiefs with authority to lead their bands to a definite goal. No trail marked the way for Samuel Hearne to his copper mine. As he and his party were on foot, the provisions they carried in addition to their equipment could last for but a short time. Thereafter they would have to depend on the remorseless Barren Grounds for their food supply, and be subject to the fickle migrations of the caribou over the wide and desolate expanse. The Indians with them were the children of the wilderness, without discipline, of wayward passions, driven and tossed as the waves of the sea under every sudden gust. Hearne's problems were to secure his food as he went, to master the whims of his predatory companions, and to keep the band moving steadily on to his goal. In his two first attempts he failed dismally.

Hearne left Churchill Fort on November 6, 1769, late in the season, when the caribou had already deserted the Barrens, and he took too northerly a course to fall in even with the rear-guard. On the very first night, when he was camped between the North and Seal rivers, one of his Northern Indians deserted him, thus throwing his load upon the rest of the party. On the 9th he met several Indians going to the fort and procured venison from them, for his party had as yet killed nothing. On the 19th, when they were beyond Seal River, their English provisions were exhausted. Consequently, they struck more to the westward into low scrubby woods. Here they found no caribou, but got some ptarmigans. Two days later they were beside a small lake where they caught a few fish and killed three caribou. They then followed a north-westerly course through low scrubby pines, but got no more than a few ptarmigans. Their fare was running at half a partridge a day per man. Already Hearne's savage guides were losing interest in the expedition. Several deserted, carrying off a number of bags of ammunition and an assortment of goods. The rest decided to strike off in their own direction to join their wives and families. They pointed the way home for Hearne and his party and decamped, making the woods ring with their laughter. Fortunately for Hearne, as he made his way back, he got venison in the sheltered valley of the Seal River. He reached Churchill Fort on the 11th of December.

The conclusion arrived at was that the Northern Indians did not relish providing food in days of scarcity for Hearne's English servants, who appear to have been no great hunters. In fact they brought up the rear where there was nothing to kill. Hearne decided therefore to substitute " Home guards," that is, Crees in the service of the post. This party, under the guidance of Northern Indians who claimed to have been near the river of the copper mine, started on the 23rd of February, 1770. At first they shot plenty of caribou along

the wooded valley of the Seal River, but as they could carry little
with them they soon were in want and fell back on fishing at the
head of a large lake connected with the river—probably Sethnanei
Lake. Here they decided to wait for the more congenial weather of
spring. " Our tent at this time was truly pleasant," says Hearne.
He occupied himself happily making observations, trapping martens,
and snaring partridges—three to ten a day. On 1st April the fishing
suddenly gave out, and on the 10th they " lay down to sleep having
had but little refreshment for the three preceding days, except a
pipe of tobacco and a draught of water ; even the partridges had·
become so scarce that not one was to be got ; the heavy thaws had
driven them out towards the barren grounds." The sleepers were,
however, aroused at midnight. Two deer had been killed ; and a
rare feast was spread in the small hours of the morning. "Several
days were now spent in feasting and gluttony." On the 24th a large
body of Indians came up from the south-west over the lake. They
were the wives and families out to wait for the annual goose-hunt
on the Barrens. Their men meanwhile had gone with their furs to
the fort—an interesting illustration of one phase of the fur trade of
Churchill Fort. Before the geese came, however, Hearne's party was
in the greatest of distress, living on a few cranberries of the past
season per day, this though the goose-hunters had their own store of
dried meat. By 19th May geese, swans, and ducks were in plenty
and the camp happy once more.

The course was now eastwards on the Seal River 16 miles ; then
northwards by a small stream and string of lakes to Beralzone Lake,
whose banks were wooded. Soon they entered the stark Barren
Grounds. The birds had flown to the north and famine was upon the
party. " From the twentieth to the twenty-third [of June they]
walked every day near twenty miles without any other subsistence
than a pipe of tobacco and a drink of water when [they] pleased."
On this last day relief came with the slaughter of three musk-oxen,
of which they ate raw, for it was wet and no fire could be lit. Hearne
adds naïvely :

Notwithstanding I mustered up all my philosophy on this occasion, yet I
must confess that my spirits began to fail me. [Life on the Barrens as he puts
it] . . . may justly be said to have been either all feasting or all famine ;
sometimes we had too much, seldom just enough, frequently too little, and
often none at all. . . . On those pressing occasions I have frequently seen the
Indians examine their wardrobe, which consisted chiefly of skin-clothing,
and consider what part could best be spared ; sometimes a piece of old,
half-rotten deer skin, and at others a pair of old shoes, were sacrificed to
alleviate extreme hunger.

Passing over Magnus Lake the party crossed the Kazan, Hearne's
Cathawhachaga River, whose Chipewyan name signifies " where fish
are plentiful in the river." J. B. Tyrrell, the first European in these
parts after Hearne, passed down the Kazan in 1894, and argued that
the crossing was above its inflow into Yath-Kyed (White Snow)
Lake, at a recognized track of the caribou. The fishing here was good,

and the guide proposed to kill caribou and dry meat for the voyage, but only sufficient deer came to hand to supply the daily wants of what was now a large camp. The next move was north-by-west, and north-west-by-west to an arm of the lake. Proceeding north they killed musk-oxen and many caribou and made as much dried meat as they could carry, leaving great quantities of flesh to rot. A camp of six hundred persons had gathered for the killing. By the end of July the guide decided that the journey to the copper mine was impossible that year. Accordingly, Hearne consented to winter with the Indians and attempt it in the spring. The party now moved westward and crossed the Dubawnt River below the lake of that name. On 11th August an unfortunate accident stayed Hearne's onward journey. When on the plains west of Dubawnt Lake, about 450 miles from Churchill Fort, he left his quadrant standing after an observation, while he ate a meal. The wind blew it down and broke it beyond repair. It is probable that the decision made to return to the fort in consequence of this mischance changed the attitude of Hearne's fickle companions. Certainly they allowed a band of strange Indians from the north to plunder him of almost all his equipment. Fortunately on the way back he met Matonabbee, the "famous Leader" who was to be his guide, companion, and friend upon the next journey. Matonabbee's criticism of Hearne's failure on these two journeys is what we would expect from the husband of six stalwart wives, all beyond the average height, weight, and strength—the best draft-women in the land. If the men are laden with equipment they cannot hunt, and if they do hunt and kill, who will carry the meat?

> Women were made for labour; one of them can carry or haul as much as two men can do. They also pitch our tents, make and mend our clothing, keep us warm at night; and in fact there is no such thing as travelling any considerable length of time, in this country, without their assistance. Women though they do everything are maintained at a trifling expence; for as they always stand cook, the very licking of their fingers in scarce times is sufficient for their subsistence.

The purport of this advice was that Hearne should give up hiring unreliable men to carry his equipment and take two or three wives who would be true to him and to duty. There is no evidence that the Englishman acted as suggested, but on his next journey Matonabbee himself was guide, and his six sturdy wives, to whom he added a seventh, contributed materially to its success.

Matonabbee was a Northern Indian with Cree blood. As a boy he had been about Churchill Fort, and later had acted as a hunter for the post. This may account to some extent for the steadfastness of the man and his loyalty to Hearne, which were no mean factors in the success of the voyage. More important still, he was of great stature and strength, and the most accomplished hunter on the Barrens. This was the secret of any authority he had among the Northern Indians, heedless as they were of control and discipline.

Moreover, he had shown a fine combination of courage and diplomacy in going almost unprotected to those inveterate enemies of
his people, the "Athapuscow Indians," the Crees, who, armed with
guns, were now taking possession of the Slave River and the south
shore of Hearne's Athapuscow (Great Slave) Lake. He won from
them a beneficial and lasting peace, through which a lucrative trade
was carried on by the Northern Indians as the middlemen between
the English of the post and the fur-trappers of the Athabaska region
—another glimpse of the fur trade of those parts.

All that Hearne could get in the way of astronomical instrument
to replace his ruined quadrant was an antiquated Elton's quadrant
which had been lying at the fort for upwards of thirty years. This
may well explain the fact that the lakes and other features seen on
his first two journeys are accurately placed on his map, while it is
far otherwise with those of his third voyage. Indeed Mr. J. B.
Tyrrell, himself an expert surveyor, who has edited Hearne's book
for the Champlain Society, says: "Either the Elton's quadrant
carried by him was quite useless, or else he did not make use of it at
all." Dr. John Richardson, who traversed a portion of the Hearne
country with Captain John Franklin in 1821, is less severe:

> The fact is, that, when we consider the hardships which Hearne had to
> endure, the difficult circumstances in which he was frequently placed, the
> utter insufficiency of his old Elton's quadrant as an instrument for ascer-
> taining the latitude, particularly in winter, with a low meridian sun, and a
> refraction of the atmosphere greatly beyond what it was supposed to be
> by the best observers of the period, and the want of any means of estimating
> the longitude, except by dead reckoning ; this reckoning requiring an exact
> appreciation of distances, as well as direct courses, circumstances evidently
> unattainable by one accompanying an Indian horde in a devious march
> through a wooded and mountainous country ; we shall not be inclined to
> view with severity the errors committed.

Matonabbee and Hearne left Churchill Fort on December 7,
1771, with one of the Indian's wives in attendance. They passed
swiftly north-westward across Seal and Egg rivers and, turning to
the west, crossed Lake Beralzone of his last trip. Thereafter they
"traversed nothing but barren ground with empty bellies." On
Nueltin (Island) Lake, from which the Little Fish River flows into
the sea, Matonabbee found the rest of his wives, who had waited here
while he and his favourite spouse visited the fort. Hence, the course
lay north-westward and westward on the Barrens, but not very far
from the woods. From time to time the party killed enough meat
to eat fresh and to dry some for their further progress. On 6th
February they crossed the Cathawhachaga (Kazan) River, and three
miles beyond they traversed Cossed Whoie (Partridge Lake), our
Kasba Lake, and later The-Whole-Kyed-Whoie (Snow Bird Lake)
and, bearing southward, Wholdiah Lake. Here, in the winter resort
of the caribou, they joined a large tent of Northern Indians living in
plenty. Continuing westward on 20th March they met Indians
on their way to Churchill Fort. On 8th April they arrived at a

small lake, Theleway-aga-yeth (unidentified, but probably in the unexplored valley of the Thelon River). This closed their westward course. Here preparations for the journey northward were made—meat dried for provisions, birch bark and wood secured for canoes, and tent poles cut for the summer on the treeless Barrens and to be converted in the autumn into snow-shoes.

On 18th April the northward course began. At Clowey, an unidentified lake to the east of Great Slave Lake, the canoes for crossing the rivers and lakes were built out of the material already prepared. There were upwards of two hundred Indians here, like Hearne's party, building canoes. On 20th May a move was made northward to Partridge Lake, identified by J. B. Tyrrell as a small lake between Artillery and Clinton-Colden lakes. The next move was given both in Hearne's book and in his map as northward to Peshew (the Cree for cat) Lake. We would expect this to be Clinton-Colden Lake, but this is not far enough north, and besides, Hearne represents himself as crossing a lake identified as Aylmer Lake still farther north. L'Abbé Emile Petitot says that Cat Lake is the translation of the Déné name for Walmsley Lake, and Tyrrell is inclined to think that Hearne veered south-westward to this lake but failed to note the change of direction. It seems safer to adhere to Hearne's narrative and to reject Tyrrell's identification of Partridge Lake as not fitting in with either Hearne's book or map. Artillery Lake seems much more likely, both from its size and position. We argue accordingly that Hearne crossed this lake near its westerly stretch and passed northward to Walmsley, i.e. Cat Lake. Here in the wilderness he was cheered by letters from Churchill Fort and England, and a two-quart keg of French brandy delivered to him by a Chief Keelshies, who traded the furs of Great Slave Lake region and conveyed them across the Barrens to trade with the English at the fort.

At Cat Lake the last dispositions for the advance were made by Matonabbee. The astute guide had gathered the Indians around him in large numbers, and won their obedience by planning war upon the Eskimos at the mouth of the Coppermine River. From the lake the women and children were to make their way in a leisurely manner northward, while the striking force was to move to its objective. Of his wives Matonabbee chose two, who had no children, to accompany him. They passed northward through Thoy-noy-kyed—probably Aylmer Lake, as Richardson makes it—to Congead Lake, identified by Richardson as Conwoyto or Rum Lake, so-called because Hearne here gave the Indians some of his liquor, the memory of which lingered to Franklin's day. At Conge-catha-wachaga River, and apparently Lake, a halt was made to kill caribou, which were plentiful here out on the Barrens at this time of the year, viz. the end of June.

Hearne was now roughly about sixty miles east of the valley of the Coppermine River and about one hundred and fifty from the Copper Hills. These hills are the centre ridge of three ranges which run across the course of the river. Before it comes to them, the

Coppermine flows in a wide valley and over a shallow gravelly bed—a broad but swift stream. At these ranges it is hemmed in and pours its waters through in as many rapids. The lowest rapid, about eight miles from the Polar Sea, was frequented by Eskimos in summer for its abundant supply of salmon. The objective of Matonabbee's war party was this Eskimo encampment. To reach it, however, they must pass by the copper ridge, the goal of Hearne's voyage. At Conge-catha-wachaga they met with Copper Indians and enlisted them against the Eskimos. Scouts were sent out to acquaint the Indians on the Coppermine of the coming expedition. The women still with the party were now left to make dried meat unto the return of the men.

The war party reached the Coppermine near the Sandstone Rapids, where the river breaks through the first range of hills. Hearne surveyed the stream as best he could as they made their way downwards under the shelter of hills and cliffs. Soon scouts came in to report five tents of Eskimos at the " Falls," the most northerly of the rapids. The warriors now put on their war-paint and prepared for the fray. Hearne's map to the contrary, they went down the west side of the river under cover of rocks and hills to within two hundred yards of the Eskimo tents, when a halt was made to put on the last daubs of paint.

Finding all the Esquimaux quiet in their tents, they rushed forth from their ambuscade, and fell on the poor unsuspecting creatures unperceived till close at the very eves of their tents, when they soon began the bloody massacre, while I stood neuter in the rear. In a few seconds the horrible scene commenced ; it was shocking beyond description ; the poor unhappy victims were surprised in the midst of their sleep, and had neither time nor power to make any resistance ; men, women, and children, in all upward of twenty, ran out of their tents stark naked, and endeavoured to make their escape ; but the Indians having possession of all the landside, to no place could they fly for shelter. One alternative only remained, that of jumping into the river ; but as none of them attempted it, they all fell a sacrifice to Indian barbarity.

Seven other tents on the east side were plundered ; most of their inhabitants had made good their escape.

Hearne could now return to his survey, as may be judged, in a somewhat perturbed state of mind. As he stood on the ridge some two hundred feet high above the scene, which he named the Bloody Fall, he could see the Arctic Ocean stretching from the north-east to the north-west, with islands breaking the horizon. Dr. Richardson, who was here with Captain Franklin in 1821, suggests that he may not have gone any farther, especially as the Indians would be reluctant to go beyond the scene of their attack. Hearne, however, tells us that he went to the mouth of the river, that the tide was out and the water sweet. He knew that it was the sea by the seals and by the heaps of whale bones left by the Eskimos. Moreover, he judged by the scoring of the ice that the tide rose twelve to fourteen feet. As the tide here is but slight, if really on the spot, he may have taken the limit of the spring flood for tidal marks. More serious is his statement that the sun was shining at midnight, for Captain Franklin, who was there at the same time of the year in 1821, gives irrefragable evidence to the contrary.*   Hearne may be excused for not having taken observations under the circumstances.   Basing his conclusion on his estimate of the length of his journey from his last observed point, Conge-catha-wachaga, where he was two and a half degrees out, he put the mouth of the river and the Arctic coast in 71° 55′ North Latitude, when it is really 67° 48′.   He thus placed the Arctic shore four degrees too far to the north.   In spite of these inaccuracies, Captain Franklin felt free to write : "Several human skulls which bore the marks of violence, and many bones were strewed about the ground near the encampment, and as the spot exactly answers the description, given by Mr. Hearne, of the place where the Chipewyans who accompanied him perpetrated the dreadful massacre on the Esquimaux, we had no doubt of this being the place."

Hearne's attention was now turned to the copper mine, which he reports as being twenty-nine or thirty miles to the south-east from the mouth of the river.   So far from the copper lying in lumps like so many stones, the whole party in four hours found no more than one lump of any size, viz. four pounds.   After copper, trade. An attempt was made to win the Copper Indians to traffic with the fort, but the distance was too great, and the Northern Indians would plunder them on the way.   Any trade would necessarily be done with the Chipewyans for middlemen.

On the return journey the women left behind were found near Rum Lake, and the rest of the following farther south.   Turning more to the west, the party crossed the Coppermine at Point Lake, and headed for the fur regions about Great Slave Lake.   At Mackay Lake Matonabbee trafficked with Dogribs for their peltry, and Hearne found beaver abundant.   He was now about to enter a region in which the Déné tribes were being harassed by " those brutes," the Crees, who ever since they had acquired guns had been occupying the successive beaver regions from the lower Churchill to the Mackenzie River.   South of his No-Name Lake, which appears to be Mackay Lake, he came to Anaw'd Lake, that is, Enemy Lake.   This may be taken as the limit of the Cree depredations northward. Following a string of small lakes southward, the party reached the Athapuscow, that is, the lake with a reedy delta, our Great Slave Lake, and crossed on the ice.   South of it they came upon the tracks in the snow of a Dogrib woman.   She informed them that she had been carried off by the Crees from the western limits of her tribe, which would be far down the Mackenzie.   She had escaped from her captors and, with the meagrest of equipment to begin with, had provided for herself comfortably through a whole winter, lost in the wood.   Hearne reached the Slave River not far from the falls near the later Fort Smith ; he followed it up, hoping to find the Crees,

---

* The incorrect statement may be due to the Bishop of Salisbury, who edited and published Hearne's account after his death.

whom he calls the Athapuscow Indians. Disappointed in this, his party hunted happily in a land of buffalo, wood caribou, and moose, as well as beaver, and laid up provisions for the journey eastward. They then wandered on to Thelwey-aza-yeth, the point at which they had turned northward on their outward voyage. As they went they met parties who were playing the part of middlemen between the Indians of the Slave River region and Churchill Fort. However, Hearne says that some of the Crees used to visit the fort annually, doubtless from our Athabaska Lake and by the Churchill River, keeping in the Cree country. There is thus abundant evidence that long before the Montreal fur-traders entered the Athabaska and Slave River regions a thriving commerce existed between those parts and Fort Churchill. Passing through the country traversed on his outward journey, Hearne reached the fort in June 30, 1772, just about the time when Matthew Cocking was reaching York Fort with his report on the intrusions of the Montreal traders into the Company's preserves on the River Saskatchewan. It was the beginning of a new chapter in the history of the Company; one in which they planned to meet keen competition by pushing their forts far into the interior of the country. So satisfied were they with Hearne's conduct of the exploration of the Coppermine that they placed him in charge of the new venture.

Samuel Hearne's character has been compared unfavourably with that of the masterful Alexander Mackenzie on the ground that he was passive, unable to make the Indians do his will, and that he contented himself with drifting with them to his objective. A just judgment must, however, take into consideration the conditions under which the two men performed their respective tasks. Mackenzie had little or no need for a guide, the broad stream marked out his course. He travelled with canoes which carried his goods and an ample supply of provisions even for his return trip. His party were the disciplined servants of the Company. Hearne's path was across the trackless Barrens, his food supply the small quantity which his women could carry over and above their equipment; his Indians the wayward children of the Barren Grounds. In this light his is one of the most remarkable achievements in the history of the North-West. He mapped out, however defectively, much of the wide territory between Churchill Fort, the Arctic at the mouth of the Coppermine River, and Great Slave Lake and the Slave River. Many of his names figure on the map of the Canadian North-West to this day. Some of the places were not viewed again by European eyes for a century and a quarter; some are still unvisited. Then, too, Hearne gave a rude shock to the theory that if we could get round the north-west promontory of Hudson Bay a course would be found south-westward and through a milder clime to the Pacific Ocean. Even if he put it four degrees too far north, he fixed the south shore of the Polar Sea, and thereby conditioned all future search for the North-West Passage.

Two years after Hearne's return he was commissioned to inaugurate the new policy of the Hudson's Bay Company in the face of the competition from the Montreal fur-traders in the hinterland of York Factory. Along with Matthew Cocking he was sent up country to establish the first inland post in these parts ; he built Cumberland House near the Saskatchewan, where the water-way to the Churchill and Athabaska breaks away northward (1774). He was in charge of Churchill Fort, in the stone fort which passes under the name of Fort Prince of Wales, when the French under La Pérouse captured the post in 1782. The failure to defend such a strong position has been put down to the weak passive disposition of the explorer to the Coppermine. It is true that the fort was elaborately armed, but it was beyond the few inmates to man it. Moreover this was but another case of servants of the Company, hired to trade, being reluctant to risk life and limb playing the part of soldiers in the face of a trained enemy—all on traders' pay without any assurance of pensions. La Pérouse took Hearne home as a prisoner, but was so struck with his accomplishments that he returned the manuscript of his book to him on condition that he should publish it. After another short period at Churchill Fort Hearne retired to England in 1787. His last years were spent preparing his book for the press, but he died in 1792 with it unfinished. The work was edited by John Douglas, Bishop of Salisbury, to whom many of its inaccuracies and omissions may be due. First accounts of his journey appeared in the Introduction to Captain Cook's *Third Voyage*, written by Douglas, 1784. Another brief account appeared in the next year in Pennant's *Arctic Zoology*, and his map was included in Pennant's *Supplement to the Arctic Zoology*, 1787.

Mr. Alexander Dalrymple, a noted hydrographer of the day, and afterwards at the Admiralty, attacked Hearne on the ground that his distances going to the Coppermine did not tally with those of his return. Dalrymple was of the school which believed in a comparatively southerly passage to the Pacific ; he was concerned that Hearne's discoveries falsified his theories. His persistence in pressing his views and his influence with Admiralty circles led to the instructions given to Vancouver to trace every inlet on the western coast to its head. The result was disastrous for Dalrymple's theory. Thereafter Hearne's indication of the position of the Polar shore at the mouth of the Coppermine was accepted as the definite delimitation of the continental coast at that point. The true latitude and longitude were made known through Captain Franklin's exploration of 1821.

5.—THE HUDSON'S BAY COMPANY BUILDS POSTS INLAND—THE PEDLARS AND THEIR "GENERAL PARTNERSHIPS," 1774–87

The summer of 1774 saw a new phase inaugurated in the history of Rupert's Land. The Hudson's Bay Company abandoned its policy, century-old and altogether profitable, of persuading the

Indians to bring their furs down to the forts by the Bay. It built the first of a long line of posts inland. It now brought its goods by the very water-ways used by the natives to set them down, so to say, at their door. The issues must be kept clearly in view. It was not simply a matter of saving the trade and maintaining dividends. The Pedlars trading freely in the chartered territory constituted something more than a trade opposition. They robbed the Company of its monopoly. Without process of law they declared the Charter null and void. Supposing that the Governor and Committee could have arrested them and haled them before an English court, the matter would not have ended there. It would have been dragged by the Pedlars, who would have assumed the pose of martyrs, into the arena of politics, and the American colonies, particularly Quebec, New York, and Massachusetts, would have brought pressure to bear on Imperial Parliament to quash the Charter. They would have found means to rally the manufacturers of England in support, as Arthur Dobbs had done a quarter of a century before. Where Dobbs had failed they would probably have succeeded. The Company avoided an appeal to law, sound though its position was so far as legal documents went. It took the safer if far slower course of occupying its lands in the interior as well as on the coast, of winning back its trade and, if possible, of driving the Pedlars out of the country. In the course of time the sheer necessities of their business forced the Pedlars to unite in the North West Company. There followed long years of struggle between the two companies, fort ranged against fort, factor facing wintering partner. In the first forty-one years the English Company's policy of squeezing the Pedlars out of its territory gave little promise of success. Indeed, at the end the Pedlars appeared likely to be the victors. In the midst of the struggle which had now taken on the aspect of war the English Company reorganized for victory. In the following five years the balance began to swing in its favour. The fight was not pressed to a decision. In 1821 the two companies united. Thenceforth the Northwesters and the Company men proclaimed with one voice their title to the soil and their monopoly of the trade as indisputably valid in virtue of the Charter. Moreover, all were now agreed that the chartered territory was much more than a strip of land along the Bay—that it comprised the valleys of all the rivers flowing into Hudson Bay. In the years under consideration, 1774-1787, the two parties to the struggle were creating their organizations and occupying the ground preparatory to the long struggle.

The Governor and Committee of the Hudson's Bay Company did not wait for Matthew Cocking's report on the policy necessitated by the presence of the Pedlars inland in increasing numbers. On May 18, 1773—the day before Cocking reached the Forks of the Saskatchewan—they decided, after reading a letter from Andrew Graham, temporarily in charge of York Fort, and after a consultation with Isaac Batt, who had been inland almost every year for eighteen years, to take the revolutionary step of establishing a post in the interior. It was decided to place Samuel Hearne, newly returned from his exploration of the Coppermine and Slave rivers, at the head of the enterprise, and to give him Matthew Cocking as his second, and Isaac Batt, about to return, and James Allen, another experienced traveller inland, for support. The working out of the details were left to Ferdinand Jacobs, Governor of York Fort.

On June 23, 1774, Samuel Hearne left the factory to inaugurate the new policy. He had with him Robert Longmoor, who was to have a long and successful career in the interior, and Robert Garret, for house carpenter. The conveyance of the goods was entrusted to " a Leading Indian and his young men," assisted by two Home Indians. On 2nd July Isaac Batt and Charles Price Isham, half-breed son of the late Governor, left with another consignment of goods entrusted to another band of trading Indians with five canoes. Two days later Matthew Cocking left with two English servants and five canoes to join his chief. On the following day two labourers, Sclater and William Flatt, went off with five canoes, and on 9th July James Banks and Robert Flatt with five canoes. A sixth consignment was sent off, after the ship arrived, in charge of Robert Davey.

The Indians engaged to take these successive consignments of goods to the new post took a different view of building posts inland from that of the Company. Every group wanted a trader in its midst, with the laughable result that the bands entrusted with Cocking and Batt and their goods carried them off to another part of the country, and Samuel Hearne's medicine chest spent the winter far out of the reach of Hearne himself.

Hearne's party left York Fort in five small Indian canoes. The cargo consisted of 180 lb. of tobacco, 130 lb. of gunpowder, 2 cwt. of shot and ball, 6 gallons of brandy, 6 gallons of white waters, and " some other trifling articles of Trading goods, and a few Necessary stores such as hatchetts, augers, etc., for erecting the House." The provisions consisted of no more than two pecks of oatmeal and twelve pounds of biscuits. On his voyage to the Coppermine, Hearne had learned to live on the country. He meant to do so now.

The intention was to build somewhere on the Saskatchewan, possibly at Pasquia (The Pas). The route taken was by the Hayes and Fox rivers, and thence by the middle route to the Nelson and by the present Armstrong River and Lake into the Grass River route. This brought Hearne out on Cumberland Lake, which he scrutinized carefully. He came to that spot on the island made by the lake and the Saskatchewan River, at which an arm running in from the river almost divides the island in two—the place at which the Indians going from the Saskatchewan region northward to the Churchill, or to York Fort, portaged from the river into Cumberland Lake. Hearne's party crossed the four hundred yards of the portage and continued its survey down the great river to below Pasquia. Hearne noted the then unoccupied house of the Pedlar Bruce on the left bank opposite the mouth of the Carrot River and the ruins of the French Fort Pasquoyac on the right bank immediately below the present Pasquia River. Not content, he returned up the Saskatchewan and into Cumberland Lake by the Tearing River at the eastern extremity of the island and running from the lake into the great river. Skirting the north shore of this island for two of his miles, he came to a fine bay to the east of the portage. Here the bank was dry, and a convenient supply of wood for building and for fuel was found, while there were fisheries in the lake. Hearne chose this as the site for his post. The reason given was that at Pasquia he would have had but one group of Indians around him. Here he would have three, presumably the Pasquia and Carrot River Indians, who could come in by the way of Saskeram Lake, as did Cocking in 1772 ; the Sturgeon Indians, who frequented the river of that name flowing into Cumberland Lake ; and the Indians on the west end of the Grass River route to the north. That the post would be almost on the Saskatchewan water-way and on the routes north to the Churchill and north-east to York Fort must also have been a deciding factor. At any rate, Samuel Hearne built his post, Cumberland House, here. It says much for his strategic insight that it is with us still—the oldest permanent settlement in the present Province of Saskatchewan.

It took Hearne's men but four days to erect a log-tent, caulked with moss, which should be their lodging-place for the winter. Thereafter a temporary store-house was built on the east end of the hut, making a building of twenty-eight feet by fourteen. Different consignments of goods came up, the last, sent off after the arrival of the ship, reaching Cumberland House on the 15th of October. It was a cause of anxiety that neither Matthew Cocking nor Isaac Batt was heard of. The trading Indians, who undertook to bring these servants and their goods up, were from the basin of Lake Winnipegosis. They therefore took a different route from that of Samuel Hearne. They continued up the Hayes River by that part of it known as the Hill River, and passed through Knee Lake and Oxford Lake ("called Pathepaco Nippee or Bottomless Water," the Holey Lake of the Company's men in the days when this became the regular route from York Fort inland). They came down the Echimamish River into Sea River, the east branch of the Nelson, and ascended the part of it known as Jack River. Here they saw a Canadian post.

Two Canoes of Pedlars wintered there & left this summer ; they carried off a great part of the York Fort half Home Indians Furrs. They were almost starved for want according to the Indians accounts ; the Natives, one of which killed himself with excess of Liquor, leaving them in the Fall as soon as the Liquor was expended & never coming near them till the Spring. One of the Pedlar's men was drowned going a-fishing in a Canoe.

On 28th July the two parties were at the Grand Rapids of the Saskatchewan, in " the Canadian's Pedler's track." They passed upstream to Cedar Lake and Mossy Portage, which leads to Lake Winnipegosis. Here Cocking's and Batt's Indians left them and

went off to their own country to the south-west, not without promises
to send men with canoes to take them to Pasquia. The argument
that they had been paid in goods to take them to their destination
fell on deaf ears. Cocking fell to lamentations over the new manners
of the natives. " Now the Pedlars are become so numerous in their
Country their Natures are quite changed, being indifferent whether
they please the Chiefs at the Factories or not." When the promised
Indians came, it was not to take them to Pasquia, but to their own
country, for their overpowering ambition was to have a trader in
their midst. The Englishmen had perforce to resign themselves to
the will of the natives. Lake Winnipegosis was crossed and the
Red Deer River ascended. For at least two years that river had
been occupied by an old trader, " The Deer," his master being
Blondeau, who had latterly been wintering at the so called Isaac's
House on the Saskatchewan below La Corne. Cocking's party crossed
Red Deer Lake and continued up the river. Sixteen miles from the
lake they came on the Canadian House, unoccupied. Twenty-five
miles beyond they left their canoes and travelled up the river valley.
Following up a tributary, probably the Etoimami, they reached a
branch of the Assiniboine River, and so to " Witch Lake," the present
Devil's (Spirit) Lake, out on the prairie, twenty-five miles north-
west of Yorkton.

During the autumn word reached Cocking that Blondeau had
built a post at Steeprock River on the shore of Lake Winnipegosis,
south of Red Deer River. Farther to the south, on or near to the
same lake, was Bruce with five canoes (possibly at the post on Shoal
River, the outflow of Swan Lake, of which Peter Fidler says that it
was occupied in 1780). It was not to be expected that the Indians
of these parts, though they had gone down to York Fort for wellnigh a century, would continue to do so with these posts at their
door. With but few goods and little or no brandy, Cocking's dealings
with the Indians were far from easy. After a troubled winter, he and
his band returned to the Red Deer River and made their canoes for
the journey to York Fort. When the party reached the Grand
Rapids of the Saskatchewan, they met the Pedlars and got a lesson
in easy methods of transportation. The packs were carried on the
backs of the Canadians " with a strap that lays across the Forehead,
better than the Natives carrying across the Breast [which] gives
pains in those parts, often spitting of blood." At this place Charles
Paterson, Frobisher's representative, offered Isaac Batt £30 a year,
all found, to desert the Company. Not less tempting to the tired
English servant was the fact that he would no longer have to carry
goods across the portages; the voyageurs would do that, while he
played the gentleman. Batt accepted and engaged himself for three
years, the salary due him by the Hudson's Bay Company to be paid
to him in addition on his reaching Grand Portage. Isaac Batt
passed out of the Saskatchewan into Lake Winnipeg in the enjoyment
of his new-found status of gentleman while Matthew Cocking made
his rueful way to York Fort.

The difficulties encountered by the Hudson's Bay Company in getting its goods up to its first inland settlement indicate the handicap which it had imposed upon itself by adhering to its old and profitable system of business and postponing all preparation for competition in the interior until the crisis should actually be on. A new organization had to be devised and raw recruits trained, so to say, in the midst of the campaign, and at great cost.

A month after Hearne finished his log hut the Pedlars came up the Saskatchewan on their way to their wintering-grounds. The two Frobishers (Joseph and Thomas) and their partner Charles Paterson, with François in their company, came — the first of many generations of callers at Cumberland House. Holmes and another Pedlar remained with the canoes nine miles away. The Frobishers brought Robert Flatt, one of the two men in charge of the fifth consignment of goods from York Fort. He had been deserted by his Indians and was found in a pitiable plight. The Frobishers would accept no more than thanks for the kind deed. Hearne supped with his visitors and learned much about the methods of his rivals and the disposition of their forces for that trading season. Louis Primo had been left by Joseph Frobisher at Portage du Traite in the spring to build a house unto their arrival that autumn. The Frobishers were on their way to occupy it. Their partner Paterson, with François, was going up the Saskatchewan with twelve canoes and sixty men. These two, while in friendly association, were probably connected with different firms in Montreal—Paterson, of course, with the Frobisher-McGill partnership, and François probably with Finlay. François, as has been seen, had come inland the year before independently of Blondeau, but had entered into an arrangement and occupied what came to be called Isaac's House jointly with him. Holmes seems to have been with the Saskatchewan party of this season. As the Cumberland Journal of 16th December speaks of " Messrs Paterson Homes and Franceways houses," two, more probably three, posts were now in operation, presumably Isaac's House and one or two of the three contiguous forts some twenty-three miles farther upstream and about two miles above the present La Corne. The explanation of the Frobishers' establishment of a second post would be that other Pedlars, including Peter Pangman, had come in and built above them; the Frobishers would go up and build beside them. The remains of these contiguous posts lie on the left bank of the river at the site indicated. In addition, the Frobishers had left a trader at Pasquia. Thus the Pedlars were on all the water-ways converging on Cumberland House, save the Grass River route. Farther afield Blondeau was at Steeprock River and Bruce in the valley of the Swan River. South of these, namely, at Fort Dauphin and on the Assiniboine, were traders with twelve canoes. In the midst of all these Pedlars' forts, which must have been manned by not less than 160 men, Cumberland House with its garrison of eight men was like a lone blockhouse besieged by the foe on every side. But the wealth and stability of the Great Company in England, its easy and cheap approach to the Bay, its convenient bases there, its short line of transportation to the fur forest, and not least, its long retention of the respect and the friendship of the Indians, must not be left out of the picture in judging the probable course of the struggle.

The conditions under which the Hudson's Bay Company could succeed in competition with the Pedlars were laid down, as always, by the aggressors. It adopted progressively the methods of its rivals, but persistently modified them in keeping with its own traditions and principles. It built, not one, but many posts inland. It took a number of French-Canadians into its employ, but deliberately limited their numbers and preserved the English character of its service. Its posts in the interior had, of necessity, to be run much as those of the Pedlars, but the discipline of the posts on the Bay, and the rule of civility to the Indians, were maintained. Prayers were read on Sunday almost as regularly in the interior as on the Bay. Posts were multiplied, but the extravagant numbers manning the Pedlars' forts were not to be found in them. The conditions inland led the servants to take unto themselves young Indian women, and a dusky progeny grew up about the posts; but the Company never openly accepted responsibility for their upkeep as did the Canadians. The mobility which the Pedlars attained by the use of canoes forced the adoption of such light craft by the English. At first Indians were employed to build them, but they proved too uncertain in their delivery, and the Company's men learned to do the building themselves, and all became expert canoeists. But the use of canoes implied a large number of servants, and to this the Company was averse. The Governor at Albany continued the use of boats, accepting canoes only as a supplementary service. The boats imposed severe labour at the portages and in shoal rivers, and implied a slower transportation, but they carried a cargo nearly three times greater than the Pedlars' canoes, were safer and less frequently delayed on the lakes, and with a favourable wind made good progress upstream on the larger rivers.

The Pedlars imposed upon the Company new practices in the matter of liquor. With their long line of transportation, only articles easy of carriage and bringing a large profit would pay. On the outward journey peltry met these conditions admirably. In ninety-pound packages it was carried easily over the portages, and it fetched high prices in the English market. Rum played a like part on the inward voyage. In the highly concentrated form of " high wines " it was carried in small kegs easily managed at the carrying places. At the forts it was watered to anything from four to eight times its quantity for service to the Indians. Thus a small quantity taken in brought a large return in furs. While the Pedlars took the usual trading goods—guns, ammunition, knives, cloth, and the like—they reaped from these nothing like the profit secured by rum. The corner-stone of their trade was rum. The part played by brandy in the English Company's business had been small hitherto. In keeping with the ideas of the time, every servant received his weekly allowance ; he could purchase more if he wished. Indians who rendered any special service might be given a treat. Brandy played a special part as a reward to hunters who provided provisions for the fort. From the times of competition with the French, Leaders whose bands brought down a good cargo of furs were given brandy for themselves and their young men ; also, brandy was traded for the small furs. It was assumed at York Fort that these practices would avail inland, that no very large quantity of liquor would be needed above the allowance for the servants. But 185 gallons were set aside for the inland expeditions. Actually Hearne had but 45 gallons—which could be watered, two parts of brandy to one of water, to say 68 gallons—for the service of the House and of the Indians for one year. The most reliable figures for the Pedlars' trade come from the following year—1775. The McGill-Frobisher-Blondeau partnership brought in 1,000 gallons of high wines for their service and for the Indians—this in twelve large canoes of the type used on the Great Lakes. That year no less than thirty-three canoes of half that size came into the Saskatchewan. It seems probable that the canoes of all the Pedlars put together brought in about as much high wine as the Frobisher canoes had when leaving Montreal, namely 1,000 gallons. When watered to four times its quantity it would be 4,000 gallons.

Such was the power gained by the Pedlars over the Indians by their large outpourings of rum that the Hudson's Bay Company was forced out of its moderate practices. For three years the regulations with regard to brandy in force at York Fort were observed at Cumberland House. The relaxation of the rules came in 1777. Matthew Cocking, Hearne's successor, wrote on 29th May :

> The Pedlars always Trading Liquor for Beaver as well as all other kinds of Furrs, I have found it absolutely necessary to deviate from the Rule that has been long observed at York Fort, so far as to Trade Liquor for some Beaver with Indians when they had no other kinds of Furrs to Trade ; The Rule of not trading Liquor for Beaver may be followed at the Companys old Settlements, because any other place of Trade may be too far distant to carry their Furrs away [to]. However at this place if an Indian cannot Trade his Furrs in such articles as he chooses, He can in a Short time reach some one of the Peddlers Settlements, or keep his Furrs to trade with them as they pass. Besides there are some Indians who kill little or nothing except Beaver in the Furr way, and these must either have Liquor traded with them or else must have it given them Gratis, which would be an Expence more than this place could bear and would even then Answer no good purpose.

While the Company's servants thus adjusted its practices to what they took to be the need of the situation, they held views of the trade in rum which stand in marked contrast with those of the Pedlars. Duncan M'Gillivray of the North West Company asserted that the Indians of the Saskatchewan would not " work beaver " with vigour but for their desire for liquor. With the buffalo to provide an ample supply of food and clothing, they looked to the Europeans for little but ammunition, tobacco, and rum. In his view rum was the incentive to industry. In contrast, the Company's servants regarded the liquor traffic as a definite handicap to the fur trade, for, as is often stated in their Journals, as soon as the Indians got a few furs, they left off hunting to take their booty to the forts, which often were many miles away, to procure a drink of rum. Then, too, as was natural where so few men manned the forts, they regarded drunken Indians as a menace to their safety. That they had so few clashes with the natives, drunk and sober, compared with the Pedlars, argues either that they were more cautious in managing them or that liquor played a smaller part in their trade.

A letter written in 1787 to the Governor-General of Canada by William Tomison, then chief at Manchester House and in a general way responsible for all the Company's inland posts, tinged though it is with bitterness at the success of the Pedlars, expresses the views held by the Company's servants of the Pedlars and their traffic in rum. (Tomison had no less than three Canadian forts to contend with: the North West Company's, Peter Pangman's, and Donald MacKay's, though MacKay leaned somewhat on him for support in his competition with his fellow-Canadians.)

Good Sir :—We the Servants of the Honourable Hudson's Bay Company have of late years received very ill treatment from a set of lawless men that has passed from Canada for trading in the interior parts of Hudson's Bay ; it has been a long standing Custom since the Company's first settling in Hudson's Bay to give large Credits to the Indians, but now of late years by the great quantity of Rum they bring from Canada which this sett of Men despersed amongst the Company's Creditors [debtors] in all parts along the Bay, Debauching the Natives into a state of insensibility and takes from them by force what they cannot obtain with Goods, this I call Robbery and defrauding the Company of their property, but we hope for the time to come that better regulations will be made for such an undertaking, and not to a set of Men that neither regards King or Government. Mr. Donald MacKay has suffered much by the treachery of Mr, Frobisher's Partnership. I myself have been threatnd to be shot by Wm. Holmes ; it grieves us to see a Body of Indians destroyed by a set of Men merely for self Interest, doing all in their Power to Destroy Posterity, so we hope that your Excellency will make such regulations as will preserve Posterity and not be Destroyed by fiery double Distilled Rum from Canada. If such eveils is not remedied, Complaints must be made to the Government of great Britain, which we hope that Just and Honourable Body will take onto consideration.

The letter was signed by William Tomison and George Hudson, chief at Cumberland House. Probably Donald MacKay was to take it to Canada.

Tomison was no advocate of temperance before his time. He had no quarrel with the allowance of brandy provided for the Company's servants, and saw no harm in Indians enjoying alcoholic pleasures on occasion. But in his determination to make the Company's business a success, he would prevent these from being carried to the point of hurting the men as servants or the Indians as trappers for the Company. In his eyes the traditions of York Fort in the matter of liquor not only protected the Indians from harm, but were sound business. That his views were essentially those of the Company itself became evident later when the Company promised that great philanthropist William Wilberforce to eliminate liquor from its trade should he secure an Act of Parliament prohibiting the sale of spirituous liquors to the aboriginal populations of the Empire. After the union of 1821, when the Company had the trade of the country wholly in its control, it returned to its early traditions and confined its barter to goods.

There is ample evidence that in this period of raging competition the Company enjoyed as of old the goodwill of the natives, and was looked to by them for the necessaries, particularly the heavy articles, of which the Pedlars carried no great abundance. What with its employment of comparatively few men in the inland posts, its short lines of transportation from the Bay, its cheap freightage overseas, the quality of its goods, taken as a whole, and its reasonable and stable prices, its entry into close competition with the Pedlars was far from a forlorn hope. Incidentally it kept active its claim to the whole basin of Hudson Bay and to the monopoly of the trade as defined in the Charter.

Cumberland House was in the forest belt. No great herds of buffalo to provide food for the post ; only fish from the lake, geese from the marshes in autumn and spring, and moose and deer when they could be killed. In the first autumn the fort fared tolerably well on fish and venison, including dried meat brought in by the Indians. Some dried buffalo meat was brought by natives coming down the Saskatchewan. As the winter wore on the supplies of venison fell off, for it always took the Indians some time to become regular purveyors to a post ; fish grew very scarce. The post was put on rations, two scant meals per day in December, and in January a small handful of dried meat and about four ounces of other meat per man each day. In February even this was reduced. Partridges, rabbits, fish, all failed. Hearne could scarcely persuade his men that they would not die of starvation. The slaughter of five moose by Indians relieved the tension on 10th February. Geese appeared before the middle of April, and when the ice disappeared the Indians began to come in once more with provisions.

The two Frobishers in their fort on the Churchill River at Portage du Traite were in a yet more sorry plight, for no supplies of dried buffalo meat could come to them from the Saskatchewan. They reduced their numbers by sending five French-Canadian servants to winter in their post on the prairies. These came to Cumberland House on 16th December " on their Journey to Messrs Paterson Homes and Franceways houses." They returned from the land of plenty in the middle of May on their way to rejoin their masters.

In the spring the Frobishers placed Primo in charge on the Churchill and left for Grand Portage. When they passed Cumberland House it was closed and Samuel Hearne on his way to York Fort with the few furs which he had gathered. He felt that his Company could not succeed with a single post inland, and that surrounded by

Pedlars. Other settlements must be made, but, as he wisely pointed out, not till the problem of transportation had been solved. Indians had promised him to build three canoes ; only one was forthcoming. Resort was again had to the Indians and their small canoes. A flotilla of twenty canoes took the Grass River route for York Fort, Hearne in their midst. He returned in the autumn, but was followed by Matthew Cocking with word that he was appointed Governor at Prince of Wales's Fort on the Churchill. He hastily embarked for York Fort, leaving Cocking in command of Cumberland House (October 6, 1775).

Eight days later Cocking was faced with an invasion of Pedlars —twenty-three canoes gone, or about to go, up the Saskatchewan, under several masters. Charles Paterson, Jean-Baptiste Cadotte, Blondeau, and Peter Pangman can be named for certain. James Finlay may have been of the number. Ten canoes came to the House on their way to the North. The two Frobishers and Alexander Henry owned these.

Henry was a " new adventurer " in these parts. He told Cocking that he was anxious to see the west before retiring from the Upper Country, and that, in addition, he hoped to recover his due from some Indians who had left Lake Superior to escape paying their debts. The narrative of his journey to the Saskatchewan and to the Churchill, embodied in his *Travels and Adventures*, gives an interesting picture of the scene in the wooded north and on the Saskatchewan during this trading season. He and his partner Cadotte left Sault Ste. Marie with four large canoes, which had brought up £2,236 worth of goods from Montreal, and with eight smaller craft laden for the most part with provisions. Following the north shore of Lake Superior, doubtless to leave some goods at Henry's post at Michipicoton, they reached Grand Portage, the meeting-place of the traders from Montreal and the winterers from the interior. Here Henry found " a state of extreme hostility, each pursuing his interests as might most injure his neighbour. The consequences were very hurtful to the morals of the Indians."

As the rivers of the interior were shallow, Henry abandoned his large canoes from Montreal and procured the necessary smaller craft, about half their size. It took his party seven days of severe and dangerous exertion to get the goods and canoes to the Pigeon River at the far end of the portage. On the 8th of July they were paddling westward. Soon they were across the height of land and floating downstream. They crossed Rainy Lake and passed down Rainy River and through the Lake of the Woods, trading with the Indians for provisions—fish and wild rice—wherever and whenever they were found. The newcomers were finding the problem of securing food along the water-way a pressing one. At the mouth of the River Winnipeg they made their first acquaintance with Crees and secured more rice and dried meat from them.

On 18th August Henry entered Lake Winnipeg. He had followed the eastern shore but a short distance when he came upon Peter

Pond, who was joining the rush of the traders into Rupert's Land. When across on the western shore he was overtaken by Joseph and Thomas Frobisher returning from Grand Portage with the goods for the trade of the impending season. With them was Charles Paterson, the representative of McGill in his partnership with the Frobishers. The party now consisted of three rival firms. Their thirty canoes and a hundred and thirty men passed along the lake and up the Saskatchewan all too slowly, for it was very stormy weather. Henry's party was already short of provisions and spent a day in the neighbourhood of old Fort Bourbon, for there was good fishing at that end of Cedar Lake. Henry says : " At Cumberland House, the canoes separated ; M. Cadotte going with four to Fort des Prairies ; Mr. Pond with two, to Fort Dauphin ; and others proceeding on still different routes." As there were no " still different routes " to take at Cumberland House, the separation must have taken place at Cedar Lake. The unnamed " others " would be Peter Pangman and two Frenchmen, both newcomers. The prospect of six rival Pedlars on the Saskatchewan brought about something of a dispersal to different fur regions and some agreements between those in one locality to form " common concerns." Peter Pond crossed Mossy Portage and passed through Lake Winnipegosis and up Mossy River to his Fort Dauphin, which he places on Lake Dauphin itself. As John Cole in Pangman's service was at Pangman's Fort Dauphin, for he passed up the Saskatchewan in July of the following summer, Pond was in opposition—unless an agreement had been made to form a pool here. The two Frenchmen appear to have agreed to act together on Swan River, where the Cumberland House Journal reports their presence. Word was brought that the Indians had plundered them of all their goods. " These Canoes it seems belonged to two French Men (new Adventurers this way) who had proposed to have Wintered with the rest at the upper Settlement, but being left on the road are supposed to have changed their Intent." There can be little doubt that one of these was Jean Étienne Waden, formerly trading on Lake Superior. He secured a licence for two canoes to Grand Portage in 1773, and again in this year (1775). In 1778-79 he may have been in the lower settlement of that season on the Saskatchewan ; certainly his representative Gebosh was in the uppermost settlement, that at Eagle Hills. In 1779 Waden penetrated to Lac la Ronge, as will appear. Finally there was a Frobisher post somewhere beyond Lake Winnipegosis. A " Master " along with Isaac Batt was to winter at some place to be agreed upon with the Indians.

Those going up the Saskatchewan—Henry says four rival interests—eliminated what would have been a ruinous competition by forming a " common concern." Of three of these there can be no doubt : Cadotte, Henry's partner, with three canoes; Peter Pangman, who is reported at Cumberland House as having broken away from the pool in the spring and as camped outside of the palisades trading for himself; and Paterson (with Blondeau for interpreter), representing the McGill-Frobisher combination. The fourth would be James Finlay, if Henry is correct in placing him at Fort des Prairies on the Saskatchewan during this season. An alternative would be William Holmes, if he was not in Frobisher's service. But then again, Henry may have counted the McGill-Frobisher " common interest " as two. All of these would scarcely be in one post. Indeed, as has been seen, Samuel Hearne attributed more than one house to the Frobisher partnership alone, namely, as has been argued, the so called Isaac's House first built by Blondeau, and a post about five miles above the site of La Corne's post and on the north bank. The other traders would be in the post reported by Henry as contiguous to it.

Alexander Henry and the two Frobishers were going into the forest region north of Cumberland House. Here again it was decided that a " common concern " should be formed. Alexander Henry to the contrary, this decision must have been taken before Cumberland House was reached, for, when the Frobishers and Henry arrived, their ten canoes were in Cumberland Lake ready to go north and eighteen of the twenty-three canoes for the Saskatchewan had already passed up the river.

Leaving Cedar Lake on the 6th of October, Henry and the Frobishers hastened up the river, for the winter was setting in early and the ice might form before they could reach their destination. All went well until Henry came to Pasquia. At that fishing place of the Indians a huge Indian chief, Chatique by name, of corpulent body and violent temper, forced him to pay toll as he passed—" three casks of gunpowder, four bags of shot and ball, two bales of tobacco, three kegs of rum and three guns, together with knives, flints and some smaller articles." Not satisfied with this, Chatique came next morning in a solitary canoe down on Henry's canoes and exacted another keg of rum. Evidently the huge chief knew how to take advantage of a newcomer.

The Frobishers and Henry called at Cumberland House, doubtless to ascertain the attitude the Hudson's Bay Company would take towards them. Matthew Cocking, now in charge there, adhered to the principle of civility, which had been the guiding star of the English Company in treating the Indians, and was now to be extended towards the Canadians. " Though unwelcome guests," says Henry, " we were treated with much civility." If rivalry there must be, it will be kept within bounds ; the game will be a gentleman's game. The entry of Cocking's Journal of 15th of October, the day after the Pedlars arrived, runs :

I have shown the Masters so far civility as to desire their eating with me. They speak of several Canoes of their People left on the road, whom they expect, some to reside below and others above the Sea [Winnipeg] Lake ; that six of their People were killed by the natives below the Sea Lake, four in the Winter and two as they were going down [to Grand Portage] in canoes ; that one man was lost by a Canoe oversetting upon a Fall in going down. These Losses of men, they say, have frightened the Canadians, several of their old servants having quitted, and that they found much difficulty in procuring fresh Men ; That they lost one Canoe, new, in coming up in the Sea Lake, and the Goods with one Man were lost by its filling in a great Swell.

The Frobisher party passed through Cumberland and Namew lakes and ascended the Sturgeon-Weir River, which the voyageurs called La Rivère Maligne, because of its many wicked rapids. The intention, as the Cumberland House Journal shows, was to winter on Beaver Lake, now known by the Cree equivalent Amisk Lake. At the end of a day's journey on the lake, and just in time, for it froze during the following night, the spot for building was reached. It was blessed with a good fishery, and was doubtless therefore chosen rather than Portage du Traite, where the Frobishers had almost been starved to death in the previous winter. On Peter Fidler's map the sites of three posts are indicated. Henry's narrative shows that the site of his post was neither at the outflow nor inflow of the Sturgeon-Weir River, where two of Fidler's houses are placed. It probably was at Fedler's site on the east shore of the lake where a small stream enters it, and where there is a good fishery to this day.

The Frobishers and Henry were experienced winterers, and organized their forces with great understanding. Their forty men were divided into three gangs. The first was detailed to build the houses. These were ranged in the form of a quadrangle to make a defensible fort. The masters' house and the store were in the front, facing the lake. One servants' house was on each side and two were in the rear. The group of buildings practically formed a block-house. Two gangs were detailed to fish. The fishery would be productive at this time of the year. The superfluous supply of fish would freeze when taken and would be stored unto the day of scarcity, which usually came in February, when the fish retired to the deepest depths of the lake. The fare, save for a rare supply of venison brought in by the Indians, was fish—morning, noon, and night, fish—without vegetables or bread, and without relish. Here, as at Portage du Traite the year before, it was thought wise to send some of the men off to the plains, that land of plenty, for the winter. On 23rd October fourteen passed by Cumberland House on their way to Fort des Prairies.

In January Alexander Henry himself left to visit Cadotte and his partners at the prairie fort on the Saskatchewan. For sheer friendship Joseph Frobisher walked with him—Henry says 120, but really 65 miles—to Cumberland House. (Henry's distances and dates are wholly unreliable.) Cocking received them again with civility, but had nothing but fish, and again fish, with which to play the host. Such was life in the forest belt of the north.

Henry now passed on up the Saskatchewan. His story, which was written many years after, for his book was published in 1809, is vague ; the ground covered is without distinctness, and his time and distances are exaggerated to a ridiculous degree—so much so that it is very difficult to trace his steps. Heavy storms heaped up the

snow on the frozen river, which was his road. Progress was painful
and slow. The party was soon reduced to travelling on scant fare—
a small cake of chocolate boiled in water. They walked on in grim
earnest, death following their footsteps, as Henry felt. But death
had preceded them in a way which proved life to them. The bones
of a red-deer left by the wolves were found and, most luckily, a whole
carcass frozen in the ice through which the beast had broken, but
had been kept from sinking by its broad antlers. In about eight days
Henry reached Nipawi, where he saw " the old wintering-ground of
Mr. Finlay, who was now stationed at Fort des Prairies." On the
twenty-first day out from Cumberland House, Fort des Prairies was
reached. As the so called Isaac's House, the more easterly of
Frobisher's two posts, was occupied this winter, it must be the post
to which Henry came.* Here Henry was hospitably entertained by
his partners. The fare was in great contrast with that at Beaver
Lake and Cumberland House. " My friends . . . covered their table
with the tongues and marrow of wild bulls [buffalo]. The quantity
of provisions which I found collected here exceeded everything of
which I had previously formed a notion. In one heap I saw fifty ton
of beef, so fat that the men could scarcely find a sufficiency of lean."
Much of this meat would be dried and, along with the supply traded
with the Indians, would provision the canoes with pemmican for
their swift course towards Grand Portage.

The fort had two gates, one towards the river and the other facing
inland. It stood on one of the most beautiful spots on the Saskatchewan. The river flows through a pleasant meadow about two miles
wide. As one stands on the right outer bank, which is precipitous,
one looks across the meadow a mile and a half to where the fort stood
and to the silver stream, broken by a wooded island. About half
a mile beyond, the left outer bank slopes gracefully upward, adorned
by a thick forest. Now facing southward, one sees a rolling country
gradually subsiding into the level prairie.

Henry was eager to see the plains and Indian life upon them.
In company with Mr. Paterson and Mr. Holmes he left to visit the
Assiniboins. "We departed at an early hour and after a march of
about two miles ascended the tableland " is Henry's description of
his start from the fort. He passed through a lightly wooded stretch
of hillocks and came to a " Moose River," which he says flowed
eastward to Lake Dauphin. This must be the Carrot River, some
thirteen miles to the south, which runs eastward and into the
Saskatchewan at The Pas. He found the prairies broken here and
there by islands of woods. The Indian world on the plains—a world
of great and disciplined camps, with abundant food—must have
seemed a great contrast to the silence of the wooded north, with its
few scattered families on the verge of starvation. Caught in a
blizzard, the party took refuge in an island of woods in a sea of snow.
A buffalo herd also stampeded to it for shelter. So numerous were
the wanderers on the plains they threatened to crush Henry and

* Its remains are in NW¼, sect. 18, tp. 49, 2.15, W2, north of Melfort.

his party in their encampment. Some of the intruders had to be shot for sheer protection, and dogs were set on the rest to keep them off.

The Indians visited were encamped in a similar island of trees upon the plains somewhere south of Melfort. There might be a hundred tents or more in what Henry calls the village. The authority of the chief maintained something approaching to an orderly society. The councils were large and solemn. The people submitted themselves to their leaders and accepted discipline for their delinquencies. A guard watched over the visitors night and day. Food was in abundance. In one day's hunt seventy-two buffalo were killed in a pound. Thereafter the women busied themselves, some cooking, some making dried meat for the day of scarcity or to be traded at the fort. There followed dance upon dance, feast upon feast. At the banquets a whole buffalo tongue was provided for each guest—a full dinner-pail, surely. Henry remarks that these people required nothing from the traders. They had all they needed in the buffalo. Its flesh was their food ; its hide made their clothing ; its sinews provided their bowstrings ; its belly served for their kettles. Droves of horses grazed peacefully on the plains, the swift servants of the village in travel and in war.

When the whole village set out for the fort with Henry and his companions, it was joined by another of a like size. Travelling together, the two formed a picturesque array. A band walked in front to trample down the snow for the dogs, which drew the property of their masters along on *travois* ; another followed as a guard ; then came hundreds of dogs with the women for drivers bringing the meat to be traded at the fort, as Henry says, not for the necessaries for a grim struggle to live, like the Indians of the northern forest, but for beads and baubles, for ammunition or for luxuries such as rum and tobacco. The prices of the goods at Fort des Prairies are given as follows :

A gun	.	.	.	.	.	20 beaver skins.
A stroud blanket	.	.	.	.	10	,,
A white blanket	.	.	.	8	,,
An axe of 1 lb. weight	.	.	.	3	,,
½ lb. of gunpowder	.	.	.	1	,,
The balls	.	.	.	.	.	1	,,

But the principal profits accrued from the sale of knives, beads, flints, steels, awls, and other small articles. Tobacco, when sold, fetched one beaver skin per foot of Spencer's twist, and rum, not very strong, two beaver skins per bottle. But a great proportion of these commodities were disposed of in presents.

While a large trade in provisions was carried on, the furs taken at the post were no less important. " The quantity of furs brought into the fort was very great. From twenty to thirty Indians arrived daily, laden with packs of beaver-skins." Henry must be referring to the period of the spring trade, for during the winter the post would have few visitors.

It seems probable that Henry did not return to Isaac's House, though he refers to the post to which he came by the same descriptive title—Fort des Prairies. It is not likely that he would leave the Frobisher's second fort unvisited, especially when it could be reached easily from the plains. He inserts a footnote : " This fort, or one which occupied a contiguous site, was formerly known by the name of Fort aux Trembles," that is, Poplar Fort. There is no trace of a second post at Isaac's House, but the ruins of three forts, one very large, on contiguous sites lie on the left bank of the river about twenty-four miles upstream, and about five miles above the site of La Corne's Fort. One must be the Frobisher post and the others those of the rival traders, among whom was Peter Pangman.

The contrast of that land of plenty, the prairies, with the forest region was driven home to Alexander Henry when he returned to his fort on Beaver Lake. The fishery was giving out and the inmates often went supperless to bed. When they left in the spring for the fort at Portage du Traite on the Churchill they had no greater stock of provisions than a single supper each, and were forced to live by fishing by the way. Consequently they travelled northward but slowly. The lack of provisions in the wooded belt and the abundant supply of meat, both fresh and dried, by the prairies constituted the physical conditions which dictated combination on a large scale. The inclusive partnership of the Frobishers brought the provisions of the plains of both the Assiniboine and the Saskatchewan rivers to the support of the canoes of the wooded north, and thus created the system of transportation which contributed greatly to the success of that great " General Concern," the North West Company.

Alexander Henry returned to the fort on Beaver Lake on April 9, 1776, doubtless with the news, which must have been in part the object of his journey, that the partnership was working as planned and that pemmican would be to hand to take the northern canoes on their way towards Grand Portage. On the 12th Joseph Frobisher left for the fort at Portage du Traite, where he had carried through his great raid on the trade of Churchill Fort, and where he had wintered during the subsequent season. Thomas Frobisher and Henry followed in a leisurely manner. They had expected to find " a particular band of Indians " at the fort. Failing to do so, they decided to seek them up the Churchill River. Beyond the Rapide du Serpent, at what would appear to be the outlet of Primo Lake, probably where Primo had his winter quarters, they came on them. The band, composed of Chipewyans from Lake Athabaska, accompanied them back to Fort du Traite, where the traders' goods lay. The bartering went on for two days. " On the third morning this little fair was closed ; and, on making up our packs, we found that we had purchased twelve thousand beaver-skins, besides large numbers of otter and marten." Henry exaggerates here, as usual. The remaining goods were left with Thomas Frobisher, who, it was planned, was to proceed to Athabaska. Henry and Joseph Frobisher went out with the furs to Grand Portage. Thence Henry went on to Montreal, and now contented himself with the life of a capitalist. During a trip to England and Europe he made a proposal of a flamboyant kind, to institute nothing less than a transcontinental mail from the Atlantic to the Pacific, at an operating cost of £13,320 per round trip. His subsequent voyages to the Upper Country did not take him beyond Michilimackinac. He died in 1824. Joseph Frobisher returned to winter on the Saskatchewan.

Alexander Henry has omitted from his narrative an incident which would have revealed to the public the none too reputable methods resorted to by the Pedlars in their competition with the Hudson's Bay Company. Cumberland House, it has been seen, was like a lone blockhouse besieged by enemies. Its only resort was to attempt sallies—to send out servants with assortments of goods, to meet the Indians before they reached the posts of their rivals, to trade with them and, if possible, bring them on to the House. This was but another case of the English Company adopting the methods of their rivals. In the spring Robert Longmoor was sent northward to bring the Indians down to Cumberland House. He met them north of Beaver Lake and all came to the Frobisher-Henry fort. Two Indians who had promised to take their furs to Cumberland House told Longmoor to carry them for safety from their tents to his. As a second bundle was being carried past the fort Henry accosted Longmoor, asking what was in the bundle. Longmoor replied that that was his own affair. Henry thereupon, with oaths, ordered four men to take the parcel into the fort. A struggle ensued during which the Englishman was dragged to the door of the fort without his leaving hold of the bundle. Joseph Frobisher intervened with threats and ordered the men to take the package within. Now began an altercation about the rights of the two parties. The Pedlars told Longmoor that he had no right to come upon their plantation to trade and, in particular, to entice any of the Indians there to trade with him, or to try to hinder them from trading with themselves. Longmoor replied that as a servant of the Hudson's Bay Company he had the right to go to any point within their limits to which his superior officer ordered him, and hinted that the Pedlars were interlopers. Frobisher then said that that particular bundle might be taken away but none other. When Longmoor went for a third he found that the Indian owner had been taken into the fort. There followed a message from the Pedlars requiring Longmoor to return the bundles to their owner. He replied that he would receive no messenger ; let the owner himself come. The messenger replied that he could not come for he was in confinement. Longmoor went into the fort to be assured of the fact. The owner implored him to give up the furs, and so release him from prison. Longmoor gave up the furs. He had observed that the Pedlars got the Indians drunk and at night sent their men into their tents to take their furs into the fort. He therefore asked to speak with Frobisher, and charged him with pillaging the natives, and giving nothing for their furs but a spell of drunkenness. Frobisher replied it was none of his business.

The altercation closed with Frobisher calling Longmoor a " dirty Rascal." At their meeting in the next year Frobisher made a sort of apology to Longmoor and laid all the blame for the incident on Alexander Henry.

A similar sally up the Saskatchewan beyond the Pedlars' settlement was made from Cumberland House by William Walker, to meet the old Indian customers before they reached the Pedlars' houses. Paterson sent a foot of tobacco to him and invited him in. Walker replied that he did not " chuse to come in without Patterson had himself attended on him." Strict social etiquette on the Saskatchewan in 1776 ! Peter Pangman was tented outside the palisades, for the temporary partnership had broken up, and he was trading for himself. He had a conversation with Walker and told him that he and another master intended to open a post farther up on their joint account. Possibly the reference was to Peter Pond, who was at Fort Dauphin, hitherto the scene of the operations of Fulton, Pangman's partner. Walker's sally brought 277 beaver worth of furs into Cumberland House.

In the following season, 1776–77, the Pedlars had two settlements on the Saskatchewan. The lower one was the so-called Isaac's House, Isaac Batt being employed there later ; the upper one was at Sturgeon River, about four miles west of Prince Albert. Before passing up to this last site they were reluctant to come to terms with one another. At length, convinced that competition would be ruinous, they entered into a " common concern " for the season, abandoned the three settlements at La Corne, and moved up to a site about an eighth of a mile below the mouth of the Sturgeon, also known as the Net-setting River. On the south the prairies, which were known as late as Captain Franklin's time as " Holms' Plains," made a sort of bay in the forest and reached the river. The site promised furs from the north and buffalo meat from the south—just what was wanted for a Fort des Prairies. Hence the flocking of the Pedlars to the region. Peter Pond, possibly in association with Pangman, was of the number. The post figures on his maps as Fort Pond, Fort la Prairie, and Sturgeon Fort. Joseph Frobisher was also here, for Longmoor, when on a sally from Cumberland House, received the Pedlar's excuses here for the incident of the previous spring.

On his return to Cumberland House, Longmoor reported the situation on the Churchill River as the Pedlars had explained it to him. Thomas Frobisher was on that river (according to Peter Pond's map, on Ile-à-la-Crosse Lake, on the peninsula where the Hudson's Bay Company's post now stands). He had sent a packet overland (the first use in history of the track by Green Lake to the Saskatchewan), and as a result his brother Joseph was going north by way of Cumberland House to meet him (with provisions). Joseph made his post on Beaver Lake, occupied during that season by Captain James Tute, the base from which to proceed deep into the forest belt.

This season the copartnership of the Pedlars on the Saskatchewan worked no more smoothly than before ; by spring it was disrupted. Then, too, their relations with the Indians were not always happy. Three of their men were killed. The Pedlars claimed that this was at the instigation of Charles Price Isham, the half-breed son of the late Governor of York Fort. Their charge was duly recorded in the Cumberland House Journal and thus came under the eye of Humphrey Marten, Governor of the fort. He promptly ordered all servants inland to avoid everything that could be construed as tending to a rupture with the Pedlars. Next spring the Committee in London wrote out : " We are sorry to hear of the deplorable Fate which befell Two of the Canadian Traders. We approve of your caution respecting Charles Isham, but hope he has not given any cause to confirm their suspicion of his being accessory to those Mens death."

In the spring Frobisher, in keeping with the plan to meet his brother, arrived at Beaver Lake and took all the men there with him to the fort at Portage du Traite. Matthew Cocking sent up Robert Davey to watch and protect Indians coming down to Cumberland House. The treatment of Davey by Frobisher stands in sharp contrast with that meted out to Longmoor in the previous year. He was pressed to partake of the Pedlars' hospitality, and told that he might trade with the Indians without let or hindrance. At the same time Frobisher protested that he was not eager to amass a fortune, and as he had plenty of goods he would offer them to the Indians at such a low price that Davey could not possibly do any business. Commenting on this, Matthew Cocking reports a statement of Frobisher's, overheard by Isaac Batt, that in 1775–76, the fifth year of his operations, he had cleared £9,000 and upwards. " This is seemingly not to be discredited when the large Quantities of Furs carried down by him are considered." When Davey went up the Churchill to meet the Indians, Frobisher followed him. Eight days' journey upstream they met Primo coming down with four canoes of furs from Thomas Frobisher. Twenty-eight canoes of Indians were with him, some of them belonging to the men Davey was in search of. Frobisher clothed the English Leader and his wife and got the man drunk without winning him over, for when they arrived at Portage du Traite he and his men left their furs with Davey at the Portage and went off to the fort, which stood on the opposite side of the river. As they brought nothing they were given nothing. They finally accompanied Davey to Cumberland House. With 63 beaver worth of goods, Davey's sally brought in 175, made beaver, in furs, and his Indians brought 688 worth of their own. The success of the sally encouraged Cocking to renew his plea of the previous year for a post farther inland, adding : " What has happened this year seemingly proves that if the Company had convenience of Carriage to Transport, the Pedlars would soon be ruined, for the Company's goods may be traded at such a rate as to undersell them much in most articles." Frobisher went out with seven canoes of furs, including those of his brother.

When Cumberland House was built the Pedlars passed up the Saskatchewan in the second week of October. The Hudson's Bay Company's men argued that if they could not come in sooner, their operations would be limited to the Saskatchewan below its Forks, and that if the Company built a post on the prairies above them it would secure an adequate control of the trade. In this they were mistaken. The Pedlars had passed the Forks to Fort Sturgeon in the region of Prince Albert—the next point where the prairies and forest met. As for the English Company, its difficulties in getting goods up to the interior were being gradually solved, and it was now ready to build on the prairies behind the Pedlars' settlement. On July 21, 1777, Humphrey Marten issued written orders for a temporary post on the buffalo hunting-grounds to secure provisions and to prevent the Pedlars from having dealings with the "Upland Indians." However, Joseph Hansom, who was temporarily in charge at Cumberland House after Cocking left to be Governor of Severn Fort, contented himself with simply carrying on, all the more, perhaps, as his post was more closely beset than during the previous years, and all his goods would be needed to hold the Indians. Captain Tute, of the Frobisher concern, with St. Germain for Pangman, and four canoes held the post on Beaver Lake to the north, and John Ross, in the Pangman service, was at Pasquia to the south-east.

Captain Tute came to Cumberland House, on his way in, short of food, and begged a supply. Hansom wrote : " I asked [him] in and in every respect used him kindly as becomes Englishmen, one to another in this part of the world ; . . . finding them really in want, I comply'd with his request and gave them 20 lb. of dried meat, 1 Bag of Pimmacon and one Bladder of Fat, which they was very thankful for and offered Payment for the same, but I told them the Honorable Hudsons Bay Company did not desire any such payment, only if any of their Servants should pass their Way and be in need, hope they will Comply with the same favour." This the Pedlars did on several occasions. The time when the bitterness of the struggle was such that the men from Montreal were capable of devising means to prevent the Englishmen from securing provisions and of quietly sitting by while they starved to death was not yet. Peter Pond and William Bruce visited Cumberland House a week later on their way up the Saskatchewan.

The murder of an Indian at Fort Sturgeon by a French-Canadian led to a correspondence with Hansom at Cumberland House, in which he was requested to arrest the murderer, who had gone off in that direction. Indeed, he had already visited the post on the way to Pasquia. The signatures to the letter dated at " Sturgeon River Fort " were Booty Graves, Charles McCormick, William Bruce, Peter Pond, Peter Pangman, Nicholes MaTure [Montour] Bartw. Blondeau. Joseph Frobisher had left the Upper Country for good. Holmes must have been in Montreal this winter, or may have been at Isaac's House, if it were occupied.

In April 1778 William Tomison took charge of Cumberland

House, Joseph Hansom acting as his second. For some thirty years Tomison was the dominating influence in the Hudson's Bay Company's service at York Fort and on the Saskatchewan. Trained to discipline as a labourer at York and Severn forts, he enforced discipline at Cumberland House and at the forts farther inland which he built. A severe critic of his men and swift to displace an inefficient servant, he none the less was capable of winning a willing obedience. Easily moved to anger by the shortcomings of the men, he was sufficiently in command of himself to recognize that faithful service atones for occasional aberrations. He maintained in the forts under his supervision something more than a semblance of the discipline which prevailed in the forts by the Bay. Thus he rendered great service to the Company, for by continuing the tradition of civility to the natives he won their respect; the forts of the Company, though manned by comparatively few men, were secure from attack, and the Company's men passed to and fro, it might be too much to say without danger, at least without loss of goods or of life. It is probably to the credit of Tomison that he incurred the enmity of the Pedlars. Their maledictions are the measure of his success in opposing them. While he never yielded to them when the interest of the Company's trade was involved, he continued the policy of civility to the intruders and reaped its reward. In the June after his arrival three Canadian canoes from Beaver Lake reached Cumberland House in distress for want of provisions. Tomison replied that he was not at liberty to supply them as a matter of business, but, having known the great necessity of want of food himself, humanity would not allow him to let them go without a small supply. While thanking him, the Pedlars informed him that Hansom, his second, was up towards Beaver Lake with more furs than he could bring in his canoes, and in great need of provisions. Tomison was thus enabled to send men off for the relief of his officer.

On September 22, 1778, Tomison arrived from York Fort, after taking the furs down, with renewed orders to build on the prairies, and with goods and men for the enterprise. He must have calculated that he was three weeks before the Pedlars and would get to the Indians before them, but Pangman and Bartholomew Blondeau passed the House the day before his arrival. The Pedlars had speeded up their transport by a fortnight and more that they might build still farther up the North Saskatchewan—this without abandoning the fort at Sturgeon River, which was now known as the " Lower Settlement." They established a post in the region of the present Silver Grove and, apparently, Blondeau four hundred yards below them. Here the great northern fur forest veered away from the river and the prairies crossed to the northern bank. The forts were on the track of the Wood Crees coming from the Thickwood Hills and from the upper valley of the Sturgeon River and its tributary the Shell— a great fur field—while to the south and west the prairie home of the buffalo stretched out like a sea whose farther shores were unknown. There would be both furs and provisions in abundance.

This post was known as the " Middle Settlement "—in the parlance of the voyageurs, Fort du Milieu.

Not content with this advance, the Pedlars went up the river past the Elbow to the Eagle Hills. One built " the Pidgeon's House " on the left bank of the river, a little east of south of Ruddell station on the Canadian National Railway. Peter Pangman built above, also on the left bank, nine miles below the mouth of the Battle River, on a beautiful " bottom " below the hill which is the outer bank. This was known as the " Upper Settlement " and " Pangman's Fort." On the other side of the river the Eagle Hills swerve away from the river westward. Once more the Pedlars were constrained to form a pool, with some one trader in command at a fort, but all sharing the returns in proportion to the goods thrown in. Thus Blondeau abandoned his half-built house at Silver Grove and erected another four hundred yards upstream, where the other Pedlars were, while at the Eagle Hills the trader at Pidgeon's House, in the course of the winter, went and lodged himself in Pangman's Fort, where McCormick appears to have had some authority, with John Cole for interpreter.

On 27th September Robert Longmoor left Cumberland House with 2,406 beaver worth of goods to build as far up as he could, if possible between the more distant Indians and the Pedlars. About a fortnight later Philip Turnor, formally appointed " Surveyor for settling the Latitudes and Longitudes, Courses and distances of the different Settlements Inland," reached the House, too late to be of the party. Longmoor had but eleven men with him, among them Isaac Batt, Charles Isham, Malchom Ross, and Mitchell Oman. On 18th October he put up on the south side of the North Saskatchewan, opposite the Pedlars' lowest settlement, that near Sturgeon River. His journey beyond was made difficult by the ice in the river. He broke his way through from time to time and reached what was spoken of as the " Middle Settlement " on the 23rd. The condition of the water and the treeless banks of the river for a hundred miles upstream warned him not to attempt to go farther. Moreover the Pedlars assured him that they would follow him wherever he should go. When Blondeau offered him his half-built house the offer was wisely accepted.

Philip Turnor, who joined Longmoor on 19th March, gives the personnel of the Pedlars' settlement and the trade relations of the men. There were three trading houses within two hundred yards, exclusive of Longmoor's, which, it has been seen, was four hundred yards down the river, " one in possession of Gebosh in trust for Wadding [Waden], one in possession of Holmes and Graves and another in possession of Nicholas [Montour] in trust for Blondeau, likewise about ten small Houses every one of their men being a trader "—that is, the men took goods out to trade for their masters. Holmes informed Turnor that all the Canadian traders on the Saskatchewan except Blondeau were in a " General Partnership," and they expected that he would soon join them. The traders at the

Upper Settlement, which was first established by Pangman, were McCormick, Graves, Pangman, Blondeau, Holmes, Grant, and Gebosh. McCormick, Gebosh, and Graves hauled their goods up after the river was frozen. When the Pedlars arrived in the autumn Blondeau and Pangman were in partnership, as were Holmes and Grant.

It was Longmoor's misfortune that he arrived after the Pedlars, for they had secured all the provision of the Indians in those parts, and his party was without food. Isaac Batt and Malchom Ross were dispatched to bring in any Indians who might have meat. But meagre supplies were procurable, and at extravagant prices, for the savages knew the value of competing traders in their midst, and gauged correctly the necessities of Longmoor's case.

Of course, there was no benevolence in the Pedlars' offer of Blondeau's house. With Longmoor under their immediate observation and in the disadvantageous position below them, they counted on preventing him from getting provisions and furs, for most of the Indians would have to pass by their post to reach him. Longmoor's game was to send men out with tobacco and goods, to trade with the natives and, where possible, induce them to come in. This the Pedlars countered by sending out ample supplies of tobacco and rum, and by insisting that the furs of Indians who took their liquor were, by that fact, theirs by right. On one occasion a large band was coming in to Longmoor's house. The Pedlars, to intercept it, sent out eighteen Frenchmen—six more men than were in the whole of Longmoor's household—armed with guns and pistols and bearing tobacco and ten gallons of rum. On Longmoor's protesting against the use of force, he was told that the furs of Indians who smoked their tobacco and drank their rum were theirs, and they would take them by force if necessary. This they were not only capable of doing, but they could easily do, for there were one hundred and twenty men in their houses and but twelve in Longmoor's all told. When this band got as far as the Pedlars' houses they were made to drink, and their horses and furs were taken and locked up within the stockades. Longmoor with one of his men appeared upon the scene, and protested that they were robbing the Hudson's Bay Company of its property and stealing from the Indians. Holmes beat Longmoor's man cruelly. It should be said that, a few days after, the Pedlars came to Longmoor's house and returned the tobacco which the Indians had accepted from his men before the Canadians came to them. They made excuses for their men's actions, saying that they had been in liquor ; that it would not happen again, and Longmoor could trade where he chose. They must have felt, on second thoughts, that there was a vast difference between asserting their right to trade within the Chartered Territory and preventing by force the Hudson's Bay Company itself from trading freely there. Nevertheless the practice continued. As soon as Indians arriving partook of the first gift of rum, willy-nilly, they had to give up their furs and see them locked up, so that the only way to get their worth was to take it in goods or rum from the Pedlars. At times the Indians themselves were locked up till they were willing to trade their furs.

Longmoor found that the Pedlars set the pace for him in every way. His men were sent out with tobacco and goods to trade with the more distant Indians. It was in vain ; the goods would be brought back ; there were none willing to trade. Longmoor entered it ruefully in his Journal : " Indians will not trade out [*i.e.* away from the fort] without Liquor and that is dangerous "—meaning that when crazed with drink the savages would rob and might kill the trader if he refused them more liquor.

Not only was the Company's trade being spoilt, Longmoor felt, but the natives were being wronged and destroyed : " It is a great pity such a body of Natives should be destroyed by a parcel of wild fellows Such as MacCormick, going about Sword in hand, threatening them to make them trade with him whether they will or no." Such treatment of the natives by the officers in the Pedlars' forts, issued in their men making light of perpetrating violences upon the savages. The natural result was that the natives at times took their revenge in one form or another. In the winter of 1776 four of the Pedlars' men were killed on the Assiniboine River—and two more as the canoes were going out. In that year also Pedlars were plundered on the Swan River. In 1777, at Sturgeon Fort on the Saskatchewan, three men sent out among the Indians lost their lives, the reason given being the maltreatment of natives when at the fort. Alexander Mackenzie, referring to the year under consideration speaks of " the improper conduct of some [of the Pedlars] which rendered it dangerous [for them] to remain any longer among the natives." It was not so with the men of the Hudson's Bay Company. Years of practice at the forts on the Bay in civility to the Indians served the Company's men in good stead ; for a quarter of a century lone servants of the Company had travelled through the land unafraid ; in the wild scenes of opposition, relations with the natives remained as of old ; there was no real reason for fear. Philip Turnor noted the attitude of a very large band of Indians who came in on horseback with thirty horses well-loaded and a great number of dogs. They passed the Pedlars' settlement by, saying that " they did not come to trade with them, but with Robert Longmoor. . . . The Englishmen were their Countrymen."

The nemesis of the policy of the Pedlars towards the natives, and especially of their recklessness in trading rum, came in this year at the uppermost settlement, the post at Eagle Hills. Mackenzie narrates the incident as the natural result of misconduct :

Most of them who passed the winter at the Saskatchewan, got to the Eagle hills where, in the spring of 1780 [1779], a few days previous to their intended departure, a large band of Indians being engaged in drinking about their houses, one of the traders, to ease himself of the troublesome importunities of a native, gave him a dose of laudanum in a glass of grog, which effectively prevented him from giving further trouble to any one, by setting him asleep for ever. This accident produced a fray in which one of the traders and several of the men were killed, while the rest had no other means to save themselves but by a precipitate flight, abandoning a considerable quantity of goods and near half of the furs which they had collected during the winter and spring.

The details, as reported by the Pedlars at the time, may be gathered from the journals of Longmoor and Philip Turnor. The laudanum was given in two doses, by McCormick and Gebosh, the latter being unaware of the action of the former ; hence Mackenzie's term "accident." In addition, McCormick had cut the Indian's tent in pieces. This was in the autumn, and led to a concerted design against the Pedlars. In the spring five tents of Indians camped upon the hill behind the fort, and, to pick a quarrel, stole a horse. At this Cole threatened to shoot all the horses of the Indians if it were not returned. One of the young men said he would first shoot Cole at the door of his house. An old Indian came in and warned the people of their danger, but McCormick refused to smoke the pipe of peace with him, saying that he should put on petticoats, for he was no more than an old woman, and that he would cut out his tongue. The interpreter refused to transmit the threat to the Indian. Cole was therefore called in and did so. At this the old Indian went up the hill in high dudgeon, and the whole body of Indians, increased now to twenty-five tents, one hundred and twenty men, came down to the fort, but quietly. They watched the traders sorting their furs and packing for departure. Suddenly, one of them, who had kept his eye on Cole, shot him. One of Pangman's men forthwith chased him, only to be shot in turn. Upon this, both sides flew to arms, and something like a general engagement ensued, the Indians firing from the bushes and the hill, the Canadians from the corners of their houses. When the Indians' fire became hot, all the Canadians took to the houses ; an Englishman, Jacobs, and a Highlander, Fisher, alone continued at their post. These men, by raising a flag of truce, brought about a cessation of arms. It was agreed that the Pedlars should make a gift of five kegs (forty gallons) of rum. On Friday they gave the savages another keg, and made the offer to surrender all their goods, provided they could take away the furs. The answer came from the Indians that they would have all the goods and kill all the men. Probably under cover of darkness two canoes of furs were loaded and dispatched downstream in the care of Gebosh. Finally the Indians took possession of the houses, the goods and the remaining furs, but the men were allowed to make their escape.

The terrible news brought by Gebosh created great alarm at the "Middle Settlement" for the Indians were expected to come down and attack it. All prepared for immediate departure. The French-Canadian servants, seeking for a scapegoat, laid the blame for the disaster on the Hudson's Bay Company's men. Gebosh stirred up feeling among the excitable Frenchmen by accusing the English of egging the Indians on. A menacing attitude was assumed towards Longmoor and his men, and their lives were threatened. Graves, Pangman, and McCormick, however, kept their men under control, and advised the Englishmen to leave at once, all the more as their goods were already traded. Longmoor wrote : "We are of opinion that we have more friends than enemies amongst the Indians, but none the less think it prudent to leave the place as soon as possible, as, should the Indians come upon the Canadians we should share the same fate, the Frenchmen being as much to be feared as the Indians, being a set of abandoned Villains." In the circumstances, Turnor decided not to try to go up to the Upper Settlement to take its latitude and longitude.

Latterly Longmoor had had greater success in trading. In the spring Indians had brought him large supplies of provisions, in fact more than his canoes could take. Six horses were sent down to the lower settlement loaded with provisions, and an additional canoe secured there. Graves offered to take down four large parcels, likewise of provisions. Even so twelve hundredweight was abandoned. So ended the occupation of the house at Silver Grove. For lack of a name, the Company's men afterwards called it Upper Hudson House, in distinction from the Hudson House built by Tomison farther down the river in the following autumn.

It is not possible to trace all the influences of the disaster at the Eagle Hills upon the Pedlars and their system of business. Followed as it was by other attacks on their posts, it was concluded that a general rising of the Indians against them was at hand. This alone would counsel union. But the unfortunate event was due in part to the recklessness of the rivalry of Pedlar with Pedlar, and of all the Pedlars in competition with the Hudson's Bay Company. Such recklessness must have been accentuated by the necessity under which the individual Pedlar or group of Pedlars laboured to meet their several creditors at Grand Portage with furs enough to square accounts and leave a favourable balance. It is apparent that Joseph Frobisher, when in the country, was an advocate of union or pools. The form these took was local and temporary. They were for the season, and applied to the individual posts which the rivals occupied as one. An individual became master of the post, and conducted the trade. In the spring the furs and the provisions were divided to the partners in proportion to the goods thrown into the pool. This was all to the good so far, but it did not relieve the individual Pedlar from the necessity of having an adequate supply of furs to turn over to his creditor for the goods provided by him. In this situation discontent with the management of the pool, as well as personal factors, tended to disrupt the arrangement before the winter was over. Peter Pangman, for example, in 1775 broke away and began to trade for himself. The remedy, of course, was to get the merchants who supplied the goods into a "general concern." This would immediately relieve the winterer from the intolerable pressure. It is not known that these were the views of Joseph Frobisher. There is no more evidence than that he and his brother Benjamin were prime movers in the formation of the "general concern" which was the root from which the North West Company grew.

The need for unity in the interior was accompanied by a similar necessity in the valley of the St. Lawrence. The supporters of the winterers were drawn into an ever widening partnership. In particular, firms like Simon McTavish & Co., and like McBeath & Co., quondam supporters of Peter Pond, who had connections with Detroit, the chief source of the corn needed for the provisioning of the canoes at Grand Portage, were brought in. McTavish's system of batteaux running out from Detroit to Montreal, and to Michilimackinac and Grand Portage, must have been a great acquisition to the partnership. All the agreements involved in creating what was called a " general concern " must have been worked out at Grand Portage, and as the Frobisher brothers, Benjamin and Joseph, were the ones most familiar with both the Upper Country and the Montreal end of the trade, it may be argued that they were the geniuses behind the movement towards unity. The extent to which their structure had grown may be gathered from a statement of Duncan M'Gillivray in his *Some Account of the trade carried on by the North West Company :*

In the year 1779, nine distinct parties entered into an agreement for one year to make the whole trade a common concern. It was divided into shares and the profits were divided in proportions mutually satisfactory ; each furnishing the outfit and paying expenses proportioned to his interest in the trade of the association ; see agreement entitled " Articles of General Co-partnership at Grand Portage. 1779."

William Grant, under date of April 24, 1780, reported to Governor Haldimand that the agreement of 1779 was continuing for the season 1780–81. Most valuable of all, he added the names of the firms in the " common concern " :

Todd & McGill	2 shares		
Ben. & Jos. Frobisher . .	2	,,	
McGill & Paterson	2	,,	The North West [sic]
McTavish & Co.	2	,,	is divided into sixteen
Holmes & Grant [Robert]	2	,,	shares all which form
Waden & Co. [St. Germain]	2	,,	but one Company at
McBeath & Co.	2	,,	this time.
Ross & Co. [Pangman] . .	1	,,	
Oakes & Co.	1	,,	

Grant also indicates that a factor making for unity was the control of transportation into the Upper Country exercised by the Government during the War of American Independence.

The prospects before the " General Co-partnership " were bright. Great success had attended the Canadians in their attempt to win the fur trade of the Churchill and Athabaska regions from the Hudson's Bay Company. In 1776 Thomas Frobisher had wintered at Ile-à-la-Crosse Lake, on the peninsula south of the entrance to Deep River (Aubichon Arm), which was the water-way leading to

Athabaska. In 1778 Peter Pond had been supplied with goods by the partnership on the Saskatchewan, and had passed along this water-way over Methy Portage, and down the Clearwater and Athabaska rivers, and had built about forty miles from Athabaska Lake and been most successful. Sir Alexander Mackenzie says:

[He] saw a vast concourse of the Knisteneaux [Cree] and Chepewyan tribes, who used to carry their furs annually to Churchill; the latter by the barren grounds, where they suffered innumerable hardships, and were sometimes even starved to death. The former followed the course of the lakes and rivers, through a country that abounded in animals, and where there was plenty of fish: but though they did not suffer from want of food, the intolerable fatigue of such a journey could not be easily repaid to an Indian: they were, therefore, highly gratified by seeing people come to their country to relieve them from such long, toilsome and dangerous journies; and were immediately reconciled to give an advanced price for the articles necessary to their comfort and convenience. Mr. Pond's reception and success was accordingly beyond his expectation; and he procured twice as many furs as his canoes could carry. They also supplied him with as much provision as he required during his residence among them, and sufficient for his homeward voyage. Such of the furs as he could not embark, he secured in one of his winter huts, and they were found the following season, in the same state in which he left them.

Thus Pond was able to solve the pressing problem of provisions with which to bring out his furs. The brush country west of his post abounded in red deer and buffalo, while the Chipewyans to the east would bring in pemmican made with caribou meat. Pond returned to his post in 1779. In 1780–81 he wintered at Michilimackinac.

Pond's entry into what he took to be the watershed of a river flowing into the Pacific, opened a wide vista for the Canadian traders. The views held by members of the copartnership of 1780 may be judged by the scheme, already referred to, submitted by Alexander Henry to Mr. Joseph Banks under the date of October 18, 1781, for his " perusal and amusement." It is nothing less than a sketch of the route across the continent from the Atlantic to the Pacific with a plan for exploration down our Slave River

until you come to the Sea [Pacific Ocean]—which cant be any very Great Distance, Suppose it should be Thirty, or Forty Degrees of Longitude Unless, some Accidents should Entervene, it can be done in Thirty days, which will be in July. Here an Establishment may be made in some Convenient Bay, or Harbour, where Shipping, may come to. In the mean time a Small Vessell may be Built, for Coasting, and Exploaring the Coast, which can be no Great Distance from the Streight, which Separates the two Contenants. . . . There are many National advantages which may Result from Discovering and Surveying these Remote unknown Parts of America, and having a Communication, from other Rich Country's in the East and easily, Conveyed across to Hudsins bay, where British Manufactorers, might be sent, To Thousands on the Continent & fetch large Profits & A Valuable New Commerce be opened and Secured to his Majesty's subjects—as there is at Present no appearance of a North west passage, for Ships.

This grandiose scheme, which was afterwards taken up by Alexander Mackenzie, came, of course, from the fertile mind of Peter Pond. It enables us to see the bright prospects which appeared to be before the copartnership of 1780, which Duncan M'Gillivray tells us was to last for three years.

For all its bright prospects the partnership had to face the whirlwind raised by the Pedlars on the Saskatchewan. The hostility of the Indians spread to the Assiniboine River, where two posts were destroyed in the autumn of 1781. Only the story of Fort des Trembles, on the north bank of the river about five miles above our Portage la Prairie, has been preserved. According to John Macdonell's *Some Account of Red River*, Messrs. Bruce and Boyer were concerned. Bruce was among the roughest of the Pedlars. He shifted, or was shifted, from post to post, for, as the Frobishers explained to Cocking, his severe method of treating the natives prevented his twice residing in one place. According to Alexander Henry the younger

the Indians concerned were Crees, Assiniboines, and Bas de la Rivière Indians ; 90 tents were at the house. The affair took place soon after the arrival of the canoes in the fall of 1781, while the people were still building. Out of 21 men present, 11 hid themselves ; the remaining 10 defended themselves bravely, drove the Indians out of the houses and fort, and shut the gates. They lost three men—Belleau, Fecteau, and La France. They killed 15 Indians on the spot, and 15 more died of their wounds. The place was instantly abandoned, canoes were loaded, and all hands embarked and drifted down to the Forks.

These tragic incidents led the traders to believe that the Indians were united in a conspiracy to drive them out of the country. In their view they were saved from this disaster by the terrible epidemic of small-pox which broke out that autumn. The infection was brought from the south by the Saulteurs and Sioux, who are said to have attacked Whites in American territory stricken with it, and to have become victims themselves by wearing their clothes. The Sioux passed it on to the Indians of the Plains as far as the Rockies and beyond, the Saulteurs to the savages of the forest northward to its extreme limits. It was on the river Assiniboine at the time of the attempt on Fort des Trembles. As the fugitives were leaving the fort two Indian lads came in from the direction of Fort Dauphin and asked leave to go with them. They proved to be victims of the small-pox. Bruce dropped downstream to the Forks. He seems to have been wintering there when he died of the disease. In support of the Pedlars' view that the scourge saved them from an uprising of the Indians is Peter Fidler's account of the plans of the Indians of the upper Assiniboine River to attack a post which stood on the Shoal River, the outflow of Swan Lake. They were stricken by the scourge while on the way and the fort was saved.

Meanwhile the Hudson's Bay Company was quietly developing its defensive offensive against the Pedlars. On October 5, 1779, William Tomison, Chief at Cumberland House, but in an informal way already responsible for the Company's affairs on the Saskatchewan, reached the Canadian Settlement near the Sturgeon River.

He had the good fortune to be there before the Pedlars arrived, and was able to trade both furs and provisions from the assembled Indians without interference. Two days later he arrived at the point where he intended to winter, fourteen miles below Longmoor's house of the previous year. The spot on which he decided to build * was a few yards back from the left bank. It was well chosen. Across the river lay a considerable prairie, the present Lily Plain, sheltered on all sides by wood—the resort of the buffalo from the winter's blasts. Some provisions at least would be got near at hand. A short distance back from the site of the house ran a track used by the natives travelling from the fur field of the Thickwood Hills down to the mouth of the Sturgeon River. The first task undertaken was to cut a pathway back from the river to this track. Longmoor and Malchom Ross were then sent out to gather provisions from the Indians. The first house built was thirty-seven feet long and twenty-seven broad. Others were added later; for the most part they ran along the palisades. In keeping with the practice at the older forts of the Company, in time a garden was made—probably the first on the North Saskatchewan River. To distinguish it from other posts, William Tomison called it Hudson House.

Mr. Holmes had followed Tomison up the river ; he arrived at Hudson House ten days after him. Soon Captain Tute came overland with horses and built a small house close by, but it was no more than a feint at occupation. Tute went on to the former Middle Settlement, that is, at Silver Grove, and took to the Lower Settlement at the Sturgeon River all the material there. Longmoor understood that an Indian had died suddenly in drink at Sturgeon Fort, and that the Pedlars were alarmed lest it should become the occasion of another attack. They therefore kept their men concentrated at that one point. For once the Hudson's Bay Company enjoyed the position they had desired—a post standing between the Indians of the upper Saskatchewan and the Canadian House. Holmes tried to play on the feelings of Tomison as Master of Cumberland House, and to bring him to abandon his advantageous position ; he wrote to him to say that he had word that Cumberland House had been destroyed by the Indians. Tomison knew the relations subsisting between the Company's men and the natives were such that the report must be nothing but a ruse. Moreover, he had had recent experience of the resort to falsehood by the Pedlars' men. Outrunners stole the furs of Indians camped at the House, and assured the owners that it was done by the Company's servants. Isaac Batt was, however, dispatched to Cumberland House to inquire concerning its welfare.

By January trade had gone so well that goods were running short at Hudson House—this in spite of a few Canadians occupying the old Middle Settlement fourteen miles above. Accordingly Tomison returned to Cumberland House, his real charge, and sent off goods to Longmoor, whom he had left in his place. Longmoor

* The remains are in NW¼, sect. 16, tp. 48, r. 2, W3, in the Nesbitt Forest Reserve.

kept men watching the track leading to the Canadian House up-stream. The winter was spent by both sides moving men about against one another as on a chequer-board. In the spring Longmoor made a real contribution to the facilities for transportation which the Company still sadly lacked, by managing to get ten canoes built at Hudson House, one very large one and one medium sized. During the summer his post as well as Sturgeon Fort was closed.

When Longmoor returned in the autumn he found the Canadian Sturgeon Fort burnt down by the Indians. When the Pedlars came up they built "a little below their old House." The remains of a post three miles below, and on the left bank of the river opposite Betts Island, a mile and a half above the bridge at Prince Albert, must mark the new site.* The Canadians were not occupying the former Middle Settlement in force during these years, but sending up men and goods overland in the winter to gather provisions and furs, these being immediately sent down to the Lower Settlement. This policy must have been due to a fear of the Indians which was not without justification, for it was more than likely that they would attempt to renew the joy of plundering a post. Indeed, the men who had captured the Eagle Hills Post appeared before Hudson House in March, 1781, and began chopping through the palisades and gate. Robert Longmoor kept his men in hand. He waited till the first gun was pushed through to shoot, when he promptly broke its barrel. Then, as the Indians came in, he took their guns and bayonets and knives from them, with the threat that if one English-man were killed he would not spare one Indian. He locked up the four ringleaders in the house, and apparently began to trade. That over, the prisoners were released. What with the English coming on the ground before the Pedlars, and occupying a site apart from them, and enjoying the good will of the Indians as a whole, Hudson House was doing well. So also was Cumberland House. The returns for this year were 6,887, made beaver, from the former and 8,445 from the latter, making 15,332, made beaver, from the Inland Posts.

In contrast, the next season, 1781-82, was one of disaster. The Indians had burnt the plains to the south of the various forts to keep the buffalo far out and thus to enhance the value of their pro-visions. It injured themselves as much as the traders. Amid great scarcity of food at Hudson House, starving Indians came in to be fed, and were fed, though it involved sacrifice. In the midst of the dearth of food, the small-pox came.

First contact with the stricken Indians was made by a band of five servants. Isaac Batt and Mitchell Oman were sent out in mid-October with ammunition and goods to forage for themselves and do what trading they could. They went up the river in canoes. Oman gave David Thompson an account of what he saw.

We proceeded about 150 miles up the River to the Eagle Hills, where we saw the first camp and some of the people sitting on the beach to cool

---

* In SW¼, sect. 6, tp. 49, r. 25, W2.

themselves ; when we came to them, to our surprise they had marks of the small pox, were weak and just recovering, and I could not help saying, thank heaven we shall now get relief [from hostile Indians]. For none of us had the least idea of the desolation this dreadful disease had done, until we went up the bank to camp and looked into the tents, in many of which they were all dead, and the stench was horrid. Those that remained had pitched their tents about 200 yards from them and were too weak to move away entirely, which they soon intended to do ; they were in such a state of despair and despondence that they could hardly converse with us, a few of them had gained strength to hunt which kept them alive. From what we could learn three-fifths had died under the disease. Our Provisions were nearly out and we had expected to find ten times more than we wanted, instead of which they had not enough for themselves. They informed us that as far as they knew all the Indians were in the same dreadful state, as themselves, and that we had nothing to expect from them. We proceeded up the River with heavy hearts ; the Bisons were crossing the River in herds, which gave us plenty of provisions for the voyage to our wintering grownd. When we arrived [there] instead of a crowd of Indians to welcome us, all was solitary silence ; our hearts failed us. There was no Indian to hunt for us ; before the Indians fell sick a quantity of dried provisions had been collected . . . upon which we subsisted until at length two Indians with their families came and hunted for us. These informed us, that the Indians of the forest had beaver robes in their tents some of which were spread over the dead bodies, which we might take and replace them by a new blanket and that by going to the tents we would render a service to those that were living by furnishing them with tobacco, ammunition, and a few other necessaries and thus the former part of the winter was employed. The bodies lately dead, and not destroyed by the Wolves and Dogs, for both devoured them, we laid logs over them to prevent these animals.

The Indians nearer the forts, where the prairies had been burnt, were in a pitiable plight. The bands with the scourge upon them, and starving, turned their faces to Hudson House to find relief. Some were stricken with death before they could reach the sought-for haven. One band was almost there when it was cut down, save for two little boys. These managed to get in. Doubtless, Longmoor gave presents to Indians to adopt them. Those that came in starving were fed, when there was but little to eat at the fort. The dead Red Men were buried by white hands. Amid it all the trade in furs continued.

The first news of the scourge as in its neighbourhood reached Cumberland House in December. A few days later men arrived from Hudson House with reports of the pitiable situation up the Saskatchewan. William Tomison manifested his keenness as a trader in his Journal's entry for the next day—" smaoking everything belonging to them with the Flour of Sulphur to prevent any effect from them to the Natives." * In the interest of the trade the scourge must be kept away from the Indians at all hazards. But this keen trader of hard exterior, the doughty champion of the Company against the Pedlars, could harbour soft feelings within. Indians

* Fumigation with sulphur and the succession of airings in the sunshine at the several posts and in London would have the effect of disinfecting the furs before they would reach the market. This would also go far to explain how it was that no European servant of the Company took the disease.

stricken with small-pox were taken into the fort and nursed. One man was told off to care for them. When the house could take no more, a camping-ground was arranged for the sick. When there was scarce enough fish to provide for the mess at the fort, a share was given to the starving natives. When it was all that the service could do to get wood enough to keep the fort warm, the wood-cutters were ordered to furnish a supply for the Indian isolation camp. Let it be said, the Company's servants in the day of trial were not found wanting. It may well have been the same with the Pedlars ; unfortunately no record of their doings has survived.

It will remain a mystery how the Englishmen escaped all infection. There seems to be evidence that their young squaws died. Isham, the half-breed, was stricken at Hudson House, but survived. The English cared for the sick, buried the dead with their own hands, took in the furs of the stricken and the dead, on the principle of business as usual, but none were caught by the scourge. Of the Pedlars, William Bruce and Captain Tute, at least, as Tomison reports, fell victims, and many of their men.

As if the small-pox, which decimated its trappers, were not disaster enough for the Hudson's Bay Company, it was made to suffer in the last stage of the War of American Independence, when France had thrown herself upon the side of the colonies in revolt. In 1782 the French admiral, Jean François Galaup, Comte de la Pérouse, entered Hudson Bay on a raid, captured the mouth of the Churchill River and blew up the fortifications of Prince of Wales's Fort. Passing on to the Hayes, he took York Fort and burned it to the ground. Scarcely less disastrous was the mishap of the following year. Tomison had gone down with the furs to York Fort, but no ship appeared on the horizon, though he waited long. At last, in despair of her arrival, and in dread of being caught on his return journey by the rivers freezing, he left. A week later the vessel cast anchor in Five Fathom Hole. The deplorable result was that the inland posts lay without the means of trading, nor even of sustenance, for Tomison had to purchase even ammunition for the hunters of the forts from the Pedlars. All the while the goods and the ammunition lay idle at York Fort.

Nor was all this the full measure of the disasters of the time. In October 1781 the Council at York decided that it was highly expedient to take the aggressive against the Pedlars on the Churchill River and in Athabaska, and ordered that settlements be made in those parts. Had this policy been immediately carried out, the Company would have entered into that rich fur field whilst its former relations with the trading Indians were fresh, and before the Pedlars had weaned them from their old loyalty, and would have won the natives at large to their support. This succession of disasters postponed the enterprise for many seasons. When the Englishmen did go in, they went as strangers and found great difficulty in effecting a footing. The Company paid no dividends for the years 1783, 1784, and 1785. Till 1778 the dividend stood steadily at 10 per cent.

Till 1782 it ran at 8 per cent. It took three years to recover from the disasters of 1781–83.

The epidemic of small-pox was at first sight deliverance for the Pedlars from the hostility of the Indians. It proved, however, disastrous to their trade. It swept away the men who trapped the furs, and scarcely less important, the men who hunted to supply venison to the forts, and made pemmican for the canoes. All unconscious of the sudden misfortune, the merchants of Montreal sent in the usual consignments of goods in the autumn of 1782 and met with great loss. Even in the wooded north the losses were, according to Alexander Mackenzie, very heavy. The stricken Indians fled to the deepest recesses of the forest in the vain hope of escaping from the scourge, and there was no trade. The party which was on the Athabaska River in 1782–83 returned with but seven packages of beaver.

The hostility of the Indians and the epidemic of small-pox were not the only difficulties which the Canadian copartnership of 1780 had to face. There was disintegration within the common concern itself. It did not hold together for the three years set by the agreement. Duncan M'Gillivray says : " As the members of the Association looked forward to the termination of a common interest, this agreement was not productive of all the benefits proposed. At the end of two years it was discontinued." The disintegration was, doubtless, due to personal factors, but it would be accentuated by the losses incurred. We may judge that Peter Pangman on the Saskatchewan was playing his own game, for he was left out of the common concern at its renewal in 1784. Another partner in disfavour was Peter Pond, for he was only allowed one share when his actual achievements would appear to have entitled him to two. In the autumn of 1781, for some reason, he did not return to his wintering ground on the River Athabaska. Most probably an early winter and frozen rivers stayed his progress when he was no farther than the Churchill River. He went to Lac la Ronge and ensconced himself beside Étienne Waden who had occupied his post, probably on the Waden Bay of the survey maps, since 1779. From Alexander Mackenzie's statement it is clear that the two traders were in a common concern. Waden's goods being provided by his supporters and Pond's by his, but the two men were to act in conjunction. Mackenzie, who appears to have been none too friendly to Pond, describes Waden as " a Swiss gentleman of strict probity and known sobriety." The two, however, quarrelled. Allowances must be made for the loneliness and the silence of life in the forest during winter, and for the trial to body and mind alike of a monotonous diet of fish. The strain would grow intenser as the winter wore slowly on, especially for such a high-strung temperament as was Peter Pond's. Add to this the habitual recourse of the Pedlars to violence. Unfortunately the only information concerning the resultant tragedy comes from the affidavit of one of Waden's men, presented by the widow Waden to Governor Haldimand along with a plea for justice. It brings

Pond's clerk, Toussaint le Sieur, as well, into the fracas. In February
Pond and Waden had fought. In March they were quarrelling of an
evening. At night the deponent heard the report of two guns. On
coming to Waden's house he saw Pond and Le Sueur leaving. Within
lay Waden, his thigh bone broken and blood flowing profusely.
The poor man was too weak to explain the tragedy before he died.
That Pond and Le Sueur went away leaving the wounded man to
his fate, if true, is damning evidence. Mackenzie says that Pond
was tried in Montreal and acquitted. No trace of the trial can be
found. It seems probable that the lawyers of the Crown decided that
the deed took place beyond the jurisdiction of Canada. There the
matter must be left.

This tragedy in the unpoliced woods of the north must have been
one of the factors leading to the disruption of the copartnership of
1780. In the year 1782-83 we find two groups of Canadians competing for the trade of Athabaska. Only the smaller group reached
the wintering-ground. Even so, they came back, as has been seen,
with but seven packages of beaver, for the small-pox was now raging
among the Indians of the forest. Pond, who represented the larger
group of traders, wintered on Thomas Frobisher's old ground of
1776-77, at Ile-à-la-Crosse, which, placed as it was at a vantage
point, had been occupied ever since. He was in Athabaska for the
season 1783-84. When he came down to Grand Portage he found
that the common concern had been renewed on the first of January
of the year 1784, and the North West Company launched.

The North West Company of 1784 was an attempt to unite all
the winterers inland and all the larger capitalists in Montreal
interested in the trade of the North-West in one great " concern "
which should co-ordinate the various branches of the trade—the
capitalists, who supplied the goods and disposed of the furs, with the
winterers, who may be considered as the " producers " of the peltries.
In the " interior " it co-ordinated the fur trade of the northern forest
with the pemmican trade of the prairies. The misfortunes and
antipathies of the years just past eliminated a number of the men
who had been in the partnership of 1780. Forrest Oakes had
recently died. Boyer, his partner, appears to have fallen into the
position of servant in the new concern. Waden was dead, and his
partner, Venant Lemer St. Germain, was eliminated. McBeath, who
had been supplying Peter Pond with goods, received two shares,
but Pond himself, whether because of his poverty or because of
disfavour due to his refractory temper and his implication in Waden's
death, received but one. One's sympathies go out to Pond. He had
been pioneer in the richest of the fur fields for six years and had had
his seasons of spectacular returns. But all the while he had been
much more than a crass fur-trader. His restless mind had explored
the possibilities of the north. He had questioned his Indians and
learned what tribes lay in the beyond, and what sort of country.
He had watched the exploration of the Pacific coast which was
leading to a profitable trade with China and would bring the far west

within the pale of civilization. Amid the physical difficulties of the trader's crude shack in winter—little paper, frozen ink, and what not ?—he was making sketch-maps of the western country which are to this day a source for the history of the trade and a record of the speculations of the time. His imagination was exploring the way to the Pacific and laying the foundation of Sir Alexander Mackenzie's later triumphs. It does look as if this ill-educated intellectual among the traders was thrown to the ground in the wrestle with the capitalists.

Then, too, Peter Pangman's claims were ignored, whether because he had come through the seasons of difficulty without capital, or because he had been playing his own game while still in the partnership of 1780. He was entirely excluded from the new concern. It was the men with large capital or credit who got the lion's share. Holmes, the winterer, got one share ; Grant, his supporter, two. The Frobisher and the McTavish firms in 1780 had each two shares ; they now had three each. The McGill firm withdrew from the trade, but two new men, Patrick Small and M. Montour, appear with two shares each. These shares, with McBeath's two and Pond's single share, make sixteen—the same number as in 1780. The agreement of 1784 was drawn to last for five years, thus giving it a measure of stability lacking in the earlier agreements.

In revenge for his exclusion from the "common concern," Peter Pangman persuaded the firm of Gregory and McLeod, whose interest in the trade of Detroit was in jeopardy because of the triumph of the American Revolution, to transfer their efforts to the trade of the North-West and become the centre of an opposition to the North West Company. This inaugurated the fiercest competition the North-West had yet seen. The greatest need of the new concern was for vigorous supporters in the interior ; it says much for the judgment of Gregory and McLeod that they found it in Alexander and Roderick Mackenzie.

Alexander Mackenzie was born in 1764, two miles out from Stornoway in the Scottish Isle of Lewis. After his mother's death the lad of about ten years of age came out with his father to a relative in New York. When the American Revolution broke out the father enlisted in the King's forces, and the boy was sent to Montreal where he continued his schooling. At about fifteen years of age he entered the service of Gregory, McLeod & Company. He so far approved himself to the firm as to be given an "outfit" for trade at Detroit. When Pangman drew the firm into the venture to the North-West, and the call was for reliable and venturesome spirits, Mackenzie was given no less a position than that of wintering partner and sent into the interior. Alexander's cousin, Roderick Mackenzie, had arrived in Montreal in the autumn of 1784, and was enlisted as an apprenticed clerk along with James Finlay, the son of the pioneer trader on the Saskatchewan. That scene of bustle and jollity, Grand Portage, in July 1785, when first the new concern entered the Upper Country, must have been greatly enlivened by the presence, so to say, in the panoply of war, of the agents and wintering partners of the two rival companies. The new concern was represented by John Gregory its agent, by Peter Pangman its moving spirit, and by John Ross his partner—assembled at its " one hangar or store warmly put together and sufficiently spacious for the purpose of the season." Soon the hour of dispersal came. John Ross went off to Athabaska with his clerk, Laurent Leroux, a man of experience, trained in the trade of those parts. He built his post close beside Peter Pond's establishment on the Athabaska River and had the redoubtable Pond himself for his opponent. Alexander Mackenzie went to the Churchill River, and lodged himself at Ile-à-la-Crosse at close quarters with Patrick Small, who occupied Pond's old fort on the peninsula south of the water-way leading to Athabaska.

Peter Pangman's special sphere was the Saskatchewan. Here he took a surprising course ; he built on the South Saskatchewan. The South Branch, as it was called, had hitherto been ignored by all the traders. As a whole, it offered little promise either of peltry or of provisions. Its long sweep through the bald prairies offered no home for beaver, nor for the more precious fur-bearing animals. While its banks were frequented by buffalo in summer, they were deserted in winter, for even those hardy denizens of the plains sought the park grasslands of the north in the winter, as affording at once grazing and shelter from the blizzards. While this was so of the South Branch as a whole, it was not true of the last sixty miles of its course to its confluence with the North Branch, for the forest crossed the North Saskatchewan at two points, near the so-called Upper Hudson House and below the Sturgeon River. The woods between the two rivers were tolerably open and, so to say, broken by bays of the great sea of grass. They thus offered a happy wintering-ground for the buffalo herds. In these parts provisions would be in plenty.

Subsequent history shows that peltry would not be lacking. The prairie to the east led to the bush country of the upper valley of the Carrot River. Moreover, the Wood Crees of the Thickwood Hills appear to have crossed the North Branch near Upper Hudson House, and to have met the Indians of the plains at what was later called Gardepuy's Crossing to trade their furs for the provisions and other products of the prairies. At any rate, Matthew Cocking, crossing at that point in 1772, met a considerable group of Indians, and subsequent houses on the South Branch carried on a successful traffic in furs.

In his first winter in opposition, 1785–86, Peter Pangman built a house about forty miles up the South Branch immediately below a group of islands clothed with poplar. Hence the name Fort des Isles. Its remains lie on the right bank of the river three miles above Fenton Ferry. Holmes of the North West Company had built at the spot during the summer. Holmes had also built a post on the North Branch, two hundred yards above the Battle River. Pangman had not men enough to occupy a post beside him, but sent a party to tent hard by, and do what trade it could. They were there for three months before they got a skin, for Holmes got the Indians within his palisades and locked them in until all their furs were traded. Only when the savages rose up and threatened to kill him, did Holmes give his opponents a chance to trade. The Indians must have then taken revenge by carrying their furs to Pangman's men, for in May these passed Hudson House with eleven packs of furs.

William Tomison, ever alert, now decided that the Hudson's Bay Company should have a house on the South Branch. In the early spring of 1785 the site was chosen. It was on the right bank of the river, on a beautiful level with a hill in the background to the south. It stood at Gardepuy's Crossing near the borders of the woods and the plains, and where an Indian track crossed the river ; it was devised to cut the native traders off from the posts of Pangman and Holmes. Cellars and chimney heaps mark the site to-day. Pangman and Holmes immediately abandoned their newly-built forts, and built on a slope on the left bank about four hundred yards below. Ruins in the present Forest Reserve indicate the site. All these passed under the name of South Branch House.* When Mitchell Oman came up the river with the winter's goods from Cumberland House to the English Company's post, M. Montour held the North West Company's fort. A few days after, Pangman brought a large cargo to the master of his post.

But during this, the second season of the Canadian struggle, attention was directed to fur-bearing regions far up the North Branch. To begin with, a third Canadian company was in the field. While the North West Company had gone far towards gathering the Pedlars on the Saskatchewan into a general concern, there were still parties in opposition in the nearer fur fields, where there was some hope of success for these weaker firms. In the Nipigon region Alexander Shaw and Donald MacKay were holding their own. In 1784 this concern invaded the Saskatchewan in the person of Donald MacKay. He came in late, however, and was halted by the frozen river some twenty miles below Nipawi, at the lower end of the tracking ground. He built a post there on the north bank, but gathered no more than three packs of furs. He was able, however, to prepare plans for a post far up the Northern Saskatchewan. He built on Pine Island, on the left side of the river, opposite the mouth of the Big Gully and north of the present Paynton on the Canadian National Railway.† MacKay was in happy relations with the men of the Hudson's Bay Company, and William Tomison, by agreement, sent up men in the summer to build beside him. Tomison named his post Manchester House. The North West Company and Peter Pangman each followed suit. As if that were

---

* The sites of these South Branch Houses are indicated by their remains. The Hudson's Bay Company's house was on river-lot 13 and in NE¼, sect. 35, near the boundary of townships 44 and 45, range 1, west of the third meridian. The North-West Company's fort stood in NW¼, sect 2, tp. 45, r. 1, W3.

† The remains of a fort may still be seen on this island, locally known as Spruce Island ; they are in SE¼, sect. 6, tp. 49, r. 21, W3.

not enough, a lone Frenchman, by name Champagne, built also.
The presence of four Canadian posts on that single island shows how
far the North West Company of 1784 fell short of achieving a general
partnership.

The tenseness of feeling at the " upper settlements " on the
Saskatchewan that winter led to strange courses.   William Holmes
had elected to occupy personally his house at the Battle River,
doubtless congratulating himself on having the field to himself.
He was deceived.   Pangman, MacKay, and William Tomison for
the Hudson's Bay Company, sent parties to camp over against and
around his fort.   These three parties, resorting to every hostility
against one another on Pine Island, agreed to act together at Battle
River should Holmes begin firing upon them.   At Pine Island Pangman inveigled Indians to take furs due to Manchester House to him.
William Tomison boldly faced him in his own fort, and brought him
to an agreement that all such furs be privately transferred to him.
Never a party left one house to meet Indians coming in but parties
from the other posts came scurrying after them in the hopes of
spoiling its trade.   Tomison pours out his lamentation : " It is not
possible to please the natives when there is so many houses to go to,
the Canadians giving the same quantity of Liquor for 20 skins that
they used to give for 50."   All parties sent men out with goods to
winter with the Indians.   That the Canadians did not always
succeed in establishing pleasant relations with them is suggested
by the fact that one of their number was murdered out on the plains.
There were lively times in the no-man's-land between the several
posts, with violent men scrambling for the Indians and their furs ;
and it may almost be said that it was due to chance rather than
virtue that the traders came through the winter without bloodshed.

The financial strength of the North West Company enabled it
to occupy several posts with the intent of dividing the trade. Not
only did it aim at holding the Battle River post without an opposition, but it built a post some fifty miles above Pine Island with a
view to cutting off the Indians of the Beaver River from its rivals
on the Island.   The post stood on the right bank of the river about
north of the present Maidstone.   Donald MacKay, however, built
a small house within a hundred yards of it.   Once, when it was
reported that Swampy Ground Assiniboins from the Saskatchewan
west of the present Edmonton, who had taken tobacco both from
MacKay and Tomison, were heading for this uppermost post of the
North West Company, the two traders united to form a flying
column to intercept them ; they marched all through the night and
arrived at dawn only to find themselves the victims of a false
report.

This frontier post of the North West Company was held by
Edward Umfreville, formerly accountant for the Hudson's Bay
Company at Severn Fort.   A man of considerable talent, he was
made second at Severn Fort immediately on his engagement in 1771.
Andrew Graham, his Chief, reported him as a " pretty accountant "

and likely to do well if properly handled. Though a comparative new-comer in 1773, he drew up an elaborate " Proposal for the better regulation of the intended expedition Inland " to establish a post. Samuel Hearne even visited him at Severn to consult him before leading his party to Cumberland House. In 1776 he became second at York Fort. Possibly because he regarded even this promotion as much too slow, he left the Company's service in 1779. In 1784 he appeared in the employ of the North West Company, and was engaged to discover a new route, one wholly in British territory, from Lake Nipigon to Winnipeg Lake. It was not his fault that a practicable water-way was not found. He passed from Nipigon into the Albany River, and by the English River to the Winnipeg. There he joined the Saskatchewan brigade and spent his first winter in the North West Company's post over against Hudson House. The following winter he was with Holmes at the Battle River, and now he was in a command of his own. This he held for two years, when he retired from the Upper Country. Two years later he published a work, *The Present State of Hudson's Bay*, in which he sought to even the score between himself and his former English employers. It is the first, but by no means the most substantial, of a long series of pamphlets, which are more or less propaganda against the Hudson's Bay Company, and which were devised to win the favour of the public for the North West " concern."

All we know of the Red River, as the Assiniboine was then called, is that one Duncan Pollock, an officer in the Gregory–Pangman partnership, was posted somewhere over against Robert Grant, who the year before was at Fort des Épinettes, Pine Fort, on the north bank of the river and west of its tributary the Pine Creek, in N.E.$\frac{1}{4}$, section 36, township 8, range 14, west of the Principal Meridian. Grant had with him William M'Gillivray, then at the beginning of a long and notable career as clerk, wintering partner and finally agent of the North West Company. The three M'Gillivray brothers, William, Duncan, and Simon, were sons of a small tenant on an estate of Lord Lovat's in Inverness-shire, in the Scottish Highlands. They had the good fortune to be the nephews of Simon McTavish, one of the chief partners in the North West Company. Educated at his expense, they owed their first steps to fortune to their interested uncle.

The new " concern's " depot at Grand Portage was soon entrusted to Roderick Mackenzie—a youth, as his *Reminiscences* and literary remains show, with a rare talent for making friends, accentuated by the gift of keeping them to the end. However turbulent the rivalry might be elsewhere, kindly feelings prevailed at " Rory's " post. A Mr. Givins was clerk in the North West Company's depot over against him. " He and I, though in opposition, were always together and separated in the Spring good friends."

In the season 1786–87 Roderick Mackenzie went to Ile-à-la-Crosse in the Churchill River region as clerk under Alexander Mackenzie, while William M'Gillivray was moved up to be Patrick

Small's assistant in the opposing North West Company's post. The two clerks built outposts in a most friendly way side by side at Lac des Serpents below Ile-à-la-Crosse Lake. Roderick writes:

On my arrival there, I fixed on a place for winter. . . . In the interval, W. McGillivray appeared well determined for opposition. His order, he said was to place himself along side of me, but he observed that he did not approve of the situation I had selected, and he was informed of a much better one not far distant, and suggested that it would be for our mutual good if I would accompany him to this place, which I without hesitation agreed to and in a few hours we reached our proposed destination, in the vicinity of a small river which promised a plentiful fishery.

" Rory," finished the year with M'Gillivray as he began it.

In the Spring, after the trade was over, my neighbour and I, after comparing notes, agreed to travel in company to our respective head-quarters [at Ile-à-la-Crosse], where our canoes arrived side by side, the crews singing in concert. Notwithstanding the surprise the chorus caused, we were both well received at the waterside by our respective employers. Mr. M'Gillivray and I lived on friendly terms ever after.

Very few of the traders were cast in this genial mould, as that very season showed. Across the watershed, on the Athabaska River, Mr. Ross faced Peter Pond as before. A scuffle took place in the spring, in which he was shot. Two of the North West Company's servants, François Nadeau and Eustache le Compte, were brought to trial in Quebec for the murder. Strictly, the Canadian courts had no jurisdiction over Rupert's Land or the North-West, and it was probably on that score that Peter Pond had escaped from punishment for the murder of Waden. There had, however, been recently several murders by British subjects in American territory not as yet organized nor even occupied—at Niagara and near Lake Champlain. After a long argument by the Law Officers of the Crown it was decided that an ancient statute, passed, in fact, in the reign of Henry VIII., bringing crimes committed beyond the jurisdiction of the courts—as, for example, overseas—before the King's Council could be construed as giving authority to the Quebec Council, sitting as a court, to try these cases. Among the cases so tried was that of Nadeau and Le Compte for the murder of John Ross. The men were acquitted. Unfortunately the affidavits in connection with the trial have not been found, and we remain in ignorance of the circumstances of the death of Ross.* That Peter Pond was in

* Dr. Bigsby, on the authority of David Thompson, says that Peter Pond " persuaded his men to rob Mr. Ross of a load of furs in open day. In the course of the altercation Mr. Ross was shot, really by accident, from a gun in the hand of a voyageur named Péché " (John J. Bigsby, *The Shoe and Canoe*, London, 1850, vol. i., p. 117). The Journal of Peter Fidler's voyage to Athabaska refers to the incident, as Ross's fort was passed on June 25, 1791 : " Ross was shot by one Peshe a canadian, by orders of Pond." Turnor's Journal of the same voyage, under date of July 22, 1791, refers to Péché without naming him, as being at the Canadian House on Great Slave Lake : " he was once within three days walk of Churchill but was afraid of going to it as he is charged with having killed a Mr. Ross." He must have taken refuge with the Chipewyans and wandered with them out into the Barrens as they journeyed to trade at Churchill Fort.

some sense responsible may be argued from the fact that Roderick Mackenzie, who cut out from his *Reminiscences* and from his copies of Sir Alexander Mackenzie's letters every bitter phrase that might give offence, says that on account of the unfortunate circumstances of Ross's death Mr. Pond " remained under a cloud." Roderick was remaining inland in charge of the post at Ile-à-la-Crosse, but when he got news of the tragedy he hastened in a light canoe to report the fact to the partners assembled at Grand Portage. " The Proprietors lost no time in communicating it to our opponents. A meeting of all concerned took place, and it was soon decided to unite the interests of both companies for their common welfare." Alexander Mackenzie, in the preface to his *Voyages*, gives a less magnanimous view :

> After the murder of one of our partners, the laming of another and the narrow escape of one of our clerks, who received a bullet through his powder horn, in the execution of his duty, they [the Northwesters] were compelled to allow us a share of the trade. As we had already incurred a loss, this union was, in every respect, a desirable event to us and was concluded in the month of July 1787.

Thus the full-fledged North West Company came into existence.

6.—THE NORTH WEST COMPANY, 1787–1800

The proprietors of the North West Company have been cast by our writers in forms somewhat larger than human, as the " lords of the North," " the lords of the Wilderness," and what not. While men like the M'Gillivrays and the Mackenzies justly capture our imaginations, we must remember that they were what they were in virtue of the power and prestige of their Company. Their achievements, while based on their personal qualities, were due to an even greater extent to the extraordinary efficiency of the concern. That they could play the lord among their servants and the Indians was not wholly because of their masterful ways, but to a very large extent was owing to the efficiency of the Company. Their skill in river navigation and in exploring, and the art with which they tamed hordes of hostile savages were acquired in the service of the concern.

Similarly, the greatness of the North West Company did not blossom out in a day. It was fashioned in the hard school of discipline of the previous ten years. The Company was the creation of masterful minds like the Frobishers and Simon McTavish, men capable of interpreting the trend of the trade, and with the willpower to solve the physical and economic difficulties which faced them. They co-ordinated the pemmican trade of the prairies with the fur trade of the forest region ; they laid their hands on the trade in provisions at Michilimackinac and Detroit to enable their transportation system to run with smoothness and precision. As the partnerships had been made more and more inclusive, their control of the trade and, what is of scarcely less importance, their ability to master and discipline their servants and even the savages increased, until, with the complete union of 1787, the Company became, always saving the presence of the Hudson's Bay Company, in a very real sense the Lord of the North. It was in virtue of this lordship of the North West Company that its proprietors could play the part of lords of the wilderness in their several departments.

The union of 1787 put an end to the fierce competition in the Upper Country. The sixteen shares of the concern of 1784 were increased to twenty, and each of the surviving partners of the recent opposition—Gregory, Pangman, Alexander Mackenzie, and Norman McLeod, a dormant partner—received one of the added shares. The partnership was to hold for five years, that is, to the end of the trading season, 1792. This eliminated competition successfully up to that time. However, the weakness of a system of temporary partnerships was that it brought on recurrent crises with every occasion on which the partnership had to be renewed. Clerks who had been trained in the Company's service but believed that they were not receiving due consideration in the renewal, in the form of promotion to be proprietor holding a share, could leave the service and take their skill and the goodwill of the Indians enjoyed by them as winterers over into the service of rival firms ready to supply them with goods. In the 'nineties the temptation to do so was very great, for the Americans were occupying the lands conceded to them by the Treaty of Versailles (1783), and pushing the Montreal merchants out of the trade of the south from Detroit and the south-west from Michilimackinac—regions in which in any case the fur-bearing animals were very largely exterminated. They naturally turned envious eyes to the rich fur fields of the North-West, and were ready to enter into partnership with any servants of the North West Company who would introduce them to the trade. Thus, in 1792, when the North West Company entered a new period of copartnership, this time for seven years, David and Peter Grant, disappointed at the positions offered them, left the service and found supporters who enabled them to appear in the North-West as an active and experienced opposition. Then, too, traders in the American area in the interior from Fond du Lac on Lake Superior, and known as the South Men, pushed up northward into the Red River and the Assiniboine regions. Finally, after the South-western Posts were formally handed over to the Americans in keeping with Jay's Treaty of 1794, firms like Parker, Gerrard & Ogilvy, and Forsyth, Richardson & Co., who were losing ground to the Americans in their old areas of trade, diverted their energies to the North-West and created a vigorous opposition to the North West Company now operating in the partnership of the seven years running from 1792-99. This partnership was renewed by an agreement dated October 30, 1795, to take effect with the trading season, 1799-1800. The renewal of the agreement so long beforehand was doubtless to enable the Company to extinguish the opposition of Peter Grant by assuring him a share in the coming partnership. Alexander Mackenzie, who was at that time a partner in the firm of McTavish, Frobisher & Co., and acting as agent travelling up to Grand Portage, was party to the agreement, but with the close of his contract with the firm on November 13, 1799, he was left with a free hand. He could thus take his vast experience and energy over to the opposition with perfect honour. In 1800 he entered into a partnership with the Forsyth and Ogilvy firms to form the " New North West Company," commonly known as the XY Company, and subjected the old North West Company to a competition such as it had not yet experienced. The necessity of renewing its partnership from time to time proved the Achilles heel, the vulnerable point, in the otherwise perfect armour of the North West Company.

The rivalry with the Hudson's Bay Company continued unabated through all these years, but it was a gentleman's game compared with that between the Montreal companies.

During the period under consideration interesting developments took place in the organization of the business of the North West Company in Montreal. In the early partnerships the various wintering partners received their goods from different firms. When these firms and their winterers were drawn into the succession of partnerships, they received shares in proportion to the number of canoe-loads of goods which they were putting into the trade. From the union of 1787, however, the firms supplying goods were either eliminated or absorbed into the Frobisher firm. After the death of Benjamin Frobisher, on April 15, 1787, McTavish & Co. united with Joseph Frobisher to form the firm of McTavish, Frobisher & Co. (November, 1787). This firm was gradually able to secure to itself the right to supply all goods required by the North West Company. This resulted in much greater unity and efficiency in procuring supplies and marketing furs for the North-West concern. McTavish, Frobisher & Co. did not only enjoy their six shares in the profits of the concern but a commission for their labours in securing and preparing the goods and selling the furs. An agreement of 1790 ran :

> That McTavish Frobisher & Coy. shall do all the business of this concern at Montreal, and import the goods necessary for the supplies, charging 5 per cent. at the bottom of the invoice, and interest from the time they fall due in England, at the rate of 5 per cent. p. annum with 4 per cent. on the amount of the whole outfit, at the close of each year, the goods, men, wages, provisions (wherever they may be purchased), cash disbursements, etc., to be included, and interest at 6 per cent. p. annum on all advances, imports excepted.

Thus Joseph Frobisher became the centre of unity in Montreal, as he had been in the Upper Country.

A similar unification took place in London. Different English firms had been supplying the goods for the North-West on credit to the Montreal firms engaged in supplying the wintering partners. As McTavish, Frobisher & Co. drew to themselves the duty of supplying all the goods for the North West Company, these English firms either dropped out or became the agents of the firm in London. Thus Phyn, Ellice & Co. had supplied goods to Forsyth in Montreal which, to the value of three shares, went to the McBeath and Pond partnership. From 1789 the goods went to McTavish, Frobisher & Co. At the same time Brickwood, Pattle & Co. were supplying the goods which represented the share of the McTavish firm. In 1805 the business in London was concentrated into the hands of McTavish, Fraser & Co., created for that purpose.

The centralization of the business interests of the North West Company in Montreal gave it a great control of conditions between that port and Grand Portage. It was necessary to have large supplies of provisions at " the depot " on Lake Superior for the canoes going into the interior or returning to Montreal. In the early days the individual traders used to be victimized by the dealers in corn and by the voyageurs needed for the canoes. It was a great gain when McTavish, who as early as 1775 had a ship on the lakes, and who had connections with Michilimackinac and Detroit, the sources of the supplies of corn, came into the partnership of 1779. Now that McTavish and Frobisher were in one firm and acting as agents of the Company, complete control of the supply of provisions at Grand Portage was attained. This made the dispatch of the canoes from the depot swift and sure.

The union of the traders in Montreal in one concern enabled them to bring pressure to bear upon the Governor of the colony in the interest of the trade. This is first noticeable during the war with the American colonists. To prevent traders from taking goods and particularly ammunition to the rebels, Governor Haldimand assumed complete control of traffic on the lakes and was refusing passes to canoes. Individual traders would have been helpless against this war measure. A memorial, dated May 1, 1779, pleading that the winterers would be starved if they did not receive the goods and ammunition necessary for the trade, secured a relaxation of the Governor's regulations. It would be much easier for an extensive and reputable partnership to secure licences than for a horde of independent traders. Accordingly the partnership of 1779 was formed, largely with this end in view. When the war was over Haldimand continued the system of only allowing the King's ships on the Great lakes. Of course, supplies for the military posts had the right of way. The regulations ran that traders must take their turn in getting their goods to the Upper Country. A petition of the merchants, dated April 2, 1785, called the attention of the Governor to the hardship involved, especially as favouritism was being shown to some merchants. As the name of neither Frobisher nor McTavish was appended to the petition, it may be inferred that union had proved strength and that the North West Company of that date could get right of way for their goods at the expense of their rivals. On May 8, 1785, Benjamin and Joseph Frobisher petitioned the Governor to be allowed to take a small vessel, the *Beaver*, up the falls (the Sault) of St. Mary's to transport their goods across Lake Superior, a request which was granted. Though they were not able to get the vessel up the falls, they got a transportation on the lower lakes, which gave them a great advantage over their opponents.

The confidence of the agents of the North West Company that they could mould the policy of the Governor in their interest is shown by their next petition. The Treaty of Versailles, 1783, had given the fur region of Michilimackinac and the South-West to the Americans, thus including all the South-western posts. Further, it drew the International Boundary along the Pigeon River, throwing Grand Portage into the United States and giving the Americans the southern side of the water-way westward as far as the Lake of the Woods. Advantage was taken of the hardship thus inflicted upon the North West Company to launch an elaborate scheme. The Company entrusted to Edward Umfreville the task of finding a water-route to the North-West which would be wholly in British territory. The route, as has been seen, was found by way of Lake Nipigon and the upper valley of the Albany River and over the height of land to the English River, which flows into the Winnipeg River below the Lake of the Woods. It proved too difficult, and was, in fact, never used. However, on October 4, 1784, the agents of the Company petitioned the Governor for a monopoly of the route for ten years, and that during that period passes be denied to traders by the Grand Portage water-way. On April 18, 1785, this extra-ordinary request was renewed in a petition presented by Peter Pond in April 1785, and was coupled with the far-reaching plans of the explorer of Athabaska :

Your memorialist humbly begs leave to inform your Honour that he has positive information from the Natives, who have been on the Coast of the North Pacific Ocean, that there is a trading Post already established by the Russians ; and your Memorialist is credibly informed that Ships are now fitting out from the United States of America under the command of Experienced sea-men (who accompanied Captain Cook in his last Voyage) in order to establish a Furr trade upon the North West Coast of North America, at or near to Prince William's Sound, and if the late treaty of Peace is adhered to respecting the Cession of the Upper Posts, the United States will also have an easy access into the North-West by way of the Grand Portage. From these circumstances Your Memorialist is humbly of opinion, that this branch of trade will very soon fall a prey to the enterprise of other Nations, to the great prejudice of His Majesty's Subjects, unless some means are speedily used to prevent it. It, therefore, becomes necessary for Government to protect and encourage the North West Company in the earliest prosecution of the proposed plan ; in order that trading posts may be settled and connections formed with the Natives, all over the Country, even to the Sea Coast ; by which means so firm a footing may be established as will preserve that Valuable trade from falling into the hands of other powers ; and under proper management it may certainly in a short time be so extended as to become an object of great importance to the British Nation and highly advantageous to this Mutilated Province.

Pond goes on to plead for a monopoly on the newly discovered route and the prohibition of passes for the old one. Thus the plan of reaching the Pacific and anticipating foreign traders on the coast was displayed to dazzle the imagination of the Governor and to win him to grant a monopoly to the North West Company. Of course the first effect of the monopoly would have been to crush the rival firm, Gregory, McLeod & Co., by excluding them from the North-West. But the petitioners humbly prayed in vain ; Governor Haldimand and the Colonial Office gave expression to the spirit of the age in refusing to grant a monopoly even for ten years. However, the union of the rival concerns in 1787 had approximately the same effect. The North West Company was now so strong that all individual traders were eliminated, and only firms with large resources could venture to oppose it. A very important aspect of its power is seen in its ability, so long as there was no opposition in Canada itself, to control the press and public opinion in the colony and to mould the policy of the Government to its will. It perfected the art of governing by propaganda, as was seen later in its long struggle with Lord Selkirk and his colony on the Red River.

Not less impressive was the organization of the trade in the Upper Country by the Company. It brought Joseph Frobisher's scheme for provisioning the brigades of canoes in their necessarily swift and unresting journeys to a perfection little short of astonishing. On the prairies, far up the Peace River and in the bush country west of the Athabaska River, pemmican was secured to bring the northern brigade well on its way. Of course the precious cargoes of fur left little room for provisions. There must be provisioning by the way. But the forest belt and Lake Winnipeg could offer little but that most perishable of foods, fish. Here was a difficulty the trader in a small way could not overcome. The great concern with fur posts in the north and pemmican (as well as fur) forts by the prairies could bring the abundance of meat on the plains in the form of pemmican to the rescue of the trader in the wooded belt. Depots for the storage of this invaluable accessory to the trade were established all along the trunk water-way. Fort Chipewyan on Lake Athabaska was stocked with the pemmican of the Athabaska and Peace rivers. From 1793, if not before, the post on Ile-à-la-Crosse was supplied with pemmican brought from the Fort des Prairies of the time on the upper Saskatchewan by dog-sleds overland during the winter. The supplies received here would be exhausted when the canoes reached the Saskatchewan at Cumberland House. For years the pemmican for the northern brigades was cached by the men from Fort des Prairies on the bank of the river somewhere about The Pas. The loss of a cache led the Company to establish its own Cumberland House alongside of the Hudson's Bay Company's post in 1793. Here the northern brigades, coming and going, received supplies for the journey to the next depot, Ile-à-la-Crosse or " The Bottom of River Winnipeg." At this last depot, about a mile and a half from Lake Winnipeg, the pemmican from the Assiniboine was stored for the brigades passing out to Grand Portage, or in to their various wintering-grounds. A supply of wild rice was held at the Rainy

Lake post in case of emergencies. Grand Portage was stocked with corn and pork fat procured in Michilimackinac and Detroit, as we have seen.

As was befitting, in a company in which winterers from the Upper Country and agents from Montreal were in partnership, headquarters were at the rendezvous at Grand Portage. In spite of its being in American territory, it was not removed until the Western Posts were surrendered under Jay's Treaty. (It was not till 1802-3 that the change was made to the mouth of the Kaministikwia River, to the site of the present Fort William.) Here, during a fortnight of happy fellowship and feasting on the luxuries brought up from Montreal, the partners, under the chairmanship of the agents, fashioned the policy for the trade-season immediately before them. All difficulties were decided by the votes of twelve shares concurring. The so-called *Minutes of the North West Company* show that the more formal decisions were drawn up in legal guise, and duly subscribed by the concurring partners, either in person or by proxy. The beauty of the system lay in that the wintering partners, who may be represented as the producers of the furs, and their agents, who were the buying and selling end of the concern, met in intimate consultation to promote the general good of the Company and to co-ordinate department with department, particularly the pemmican producing forts with those of the forest belt. It made for wisdom and efficiency, and it bred a fine *esprit de corps*. And this was shared by the servants gathered around them and participating in the pleasures of the fortnight.

An important factor contributing to the unity of spirit and ensuring discipline and efficiency was the principle embodied in the constitution of the Company, that shares could not be bought by outsiders, but were reserved as a reward for experienced and capable clerks. Partners retiring surrendered their shares to the control of the Company, which negotiated their sale to the most deserving of the servants. The fact that clerks who displayed energy and capacity could expect ultimately to be able to purchase a share and become partners led them to give their best to the concern. All ranks in the service were given their keep when voyaging or at their post. The partners, proprietors, and *bourgeois*, as they were in turn called, enjoyed privileges which enhanced their position as officers and made them the envy of the underlings. Among these was the light canoe placed at their service, in which they could go forward, leaving the freighter canoes under the care of the clerks, or they could lag behind transacting business or enjoying the pleasure of visiting the posts by the way.

" The spirit of the North-West Company " which characterized the officers of the Company was carefully instilled into the lower orders of the service. These were filled by French-Canadians or " breeds " of all shades down to the Indians themselves. They were managed with consummate skill by the *bourgeois*. Their love of song and of pomp and circumstance was given ample scope in the customs of the brigade. The crews sang as they paddled ; they camped before coming in to the important posts to shave and to dress in their most colourful garments: then came the spectacular arrival at the fort, paddles keeping time with the voyageur song. Their endurance of hard labour was taxed to the limit, but it was tempered by *régales*, libations of rum, at stated points on the route or after a specially hard day's work. A *régale* and a dance were *de rigueur* at the arrival at the wintering post. Care was taken that the food supply was ample, for the brigade travelled, like the British army, "on its stomach." Periods of wellnigh starvation were incidental to the trade, but high and low suffered alike with good-humoured patience. The supply of meat per head at the pemmican posts was eight pounds per day. The French-Canadians' love of Indian women was not forgotten. Servants could take their squaws, with the leave of the *bourgeois*, and wife and family were supported at the expense of the post. What more could the men wish for? * No wonder if they, too, breathed the North West spirit. This does not mean that there never was trouble in the service. Duncan M'Gillivray tells of a mutiny of the Athabaska brigade at the Rainy Lake post in 1794. It was doubtless due to the strain of the long voyage and, as he says, to instigation by the turbulent few. These were sent down to Montreal, where the fur-traders would combine to keep them out of employment and teach them to repent. The rest went back quietly to their paddles.

The relations of the Northwesters, high and low, with the Indians were of the best. This was largely through their connections with the squaws. The *bourgeois* usually took to himself a chief's daughter, who ordinarily made a fine combination of servant, wife, and chief lady of the fort. While their relationship might be temporary, brought to an end by the flight of the woman or the removal of the man to another fort, the squaws had a way of endearing themselves to their husbands, which often preserved the connection as long as their *bourgeois* remained in the Upper Country. When Alexander Henry the younger was on the Red River, a chief's daughter installed herself in his quarters after the festivities of New Year's evening in spite of his protests, but he came to love her and his children by her, and he took "her ladyship" and the family with him to Fort Vermilion on the Saskatchewan, and to Rocky Mountain House. Even happier were Daniel Harmon's relations with his partner. After the Indian custom, he had been offered young women by their parents anxious to get the usual presents in return, but had been obdurate. However, when at the house of his time (1805) on the South Branch of the Saskatchewan, near the present St. Laurent Crossing, he closed with an offer, making the following entry in his Journal :

* As a matter of course, the squaws, including Her Ladyship the *bourgeois'* partner, strung snow-shoes, made moccasins, and prepared and adorned leather garments for their men, and dressed leather and dried provisions out of the fresh meat brought in, and made themselves of general service to the fort.

Thursday, Oct. 10—This day a Canadian's daughter, a girl of fourteen years of age, was offered to me, and after mature consideration, concerning the step which I should take, I have finally concluded to accept of her, as it is customary for all gentlemen who remain, for any length of time, in this part of the world, to have a female companion with whom they can pass their time more sociably and agreably, than to live a lonely life, as they must do, if single. If we can live in harmony together, my intention now is, to keep her as long as I remain in this uncivilized part of the world ; and when I return to my native land, I shall endeavour to place her under the protection of some honest man, with whom she can pass the remainder of her days in this country, much more agreably, than it would be possible for her to do, were she to be taken down into the civilized world, to the manners, customs and language of which, she would be an entire stranger. Her mother is of the tribe of Snare [apparently a branch of the Thompson] Indians whose country lies along the Rocky Mountains. The girl is said to have a mild disposition and an even temper, which are qualities very necessary to make an agreeable woman, and an affectionate partner.

Harmon's relations with " my woman " and the " mother of my children," as he called her, proved extraordinarily happy. He took her with him to the wilds of New Caledonia beyond the Rockies. He did better, if better it was, by her than he first intended. He brought her out with him, married her in due form, and spent the rest of his days with her in Vermont. In this he was but following the example of Roderick Mackenzie with his squaw, and of David Thompson with his half-breed wife, Charlotte Small.

The relations of the servants with the Indian women were naturally looser, but probably not as loose as might be expected. Men were found then, as now, of all grades of character. Some assimilated themselves to the Indians and, like one Ducharme on Lake Winnipegosis, kept two squaws, apparently both fed by the outpost in which he was.

The ties which bound the men of a post to the Indian women taught the North West Company to understand the natives, and gave them a great hold on them, for the various tribes naturally traded with the forts in which their women were installed, in the partner's quarters, or in the houses of the men. Instances might be quoted to show that it was a definite policy to make capital out of these matrimonial relationships. In one case, to secure the friendship and trade of a hostile tribe, the chief's daughter was formally installed in the bourgeois' quarters. In time, however, the deadweight carried by the Company in the form of the semi-Indian families being fed at their posts became excessive. In the first decade of the nineteenth century an attempt was made to throw it off and to economize by prohibiting formal connections with the Indian women. The squaws and their children were to live outside the post and to be supported out of the wages of the men. This regulation proved impossible to enforce.

A brigade reached its wintering ground by water, of course. A halt was made before arriving, for all to shave and put on their finest colours. Then came the spectacular arrival—a procession of canoes, paddled in tune with some gay voyageurs' song ; a happy reunion with the women and children ; the display of gaudy presents purchased at the rendezvous ; and finally the *régale* and dance. Alexander Henry the younger describes a dance at Fort Vermilion on the Saskatchewan opposite the mouth of the Vermilion River in our Alberta where the posts of the English and the Canadian companies stood side by side.

Sept. 15 (1809)—We had a dance at my house, to which I invited my neighbour [Mr. Hallett] and his family. All were merry—our men as alert as if they had already rested for a month ; but we were much crowded, there being present 72 men, 37 women, and 65 children, and the room being only 22 × 25 feet made it disagreeably warm.

The forts usually stood on what was called a low bottom, really the lowest ledge of the river bank. This would be easily accessible from the river, and would afford the wood necessary for the fort. As seen from the river, a fort was a group of small log buildings protected by a wooden palisade. It would be about 150 feet square, with a gate looking towards the water and a second looking inland, each protected by a bastion from which an attack could be warded off. Within was an open space in which the Indians could be gathered before the Indian Hall in the *bourgeois'* house, which stood out toward the centre of the post. This open space was secured by building the houses along the sides of the palisades. At Pine Island Fort, on the North Saskatchewan, the houses were echeloned, that is, ran in a series of squares from the rear of the side palisades to the front gate, much as, say, the black squares touching one another run diagonally across a chequer board. The houses formed the sides of a triangle whose apex was the front gate. In the prairie regions the forts were large and heavily manned, because of the menace of the great tribes. There were eighty men at Fort George on the Saskatchewan in 1794. Only a portion of these would be resident in the fort. Some would be out hunting buffalo or trapping furs. At Fort Vermilion thirty of the servants with their families, seventy-two persons in all, were housed in seven houses, or about ten persons per tiny shack.

After the arrival of the brigade the goods were unpacked and the shop made ready for trade. The Indians flocked from far and near. They were received with great ceremony. Here is the scene at Fort George on the Saskatchewan, as described by Duncan M'Gillivray.

When a band of Indians approach near the Fort it is customary for the Chiefs to send a few young men before them to announce their arrival, and to procure a few articles which they are accustomed to have on these occasions—such as powder, a piece of tobacco and a little paint to besmear their faces, an operation which they seldom fail to perform previous to presenting themselves before the White People. At a few yards distance from the gate they salute us with several discharges of their guns, which is answered by hoisting a flag and firing a few guns. On entering the house they are disarmed, treated with a few drams and a bit of tobacco, and after the pipe has been plyed about for some time they relate the news with great deliberation and ceremony relaxing from their usual taciturnity in proportion to the quantity of rum they have swallowed, till at length their voices are drowned in a general clamour. When their lodges are erected by the women, they receive a present of rum proportioned to the Nation and quality of the chiefs, and the whole band drink during 24 hours and sometimes longer for nothing —a privilege of which they take every advantage—for in the seat of an opposition [in this case the Hudson's Bay Company in Buckingham House, over against Fort George, William Tomison in charge] profusion is absolutely necessary to secure the trade of an Indian. When the drinking match has subsided they begin to trade ; they obtain the large keg [of rum] for 30 Beavers ; long guns at 14 ; fine [strouds] at 8 per fathom ; 3 point blankets 6 ; 1 pair trenches [ice chisels for digging out the beaver] 3 ; 1 medium axe 2 ; 1 fathom Brasil tobacco 3 beavers ; 1 Spencer's twist 2 ; 20 balls 1. . . . The neighbouring Indians having got intelligence of our arrival are pouring in continually from all quarters and the Fort since that time has been a scene of drunkenness and brutality. This day in a quarrel betwixt two factions of Crees an Indian was butchered in a cruel manner—another young man was also stabbed in the neck, but it is hoped he will recover. The drinking match is therefore stopped to prevent more mischief at this time.

Similar scenes were enacted when the Indians came with their furs in the spring. The description is again Duncan M'Gillivray's.

15th April—During 3 days past Indians are pouring in continually from all quarters. There are no less than 7 different nations at the Fort ;— such an assemblage of strangers, who are in general inveterate enemies and ignorant of every language except their own, must exhibit some curious scenes, when their minds are expanded with liquor, but whatever motives of enmity influence their actions, they seem all to agree in one measure which is to get heartily drunk. They form intertaining groups arround their fires and pledge each other with a degree of satisfaction, which seems to be increased in proportion to the time they have been deprived of rum. Men, women and children, promiscuously mingle together and join in one diabolical clamour of singing, crying, fighting &c. and to such excess do they indulge their love of drinking that all regard to decency and decorum is forgotten :—they expose themselves in the most indecent positions, leaving uncovered those parts which nature requires to be concealed—a circumstance which they carefully avoid in their sober moments, and the intercourse between the sexes, at any time but little restrained, is now indulged with the greatest freedom, for as chastity is not deemed a virtue among most of the tribes, they take very little pains to conceal their amours especially when they are heated with liquor.

The Indians were equipped for the hunt on credit, and usually brought or sent in furs in midwinter, but all assembled with their spring hunt before the departure of the brigade. The servants of the Company, needed for the canoes but superfluous at the forts, were sent out to hunt for venison to supply the table and to make pemmican for the voyage, or else were equipped on credit for trapping furs, and received their reward in the price paid for their peltries at the same rate as allowed the Indians.

At every turn the Company was faced with the great cost entailed upon it by its long lines of transportation. Success was only possible because the freights carried both ways were of very great value compared with their bulk. Their packs of furs of 90 pounds weight, when brought to Montreal, were worth about £40 sterling.

The rum taken into the interior was in the form of small kegs of " high wines " of great strength, and therefore of great value, for the liquor was watered down to suit the tastes of the various tribes. Alexander Henry the younger made this entry in his Journal at Fort Vermilion on the Saskatchewan on September 15, 1809 : " We do not mix our liquor so strong as we do for tribes who are accustomed to use it.   To make a nine gallon keg of liquor we generally put in four or five quarts of high wine and then fill up with water.   [This he calls Blackfoot rum.]   For the Crees and Assiniboines we put in six quarts of high wine and for the Saulteurs eight or nine quarts." Thus the cost of transporting rum, the chief article in the trade, was low, and the profits were very high.   The profits on the wine, and indeed on all the goods, were increased by the introduction of what was known as " Grand Portage currency."   As the dollar of Montreal was counted but half a dollar at Grand Portage, the price of goods was automatically enhanced a 100 per cent., for wages calculated on the basis of the Montreal dollar would be counted at fifty cents in buying merchandise or liquor at Grand Portage.   Moreover, the additional percentage charged on the goods for transportation in Montreal currency would be doubled at that depot.

Critics of the Company have pointed out that, as it paid its servants in the Upper Country in goods, its wage bill was reduced by half by this device.   They also accuse it of encouraging the drinking habits of its men, for as the profits on rum were exceedingly high, wages were reduced in proportion.   François Alexandre Frédéric la Rochefoucault-Liancourt, son of the Duc d'Estissac, a French nobleman of a philanthropic turn of mind and much interested in the abolition of slavery, visited Canada in 1797.   His inquiries drew his attention to the methods of trade of the North West Company. It is not known how he came into the possession of the Journal of an Italian Count, Andreani by name, who had travelled in the Upper Country in 1791.   La Rochefoucault-Liancourt's conclusions were so far in agreement with those of Andreani that he included in his book what appears to be a free transcription of the part of his Journal dealing with the North West Company.   A passage discussing the men's wages runs :

As the men employed in this trade are paid in merchandize which the Company sells with an enormous profit, it is obvious at how cheap a rate these people are paid.   They purchase of the Company every article they want ; it keeps with them an open account, and as they all winter in the interior of the country and beyond Lake Winnipeg, they pay as a consequence excessively dear for the blankets and the clothes which they bring with them for their wives.   These servants of the Company are in general extravagant, given to drinking and excess ; and these are exactly the people whom the Company wants.   The speculation on the excesses of these people is carried so far, that if one of them happened to lead a regular sober life, he is burdened with the most laborious work, until by continual ill-treatment he is driven to drunkenness and debauchery, which vices cause the rum, blankets and trinkets to be sold to greater advantage.   In 1791, nine hundred of these menial servants owed the Company more than the amount of ten or fifteen years pay.

Andreani fortifies his account by an elaborate statistical statement devised to show that the Company would be operating at a loss did they not thus exploit their servants. He balances what he takes to be the cost of the goods purchased in England and the cost of the service against the sales of the furs. Unfortunately for the argument, many of the figures are palpably wrong. The 400 men with the canoes plying between Montreal and Grand Portage as given in the text become 1,400 men in the statistical scheme and swell the cost of the service proportionately. The value of the goods purchased in England is given at £16,000, but Alexander Mackenzie gives it as £40,000 for 1788, and Duncan M'Gillivray, agent for the Company, writing about 1808, gives the average for the years previous to 1807 at the same figure. Most vitiating of all, the goods—rum, tobacco, and much else—purchased in Montreal do not figure in the account.

Lord Selkirk, who met Andreani in Switzerland, adopted his argument as light-heartedly as La Rochefoucault-Liancourt. He also leaves out of account the cost of the goods purchased in Montreal, and he reduces the value of the goods purchased in England to £10,000, though in another part of his pamphlet, *A Sketch of the British Fur Trade*, he puts it at £30,000, much nearer the actual figure. Apparently the noble lord considered the specious argument much too good propaganda to be passed over. All the same, there is substantial truth in the view that the reduction of the wages of its servants by exploiting them through its trade system helped the Company to discount the disadvantages imposed on it by its long line of transportation, and contributed to putting its business on a profit-making basis.

Another serious disadvantage under which the Company laboured was the length of the time during which its capital was locked up in its purchases before the returns could be realized. Here the Hudson's Bay Company, with its short route by water to York Factory, near the edge of the fur region, was in a much more advantageous position. Their goods bought immediately before shipping in May reached York Factory in August and were on the Saskatchewan, say, in September. The returns in the way of furs passed back in the following summer and reached London in the late autumn. The goods for the North West Company left London in the spring or at best the summer, arrived in Montreal in the summer or autumn, but did not leave for the North-West until the following May, to arrive on the Saskatchewan in September. The Canadian Company had, therefore, to pay a year's interest on its outlay because of the long channel through which its goods passed from England to the North-West.

Because of all the disadvantages under which the Company was labouring, it was necessary for it to secure the largest possible amount of furs to meet costs and pay dividends. Canoes must come out with full freights of peltry. This meant great slaughter of the fur-bearing animals in the region occupied by a fort. A " beaver region " would be depleted of its furs in four or five years. This reckless policy was accentuated when the Company brought in bands of Iroquois who, unlike the natives, had no interest in preserving the animal life of the district, but used steel traps, which killed off old and young indiscriminately. The keen competition with the Hudson's Bay Company was another factor working in the same direction, for if animals—for example, breeding mothers—were left, the rival company might secure them. The result was that the two companies moved up the Saskatchewan from one beaver region "ruined" to the next as yet untouched. This is in sharp contrast with the situation when the Indians took their furs down to the Bay. Without intentionally aiming at a closed season, the effect of one was attained. The trappers left the wintering ground in the early spring when the young were being born, and did not return until the late autumn when they had become independent of the life of their parents. The profligate policy now in vogue forced the North West Company farther and farther afield, and in so doing accentuated the handicap imposed upon it by its long lines of transportation.

The more one looks into the difficulties under which the North West Company laboured the more one appreciates the genius of men like the Frobishers and McTavish, who overcame them by fashioning out what was probably the most efficient organization on the continent of its day. That goods leaving Montreal in May and furs leaving Athabaska at about the same time should meet year after year without fail on the shores of Lake Superior, or at Rainy Lake, and be exchanged and the crews reach their winter homes at the two extremes almost with the regularity of ocean liners was surely a triumph of human organization over the inescapable obstacles and vagaries of nature.

Much as the North West Company owed its success to the spirit of enterprise shown by its proprietors and to the remarkable efficiency of its constitution and system of business, it owed more to the rising price of furs in the London market, due to the increasing wealth of the middle class in England and to changes in fashion. Manifestly, it could not have gone so far afield in the decades before the middle of the eighteenth century, when prime coat beaver was realizing but 5s. per pound weight, and prime parchment beaver was bringing but 6s. It was the good fortune of the Pedlars, when they entered Rupert's Land in 1770, that these types of fur were good for 9s. 8d. and 12s. 2d. respectively. The enhanced prices made it possible to bear the great cost of transportation from Montreal. It was the good fortune of the North West Company, when it was formed in 1784, that there was a further rise in the price of parchment beaver to 19s. 3d. Other furs were following the trend of the market. Martens brought 5s. 8d. per skin in 1770, and 11s. 1d. in 1784 ; prime otter, 17s. and 39s. 6d. per skin in those years ; the finest of black bear skins rose from about 36s. 6d. to near 87s. 6d. Obviously, the higher the prices realized in the London market, the farther west the Northwesters could go, still making their trade pay. So too with the Hudson's Bay Company. The increased cost involved in the policy of operating posts inland was met by the rise in the prices secured in the London market for their furs.

None the less the North West Company's continuing problems were the cost of their long lines of transportation and the depletion of the fur fields by their reckless methods of exploitation, forcing them farther and farther afield. It was these problems that turned the attention of the proprietors of the Company in the frontier department of Athabaska, Peter Pond and Alexander Mackenzie, to the possibility of finding an easy water-way to the Pacific by the Slave River and what is now known as the Mackenzie, and an entry into the marine fur trade of the western coast.

7.—THE PACIFIC WEST AND ITS INDIANS *

The Pacific West of Canada stands out in marked contrast with the open plains of the North-West. It may be described as a rugged upland region with double ranges of mountains forming its ramparts to the east and to the west. Facing the prairies there are the Rockies, flanked by a second range often called the Selkirks, but strictly a series of mountain masses isolated by the intervening valleys of great rivers. The mass immediately north of the International Boundary is formed by the Purcell Range to the east and the Selkirks proper to the west. These two merge into one in the north, but in the south are divided by Kootenay Lake, a feature in the valley of the Kootenay River. The two groups form what might be called an island of mountains, for the Columbia River running northward on their eastern flank sweeps westward, isolating them from mountains farther north, and turns to follow a southerly course along the western slope of the Selkirks, while the waters of the Kootenay from within two miles of the source of the Columbia lap the southern portion of the eastern flank of the Purcell Range, passing round its southern slopes to form Kootenay Lake between the two ranges, and finally breaking its way westward past the southern spur of the Selkirks into the Columbia River. A canoe could pass around the whole mountain mass save for the portages, of which the most prominent is but five miles. A third range, parallel to these two, is the Gold Range isolated from the Selkirks by the River Columbia to its east. Between the Columbia and the Fraser are the Cariboo Mountains, which might be described as the convergence of the three ranges mentioned above. The River Fraser flows northward along their eastern flank, breaks its way past their northern spur to turn southward and flow along their western slopes towards the sea.

On the west the ramparts of the rugged upland against the ocean consist of the Coast Range, through which the Fraser forces its turbulent way, and what is often regarded as a submerged chain of mountains whose heights constitute the islands of the coast, particularly Vancouver Island and the Queen Charlotte Archipelago.

* This and subsequent sections on the Pacific Slope are illustrated by Sketch-map No. 9 at p. 362.

The physical features of the Pacific West which call for particular attention are such as have contributed to the vegetable and animal life, which have constituted the food supply or have provided the various domestic necessaries of man, and which have enabled him to live in something like society. Of these, that which has influenced the climate, the vegetation, and animal and human life most is the Pacific Ocean. Its effect on the various parts of the country is, however, greatly modified by the successive mountain ranges. It is to these that we owe the variation in moisture which makes the coast a dense forest and the interior plateau to some extent a " dry belt." The warm waters of the sun-beaten " Japanese current " drift north-eastward towards the continent of America much as the Gulf Stream does towards Europe, but a cold Arctic current intervenes between its benign atmosphere and the land. The winds which are charged with moisture as they pass over this Japanese current are chilled when they cross the Arctic flow and strike upon the coastal range. Hence the heavy precipitation running from sixty inches of rain in the south to one hundred in the north. This makes the belt along the coast a land of gigantic trees and almost impenetrable underbrush. But, save up the river-valleys, these rain-bearing winds do not penetrate through the Coast Range. Between the Coast Range and the foot of the Gold and Cariboo mountains the precipitation diminishes from fifty inches to ten. Hence " the dry belt "—a land of open woods alternating with grassy and even barren spaces. On the American side of the boundary this area becomes the arid plain of the mid-Columbian valley. The whole region is marked by the comparative calmness of many of the valleys, especially in the south, and the surprising mildness of their climates. In contrast, the upper streams of winds from the ocean, usually called the Chinook winds, carry their moisture over the Coast Range and deposit it mostly as snow upon the eastern ramparts of the uplands, upon the Gold and Cariboo ranges, on the Selkirks, and, in a lesser degree, on the Rockies. These ranges are consequently heavily wooded on their lower slopes and snow-laden on their heights, and the Rockies in particular become the source of great rivers—of the Saskatchewan, the Athabaska, and the Peace ; rivers flowing eastward, and in the United States the River Missouri ; while the Columbia, the Fraser, the Skeena, the Stikine, and the Yukon empty their waters into the Pacific Ocean.

Looked at in the large, there are two distinct areas in the Pacific West, the wild region by the shore of the sea, with its moisture often more than ample—a region of dense forests—and the comparatively dry and open but, under the circumstances, surprisingly mild upland between the mountain ramparts to the east and to the west.

Certain influences come in to make a well-defined third region. Between the Gold and Cariboo ranges on the west and the Rockies on the east the precipitation runs in the neighbourhood of thirty inches, making those parts a fine but scarcely a dense forest region.

Moreover, the Rockies become lower and more open to the north. The openings permit the Arctic airs of the Mackenzie basin to penetrate on occasion westward. The mountain ramparts, too, spread out to meet one another. Hence that bleak and shaggy region of forest, of glen and lake and stream, which the fur-traders not inappropriately called New Caledonia.

Of these three regions the strip on the coast is very different from anything to be seen in the North-West. It might, however, be supposed that life in the forest of New Caledonia would be not very different from that in the forest belt of the North-West and, similarly, that existence in the dry belt would be much like that of the prairie region. Not so, for in a way hitherto unmentioned the Pacific Ocean influenced life in almost the whole of the country west of the Rockies. It provided such an abundant supply of fish on the coast that the aborigines could live in large villages and develop, if not tribal, at least community instincts, primitive social customs, and a barbarian culture. Of these fish different species of salmon travelled upstream far inland, and could be caught in abundance at favourable points in the rivers, particularly at the rapids and cascades. Thus many parts of the dry belt and of the forest region of New Caledonia could support a population living together in considerable numbers, the like of which was never found in the forest belt east of the Rockies. Accordingly, the Indians of the Pacific West, taken as a whole, acquired sedentary and social habits unknown in the North-West. East of the Rockies the natives lived by the hunt, supplemented in the forest belt and on the Barren Grounds by fish; but west of that range they lived on fish, supplemented at the appropriate seasons by their hunt. Taken as a whole they acquired sedentary habits, and developed social customs and a culture much superior to those of the North-West. Even on the arid plain of the Columbia a life approximating closely to that on the prairies was greatly modified and, so to say, socialized by the savages living together in great numbers during the fishing season and through the winter.

Three areas call for particular attention as having each a history of its own—New Caledonia, the valley of the mid-Columbia with its tributaries, and, finally, the coastal strip with its islands. In this order were they permanently occupied by Europeans.

New Caledonia is defined by Father Adrien-Gabriel Morice as " lying between the coastal range and Rocky Mountains, from latitude 51° 30′ to 59° of latitude north." It therefore included the northern section of the eastern forest and of the dry belt.

The region is mostly mountainous, especially in the north, where lines of snow-capped peaks intersect the whole country between the two main ranges. Endless forests, mostly of coniferous trees, and deep lakes, whose length generally exceeds their breadth, cover such spaces as are not taken up by mountains. The only level or meadow lands of any extent within that district lie on either side of the Chilcotin River [that is in the dry belt]— where excellent bunch grass affords lasting pasture to large herds of cattle and horses.

In the north the forest is largely of spruce, the home of moose and caribou, while in the south it is of the Douglas pine, the favourite range of deer. Over the whole region poplar, aspen, and willow abound by the lakes and streams, affording an ample food supply for beaver. Other fur-bearing animals are the grizzly and the black bear, the marten, fisher, otter, and mink. Hence the reputation of the district in fur-trading circles. The Indians of the region do not seem to have made much of the smaller animals for food, save that beaver was the relished meat at their ceremonial feasts. They confined their hunt to large game and to the geese and ducks which thronged the lakes in season. Berries, particularly the service berry, offered an important supplementary article of food. These were cooked and compressed into flat cakes and kept for times of emergency. The staple fare, however, was fish such as trout, white-fish, land-locked salmon, and carp found in the lakes; but above all, salmon coming up from the sea to spawn. These last were caught in great abundance in August and September, and dried and stored for future use. The natives, save in the seasons for the hunt of big game and of the local fishery, were to be found in villages by the lake sides and by the streams at spots favourable for the catch of salmon. Apart from their constant blood-feuds, their wars were for the possession of these fisheries. Father Morice mentions a case to the point. The Western Babines were suddenly deprived of their means of sustenance by the fall of a precipice into their river, which prevented the salmon from passing up. They marched in a body and seized the nearest fishing-place from the Tsimshian tribe below.

The centre of the life of the people was the village at or near the fishery. From it the natives went out at the proper season to gather berries, or hunt wild game, or catch the fish of their lake. Life was much less assiduous here than in the forest belt of the North-West, but none the less it was subject to periods of starvation, partly due to the recklessness of the people, but often owing to the failure of the salmon to come up to lakes so far upstream.

The shores of the salmon streams of New Caledonia and the lakes connected with them were, in the main, the habitats of the various groups of people. First of all there was the Fraser River, along whose banks from the Chilcotin and Blackwater upwards villages stood at rapids and cascades where the fish were easily caught. An important tributary was the Nechako, into which streams drained Stuart Lake and Fraser Lake. The fur-traders afterwards built their posts near the outflow of these lakes, as being spots at which salmon were secured in large quantities, and where Indian villages were near. Daniel Harmon's Journal of September 2, 1811, runs :

We have now the common salmon in abundance. They weigh from five to seven pounds. There are, also, a few of a larger kind, which will weigh sixty or seventy pounds. Both of them are very good, when just taken out of the water. But, when dried, as they are by the Indians here, by heat of the sun, or in the smoke of a fire, they are not very palatable. When salted they are excellent. As soon as the salmon come into this lake, they go in search of the rivers and brooks, that fall into it ; and these streams they ascend so far as there is water to enable them to swim ; and when they can proceed no farther up, they remain there and die. None were ever seen to descend these streams. They are found dead in such numbers, in some places, as to infect the atmosphere, with a terrible stench, for a considerable distance round. But even when they are in a putrid state the Natives frequently gather them up and eat them, apparently, with as great relish, as if they were fresh.

The run of salmon which afforded a food supply to the people in the north came up the Skeena River and its tributaries, for example, up the Babine River to Babine Lake, and in the upper reaches of the Skeena to Bear Lake. Lakes whose outlet was eastward—as, for example, McLeod Lake, drained by the Pack River into the Parsnip, one of the principal branches of the Peace River—had no more than their native fish to offer the people who frequented their shores.

New Caledonia was the home of the western branch of the Déné stock, separated by the Rockies from their kindred in the east. Indeed, two tribes still frequented both sides of that range. The Nahanies, " People of the setting sun," connected with the group of the same name whose habitat was north of the upper waters of the Liard, the chief tributary of the Mackenzie River, occupied the sources of the Nass, Stikine, and Taku rivers flowing westward, and of the Teslin running northward into the Yukon. They were found on Dease Lake, whose waters flow into the Liard.

The Sikanies, " People of the rocks," were originally on the upper Peace River, but were driven across the Rockies by their kindred tribe, the Beavers, armed with the White Man's gun. In their new home they either did not adopt the fishing habits of their neighbours or were too weak to seize on their fisheries. The precariousness of their existence is well described in Harmon's Journal, kept when he was at Dunvegan on Peace River :

The Sikanies are a quiet inoffensive people whose situation exposes them to peculiar difficulties and distresses. When they proceed to the west of the mountains the Natives of that region [the Carriers] attack and kill many of them ; when they are on this side, the Beaver Indians and Crees are continually making war upon them. Being thus surrounded by enemies, against whom they are too feeble successfully to contend, they frequently suffer much for want of food ; for when on the west side, they dare not, at all times, visit those places, where fish are in plenty, and when on the east side, they are frequently afraid to visit those parts, where animals abound. They are compelled, therefore, oftentimes to subsist upon the roots, which they find in the mountains, and which barely enable them to sustain life ; and their emaciated bodies frequently bear witness to the scantiness of their fare.

This afflicted people frequented the Parsnip and Finlay rivers which unite to form the Peace, and traded at the forts on McLeod Lake and Bear Lake. With the Nahanies they represent the grade of culture of the Eastern Dénés at their lowest, for they earned their sustenance by the uncertain hunt of game on the shaggy slopes of the Rockies and roamed through the forests in scattered families.

The tribes whose life was typical of New Caledonia were the Babines, the Carriers, and, to a less degree, the Chilcotins. The Babines received this name from the French word *babine*, the chop or lip of an animal. They were so called because they wore a plug of bone or of hardwood between the teeth and the lower lip. Their main territory was about Babine Lake and River, and the Bulkley River and Lake to the east, whose waters flow into Stuart Lake.

The Carriers were called *Porteurs* by the French-Canadians because of the tribal custom of widows carrying a portion of the bones of their cinerated husbands on their backs for the space of their mourning. They were a numerous tribe, having, it is claimed, seven subdivisions. The fur-traders found their villages about Stuart and Fraser lakes, at the confluence of the Nechako and Fraser, and about the Quesnel and Blackwater. Finally the Chilcotins occupied the dry belt between the Coast Range and the Fraser, where they secured a precarious food supply by the river and lake which bear their name.

A somewhat ample food supply enabled these groups of the Western Dénés, especially the Carriers and Babines, to live in villages of considerable size and within easy reach of one another. They did not, however, develop any real tribal life, and had no tribal chief. The village was the pivot of their society, so much so that village was often at variance with village within the same tribe. Even so, the individual group might have no head, though apparently an outstanding character, like " Old Qua " of Harmon's Journal, might have a position not easy for the fur-traders to distinguish from that of a chief. The village society was made up of hereditary noblemen, who owned each his portion of the well-defined territory of the village, and of a lower class who hunted with and for them. The nobleman and these his dependents lived in a large house, its framework of poles covered with bark, and with the usual open roof for the smoke to pass out, and with a door at either end. For the sake of warmth the floor was more or less underground. Each family occupied its own portion of the house, with its own fire and its own storage for food. Those in want were supplied out of any superabundance among their associates. It shows a very considerable development of the social instincts that the household and village were harmonious within themselves, and that the settlement acted as a unit in its peaceful or warlike relations with its fellows. This solidarity of the village and its comparatively large population seemed a standing menace to the traders, for they never knew when a difficulty between themselves, or their servants, and the savages might lead to an assault of the whole community upon their fort.

There was an intertribal trade between the coastal tribes and the Carriers and Babines. Copper, garments made of sheep's wool, and the much-prized sea shells, which strung together like wampum constituted the currency of the savage, passed from tribe to tribe up the Skeena to the Dénés. It may be surmised that types of fur or leather not easily procured by the sea made up the return trade. The mode of communication and transport, where feasible, was with canoes made of aspen wood or cedar bark. Alexander Mackenzie found a trade, probably of long standing, in progress between the Carriers of the Fraser River and the coastal tribes. He took its beaten path along the River Blackwater to the sea.

The second cultural area may be defined as the arid mid-Columbia and its tributary valleys. This region, like New Caledonia, included a portion of the eastern forest—the upper Columbian and Kootenay valleys—and of the dry belt of our British Columbia—the valley of the Okanagan, north and west up to the Thompson and Fraser rivers. At the Chilcotin it touches the southern border of the Déné country. Towards the middle of the nineteenth century it was cut in two by the International Boundary, and became subject to two diverse political systems. Thereafter there was the British North and the American South, each the scene of a development of its own. Up to that time, however, the region must be considered as one, with a history in which the story of the north, our southern British Columbia, was but an episode in the history of the Columbian valley. Accordingly, the whole region must be envisaged, however briefly, to understand the course of events.

The region is drained by two streams—the Fraser, with its tributaries the Thompson and Lilloet, and the Columbia, with its many branches, the Kootenay, the Okanagan, the Pend d'Oreille (Clark's Fork), the Spokane, the Snake (Lewis), the Yakima, and the Willamette. The upper Columbia and Kootenay rivers appear principally as the water-ways by which the fur-traders came into the country from the east. The Fraser with its many wild rapids and cascades and its iron-bound perpendicular banks will only demand attention—at least before the gold rush of 1858—as the scene of two courageous attempts to find in it an easy path to the sea. The Thompson and Okanagan region and the plains of the Columbia, in the mind of the fur-traders, was a well-defined area. Its vantage points were occupied by more or less permanent fur-trading forts long before the coast saw anything more than a post at the mouth of the Columbia, playing the part as the depot for the traffic in peltries inland.

The vegetation in the British Columbian upland was plentiful, and consequently animal life was abundant. There were timbered heights with little undergrowth, passing over into park grasslands, and grassy valleys. Only in the Okanagan valley did the sandy wastes of the mid-Columbian valley appear. While some of the aborigines subsisted upon game and the fish native to the lakes and streams, the greater part of them was to be found, at least during much of the year, by the banks of the salmon-bearing Fraser and Thompson rivers. They constituted, as Mackenzie and Simon Fraser learned, large and dangerous communities.

The scene on the banks of the Columbia was much more desolate. What were called the Great Plains stretched westward from a point about two hundred miles from the sea—from the Dalles and the Falls of the Columbia :

> The aspect of the country becomes more and more triste and disagreeable ; one meets at first nothing but bare hills, which scarcely offer a few isolated pines, at a great distance from each other ; after that, the earth stripped of verdure, does not afford you the sight of a single shrub; the little grass which grows in that arid soil, appears burnt by the rigor of the climate. The natives who frequent the banks of the river, for the salmon fishery, have no other wood but that which they take floating down.

Consequently game was not plentiful. No great herds of buffalo nor of red deer or antelopes here. No beaver either, save in the valleys of tributaries like the Snake (Lewis), the Spokane, the Pend d'Oreille (Clark's Fork), the Okanagan, and the Kootenay, where the willow and the poplar appear. It would have been a land dispeopled by nature had it not been for the salmon swarming up the rivers in season to spawn. The population gathered in large communities, as the fur-traders found to their cost, by the rapids and falls especially where the catch was easily got ; they laid up large supplies of dried fish, which constituted the staple food supply during the rest of the year. A supplemental fare was to hand in certain roots and in such animals as fell to their arrows in distant wooded heights to which they migrated for the hunt. The people in the village had a strong sense of property in the river as a water-way and in the portages past the falls and rapids.

The tribes which occupied the present British area were of two stocks, the Kutenai and the Salish. The Kutenais were originally east of the Rockies, probably in the Montana of to-day, and with their neighbours of that time, the Snakes, were early the happy possessors of horses secured from tribes on the plains west of the Mississippi, and originally from the Spaniards in Mexico. In the second quarter of the eighteenth century the two tribes, fighting on horseback, were victoriously forcing their way into the valley of the South Saskatchewan, when the Piegans with the White Man's guns procured by their allies the Assiniboins and Crees at the Hudson's Bay Company's factory by the Bay, drove them back and even pushed them across the Rockies—the Kutenais into the upper valleys of the Columbia, the Snakes into uplands of its tributary, the Snake (Lewis). Both tribes were loath to forgo the joys of the buffalo hunt, and used to return to the east of the Rockies during the summer to renew their ancient life, though it cost many a bloody fray with the Piegans, mostly disastrous to those whose weapons of war were still perforce the antiquated bow and arrows.

The Salish tribes of the uplands, while connected linguistically with their kindred of the coast, were very different in their manner of living, for they had to conform to wholly different surroundings. In the western uplands were the Lilloets, on the Fraser and on its western tributary which still bears their name. The Shuswaps occupied the banks of the Fraser south of the Chilcotin Dénés and the wide area including Shuswap Lake extending to the valley of the Columbia. South of these were the Nilakyapamuk or Thompson Indians on the river named after David Thompson on the misinformation that the explorer of the Columbia was on its upper waters. Still farther south and extending beyond our International Border to the confluence of the Columbia with the river of their name, were the Okanagans with outlying subdivisions downstream to the region of Colvile. Finally there were the Flatheads, so called because they did not flatten their heads but left them as in nature to contrast with the tribes to the west who compressed their heads in one way and another to a point. Various subdivisions of this tribe were found by David Thompson on his Pend d'Oreille River (Clark's Fork) and the Spokane. Other groups lay opposite these on the right bank of the Columbia. The Shahaptin family occurs under various names, the Nez Percés on the Snake (Lewis) River, once called by their name, and the Columbia ; the Umatilla, the Walla-walla, and Yakima on the rivers so called. This family occupied the western portion of the plains of the mid-Columbia to the Dalles, where they met the Chinookan family of the coastal forest region.

Of all the tribes in the Columbian valley east of the Coast Range it may be said that their life was like that of the Prairie Indians. It was, however, modified by the fact that salmon was their staple article of food, and that they lived, temporarily at least, in village communities of varying size near the fisheries on the river. Yet the village community did not attain to a normal development because of their seasonal changes of residence. For example, the Okanagans lived in houses by the river with several families apiece much as did the Dénés. Their winter villages, however, were on some secluded stream by the mountains where the supply of wood would be ample. With spring these villages broke up and the families scattered for the season's hunt, to reunite in large numbers at their fishery about the middle of June. Now followed a period of great industry, fishing and curing the year's supply, accompanied by a complete abandonment to the joys of a crowded camp. " Gambling, dancing, horse-racing and frolicking, in all its varied forms are continued without intermission ; and few there are, even the most dull and phlegmatic, who do not feel, after enjoying so much hilarity, a deep regret on leaving the piscatory camp on these occasions," says Alexander Ross, who lived among them. The fishing season over, the community removed to the mountains for the hunt of large game, and after a month or six weeks returned to its winter quarters. Certain uncultivated vegetables and bread made of moss added to its means of subsistence. Such intertribal trade as was carried on was along the Columbia, and consisted of buffalo skins and the like passing downstream, and roots and shell ornaments being taken upward.

The Pacific coast is a region by itself. It has been formed by a depression of the earth's crust in which the valleys were flooded by the sea and transformed into inlets. The Coast Range and the heights of submerged mountains, which remain above water as so many islands, rise for the most part abruptly from the ocean. The large bodies of land—Vancouver Island, Moresby, and Graham of the Queen Charlotte Archipelago, the Prince of Wales group and Baranoff, both in Alaska—form an outer sea-wall broken through by the Strait of Juan de Fuca to the south and by Queen Charlotte Sound and Dixon Strait in the centre. Within lie inland seas dotted and separated by innumerable islands. " The sheltered channels are so continuous that the larger dug-out canoes can be brought safely from Skagway [Alaska] at the mouth of the Chilkoot River to Victoria, provided favourable weather is waited for before crossing the two or three more exposed stretches of water." The coast-line of the mainland and the islands is immense. On it was strung, as so many beads, a great number of villages all looking towards the sea or channel whence came their food supply.

The water teemed with life—whales, porpoises, sea-lions, seals, sea-otter, and of the fish, halibut, cod, herring, and, in their several seasons, the various species of the migratory salmon. All these in the sum provided—fresh and cured—a great abundance of food. Consequently the aboriginal population was greater here than in any part of what is the Dominion of Canada to-day. Duncan M'Gillivray in 1808 estimated the total Indian population between Labrador and the Rockies at fifteen thousand. Lewis and Clarke believed that there were twelve thousand Indians in the two hundred miles of the Columbia which belong to the coastal area.

The coastal West may be defined as the western slope of the Coast Range, including the thousand and one islands which adorn its seas. The winds of the Japanese current are chilled by the mountains and yield their moisture in an abundance of rain. Hence the forest of gigantic trees and the almost impenetrable undergrowth which clothed the land. Douglas fir and red cedar (*thuja gigantia*) prevail in the south, hemlock and sitka spruce in the north. These forests played a very large part in the life of the people. Apart from affording animal food by way of supplement to fish, they provided most of the necessaries for housing and clothing the population. From them came the large dug-out canoes in which the people gathered their daily food.

[The] cedar-tree has had a unique and far-reaching influence in the lives of the littoral tribes, and has been more potent in shaping the lines of their culture than any other single factor of their environment. It was to them much what the cocoa-nut palm was to the South-Sea Islanders. From its outer bark the men constructed their ropes and lines, coverings for their dwellings, their slow matches or "travelling fire" and many other things. From its inner bark their wives wove their garments for themselves and their children, made their beds and pillows, padded their babies' cradles, fashioned the compressing bands and pads for deforming their heads, besides applying it in a multitude of other ways. From its wood the men built the family and communal dwellings, made such furniture as they used—tubs, pots, kettles, bowls, dishes, and platters ; fashioned their graceful and buoyant fishing and war canoes, their coffins, their treasure-chests, their ceremonial masks, their heraldic emblems, their commemorative columns, their totem poles and a host of other objects. From the branches of the younger trees they made their most enduring withes and ties and from its split roots their wives and daughters constructed the beautiful water-tight basketry of this region. There was practically no part of this wonderful tree which they did not apply to some useful purpose or other.

With an abundant supply of food came a large population. With ample means in the forest for the needs of the community came a cultural life which stands by itself among the aboriginal peoples of Canada. There came also a well-developed, if primitive, social organization. The villages were large, and made up of many wooden houses in which several families lived as one. They were likewise comparatively permanent and lent themselves to the development of a strong community life. Not skill as a hunter as on the Barren Grounds, not achievements in war as on the prairies, but wealth and property gave distinction in this society. There were definite classes in the community. The chiefs and their relatives formed the highest rank. There was a middle class whose members held their position because of their wealth. There was a class of dependents and, finally, of slaves. Each village had a well-defined territory, and each well-to-do family its hunting-ground. The sense of property was much keener than among the Indians of other areas. The great numbers which the abundant food supply enabled to live in compact communities gave the tribes a sense of their power in their contacts with the small bands of European traders who came to them. The ample provision for their needs found in their coastal home made them independent in the face of European goods, save for copper and iron and the trinkets which fascinate all savages. Their sense of property, in the land, in the woods, in the grass, and even in their springs of water, brought about clashes with the White Men who naturally felt free to help themselves out of the prevailing abundance, while the desire to possess, which was ingrained in this plutocratic people, subjected the traders, not simply to sly pilfering, but to plunder and massacre on a large scale.

The tribes of the coastal west, living on its mediterranean seas, are distinguished by their languages. Tsimshians were mainly on the Nass and Skeena rivers—" their villages extending for quite a distance up these rivers into somewhat different environment and a less humid climate ; they maintained, however, a life quite similar to that of the coast people, securing through trade those products which are naturally limited to the sea." They carried on a trade with the Dénés of New Caledonia to the east.

The Haidas occupied the Queen Charlotte Archipelago. South of these two tribes were the Wakashan, divided into two groups, which may be said to have each had a language of its own—the Kwakiutl and the Nootka. Kwakiutl held the coast from Douglas to Burke channels, with an isolated Salish group on Burke Channel and the Bella Coola River. They also held the northern part of Vancouver Island. Their kindred the Nootkas held the whole of the south shore of the island, being cut off from tribes on the north by the dense forests of the interior.

The Salish were a widely spread stock. Their inland kindred have already been placed. Many coastal groups were to be found from the lands of the Kwakiutl on the north to the valley of the Columbia.

The coastal belt of the Columbia was two hundred miles wide, extending to the Dalles and the Falls. It was occupied by the tribes of the Chinookan family.

The very interesting and, from the point of view of the fur trade, very wealthy Pacific West remained unknown in any real sense to the people of Europe till the last third of the eighteenth century.

8.—THE RUSSIAN AND SPANISH APPROACH TO THE NORTH-WEST COAST, TO 1779

While Frenchmen interested in geography were dreaming of reaching the Western Sea by a quick march across the continent of America, and while the officials and the fur-traders of French Canada were slowly exploiting fur region beyond fur region, Russian Cossacks and fur-traders had reached across Asia to the shores of the Pacific in what Hubert H. Bancroft calls " a century sable-hunt round the world." Okotsk, on the coast, was founded as early as 1639. Thereafter attention was centred on the north-east, on the Arctic shore; but the possession of Kamchatka from 1706 laid the foundation of Russian interest in the exploration of the Pacific. In 1728 Vitus Bering, a Dane in the Russian navy, with a very able second in command, Alexei Chirikov, sailed in the ship *Gabriel* through Bering Strait and rounded East Cape. " He was of opinion that the coast must continually run from that Cape to the West, and if this was the case, no connection with America could take place." The strait between the continents was given Bering's name. In 1741 the Russian Government fitted out a truly scientific expedition at great expense. Its object was to reach America. Petropavlovsk in Kamchatka was the starting-point. Bering commanded the *St. Peter* and Chirikov the *St. Paul*. They sailed on 4th June (O.S.). Misled by a map by Louis Delisle, which embodied mere conjecture, they ran south-eastward towards the fictitious land of Juan de Gama, but were separated near the fiftieth degree of latitude. Both commanders now took a north-easterly course. Chirikov was the first to sight land. He put it in lat. 55° 36' north, which would make it the Prince of Wales Archipelago, near the southern extremity of Baranoff Island, on which Sitka now stands. At noon of 16th July the next day he was in lat. 56° 15', somewhere north of Sitka. That day Bering reached land in lat. 58° 30', in sight of Mt. St. Elias. Chirikov attempted a landing, but lost the crews of two small craft sent on shore and there massacred by the Indians. Thus deprived of his boats he abandoned the exploration. As he sailed homeward he lost sight of land at what must be Cape Elizabeth, the southern extremity of Kenai Peninsula, not to see it again until he came to the Aleutian Islands.

Meanwhile Bering watered his ship at Kayak Island off Cape St. Elias. He then sailed northward and westward, but saw little of the coast. He passed the present Chirikov Island and sighted the Aleutians. With his crew so stricken with scurvy as to be scarcely able to navigate the ship, he decided to land on Bering Island of the Commander Group over against Kamchatka. Distressed with scurvy, he " was carried on shore . . . on a hand-barrow, which consisted of two poles bound round with ropes and well secured from the open air." He died on 8th December (19th, N.S.). A wild storm drove the *St. Peter* ashore and buried it in sand. Such of the crew as survived the dread disease built a small craft out of its timbers and reached Petropavlovsk safely in the following summer.

The discoveries made by these two commanders gave Russia its first and somewhat frail title to Alaska. The claim was, however, made substantial by the flourishing fur trade and by the settlements which followed in the train of discovery. The castaways on Bering Island had lived on the flesh of sea-otters, and had brought their skins home with them. The beautiful pelts brought about immediately a fur trade with the island. In 1745 traders reached the Aleutian Islands, and in 1763–65 Kodiak Island east of the Alaskan peninsula. The course of the trade was from island to island in search of sea-otters, the mainland continuing unexplored. This advance of the Russians to America synchronizes with the activities of La Vérendrye and his successors in the fur region known in the French documents as La Mer de l'Ouest, our Lake Winnipeg.

Although the Spaniards had led the world of Christopher Columbus's day in exploration and colonization, they had now for more than a century and a half lain torpid by their tropical seas. According to their views, their discovery of the Pacific had given them an indisputable title to the whole coast of the Americas—a title based, at its outset, on the Treaty of Tordesillas with the Portuguese (1494) and the papal bull of Alexander VI. sanctioning the division of the world, as recently discovered, between the two nations. They should, therefore, have protested against the inroads of the Russians. That they did not do so suggests that they were tacitly aware that discovery followed by trade and settlement gave the intruders a sound claim to the areas reached by them. It was to set a limit to the encroachments and to strengthen their paper title by actual discovery and settlement that they inaugurated an era of expansion northward from Mexico. Roused by news of the Russian advance, and quickened by a fresh missionary impulse, they explored the coast of California—founding settlements and missions at San Diego, north of the present Mexican border, in 1759, at Monterey in 1770, and at San Francisco in 1776. In that year Peter Pond occupied his Fort Sturgeon above our Prince Albert and Thomas Frobisher was at Ile-à-la-Crosse, while the Hudson's Bay Company had but two years earlier inaugurated the policy of establishing posts inland and pressing westward.

Thus at the beginning of the last quarter of the eighteenth century our Pacific coast was being approached from Asia, from Mexico,
and from two points on the east of the continent—Hudson Bay and
Montreal. The movement of the English westward was slow, the
fur-traders passing from one beaver region "ruined" to the next
whose furs were untouched. Moreover it was by a difficult overland
journey with the mountain masses of the Pacific before them. The
progress of the Russians was similarly due to the lure of furs—the
precious sea-otter skins. While their way was by sea, and therefore
easy, it was made difficult and dangerous by ships which were
home-made—little more than timber tied together with thongs.
The Spanish advance was under political and religious impulses—
to protect their settlements and their missions from the foreigner
and the heretic. With good ships and seamen trained in the Spanish
Navy and in the overseas trade the race was easily theirs.

In 1774 Juan Perez, who had played a distinguished part in effecting the Californian settlements, was ordered by Don Antonio Maria
Bucarelli, Viceroy of New Spain, to make land as far north as the
sixtieth degree of latitude. He was given a long legal formulary to be
used in taking possession of the country. He was to follow the coast
on the homeward voyage. He left San Blas in the *Santiago* with a
crew of eighty-eight men. Estevan José Martinez, of whom we shall
hear much, was his pilot. The friar Juan Crespi went on board at
Monterey and became the historian of the expedition. On 16th July,
in lat. 52° 41', Perez was making for land and preparing a cross
to be erected as he formally took possession of the country. On the
17th he made his lat. 53° 3' north. Next day, at half-past eleven,
he saw the coast indistinctly. On the 19th he sighted a cape at which
the shore turned from NNW. to NE. and was low lying. He was
on the west coast of Queen Charlotte Islands. He followed it northward until it began to run to the east. He was now at their northern
extremity. The natives—they would be Haidas—aware of the
presence of the Spaniards, made many fires for a welcome, and came
out cautiously in their canoes made of one piece of wood " very
well hewn." They refused to go on board, but willingly entered into
trade, offering "fish dried like cod but whiter . . . a well-plaited
rush hat of several colours . . . a very pretty little mat a yard
square, woven of fine palms of two colours, white and black, which
being woven in little squares, makes a very good and handsome piece
of work "—typical Haida work, no doubt. On the 21st the explorers
were beyond the cape which is the north extremity of the islands,
and which they named Santa Margarita. They were in Dixon
Sound heading eastward and could see a peak of land to the north—
Prince of Wales Archipelago. As before, the natives came out to
them, but only two had the courage to go on board the ship. During
the next two days the Spaniards were becalmed and drifted out to
sea. They were then driven by the wind southward to the point at
which they first sighted land—a low-lying coast, south of which they
saw " San Christobal," the highest peak of the islands. On the 25th

an east wind carried them out to sea. They were still in sight of
land on the 20th, but lost it thereafter. They must have seen most
of the west coast of the Queen Charlotte Islands.

It was 6th August when Perez made land again. The latitude,
as he made it, was 48° 52′ N. Two days, however, passed before he
could come in and anchor. Even then he was " waiting until the
next day to go ashore and plant the holy cross there and take possession of the land " in the name of the Spanish King. The roadstead
had the shape of the letter C, and afforded little protection from the
winds. It was the south of Nootka Sound near the cape which is
its extreme limit, San Estevan, as they called it. The Indians who
came out to them in canoes would be the Nootkas, of the extensive
Wakashan group of tribes. They made trifling exchanges of articles.
One savage stole two silver spoons from the pilot Martinez, spoons
which figured later in the Nootka Sound Controversy. Next morning,
as preparations were being made to go ashore for the formal ceremony
of taking possession of the land, a strong wind and heavy swell
forced Perez to cut loose from his moorings and put to sea. He was
in sight of the distant coast as he sailed southward, but missed the
present Juan de Fuca Strait. On the 11th he sighted the present
Mt. Olympus, naming it Santa Rosalia. With a north-west wind he
sailed eastward in the hope of being able to plant the holy cross and
take possession of the land, but fog and a strong south-east wind
forced him to put about. Thus he missed the Columbia River.
He was able to see the coast from time to time as he sailed southward. On 27th August the expedition was safe in the harbour of
Monterey—the land which they desired still untrodden by Spanish
feet, the long formulary for taking possession still unread, and the
holy cross, the symbol of claims to be made for Christ and the King,
still lying in the ship.

The *Santiago* was sent back next year under Bruno Heceta,
a naval lieutenant, and with Juan Perez for sailing-master. She was
accompanied by a small schooner, the *Sonora*—thirty-six feet long,
twelve feet wide, and the depth of her hold eight feet—her commander Lieut. Juan Francisco de Bodega y Quadra. The landfall
of the expedition was in 48° 26′ N. lat., where it was expected the
Strait of Juan de Fuca would be found. Indeed, Heceta coasted in
search of it southward to Point Grenville (in the state of Washington)
in his lat. 47° 23′ N., really 47° 20′. On 14th July he landed, and
erected a cross, thereby staking out the Spanish claim. The *Sonora*
meanwhile had passed an island, Isla de Dolores, so called for its
forlorn appearance, and reached the coast slightly north of the
Santiago. Her commander Quadra sent a party ashore for water,
only to see it massacred. The spot has been called Martyr's Point,
and the name Isla de Dolores changed to Destruction Island.

Heceta and Quadra were parted at sea by a storm. An outbreak
of scurvy led the commander-in-chief to return. However, he took
a course as far north as possible and sighted land in 49° 30′ N. lat.
in the region of Nootka Sound. On 12th August, two days later,

on a southerly course he saw a light, which may have been at Clayoquot Sound. He missed the present strait of Juan de Fuca. Passing the Isla de Dolores, he discovered an opening in the coast, with a strong current suggesting a strait or a river. It was in 46° 17′ N. lat., as he made it, and was none other than the Columbia River, whose estuary is in N. lat. 46° 15′. Heceta called it Rio San Roque and the bay at its mouth Assumption Bay. Too many of the crew were down with scurvy to make a landing possible. Accordingly the ship passed southward ; it reached Monterey at the end of August.

Meanwhile the *Sonora* under Quadra, and with Alferez Antonio Maurelle as pilot and keeper of the log, had been brought by favourable winds to a landfall in 57° 2′ N. lat., as it was calculated, *i.e.* in the region of the present Sitka, within sight of the mountain called Edgecombe by Captain Cook. The ship passed northward, and at one point, De los Remedios (57° 18′ N.), Quadra took possession of the land. His crew stricken with scurvy, he turned his prow homeward in 58° N., keeping land in view as far as might be. Possession was once more taken at what was called Bucarelli (55° 17′ N.), an inlet of Prince of Wales Island. Quadra sighted the Queen Charlotte Islands and Vancouver Island, and from time to time got views of a distant coast. He was able to examine it more closely from the forty-fourth parallel of latitude southward. He discovered a bay, named after him Bodega Bay.

The Spaniards had now penetrated northward to the region discovered by the Russians, and had acquired such claims as first discovery could give to a vast stretch of coast, but their examination was so superficial that they were not aware that much of the coast which they had seen was not the mainland at all, but a succession of islands. In 1779 a third expedition was sent out to explore still farther north. It reached the sixty-first degree of north latitude at our Prince William Sound. Satisfied with thus fortifying its vague claims by actual discovery, the Spanish Government issued an order to cease exploration, but for some reason, perhaps because it thought its claim good in any case, it did not announce the discoveries and did not proclaim to the world the Spanish possession of the territory seen. The fact of the voyage of 1774, however, was known in Britain from Spanish sources in 1776.

9.—ENGLISH EXPLORATIONS AND FUR TRADE OF THE NORTH-WEST COAST, 1778-88

The English now appear upon the Pacific coast in the person of Captain James Cook—a type of Briton of which we find representatives in every age after the reign of glorious Queen Bess. While their base was " the island set in the silver sea," their life was on the Seven Seas out in the wide world. Born in a humble cottage, at Marton, in the parish of Grimsby, in Yorkshire, on October 27, 1728, Cook first found his sea legs in the mercantile service on the North Sea. At twenty-seven years of age, with the Seven Years War impending, he entered the British Navy and continued in the service till his tragic death. He figures in Canadian history at more points than one. As sailing-master of H.M.S. *Pembroke* he was present at the capture of Louisburg in 1758. In the following year he sailed up the St. Lawrence with Admiral Durell's squadron, and was of the party which surveyed the dangerous " traverse " at Ile d'Orleans ; he thereby enabled Sir Charles Saunders's fleet to pass upstream to Quebec. His ship played its part in the various movements on the river during the siege of that fortress ; for example, in the feint below Beauport, on the evening before Wolfe's famous scaling of the cliff and his victory on the Plains of Abraham. At the end of the campaigns which brought about the conquest of Canada, Cook was granted " fifty pounds in consideration of his indefatigable industry in making himself master of the pilotage of the river St. Lawrence." During the winters when his new ship, H.M.S. *Northumberland*, lay in Halifax harbour, Cook, "without any other assistance than what a few books and his own industry afforded him," devoted himself to the higher mathematics and astronomy necessary for a " complete navigator." From this time he served under the flag in all parts of the world. In 1763–67 he was surveying the coasts of Nova Scotia, and in particular of New-foundland, making charts which are said to be useful to this day. In 1768–69 he was on the Pacific Ocean conveying a group of scientists on behalf of the Royal Society to observe the transit of Venus at Tahiti. It will be remembered that Mr. Wales was sent to Churchill Fort on Hudson Bay for the same purpose, and probably there trained Samuel Hearne in the art of astronomical observation. Mr. Alexander Dalrymple, hydrographer to the East India Company, and afterwards the critic of Samuel Hearne, had been proposed as commander of the expedition, but the Admiralty's final choice was Cook, who was placed as 1st Lieutenant in charge of H.M.S. *Endeavour*. On the homeward voyage, after a vain search for the mythical Antarctic continent, Cook sailed round the coast of New Zealand and charted it. After doing the same for the east coast of Australia, he passed round Cape of Good Hope, and thus completed his first circumnavigation of the world.

In 1772 Captain Cook, as he now was, sailed in H.M.S. *Resolution* by way of Cape of Good Hope to determine the existence of the Antarctic continent. He showed that the southern Pacific was an open sea. He then revisited New Zealand and discovered a multitude of islands in what is now known as Australasia. The return was by Cape Horn. Cook's Journal of this voyage was prepared for the press by the Rev. John Douglas, Canon of Windsor, and later Bishop of Salisbury, who afterwards edited Samuel Hearne's *Journey . . . to the Northern Ocean.*

During these voyages Captain Cook had brought his masterly mind to bear on the problem of scurvy, the scourge of navigation on the high seas. Not the least contribution to exploration on such a distant coast as the American West was his discovery of a diet which kept his crews comparatively free from the dire disease which maimed all the Spanish explorations of that coast, comparatively short as was the distance which they had to traverse. Finally, Cook's voyages so stimulated interest in geographical exploration that it was determined to attack the question of the North-West Passage, dropped since Arthur Dobbs's day. Now that the problem of the health of the crew upon a long voyage was assured, its solution appeared possible by penetrating from the west through Bering Strait eastward to Hudson Bay. Captain Cook was felt to be the logical choice for the command of the expedition. In H.M.S. *Resolution*, accompanied by H.M.S. *Discovery*, commanded by Captain Clerke, he sailed round Cape of Good Hope and revisited New Zealand. At Tahiti he provisioned his ships with wood and water for the northern voyage. In February 1778 he discovered islands which he named after the Earl of Sandwich, then at the head of the Admiralty. These islands later figured greatly in the history of the American coast as the happy base for many trading expeditions to that distant shore.

The secret instructions of the Commissioners of the Admiralty to Captain Cook ran, that he was to proceed in as direct a course as possible from Tahiti to New Albion, that is that part of the American continent visited by Francis Drake in 1579, endeavouring to fall in with it in the forty-fifth degree of latitude. " You are also, in your way thither, strictly enjoined not to touch on any part of the Spanish Dominions in the Western continent of America, unless driven by some unavoidable accident. . . . And if, in your farther progress to the Northward, as thereafter directed, you find any subjects of an European Prince or State, you are not to disturb them, or give them any just cause of offence, but, on the contrary, to treat them with civility and friendship." In spite of the later Spanish interpretation of this instruction, the implication is that the Spanish territory was on this side of New Albion, but Spaniards, if found beyond, were to be treated with friendship. The wording is due to the fact that the Spanish policy of not publishing their northern discoveries and that they had taken possession of the land in the name of Spain left the English ignorant of what they had done. Cook knew no more than that there had been voyages northward. He obeyed his instructions to the letter, and visited no Spanish settlements on his way to New Albion, nor did he meet any Spaniards north of the forty-fifth degree of latitude. The instructions went on to say that Cook was next to proceed northward to the sixty-fifth degree of latitude, making the necessary observations without any minute exploration, but from that point to search any river or inlet which might lead to Hudson or to Baffin Bay. Finally, he was to go to some port in Kamchatka or elsewhere to winter and to return in the spring to his task.

On March 7, 1778, Captain Cook made his landfall in 44° 35′ N. lat., on the coast of Oregon within sight of a cape from which he was driven by a storm, hence his name Cape Foulweather, which is still on our maps. Returning, he coasted northward till he seemed to see a harbour, and as if smiling at his deception, he called the cape standing to the north Cape Flattery. It stands under that name to-day, the promontory south of the entrance to Juan de Fuca Strait, but Cook was too far south to perceive the opening. " We saw nothing like [the pretended strait of Juan de Fuca], nor is there the least probability that ever any such thing existed." A fierce gale right on shore forced him to stand once more to sea. On the morning of the 29th he made his next landfall in 49° 29′ N. lat. Passing between Breaker's Point on the south and Woody Point on the north, Cook entered a sound which he named King George's Sound, but afterwards changed it to Nootka Sound from what he took to be the native name. The ships were sailed into its north-easterly arm to " Friendly Cove," now Resolution Cove, on Bligh Island. Here Cook achieved an intimacy with the natives such as Perez had not known when at the extreme southern limit of the sound, for he was there but a day and did not leave his ship. A camp and an observatory were built on shore, and the crew were set to the task of refitting the vessels. The natives visited the Englishmen daily, and an informal trade began in which the savages secured iron and copper on which they laid great store, while the crew obtained curiosities and furs —skins of bears, deer, foxes, wolves, and, most important of all for history, sea-otters. Cook found the people expert traders who tried to engross the trade with the ships by keeping off all the neighbouring tribes, for whom they would fain play the part of middlemen. They subsisted on abundant supplies of fish—particularly sardines, which came in at that season in shoals. These they cured for future use. At other times they hunted animals on land and in the sea. They lived in houses, several families in each house, in villages of about a thousand people. They had a well-developed sense of property, and would not allow the Englishmen to gather wood, or grass, or even to take water, without payment. Cook visited villages west and north of Bligh Island, which he circumnavigated. Altogether it must have been an interesting and happy interlude in his long voyage.

Captain Cook's instructions ran : " You are also, with the consent of the natives, to take possession in the name of the King of Great Britain of convenient situations in such countries as you may discover, that have not already been discovered or visited by any other European power . . . setting up proper marks and in-scriptions, as first discoverers and possessors." As the Captain did not take possession of Nootka Sound it may be argued that in not doing so he followed his instructions to the letter, for the Spaniards under Perez had visited the region four years before. Towards the end of his sojourn there, evidence of their presence appeared in the form of the two silver spoons which had been stolen from Martinez, the pilot of Perez's expedition. They were bought of Indians who came up from the south.

When Captain Cook left Nootka Sound on 26th April he ran into foul weather which obliged him to keep off-shore, but from 55° 20' N. lat. he coasted northward, sighting a cape and mountain which he named Edgecombe. His course up the coast of Alaska can be traced by names which still figure on our maps—Cape and Mount Fairweather, Prince William Sound, and Cook's Inlet. Because of its swift current the inlet was mistaken by the navigator for the estuary of a large river, Cook's River as it was called. This illusion set the fur-traders in the Athabaska country speculating as to whether it might not be—indeed they concluded that it was—the mouth of the as yet unexplored Mackenzie River, and Peter Pond and his successor, Alexander Mackenzie, planned a journey whose end proved to be at the Polar Sea. Cook himself must have argued that the inlet was at a strategic point, for he took possession of it in the name of the King.

Captain Cook explored carefully the whole coast of Alaska and through Bering Strait and north-eastward until he was forced by ice at Icy Cape to retrace his course. His delineation of the north shore of Alaska to Icy Cape, coupled with Samuel Hearne's fixation of the Polar shore as at the mouth of the Coppermine River, gave geographers a more complete idea of the northern coast-line of the continent.

Captain Cook returned to the salubrious shores of the Sandwich Islands for the winter months. He came to a tragic end there on February 13, 1779, at the hand of the natives. Captain Clerke took command of the expedition and made a second but equally futile attempt to trace out the North-West Passage by way of Bering Strait. When at Macao, the Portuguese colony near Canton, on the way back to England, some of his officers and men realized astonishing prices for sea-otter skins traded with the natives for the merest trifles. The best brought 120 dollars a skin. This created something like a rage among them to return to the American coast and build up a fur trade with China. The wealth to be so gained was advertised by the publication of the official account of the expedition in 1785. It was particularly noted that Cook's party got sea-otter skins at Nootka Sound, at Prince William's Sound, and at Cook's Inlet. Thus was inaugurated the English fur trade of our Pacific coast. Many of the men who initiated it—Portlock, Dixon, and Colnett—were actually of Cook's expedition, and so, in a sense, trained for their careers as fur-traders. Moreover, Vancouver, who was chosen by the Admiralty for its next voyage of exploration, and who delineated the Pacific coast, we might almost say, to its last inlet, was an officer under Cook on this his last voyage. Truly the great navigator left his impress on the history of our western shore.

All was not plain sailing for the Englishmen who followed in the wake of Captain Cook. The East India Company had the monopoly of trade to China, the market for the sea-otter furs of the American coast. The South Sea Company controlled the trade to the islands of the South Pacific. Accordingly, English adventurers to the north-west American coast were driven to devious ways of conducting their trade. It was natural that the first to rush in should be a captain, James Hanna by name, who in his ship in the roads of Macao had the opportunity to know of the prices which had been secured by the men of Cook's expedition in the fur mart of Canton. It is not known whether he had a licence from the East India Company to sail to China, and stretched it to cover his trip to the new-found fur field, or whether he sailed under Portuguese colours from Macao, the Portuguese colony facing Hong Kong and at the mouth of the bight leading up to Canton. He reached Nootka Sound in August 1785 in a brig of fifty tons. The natives attempted to storm his vessel, but he drove them off with considerable slaughter—the first of a long series of bloody clashes on the part of the White Men with the Red Men of the coast, who because of their numbers dared to be hostile. This clash, however, so far from hindering Hanna in his trade, enabled him to carry it on quietly and successfully. He left at the end of September with a cargo of 560 sea-otter skins, which he sold in Canton by way of Macao for 20,600 Chinese dollars, and thus realized something like a fortune.

The next to rush in were Captains Lowrie and Guise, who were fitted out for their voyage by merchants in Bombay, among whom was one James Strange. They probably sailed under the protection of a licence of some kind from the East India Company. In two small vessels called snows, the *Captain Cook* and the *Experiment*, they reached Nootka Sound in June 1786. They coasted northward and discovered Queen Charlotte Sound, which they named after the Queen. Thence they proceeded to Prince William Sound. They then returned to Macao, and in 1787 sold their 604 sea-otter skins for 24,000 Chinese dollars. These two vessels were the first of six which sailed our coastal seas that year in search of peltries. The rush to the new Eldorado was now on.

Captain Lowrie left his surgeon John MacKay at Nootka Sound to recover from a sickness, but also to learn the native tongue, and to ingratiate himself with the natives and secure their furs for him on his return. He was the first White Man to winter in these parts. He took a squaw to wife, and established happy relations with the natives. Consequently, when Captain Hanna appeared again in the ship *Sea-otter* (120 tons) at his former happy trading-ground, he found the peltry of the region pre-empted by MacKay. Of necessity he went farther afield. He coasted northward to the fifty-third degree of latitude, discovering and naming Smith Inlet and Fitzhugh Sound. He returned to China with 400 skins, many of them of little value, so that he only got 8,000 dollars for his cargo.

Here falls in, by way of interlude, the voyage of Jean-François de Galaup, Comte de la Pérouse, the French navigator. During the war between France and England, in which the French Navy had done so much to help the American colonists to achieve their independence, he served his country with distinction, capturing forts Churchill and York on Hudson Bay (1782). In 1785 he was dispatched by the

French Government to attempt to discover the North-West Passage from the west, and to explore the north-west coast of America, much as Cook had done. In command of the *Astrolabe* and the *Bousserole* he reached the coast near Mt. St. Elias in Alaska on June 23, 1786. His six weeks of exploration northward are not a matter of great concern, as also his hasty voyage southward along our coast. What really is of importance is that his report of the Russian operations roused the Spaniards to the fresh activity which led to the clash with England over the possession of Nootka Sound.

In June 1787 Captain Charles William Barkley appeared on Nootka Sound in the *Imperial Eagle*, a fine ship of 400 tons from London and Ostend by way of Cape Horn. He was an ex-officer of the East India Company, and he escaped from the monopoly of his late employers by sailing from Ostend in the Austrian Netherlands under the Austrian flag. He persuaded John MacKay, the first Englishman to winter on the Pacific coast, to act for him in spite of his obligations to Captain Lowrie. Thus Barkley secured a fine lot of sea-otter skins. Passing down the coast of Vancouver Island, which was still thought to be the mainland, he traded in Barkley Sound, which he so called after himself. Farther south he opened up a strait which he believed to be that of Juan de Fuca, and which he so named. Still farther south he sent out a boat's crew to trade for him on the mainland at the mouth of a river near the spot at which the men from the *Sonora* had been killed. The appropriate name Destruction was given to the river, but was later transferred to the Spanish Isla de Dolores. It thus marks the bloody neighbourhood out for us to this day. The 800 sea-otter skins collected by Captain Barkley were sold in Canton for 30,000 Chinese dollars, bringing a very handsome profit. Before embarking at Ostend, Barkley had married Frances Hornby Trevor, an English lady of seventeen; he brought her with him on his voyage—the first European lady on the north-west coast of America.

In the same year the representatives of " The King George's Sound Company " appeared upon the Pacific scene. The title of the Company was taken from Captain Cook's original name for Nootka Sound. The Company secured itself against intervention by the East India and the South Sea companies by procuring licences from both. It had good backing, and its expedition attracted the interest and support of geographers and scientists. Its first ships were the *King George*, 320 tons, in command of Captain Nathaniel Portlock, and the *Queen Charlotte*, under Captain George Dixon. Both commanders, as has been seen, were acquainted with the west coast of America through participating in Captain Cook's voyage. They made the Sandwich Islands their base, and reached Cook's Inlet on July 1786, where they came upon a temporary camp of Russians, the spear-head at that date of the Russian movement eastward. In August they ran eastward to Prince William Sound, but were prevented by contrary winds from reaching it. They then coasted southward, sighting Mt. St. Elias and capes Fairweather and Edge-

combe. Their intention was to winter at Cook's Friendly Cove in
Nootka Sound, but baffled by the winds, they gave up the plan and
sailed to the Sandwich Islands. So far the expedition, though not
absolutely unsuccessful, was altogether disappointing. The crew
consoled themselves with the prospect of enjoying the flesh-pots of
the Sandwich Islands. " We comforted ourselves with the hope of
many a delicious regale among the hogs, yams and other good cheer
of Sandwich Islands."

Next year, 1787, Portlock and Dixon arrived in Prince William
Sound towards the end of April. They fell on Captain John Meares,
who had spent the winter there in great distress. Portlock in the
King George remained in the sound, while Dixon in the *Queen
Charlotte* was sent southward to trade along the coast. The Englishmen were feeling their way to the best methods of trade upon an
inhospitable shore whose population, especially in the north, was
sparse, settled only in villages few and far between. All the furs
at any one settlement could be gathered in the trade of a day.
From Portlock's ship in the sound boats were sent in different
directions to scour the shores. This proved unprofitable. Dixon's
method stands in sharp contrast. He passed down the coast from
village to village. The natives came out to him in their canoes, and
usually traded all their furs worth having in a single day. William
Beresford, Dixon's assistant trader, whose letters to a friend constitute the report of the voyage, wrote : " Thou mayest see by the
whole tenor of my last, that our coasting along these islands was the
best and most expeditious method of trading we could possibly have
hit upon." So it was, and it therefore remained the practice of the
traders for wellnigh a half-century. When necessary, parties would
be sent ashore for wood and water, and for timber to make spars,
and for other necessaries for the ships.

Place-names on our maps will suggest the course followed by
Dixon. He coasted southward to Queen Charlotte Islands. He was
far enough in the strait between these islands and Prince of Wales
Archipelago to see a point far within which he was later to conclude
must be the continental coast. The name Dixon Sound was bestowed
on the strait next year by the geographer, Sir Joseph Banks. Dixon
gave their names to North Island and to Clark's Bay at the entrance
of the strait and, passing down the western shores of Queen Charlotte
Islands, to Hippa Island and Rennell Sound, and at their southern
extremity, to Cape St. James, for the day of its discovery. He now
passed round this cape and ran up the east shore to beyond the
fifty-third degree of north latitude, far enough, as he thought, to see
the point of land seen far in from Dixon Strait. He concluded that he
had been all along following the shores of a series of islands. These
he called, after his ship, the Queen Charlotte Islands.

As for the trade—on 2nd July, Dixon had been in the bay on
North Island, which he called Cloak Bay because of the remarkable
trade in cloaks made of sea-otter skins which he had carried on in
it—William Beresford wrote :

A scene now commenced, which absolutely beggars all description, and with which we were so overjoyed, that we could scarcely believe the evidence of our senses. There were ten canoes about the ship, which contained, as nearly as I could estimate, 120 people ; many of these brought most beautiful beaver cloaks ; others excellent skins, and, in short, none came empty handed, and the rapidity with which they sold them, was a circumstance additionally pleasing ; they fairly quarrelled with each other about which should sell his cloak first ; and some actually threw their furs on board ; but we took particular care to let none go from the vessel unpaid. Toes * were almost the only article we bartered with on this occasion, and indeed they were taken so eagerly, that there was not the least occasion to offer anything else. In less than half an hour we purchased near 300 beaver skins of an excellent quality ; a circumstance which greatly raised our spirits, and the more, as both the plenty of fine furs, and the avidity of the natives in parting with them, were convincing proofs that no traffic whatever had recently been carried on near this place, and consequently we might expect a continuation of this plentiful commerce. That thou mayest form some idea of the cloaks we purchased here, I shall just observe that they generally contain three good sea-otter skins, one of which is cut in two pieces, afterwards they are neatly sewed together so as to form a square, and are loosely tied about the shoulders with small leather strings fastened on each side.

Beresford could not be expected to get an adequate knowledge of savages whose language was unknown to him, but he tried to spell out their social relationships.

Though every tribe we met with at these islands is governed by its respective Chief, yet they are divided into families, each of which appears to have regulations and a kind of subordinate government of its own : the Chief usually trades for the whole tribe ; but I have sometimes observed that when his method of barter has been disapproved of, each separate family has claimed a right to dispose of their own furs, and the Chief always complied with this request ; whether or no he receives any emolument on these occasions I cannot determine.

Off Vancouver Island Captain Dixon met with two ships of his own Company, the *Prince of Wales* commanded by Captain James Colnett and the sloop *Princess Royal* under Captain Duncan, out from Nootka Sound two or three days. On the way from England these ships had spent some time capturing seals on Staten Island at the extremity of the South American continent, where the Company proposed to establish a seal fishery and to form a base for their trade to Nootka Sound. Mr. John Etches, brother of the managing owner, Richard Cadman Etches, was on board and reported that they had been at Nootka Sound but got no trade, for Captain Barkley of the *Imperial Eagle* had arrived there a month before them. Captain Duncan and Mr. Etches made a copy of Dixon's chart, and, on his advice, proceeded to the east coast of the Queen Charlotte Islands. Duncan made the passage of our Heceta Strait, and proved that Dixon's view that it was a strait separating an archipelago from the mainland was correct. Dixon steered for Canton, where he sold " 2,552 otter skins, 434 cub, and 34 fox " for 50,000 Chinese dollars. He took on a load of tea and sailed for England.

* Toes are links of a chain.

These expeditions did not simply inaugurate the English marine fur trade on the north-west American coast. They discovered many parts untouched by the Spaniards, who, in any case, had not yet made public such explorations as they had made nor their claim to possession. Besides, the English seamen had gone some distance towards establishing the right of England to trade in these parts— a more substantial title than that based on simple discovery.

10.—ENGLISH AND SPANISH CLASH AT NOOTKA SOUND, 1788-89

Trading on the Pacific coast called for some base of operations. Here Nootka Sound with Cook's Friendly Cove offered itself. This last was a protected harbour. Its climate was mild, and the sea was open all the year round. Moreover, it was a good mart for sea-otter skins. Accordingly, Captain John Meares, now in Canton after a distressful winter at Prince William Sound, which proved that the north was no place for wintering, made plans for an establishment at the Cove.

The story of Meares's venture is told in his *Voyages made in the years 1788 and 1789 from China to the North-West Coast of America*, published in 1790, including its appendices, and in his notorious *Memorial*, of which more anon. Unfortunately, although Meares used his daily journal in writing the book, it was composed in the height of the Nootka Sound controversy, and is marked not only by a spirit of violent partisanship, but it shows that the author was capable of wilful deception, to the point of changing his documents to enhance his importance and to establish his claims. It is possible, however, by checking his statements by those of others as well as of himself, to reach the substantial truth.

Meares arrived in Nootka Sound on May 23, 1788, in the ship *Felice*, apparently prepared to fly either the British or the Portuguese flag as occasion might require. The crew and the labourers for his establishment were English, Portuguese, and Chinese—the first Chinese to reach the Pacific coast, at least in historic times. Maquilla, the chief of the region and Captain Cook's friend, readily granted him " a spot of ground in his territory " for the house in which the party to be left on shore could live and work. On the 28th, that is, in say four days, the building was " completely finished "—no very elaborate establishment, surely, in spite of Meares's grandiose description :

On the ground floor there was ample room for the coopers, sailmakers and other artizans to work in bad weather ; a large room was also set apart for the stores and provisions, and the armourer's shop was attached at one end of the building and communicated with it. The upper story was divided into an eating room and chambers for the party. . . . [The house] appeared to be a structure of uncommon magnificence to the natives of King George's Sound.

The savages had worked readily with Meares's men, and received their wages in beads or iron when the bell rang in the evening.

A strong breast-work was thrown up round the house, enclosing a considerable area of ground, which, with one piece of cannon, placed in such a manner as to command the cove and village of Nootka, formed a fortification sufficient to secure the party from any intrusion. Without this breast-work, was laid the keel of a vessel of 40 or 50 tons, which was now to be built agreeable to our former determinations.

In fact, the carpenters were at work on the frame of the ship during the voyage out. Meares's *Memorial* adds that he "hoisted the British Colours" over his fort. "Good harmony and friendly intercourse" subsisted between the Englishmen and the natives. Some savages, for example, Callicum, Maquilla's chief man, grew much attached to Mr. Meares.

All the while trade was being carried on with the natives. At first Meares had fixed his prices for everything, but in the end he adopted the savage method of trading.

Whenever Maquilla or Callicum thought proper to make us a present, one of their attendants was sent to request the company of the Tighee or Captain on shore. . . . On our arrival at the habitation of the chiefs, where a great number of spectators attended to see the ceremony, the sea-otter skins were produced with great shoutings and gestures of exultation, and then laid at our feet. The silence of expectation then succeeded among them, and their most eager attention was employed on the returns we should make.

The traders took pains to make a satisfactory gift in return, for it ensured a swift departure to make a fresh hunt for furs. Maquilla on his side played the part of middleman, keeping other tribes from coming in to trade, but bringing in their furs himself to the traders. When the trade of the Sound dwindled, Meares ran down the coast to Clayoquot Sound, where he named the cove, hard by the village of Wicananish its chief, Port Cox. Here a magnificent harvest of furs " of the most beautiful kind " was gathered in return for presents. A formal treaty was made with Wicananish by which all the furs of the region should be held for Meares, and the Indians in return should have common access to his ship. Here again the chief became the middleman for a large region, securing its furs for the trader.

Proceeding down the coast, Meares reached the Strait of Juan de Fuca and the island of a chief named Tatooche, off Cape Flattery. According to the *Voyages* he found the chief surly and the natives hostile, but the *Memorial* runs :

He also acquired the same privilege of exclusive trade from Tatooche, the chief of the country bordering on the Straits of John De Fuca, and purchased from him a tract of land within the said Strait, which one of your Memorialist's officers took possession of in the King's name, calling the same Tatooche, in honour of the chief.

This may safely be eliminated, at least from this point of the story, as untrue. Concluding that Wicananish had already drawn all their furs from this tribe, and unable to find a harbour, Meares sailed along the coast southward.

The next definite point reached was Destruction Island, beyond which Meares searched for the River "Saint Roc." He came within view of a bay which promised to reveal it, but he finally decided that there was no such river. Accordingly he named the cape, which, as it was later discovered, is north of the mouth of the Columbia River, Cape Disappointment, and the bay he called Deception Bay. It would appear that he was very near the estuary of the Columbia River, which may have lain concealed behind its line of breakers and its bar. Meares's vagueness suggests, however, that he may have fabricated his account, for he should have observed the river which at that time of the year would be in flood. He says : " We can now with safety assert that no such river as that of Saint Roc exists." Meares's conclusion, as he sailed southward to Cape Grenville and Cape Lookout, was: "Not a human being appeared to inhabit the fertile country of New Albion."

As he returned, Meares entered Barkley Sound and anchored in a harbour named by him Port Effingham, where he attended to the needs of his ship. At this point in his narrative, though it has little to do with it, for Meares is about fifty miles away, he adds a suspiciously conspicuous item to his story. " It may not be improper to mention that we took possession of the Straits of John de Fuca, in the name of the King of Britain, with the forms that had been adopted by preceding navigators on similar occasions." He goes on with the story of his trading, and then tells of sending off the longboat under Robert Duffin on 13th July, whose instructions are given as his Appendix No. III. They include orders to explore the Strait of Juan de Fuca and to take possession of the strait and the lands in the name of the King and Crown of Great Britain. By the 17th the boat had got no farther than into the strait, and with little or no trade, when a desperate encounter with the natives took place. Some of its crew were seriously wounded. As Meares says later, " We had never had any intercourse with the inhabitants of the straits." Certainly the crew of the longboat had none worth mentioning. We may conclude that the story of taking possession of the straits is a fabrication devised to re-enforce the title of Britain to those parts and to induce the British Government to back the exalted claims asserted by Meares.

On 27th August our adventurer, then in Nootka Sound, was joined by his subordinate officer, Captain W. Douglas, in his ship the *Iphigenia*, with supplies from the Sandwich Islands. On 17th September the *Lady Washington*, 100 tons, from Boston, commanded by Captain Robert Gray, arrived, Nootka Sound being her rendezvous with the *Columbia Rediviva*, whose captain was John Kendrick. This was the first expedition from the United States to this fur region. Haswell's Log of the *Lady Washington*, under date of Monday, 15th September, says of Meares's ships, " fitted from Macao in China and under Portugeese Coulers." On the 20th the ship built by Meares's party was launched in the presence of the crew of the American vessel and of the astonished natives. It was named the *North West America* and, Meares says, was launched under the British flag. Haswell is silent on the point, but later the Americans asserted that it was under Portuguese colours.

Meares was now making his arrangements for the next year's trade and settlement. He informed the chief Maquilla and his following that he would return to them the next spring with others of his countrymen and would build more houses. They promised to have plenty of furs for his return. Meares says, though it may be no more than a frill added to his story to enforce his claims and those of Britain, that Maquilla did obedience to him as his lord and sovereign and took his tiara of feathers from his head and placed it on the Englishman's brow. Instructions were given to Captain Douglas to proceed to the Sandwich Islands for supplies, taking care to salt his pork, "following the method which Captain Cook directs"; to return to Nootka Sound with his consort the little *North West America* about the 1st of April, and then to explore and trade about the west coast of Queen Charlotte Islands from Cape St. James northward, while Captain Robert Funter in the *North West America* should trade on the east side. The ships were to return to meet Meares in Nootka Sound in the autumn of the year (1789). Meares himself sailed on September 24, 1788, for Macao. The Americans afterwards asserted that he sent the boards of the sides of his house to the Sandwich Islands, and that he gave the roof to Captain Kendrick.

A few days after Meares's arrival at Macao two ships of the King George's Sound Company, the *Prince of Wales* under Captain Colnett and the *Princess Royal* under Captain Duncan, also arrived from the north-west coast of America, with Mr. John Etches, brother of the managing owner, on board. Meares and Etches entered into an arrangement to form a joint-stock company for the next trading season. As the *Prince of Wales* had been chartered to take tea for the East India Company to England, she passes out of view. A ship newly purchased, the *Argonaut*, was put under her recent captain James Colnett. Captain Thomas Hudson replaced Duncan on the *Princess Royal*. The two ships were supplied with goods for a trade of three years, and the frame of a 30-ton vessel was procured to be completed on the American coast. The ships took on artificers of different kinds and some twenty-nine Chinamen to effect a "solid settlement," presumably on Nootka Sound. In the mind of Captain Meares the advantage of the partnership lay in the elimination of competition and in the ships sailing with licences from the East India and the South Sea companies—good till 1790. There may be doubts as to the English character of Meares's former expedition, for he, on occasion at least, used the Portuguese colours, but this venture of 1789 was indubitably English, combining such rights of trade or settlement as had been acquired by both Meares and the King George's Sound Company by their previous voyages. The partners were bent on extending those rights by a "solid establishment and not one that is to be abandoned at pleasure," says Meares. It was to play the part of a base for their trade, at least during the summer. The mild climate of the Sandwich Islands, with their superabundant food supply was still thought preferable for the ships in winter. In the early summer months of 1789 these two vessels were following one another to the American coast with every prospect of a lucrative trade, as the adventurers, all unaware of what was transpiring at Nootka Sound, congratulated themselves.

When La Pérouse reached Monterey in September 1786, he reported the activities of the Russians in the north to the Spaniards. Estevan José Martinez, who had been a pilot in the expedition of Perez in 1774, was forthwith commissioned to investigate. He returned from the coast of Alaska in the autumn of 1788 and informed the Viceroy Don Manuel Antonio Florez, on the authority of a boastful Russian, that the Czar intended to occupy Nootka Sound the very next year to check the fur trade of the English. The Viceroy promptly sent him back to Nootka to pre-empt the region for the Spaniards. In due time, yet after Martinez had sailed, the Spanish Government gave its approval to the plan. While this movement had the Russians immediately in view, it envisaged the English, and especially the Americans. The American ship the *Columbia Rediviva*, in distress on its way to the north-west coast of America, had put into a port of the Spanish island of Juan Fernandez early that year. The Governor had relieved the ship and allowed it to proceed. For this he was cashiered by his chief, the Viceroy of Peru. In a letter quoted in part in Manning's "Nootka Sound Controversy" (*Am. Hist. Assoc. Ann. Report*, 1904, p. 302) Florez said with great insight that the object of the Americans who had touched at the island of Juan Fernandez was to obtain a foothold on the Pacific coast.

We ought not to be surprised that the English colonies of America, being now an independent Republic, should carry out the design of finding a safe port on the Pacific and of attempting to sustain it by crossing the immense country of the continent above our possessions of Texas, New Mexico, and California. Much more might be said of an active nation which founds all its hopes and its resources on navigation and commerce . . . it is indeed an enterprize for many years, but I firmly believe that from now on we ought to employ tactics to forestall its results ; and the more since we see that the Russian projects and those which the English make from Botany Bay, which they have colonized, already menace us.

These views were embodied in the instructions given to Martinez. He was to sail with the *Princesa* and the *San Carlos* to Nootka Sound in early February. In March a supply ship, the *Aranzazu*, was to follow. Captain Cook's plan of Nootka Sound was to be his guide. A settlement was to be formally established to make manifest the sovereignty of Spain over the region. Commanders of Russian or English vessels which might arrive were to be received

with the politeness and kind treatment which the existing peace demands, but should be shown firmly the just ground for our establishment at Nootka . . . if . . . the foreigners should attempt to use force, you will repel it to the extent that they employ it, endeavouring to prevent as far as possible their intercourse and commerce with the natives . . . 13. To the English you will demonstrate clearly and with established proofs that our discoveries anticipated those of Captain Cook, since he reached Nootka, according to his own statement, in March of the year 1778, where he purchased (as he relates in Chapter I, Book 4, p. 45 of his work) the two silver spoons which the Indians stole from yourself in 1774 . . . 14. You will have more weighty arguments to offer to vessels of the Independent American Colonies, should they appear on the coasts of northern California, which hitherto has not known their ships. [Here the relief of the American ship at Juan Fernandez is mentioned.] 15. In case you are able to encounter this Bostonian frigate [the *Columbia Rediviva*] or the small boat which accompanied her [the *Lady Washington*] but was separated in the storm, this will give you governmental authority to take such measures as you may be able, and such as appear proper, giving them to understand, as all other foreigners, that our settlements are being extended to beyond Prince William's Sound, of which we have already taken formal possession, as well as of the adjacent islands, viz. in 1779.

When it is recalled that the Spanish Colonial System excluded all foreigners from trade with the colonies and from the area of Spanish sovereignty, it will be apprehended that the occupation of Nootka Sound, as proposed, raised a question which affected not England alone but all other nations, and involved their exclusion from the region and from its trade. It was an American question just as much as it was an English question.

Martinez carried out his instructions with a remarkable combination of promptitude, firmness, and subtlety. On May 5, 1789, he brought his ship, the *Princesa*, to anchor in Nootka Sound. He forthwith built his fort and constructed a battery to protect the harbour. No mention is made of Meares's establishment. To all appearance it was no longer standing. On the Spanish officer's arrival there were two ships in the Sound—the American *Columbia Rediviva*, under Captain Kendrick, some distance up the Sound, and Meares's second ship, the *Iphigenia*, commanded by Captain Douglas, who, according to his instructions, had returned in company with the *North West America* under Captain Funter from the Sandwich Islands. She lay in Friendly Cove itself. Martinez's duty was, while showing every civility, to bring their captains to accept the Spanish sovereignty of the region. He had little difficulty with the Americans. Captain Kendrick, and later his subordinate Captain Gray, who at the time was absent with his ship, the *Lady Washington*, played the part of individualists. To make their present venture a financial success, they sacrificed any rights the United States might have through their trade with the natives during the previous winter and any claim they might have to return to trade in the future. They acknowledged the sovereignty of Spain, attended the elaborate ceremony of taking possession of the region in the name of the Spanish king (24th June) and drank to His Majesty's health. In return for thus conceding the main point, their expedition was allowed to go on peacefully with its trade. It is highly probable that the astute Americans entered into some sort of partnership with Martinez. Robert Duffin, one of the least unreliable of the English witnesses, says that Captain Kendrick traded for Martinez "on shares." On these terms the Americans at Nootka Sound supported Martinez whenever it was necessary, as witnesses to his documents, as navigators of the captured ship *North West America*, as bearers of his furs to Macao, and finally, when the diplomatic crisis came to its height, as evidence to prove his humanity and justice and to enable him to make good his assertions against the English. Kendrick and Gray thus saved their present venture from disaster by throwing to the winds the future good of the trade and the rights of their country, for the terms on which they were allowed to continue their trade made a permanent and free American trade impossible. As it was, their voyage was scarcely a success, and Martinez had asserted Spanish authority over against America in their persons and had effectually closed the door to all future voyages. He had carried out his instructions triumphantly so far as the Americans were concerned.

Martinez now had to face a succession of four English captains, who could, of course, claim the rights arising from a much older traffic in those parts than could the Americans. He ended by seizing their four ships in turn. It is not necessary to analyse the mass of conflicting evidence as to the rights or wrongs of the individual seizures. Throughout, Martinez was carrying out his instructions, to win an acknowledgement of the sovereignty of Spain and to prevent trade with the Indians supposed to be subject to her. He showed himself master of the firmness and guile called for by his task. Captain Douglas had arrived from the Sandwich Island, with the *Iphigenia* in Nootka Sound sixteen days before Martinez. Captain Funter, in the *North West America*, came in immediately thereafter and proceeded on a trading trip to the Queen Charlotte Islands, as planned. He was followed by the American Captain Gray in the *Lady Washington*, before Martinez appeared upon the scene. When the Spanish ship, the *Princesa*, came into port Captain Douglas thought it wise to run up the Portuguese colours on the *Iphigenia*, though her crew was predominantly English. Martinez, to commence with, showed Douglas the civility and friendship enjoined in his instructions, but on 8th May he called for the *Iphigenia's* papers. Her officers, as he asserted, gave unsatisfactory explanations of the English ship sailing under Portuguese colours. Fastening on a clause in Douglas's instructions bidding him, if attacked, to resist force with force, Martinez as good as accused the captain of being a pirate sailing under false colours, and anchoring in Spanish Dominions. This may have been due, as is stated, to a wrong interpretation of the paper drawn up in a foreign language. The fact remains that Martinez made the officers of the *Iphigenia* prisoners. He then prepared the vessel for a voyage either to San Blas in Mexico, or for a trading trip on the coast; but, as it proved, he had no crew with which to man her. This would suggest that Martinez hoped, by a show of violence, to come to an agreement with Douglas such as he had made with the Americans, to acknowledge the Spanish rights, and to go on a trading voyage on shares with him, but the English captain confined himself to making explanations of his sailing under Portuguese colours and to passive resistance. The alternative now open to Martinez, seeing that he could not man the ship, was to release her, but to take bonds for the payment of her value should the Viceroy of Mexico declare her a lawful prize. Accordingly, he replaced the supplies and goods taken on her, as the Englishmen claimed, only in part. Finally Captain Douglas sailed out of port with a salute from the Spanish battery. Martinez was thus rid of his first Englishman, obdurate but not likely to return, and held in his hand a bond equal to the value of the ship. The supplies and goods he replaced on her could not have been on an ungenerous scale, in spite of the statements of the English, for Douglas says he had " no idea of running for Macao with only between 60 and 70 sea-otter skins on board." And he sailed north on a fur-trading cruise.

Captain Douglas had under his command the schooner *North West America*, built by Meares in Friendly Cove, and in charge of Captain Funter, and now on a trip for furs, as we have seen. Martinez tried to persuade Douglas to give him a letter for Funter requiring him to sell the schooner to the Spaniard at a price to be set by his American friends. Douglas replied that she was not his to sell, but he went so far as to write to Funter to say that he must act on his own judgment in the circumstances. When Funter came into Friendly Cove on 8th June he refused to consider the sale, the ship not being his. Martinez then seized her on the same plea as he had alleged for the seizure of the *Iphigenia*, but this time he kept the ship, for she was so small that he was able to make up a crew. He named her *Gertrudis*, placed her under the command of David Coolidge, mate of the *Lady Washington*, and prepared her for a fur-trading expedition. He now offered Funter half the furs gathered, if he would go as her pilot and take the ship to the ports of the coast rich in furs, but the Englishman remained obdurate.

Strictly, there had been no affront to the British flag in these two seizures, for both ships were sailing under Portuguese colours, it would seem. The English had mismanaged their case in not flying their own flag. In great contrast, Martinez had handled matters, so far, with great skill. He had avoided an insult to Britain, yet rid himself of one English ship and converted another to his service. Besides his own, he had brought into his service two American vessels under their own flag, and an English schooner flying the Spanish colours and commanded by an American—all gathering furs in whose profits he had at least a share.

But, as we have seen, there were two English ships fast approaching Nootka Sound—the *Argonaut*, under Captain Colnett, and the *Princess Royal*, in the charge of Captain Hudson, owned by the joint-stock company formed by Etches and Meares in Canton, sailing under licences granted by the East India and the South Sea companies, and flying the British flag. The first to arrive was the *Princess Royal*. She entered the Sound on 15th June. Captain

Hudson was received at the outset with the prescribed civility and friendship, and responded to it better than his predecessors, or perhaps Martinez felt that he must be more cautious. Certainly the log of the Spanish *Princesa* runs that Hudson stated that " he had acted in the belief that this port as well as the coast belonged to the English crown, as discoveries made by Captain James Cook. However I [Martinez] convinced him . . . that I had anticipated Cook by three years and eight months . . . he could confirm this by . . . Joseph Ingraham [the American], who had noted it in his log from the knowledge he had gained from the Indians of the region." When the Spaniards took formal possession of the land, nine days later, a splendid banquet was given by Martinez on board the *Princesa*, and foreigners of the English nation and the " American Congress " drank to the health of His Most Catholic Majesty, the King of Spain. No doubt Captain Hudson was the chief Englishman present. These happy relations led the Spanish commander to give the English captain a circular letter requiring Spanish commanders, whom it might concern, to allow him to pass on. When the *Princess Royal* sailed out of port on 2nd July, Martinez must have congratulated himself upon having successfully lived up to his instructions and on having easily disposed of a vessel sailing under the British flag.

As Captain Hudson passed out to sea he came upon Captain Colnett in the *Argonaut*. Thus Martinez was forced once more to address himself to the problem of carrying out his instructions in the face of an English captain sailing under his country's flag. Colnett had been an officer in the British navy, and had sailed under Captain Cook during his second circumnavigation of the world. He was one of those Englishmen of unbending will to whom, in spite of their many faults, the Empire owes much. He was conscious that in Nootka Sound he was in waters in which many Englishmen had sailed unmolested during the past four years, that the fur trade of those parts was the creation of his fellow-countrymen, that Meares had had an establishment in Friendly Cove the year before, and that he himself was there under instructions to found a more permanent settlement. So far was he from cloaking his design, that he asserted that he was a servant of the Crown, and that the establishment intended was to be a colony. A clash was therefore inevitable. Just how it came about is of minor importance.

Writing nine years later, when passions may be presumed to have subsided somewhat, Colnett said that his ship was met at the mouth of the harbour by two Spanish launches with Martinez and a boat from the American ships which were in port at the time ; that, when he learned of Spanish warships lying within, his desire was to sail away, doubtless to make his establishment elsewhere, that he was enveigled into port by a tale on Martinez's lips of distress and of great want of supplies, and by a promise given by the Spanish commander on his honour that he would be allowed to sail after the needed help was given, and finally that the warships were there only to forestall the Russians. At last persuaded, he entered the port and gave the needed assistance. Civilities followed to the extent even of Martinez offering a launch to tow him out of harbour, but when the hour of departure came, he was required to take his papers to the Spanish commander, who, without being able to read them, threw them on the table, asserting that he should not sail until it should please him ; at the end of the altercation he was brought to the ground by a blow, was made a prisoner, and his ship was seized. The story in the log of the *Princesa* runs that Colnett had gone in the morning upon an expedition spying upon the Spanish fort ; that he refused to show his papers when asked for them, but stated that he was the governor of a colony ; that Martinez said he could not be allowed to make a settlement, and would not allow the launch to help him out of port till he showed his passport ; that Colnett refused, saying he might fire upon him if he wished ; that he was a G—d d—d Spaniard. For this insult he was seized and his ship with him.

It is not necessary to reconcile these stories in their details, Martinez may have been stung by the insult and in his anger may have resorted to violence. The substantial cause of the seizure of the man and the ship, it is clear, was that Colnett refused to be amenable to the commands of the Spanish commander or would not recognize his right to rule in those parts and to assert the Spanish title. In so doing he risked his chance of making a prosperous voyage, but he conserved for his king and country their claim to continue trading without let or hindrance, and their complementary right to establish settlements in the interest of that trade upon a coast hitherto neglected by the Spaniard, but exploited by English-men. Even in the temporary insanity which the excitement of the clash brought upon the English captain he never surrendered the rights of Britain in those parts. Thus he precipitated the Nootka Sound crisis and contributed to the decision, all important for subsequent history, that the North Pacific coast was to be open to English-men, and by implication to the Americans, who were frequenting it for trade and settlement.

When Captain Hudson returned in the *Princess Royal* to Nootka, on 13th July, Martinez, now definitely embarked on the Viceroy's bold policy of asserting the rights of Spain, took him prisoner in spite of the civilities of the past, and seized his ship. The extent of the cruelties of the Spaniards and of their appropriation of the Englishmen's goods need not detain us. Martinez seems to have acted in a businesslike way, carefully making all inventories necessary. He finished by sending the two English vessels to San Blas, subject to the decision of the Viceroy, as to whether they were good prizes or not. He carried out his instructions to the satisfaction of the Spanish Government, but his actions raised a vital issue between England and Spain.

II.—THE CLASH BETWEEN ENGLAND AND SPAIN OVER NOOTKA
SOUND, 1789–90—THE NOOTKA SOUND CONVENTION, 1790

Word of the incidents at Nootka Sound came to the Spanish
Government by its own short route through Mexico in a series of
straightforward official documents formally drawn up by Martinez
and forwarded by the Viceroy.   The news could only reach England
by the indirect way of China, and even so through unofficial and, as
it proved, unreliable channels.   First rumours current in Spain
were reported on January 4, 1789, to the British Foreign Minister
by Anthony Merry, *chargé d'affaires* at Madrid.   They were to the
effect that an English vessel had been seized by the Spaniards.
Merry asked the Spanish Prime Minister, Count Floridablanca, for
information, but got for answer that the Spanish Minister in London,
the Marquis del Campo, would impart the circumstances to the
British Foreign Office.   But when Del Campo's statement was presented on February 11, 1790, it included no information other than
that Martinez had found two vessels in Nootka Sound belonging to
a Portuguese, and that an English ship (the *Argonaut*) had arrived
on the 2nd of July.   It went on to ask that His Britannic Majesty
should punish such undertakings, so as to restrain British subjects
from enterprises in Spanish domain.   As has been seen, the issue
between the two countries was not really raised till the British flag
was hauled down on Captain Colnett's ship.   Compared with this,
the question whether the *Iphigenia* and the *North West America* were
sailing under the Portuguese flag or not was of little importance.
The British Government, still ignorant of details, put the seizure,
as they were informed, of a British vessel in time of peace to the
front of their reply and demanded " a just and adequate satisfaction."
The vessel must be restored.   Thereafter the question of Spanish
sovereignty could be discussed.   The firmness of the reply came
as a surprise to the Spanish Government, which probably over-
estimated its own strength renewed under the efficient administration of the late King Charles III., while it exaggerated the humiliation
of England due to her loss of the American colonies.

On 20th April Del Campo replied for his government that the
Argonaut had been released by the Viceroy of Mexico on the ground
that its captain, Colnett, had been unaware of the sovereign rights
of Spain on Nootka Sound, that the matter was therefore closed.
All the while the Spanish fleet was being prepared for active service.
The British also began to prepare what was called " the Spanish
Armament."   At this point Captain Meares arrived from China and
proclaimed the indignities cast upon the English at Nootka.   That
his house had been built in four days, and that it had been taken
down and the boards shipped to the Sandwich Islands in his own
ship, the *Iphigenia*, did not prevent him from giving a flamboyant
description of his establishment, of his treaties with the Indians,
and of the territories of which he had taken possession in the name

of the King. In the absence of more accurate information withheld by the Spanish Government, this propaganda had its designed effect, and raised the war spirit of the nation. Meares embodied his claims in a *Memorial* dated 30th May, which he presented to Parliament. Thus the public was whipped up to the support of the Government, which had already taken vigorous action. On 5th May King George III. had sent a message to Parliament : " No satisfaction is made or offered, and a direct claim is asserted by the Court of Spain to exclusive rights of sovereignty, navigation and commerce in territories coasts and seas in that part of the world. . . . Spanish armaments are being raised." The House of Commons followed the King's lead by voting £1,000,000 " to enable His Majesty to act as the exigencies of affairs might require." Orders were given to equip the fleet, while the support of Britain's allies, Prussia and Holland, was secured, and other European powers sounded with a view to their co-operation, more or less active. Thus the issue raised on Nootka Sound by Martinez's instructions, and his action on the one side, and Captain Colnett's stubborn insistence on Britain's rights on the other, brought the two countries face to face with war.

Yet there were dangers on the horizon for both nations. These caused the several governments to consider the ways of caution. The British Ministry feared that, if it should press Spain too far, the ancient Family Compact would be revived and bring France to the enemy's side. The Spanish statesmen, too, had their fears. France was now in the early phase of the Revolution and could not be relied upon as when her monarch's authority was unquestioned. She might adhere to the Family Compact, but would she act effectively in keeping with it ? Then, too, there was a movement in the Spanish Colonies looking for independence. Should it come to war, England would support with all her power the formation of a free South America, for it would open a large and coveted market to her commerce. The more distant issues commanded moderation and compromise. Accordingly the question at issue was settled by the slow machinery of diplomacy. Britain insisted on an indemnity for the insult to the flag and for the losses inflicted on the traders in the seizure of their ships, before the issue between the two nations as to the sovereignty should be discussed. Get back to where we were before the wrong was done, and we will discuss the issues between us, was the attitude. Spain demanded a settlement of the question of sovereignty by arbitration ; thereafter the extent of the wrong done could be judged. In the matter of the indemnity Britain waived what might be due for the insult to the flag. As to the claims for the *Iphigenia* and the *North West America*, since there were doubts whether they were entitled to British protection, for it was claimed that they were flying the Portuguese flag, that could be settled by a commission of inquiry.

On July 24, 1790, the Spanish minister, by agreement, made a declaration for his Sovereign, on one side, that he was persuaded that under the same circumstance His Britannic Majesty would have acted as the Spaniards had done, and that the Spanish King was accordingly willing to make restitution and to indemnify the parties who had suffered the loss. The British Minister at Madrid, Alleyne Fitzherbert, for his Britannic Majesty, on the other side, made a declaration that he would be satisfied with the Spanish declaration and the performance of the promises made in it. Thus Britain contented herself with the simple release of the ships and an indemnity to the traders, to be fixed by a commission of inquiry. In 1793 a court of arbitration fixed the sum at 210,000 Spanish dollars.

Further negotiations over the question of the sovereign rights of Spain were greatly facilitated by the general European situation. The adherence of the French Assembly to the Family Compact, followed by preparations for war, caused Britain to take a moderate course, lest her ancient enemy across the Channel should range herself upon the Spanish side. However, the tardiness of the Assembly in adhering to the principle of the ancient Family Compact, and its determination to rewrite that Compact in terms of a " defensive and commercial " alliance, accompanied as it was by the Spanish dread of the progress of the Revolution, brought home to Floridablanca, the Spanish Prime Minister, the fact of the isolation of Spain. Moreover, he knew that the Spanish treasury was empty, and the people restive. He became convinced that the situation called for friendship and even an alliance between Spain and Britain. He therefore made a last attempt to carry his point in the matter of the sovereignty of Spain at Nootka by offering Britain an alliance should this be conceded. Britain, however, now armed for war, remained firm on the point. None the less, the British Ministry intimated that it would not expect a settlement at the expense of the dignity of the Spanish King. The claim for exclusive sovereignty, however, must be dropped. Had not Spain tacitly acted in reference to the trade and settlements of the Russians on the principle that these entitled them to peaceful possession ? Why not the same for Great Britain and her subjects ? Fitzherbert presented a draft of a convention in this sense, and allowed the Spanish Court ten days for its acceptance, with the alternative of war. With minor changes conceded to the Spaniards, it was accepted, and the question which had at one time threatened a European war was settled.

The first article of what is known as the Nootka Sound Convention restored, not to Britain, but to " the subjects of His Britannic Majesty," the buildings and tracts of land of which they had been dispossessed. The second sketched arrangements for the restitution of the buildings, vessels, and merchandise, failing which, a just compensation was to be given. In the third, the parties signatory " agreed that their respective subjects shall not be disturbed or molested either in navigating or carrying on their fisheries in the Pacific Ocean or in the South Seas or in landing on the coasts of those seas in places not already occupied, for the purpose of carrying on their commerce with the natives of the country or of making establishments there." The next three articles placed restrictions upon the freedom thus granted to England. The English were prohibited from illicit trade with the actual Spanish settlements, and were not to go within ten maritime leagues of any part of the coast already occupied by Spain. In the area under discussion the subjects of both Crowns " shall have free access and shall carry on their commerce without disturbance or molestation." Finally, the right of temporary settlement for the purpose of trade was granted to the English in South America south of the coast actually in the control of Spain, where, it will be remembered, the King George's Sound Company had occupied a post for a season on Staten Island. The seventh article arranged that no acts of violence should be perpetrated upon the subjects of either Crown violating the Convention, but differences must be settled amicably by negotiations between the Home Governments.

The Convention was signed on October 28, 1790. It put an end to the claim that simple discovery could bring the spacious coasts of north-west America within the exclusive colonial system of Spain. Englishmen, by inaugurating a fur trade in a land in the strict sense unoccupied by Spain, had an indefeasible right to carry on that trade and, if necessary, make settlements in its furtherance. By inference, and in fact, the rights won by Britain for herself were made the rights of any other people, as, for example, the Americans, who might have entered into the trade, and who might make settlements. In the lap of this agreement lay the whole future of the north-west coast.

Unpleasant aspects of the Nootka Sound crisis are the gross misrepresentations of Captain Meares, the fierce war spirit which they created, and the pride with which the inflamed imagination of the public proclaimed what was regarded as the humiliation of Spain. This is strikingly illustrated by a painting by R. Dodd, which was broadcasted to the nation in the form of an engraving published in 1791. In the foreground Captain Colnett is represented as proceeding in a boat to the *Princesa*, while Martinez stands in his boat with drawn sword ordering his men to seize the Englishman. Behind the boats, to the right, the *Princesa* is wreathed in the smoke of battle. On the left lies the *Argonaut*, the Spanish flag being raised at her stern, and in the distance the American ships float at anchor. In the centre background, on a high promontory, stands the Spanish fort dominating what appears to be Meares's two-storeyed establishment. The title of the engraving is " The Spanish Insult to the British Flag at Nootka Sound." The long subscription breathes the spirit of the nation at the moment :

The substance of this transaction is already well known to the Public, all that need be here related is the treacherous behaviour of the Spanish Commodore, who under the mask of friendship decoyed the English traders into port giving Captain Colnett of the *Argonaut* his word and honor, that he should not be molested in his Commerces ; but the next day the Captain in going on board the Spanish Frigate in his Boat, was made a Prisoner, and had his sword taken from him, his Boats Crew were beaten and very ill-treated by the Spaniards, and threatening to hang him at the yard arm, if he did not surrender up his Ship, which he with true British Spirit refused to do, unless fired into with shot, but resistance was in vain against the power of numbers ; the Spanish Commander then sent an armed force on board the *Argonaut*, with three Priests, who hauled down the English colours and hoisted their own, the Priests sprinkling the decks with Holy Water took possession for the King of Spain. This and other aggravating circumstances roused the spirit of the English Nation, the event of which has been a speedy equipment of the most powerful Fleet in the World, which by only showing as the bulwark of National liberty, the Spaniard has been reduced to reason, while surrounding nations are held in awe.

In the light of the fevered imagination of the public the action of the British Government was sober and reasonable. It is true it mobilized the fleet and presented the draft of the Convention practically in the form of an ultimatum, but it demanded no transfer of sovereignty, nor even an indemnity for the insult to the flag. It demanded, and was given, compensation for losses suffered, and the acknowledgment of the right of Englishmen to sail along the north-west Coast of America as heretofore, and unmolested.

Martinez had abandoned Nootka in 1789, but the Spaniards reoccupied it in 1790, and in the three following years a considerable Spanish establishment grew up. In August of 1792 Captain Vancouver arrived in H.M.S. *Discovery* to take over from Don Juan Francisco de la Bodega y Quadra, now the Spanish Commander at Nootka, the property of Captain Meares. Vancouver's relations with Quadra were of the most cordial. The ceremonious receptions and banquets became friendly affairs, although the business proceedings partook somewhat of the nature and the leisureliness of a game of chess. Quadra's first communication, with its enclosures, entered into the rights and wrongs of the whole difficulty at Nootka Sound, and justified Martinez in all his actions, asserting that Spain had nothing to deliver up, no damage to make good. Yet the Spanish commander asserted that he was prepared, without prejudice to the legitimate rights of Spain, to deliver to England the houses, offices, and gardens occupied by him, and to retire to a settlement recently effected on the Strait of Juan de Fuca. Vancouver replied that he was not authorized to enter retrospectively into the rights of the several Governments, for that had been settled by the Convention, that he had been commissioned simply to receive territories as defined in that instrument. He referred to a letter from the Spanish Prime Minister to the commander at Nootka requiring him to put the English officer " in possession of the buildings and districts or parcels of land which were occupied by the subjects [of his Britannic Majesty] in April 1789 as well in the port of Nootka . . . as in the other, said to be called Port Cox [Clayoquot]." Quadra replied offering him the small plot of ground said to be owned by Captain Meares. Vancouver tells us in his *Voyage* that he " could not entertain an idea of hoisting the British flag on the spot of land pointed out by Senor Quadra, not extending more than a hundred yards in any direction." He shared with the people in England the illusion based on Meares's misrepresentations that he had had a large establishment, and had acquired great territories. In reply, he fell back again on his Instructions. Quadra replied that he was willing to leave Vancouver in possession, but could not formally deliver up the territory. It was finally arranged that Nootka should remain for the present in Spanish hands, but that the whole matter should be referred to the several home governments. Accordingly, Vancouver sailed away on 13th October to winter in the Sandwich Islands, and return to his survey of the coast and to await instructions for the transfer of the property of the Englishmen into his hands. He was back in Nootka Sound on September 2, 1794, after completing his survey, but the expected instructions were not awaiting him. After waiting for them for six weeks in vain, he sailed away to England.

The continued friendship of Spain and Britain made for a final friendly agreement. It was signed on January 11, 1794, and arranged that both parties should abandon Nootka. To carry out these terms an English Commissioner, Sir Thomas Pierce, and a representative of Spain, Manuel de Alava, met at Nootka. The Spaniards destroyed their buildings, and on March 23, 1795, after a final formal ceremony, the commissioners, each for his own nation, abandoned the Sound to its aboriginal inhabitants.

The north-west coast of America was thus left open to such nations, Russian, British, American, or Spanish, as had developed trade interests. Spain, her energies already largely spent, laid little stress on the resources of the north. She became deeply involved in Europe, in the wars of the Revolution and of Napoleon. She never returned to these waters. The Russians persistently developed their marine fur trade, and slowly moved southward. Competition was proving ruinous to traders and natives alike, and the farther afield the operations were, the greater the need for capital and for unity. In 1799 a union of interests took place under the name of the Russian Fur Company. The enterprising and forceful, if diminutive, Alexander Baranof had established a post on Norfolk Sound six miles north of the present town of Sitka. He thereby pre-empted the coast for the Russians southward to the Prince of Wales Archipelago.

The territory to the south of the Russian sphere continued to be a fur field open to the British and Americans alike. Trade and settlement will be the determining factors in defining the possessions of the two peoples. Americans and Britons alike owe much to Captain Colnett, whose perspicacity and obstinacy raised the issue as to whether the Pacific coast should be as open to traders as in the past, and who thus contributed to a final settlement momentous to both the American Republic and the British Empire.

12.—THE FUR TRADE OF THE PACIFIC COAST—EXPLORATIONS BY AMERICANS AND BY CAPTAIN GEORGE VANCOUVER, 1790-94

The history of the Canadian Pacific coast during the decades after the decision that it was to be open to all comers for trade is summed up in the marine fur trade. At first ships of various nations came to its waters. For example, in 1791 a French, at least two English, and five American ships, that can be named, were on these coasts, not to mention the Spaniards at Nootka. The European nations ran into the tense period of the wars of the French Revolution, while Great Britain, in particular, girded up her loins to overthrow the would-be master of the continent, Napoleon Bonaparte. The wars were not simple military struggles—armies against armies and fleets against fleets—but commerce was pitted against commerce. While the extension of the British Empire through the victories of her fleets and armies went on apace, the expansion through emigration and the investment of capital in the more distant parts of the world were definitely checked. A sharp contrast is presented by the United States. They played the part of a neutral nation and, of course, emphasized the claims of neutrals to trade with all belligerents; they seized the golden hour to develop their interests on the high seas. This situation on the Atlantic was reflected on the distant Pacific coast in the gradual disappearance of English ships from the trade in furs and the predominance of American vessels in its waters. It might be added that the enterprise, astuteness, and perhaps the lack of commercial scruples on the part of the Yankees, were factors contributing to this result.

In the first years after the Nootka Sound controversy broke out the north-west coast was finally delineated. Apart from certain explorations conducted by the Spaniards before they evacuated the Sound, this was accomplished by the survey of Captain George Vancouver under the instructions of the British Admiralty, and partly by the casual discoveries of fur-trading ships. We get a view of the operations of the fur-traders as such, and of the rôle which they played as explorers in the log-book of the ship *Columbia Rediviva* of Boston, while the most striking example of the official explorer is to be found in the person of Captain Vancouver, who placed his operations on record in his *Voyage of Discovery to the North Pacific Ocean*, published in 1798.

The *Columbia Rediviva* left Boston on her second voyage to the north-west coast of America on September 28, 1790, about a month before the Nootka Sound Convention was signed. She was under the command of Captain Robert Gray, and was fitted out for a cruise of four years. Captain Gray was under orders to visit no Spanish settlement save in case of grave need. As the first voyage of the ship had not been very successful, some of her outfitters had withdrawn, but others were found with the courage to try the venture anew. Before the ship reached her trading-ground many of her crew were stricken with scurvy ; " their gums quite putrid and legs as big round as their bodies quite numb." Carefully avoiding the Spanish settlement on Nootka Sound, Captain Gray cast anchor in Clayoquot Sound (Cox's harbour). About 300 natives came out to him in the course of the day in canoes made from the body of a tree with stern pieces fixed on. Their dresses were skins or blankets made of dog's hair. To the great relief of the scurvy-stricken crew, they brought " plenty of fish and greens." " Spruce tea boil'd from Boughs " was made—an excellent antiscorbutic, as Jacques Cartier had found during his winter at Quebec. Wincananish, the chief of the place, came out to trade, and many otter skins were exchanged for copper and blue cloth. By the 17th the trade was over and the crew ready for sea again. Captain Gray passed by Nootka Sound and cast anchor again in a small cove, " Columbia's Cove," in " Chickleset," our Nesparti Inlet, near Captain Cook's Woody Point, now known as Cape Cook.

We laid in this harbour till the 26th., [runs the log] during which time got many Sea otter and land furs . . . in exchange for Copper, Iron and Cloth, (with Beads, fish Hooks and such small stuff), kept the Ship supplied with various kinds of fish and greens, with a few deer. These Natives were generally arm'd with Bows, arrows and spears. . . . Their women were more Chaste than those we had lately left. But still they were not all Dianas. During our tarry here I visited one of the villages in the Sound, found the Natives busily employ'd building Canoes, and packing provisions against the ensuing Winter. They treated me quite friendly. They dry their fish in the sun, and then pack it in neat wooden boxes.

The *Columbia Rediviva* now sailed back south-eastward. Avoiding Nootka Sound again and passing Clayoquot Sound and Barkley Sound, Captain Gray cast anchor abreast of the village of Netenatt, about fifteen miles beyond. " Vast many Natives came off, with Sea Otter and other Furs, which we purchased with the same articles as before " is the entry in the log. At the entrance to the Strait of Juan de Fuca, off Tatooche Island on the south shore, many otters, and halibut and salmon in abundance were secured. Retracing his course north-westward, Captain Gray passed round the extremity of Vancouver Island to " Barrett Sound," our Houston Stewart Channel in the Queen Charlotte Islands, where he remained for a week. The log runs :

During which time we purchas'd a good lot of Sea Otter and other furs chiefly for Iron and Cloth. Copper was not in demand. The boats were sent frequently after wood and water, but were always well arm'd. . . . The females was not very chaste, but their lip pieces [described as " looking very gastly "] was enough to disgust any civilized being. However some of the crew was quite partial.

The traders do not seem to have got supplies of fish in the north.

The *Columbia Rediviva* now ran up our Hecate Strait east of Queen Charlotte Islands, keeping close to the mainland. The entry in the log for 23rd July runs : " Spoke the Brig *Hope*, Joseph

Ingraham master from Boston, on the same business as ourselves."
Ingraham had been out with the *Columbia Rediviva* on her former
voyage. On the 30th the natives informed them "that severall
English vessels [probably the *Grace*, Captain William Douglas, and the
Gustavus, Captain Thomas Barnett, and perhaps others] had visited
not long since." Yet the Americans got "a good lot of furs." They
now ran across to the east coast of Queen Charlotte Islands, probably near Cumshewa Inlet, where a chief, "Cumswah," brought them
several fine otter skins. "Only four Indians made their appearance
and I believe there was no villages in the vicinity."

Running before a south-easterly gale up the strait between the
Prince of Wales Island and Gravina Island, the *Columbia Rediviva*
found safety at the western entrance of Revillagigedo Channel
(otherwise Tongass Narrows). She then passed across Clarence
Strait. Off the east coast of Prince of Wales Island, Gray got
"plenty of fine otters." He was now in a region which had been
visited by a brig *Hancock* of Boston. For some trifling offence, her
master, Samuel Crowell, had fired upon the Indians and killed a
number. The boat's crew of the *Columbia Rediviva*, on 12th August,
paid a sad toll for this reckless conduct, for, on landing, a Mr.
Caswell and his two men were killed. Caswell's was the only body
recovered. His burial next day brought a rare touch of colour to the
dry entries of the log. While the body was being taken ashore the
minute guns of the ship proclaimed the sorrow of the crew.

Captain Gray performing the divine service ; we enter'd [*sic*] the remains
of our departed and much beloved *friend* with all the solemnity we was able of.
The place was gloomy, and nothing was to be heard but the bustling of an
aged oak, whose lofty branches hung wavering over the grave, together with
the meandering brook ; the Cries of the Eagle, and the weeping of his friends
added solemnity to the scene.

On the north shore of Queen Charlotte Islands Captain Gray fell
in with the *Hancock* anchored in Masset Inlet. At Parry Passage
farther west the *Hancock* left a man to live with the Indians and
collect furs, but he soon tired of their disgusting life and got away
at the first opportunity. This experiment, often tried by the traders
on the west coast, always ended in failure. The contact of the White
Men with the Red was confined to trading from or on the ships.
Coming south through Hecate Strait, Captain Gray returned to
Cumshewa Inlet, doubtless expecting the Indians there to meet him
with a large body of furs collected since his first visit, but Captain
Ingraham in the *Hope* had been there for a fortnight and had gathered
the harvest. When Gray was south-east of the islands, a canoe
brought many prime furs a great distance out to meet him.

By 28th August the *Columbia Rediviva* had run down the south-
westerly coast of Vancouver's Island, leaving Spanish Nootka Sound
as heretofore unvisited. At Clayoquot Sound Captain Gray found
his Company's other ship the *Lady Washington*. Her captain,
John Kendrick, had also been up among the Queen Charlotte Islands,

and had had an encounter with the Indians of Barrett's (Houston Stewart) Sound, and had killed upwards of fifty. At Clayoquot many sea-otter and other furs and much fish were procured.

After a short but very successful visit to the entrance of Juan de Fuca Strait, Captain Gray went into winter quarters in Clayoquot Sound. In this he is the exception, for the ships usually sailed to China at the end of the season. Though relations with the Indians were at first good, before the end of the winter a Sandwich Islander in the crew stirred the savages up to massacre the whole complement of Americans. At the last minute, however, he repented and revealed the plot. The disaster was thus avoided. Notable, too, was the building of the sloop *Adventure*. She was placed under the command of Robert Haswell, Captain Gray's first mate. Though the plot of the Indians had been frustrated, as the two ships left the sound in the spring, Captain Gray revenged himself for it by destroying 200 houses in the village of Opitsitah. The keeper of the ship's log could not restrain his pen from a comment: " It was a command I was no ways tenacious of, and am grieved to think Capt. Gray shou'd let his passions go so far."

The *Adventure* sailed northward to gather furs in the Queen Charlotte Islands. The *Columbia Rediviva* ran southward as far as Cape Mendocino for the operations of a new season. Captain Gray returned northward without recognizing the Columbia River. He bespoke H.M.S. *Discovery* under Captain George Vancouver and H.M.S. *Chatham* under Lieutenant William Broughton. The Englishmen also had passed the Columbia by unperceived. After going northward as far as Cape Flattery, Captain Gray returned southward to Gray's Harbour. Continuing southward, on 12th May he discovered and entered a great river which he named the Columbia after his ship. " Vast many canoes " came out to the ship, bringing much peltry. In spite of a happy trade, perhaps simply moved by greed, the Indians, as the Americans thought, prepared to attack the ship.

At midnight we heard them again, and soon after as it was bright moonlight, we see the canoes approaching to the Ship. We fired severall cannon over them but [they] still persisted to advance with the War Hoop. At last a large canoe with at least 20 Men in her got withing ½ pistol shot of the quarter, and with a Nine-pounder loaded with langerege and about 10 Muskets, loaded with Buck shot, we dashed her all to pieces, and no doubt killed every soul in her. I do not think that they had any conception of Artillery. But they was too near us for us to admit of any hesitation how to proceed.

Such is the entry in the ship's log.

The estuary of the river into which Captain Gray had found a lucky entrance extended as far as the eye could see. As he sailed upwards the natives followed the ship along the shore. Some came off and traded furs and salmon. As they contemplated the ship with astonishment, Gray concluded that his were the first civilized men the savages had seen, and that no Europeans had been in the river before him.   The Americans afterwards laid great stress on this discovery of the Columbia as a ground for their claim to the Oregon.

Captain Gray anchored opposite a large Chinook village, " 5 leagues from the entrance " of the river, and lay there for a week putting his ship into good order.   He made an attempt to sail farther up, but failed through missing the channel and encountering shoals. He concluded that sea-otters, the objects of his search, could not be procured in the fresh water of a river, and sailed away on the 20th May.   However, Boit, who kept the log, noted the value of the region for the fur trade, and for settlement.

> This River in my opinion, wou'd be a fine place for to set up a *Factory*. The Indians are very numerous, and appear'd very civil (not even offering to steal).   During our short stay we collected 150 Otter, 300 Beaver, and twice the Number of other land furs.   The river abounds in *Salmon*, and most other River fish, and the Woods with plenty of Moose and Deer, the skins of which was brought us in great plenty, and the Banks produces a Nut, which is an excellent substitute for either bread or Potatoes.   We found plenty of Oaks, Ash, and Walnut trees and clear ground in plenty which with little labour might be made fit to raise such seeds as is necessary for the sustenance of inhabitants, and in short a factory set up here, and another at Hancock's River [Masset Inlet], in Queen Charlotte Isles, wou'd engross the whole trade of the N.W. Coast with the help [of] a few small coasting vessells.

In these words Boit sketched almost prophetically the future of the estuary of the Columbia and of the trade of the west coast.

This voyage of Captain Gray may be taken as an epitome of the fur trade of the Pacific coast.   The *Columbia Rediviva* met the sloop *Adventure*, according to agreement, on Queen Charlotte Sound, but she struck a rock, and Gray had, as we may judge reluctantly, to put into the Spanish post on Nootka Sound for repairs.   The Spanish commander gave the Americans every assistance, so that they were able to continue their cruise.   Finally, Captain Gray sold his sea-otter skins in Canton for 90,000 Chinese dollars, averaging 45 dollars each.   " The land furs sold quite low, in proportion."   A cargo of tea, silk, some sugar, and china was taken on board, and the ship closed her eventful cruise on July 25, 1793, in Boston harbour.

It was characteristic of the fur trade on the Pacific coast that several clashes between the Americans and the natives had occurred. This hostility between traders and natives increased rather than diminished with the years.   It is in sharp contrast with the, on the whole, happy relationships found in the trade of the North-West. To some extent this may be due to the general attitude of the American to the Indian, but much lay inherent in the circumstances.   The posts in the North-West were comparatively permanent, and the Whites settled down to happy relations with the Indians.   Connections with the Indian women were far less casual.   Because more lasting, they were more respectable, and issued in a half-breed stock which bridged the gap between the White and the Red Man, and led to mutual understanding.   All the circumstances tended in the same direction. The Whites in their frail forts, or journeying in their fragile canoes, were at the mercy of the savages. They therefore fostered methods of conciliation. Contrast with this the Whites on the Pacific coast. Passing from inlet to inlet, rarely leaving their ships, with no contact with the natives other than in trade carried on over the sides of the vessel, they probably often misunderstood the movements of the savages and had no way of anticipating their moods. Secure upon their ships, usually protected with a netting to prevent the savages from boarding save one at a time, when they saw the Indians in manœuvres which they took to be hostile, they simply shot them down. Moreover, the savages of the coast, massed in villages and much given to wars of plunder, were often emboldened by their numbers to take the aggressive, and laid themselves open to be dealt with mercilessly.

If this contrast is not to the honour of the maritime fur-traders of the West, it is to their credit that rum played little or no part in their traffic. When furs worth 45 Chinese dollars each could be secured for a few nails, for a little iron or copper, or for a small piece of cloth, there was no need for the fiery liquor. The ships could carry large quantities of the heavier goods, while the canoes and portages of the North-West put a premium on " high wine " because its value was so great and its bulk so inconsiderable. At any rate, rum was not the corner-stone of the coastal trade, as it was of that of the Canadians in the North-West.

If the fur-traders did much on their voyages to reveal different parts of the maze of islands and inlets of the mediterranean sea of the Pacific coast, only expeditions organized by the governments of the nations interested could delineate the shore-line satisfactorily. During the years in which the Spaniards occupied Nootka, they did much, but to the English world at any rate, Captain George Vancouver has been the real delineator of our Pacific coast, not simply because he was of our blood, but because the scientific results of his voyage were immediately published to the world and in the language we can read.

To understand the task assigned to Vancouver we must recall the geographical information and the theories of his time. The publication of the official narrative of Captain Cook's third voyage in 1784 gave the world definite knowledge that the south shore of Alaska offered no water-way to the Arctic Ocean or to Hudson Bay, unless it might be by river from Cook's Inlet. This led the fur-traders in Athabaska to raise the question whether they might not reach the Pacific by paddling down the Slave River to Great Slave Lake, and thence down the large river known to flow from it. Alexander Mackenzie gave the answer in the negative by his voyage of 1789 to the shore of the Polar Sea. A Captain John Frederick Holland was simultaneously discussing with Alexander Dalrymple, hydrographer of the East India Company, a plan for just such a voyage as Mackenzie made, which could have brought no other answer than that of the fur-trader, but it shows the interest taken in certain circles in England closely associated with Admiralty in the question of the North-West Passage as it stood at the time. News of Mackenzie's voyage and his location of the north shore of the continent so far north would only reach England in the autumn of 1790, and then would be confined to a narrow circle. Very important information had been given to the world by Samuel Hearne, who had journeyed to the shore of the Polar Sea at the mouth of the Coppermine River, an account of which had been published in 1784 by Dr. Douglas in his Introduction to the official report of Captain Cook's third voyage. A similar account appeared in Pennant's *Zoology* of the same year. Hearne had shown that there was no sea between Fort Churchill and the Arctic Ocean at the mouth of the Coppermine. This should have set to rest the ancient theory that, if only one could slip round the northernmost promontory of the continent, one could sail south-westward by increasingly pleasant waters to the mild climate of the Pacific Ocean, and so to China. But views cherished from of old die hard. Sir Alexander Dalrymple defended the accepted theory, of which he was the victim, by throwing doubt on the veracity of Hearne's narrative. Men in such a frame of mind twist new facts into their service. Fresh information was coming in from the fur-traders on the Pacific coast that the region was a maze of islands and inlets. This could only mean, the theorists said, that Da Fonte's or Juan de Fuca's strait existed unexplored somewhere among these inlets and south of the Alaskan coast, so carefully surveyed by Captain Cook. It was claimed that the space between Repulse Bay north of Hudson Bay and the Pacific was one vast archipelago. Alexander Dalrymple, with Hanna's account of the exploration of Fitzhugh Sound before him, argued that this Sound was Da Fonte's strait, and that it would lead a long way towards Hudson Bay, and that the river thought to flow into it would prove a valuable water-way for trade to China. In a pamphlet entitled *Plan for promoting the Fur Trade and securing it to this Country by uniting the operations of the East India and the Hudson's Bay Companys* (London 1789) he advocated a union of the East India and the Hudson's Bay companies to prosecute the trade of the Far East by taking advantage of this route across the northerly part of the continent. Such a short line of communication would give a complete control of the trade to the English.

These futile speculations are only of importance in so far as they help to explain Vancouver's instructions, dated March 8, 1791, so far as they had to do with exploration. Among the objects which he was to keep in view was

1st, The acquiring accurate information with respect to the nature and extent of any water-communication which may tend, in any considerable degree, to facilitate an intercourse, for the purpose of commerce, between the north-west coast, and the country upon the opposite side of the continent, which are [*sic*] inhabited or occupied by his Majesty's subjects.

The next object in view had to do with the clash of the nations on the Pacific coast.

2ndly, The ascertaining, with as much precision as possible, the number, extent and situation of any settlements which have been made within the limits above mentioned [between latitude 60° north and 30° north] by any European nation, and the time when such settlement was first made.

Returning to the first object the Instructions ran on :

It would be of great importance if it should be found that, by means of any considerable inlets of the sea or even of large rivers, communicating with the lakes in the interior of the continent, such an intercourse as has been mentioned could be established ; it will therefore be necessary, for the purpose of ascertaining this point, that the survey should be so conducted, as not only to ascertain the general line of the sea coast, but also the direction and extent of all such inlets, whether made by arms of the sea, or by mouths of large rivers, as may be likely to lead to or facilitate, such communication as is above described.

Vancouver was to pay particular attention to the Strait of Juan de Fuca. " The discovery of a near communication between any such sea or strait, and any river running into it or from the lake of the woods [!] would be particularly useful." Failing here, he was to investigate Cook's River to the north with a similar intent. In short, working from the Pacific coast, Vancouver was to try to find the water-way to the rich markets to China, which had been the dream of Henry Hudson and his successors, and which Groseilliers and Radisson had promised the English when the Hudson's Bay Company had secured its charter. All search for it from the shores of Hudson Bay, including that inaugurated by Arthur Dobbs in the middle of the eighteenth century, had failed. The hope now was that it might be found in one of the inlets of the western coast, and that the dream which had haunted the English since the day of Martin Frobisher might be at last realized in an English route to China calculated to make England mistress at once of the American fur trade and of the traffic to the Far East. Vancouver's " Additional Instructions " had to do with the conclusion of the controversy with Spain. He was " to be put in possession of the buildings, and districts, or parcels of land . . . which were occupied by his Majesty's subjects in the month of April 1789, agreeable to the first article of the late convention." A letter from the Prime Minister of Spain to the commander at Nootka was added to ensure the restoration required. This part of Vancouver's mission has already been dealt with.

Vancouver's training fitted him eminently for the tasks before him. He was born about 1758. In 1772 he was placed as " able seaman " under Captain Cook in H.M.S. *Resolution* on his second voyage, and, as midshipman, had been with him on the Pacific coast during his last exploration. He had been lieutenant in the sloop of war, the *Fame*, and was with Admiral Rodney when he won his great victory over the French in the West Indies in 1782. He must have approved himself to Admiralty, for he was chosen to command an expedition for discovery in the South Seas, but the sailing of his ship was suddenly cancelled because of the mobilization of " The Spanish Armament " to meet the crisis precipitated by the clash of the English and Spanish on Nootka Sound. Armed with his varied instructions, Vancouver sailed in H.M.S. *Discovery* from Falmouth on April 1, 1791, bound for the Pacific coast. He was accompanied by Lieutenant W. R. Broughton, in command of H.M.S. *Chatham*, the armed tender to the *Discovery*. He passed round Cape of Good Hope and explored parts of Western Australia and New Zealand, and visited the Sandwich Islands, familar ground to him. He was still in seas known to him when he reached the American coast south of Cape Mendocino and passed Captain Cook's capes Gregory, Perpetua, and Foulweather. Anxious to find a port at Captain Meares's Deception Bay, under the brow of Cape Disappointment, for " the country presented a most luxuriant landscape," Vancouver approached to within two or three miles of the land. Here was indeed a river— the Columbia—which later proved a water-way for the fur-traders from the interior lakes of Canada, including the Lake of the Woods, just what Vancouver was sent out to discover, but he saw only a line of breakers from shore to shore. " Not a little disappointed we resumed our route " he remarks, in his *Voyage of Discovery*. The explanation of Vancouver's failure to see the River Columbia may perhaps be found in Lieutenant Broughton's survey of it during the following year. " The breakers were so shut in with each other as to present one entire line of heavy broken water from side to side across the channel." Proceeding northward, Vancouver spoke the American ship *Columbia Rediviva*, whose Captain Gray thereafter passed southward, as has been seen, and entered the stream which he named the Columbia.

Passing round Cape Flattery, Vancouver entered the Strait of Juan de Fuca. Here his contribution to the annals of discovery really began. A succession of names indicates the waters carefully charted by him as he traced every inlet to its head—Port Discovery, after his ship ; Hood's Channel, after Admiral Hood ; Puget Sound, after the second lieutenant of the *Discovery* ; Admiralty Inlet ; and west of it Whidbey's Island, after an officer of the ship. On 4th June, the King's birthday, when in a channel west of the south end of Whidbey's Island, and on which stands the present city of Everett, in the State of Washington, Vancouver formally proclaimed England's possession of

the coast on that part of New Albion in the latitude of 39° 20' north and longitude 236° 26' east, to the entrance of this inlet of the sea, said to be the supposed straits of Juan de Fuca ; as likewise all the coast, islands etc. within the said straits, as well on the northern as on the southern shores ; together with those situated in the interior sea we have discovered.

He gave the branch of Admiralty Inlet on which his ship lay the significant name of Possession Sound, and he called the country, which would extend from a point between San Francisco and Cape Mendocino northward, New Georgia. The name remains with us

in the Strait of Georgia, applied to the southern channel between
Vancouver Island and the mainland. The year before this strait
had been called by the Spaniards Gran Canal de Nuestra Señora del
Rosario la Marinera—a preposterously long name, from which the
geographers have mercifully delivered us.

As Vancouver proceeded northward—from Point Roberts, south of
the present International Boundary, and so named by him—a shoal
which he tried to cross time and again kept him seven or eight miles
out from the mainland. " All our endeavours [to pass over it] were
exerted to no purpose." As his party were in boats, they ran westward to the opposite shore for the night, and on 13th June reached the
shore of the mainland at the south extremity of Burrard Inlet, Point
Grey, which he so named after a distinguished naval officer, his
friend. By taking this course Vancouver missed the three mouths
of the Fraser River. Two of them he saw from a distance and took
to be small bays. Near Point Grey he afterwards met the Spaniards
in the *Sutil* and *Mexicana*. They had anticipated him in the exploration of the region, and reported having seen driftwood such as indicated a river, and that they had called the stream Rio Blancho
" in compliment to the Prime Minister of Spain." As he moved up
the coast Vancouver named Burrard's Inlet after a naval officer,
Sir Harry Burrard, and Howe's Sound and Jervis's Channel after
the admirals of those names. All this exploration was done with
boats. When on the way back to the ships Vancouver met the
Spanish vessels, the *Sutil* commanded by Don D. Galiano and the
Mexicana under Señor Don C. Valdes. These officers were out completing a survey initiated a year before by their senior officer Señor
Alexandro Malaspina. They expressed their surprise that he had
not noticed the Rio Blancho.

The Spanish officers informed Vancouver that Señor Quadra
awaited him at Nootka Sound for the conclusion of the diplomatic
episode. Accordingly, the Englishman, on regaining his ship, sailed
through our Strait of Georgia, naming Desolation Sound for its
dreary appearance, and Bute Channel (Inlet) after the Marquis of
Bute. The passage farther on he named Johnstone Strait after an
officer of the *Chatham*, and inlets running northward he called Long-
borough's and Knight's. As he passed through Queen Charlotte
Sound he surveyed Smith's Inlet and explored Captain Hanna's
Fitzhugh Sound, but was unable at this time to reach its limit.
Vancouver now bore away down the south-westerly coast of Vancouver Island to Nootka Sound to meet the representative of Spain,
and to take part in what he expected would be the closing chapter
of the Nootka Sound crisis. In this his first season of exploration
he had put it beyond a shadow of a doubt that none of the inlets
running into the mainland from the Strait of Juan de Fuca led to a
great inland sea or offered an approach to Hudson Bay.

We have already noted the friendly spirit in which Vancouver
conducted his dispute with Quadra as to what was to be surrendered
to him. This friendliness was registered in the name which they

gave to the land on which they stood and which was known now
to be an island. They called it Vancouver and Quadra Island. Only
Vancouver's name is now attached to it. After the two commanders
had failed to agree as to what was to be done in the matter of the
surrender of the property and the territory belonging to the English,
they decided to await instructions from their several Governments.
Quadra sailed away first. Vancouver followed on 13th October
accompanied by Broughton. His intention was to view the southern
coast and report on such Spanish settlements as might be on the
coast running south to Monterey. The task of surveying the Columbia
River, whose existence was now known through Captain Gray, was
assigned to Broughton. That officer did not get his ship past the
breakers at the mouth of the river without difficulty. Within the
estuary he found the villages deserted, the Indians being away at
their seasonal hunt. The *Chatham* cast anchor about a mile and a
quarter from the inner shore of Cape Disappointment, off a point on
which was a deserted village. In the bay to the north-west lay an
English schooner, the *Jenny*, in command of Captain James Baker ;
hence the name Baker's Bay placed by Broughton on his map.
On the 22nd the *Chatham* was moved up to a position about three
miles north-by-west from a promontory which he named Point George.
Next day the boats were sent out to survey what Broughton regarded
as the estuary of the river rather than the stream itself. Captain
Gray's name, Point Adams, for the promontory across the mouth of
the river from Cape Disappointment was retained, as was natural.
As the survey proceeded the *Chatham* was moved upstream to a
position close to the north shore and about opposite Fort Astoria
of subsequent times. As it was deemed that the vessel could not go
farther with safety, boats were provisioned and sent off to complete
the survey. The various features were carefully named. The point
at which Captain Gray had turned was called Gray's Bay. At a
sandy point on the north bank of the river formal possession of the
river and its region was taken " in his Britannic Majesty's name."
Of course, without trade and settlements following, such a ceremony
could not establish the sovereignty of Britain any more than a similar
procedure on the part of the Spaniards had availed to keep the
English away from the Pacific coast. Broughton called the spot
Point Vancouver after his commanding officer. It has been identified
as the present Cottonwood Point, nearly opposite the railway station
of Corbett, Oregon. Looking across the river south-eastward
Broughton saw a mountain remarkable for its magnificence and
clothed in snow from its summit. This he named Mount Hood after
the Admiral of that name. Having charted the river for some ninety-
two miles above the position of his ship, Lieutenant Broughton returned and sailed to join Vancouver at Monterey. Thence he was
sent with dispatches to England by way of Mexico, Lieutenant
Puget taking command of the *Chatham*. The ships wintered in the
Sandwich Islands.

Exploration next year began in Fitzhugh Sound, the survey

of which had been left unfinished when Vancouver sailed to Nootka
to meet Quadra.   The inlets in the coast north of this, with their
numerous branches, were explored to their extremities in boats.
Burke's Canal was called after the Irish orator.   Dean's Channel
and King Island were so called after Rev. James King, dean of
Raphoe, the father of Captain James King who had sailed with
Vancouver under Captain Cook on his last voyage.   Vancouver
followed Dean's Channel west of King Island, while James Johnstone, sailing-master of the *Chatham*, followed Burke's Canal on the
east side of the island to Point Menzies, named after the surgeon of
the expedition at the time.   When Vancouver got to the north-
easterly shore of King's Island, he followed the channel south-
eastward, and came upon Johnstone's track at Point Menzies.
Here Burke's Canal bifurcates to form the South and North Bentinck
Arm, the latter ending at the mouth of the Bella Coola River,
Alexander Mackenzie's course to the sea coast.   On 1st June Johnstone was at the head of the Arm, all unconscious that Alexander
Mackenzie was fast approaching it from the east and would reach
it on 20th July.

Meanwhile Vancouver returned to Dean's Channel and explored
it to its limit, and, as he returned down the channel, explored Cascade
Inlet opposite the point of King's Island at which Alexander Mackenzie turned his face homewards.   Returning to the ships, the
explorers sailed through Milbank Sound.   Parties in boats charted
the present Fraser Reach east of Princess Royal Island, Gardiner's
Canal, and Grenville Canal, and Chatham Sound.   On 20th July
Vancouver was sailing in a wide channel east of the upper portion of
the Queen Charlotte Islands, our Hecate Strait, and beating up
against contrary winds to continue his explorations with unabated
care.   On that day Alexander Mackenzie reached the waters of the
Pacific at the head of North Bentinck Arm.   Dalrymple's dream
that the fur-traders could cross to the Pacific had so far come true,
but Vancouver had already proved that the inlets from the west
ran far short of his theory, and Mackenzie's voyage showed that the
overland journey was long, that the mountains were massed over
a wide belt, and that the rivers were of the most turbulent.   Nevertheless the North West Company, under the influence of Mackenzie
and of Duncan M'Gillivray, will attempt to enter the fur regions of
the west coast from across the continent.

Continuing his task, Vancouver charted Port Essington, the
opening south of our Prince Rupert into which the Skeena River
pours the waters of northern British Columbia, the New Caledonia
Department of the North West Company.   Farther north he
examined and named Observatory Inlet, including our Nass Bay on
it, into which the Nass River flows, and Portland Canal, the northern
limit of British Territory as it is to-day.   In Alaska he charted and
named the Prince of Wales Archipelago, and concluded his exploration of 1793 with the remark: " Should the information we have
thus obtained reach Europe, there will no longer remain a doubt as

to the extent or the fallacy of the pretended discoveries said to have been made by De Fuca and De Fonte."

In 1794 Vancouver returned to his task, beginning with Cook's Inlet. This he found to be no more than an arm of the sea : " This can no longer be considered as a *river* ; I shall therefore distinguish it henceforth as an inlet." Turning eastward he surveyed the coast of Alaska to the limit of his exploration of the previous year. After returning to Nootka, only to find that no instructions from the Government had arrived, he visited various Spanish settlements on the west coast of America as far as Valparaiso, rounded the Horn, and arrived in the Thames on October 20, 1795. His next years were spent in the preparation of the official account of his voyage, but, before it was completed, the indefatigable explorer, who may not have endured the hardship of his four years afloat unimpaired, was stricken down by death. He was buried in the churchyard of St. Peter's, Petersham, on the Thames above Richmond, on May 18, 1798. His brother gave the last touches to his *Voyage of Discovery to the North Pacific*, and published it in the autumn of that year.

13.—THE APPROACH TO THE PACIFIC FROM THE EAST— ALEXANDER MACKENZIE, 1789-93

For wellnigh two centuries the Search for the Western Sea had been urging French and English westward, ever deeper into and farther across the wide American continent. Jacques Cartier and, after him, Samuel de Champlain had marked out the valley of the St. Lawrence as the line of progress. Henry Hudson, and later Groseilliers and Radisson and the Hudson's Bay Company, had sought the illusive sea by way of Hudson Strait and Bay. A great stride forward was made by Henry Kelsey for the Hudson's Bay Company when he reached the plains east of the South Saskatchewan. His sole object, however, was to increase the trade of his Company, and his very success stayed further advance. The next step forward was made from the valley of the St. Lawrence by the La Vérendryes. They reached the Missouri and the Black Hills of South Dakota on a south-westerly course, and the Forks of the Saskatchewan in the north-westerly direction. This last was, however, an advance of not much more than fifty miles westward beyond the longitude reached by Kelsey. There followed the great stride made by the Hudson's Bay Company in the person of Anthony Henday, when he penetrated to within sight of the Rockies in 1754. Other servants of the Company came after him, but here, as with Henry Kelsey, the horizon was limited by the fur trade. In any case, the advance from the valley of the Saskatchewan would have been checked by the mountain mass of the Rockies.

The situation was wholly changed when the Pedlar, Peter Pond, crossed the watershed of Hudson Bay at Methy Portage and entered a system of rivers whose inflow into the ocean could be no more than surmised. Fresh incentives to push on came into play. One such lay in the fur trade itself. The cost of transportation from Montreal to the valley of the Athabaska was such, that the question arose, whether that river and the Slave into which it flows would not afford an easy and a cheap communication with the Pacific Ocean. A no less potent motive for exploring these rivers was the hope that they would lead into the marine fur trade, in which great wealth was now being found.

Immediately after the union of the fur-traders of Canada in the " concern " of 1787, two masterly characters were engaged in the trade of the North West Company in far Athabaska—Peter Pond and his junior colleague Alexander Mackenzie. There were many likenesses both in the outward circumstances and the inward characteristics of these two men. Pond had pushed far northward through the forest belt ; Mackenzie pressed on from the point thus reached to the beyond—to the Arctic and the Pacific Oceans. Pond had little or no interest in Montreal ; neither had Mackenzie, for only a few years of his youth had been spent there, as a clerk. Both men were at the far end of the long line of communication by which goods came overland ; both felt the weight of its handicap. In Mackenzie's case, the one persistent motive of his life was to free the trade of Athabaska from the cost of the long journey from Montreal. Both men were impressed with the wealth to be won in the new-found fur trade of the Pacific coast ; both bent the more than usual gifts of their natures to reach the dazzling goal which their imagination pictured on the distant horizon. Both were passionate souls, ready to ride over all opponents who stood in their way. Witness Mackenzie's fierce fight in the XY Company with his former Company, the North West concern, and the extreme lengths which he allowed himself in opposing Lord Selkirk. Over against these stand Pond's violent relations with Waden and with Ross.

Pond's last years in the North-West were devoted to picturing his conclusions and his dreams upon a succession of maps. His notes are a confused mass of scientific observations and clever inferences, made by an illiterate man. Through them all runs the question of the relation of the Pacific Ocean to the water-system on which he traded. Where would the great Slave River, running northward from Athabaska, take him to ? From the beginning Pond was sure that it had some relation with the Pacific. The winds from the west brought up great clouds as from the salt sea, while those from the south-east gave clear skies.

There remains no more than 74 degrees between Arabasca [Athabaska] and Bearing [Bering Strait] which is nothing to the distance between the great carrying place [Grand Portage] and Arabasca. This I know to be a fact. Could the exact distance be come at I would not believe [it] to be more than 60 degrees.

In fact the valley of the Slave is only about twenty degrees from the Pacific, and sixty-six from Bering Strait. Pond's early maps reflect the information conveyed to him by the natives ; the Slave River is made to flow out of Great Slave northward into the Polar Sea. His later maps were influenced by Captain Cook's conclusion that a great river flowed into the Pacific at " Cook's River," the present Cook's Inlet. Accordingly, they show the Slave River as emptying itself into the Pacific.

But Peter Pond's position in the North West Company was uncomfortable, owing to the unfortunate circumstances of the death of John Ross, and he did not remain to put his speculations to the proof. In 1789 he came down to Montreal, sold his share in the Company, and left the country. When in Quebec, he urged his later and less accurate view of the course of the Slave River ; the Rocky Mountains ended in lat. $62\frac{1}{2}°$ N., and the river passed by them, in lat. 59° N., to the Pacific. His hearer, Mr. Isaac Ogden, argued that it was none other than Cook's River. Isaac conveyed these conclusions to his father, Mr. David Ogden in London, and added : " Another man by the name of McKenzie was left by Pond at Slave Lake [sic] to go down the River and from thence to Unalaska and so to Kamskatsha and thence to England through Russia. If he meets with no accident you may have him with you next year." Thus the plan of the exploration was Peter Pond's ; the execution of it was left to Alexander Mackenzie.

A correspondence published in the *Report of the Public Archives of Canada* for 1889 shows that interest in an English route by the North-West Passage or through the continent was keen at this juncture, and that plans for a fresh search for it were being considered. They came to nothing. One part of the scheme was that a Captain Holland should pass down the Slave River to the Pacific. Mackenzie's voyage of 1789 gave this proposal its quietus. Alexander Dalrymple was a chief advocate of the proposed exploration, and was in communication with Mr. Samuel Wegg, Governor of the Hudson's Bay Company. He reported that the Company was prepared to put its sloop at the disposal of a renewed search for a communication with the Pacific, and would bear the cost, if the Admiralty would send out " a proper Person " to be in command. This would suggest that the English Company also was interested in finding a way to the fur field of the Pacific and that its dispatch of its surveyor, Philip Turnor, in 1790, to explore the Athabaska region may have had for its ulterior motive the hope of finding an entry into the marine trade of the Pacific coast. Unfortunately, the Minutes of the Committee for these years are lacking, and therefore the policy envisaged is unknown. The fact that Captain Holland was to explore the Slave River for the Admiralty indicates that the belief of the proprietors of the North West Company that Turnor went out supported by Admiralty had no basis in the truth. In any case, Alexander Mackenzie's expedition forestalled all comers.

Mackenzie took the torch from Peter Pond's hand and pressed on with a masterfulness, self-control, and judgment all his own. Yet his achievement in reaching the Arctic—and that in a single summer—must not be overrated. Many factors were in his favour, as compared with Samuel Hearne, for example. The course of his exploration was marked out by the great river, which he had simply to follow downstream. The means of conveyance was the easy and swift canoe, loaded with enough provisions to allow of stores being cached by the way for the return voyage. Mackenzie had a band of disciplined servants, simple-minded and trained to obedience, and toughened by many a similar voyage. None the less, he deserves all credit for the tirelessness with which he pushed his way northward, and for his masterly handling of his men.

The party included four Canadians, two of whom were attended by their Indian wives, and a German, and as guide English Chief, formerly of the band of Matonabbee, Hearne's faithful supporter. The Chief brought his two wives and two followers, respectively to serve and to hunt. Moreover, Laurent le Roux, the trader on Great Slave Lake accompanied it in his own canoe as far as his post. Roderick Mackenzie had come from the Churchill Department to take charge of Athabaska during the absence of his cousin. His new post, Fort Chipewyan, on the south shore of Athabaska Lake, was the point of departure.

On June 3, 1789, at 9 a.m., the party embarked. The course as far as the post on Great Slave Lake was already known. It ran twenty-one miles westward, and nine north-north-west across Lake Athabaska, into and down a river leading from the lake to the point at which Peace River becomes the Slave ; then down the Slave River past the Portage des Noyés, where Cuthbert Grant in 1786 had lost five men and two canoes in the rapids. At the delta of the river, as it enters Great Slave Lake, it followed a small branch to the east down to the lake and then ran eastward within a long sandbank to the house occupied by Le Roux. This was sheltered from the broad waters of the lake by a row of islands. It was now the 9th of June.

Henceforth the course would be into the unknown. That there was a great stream flowing out of the west end of the lake northward had been ascertained by the fur-traders, but its actual position had to be found. Moreover, the lake beyond the islands was still an unbroken mass of ice. During the disappointing delay, Mackenzie took good care to find fish and fowl for the daily fare, so as not to entrench upon the pemmican provided for the voyage. On the 15th the journey was resumed. The course was dictated at first by the open water, as there was still ice on the lake. It ran north-eastward from island to island till a crossing of the lake was effected, when it turned westward and south-westward. Several bays were entered, in the belief that they would lead to the river. Once the coveted stream was found the course was unmistakable. Real danger lay in the possible hostility of Indians and Eskimos, to whom they would appear as enemies coming suddenly upon them. When strange Indians—Slaves (Beavers), Dogribs, and Quarrellers (Squint-eyes)—were met, Mackenzie showed that he knew how to disarm their panic, as well as how to allay the fears of his own crew. The dread of the Eskimos, whom Captain Franklin in 1824 found so intent on plunder, proved needless, for they were away at their summer hunt.

On 10th July Mackenzie was at what proved to be the delta of the river, where he took the middle channel. On the following day he visited deserted Eskimo houses, and found pieces of whalebone scattered about their fires. He then reached what he took to be a lake. On an island in it he climbed a hill, only to see " solid ice, extending from South-West . . . to the Eastward." The next day the water rose at the encampment, so that the baggage had to be removed. On the 14th, a school of whales was seen from the island on which the party had been camping. Mackenzie therefore named it Whale Island, and reckoned it in 69° 14' north latitude. Under that name it marks to-day the limit of his journey. On the following day the water rose upon the baggage. Mackenzie concluded definitely that it was the tide, that he had reached the Arctic Ocean, and that it was a frozen sea. The voyage had no further interest for him. Moreover, the crew was getting out of hand, and the provisions, which were to hold out until he reached his nearest cache, were running short. The laborious journey homeward against the current therefore began. On 12th September Fort Chipewyan was reached, and the great journey, as a journey, successfully ended on its one hundred and second day.

Mackenzie's narrative of his voyage leaves the impression that his motive was simple exploration. His plans were really those of a fur-trader and resulted ultimately in the expansion of the trade northward. But he had intended to achieve more far-reaching results. Captain Holland, writing in Quebec on November 10, 1790, about two months after the news of Mackenzie's voyage would have been received, indicates what was the plan of the North West Company in sending Mackenzie down the Slave River. " The last accounts we have from the Slave Lake have been obtained through the medium of M. Mackenzie, a Person Employed by the Merchants of Montreal (self Entitled the North West Company) in Exploring one of the Outlets Issuing from that Lake and supposed by them, to have communicated with the Western Ocean, the contrary of which he has discovered. . . . Their Views in taking these pains proceed from the hope that if they succeed in penetrating to the Ocean, Government may be induced to grant them a Charter and Exclusive Right in the Lucrative Furr trade to those parts." Holland, because of his connections with the Government and his interest in exploration to the Pacific, would be well informed. Now, and to the end of his life, the aims of Mackenzie were to enter upon the trade of the Pacific, to secure, to that end, the short line of transportation by Hudson Bay, and to obtain a charter from the Government which would give the Company rights similar to those possessed by the Hudson's Bay Company.

From this point of view his voyage, through no fault of his, was a complete failure. No wonder that he called the river, which others named after himself, the River Disappointment. No wonder that he wrote to his cousin Roderick from Grand Portage on July 16, 1790, after making his report : " My expedition was hardly spoken of, but that is what I expected." None the less, he had performed a great feat. He had extended the world's knowledge of America, and placed a fresh part of its Polar Shore on the map. In conjunction with Hearne's indication of the course of that shore at the mouth of the Coppermine River, this showed the general trend of the coast westward.

Mackenzie was the last man to accept a first defeat as final—least of all with such great aims in view. He was now bent, so to say, on forcing his way to the Pacific by a voyage westward up the Peace River. At the same time he was speculating as to other possible routes. In March 1792, when in winter quarters preparatory to his start, he wrote to Roderick, whom he appears to have stationed at Great Slave Lake to make inquiries : " I hope you will make all possible enquiry regarding the country of the Beaver Indians as well as of the country of the Slaves, and more particularly regarding a great river [our Yukon] which is reported to run parallel with, and falls into the sea to the westward of the River in which I voyaged."

On October 10, 1792, Mackenzie left Fort Chipewyan on the first stage of his second search for the Pacific. He passed, as before, by the Pine River into the Peace, but this time turned upstream. As he passed, he noted Peace Point " from which, according to the report of my interpreter, the river derives its name" (1782). On the 17th he was at Vermilion Falls, and the next day reached " the old Establishment," the first on this river and built by Boyer some six miles above Boyer's River. It was on the north bank. Passing on, he overtook Mr. John Finlay, the proprietor in charge on the Peace, and, forty-one of his miles beyond the Old Establishment, reached his fort (Du Tremble)—the New Establishment. This post was in occupation during the previous season, for Mackenzie says : " We landed before the house amidst the rejoicing and firing of the people, who were animated with the prospect of again indulging themselves in the luxury of rum, of which they had been deprived from the beginning of May." Mackenzie hastened on past McLeod's Fort, a frontier outpost occupied during the previous season, to the spot at which he proposed to winter. It was on the right bank of the river about two miles beyond its confluence with Smoky River. From Fort McLeod two men had been sent up in the spring to make the first preparation for building. Here Mackenzie spent the winter in the simple part of fur-trader. In the following May he sent down six canoes of furs. Meanwhile he had made preparations for his journey. His canoe was " twenty-five feet long within, exclusive of the curves of stem and stern, twenty-six inches hold, and four feet nine inches beam. At the same time she was so light, that two men could carry her on a good road three or four miles without resting." The freight weighed three thousand pounds. The crew numbered ten—seven French-Canadians, two Indians, and a Scot, clerk to the Company, Alexander MacKay, who afterwards went out to the Pacific coast with John Jacob Astor's expedition and lost his life at the destruction of the *Tonquin.*

On Thursday, 9th May, the journey began in which Mackenzie's genius for command, his courage, and his tenacity were to be tested to their utmost. Nothing but a more careful study of the details of his narrative than is possible here can do justice to the man. While he was necessarily to follow his water-way as before, inasmuch as he was ascending and not descending, many perplexing alternatives would face him. The peoples beyond the Rockies, more or less sedentary in their villages, would be hostile, and because of their numbers would be able to overwhelm him at will. His crew would quake with fear. Only a masterly man, and one endowed in the superlative degree with self-control and judgment, could have made his way, as Mackenzie did, to the desired end. The large supplies of provisions and of rum carried in the canoe made his task easier, for the men were usually well fed, and they were treated to a " regale" of rum after any specially hard day's journey, or when great difficulties had been overcome.

On the 16th the party reached the Sinew (the present Pine) River, flowing into the Peace from the south. Mackenzie noted : " This spot would be an excellent situation for a fort . . . as there is plenty of wood and every reason to believe that the country abounds in beaver." It was also a good buffalo country, thus making an ideal location from the fur-trader's point of view. " The land above the spot where we encamped spreads into an extensive plain. The country is so crowded with animals as to have the appearance, in some places, of a stall-yard." In fact a post was placed here within a few years. David Thompson visited it in 1804 under the name of Rocky Mountain House. (It must not be confused with the later Rocky Mountain Portage House at the Peace River canyon.) The river above flows through a valley so narrow as to leave practically only the stream running in rapids between banks 700 to 1,150 feet in height. Progress was possible only by tracking, and at times along the top of the cliffs.

My present situation on a cliff was so elevated that the men, who were coming up a strong point, could not hear me, though I called to them with the utmost strength of my voice to lighten the canoe of part of its lading. And here I could not but reflect, with infinite anxiety on the hazard of my enterprise : one false step of those who were attached to the line, or the breaking of the line itself, would have at once consigned the canoe, and every thing it contained to instant destruction : it, however, ascended the rapid in perfect security, but new dangers immediately presented themselves, for stones, both great and small, were continually rolling from the bank, so as to render the situation of those who were dragging the canoe beneath it extremely perilous ; besides, they were at every step in danger, from the steepness of the ground, of falling into the water : nor was my solicitude diminished by my being necessarily removed at times from the sight of them.

This must serve as only one example of the physical difficulties and dangers, infinite in variety of detail, which only the long experience of the crew and the commander's indomitable will could have overcome. Through it all, the health and strength of the men remained unimpaired. The canoe, battered and broken again and again, was as often repaired and gummed, until it was so heavy and rickety that it could scarcely be carried over the portages. The men chose rather to risk their lives in the descent of the Fraser than try to portage the canoe.

On the evening of the 20th the party had reached the eastern edge of the canyon of the Peace River, having done twenty-eight miles in four days. They were now in the neighbourhood of the fort known as Rocky Mountain Portage, established by Simon Fraser twelve years later. Peace River canyon forms two sides of an isosceles triangle whose apex points southward. As the river runs through some twenty miles it falls 270 feet. Hence the portage of about twelve miles over very difficult country, which forms the base of the triangle. On the 24th Mackenzie was on the river at the western end, having taken three days to traverse the twelve miles. On the 31st he reached the confluence of the Finlay, coming from the north, and the Parsnip, flowing in from the south ; the two streams uniting to form the Peace River. Hitherto the great river had been the guide. Now the judgment of the man was to be tested. His own theory of his course to the Pacific pointed out the Finlay as the way ; then, too, its broad stream was inviting, the rapids of the Parsnip repellant. But an old Indian at his winter quarters, who had been on war parties in this region, had told him of a great river flowing westward, and had cautioned him not to take this northerly branch, for it was soon lost in many wild streams among the mountains. In spite of the protests of the canoe-men, and in the teeth of his own theoretical leaning, Mackenzie followed the old Indian's directions and took the true but difficult way indicated by the Parsnip. Unfortunately, as they ascended, he missed the Pack River coming in from McLeod Lake, which would have offered a comparatively direct and easy route by the Giscombe Portage to the Fraser. Simon Fraser later suggested that the hard-wrought explorer was at the moment enjoying, in the manner of the *bourgeois*, the luxury of a quiet nap in his canoe while the voyageurs toiled on. On 7th June they were near the source of the Parsnip and the Height of Land, and were anxiously asking : What next ? They came on a small band of Indians whose hostility and whose studied silence Mackenzie disarmed by a few presents and by quietly camping beside them. On the second day they began to be communicative, and finally provided him with a guide. Passing through a lake, which he took to be the source of the Parsnip, Mackenzie portaged into another small lake, whence he began to descend towards the Pacific. The stream (our James Creek) more than earned its name, still on some maps, " The Bad River." It led them, at times wading through swamp up to the middle of their thighs, at last to a navigable stream, the Herrick Creek of to-day. A little farther down, this is joined by another stream and forms the McGregor River, which is the north branch of the Fraser. This was followed some twenty-five miles down to the Forks. Here Mackenzie entered the main stream of the Fraser, which by the way he took to be the Columbia. It was necessary to portage at some parts of the upper Fraser canyon, below the later Fort George. "The labour and the fatigue beggars description," says Mackenzie. On 20th June he would pass the Blackwater River on his right.

Mackenzie was now in an entirely new Indian world—one unknown to the fur-traders of the east, as they were unknown to it. Its Indians had an abundant food supply in the salmon of the river during the season. Accordingly they built more permanent homes. When he saw the first one he remarked, " the only Indian habitation of this kind that I have seen on this side of Michilemakina." It was thirty feet by twenty, and had three doors and three fire-places with beds on either side of them, and, behind the beds, a sort of manger in which to keep fish. Within was a great crate for catching fish. At the fisheries along the river large villages stood in which the people lived during the season when making and curing their catch and during the winter. At other times they would be away hunting in their territory. These people presented a great contrast to the Indians of the Plains, not only in numbers but in their sense of ownership of the land and of the river from which they got their food supply. Hence their hostility to the stranger who came down upon them. Each group told Mackenzie that the next people below were malignants and would murder him. Moreover, these Indians had never seen the Whites ; they knew of them only by wild stories of their misdeeds at the coast. To meet them and win their goodwill taxed Mackenzie's talent to the utmost. Then, too, the terror aroused by their hostility was like to cause the Canadian crew to break out of hand. His control of them is one of the finest parts of Mackenzie's story.

On 21st June the party passed the Quesnel River on the left and came to its first real encounter with this new type of Indian—in this case a Carrier tribe. When one of the natives saw the strange party, he gave the alarm and brought his people to the bank of the river armed with bows, and arrows, and spears. Mackenzie kept his canoe stationary in midstream. The interpreters warned him that the Indians were threatening instant death, should he land. He therefore passed to the other side and camped.

I therefore formed the following adventurous project, which was happily crowned with success. I left the canoe, and walked by myself along the beach, in order to induce some of the natives to come to me, which I imagined they might be disposed to do, when they saw me alone, without any apparent possibility of receiving assistance from my people, and would consequently imagine that a communication with me was not a service of danger. At the same time, in order to possess the utmost security of which my situation was susceptible, I directed one of the Indians to slip into the woods, with my gun and his own, and to conceal himself from their discovery ; he also had orders to keep as near me as possible, without being seen, and if any of the natives should venture across, and attempt to shoot me from the water, it was his instructions to lay him low : at the same time he was particularly enjoined not to fire till I had discharged one or both of the pistols that I carried in my belt. If, however, any of them were to land, and approach my person, he was immediately to join me. In the mean time my other interpreter assured them that we entertained the most friendly disposition, which I confirmed by such signals as I conceived would be comprehended by them. I had not, indeed, been long at my station, and my Indian in ambush behind me, when two of the natives came off in a canoe, but stopped when they had got within an hundred yards of me. I made signs for them to land, and as an inducement, displayed looking glasses, beads, and other alluring trinkets. At length, but with every mark of extreme apprehension, they approached the shore, stern foremost but would not venture to land. I now made them a present of some beads, with which they were going to push off, when I renewed my entreaties and, after some time, prevailed on them to come ashore, and sit down by me. My hunter now thought it right to join me, and created some alarm in my new acquaintance. It was, however, soon removed, and I had the satisfaction to find that he, and these people perfectly understood each other. I instructed him to say everything that might tend to sooth their fears and win their confidence. I expressed my wish to conduct them to our canoe, but they declined my offer ; and when they observed some of my people coming towards us, they requested me to let them return ; and I was so well satisfied with the progress I had made in my intercourse with them, that I did not hesitate a moment in complying with their desire. During their short stay, they observed us, with a mixture of admiration and astonishment. We could plainly distinguish that their friends received them with great joy on their return, and that the articles which they carried back with them were examined with a general and eager curiosity ; they also appeared to hold a consultation, which lasted about a quarter of an hour, and the result was, an invitation to come over to them, which was cheerfully accepted. Nevertheless, on our landing, they betrayed evident signs of confusion, which arose, probably, from the quickness of our movements, as the prospect of a friendly communication had so cheered the spirits of my people, that they paddled across the river with the utmost expedition. The two men, however, who had been with us, appeared, very naturally, to possess the greatest share of courage on the occasion, and were ready to receive us on our landing ; but our demeanor soon dispelled all their apprehensions, and the most familiar communication took place between us. When I had secured their confidence, by the distribution of trinkets among them, and treated the children with sugar, I instructed my interpreters to collect every necessary information in their power to afford me.

Mackenzie's position a little farther down the river was perilous and perplexing in the extreme, not only from the hostility of the Carriers, at the later Fort Alexandria (the farthest point reached), and the reported malignancy of the Shuswaps beyond, but because his own crew was getting beyond control with terror. Yet in the hour of danger his judgment remained unimpaired. From such information as he gathered, he concluded that the Fraser lower down would often be unnavigable because of its rapids and cascades, that in any case its course was too long for the provisions in hand, now greatly diminished, that there was an easy Indian trade path along the Blackwater—his Westward River—to the coast, which was much nearer that way than by the Fraser. He writes : " If the assertion of Mr. Mears 1790 be correct it cannot be so far as the inland sea which he mentions within Nootka must come as far east of 126° W. longitude." Meanwhile he had collected bark and built a new canoe for his return.

On 4th July the overland journey was begun. As carefully traced in modern times, it ran along the Blackwater River, at first on its northern bank, then on the southern, and finally to the height of land. It turned south-westward to cross the Salmon, or Dean, and Takia rivers, and then southward to the Bella Coola River, at a village at its confluence with the Kahylekt. Here the reception was so kindly, compared with communities later visited, as to lead Mackenzie to name it " The Friendly Village." Canoes were obtained for the journey down the Bella Coola to the coast. The whole party was feasted on salmon at successive villages along the river. At one, Mackenzie saw four heaps of three to four hundred fish each, and sixteen women at the work of cleaning and curing. This abundance was more than welcome, for the party was now receiving but two-thirds of its usual daily rations. The treatment received at this village on the return earned it the name of " The Rascal's Village." On 20th July Mackenzie was on an arm of the long-dreamt-of Pacific. English seamen had been there before him. Vancouver's expedition, exploring the coast and its many inlets, had recently passed northward. James Johnstone, the sailing-master of the *Chatham*, had explored the North Bentinck Arm, and visited the village near the mouth of the Bella Coola on 1st June, forty-eight days before.

Mackenzie procured a large canoe at the village and ran down the North Bentinck Arm in the hope of reaching open sea. He passed through Labourchere Channel to Dean Channel and down this last past Cascade Inlet to a point a short distance north-east of Elcho harbour. Here he landed at a deserted village by a great rock. He gives the latitude as 52° 20′ 48″ N. " I now mixed up some vermilion in melted grease and inscribed in large characters, on the south-east face of the rock on which we slept last night this brief memorial : ' Alexander Mackenzie, from Canada, by land, the twenty-second of July, one thousand seven hundred and ninety-three!' " He was the first to cross the broad American continent overland—no mean feat in the circumstances.

With supplies of salmon secured from the villages as they passed homeward, Mackenzie's party reached their first cache, and so from cache to cache. Their new canoe near the Blackwater River brought them swiftly on their homeward way. None the less, at Rocky Mountain Portage they were at the end of their pemmican. However, they were now entering a land of plenty, of buffalo and red deer in herds. Moving placidly down the Peace River, all anxieties over and abundance to eat, they gave rein to their appetites. Although they had had a hearty meal at one o'clock, between six in the evening and ten next morning the party of ten persons and a large dog ate the carcase of a red deer weighing 250 pounds. And so, happily, to their starting-point near the Forks of the Smoky River by 24th August, and to Fort Chipewyan, where they spent the winter of 1793-94.

In August 1794 Alexander Mackenzie was at Grand Portage. So was Duncan M'Gillivray, at that time but a clerk in the Company. There is no record of any discussions between them, but it may be presumed that the explorer's ideas reached his junior, and began that process of education which was to lead him to take up Mackenzie's plans and to cross the Rockies himself seven years later, and later still, to inaugurate what may be called " the Columbian enterprise."

It is of great importance for understanding Mackenzie, and interpreting his subsequent history, to grasp the ideas seething in the mind of this confident and aggressive young man of but thirty years of age—all the more as he pitted himself against Simon McTavish, the great mandarin of the North West Company. Nowhere are they to be more clearly seen than in the Report which the Lieutenant-Governor of Upper Canada, John Graves Simcoe, made to the Lords of the Committee of the Privy Council for Trade and Foreign Plantations after a conversation with him as he passed through to Montreal. [Mr. Mackenzie] :

describes the communications between upper Canada and this Ocean [the Pacific] to be practicable, similar methods being pursued by which the Northwest Company have already extended their factories over the internal Parts of the Country. The height of land between the *Peace River* which he ascended to its source and branches of the great River which he supposes to be the River of the West, not being more than seven hundred yards. The Traffic which may be carried on by this rout [sic], will undoubtedly strike your Lordships as a matter of great importance, but it appears from the observations of Mr. Mackenzie who seems to be as intelligent as he is adventurous, That to carry on this Commerce to National Advantages, the privileges and rivalship, the claims and monopoly of great Commercial Companies must be reconciled and blended in one common Interest. His observations on this head which particularly attracted my attention were that the most practicable Rout to the Northwest was thro' the territories of the Hudsons Bay Company, that by this route from Great Britain all the Navigation from Montreal thro' the Chain of Lakes and their immense Communication to the more distant part or the interior Country and its consequent Carriage, would be saved, but that on the other hand the people of Canada being infinitely more capable of the hardships of the Indian life, and all the vicissitudes and dangers incident to the Trade, than Europeans, from thence, must draw those supplies of men without which It would not be possible to pursue the Commerce. The Northwest Traders would find it their Interest to collect all the most valuable of the Furs, now brought from the Interior parts of America, and to pass them down the streams which fall into the Pacific Ocean—and this, Mr. Mackenzie says, they could do with much less Expence and difficulty than bringing them thro' the St. Lawrence. In respect to the Valuable Furs on the coast of the Pacific Ocean, his ideas are that a post at Cooke's River and another at the Southerly limit of the British Claims would probably secure the whole Traffic and as this cannot be done in any other manner than by conciliating the affections of the natives, it is natural to suppose that the habits of a people long accustomed to the manners and disposition of the Indians, will be found to be of the greatest consequence to promote so desirable a purpose ; the Crews of Trading Vessels seem by no means fit for this traffic and the [Russians] have severly felt their ignorance of its Customs. The East India Company, who possess the Privilege of the Chinese Market, It is to be presumed, would find the Utility of these Establishments and he seems to apprehend the diminution of the Quantity of Silver sent to China in Consequence of the increase of the Fur Trade would be a national advantage. The knowledge that by Hudsons Bay the rout is practicable and most convenient not only to the further Lakes but to Lake Superior, may be of importance to Great Britain, as a maritime Power— and possibly in case of necessity, might be of consequence to the safety of Upper Canada.

Here is a scheme which, had it been accomplished at the time, would have changed the whole history of the Pacific Coast. It involved the use of the matchless personnel of the North West Company, the valuable short route of the Hudson's Bay Company to the more distant fur regions and to the Pacific, the occupation by Britain of the rich maritime fur area of the Western Coast, and the development of a valuable trade with China. When Mackenzie pleaded with the Government for a charter, it was because he believed that nothing short of a great chartered company, with a monopoly like the East India Company and the Hudson's Bay Company, backed by the Imperial Government, could carry through such a vast enterprise. When he opened negotiations in 1804 with the Hudson's Bay Company for the right to transmit goods through the Bay, he was simply working at a detail of the larger scheme. Altogether, Mackenzie is the first great Westerner—looking at the problems of the West, chiefly problems of transportation, through the windows of his post in Athabaska, and solving them through connections with Hudson Bay and the Pacific, rather than Montreal. He did not live to see his dreams realized, but shortly after his death the union of the Hudson's Bay Company and the North West Company went far towards bringing them to a happy if, so far as Britain's claims on the Pacific are concerned, a belated actuality.

CHAPTER **VI**

THE GREAT STRUGGLE BETWEEN THE ENGLISH AND CANADIAN COMPANIES BEGINS, 1787–1800 *

THE COLUMBIAN ENTERPRISE, 1800–14 †

BY 1784 and 1787 the constitution under which all the Canadian fur-traders could unite in the North West Company to present a solid front to the Hudson's Bay Company was perfected, but it took fifteen years to secure the solid front. That feature in the constitution which made the Company a temporary partnership, renewable at the end of so many years, left it open for capable and experienced servants, disappointed at their failure to be taken in as partners, to step out and form new companies in opposition. Moreover, firms interested rather in the South-West were so hampered by the regulations inflicted by the Americans in their trade, which was now in American territory, that they turned their attention to the North-West. Thus the early 'nineties saw four rival companies in the trade —the North West Company; a company established by its late servants, David and Peter Grant; the "South Men"; and the Hudson's Bay Company. By 1795 the North West Company had secured, momentarily, a solid front. But by that date the Hudson's Bay Company had solved its problems of transportation and secured an experienced service, and had extended its inland posts, so that an English post faced one or more Canadian posts all along the line. The forces were marshalled on either side for the great struggle.

The period of wellnigh a quarter of a century after the completion of the organization of the North West Company was marked by the extension of the companies' forts to the foot of the Rocky Mountains. But the farther afield the Company went, the more burdensome became the cost of transportation all the way from and to Montreal. Evidence that the Northwesters were restive under this handicap is found in Alexander Mackenzie's attempts in 1789 and 1793 to find an easy route to a port on the Pacific, and in an appeal made by Simon McTavish, when in England during the winter of 1790–91, to Mr. Pitt, then Prime Minister, to quash the Hudson's Bay Company's Charter that the North West Company might land goods in Hudson's Bay. Pitt's reply was that no monopoly could be abolished

* Illustrated by Sketch-map No. 10 at p. 426.
† Illustrated by Sketch-map No. 9 at p. 362.

without an Act of Parliament. The handicap of its long line of transportation was accentuated when the Company crossed the Rockies on what may be called the Columbian enterprise. In the hope of escaping from its burden, the Company attempted to buy out the English Company, and that failing, offered to make an annual payment of £2,000 for the right of transit for its goods through the Strait and Bay. The failure to secure relief by negotiations brought a new and embittering motive into the struggle between the North West Company and the Hudson's Bay Company. The North-westers attempted to bring their rivals to their will by a pressure which did not stop short of violence. They so far succeeded that for a number of years the English Company paid no dividends.

There followed the reorganization of the Hudson's Bay Company under the guidance of Lord Selkirk's brother-in-law, Andrew Wedder-burn (Colvile). The factors were given a share in the profits of the Company; a colony was established on the Red River to provide the Company's forts with provisions; arrangements were made to settle retired servants in the colony with a view to securing in their sons servants of the type which contributed so largely to the success of the Canadians, men acquainted with the languages and the ways of the Indians. Finally, a definite aggressive was planned to enter that richest of fur regions—the valleys of the Peace, Slave, and Mackenzie rivers. In spite of serious reverses, the reorganization accomplished its aim; the Hudson's Bay Company was paying dividends once more.

One feature of the struggle must be kept clearly in view. It was much more than a competition between the two companies. The fundamental issue at stake was the validity of the English Company's Charter. The simple presence of the Canadians trading freely in the territory claimed by the Hudson's Bay Company declared the Charter null and void. The grant of a large tract of land by the Company to Lord Selkirk for a colony reasserted the validity of the Charter and the right of the Company to the soil. This was followed by notice served by Lord Selkirk and by the Company upon the Northwesters to get out of their respective lands. Thus the Englishmen kept alive in law their claim to the country. The Northwesters were not blind to the issue. They found means on two occasions to destroy the colony.

The struggle was ruinous to all parties—to the Indians, to the fur trade, and to the two companies. It issued in a threatened dis-solution of the North West Company, the only escape from which was a union with the Hudson's Bay Company on its own terms. After the union all parties proclaimed the validity of the Charter; they all used the short and cheap route by Hudson Strait. The Imperial Government by Act of Parliament gave its blessing to the union, recognizing the whole basin of Hudson Bay as the Chartered Territory. A lease granted the monopoly of the trade with the Indians in the country beyond—the North-West Territory. Rupert's Land and the North-West entered a period of profound peace and unparalleled prosperity.

I.—FROM JAMES BAY TO THE ROCKY MOUNTAINS, 1787–1800

The Pedlars, of course, invaded the fur fields south of James Bay, the Bottom of the Bay, as the Hudson's Bay Company called it. In 1766 Governor Kitchen wrote home, with great insight : " In a few years the English will hurt the trade at Moose Fort more than the French ever did." In 1768 Humphrey Marten, Governor at Albany Fort, reported a decrease in trade due to the Pedlars. It will be recalled that Henley House was not strictly an inland post, as the Governor and Committee insisted as late as 1768, but " an establishment of Assistance to the Indians in their Journeys, and not as a means to prevent their trade being brought to Albany." In 1775, the year after the establishment of Cumberland House inland from York Fort, this insistence on the Indians coming down to the Factory on the Bay was abandoned, and the policy of inland posts and of the multiplication of posts as a means of protecting the trade from the Pedlars was wholeheartedly adopted. This resulted in a sudden transformation of the scene. Servants began explorations up all the rivers, quadrants being supplied to enable them to take the latitude of important points. For example, in 1775–76 Edward Jarvis, Master at Henley House, explored the most easterly branch of the Albany to establish its relation with the Missinaibi, the most westerly tributary of the Moose, and followed this up by penetrating, by the Missinaibi, to Michipicoton on Lake Superior, where he visited Alexander Henry's post and another in opposition to it. In 1780 Philip Turnor surveyed to the same point from Moose Fort, by way of the Missinaibi, a principal tributary of the Moose River. He was only following in the wake of John Thomas, who had penetrated as far in 1777. In this year one Moore was sent up the Rupert River to Lake Mistassini.

Ever since the destruction of Fort Charles in 1686 the Rupert River had been without an English fort, the Indians going to Eastmain or to Moose Fort. Word that the Pedlars had established themselves on Lake Nemiscau in 1774, led to the reoccupation of the river. In 1776 John Kay was sent " to build a House, or a good Logg Tent at Rupert's River, where the old Factory formerly stood." Rupert Fort, as it was called, was an outpost of Eastmain.

The valley of the Moose River was approached by the Pedlars either from the Ottawa River by Lake Abitibi or by Lake Superior from Michipicoton through Lake Missinaibi. From their respective bases at Michipicoton and Lake Abitibi they sent small parties in to build log tents among the Indians, wherever they might be. The new policy of the Hudson's Bay Company was to meet this competition by placing posts towards the height of land, which would act as shields to the fur fields behind them. In 1777 no less than three posts were established inland from Moose Fort—a temporary post at the head of Lake " Mesacogamy," reached by the French Creek ; a post on Missinaibi Lake about forty miles from Michipicoton ; and, to act as a base for it, Brunswick House on the Missinaibi, half a mile above its confluence with the Wabiskagami. It proved impossible to hold Missinaibi Lake. In the first year it was abandoned because provisions were so scarce that its garrison almost died of starvation. In the second, European provisions were provided, but the Indians, no doubt instigated by the Pedlars, assumed a hostile attitude. One even shot at an Englishman. John Thomas, Master of the house, lost his nerves and decided on retreat. The house was burned down by the Indians, and the site remained unoccupied till some time after the union of 1821. Brunswick House was not out of the reach of the Indians of Lake Missinaibi. As the Pedlars had to bring their goods in all the way round by the Great Lakes, while the transportation route of the English Company was a hundred miles in a straight line from Moose Fort, Governor Kitchen was probably just in his boast that he could undersell his opponents. Brunswick House did very well—at its best gathering more than a thousand, made beaver, without diminishing the returns at Moose Fort itself.

The plan of building as close as might be to the height of land was resumed in 1788, and a post was built on Micabanish (Brunswick) Lake. When Brunswick House was abandoned in 1790 this post was called New Brunswick.

The policy of the Company was the same for the other important tributary of the Moose, the Abitibi. The base of the Pedlars was on Abitibi Lake, log tents being built in various directions among the Indians. The Mesacogami post was an advance up the French Creek, a tributary of the Moose below the Abitibi, which the Indians said was a good water-way. It proved not to be so, and the post was a disappointment. In 1784 Philip Turnor was sent up the Abitibi to build in opposition to the Pedlars. He did not go as far as the lake, for the Indians said it would be difficult to get venison there. He built " almost in the center of the Abitibi Indians hunting ground," and " at the fork of two Rivers [the Frederick House and Abitibi rivers] about 60 [90] miles from the Lake." As the fisheries here proved inadequate, in the following season Turnor moved up the Frederick House River to "Waratowaca," Nighthawk Lake, in anticipation of the Pedlars, and built Frederick House. Abandoned in 1795, this post was reopened in 1798 ; it appears to have been in operation ever since. Turnor estimated that the post was within seventy or eighty miles of Lake Timiscaming.

The establishment of these inland posts increased the costs of the operations of the Hudson's Bay Company, but added greatly to the volume of the trade at Moose Fort. The returns in 1762–63, when that post stood alone, were 5,111, made beaver, " the largest that has been at this place for many years." In 1780 and 1781 the returns of the factory and its dependencies were above 9,000 ; in 1783 and 1784 above 10,000 ; in 1785 and 1786 above 12,000. Thereafter there was a decline. But not only was the volume increased, the furs got were of the finest quality, for the Pedlars were no longer able to pick out the best and leave the poorest to be taken by the Indians to the fort by the Bay. Moreover, the enhanced prices in the London fur market would cover the cost of the inland posts.

The development inland from Albany Fort followed the long water-way of Albany River. In 1775 Henley House ceased to function as a wayside assistance to Indians going down to Albany and became truly an inland post, " a large Mart of Trade." It was time, for there were four settlements of the Pedlars in the hinterland, one of them on Lake Mepiskawacaw, seventy miles from Henley. Very soon Henley House was good for little short of 2,000, made beaver. In the later 'eighties, when it held its field more to itself, its returns rose above that figure. In 1777 Gloucester House was built on Upashewey Lake, on the Albany, put at 243 miles above Henley House. After the hardship of the first years it proved a very successful venture. From 1782 to 1787 its returns only once fell below 4,000; in 1786 they were 5,271, made beaver. In 1779 Philip Turnor, the Company's surveyor, fresh from the Saskatchewan, surveyed the Albany as far as Gloucester House, but could not proceed farther for lack of a guide.

From this time the Company, doubtless because of its success, was offered the services of some of the Pedlars and of a number of the Pedlars' men. Some of those taken into its employ proved a great addition, especially as they knew the water-ways of the intricate country between the Albany and Lake Nipigon. Monsieur Mauganest, a native of old France, but for many years a resident of Montreal, deserves special attention. He was sent up by the Company to Gloucester House in 1779 with instructions to proceed two hundred miles farther inland. He proved a disappointment in so far as he did not get beyond that post, but he left his mark on the Company's methods of business by instructing its servants at Albany in the best ways of packing goods for the interior. It was at his suggestion that the Company introduced their famous point-blankets to the trade. He laid great stress upon the Company's servants dispensing with European provisions and learning to live on the country. George Sutherland took the Canadians whom Mauganest brought with him into the Company's service to winter on Sturgeon Lake. The poor man was brought down in the spring a wreck from starvation. Two of Mauganest's men died of inanition, and the rest saved themselves by taking employment with the Pedlars.

There were competing Pedlars on Lake Nipigon all along. In 1783 one Ezekiel Solomon, a Jew, penetrated from Nipigon, his base, to Lake St. Joseph (Pascocoggan). In 1784 James Sutherland explored the route to Lake Nipigon and the Canadian track thence to Lake St. Joseph, and in 1786 Osnaburgh House was built a few miles below the lake. It was close to the Canadian track northward and subject to greater competition than was Gloucester House. Nevertheless, in its second year it brought in 4,349 and in its third 4,823, made beaver, but this was partly at the expense of Gloucester

House, whose returns fell toward 2,000, made beaver. Pedlars in these parts were John Bartie in the earlier days, and now John Tupper, whose house was on an island in the middle of Lac Seul. Alexander Shaw and Donald MacKay were on Sturgeon Lake in 1789, MacKay having given up his enterprise on the Saskatchewan. Donald's brother, John MacKay, was on Lake Nipigon. In 1791 the two MacKays entered the service of the Hudson's Bay Company. Both figured in frontier posts.

As early as 1777 George Sutherland had wintered beyond the valley of the Albany. Passing through Lac Seul into English River, he turned northward at the first confluence, Three Rivers as it was called, and ultimately reached Red Lake, east of Lake Winnipeg. During the winter he descended the valley of Pigeon River to the lake, in what he made to be 52° 31′ north latitude. Incidentally he warned two Pedlars' houses, 120 miles to the south, of a plot among the Indians to destroy their post, and thereby saved them. In 1790 the Hudson's Bay Company built on Red Lake and on Lake Wippenaban, probably Indian Lake, on the English River. When Wippenaban was not occupied, Ball Lake above it was, the post there being known as Eshkabitchewan, from falls above the inflow into the lake. The house stood near the inflow of the Wabigoon River draining Eagle Lake, and was about two days' journey from Portage de l'Isle on the Winnipeg River, the great track of the Canadians to Lake Winnipeg. From nearly all these posts on the main water-way outposts, more or less temporary, were established in the midst of the Indians. Outposts in the district of Red Lake were very successful. More permanent posts were the one on Nipigon Lake, established by John MacKay, and one on Cat Lake, north of St. Joseph's Lake.

The result of this great activity is seen in the returns of Albany Fort. In 1763–64, a year with little or no competition from Canada, they were 10,390, made beaver ; in 1773, as a result of the incursion of the Pedlars, they fell to 3,125. By 1788–89 the new policy was bearing its fruit ; they rose to 15,125, made beaver, and here also the quality of the furs was prime, no longer the leavings of the Pedlars. This was achieved in spite of that master Pedlar, Duncan Cameron, whose canoes ran from his base on Lake Nipigon through Lac Seul to the region of Red Lake and the upper waters of the Pigeon River flowing into Lake Winnipeg.

In 1793 the Governor of Albany Fort began a great offensive against the Pedlars in the region from which the Indians had come down to his post by the Bay in the days before the invasion of the French under La Vérendrye. In a single year posts were opened on the Winnipeg River above Portage de l'Isle ; on Rainy River ; and as far afield as Brandon House on the Assiniboine. Thus, at one stroke, what the North West Company called their Rainy Lake and Red River departments was occupied by the Hudson's Bay Company. Competition with the North West Company in these areas now began in earnest.

FROM RAINY LAKE TO LAKE WINNIPEG

The region between Lake Superior and Lake Winnipeg was one of the less important departments of the North West Company at this time. It had long been exploited and, in any case, on account of the rocky nature of the ground, beaver could not have been as plentiful as they were farther north and west. La Vérendrye had knowledge of three courses leading to Rainy Lake—by the Kaministikwia and its tributary the Mattawan River and the string of lakes later followed by the Dawson route; by the Kaministikwia, Dog Lake and River, across to the Seine River flowing into Rainy Lake; and finally by Grand Portage. During the period under consideration the first two had passed out of memory. The Grand Portage water-way held the field. The portage itself was about nine miles long and involved " poses " or rests for the carriers, all the more as the ground was hilly. At its far end, on Pigeon River, Fort Charlotte stood with its stores for furs coming in and goods going out—all packed, merely passing through. The route led up the Pigeon River, across the height of land, and along the International Boundary all the way to Rainy Lake. Rainy River flowing from the lake runs immediately to rapids which end in the Chaudière or Kettle Falls, at the present Fort Frances. The Northwesters shot the rapids past the site of La Vérendrye's Fort St. Pierre on their right and portaged past the falls on the same side. They re-embarked and reached the fort which figures under the somewhat inaccurate description of Rainy Lake Fort, about half a mile farther down.

Lac la Pluie, as the post is mostly called, played an important part as the rendezvous for the Athabaska brigade, for, in order to be sure to get back to its wintering-grounds before the rivers froze, it passed over its furs to a select brigade of " porkeaters," as the voyageurs from Montreal were called, and received goods in return. Thus the post, while gathering its own scant supply of furs, was a depot for merchandise and especially for provisions. Apart from small quantities of meat, the supply of food laid up for the brigades was wild rice gathered by the Indians, as in La Vérendrye's day, from the marshes of Rainy Lake and the Lake of the Woods. The canoes of the harvesters were pushed in among the grain, the ears of which were drawn across the gunwale of their craft by a hook and were beaten with a straight cudgel, so that the rice fell into some receptacle in the canoe. When Alexander Henry, the younger, was at Lac la Pluie in 1802 with his brigade of eleven canoes, he had come from Grand Portage on two bags of corn, one and a half bushels each, and fifteen pounds of grease (pork fat). Here he received two bags of rice, one and a half bushels each, and ten pounds of grease, to take him to the " Bottom of the River Winnipeg."

The brigades now ran down Rainy River, whose beauties the traders seldom fail to extol. Duncan M'Gillivray says : " It is reckoned the most beautifull River in the North, a preference which it richly deserves, from the variety of delightfull scenes which its banks disclose at every winding." The traders passed out of the river and crossed Lake of the Woods, strange to say, without ever a mention in their Journals of Massacre Island or Fort St. Charles, memorable for their association with the name of La Vérendrye. This indicates that their route was by the islands along the east shore. The course was now past Rat Portage down the River Winnipeg, whose *décharges* and portages are referred to in terms little short of malediction. Mention is frequently made of the Dalles eight miles down, of Portage de l'Isle a mile and a half below the English River, "the track" by which the English Company's servants came in from Albany. The stretch of the river called La Rivière Blanche, from the foam of its succession of cataracts, was most frightful of all. Alexander Mackenzie says : "Here are seven portages, in so short a space, that the whole of them are descernible at the same moment." In its boiling torrents loss of life was often incurred, and usually but narrowly averted. Duncan M'Gillivray describes an incident which occurred as he passed down in 1794.

At the second *Portage de la Rivière Blanche* one off the Canoes imprudently advanced too near the Fall to unload, the most convenient landing place being already occupied by the other canoes, and after the Goods were debarked, the Upper end of it thro' some negligence was suddenly carried out by the current with the steersman suspended after it, and the foreman attempting to retain his end was also carried away before he could receive any assistance—they were hurled down with surprizing velocity thro' three successive cascades, nothing but the particular dirrection of Providence could have saved them in such immenent danger—for the Canoe was several times overwhelmed with water, & threatened every moment with being dashed to pieces in the windings of the Rocks, and after arriving in the dreadfull whirlpool below, it remained a considerable time under water. At length however the Current drove it towards shore, with the men still hanging after it, and tho' they at first seemed insensible yet after a little assistance they recovered their strength, & before night renewed their labours, with as much alacrity as if nothing had happened them, a convincing proof of the force of their constitutions.

After the trader left the last portage on the Winnipeg River, apparently Manitou Rapids, he would see on his right the high round knoll on which stood the French Fort Maurepas of 1744, "not a vestige remaining except the clearing," as John Macdonell says in 1793 as he passes by. On the opposite side of the river, at the spot known as La Pointe aux Loutres, Otter Point, stood the first storehouse of the North West Company. About two miles farther down and on the left bank stood the post known as Bas de la Rivière Winipic (Bottom of the River Winnipeg) or Lesieur's Fort, built by Toussaint Lesieur in 1792 to replace the storehouse farther up. It was about forty rods above the later Fort Alexander and two and a half miles from the mouth of the river. There were few beaver in the region, yet from 1744 till the transfer of Rupert's Land to Canada in 1870, with but a break at the conquest of Canada, it was occupied by some post or other. The reason lay in its strategic position. It was at a point which called for provisioning the brigades coming and going. Bags of pemmican, 100 to 250 in number and weighing 90 pounds each, would be brought from the Assiniboine (" Red ") River in crude boats made for the purpose. In Alexander Henry the younger's day there was a " boat fort " on the opposite side of the river in which boats might be kept for the return voyage, but mostly they were burned for their nails, and new craft made next spring at the source of the pemmican.

The Rainy River Department of the North West Company remained comparatively free from competition. Rivals could with difficulty hold their own in a region depleted of furs, and in which provisions were not easily procured. A statement in a letter of Angus Shaw seems to say that in 1789 Lesieur and a Simon Fraser, who must be distinguished from the explorer of Fraser's River, were in partnership, and one of them at Portage de l'Isle. " I wish them joy of their bargain," says Shaw. In the spring their returns were counted among those of the North West Company. They must have been starved out or else won from their lonely venture by the attractions of a fixed salary from the Company.

Into this unpromising region the Hudson's Bay Company's servants came in 1793 and, all things considered, did tolerably well. James Sutherland and John MacKay entered the Winnipeg by the English River and turned upstream. Sutherland built on an expansion of the river about eight miles above the Forks, on the opposite side of the stream from a former North West Company's fort, presumably that of Simon Fraser. The post was called Portage de l'Isle, though the portage was actually some ten miles downstream and one and a half miles beyond the English River. Sutherland had the advantage of being there before the Canadians and of committing the Indians to his post by giving them " credit." About a fortnight later La Tour arrived to oppose him for the North West Company, building where his Company's former post had stood. He tried to make up for his lateness by abundant outpourings of rum. Two days after the Canadian's arrival, Sutherland wrote : " Mr. La Towers Brandy cock still running and exceeds all I have ever seen at any of our Settlements and scarcely receiving anything for it ; only a little Rice now and then." Canadians had reported La Tour as " near a mad man," and his frequent beating of his servants confirmed the characterization. Yet Sutherland got on well with him. He refused to receive the Canadian's servants, who sought to escape from maltreatment by their master by applying for employment with the English Company. La Tour must have been impressed by the regular reading of prayers on Sundays at the English post, otherwise Sutherland could scarcely have made the entry of 18th May in his Journal : " I Baptized his Son, a boy of about 3 years of age by the name of James, his father promising to see him brought up as a Christian at Montreal." Three weeks later Sutherland set off for Osnaburgh House with 18 packs, containing 1,500 beaver worth of furs, the returns of the post manned by ten men and the master.

John MacKay determined to settle on Rainy River, " one of the beautifullest rivers I ever saw in this Country." Before fixing on his site, he visited the North West Company's post below the outflow of the river from the lake. He was received by the master, Charles Boyer, with a salute, but did not return it. Yet the two men got on friendly terms. " Mr. Boyer seemed to be a Gentleman well qualified for this business ; he speaks the Indian language extremely well and is an excellent builder of Birch rind Canoes," he notes in his Journal. Boyer reported that he made but eighteen packs at his post during the previous season. MacKay returned down the river and settled immediately below the Manitou Rapids, where there is an Indian Reserve to-day. The attraction of the spot lay in its fishery, which exists to this day. The dispositions of the North West Company were already made, and MacKay held the field to himself, disturbed by no more than friendly visits from Northwesters, including Boyer, watching over their Indians.

MacKay spent the summer at Portage de l'Isle, where he was visited by the *bourgeois* of the North West Company on their journeys to and from Grand Portage—Alexander Mackenzie, John Macdonald of Garth, Duncan M'Gillivray, Angus Shaw, and others— and by David and Peter Grant, then in opposition on the Saskatchewan and on the Assiniboine, respectively. He had little more than grog to offer his visitors, and greatly relished a repast laid before him by the Northwesters returning from Grand Portage with the luxuries of Europe. " They treated me with French Brandy, Madeira & Port wine ; likewise with a dinner of ham, tongues, beef, venison & biscuit, which were very acceptable, as I live very poor at present, having nothing but what we procure ourselves, which would not be looked upon as victuals in any other country."

Leaving Edward Clouston in charge of Portage de l'Isle for the following season (1794–95), MacKay returned to Rainy River, but arranged to put out all his effort at a new house near the mouth of the river, while he resided at his former post. Boyer left Lac la Pluie in charge of Frederic Shultz and lodged himself immediately below MacKay, all unconscious that he was leaving the Englishman a free field below. The two English posts on the Canadian track must have done fairly well, considering the small number of men occupying them. Clouston left for Osnaburgh House in the spring with forty-seven packs of furs.

In the following season the English post on Portage de l'Isle was closed. It had originally taken the place of the post of Eschabitchewan on Ball Lake on the English River. Now that the Indians of Portage de l'Isle were brought into happy relations with the English, a return was made to the former region, which was only two days' journey to the east. The new post was built on Lake Wippenaban (Indian Lake) a little closer to Portage de l'Isle. The Company's Indians went over from the Portage to hunt for the fort.

MacKay removed to his house near the Lake of the Woods and

held his own there till the season 1796–97, when the North West Company made dispositions to drive him out : " There is no less than 5 traders opposing one another to oppose me." The returns of the five posts were estimated at 2,300, made beaver. MacKay took away 1,200, and said farewell to his misnamed post of Lac la Pluie.

The Hudson's Bay Company had a small post at Bas de la Rivière, in 1800, beside the North West Company's depot. Daniel Harmon, who had just entered the Canadian Company's service and was on his way to Swan River, made this entry in his Journal under date of August 6, 1800 : " I have visited the Hudson's Bay people, whose fort is but a few rods from ours. Mr. Miller, the gentleman who has charge of it, informed me that they obtain their goods from Albany Factory ; that, in going down with their barges they are generally about forty days ; but that they are nearly twice that time in returning, in consequence of the current." About a week later Alexander Henry the younger, on his way to the Red River, made entry in his Journal : " They have a clerk and two men who pass the summer here, but talk about throwing it up this fall, as a post will not pay expenses. Their object in settling was to make packages, but, from scarcity of beavers, they have been disappointed ; and have no occasion for a depot of provisions, as they bring their fall stock from Martin's falls." This is not wholly correct. Before the Company's servants had learned the art of preserving provisions, their cache at this point for the outcoming boats was spoiled by the damp in the soil. From 1795 men were left here to keep the pemmican in a dry house and to gather provisions to take the boats on to Brandon House, and at the same time to do a little trade. Later they remained through the winter. The post was closed in 1801.

THE TWO RED RIVERS, THE UPPER (THE ASSINIBOINE) AND LOWER

The Red River Department of the North West Company was strictly that of our Assiniboine which bore the name of Red River. The brigades, duly provisioned with pemmican, passed southwestward from the mouth of the River Winnipeg, entered the Red River by its middle channel and passed Nettley Creek, called Rivière aux Morts from a massacre of Saulteurs by the Sioux. It was probably the site of La Vérendrye's first Fort Maurepas. The passing trader might, like John Macdonell in 1793, remark on the site of Frobisher's fort half-way between the Creek and our St. Andrew's Rapids ; or at the Forks of the Red and the Assiniboine he might, like Alexander Henry the younger, point out the remains of an old French post (Fort Rouge). The Forks, the site of the city of Winnipeg, had no charm for the Northwesters. They were bound for the neighbourhood of the forest belt which skirted the northern border of the valley of the Assiniboine. They traded with such Indians as were assembled at the point, sending the canoes on to trace out the tedious sinuosities of the river, while " the gentlemen " walked or rode across the plains, hunting and killing meat for the next night's encampment of their brigade. As they got towards Poplar Point they would come on the ruins of a succession of ancient forts—Blondeau's; La Vérendrye's Fort la Reine; and Adhémar's. Further on they would pass a later Fort la Reine at our Portage la Prairie, wrongly attributed by Macdonell to Repentigny (Saint Pierre). About five miles above, they would recall with bated breath the tragedy of Fort des Trembles, for the traders never knew when the Indians of the Plains might break loose upon them. So far the Northwesters would only be passing the stamping-ground of the old Pedlars, men whose ventures were on a small scale, and who did not penetrate farther into the country than they could help. Now they would enter their own field and come to Pine Fort, built in 1768 on the north bank and just beyond Pine River, in our section 6, township 9, range 13, west of the principal meridian. While the freighted canoes passed on beyond the mouth of the River Qu'Appelle " the gentlemen " might, if it were 1787 or later, visit Fort Espérance, which stood on the right bank of Qu'Appelle River, below the Big Cut Arm Creek in SE¼ sect. 32, tp. 17, r. 30, W1. In the later 'eighties it was the favourite residence of the Partner of the Department, Robert Grant, its builder. Pine Fort and Fort Espérance were within the prairie. Great herds of buffalo might be seen from their bastions. During the winter the hunters of the fort and the Indians brought in fresh meat, dried meat, and " grease," *i.e.* fat from the back of the buffalo. The men of the forts would, save for the periods of dire scarcity to which every post was subject, live literally on the fat of the land. In the spring the grease would be melted and poured on the pounded dried meat in bags of buffalo hide capable of taking about ninety pounds. Boats would be built to convey these as the supplies for the various brigades passing to and fro at Bas de la Rivière Winipic. Of course these posts had their fur trade, but most of the furs were got far up the Assiniboine.

As the Northwesters ascended the river beyond the River Qu'Appelle, the beaver region to their right, at first limited by the Riding Hills and the Duck Mountains, would broaden out to include the valleys of the Swan and the Red Deer rivers. As David Thompson rode through this region in 1797, the ground was wet " from the many ponds kept full by Beaver Dams ; . . . these sagacious animals were in full possession, but their destruction had already begun and was now in full operation." Thompson went southward to " Cuthbert Grant's House," otherwise known as Aspin House, the English for Fort de la Rivière Tremblante. This, the " Upper Post," built by Robert Grant in 1791, was the great fur fort of the Department in the 'nineties, the pemmican being procured rather from the forts on the prairies to the south. Ruins on the east bank of the river—in section 10, township 28, range 31, west of the principal meridian, south-west of Togo, Saskatchewan—probably mark its site.

Until 1793 the North West Company had things all its own way, but then came the deluge. Two men by name Grant, Peter and David, had been in the Company's service in the 'eighties. In 1789 David had been offered £100 a year as clerk, but declined and withdrew. Cuthbert Grant, who had won his spurs in Athabaska, was brought in to replace him. Peter Grant must have aspired to the position of partner. When the agreement of 1790 was drawn up continuing the Company and his claims were ignored, he also withdrew and joined David in a private venture in opposition to their recent employers. Worse still, the Hudson's Bay Company was conducting an aggressive on a wide front. In 1793 the English-men came in from Albany Factory by way of the English River into the Winnipeg. Cuthbert Grant of the Red River Department and his clerk John Macdonell, who reports it in his Journal, got word of their presence from Indians below Portage de l'Isle. They left their brigade to follow on, and went after them in the proprietor's fast canoe. They had the good fortune to have a stiff wind in their favour passing through Bonnet Lake. At the lower end they came upon the men whom they chose to regard as intruders, "having done as much in two days as they had in ten," that is, with their boats. The English party was officered by Donald MacKay—whom the Northwesters later nicknamed *le malin*, the savage—and John Sutherland. It plodded on in its boats and two canoes and passed the Northwesters, who were visiting their friends at the "Bottom of the River Winnipeg." It was, however, overtaken at the St. Andrew's Rapids of the Red River.

But Peter Grant, the free-trader, was in before them all. He had built a fort at an unoccupied spot on the left bank of the Assiniboine, two miles above the mouth of the Souris River, and had left Ronald Cameron his clerk in charge, while he went on and built another, ten miles above the Forks of the Assiniboine and the Qu'Appelle rivers, probably at Silver Creek. John Macdonell left one Augé to build immediately above Cameron. Finally Donald MacKay arrived and built Brandon House, the first of that name, above the North West Company's post. Macdonell had proceeded to his quarters at Fort Espérance on the River Qu'Appelle in the neighbour-hood of the present Welby, Saskatchewan, the post built in 1787 by Robert Grant. From this point he provided an outfit for Augé. Thus there suddenly grew up three competing posts on the left bank of the Assiniboine two miles above the Souris River. (Their ruins were noted in 1890 by Mr. J. B. Tyrrell in NE¼, sect. 19, tp. 8, r. 18, W1.) The North West Company's post was called La Souris (sometimes Fort Assiniboine), this being the site of the first of that name. In the following summer Pine Fort, about eighteen miles overland and down the river, was abandoned in its favour. Mac-donell also equipped men and sent them down the Qu'Appelle from Fort Espérance to build beside the post of Peter Grant on the

Assiniboine about ten miles above the confluence of the two rivers. In February John Sutherland, for the Hudson's Bay Company, came overland with an outfit and lodged himself beside these two posts.

As if this was not opposition enough in the river valley, the " South Men "—that is, traders from Michilimackinac, who entered the valley of the Mississippi from Lake Superior at Fond du Lac and reached the Red River from the south—made their appearance.

The relations of Donald MacKay at Brandon House and the Northwester Augé, were far from easy. Donald had been trained in the more violent ways of the Pedlars, and believed that a show of violence was not out of place in this wild country. One evening in April he saw Augé pass upstream to an Indian who had taken " debts " at Brandon House. When the Northwester was returning at dark, he challenged him, but got no answer. When he threatened to shoot, the challenge was answered, but an order to come ashore was disregarded. MacKay then fired, as he asserted, in the air. The next day he was attacked in his room in the upper storey by three of Augé's Indians, but managed to throw them down the stairs. Yet the irascible MacKay was a friendly fellow. When the North West Company's winterers, Cuthbert Grant and John Macdonell, came down in May, he invited them to Brandon House and " passed a merry evening " with them ; he even accompanied them towards their fort. Invited in to take wine with them, he accepted. He had walked into a trap, for he was placed under detention, indeed placed in irons. Required to beg pardon of Augé, he refused. He was then told that Augé would kill him ; he replied by challenging the man to a fair duel there and then. Cuthbert Grant would not permit this. MacKay was allowed to go to his duties at the fort on the following day, on condition that he return. His reply was that his arrest was illegal and that he would not return. With that the incident was closed. That Donald's actions were felt not to be in keeping with the temperament of the Hudson's Bay Company, is suggested by the fact that he was not sent back to Brandon House. The MacKay who later figured so largely at that post was John, his younger brother, at this time at the post on Rainy River. Robert Goodwin was given the charge for the following season (1794–95), with John Sutherland for second.

That winter (1794–95) Cuthbert Grant informed Angus Shaw of Fort George on the Saskatchewan, by the winter express, that his opponents were very numerous, giving him no less than fourteen posts to oppose. These, with seven belonging to his own company, amounted in all to twenty-one forts on the " Red River." Peter Grant had come in with four canoes, and the Hudson's Bay Company with five boats, and the adventure of the South Men from Michilimackinac had employed seventeen canoes. There were the three posts two miles above the Souris River. Then, too, Peter Grant built at la Rivière Coquille (our Shell River). Cuthbert Grant forthwith built beside him. Peter Fidler's survey of 1808 places these posts on the left bank of the Assiniboine one mile below Shell River. In the late autumn John Sutherland came upstream and built over against them, so that here also there were three rival posts.

One of the ways by which the North-westers were able to worst their rivals was by building additional posts. With a large retinue of servants and plenty of goods, they could thus force their opponents to the expense of maintaining a whole row of posts. Macdonell re-opened Fort Montagne à la Bosse (Hump Mountain), " frequently established and as often abandoned," as he says. It stood immedi-ately east of Gopher Creek in sect. 11 or 12, tp. 10, r. 25, W1, some three miles north of Routledge on the Canadian Pacific Railway. Peter Grant felt it necessary to build beside it. The value of the posts here lay in their position close to wintering-grounds of the buffalo. Their returns were largely in provisions. Goodwin, master at the Hudson's Bay Company's Brandon House, could not provide the men for an additional rival house here. In any case, he was getting the provisions necessary for his comparatively small crew, and did not have to provide supplies for northern brigades as did the Canadians. But when the North West Company built at Portage la Prairie, with William McKay in charge, he sent a party down under William Linklater to build beside him, for furs came in at that point from the White Mud River and the bush country towards Lake Dauphin.

The Northwesters had other means at their disposal than building forts. With men who knew the Indian languages in their service, they could send parties out *en derouine*, as it was called, as Pedlars trading with the Indians in their camps and often getting the furs as soon as killed. Here the Hudson's Bay Company was seriously handicapped, for few of its men, as yet, knew the Indian tongue.

Among the twenty-one posts referred to by Cuthbert Grant would be those on the Swan and Red Deer rivers, which were in the part of his Department from which the majority of the furs were secured. In 1787 the North West Company had built on the left bank of Swan River about twelve miles above Swan Lake. Three years later Charles Price Isham had come in from York Fort and built for the Hudson's Bay Company on the right bank about one-eighth of a mile above Grant's house. In 1793 Grant built upstream near Thunder or Bird (strictly Thunderbird) Mountain to cut the furs off from the English Swan River House. In the following year Isham replied by building Somerset House two miles above it and near the confluence of Thunder Creek and the Swan River. Thus there were four forts in this river valley. Not content with this, Isham took goods in by pack-horse from Swan River to the Elbow of the Assini-boine, and built Marlboro House there, very near the later Fort Pelly. Add to these the posts of the North West Company and those of the South Company, which, according to Peter Fidler, built over against the Hudson's Bay Company's Swan River House and their Somerset House ; possibly also a South Company's post on the Red Deer River beside the North West Company's, opposite the mouth of the Etoimami, where there are the remains of a second post unaccounted for. As if this was not chaos enough, forts were multiplied on the upper Assiniboine. In the following year (1795–96) the North West Company had built Fort Alexandria, about sixteen miles overland westward from the Elbow. Isham abandoned Marlboro House and built Fort Carlton a hundred yards from it. There were still three forts at Shell River, and the three near the Souris River became four when Barkey, for the South Men, built between Brandon House and the North West Company's Fort la Souris.

Things became crazier still in 1796, when the Brandon House outrunners under Sutherland abandoned Shell River, ascended the Assiniboine to the Elbow, and built Albany House, a mile above the abandoned Marlboro House. There were now two forts of the Hudson's Bay Company, one supplied from Albany and the other from York Fort, within fifteen miles of one another, and necessarily interfering with one another's trade—this at a crisis when, on account of European wars, the English Company had difficulties in recruiting servants and when its plan to take the aggressive in that richest of all the fur fields, Athabaska, was being postponed for lack of men. Nothing could show more patently the shortcoming of the Hudson's Bay Company scheme of leaving each Governor to follow his own devices in his sphere, without consulting his colleagues. In the struggle with such a highly co-ordinated body of men as was the North West Company, there was a crying need for something like a general staff, surveying the whole field and taking the aggressive where the greatest results could be attained, and preventing all overlapping.

This year there were five posts on the upper Assiniboine within a stretch of sixteen miles as the crow flies—the North West Company's Alexandria and York Fort's Carlton House ; three miles to the east the North West Company's and Peter Grant's houses ; and at the Elbow, Albany House. Yet Sutherland got twenty-three packs of furs, ninety pound each, at this last post. The situation became easier in 1796–97 when Grant's opposition ceased and when York Fort abandoned its posts on the Swan River and the Assiniboine in the spring of 1800. There were now but three interests in this fur region—the North West Company, the Hudson's Bay Company, and the " South Men," whose posts for the most part elude the historian's grasp.

The most permanent feature in the landscape was the group of posts two miles above the confluence of the Souris and the Assiniboine. For thirty years there were posts at or near this point, due to its strategical position. An interesting feature in their trade was their traffic with the Mandans on the Missouri River. It could not bear the cost of maintaining forts in those distant parts. It remained to the end a trade of Pedlars who dared the difficult and dangerous *traverse* across the prairies. All the companies engaged in it. There were years when the volume of furs at Brandon House was kept up by the profitable returns of the outfits to the Mandan country. In 1797 David Thompson crossed the open prairies from the North West Company's Fort la Souris, in the dead of winter, to ascertain the relation of the Missouri to the International Boundary. He has left in his *Narrative*, published by the Champlain Society, a very important, if brief, account of the Mandans and their history. The interesting life of this people—their villages, their social life, and their lascivious ceremonies—brought the traders, for example Alexander Henry the younger in 1806, across the plains simply for diversion.

Next to the posts above the Souris, the North West Company's Fort Espérance ranks as more permanent than its fellows. Built in 1787 by Robert Grant, it figured in 1816 in the struggle with Lord Selkirk, and was only replaced at the Union of 1821, when its rival, the Hudson's Bay Company's Beaver Creek House, twenty miles to the south-east, near the later Fort Ellice, filled its place in the united company.

Most of the fur-traders who figured in the period under observation—Robert Grant and Cuthbert Grant of the North West Company, and Peter Grant the free-trader—are little more than names in the history of the West. Because of his journals John Macdonell comes more clearly into view. His Journal of the voyage from Lachine to Fort Espérance gives a detailed account of the route from the point of view of an interested young fur-trader going to take a position in the Upper Country. Its continuation as the *Red River Journal* and his sketch of the " Red River " make him of considerable importance to the historian. Quartered mostly at Fort Espérance, he was at Fort la Souris when David Thompson was equipped there in 1797 for his journey to the Mandans. In 1799 he became a wintering partner. Big John Macdonell, as he was called, was the brother of Miles Macdonell, the first Governor of Lord Selkirk's colony. His love of the prairie country was such that on retiring in 1812 he contemplated taking land in the colony and settling there with his half-breed wife and family.

John MacKay of the Hudson's Bay Company's Brandon House reveals himself in the Journals of his post as an intelligent and successful trader, and able, while serving his employers well, to win the respect of his opponents by his even temper and humane disposition. His son, John Richard MacKay, and his grandson William, served the Company with distinction in their respective generations.

Another efficient servant of the Company, John Sutherland of Albany House, deserves mention because of the virtues of his squaw. When occasion called for it, she contributed to the success of the post by her skill and industry in curing skins and making pemmican. Yet she must have been somewhat of a " high-brow " among her fellows. After a visit, the Northwester Daniel Harmon of Fort Alexandria sang her praises in his Journal : " He has a woman of this country for a wife, who, I am pleased to find can speak the English language tolerably well. I understood also that she can both read and write it, which she learned to do at Hudson's Bay,

where the Company has a school. She speaks likewise the Cree and
Saulteux languages. She appears to possess natural good sense, and
is far from deficient, in acquired knowledge."

The present Red River was given little consideration by the
earliest fur-traders. They passed it by in favour of the Assiniboine,
with its fine combination of buffalo meat secured from the prairies
to the south, and furs secured in the forest belt to the north. However, it was frequented by the " South Men," who came in through
the United States and penetrated to the Assiniboine and accentuated
the opposition there. Before 1789 Peter Grant, then a clerk in the
service of the North West Company, built a fort on the right bank
of the Red (near the present St. Vincent, Minnesota) opposite the
mouth of its tributary, the Pembina River—Alexander Henry says
" the First establishment ever built on the Red River." In 1789
he was on Red Lake (Minnesota), drained by a river of the same name
into the Red River. In 1796 Charles Chaboillez built a fort on the
Rat River, which flows into the Red twenty-two miles above the
Forks (the site of Winnipeg to-day). The following year he transferred his post to the south side of the mouth of the Pembina River,
where the town of Pembina now stands and opposite Grant's old
site. Here David Thompson, on his mission placing the forts of the
North West Company in their exact relation to the International
Boundary, visited him in 1798. Thompson, by observation, found
the fort to be in lat. 48° 58′ 29″ N., and therefore south of the
border. From this, as the central fort, many parties were sent out
over a wide area to the south, in what is now American territory.
Their outposts, apart from gathering furs, acted as a screen thrown
out to protect the sacred precincts of the North West Company
from the aggressions of the " South Men." One such was at the
mouth of the Salt River (North Dakota). Another stood at the
confluence of the Clearwater and Red Lake rivers in Minnesota, close
to the present site of Red Lake Falls.

THE BASIN OF LAKE WINNIPEG

Lake Winnipeg was not of special interest to the fur-traders save
as a water-way along which, with an anxious eye for its treacherous
storms, they moved to their wintering-grounds. The country immediately west was, however, a good region. Three small brigades,
passing northward from the depot at the " Bottom of the River
Winnipeg," left the lake by the Dauphin (the Little Saskatchewan)
River and passed through Lake St. Martin to Lake Manitoba, which
they would cross to its north-westerly extremity. Here Meadow
Portage would lead them into Lake Winnipegosis. Across the lake
in the westerly direction is the inflow of the Mossy River which
drains Lake Dauphin. La Vérendrye's Fort Dauphin had been on
the right bank of the river about three-quarters of a mile upstream,
where the remains of several forts may be seen. Judging by Peter

Pond's rude map of 1790, his Fort Dauphin was at the north-west angle of Dauphin Lake. The sites of the post continued to be changed. In 1797 David Thompson waited four days at Meadow Portage for a canoe of his brigade to go up to the fort and return to the mouth of the river. The post must have then stood, as on his map, on the left bank of a stream flowing into Lake Dauphin from the south— probably the Valley River where Mr. J. B. Tyrrell found remains on the right bank about two miles in a direct line from the lake. This may well have been the site of Peter Pond's post. In 1800 Daniel Harmon places the North West Company's establishment at the mouth of the Mossy River, facing Meadow Portage and at the site of the old French fort. The XY Company, possibly the South Men before it, built beside or over against this post.

The two other brigades would pass on from Prairie Portage and glide to the northern end of Lake Winnipegosis and then westward. The one would enter Shoal River to the south for the Swan River district, while the other would keep to the north-west and ascend the Red Deer River. The forts on these two rivers flowing through the forest region north of the Assiniboine have been mentioned in connection with the Assiniboine.

THE WOODED NORTH—THE RAT COUNTRY

The North West Company's large brigades of canoes—for the Saskatchewan Forts des Prairies, for the English (Churchill) River Department, and for Athabaska—were provisioned at the " Bottom of River Winnipeg " with Red River pemmican for the voyage to Cumberland House. At times the storms on Lake Winnipeg stayed their course till their provisions were about exhausted, when the journey up the Saskatchewan would be made on starvation allowances. In fine weather the lake became a sort of race-course on which the Athabaska brigade, in the best of form after its long and arduous journey, gloried in the display of its superiority over the others. In 1794 this " Northern brigade " challenged the Fort des Prairies men, as Duncan M'Gillivray tells us.

Our people were well aware of the disadvantages they laboured under (being about ⅓ heavier loaded than their opponents) but they could not swallow the haughtiness and contempt with which they thought themselves treated, and tho' they could flatter themselves with no hopes of success from the event yet they resolved to dispute the Victory, with the greatest obstinacy that their opposers might not obtain it without the sweat of their brows. In consequence of this determination the two bands instead of camping according to orders, entered the lake at sunset, the one animated with the expectation of victory, and the other resolved if possible, not to be vanquished. They pursued the voyage with unremitting efforts without any considerable advantage on either side for 48 hours during which they did not once put ashore, till at length, being entirely overcome with labour and fatigue, they mutually agreed to camp where we found them, and cross the Lake together. . . . On the second night of the contest one of our steersmen being overpowered with sleep fell out of the stern of his canoe which being under sail advanced a considerable distance before the people could recover from the confusion that this accident occasioned ; in the meantime the poor fellow almost sinking with the weight of his cloathes cried out to 2 canoes that happened to pass within a few yards of him to save his life *pour l'amour de dieu* ; but neither the love of God or of the blessed Virgin, whom he powerfully called to his assistance, had the least influence on his hard-hearted countrymen who paddled along with the greatest unconcern, and he must have certainly perished if his own canoe had not returned time enough to prevent it.

The brigades passed up the Saskatchewan, portaging three miles past the Grand Rapids near its mouth and crossing Cedar Lake. At times they lost their way in the many muddy channels of the river in the region above. During the early days, when the men from Montreal were reaping golden harvests by simply lodging themselves on the lines of the Indian trade to York Factory, the west end of Cedar Lake was a favourite site for forts, and Pasquia, the spot known to-day as The Pas, was of great importance. Now that the struggle with the English Company was centred far up the Saskatchewan, these regions had lost their importance. Until 1793 Pasquia enjoyed a lingering interest in the eyes of the Northwesters, for at some spot in the neighbourhood, revealed only to the guides, the pemmican from the Forts des Prairies lay cached to take the brigades to their destination. Failure to discover the cache one year made other arrangements necessary. Accordingly, in 1793, under William M'Gillivray's directions, a depot was built at the narrows of Cumberland Lake, but the Company decreed a post called Cumberland House, beside the Hudson's Bay Company's post of that name. Here the pemmican from the Saskatchewan was stored to provision the northern brigades going out to the Bottom of Lake Winnipeg and all the brigades going in to their wintering-grounds.

The Athabaska and English River brigades would make their way north-eastward through Cumberland and our Namew lakes, at that time thought of as one, to the Sturgeon-Weir River, the Rivière Maligne of the voyageurs. At its confluence with the Goose or, as the Northwesters called it, the Rat River, a portion of the English River brigade would pass up the latter to what David Thompson calls the Muskrat country—"Les Rats" of the voyageurs.

Strictly the Muskrat country lay east of the Sturgeon-Weir and between the Nelson and the Churchill, but the earlier fur-traders of the region linked up the lower valley of the Churchill as far as Reindeer lake with it. The Indians here had long had close relations with the English at York Factory, for they could pass down the Grass River route, or down the Burntwood River through the lake of that name and Three Point Lake to Split Lake on the Nelson, and so to the factory. An interesting struggle between the North West and the Hudson's Bay companies for the peltries of the region began in 1783. The region was sparsely populated ; small groups of Indians gathered in autumn and in spring at points favoured with a fishery. The plan was to send in a single canoe to winter at one of these places of assembly and gather from the Indians the furs of their hunting-ground. In time a succession of small forts lay on the various water routes. When in 1786 Malchom Ross followed the water-way from Churchill Fort to Cumberland House, he got first news of a Canadian house on the Churchill, when he was near the confluence of that river with the Kississing, the Forks of William M'Gillivray's Journal of 1789. It would be the post on Pukkatawagan Lake three and three-quarter miles above the falls, the building of which David Thompson attributes to Mr. Baldwin. The post stood, according to Thompson, on the north shore near the entrance to an arm of the lake. Ross reports Louis Primo, formerly with the Hudson's Bay Company, as in charge for the summer and awaiting the arrival of the season's canoe. Proceeding up the Kississing River, he met the expected canoe under the command of " Jurial Baldwin," who asserted that his Company had taken 13,000 skins out of the Muskrat country in the spring. Baldwin's post on Pukkatawagan Lake was probably newly built, for Ross passed the house occupied by him during the previous winter on Lake Kississing. Portaging from the upper waters of the Kississing into a stream flowing towards the Saskatchewan, Ross passed through Athapapuskow Lake and entered the Grass River track from York Fort at its outflow. Here he got word that another Canadian canoe had gone down the Grass River route towards York Fort. Its destination was probably the first house on Reed Lake, which David Thompson places at its west end. In one of its earliest years William M'Gillivray was at this post, according to David Thompson. Mr. Patrick Small must have been the first Northwester in these parts, for the river flowing out of Athapapuskow Lake into Goose Lake was known as Mr. Small's River.

In the year 1787 the union of the Gregory–McLeod–Pangman–Mackenzie concern with the North West Company took place. A superfluity of officers and men must have been one of the results. Hence an aggressive into the Rat Country. Alexander Mackenzie wrote Roderick Mackenzie, who was to winter at Ile-à-la-Crosse :

I now enclose you sundry papers which you will peruse with Mr. Thomson [Robert Thompson]. You will advise him to be cautious in every respect where he is going to. The English are badly inclined. They told me that if I should send any men to the place where *La Grosse Tête* had passed the winter, M. Thomason [William Tomison] would go himself at the head of a party, seize upon the goods, take the men prisoners, and send all to Hudson Bay, adding, if any resistance was offered, that no mercy would be shown. But Mr. Thomason was not then aware of the coalition of the two companies, and I did not think proper to tell him of it. However Mr. Robert Thomson ought to build a fort this Fall.

This, as it proved, was no more than bluster on the part of a faithful guardian of the interest of the English Company. It was a fresh assertion of the rights conferred by the Charter.

The situation in 1789–90 is brought into clear light by the Journal of William M'Gillivray. After his apprenticeship under Robert Grant on the Assiniboine, he was entrusted with the post on Reed Lake in the Rat River region. Thereafter he was at Pukkatawagan Lake on the Churchill, reached by the Kississing route, and had La Grosse Tête as one of his chief Indian traders. Thompson was to go to Reed Lake. However, he passed beyond and built an outpost at " Lac d'Outard." Judging by the number of his portages, this may have been Paint Lake, where we find William McKay in 1792–94.

M'Gillivray's may be taken as a typical post in the northern forest. Indians were few. But forty men, all told, came to the autumn muster at the fort and were equipped for the hunt. Whole weeks might pass without a savage trader appearing. After the muster the Indians scattered to hunt in bands of not more than a tent or two. If venison was killed, a messenger came in, often several days' travel, to the post, and men were sent out to bring it in. Trusted servants were assigned to bands whose fidelity was doubtful, to stimulate them to hunt, and to see that their peltries came in to M'Gillivray, who had equipped them on credit. In the dead of winter M'Gillivray himself took a journey of six days each way to within a day of Portage du Traite. He visited the various bands and urged them to industry. Twice during the winter letters passed between him and Mr. Robert Thompson, who was six days' journey to the east. Relations with the savages were happy, and M'Gillivray, with a very few men, could live among them without occasions of alarm. In truth the White Men were welcomed and cherished by the savages, for their guns and ammunition, and their iron implements greatly lightened the task of securing food and furs. Then, too, there was rum, a great incentive to friendship, and to industry, as the Northwesters professed to believe.

M'Gillivray says that half of the Indians at the autumn muster at his post had been to the English Factory at Hudson Bay that summer. They had, of course, been equipped on credit, and were reluctant to trade their furs with him. " I am afraid they will wish to go and pay in the Spring. However, if they do, it will be because I cannot prevent them, as I shall use promises and menaces (if Goods fail) to deter them from their purposes." He adds that the Indians might never trouble themselves as to when they might pay their " credits," that were they seven years absent from the Bay they would carry their peltries, due to the English, before they died. " They are naturally lazy and great ivrognes [drunkards] & when they can get Rum so near they'll hardly go a greater distance for it." What with plentiful outpourings of rum, and considerable bullying of the Indians, M'Gillivray's winter was a successful one—to a large extent at the expense of the Hudson's Bay Company. He left after the usual spring muster for trade, with two large canoes and one small one loaded, indeed overloaded, with peltries—fifty-eight packs and six kegs of Castorum in all.

M'Gillivray's post cut off the trade of the Crees going down from the Churchill to the English at the Bay. He had hoped to get also possession of the furs of the Chipewyans, north of the river, who used to go across the Barrens to Fort Churchill. In this he was disappointed, for that timid people were afraid to come to him into the Cree country.   A few did actually arrive, and M'Gillivray made arrangements with them to build on Reindeer Lake (Lac des Caribou) next year.   The site of this post is indicated by David Thompson as on the point on the west shore two miles east of the mouth of the Paint, our Vermilion River.   Life at this post in a most desolate region must have been very trying, and the site was soon abandoned, but it may well have served its purpose by making connections with the Chipewyans passing far to the north over the Barrens to Fort Churchill.   Connections once made, they could be drawn down to the forts built later at the outflow of the Reindeer River from the lake.   After a third winter in the Rat Country, M'Gillivray bought Peter Pond's share in the Company and became Wintering Partner in charge of the whole English River Department, with Ile-à-la-Crosse for headquarters.

Of the traders in the Muskrat Country in these early times David Thompson alone is remembered.   He traced out most of the water-ways of the region.   Though the Grass River route from York Factory was frequented and even described long before him, the cross-route from Reed Lake by the File River into the Burntwood River, the course by that river from the Nelson to the Churchill, and finally the route from the Churchill by the Reindeer River and Lake, and by the Black River to the eastern shore of Athabaska Lake, were first traced by him and the country described.   It is said that mining companies interested in those parts pay large sums for copies of his *Narrative*, skilfully edited by Mr. J. B. Tyrrell, who has himself explored many of the water-ways described.

David Thompson was born in Westminster in 1770 of humble parents.   Left an orphan when but two years old, he had the good fortune to be placed in the Grey Coat school there, by the intervention of a kindly gentleman.   It had been the custom of the Hudson's Bay Company from early in the eighteenth century to look to that charitable institution for promising lads to be apprenticed and trained for the office of " writer " or accountant in the overseas service.   Thompson was chosen for his knowledge of mathematics, probably because the Company was taking a more pronounced interest in the surveying of its territory and intended to have him trained with that end in view.   In May 1784 he sailed for the new Churchill Fort, built after the destruction of the stone Prince of Wales's Fort by the French two years before.   There he spent his first winter overseas, with no very definite task assigned to him. He spent the following season at York Fort, assisting the accountant and learning at once to be writer and trader.   His *Narrative* shows that at this early stage he was deeply interested in the phenomena of nature and in the plant and animal life around him.   A year later he was fitted out with " a trunk, a handkerchief, shoes, shirts, a gun, powder, and a tin pot or cup," and sent off, one of a band of forty-six under Robert Longmoor, bound for the posts on the Saskatchewan.   He was placed under Mitchell Oman at the South

Branch House, on the South Saskatchewan, some ninety miles north of Saskatoon. The Journal of the post for that year is in his boyish hand, and ends : "This Journal kept by David Thompson." He spent the summer of 1787 at Hudson House, and was assigned to Manchester House for the following winter. On 9th October he was sent out, one of a band of fourteen, to winter among the Piegans, " to endeavour to learn the language." He learned much more, for he afterwards embodied in his *Narrative* precious information on the manner of life and the early history of the Piegans. After another summer at Hudson House, he had the misfortune to have his leg crushed against a log by a sled, apparently as he came down the mouth of the Big Gully opposite Manchester House. This was in December. For long the fracture defied what surgical skill that old fur-trader William Tomison could muster for its treatment, and only in the following summer did the bones appear to have grown together. This accident closed the door for the time being to a development which was wholly in keeping with the genius of the young man. The Company had arranged for Philip Turnor to spend the winter of 1789–90 at Cumberland House, and to train Thompson in survey-ing, to be his companion and assistant during his journey to Atha-baska. The young man proved an intelligent pupil, but during the course of the winter it became apparent that his leg could not stand the strain of the journey, and Peter Fidler was hastily summoned from the South Branch House, for a short course in surveying, and to take his place. The extent of Thompson's grief may be judged by the ungenerous grudge against Fidler which he appears to have harboured for many years. After another winter at Cumberland House, and one at York Fort, he was placed under William Hemmings Cook, master at Chatham House in the Rat Country, and his career as an explorer and surveyor began in earnest. It was the misfortune of David Thompson that there were conflicting views within the service of the Hudson's Bay Company. William Tomison, as Chief Inland, was straining every nerve to uphold the Company's cause on the Saskatchewan. Joseph Colen, in charge of York Fort, was greatly concerned at the inroads of the Northwesters into the Rat region, the home country of his fort. The Committee in London stood for occupying Athabaska, the richest of all the fur regions. Had an adequate number of servants been sent out during the previous years, these three objectives might have all been reached, but the Committee found it impossible to get them. With too few men, particularly with too few experienced men, there had to be a choice between these policies. The men on the ground naturally threw their forces into the struggle near at hand, and David Thomp-son, who had set his heart on exploration, found himself greatly hampered.

In 1790 the Committee's policy held the field, and Philip Turnor, who had been sent out for the purpose, spent the winters of 1790–91 and 1791–92 in a preliminary exploration of the route to Athabaska and Great Slave Lake. Meanwhile Joseph Colen was able to develop his policy of occupying the fur region immediately south and west of York Fort. The North West Company had built on Cross Lake and Lake Sipiwesk, and William McKay was in a post on Paint Lake, thus occupying the immediate hinterland of York Fort. In the autumn of 1790 Colen sent in James Spence to build on Split Lake. The post was called Lake's House after the Governor of the Company. He placed his fort at the inflow of the Burntwood River. The next year Colen sent William Cook in to oppose McKay. He built Chatham House on Wintering Lake near by. McKay countered by building a small post beside Cook's to keep the Indians from going to him. In the following summer, 1792, Turnor got back to Cumberland House, and it was the intention to send a trading expedition to Athabaska in 1793 or 1794. While at York Fort waiting for his ship, Turnor undertook to escort Indians with goods to Chatham House, and incidentally to survey the route. On his return he met Spence at the mouth of the Burntwood River and got information as to its course.

The Indians say it is navigable up to a carrying-place which leads into the Churchill River. If it should be found practicable to get up this river into the Churchill water, it would miss the part of the Churchill which is reported to be so bad and would be a much nearer way to Isle-à-la-Crosse than by the way of Cumberland House ; besides there is some reason to expect a passage will be found into the East end of Athapiscow Lake by the way of the Deers [Reindeer] Lake.

This led to the determination to find a short water-way to Athabaska, by Reindeer Lake, to be all the Company's own.

Colen, doubtless to ingratiate himself with the Committee, instructed David Thompson to explore the Nelson and the proposed route to Athabaska. The natural course would have been to send him up the Burntwood River, say to the region of the North West Company's post on Pukkatawagan Lake on the Churchill, to winter there, midway between York Fort and Lake Athabaska, and to get into relation with Indians who might act as guides for the remainder of the way to Athabaska. But Colen was not interested in the Athabaska project, nor inclined to send his men to oppose Canadian posts which were cutting into the Churchill trade. His concern was the trade of York Fort. Thus while instructing Thompson to explore for the route he sent him, as has been seen, under William Hemmings Cook of Chatham House, out of the way up the Nelson to Sipiwesk Lake. Thompson chose a promontory on the north shore of the lake for his winter quarters, and doubtless supported his chief in opposing Mr. McKay. Nothing daunted by the stupid disposition of him by Colen, Thompson set off from Lake Sipiwesk in the spring, equipped out of the slender resources of his post. He overcame the disadvantage of his starting-point by journeying by devious streams to the Burntwood River. He took the Cross Portage from Sipiwesk Lake to Sabomin Lake, portaged from it to Landing Lake, and thence took his " Thickwood Carrying Place," our Thicket Portage, to Chatham House, which stood before him at the extremity and on the southern shore of a peninsula which extends from the west far into the Wintering Lake. From the west end of the northerly arm of the lake he entered a creek and portaged from it into Paint Lake, on the Grass River route. McKay's post stood on the left of Thompson's first course on the lake, within a mile and a half of the portage. By a series of streams and portages Thompson got into the Burntwood River track at his Pipestone (our Pipe) Lake. He had at last reached the water-way whose exploration was his object. Passing upward through Three Points and Burntwood lakes to the source of the river, he crossed a portage of 1,705 yards into the Kississing River, the track of the Canadians, and into the waters of the Churchill. He now ascended the Churchill, portaged past the Pukkatawagan Falls into the lake of that name, noting Baldwin's house on his right about three and three-quarter miles to the west, and at the entrance to something like a lake. Taking the southerly arm of the Churchill, known as Duck Lake, he steered for Duck Portage, which would bring him back into the Churchill, and noted White's House, an outpost from the North West Company's Pukkatawagan House, one and a half miles east of the portage. Pressing on up the Churchill, he reached Reindeer River, and ascended it to a point said by his guide to be within four days of the lake. He had covered something more than half the distance to Lake Athabaska, but was without provisions and no guide could be procured. What a difference it would have made to have had the Churchill for his starting-point! He was forced to retrace his steps, and reached the Nelson River by the Burntwood, and so to York Fort. Even though he had had to make his way across the Muskrat Country to do it, he had gone a long way on the route to Athabaska. Incidentally he had shown that Canadians had not yet penetrated to the Burntwood River.

An expedition to Athabaska was ordered by the Committee for 1794. Malchom Ross, Turnor's companion, was to be in charge, and Peter Fidler and David Thompson with him. The party was to be equipped at Cumberland House. Thompson was sent up to Buckingham House to survey the Saskatchewan, and to return to Cumberland House in time for the start. Malchom Ross wintered at Cumberland and, to procure provisions for the expedition, went up to Nipawi to organize the Indians for a buffalo hunt. But there were two Canadian posts there, David Grant's under a Mr. James Porter, and the North West Company's under A. N. McLeod. No Indians could be got, and Ross returned with an empty hand. When the time came for choosing the servants to go to Athabaska, the men at Cumberland House refused to go. Colen laid the blame on William Tomison, Chief Inland. Fundamentally the difficulty lay in the lack of experienced servants. When the expedition to the North fell through, Ross and Thompson took a canoe of trading goods at Cumberland House and went off to winter in the Rat Country. They went in by the Cranberry Portage to Reed Lake, where Thompson left Ross to build while he took furs down to York Fort and brought up goods. As he went on he noted " White's house," a quarter of a mile from the Crooked River (Little Swan), which he took northward to get into the Burntwood water-way. In Limestone Lake he found Hudson's Bay Company's men from Fort Churchill established near the tip of the promontory which runs far northward into the lake. Apparently the Fort Churchill people were not averse to entering the domain of York Factory, if only they could keep up the volume of furs passing through their post, which was being diminished by the aggressive of the Northwesters in the Rat Country and in Athabaska. In Burntwood Lake Thompson passed the North West Company's post in which Robert Thompson had spent the previous winter. On the next lake, Three Points Lake, he found Mr. William Sinclair of the Hudson's Bay Company's service at Churchill building. He himself returned from York Factory by the Grass River through Paint Lake, where William McKay had wintered, to Reed Lake House, to Mr. Ross. The post was in lat. 54° 36′ 17″ on the south shore, south of the mouth of the narrows made by a large island. The North West Company abandoned White's House and built over against the English post.

The Hudson's Bay Company had not in the meantime given up the search for a route of its own to Lake Athabaska. If the exploration was denied to Thompson, it was entrusted to Peter Fidler, his fellow-scholar under Turnor. Fidler had been with Turnor to Lake Athabaska. In 1793 he was at York Factory, whence he was sent to Churchill Fort to explore the Seal River north of Fort Churchill, in the hope that its water-way would lead directly west to the desired goal. Fidler discovered, as his map shows, that that route turned southward and led into the Churchill at South Indian Lake. He surveyed the Churchill to its mouth, but that river was too difficult to become a highway to the West, though it was used for the outposts from Churchill Fort. Thompson's discontent with the Hudson's Bay Company was probably increased when Fidler was given the task which had been in the first place assigned to him. At any rate, when these two passed one another on the Churchill River route in 1805 they did not speak.

It has been seen that William M'Gillivray in 1790 proposed building on Reindeer Lake to win the trade of the Chipewyans, who passed across the Barren Grounds to trade at Churchill Fort. The post was built on the west shore of the lake, two miles east of the Vermilion River. It was occupied for no more than two or three years. In 1793 the North West Company built on a lake which might be regarded rather as the extreme southerly limit of the lake, doubtless drawing the Chipewyans down to it. Messrs. Simon Fraser the elder and Alexander Fraser occupied it. But for Joseph Colen's interest in the region immediately in the rear of York Fort the Hudson's Bay Company might have been here in 1792. It was not till 1795 that reasonable steps were taken to establish a post from which the exploration to Lake Athabaska could be carried out with some prospect of success. In that year

Thompson and Ross were detailed to build on the Churchill. Thompson built on Duck lake, a short distance south of Duck Portage; the North West Company followed him, and, abandoning the old site on the north shore of the lake, built a small outpost beside him. To make things worse a party from Fort Churchill occupied the same ground for a part of the winter. Ross built Fairford House, about a mile east of the confluence of the Reindeer River with the Churchill. In the following spring Thompson started from Fairford House with an equipment, largely of his own devising, to find the much-desired route to the eastern extremity of Lake Athabaska for his Company. He passed up Reindeer River, and over a portage to its expansion below Reindeer Lake, noting the house occupied by the Frasers on his right. Following the western shore of Reindeer Lake itself, he passed the old Canadian post and came to our Canoe River, which he followed to Wollaston Lake. Thence he ran downstream by " Black River," our River Fond du Lac, through Hatchet and Black lakes, to the point on Athabaska Lake to which Turnor had surveyed. On the way home, through his Indians being inexpert with canoes, he was carried over a cascade and almost drowned. He found the region a land without inhabitants or game, at least at that time of the year when the caribou would be on the Barrens, so that he almost succumbed to starvation. A fortunate meeting with Indians who had a little meat supply enabled him to reach Fairford House in safety. Thompson had found a route to Lake Athabaska which the English Company might have for its own. It was not as easy as was desirable, for the Canoe River from Reindeer Lake to Wollaston Lake was extremely shallow. Supposing that it could be used, it would be necessary to secure provisions by the way for the passing craft. It was probably to make certain of this and, if the prospects proved good, to form a station on the route, that Ross and Thompson returned that autumn and built Bedford House on the western shore of the lake on Vermilion Point, a conspicuous pine-clad promontory south of the old Canadian Post. The plan brought nothing but disappointment. The country was little frequented by moose or caribou and wellnigh untrodden by man. The fishery provided no more than a bare existence. What with the difficulties of the water-way itself and the impossibility of securing provisions by the way, no attempt was made to use it.

In the following spring David Thompson's contract with the Company lapsed. Disappointed at his experiences at the hand of Colen, and without faith in his future with the Company, he left Bedford House on foot and arrived at a new house built by the Canadians the previous autumn at the outlet of the lake, doubtless to be nearer to the English post, and there offered his services to the North West Company. In this Thompson, for all his disappointments, was scarcely fair to the Hudson's Bay Company. After all, he owed his training as a surveyor to the Company which had placed him under Philip Turnor. The set of surveying instruments which he took away with him was a gift from the Committee " for his sole use and benefit," and after his last exploration his salary had been raised to sixty pounds.

Thompson reached Grand Portage in July 1797, at a very favourable juncture. Jay's treaty of 1794 had prescribed the surrender of the Western Posts to the Americans and foreshadowed their occupation of their territory up to the boundary fixed by the treaty of 1783. Grand Portage itself was on American ground. What of other posts occupied by the North West Company? Thompson was retained in the first place to ascertain their position. He had already surveyed for the Hudson's Bay Company the York-Saskatchewan route and the Rat River Country and to Lake Athabaska. With a thoroughness characteristic of the man he continued this survey southward. He traced the North West Company's route from Grand Portage to Lake Winnipeg, and by Dauphin (Little Saskatchewan) River to lakes Manitoba and Winnipegosis. He ascended Swan River, visited the North West Company's post on Red Deer River, and passed down the Assiniboine to Fort la Souris. Thence, as has been seen, he crossed the prairie to place the Missouri River on his map, and returned. He then went down the Assiniboine and up the Red River to Pembina, and showed that the Canadian post there was in American territory. The treaty of 1783 drew the International Boundary from the North-West Angle of the Lake of the Woods to the Mississippi. In the course from Pembina to Lake Superior he practically discovered the source of the great river, and showed it to be farther south than had been supposed. After surveying the south, the east, and the north shores of Lake Superior he arrived at Grand Portage on 7th June to report, having accomplished a journey of four thousand miles in less than a twelvemonth. Thereafter he was sent as a fur-trader up the Churchill, and thus enabled to carry his survey westward from the Rat River Country as far as the valley of the Athabaska.

If the attempt of the Hudson's Bay Company to find a short route of its own to Athabaska Lake proved a failure, its defence of the Rat Country was a complete success. The natives of the region were Half Home Indians, long accustomed to trade with the Englishmen; they rallied to their posts. Moreover the Company, enjoying the short and cheap lines of communication, could offer the Indians a more generous trade than the Canadians, and, above all, could come in earlier and commit them to itself. The plan was to open a post for a year or two, now in this, now in that part of the region, and thus to keep the various bands of Indians in happy relations with the Company.* Sir Alexander Mackenzie wrote of the Rat Country

* *From York Fort :* Chatham House on Wintering Lake during the seasons 1791–93; Sipiwesk House on Sipiwesk Lake, 1792–93 ; Wekusko Lake House, 1793–94 ; Reed Lake House, 1794–95 ; Wegg's House on Setting Lake at the inflow of Grass River, 1795–96 ; Duck Portage House, 1795–96 ; Hulse House on Long Lake, 1796–97 ; Burntwood Lake House, 1796-97 ; Lake's House on Split Lake, 1796–97 ; Bedford House on Reindeer Lake, 1796–97 ; Reindeer Lake House, 1798–99 ; Setting River House, 1798–99. *From Churchill Fort :* Granville House on Granville Lake, 1794–96 ; Carlton House at the confluence of the Kississing and the Churchill, 1796–98. In 1799 the Company's interests in the valley of the Churchill were entrusted to Churchill Fort.

before 1801 : " The traders from Canada succeeded for several years in getting the largest proportion of [the Indians'] furs, till the year 1793, when the servants of the Hudson's Bay Company thought proper to send people amongst them (and why they did not do it before is best known to themselves) for the purpose of trade. . . . From the short distance they had to come, and the quantity of goods they supplied, the trade has, in a large measure, reverted to them, as the merchants of Canada could not meet them on equal terms."

THE UPPER VALLEY OF THE CHURCHILL (ENGLISH) RIVER

The North West Company's English River and Athabaska brigades, which we left at the Sturgeon-Weir River, would ascend that malign stream, with the usual maledictions at its terrible rapids, to Beaver Lake, where Frobisher and Alexander Henry were quartered in 1775–76.   They would follow their predecessors by stream and lake to Portage du Traite.   Frobisher's fort might have disappeared, but the memory of his coup is preserved to this day in the name of the portage.   Here the canoes for the Reindeer Lake post would turn down the Churchill.   The main brigades would ascend through a succession of narrow lakes, widenings of the river, by many rapids and portages to the site of the present Stanley Mission on the right.   On the left the Montreal (Rapid) River pours the waters of Lac la Ronge into the Churchill.   Canoes would leave for the post on that lake.   The main brigade would pass on to the fort and depot on Lake Ile-à-la-Crosse, headquarters of the English River Department.

The fragment of a Journal kept by William M'Gillivray gives a clear view of the management of the Department, as in 1793.   The fort over which M'Gillivray presided was south of the " Deep River " (the present Aubichon Arm of the lake), the water-way to Athabaska, on the peninsula which had been occupied by Thomas Frobisher and Peter Pond, and on which the Hudson's Bay Company's post stands to-day.   Sir Alexander Mackenzie says it was on a low isthmus five miles from the point at which the course turned westward towards Deep River.   The site had been long occupied, for M'Gillivray says : " The firewood is so distant now that it is almost impossible for the men to carry it home."   Here Mr. William M'Gillivray, who had bought Peter Pond's share when he retired, presided over his Department as Wintering Partner.   To begin with he was simply a trader for the people of the region—mostly Crees but some Chipewyans.   As such he conducted his trade much as at his post in the Muskrat region, but there was a larger Indian population here.   In addition he had the duties of supervisor of the forts of the Department.   He had to co-ordinate the business of all the forts, and especially to see that provisions were secured during the winter not only for his own canoes in spring, but for the Athabaska brigades going out and coming in.   The forts in the Rat region were so distant that they were left to care for themselves, so that M'Gillivray's immediate concern was with the posts on Reindeer Lake, Lac la Ronge, and Lac d'Orignal (Moose Lake), and with outposts at Green Lake and Waterhen Lake. A winter express reported the wants and superfluities of the several stations. As a result Simon Fraser the elder received certain goods needed at his post by the return express, and forwarded certain articles needed at Lac la Ronge in the spring by a special midwinter express. The post on Green Lake, and at this time especially that on Lac d'Orignal, besides gathering the furs of the several regions, acted as links connecting the English River Department with that of the Forts des Prairies (Saskatchewan). The canoes for Green Lake crossed Ile-à-la-Crosse Lake eastward from the depot and ascended the Beaver River coming from the south. They left the river at its great bend and continued southward into Green Lake. The fort stood on the east shore where the narrows broaden out into a lake. It was first occupied in 1782.

The canoes for Lac d'Orignal ascended the tortuous Beaver River from the great bend to the outflow of our Moose Lake (Lac d'Orignal), whence the goods were usually portaged to the lake, the canoes being taken up the shallow stream empty. The fort stood on a large point south-east of the entrance to the lake. It was in a rich beaver country, and was also within easy reach of Fort George on the North Saskatchewan, the Fort des Prairies of the time, about thirty-five miles to the south and a little east. In 1792 M'Gillivray had been hard pressed for provisions. For some reason they were short at The Pas, and he had to make his way as far as Montreal (Rapid) River, fishing at the successive encampments. The delay meant that he was almost caught in the ice. This must not occur again. He arranged to build a post at the narrows of Cumberland Lake, north-east of the English post. Incidentally, it would cut off from the enemy provisions brought down from the Indians of the north, but it was devised to be the "depot" for Saskatchewan pemmican for the brigades. The plan was changed, and the North West Company's Cumberland House, as has been seen, was built beside the English House. M'Gillivray also aimed at diminishing the hardships of life in the wooded north by bringing pemmican overland from Fort des Prairies. Here the fort on Lac d'Orignal played its part. Pemmican was brought overland from Fort George and taken down to Ile-à-la-Crosse by canoes in the spring. The value of this for the English River posts was proved within a year. In the spring of 1795 the men at Green Lake were starving—in fact, making soup out of the fish bones cast out in the autumn. Relief came with an emergency supply of pemmican from Fort George. The pemmican from the Saskatchewan was also intended to provision the Athabaska brigades going out and in. When M'Gillivray left in the spring of 1793, there were thirty-six bags of pemmican waiting for them and 800 pounds of pounded meat and grease (fat) in storage to be mixed and made up ready unto their return. It was this co-ordination of post with post within the Department, supervised by a

Wintering Partner, and again of Department with Department, which made it possible for the North West Company, handicapped as it was by its long line of transportation, to achieve its notable success, even in so distant a region as the basin of the Mackenzie.

The English River Department was a very profitable one for the North West Company, all the more as most of its peltry was beaver of prime quality. William M'Gillivray gives the following as the returns for 1792–93 :

Lac d'Orignal	64 Packs		4 Canoes	
Isle a la Crosse & Poule D'Eau				
[Waterhen Lake]	89	,,	5	,,
Lac la Ronge	52	,,	1	,,
Lac des Caribou				
[Reindeer Lake]	79	,,	3	,,
Rat River	79	,,	3	,,
Maskegon				
[Nelson River]	29	,,	2	,,
[Total 392		,,	18	,,]

Further light is thrown on the English River Department by David Thompson's Journal of 1798. The year after his remarkable survey of the posts of the south he found a small post occupied by one Roy at the mouth of the Rapid, now the Montreal, River which flows into the Churchill opposite the present Stanley Mission. He passed up the Rapid River to Lac la Ronge to survey the lake. About eighteen miles down the eastern shore he camped at the old fort occupied by Simon Fraser in 1795–96, the post of Alexander Fraser in M'Gillivray's time. Thompson estimated that it was about eight miles from the southern extremity of the lake. Sailing a little south of west he reached a point of islands in the middle of the lake, and then ran S70W twelve miles to the new settlement occupied by (Joseph) Versailles. This would be at the inflow of the Montreal River, where the Hudson's Bay Company's post now stands. On his return Thompson coasted along the west shore, noting its many bays running westward.

Passing up the Churchill, Thompson came to the North West Company's new post of Ile-à-la-Crosse, which he found on the promontory north of the Deep River. The move must have been made to be near an ample supply of wood. Running east by south from this post, Thompson entered the Beaver River and followed its course upward till he came to the outlet from Green Lake. He visited the North West Company's post two-thirds of a mile east from his entry into the lake and took its latitude. To put the Saskatchewan in its right relationship to the valley of the Churchill River he now passed overland to Fort George and then travelled by the trail of Angus Shaw's time to Lac d'Orignal, meeting his canoes on the Beaver River where the stream from the lake enters it. Proceeding up the Beaver River, and then " Beaver Lake Brook," he portaged to waters flowing into the Athabaska River and entered Lac la Biche by a brook. Passing one mile westward along the shore of the lake he built his post, probably in what is now the north-east corner of the Hudson's Bay Company's reserve. David Thompson wished to get Lac la Biche in proper relation on his map with the Saskatchewan. He therefore journeyed overland to Fort Augustus on the North Saskatchewan and took its latitude. Thence he reached Pembina River, which he followed into the Athabaska. Passing down the Athabaska, he ascended the Lesser Slave Lake River to the lake. Returning to the Athabaska, he followed it to its confluence with the Clearwater, in fact to the track of the Athabaska brigade. He ascended the Clearwater, crossed the Methy Portage, and arrived at Ile-à-la-Crosse, where he met his canoes which had come down the Beaver River. While at the post he took unto himself Charlotte Small, *en façon du nord*, that is, without a clergyman in a land without churches. She was the half-breed daughter of Patrick Small, who had preceded William M'Gillivray as Wintering Partner in the Department. The honeymoon trip was strictly on business, with the canoes to Grand Portage and thence to Fort George on the Saskatchewan, where Thompson began his great map.

Till 1799 the North West Company had had no rivals in the valley of the Churchill River above Portage du Traite. What with disastrous years in the early 'eighties, the shortage of men in the 'nineties, and the factors of York and Churchill concentrating their attention on the Rat Country, the Hudson's Bay Company had left the field farther inland unoccupied. In 1799 the Committee put an end to the conflict between York Fort and Churchill by ordering the former to withdraw from " the Athapascow Country," as the region was often called, and provided Churchill Fort with the men necessary for a push up the river, not without " disagreeable apprehensions." "We find by experience that Men have an insuperable Objection to engage for Churchill on Account of the scarcity of Provisions when Travelling Inland." Thomas Stayner, the Governor, was ordered to exert himself to the utmost to make the plans he had advocated a success.

A succession of boats with ample supplies of goods made their way up to Ile-à-la-Crosse. There William Linklater built a short distance from the North West Company's post. William Auld went on to Green Lake, and built Essex House beside the Canadian post there. Peter Fidler had charge of the party going up the Beaver River. He entered " the Barren Grounds River " (Chitek River), a tributary flowing from " Barren Grounds Lake " (*i.e.* Prairie, the present Meadow Lake), and built Bolsover House. Fidler himself followed the course taken by David Thompson the autumn before, and built Greenwich House beside the North West Company's post on Lac la Biche. In the course of the winter he passed down the Lac la Biche River and followed the Athabaska to its confluence with the Lesser Slave Lake River, where he found a Canadian post occupied. The invasion of the Englishman into these parts opened a new chapter in the relations of the Hudson's Bay Company with the men from Montreal.

THE SASKATCHEWAN

The brigades of the North West and the Hudson's Bay companies had the Saskatchewan for their common route. The craft of the two concerns must have seemed ridiculously unlike as they travelled up the river, as they did occasionally, together. The Canadians glided along gracefully in their canoes, each equipped to carry twenty-five pieces, and propelled by five to seven men. Their labour at the Grand Rapids would be greatly eased by the lightness of their craft. The Englishmen had an equipment in which their character was expressed. They faced the swift waters of the Saskatchewan with boats carrying forty pieces.* It was hard work and slow, but the scheme was not as stupid nor as slow as it might seem, for the boats were much safer on the lakes, and could bear sail on lake and river when the canoes dared not. Besides they carried nearly double the freight with the same number of men. The two brigades would get pemmican at Cumberland House (the Canadians before 1793 from a cache on the Saskatchewan about The Pas), but just enough to take them to the first prairies. At La Montée (from the French *monter*, to mount), forty miles west of Prince Albert, the officers would leave the canoes and take to horse to " run " buffalo and red deer upon the plains and convey the fresh meat to the canoes making their toilsome way upstream. The pleasant change made this journey the happiest in all the North-West. As the years passed, the Fort des Prairies to which the brigades were bound receded westward, from denuded beaver country to untapped regions above.

The union of the North West Company and the Gregory-McLeod concern brought a sudden change in the scene. The now full-fledged North West Company faced a single rival in the Hudson's Bay Company. Pangman's post on the South Branch was closed, leaving a fort on either side of the river in opposition the one to the other. Holmes's post immediately above the Battle River was thrown to the discard, as also Umfreville's above Pine Island. Donald MacKay withdrew from his private venture, to return to the Nipigon Country and ultimately to enter the services of the Hudson's Bay Company. Thus Peter Pangman presided over his own post on Pine Island in opposition to Manchester House of the English Company.

Pangman's post, as the ruins indicate, was about 160 feet square. It would have the usual two gates ; as it was on an island each would face its branch of the river. The Wintering Partner's house was in the centre. Between it and the north palisade was the store

---

* The first boat in use by the Hudson's Bay Company on the Saskatchewan for transportation was built at Manchester House in 1788. It was to take the pemmican downstream to Cumberland House. It was probably the difficulties experienced on the sandbars which led to the adoption of the pattern of the York boat, after the style of the canoe, with both ends shaped as a bow. The boats from Albany on the Assiniboine appear to have been flat-bottomed. Hence the name " York boat " for those on the Saskatchewan. Their use on the route to York Fort began shortly after 1797.

and a *glacière*, a house in which fresh meat was heaped up in the winter and finally covered with water, which immediately froze and thus gave the post a supply of fresh meat up to the departure of the brigade for Grand Portage. From the line of the palisades the houses on either side ran chequer-board fashion diagonally across the fort to the western gate. Thus there was a triangular open space within the palisades and in front of the Proprietor's house. Here the Indians would gather, but would be under observation, and if the occasion called for it, as was the case one day, would be under fire from the huts on every side. At the ceremonial entry of a band, the chief and his councillors would be received with a fusillade and pass from the gate to the " Indian Hall " before them to smoke the pipe of peace and hold a council with the Wintering Partner in his own home. Here also the ceremony of clothing the chiefs whose bands had brought in a satisfactory quantity of furs would take place in the spring. The traders had the eye to choose safe but beautiful sites for their forts. Across the waters of the river laughing in the sunshine, down towards the Big Gully, the steep banks rise into wooded hills which seem to shut off this spot from all the rest of the world. Not so for the traders, for beyond upon the plains to the west and south great equestrian tribes, warlike and pitiless, roamed—Crees, Assiniboins, Gros Ventres, and Blackfeet. Beyond these the strong woods of the Battle River valley were peopled by beaver-hunting tribes ; on the north and east lay the great fur belt. The beaver hunters from these parts were received at the forts with great ceremony and with an open hand ; their chiefs were clothed and given rum and ammunition in proportion to the wealth of fur they and their bands brought. In contrast, when the *Gens du large*, the people of the plains, came they were received with dignity, yet with secret fear, for they would appear in great force, and bring but coarse skins of buffalo and wolves, not the kind to broach the kegs of rum or open the stores of the trader. They were given more than their due lest relations should become strained.

About one mile upstream, on the same island, stood the rival English post, Manchester House, whose relations with the various tribes would not differ materially from those of their neighbours. Yet there was a difference. The strict discipline of the servants and the long tradition of " civility " towards the savage customers as seen in the forts on the Bay were to be found essentially unimpaired in the posts inland. These were re-enforced by the prudence dictated by the fact that the English posts were held by a comparatively small number of men. The result was that while Canadian servants were struck down by the savages, one from Pangman's post as recently as 1787, the Englishmen had moved up and down in the same danger with comparative safety. They had frequented the valley of the Saskatchewan since Henday's voyage in 1754, and up to 1791 no English blood had been shed by savage hands. Men had wintered with Blackfeet and Bloods and Piegans under the shadow of the Rockies and returned not only in safety but undespoiled. But in the summer of 1792 the first Englishmen fell. Isaac Batt was going out from Manchester House with a full equipment to hunt on the plains south of the river. Two strange Indians who had been at Pangman's post offered to go with him. His thirty-five years of safety among the natives must have blinded him to the danger. He accepted. Batt's squaw, his three boys, and a lad, John Thompson, were of the party. Out on the prairie, while handing a pipe to one of the men, Batt was shot by the other. He and his squaw were stripped of their clothing and their whole equipment was carried off. John Thompson returned unharmed. William Tomison regarded Batt as guilty of great imprudence and charged James Gaddy, Master of the House during the summer, with culpable neglect of his duty in " suffering him to go a hunting on the South side of the River with such unknown Villians."

In the autumn of 1793 a real crisis came in the relations of the trading-posts with the Indians. It was due to the traffic in arms. From the beginning tribes in intimate relations with the forts procured firearms and went on the war-path against the more distant tribes, and shot their ill-armed warriors down pitilessly. In this way the Crees had driven the Chipewyans out of the valley of the Churchill, and the Gros Ventres or Fall Indians from their original hunting-grounds at Nipawi and east of the South Saskatchewan, westward to the plains beyond the Eagle Hills. True, these Fall Indians could come to Manchester House and secure arms, but the only furs procurable on the plains were wolf and fox skins, and these were of no great value to the fur-traders. In contrast, the Crees came to the posts with beaver and other prized furs, and could trade all the guns and ammunition they desired. Thus the Fall Indians continued the prey of their well-armed foes. In the summer of 1793 Crees trading at the South Branch houses and at Swan River took the war-path westward. They discovered a band of Fall Indians near the South Saskatchewan over against the Moose Woods. " They watched their opportunity and, when the others retired to rest unsuspicious of danger, they fell upon them like hungry wolves and with remorseless fury butchered them all in cold blood except a few children whom they preserved for Slaves." It was probably to obtain arms for revenge that the Gros Ventres now formed the design to attack the traders " whom they considered as the allies of their enemies." They came to the bank of the river at Pine Island, leaving their horses with their boys. The traders took them across in boats. Once in the North West Company's fort they gave up the pretence of trading and became insolent. James Finlay, Mr. Pangman's successor as Wintering Partner, was in charge and was for placating them with ample presents when James Hughes, a young clerk, doubtless from the door of the Indian Hall, cried, " Aux armes, to arms, men." Caught in the centre of the fort, as in a trap, the savages turned and fled. Men and women dropped their clothing and swam across to their steeds. Four were killed or died of their wounds. The savages had managed, however, to strip some of the servants of their equipment and to drive off some of the horses of the fort. They were even more successful at Manchester House, which was held by but few men, for it was now no more than an outpost of Buckingham House, recently built. They stripped the men of their clothing and carried off almost all the goods in the storehouse.

Encouraged by this success they attacked the houses on the South Branch in the summer following, when they were lightly manned. The attack was a complete surprise for the Hudson's Bay Company's post. James Gaddy, who appears to have been the Master, was away at the Birch Hills; Magnus Annal was breakfasting at the Canadian post. Hugh Brough, with the interpreter, was out after the horses. When a cavalcade of Indians came in sight the interpreter warned him that they were on the war-path and fled. Brough quietly awaited them, and was shot down and scalped. Magnus Annal was taken as he returned from the Canadian post and killed. Only J. C. Van Driel and William Fea and a few Indian men, women, and children were in the fort. Apparently the Englishmen at this post had felt so secure among the natives that they had built no bastions and made no provision for shooting from the palisades. Surveying the scene from the top of the house, Van Driel concluded that he could not defend the place against what he estimated to be a hundred Indians. He had already locked the gates, and when the savages set fire to the palisade he sought safety under rubbish in one of the cellars of the first fort now in the garden. Fea hid in another cellar, but was discovered and killed. " Even the women and children did not escape the merciless cruelty of the miscreants." In the evening Van Driel secured a canoe and fled to Nipawi.

The North West Company's post also was held by but a summer garrison, but all the men appear to have been at home. More distrustful of the Indians, the builders had erected bastions at two corners of the palisades and galleries over the gates. Moreover one of the men had been across the river on the English side and gave the alarm, while the Indians would lose time crossing the stream. All was ready for the attack of the enemy when he began to fire from the shelter of the woods. When an Indian chief stepped out to advance to the palisades he was shot down. This brought about a sudden revulsion of feeling among the savages; they took to mourning for the dead, abandoned the attack, and carried off their wounded. The fort was saved, but Louis Châtelain, the Master, thought it prudent to carry off all his goods and equipment and to abandon the post.

The crisis brought about the abandonment of the forts on Pine Island in 1793 and on the South Branch in 1794. In place of the latter, forts were erected in the neighbourhood of La Corne. The Canadians built Fort St. Louis, apparently so called after La Corne's Fort, in 1795, on the right bank of the Saskatchewan immediately below Peonan Creek; and the Hudson's Bay Company Carlton

House, a mile and a half downstream, and on the opposite bank of the river, in 1796. The successors to Pine Island Fort and Manchester House had already been built, in 1792, far up the North Saskatchewan, forty miles by river above the present boundary of the provinces of Saskatchewan and Alberta. They stood on the left bank of the river, the North West Company's Fort George on the east side of a deep creek and the English Company's Buckingham House on the west side. Angus Shaw, who had built the Canadian post on Lac d'Orignal of the Churchill River Department, came across and built Fort George ; Buckingham House was built by the ever-present William Tomison. John MacDonald of Garth, who followed Shaw across from Lac d'Orignal, describes the site. The fort stood " upon the margin of a fine hummock of Pine—upon a rising Hill or Bank with the noble Saskatchewan in front—with banks of Strong Woods for perhaps a mile in breadth & twenty in length along the river, . . . a shelter for the different kinds of deer, particularly the Moose Deer." Indeed, the region is known to this day as Mooswa, and Mooswa Creek, six miles below, was a favourite place with the Indians and the Englishmen twenty-five years before for building canoes for the journey to York Fort.

John MacDonald of Garth—so called to distinguish him from the other MacDonalds and Macdonells in the North-West of his time—will always be associated with the valley of the Saskatchewan at this epoch. His *Autobiographical Notes*, written in the boastfulness of old age, if at times inaccurate, are always colourful ; they show a sensitiveness to the beauties of the scene such as is to be found in no other document.

" [1793] In May we made all due preparation in puting canoes in order —making Batteaux, making Pemican—and packing Furs—& by the 15th were all ready to embark for our rendez-vous at Grand Portage—all afloat upon the Grand Saskatchewan, then at high water from the melting of Snows from the Rocky Mountains & all its tributary streams. It was a Grand Sight to me to see such a Grand River, the innumerable herds of Buffloes & Deers & many grizle Bears on its Banks feeding & crossing in such numbers that we often got our canoes amongst them & shot hundreds without need. There lay sometimes upwards of a thousand dead on some low points drowned when crossing in the Spring on the ice & washed ashore. Amongst them were to be seen often the Bears feeding upon the carcases. We, of course, shot as many [buffaloes] as were required for our own food & took on board as much as would feed us while it kept fresh and good, generally until we got to Lac Winipeg."

Another clerk, Duncan M'Gillivray, brother of William and Simon, and nephew of Simon McTavish, agent of the Company, will always be associated with Fort George. His Journal kept at that post in the trading season 1794–95 throws a flood of light upon life within the palisades, upon its gaieties, unblushing misdeeds, and more particularly upon the workings of a Fort des Prairies, on the edge of the beaver region to the north and the buffalo range to the south.

Duncan's Fort George presents a vivid contrast with William

M'Gillivray's post deep in the northern forest. To begin with, it was in a land in which the abundant food supply found in the herds on the prairies supported great bands of Indians. At any moment one of these might fall upon the post and overpower it, as the Gros Ventres had done the summer before at Pine Island. Anxiety at the *Gens du large* is written across the pages of Duncan's Journal, whereas William M'Gillivray's shows a post wrapped in the quiet of the deep forest. The canoemen not needed for the routine of the fort were equipped to trap and trade on the same terms as the Indians, or were sent out to procure venison for the fort, but were all kept within easy call of the post in case of danger. For a trial of strength Fort George could muster eighty men. There was an equal number of women and children within the palisades; as it were, a populous city when compared with William's slumbering village.

In the forest of the north the weapons of the White Men helped the savages in their stark struggle to exist, while on the plains Indians had no need of the White Man's goods :

> The Inhabitants of the Plains are so advantageously situated that they could live happily independent of our assistance. They are surrounded with innumerable herds of various kinds of animals, whose flesh affords them excellent nourishment and whose Skins defend them from the inclemency of the weather, and they have invented so many methods for the destruction of Animals, that they stand in no need of ammunition to provide a sufficiency for these purposes. It is then our luxuries that attract them to the Fort and make us so necessary to their happiness. The love of Rum is their first inducement to industry ; they undergo every hardship and fatigue to procure a Skinfull of this delicious beverage, and when a Nation becomes addicted to drinking, it affords a strong presumption that they will soon become excellent hunters. Tobacco is another article of as great demand as it is unnecessary. Custom has however made it of consequence to them as it constitutes a principal part of their feasts & Superstitious ceremonies, and in their treaties of peace and councils of War, a few whiffs out of the medicine pipe confirms the articles that have been mutually agreed upon. As for ammunition it is rendered valuable by the great advantage it gives them over their enemies in their expeditions to the Rocky Mountains against the defenceless Slave Indians who are destitute of this destructive improvement of War. It is also required to Kill Beaver, but if the Fur Trade had not allured adventurers to this Country there would be no necessity for hunting this animal. The rest of our commodities are indeed usefull to the Natives, when they can afford to purchase them, but if they had hitherto lived unacquainted with European productions it would not I believe diminish their felicity.

The very self-dependence of the *Gens du large*, the people of the plains, made them reckless in their dealings with the White Men, while their numbers gave them a sense of power and a pride which the traders took great care not to offend. At the same time, these were on their guard to check the first display of arrogance in individuals. To this end a band of bullies was kept at call within the fort, and the officers themselves were not slow to inflict punishment with their own hands. For example, Gros Blanc, who had previously inflicted an injury on Duncan, ventured to come to Fort George to trade. The offended clerk, hearing of his presence, entered the hall where the principal men were assembled, sprang on the great chief, and " offered him an indignity which he will always remember with anger and resentment," with the result that Duncan was presented immediately with a horse and some finely ornamented robes, leggings, and the like, as a peace offering from the band, and finally Gros Blanc himself adopted him as his brother. In a society which respected nothing but brute force, and which lived by the canon of an eye for an eye, a tooth for a tooth, blood for blood, the display of resentment and the revenging of insult were taken as normal, indeed, were accorded respect, as all the traders knew.

The traffic in arms might win the friendship of the tribe about a fort, but that same tribe grew jealous the moment the traders tried to open up a trade with nations beyond, helpless before the guns traded at the fort. M'Gillivray tells of the Kutenais, whom the Piegans had driven from the upper waters of the South Saskatchewan to beyond the Rockies, making many attempts to get through the territories of their victors to Fort George :

> The Gens du Large and all the other nations in this neighbourhood wishing to retain an exclusive trade among themselves, have hitherto prevented the Intentions of this Band, of commencing a friendly intercourse with the Fort in order to exclude them from any share of our commodities, which they are well aware would put their enemies in a condition to defend themselves, from the attacks of those who are already acquainted with the use of arms.

The traffic in rum also put the traders in a precarious position, especially as " the presence of an opposition," in this case the Hudson's Bay Company in Buckingham House across the creek, made their gifts recklessly lavish. When hostile bands in large numbers happened to come to the fort at the same time, none could tell what would be the outcome of a drunken brawl between individuals of the different tribes. Crees, Assiniboins, Blackfeet, Piegans, all traded at Fort George. Next year (1795) Mr. Shaw built Fort Augustus at the confluence of the Sturgeon River with the North Saskatchewan, to accommodate the beaver-hunting tribes, leaving Fort George to the *Gens du large*. He aimed at thus avoiding the chief enmities among the savages.

The ordinary routine of a prairie fort has been already described. It comes as a surprise that the furs of the finest type gathered on the Saskatchewan fell not far short of the harvests of the Athabaska region. The returns for Fort George in 1794–95 were 325 packs of 90 lb. each. Not less important were the 300 bags of pemmican of the same weight, sent down in boats to Cumberland House to meet the needs of the brigades passing that depot, out and in. Moreover Fort George was supplying the needs of the English department to the north. On 9th February an express was sent north-eastward to Green Lake and the Churchill River, doubtless with a supply of pemmican for the northern brigades at Ile-à-la-Crosse. On its return it brought goods from Green Lake, much needed for the summer trade at Fort George.

The relations of the Northwesters at Fort George with their

rivals at Buckingham House might be described as cold—or, in diplomatic language, as strictly correct. The existence of the two forts almost side by side made for safety from attack at the hands of any band of Indians which might break upon them. When a fire caught in Buckingham House, the Northwesters turned out and helped to extinguish it, in return for which they received a courteous letter from Mr. Tomison and an invitation for all hands to a dance and to what the English regarded as delicious punch. The festivity over, relations returned to the *status quo ante*. MacDonald of Garth reports a clash over a well, which the English had dug in the creek and from which by their courtesy the people of Fort George got a supply of water much nearer to hand than the river. In a period of drought the English forbade the Northwesters to use their well. That blusterer John MacDonald of Garth was sent to bring Mr. Tomison to reason. " He would not listen to any reason, indeed I had little to give him," says John, " but that if he would not give us our wants that either of us must pay a visit to the bottom of the well. This argument rather startled him & we got our share of the water ever after."

The farther afield the fur-traders went the more the competition was felt. Of this M'Gillivray was conscious. He had been at Grand Portage when Alexander Mackenzie passed through, after his journey to the Pacific, and may have already been won to his view of the necessity of union, especially in the face of the great tribes of the plains. " Methinks that this consideration alone might have some influence with the Hudson's Bay Company to induce them to adopt some terms of agreement with the North West Company. . . . I imagine that the latter would not be averse to some kind of union from a conviction of its general utility to both parties ; indeed the mutual advantages that would arise from it, are so evident that they will naturally occur to every person who has any knowledge of the Country." In this passage Duncan M'Gillivray struck the key-note of his subsequent policy as agent of the North West Company.

The opposition of Peter and David Grant throws its shadow across the pages of M'Gillivray's Journal. In 1793–94 David Grant had a clerk, James Porter, in a post about a mile above Finlay's Falls at Nipawi. The North West Company placed A. N. McLeod beside him. Malchom Ross of the Hudson's Bay Company came up to procure provisions for the proposed expedition to Athabaska, but lacking goods and unable to get Indians to hunt for him, for all were pledged to one or other of the two posts, he returned to Cumberland House empty-handed. Grant built a second post at the Sturgeon River, immediately west of Prince Albert. Angus Shaw placed John MacDonald of Garth beside him. James Bird, now at the beginning of long and honourable service with the Hudson's Bay Company and in charge of its South Branch House, for lack of goods, contented himself with sending a party to tent over against these two posts and to collect the debts of Indians who had taken credits from him. One effect of Grant's opposition was that the Fort des Prairies Department of the North West Company was divided into an upper and a lower department. James Finlay was placed in charge of the lower one.

David Grant returned to his forts in 1794, but the pressure of the North West Company made it a disastrous venture for him. Duncan M'Gillivray gives an interesting insight into the difficulties which beset individual adventurers who dared oppose his Company. Apart from the capital necessary to compete with such a strong concern, there was the impossibility of getting reliable servants :

[David Grant at the Sturgeon River] is said to be quite distracted, having no person in his service in whom he can place confidence, his interpreters and most of his men being composed of Rascals who have formerly been expelled the Country for misconduct ; it cannot therefore be expected that people of this disposition will exert themselves with fidelity or honor in the service of their employers.   Sometime before the Holidays David received accounts that Roy his representative at Nipawi [Châtelain holding the North-West Company's post over against him] being entirely addicted to drinking, squandered away the Goods with great profusion to his companions and favorites :—upon this he resolved to visit that place to remonstrate with Roy for his bad conduct, leaving Dumay to superintend affairs at Sturgeon Fort in his absence.   Dumay did not long enjoy this situation for La Verdure an old offender, usurped his authority, deprived him of the Keys, and became master of the Goods and before Mr. Grant could be apprized of this revolution he expended 7 or 8 Kegs [of High Wines] in company with some of our People, whom he generally invited to partake of His liberality. In short David's situation is so disagreeable as can well be imagined ; his men disobey and desert him ; his goods are lavished away in his absence ; and his mind so perplexed and confused that the men suppose *qu'il a perdu l'esprit*, according to their own phrase.

Duncan is discreetly silent about any part the Northwesters may have played in creating disaffection among Grant's men.   The disastrous result of this season's trade and the promise of the Northwesters to make Peter Grant a proprietor in their Company brought this opposition to a sudden end.

Mention may be made of forts of the North West Company which the English Company's servants believed were built to cut off the trade of Cumberland House. In 1790 Mr. William Thorburn built at Nipawi, on the right bank of the Saskatchewan, half a mile below Finlay's Fall. Possibly because this was too far up to accomplish its purpose, he built next year (1791) on the left bank of the river opposite the west end of the island at the mouth of the Petaigan River. The post was called Hungry Hall, as Peter Fidler says, " on account of the Poor living they had there." Fidler calls the rapids about three miles below Thorburn's Fall. The name survives in the present form of Tobin Rapid. When Thorburn returned for a second year (1792–93) at his post of the lean fare, Malchom Ross was sent up from Cumberland House to build beside him.   The establishment of the North West Company's Cumberland House in 1793, beside the Hudson's Bay Company's post, made Thorburn's establishment superfluous.

Far up the North Saskatchewan, as on the Peace River, the

posts moved ever more and more westward towards the Rocky Mountains. As has been seen, in 1795 the North West Company built at the confluence of the Sturgeon River (of Alberta) and the North Saskatchewan. Two rival posts like Fort George and Buckingham House soon destroyed the fur animals in their immediate vicinity. In 1794 Angus Shaw's attention was directed to the wealth of beaver at the mouth of the Sturgeon. The report ran that it was " a rich and plentiful Country, abounding in all kinds of animals, especially Beavers and otters, which are said to be so numerous that the Women and Children kill them with sticks and hatchets. The Country around Fort George is now entirely ruined." Accordingly, Shaw established Fort Augustus on the left bank of the Saskatchewan about a mile and a half above the confluence. William Tomison followed and built Edmonton House (the first of that name) within a musket shot of the Canadian post. The country did not belie its reputation, but the Indians were troublesome. In 1798 two Indians arrived at Edmonton House with nothing to trade. Tomison refused to give them anything and turned away. Moved to anger, one of them gave him " a Cruel Stab in the inside of the left Knee, which almost went through." As the injury left him for the time disabled for arduous travel, he took ship from York Fort for England.

By 1799 the region was depleted of its furs. In that winter plans were made to remove the two forts to the site of the present Edmonton. The houses were built and the goods transported to them in the spring of 1801. This winter was also the last in which Fort George and Buckingham House were occupied.

Part of the new alignment of the posts was the establishment of the North West Company's Rocky Mountain House and the Hudson's Bay Company's Acton House, in 1799, on the left bank of the North Saskatchewan a little over a mile above the mouth of the Clearwater. While the forts were in the midst of the Piegans, both companies hoped to draw the Kutenais to trade with them. Looking out upon the Rockies from his window, Duncan M'Gillivray, now a partner in the North West Company and soon to become its agent, began to dream of entering into the fur trade of the Pacific coast. In the autumn of 1800, as David Thompson, who had come to winter at Rocky Mountain House, reports : " Mr. Duncan M'Gillivray came and wintered also, to prepare to cross the mountains." It was the beginning of what may be called the North West Company's Columbian Enterprise.

2.—THE COLUMBIAN ENTERPRISE—THE NORTH-WEST COMPANY'S APPROACH TO THE PACIFIC COAST BY FRASER RIVER FROM PEACE RIVER, 1800–8—SIMON FRASER

Alexander Mackenzie, the first Canadian fur-trader to reach the Pacific coast, reached Montreal in September 1794, the year after his voyage. The object of his journeys to the Polar Sea and the

Pacific had been to relieve the trade of distant Athabaska from the burden of the long line of transportation from Montreal. His explorations showed that the frozen shore of the Polar Sea and the difficult passage across the Rockies offered no immediate solution of his problem. His attention was now turned to the route through Hudson Strait as offering cheap transportation to the more distant North-West. As the Charter of the Hudson's Bay Company stood in the way, he advocated a union of all the British fur-trading interests, meaning the North West Company and the Hudson's Bay Company, in one powerful concern operating under a charter from the Imperial Government. He urged that this great combination could enter into the fur trade of the Pacific coast by Hudson Bay and the overland route, and bring the whole fur trade of the continent into the hand of the British nation. It was the scheme of a vigorous and penetrating mind, which believed that every obstacle can be overcome and the most distant goal reached by clear thinking, hard work, and judicious organization. There were indeed many difficulties in the way of his scheme, and not the least of these was the North West Company with its interests deeply rooted in Montreal. Mackenzie had earned a name for himself and his Company by his astonishing achievements as a voyageur, but he came on trouble in his own camp. He was hurt by the slight stress laid on his explorations by the agents of the Company, prince among whom was Simon McTavish. It has usually been thought that Mackenzie and McTavish were of incompatible temperaments. This may well have been, but there was more in their quarrel than personal dislike. Mackenzie was the visionary radical calling for a policy which would make drastic alterations in the machinery of the Company, including the relegation of Montreal to a comparatively subordinate place in the transcontinental trade. McTavish was the old man, conservative by instinct, insisting that well should be let alone, wedded to Montreal, and distrustful of the dreams of the younger man. Unfortunately we know but little of the discussions at the successive rendezvous at Grand Portage. It may be inferred that it was to silence Mackenzie that he was taken into the firm of McTavish, Frobisher & Co. and began his annual journeys as agent of the North West Company to the meeting of the Company on Lake Superior. David Thompson, who had come to join the North West Company, met him in 1797 at Grand Portage along with his fellow-agent William M'Gillivray, also a partner in McTavish, Frobisher & Co. He describes them as " gentlemen of enlarged views."

From the nature of the man, and from subsequent events, we may judge that Mackenzie was not silenced by being made agent, but continued to advocate his far-reaching scheme. He had a large following among the winterers, but William M'Gillivray was definitely opposed to him. As the time drew near for the renewal of the agreement which constituted the North West Company, Mackenzie was in a very uncomfortable position. Nothing is more distressing to an energetic spirit with great purpose than to be in a place of responsibility, yet unable to carry out his views. When, after the surrender of the posts in American territory in 1796, the traders of the South-West pushed into the North-West, constituting oppositions gravely menacing the business of the North West Company, the danger was that Mackenzie might leave the Company and join them. It has been suggested as an explanation of the termination of his agreement with McTavish, Frobisher & Co. and his abandonment of the North West Company that he was not allowed to renew his contract, because he had been trafficking with and encouraging the Ogilvy and Forsyth firm in their opposition. This is on the face of it highly improbable. Much more convincing is the view that Mackenzie had not been silenced, but had been winning the Wintering Partners to his scheme for securing the use of the short route by Hudson Bay. Roderick Mackenzie tells us that there was a serious discussion at the rendezvous of 1798. " It was resolved unanimously by the wintering partners that, Mr. Mackenzie, having their sole confidence, they could not dispense with his services, therefore that every means should be adopted to retain him, but unfortunately the best endeavours of his friends were of no avail, for he retired in November and crossed the Atlantic." There is room for the inference that Mackenzie did not do this willingly, and that he was thrust out of his position by the refusal of McTavish to renew the agreement of the firm with a man whose policy threatened to set aside the Montreal route in favour of Hudson Bay. If Mackenzie retired of his own accord it was a grave error of judgment. Apart from the fact that his association with the opposition involved him in severe financial losses, he discarded the one business organization capable of realizing his plans for a transcontinental fur trade. Time and tide were in his favour. McTavish was falling into the background, indeed, was to die within five years. It is true that William M'Gillivray was the personal embodiment of the ideas of his uncle, Simon McTavish, but, as time was to show, he was capable of being converted by the ambitions of the Company.

Mackenzie's ideas were not forgotten by the winterers, but were taken up by no less a person than the ardent and ambitious Duncan M'Gillivray, William's younger brother. Duncan's years as a winterer were spent in the Upper Forts des Prairies far up the Saskatchewan and in sharp competition with the Hudson's Bay Company. As a clerk in Fort George, with the English Buckingham House facing him across a gully, he wrote in 1795 : " I imagine that the [English] would not be averse to some kind of a union from a conviction of its general utility to both parties ; indeed, the mutual advantages that would arise from it are so evident that they will occur to every person who has any knowledge of this Country ; it would therefore be superfluous to point them out to you, who are so well acquainted with all Branches of the Fur Trade." As a clerk, and finally as Wintering Partner in one of the most distant departments of the Company, M'Gillivray had seen the posts on the Saskatchewan pass from fur region to fur region, ever farther afield.

Finally, under his admired chief Angus Shaw, on the verge of retiring, Rocky Mountain House had been built at the foot of the Rockies (1799). Looking out from this fort, M'Gillivray must have asked himself whether, having come so far, he was to go no farther. It was his nature to answer " Forward." The fur trade needed new beaver regions as the old were ruined. Besides, there were the immense possibilities of the fur trade of the coast. The pressure of the cost of transportation to his distant posts and the lure of the Pacific trade made M'Gillivray appreciate the schemes of Alexander Mackenzie and adopt them as his own. He assumed the mantle that had fallen from Mackenzie's shoulders and became the promoter of " the Columbian enterprize," and the advocate of its concomitant necessities, union or some understanding with the Hudson's Bay carrying with it the use of the short and cheap route to the fur market of England by Hudson Strait. The lapse of time and his blood relationship with the partners of McTavish, Frobisher & Co. made it possible for him to win all parties in the North West Company to a scheme which had only brought division when advocated by Mackenzie.

We know from David Thompson that Duncan M'Gillivray went to Rocky Mountain House in the autumn of 1800 " to prepare to cross the mountains." He had with him what was believed to be the only copy in Canada of Vancouver's *Voyage of Discovery to the North Pacific Ocean*, which had been published in the autumn of 1798. Part of his preparation was copying extracts from the work to serve him when on his coming voyage. Thompson's copy of these extracts are in his Journal of 1801 in the Public Library at Vancouver. Other preparations took the form of two preliminary voyages manifestly undertaken to acquire information as to the passes across the Rockies. M'Gillivray travelled up the left bank of the North Saskatchewan, across to the Brazeau, and over the height of land into the valley of the Athabaska. When he turned he was in the latitude of our Athabaska Pass, though to reach it he would have had to follow the stream on which he was down to the Athabaska River and thence up that stream and its tributary, the Whirlpool River, to the height of land. During the other journey which he took in the company of David Thompson he followed the Bow River upwards to the steep cliffs of the Rocky Mountains near the present town of Exshaw over against White Man's Pass. Thompson's Journal in the Vancouver Library shows that M'Gillivray was too unwell in the spring to undertake the journey across the Rockies, but not so ill as to be prevented from supervising the preparations. James Hughes, a Partner, and David Thompson, a clerk, were accordingly given the task, Thompson taking with him a copy of the extracts from Vancouver's *Voyage*. The party, which included James Hughes and seven men travelling on horseback or in canoes, went up the Saskatchewan from Rocky Mountain House some forty miles to the Sheep River, which they followed towards its source. Ultimately the country became too rough for the horses to go on. The river proved equally impossible, for it was in its spring flood, and the water was over the low banks up to the cliffs behind them, so that there was no shore from which to draw the canoes upstream. Defeated, the party returned and reached Rocky Mountain House on 30th June.

At some subsequent time during that summer Duncan M'Gillivray conducted in person the exploration planned. Unfortunately there is no record of the journey save Thompson's statement that he (Thompson) led an expedition in 1801 to the upper waters of the Kootenay (M'Gillivray's River). But the fact of it is known from a letter written by Lieutenant-Governor Milnes to a John Sullivan of the Colonial Office on September 9, 1803, introducing " Mr. M'Gillivray," then going to England : " He will also have the honor to lay before you a complete Chart of the Indian Country which has been explored by [the North West Company] in following up the spirited Enterprise that was undertaken by Sir Alexander Mackenzie, who formerly belonged to the Company." This enterprise is referred to in a letter by Sir Alexander Mackenzie to John Sullivan, dated October 25, 1802, as " an attempt made by one of the partners of the old Fur Company to penetrate in a more Southern direction than I did to the river Columbia, in which he failed through ill-health." A subsequent expedition was led by a second partner, who would be Duncan. M'Gillivray's steps can be traced with considerable assurance by means of David Thompson's map and by the place-names which prevailed in subsequent years. He probably crossed the Rockies from the point on the Bow River reached the autumn before, for Thompson has entered clearly on his map the creek that comes down to the Bow in the neighbourhood of Exshaw ; the Rockies under the name " Duncans Mountains " ; and, very distinctly, the branch of the Kootenay River reached from White Man's Pass, entered as " M'Gillivrays River." (White Man's Pass, so known to the Indians on the west side, probably got its name by being the pass by which the first White Man, to wit, Duncan M'Gillivray, entered the country.) The limit of M'Gillivray's voyage was probably Kootenay Lake, for it figures on one of Thompson's maps as " McGillivray's Lake." Though it was the practice then to name rivers and the like from their first explorers, as, for example, Mackenzie's, Finlay's, and Fraser's rivers, it might be argued that these names were given by Thompson in honour of his chief; but M'Gillivray could scarcely be flattered by Thompson's calling the portage two miles long from the Kootenay River to the upper Columbian lake in which the Columbia River takes its rise, " McGillivrays Portage," as he does in his *Narrative*. Rather it was the portage by which Duncan passed into the valley of the Columbia. Finally, the pass by which he returned was the Athabaska Pass, where a striking pinnacle at the height of land bore afterwards the name of M'Gillivray's Rock. Gabriel Franchère passed it in 1814 and says : " Mr. J. Henry, who first discovered the pass, gave this extraordinary rock the name of M'Gillivray's Rock, in honour of one of the partners of the North West Company." Ross Cox, who also passed by, writing much later, for his book, *The Columbia River*, was not published till 1832, when Duncan M'Gillivray would be forgotten, in a footnote makes a gloss on the name : " This is called M'Gillivray's Rock, in honour of the late Wm. M'Gillivray, a principal director of the Company." All these geographical names really mark the course taken by M'Gillivray one way or the other.* John Stuart (with Simon Fraser on Fraser River in 1808) asserted in 1843 that " D Thomson and MacGillivray crossed [the Rockies] in 1801 & 2 " [1801].

The importance of Duncan M'Gillivray's journey does not lie in any discoveries he may have made so much as in the fact that he and the North West Company were feeling their way to the Columbian enterprise as early as 1800–1. In 1802 M'Gillivray left the interior to enter the firm of McTavish, Frobisher & Co. (soon to be known as McTavish, M'Gillivrays & Co.) and to become their representative travelling up to Fort William, now the rendezvous, to meet the winterers in the annual meeting of the North West Company. Thus when Simon Fraser went into New Caledonia and explored the Fraser River, and when David Thompson crossed over into the valley of the Columbia, they were carrying out a policy framed by the proprietors of the Company, with Duncan M'Gillivray in the chair.

The Columbian enterprise was not pushed in the years immediately subsequent to M'Gillivray's first attempt. This was doubtless due to the need of men and capital during the fierce struggle with the XY Company, but also to the fear that the enterprise would bring financial loss, if the furs were to be carried all the way across the continent to Montreal. In his *Some Account of the Trade carried on by the North West Company*, written by Duncan M'Gillivray in the months before his death in April 1808, and when Fraser's posts in New Caledonia had been built, he says : " The trade as it is carried on at present beyond the mountains, instead of getting any profit, is a very considerable loss to the Company, as the Furs did not pay for the transport to Montreal, where they were shipped." Thus Duncan M'Gillivray and his Company became converts to Alexander Mackenzie's view that the possession of the short route by Hudson Bay was an integral part of the policy of reaching the Pacific. Accordingly, we come upon the first of a series of attempts made by the fur-traders of Montreal to get control of the Hudson's Bay Company, or at least to share in that precious part of their monopoly, the short direct and cheap route from the North-West to the London market. In 1804 Edward Ellice, the London representative of the XY Company and after the union of that year of the North West Company's system, made an all but successful attempt to buy out the English Company. When this failed the alternative was to purchase the right to use the Hudson Bay route. On July 6, 1805,

* This argument is inferential, and therefore to some extent precarious. It has been disputed by no less an authority than Mr. J. B. Tyrrell, in the *Canadian Historical Review* of March 1937. My reply in the June number reviews the evidence.

the annual meeting of the North West Company at " Kaminitiquia " (Fort William) authorized its agents " to offer to the said Hudson's Bay Company a Sum not exceeding Two thousand pounds Sterling . . . a year for such transit," by way of the Nelson or Hayes River, on condition of doing no trade in the region around the Bay. To effect some arrangement Duncan M'Gillivray had visited England in 1804, and he returned in 1805, and in conjunction with Mr. Thomas Forsyth, Sir Alexander Mackenzie's partner, now in the united concern, carried on the negotiations with the Hudson's Bay Company. These efforts proved futile. The effect of the English Company's refusal to meet the wish of the Canadians must be left for treatment in another connection.

It says much for the eagerness of Duncan M'Gillivray and the North West Company for the Columbian enterprise that, despite their failure to secure the short line of transportation, they went on with the policy of advance across the Rockies and to the Pacific coast. They must have been confident that careful management would overcome their difficulties. In the light of this, reforms and economies recorded in the so called *Minutes of the North West Company* may well be noted. In 1804 a resolution was passed abolishing " the practice of the use of Light Canoes by the Proprietors." The Wintering Partners were required to travel with their freight canoes and to have no more than one man in attendance, under penalty of £50. A light canoe, however, was to pass downward bringing the letters and accounts in advance, that the necessary preparations at the rendezvous for dispatching the outfits could be made. Another resolution dealt with the price of goods at the rendezvous. It was increased to 23 per cent. on the cost of all goods at Montreal (calculated in Grand Portage currency). The prices of goods given to clerks at a reduced rate were also raised. The allowance of £20 in cash to clerks in lieu of equipments was abolished as having been the source of abuses. The resolution making these changes was first adopted in 1803 but reaffirmed in 1804 and 1805. At this last date it is the item in the Minutes preceding the resolution to make an offer to the Hudson's Bay Company for the right of transit through the Bay. Next year a drastic resolution was passed requiring the expenses of the posts to be reduced by preventing the servants of the Company from taking squaws to themselves and thereby burdening the Company with the support of a swarm of half-breed children. Squaws and their children must live outside of the fort, and at the expense of the men. Proprietors were to be subject to the penalty of £100 if they failed to enforce this rule. It was easy to put this drastic resolution in the Minutes. Its enforcement was an entirely different thing. Simon Fraser, in 1806, while rebuking his clerk James McDougall for allowing an *engagé* to take a certain squaw, expresses his doubt of the regulation ever being seriously put into force. To effect further savings a fresh schedule of wages was drawn up to be rigidly enforced to obviate " the great loss and injury of the Concern." Finally, the loss to the Company through the servants sending down *pacquettons*—small packages containing furs—and carrying on a trade at the expense of their employers was to come to an end. These numerous attempts at economizing can hardly be without their bearing upon the policy of the Company of entering a region in which the costs were certain and the returns, at any rate at the beginning, problematical.

The advance to the Pacific was on a wide front. The form which it took was the establishment of posts for trade west of the Rockies to be bases from which the coast could be reached. It was due to the influence of Mackenzie's voyage that the first steps were taken on the Peace River frontier, and in part along the track explored by him. The decision must have been made in the summer of 1804, before the union with the XY Company on 5th November of that year. Sir Alexander Mackenzie, who then re-entered the concern, would thus have nothing to do with it. It must have been due to Duncan M'Gillivray that the forward policy was then adopted. Pursuant to orders, Simon Fraser was on the Peace River at its Rocky Mountain House in the summer of 1805 taking the first steps.* A preliminary survey of the upper valley of Peace River was made. Fraser followed Mackenzie's track up the Parsnip River, for his Journal of the following year (1806) points out two of Sir Alexander's encampments noted by him in the previous summer. However, he diverged to the right at the Pack River, the tributary of the Parsnip, which Mackenzie had missed, Fraser suggests, during a nap. By this he reached what came to be called McLeod's Lake. Here on a peninsula formed by the outlet of the lake and the inflow of a stream from the west he established an outpost. The Indians of the region were Sekanais. The first post in the present British Columbia was Rocky Mountain House, later moved to the present St. John's. This was the second.

The small post built on McLeod Lake was left in charge of a few French-Canadians under one Lamalice, but they quarrelled, and the post was like to go under. James McDougall, Fraser's clerk, went up in January to take charge. When Fraser returned in the autumn down Peace River, along with John Stuart, he established a post at Rocky Mountain Portage at the lower end of the Peace River canyon and on the south bank at the present Hudson's Hope. It was, of course, built for its own trade, but at the same time to be

* David Thompson had surveyed Peace River the year before for the North West Company. The uppermost fort at that time (1804) was Rocky Mountain House. He mentions " the Old Fort of Mr. McLeod," that near Whitemud River, occupied the winter before Alexander Mackenzie's journey ; Horse Shoe House ; Fort Vermilion, then sixty-seven miles above the present place of that name, which is on the opposite side of the river from Fort Liard (Mr. John Clarke was in charge) ; the abandoned " Aspin Fort," that is, Fort du Tremble, the " New Establishment " of Alexander Mackenzie's time, and Fort Liard, Mackenzie's " Old Establishment " ; and finally " the house of the Grand Marais, now deserted." At that time W. F. Wentzell had a post on Red (Mikwa) River, the successor to the house at Grand Marais. It was the last winter of the struggle between the XY and the North-West Companies, but Thompson is silent about the posts of the former concern. The Hudson's Bay Company had had a frail tenure at Mansfield House over against Fort Liard. See Sketchmap No. 9 at p. 362. Fort St. John, the St. Mary houses, and Fort d'Epinette and Colvile House on the map date from the later struggle between the North West Company and the Hudson's Bay Company, treated at p. 600 *et seq.*

a base for the forts beyond the Rockies. This was the third post built in our British Columbia.

When McDougall was at McLeod Lake, during the spring of 1807 he journeyed three and a half days overland to what he called the Carriers' Lake. This can be no other than the later Stuart Lake, sixty miles, as the crow flies, to the south-west. The lake abounded in fish at certain seasons, and its waters flowed in a small stream (the Stuart River), as Fraser thought, into "the Columbia River," for such he took the Fraser to be. The knowledge of this lake, of its outlet, and of its food supply thus gained, will explain Fraser's movements in the following summer. The furs sent down by McDougall in the spring from McLeod Lake made up fourteen packs, superior to anything Simon Fraser had seen in Athabaska, being quite black. This was a happy augury for a district soon to be called New Caledonia because of the wildness of its scenery.

During the winter Fraser got news at Rocky Mountain Portage House of the upper waters of Finlay's River and beyond, that one could reach Bear Lake with no very great difficulty, that salmon came up to the lake from the sea, and that its outlet led to another and a much larger stream "that glides in the north-west direction," but whose navigation was impossible ; that by trading with their relatives on this river the Indians got "iron works." (Bear Lake later became the site of a post, Fort Connolly.) The river was the Skeena, and the iron utensils and implements must have been obtained from trading ships on the coast near the present Prince Rupert. There is much evidence that the Indians were keen bargainers in an intertribal commerce reaching far inland. Fraser's forts beyond the Rockies, whose establishment was now planned, were intended to divert this trade to the North West Company.

As the season was backward it was 21st May before the expedition of 1807, officered by Simon Fraser and John Stuart, got away. It embarked in the two canoes which had brought the furs down from McLeod's Lake, but these proved crazy craft, and the crew was without experience—all of which added greatly to the distresses of the journey. On 6th June it was at the Pack River, putting the provisions and goods necessary for their journey to the supposed Columbia River *en cache*. Fraser proceeded to the post at McLeod Lake, and was there welcomed by McDougall on the forenoon of the next day. His first preoccupations were to get the necessary wood and bark to build two really good canoes, and to secure the necessary guides. The wisdom of getting into relations with the people by first establishing a fort was evidenced by the ease with which these were procured. Fraser had determined to build a post on the Lake of the Carriers (Stuart Lake), whose people McDougall had visited a few months before. The overland route was thus known, but it was too arduous without pack-horses. The simplest water-way would have been from McLeod Lake up its contributory stream, the Crooked River, to Summit Lake and thence by the Giscombe Portage of two miles to the Fraser River ; but through the ignorance or probably the reticence of the Indians, no suggestion of its existence was got. A constant preoccupation was provisions. McLeod Lake afforded little fish, scarcely enough for the sustenance of the men at the post. However, dried fish was procured from Carp Lake, which lay southwest from the post, so that it was not necessary to consume the provisions set apart for the expedition.

On 23rd June Fraser's party took the route back to the cache at the mouth of the Pack River. Thence it traced the Parsnip southward to its source and over the height of land to the Bad River, down which it passed to the Fraser. The journey proved not less trying than it had been to Alexander Mackenzie. Moreover it was a very roundabout way, and Fraser was chagrined on reaching the watershed to hear of the short route which he might have taken up the Crooked River. On reaching his " Columbia River " he passed downstream to its confluence with the Nechako, noting that its banks were as beautiful as those of the Rainy River. Leaving the main stream, he ascended the Nechako northward to its forks with the Stuart River, where he first met people of the tribe whose trade he was seeking. Taking the river on his right, our Stuart River, he reached the Lake of the Carriers, our Stuart Lake, the first objective of the journey. McDougall had visited it in springtime, when fish were plentiful and all nature was fair, but now no fish were to be caught, and even the natives were starving. The savages were greedy for the goods which Fraser brought, a happy augury for the future trade of the post, but Fraser notes, doubtless with regret : " They are independent of us, as they get their necessaries from their neighbors who trade with the Natives of the sea-coast," *i.e.* by way of Babine Lake and River and Skeena River.

Fraser and Stuart set themselves at once to the task of building a fort, all the while waiting anxiously for the salmon to come up the river and supply provisions for a further journey. The site chosen was in a beautiful bay immediately north-east of the outlet of the lake. The fort, known at first as Stuart's Lake, but later as St. James, was the fourth post, and is apparently the oldest permanent European establishment in our British Columbia, for it is occupied to-day. The traders of after times sing the praises of its lake, called after Fraser's companion, Stuart's Lake. For example, John McLean forgot his fault-finding with his Company and most of its servants, and broke into praise of its beauties :

The lake is about fifty miles in length, and from three to four miles in breadth, stretching away to the north and north-east [north-west] for twenty miles. The view from the fort embraces nearly the whole of this section of it, which is studded with beautiful islands. The western shore is low, and indented by a number of small bays formed by wooded points projecting into the lake, the background rising abruptly into a ridge of hills of varied height and magnitude. On the east the view is limited to a range of two or three miles by the intervention of a high promontory, from which the eye glances to the snowy summits of the Rocky Mountains [*sic*] in the distant background. I do not know that I have seen anything to compare with this charming prospect in any other part of the country.

The population of the region was comparatively numerous. It was largely sedentary, being settled in villages about the lake. The area occupied by each tribe, or rather subdivision of the tribe, was well-defined, as also the hunting-ground of each family. The people lived on the fish caught and cured in the season and to some extent on the proceeds of the hunt in its season. They offered a good market for the traders' goods, as soon as they should learn to " work beaver." At first there would be no great stimulus to this industry beyond the desire for the traders' goods, but when the love of ardent liquors became deep-seated it would, according to Duncan M'Gillivray's philosophy, become the incentive to industry, and make the harvest of furs an assured one.

The relations of the traders with the people were happy at the outset, but with so large a population massed in villages and conscious of its overpowering numbers there was always the danger of a sudden and passionate eruption of hostility over some passing incident. In this Stuart Lake may be taken as typical of the posts in New Caledonia. The fur trade on the lake became lucrative, especially after 1821, when the peltries were sent to the Columbia by canoe and pack-horses, and were shipped to England by way of Cape Horn.

At the moment, however, things were very uncomfortable for Fraser and Stuart, for it was not the season for salmon. Other fish could not be procured in quantities necessary for life, and berries were wellnigh all that could be found to keep flesh and bones together. The situation became very anxious, for the salmon failed to appear when expected. Fraser therefore scattered his force, sending Stuart with a party overland to a lake called Natleh, about forty miles to the south-west and subsequently known as Fraser's Lake, where salmon were supposed to be plentiful. Stuart was to view the country and run down by the little stream flowing out of the lake into the Nechako River, and by this last to its confluence with the Stuart River. There he was to meet his chief. Fraser left Stuart Lake on 3rd September for the place of meeting. He had desired to procure provisions enough to continue on to the " Columbia," and down that stream to the " Atnah " (Shuswap) tribe, at the point where Mackenzie had left it, but as none could be procured, the two traders returned to Natleh Lake, and there built a post on a large bay immediately south of its outlet. The run of the salmon now commenced, and all were kept busy laying up a store of dried fish. On this body of water of about thirteen miles in length, one of the many elongated lakes among the mountains, Indian villages attested to the abundance of the food supply. Moreover the prospects for beaver were good, but the autumn canoes with goods from the east failed to reach New Caledonia. There was nothing to trade with the Indians for supplies or for beaver. The fare at the forts that winter was bad, but the trade must have been even worse.

Next year (1808) two canoes of goods arrived with reinforcements in the persons of Maurice Quesnel and Hugh Faries. Trade for furs and for provisions alike began in earnest in the new department. Fraser was enabled to establish a post, Fort George, at the confluence of the Fraser and the Nechako rivers, Faries in charge. The site was below the Forks and on the right bank. The Indians of the region were the most southerly of the Carriers. They were not as numerous as at the other posts, but there were prospects of trade, and the fort would act as a base for the advance down the river to the coast, which was an integral part of the policy of crossing the Rockies.

Fraser now turned his attention to the exploration of his "Columbia River." With provisions in the form of dried salmon, and with goods with which to pay for such necessaries as should be wanted on the way, he "embarked at Fraser's River," that is, on the small stream which flowed out of Fraser's Lake, on May 22, 1807. He ran down the Nechako to its confluence with the "Columbia" (Fraser) River, to Fort George. After a short stay, during which he would make his last preparations, he started on his great venture on 28th May with two of his officers, Messrs. Stuart and Quesnel, a crew of nineteen men, and two Indians, manning four canoes. The story of his daring journey is told in detail in his Journal. While his account lacks the clarity and vivacity of Sir Alexander Mackenzie's narrative of his two journeys, it is an absorbing tale of endurance to the limits of human flesh, of a courage which would have been regarded as reckless and suicidal but for its marvellous success, and of hairbreadth escapes, not only from the clutch of the pitiless stream, but from the perils of the no less pitiless cliffs which bordered it, for at many points the portages were scarcely less dangerous than the rapids and whirlpools. Take for an example Fraser's never-to-be-forgotten experiences in the Cottonwood Canyon on the first day of June :

At an early hour this morning all hands were up and soon after the natives appeared in several directions some of which came to us ; however by 5 a.m. Mr. Stuart myself and six men went to visit the rapid again while the others remained to take care of the baggage and Canoes ; we found the rapid to be about 1½ mile long and the rocks on both sides [of] the River contract themselves in some places to either 30 or 40 yards of one another ; the immense body of water passes through them in a zig-zag & turbulent manner forming numerous Gulphs and whirlpools of great depths. However as it was deemed impossible to carry the Canoes ; it was the general opinion that they ought to be run down ; indeed there was no other alternative than either that or leaving them [the canoes] here ; Mr. Stuart remained at the lower end with Legarde and Waka, to watch the Natives while the others were running the Canoes down ; though they [the Indians] appeared peaceable, it would not be prudent to allow the people to run down the Canoes under such a steep and rocky bank without having a guard above, as it would be in the Indians' power to sink them all to the bottom, were they ill-inclined and I returned to the upper [end] to see the people embark ; accordingly five of the best men embarked with only about 11 or 12 pieces, they immediately entered the rapid, but the whirlpools below the first cascade made them wheel about and they remained a considerable time without being able to move one way or the other, and every moment on the brink of eternity ; however, by the outmost exertions they went down two others [rapids] till between that and the fourth which is the most turbulent the eddies and whirlpools caught [hold] of the canoe and spite of them brought [them] ashore in a moment and fortunately it was it so happened, or that they were not able to get out again for had they [gone] down the fourth cascade it would have been more than likely they would have remained there. Seeing it impossible to go any farther they unloaded upon a small point in a very steep and high and long hill ; upon my way down to see what had become of the people I met Mr. Stuart coming up who informed me of the situation, he having seen them from the lower part of the rapids ; we went down immediately to the place they were thrown ashore which we reached with much difficulty on account of the steepness of the banks ; I often supported myself by running my dagger into the ground to hold myself by it ; happy we were to find all hands safe after such eminent [sic] danger. With much difficulty a road was dug into the hill with a hoe, about the breadth of one foot wide and a line tied to the bow of the canoe and brought up an extra-ordinary bad and long bank ; had any of those that carried the canoe missed their step all would have tumbled into the River in spite of those that hauled the line ; and when that was effected the baggage was brought up and by the time the remainder of the canoes were unloaded night came on. . . . The tremendous gulphs and whirlpools which are peculiar [to] this River is ready every moment to swallow a canoe with all its contents and the people on board, and the high and perpendicular rocks render it impossible to stop the Canoe or get on shore even was it stopped. . . . In the present state of the water I pronounce it impracticable.

It was nevertheless determined to carry three of the canoes over this portage and as far as possible proceed by water. Horses were procured from the Indians, but so steep was the declivity to the river that one horse was precipitated to the bottom, breaking Mr. Stuart's desk with the loss of his papers and medicines. This was in the country of the Atnahs.

Farther on the carrying-places were at times scarcely less perilous than the rapids. A portage is thus described in the version of the Journal published by L. R. Masson and under date of the 4th of June :

After passing safely through the dangerous rapid at the spot, the men returned by land for the baggage. This task was as difficult and dangerous as going by water, being obliged to pass on a declivity which formed the border of a huge precipice, on loose stones and gravel which constantly gave way under their feet. One of them, who had lost the path, got into a most intricate and perilous situation. With a large package on his back, he got so engaged among the rocks that he could neither move forward nor backward, nor yet unload himself, without imminent danger. Seeing this poor fellow in such an awkward and dangerous predicament, I crawled, not without great risk, to his assistance, and saved his life by causing his load to drop from his back over the precipice into the river. This carrying-place, two miles long, had so shattered our shoes that our feet became quite sore and full of blisters.

Reviewing the whole journey, one feels that by the test of sheer physical endurance and of the will to overcome difficulties at which the bravest might quail, the achievements of Simon Fraser must rank above those of Alexander Mackenzie. Moreover, Fraser's mastery of his crew and his management of the Indians along his route are on a par with the skill of his predecessor. He was past-master in the art of obviating hostilities and of winning the successive tribes to his will. He usually sent word ahead that he was coming. Thus

his party did not break suddenly upon strangers and in the light of
an enemy effecting a surprise, but rather as visitors to be entertained.
Even the Atnahs, whose attitude of hostility turned the intrepid
Mackenzie back on his steps, became Fraser's friends and provided
him with a guide who acted as mediator between him and the tribes
farther down the stream.

On 5th June the " Chilk-ho-tins " (Chilcotins), a Déné tribe,
were reached, the considerable river passed on the right being
doubtless the river which bears their name. On the 9th the party
came to the fearsome *rapide couvert*, one of the worst canyons on the
upper Fraser :

> Here the channel contracts to about forty yards and is enclosed by two
> precipices of immense height which, bending towards each other, make it
> narrower above than below. The water which rolls down this extraordinary
> passage in tumultuous waves and with great velocity had a frightful appear-
> ance. However, it being absolutely impossible to carry the canoes by land,
> all hands without hesitation embarked as it were *à corps perdu* upon the
> mercy of this awful tide. Once engaged, the die was cast ; our difficulty
> consisted in keeping the canoes within the medium or *fil d'eau*, that is clear
> of the precipice on one side and from the gulfs formed by the waves on the
> other. Thus skimming along as fast as lightning, the crews, cool and deter-
> mined, followed each other in awful silence, and when we arrived at the end,
> we stood gazing at each other in silent congratulation at our narrow escape
> from total destruction.

The next day the river was reported as wholly impracticable.
The canoes were stored on a scaffold and the superfluous equipment
and goods placed in two caches. On the 11th the party moved
forward, each bearing his own package of indispensable equipment
to the amount of eighty pounds weight. Hoping against hope,
Fraser and Stuart visited the river to see if it might be practicable.
" The channel was deep, cut through rocks of immense height and
forming eddies and gulfs which canoes could not even approach with
safety." They turned away, bracing themselves to endure the long
trudge before them. That day they began to meet the " Askettihs,"
presumably the Lilloets. On the 14th the party shaved and donned
their best apparel for the ceremonial entry into the metropolis of
the tribe at the confluence of the Fraser with another stream, probably near the present Lilloet. They were received with great show
and a genuine hospitality, being ferried next day across to the
village, " a fortification of 100 feet by 24 surrounded by a palisade
eighteen feet high, slanting inward and lined by a shorter row
which supports a shade [roof] covered with bark, constituting the
dwellings." Several European articles, including a new copper tea-
kettle, were seen. The savages drew for them a rough chart of the
country down to the sea and, not without a show of reluctance,
traded a canoe and a small supply of dried salmon. Next day a
second canoe was secured, and a portion of the party was now able
to proceed by water.

Fraser came next to the country of the Hacamaugh Indians,
and on the 19th to their principal seat at another confluence of

rivers, at the present town of Lytton. He had been hearing of this second river running on the east but towards his own " Columbia River," and that White Men were on it. Believing these to be David Thompson and his party, who were to advance to the coast on a more southerly course, and were in fact on the Columbia, he named the inflowing stream Thompson's River. The people proved very hospitable and traded canoes, so that once more the whole party was on the water. Soon the navigation became wild. At a cascade a canoe with all its goods was lost; however, the crew managed to come through alive. On the 22nd they were beyond these rapids and at Anderson River, near the present North Bend, not without further accidents and much travail at the portages. They had again to abandon their canoes. The country was more terrifying than anything yet seen :

It is so wild that I cannot find words to describe our situation at times. We have to pass where no human being should venture ; yet in those places there is a regular footpath impressed or rather indented upon the very rocks by frequent travelling. Besides this, steps which are formed like a ladder or the shrouds of a ship, by poles hanging to one another and crossed at certain distances with twigs, the whole suspended from the top to the foot of immense precipices and fastened at both extremities to stones and trees, furnish a safe and convenient passage to the Natives ; but we, who had not the advantage of their education and experience, were often in imminent danger when obliged to follow their example.

Below this they came to a chief, Spezzum, whose name still figures as that of a place.

On 28th June Fraser's party were among the " Achinrow nation," and at the point from which the river is navigable to the sea, which would be the present Yale. Fed with abundance of salmon, they were conveyed down the river in the canoes of their savage hosts. On 1st July they were within tidal waters. Fraser notes the large population. He was astonished at the sight of a house 640 feet long in a village near the present New Westminster. In this populous region, however, he was not accorded the barbaric hospitality experienced thus far. The people were the fierce Cowichans. It was practically by force that Fraser secured a canoe for the last stage to the sea. On 2nd July, at Musquam, at the northerly mouth of the river, he cast his eyes on the waters of the Gulf of Georgia " running in the south-west and north-east direction." Fraser made the latitude 49° north. As he knew that the Columbia was in 46° 20', he became aware that all his exertions had not brought him to the exact goal aimed at. His " Columbia " was not the river of his dreams. (The traders called it Fraser's River.) That mattered little so far as the advance of the North West Company westward was concerned. Grievous disappointment lay in the fact that the pitiless rapids and perilous portages, involving almost superhuman labour, defeated the hope of the fur-traders for an easy line of transportation to the coast and postponed the day when the merchants of Montreal could enter into the maritime fur trade. The result was that Fraser's journey, in many ways more remarkable than that of Alexander Mackenzie, did not leave any definite impress on the history of the country.   Notable as his voyage is as a human achievement, it pales in significance before the comparatively uneventful exploration by David Thompson of his " Kootenay," our Columbia River, for this was a practicable water-way for the traders, one whose record is woven into the fabric of the history of the land.

Fraser and his party had a much less eventful journey homeward and arrived at Fort George on 6th August.

3.—THE COLUMBIAN ENTERPRISE—THE NORTH WEST COMPANY'S APPROACH TO THE PACIFIC COAST BY COLUMBIA RIVER FROM THE SASKATCHEWAN, 1805–11—DAVID THOMPSON

While Simon Fraser was establishing his posts beyond the Rockies on the Peace River frontier, preparations were being made for the advance towards the Pacific from the Saskatchewan border. In 1805, the year in which it was decided to ask the Hudson's Bay Company for the right of transit for goods through their Bay, the North West Company gave its first orders.   Accordingly, in the summer of 1806 Jaco Finlay, a half-breed, went to blaze a trail through the pass leading from the headwaters of the North Saskatchewan to our Columbia River.   The pass has been named Howse after a Hudson's Bay Company's servant at Acton, their Rocky Mountain House, who used it later.   David Thompson, who had now approved himself to the North West Company as surveyor and explorer, was chosen to lead the advance.   He received his Instructions at the rendezvous at Kaministikwia in 1806, Duncan M'Gillivray in the chair.   Thus the Columbian enterprise, as first planned in 1800, was at last under way.

It has been argued that the Columbian enterprise was the result of the American expedition to the Pacific commanded by Lewis and Clark.   Rather it arose out of Alexander Mackenzie's spectacular voyage to the Western Sea and his scheme to go in and take possession of the coastal fur trade.   The subsequent expedition of Lewis and Clark could be no more than an additional incentive. The enterprise was the fixed policy of Duncan M'Gillivray when he was Wintering Partner on the Saskatchewan and during his years as agent for the Company, and it was finally launched in his last year but one, for he died on April 9, 1808.   It was the preoccupation of Duncan's last months, for during the early part of 1808 he was writing his *Some Account of the Trade carried on by the North West Company*, a plea, in keeping with the scheme of Alexander Mackenzie, for the Imperial Government to come to the support of the Company in its new venture.   This lucid little sketch was paragraphed and worked over by the hand of William M'Gillivray in 1809, and was finally published in 1811 under the title of *On the Origin and Progress of the North West Company*, in a form adapted to that date.   In the first place Duncan sketched the history of the Canadian fur trade in the North-West up to the formation of the North West Company. He then elaborated a defence of the Company's sale of liquor to the Indians. This was intended as a reply to the attempt of William Wilberforce and Lord Selkirk to induce the Imperial Government to prohibit the sale of alcohol to the aborigines of the Empire. M'Gillivray showed that in periods of opposition the sale of rum had been enormous, but that under the practical monopoly of the North West Company it was in the interest of the Company to reduce it, and that it had actually been brought down to a very modest figure.

In the years 1802, 1803 and 1804, those of the greatest struggle in the North West [*i.e.* with the XY Company] the average expenditure of the North West Company was 14,400 g.s. [*i.e.* in the concentrated form of " high wines "] and that of the opposed party at least 5,000 (totalling) 19,400 g.s. . . . while the trade is confined to a single company, that company is bound by every motive which self-interest can supply to preserve the savages from wars, drunkenness, idleness or whatever else would divert them from the chase and lessen the quantity of skins annually received at the different posts.

M'Gillivray then dwells on the great influence of the traders in keeping the Indians loyal to the Crown and away from the Americans. He displays the wide range of forts, " 84 in number," maintained by the Company, from those on the Straits of Belleisle to three on the west side of the Rockies. (No doubt McLeod Lake, Stuart Lake, and Fraser Lake are intended.) Emphasis is placed on the value of the trade to the commerce of Britain. English manufactures taken for it averaged £35,000 sterling ; the duties paid amounted to £15,000 sterling. Finally, the importance of the Columbian enterprise is explained and emphasized and a plea entered that the Imperial Government come to the support of the Company.

Not satisfied with the immense region on the eastern side of the Rocky mountains throughout which their trade is established, they have commenced a project for extending their researches and trade as far as the South Sea ; and have already introduced British manufactured goods, among the natives on the Western side of the Rocky mountains ; intending at some future period to form a general establishment for the trade of that country on the Columbia river, which . . . receives and conducts to the Ocean all the waters that rise west of the Mountains. The trade as it is carried on at present, beyond the Mountains, instead of yielding any profit, is a very considerable loss to the Company ; as the furs will not pay for transport to Montreal, where they are shipped ; nor can any establishment be formed immediately on the side of the Western Ocean ; as the natives in consequence of some very ill treatment by some American adventurers, trading on the coast about ten years ago, are extremely hostile to the whites. But this prejudice will yield to the Superior convenience of a hatchet and a gun, over a sharp stone and a bow and arrow (with which the Indians will become gradually acquainted) and to the kindness and fair dealing of those who intend to make permanent establishments among them. Should the Company succeed in this project, a new field will be open for the consumption of British manufactured goods ; and a vast country and population made dependant on the British Empire. It is conceived however that all this cannot be accomplished without the aid of the British Government, which will scarcely be withheld from an effort of such commercial and political importance.

M'Gillivray does not say what he wishes of the Government. When the pamphlet was published in 1811 a definite plea was made for a charter for the North West Company. This is nothing more or less than Sir Alexander Mackenzie's scheme of a charter which would free the Company from the monopolies of the East India and South Sea companies and permit it to sail on the southern seas and to China, and, it may be inferred, would incidentally assist the Company in negotiating an arrangement with the Hudson's Bay Company for transit of goods through Hudson Strait—a chartered company negotiating with a chartered company on equal terms. M'Gillivray's sketch shows that his " concern " was deeply committed to the Columbian enterprise and that its policy was to establish a succession of posts which would win the friendship and co-operation of the transmontane Indians until it should be safe to establish a depot on the Columbia near the coast. In keeping with these principles Fraser had built his forts in New Caledonia, and David Thompson was completing his second winter of trade on what he called the Kootenae River, but which proved in fact to be the Columbia.

In many ways David Thompson was the right man for the Columbian enterprise. He could survey, as none other could, the intricate country created by a tangle of mountains, and few Wintering Partners were more expert in solving the problems of an unexpected situation. But he does not appear to have been of a masterful nature. His interest lay in mapping out the land as he went and in doing his duty as a fur-trader, but if we may judge by his Journals he was scarcely conscious of the great enterprise committed to his charge. Hence the leisureliness—from the point of view of the British Empire the disastrous leisureliness—of his advance to the sea as compared with that of Simon Fraser. However Thompson may have conceived of it, there can be no doubt of the purpose of his enterprise as in the minds of the North West Company. James Bird of the Hudson's Bay Company's Edmonton House could have done no more than report the views of his neighbour at the Canadian Fort Augustus when he wrote to the factor at York Fort on December 23, 1806 :

> Mr. David Thompson is making preparations for another attempt to cross the Mountains, pass through [the Kutenai country] and follow the Columbia River to the Sea. He is to have eight Men with him, and the object of his enterprise is said to be, to ascertain positively whether a Trade can be formed with that Country valuable enough to be worth pursuing thro the difficulties with which it must be attended, and if it should, the uniting of the commerce of the two Seas.

John MacDonald of Garth, Duncan M'Gillivray's successor as Wintering Partner in the Department of Upper Forts des Prairies at Rocky Mountain House, supervised the preparations for Thompson's expedition. In 1806, that is, when Fraser was making his first transmontane exploration from the Peace River frontier, MacDonald sent the half-breed Jaco Finlay to open a path through the pass at the source of the North Saskatchewan. Finlay was instructed to build canoes on the river beyond, to be ready for Thompson's use. As it proved, he made but a footpath too narrow for pack-horses, and the work might well have been left undone.

On May 10, 1807, Thompson started from Rocky Mountain House with the equipment and goods for his new forts, and the added burden of his wife and family. A preliminary danger lay in the possible hostility of the Piegans. This powerful tribe, whose hunting-grounds stretched along the eastern slope of the Rockies, had proved friendly to the Company so long as it kept east of the mountains, for they obtained at its forts the arms which made them a terror to the tribes west of that range. With these munitions they had been able effectually to bar the way of the Kutenais to the posts of the traders, where they could have secured guns—the only means of defence against those who preyed upon them. It could be taken as certain that the Piegans would become hostile to the traders as soon as they should attempt to pass through and arm their hitherto defenceless victims. Thompson says : " The murder of two Peagan Indians by Captain Lewis of the United States, drew the Peagans to the Mississouri to revenge their deaths ; and thus gave me an opportunity to cross the Mountains by the defiles of the [North] Saskatchewan River, which led to the headwaters of the Columbia River." Finan MacDonald went forward with five men in a large canoe up the river to a fine meadow, " The Kootenay Plain," on the north bank and among the foothills. Thompson's means of conveyance were ten horses. They carried three hundred pounds of pemmican and some baggage, and they were needed to carry everything over the height of land to the Columbia. On 5th June the canoe left this plain to go to the limits of navigation. The next day it left the main stream, which came from the north-north-westward, and took a small tributary flowing in from the south, but it could proceed no more than four miles. It returned to the plain for the remainder of the goods, while Thompson lay there among the mountains awaiting them. " Here among their stupendous and solitary wilds covered with eternal Snow, and Mountain connected with Mountain by immense Glaciers, the collection of Ages and on which the Beams of the Sun makes hardly an Impression when aided by the most favourable weather, I stayed for fourteen days more, impatiently waiting the melting of the Snows on the Height of Land." At last Thompson sent for his men and for the horses resting amid the pleasant pastures of the Kootenay Plain. On 25th June, leaving Finan MacDonald with part of the goods, the main party advanced in the face of the perils of the pass and beyond it along the course of the Blaeberry River, foaming in the spring flood down its shallow bed. Their progress was of the slowest. On one day they advanced but one and three-quarters of a mile, for Jaco Finlay's footpath through the woods was useless for the pack-horses. The animals grew weak for lack of pasture, for the grass had not yet began to grow. For the same reason big game was not to be found, and there was no chance to replenish the larder by hunting by the way. Provisions began to be exhausted. The famished party had to condescend to eat dog. On 30th June they encamped on the banks of the Columbia. " Thank God," says Thompson, though he had but six pounds of pemmican to go on. Jaco Finlay's canoes, built here the summer before, were no better than his road, so it proved impossible to hasten on. Accordingly Thompson began to build new craft, while he waited for the rest of the goods to be brought over " The Mountain Portage." Meanwhile fishing proved fruitless. After a week some Kootenais were found and engaged to hunt. At last, on 11th July, all was ready for farther advance.

About a hundred miles upstream, that is, in a southerly direction, brought Thompson to his Kootenae (Windermere) Lake, the lower of the two Columbian lakes which are the source of the great river. Evidently he was aiming at reaching M'Gillivray's River (the Kootenay) by way of M'Gillivray's Portage and following its westerly direction towards the sea. Progress was, however, stayed by the difficult position in which the trader found himself. " From the State of the Country and the Situation of my Affairs I found myself necessitated to lay aside all Thoughts of Discovery for the present and bend my whole aim to an establishment for Trade." This would, of course, bring a traffic in provisions as well as furs. The situation was not relieved when the salmon came up to the lakes to spawn, for they were so far spent as to be unfit for food. The party was reduced to eating a dead wild horse, but this proved most obnoxious fare.

Thompson's decision to stay at the " Kootenay Lake " and build a post was probably an error in judgment on his part, for had he managed to push on he would have met a band of Kutenais coming towards him, and his wants would have been so far supplied by them as to enable him to reach the objective set for him by Duncan M'Gillivray, namely, to reach M'Gillivray's River (the Kootenay) and to build there. Thompson was not unconscious that he was falling short of his instructions, for he says : " What a fine opportunity was here lost of going to the Flat Bow Country [the valley of the Kootenay, south of the lake of that name] from the embarrassed Situation of my Affairs." A fine opportunity was indeed lost, for the valley of the Kootenay was more thickly peopled, since the Indians there obtained an abundant supply in season of fish from the river, and at other times of buffalo meat from the prairies beyond the mountains. There Thompson would have done a better trade, lived in greater comfort, and his base for farther advance would have been nearer the coast.

Thompson pitched on a spot at the outflow of the Columbia from Lake Windermere on which to build. It was on a bank some 240 feet high and " not far from the fine log building which has been erected as a memorial there, at the joint expense of the Canadian Pacific Railway and the Hudson's Bay Company, and which was dedicated with fitting ceremonies in the late summer of 1922." When the Kutenais arrived from the Kootenay River they pointed out that the position chosen was indefensible. The trader therefore removed to a spot two miles down the river and north of the lake, where another stream, our Toby Creek, comes in from the Selkirks on the west and forms a defensible peninsula. The post was built on a bank only twenty feet above the stream, which thus afforded an assured supply of water. A hall for Thompson and a house for the men were erected, as well as a ball-proof stockade, with bastions running out to the steep bank and affording the opportunity of drawing water. The post was called Kootenae House.

True to Thompson's surmise, a war-party of Piegans arrived in November to destroy what they must have regarded as an arsenal for arming their foes. By this time the fort had been supplied with dried provisions and could draw its water from the river in the secret of the night. It was able to stand what was practically a siege. A subsequent war-party was bought off before its arrival by a very ample gift of tobacco.

Soon after his settlement, David Thompson received from a Kutenai chief a copy of an, under the circumstances, amazing document, purporting to be signed by Lieutenant James Roseman and Zachary Perch, Commanding Officer at " Fort Lewis, Yellow River, Columbia, 10th July, 1807." Such copies were given to various chiefs who appeared at the fort for trade, to give to British Traders to inform them of the regulations subject to which they might trade " within our Territories," these territories being defined as " the Mississouri, Red River and all the Lands westward to the Coast of California and the Columbia River with all its Branches of which we have now taken possession "—meaning by the cession of Louisiana. No flag was to be displayed in any manner, or given to the natives, save the American flag. " 6th, As all Indian Traders in the American Territory enjoy the Protection of America and its salutary Laws, Justice requires that they shall contribute towards the Armed Force that Protects them." This was to be done by paying the import and export duties indicated at the nearest customs house. As the nearest American soldier and customs officers were about a thousand miles away, and David Thompson was the sole European occupant of the valley of the Columbia, he may be excused for treating the American claims as, for him, non-existent. This remarkable document was probably the fabrication of some fur-traders who hoped to intimidate Thompson into giving up the Columbian enterprise, for there were no officers in the American army of the names given, and " Fort Lewis, Yellow River, Columbia " appears to be as mythical as the officers themselves.

Finan MacDonald arrived in the autumn with the goods for the post, so that Thompson was able to make an extended excursion in the spring along the course marked out for the previous summer. He crossed M'Gillivray's Portage to the Kootenay, which he calls M'Gillivray's River and also names the Flatbow. He ran downstream beyond our International Boundary and past the Tobacco River in Montana to the Kootenay Falls. Portaging past them, he came on a camp of Flatheads and Kutenai at or near the present Bonner's Ferry in Idaho. By 14th May he had continued his course downstream to the Flatbow or Kootenay Lake at the present Kootenay Landing. He now returned to the Flathead camp. Because the river was in flood, he took to horse and rode over the hills through the terrible country traversed to-day by the Canadian Pacific Railway. Passing Moyie Lake, he came to the Kootenay River once more, near the present Fort Steel.

Thompson was back at Kootenae House in time to take out his furs to the Saskatchewan. On his return with goods in the autumn he was able to send Finan MacDonald to establish the post on M'Gillivray's River which had been his objective of the year before. It was built at Kootenay Falls, Idaho. Thus in 1808 the point was reached which was aimed at in 1807, but it was only established as an outpost, Thompson remaining in the rear at Kootenae House. In all this, his conduct of the Columbian enterprise, Thompson was falling short of the wise and pushful policy of Simon Fraser in prosecuting the enterprise on the Peace River front and pushing to the ultimate goal, the Pacific, as soon as might be. Fraser built four forts in his first year and devoted the following summer to exploring the Fraser River to tidal waters. In two years the possibilities of that route to the ocean were known. To begin with, Thompson built his first post short of the Kootenay River, where he was to establish his base, and when he did place a post at Kootenay Falls he treated it as a mere outpost. Finally, instead of using the summer to explore the route by the Columbia to the ocean, and thereby giving direction to his Company, he spent the months favourable for exploration in taking the furs out. Thus the seasons went by without the Company achieving its main object—the establishment of a depot on the coast which would reduce transportation costs, make the trade pay, and pre-empt the Pacific coast for Britain.

In the spring of 1809 Thompson took out the furs, but went no farther than Fort Augustus, for he was to make another advance, presumably towards the coast; but from the point of view of the policy of his Company he was guilty of another error in judgment in not pursuing his exploration of Kootenay (M'Gillivray's) River, downstream beyond Kootenay Lake—reached eighteen months before. Had he done so, he would have found an easy and short course to the broad Columbia, with a comparatively smooth way before him to the coast. Instead, from our Bonner's Ferry below the Kootenay Falls, and as the crow flies about forty miles from the lake, he abandoned the easy course by canoe for tedious travel overland to the Pend d'Oreille Indians at the lake of their name. The most natural interpretation is that he sacrificed, or at least risked, the more distant goal for the immediate prospects of trade with these Indians. He arrived on the lake on 8th September and crossed it to the neighbourhood of Clark Fork (River) and there built his post. " The site has been identified as a rather rocky point of land about two miles from the main channel of Clark Fork River and a

half-mile from Memaloose Island, and locally known as Sheepherders
Point " (T. C. Elliott). Here Finan MacDonald was in charge during
the subsequent winter. It was called Kullyspell House from a band
of Indians. Thompson rejoiced to find the Indians without guns,
and carried on a lively trade in that article. " All those who could
procure Guns soon became good shots, which the Peeagan Indians,
their enemies in the next battle severely felt, for they are not good
shots, except a few." Thus not only did Thompson take an indirect
and difficult route towards the coast, but he armed the Indians of
the new post, so that they won a notable victory over the Piegans.
The result was that the defeated Indians became his mortal foes,
waylaid him on his pressing journey to the coast next year to forestall John Jacob Astor's expedition to the mouth of the Columbia,
and prevented him from reaching the Pacific coast before the
Americans.

Having achieved his immediate object, viz. trade, by establishing
Kullyspell House on Pend d'Oreille Lake, Thompson turned his
attention to the policy of reaching out towards the coast. He
followed down the river flowing out of the lake, which he called the
Saleesh, but which is now known as Clark Fork, but he found its
course impossible and speedily returned. He then turned his mind
once more to the fur trade. He went to M'Gillivray's River to meet
the canoes coming in with goods under the charge of James Mac-
Millan. Later in the autumn he turned his back to the sea and built
the fourth trading post in the Columbian Department, Saleesh
House, at Thompson's Prairie in Montana, and wintered there with
James MacMillan. In the spring (1810) he made a second futile
attempt to reach the Columbia by Clark Fork. In turning away
from the Kootenay he had missed his path. He now went out with
the furs.

There is reason to believe that Thompson's heart was not in the
Columbian enterprise. To begin with, he might have sent his clerk
MacMillan out with the furs and in person pushed his exploration
to its goal, but, most eloquent of all, he took his family across the
Rockies with him, as Alexander Henry the younger, who was on the
Saskatchewan at the time, says, with the intention of leaving the
country. Evidently this expert surveyor and map-maker had in no
sense grasped the importance of the enterprise entrusted to his care.
Although a Wintering Partner in the North West Company, he
showed nothing of the vision which made for the greatness of the
proprietors of the Montreal concern, and which achieved the successes of that great Company. At Rainy Lake, the depot for the
Columbian as well as the Athabaskan Department, he must have
received something of a shock at the news of the movements of the
Americans to occupy the mouth of the Columbia, and at the order
to return immediately to his task of making a way down that stream
to the coast in anticipation of their designs.

In the negotiations which ended the War of Independence and
issued in the Treaty of Versailles, 1783, the Earl of Shelburne, then

at the head of the British Ministry, had conceded to the Americans as a boundary line the water-way from the Pigeon River on Lake Superior to what has since been defined as the North-West Angle of Lake of the Woods, and thence along the forty-ninth parallel of latitude running, as it was believed, to the Mississippi River—this when there were no Americans in the wide territory between it and the valley of the River Ohio. "Scarcely an American settler had carried his axe across the Ohio when the Treaty was signed. Save for a few hundred *habitants* in the old French towns along the Illinois, the only White Men within this immense territory were Canadian traders with the Indians," as an American writer puts it. British garrisons in a number of posts such as Detroit and Michilimackinac should be added. The anger of Britain at Shelburne's concessions registered itself in the vote of the House of Commons—207 to 190—of 22nd February censuring the Government for the terms of the peace. However, there was no intention thereafter to tear up the treaty. Governor Haldimand held on to the Western Posts lest the Indians, in their anger at being left to the mercy of the Americans, should break out into ruthless warfare. The Northwesters, however, clung to the hope that something would turn up to keep the South-West, as it was called, under the British flag. The trade of the lower Ohio and of the upper Mississippi valley had for long followed the easy and economic lines of transportation by water through Lake Michigan and by Michilimackinac and the St. Lawrence to or from Montreal. Indeed, it is conceivable that, had steam transportation by land not come in to surmount the physical obstacles between the Atlantic states and the American North-West, this situation might have remained to this day. At the time of the treaty the administration of the United States was not in a position to take over their north-western frontier, nor to assume control of the Indian tribes to whom King George was a father and protector and the American colonists inveterate enemies. Thus it came about that the British continued to hold the Western Posts for another decade.

But nothing turned up to maintain the hold of Britain upon the wide fur region conceded. On the contrary, the Americans conquered the Indians and demanded the surrender of the posts. This, along with many factors beyond the horizon of this volume, led to the negotiations in London associated with the name of John Jay, Chief Justice of the United States, and at the moment Plenipotentiary Extraordinary to Great Britain. In the area of the discussions in which this volume is interested, the concern of the British Government was to protect the trade of Canada while surrendering the posts and making good the International Boundary as agreed upon in 1783. *The Project of Heads of Proposals to be made to Mr. Jay* runs : " The cession (of the Posts) is not to be considered as interrupting the usual course of Communication and Commerce between the Two Canadas and the Indian Nations." This principle was gained by the British and its limits defined in Jay's Treaty, concluded on November 19, 1794. The second article arranged the cession of the Western

Posts on or before the first day of June 1796. The third article runs :

It is agreed that it shall at all times be free to His Majesty's subjects and to the citizens of the United States . . . freely to pass and repass by land or inland navigation, into the respective territories and countries of the two parties, on the continent of America (the country within the limits of the Hudson's Bay Company only excepted) and to navigate all the lakes, rivers and waters thereof and freely to carry on trade and commerce with each other. . . . No higher or other tolls or rates of ferriage than what are or shall be payable by natives, shall be demanded on either side ; and no duties shall be payable on any goods which shall merely be carried over any of the portages or carrying-places on either side, for the purpose of being immediately re-embarked and carried to some other place or places.

The intention, it is plain, was to give equal rights to both nations in the Indian trade of the Upper Country outside of the limits of Rupert's Land.

The American public regarded Jay's Treaty as something near a betrayal of their interest as far as the Western Posts were concerned, for if the Canadians were allowed the right of free entry, the advantages in their favour in the form of the cheap water-routes were so great that the furs of the American North-West would continue to be gathered by them and shipped to England by way of Montreal. Devious ways were resorted to in order to nullify this article of the treaty. The Canadian fur-traders, hard hit by them, sent in memorials to their Government seeking redress for the infractions of the treaty. The Americans are accused of charging much higher duties up country than at their Atlantic ports. They are said to have established a vexatious system of passes— in one case, at any rate, denying licences to any but American nationals. Regulations were introduced requiring rum to be imported in nothing but large casks, when it could be conveyed in canoes and over the portages only in small kegs. " A Systematic Plan to drive the British Indian Traders from the American Territory by every species of vexation " one memorial characterizes these regulations. Finally, in 1808 the Americans fired upon a brigade of the boats of the Michilimackinac Company in the middle waters of the Niagara River, pursued it out into the lake, and seized it. It made the situation worse that the United States had purchased Louisiana from France in 1803, and the difficulties heretofore experienced east of the Mississippi were now encountered in the country west of that river. This region, of course, did not come under the terms of Jay's Treaty.

It was this harassing situation that drove the traders of the South-West into the Canadian North-West, and issued in the formation of the XY Company. In the hope of conserving their trade with the Indians of the valley of the Mississippi, traders who remained in the trade of the South-West from Michilimackinac tried to overcome the handicap imposed upon them by the Americans by uniting in one great " concern," the Michilimackinac Company, modelled after the North West Company. It was in vain. The embarrassments inflicted upon these traders constituted a golden opportunity for John Jacob Astor, a German who had migrated to London and thence crossed the Atlantic to make his fortune. To his genius must be ascribed the organization of the American fur trade in a system scarcely less virile or aggressive than that of the North West Company itself. Jay's Treaty enabled him to enter the Canadian trade as far as he might desire, but he found the Michilimackinac Company too powerful for him. Taking advantage of their difficulties, he made an offer to the American Government to divert the whole of the trade of the South-West into American channels if only the Government would support him. With their countenance he obtained a charter from the Legislature of the State of New York incorporating the American Fur Company with a capital of one million dollars. In 1811 he was able to get control of the Michilimackinac Company, and formed an association known as the South West Company with intimate relations with the North West Company. The advantage of it lay in that the South West Company could buy much of its goods through the agents of the North West Company in Montreal, but also bring to the trade American wares bought in New York, which would, of course, be free of duty on entering American territory again.

Not content with his grip of the fur trade of the " old North-West," and the South-West, Astor decided to lay his hand upon the marine fur trade of the Pacific coast. Associated as he was with the fur-traders in Montreal and the agents of the North West Company, he cannot have been unaware of their Columbian enterprise. To the Northwesters his venture on the Pacific coast must have seemed nothing less than an attempt to " jump their claim." To the historian it was all of this, but it was something more. It registered the interest of the American people in the Pacific West. That interest began with ships from Boston engaged in the marine fur trade, but it was greatly increased by the acquisition of Louisiana. Spain had agreed to the retrocession of that region to France on the understanding that it was not to be alienated, but Napoleon startled the Americans who were negotiating with him for the freedom of the trade of the Mississippi by offering to sell the whole country (1803). The young Republic might have found it difficult to face the sum required did not the sale of its lands offer an ample ultimate return. The Americans immediately set themselves to examine their new estate and to warn off intruders. In 1805–6 Lieutenant Zebulon Montgomery Pike ascended the Mississippi and warned the North-westers on the headwaters of the Red River, at Sandy and Leech lakes, that they were plying their trade in American territory. Then, too, President Jefferson organized an expedition commanded by Meriwether Lewis and William Clark with a view to exploring the connections of Louisiana with the Pacific coast. This party ascended the Missouri, noting the successive places of settlement occupied by that interesting people, the Mandans, and it wintered in quarters called Fort Mandan immediately below the village occupied by the remnant of the tribe (1804-5). It then ascended the river and passed over into the watershed of the Columbia at the sources of the Snake River, which was named the Lewis. It spent the winter of 1805-6 at the mouth of the Columbia in the region first discovered by Captain Gray. The expedition heightened the interest of the American public in the Pacific, as no doubt it was intended to do. Its most practical outcome came through the genius of that master organizer of the fur trade, John Jacob Astor. His scheme was the American edition of the dreams of Sir Alexander Mackenzie and Duncan M'Gillivray—to establish a string of forts along the Missouri and the Lewis rivers to the coast ; to establish a depot at the mouth of the Columbia ; and to engage in the marine fur trade of the coast, selling his peltries in the markets of China. It was in Astor's favour that American ships could sail on the Pacific and enter the marts of the Far East without coming to terms, as the North West Company would have to do, with the East India Company. Astor communicated his plans to President Jefferson, and was promised every protection from the Government. He like-wise approached the North West Company, in the hope of avoiding competition, and offered them one-third of the interest in the trade. This Company, as has been seen, was aiming at the same goal as Astor, and at this time very near gaining it, for David Thompson had established or was establishing his posts on the Columbia and the Kootenay rivers and on Pend d'Oreille Lake. Moreover, the Company was making a bid for a charter from the British Government, granting them a monopoly of the trade and the right to enter the Chinese market. They ultimately declined the American offer. By June 1910 Astor's plans were perfected under the name of the Pacific Fur Company. No time was lost or could afford to be lost. In that very month arrangements were made for a land expedition by way of the Missouri and along Lewis and Clark's course to the Pacific coast, and for a second trading party to go by ship round the Horn, meeting the overland expedition in the estuary of the Columbia. Washington Irving sketches Astor's far-reaching plans :

His main establishment once planted at the mouth of the Columbia, he looked with confidence to ultimate success. Being able to reinforce and supply it amply by sea, he would push his interior posts in every direction up the rivers and along the coast, supplying the natives at a lower rate, and thus gradually obliging the North West Company to give up the competition, relinquish New Caledonia, and retire to the other side of the mountains. He would then have possession of the trade, not merely of the Columbia and its Tributaries, but of the region farther north, quite to the Russian possessions. Such was a part of his brilliant and comprehensive plans.

The North West Company was aware of Astor's scheme in 1809, but it seems to have believed at first that it would come to nothing. By January 1810 its agents and partners in Montreal were in a panic. The distance overland made it difficult for anything to be done to arouse Thompson out of his ill-judged leisureliness, if such it was, in reaching forward to the coast. To begin with, the North West Company had recourse to the British Government. In March, and again in June, McTavish, Fraser & Co., their agents in London, had Astor's plans laid before the Secretary of State for Foreign Affairs. Unfortunately for them, England was passing through months of great commercial and political embarrassment, for the war with Napoleon was coming to its climax. At any rate, nothing was done. On 10th November the Northwesters appealed, over the head of the Minister, to the Government in the person of the Prime Minister himself, Lord Liverpool, reporting by a letter that Astor's expedition had actually sailed :

> I fear it may be almost too late to accomplish the object which the North West Company had in view, if they could have obtained the Sanction of His Majesty's Government in sufficient time. That object was to establish settlements on the Columbia River, and so to secure the right of Possession to Great Britain before the arrival of the Americans. Still, however, this object might probably be accomplished and His Majesty's right to the Territorial possession of the Northwest Coast of America preserved, if one of His Majesty's Ships could immediately be despatched to take formal possession of and establish a Fort or Settlement in the Country. The American Ship is to make a trading Voyage on her way along the Coast of South America, and His Majesty's Ship would probably get to the Columbia River before her. . . . If the Plan which I have presumed to suggest should be adopted, and one of His Majesty's Ships sent to take possession of the Country in Question, the North West Company would send an Expedition across the Continent to meet her and to form trading Establishments under the protection of His Majesty's Fort.

If His Majesty's Government had failed to occupy the Columbia when it might have done so without seeming to forestall the Americans, they were not likely to take the step at the eleventh hour, when it could only be interpreted as an act of hostility—all the more as their preoccupations in Europe bade them borrow no fresh troubles. At any rate, they failed to come to the rescue of the North West Company's Columbian enterprise. In sharp contrast with this is the fact that the American Government had sent warships to guard Astor's craft, the *Tonquin*, when she put to sea on 10th September.

On the 22nd of July, that is, fifty-one days before the *Tonquin* sailed from New York, David Thompson arrived at the depot at Rainy Lake, intending to leave the interior on furlough. The canoes which left Montreal in May must have brought him the orders which turned his face once more towards the Rocky Mountains and the Columbia River. While we have no record of the exact terms, we can make no mistake in believing that he was ordered by the panic-stricken agents of the Company to hasten to the mouth of the Columbia, take possession of the region in the name of Great Britain, and, if possible, build a post before the arrival of the Americans. Thompson's *Narrative* is naturally silent on the point, for it was written when the Oregon was about to pass into the undisputed possession of the United States. His Journals kept from day to day do not explain the wider issues of his sudden return to the Columbia, but that return, coupled with the documents which show the frenzied efforts of the Company to anticipate the American settlement at the mouth of the Columbia, is sufficient evidence of the nature of his instructions. After he had taken his family back and had left it at Fort Augustus on the Saskatchewan, he was proceeding on horseback towards Howse Pass at the headwaters of the Saskatchewan, the route he had hitherto taken to the Columbia, while the canoes were ascending the river to the traverse across the mountains. Thompson was now to pay the price of his policy of not following the river from Kootenay Lake towards the sea, but diverging to the Flathead tribes on Pend d'Oreille Lake. His arming of these tribes against the Piegans had resulted, as has been seen, in a severe defeat of this people and their determination that no more guns and ammunition should be taken by the traders through their country to equip their mortal foes. They dogged the canoes as they ascended to within twenty miles of the mountains, and finally showed themselves in a menacing manner. The canoemen, who do not seem to have known just where their *bourgeois* was, and were without his steadying influence, returned to Rocky Mountain House to await events. When Thompson came to know of the hostile presence of the Piegans, as he says, he " rode for his life." No Alexander Mackenzie or Simon Fraser this, but a scholarly surveyor, not without an element of timidity in him. In this the crucial hour of his life, David Thompson was weighed and found wanting. He proved himself as without that " spirit of the North West Company," which by argument, by bargain, or by sheer masterfulness, won the savages to its will and forced its way through to its goal. This retreat of Thompson imperilled his chances of reaching the Columbia before the Americans. It was now the fourth week of September. Had he got through with all his men and goods he would have been, according to his instructions, paddling down the Columbia early in October, and he would have reached the mouth of the river and had his fort built in time. On their arrival the Americans would have been greeted by the British flag floating on the Oregon.

On 5th October Alexander Henry the younger arrived at Rocky Mountain House to reopen the post, which had been temporarily closed. He was surprised to find it occupied by Thompson's brigade, which had been quartered there since 24th September. " Mr. Thompson had not been seen since he left Upper Terre Blanche House [above Edmonton] on the 15th of September." The Piegans soon came into the fort and displayed no happy mood. Henry, however, proved himself equal to the situation. On 11th October he ostentatiously sent the Columbian canoes downstream as though they were returning to the lower fort. By plentiful outpourings of rum he got the Piegans into a deep drunken slumber during which the canoes passed the fort by night upwards towards the mountains where Thompson was supposed to be. Next day he was "astonished" at the arrival of William Henry, Thompson's clerk, with three

Rocky Mountain House canoes from the east. Alexander Henry's entry runs :

He informed me that on their way up they [*i.e.* Thompson and William Henry on horses] followed an old route which they hoped would bring them to the Saskatchewan at this place, where he [Thompson] expected to use his canoes ; but instead of that, they had sighted the river near the first ridge of mountains . . . where they fell in with the horses belonging to the four tents of the Piegans. This alarmed them and made Mr. Thompson suppose he was watched by the Indians and that his canoe had been stopped below ; he therefore sent an express to Bercier, at the Kootenay plains, telling him to come down with the horses [for the traverse] and follow him quickly to the North branch [the Brazeau River] by the interior route.

Alexander Henry's narrative continues : " I immediately sent Clement on foot to stop the canoes until further orders from Mr. Thompson." Next day Alexander Henry went downstream to see Thompson and found him on the left bank of the river " on the top of a hill 300 feet above the water, where tall pines stood so thickly that I could not see his tent until I came within ten yards of it. He was starving, and waiting for his people—both canoes and those men who were coming down with his horses."

No doubt the two partners discussed the possibility of still passing through to the Columbia by Howse Pass. Henry would urge that the men had passed up with the canoes and that all that was wanted was a courageous leader. Thompson would, however, show that without the horses at the portage it was useless to proceed, and moreover there was the danger from the Piegans. He must have insisted that the safest and indeed the only course left was to await the arrival of the canoes and the horses, and to make a way to the Athabaska Pass, known since Duncan M'Gillivray's day, and traversed recently by a band of " freeman." There would be no danger from the Piegans on this route, and doubtless he asserted there would be ample time to reach the Columbia and follow it downstream to the mouth. Thompson's hasty retreat and his ill-judged recall of the horses from the traverse of the mountains made the original route no longer the surest, and in any case it was not the safest way. Henry concludes : " It was therefore determined that the canoes should be ordered to return below as privately as possible, to avoid any misunderstanding with the natives." Thompson says helplessly and in self-defence : " There was no alternative." None the less much precious time was lost.

Thompson, his clerk William Henry, and his men, their goods on pack-horses, now turned to make their way through a pathless country. Much time was lost cutting a road through the brushwood to what afterwards was known as the Grand Traverse (Athabaska Pass). Thence Thompson with but a small portion of his goods trudged on snowshoes—for winter was now upon him—over the pass and down the Wood River to the confluence of the Canoe River with the Columbia. At this spot, known later as Boat Encampment, the great river sweeps round the Selkirks and takes its course southward. It was now 18th January, but the winter was mild and the river was " open and only a chance bridge of ice over it."   Had Thompson had all his men and goods with him he might possibly have attempted a dash downstream. As it was he was in a quandary, which he describes himself :

> Our voyage to the Sea was to proceed down the River but having only three men . . . being the Men that had the courage to risque the chances of the Voyage, we were too weak to make our way through the numerous Indians we had to pass. . . . In order to augment my number of men I had to proceed up the River and to the Saleesh [Flathead] country to where I knew I should find the free hunters, and engage some of them to accompany me. This gave us a long journey of hardship and much suffering.

Ever cautious and leisurely, he settled down for the winter, expecting the rest of his party to bring the goods over to him. Of course, they were held back by the deep snow of winter in the pass. When they failed to appear by 17th April, " as necessity urged [him] on," to use his own phrase at a later stage of his journey, he worked an arduous way in a cedar canoe of his own making up the river to the terminus of his familiar traverse over Howse Pass and up to the source of the Columbia, which he reached on 14th May. Thence he crossed M'Gillivray's Portage to the Kootenay River, which he followed to its south-eastern bend at the present Jennings, in the State of Montana. Procuring horses from the Indians, he travelled overland to his Saleesh House on Clark's Fork, taking into his service as he went a number of freemen to raise his party to the strength necessary for his journey through the populous tribes between him and the coast. Arrived at the post, he had to take precious time to build another canoe.

Now at last we find David Thompson in a hurry. The river was in flood and under ordinary circumstances would have held him back, but though it rushed through the woods " in a fearful flood," he ventured it in his canoe :

> We saw the risque before us, but we were all experienced men and kept the waves of the middle of the River. . . . We continued under the mercy of the Almighty and at sunset put up ; each of us thankful for his preservation ; and as the morrow did not promise anything better, and necessity urged us on, my poor fellows before laying down said their prayers, crossed themselves, and promised a Mass to be said for each, by the first priest they should see.

He passed through Pend d'Oreille Lake and downstream to the present Cusick in Washington. His former explorations of the river had shown him that he could not follow it on to its inflow into the Columbia. He therefore crossed overland to Spokane House, built the autumn before by Finan MacDonald, the fifth post in the Columbian Department. Its site was " at the junction of the Spokane and Little Spokane rivers, ten miles north-west of the city of Spokane." Continuing overland on 19th June he reached the Columbia at the Kettle Falls, forty-one miles south of the Canadian border. He had taken sixty-three days to reach this point from Boat Encampment. The journey down the river would not have required more than six days. Precious time was now consumed finding wood and making a cedar canoe, his third in three months. At last, on 3rd July, he was on the broad waters of the Columbia, his party numbering eight French-Canadians and two Iroquois, with two men of the region as guides and interpreters. His note-book runs : " We set off on a voyage down the Columbia to explore this river in order to open out a passage for the interior trade with the Pacific Ocean."

Thompson's apprehensions of danger from the large Indian population along the river proved an illusion. The summer villages were many and some very large, so large that it is difficult to believe that the nine men now with him could be much safer than the three whom he had at Boat Encampment would have been. The White Men had only to land at the villages, smoke with the Indians in Council, promise them guns, and receive their hospitality with courtesy, to be sent off downstream with their good wishes. On one occasion Thompson says : " After smoking some time they prepared to give us a Dance, that we might have a safe voyage to the sea and in like manner return to them. The Chief made a short prayer."

At the junction of the Shahaptin (Lewis) River, on 9th July, Thompson erected a pole and tied to it half a sheet of paper with something like a proclamation. " Know hereby that this country is claimed by Britain as part of its territories, and that the N.W. Company of Merchants from Canada finding the factory for this people inconvenient for them do hereby intend to erect a factory in this place (by arrangement with the Chief) for commerce with the country around. D. Thompson." This was, of course, a desper-ate attempt at the eleventh hour to carry out towards its completion Duncan M'Gillivray's Columbian enterprise. Thompson explained to the chief of the region that " the way they brought the goods at present obliged him to cross high mountains and through hostile people. . . . They now sought a short safe way, by which all the articles they wanted would come in safety." The very next day, somewhere near John Day River, he entered in his Journal : " Heard news of the American ship's arrival." The phrase is alto-gether impersonal and curiously silent as to significance of the news. We must not infer from it that Thompson was not attempting to reach the coast before the Americans, for it shows that he was aware of Astor's expedition. On 15th July, his twelfth day on the Columbia, Thompson arrived at the post—Astoria—which the Americans were building. Towards midday in his large canoe with a flag at its stern he rounded the point above the fort—Tongue Point. His British flag was displayed too late, for the Stars and Stripes was already floating on the breezes of the Oregon and the American claim staked.

That summer Thompson passed up the part of the Columbia

which he was to have followed on the way down and completed his survey of the stream. He wintered at his Saleesh House and travelled as far as Missoula in Montana. On 12th August of 1812 he arrived at Fort William with his furs and the report of his failure. The significance of that failure is, of course, much more apparent to-day than it could possibly have been at the time. To all appearances Thompson was bent on leaving the Upper Country, and certainly the proprietors made generous arrangements with that end in view. Their Minute runs : David Thompson " now going down in rotation shall be allowed his full share for three years after this outfit and one hund^d. Pounds besides—that he is to finish his Charts, Maps etc. and deliver them to the Agents in that time, after which he is to be considered as a retired Partner and enjoy the Profits of one hundredth [*i.e.* his share in the Company] for seven years—the Hund^d. [pounds per annum] is meant for compensation for making use of his own instruments and for furnishing him with implements for drawing, writing etc."

David Thompson will always stand out beyond his fellows in the eyes of the historian and geographer however much the Canadian patriot may deplore Britain's failure through him to establish a first claim by settlement to the Pacific coast of the Oregon. None, except perhaps John MacDonald of Garth, saw the beauties of the North-West landscapes as he did. Not only did he survey its rivers and observe the physical features of the land in detail ; he noted its trees and the manner of their growth; he studied its animals and its fish, and he has left us vivid pictures of their habits, and of the ways of the savages in catching them. Above all he loved to sketch the peoples he met, their physiognomy, their character and habits ; and he has given to us in his *Narrative* priceless glimpses into their past history. His greatness as a surveyor and geographer is attested by his Journals and his *Courses* and by his " Map made for the North West Company in 1813 and 1814," which marks his last connection with the " concern." It embraces, it is true, the surveys of Philip Turnor, of Sir Alexander Mackenzie, and of John Stuart of New Caledonia, Fraser's companion on his journey to the coast, but its main feature is that it embodies his own life's work as a surveyor, his explorations when with the Hudson's Bay Company as well as the systematic survey of his years with the North West Company. The map used to hang in the dining-hall of the Company at its rendezvous, Fort William, and doubtless it played an important part in the deliberations of the Partners. It is to-day a priceless source of exact knowledge to the historian of the North-West, and is a monument to the most intellectual in the long and distinguished line of the Wintering Partners of the North West Company.

From 1816 to 1826 Thompson must have been in his element as British representative on the Commission which delineated the boundary between Canada and the United States as far as the Lake of the Woods. Thereafter he followed his profession at Terrebonne, near Montreal, and at Williamsburg in the county of Glengarry.

His large family by his half-breed wife Charlotte Small, whom he brought out with him to Canada, and his devotion to his sons, setting them up in business and paying their debts when they failed, brought him in his old age to extreme poverty. He died at Longueuil, near Montreal, on February 10, 1857. He lived to see the last phase of the struggle between the British and the Americans for the Oregon, and the final surrender of the forty-ninth parallel of latitude as the International Boundary. His attempts to place his knowledge of the geography of the Oregon before the British Government to enable it to stand firm against American aggression would be more pleasing to contemplate if he had reached the Pacific first and had built his fort before the arrival of Astor's party, and had thereby given his king and country a first claim, based on settlement, to the whole valley of the Columbia.

The Hudson's Bay Company's factors were interested observers of the North West Company's Columbian enterprise. They saw the physical difficulties involved and were dubious as to the possibility of making it a commercial success. In particular, they were aware that it would incur the hostility of the Piegans. They decided to " wait and see." When it appeared that the North West Company was going to make it a success they became less critical. In 1810 Joseph Howse offered to conduct an expedition across the Rockies and was given the necessary assortment of goods. Very soon grave fears for his safety were entertained. Howse wrote that a battle had been fought between the Piegans and a party of Flathead Indians with whom David Thompson's clerk, Finan MacDonald, was in company, and that the Piegans had been defeated with the loss of fourteen men ; that, in consequence, " they were laying in ambush for him or any White Man who might attempt to convey goods [including ammunition] to the Flatheads." News gathered from the Piegans ran that a band of braves was on the Kootenay River watching for Howse. James Bird at Edmonton House lamented the impossibility of bringing assistance to his subordinate in his isolated position.

But Howse acted at once with caution and courage. He stayed where he was until he received word that the way before him was safe, when he went on to the Flathead country. He made a good success of the trading season. His safe return may be attributed in part to the precautions taken by James Bird. William Flett and a party were kept at Acton House with the special purpose of keeping relations with the Piegans friendly. By dint of good management Flett brought their chiefs to a definite promise not to molest Howse as he returned.

Joseph Howse brought out thirty-six bundles of good furs, at a profit of 75 per cent. He emphasized his belief that there was an abundance of furs in a wide region around his winter quarters and offered to return. But, as will be seen, the Company was fast approaching a crisis in its struggle with the North West Company. The distant enterprise was abandoned. The Governor and Committee, however, showed their appreciation of Howse's services by voting him " £150 as a Gratuity for his past and an encouragement for his future exertions."

4.—JOHN JACOB ASTOR'S COLUMBIAN ENTERPRISE—THE STRUGGLE FOR THE TRADE OF THE COLUMBIA, 1811–14

The struggle for the Oregon began in 1811. On the surface it was a contest between an American and a British fur-trading company. The underlying issue was whether the valley of the Columbia should be American or British. In the Nootka Sound controversy Britain, hampered rather than helped by the American traders, had successfully asserted against Spain the principle that discovery alone could not give title to so vast a region as the Pacific North-West. She thereby won, not only for herself but for all with actual interest in the country, and therefore for the Americans as well as the English, the right to trade and to settle. In 1811 the North West Company by its discoveries and its line of trading posts—at the Kootenay Falls, Pend d'Oreille Lake, Thompson's Saleesh House, and Spokane House—had gone some distance towards giving Britain title to the parts of the present states of Idaho, Montana, and Washington affected. Not by Captain Gray's discovery of the estuary of the Columbia so much as by John Jacob Astor's establishment of Astoria did the Americans go the same distance, but no greater distance, towards securing a valid claim to the mouth of the Columbia. The issue in the foreground, however, was whether Astor's Pacific Fur Company could drive the Northwesters and, for that matter, rival Americans out of the region west of the Rockies. The main scene of the struggle was south of the forty-ninth parallel of latitude. Its details, fascinating as they are, cannot be of concern here. It must, however, be indicated how far Astor's company occupied the ground, particularly north of the present International Boundary, how it was forced to sell its property to its rivals, and the extent to which the transaction between the private corporations affected the rights of the American nation to the Oregon. Incidentally, some attention must be given to the methods of trade which proved successful in the Pacific West and to a number of traders, such as John Clarke, Alexander Ross, and Donald McKenzie, whose careers enter into the fabric of the history of the Canadian West.

Astor's design was, in the first place, to expel all rivals from the maritime fur trade. What with the monopoly enjoyed by the East India Company and the absorption of Britain in the European struggle with Napoleon, the coastal traffic was practically abandoned by the English. Astor had really to deal with citizens of his adopted country. They were carrying on the trade much as from the beginning. They effected no settlements, but passed from harbour to harbour in the mediterranean seas and on the outer coast. They gathered their furs, above all the precious sea-otter skins, at each stopping-place in the course of a few days, the exchange mart being their ship itself. They passed to Canton, usually by way of the Sandwich Islands, disposed of their peltries in the Chinese market, and took on cargoes, chiefly of tea, for the home port, mostly Boston. As the prices secured for peltries in Canton were now low, their fur traffic might have died of inanition but for the trade with the Russians, who had to look abroad for goods and even for provisions. The Americans accordingly completed the outgoing cargo of their ships, for the goods for the fur trade were not of large bulk, with supplies for the Russians, and thereby earned the additional profit necessary to make their ventures sure of success. Astor's plan was to make the settlement on the Columbia the base of supplies for his ships engaged in this maritime trade and to secure an exclusive contract with the Russians to provide them with their needed goods and provisions. With this his own success would be assured, while his rivals, deprived of the Russian traffic, would be driven from the Pacific coast. That the policy was a far-seeing one is proved by its adoption later by Governor Simpson of the Hudson's Bay Company and by its complete success in eliminating his American competitors.

Through disasters to his ships and because of the short tenure of life enjoyed by his Pacific Fur Company, Astor was not able to give his design a fair test. In keeping with instructions, the ship *Tonquin*, after landing the party for the Columbia, and but a portion of the goods for the fort, left for a trading cruise. Its captain, J. Thorn, was without experience of the trade and obstinate, a combination that has ruined many a promising enterprise. He ran up the south-west coast of Vancouver Island to Clayoquot Sound and there, in Templar Channel near the Indian village of Echatchat, began traffic with the natives. Somehow he fell foul of them. They seized the ship and killed most of the crew. As a last desperate measure some one set fire to the magazine and blew up the vessel, Whites, Indians, and all. Accounts of a disaster from which no Europeans escaped are necessarily vague and conflicting. Alexander Ross and Gabriel Franchère, Astorians who have left vivid accounts of their experiences on the Columbia, report the account of the Indian who gave a de-tailed story to the fort, but contradict one another at many points. Evidently Captain Thorn and the Indians disagreed over the trading and the captain subjected his dusky customers to rough handling. When they returned later they dissembled their anger and were received cordially and without the precaution (which had been taken in the first instance) of admitting the savage traders at but one point through the boarding nets which were used to guard the ship. The account of the log of the *New Hazard*, a vessel on the coast at the time, describes the tragic end.

A large number of Indians came on board the *Tonquin*. Captain Thorn desired them to go away. They would not. He used some authority to get them off, when they attacked him. Finding it vain to regain his ship, the Captain with one other ran and set fire to the magazine, which blew her stern out and she went down stern first. About one hundred Indians were killed, blown up and sunk. One of the boats was on shore with six men, who finding they had no refuge from the Indians, set out for the Columbia River, it is supposed ; but going ashore at Classet [at Cape Flattery] were shot by the Natives.

Ross and Franchère agree that the captain, who came on deck unarmed, was killed at an early stage. They attribute the explosion to some other, and Franchère says that it took place next day when the Indians, driven off at the first encounter, returned and were exultant at their capture of the ship. The first to be killed in this sad affray was Alexander MacKay, companion to Sir Alexander Mackenzie on his memorable voyage to the Pacific. He had enlisted as a partner in Astor's Pacific Fur Company and had come with the *Tonquin* from New York.

Astor's second ship, the *Beaver*, arrived at Astoria during the following year. Leaving supplies, it passed northward to Sitka, trading as it went. Here Mr. Wilson Price Hunt, Astor's representative, concluded a promising agreement (first sketched at St. Petersburg) with Baranoff, the Russian Fur Company's representative. To take payment in seal skins for the goods which he furnished, he went on to the island of St. Paul in Bering Sea. As he was thus delayed till late in the season, he did not return to Astoria, as had been arranged, but sailed to the Hawaiian (Sandwich) Islands, whence he sent his furs to be sold in Canton, intending himself to return to Astoria in Astor's ship of the following year. When this, Astor's third vessel, was lost off the Sandwich Islands, not only was he stranded, but the partners of the Pacific Fur Company at Astoria were put in a very difficult position. Intent on making the Columbian enterprise a success, they were greatly chagrined at the course of the maritime venture. Captain Thorn had insisted on keeping a considerable part of the goods for Astoria on the *Tonquin*, as being safer on board than exposed on the shore. They were, of course, lost with the ship. Mr. Hunt failed to return with the *Beaver*, and the third ship—the *Lark*—was awaited in vain. The results were a sense of neglect, doubts of the efficiency of Astor's management, and uncertainty as to the ultimate success of the company which, if we may trust Alexander Ross's opinion, contributed to the final issue.

At the outset the partners at Astoria took up their task not only with vigour but with the certainty of success. After a preliminary exploration by Donald McKenzie a post was established on the River Willamette near the present McKenzie River, named after him. It stood on a beautiful prairie " abounding in beaver, elk, and deer." The first party for the more distant interior took advantage of the company of David Thompson to ascend the Columbia with him as he returned. They managed to get past the menacing crowds of savages at their fishing villages by the rapids and cascades. Thompson, however, left them before they reached the confluence of the Columbia and the Snake (Lewis) rivers and made his way to Spokane House. The Americans ignored the proclamation of the region as British, which he had posted at the forks, and proceeded to the

mouth of the Okanagan River, six hundred miles, Ross says, from
Astoria. This was the first fur region to be seen, for the Columbian
desert below it had nothing to offer in the way of peltries. Here,
on the east bank of the river and half a mile from the Columbia,
they built a post. It was at a strategic point of great importance
for the fur trade of the interior. Canadian interest in this fort is
two-fold. It was from this point and by the Americans that the
uplands between the rivers Fraser and Columbia in the present
British Columbia were first explored. Here too Alexander Ross,
the historian of the Columbian valley, afterwards sheriff and what
not at the Red River Settlement and finally its historian, served his
apprenticeship as a fur-trader. He was in Upper Canada when he
first heard of Astor's plans for a Pacific Fur Company and went to
Montreal to enlist in its service as a clerk. He arrived in the Columbia
on the *Tonquin* and assisted at the founding of Astoria. Endowed
beyond the ordinary with a keen and critical perception, he wrote
books of great interest and sketched word-pictures whose colour
has not faded with time. He was present at many of the most important scenes in the history of the twelve years after the founding
of Astoria, and even when absent writes with an authority diminished
only by his incurable love of criticism and caricature. Moreover,
during his Astorian period he was stationed as clerk at Fort Okanagan, and he has given us a short but intimate sketch of the Indian
tribe after which the region and the post were named. Here, in the
fashion of the fur-traders, he took to himself an Okanagan squaw,
which may account for the unusual warmth of his picture of the
women of the tribe. " They have an engaging sweetness, are good
housewives, modest in their demeanour, affectionate and chaste,
and strongly attached to their husbands and children."

During the winter of 1811–12 Ross, as clerk, was in charge of
Fort Okanagan, while David Stuart, the partner and his chief, with
his clerk Ovido de Monterey and two men, proceeded northward with
pack-horses purchased from the Indians as he came up the river.
Stuart and his party were the first White Men to penetrate into the
region between the Fraser and the Columbia. They followed the
valley of the Okanagan past its lakes to the height of land, and after
travelling for some time among the Shuswaps, reached the Thompson
River, among whose Indians they sojourned till February. They did
not leave without arranging to establish a permanent post the
following winter. During the summer, while Stuart was taking the
furs to Astoria, Ross came north and camped among the Shuswaps
on Thompson River " at a place called by the Indians Cumeloups
[Kamloops], near the entrance of the north branch [of the Thomp-
son]." He carried on a brisk trade and has given us a lively picture
of his departure.

One morning before breakfast I obtained one hundred and ten beavers
for leaf-tobacco, at the rate of five leaves per skin ; and at last, when I
had but one yard of white cotton remaining, one of the chiefs gave me twenty
prime beaver skins for it. Having now finished our trade, we prepared to

return home ; but before we could get our odds-and-ends ready, Boullard, my trusty second, got involved in a love affair, which had nearly involved us all in a disagreeable scrape with the Indians. . . . Unknown to me, the old fellow had been teasing the Indians for a wife, and had already an old squaw at his heels, but could not raise the wind to pay the whole purchase money. With an air of effrontery he asked me to unload one of my horses to satisfy the demands of the old father-in-law, and because I refused him he threatened to leave me and to remain with the savages. Provoked with his conduct I suddenly turned round and horsewhipped the fellow, and, fortunately, the Indians did not interfere. The castigation had a good effect ; it brought the amorous gallant to his senses—the squaw was left behind.

In August, after bringing the merchandise up to Fort Okanagan, Mr. Stuart came north to keep his promise to the Indians and built his fort at Kamloops. The North West Company sent Mr. Joseph Laroque, a clerk, to build a post beside him. When Alexander Ross came up to spend the New Year with his chief he found the rival traders " open and candid, and on friendly terms." Kamloops was a natural stage in the approach to New Caledonia from the south, and Stuart sent out parties in all directions—north to Fraser's River and two hundred miles up the Thompson. Doubtless the North-westers were anxious lest the Americans who, by the way, had intro-duced the use of the pack-horse to the trade, should penetrate to their northern stronghold, New Caledonia. Ross had trying experi-ences as he journeyed homeward through the deep snow of midwinter.

Farther south the Astorians made a point of placing their posts over against the forts of the North West Company established in David Thompson's time. This task was committed to John Clarke. He was an American who had engaged himself to the North West Company when but eighteen years of age. He built " Fort Clark," one of the earliest posts on Mackenzie River, and later served on the Peace River. He is said to have been described by Astor as " the brightest star in the Columbian constellation." Ross says that he was extravagant and " to be called by the Indians a generous chief was his greatest glory." Pompous and impressed with his own valour, Clarke commanded in a high degree the subtle art of leading others to take him at his own estimate. When none could resist him, he could swell with courage and even be ruthless, but in the hour of crisis he was apt to deflate and prove craven.

Donald McKenzie stood in sharp contrast. Said to be a relative of Sir Alexander Mackenzie, he had enlisted in Montreal for Astor's overland expedition. He had none of Clarke's ambition to outshine his fellows, but his perception of Indian character and his frank appeal to the childlike pride of the savages brought him triumphs which must have been the envy of more pretentious men. Above all, he knew the admiration of the Indians for prompt courage in the hour of danger, and his judgment as to when or how to play upon it never failed him. All that McKenzie was to the Indians he was to his White fellow-traders. Clear seeing, just, firm, kind, yet masterly, he is one of the finest characters in the history of the fur trade. When Astor's overland expedition came by misfortune in the drought-stricken uplands of the headwaters of the Snake River and broke into three parties, which were to provide for themselves as best they could on the way to the fort at the mouth of the Columbia, McKenzie's was the only group to arrive in safety. At the critical hour he addressed his little band : " Now, my friends, there is still hope before us ; to linger on our way, to return back or to be discouraged and stand still, is death. . . . Let us persevere and push ahead and all will end well ; the foremost will find something to eat, the last may fare worse." They pressed on and came through, tattered and torn, but safe to the last man.

In 1812 McKenzie and David Stuart joined forces with John Clarke that the numbers of their united party might overawe the throngs of Indians in the fishing villages by their water-way into the interior. None the less the party got into difficulties portaging at the cascades. The Indians presented a formidable front. Parley proved useless. Clarke " stood appalled and almost speechless " behind a rampart of bales of goods hastily improvised. McKenzie, in sharp contrast, took David Stuart for a quiet stroll through the Indian camp and was unmolested. He saw a stolen rifle in a chief's lodge. He forthwith walked in with his four companions and demanded it. When told that it was not there, he set himself to cutting up the robes in the tent with his dagger in an ostentatious search for the stolen article. It was immediately produced and surrendered. McKenzie now beat a hasty retreat, but not without upbraiding the assembled crowd for its dishonesty. Returned to the rampart of bales, he found Clarke still paralysed with fear. Donald gave his word that he would lead the party over the portage in safety. Clarke, doubtless greatly relieved, surrendered the command, and McKenzie, by a judicious disposition of his men, got men and goods all over and away without loss.

When Clarke was on the return journey next spring, ignorant and regardless of Indian character as he was, in lordly style he displayed a silver goblet before the eyes of a small band of savages. It was, of course, stolen that night. The bombastic but humiliated trader searched out the culprit and there and then hanged him. When the whole tribe gathered to avenge the wrong, Clarke's march took on the aspect of a flight. When these two men reappear in these pages, Clarke as representative of the Hudson's Bay Company in Athabaska, and McKenzie as the Company's factor and finally as Governor in the Red River Settlement, they will be found true to form.

Clarke built a post contiguous to the North West Company's Spokane House, near the junction of the Spokane and Little Spokane rivers, and in the charge of James MacMillan, who also will reappear in the Red River Settlement. Here he and his rival, if we can trust Alexander Ross, who visited the post, resorted to all the chicanery to which the bitter struggle of the Northwesters with the men of the XY Company had habituated the fur-traders. " Each party had its manœuvring scouts out in all directions watching the motions of the Indians, and laying plots and plans to entrap or foil each other.

He that got most skins, never minding the cost or the crime, was the cleverest fellow." Cox, who spent most of the winter in the post, on the contrary, reports a friendly agreement not to give rum to the Indians. " In other respects also we agreed very well with our opponent, and neither party evinced any of the turbulent or lawless spirit, which have so ferocious an aspect to the opposition of the rival companies on the east side of the mountains." Ross Cox established a post among the Flatheads some distance below the Saleesh House of Thompson, now under Finan MacDonald, where Russel Farnham was left in charge for the winter. The following winter Cox himself was forty miles farther up beside the North West Company's post.

The Canadian post among the Kutenais was now on the Kootenay River above the Falls, Thompson's post below Lake Windermere being abandoned. Here John MacDonald of Garth wintered in 1811–12. Nicolas Montour was now in charge. Clarke sent François Pillet to build over against him. Perhaps because the two men in command of these rival posts were excitable Frenchmen, lively scenes were witnessed, as Ross Cox testifies. " Mr. Pillet fought a duel with Mr. Montour of the North-West, with pocket pistols, at six paces ; both hits ; one in the collar of the coat and the other in the leg of the trousers. Two of their men acted as seconds, and the tailor speedily healed their wounds."

Donald McKenzie led an expedition up the Snake River to find a cache of goods left by the unfortunate overland party. He established a post at a spot not yet identified, but speedily convinced of the inadequacy of that measure he abandoned it. That region was too vast, drought-stricken, and treeless to support anything but the sparsest of populations. Little or nothing could be expected of its wretched people. Yet the streams were lined with willow and poplar, and the beaver population, though scattered over a wide area, was considerable. Not forts but trapping parties ranging over the spacious region was the method finally adopted for exploiting the fur resources in sight.

The misfortunes which befell the Pacific Fur Company were great, but such as might be expected at the initiation of an enterprise in a distant land whose difficulties and whose problems lay beyond the experience of the traders. Moreover, these were balanced by equal successes. What broke the back of the enterprise was the war of 1812 between Britain and the United States. It was as unexpected as it was disastrous. News of its outbreak reached John Clarke and Donald McKenzie at Spokane House, when the Northwester John George McTavish arrived from beyond the Rockies with the goods for his Company's post. It reached Astoria through McKenzie on January 13, 1813, and led Duncan MacDougall, the partner in charge, to decide on the dissolution of the Company. Northwester McTavish and Joseph Laroque arrived at the American post on 11th April, to await the consummation of the plans of their Company. It had been the definite policy of the Northwesters as early as 1805 to reach the mouth of the Columbia and to establish there a base for the inland and maritime fur trades. Through the leisureliness of David Thompson, John Jacob Astor had been able to jump in before them and to stake out a claim for himself and for the American Republic. The agents of the North-West Company saw in the war the means of retrieving the situation. The rendezvous at Fort William to which David Thompson reported his failure to anticipate the Americans decided to send a ship out by way of Cape Horn as well as an expedition overland, and on 18th August the agents wrote McTavish, Fraser & Co., Inglis, Ellice & Co., and Sir Alexander Mackenzie, in London, explaining the necessity of the situation. The scarcity of furs east of the Rockies made it obligatory to hold the new beaver region found to the west.

> The progress already made by the American Party who have established themselves in the River renders this determination on our part absolutely necessary for the defence of our only remaining Beaver Country and we know from dear bought experience the impossibility of contending from this side of the Mountains with people who get their Goods from so short a distance as the Mouth of the Columbia is from the Mountains.

The Government must come to the support of the Company with a warship, and the Company's vessel must be given a " Letter of Marque." When the London connections of the firm laid the matter before the Government, this policy was given a broader and more national aspect. They had petitioned the Government the year before for " an exclusive charter " to trade across the continent and by the Pacific Ocean " within the limits of such parts thereof as belong to your Majesty " (an allusion to Broughton taking possession of the Columbia and Vancouver of Puget Sound in the name of the King). Their plea still remained under the consideration of the Government. Meanwhile they had sent an expedition (David Thompson's) to the mouth of the Columbia, and " another and more numerous party had been despatched across the continent this season " (that of J. G. McTavish); and a ship was being prepared for the ocean voyage. They prayed that permission be given to arm her.

The Government, which a year before declined to run the risk of a clash with the United States by helping the North West Company to forestall the Americans on the Columbia in a time of peace, now acted with promptitude. The Company's ship, the *Isaac Todd*, left Portsmouth in March, 1813, with other ships and under a strong convoy, and with H.M.S. *Phœbe* specially detailed to care for her. Donald McTavish and the redoubtable John MacDonald of Garth, Wintering Partners, sailed on the *Isaac Todd*. The latter was transferred to the *Phœbe* at Rio de Janeiro, and to H.M.S. *Raccoon* at Juan Fernandez, for it was believed that the *Phœbe* was too deep a ship to cross the bar of the Columbia. As the *Isaac Todd* was a slow sailer and the matter was pressing, the *Raccoon* sailed away and was bounding on towards America when J. G. McTavish arrived to await the Company's ship. He did not come with an overpowering force to capture the fort. Indeed he was dependent on the Americans for his supplies. His presence simply brought the Astorians face to face with the hard facts of the situation. Astor's third ship, the *Lark*, was due. Should it not arrive they would be without supplies. Britain's command of the seas robbed them of the hope of any subsequent vessel getting out of New York to come to their relief. Moreover, the maritime expedition of the North West Company would soon be upon them. They might, of course, use their goods to purchase horses and provisions by the way, and venture the transcontinental journey. The distressful experiences of Astor's overland expedition must have made it easy to put this alternative out of consideration. Besides, the North West Company, with their Indian hangers-on, could easily bring disaster upon them. By the end of June all the partners of the Pacific Fur Company were assembled at Astoria. They took the course which any merchant would take who saw himself faced with bankruptcy in the not very distant future. On 1st July they decided to carry on in the meantime till June 1, 1814. If the situation was not improved in the intervening eleven months, they would effect a sale of their property, goods, and furs to the North West Company and wind up their business—a course which they felt free to do, for were they not partners, and, although Astor had provided the capital with which they carried on, were they not provided by him with power to act as circumstances might require. As the *Isaac Todd* failed to arrive, McTavish returned with this news to his post. On 7th October he returned with Angus Bethune bearing a letter to Duncan MacDougall from his uncle, Angus Shaw, informing him of the sailing of the *Isaac Todd* and H.M.S. *Phœbe* in March. He was followed by Northwesters gathering to meet these ships. John Stuart of New Caledonia explored a route southward to Fort Okanagan and arrived on 11th October. On the 16th the Astorian partners, as they felt perfectly free to do under the constitution of their Company, sold all their property to their rivals on the basis of 10 per cent. above the original cost and charges. They then dissolved their partnership. A month later another couple of Canadians arrived to find that their " concern " had occupied the coveted fort three days before. About ten days later another partner arrived, John MacDonald of Garth, on H.M.S. *Raccoon*. The event proved that the Astorians had acted wisely, for they realized on their property in good bank drafts in time to save it from falling into the hands of the warship as lawful booty. So passed away Astor's grandiose scheme to win the trade of the Pacific West for his Company. This phase of the struggle for the Oregon ended with the British Company in possession.

Did the American Fur Company, in selling their property to the North West Company, a British concern, surrender the title of the United States to the mouth of the Columbia ? Did it, in building a fort on the river, create it American territory for all time ? The American Government claimed that it did, and that the sale did not transfer the title to Britain. Captain Black of H.M.S. *Raccoon*

was not, like the Astorians, a private individual, but, in his capacity
as an officer in the Royal Navy, a representative of His Majesty
King George.   When he reached the river and entered the fort now
in possession of British subjects, and when he ran up the British flag
and formally took possession of the country in the name of the
King, did he give Britain title to the region ?   The American Government claimed that he did not and could not.   They had inserted a
clause in the Treaty of Ghent—which brought the war of 1812 to a
close on December 24, 1814—by which all territories and places taken
by either side during the war were to be restored at the peace.   In
July 1815 James Monroe, their Secretary of State, informed the
British Embassy at Washington that steps were being taken to
assert the American claim to Astoria, and asked for papers authorizing those in charge to return the post to America.   No papers
were forthcoming.   The British view was that Astoria was
not captured in war, but passed to British subjects by a
commercial transaction.   In September 1817 the American
Government dispatched the sloop of war *Ontario* to occupy
the place, thus facing the British Government with an impending *fait accompli*.   Lord Castlereagh proposed for England
that the matter of the title be settled by arbitration.   Mr.
Richard Rush for the United States declined, insisting that there
was no reason for questioning the title.   Lord Castlereagh regretted
the course followed by the American Government and, to avoid a
clash, expressed Britain's willingness to have the Americans take
possession pending the settlement of the question of title.   " Indeed,
the British Government displayed a magnanimous desire to avoid
any hostile collision between the representatives of the respective
governments in those distant parts " is the comment of the American
historian, H. H. Bancroft.   In the presence of the American sloop of
war *Ontario* and of H.M.S. *Blossom* the surrender of Fort George, as
Astoria was now called, was accomplished, and the Stars and Stripes
once more floated on the breezes of the Oregon.   Yet when the
American ship disappeared from the scene, the British Company
remained as before in possession.   The question of the title had
still to be settled.   As the two governments were not able to come
to an agreement, and the United States had refused to go to arbitration, a *modus vivendi* was sought and arrived at on October 20,
1818.

> Any country that may be claimed by either party on the north-west
> coast of America, westward of the Stony Mountains, shall . . . be free and
> open for the term of ten years from the date of the signature of the present
> Convention, to the vessels, citizens and subjects of the two powers ; it being
> well understood that this agreement is not to be construed to the prejudice
> of any claim which either of the two high contracting parties may have to
> any part of the said country, nor shall it be taken to affect the claims of any
> power or state.

Thus the settlement of the question of the title to the Oregon
was deferred.   Meanwhile, by a treaty between the United States

and Spain, the 42nd parallel of latitude was made the north boundary of Spanish California, and the Spanish King " ceded to the said United States all his rights, claims and petentions to any territory east and north of the said line." Thus claims real or imaginary which Spain might have to the north-west coast passed to the United States.

In 1821 another boundary question arose, through the claim asserted by the Czar of Russia in an imperial ukase to the whole of the Pacific coast of the continent down to the 42nd parallel of latitude. In 1824 and 1825 treaties between Russia and the United States and Britain fixed the southern boundary of Russian territory in America at 54° 40' north latitude. This line became the northern boundary of any British Settlements which might be on the coast. It is to-day the northern limit of British Columbia at the coast.

Chapter VII

A PERIOD OF VIOLENCE, 1800–21—LORD SELKIRK'S COLONY, 1812–18

DURING the eighteenth century the competition of trader with trader, and of company with company, was, on the whole, carried on within the limits of the legitimate. The first score of years of the nineteenth century saw a marked change. The domestic feud between the old North West Company and the New North West, the XY Company, as it came to be called, habituated the men of both parties to deeds of violence. After the union of these two companies in 1804 the same rude and even bloody methods were resorted to by the men from Montreal against the Hudson's Bay Company and against Lord Selkirk's colony on the Red River. Finally the Hudson's Bay Company was driven to resort to brute force to defend its property. At length the long and at times bloody struggle ended in the Union of the Canadian and English companies in 1821, and in the inauguration of a generation of peace.

I.—THE XY COMPANY AND THE TRADITION OF VIOLENCE, 1800–4

The North West Company had been subjected to intermittent competition with traders from the St. Lawrence, but with the perfection of its organization it found this no serious menace. The intruder would have but little capital at his back, and would have to employ for the most part the cast-off servants of the large company, mostly drunken and unreliable men. He would find himself opposed to a select band of " bullies " whose sole task was to defend the " concern " and to overawe the rival, his servants, and his Indians by the menace of violence. In the course of time the Northwesters, though themselves in the strict sense of the term intruders in the chartered realm of the English Company, began to act as if they had the sole right to the trade in those parts. For example, a Monsieur Dominic Rousseau of Montreal, about 1802, sent a Monsieur Hervieu, as his clerk, with an assortment of goods to trade on the shore of Lake Superior. He camped about a gunshot from the rendezvous to catch the trade of the servants of the large " concern." Duncan M'Gillivray, who was about to enter the firm of McTavish, Frobisher & Co., the agents, bade him decamp, on the ground that he had no right to be there. Hervieu naturally asked what title the North West Company had to the exclusive possession of the country. Later M'Gillivray returned with Archibald Norman McLeod and a retinue of servants and replied that he would show him his title, and with his dagger he tore Hervieu's tent from top to bottom. McLeod followed suit, throwing down the tent and upsetting the chest of merchandise.

In 1806 Rousseau renewed his attempt to enter the trade, and sent a Monsieur Delorme inland by the Grand Portage route, now disused, for the Northwesters were at this time travelling from Fort William by the Kaministikwia–Dog Lake–Seine River route. Alexander MacKay, formerly clerk to Alexander Mackenzie, but now a *bourgeois*, with a band of servants, threw trees down across the narrow streams and made it impossible to proceed. The Northwesters would have none enter the country by any route, used or disused. The land, or rather its trade, was theirs. As such deeds of violence were regarded as but manifestations of " the North West Spirit," and were a matter of boast in the Company, they would tend to become more frequent. Violence would outstrip violence as the years passed. The bitter oppositions of the years 1798 to 1804 proved a long schooling in wrong-doing, which stamped itself upon the succeeding years.

The difficulties thrown by the Americans in the way of the trade to the South-West from Michilimackinac after the surrender of the Western Posts in 1796 have been mentioned. One result was that firms dealing hitherto with the American Indian Territory turned their capital and energy towards the Canadian North-West. Forsyth, Richardson & Co., whose interests were chiefly in the hinterland of Detroit, and the house of Parker, Gerrard, and Ogilvy, whose trade extended from Michilimackinac by way of Fond du Lac on the western shore of Lake Superior into the Mississippi region, turned their attention north-westward. In 1793 the Forsyth Company was in the country north of Lake Superior. An agreement dated October 20, 1798, drew additional men and capital to the enterprise. It names Pierre Rocheblave, Alexander Mackenzie (not Sir Alexander), John McDonald, James Leith, John Wills, and John Haldane as Wintering Partners. This company was dubbed the " Little Company " by the Northwesters, and the " Potties " (from *potée*, pot, a small measure, here a term of contempt).

From a diary of David Thompson, kept at Fort George on the Saskatchewan, it is known that the canoes of the " Little Society " with Mr. Mackenzie were in that neighbourhood in September 1799. That company's fort was built on Fort Island some twenty miles west of Fort George. The North West Company and the Hudson's Bay Company abandoned Fort George and Buckingham House respectively, and built their Fort de l'Isle, or Island Fort, beside them. The diary also indicates that the Ogilvy canoes passed up afterwards on their way to the North West Company's first Fort Augustus, where they would also have the Hudson's Bay Company's

first Edmonton House in competition with them. On May 23, 1800—
according to the Journal of James Mackenzie of the North West
Company's Fort Chipewyan, now at its present site on the north
shore of Lake Athabaska—" the Potties" arrived with three canoes
and proceeded to build on the Little Island near the fort.   On 26th
May the Ogilvy people were also in that region.   During the summer
both parties were on Peace River.   On 15th October of that year
John MacDonald of Garth and Duncan M'Gillivray, in a joint
letter, dated Fort Augustus, reported that the opposition had gone
to Lake Athabaska with six canoes by way of the Pembina River.
The use of the Saskatchewan water-way to reach the north country
may be explained by the abundance of provisions on that route as
contrasted with the Churchill River, and by the fact that they could
not get guides for the usual track.

The rivalry of the two small companies with one another and
with the great North West and Hudson's Bay companies was
ruinous.   Accordingly they coalesced in 1800, and drew into the
combination Sir Alexander Mackenzie, who had been pushed out
of the McTavish–Frobisher firm in November, 1799, and so out of
the North West Company.   The new " concern " passed under the
name of New North West Company.   The goods of the old Company
were marked NW ; the new Company chose to mark its bales XY.
Hence the common appellation in the Upper Country—the XY
Company.   Naturally its constitution and methods of business were
those of the very successful old Company.   Its rendezvous was
Grand Portage, the old Company having removed to the mouth of
the Kaministikwia after Roderick Mackenzie had rediscovered the
route up that river and by Dog Lake and Seine River to Rainy Lake
—an all-British water-way. (From 1807 the rendezvous at Kaministikwia was called Fort William after William M'Gillivray, the Company's agent.)   The depots and posts of the new Company were
placed beside or near those of the old.   Its Rainy Lake depot was
about half a mile above the old Company's post, and very near to the
falls.   The ruins of a post reported to be on the opposite side of the
river, over against the North West Company's Bas de la Rivière
Winipic, may mark its depot there.   Pemmican for its northern
brigades had to be secured in the Assiniboine River.   It built its
Fort la Souris on the right bank of that stream and opposite the
North West Company's fort of the same name and the Hudson's Bay
Company's Brandon House.   The Canadians moved across and built
immediately above, to overawe the Indians.   The XY Company
built its Fort Qu'Appelle, probably marked by ruins on the opposite,
the north, bank over against the old Company's Fort Espérance.
On the upper Assiniboine it built about five miles above the North
West Company's Fort Alexandria, and on the Red River a little
below, and finally actually beside, their post at the mouth of the
Pembina River.   There was also an XY Fort Dauphin.

A vigorous push was made on the Saskatchewan, not only for
its furs but for the pemmican necessary for the northern brigades.

There is no record of an XY Cumberland House, but the post built in 1798 by the Little Company, half a mile below the Canadian Fort St. Louis and the same distance above the English Carlton House, on the left bank, was probably occupied, as also its post two miles above the Sturgeon River, both the old and the English companies building posts at the Sturgeon itself in opposition. For reasons to be mentioned later, the old post of the Little Company on Fort Island now occupied in force, with a Canadian and an English house beside it, was the most notable of the new Company's posts on the Saskatchewan.

Both the North West Company and the Hudson's Bay Company had been making changes to meet the new situation. In the spring of 1802, or immediately thereafter, the first Fort Augustus and the first Edmonton House were abandoned and new posts built during the winter at the present city of Edmonton, on the flat below the site of the Parliamentary Building.* These two posts, whose site is now in the centre of a capital city, were probably the first to grow grain in the present Province of Alberta. The year the post was removed to Terre Blanche men were sent back to Fort Augustus to cut the barley there.

In 1800, apparently to escape from the increasing competition on the North Branch, Peter Fidler, for the Hudson's Bay Company, conducted the first expedition far up the South Branch, and built Chesterfield House on the left bank of the river immediately below the mouth of the Red Deer River of Alberta. The object seems to have been to draw the Blackfeet and Piegans away southward, and the Indians of the Missouri northward. The North West and the XY companies followed him and built on contiguous sites. Fidler had old connections with the Blackfoot tribes and seems never to have been in great danger, any farther than the large bands of the

---

* The situation in 1800–1 is shown in a letter of James Bird, the H.B.C.'s officer in charge of the Saskatchewan, dated Feb. 19, 1801. The H.B.C. and the N.W.Co. had multiplied outposts to cripple the trade of the two weak companies in opposition. Bird mentions Acton House (where was also the N.W.Co.'s Rocky Mountain House) ; Pembina River (on the Saskatchewan where was the portage to the Pembina River, taken by one of the opposition companies to go to Athabaska, at or near the N.W.Co.'s Boggy Hall in N.E. ¼, sect. 3, tp. 47, r. 9, W5, and possibly an opposition post) ; Nelson House (at or near the N.W.Co.'s White Mud House which David Thompson's survey would place in sect. 30, tp. 51, r.2, W5, about 30 miles west of the present Edmonton) ; Edmonton House (No. 1, where was the N.W.Co.'s Fort Augustus No. 1 and an Ogilvy Post at Sturgeon River 20 miles east of the present Edmonton) ; and Fort Island (where the N.W.Co. and the Forsyth firm were lodged). The low returns being received called for economy by concentration. Nelson House, so called after the Battle of the Nile, was closed in 1801. David Thompson's itinerary of his journey from Rocky Mountain House to Fort Augustus (No. 1, where Edmonton House would then be) shows that that post was open in Sept. 2, 1801. In the following summer or immediately thereafter Edmonton House No. 2 was built on the low river bottom below the present parliamentary building. It would serve the Indians of both Edmonton House No. 1 and Nelson House. (Here also the second Fort Augustus was placed.) The earliest journal of this post in the H.B.C.'s Archives is that of 1806–7. It gives no suggestion that the house had recently been built.

With regard to the continuance of the name Edmonton, the Governor and Committee insisted that it was confusing to have the names of the forts changed with a change of site. When in 1810 the post was removed to the mouth of the White Earth River (in sect. 58, tp. 16, r. 4, W4, where the remains can be seen) it was still Edmonton (No. 3). When it was brought back to the site of the present capital of Alberta in 1812, it was still Edmonton House (No. 4). The journals of Edmonton No. 2 and No. 4 agree in the time taken by the boats from the mouth of the Vermilion River to the House, viz. 11 or 12 days. Both Houses relied on the fishery of " God's Lake," David Thompson's Manitou Lake, the present Lake St. Ann.

people of the plains, conscious of their power, were a constant peril, and the feuds of tribe with tribe. Moreover, the South Saskatchewan was no beaver region, except in so far as the Piegans might bring that valuable peltry from the upper regions of the Red Deer River. In 1801–2 the North West Company, which had had its difficulties with the great bands and had secured but poor returns, abandoned their fort, leaving Fidler and the XY people on the spot. Apparently the posts remained unoccupied till Joseph Howse of the English Company and John MacDonald of Garth of the North West Company came to them in 1804–5. Thereafter the position was abandoned, for the Indians proved very troublesome.

The New North West Company had a depot at Ile-à-la-Crosse Lake, probably where ruins remain west of the mouth of the Beaver River across the lake from the old Canadian and English posts ; also an outpost at Green Lake. It made a special effort to capture the rich fur region passing under the name of Athabaska. It built its depot alongside of Fort Chipewyan. It maintained two and ultimately four posts on Peace River. It built beside the North-westers on Great Slave Lake, at Fort Liard on the Mackenzie, and as far north as their post on Great Bear Lake. Add to this far-flung line of posts that every fort was crowded with men, with bands of bullies to stand up to the bullies of the old Company, and some idea will be got of the vast capital put into the new venture. Nothing but the high prices fetched by furs in the London market could justify the old Company in its lavish expenditures in defence.

Two things money could not buy for the New Company—a sober and experienced service, trained to economy and with an adequate knowledge of the country ; and contact with the natives in the face of the menace of their former masters. Failure to secure these must bring disaster.

The more permanent effects of the struggle command attention. In the fierce competition the traders whose posts stood side by side led a cat-and-dog life in which principles of honesty and fair play had no part ; men in ordinary circumstances inclined to be honour-able became steeped in dishonour. Take two illustrations from the Journal of the very likeable and unblushingly frank Alexander Henry the younger, quartered in the North West Company's post at Pembina on the Red River. " Grosse Gueule and myself had a serious dispute ; he wanted to give his furs to the XY, which I prevented at the risk of my life ; he was advised by them to kill me." " I went to the upper Tongue River to meet a band of Indians returning from hunting beaver, and fought several battles with the women to get their furs from them. It was the most disagreeable derouine I ever made. It is true it was all my neighbours debts," that is, due to the XY fort for equipment given.

When menaced by opposition the Northwesters sought to avoid concentration of the trade at their posts by sending out pedlars to deal with and even to live with the Indians in their camps. Such parties sent *en derouine*, as it was called, were like to meet their opponents out in the open on the same errand ; clashes were inevitable, and violent deeds not exactly rare. One case is notorious and had a notable influence upon legislation and the law courts. The deposition of a North West servant, Alard, of August 2, 1802, tells the following story. He was wintering at Fort de l'Isle, the Island Fort, on the North Saskatchewan, successor of Fort George, and some twenty miles west of it, with a Mr. James King (a former XY bully whom the North West Company had enticed into their service) and two other men. He left to gather the furs due to the Company by one Lecendre, a free man, and certain Indians, five days' march away. Rocheblave of the New Company sent out his clerk, Lamothe, from the neighbouring fort on a similar errand. The two parties travelled together to the Indian camp. On the way King suggested that they should come to some agreement about the credits in the shape of furs to be got from the savages. Lamothe consented. On their arrival each slept in an Indian lodge whose occupants were traders at his own fort and, by the agreement, were acknowledged as such. In the morning King gathered the furs of his people, but then went over to the lodge in which Lamothe was quartered and demanded furs alleged to be due his Company from the Indian there. He was told that Lamothe had taken all. Lamothe was required by King to surrender them to him. Lamothe asked if he would surrender them were he in his place. King replied " No." Lamothe then said, " Then you will not have mine." King said he would take them. Lamothe replied, " Do not force me to do what I do not wish to do." King reached forward as though to seize the beaver skins. At that moment the deponent passed out of the tent, but immediately heard a pistol shot. He returned at once and saw King on the ground and Lamothe with his pistol as though about to shoot again. On his interfering Lamothe threatened him. Shortly afterwards the young man was overcome with grief and, weeping, said : " All this comes of ill advice." He had been warned against King before starting. As a result of this and other deeds of violence, Richardson of the New Company, one of the sanest minds in Montreal, a past member of the Legislative Assembly and soon to be appointed a member of the Executive Council, was appealed to by the Governor-General of Canada for advice. He states the case for Lamothe :

A clerk of the Old Company, confiding in his superior strength, and accompanied by Servants, insisted upon taking from a Young Man, a clerk of the New Company then without assistance, some Furs which he previously received in payment from an Indian. The Young man remonstrated against the injustice, and warned the other of the consequences, as he was determined to protect the Property in his charge at all hazards ;—The other still persisted and laid hold of the Furs to take them by Force, when the clerk of the New Company fired and killed him whilst in the act of what *he* considered a Robbery.

Richardson took the occasion to air the grievances of his Company :

The New Company upon the commencement of its operations was viewed by the other with a jealousy and rancour improper in Subjects of the same Empire, pursuing a legal and open Trade. . . . [They] had to expect every obstacle which the Old could throw in their way. . . . The most false and malicious impressions have been made upon the minds of the Indians regarding them, whereby the lives of their Associates, Clerks, and Servants, with property in their charge, are endangered. The Indians have been stimulated to commit actual pillage, and to fire upon Canoes of the New Company. Attempts have been made to debauch and entice away their Clerks and Servants (in some cases with effect), and a Clerk so debauched from their Service afterwards employed treacherously to impose other persons *therein*, who were then ignorant of such treachery. The Property of the New Company has been pillaged and stolen in the interior Country, in some cases by some of the Associates, Clerks, and Servants of the Old. Their property has also been destroyed by underhand Arts. These are severe charges but strictly true, and the dignity of the Government, as well as the safety of many of His Majesty's Subjects, requires that means should be fallen upon to prevent a recurrence with impunity of such illegal Acts from any quarter.

Richardson concludes with almost prophetic insight, " Retaliations may become frequent—Force may generally prevail over justice—The consequences may be dreadful to contemplate, and the Fur Trade must in the end be annihilated, if a competent Jurisdiction is not established in the Canadas, for the Investigation of Crimes and criminal offences, committed in the British part of the Indian Country." He suggested a military post at Kaministikwia with a resident magistrate.

Chief Justice Alcock was of opinion that Lamothe could be tried in Canada " if the death happened in a part of the British Territory not comprised in the Hudson Bay Charter." Richardson, consulted again, agreed, but pointed out that Alcock avoided giving an opinion as to whether the spot were in Upper Canada or the Hudson's Bay Territory :

For my part I am confident, that the Place in question is in the Territory of Hudson's Bay and not in the Upper Province. . . . That Territory is bounded by the *Height of Land* which separates the waters falling into Hudson's Bay from those falling into the Lakes, the St. Lawrence and the Atlantic Ocean ; and where *that* is doubtful, the 50th degree of North Latitude was to be the boundary.

A Grand Jury found a true bill against Lamothe, and the young man actually came down to Montreal ready to submit to trial, but when it appeared that he might languish in gaol while the lawyers were settling the question of the jurisdiction of the Canadian Courts, he returned to the Upper Country beyond the reach of the Law.

The upshot of it all was the Canada Jurisdiction Act, passed through Imperial Parliament in August 1803. " All offences committed within any of the Indian Territories or parts of America, not within the limits of either of the said Provinces of Upper or Lower Canada [therefore inclusive of the Chartered Territory] or of any civil government of the United States of America, shall be, and be deemed to be, offences of the same nature, and shall be tried in the same manner and subject to the same punishment as if the same had been committed within the Province of Lower or Upper Canada."

The second clause gives the Governor or Lieut.-Governor of Lower Canada power to authorize persons resident " to act as Civil Magistrates and Justices of the Peace," within the limits defined in the first clause, to hear crimes and offences and to commit the guilty who may be " conveyed to Lower Canada to be dealt with according to the law, and it shall be lawful for any person or persons whatever to apprehend and take before any person so commissioned . . . or to apprehend and convey or cause to be safely conveyed with all convenient speed to . . . Lower Canada any person or persons guilty of any crime or offence, there to be delivered into safe custody for the purpose of being dealt with according to the law." This well-intentioned clause was needlessly wide and left it open for an unscrupulous trader to arrest his opponent and take him down to distant Montreal, probably to be released by the courts there—a procedure much to the advantage of the trader who effected the arrest, for he had got his rival out of the country meanwhile. The third clause permitted the Governor to fix the place of trial in Upper Canada, if he thought the circumstances called for it.

Under the act Duncan and William M'Gillivray, Roderick and Sir Alexander Mackenzie, and John Ogilvy, were appointed Justices of the Peace. Their names figure as such in the Quebec Almanack of 1805. It is to be noted that no officer of the Hudson's Bay Company received any such appointment at this juncture. The Act really envisaged the struggle of the two Canadian companies— a struggle which thus left its impress on subsequent history.

The struggle between the two Canadian companies proved a misfortune for the Hudson's Bay Company. Till then the relations between the English and the Canadians were not unhappy, though they cannot be said to have been cordial. In Alexander Henry the younger's Journals of the Red River posts his English opponents scarcely figure. In 1808, when Henry went to Fort Vermilion on the Saskatchewan, he found the rival posts within one palisade. The site for the post at Terre Blanche, which took the place of Fort Vermilion, was chosen by the representatives of the companies in consultation, and again the forts had a common palisade. At Fort Vermilion Henry invited his neighbour Mr. Henry Hallett to breakfast soon after his arrival, and together they drew up a list of the Indians trading at the several posts and agreed each to have dealings with his own Indians only. Such reasonable relations were a survival beyond the rough times of the XY troubles, from the last decades of the eighteenth century.

When the age of violence began the English Company's servants were helpless. They had received repeated instructions to avoid everything that might lead to a clash with their rivals. Moreover, as they received fixed salaries, which they drew whether the furs gathered were many or few, there was no incentive to risk life or limb to secure larger returns. This very pacifist attitude, however, gave their rivals a free field for plunder.

It was the further misfortune of the English Company that

their long-delayed entry into the trade of Churchill River and the Athabaska country synchronized with the growth of the trade war between the two Canadian companies. The old North West Company met the new company and the Englishmen with the same un-measured violence. The doings in Athabaska mark the beginning of a new phase of the rivalry of the men of Montreal with the men of Hudson Bay.

Peter Fidler had organized the Hudson's Bay Company's interest on the upper Churchill in 1799, establishing posts at Île-à-la-Crosse, at Green Lake, and at Meadow Lake. He himself wintered in the Athabaska watershed, at Greenwich House on Lac la Biche. In 1802 he crossed Methy Portage and built Nottingham House on an island three-quarters of a mile from Fort Chipewyan, as it then stood. The " racket " between the two Canadian companies was at its height, and Fidler had as good as lodged himself between the firing lines.

All parties needed the pemmican of Peace River to ease the hardships of life on Lake Athabaska and to provision the outgoing canoes. The XY Company had already built posts at Grand Marais and below the Vermilion Falls, that is, near Mikwa ("Red") River, a tributary of the Peace. Peter Fidler sent Thomas Swain to establish himself at the North West Company's post next above, viz. at the Old Establishment (Fort Liard). There he built Mansfield House. At that very time the XY men were seeking to effect a lodging there also. Peter Fidler sums up their experiences. The Old Company circulated such infamous stories about them that the Indians would not let them stay. They were obliged to come down the river again and remain at their first house below the Falls. " This is the 3rd Summer that the New Co. has attempted to build there & as often drove down by the Indians." The reception ac-corded to Swain by the natives was very different. " On our People arriving amongst them, they was very willing that we should build there, as they have still some distant knowledge of the Churchill people, which was much in our favour. Formerly all the Beaver Indians used to go down to that Settlement to Trade, but at present there are only 3 old men living who have been there." This indicates that, had the Hudson's Bay Company entered Athabaska with or soon after the Pedlars, they would have received a welcome from old customers, and could have established themselves with the greatest ease. In 1791–92 Philip Turnor was accorded a welcome by the natives ; they greeted with satisfaction his promise of establishing posts in those parts. It was a different story ten years later. Fidler wrote :

We are comparatively speaking but strangers to the Indians, altho' they have long Traded at Churchill Factory. Our being here in the winter of 1791 & our Telling them that we would return the same summer following with plenty of Goods & to build houses in their Country which they were very glad off, but our not keeping our word in that respect, makes them dubious that we shall again abandon them to the mercy of the Canadian Traders, and Should they trade with us this winter entirely, they say they would be very badly used by them.

Fidler told them that his Company was there to stay ; the North-westers assured them that, as on the former occasion, it was there but for the winter. Though Thomas Swain was welcomed by the Indians, the Northwesters saw to it that he did not get any meat from them. In dread of starvation, he abandoned the post, Mansfield House, and returned to Athabaska. Peter Fidler was forced to dry fish for the outward journey in the spring. While he was able to hold out in Nottingham House, he did not do much more. The old Company had men who knew the Indian languages and could live with them or go out to them with the certainty that by friendship, or by a show of violence, they could bring the furs, or the Indians with their furs, past Nottingham House to Fort Chipewyan. Indians who traded with the English were maltreated. James Mackenzie, the master at the old Company's House, "very ill-used the boy & beat him much for paying us part of his credit."

Fidler's Journals show how ruinous the struggle was to all parties. Such plentiful gifts were made by the traders to the Indians to keep their trade that profits were greatly reduced. Worse still, the Indians, getting so much in gifts, did not exert themselves to " work beaver," or even to gather provisions. All parties lamented their indolence. The old Company suffered from this scarcely less than its rivals. In the spring of 1803 one master came in from an outpost on Athabaska River with 11 packs, the returns for 44 pieces, that is, 90-lb. packages, of goods ; another from Peace River with 4 packs, the returns for 25 pieces. The total returns for the Department were 182 packs, the returns for twenty-eight loaded canoes. Fidler adds : " How different the times now from 4 years ago [1799–1800] when they went in with only 15 half loaded Canoes and the Spring following went out with 648 Packs of 90 lb. each of excellent furrs." If the struggle was ruinous for the North West Company, it was devastating for its rivals. In the first year the XY Company took in seven canoes, and ten in the following three years ; the returns for this ample supply of goods were, 1800—2 packs; 1801—10 packs; 1802—31 packs; 1804—84 packs. Fidler's returns in 1803 were 6 small bundles containing 253 beaver worth of furs.

In 1803–4 the XY Company was able to occupy four posts on Peace River. The Northwesters had five. The English Company none. Fidler sent Swain rather to Great Slave Lake. He proved able to stay on in the face of two rival posts, but gathered no more than 218 beaver worth of furs. Fidler got a few more than that at Nottingham House, the total returns being about 463 beaver worth. This year the servants in the employ of the two Canadian companies outnumbered the English Company's five to one.

The success of the North West Company in bullying the Indians, so that they dared not trade with its rivals, may be attributed to the innate timidity and to the individualism of the Chipewyans. Such a policy would have failed on the Saskatchewan with its great war-like tribes. In the summer of 1804 even the Chipewyans broke out in protest. They attacked the old Company's fort at Fond du Lac, near the eastern extremity of Lake Athabaska, and killed the two men in charge, their wives, and their children. Another party killed four men within five miles of Fort Chipewyan. But the campaign of violence went on. The XY men replied to violence with violence. In the winter of 1804–5 McDonell shot the master of the North West Company's post on Great Bear Lake during a quarrel over Indians. Five weeks later an express arrived at Fort Chipewyan, by way of the Saskatchewan and Peace River, bearing a circular to the proprietors of both Canadian companies announcing the union of the North West companies, old and new, and that the mad struggle was at an end.

The losses suffered by both companies had been such that union was simple wisdom. If the antagonism of Simon McTavish and Sir Alexander Mackenzie was a contributing factor to the quarrel, it would have been removed by McTavish's death on July 6, 1804. The scandal of a struggle which had issued in the murder of King, and lawless deeds in an unpoliced land, was ended by an agreement signed on November 5, 1804. The firms and Wintering Partners connected with the two concerns entered into an association for twenty years under the name of the North West Company. There were to be one hundred shares, seventy-five allotted to the old Company and twenty-five to the new. The Wintering Partners of the XY Company thus brought in were Pierre Rocheblave, Alexander Mackenzie (" The Emperor," not Sir Alexander), John McDonald, James Leith, and John Wills. The corresponding firms were Forsyth, Richardson & Co., in which Sir Alexander Mackenzie was a partner, in Montreal; and Phyn, Inglis & Co., soon to become Ellice, Inglis & Co., in London. These firms were to get one-fourth of the business of purchasing supplies and one-fourth of the returns. The Forsyth firm was to share the agency with the firm of McTavish, M'Gillivrays & Co. in Montreal.

A notable feature of the agreement was the sixth article, which envisaged the possible absorption of the Hudson's Bay Company.

2.—THE CAMPAIGN OF VIOLENCE AGAINST THE HUDSON'S BAY COMPANY, 1804–10

The North West Company, after the disappearance of the English Frobishers, became increasingly not so much a Scottish, as a Highland Society. Its Wintering Partners, and even its agents, were McTavishes, M'Gillivrays, Mackenzies, MacDonalds, McLeods, Camerons, Campbells, and the like. In a new land all the feuds of the several clans were forgotten, and the heterogeneous loyalties represented by these names disappeared, or rather were fused into a common loyalty to " the concern," the North West Company. All the old enmities were absorbed in a common enmity towards its sole remaining rival, the Hudson's Bay Company. The pride which one clan in the Highlands took in its raids upon its neighbours reappeared in the unpoliced West in the joy which these Highlanders found in the depredations committed by the members of the concern upon its foe.   The lack of fair play and honesty was no more evident in the Canadian West than in the Highlands of Scotland before the clans were subjected to law and order.   The habit of resorting to brute force during the struggle between the two Canadian companies rekindled in these Highlanders the traditional glory in deeds of valour, and the success of the resort to force in bringing the XY Company to heel, bade them continue in the same course in their dealings with the Englishmen.   The knowledge that these would not retaliate, and because of their small numbers could not strike back, eliminated even the necessity for prudence, all the more as there were no Courts in the land to which the injured could appeal.

Within a fortnight of the arrival of the news of the union of the old and the new North West companies, Peter Fidler at Nottingham House in Lake Athabaska, wrote in his Journal :

> Mr. [James] McKenzie sent a note over desiring my company to tea—but on Purpose to tell every bad story they could, in order to make us leave this Quarter—and among many things Mr. [A. N.] McLeod told me that we had no right to come into this Quarter for the purpose of Trade & that they would act with the greatest of rigor towards us, in order to expel us hence, & afterwards that the proprietors of the N.W. Co. were resolutely determined that the Servants of the Hudson's Bay Company should walk over their Bodies rather than they would allow an Indian to go into the Hudson's Bay Company's House.

Two days later the Canadians set fire to the wood which had been prepared by Fidler for building a new house.   When Fidler reached Ile-à-la-Crosse on his return in the autumn, he was informed that the Northwesters had destroyed the Company's garden at Green Lake and burnt the house to ashes.   When he arrived at Nottingham House in the autumn he found a Canadian block-house built within 200 yards of his post.   As though that were not enough, a tent was set up four yards from the corner of his fort.   During the summer the Canadians had destroyed the fort's canoe to prevent the Englishmen from going to the Indians.   Samuel Black, a young man without the shadow of self-respect in his make-up, but intent on winning the approval of his Highland chief, had been told off to play the gad-fly to Fidler.   He lodged himself in the block-house and then put up the tent beside the very palisade of Nottingham House, the better to play his part.   In fairness, it should be said that when Fidler protested to Mackenzie against the tent, it was withdrawn. When the nets were not procuring fish enough to provide for Nottingham House, and men were sent off to shoot geese, Black followed and shouted at the birds to make them fly away.   Worse still, he pulled up the principal part of the vegetables in the garden, and prowled about at unearthly hours of the night, suddenly shouting or discharging guns to alarm the inmates of the English House.   The upshot of it all was that not a single Indian came to Fidler's fort, and the

supplies of meat, which the natives must supply, failed.   In dire
necessity Fidler entered into an agreement with Mackenzie, the
principal feature of which was that he was to refrain from trading
with the Indians, while Mackenzie was, in return, to give him 300
large beaver skins and 200 beaver worth of other furs before his
departure in the spring, with six bags of pemmican and the flesh
of ten moose during winter for his table.   Though the Englishman
adhered strictly to the agreement, Black continued on the watch
in his block-house, and did not cease from playing the rôle of gad-
fly.   In the spring Mackenzie refused to give the furs contracted for,
and Fidler left for York Fort empty-handed.   " We are so very few
—they so numerous," he wrote helplessly in his Journal.   The
Hudson's Bay Company forthwith abandoned its Athabaska enterprise.

Not content with this triumph, the North West Company carried
its campaign of violence into many of its other departments, the
actors being for the most part men trained to lawlessness in the school
of Athabaska.   Meanwhile, and indeed before the union of the two
Canadian companies, fresh policies were being devised in Montreal
and London.

In the heat of the struggle between the two Canadian companies
Alexander Mackenzie found time to publish his *Voyages* (1801).
In the concluding pages he elaborated his views about the fur trade
of the continent, including a chartered company using the Hudson
Bay route to reach the marine fur trade of the Pacific coast.   In the
following year he received the honour of knighthood at the hands of
the King.   The conspicuous position in which he now stood offered
some promise of enabling him to win the Government to his views,
and to create the desired chartered company.   After a preliminary
conversation with Lord Hobart, he laid his scheme before the
Government, under the title *Preliminaries to the Establishment of a
permanent British Fishery & trade in Furs etc. on the Continent &
West Coast of North America* (1802).   There should be " a supreme
Civil & Military Establishment " at Nootka Sound ; there should
be passed a Parliamentary Act overriding the monopolies of the East
India and South Sea Companies to the trade of the Pacific so far as
to give the proposed chartered company entry into the markets of
China, or, as an alternative, a " license irrevocable and unlimited "
should be granted by these companies to his proposed General
Fishery and Fur Company.   Further, the Hudson's Bay Company
should grant to it " a license of Transit irrevocable and unlimited "
through Hudson Bay.   The fourth article was drawn with the trade
war actually going on in view.   " The two Companies already
embarked in the Fur Trade from Montreal, including their several
connections in London must find their interest in coalescing . . .
there is not the least reason to doubt, That under such Licenses,
1st of Fishing Trade & Navigation & 2nd of Transit, they would
unite themselves & succeed equally to their own proper & to the
public advantage."

Sir Alexander Mackenzie went over to Montreal and laid his scheme before the North West Company, but failed to win them to it. He then urged General Hunter, Lieutenant-Governor of Upper Canada, to advise the Home Government to give the charter to one or other of the two contending companies, on the understanding that the one securing the charter should offer licences to the members of the other company. Thus those who accepted would be drawn into the combination, and those who did not would be excluded from the trade by the Act of Parliament granting the charter. General Hunter, however, proved uninterested in the scheme.

Had Mackenzie got his Chartered Company, he would have been able to end the struggle between the old and new North West companies with honour. The right of transit through Hudson Bay and on the Pacific to China would have enabled the Canadians to enter into the trade of the Pacific slope with some assurance of success. It would indeed have been a triumphant realization of his dreams. Moreover, it would have placed him in a commanding position in the fur trade of Montreal.

Mackenzie was endowed with great inventiveness. When he failed to secure the support of the Government, he turned to find his charter by securing control of the Hudson's Bay Company. Edward Ellice was enlisted for this enterprise. He tried to buy sufficient stock in the English Company to enable him to bring it into line with the new North West Company, and to win for it the short and cheap line of transportation through the Bay. It was thought that £103,000 would accomplish the purpose. Meanwhile, Mackenzie wrote the Governor and Committee asking for friendly negotiations. They moved slowly. The union of the two Canadian companies took place in November. In the light of the above plans of Mackenzie, it becomes clear why a clause in the agreement of union envisaged the absorption of the Hudson's Bay Company.

All the while Duncan M'Gillivray, now agent of the old North West Company, was working on independent lines towards the same ends. As has been seen, he had become a convert to Mackenzie's views of the gain to be found by entering into the fur trade of the Pacific. He knew that the plan could not be a commercial success if the goods and the furs had to be transported across the whole continent between Montreal and the mouth of the Columbia. In the summer of 1804—again before the union of the two Canadian companies—he went over to England and wrote the Governor and Committee of the Hudson's Bay Company asking to enter into negotiations with them " to concert arrangements for the better regulating of the Indian Trade in America." But Duncan did not take this step without having taken action which he thought calculated to bring the English Company to a yielding frame of mind. The North West Company had recently leased the King's Posts in Quebec on the north side of the lower St. Lawrence. In the summer of 1803 it dispatched the ship *Eddystone*, under Captain Richards, recently in the employ of the Hudson's Bay Company, on an expedition into Hudson Bay. Charlton Island was made the depot, and thence posts were established on the mainland—on Hayes Island at the mouth of Moose River and on Rupert River. The Governor and Committee received word that the *Eddystone* was heavily armed, and that Richards was commissioned to assert the North West Company's right to trade in the Bay by force if necessary, that John George McTavish, Simon's nephew, was in charge, that Angus Shaw had crossed overland to join him, and that a leaden tablet had been placed upon a tree before the fort built on Charlton Island : " This Island of Charlton taken possession of by Angus Shaw Esqr. 1st day of September 1803 for the benefit of the N. West Company in the presence of Captn. Richards and the following gentlemen being British Subjects—Captain Sarmon Mr. McTavish, Mr. McDougal, Mr. Folster." Theodore Roosevelt is said to have had as a guiding principle, " Go easy and carry a big stick." Duncan M'Gillivray was ready to enter into friendly negotiations with the Hudson's Bay Company, and the expedition to Charlton Island was the big stick intended to bring the Englishmen to reason. The Governor and Committee followed a policy of procrastination with M'Gillivray, as with Mackenzie, and the union of the two Canadian companies was effected before the discussions began. Hence both parties to the union envisaged bringing the English Company to terms and stood behind the sixth article of their agreement, looking to the absorption of the Hudson's Bay Company. But it must have become apparent very soon that Ellice's plans, whatever they were, for purchasing the controlling stock in the English Company were not to succeed. The immediate objective aimed at became therefore the right of transit for the Canadian Company's goods through the Bay.

The Minute of the Committee of the Hudson's Bay Company agreeing to meet with M'Gillivray, and Governor Lake's notes prepared with a view to the discussions, show that M'Gillivray's phrase " to concert arrangements for the better regulating of the Indian Trade in America " suggested an agreement to minimize clashes in the conduct of the trade. When the conference was held, on January 30, 1805, M'Gillivray confessed that that was a minor consideration, " that the North West Company conceived that they had a right to navigate and traffic in the Bay and that they wished to ascertain whether it would meet with the acquiescence and support of the Committee." The answer given was that this was so different a matter from what had been suggested in M'Gillivray's letter, no answer could be given ; let the definite proposal of the North West Company be put in writing. A few days later the proposal was submitted over the signatures of Duncan M'Gillivray and Thomas Forsyth, Sir Alexander Mackenzie's partner, for Sir Alexander was now in Canada. It was that the North West Company proposed to extend its trade beyond the Rockies and, if practicable, to the Pacific Ocean ; that this would be greatly facilitated if they had a transit through Hudson Bay by York Fort to Lake Winnipeg ; that it was not thought that this would injure the trade of the English Company ; that in any case, as British subjects, the Canadians had the right to trade in and through the Bay ; and that they intended to avail themselves of it, but as an inducement to the Hudson's Bay Company to meet their views they would agree to withdraw from the posts which they had established at Charlton Island and on the mainland. Minor matters looking to the advantages of the trade could be considered thereafter.

The answer of the Committee ran that the transit would strike at the very root of its trade and that the proposal was to pass through their territory, yet offered no guarantee that the Company's trade would not suffer. In the following July (1805) M'Gillivray, as agent, met with the Wintering Partners at Kaministikwia. There he would receive a report on the practicability of the Churchill River route to the interior made by David Thompson, who had been sent to winter on the South Indian Lake, as far down that river as any Northwester had ever been. From the difficulties of the route, the report must have been none too encouraging. At any rate, William McKay, the Proprietor in the Lake Winnipeg Department, was instructed to examine the possibilities of the routes to Port Nelson. In the spring of 1806, he ran down the Nelson to its estuary. At that point his Journal ends. He probably returned by the Hayes to report on that route. These movements of the Northwesters are explained by statements made by some of them to the servants of the Hudson's Bay Company, that they expected a ship to bring their goods either to Churchill River or to the Nelson. Meanwhile, the decision of the Proprietors assembled in 1805 ran : " The Agents of the Concern shall be & they are hereby authorized and directed to offer to the said Hudson's Bay Company a sum not exceeding Two thousand pounds . . . a year, for a period to be agreed upon, provided they consent that the North West Company shall establish a free communication with the interior Country by Nelson or Hayes' Rivers without being Subject to any interference or molestation whatever," the North West Company agreeing to abandon its posts on the Bay. With the authority thus given, M'Gillivray returned to England, and in November made the proposal as above, the agreement to last for seven years. The final answer of the Governor and Committee was that they could not, consistently with their Charter, which required the whole of their trade to be carried through Hudson Strait, make an agreement with a Company whose traffic would not conform to this condition.

The incursion of the North West Company into Hudson Bay was of little importance in itself, for, in spite of the threats of M'Gillivray, it was not repeated, and no attempt was made to summarily establish a transit. None the less it proved epoch-making, for it led the Hudson's Bay Company to appraise its legal position under the Charter, and this, in turn, led to views which affected profoundly its subsequent policy. With a view to a possible prosecution of the Northwesters in the Bay, a case was laid before prominent lawyers, including Messrs. T. Erskine, V. Gibbs, and Sam. Romilly. These doubted whether it was within the power of the Crown to appropriate the trade and commerce with countries abroad, whether newly discovered or not, and referred to a resolution to that effect adopted by the House of Commons on the 18th January, 1693/4. They therefore advised against prosecution. To the question whether under the Charter the Company was legally in possession of the islands within the Bay, the answer was given : "We take it to be settled law that the King may grant newly discovered countries. . . . We see no reason to doubt the legality of the Company's title to such islands and adjacent land." As this principle, that it was within the prerogative of the King to grant lands out of the Royal Domain, was acted upon by the Colonial Office far into the nineteenth century, it may be taken that the lawyers gave a sound opinion. The Company now perceived that its most secure privilege was not its monopoly of the trade (it did not prosecute the Northwesters) but its possession of the soil, as will appear when the history of Lord Selkirk's colony is considered.

The violences perpetrated by the men of the North West Company upon the Indians and servants of the English Company, initiated in the first place to drive that Company out of the Churchill River and Athabaska, became very general. No doubt the first aim was simply to cripple a rival, but in view of the attempt of Ellice in 1804, and then of Sir Alexander Mackenzie in 1808, to get control of the English Company, and in view of the manifest desire of M'Gillivray to secure a transit through Hudson Bay, there is much to be said in favour of Lord Selkirk's assertion that there was a deliberate campaign on foot to bring the Hudson's Bay Company to the will of and under the control of the North West Company.

After the coalition of the Old and New North West Companies . . . the ferocious spirit which had been fostered among the clerks and servants of the two Companies by six years of continual violence, was all turned against the Hudson's Bay Company : and there is reason to believe not only that a systematic plan was formed for driving their traders out of all the valuable beaver countries, but that hopes were entertained of reducing that Company to so low an ebb, as in time to induce them to make over their chartered rights to their commercial rivals.

Selkirk backs his statement with ample illustration. In 1806, in May, when the furs of the season would be packed and ready for shipment, Mr. John Haldane, formerly Wintering Partner of the XY Company in Athabaska, now in the Red Lake district east of Lake Winnipeg, broke into the English company's outpost at Bad Lake about midnight with a superior force. The Master, William Corrigal, who was in bed, was overawed with arms, while the Northwesters made away with 480 beaver skins. When Corrigal protested to Haldane, he was told : " He had come to that country for furs, and that furs he was determined to have." Haldane's men took the furs to Fort William and there sold them to their masters. At an outpost of Corrigal's house two similar raids were made, in which the Northwesters carried off fifty beaver skins and a considerable quantity of cloth, brandy, tobacco, and ammunition. That autumn Mr. Alex. Macdonell, who was later to earn ill-fame by his violence towards the Red River Settlement, fell upon the Hudson's Bay Company's servant, John Crear by name, at Big Fall near Lake Winnipeg, charged him with trading with an Indian indebted to the North West Company, broke open the warehouse, felled its guardian to the ground with the butt end of his gun, stabbed another in the arm dangerously, and rifled the warehouse. The furs at that time of the year were few and poor. More valuable booty was taken in the shape of two bags of flour, a quantity of salt pork and beef, dried meat, and a new canoe belonging to the Englishman. Macdonell's men returned in February and made away with a great number of valuable furs, and the Northwester himself obliged Crear to sign a paper stating that he gave them of his own free will.

In 1808 at Reindeer Lake in the English (Churchill) River Department, that redoubtable Northwester, John Duncan Campbell, fell on William Linklater as he brought in a hand-sled of valuable furs, took hold of his snowshoes and threw him on the ice, and made off with the booty. Campbell had carried through a similar piece of violence at Ile-à-la-Crosse in 1805. This conduct, so far from bringing censure on him, led to his being placed in charge of Ile-à-la-Crosse, the central fort of the department, which was crowded with servants, to overawe the mild and easy-going Peter Fidler in the English house. A watch-house was built at Fidler's gate to keep the Indians away, and it was manned with bullies under the reckless Samuel Black. These carried off Fidler's firewood, destroyed his garden, made away with the fishing lines and nets by which alone he could live. Finally, Black forbade the Englishmen to leave the house, and so terrified them that the post had to be evacuated. It was forthwith burned to the ground by the Northwesters. The men from Montreal explained such deeds as simple retaliation in a trade war, but as the English Company's service was always in a great minority, and as their general attitude was that they were paid to trade and not to fight, the conclusion must be that the plea was no more than a smoke-screen to conceal the true nature of their deeds from the public.

In these years the Canadians learned that the Canada Jurisdiction Act was a potent instrument in their hand against their English rivals. The Act envisaged the appointment of men in the Indian Territory as Justices of the Peace, and, as has been seen, five Proprietors of the North West Company were appointed such under its provisions. They do not seem ever to have acted. At any rate, in 1809 Duncan M'Gillivray was dead ; Ogilvy had retired ; and it was doubtful whether two of the five had ever taken the oath of office. Accordingly, on March 9, 1809, William M'Gillivray applied for the appointment of Angus Shaw and that embodiment of violence, Archibald McLeod, as Justices of the Peace, and their names soon figure as such in the Quebec Almanac. In the autumn of that year Aeneas Macdonnell, a clerk of the North West Company, held an outpost at Eagle Lake, east of the Lake of the Woods, within forty yards of the English house, held by William Corrigal. He observed an Indian dealing with Corrigal at the lake-side. On the plea that the Indian was indebted to his Company, Macdonnell came down on him armed with a sword, and seized not only his canoe but also the English Company's goods given him on credit. Corrigal ordered two of his men, James Tate and John Corrigal, to go into the water to secure the canoe and the property. Macdonnell struck at Tate, who was unarmed, and therefore no aggressor, and cut him severely across his wrist and in the neck. John Corrigal took to the water, but finding it too deep came to shore. With his sword Macdonnell cut him at the elbow to the bone. Another Englishman had his shoulder dislocated. Meanwhile Corrigal's servants got their arms. One of them, John Mowat, had been struck by Macdonnell with his sword, and when the Northwester came at him a second time, he shot him. Word of the deed was sent to Haldane, Macdonnell's chief, and to Fort William where was Archibald McLellan. These men arrived at Corrigal's post with an armed posse. Mowat acknowledged his deed and consented to surrender. It was agreed that two of Corrigal's men, James Tate and John Corrigal, should go, if necessary, to Montreal as witnesses for the defence. Mowat was taken to Rainy Lake in October and to Fort William in June of next year, suffering all the while the hardships of a convict. At Fort William Angus Shaw, the weather-beaten old Northwester, appeared in the capacity of Justice of the Peace. Mowat protested against appearing before a magistrate anywhere but in Montreal, but was placed in irons and, now a sick man, lay unattended, though there was a doctor in the place. Although canoes had left for the St. Lawrence before, it was not till 17th August that he was sent down. When the three servants of the Hudson's Bay Company reached Montreal, Tate and Corrigal, so far from being treated as witnesses, were arrested—Tate at the office of no less a person than William M'Gillivray himself, on the charge of aiding and abetting Mowat in the murder of Aeneas Macdonnell. The Grand Jury, however, threw out the bill against them. In spite of the testimony of Tate and Corrigal, Mowat was sentenced to prison for six months and to be branded on the hand with a hot iron. In the final issue it appeared that the Canada Jurisdiction Act could be invoked against the servants of the Hudson's Bay Company for actions taken in sheer self-defence during a fracas initiated by the men of the North West Company—a result far from what was contemplated when the legislation was passed—and that William M'Gillivray was capable of playing his part in thus turning justice awry.

The pressure put upon the Hudson's Bay Company in this bitter struggle affected its prosperity, as doubtless it was intended to do. True, the average value of furs taken out in the five years 1807–11 was higher than that of the preceeding years, 1801–6, the figures being in pounds sterling 15,468 to 14,949, but the expenses entailed were increased out of all proportion. With the possibility of an outbreak of violence at almost any point, the forts had to be manned far beyond the necessities of the trade. In former days there would be times when the fort was almost untenanted, for the men would be out meeting the Indians and gathering furs. Now the posts had to be kept manned for a defence. Parties of one or two white men with a few inferior servants used to pass to the Indian camps in safety. Now they must go strong enough to face any eventuality. The cost of the service and of provisioning the forts must have been very great. In fact the Company came to the crisis aimed at by its Canadian rivals. The Northwesters later published it, seemingly with glee, that Hudson's Bay Company stock fell to between £50 and £60 for the £100 stock which at one time was going at £250. Certainly Sir Alexander Mackenzie, with William and Simon M'Gillivray's support, began to plan a purchase of shares, with a view to gaining the control of the Company. As the transfer of stock had to be reported and agreed to by the Governor and Committee, it was necessary to find some person trusted by the Committee to play the game of the Northwesters. Mackenzie believed that he had his man in Lord Selkirk.

Thomas Douglas, fifth Earl of Selkirk, was born in 1771, that is, about the time when the English Montreal traders were first invading the Saskatchewan. The deaths of his elder brothers—so many barriers between him and the title—and in 1799 of his father, brought him the title and all the estates and wealth attached to it, when he was in his twenty-eighth year. Selkirk was one of those characters about which contemporaries held the most varied and conflicting opinions and which in after time constitute an enigma to historians. This is because his nature and interests were highly complex. To understand his lordship it must be remembered that many British nobles took the management of their estates and their money with high seriousness and did not think it beneath the aristocracy to engage in " big business." On the contrary, they prided themselves on the acumen with which they handled their affairs. Lord Selkirk was not above devoting himself with zeal to the agricultural interests of his estates, or to a deal in stocks if it promised success, or again to speculating in land in the colonies, if it would ultimately enrich the family. Many of his enemies in Canada, among whom Bishop Strachan may be counted, took delight in picturing him as a plunger in stocks and as a reckless land speculator. A calm judgment requires us not to condemn this in Lord Selkirk unless we are ready to damn it in all others of his and of our generation. Then again, Selkirk was a patriot and philanthropist. When his brothers were alive and the title seemed beyond him, he was given an education in the comparatively humble University of Edinburgh, which should prepare him for an honourable career in his native land. He appears to have looked forward to law as a profession. In his student days he associated himself with " The Club," a group of the brightest young men at the university. Francis Jeffrey, the most famous essayist and reviewer of his generation, Dugald Stewart, the outstanding

Scottish philosopher, and no less a genius than Walter Scott, the novelist, were members. It says much for Selkirk that in the dark days of the Red River Settlement troubles, these men believed in him and were his staunchest allies. The little group of students which constituted "The Club" cherished literary interests and a humanitarian enthusiasm which were to be their pride in after life. While Selkirk was of one mind with them "he was by no means carried away by the deluge of revolutionary thought."

In 1792 he was in Paris observing the revolution rapidly developing in France, "with sympathy but not without reserve." With Sir William Hamilton, soon to be one of Scotland's foremost philosophers, he visited Italy, and in 1794, when in Switzerland, he made the acquaintance of Count Andreani, whose penetrating criticism of the North West Company, based, as has been seen, on inaccurate statistics, he adopted as his own and used in his later attack upon that "concern," published as *A Sketch of the British Fur Trade* (1816).

Selkirk's support of movements such as Catholic Emancipation in Ireland led him to look beneath the surface to the human misery out of which the discontent of the day arose. It is characteristic of the man that his interest in Ireland led him to visit that unhappy island. Subsequently a curious and somewhat unperceiving sympathy with the Catholics and with the Irish runs through his career, leading him at times to strange misjudgments. The remedy for the prevailing ills he found in emigration. True to his nature, he immediately produced a scheme to meet the crisis.

Selkirk's "Proposal tending to the Permanent Security of Ireland," forwarded by him to Lord Pelham, Secretary of State, before April 4, 1802, and his "Observations Supplementary" to it, presented on that date, deserve more attention than they have received, for they help one to understand not only the man, but his interest in the fertile region about Red River. It should be borne in mind that the situation in Ireland to which his lordship refers was that after the Rebellion and the Act of Union which was carried through with the promise of Catholic Emancipation—a promise which Protestant George III. refused to implement. The hostility of the Irish to the British—a standing danger to the Empire, as Lord Selkirk averred—could be allayed not by coercion but only by the slow process of conciliatory legislation and humane administration. These processes could be greatly accelerated by an emigration which would take out of the country people embittered by poverty and would make them prosperous, contented, and loyal in a British colony overseas, expressly set apart for Irish Catholics. It was the most energetic of the Irish who refused to submit to the poverty of their circumstances and agitated against the British Government. These would be the first to avail themselves of such a scheme of emigration. By going overseas they would rid the Government of a troublesome element at home and smooth its path. Moreover, a mass movement out of Ireland would create a vacant space into which loyal and energetic Scotsmen could be moved. Thus the Protestant element in Ireland would grow till it counterbalanced, in a measure, the Catholic, while the British Government would have a constantly increasing support in the country itself, and its hold upon it would become secure. So much for the Irish end of the scheme. The American end envisaged the formation of an Irish Catholic colony within the Empire strengthening the British hold on America. As there was not sufficient vacant space for such a scheme near the Atlantic coast of British America, it must be far in the interior.

At the Western extremity of Canada upon the Waters which fall into Lake Winnipeck &, uniting in the great River of Port Nelson, discharge themselves into Hudson's Bay, is a Country which the Indian Traders represent as fertile, & of a Climate far more temperate than the shores of the Atlantic under the same parallel. . . . Here, therefore, the Colonists may with a moderate exertion of industry be certain of a comfortable subsistence & they may raise some valuable objects of exportation—

Hemp, for example, which is supplied to Europe at present from similar climates in the Russian Empire. Selkirk went on to elaborate an argument, which he must have drawn from Mackenzie's *Voyages*, published the year before. Indeed his plea, if granted, would have put the objects for which Sir Alexander was at that very time striving into his hand. One cannot but wonder whether the two men had not already met, and whether they were not at this early date (1802) working as they did in 1810 hand in glove. The great impediment to the colony, the argument continues, would appear to be the monopoly of the Hudson's Bay Company, for the route to it would be by the Bay and up the Nelson River. That Company would hardly give up its rights without compensation. This, however, could be secured by charging a licence fee from every trader going into the country, and handing over to the Company from the proceeds what would be equal to the average dividend of past years, as a recompense for annulling the Charter. The individual trader would be confined by his licence to a limited area, and would thus reap all the advantages

now divided between the Company and its competitors and would have the benefit of the short route by the Bay which would enable him to carry on his business at one fourth of the expence to which the Canadians are subject. . . . If these indefatigable Canadians were allowed the free Navigation of Hudson's Bay, they might, without going so far from Port Nelson, as they now go from Montreal, extend their traffic from Sea to Sea, through the whole Northern part of America, & send home more than double the value that is now derived from that region. . . . Many other Commercial advantages might be derived from the proposed Colony. It is asserted that a valuable fishery might be carried on in Hudson Bay & Straits. . . . It appears particularly that the branches of the River of the West or Columbia interlock not only with the heads of the Missouri, but with the Waters of Lake Winnipeek. A Communication might therefore be opened & a Post established on the Pacific Ocean, from which many of the advantages would arise which were formerly expected from the discovery of a North-West passage.

Finally, the cost of administering the colony would be met by the balance from the proceeds of licences and by duties levied upon this wide trade. The Imperial Government, however, would pay the cost of the passage of the Irish immigrants to their new home.

Nothing came of the proposal. The Ministers of the Crown were against aiding any particular class of people to emigrate, and against giving them particular privileges. Further, Lord Hobart wrote on May 27, 1802, "What Lord Selkirk says of the Fur Trade is very true, and the Canadians now trade to the very out-Posts of the Hudson's Bay Company—But I should be adverse to interfere in that trade which takes such good care of itself. There is such a thing as *Salutary neglect* which in such cases beats all the care in the world."

This scheme of Selkirk's has been displayed in detail, because it throws a flood of light upon the character of the man—his patriotism, his profound interest in the problems of the State, his deep insight into the causes of the present discontents; most creditable of all, his mind leaping across barriers innumerable to provide a solution. All the difficulties at home, the intractable Irish character, the prejudice of the Irish administration against emigration, the inertness of the English statesmen of the day—all the obstacles abroad, the rigour of the climate at the Red River, the toilsome and perilous lines of transportation, the monopoly of the Hudson's Bay Company—all are lost sight of in the vision of a rejuvenated and loyal Ireland, and a prosperous and happy Irish Catholic colony in America. There is no suggestion in the scheme of any gain to the noble lord, though it may be assumed that he would have taken up land in the proposed colony. On the contrary, he professed to be ready to devote himself to it as a patriotic enterprise worthy of all his exertions. "Deeply impressed with the importance of these views, the Memorialist would not hesitate to devote his personal exertions and the best years of his life to the Service of his Country." This is the Selkirk, best known by his work, published three years later, *Observations on the Present State of the Highlands of Scotland with a view of the causes and probable consequences of Emigration*, 1805. It is an admirable Lord Selkirk, but in justice to William M'Gillivray, his arch-opponent, and to the North West Company, it must be borne in mind that the Lord Selkirk who crossed their path was a shrewd man of business who expected a humanitarian enterprise to enhance the wealth of his family. The way in which Selkirk the philanthropic colonizer and Selkirk the land speculator came to be blended is clearly seen in the steps taken by him when it became apparent that the Government would not undertake the scheme of an Irish Catholic colony on the Red River. He decided to promote emigration with his own resources, and to this end applied for grants on Prince Edward Island and at the Sault Ste. Marie at the entrance to Lake Superior. He was granted the eastern peninsula of the island, and in August 1803 landed 800 settlers from Argyle, Ross-shire, Inverness, and the Isle of Skye upon it—emigrants "whose views were directed to the United States but were thus saved for the British Empire."

3.—THE REORGANIZATION OF THE HUDSON'S BAY COMPANY, 1810–11

The pressure of the North West Company upon the Hudson's Bay Company was not without its effect. Dividends had run during the latter part of the eighteenth century at 8 per cent. In the first eight years of the nineteenth century they were 4 per cent. From 1809 until 1814 no dividends were paid. The Northwesters claimed that the Company's stock which had once sold for £250 was selling in 1810 at from £50 to £60. Indeed, it was this situation that gave Sir Alexander Mackenzie his hope of capturing stock sufficient to control the Company and win for the Northwesters the use of the route by Hudson's Strait and the entry into the fur trade of the Pacific slope. The crisis bade the Governor and Committee reorganize. Plans were drawn up by more than one member, but the scheme of Andrew Wedderburn, better known by the name of Colvile, proved the acceptable one. Wedderburn was brother-in-law to Lord Selkirk and had only recently been elected to the Committee. He proved himself one of the ablest men who ever held office in the Company. He became Deputy-Governor in 1839 and was Governor from 1852 to 1856. His scheme was adopted in the spring of 1810. The reorganization aimed at securing a better supervision of the trade, at giving the servants a more definite interest in increasing the returns, and at thereby making them stand up against the depredations of the Northwesters. The better supervision was to be secured by appointing two Superintendents, attached to no particular fort, rather supervising the interests at large of the Company in the several regions—Albany and Moose, and York and Churchill. The former Albany and York regions were subdivided by creating the Saskatchewan and Winnipeg regions into factories, with a Chief Factor, responsible for the several subordinate posts—York, Churchill, and the Saskatchewan under the western superintendent, and Albany and Winnipeg under the eastern. The incentive to greater energy in increasing the trade was assured by giving the servants a share in the profits. For this purpose a distinction was made between the trading and the administrative services. One-third of the profits in a " factory," in the sense of the scheme, were given to the Chief Factor, and one-third was divided out to the trading officers under him. The last third went to a general fund which was distributed among the superintendents, accountants, and the like who were not directly connected with trading. This plan involved a reduction of the fixed salaries. Minimum salaries were paid, the same to be increased by the share in the profits of the trade as above.

It was hoped that the servants would thus be moved to greater energy in opposing the Canadians. The circular explaining the scheme went carefully into the extent to which the Company's servants could meet violence with a show of brute force.

We have always been and still are desirous that you should avoid all occasion of violent conflict with any commercial rivals ; we have no wish to give any molestation to other Traders, so long as they are content to act on the principles of fair competition. On these principles we have formerly directed, that you should by no means be guilty of any act of aggression against the Canadian Traders. To these principles we still adhere ; but forbearance must not be carried so far as to invite aggression. It appears that in numerous instances the Servants of the Company have yielded to the violence and threats of the Canadians, and have allowed the property of the Company to be pillaged, or have been deterred from the exercise of their duty in the manner most advantageous for their employers. Such abject submission is very different from that moderation which we have recommended. The spirit of aggression and illegal violence by which the Canadian Traders appear to be actuated can only be repressed by determined firmness on the part of the Company's Servants ; and we shall consider as undeserving of our Favor any Officer who shall betray weakness or timidity in defence of the Company's just Rights. We expect that you will defend like men the Property that is entrusted to you ; and if any person shall presume to make a forcible attack upon you, you have arms in your hands and the Law sanctions you in using them for your own defence. The peril is on the head of the aggressor. We should very much regret if you were to go one step beyond what the Laws of your Country will fully justify.

The circular adds that no more servants from the Orkneys will be sent out but men " from the Western Islands and Coast of Scotland, where the people are of a more spirited race than in Orkney."

In the circular it was stated that the cost of European provisions had reached an amount which was equal to a handsome dividend. It must be diminished. There must be cultivation at the posts—potatoes, Indian corn, grain—and the quantity of imported flour must be reduced. The opinion that provisions should be grown in the country left the way open to Lord Selkirk's ambition to found a settlement in the prairie region.

Part of the scheme of reorganization was the establishment of the colony on the Red River. It would give a supply of provisions within the country and at greatly diminished cost. Then, too, for twenty years—mostly years in which England was engaged in war—it had been difficult to get suitable servants. The colony promised a steady and cheap supply of labourers in the more distant future. These views of the place of the colony in the reorganization are nowhere found expressed in the documents ; they are written large in the course of events.

Nine months after the scheme of reorganization was adopted by the Governor and Committee, it was " Resolved that Mr. [Andrew] Wedderburn [Colvile] be desired to request Lord Selkirk to lay before the Committee the Terms on which he will accept a Grant of Land, within the Territories of the Company." (1811, Feb. 26.)

Lord Selkirk's reply was that he should be given a tract of land on condition that he should secure, from the commencement of 1812, two hundred effective men each year ready to embark on the Company's ships for service overseas, that the Company should continue to enjoy the right to settle and trade in any unoccupied site within the colony, that his Lordship would grant 200 acres to any officer recommended to him by the Governor and Committee, that the grants to all settlers should preclude them from infringing upon the monopoly of the Company, but that they should be free to import goods and export produce through York Fort. The Company was to provide accommodation in its ships and charge no more than the usual freight. The bulk of the goods was not to be broken in transit, and all exports were to be housed in the Company's warehouses in London, paying the usual rates, and to be sold at auction there. Export and import duties of not more than 5 per cent. might be levied, but the proceeds were to go to a separate fund devoted to the Police and Civil Government of the colony, to the improvement of communications between York Fort and Lake Winnipeg, and " to all such other purposes as the Governor and Committee shall deem necessary for the improvement of their Territories and establishments in North America." The Governor and Committee were to have absolute control of the fund, but were not to put the money into the profit account.

The proposal was considered at a General Court, which adjourned. At a second General Court held on May 29, 1811, it was accepted by stockholders representing " £29,937," the votes to the contrary representing " £14,823, 19s. 11d." Two old stockholders representing £12,233, 6s. 8d. were among the contrary-minds, with Sir Alexander Mackenzie, who held £200. Recent purchases by Northwesters (John Inglis, £1,000, and Edward Ellice, £1,293, 13s. 3d.), as being held for less than six months, were not entitled to vote ; as also £100 held by one Capel Cure; making £2,693, 13s. 3d. of stock disqualified. The Governor, Deputy-Governor, and the seven Committeemen were in favour of the Grant ; and three stockholders (exclusive of Lord Selkirk) representing £4,936 ; Lord Selkirk's vote represented £4,087, 10s. of stock. Three stockholders present failed to record their votes. The Northwesters asserted that Selkirk had bought stock to the extent of £40,000 of the total, given by them as £100,000. " His Lordship may be considered as possessing an unlimited influence and controul in the management of the affairs, and the disposal of the property of the Company." In other words, Lord Selkirk got control of the Company and voted himself the Grant of 116,000 square miles of fertile lands. The Minutes of the General Court show the contrary. The votes of Selkirk and his brother-in-law Andrew Colvile represented no more than £8,561, 13s. 4d. Selkirk's other brother-in-law, John Halkett, who held considerable stock, was not present and did not record his vote by proxy. Selkirk's large purchases of stock came after he had received the Grant. His interest in the Company was intensified by the scope which it gave to his aims as a colonizer.

A signed " Protest " was presented by the six non-contents, three of whom were connected with the North West Company. It insisted that the Grant should have been offered at a public sale, and that Lord Selkirk was making no adequate return for the large concession ; the scheme had no " other motive than to secure to the posterity of the Earl, at the expense of the Stockholders of the Company, an immensely valuable landed estate " ; the Colony would be damaging to the fur trade, for the colonists would soon carry on a private traffic in furs through the United States. The Protest claimed to be " signed by every member present at the meeting except Lord Selkirk and the members of the Direction." The Minutes show that this was not true. When the Protest failed to stay the Grant, the Northwesters raised the cry that the Indians would be hostile, and that Lord Selkirk would be exposing the colonists to inevitable slaughter.

After the first crisis in the affairs of the colony, the Hudson's Bay Company explained the origin of the colony to the Colonial Minister.

> The servants of the Hudson's Bay Company, employed in the fur-trade, have hitherto been fed with provisions exported from England. Of late years this expense has been so enormous, that it became very desirable to try the practicability of raising provisions within the territory itself. . . . It did not appear that agriculture would be carried on with sufficient care and attention by servants in the immediate employ of the company ; but by establishing independent settlers, and giving them freehold tenures of land, the company expected that they would obtain a certain supply of provisions at a moderate price. The company also entertained expectations of considerable eventual benefit from the improvement of their landed property by means of agricultural settlements. . . . With these views, the company were induced in the year 1811 to dispose of a large tract of lands to the Earl of Selkirk in whose hands they trusted the experiment would be prosecuted with due attention, as the grant was made subject to adequate conditions of settlement.

The colony was therefore an integral part of the reorganization of the Company, and, in proportion as it promised success, would meet with the hostility of the North West Company.

A feature which does not appear on the surface, but which was of great importance in the sequel, was that a successful colony would proclaim the title of the Company to the soil.

The legal document conveying the land to Lord Selkirk received the Company's seal on June 12, 1811. The area described was about 116,000 square miles, in what is to-day Manitoba, Saskatchewan, North Dakota, and Minnesota. The boundary followed the parallel of North latitude 52° 30′ from the western shore of Lake Winnipeg to Lake Winnipegosis ; thence it ran south to 52° North latitude, which parallel was followed westward to the Assiniboine River. The lower Swan River posts were north of this line, and therefore outside of the Grant ; but Somerset House and its Canadian rival post at Thunder Hill were south of it, as well as Fort Alexandria and the Hudson's Bay Company's Carlton House, which stood in 51° 58′ North latitude. From the Assiniboine the boundary ran due south to the height of land which separates the waters which flow into Hudson Bay from the valley of the River Missouri, that is, well into the United States. The North West Company's forts Espérance on the Qu'Appelle River and La Souris, along with the Hudson's Bay

Company's opposing houses—the later Fort Qu'Appelle, and Brandon House—were east of this line and therefore in the area granted. The height of land was the southern boundary till the water-way from Grand Portage to Lake Winnipeg was reached. This water-way, under the name of " Winnipeg River," was the boundary as far as Lake Winnipeg. Rainy Lake Fort, being north of the route, was outside of the Grant, but Fort Alexander (Bas de la Rivière Winipic) on its left was within it. The North West Company's forts—Dauphin, Gibraltar * at the confluence of the Red River and the Assiniboine, and Pembina—were roughly on a line running south-east and south through the centre of the Grant.

One-tenth of the area granted was to be set aside for the settlement of persons, as already described, connected with the service of the Company.

Lord Selkirk and his heirs were required to settle a thousand families in the colony within ten years, otherwise the grant was to become null and void. A token payment of ten shillings was made for the land conceded.

In 1807 Lord Selkirk had married Miss Jean Wedderburn-Colvile. It has been thought that the connection of the family with the Hudson's Bay Company brought about his lordship's interest in the fur trade. It was the reverse. In 1808 Selkirk was in some sort of relation with Sir Alexander Mackenzie, and was purchasing stock in the Hudson's Bay Company. The Wedderburn-Colvile connection was drawn thereafter into the Company, and by him. The entries in the Company's Stock-Transfer Book throw a curious light on the matter. On July 6, 1808, Sir Alexander Mackenzie bought £1,800 of stock ; on the 13th Selkirk made his first purchase, and by May 24, 1809, had acquired £4,087, 10s. of stock. At this point Andrew Wedderburn [Colvile] stepped in, and in June and July secured £2,674, 3s. 4d. of stock. In August John Halkett, Selkirk's other brother-in-law, began his purchases, and before the end of September had acquired £3,717 of stock.

The purport of these purchases must remain largely a matter of surmise. A letter from Sir Alexander Mackenzie to his cousin Roderick, written from London in April 1812, mentions a verbal understanding with William M'Gillivray to invest £30,000 in Hudson's Bay Company's stock, and shows that Lord Selkirk had been busy purchasing, as he understood it, for him. This is confirmed by letters from Mackenzie to Selkirk in 1808 ; Mackenzie was finding difficulty in getting stock, because the influence of the Secretary was being exercised against him, and because he had no ready money. He was expecting Selkirk to purchase. Mackenzie's letter is further borne out by an entry in the Minutes of the North West Company. In

* John MacDonald of Garth, head of the Upper Red River Department, claims to have built and named Fort Gibraltar in 1807, but the post was in the Lower Red River Department, the sphere of Alexander Henry the younger, and had not been built when Henry left it in the spring of 1808. MacDonald may have suggested its building. John Wills was placed in charge of the Lower Department in 1809. A tradition prevailed in the Red River Settlement that the fort was built by Wills. It stood at the confluence of the Assiniboine and the Red, but faced the Red River.

July 1811 £1,500 were voted " to enable the agents . . . to purchase on account of the concern Hudson's Bay stock . . . with a view of establishing an influence in the Committee of the said Company—in order to establish a Boundary line with them in the interior Country." Negotiations were going on for a division of the fur country. As the English Company was then paying no dividends, the Northwesters hoped for a favourable agreement; they came very near asking for all the fur forest except the valleys of the Moose and Albany, and offering the rest to the Englishmen. In the final issue the Hudson's Bay Company refused to consider any scheme which might cast doubts on the validity of the Charter. To get entrance for the Northwesters into the Company and on the Committee, that they might influence the stockholders to grant terms favourable to them, is established as the aim of the Northwesters in the purchases. It can hardly be doubted that they, and Sir Alexander Mackenzie in particular, had the acquisition of a free transit through Hudson Bay to the fur fields of the West also in view.

But what of Lord Selkirk ? His scheme of 1802 for an Irish colony on the Red River shows that he had accepted Mackenzie's ideal of a unified British fur trade extending to the Pacific and using the short route by the Bay. It may be surmised that Mackenzie, to gain his ends, held out some hope to his lordship that mutual co-operation would open up the way for his colony on the Red River. At the same time, Selkirk may well have argued shrewdly that his association with the arch-Northwester would induce the Hudson's Bay Company to offer him the land on the Red River for an agricultural settlement, which, on the face of things, would be of great advantage to that Company.*

The course of events soon destroyed the strange alliance between the great fur-trader and the great colonizer. The ability of Andrew Wedderburn [Colvile] was quickly perceived in the Hudson's Bay Company, and in January 1810 he was placed on the Committee. In the months immediately succeeding, the Committee was engaged in reorganizing the Company's trade, and Colvile's scheme was accepted as offering greater promise of bringing the stockholders through the crisis than others laid before them. A part of that scheme was to promote agriculture at the Company's forts, that provisions should be procurable in the country and at a low cost. It was but a short step from that to establishing an agricultural colony to furnish supplies and men to the fur posts. Hence the request of the Committee conveyed to Lord Selkirk for the terms on which he would accept a grant of land ; hence also the Grant of June 12, 1811.

His happy arrangement with the Hudson's Bay Company for a

---

* Lord Selkirk has put it on record in a letter that Andrew Colvile (his brother-in-law and an influential member of the Company's Committee) objected strongly to his proposed dealings with Mackenzie. It may be inferred that it was Colvile that got his much-desired colony for Selkirk, and, for the Company, an agricultural settlement that proved in the course of time a veritable handmaid to it.

colony on the Red River would tend to break Lord Selkirk's association with Sir Alexander Mackenzie's scheme. The fierce attack on
his lordship by the Northwesters who had bought stock between the
first and the second General Court, and so acquired a place at the
meeting which dealt with the Grant, revealed a deep-seated hostility
to colonization, and put an end finally to Selkirk's association with
Mackenzie their leader.

The propaganda of the Northwesters has led people to believe
that Selkirk got control of the Hudson's Bay Company by keeping
the stock he was buying, with or for Mackenzie, and then pushing
the Grant for a vast estate of 116,000 square miles through the
Court, to the detriment of the Company and with the hope of
enhancing the wealth of his family. The transfer of stock as indicated in the Stock-Transfer Book of the Company dispels this
illusion. When the Grant was made to him, Selkirk owned no more
than the £4,087, 10s. which his vote in the General Court represented.
Nor was the vote carried by a combination of the three brothers-in-
law, for Halkett did not vote.

After the Grant was made to him, Selkirk made large purchases
of the Company's stock. Between June 19, 1811, and January 7,
1812, he acquired £18,272, 6s. 2d. worth. Towards the end of his
life he had an interest of £26,000 in the Company. The allegation
of the Northwesters that he owned £40,000 of stock at the outset,
and in virtue of it drove the Company to work his will, does not bear
investigation. The driving force in the Committee was Andrew
Colvile, a man whose judgment throughout proved sane and shrewd.
Lord Selkirk's name appears but rarely in the Minutes of the Committee. He was never a director of the Company. The sympathy
of the Committee with the colony lay in the nature of things. It
was part of their scheme to put the Company on its feet. Thus,
the North West Company directed its enmity against the Company
and Lord Selkirk's colony alike.

4.—LORD SELKIRK'S COLONY—GOVERNOR MILES MACDONELL,*
1812–15

In launching his colony Lord Selkirk had taken the risk of great
loss, for he was responsible to finance the migration and the government of the settlement till it should become a success. The immediate expense was certain ; the financial gain would necessarily
be problematical. There might be more immediate returns in the
dividends of the Hudson's Bay Company, and the Company's right
to the soil would be asserted. The final profit would come in the
enhanced value of the land around a prosperous settlement. Meanwhile Selkirk's interest in emigration as a remedy for the ills of the
homeland would bring him satisfaction. He took care to assure
himself that the Grant was legal and, not less important, that the

* Illustrated by the inset of Sketch-map No. 10 at p. 426.

colonial institutions—the Council and the system of justice to be established—would bear the stamp of legality.   He consulted lawyers of high standing—Samuel Romilly, G. S. Holroyd, William Cruise, J. Scarlett, and John Bell—and was told that the grant of the soil to the Hudson's Bay Company conveyed by the Charter was good in law.   Their judgment here was sound, and has been borne out by history.

The lawyers went on to say that the holder of the grant in fee-simple " will be entitled to all the ordinary rights of landed property as in England, and will be entitled to prevent other persons from occupying any part of the lands."   The bearing of this opinion on the history of the colony will be apparent.   The lawyers were also of opinion that the privilege of civil and criminal jurisdiction granted in the Charter, when passed on to his colony by the Governor and Committee, could be legally exercised by a Governor and Council acting as judges, and proceeding according to the laws of England, and that the Company could appoint a sheriff, and the sheriff, in turn, could " call out the population to his assistance and . . . put arms into the hands of their servants, for defence against attack, and to assist in enforcing the judgments of the Court," while the Governor in the Hudson's Bay Company's Territory could appoint constables and other officers for the preservation of the peace. Finally, " all persons will be subject to the jurisdiction of the Court, who reside or are found within the territories over which it extends." Lord Selkirk's inquiry as to whether the Canada Jurisdiction Act gave the Canadian Courts jurisdiction in the Chartered Territory was answered in the negative.   In this particular judgment the lawyers erred, inasmuch as that Act would be in force until the " civil jurisdiction " sketched above became a reality, but all that they said about the legality of creating a system of Justice under the Charter will be accepted without demur by the Imperial Government in 1821.   It may, therefore, be taken as sound in 1811.   Thus Selkirk had every reason to believe that he was building his colony on a legal basis.   Unfortunately for him legality is not the final canon of right in Government.   There are factors which may best be described by Bismarck's famous term " imponderables," and of those the most important is the tacit acquiescence in the system of government by the people beneath it. This acquiescence the Northwesters within Selkirk's Grant, with grim determination, refused to give.   Therein lay the greatest obstacle in the path of the colony.

Selkirk now turned to find a Governor for his colony.   It was intended to send him out in 1811 with a party of servants, potential, but not actual settlers, to prepare for the arrival of the settlers themselves in 1812.   The Governor chosen was Miles Macdonell, then about forty-four years of age.   He had been born in Inverness, Scotland, had gone with his father to the Colony of New York, had been taken to Canada after the American Revolution, and had settled with United Empire Loyalists at St. Andrew's, near Cornwall.

At this time he was a Captain in the Royal Canadian Volunteers. He received his commission as Governor, not from Lord Selkirk, but from the Governor and Committee of the Hudson's Bay Company, so that he should exercise the authority of the Chartered Company itself. His position was further strengthened by a formal appointment (December 1811) under the hand of the Governor-General of Canada, as a Justice of the Peace. A number of the Company's officers, among them William Auld, Thomas Thomas, and William Hillier, were made Justices of the Peace at the same time—this under the Canada Jurisdiction Act.

Macdonell's instructions, however, came from the pen of the noble lord. After necessary directions concerning the voyage and the management of the men, he was required to choose the site of the colony between the mouth of the Red River and its forks, probably at " Pelican Ripple " (the rapids at St. Andrew's), and to put himself in communication with the Company's posts at Pembina, and especially Brandon House, from which he would procure necessary supplies, such as horses, seed potatoes, and perhaps some grain seed. He was to go cautiously before the Indians, and, if they showed signs of jealousy, he was to purchase the land, preferably by promising annual gifts to them, but a better security would be the awe which they would entertain for a strong and well-guarded post. With the servants he was to cultivate land, as possible, in the immediate neighbourhood of the fort, so as to have as large a harvest as might be at the arrival of the settlers. It will be noted that the question of the system of Government was postponed for more mature consideration. The instructions envisaged no more than the preparations for the establishment of the colony.

During the summer (1811) Lord Selkirk's agents were recruiting labourers for the settlement and for the Hudson's Bay Company. It reveals his lordship's sympathies that he sent Miles Macdonell to visit Ireland. A considerable body of men were expected from Sligo and from " the famous town of Killaloe." Writers (clerks) were enlisted in Glasgow. So many failed to come to the muster that the recruiting agents here ventured to offer exorbitant wages in spite of their instructions. Orkney men also were being engaged. The agreements were for three years with the bonus of a lot of 100 acres in the colony on the conclusion of the contract, if satisfaction had been given.

Simple prudence called for the arrival of all on the Red River in the autumn, so as to ensure the completion of the preparations for the coming settlers and, in particular, the reaping of a harvest before their arrival a twelvemonth later. Macdonell expected to leave the Thames " very near to June 4th or 5th "—about the usual time of sailing. The ships, however, were only ready on 15th June. It was the ancient custon for the Governor and Committee to supervise the departure in person and to dine at Gravesend in state at the Company's expense. This year thirty-four gentlemen of the Company and of its ships dined at the Falcon Inn, with appropriate toasts and speeches.   In truth it was no ordinary occasion for the Company of Adventurers.   It was the inauguration of a new policy.   At the close of the meal Mr. Berens, the Deputy-Governor, handed Miles Macdonell his commission as Governor of " Ossiniboia," and the Earl of Selkirk wished his representative a successful mission.   It was a time of war and convoys were necessary.   The ships of the Company, along with many others, were to be guarded by men-of-war up the east coast of England.   The convoys were delayed ; the ships to be guarded assembled slowly, when every day counted for Selkirk's plans.   Then, too, head winds prevailed.   On 25th June the ships had to put into Yarmouth, and were only able to proceed on 5th July.   It was not before 17th July that they arrived, by way of Stromness in the Orkney Isles, at Stornoway in the Isle of Lewis, the rendezvous.   There delay followed delay.   There was trouble with the men, for Macdonell tried to reduce the injudicious wages offered by the agents to the Glasgow men.   He also tried to save money for the Company by putting the two clerks for the James Bay region in steerage with the labourers, and the rest in a mess by themselves inferior to that of the officers.   He thus aroused suspicion and discontent when happy relations were of the first moment.   Moreover, the Northwesters were already plotting mischief—to use their own phrase, " defeating the Colony in Britain."   A letter in the *Inverness Journal* above the signature of " A Highlander," but in truth by none other than Simon M'Gillivray, was distributed in the Orkney Isles and in Lewis to strike terror into the hearts of the men engaged.

> To reach this comparatively milder Climate [from Hudson Bay] the emigrants must first traverse the inhospitable regions in the vicinity of Hudsons Bay and perform a voyage of 2000 Miles [it is not 700] of Inland Navigation—stemming strong currents and dangerous rapids & carrying their boats and cargoes over numerous portages.   This voyage I do not think they can possibly perform in the present season for the frost will be approaching before they can reach York Fort, where I fancy they must pass the next winter, and if so, Mr. Editor, it is my firm belief that many of them will perish before the Spring from excessive cold and from want of food. . . . In addition to this [when they arrive at their destination] they will be surrounded by warlike Savage natives . . . who will consider them as intruders come to spoil their hunting ground, to drive away the wild animals and to destroy the Indians as the white men have already done in Canada and the United States. . . . Even if [the emigrants] escape the scalping knife, they will be subject to constant alarm and terror.   Their habitations, their Crops, their Cattle will be destroyed and they will find it impossible to exist in the Country.

Imagine the unrest this grave warning from one who apparently knew the country would awaken in the minds of the men assembled at Stornoway, ready to launch out into the unknown.   Some of them had received a year's advance of wages to equip themselves for their journey.   Conscience would say Stay by the contract, Stay. Men in the interest of the North West Company came to them to say Run, Run for your lives.

Alexander Mackenzie had been born two miles out of this very

Stornoway, and an aunt of his was married to one Reid, the Customs Officer of the place. Reid told the men that Macdonell had no power to make them embark, that he could only do so by a process at law for non-performance of contract. Many of them had been drinking deeply and were ready enough to hide and escape. Macdonell had to get the assistance of marines and seamen from the men-of-war to get those whom he could find to the ship, the *Edward and Ann*, which was moored close inshore. Finally, when Reid came on board to inspect the muster of the people, his clerk told them publicly that, if any were unwilling to go, they were free to pass on shore. There was something like a stampede over the ship's side. Some got ashore in Reid's boat, some in the craft of one Captain John McKenzie, son-in-law to Reid, who had been recruiting among the men for war service and was only prevented from coming on board by Macdonell's firmness. Doubtless the Captain's canvass was that any who joined the King's colours would be out of the reach of Lord Selkirk's wrath. Macdonell wrote to Selkirk: " This, my Lord, is a most unfortunate business," and indeed it was, the first blow struck at the colony by the Northwesters.

Every day of delay, as the writer to the *Inverness Journal* knew, was a misfortune. The collector Reid imposed several days' delay by insisting on all the extreme formalities of the Customs. " Captains of Ships with their papers—Surgeons with their Deplomas, List of Medicine Chest all ordered ashore & a List of passengers & Ships Company required to be given with the most rigid scrutiny." The ships would not be cleared till it was all through. In the end ninety labourers, fourteen writers, and an Irish priest named Charles Bourke, made a total of one hundred and five. It was 26th July before the anchor was raised—the latest departure for Hudson Bay on record up to that time.

But the Northwesters were not content with attempting to defeat the colony at its start from Britain. They began at once to stir their Wintering Partners to action against it. Simon M'Gillivray, William's brother, hitherto in the firm of McTavish, Inglis & Co., London, the English agents of the North West Company, had been taken into the Montreal firm of McTavish, M'Gillivrays & Co., the agents of the concern. He seized the occasion to write, on April 9, 1812, to the Wintering Partners, who would assemble at Fort William in July following : " By the Inverness newspapers . . . you will see that I have given his Lordship [Selkirk] some annoyance through the medium of the press and I have reason to hope that the ' Highlander's Letters ' will, in a great measure, prevent him from getting servants or emigrants from the Highlands of Scotland. . . . The committee of the Hudson's Bay Company, is at present a mere machine in the hands of Lord Selkirk, who appears to be so much wedded to his schemes of colonization in the interior of North America, that it will require some time, and I fear cause much expense to us, as well as to himself, before he is driven to abandon the project, yet *he must be driven to abandon it,* for his success would strike at the very existence of the trade." This, the official North West view of the colony and the instigation to work for its failure, would reach the most distant forts of the Company in the autumn of 1812.

Even nature failed to smile upon the expedition. Head winds baffled it much of the way. At the entrance to the Bay a redistribution of the men for the various factories was made. The *Prince of Wales* steered for James Bay and the Southern Department. The *Edward and Ann,* and the *Eddystone,* with the men for the Red River, headed for York Factory. The *Edward and Ann* arrived on 24th September after a passage of sixty-one days—" the longest ever known and the latest to Hudson's Bay." So late was it, the whole body of men had to winter at York Factory. The *Eddystone* arrived two days later. As she could not continue to Fort Churchill her Churchill passengers had also to be accommodated at York Factory during the winter, accentuating the hardship which the others must suffer. " Of all the occurrences which have opposed themselves this year the late arrival here is the worst in its consequences," wrote Miles Macdonell to Lord Selkirk. As navigation to the interior was now impossible, the workmen had to winter on the Bay, but, worse still, they could not reach the Red River in time to break the sod and secure a harvest unto the arrival of the settlers in the following autumn.

The large body of servants come in by the ships could not be accommodated at the York Factory. Log huts were built on the north side of the Nelson River opposite Seal Island. Here, twenty-three miles from the factory, across the peninsula formed by the Nelson and the Hayes, on a narrow flat protected from the northerly blasts by a high wooded bank, " Nelson Encampment " was formed. Two groups of huts, one for Selkirk's men under Macdonell, and the other for the Company's servants under William Hillier, were built of logs. The hardships of the long-drawn winter need not be sung again. John McLeod says in his Journal : " [We] passed as comfortable a winter as could be expected under such circumstances." Curiously not so much is heard of sufferings from the cold as of recurrent difficulties over the food supply. The spot was considered favourable for a caribou hunt, as the herd passed close by on its autumn migration southward to the forest, but only small bands passed that way this year and but a scant supply of fresh meat was secured. Much of the food supply had to be brought from the Factory, not without misunderstandings, as it proved, between the officers at the post and the men of the encampment. It is of more permanent significance that Macdonell never succeeded in establishing an ascendency over his charges. He could not prevent the Irish from quarrelling among themselves and with the Orkney men. When scurvy broke out he had difficulties in persuading some to take a brew of spruce such as had saved Jacques Cartier's party at Quebec. One cast-off servant of the Company, William Finlay, insisted on putting his faith on porter, cranberries, and port wine, and refused to partake of the proffered remedy.   Only one man actually died of the scourge.   Macdonell likewise failed to win the hearty support of the officers at York Factory, William Cook and his subordinate, Geddes.   Not trusting their judgment, he had taken the fractious Finlay into the employ of the Settlement.   He reaped his reward in a mutiny.   From February to May the mutineers were beyond control. Only when the Company's Superintendent, William Auld, came to the rescue in the spring and refused provisions, were the rebels brought to terms.   At last, on 22nd June, the encampment was broken up, and on 6th July the party, which was to break the first sods for the colony, started, twenty-two strong, up the Hayes River for its destination.

All through this and subsequent voyages Macdonell studied the route from York Factory to Red River, noting the improvements necessary to make it an easy water and land route to the colony. Here and there he would note spots where little establishments could be made, vegetables grown for food supply, and cattle kept to draw the goods across portages.   But through it all one of the Governor's great weaknesses of character appears—an optimism that made light of every difficulty.   Here, only a few loose stones need be removed to make the water-way easy for canoes ;   there, a good channel for boats might be made at little cost by removing and blasting some rocks.   Even at Flat [" Rock "] Fall, which he admitted would be difficult to improve, " A Canal of 14 yards cut through a solid rock behind the point would serve."   It had been well for the Governor if this contempt for the difficulties in his path had been confined to the physical.

The journey was not eventful.   At Oxford House, Macdonell saw a bull and heifer, one year old, and coveted them for the colony. Selkirk had provided eight head of cattle at Stornoway, but amid the difficulties of that rendezvous the Governor had left them behind. He was not one of those masterful men who bend circumstances to their will.   Now more conscious how sad the state of an agricultural colony would be without cattle, he took these two along with him in the boat.   They took readily to their novel mode of travelling. " Find the cattle very tractable ;   they jump out and into the batteau of their own accord."   So the beasts journeyed on to the Red River. They are said to have been named Adam and Eve ;   they were ex- pected to multiply and replenish the earth, that the settlers might ultimately have milk and meat on their daily board.

At noon on 29th August, Macdonell's party—the Governor, A. Edwards, the physician, and eighteen labouring men, six of them Scotsmen, mostly from Ross-shire, four from the Orkneys, and eight Irishmen, mostly from Killaloe and Sligo—entered the Red River.   The Governor's hopes ran high, and it is clear that he was enjoying, even in this unpeopled region, the pomp of power.   By disposition he always saw the rosy dawn and persistently forgot the toil of the heat of day.   It may be conceded that it is exhilarating to be the founder of a colony and to play the part of first Governor, but all colonies come into being with travail, and the perils of the birth of Red River Settlement were to be such as no other British colony has ever known. Fortunately for the happiness of Miles Macdonell, he was unconscious of all save the intoxication of the moment.

At four in the afternoon the party reached an outpost of the Hudson's Bay Company, Fort William by name, built that spring on the east side opposite " an old Establishment abandoned," possibly Frobisher's fort. At the foot of the rapids now known as St. Andrew's and in the neighbourhood of the present Lower Fort Garry, they were met by horses sent by Mr. Hugh Heney, in charge of the English Company's post at Pembina, but now awaiting the Governor at the Forks of the Red and Assiniboine rivers. Accompanied by Mr. Edwards, the surgeon, Macdonell took to the saddle and rode up the west side.

After leaving the river bank entered a fine plain as level as a bowling green covered with a fine sward of grass, knee high—here and there a clump of wood, as if planted for ornament by the hand of man, partridges rising before us in coveys each side of the path. Ducks and Geese fly about us. This plain extended close to the Forks, which we reach at 2 o'clock P.M. Messrs. Wills and [Alex] McDonell received us at the gate of the N.W. Co. Fort, and asked us in.

The boats arrived before sunset and unloaded on the east side, where the Hudson's Bay Company's men under Messrs. Hillier and Heney were camped. At the very outset the Governor's relations with the Northwesters were of the most cordial, for Alexander Macdonell at Fort Gibraltar was his cousin. On Tuesday, 1st September, Messrs. Wills, A. Macdonell, and Benjamin Frobisher, called on him and invited him along with Hillier to dine. " We passed a very pleasant evening and only returned at 1 in the morning," across the Red River. The next morning the Governor spent sorting the stores. In the afternoon, his Journal runs :

Went out with all the gentlemen here of the N.W. Co. mounted and a number of followers about 18 altogether, freemen, servants, Indians, every one that could muster a horse—running races with each other. I invited them to be present the next day at the ceremony of delivery and seizin of the land—which was fixed to take place to-morrow at 12 o'clock.

The hour appointed for the ceremony was announced by a gun. The gentlemen of the North West Company's Fort Gibraltar, Wills, Macdonell, and Frobisher, crossed over to the east side, but they had refused their servants permission to attend. With due form, an officer's guard and colours flying, William Hillier and Hugh Heney, mentioned in the Grant to Lord Selkirk as appointed attorneys to act for the Hudson's Bay Company, read the Grant in English and in French in the presence of the people assembled, viz. the adherents of the English Company, the labourers of the colony, the three Northwesters and a number of free French-Canadians and

Indians, and transferred " Assiniboia " to Lord Selkirk in the person of his representatives Miles Macdonell and Kenneth McRae. Thereafter they read the Commission of the Company appointing Macdonell Governor of Assiniboia, and he formally assumed office. Seven swivels, that is, guns turning on a pivot, were fired and three cheers were given. The gentlemen assembled at the Governor's tent, partook of a cold snack and drank appropriate toasts. A keg of rum was broached for " the populace." When all was over Macdonell crossed with Edwards to the North West Company's fort. It is significant of his policy that he spent his first evening as Governor on the site of his colony in conviviality with his potential enemies, and left the officers of the English Company, those upon whose friendship he must rely for support in the heat of the struggle, to the silence of their camp on the east side of the river. Next day, the earnest task of governing began.

The first and most pressing problem of an incipient colony is its food supply—a problem which at some time in every year faced the fur-traders' posts in this land of alternating feast and famine. The Governor and what he chose to call his staff (*i.e.* his surgeon, Edwards) and his less than a score of men were without provisions. The Hudson's Bay Company's posts of the region were to have had a supply of pemmican ready, but there was little even for their own brigades going up the Assiniboine. Catfish caught in the river and a liberal supply of potatoes bought of Mr. Wills at Fort Gibraltar tided over the scarcity of the day. But if want was felt when there were but a score of precursors on the spot, what could be done when the colonists themselves, now in the act of leaving York Factory for their future home, should arrive ? Selkirk had wisely planned a year of preparation which would have provided some houses and cultivated fields, above all a harvest awaiting the settlers. The continental war, which necessitated a convoy, the difficulties at Stornoway the scene of the first opposition to the colony by the Northwesters, and the baffling winds of the North Altantic had turned a well-devised scheme awry. When the settlers would arrive in November there would be not a house to receive them, not a grain of wheat garnered, nothing but mile upon mile of russet brown prairie. Here was indeed a situation to tax the alertness and energy of the Governor and his power to bend circumstances to his will. He put his hope, as all the people of the plains were wont to do, in the buffalo. At this time of the year the eastern herd was grazing its way southward to its winter home in the scrubby regions extending from Pembina at our International Boundary to the Grand Côteau de Missouri. On the 6th the Governor's two large boats, with most of his men, passed on in charge of John McLeod and along with Mr. Heney to Fort Skene, as the Hudson's Bay Company's post near the mouth of the Pembina River was called ; it stood on the edge of the herd's winter grazing grounds. Macdonell himself remained for the moment to choose the site of the settlement. After breakfasting with the gentlemen of the North West Company, he passed down the west bank of the river, expecting to find suitable land near the foot of the rapids at the present St. Andrews, but he decided against the spot. Farther down the land grew more and more unpromising. Returning up the river, he chose " a point of some extent of burnt wood fit for immediate cultivation which likewise contains green woods for building ; and a little below the Forks." This will be called after Selkirk's family name, Point Douglas. It is the promontory formed by a bend in the river little more than a mile below the North West Company's Fort Gibraltar and east of the present Union Station, Winnipeg. The Canadian Pacific Railway crosses the Red River at its extreme limit. Next day, a diminutive procession on horseback, with the cattle and the few men who were to be left to break the sod, made its way to the spot. " [It is] rough and foul with weeds, brush and underwood but the soil appears to be excellent," says Macdonell. He placed the workmen under Mr. Charles Price Isham, the old servant of the English Company taken into his employ, gave ammunition to five Indians to hunt for them, and prepared to follow his party to Pembina. A quantity of pemmican was left for the journey of the coming colonists. Provided with a horse, some potatoes, and a keg of salted catfish procured at Fort Gibraltar, and with the cart of a French-Canadian freeman, Peltier, the Governor set off for Pembina, in the company of Alexander Macdonell, who was in charge of the North West Company's post there. He took what was probably already a well-defined route up the Assiniboine, and crossed that river at the " Passage " at the White Horse Plain of later date. Then, travelling southward, he crossed the rivers Sale and aux Gratias, beyond which he reached the banks of the Red River once more. Following it upward, he came (12th September) to the Hudson's Bay Company's post somewhat north of the Pembina River, where he found John McLeod had arrived with the colony's workmen. It is significant that the Governor merely called on Mr. Heney and went on to lodge with Alexander Macdonell at the North West Company's post, scarce half a mile beyond in the northerly angle made by the Red and the Pembina rivers. Clearly, he was cultivating the friendship of the Northwesters and taking little pains to win the Hudson's Bay Company's officers to his support. Next day the Governor and his cousin rode out to select the site for a fort—a necessity here, for it was on the borders of the Sioux country. He chose the south angle of the confluence of the Red River and the Pembina, opposite the North West Company's post, which thus stood between the posts of Lord Selkirk and the English Company. Thereafter he went down to Fort Skene, Heney's post, to send the workmen up. The river afforded for the present an abundant supply of catfish, but fresh meat must also be secured. Some was got from Heney, but, as Governor, Macdonell did not wish to be dependent, perhaps wished to show his independence of the Hudson's Bay Company, he retained a number of hunters to " run " buffalo. Among them was Lagimonière (Lagimodière), the ancestor of Louis Riel on his mother's side, who had first come to these parts in 1801, and in 1807 had brought out his wife, the first European woman in the North-West. He proved the most successful and reliable of them all.

Building went on slowly, for the workmen were strangers to the axe. Lord Selkirk had arranged for a band of expert French-Canadians from Montreal, but it failed to appear upon the scene, the Northwesters said, because their agents had bought up all the bark, and no canoes were to be had. It was 27th December before the Governor got into his own quarters.

At this stage the North West Company, in the person of Alexander Macdonell, was the reverse of hostile. He put two men and a horse at the disposal of the Governor for the building of the fort. Governor Macdonell's policy was to secure the most cordial relations possible with the Northwesters, and in this he was, for a number of months, entirely successful. He did little to cultivate the loyalty and win the support of the Hudson's Bay Company's officers. Indeed, a very few days after his arrival at Pembina he had his first clash with Heney. He regarded the colony as quite separate from the Company, while Heney was concerned to retain all the traffic of the region in the hands of his own post. When the Governor entered into direct relations with a French-Canadian freeman, Joseph Cire, and bought 125 lb. of fat, 316 lb. of pounded meat, and 317 lb. of dried meat, though the price paid was the same as he was giving, Heney protested against the meddling with the meat trade. (The Governor must have been annoyed with the man from the beginning for handing over to Hillier, established at the post near the mouth of the Red River, all the potatoes intended for the colony, which had been brought in from different English posts. This must have been in the autumn, when Selkirk's men did not arrive.) When Macdonell offered him the half of the pounded meat, Heney first accepted and finally declined it : " He had meat enough." Manifestly relations were difficult, possibly as the result of the Governor passing by the English post to quarter himself with the Northwesters, but, apart from that, the question was raised by this incident : Was the colony free to trade in other articles than fur with the people of the place? Heney's position gave the reply in the negative. Much pleasanter were Macdonell's relations with Brandon House, across the prairies, on the Assiniboine. Every call made on this post for horses and goods was met in a cordial spirit. Likewise happy relations were easily established with the freemen (French-Canadians detached from any fur company), and with the Indians. The latter pestered the Governor with their much begging, but were easily conciliated with a few presents, more especially in the form of tobacco and rum.

On 4th October Macdonell was back at the Forks to supervise the work at Point Douglas. A good deal of hay had been made, but very little land cleared. It had been impossible to get any ironwork made, doubtless because blacksmiths engaged in Scotland had deserted at Stornoway. There was no blacksmith at the North West Company's post. Not even harrow-teeth could be made. The workmen were living on catfish, of which a tolerable supply was obtained from the river. Mr. John Richard MacKay of Brandon House added to their comfort by sending down four bags of pemmican, in all 298 lb. Soon the Governor was able to sow twelve gallons of winter wheat : he had to do it himself, for none of his men had ever grown grain. He covered the seed with a hoe, for no harrow was to be had. From the night frosts and the late sowing he feared it would not succeed—and he proved right. In any case, winter wheat cannot be grown successfully in those parts.

Cordial relations continued with the Canadian fort. For example, the seed-grain, liquor, and ammunition were stored, and seventeen kegs of potatoes were purchased at it. Macdonell dropped downstream to visit Mr. Hillier in his post somewhere near the present Selkirk. He found that Heney had already written him about the Governor's " being too frequently with the N. W. Co " and about his trading in meat. Hillier in reply had ordered Heney to give no goods to the Governor with which to trade. Placated by this visit of courtesy, he now offered to himself supply all that might be needed. When Macdonell returned to Pembina, on the 18th, he found that Heney had given written orders to the reliable John McLeod to leave the colony's service and to build an outpost at the Upper Forks (the Turtle River), with Bostonais Pangman, a halfbreed, for interpreter. As the labourers from overseas did not know how to build mud chimneys such as were in vogue in the North-West, the Governor sent to Heney for a skilled hand ; the request was refused. His Journal for the 22nd indicates Macdonell's plight. " Resolve to send for Mr. Hillier. I have no goods to pay for provisions,—cannot stoop to ask any from Heney who perhaps would refuse." The policy of coddling his possible enemies and neglecting the friends on whose co-operation his success depended, had already brought the Governor into a difficult place. As the end of October approached, the problem of provisions grew serious. Several of the men with families, like the Company's old servant Isham, were sent out on to the plains to be near the buffalo, and thereby reduce the demand for food at the fort. Macdonell's entry of the 27th in his Journal begins with the ominous fact that the fishing had come to an end for the season—one pike caught in three days. This is followed by the scarcely less alarming announcement that the colonists had arrived.

At 12 o'clock heard firing at the Hudson's Bay Company's fort and observed a string of boats coming up from there, which turned out to be our people so long expected from below, in 9 Boats. In the leading boat the Bagpipes played, and the British Flag was displayed. We received them on landing with a guard of ceremony. On the Bank a discharge from a swivel and small arms . . . my people pitched their tents and covered a good deal of ground.

The Governor's exhilaration at the pomp of the moment might well have been chilled by the thought of the number of mouths to be fed and the provisions that were lacking.

The party of settlers had been recruited in the west of Ireland and in the Hebrides. Their rendezvous was Sligo. The leader of the expedition was Owen Keveny, a man of "steadiness, activity and integrity," but a firm disciplinarian. Their voyage has been briefly chronicled by Thomas M'Keevor, the physician placed in charge, and illustrated by a number of woodcuts. It may be taken as typical of many such voyages to come, and may therefore be briefly described. It was on 24th June about four in the afternoon that the good ship *Robert Taylor* weighed anchor in Sligo Bay, having on board Lord Selkirk, who had personally supervised the embarkation of his servants and of the colonists. As the wind outside proved fair, Selkirk and his companions took leave at six o'clock. One has to have travelled by an emigrant ship to know the anguish of those who may be leaving their homeland and never to see it again. If it is so with our modern come and go, what must it have been for those who were going deep into the continent to the isolation of a lone colony to be started on the prairies ? Of this, however, the physician says nothing, but, though only on a round trip, he drops into sentiment. " On the one side I beheld the vast and widely extended body of waters, over which the moon was just beginning to throw a diffused and silvery light, on the other appeared my native-land, like a dusky streak, stretched along the verge of the horizon. . . . The solemnity and stillness of this calm repose of nature was only interrupted by the soft splash of the light wave against the head and sides of the vessel, and occasionally by the slow and solemn voice of the captain giving his commands to the helmsman." On 2nd July, in lat. 57° 43′ N., the Company's ships, the *Eddystone* and the *King George*, were sighted, but being slow sailers they were outdistanced by the *Robert Taylor*. In the course of the voyage trouble arose between the Scots and the Irish, due to one Andrew Langston who had done something to recruit the immigrants and had been somewhat petted by Lord Selkirk. He asserted roundly that they were not being treated in keeping with his lordship's orders and, in particular, that the Scotsmen were being better cared for than the Irish. The result was a general turbulence on board. Keveny handled the situation with a firmness commended by Lord Selkirk, who, however, tempered his praise with the old adage that *sauviter in modo* should accompany *fortiter in re.*

When well within Davis Strait, ice began to be seen. Ice-anchors and boat-hooks were got ready in case of need. For a number of days the weather was so thick, no observations could be taken, and the people scarce knew where they were. At the mouth of Hudson Strait a great iceberg lay before them. The ship missed stays and ran straight for it.

In a short time we were all on deck ; and here the appearance of our situation was awful in the extreme ; the shouting of the men, the rumbling of the cordage, the tremendous mountain of ice, on which we every moment expected to be dashed to pieces, contributed to render the scene the most terrific that could well be imagined. . . . We were not ten yards from it, when fortunately a light breeze springing up, the sails filled, and in a short time we were completely clear of this frightful mass.

Soon the ship was leaking from the impact of the icefloes, for some of the copper was torn from her bottom. Resort was had to the pumps. After two days' delay by this mishap, the *Eddystone* and *King George* came up to the *Robert Taylor*. The last two were anchored to the same icefloe, and a party crossed to the *King George* for tea and refreshments followed by a dance on deck, the music being provided by a rawboned athletic Highlander. The ships were greatly delayed by ice in the Straits. When they could find a " vein of water," or when the ice was loose and straggling, some progress was made. When anchored to the floe, the tedium was relieved, now by a white bear hunt, now by visits from the Eskimos. The course was along the north shore. At last Cape Digges was reached. Here a party landed to climb the promontory. In four more days—*i.e.* after twenty-three days for the 450 miles of the Strait—they reached Mansel Island within the entrance of the Bay. Here the ships prepared to part. Langston, the mutineer, was put on the *King George*. Twenty merino sheep were brought over from her to the *Robert Taylor*, for the *King George* was to go to Churchill to bring boats thence to York Factory for the voyage inland. Altogether Keveny showed insight and decision.

The Bay was crossed with no more than the inconvenience of the fog and of a fearful gale. In the midst of the confusion of the storm a Mrs. Maclean gave birth to a daughter. Two days later, on 26th August, the ship lay quietly at anchor in view of York Fort. The voyage was as long as that of the previous year—sixty-one days. The start a month earlier made all the difference between success and failure. Then, too, things were well in hand this year at the Fort. Mr. Kenneth McRae was there to receive the people for the Governor. Soon the *King George* brought boats from Churchill, so that the whole party could start together for the interior. However, lest confusion should arise at the portages, they left in detachments of three or four boats, in all eleven, one day apart, Mrs. Maclean and her infant bringing up the rear in a canoe. York Factory was rid of them on 9th September, and the Governor received them *en masse*, including the Maclean baby, at Pembina, as has been seen, with due ceremony on 27th October.

Miles Macdonell showed at his best in this crisis created by the arrival of the colonists at Pembina before any preparations could be made for them. The houses necessary were erected as soon as might be ; there was some sickness among the people when they were still in their tents. The hunters were kept busy out on the plains. When the buffalo were two or three days' journey away, temporary camps were formed for collecting meat, and the servants were employed bringing it in on carts or sleds, not without occasional suffering from frozen features and even frozen limbs. When times of scarcity came, as they always did at the posts when the buffalo wandered out of reach, a reserve of oatmeal was drawn upon for the moment, or else supplies were borrowed from the companies' posts. This was specially the case in the depth of the winter. " Feb. 2 [1813] Not a morsel to give our people ; borrowed 59 lb meat from N. W. Co. which was immediately issued. In the evening 4 sleds of meat arrived from Lagimonière."

Then, too, while asserting the freedom of the colony to trade for meat, the Governor secured happier relations with the Hudson's Bay Company's officers. Hillier had come up to Heney's post, and taken charge over it. He supplied Macdonell with the goods to trade, loaned meat to him, and when himself in difficulties, borrowed of the Governor. When his fort had completed its supply of meat for the season, he directed the rest to the colony. Looking forward to the scarcity of the summer and autumn, Hillier and Macdonell wrote letters to the Company's posts at the Swan and Assiniboine rivers and on the Saskatchewan, to forward pemmican to the Jack River post to be taken to the colony during the summer. Finally, Hillier took some of the women and children to his post for better care. All this Macdonell accomplished without giving offence to the Northwesters, on the contrary, while drawing Hillier along with the Northwesters into the little society gathering around the Governor. French-Canadians from the Canadian post helped to bring in the flagstaff for the fort, and when it was erected fifty-five feet of it above the ground and the flag hoisted, took part in the salute with guns and in the cheers from the people. Both Hillier and Alexander Macdonell were present, and spent the evening in dance at Mrs. Maclean's. The fort was named Fort Daer, after the title of the heir of Lord Selkirk. Next day was Christmas. " Play at Hurl [hockey] on the ice with the people of the 3 forts. We all dine at Mr. Hilliers, dance to the Bag Pipe in the evening—very pleasant party." Altogether the Governor's policy of freeing the colony somewhat from its association with the English Company, and keeping on cordial terms with the Northwesters was succeeding admirably. But one factor had been lost sight of both by him and the local men of the North West Company, who seem to have enjoyed the zest added to their lonely life by the society of the leading colonists—viz. the machine of the " concern," the Agents and the Proprietors, who would be more concerned about the interests of the Company than the attractions of Red River Society.

The scene changed towards the end of February. Word came in from John McLeod of the English outpost at Turtle River, which was getting two-thirds of the trade, that the person in charge of the North West Company's post, which had been built there to watch him, was inciting the Indians against the colony and the Company, saying that, if they did not prevent the colony from being established, they would very soon become slaves, that they should drive the settlers from the country, that to begin with they should claim the land as theirs and negotiate terms of purchase at a very high price. This hostile propaganda was sent out from the North West Company's post at Rainy Lake. McLeod, however, with the help of Bostonais Pangman, his half-breed interpreter, was able to win the Indians over to his side by saying that, if the colony and the Company were driven out, the Northwesters would become masters of the Indians—a point of view the astute savages readily appreciated. Hard upon this news, Dugald Cameron, from Bas de la Rivière Winipic, arrived at the North West Company's post across the Pembina from Fort Daer. He breakfasted and dined with the Governor and, on one occasion, was shown a copy of the Hudson's Bay Company's Charter to convince him of the rights of that Company, and the legality of the Grant to Selkirk. Soon the freemen, who had been the salvation of the colony and appeared to have been hitherto contented to find in it a new market for their meat, were reported to be plotting to drive the colonists out. They even refused to bring in meat for which they had already received credit. While Macdonell continued his good relations with the Northwesters—he even brought Alexander Macdonell, when sick, to Fort Daer to be cared for—he was thrown back on Mr. Hillier for counsel and support. But Hillier had to return to the lower post, Fort William, leaving the hostile Hugh Heney once more in charge at Fort Skene. The Governor was left to face his troubles alone. Dugald Cameron soon perceived the weakest point of Miles Macdonell's administration—his failure to achieve an ascendancy over his own people. He fomented the discontent of the workmen and settlers, and even won a member of " the staff," Kenneth McRae, to his schemes. On July 17, 1813, Miles wrote Lord Selkirk : " My situation all last winter was uncomfortable in the extreme. Surrounded without by enemies ; and within dissatisfaction spreading from the officers among the people, I could not venture to be for an hour absent from the Fort for fear of what might happen." This is an exaggeration, in that the situation depicted did not develop till February.

The lack of loyalty and obedience on the part of the servants and settlers of the colony may be attributed partly to the hardships they were enduring, and partly to the undisciplined character of many of the men. But it was also due to the Governor. His junketings with the Northwesters and the Macleans were in sharp contrast with the drudgery and toil required of the rest of the community. In any case, there was no *camaraderie* between the Governor and the governed, none of that respect and trust based on friendship which lead to implicit obedience. Slackness, grouching, and even rank flouting of orders were common. When, therefore, Cameron began to contrast the happy lot of settlers in Canada with the miseries of life in the colony, he found ready listeners—all the more as on the other side Heney was playing the part of unconscious ally, fomenting discontent and helping the mutinous. Cameron left on 18th March, but not without having won Alexander Macdonell to his policy. On 18th April the Governor wrote his cousin to say that he had full knowledge of his intrigues. He replied denying the charges against himself and Dugald Cameron. Next day the Governor ordered all intercourse with the North West Company's fort to come to an end. His policy of conciliating the Northwesters had completely broken down. So long as he had had to do with the men of the local fort it promised success, for the Governor and the colony added much to the enjoyment of life, but the machine of the concern was impervious to such allurements. The colony would be the means of rehabilitating the Hudson's Bay Company. It must, therefore, be harassed, if possible destroyed.

In early May the Governor was busy burning the brush about the fort, clearing the ground for a garden, sowing wheat, Indian corn, and garden seeds. The corn, wheat, and barley proved a failure because of drought. Moreover, the seed was of the poorest. The problem of food supplies was still pressing. Peter Fidler of Brandon House came to the rescue with a cart-load of pemmican, and of potatoes for seed. On 14th May, a party of nine men and six women with children was sent down to the Forks. Soon Fort Daer was all but tenantless.

At the Forks the Governor busied himself planting Indian corn, wheat, oats, and barley with a hoe. Fifty kegs of potatoes was the measure of that vegetable put in the ground. Some ploughing was done for turnips and buckwheat, until the plough broke. Charcoal was forthwith burned, and a forge set up to make and repair farm implements. Food continued scarce through the summer, but Peter Fidler at Brandon House once more came to the Governor's assistance with sixty bags of pemmican, 90 lb. each, sent down the river. Fish was secured from the Red River.

Relations with the Canadian fur-traders were distant. Accounts were settled with the North West Company, in the person of Mr. Frobisher at Fort Gibraltar, but the old intimacy was now at an end. Under the orders of Mr. Heney, John McLeod was building a post on the east side of the Red River opposite the Forks, where St. Boniface now stands. Macdonell, persistently overlooking the possibility of violence from the Northwesters, and emphasizing his independence of the English Company, wrote to Lord Selkirk that the post was a nuisance and asked to have it removed. Accordingly, it was not occupied. On the last day of May Peter Fidler arrived to survey the lots for the settlers, a task which took him not more than three days, on his way to York Factory. Mr. Maclean, the gentleman among the settlers, was apportioned " a farm," the other settlers got lots of 100 acres each. The lots were made four acres wide at the river-front, the three acres frontage as in Quebec being considered too narrow. The settlers began to build, and the gardens of Fort Douglas were picketed. A fold was made for the sheep, whose numbers had fallen to fifteen ewes, two rams, and one lamb. The lambs born in the winter had perished. As to the cattle—Peter Fidler, " very ready at all times to contribute every assistance," had bought a bull, a cow, and a heifer, at the North West Company's Fort La Souris, opposite Brandon House, for the enormous sum of £100. These added to Adam and Eve and their calf made the total cattle population six heads. Macdonell was not unaware of the pressing need of cattle in the Settlement. During the winter a number of buffalo calves had been secured, doubtless with a view to a cross with the European bull, but they had died for want of milk. Fort Douglas was begun, and a road cut to it from the river. In addition to some local inquirers, six Canadians came all the way from the Saskatchewan to ask for lots. Manifestly there was a real place for the Settlement in the life of the people of the land. The expansion of the area under cultivation would speedily solve the problem of the food supply. Stocking the colony with cattle constituted a much more difficult problem, however. A second band of settlers was leaving Britain. The future was full of promise. All that was needed was the peace indispensable for normal development.

The menace of the Indians, harped on by Simon M'Gillivray, did not exist. While no Indian treaty had yet been made, the question of Indian title was not forgotten. Originally—in the time of La Vérendrye—the region had been the hunting-ground of the Assiniboins. These had been decimated by the small-pox in 1780, and had concentrated to the west, on the open plains and about the fur-traders' posts on the middle and upper Assiniboine. Saulteurs had, by their permission, drifted in down the valley of the Red River. Macdonell wrote Selkirk : " I am at a loss in what manner to make a purchase from the natives. Those here do not call themselves owners of the Soil, although long in possession. . . . A small annual present will satisfy [them] and should the others make a claim a present will satisfy them also. In all these matters I stand alone, there being no person to advise with. I should wish therefore to hear further from your Lordship on the Subject."

On 18th July Macdonell left Mr. Maclean in charge of the colony and journeyed for York Factory to meet a new band of immigrants, usually referred to as the Kildonan Settlers. In reply to his request made in the winter, a considerable supply of pemmican came down to Jack River post from the prairie forts, to be forwarded to the colony. Macdonell felt the need of a depot at the lower end of Lake Winnipeg for such supplies, and for the goods from the factory. While passing, he chose a site on the narrows near Mossy Point at the outlet of Lake Winnipeg. It would be equally convenient whether the Nelson or the Hayes were finally chosen as the transportation route. At York Factory there was disappointment for the Governor. The large body of immigrants from Kildonan reached the Bay by the *Prince of Wales*, but it had been stricken with fever on the voyage. Captain Turner, therefore, hastened to Fort Churchill, where he landed them forthwith, refusing to bring them on in that state to York Factory. Thus, on this group also, a winter's sojourn in extemporized huts by the shore of the Bay was inflicted. The Governor could only return to the colony unaccompanied, without even receiving all the letters which came out in the ship.

The attitude of William Auld, the Company's Superintendent, to the Governor was now greatly changed. He had seen a letter from him to Lord Selkirk, which was critical of his administration.

This would explain much, but not all. Mr. Auld believed that the colony was in some sense within the sphere of his governance, and was bitterly opposed to Macdonell for keeping it apart from the Company and courting the friendship of the Northwesters. This comes out clearly in connection with Lord Selkirk's letters to Macdonell, which failed to reach him at York Factory. Some Auld opened. One was marked to be opened by the Governor only. Auld resented Lord Selkirk's keeping him out of the discussion concerning the colony. He knew that Selkirk was appointing Owen Keveny and William Hillier councillors to the Governor, Miles Macdonell. He constituted a Council himself at Fort Churchill, which decided to suspend the delivery of the packet till further orders, rather than deliver it to such an indiscreet man as the Governor. Thus Auld in resentment assumed a supervision over the colony which was not his to take. (For this rash assumption he was dismissed from the service.) The antipathy now harboured by him to the colonists is further seen in his letters. " Only 17 sick were on the list when I left, but the rest are the laziest dirtiest devils you ever saw." He speaks of the necessity of getting back to Fort Churchill " to manage the d—d savages from Scotland."

Macdonell was back in the colony on October 15, 1813. His early concern was to receive Peguis, the Saulteur chief, and give him presents. The Governor found that Maclean had carried on well in his absence, only using two bags of a precious reserve of oatmeal. The shell of a house—fifty-four feet by twenty-one—the beginning of Fort Douglas, had been put up. Its site was at the base of Point Douglas, where the bend of the river which formed the point began. It faced upwards towards the Forks and the North West Company's Fort Gibraltar. The dogs had killed five sheep and a lamb. The bull which Fidler had bought of the Northwesters had become so vicious that it was decided to kill it for meat. This proved unfortunate, for in the following winter Adam went down to the hole in the ice on the river to drink and, falling in, was drowned. His fate was a mystery, until the body was seen afloat after the ice went out in the spring. Happily, a bull calf was left by him to perpetuate the herd. The harvest proved disappointing. It consisted for the most part of potatoes, the yield being forty-five to fifty kegs for each measure planted. The turnips were huge. The oats grew well but, being planted late, were affected by the frost. The wheat, pease, beans, Indian corn, rye, and hemp, were a complete failure. It was necessary to again occupy Fort Daer on the Pembina River, and to secure a food supply from the buffalo herd.

On 25th October the Governor reached Fort Daer from the Forks in the wake of the settlers, leaving Mr. Maclean, his family, and six men at Fort Douglas. He devoted the winter to superintending the meat supply. The people were now trained to the task of bringing the meat in, and were more contented. The disaffected Edwards had been replaced, as physician, by George Holdsworth. Not only the Indians, but the freemen and half-breeds were well disposed.

Lagimonière and Peter Pangman's half-breed son, Bostonais Pangman, were among the hunters engaged. Thus the Governor's second winter was much happier than his first. Not the least important factor working to this end was the abandonment of their posts at the Pembina by both fur companies. The competition with the colony for meat led them to retire. The Governor was thus relieved of their hostility, but, even more important, he was thrown back upon a life in common with his people. No junketings with the fur-traders this year, but happy festivities in which Governor and people both took part. At the first New Year season the people were sullen. This year there was a happy *camaraderie*, as Macdonell's Journal shows. " 1814, Jan. 4, Assembled our people ; Mr. Sinclair asks for a Holiday for them and also some liquor to give them to drink. Had the H. B. Co's Charter read to them ; also the grant to the Earl of Selkirk and my commission as Governor of the Territory, fired off the 2 [three-pounders] and gave 3 cheers at the close. The people enjoyed themselves much and kept it up the greater part of the night. The gentlemen did the same." On 4th February Macdonell wrote to Auld : " I feel myself transported into a terrestrial Paradise in comparison to my situation last winter." And again to Lord Selkirk on 25th July, " We passed upon the whole an agreeable winter, very different from the former. The greatest unanimity and cordiality pervade all ranks of our little community." These happy relations may have deceived Macdonell into believing that his people would stand staunch behind him in case of a struggle with the North West Company. Certain it is that he was meditating a Proclamation prohibiting the export of pemmican from Assiniboia, which was sure to precipitate a struggle with the Northwesters.

There were many reasons in favour of such an embargo. William Auld, who collaborated with the Governor on the scheme, when he was at York Factory, placed them on paper on May 13, 1814. It was " an indispensible duty imperiously pressing on Captain Macdonell, not only to provide for his people, but to prevent a scarcity happening among them, more especially in so remote a situation as precludes all possibility for looking for assistance from any other quarter." The provisions carried off by the traders would provide for the colonists on their own farms at the Forks, for the Indians and freemen would bring it in, but, just because the traders were getting it, the colonists had to abandon their homes and the work which should be done on their lots in the shape of ploughing, while gathering wood was neglected and the colony not progressing as it should. Moreover, they were calling on the Hudson's Bay Company for English provisions, and thereby dislocating its usual business and causing expense. The provisions gathered by the Northwesters were not only to the damage of the colony, but of the Hudson's Bay Company, for the Company's posts in the north must send provisions to the colony, and thereby hamper themselves in their competition with their rivals. Moreover, the pemmican which should have gone to the English posts on the Assiniboine had been diverted to the colony to the great suffering of the men at those posts. Let the colony prohibit the exportation of provisions and erect a post for gathering supplies on the Qu'Appelle, and it would become self-sufficing and cease to hamper the English Company in its competition with the Canadians. In this argument, the embargo appears less as an offensive movement against the North West Company than as a necessary safeguard of the interests of the colony and a defensive policy for the Hudson's Bay Company, to prevent it from being hampered by the call of the colony for provisions. It was devised at once to make the colony self-sufficing by securing for it the meat trade of the area covered by Selkirk's Grant and to free the English Company from the handicap which the colony imposed upon it in its competition with its powerful rivals. None the less the Northwesters may be excused for considering it as a definite attack upon their trade, for the pemmican of the two Red Rivers was needed at Bas de la Rivière Winipic to provision their northern brigades for the journey out to Fort William on Lake Superior. They would take it, or profess to take it, as directed solely against them. Macdonell's experience when leaving Scotland should have apprised him of the bitterness of their opposition. Moreover, his correspondence with the Agents of the North West Company in the summer of 1813 should have shown that they saw the colony as nothing more or less than a device to destroy their business. On 1st June he had written to the Proprietors of the concern protesting against the conduct of Alexander Macdonell and Dugald Cameron at Pembina. William M'Gillivray had replied repudiating the charge and refusing to regard the colony as different from the Hudson's Bay Company. "How you can hold out that the views of Lord Selkirk and of course his Agents are merely agricultural is to us unaccountable, when we are told that the engagements of all his people oblige them to be drafted into the service of the Hudson's Bay Company whenever that concern stands in need of them for the purposes of the Fur Trade." * He saw the colony truthfully as a coming reservoir of servants and provisions for the English Company to enable it to succeed in its competition with his own " concern." If he could persuade the settlers to disperse, he would protect the North West Company against the reorganization for efficiency on the part of its rival, of which the colony was one feature. The Governor thus stood in a precarious position, with the growing hostility of the North West Company on the one side, and no great zeal for him on the part of the servants of the English Company on the other. Yet he was so oblivious of all the difficulties that he was planning a course of action—and that without the organization to meet a crisis—which could only enrage the North West Company against the colony.

Miles Macdonell appears to have been less interested than Auld

---

* The reference is to a condition in the agreement between the Company and Lord Selkirk that he should procure recruits for its service up to a hundred men per annum. The contracts with the men were drawn so as to allow of their allocation to either service on arrival at York Fort. There can be little doubt that Selkirk expected to be able ultimately to secure at least some of this labour in his colony.

in the benefits which an embargo would confer on the Hudson's Bay Company, and more concerned with the food supply of an increasing colony, and with ridding himself of the presence of the North West Company in his domain. Writing from York Factory to Lord Selkirk on September 10, 1813, he discusses the possibility of accommodating as large a body as 250 immigrants. " When once arrived in Red River I shall undertake to feed them. I am now determined that the N. W. Co. shall not take more provisions from store, than what will carry out their people who winter in Red R. and when they find themselves subjected to this they may not perhaps think it an object to continue there." The embargo on the export of pemmican, then, was devised to provide the food for a large incoming body of settlers, but the Governor, knowing the difficulties it would occasion to the Northwesters, who had intrigued against him and his colony, was happy to think that it would incidentally rid him of their presence. While he does not say it, he may have wished the Hudson's Bay Company also to depart, for, as has been seen, he had asked Lord Selkirk to use his influence to have Heney's post at the Forks removed.

Meanwhile Lord Selkirk was concerning himself with the institutions of the colony. In 1812 he communicated to Lord Liverpool, then Prime Minister, the plans for a colony on the Red River. His lordship, in his reply, made no suggestion that the scheme was inconsistent with the views of policy entertained by His Majesty's Government. A similar communication, including a statement with regard to Selkirk's title to the land, was made to Lord Bathurst, the Secretary of State for the Colonies, and to the Earl of Clancarty, the President of the Board of Trade, neither of whom expressed any objection to the colony. Selkirk believed that they approved of it. When war with the United States broke out Selkirk applied to Lord Bathurst to obtain a supply of arms and ammunition and a few light fieldpieces for the defence of the Settlement. Selkirk says : " The readiness with which this was granted, led me still further to feel confident that my undertaking was not disapproved of." Finally, the settlers who arrived at Fort Churchill in 1813 came with the light field-pieces, and were protected by the *Jason*, a British warship.

Believing then that his title was sound at law and that the British Government did not deny its legality, on the contrary, approved of his colony, Selkirk was considering a first sketch of its system of government. Miles Macdonell, on May 31, 1812, in view of his troubles at Nelson Encampment, had written his lordship that the situation called for a military Governor with a Commission from the Crown, and a force of, say, fifty mounted infantry behind him. Selkirk's reply, dated June 13, 1813, was particularly appropriate in view of the scheme of an embargo on the export of pemmican brewing in the Governor's mind. A military government was at present out of the question. The Canada Jurisdiction Act did not apply to the Chartered Territory, but it would not remain long so, if the Company did not proceed to exercise the jurisdiction legally vested in it so as to adequately redress wrongs committed in its region. None the less the Governor must take the utmost care not to exercise his authority in a violent or invidious manner, lest he raise a clamour which might lead to the annulment of the Charter :

If you keep clear of any unnecessary collision with the N.W. Co. (remaining as to them decidedly on the defensive) I do not apprehend any material difficulty or obstacle against your taking upon yourself all the powers that are necessary for maintaining the internal policy of the settlement ; and the Commission which you already hold from the Company appears to be sufficient warrant to you for doing so. By the Charter, the Governor of any of the Co's establishments *with his Council* may try all causes, civil or criminal, and punish offences according to the law of England. You have, therefore, authority to act as a Judge, but to do this correctly, it is necessary that you have a council to sit as your assessors, and also that you try by Jury all cases which in England would be tried by a Jury.

Even if the number of twelve should prove impracticable, something of a jury should be impanelled. The position in which the colony stood, according to Lord Selkirk, in relation to the two fur-trading companies is carefully defined. All persons within the Grant are subject to the Governor in the matter of wrong-doing. If the English Company's servants claim protection and redress for violences committed within the limits " you cannot refuse to interfere, and the delinquents should be brought to punishment in the same manner as if they had attacked the settlers ; but you must take care to deal with perfect impartiality between the servants of the two Companies. Indeed, on all occasions of collision with the N.W. people, it will be advisable to be very sure of your ground and to have a case very well made out, before you take any strong measures."

Selkirk now turns to his property rights in virtue of the Grant. He is not oblivious of the Common Law rights which the North West Company might have gained by the occupation of a spot uninterruptedly for twenty years or more. Where they have not occupied for twenty years or more they can be summoned to remove. " Even though this summons should not be followed by effective removal, yet it will be sufficient to interrupt prescription, and this ceremony ought, therefore, to be used in every case where the N.W. Co. have possessed a post within our limits for nearly 20 years, but has not beyond that period. The summons must be made before a number of witnesses so as to secure that the memory of the proceeding shall not be lost."

To make the Governor's authority effective, Selkirk gave Macdonell permission to issue commissions modelled after his own, to " Councillors of the Territory or District of Ossiniboia "—to Mr. Keveny as first in Council, or second in command ; to Dr. Lassere (who unfortunately died of the fever on the way to the Bay) ; to Kenneth McRae, and to Archibald M'Donald, and, with Mr. Auld's permission, to the Chief Factors of East and West Winnipeg departments of the Hudson's Bay Company. A sheriff must be appointed, and Keveny's name was suggested. Finally, trusted men among the indented servants could be officered and trained, and a little extra pay given them to act as constables.

The course sketched by Lord Selkirk was simple wisdom. Miles Macdonell received the letter on December 31, 1813, forwarded from Fort Churchill and York Factory.* Yet he launched his proclamation of an embargo nine days later, on January 8, 1814. He should have, according to his instructions, kept on the defensive and set aside his plan of an embargo, even if he regarded it as essentially defensive, for it was only too likely to precipitate the conflict with the North West Company against which Selkirk had warned him. Above all, he should have postponed all conflict until the people had settled down to co-operation with its government and had attained to some degree of trust in its power to do justice to them and to protect them, so that in the hour of trial they would have stood staunchly by their Governor. But this is asking too much of Miles Macdonell, who had had no administrative experience and, failing that, had not the sober vision to see the situation in the true light of day. Crass blindness to the obstacles in his path and overweening trust in his own power and the prestige of his office were to be the undoing of the man.

Macdonell's Journal of January 8, 1814, runs : " A Proclamation which had been some time in contemplation I had put up today on the South gate which was just hung (this prohibits all export of provisions of what nature so ever for one year from this date and also advertises the name and limits of the Territory of Assiniboia). . . . Gave a dance this evening to the people ; the gentlemen, men and women enjoyed themselves and encroached on the Sabbath." The entry reflects the light-heartedness of the Governor's action. The Proclamation envisaged in the first place the supply of food necessary for the large body of incoming settlers. But if the embargo could be successfully enforced, Lord Selkirk's title would be made good in practice, as it was believed to hold good in Law. Finally, the Governor expected that the North West Company, and perhaps even the Hudson's Bay Company, would go elsewhere for their

---

* Professor Chester Martin infers that Macdonell had not received this letter, that it was the one returned by Auld to Selkirk unopened. (*Work of Lord Selkirk in Canada*, p. 56 and p. 67). But Macdonell's letter to Auld of February 4, 1814 (*Selkirk Papers*, p. 951), runs : " I am instructed to form a council," and his report of what he was doing in the matter shows that he had received the letter. It was probably among those left at Fort Churchill and forwarded by the winter express which, Macdonell's Journal shows, reached him on 31st December. " Recd my letters from the Earl of Selkirk brot [brought] by Mr. Sinclair." Spencer was appointed of the Council on 8th February (*Selkirk Papers*, p. 966). On 8th March Macdonell writes the agents of the N.W. Co. that the Jurisdiction of Lower Canada does not extend to the Western Country (*ibid.*, p. 967f.). Finally, in his letter dated Red River, 25th July, written before the unopened letter could have come back to him from England, Macdonell says : " Your Lordship's communications reached me 31st December. Nos. 1, 2 and 4 all had been opened and read by Mr. Kivney. Mr. Auld returned No. 3 to your Lordship. . . . I made out a notice in the form of a proclamation to prohibit the export of provisions to a certain extent. It had been written before the receipt of your Lordship's letters and, notwithstanding the cautions recommended in the Judicature Instructions, I issued it on 8th January, judging that remissions might always be granted according to circumstances " (*Selkirk Papers*, p. 1188).

pemmican and rid him of neighbours whose intrigues disturbed him.

It would be well to keep the bearings of the embargo clearly in mind. First as regards the season 1814–15 to which it applied—there was no intention of confiscating the pemmican gathered at the posts that winter without compensation. All pemmican taken was to be " paid for by British Bills at customary rates." Pemmican gathered within the area granted to Lord Selkirk, viz. at Pembina and in the upper waters of Red River to the height of land—territory now in the United States—came under the embargo, but that secured on the upper waters of the Qu'Appelle River, now rapidly becoming a chief source of supply, could pass freely down the Assiniboine and Red rivers to its destination. The hardship inflicted was therefore confined to Fort Gibraltar at the Forks and the Post on the Assiniboine at the Souris River, and Fort Qu'Appelle, about a score of miles up the Qu'Appelle from the Assiniboine. Enough pemmican to enable the fur-traders at these posts to reach their destination was to be exempt from the embargo. But surely it was an injustice to lay hands on the pemmican needed to take the northern brigades to Fort William, especially to do so without sufficient notice for effectual measures to be taken to secure supplies of pemmican from farther afield, from Swan River, Red Deer River, or possibly from the Saskatchewan. Had sufficient notice of the embargo, however, been given, it involved no more hardship than that involved in collecting the amount of pemmican gathered within Assiniboia without its bounds, say, on the upper Qu'Appelle and the Saskatchewan rivers. This would involve some additional cost, but it would in no sense destroy the trade of the North West Company. Evidently Macdonell calculated on his teasing his neighbours into readjusting their business to his embargo, especially as it was to be enforced and, as we shall see, was enforced upon the Hudson's Bay Company as well as on the rival concern. Much can, therefore, be said in favour of the embargo as a measure to protect the coming settlers—nothing can disguise the unwisdom of precipitating at this early stage a struggle with the North West Company—especially as it gave the Northwesters, who were ready to take any means whatever to undermine the colony, excellent material for propaganda against the Hudson's Bay Company and Lord Selkirk. They denied that the territory involved was included in the Charter ; they questioned the legality of the grant to Lord Selkirk, and insisted that the colony, and in particular the embargo, was a villainous device to destroy their trade in the interests of the English Company by destroying their system of transportation. Thus they made the issue the survival of the North West Company's business. As this was of the utmost importance to the colonies on the St. Lawrence, all Canada got behind the Company in its campaign against the colony.

Two days after the issue of the Proclamation at Fort Daer, Messrs. Sinclair and Stitt were sent off with copies for the several posts. On 1st February they returned. They had served the notice of the embargo on the English Brandon House. Hillier was in charge and accepted it, but refused to accompany the party across the river to post the Proclamation at Fort la Souris of the North West Company. John Wills, in charge there, denied the legality of the Proclamation and refused to allow it to be posted on his gate. He would not recognize any authority as residing in Miles Macdonell. However, he took copies to send to the Proprietors at Swan River, Fort des Prairies, Cumberland House, and Winnipeg River. This last was the only one of these posts within Assiniboia. Thus the struggle was on.

The Governor knew that it was, but took it light-heartedly. He wrote Auld on 4th February : " I have sufficient force to crush all the Northwesters in this river, should they be so hardy as to resist openly my authority. On the general rendezvous of their Northern canoes in Spring at Winipic River, their great numbers and the desperate situation of their affairs might possibly induce them to make a violent effort—but I cannot imagine that the *Bourgeois* can prevail on their men to act against us in that way. Whatever may happen I am determined that my authority shall not be trampled on."

Only now did Macdonell begin to concern himself with the institutions of government recommended by Lord Selkirk. The very day of the return of his messengers, he appointed John Spencer sheriff, to serve necessary warrants on any who should disobey the embargo. He also appointed a Council, but with no idea of making it a part of the governing machine. He wrote Auld on 4th February : " It seems . . . that a Council is indispensably required to fill up the letter of the law." It was, therefore, no more than a shadow of a council. Its members were George Holdsworth the surgeon, John Spencer the sheriff, Archibald McDonald, who had come out with the emigrants of 1813 and was at Fort Churchill, but would arrive in the course of the summer. Auld's permission was asked to have Hillier of Brandon House and Sinclair of the Winnipeg Department serve.

Word reached Macdonell at Fort Daer that the North West Company would resist the embargo with force, and at Fort Douglas (14th May) that Alexander Macdonell was trying to induce the Indians to assemble at the Forks with that end in view. On the 19th the Governor knew that a boatload of North West Company's pemmican from Fort la Souris was coming down the Assiniboine. He swore in four constables (apparently the first to be sworn in) and sent off a guard to watch the river. These reported armed French-Canadians in numbers. The Governor then sent out an armed demonstration with two brass fieldpieces. So far were the Indians from supporting the enemy, Peguis came in and left a pipe of peace with the Governor in token of his friendship. On the 21st, Spencer the sheriff proceeded up the Assiniboine. Meanwhile Mr. Wills had come down from Fort la Souris and was in conference with the Governor. On the 24th the sheriff returned with the North

West Company's boat and two of its crew as prisoners. The pemmican had been secreted somewhere on the bank of the river. The prisoners informed the Governor of the spot where it would be found. On the 27th the sheriff brought it in—ninety-six bags in all. The servants of the North West Company on oath stated that they had been ordered to secrete it. Macdonell, however, offered the pemmican to Mr. Wills if it was needed for the upkeep of the fort. The offer was not acknowledged. (Afterwards loud complaints were made to the Government of Canada that the seizure of the pemmican left Fort Gibraltar in a state of starvation.) On the 29th word came in that the North West Company's pemmican from Swan River and Fort Qu'Appelle had been unloaded at Fort la Souris instead of being brought through as usual—this till a sufficient armed force should be gathered to pass it down safe from being requisitioned. Two days after the Governor wrote Mr. John Pritchard, the clerk in charge at that post, and sent the sheriff accompanied by Mr. Howse, of the English Company's Saskatchewan district, to seize the provisions from Fort Qu'Appelle, but not those of Swan River, as he was uncertain whether that post lay within Assiniboia.

On 1st June the Northwesters, at the behest of Mr. Wills, began to gather. Dugald Cameron arrived from Bas de la Rivière Winipic. On 3rd June the Hudson's Bay Company's brigade came down from Brandon House and delivered up 190 bags of pemmican, 80 lb. per bag. This was stored in the garret at Fort Douglas. In this act the English Company honoured the Proclamation. Mr. Stitt, in whose charge it was, received written permission to depart with the portion necessary for his voyage. The Northwester Wills proposed that his Company should be allowed to bring its pemmican down and store it at his fort till the Wintering Partners should gather (when, of course, they would be in such force that the Governor would not dare touch it). The proposal was declined, more especially as Wills was building a blockhouse commanding the navigation of the river. Wills forthwith removed the beginnings of the blockhouse. All parties, while standing for their several rights, were reluctant to go to extremes. On the 9th the Northwesters applied for permission to take out the Swan River pemmican as not coming from within bounds ; they received it. On the 13th Dr. McLoughlin arrived and with him Duncan Cameron and John McDonald of Fort Dauphin. A conference was held on the road between forts Gibraltar and Douglas. The demand was that all the North West Company's pemmican should pass through. It was refused. The Governor had, however, kept the discussions friendly in tone, and when the Northwesters requested his piper for a dance, he was granted. Next day the Governor showed the Northwesters round the settlement, such as it was, but no agreement was reached. On the 15th word arrived that Mr. Howse had been seized by a party of Northwesters and taken to Fort Gibraltar. The Governor demanded his release, but in vain. When, therefore, Alexander Kennedy of the North West Company was passing up the river with twenty men and two canoes on the way to strengthen the force in Fort Gibraltar, the Governor seized the canoes and the arms. The men were released on the promise not to serve against the colony, but the arms were retained. Macdonell now placed a guard on the river. On the 17th a force was sent out to meet the pemmican seized at Fort la Souris and to bring the sheriff home safely. That day John MacDonald of Garth, the North West proprietor in charge of the Columbia, arrived and opened negotiations. He pointed out the shortage of provisions for his concern at Fort William because of the American War, that they needed all their pemmican and more, and suggested that his Company should send ten canoes to the Bay to bring up oatmeal and that it should also procure 175 bags of pemmican the coming winter to relieve the situation in the colony. If only the Governor would let them have their pemmican, which was indispensable for the transportation of the northern brigade; this conceded, hostilities would cease. The Governor agreed to this immediately (17th June). The next day the sheriff Spencer arrived in two boats with part of the pemmican from Fort la Souris. In keeping with the agreement it was sent to Fort Gibraltar. The sheriff was so chagrined at the issue that he forthwith resigned as sheriff and as councillor. Next evening there was a general dance at the North West Company's post. The day after, John MacDonald of Garth and the other Northwesters dined with the Governor.

On 21st June the Kildonan settlers arrived from Fort Churchill. They had trudged the weary way from that post to York Factory, and thence had voyaged by boat and portage to their new home at the Red River—thirty-one men, three women, and seventeen girls, making fifty-one persons in all. Archibald McDonald, their supervisor, reported no provisions at York Fort. Accordingly the clause of the agreement with the Northwesters requiring them to send canoes to the Bay for provisions fell to the ground. The Northwesters, however, kept the pemmican which was in their possession. On 15th July, after the Northwester brigades had proceeded on their way to Fort William, the rest of the North West Company's pemmican from Brandon House, where it had been temporarily stored, was brought down. Macdonell took 100 bags and sent 176 to Fort Gibraltar.

So ended the first stage of the "Pemmican War." It was something of a triumph for Miles Macdonell. He had won an inferential recognition of the rights of the Charter and of the Grant to Lord Selkirk. He had inflicted an injustice on the North West Company in placing the embargo on pemmican with such little notice. That wrong was partially righted when the Northwesters went off with a satisfactory supply, and no need to send canoes to the Bay. He had also carried the day over the Hudson's Bay Company. Though he had written Auld that the embargo was not directed against the Company but the Canadians, he kept its pemmican for the use of the settlers. He remarks: "Mr. Auld on his return here . . . was not pleased at my taking so much pemmican from the Company.

Mr. Stitt surrendered 190 bags and a quantity of Fat—he left [here] with 14 men and took away 102 bags of Pemican 10 kegs Fat &c."

The Governor now turned to the task of placing the new colonists. They were given lots of 100 acres down the river bank from Fort Douglas. Peter Fidler, since the beginning of May, had been surveying the lots. To bring the people close together the frontage on the river was reduced from four to three acres. The new settlers soon planted forty-two kegs of potatoes. They were most industrious and cheerfully engaged in building their houses. Macdonell wrote to Selkirk : " I have found them, as your Lordship remarks, tractible and disposed to listen to advice for their own good." This was the true commencement of Red River Settlement. " Till these people came, there was scarcely a person permanently established here ; those of 1812, old Neil McKinnon, Angus McDonald, Smyth &c., did very little and were always doubtful of the issue. The servants we had cared not in general how little they wrought or in what manner it might turn out so long as they were paid their wages. None of them cared for settling on lands."

This spring seven kegs of barley, four of wheat, and five or six of oats were sown, also Indian corn, buckwheat, and nearly 300 kegs of potatoes, " promising very different from the crops of last year." Green pease were eaten on 1st July. The sheep were reduced to two Rams, nine Ewes and four lambs. Their wool was sent down to York Factory for export. Light and therefore easily carried but valuable, it promised, as Lord Selkirk fondly thought, to be one of the exports of his colony. The census of the cattle revealed three cows, one of them a two-year-old heifer not in calf, a one-year-old bull, and two bull calves. The French-Canadians were proving interested in the Settlement, and though their habits were not those of settlers, were looking for something like a permanent home. Some were already as good as settled at Pembina, some at what came to be known as the White Horse Plain. Others hoped to settle at the Forks. Macdonell suggested to Lord Selkirk that a good priest would be the means of " bringing them quickly to a regular mode of life." Mr. John Pritchard of the North West Company at Rivière la Souris, and Mr. James Bird of the Hudson's Bay Company on the Saskatchewan, were contemplating settlement in the colony. In truth, there was a real place for Lord Selkirk's scheme in the needs of the country.

The problem of supplies for the coming winter was by no means solved by such pemmican as the embargo had brought into the Governor's hands. The settlers would have to go to the plains once more. There had been but little snow during the previous winter, and the French-Canadians and half-breeds had been able to hunt buffalo with their horses all through the winter. This was disliked by the Indians, who preferred hunting, as of old, on foot, and with bows and arrows, for that method did not frighten their prey into scampering to distant parts. Accordingly on July 21, 1814, Governor

Macdonell issued a Proclamation prohibiting "running" buffalo with horses ; this he did only after consultation with the Northwesters at Fort Gibraltar.   They accepted it as for the good of all parties, for shooting buffalo from horseback used to stampede them into a wild run, often beyond the reach of the forts.   It was their interest as well to keep the herds close in.   Accordingly, they posted the Governor's Proclamation on the gates of Fort Gibraltar.   The freemen and half-breeds, who profited by keeping the buffalo far out and thus having the meat trade in their hands, would be known to dislike the Proclamation.   It does not appear that at this stage the Northwesters intended to foment their discontent.

On 25th July the Governor left for York Factory.   While on this voyage his preoccupation was with the " winter road."   Easy communication with the Bay was essential to the success of the colony. The portages were to be made easier, establishments with settlers, producing provisions and keeping cattle and carts for the portages, were to be placed at vantage points—all facilitating traffic in summer ; but it was contemplated that sleds could run on the rivers and lakes in winter provided there were stations with supplies by the way. The Company was to give the Hill River House for this purpose, and something of a depot, set apart for the settlement, was to be established at the Rock.   Macdonell kept watching for the strategic sites.   On the return he fixed the site of the Rock House.

When at the factory the Governor was incapacitated by a nervous breakdown verging on insanity.   The excitement of the past months, the utterly involved state of the colony's accounts and its goods, the hostility of Auld and the Hudson's Bay Company's men at the factory, culminating in what seems a plot to get rid of him, the sense that the struggle with the Northwesters was only beginning, may all have been contributing factors.   " I am about distracted on account of the state of [Red River Settlement] matters here," he writes in his Journal.   He was even induced momentarily to place his resignation in the hands of Auld.

The ships the *Rosamund* and *Prince of Wales* arrived on 2nd September with fourteen men and one woman for the colony. At Knee Lake, on the way up with them, the Governor learned that the Northwesters, armed with a warrant from A. N. McLeod, Justice of the Peace in the Indian territory, had arrested Spencer, the sheriff, on a charge of larceny, and had carried him off to Montreal for trial.   On his arrival at Fort Douglas, 20th October, he knew that the Company had repudiated the agreement of 17th June, and would not implement their promises in the matter of fat to come down from Fort la Souris.   The truth was that the North West Company at its rendezvous at Fort William refused to recognize the arrangement.   If the Wintering Partners at the Settlement had felt that the Governor was really trying to solve the problems of the colony's food supply and were therefore ready to meet him half-way, not so William M'Gillivray, and A. N. McLeod, and those who looked on the colony as a disguised attack on their own concern. The action taken at Fort William is thus described in the Minutes of the occasion :

. . . The Gentlemen of the neighbouring Departments . . . assembled with their men and Mr. Miles was very near paying dear for his temerity, but being averse to commencing actual Hostility and wishing to know the sentiments of the Concern at large in this extraordinary transaction, they entered into a compromise that he should keep 200 Bags and give up the remainder. Thus the matter ended for the time, not, it must be confessed to the Credit of the Concern—and in consequence of what past at the meeting [at Fort William], it is not probable that a similar attempt will be equally successful—a full determination was taken to defend the Property at all hazards and all the Wintering men being assembled for the purpose, the true state of the case was explained to them and the impression it made, it is hoped, will render it a dangerous service to any man who may presume to plunder them—a feast of 13 [measures] of liquor and Provisions was given to them on the occasion. The men of Red River and four of those from Fort Dauphin who had behaved ill on the seizure of the Provisions were pointed out to them and disgraced.

The Minute points to future action in defence of the rights of the concern. In fact, the deeds of the proprietors indicate the determination to undermine the authority of Governor Macdonell and to disrupt the colony. The arrest of Spencer, the sheriff, was, so to say, the first shot fired in the attack. Alexander Macdonell, on the way back to his post on the Qu'Appelle River, in a letter dated Portage la Prairie, August 5, 1814, wrote John MacDonald of Garth :

You see myself and our mutual friend Mr. [Duncan] Cameron so far on our way to commence open hostilities against the enemy in Red River ; much is expected from us if we believe some—perhaps too much. One thing [is] certain that we will do our best to defend what we *consider* our rights in the interior ; something serious will undoubtedly take place ; nothing but the complete downfall of the Colony will satisfy some, by fair or foul means—a most desirable object if it can be accomplished. So here is at them with all my heart and energy.

When the Governor saw that the struggle was on again he served notice (21st October) on the North West Company at Fort Gibraltar to quit the property of their landlord Selkirk. Similar notices were served on Fort Alexander (Bas de la Rivière Winipic), on Fort Dauphin, on Rivière la Souris, and on the post on the upper Assiniboine. Of course the North West Company, which was making a strong bid for the support of the public, made it appear that the intention was to drive them out of their forts. In truth, the serving of these notices did no more than preserve the title of Selkirk to the land and prevent the Northwesters from gaining squatters' rights to the sites.

The position of the Governor, as the struggle drifted to an issue, was far less reassuring than it had been the year before. With an increased population the problem of provisions was as pressing as ever. The servants of the colony were shiftless workmen and the earliest settlers were few. Besides, instead of staying at the Forks and effecting improvements, they had to spend more than half of

the year at Pembina seeking on the plains the bare necessities of life.
Thus their crops afforded but a small relief to the incoming settlers.
The cattle were too few to be reckoned as a help. On 22nd October
the Governor sent some of the men and their families once more to
Pembina. A cow was sent up to provide milk for buffalo calves, with
a view to a cross with the European bull, in the hope of securing
a herd of cross-bred cattle for the settlers. In the middle of January
the situation became acute. Although the Indians tried to stop them,
the half-breeds insisted on running buffalo on horseback, and the
herds were driven far afield. The settlers at the Forks were sent out
to the plains on pain of having their food supply cut off. The
situation at Turtle River was acute, due to clashes with half-breeds.
Macdonell describes it in *A Sketch of the Conduct of the North West
Company*, an *apologia pro vita sua*, prepared later :

> [The Proclamation] was deemed a measure beneficial to the country,
> which would facilitate in general the procuring of provisions, that certain free
> Canadians and half-breeds . . . who made a practice of hunting the buffalo
> at all seasons should be restricted. The North West gentlemen who passed
> the Summer in our vicinity, Mr. Wills, J. Dougald Cameron, and Seraphim
> Lamar, encouraged me to give out an order against this practice, which I
> did before I left the Settlement to go to York Fort. The people in general
> were well pleased with the restriction, as only a few of these [the half-breeds]
> had hunting horses, about five or six, the chief of whom was Beaulino, the
> North-West hunter. This order remained on the North-West gates, at the
> Forks and Brandon House [*i.e.* at Fort la Souris], till taken down by the
> orders of Mr. Cameron. After his arrival he informed the free Canadians that
> they should not be restricted in any way. In contradiction to this, he was
> heard to declare early in the Fall, that it was formerly no crime in the freemen
> to hunt for the colony, but that he would take good care they should not do
> so in future. . . . Repeated accounts reached us from Fort Daer (Pembina)
> that the cattle [buffalo] were driven from our hunters by Beaulino the North-
> West hunter, and others running them on horseback, on which account they
> were not getting much meat. Our people at Turtle River, and Mr. McLeod
> the Hudson's Bay trader there, made repeated complaints of the same
> nature ; that our hunters could not kill a sufficiency of cattle ; that when
> they would be crawling on their bellies after a herd of buffaloe on the snow,
> a party of horsemen would come before them and drive away the herd ;
> that my immediate interference was required, or the consequences would be
> serious. The natives also complained of this mode of hunting, as they had
> not horses, and their fear of the Sioux would not admit of their pursuing after
> the cattle far. It appeared that the North-West were determined to counter-
> act us in every way ; their hunter Beaulino, who always kept 10 or 12 horses
> for running cattle, was the principal aggressor.

Macdonell went up to quell the rising storm. The Indians rallied
to him out of anger at the half-breeds, who openly avowed that they
were acting on the instigation of the North West Company. " In
every act they were headed by the N. W. Clerks " runs Macdonell's
Journal. The Northwesters even drew up a petition for them to the
Prince Regent, in which they (the half-breeds) claimed the land as
theirs, and asserted that it was being taken away from them along
with even the right to hunt. The half-breeds were led to believe
that they were the owners of the soil—" the free half-breeds of Red
River." The men from Canada thus recklessly sowed the wind

The next generation would reap the whirlwind in the Riel Rebellion of 1869.

The freemen had been told that Miles Macdonell and his settlers would be driven out of the land. They had been advised to get the largest amount of credit possible from the Governor, for they would not need to repay it. Macdonell found that hunters equipped by him refused to bring in their meat. He thereupon required his servants to bear arms. McLeod, with an armed force, began to seize the meat, but was taken prisoner and subjected to many indignities. Bostonais Pangman, who had been a tower of strength to him the previous winter, proved to be now the leader of the half-breeds.

The sufferings of the new settlers throughout the winter were very great and brought disillusionment in their train. Cameron strutted about Fort Gibraltar and among the immigrants as an officer of the King in the uniform of the Canadian Voltigeurs (though the corps was now disbanded). He impressed them as one having authority. He insinuated abroad doubts of the legality of the Hudson's Bay Company's Charter and Lord Selkirk's Grant, and consequently doubts of the value of titles to the lots taken up by the settlers. Worst of all, he created fears of merciless attacks from the Indians. Settlers came to him to make inquiries, and were told of the happy lot of immigrants in Upper Canada. They were offered a free passage in the North West Company's canoes to that land of prosperity and ease. Many settlers accepted. Of course, Selkirk had no lien on them, save for such indebtedness as had been incurred for the passage and for goods supplied. That indebtedness, however, could be thrown off by flight to Canada. Then, too, the contracts with the workmen who came out in 1812 were about to lapse. Here again Selkirk had no lien on the men save for indebtedness. His lordship places all the blame on Cameron. Legally the onus for default would lie on the colonists and servants. At most Cameron was but implicated in a conspiracy to defraud.

It would have been well for the reputation of the North West Company had Cameron been contented with this great success, but he was determined to capture the Governor. He procured a warrant from A. N. McLeod, who held an appointment as Justice of the Peace under the Canada Jurisdiction Act, charging the Governor with breaking in and stealing pemmican, and was prepared to resort to violence to effect his arrest, and to destroy the colony. With such an intrigue on foot it was folly in Macdonell to leave the settlers at the mercy of Cameron and to spend eleven weeks in the south facing the half-breeds, as has already been told. On 3rd April, four days before his return, the conspiracy came to a head. Settlers, at the instance of Cameron, carried off the artillery supplied by the Imperial Government from the store at Fort Douglas, where it lay dismounted. Cameron, with Cuthbert Grant and William Shaw, two half-breeds in his employ, came out of the woods with an armed band to escort the cannon to Fort Gibraltar. Thus the conspirators drew the teeth of the Governor. Macdonell had been training the settlers to arms during the autumn, but Cameron had undermined the loyalty of many. No inconsiderable number, however, stood true, and were prepared to defend the Governor. The North West Company's partners now began to gather, their canoes bringing half-breeds and Indians even from the distant Saskatchewan—the men to overawe all opposition, and the canoes to afford transportation for the fugitive settlers. On 7th June forty-two men and some women passed down the river, protected by an armed band patrolling the west bank. This band drove off the colony's precious cattle to Frog Plain. The all-important bull was killed for meat, a quarter being sent to Duncan Cameron at Fort Gibraltar. The rest of the beasts got clear and returned of their own accord to their byre. On the 10th a North West Company's express arrived with a hand-bill announcing the close of the American War, and the signing of the treaty of peace at Ghent. On the back of this handbill was written in J. Dugald Cameron's hand, " Peace all over the world except at R.R." That very day an attack was made on Fort Douglas, but not pressed. The only casualties were from the bursting of an old field-piece being used in the defence of the fort. It wounded Mr. Maclean severely. Now at last, in the hour of crisis, we begin to hear of the Governor's Council. They, with a number of others, agreed with the Governor that, as the main object of the enemy was to capture him, he should go into hiding (11th June). After a short period of concealment, however, he returned to his command. On 16th June, after a conference with Mr. Alexander Mackenzie (" the Emperor "), at the time agent for the North West concern, and come up from Montreal to hasten the ruin of the colony : " the gentlemen of my Council with Messrs. Fidler and Stitt wrote me an official letter that I should surrender myself to the North West company to obtain if possible, some terms for the preservation of the colony. Our men are again desponding seeing themselves so few." To avert an impending attack on the fort, Macdonell surrendered on agreement with Mr. Mackenzie that the colony should be preserved from hostility at least for the summer. The condition was not observed. On the contrary the people were told to " quit the river, the Company as well as the Colony," and the horses and other plunder were not returned. On 20th June, at 3 p.m., the crestfallen Governor was taken down the river in a light canoe accompanied by Mr. Mackenzie and Simon Fraser, whose fame as an explorer is tarnished by his presence here, and Duncan Cameron. Others of the " concern " followed in their wake. Early on the second day he was at Bas de la Rivière Winipic, where the deserters from the colony were assembled. The brigades came in one after another from the north and took each its portion of settlers. Before the Governor was taken farther, word came in of the attack by the half-breeds on the colony, and of its desertion by the remnant of the settlers. As the Governor was being conveyed across Lake of the Woods on the way to Montreal he met Colin Robertson followed by a large brigade destined to make a fresh attempt to win a position in the Athabaska region for the Hudson's Bay Company. At the rendezvous at Fort William there was jubilation among the proprietors of the " concern." " I am happy to inform you," wrote Simon M'Gillivray, " that the colony has been all knocked on the head by the N.W. Co." Another partner wrote : " I hope that things will go on better now, since the Colony is gone to the Devil." All the half-breeds present who had taken part in achieving the triumph were feasted and received large rewards in money. Bostonais Pangman was given the sword of an officer.

Neither Spencer nor Macdonell was brought to trial in Montreal. The Northwesters had learned the trick of arresting their opponents under the Canada Jurisdiction Act, and getting them out of the interior. They were concerned for no more.

Thus ended the régime of Miles Macdonell. He failed partly from the faults of his character, his blindness to obstacles in his path, and his inability to inspire trust and loyalty in his people ; from the self-confidence or inexperience which led him to make light of those institutions of Government which give cohesion to the people, and are a rallying point in the day of stress ; and partly from the inherent difficulty of his task, with a recalcitrant group like the North West Company at the centre of his government, refusing to recognize his authority. But it must be remembered to his credit that, so long as he faced only Wintering Partners of the North West Company who were near enough to perceive that he was acting in the interest of a suffering people, he achieved a somewhat spectacular success. He and his colony were really wrecked by the machine of the North West concern, too far away to be touched by pity for the settlers, bent only on beating the Hudson's Bay Company to its knees. How near it had come to success may be inferred from the power given to Lord Selkirk, when he left for Canada in 1815, to treat for an agreement with the North West Company conceding the right of transit through the Bay, but under the Charter ; necessary leases for the sites of their forts to be given at nominal rates. But its ruthless treatment of the colony inevitably stiffened the will of Lord Selkirk to persist with his plan and opened the way to retaliation—to meeting force with force.

After the Governor was taken prisoner it was hoped by the remnant of the settlers that they would be left in peace in their homes. Far from it. The half-breeds, led by servants of the North West Company, continued to harass them—stealing their horses and sniping at their houses. Finally the Indians, ever friendly, came to them to advise them to depart, and promised to escort them in safety to their craft. Boats, crowded with men and women and children to the number of about sixty, accompanied by their cattle, bore the fugitives through Lake Winnipeg to its north end, to a spot near the narrows opposite Mossy Point. Here an encampment was made and events awaited. John McLeod, trusted and respected by all, even the Indians and half-breeds, was left with two or three men to guard the crop. The half-breeds, under their leaders, servants of the North West Company, plundered the houses and burned them down. Not so the Indians. Peguis, their chief, wept over the ashes of the Governor's house. The Settlement was at an end. After the half-breeds left, silence reigned on the Red River save for the soughing of the wind in the grain.

5.—LORD SELKIRK'S COLONY, 1815–18—GOVERNOR SEMPLE—SEL-
    KIRK'S VISIT—THE COMMISSION INVESTIGATING THE DEEDS
    OF VIOLENCE

Colin Robertson, the former Northwester, who had been advising Lord Selkirk and the Hudson's Bay Company as to the shortcomings of their system and what the reorganization should be, had been chosen to bring up, as far as Lake Winnipeg, a great expedition to enter into the trade of Athabaska. At Lake of the Woods he had passed the Governor on his humiliating journey to Montreal. He hastened on to the Red River, where he walked " over the ruins of several of the houses which had been burned by the white savages." A blacksmith's shop, occupied by McLeod, was all that remained of the colony. " The [Métis] told me frankly that they had been paid by the N.W. Co. to drive away the Colonists." Robertson hastened on to what he calls Winnipeg Settlement, where the remnant was encamped. After seeing the Athabaska expedition away from the lake on its northern adventure, he brought the colonists back to their " Land of Promise " lying waste (19th August). He sent the faithful Lagimonière with letters to Lord Selkirk in Canada informing him of the re-establishment of the colony. The faithful messenger, for safety's sake, passed through the States to Fond du Lac and thence to Montreal—a remarkable feat for a lone voyageur.

Robertson, from his past sojourning in the country, knew the hard necessities of life in the West, understood how to meet them, and meet them with promptitude and with vigour. The crop of grains sown that spring was plentiful. All were set to the task of reaping it to the last grain. Fish was abundant in the river. Men were set to catch and to salt for the winter. It was early learned that buffalo were plentiful at Pembina. Servants were sent up to store pemmican unto the day of scarcity. Indians brought in supplies of dried meat. They were treated with the utmost friendliness, sold their store, and went away satisfied. Moreover, Robertson was master of the art of handling the half-breeds. Fond of extravagant dress and language, he strutted before them and played on their feelings as Duncan Cameron had done. Not a word was said of punishing them for their misdeeds. Did they know that the North West Company in Montreal was laying the blame for the destruction of the colony on them ? They replied indignantly that they had been paid by the concern to do it. Did they think the Northwesters truly cared for them ? The colony had bought their meat at a higher price and given fine blankets and goods, not beads and rum, in payment. Was it not all

for the good of the half-breeds, freeing them from the absolute control of the *bourgeois* ?   The excitable half-breeds responded to the
subtle argument and enlisted as hunters for the settlement.   Bostonais Pangman was to all appearances once more devoted to the
cause.

Robertson handled Duncan Cameron at Fort Gibraltar with equal
subtlety, for as a Northwester he had no more compunction over a
breach of the peace than had Duncan himself.   Moreover he knew,
as all the Northwesters did, that an attack, if it can succeed, is the
best of all defences.   Cameron was strutting as of old in the King's
uniform, impressing it upon the multitude that he was the King's
representative.   He must be plucked of his feathers.   When news
came in that the Northwesters of the Qu'Appelle River, under
Alexander Macdonell, had attacked John Richard MacKay in the
Hudson's Bay Company's post there Robertson decided to act.
His men seized Cameron when he was taking a quiet walk on the
prairie towards Fort Douglas.   Robertson himself took possession
of Fort Gibraltar (15th October).   This was done with no other
object than to teach the half-breeds that, in spite of his uniform,
Cameron was not the man he set himself up to be.   The Northwester in captivity proved a very meek bird, promised to order all
attacks on Fort Qu'Appelle to cease, and neither directly nor
indirectly to seduce the settlers from the colony.   He was forthwith given his liberty and his fort was returned to him unimpaired.
It is significant that he did not wear his uniform again for months.
Robertson was enough of a charlatan himself to know how to treat
the charlatanry of his opponent.   He wrote " Glittering Pomposity
has an amazing effect on the Freemen, the Métis [half-breeds], and
the Indians."   Of course the North West Company's agents in
Montreal published this episode as a gross act of violence perpetrated
on a mild Wintering Partner taking a quiet walk into the country.
(They said nothing of the attack on MacKay.)   But Robertson was
enough of a Northwester not to care what was said abroad of his
deeds in the interior.   In his mind his opponents must be beaten at
their own game.   His oft-repeated motto was, "When among wolves,
howl ! "

On 4th November a new band of settlers, eighty strong, reached
the colony.   William Semple came with them.   He held a commission
from the Governor and Committee as Governor-in-Chief of Rupert's
Land, and he was to take over the supervision of the colony.   He
thus superseded Robertson, but he wisely asked him to remain in
charge.   Semple was a straightforward, trustworthy, simple-minded
Englishman who in ordinary times would have made an excellent
ruler.   At first he willingly kept step with Robertson in the management of the colony.   As the ice began to set in, detachments of the
new settlers were sent up to Pembina to be near the food supply and
to take part in bringing it in.   It was fortunately a very mild winter.
" Mon. 8th Jan. 1816—Our cattle are feeding in the plains the same
as in the fall of the year," wrote Robertson.   The chief difficulty

encountered was that it was very difficult to bring the meat in without enough snow on the ground for sleds, for the horses of the Settlement had been made away with by the half-breeds during the troubles of the spring. None the less it was a tolerable winter for all. The half-breeds did not drive away the buffalo, and Mr. Cameron confined himself to the quiet trade of his post. Robertson took good care to pay no more than a flying visit to Fort Daer at the Pembina, and to be a faithful watch-dog. He kept his men busy rebuilding Fort Douglas and the Settlement. His chief concern was over the officers under him, for they persistently treated the Indians as a dirty nuisance, and the half-breeds as beneath the notice of a full-blooded Briton. They were too confident in their own strength to appreciate the subtle game Robertson was playing, on the assumption that to win the half-breeds was to protect the colony.

Robertson and Semple both looked with contempt on the type of religion represented by Mr. William Sutherland, the Scottish elder, who, in default of a Presbyterian minister, held prayer meetings in the Scottish homes, with much scripture reading and long prayers. Their view was that the community must have a Protestant clergyman, and for the French-Canadians a Catholic priest, but these two must not be too diverse in their practices, lest confusion should arise in the simple minds of the Indians and half-breeds. The Protestant clergyman should therefore be a high Anglican. Semple wrote to this effect to Mr. Benjamin Harrison, a member of the Company's Committee, who belonged to the religious coterie known as the Clapham Sect and took great interest in the religious policy of his Company. Harrison tried to induce a missionary society working among the Indians of North America to adopt the Red River as a field for its activity. The recommendation of Governor Semple probably had more to do than anything else with the Presbyterians not getting a minister of their own faith to take charge of them.

On 17th December Governor Semple left to devote himself to his wider duties as Governor-in-Chief. Robertson had suggested some plan of demanding from the North West Company at their fort on the Qu'Appelle River the guns of the colony, which had been taken to that post and placed in position. If Alexander Macdonell could be overcome, the colony would be safe, for the danger was that he would rally a large band and descend on it in the spring. Robertson waited eagerly for news, but the Governor contented himself with demanding the guns, and sat quiet under the refusal. Perhaps his force was not strong enough. If so, no demand should have been made, for his quiet accepting of the refusal added prestige to Alexander Macdonell in the eyes of the half-breeds. It is more probable that the Governor, new to the country, himself upright and law-abiding, could not reconcile himself to an attack that could not easily be justified before the law.

At the end of January Cameron approached Robertson with a view to a visit to Fort Qu'Appelle, protesting that his sole object was peace. He feared lest Robertson might seize him on the way, but he was told that he could go in perfect security. He returned on the 7th of March and soon was strutting about once more in his regimentals. A number of half-breeds from outlying districts began to come in to him, and many rumours of his ill intentions were afloat. To test these Robertson sent a servant to Fort Gibraltar to play the discontented. Cameron offered him a free passage to Montreal. Robertson, now convinced that the Northwester had broken his word of honour, was anxious to seize the winter express whose letters would reveal the enemy's plans. As a first step he seized Fort Gibraltar and made Cameron a prisoner. No one was hurt. On Cameron's desk lay a half-finished letter to James Grant of Fond du Lac, Lake Superior, requesting him to send a band of Indians in the spring to the Red River "as they would make a handsome pillage if they went cunningly about it." Robertson then seized the express and got further confirmation that the North West Company was plotting the destruction of the Settlement in the spring. Unfortunately the colony's officers at Fort Daer, without waiting for instructions, imitated Robertson and seized the North West Company's outpost opposed to them and manned by half-breeds under Bostonais Pangman. The act threw the half-breeds over on to the side of Cameron. The indignation of Robertson at this ill-considered aggression on the part of his subordinates was great. On 28th March Governor Semple returned to Fort Douglas and gave his approval to all that had been done by Robertson. It would have been well if he had continued to follow the lead of the subtle Canadian, but Semple was too upright and straightforward to really sympathize with his subordinate's tactics, and hesitated to accept plans which really meant war. In his indecision he began to consult his Council, which included Archibald McDonald, who had perpetrated the blunder at Pembina, and Bourke, an Irishman in charge of the store. (Robertson was not a member of the Council.) Both were opposed to Robertson as pampering those rascals the half-breeds, and thwarted his plans, but they had no alternative policy save to sit and wait for the enemy. Robertson was for sending his prisoner, Cameron, away at once to the post at Jack River while the going was good, but it took the Governor long to decide that the plan was wise. Meanwhile Cameron was getting into communication with the half-breeds and winning their sympathy. Robertson foresaw the plan of the Northwesters to march down on the colony and harass it, as the year before, into leaving, but could not bring Semple to his view. On 13th March Alexander Macdonell wrote to Cameron, the letter falling into Robertson's hands. "A storm is gathering in the north ready to burst on the rascals who deserve it. Little do they know their situation. Last year was but a joke. The new nation under their leaders are coming forward to clear their native soil of intruders and assassins." The clouds gathered in May. On the 12th Alexander Macdonell and a band of his servants surprised the Hudson's Bay Company's brigade from Fort Qu'Appelle, when in difficulties at a rapid, and seized all the pemmican necessary for the English Company's Athabaska brigade. Robertson proposed an immediate counter-attack with forty men and two field-pieces to recover the provisions. He would have tried to surprise the Northwesters at some difficult point in the river, to retrieve the misfortune. Semple now showed the weakness of his character. First he would lead the expedition himself. Then Robertson was to go. Finally he decided to wait for the enemy at the Settlement. Meanwhile the Northwesters pillaged Brandon House on their way, carrying off its furs. Semple and his Council were true Britons, drifting into a war relying upon their strength, but without any clear strategical policy for the day of action. Robertson refused to be held responsible for the coming disaster, and prepared to leave the Settlement in high dudgeon. His last advice was to dismantle Gibraltar and concentrate the colony's forces in Fort Douglas—advice which was taken. The fort was demolished in four days. On 11th June he passed down the river.

The plan of the Northwesters was to pass by Fort Douglas and concentrate on the Red River below. Here they could be joined by the brigades of the north. Half-breeds marched by a route entirely out of sight to Frog Plain. The North West Company's servants, also half-breeds, under its clerk Cuthbert Grant (for the partner judiciously remained behind so as not to be in any fray that might arise), followed a track within sight of the fort. On 17th and 18th June Indians came in to warn the Governor that he would be attacked. On the afternoon of 19th June a man in the watch-tower announced that the half-breeds were in sight. They could be seen on horseback passing along the plains on a course leading from the Assiniboine to the Red River diagonally towards the lots of the settlers. The Governor said : " We must go out and meet these people. Let twenty men [volunteers] follow." Two settlers suggested that they should take the three-pounder with them. The Governor replied that he was not going to fight, but would ask the Northwesters what they meant to do. Negotiations, when the day of parleying was past ! The men snatched up their muskets and what ammunition there was to hand—some two rounds, some ten. The little band passed down the Settlement road and, as they went, met settlers fleeing in alarm to the fort. Three-quarters of a mile down, at Seven Oaks, they saw people on horseback near a clump of woods. They diverged towards it, only to find that the band was larger than first estimated, and all done up with war-paint. The Governor ordered a halt and sent for the field-pieces (belated wisdom surely), but impatient at delay he was guilty of the folly of ordering an advance. He soon stood face to face with a body of mounted half-breeds some sixty strong in war-paint, extended in the form of a crescent. Cuthbert Grant, the half-breed son of the early Northwester, was in command. The Governor extended his line. The half-breeds advanced. The Governor's forces retired a short distance. A French-Canadian, François-Firmin Boucher, rode up and asked the Governor what he wanted. " What do you want ? "

was the reply. To this Boucher answered, "We want our fort." The Governor said, "Go to your fort." Boucher replied, "Why did you destroy our fort, you damned rascal." The Governor laid hold of the bridle of Boucher's horse, saying, "Scoundrel, do you tell me so ? " At this Boucher slipped down from his saddle. The half-breeds took this as the signal for action and began shooting. A first shot instantly killed a Lieutenant Holte at Semple's side. A second wounded the Governor himself. He cried, "Do what you can to care for yourselves," but the men for the most part had crowded round him and were being shot down. Some cried for mercy, but in vain. Four effected an escape and two were spared because of old friendships. The Governor, five officers, and fourteen men were killed. It does not appear that even at the last Governor Semple had any plan of action. He went out on the spur of the moment with but a portion of his men—apparently intending no more than an interview. As he came face to face with danger he sent back for his cannon, but even then did not wait for it to come. He fell a victim to his British courage, and to his equally British aversion to planning for the future.

The Northwesters represented the "massacre of Seven Oaks" as a battle in which the Governor was attempting to seize their provision carts. The carts are nowhere mentioned as in sight, and Boucher's demand for the fort indicates that that was not the case. The evidence rather shows that there was no firing on the Governor's side. The Northwesters, however, claimed that one of their men was killed. The settlers averred that the Governor cautioned them not to fire without his command—which was never given. The North-westers asserted that the two first shots came from the Governor's party. The settlers bore evidence that the only two shots fired went off accidentally some time before, when they were still on the march. It is scarcely necessary to reconcile these conflicting testimonies. It is certain that the Governor Semple had drifted into the struggle without the precaution of a plan of action. He fell the victim of his own unpreparedness—of his strange disregard of a simple principle that the best of all defences is a carefully devised attack. The half-breeds knew better and had no scruples. They attacked.

On the 21st the colonists, now in charge of Alexander Macdonell, the sheriff, once more took to their boats and left for the north. On the way down A. N. McLeod, in the ridiculous capacity of Justice of the Peace, tried to induce Macdonell to take an oath not to return to the colony. The settlers passed through Lake Winnipeg to an encampment at the spot occupied by them in the previous year. It stood on the right bank as the narrows at Mossy Point were approached. Once more the silence of the prairie reigned on the Red River.

The proprietors of the North West Company loudly disclaimed all responsibility for what they called the Battle of Seven Oaks, but their deeds reveal the truth convincingly. Cuthbert Grant, the leader of the half-breeds, was in their employ. After the massacre John

Pritchard, now of the colony, besought him to have compassion on the women and children in Fort Douglas. Grant replied that an attack would be made on it that night, and if a single shot were fired, it would be the signal for the destruction of every soul. Macdonell, the sheriff, went to Frog Plain to surrender the fort to Grant, who immediately took possession. Alexander Macdonell of the North West Company, the schemer behind the scenes at Portage la Prairie, and the gentlemen at his side " all shouted with joy " when the news reached them. Macdonell rode off and lodged himself in Fort Douglas as possessor. The half-breeds who took part in the shooting were rewarded for their bloody deeds by the proprietors of the North West Company assembled at Fort William under the chairmanship of William M'Gillivray. True, the destruction of the colony was the work of the half-breeds, but the Northwesters were the prime movers in the conspiracy, enjoyed the fruit of the bloody deed, and rewarded its perpetrators.

LORD SELKIRK IN CANADA AND IN HIS COLONY

The next phase in the history of the Red River Settlement saw the intervention of Lord Selkirk in person, and of the Imperial and Canadian Governments. Selkirk from the outset was not unaware of the danger which the colony might have to face. As has been seen, he had sought the approval of the Imperial Government for his schemes, and he believed he had received it. He had even secured certain arms from His Majesty's Ordnance Department to defend the settlers in case of an American incursion—doubtless he also thought in the face of the natives and the North West Company. These were a part of the arms captured by the settlers and the North West Company in the last days of Miles Macdonell's rule (May 1815). In February of that year his lordship was aware of the precarious position in which the Settlement stood, and on the 18th the Hudson's Bay Company at his instance petitioned the Imperial Government, in the person of Lord Bathurst, the Colonial Minister, for a small military force to protect the colonists. The suggestion was a small party of ten or twelve artillerymen with one or two non-commissioned officers. These might be drawn from Prairie du Chien on the Mississippi, a western post then being evacuated. It was, of course, too late to do anything that might have saved Miles Macdonell, but it might have prevented the disaster in which Governor Semple bit the dust.

In that the Crown had entrusted the country to the care of the Hudson's Bay Company, it would seem natural that the Ministers should have consulted with the Company and come to its support. This course, as will be seen, was twice taken by the Government in the middle of the nineteenth century. But the most influential personage in the Colonial Office, the Under-Secretary Henry Goulburn, was bound to the agents of the North West Company in

London by intimate ties. No doubt he advised to the contrary.
Supposing that the Government were in doubt of the reality of the
situation as depicted by the Company, it would have been natural
to seek reliable information. An officer might have been sent out
to the actual field to report to His Majesty's Minister, as was done
in the case of Major Caldwell in 1848, but that seems never to have
been contemplated. What was actually done, no doubt at Goulburn's instance, was to ask information of the Governor-General
of Canada. On 18th March, Lord Bathurst forwarded to Sir Gordon
Drummond, the Governor-General, the communications from the
Hudson's Bay Company and Lord Selkirk, with instructions to make
inquiries as to the truth of the representations and, if he considered
them well founded, to furnish the protection necessary. Of course
the Governor-General had nothing to do with the Red River, and
no information was procurable save from the North West Company,
the very party at whose hand, as Selkirk feared, the colony was
doomed to suffer. Colin Robertson says that the agents of that
Company were so much in the public eye in Canada, were so hospitable to visitors, and had made such a show of public spirit during
the war of 1812, that people were wholly unconscious of their
ways in the Upper Country. William M'Gillivray himself had
brought the Company to the assistance of the Government so conspicuously in the relief of Michilimackinac, that he had been made
a Legislative Councillor in 1814 as a reward. It would, therefore,
seem the most natural thing to the Governor-General to ask, confidentially, the heads of the North West Company, whom he knew,
as he said in his reply to Bathurst, to be " persons of the utmost
integrity and respectability," what were the facts of the case. His
communication was no surprise to M'Gillivray, for the Northwesters
were kept well informed by no less a person than the Under-Secretary
of State himself. Goulburn had transmitted a copy of the Hudson's
Bay Company's request to the agents of the North West Company
in London in February, and this was duly forwarded to Montreal.
M'Gillivray, in answering the Governor - General's Secretary,
J. Harvey, repudiated Selkirk's charge " with feelings of indignation." It constituted a calumny. The facts were to the contrary ;
during the first year of the colony the North West Company had
really come to the rescue of

the innocent people who had been enticed from their homes by [Lord Selkirk's]
golden but delusive promises, and had saved them from starvation. . . . I
therefore declare that I am an utter stranger to any instigation or any determination of the Indian nations to make any attack on the settlement in
question ; but I will not take upon me to say that serious quarrels may not
happen between the settlers and the nations, whose hunting ground they
have taken possession of. . . . The arrogance and violent conduct of Lord
Selkirk's Agents [meaning, of course, Macdonell and Spencer the Sheriff]
cannot well fail to produce such a result as the quarrels above mentioned.

This letter was written on June 24, 1815, four days after Alexander
Mackenzie, Simon Fraser, and the rest of the Wintering Partners

of the Company passed down the Red River in triumph with Miles Macdonell a prisoner, arrested under the warrant of A. N. McLeod, another partner, for burglary and robbery, although the pemmican in question was to be paid for, and had been paid for under an agreement with the Wintering Partners of the North West Company. It was written about the time the friendly Indians were escorting the remnant of the settlers to their boats for the north, and when the half-breeds in the pay of the North West Company were burning down Fort Douglas and the rest of the buildings. On 16th August Sir Gordon Drummond replied to Lord Bathurst, enclosing M'Gillivray's letter and stating that it was impracticable to send a detachment of soldiers to Red River with the necessary provisions ; further, it might involve the country in an Indian war ; and he was " apprehensive that the most mischievous consequences are likely to arise from the conduct and character of the individual whom Lord Selkirk has selected for his agent, who styles himself a governor, and from whose intercourse with the persons in the service of the North West Company it is in vain to look for the spirit of moderation and conciliation." Finally, Henry Goulburn for Lord Bathurst, replying on 14th October to a second request of the Hudson's Bay Company for military protection, reported the conclusions of the Governor-General of Canada ; no force could be sent, and, moreover, the colony was already dispersed. The Hudson's Bay Company had hoped that the seizure of arms really belonging to the Royal Ordnance, as an offence against the Crown, might rouse the Government to some action. Goulburn merely said that the arms would now be collected. They were not. They were taken upstream, as has been seen, to fortify the Qu'Appelle post.

In the autumn of 1815 Lord and Lady Selkirk arrived in Canada to organize the forces of the Hudson's Bay Company, and to safeguard the destinies of the colony. The complaints of the Company against the violent proceedings of the Northwesters which had ended in the dispersion of the settlers, and a renewed petition for protection for the colony which had been re-established, so far aroused Lord Bathurst that on January 3, 1816, he sent a dispatch to Sir Gordon Drummond desiring him " without loss of time to inculcate upon the servants of the two companies the necessity of abstaining from a repetition of those outrages which have been latterly so frequent a cause of complaint, and convey to them the determination of His Majesty's government, to punish with the utmost severity any person who may be found to have caused or instigated proceedings so fatal to the tranquillity of the possessions in that quarter, and so disgraceful to the British name." Except for the implication that one company was as bad as the other, this dispatch was all to the good. Sir Gordon Drummond replied on 21st April that he would not fail to impress the matter upon the two companies. On 25th April he wrote to Lord Selkirk in almost identical terms with Lord Bathurst's dispatch, warning him that the Government would punish " with the utmost severity, any person who may be found to have caused or instigated proceedings so fatal to the tranquillity of the possessions in that quarter and so disgraceful to the British name." It may be assumed that a similar letter was sent to William M'Gillivray. Selkirk protested that his instructions to his servants had always been in keeping with the Governor's letter, and that he could prove amply that the outrages had all been on one side.

On his arrival in Canada Selkirk heard of the dispersion of the settlers, and then again, through the letters brought by Lagimonière, of its re-establishment. He immediately sent the faithful voyageur back with word that he would personally come to the colony in the spring with every means he could obtain for its protection, but A. N. McLeod at Fort William, Justice of the Peace and representative of the majesty of law and order in the Indian territories, issued an order to certain Indians to intercept the faithful voyageur. Lagimonière was robbed of his letters and his canoe, and was beaten in a shocking manner by the Indians, who received $100 from Justice of the Peace McLeod for their vicious work.

In November Selkirk had petitioned Sir Gordon Drummond for a body of soldiers to be stationed in the colony. Sir Gordon adhered to his former decision to the contrary, but gave his lordship permission to take up a small personal escort at his own expense ; he also agreed to issue a commission as Justice of the Peace to his lordship. When Selkirk received word that hostilities would be renewed against the colony, he repeated his request for protection for it in the most pressing manner, offering to give proofs of his fears, and himself to pay the cost of the troops. All was in vain. He was told that he might have no more than an escort, and that at his own expense. Selkirk, now without hope of either the Imperial or the Canadian Government taking steps to maintain law and order on the Red River, turned to devices which would protect the colony, though at his own cost. Certain regiments which had taken part in the war of 1812 were being reduced. Of the De Meuron regiment some two hundred had remained in Canada. Some eighty of these and four of the officers entered into an agreement with his lordship. They were to be paid for taking the boats of his expedition up to Red River. When there they were to be offered land for settlement. If they did not choose to take it, they were to have a free passage back to Montreal or by Hudson Bay to Europe. Some twenty of the De Watteville regiment and a few of the Glengarry Fencibles entered into a similar agreement. They were ex-soldiers, and—as Selkirk's *engagés* in the first place, and possibly later as soldier-settlers—they would afford a trained body of men capable of defending the colony. Selkirk gave them arms, as he had done with his other settlers. He informed the Government of Canada of his action. There were no legal grounds on which any could object. This large and experienced force left with Selkirk for the Upper Country in the spring of 1817.

Moreover, arrangements were made for a group of French-

Canadian settlers to take up land on the Red River and strengthen the colony.

While Selkirk was thus providing for the military protection of his colony, he was busied about many other necessary measures. One of the greatest advantages of the colony was that, when the settlers arrived at the bald prairies on the bank of the Red River, they found no forest standing between them and the soil, but could at once till the ground. Yet a grievous disadvantage lay in its isolated position ; it was very difficult to provide them with cattle. Some cattle had been ready to come with the first party, but Miles Macdonell had left them behind for lack of means of providing water for the voyage. A second consignment had been killed by the unsympathetic William Auld at York Factory, on the ground that he needed fresh meat to save his men from scurvy. In the autumn of 1815 cattle had been forwarded from Fort Albany to Osnaburg on Lac Seul, but at the break-up of the colony in 1815 they were retained at the post, and a part of them fell a prey to the Indians. Owen Keveny, who had brought them thus far, was arrested under a warrant issued by a North West proprietor, and was murdered by a North West Company's servant, Charles Reinhard, who was ostensibly taking him to Montreal for trial. Reinhard was tried at Quebec and sentenced to be hanged. Adam and Eve and their bull calf, and the bull and two cows bought of the Northwesters, were all the cattle that had actually been in the colony, and the three bulls in succession had been drowned or killed. Selkirk had hoped that the farms on Red River might be stocked with a cross between this little herd and the buffalo. This would give a speedy solution of the difficulty, but the European bull would not look at the shaggy cow of the plains. His lordship had also considered the possibility of sending sheep and cattle from his colony of Baldoon in Upper Canada to the Red River Settlement, but the way was long and none knew it, and the dangers from the rivers and the Indians were countless. He was now searching for some party willing to enter into a contract to deliver a herd on the Red River. He would give $4,000 for fifty young heifers and $1,000 commission to the agent securing them. Ewes one year old also were wanted. His lordship was not slack in this pressing matter.

At the same time Selkirk was following up the suggestion of Governor Semple that a Catholic priest should be sent out to shepherd the French-Canadians and half-breeds of the Settlement, a policy desirable on religious grounds as a means of reconciling the French freemen and half-breeds to the colony. Miles Macdonell had already broached the matter to Monseigneur Duplessis, Bishop of Quebec. On April 4, 1816, Selkirk wrote to his lordship offering to co-operate with him in sending out a missionary to be permanently resident on the Red River. The bishop replied cordially, expressing his desire to bring under his pastoral care the poor people of every tribe in the immense country between Lake Superior and Hudson Bay. He proposed to avail himself of the free passage offered, and to send a missionary out in the spring on a voyage of inquiry. A permanent mission could be established later.

The winter spent by Lord and Lady Selkirk in Canada must have been far from a happy one, apart from the gross indifference of the Government to all pleas for protection for the colony. Canadian society centred around the wealthy Northwesters, who entertained the magnates of Montreal, officers in the Government and army, and visitors from abroad, on a lavish scale. It was not in the nature of things that Montreal society should believe the stories of violent deeds in the Upper Country reflecting on their genial hosts. They would readily believe all that was told across the table of the ways of Lord Selkirk as a land speculator and as the directing force in the Hudson's Bay Company. The intervention of Lord Selkirk in person, with the prestige of his position, the glamour of wealth, and especially the gracious ways of Lady Selkirk, would insinuate it into the minds at least of the younger set that there was possibly another side to the matter. The retaining of a distinguished legal firm, Messrs. Maitland, Gordon & Auldjo, as agents of the Hudson's Bay Company gave another point of contact with the Canadian people. Up to this time the Press had been wholly on the side of the Northwesters. Indeed, their whole case was now being put before the public in a series of articles from the pen of " Mercator " in the *Montreal Gazette*. The illegality of the Hudson's Bay Company's Charter, and of Lord Selkirk's Grant, of his colony, and of the office of Governor; the justice of the claim of Canada to the North-West in virtue of its occupation by La Vérendrye and other Frenchmen, his successors; and latterly in virtue of the operations of the North West Company in a country left wholly vacant by the English Company—all this and much more was acutely argued and enforced by the astute " Mercator." A few faint voices were heard on the other side.

These preliminary skirmishes were to be followed by a battle of books carried on by men of great calibre on either side. Before he left England Selkirk was busy with his *Sketch of the British Fur Trade in North America with observations relative to the North West Company of Montreal*. As might be expected, it is more " observations relative to the North West Company " than a sketch of the British fur trade. Partisan as it is in tone, and at times inaccurate in its geography and its dates, it is the most truthful and most overwhelming of all the pamphlets called forth by the exciting struggle. Selkirk devotes himself to making public the corrupt and violent deeds in the Upper Country of the coterie of magnates who stood so high in the esteem of Canada—the dishonesty of counting the dollar at Fort William at half its value in Montreal, of paying the servants of the Company only in goods valued at 100 per cent. plus cost more at the rendezvous than in Montreal; the violence of the Wintering Partners towards free traders who, as British citizens, had as much right in the country as any one else, illustrated by an account of the ill deeds of the late Duncan M'Gillivray himself; the bloodshed in the days of the XY Company, culminating in the murder of James King, and the passing of the Canada Jurisdiction Act; the equally bloody deeds of the Northwesters since that day, the object being to drive the Hudson's Bay Company out of business; and finally the knavish use of the system of Justice of the Peace of the Indian country under the Canada Jurisdiction Act, by which the Wintering Partners were arresting their opponents in the name of the King, hustling them out of the country without any intention of prosecuting them before an impartial tribunal—all the dirty linen of the North West Company is hung out on the line for the gaze of the public. The pamphlet was published in 1816. It is an eloquent testimony to its essential truthfulness that the Northwesters never attempted a direct reply.

On the other side, the potent pen of Doctor Strachan, in many ways the most influential mind in Upper Canada, was busy preparing to expose Lord Selkirk's dealings as a land speculator to the astonishment of the country. The proud doctor and his coterie had looked askance at the large grant of land given to Lord Selkirk for his colony at Baldoon, and were not tempted to minimize its failure and the sufferings of its settlers. So far Strachan was on familiar ground, but in truth he does not say much about the matter. He was, of course, quite unfamiliar—at least when he wrote the main part of his pamphlet, *A letter to the Right Honourable the Earl of Selkirk on his Settlement at the Red River, near the Hudson's Bay*—with the situation in the North-West. When he wrote his *Postscript*, Red River settlers had been brought to Canada by the North West Company, and he was in the way of having more intimate knowledge from the tales of the suffering people. As the doctor had married into a family connected with the fur trade, and as the main part of his pamphlet is devoted to a document in circulation among the Northwesters and nowhere else, it must be assumed that he undertook the task under their influence. Indeed, after the Union of 1821 William M'Gillivray wrote to him thanking him for his "steady" support through the struggle. When Selkirk first assumed the duty of colonizing Red River he seemed, Dr. Strachan asserted, to have shrunk from taking on his sole shoulders the cost of the undertaking. He therefore drew up a Prospectus in the approved style of the land speculator, calculated to win the assistance of a number of fairly well-to-do people in the parts of Britain and Ireland from which he hoped to draw emigrants. These were invited to join with him in an enterprise which was sure to be profitable to all concerned—not immediately, but in the end. Strachan riddled the attractions held out in this prospectus to the hypothetical investors. He denied that the title of the Hudson's Bay Company and Lord Selkirk to the land on Red River was valid. Indeed, from the Forks of Red River south the grant was really American territory, he asserted audaciously. On this ground he denies that the settlement would be a British colony. Lord Selkirk was founding a colony which would fall into the lap of the Americans. He denied that the land was as good as, or of value equal to, that of Upper Canada or Nova Scotia. " The price of land to the settlers is a shameful imposition." He emphasized the difficulties of reaching Red River from Hudson Bay and from Canada by publishing a list of the respective portages and distances. The danger of massacres at the hand of the Indian was dwelt upon. The pamphlet concludes : " Let those of my fellow subjects who are determined to brave a foreign climate in quest of an independency, for the sake of their children, proceed to the Canadas, under the protection of the Government, and avoid land-jobbers as their greatest enemies." The *Postscript* is made up of a number of affidavits from settlers, who had abandoned the Red River, enumerating their sufferings and grievances. Coming from such a trusted personage as Doctor Strachan, the pamphlet was indeed calculated to damage Selkirk's reputation—so much so that the Northwesters published a Canadian edition and spread it abroad. Selkirk never answered it directly, but in the next pamphlet issued on his side, *Statement respecting the Earl of Selkirk's Settlement of Kildonan upon the Red River*, published in 1817, in the June edition, which he corrected, it was stated that the prospectus was " neither advertised, nor published, nor in any shape publicly circulated. It formed part of a sketch of which the Earl of Selkirk had a few copies printed . . . for private circulation among a very limited number of his friends, whom he wished to consult about the measures he was then entering into."

Doctor Strachan's pamphlet enables us to see the light in which Lord Selkirk stood in the eyes of contemporary Canada. He was a land-jobber, and his philanthropic schemes of colonization were simply devices by which to increase the value of the land in his hands and to amass wealth for himself and his family. Canada also saw in his lordship the principal director of the Hudson's Bay Company (though he never was on its Committee), organizing it against the North West Company, and planning a series of posts in the Athabaska region, regarded by the Northwesters as their sacred precinct. With these two features of Selkirk so prominent in the mind of Canada, official and unofficial, the finer—the philanthropic and patriotic—lines of his portrait were wholly lost to sight.

In the spring of 1816 Lord Selkirk and his De Meuron soldier-settlers were making their way towards Red River Settlement. Miles Macdonell with an advance party was at the mouth of the River Winnipeg when word reached him of the " massacre of Seven Oaks." He returned in all haste to apprise Lord Selkirk of the terrible event, and met him at the Sault on 24th July. All his lordship's plans had been laid to proceed to the colony by American territory, through Fond du Lac across to the sources of Red River and downstream to the Settlement. This route offered the advantage of avoiding a clash on the main water-route used by the North West Company. The first boats had left already, but the whole plan of travel was changed forthwith. Selkirk determined to go to Fort William and have the instigators of the destruction of his colony arrested. He tried to get John Askin at Drummond's Isle and Charles Ermatinger at the Sault, Justices of the Peace for Upper Canada, to accompany him and to issue and serve the necessary warrants. Neither was willing to face the difficult, and what they probably thought, the dirty task. Selkirk determined to act on his own authority as Justice of the Peace. On the worst interpretation he was not acting otherwise than the Northwester A. N. McLeod had done before him in the matter of Miles Macdonell. Retaliation had begun. By the most favourable view he was seeking to bring men whom he thought guilty of a criminal conspiracy to justice. He forgot, however, that it ill became him to be prosecutor and judge at one and the same time. How far he intended at the outset to seize Fort William by way of reprisal will appear from his actual doings. On 12th August, with his escort of soldiers of the King from Drummond's Isle and his soldier-settlers, he passed up the Kaministikwia in the face of Fort William and camped about a mile above, but on the opposite side. He forthwith wrote to William M'Gillivray, asking on what grounds John Pritchard, Peter C. Pambrun, and others, taken after the massacre of Seven Oaks, were held prisoners. M'Gillivray artfully replied they were not prisoners and sent them across. They told the tale of the massacre and embodied their evidence in sworn affidavits. On the ground of these, the next day his lordship issued a warrant against William M'Gillivray for treason and conspiracy, and for being accessory to murder, and sent John M'Nab and another, duly sworn in as constables, to effect his arrest. M'Gillivray quietly surrendered. After finishing a letter which he was in the act of writing, he crossed to Lord Selkirk's tent, accompanied by Kenneth Mackenzie, joint agent with him, and by John McLoughlin of the post at Nipigon, who were to give bail. To their surprise, these men too were arrested on a warrant already prepared against them. M'Gillivray asked to be released on bail. This his lordship denied him, on the ground of the seriousness of the charge. The constables were then sent across with warrants against a number of the remaining proprietors. They were found assembled at the gate, and refused to submit to arrest until M'Gillivray should be released. Captain Proteus d'Orsonnens of the De Meurons, with a body of twenty-five of his men, was in a boat at the riverside waiting to support. At the call of the constables he promptly marched his men up and stayed the Northwesters as they were closing the gates of the fort, thus resisting arrest. He pushed his way into the fort. A bugle sounded within was taken as a signal for the rest of the soldiers at Lord Selkirk's camp to come up. Captain Frederick Matthey led the De Meurons across, and possession was taken of two cannon. Although there were two hundred men or more in the place, its capture was effected without bloodshed. However, it was not occupied by Selkirk's party that night. Armed with a warrant for the purpose, the officers sealed up the papers of the North West Company and placed the arms of the fort under lock and key. The Wintering Partners under arrest, Alexander Mackenzie and Simon

Fraser, who, it will be remembered, carried off Miles Macdonell in 1815, and John McDonald and Hugh McGillis, were taken over to Selkirk's tent. They gave his lordship their word of honour to offer no obstruction to the executing of the law, and to refrain from all hostile measures. They then returned to their apartments and had the freedom of the guarded fort. That night, however, some of the seals of the desks containing papers were broken, ammunition was secreted outside the fort, and a canoe loaded with arms and ammunition was sent up the river, while a quantity of arms was concealed on the farm. On information given by a half-breed, Selkirk issued a search warrant, and four cases of guns, eight or more in each, were found. Also forty fowling-pieces, recently primed and loaded, were brought to light, and powder secreted in a swamp. Selkirk took precautions accordingly. The servants of the North West Company were made to camp on the opposite side of the river, and his soldiers occupied the ground between the fort and the river bank. Further investigation revealed thirty bales of furs from the Hudson's Bay Company's Fort Qu'Appelle, carried off by the Northwesters, their original marking " Q.R." re-marked " R.R." Many bundles of the letters which had been sealed up had been burned during the night in the kitchen fireplace. Much incriminating material, however, still remained. A list of the half-breed participants in the " massacre of Seven Oaks " showed that thirteen had received clothing by way of reward, and bales of clothing were found ready for dispatch bearing the names of thirteen who had not yet been rewarded. Selkirk took possession of bundles of papers unopened and of the bales as evidence for future use. In the Council room there was found later a copy of the letter from Justice of the Peace A. R. McLeod to James Grant of Fond du Lac inciting him to seize Selkirk's letters on the way to Red River in the hand of Lagimonière.

On 17th August, Selkirk wrote to the new Governor-General, Sir John Coape Sherbrooke, and to the Attorney-General, forwarding copies of the warrants issued, and of the affidavits, whose evidence, he felt satisfied, justified his course of action.

On the 18th William M'Gillivray and the other proprietors, with the exception of Daniel Mackenzie, were sent off for Montreal as prisoners. Struck by a storm, the overloaded canoe was swamped and Kenneth Mackenzie with five others was drowned. Selkirk decided to winter at Fort William and hand the fort over to the Government when called on so to do. So far, the partisans of Selkirk may say, his lordship had played the part of Justice of the Peace with dignity and in due form.

But issues other than those of Justice were coming up. The last of the North West Company's canoes for the interior, those for the Red River and Bas de la Rivière, were ready to leave. His lordship refused to allow them to proceed on the ground that they would only be used to equip rebels against the Government. Then, too, he was in possession of a large body of property belonging to the rival company. He appropriated what he needed at the moment, keeping, however, a careful account of it. But he considered the furs, said to be worth £100,000, as security against the loss which had been inflicted on his colony by the Northwesters, and against the pemmican and furs belonging to the Hudson's Bay Company seized on the Qu'Appelle and Assiniboine rivers. Moreover, Selkirk felt that he was now in a position to force the North West Company into agreeing to submit the whole question of mutual injuries and losses to arbitration, the two parties agreeing to restitution as the arbitrators should decide. Such an agreement, to be binding, should have been submitted to William M'Gillivray, the legal agent of the North West Company, but that redoubtable Northwester was now on the way to Montreal. Selkirk submitted it to James Chesholme, J. G. McTavish, and Jasper Vandersluys, who were mere paid clerks. They declined to agree to the proposal. He, however, made the agreement with Daniel Mackenzie, one of the Proprietors, whom he had kept with him more or less in confinement, probably because he offered to turn King's evidence. Mackenzie had bought up all the supplies at Michilimackinac in the hope of stalling Selkirk's expedition. He now entered into an agreement by which he proposed, on behalf of the North West Company, to sell these and other supplies to Lord Selkirk, who was in real difficulties over the provisions necessary for his party. His lordship accordingly took over the stores. The agreement was, of course, illegal, for Mackenzie had no power to act for his company. Under cover of another agreement, Lord Selkirk took possession of the cattle and sheep at Fort William, intending to forward them to the Red River Settlement.

All these proceedings put Lord Selkirk in a very dubious light, which was accentuated by the actions of his officers, which must have been in keeping with their instructions. On 10th September, D'Orsonnens set out with a body of men for Rainy Lake, and a month later seized the North West Company's post there, making, however, an inventory of the goods. Soon Miles Macdonell joined him. The ex-soldier and the ex-Governor planned a stroke for the recovery of the Red River. In difficulties for transport, they took such horses as were to be had at the captured post. These being insufficient, they shod the cattle and hitched them to the sleds weighed down with two small cannon and the provisions. At the beginning of the second week of December the diminutive expedition was away, leaving five soldiers to guard the fort. It consisted, according to Miles Macdonell's Journal of " 1 Govr., 1 Capt., 2 Subs . . . 25 soldiers and 10 Canadians, making a total of 38 effective men with 5 horses, 2 canon, ammunition and provisions." The additional transport consisted of " 1 bull, 2 cows and a 2 year old heifer." One ox strained itself on the ice and was killed for meat. The little bull was hitched in its place. The course lay down the Rainy River to Lake of the Woods, then westward to the War Road of the Sioux leading to Lac Roseau. Strengthened to sixty men by the adhesion of Indians, the force went down the Roseau River which enters the Red below Pembina. Cutting across the plains, it surprised Fort Daer, held by a few French-Canadians, on the last day of the year. On the northward march to the Forks a wild blizzard struck the force. All the animals gave out but a cow, which broke a road for the rest through the snow-banks. On 10th January Fort Douglas, then in the hands of " the enemy," was taken in the early hours of the morning. " Had our flag hoisted at sunrise " is Macdonell's proud entry. Archibald McLellan, the Northwester in charge, who was implicated in the murder of Owen Keveny, was kept as a prisoner. The cattle were demobilized, and, so to say, returned to civil life to form another beginning of a herd for the colony, but through the carelessness of the service they were left unwatered and the all-important bull died out on the plains. A servant, William Laidlaw, went on and seized the North West Company's fort Bas de la Rivière Winipic, where some of Selkirk's property was found. When provisions began to be scarce Peguis arrived with a supply of meat, pleased to see the land once more in the hands of his old friend Macdonell, while the faithful Lagimonière was at hand to continue his office as dispatch-bearer.

The Northwesters naturally took the seizure of Fort William and all these posts as simply acts of reprisal. When the news reached Athabaska, they seized Fort Wedderburn on the lake, and the posts at Lesser Slave Lake, Ile-à-la-Crosse, and Reindeer Lake, and A. N. McLeod, now in those parts, threatened to march down in the spring to capture the Hudson's Bay Company's posts on the Saskatchewan, and finally to recapture Red River.

It was also natural that Selkirk's action in seizing the property, and especially the furs of the North West Company at Fort William, and this military raid, which placed Fort Douglas and the posts of his rivals in his hand, should be interpreted in Canada in the light of retaliation—as a resort by his lordship to brute force and violence. From his own point of view, however, his lordship was thoroughly justified. He had been able to secure protection for his colony from neither the Imperial nor the Colonial Government. Had he remained passive his colony would have been dispersed. The military expedition under D'Orsonnens regained possession of the site of the colony and retrieved the disaster of Seven Oaks. With their homes in the possession of Selkirk's soldiers, and his lordship about to arrive with his party of soldier-settlers, the faith of the settlers in the future of the colony revived. Venture-some farmers came south over the ice of Lake Winnipeg to be in time for the sowing in spring. They were followed by the rest of the settlers and, when Lord Selkirk arrived in the course of the summer, he found his colony reconstituted and the fields promising an abundant harvest. His swift stroke had saved the day.

After the massacre of Seven Oaks, Selkirk had urged Sir John Sherbrooke to appoint a commission of inquiry, but in vain. Curiously enough, the Governor and Council, who could not be moved to action by the untimely death of some twenty British citizens at Red River, acted promptly when the North West Company's rendezvous was seized by Lord Selkirk in the name of Justice, and without the loss of a drop of blood. It was decided to withdraw all the commissions of the Justices of Peace given to the partisans on either side, and to appoint " two persons of influence and impartiality to be sole magistrates of that territory and to proceed thither to exercise their functions and with further powers, as commissioners of inquiry, to mediate between the two companies." An attempt was made to find the men in Upper Canada, in the hope that such would be impartial, but without result. Finally, Colonel W. B. Colt-man, a member of the Executive Council, at which he would from time to time rub shoulders with William M'Gillivray, was chosen, and a Major J. Fletcher was associated with him. These men made an attempt to reach Lake Superior that very autumn (1816), but it proved too late to travel. Their instructions must be carefully noted in order to judge how far they attempted to carry out the important duties imposed on them :

> Being invested with the powers of magistrates within that territory, you will possess and exercise the functions of that important office . . . to their fullest extent, by inquiry into all offences which have been or may be committed in that territory, by arresting and securing in due form of law the perpetrators thereof and by transmitting them to this province for trial. Receiving herewith also a commission of inquiry, investing you with extensive special powers, you will, as therein enjoined, diligently investigate the causes and circumstances, and take every legal measure to prevent the repetition of those dissensions which have arisen, and the outrages which have been committed against the King's peace in the aforesaid territories.

The commission was to be one of action, to arrest and send to trial those who should appear guilty. Even as a commission of inquiry it was to act " to take every legal measure to prevent a repetition of the outrages," presumably by bringing the guilty to judgment. By these instructions the doings of the members of the Commission must be judged.

Meanwhile an interesting drama was being enacted in Montreal and on Lake Superior. M'Gillivray and his associates were admitted to bail in Montreal at the home of a magistrate, who refused to so much as consider the evidence against them before doing so. Now at liberty, they devoted themselves to turning the tables on Lord Selkirk. An application was made, in the first instance to a Mr. Campbell, one of the judges of Upper Canada, for a warrant for his lordship's arrest, but the judge thought the grounds alleged in-sufficient. Chief-Justice Powell concurred in this decision. An armament of two hundred men, chiefly Iroquois, was sent to recapture Fort William, but for some reason the Indians grew recalcitrant at Sault Ste. Marie and refused to proceed. Finally a warrant, dated at Drummond's Island, was secured from a Dr. Mitchell, whom Selkirk describes as " an old man in his dotage . . . never by any chance sober after mid-day." A constable was sent to Fort William with the warrant. Selkirk wrote Lieutenant-Governor Gore that it was

" in the highest degree probable that [the warrant] had been obtained surreptitiously. The constable when asked whether he had any letters or credentials of any kind, could produce none, which confirmed the idea of his being an imposter." The noble lord therefore refused to submit to arrest. He made the further defence to the Commissioners, that he regarded it all as a ruse to get possession of his person, much as Owen Keveny had been taken by a warrant and then done to death in a lonely spot on the voyage. There was another reason which Selkirk might have alleged for refusing to be arrested by an unknown constable doing the work of the North West Company. In many cases, of which the most notorious is that of Miles Macdonell, warrants were used by his opponents for no other purpose than to rid themselves of the presence of rivals in the country. His lordship was on his way to reconstitute his colony and did not intend to be deflected from his purpose. The reaction of Selkirk's refusal to submit to arrest by this man on the Governor-General, accepting as he did the Canadian and the North West Company's opinion of Selkirk, is not surprising, but its reaction on Lord Bathurst, the Colonial Minister, is damaging to the traditions of British fair-play. With but the slightest knowledge of the circumstances, and doubtless prompted by Under-Secretary Goulburn, the intimate of the Northwesters, the minister, who passed over the tragic death of some twenty British citizens at Seven Oaks without taking any action to bring the perpetrators of the massacre to justice, ordered the most vigorous proceedings to be taken against his lordship for resisting arrest.

On 1st May Lord Selkirk left Fort William in charge of a small force. It was recaptured by the Northwesters in the course of the summer. His lordship arrived at the Red River Settlement in the third week of July, 1817. He busied himself disentangling the business of the colony. First of all there was the question of his title to the land. A great Council of Indians was held. As everything his lordship did was being misrepresented, he asked W. B. Coltman the Commissioner, now at the place, to meet with the Indians in Council and assure himself of their friendliness ; of their willingness to make a treaty by which they would be compensated for the settlement on their lands ; and of the fairness of his own dealings with them. The tradition ran that the aboriginal inhabitants of Red River were the Crees. They had, however, drifted out over the plains westward, and had welcomed in turn the Assiniboins and the Saulteurs as allies with them against the Sioux. Coltman reported that " the Cree Indians have agreed that the Saulteurs may treat for the lands as far as River aux Champignons [Muskrat River at Portage la Prairie]." The treaty thus was made principally with the Saulteurs, whose greatest chief was Peguis. It granted " all that tract of land adjacent to the Red River and Assiniboine River, beginning at the mouth of the Red River and extending along the same as far as the Great Forks at the mouth of Red Lake River, and along the Assiniboine River as far as Muskrat River." On most of this stretch the width was to be two miles from the river bank ; at Fort Douglas, Fort Daer, and the Grand Forks, it was to be six. In return the two tribes were to receive on or before the 10th day of October in each year, a quit-rent of 100 pounds of good tobacco, delivered to the Saulteurs at the Forks, and to the Crees at Portage la Prairie. The rights of the North West Company in the area were, by agreement with Coltman, recognized in the clause "Provided always that the traders hitherto established upon any part of the above-mentioned tract of land shall not be molested in the possession of the lands which they have already cultivated and improved, till His Majesty's pleasure be known." For a whole generation no one protested against this treaty. The Indians did not value the soil. They found the colony a good market for their meat and leather, and the settlers open-handed with little gifts. Hence their friendliness from the beginning.

The settlers who had fled north after the massacre of Seven Oaks had returned and were placed on their lands. The general plan of the Settlement and its position in relation to Fort Douglas and the Forks will be easily understood from the map on p. 426, which is based on Peter Fidler's survey. Each lot had a front of 10 chains, or 220 yards. It ran 90 chains, or 1,900 yards, back from the river, and contained 90 acres. Moreover, Selkirk's directions ran " each lot is to have a separate piece of woodland, containing 10 statute acres, to be laid off on the east side of the river . . . to be preserved by the occupier as woodland and not to be used for any other purpose." Selkirk went over the ground with the people. " Here," said his lordship—pointing to the lot No. 4 on which he stood—" here, you shall build your church, and that lot," said he again—pointing to the next, being No. 5—" is for a school." To some of the settlers, who had suffered great hardships in the disturbances, their lots were given free, on condition that they paid their indebtedness for goods and provisions as soon as they should be able.

" The experienced eye of his lordship saw things at a glance, and so correct and unerring was his judgment, that nothing he planned at this early date could in after years be altered to advantage. Public roads, by-roads, bridges, mill sites, and other important points were settled." In these words Alexander Ross recorded the judgment of the colonists. The parish was named Kildonan, after the original home of the settlers. As they were predominantly Presbyterian and begged for a minister, Selkirk promised him to them.

There arrived, with Selkirk, and after him, a new type of settler—the ex-soldiers—chiefly De Meurons, to the number of forty-six. They were placed on the east side of the river, within sound of the alarm given at Fort Douglas. Without individual initiative, hard drinkers, accustomed to idleness and given to brawling, the professional soldiers of those days were poor material for an agricultural colony. The De Meurons lived true to form, and earned a sad reputation at the hands of the thrifty Scottish settlers, but this must not blind us to the real contribution which they made to the colony. A disturbance to its inner quiet, they maintained it in peace in the face of foes. They were also a cause of strength to the Hudson's Bay Company in its strife with the Northwesters. Their support, as will be seen, enabled Governor Williams in 1819 to make his great capture of the North West Wintering Partners at the Grand Rapids. Thus, under the immediate supervision of Lord Selkirk, the colony was once more a reality and was taking its permanent form. With the arrival of French settlers from lower Canada it became a little Quebec, with English and French, Protestant and Catholic, living side by side, the river only between.

All along his lordship had been greatly concerned for the agricultural welfare of his Settlement. The pressing problems of agriculture in the North-West have been transportation, early autumn frosts, and drought. Selkirk was well aware of the first two of these. He strained every nerve to overcome difficulties of transportation. It had hitherto proved impossible to bring in cattle to his colony— an island of little farms set in the depth of the wilderness. When at Sault Ste. Marie on the way up, he entered into a contract with Colonel Robert Dickson, a fur-trader interested in the Mississippi valley, to bring in a herd over the plains from the Mississippi and from Kentucky. Without the low of the kine in the byre, and milk, butter, and meat on the table, the people could scarcely be contented. Hogs had already been provided. His lordship was equally anxious to procure the seed most suited to the climate. Barley seed from the Orkneys and some which grew in the most northerly fields of Sweden under the Arctic circle, had been sent out, and parsnip seed of a superior kind. A model for a mill was provided, and a colonial store opened. Though the colony was devised—by providing provisions and efficient servants, possibly, too, by growing tobacco and distilling liquor—to assist the Hudson's Bay Company in its reorganization to meet the onset of the North West Company, it was to have a sound economic basis of its own. It must produce for the English market such raw material as was light in weight and therefore easy to transport to York Factory, but of high value and likely to pay. Wool was thought of. At this time the development of manufacture by steam-driven machinery had outstripped the increase in raw materials. The English mills were calling for wool, and the price of that article was soaring. The introduction of merino sheep into Australia was laying the foundation of the wool industry of that colony. With keen perception, Selkirk dreamed of his colony becoming prosperous producing wool, which being light could easily be carried over the portages, and being valuable would bear the cost of transportation. Accordingly, he had sent out a flock of twenty merino sheep with the first party of actual settlers. But the dogs of the Settlement were a standing menace; the dispersal of the colony prevented the proper attention called for by the scheme, and finally, the settlers sent out lacked the vision and initiative to make the Red River a great wool producing country. Similarly, Lord Selkirk's attempt to guide his colonists into producing flax and hemp, similar light but valuable raw materials, for the London market failed. If there were to be anything of an export trade the water-way to York Factory must be improved and transportation organized. Selkirk planned improvements at the portages which would have facilitated summer traffic, and a winter road for sleds running on the frozen streams and over the carrying-places. The Company was to establish it as far as Lake Winnipeg, and Lord Selkirk was to be responsible for its continuation to the Settlement. Establishments along the route, with farms providing vegetables such as potatoes and storing meat, were to eliminate the risk of starvation by the way. Norwegians, apparently ex-convicts, were brought out for this work, and built Norway House to be the depot on the Lake Winnipeg. Oxford House was to be one of the intervening posts, and The Rock, on the Hill River some ninety miles from York Factory, to which water communication was easy, was to be the depot at the other end.

The real genius of Selkirk shines out in all these plans. The Northwesters might accuse him of being a rapacious fur-trader ; Dr. Strachan might expose him in the light of an unscrupulous land-jobber ; he was indeed deeply interested in the fur trade ; he was also, like many other English noblemen, interested in increasing his family fortune by speculation in land overseas ; his sympathy with the downtrodden at home had led him, in conjunction with these more self-regarding interests, to establish this colony surrounded by the wilderness, but he did not abandon the settlers to shift for themselves. He brought all his experience and intelligence to the solution of their problems. He believed he had given them an assured home market in the posts of his Company, but he also bent all his energy, as far as an intelligent gentleman farmer sitting in his armchair in England could do so, to providing the colony with a trade with the mother-country, which should make it an ecomonic success and ensure its happiness. When on the spot in 1817, he placed it under the care of his soldier-settlers, the officers on the land in the immediate neighbourhood of Fort Douglas, the privates on the east side of the river, within earshot of the bell of the fort. The colony was now on a sure foundation from which it could not be moved. With a mind essentially Anglo-Saxon in its outlook, he was interested more in the welfare of the people than in the constitution of their government. He took pains, however, to see that the Governor and Council, and the law courts, were constituted on a legal basis. Beyond that he was not concerned. He left these institutions to follow the dictation of circumstances and to frame their procedure for themselves.

Lord Selkirk's summer at the Red River Settlement must have brought him much satisfaction, but it was marred by an unnecessary wrangle before Colonel Coltman, the Commissioner appointed by the Governor-General of Canada. Coltman came fortified with a Proclamation dated May 1, 1817, issued by the Governor-General of Canada, in the name of the Prince Regent, requiring all parties to refrain from hostilities and to restore mutually posts and goods seized in the strife. At the instigation of the Northwester Partners in Red River, he required of Lord Selkirk the restoration of goods in his possession at Fort Douglas and Bas de la Rivière. Selkirk replied that he was ready to make the restoration, but that the North West Company must restore at once the goods seized in Athabaska, the furs at Fort Qu'Appelle, and the property taken by the fugitive settlers. He pointed out also that property seized by his side had always been inventoried and, when circumstances admitted of it, paid for; for example, Miles Macdonell in the matter of the pemmican seized, and again his own case in dealing with the property at Fort William which he purchased of Daniel Mackenzie, and finally in the matter of Captain D'Orsonnens at Rainy Lake. At the command of the Commissioner he made the restitution indicated, but could get in return no more than an order, signed by the North West Company's Partners, to the several Departments, to surrender goods at the moment in their possession and belonging to the English Company or to his lordship. The effect was a gross injustice, for the order, as worded, would not apply to goods and furs carried off but already out of the hands of the Wintering Partners. Selkirk's only source of redress would be in the law courts. The Commissioner thus played the game of the North West Company.

Still more unsatisfactory was the attitude of the Commissioner to the crimes committed. His instructions made him a magistrate to inquire into, arrest, and send down for trial those guilty of crimes, and in the next place to take every legal measure to prevent a repetition of the disturbances. Coltman, when at Red River, to a large extent ignored the first and not least important part of his instructions. He showed none of that sense which is the pride of the Englishman—that Justice is the corner-stone of the State. In answer to a suggestion of Coltman's that the North West Company and Lord Selkirk should come to some accommodation in the interests of peace, Selkirk replied : " Nothing could so essentially contribute to the great object of Mr. Coltman's Solicitude, the establishment of peace and good order in the interior, as examples of punishment inflicted by the Law on those who have been notoriously criminal." Rather, Coltman tried to be the friend of all parties, and openly professed his esteem for William M'Gillivray (his fellow councillor) and for Lord Selkirk. He even told the half-breeds of Red River that the Proclamation appeared to treat the violences as acts of private war rather than as robberies, felonies, or murders, and therefore they might look for " considerable lenity in the judgment to be exercised on the past offences of all who have not participated in deliberate murder." He now settled down to gathering affidavits, leaving the culprits at large, or at most binding them to appear for trial in Montreal.

In the matter of Alexander Macdonell, the chief aggressor on the

Red River, Coltman, in spite of the representations of Lord Selkirk, postponed taking affidavits until that impersonation of violence was far on his way to distant Athabaska, and he finally stated in his report :

> The warrant I issued against McDonell, could not be executed owing to his previous and unexpected escape into the interior from Bas de la Rivière, where I met him. . . . This flight certainly adds to the suspicions against McDonell, and combined with all other circumstances, calls for the most vigorous measures to bring him to trial. A similar observation appears to me also to apply in the case of Archibald Norman McLeod, against whom I likewise conceived it my duty to issue a warrant, which I sent to Mr. Fletcher at Fort William, but this also failed to be executed owing to the very short stay he (McLeod) made at that place, or at Montreal, from whence he proceeded to England.

The Justice of the Peace who had distributed rewards to the men who shot the settlers down at Seven Oaks knew enough about his conduct in the eyes of the law to feel that he was safest overseas. In sharp contrast, Lord Selkirk was arrested. He gave bail for the huge sum of £9,000, as required, for his appearance before the courts in Upper Canada. Cuthbert Grant, the leader of the North West Company's half-breed servants at the massacre of Seven Oaks, was arrested by Colonel Coltman when in the colony. He travelled to Montreal, occupying the same tent as the Commissioner and almost as a companion. True bills were found against him at Montreal, but he was allowed his freedom on a trifling bail. He escaped to the Upper Country and was never brought to trial.

Selkirk left the Red River Settlement on 9th September and reached Canada by way of the United States. When he appeared before the Quarter Sessions at Sandwich, Upper Canada, he was charged with the resistance of Dr. Mitchell's warrant, but the Bill of Indictment was thrown out by the Grand Jury. The Attorney-General now grouped all the charges against Selkirk under the head of "conspiracy" against the North West Company. Three days were taken in hearing witnesses and two with the deliberations of the Grand Jury. Apparently the verdict was going to issue in the discharge of his lordship. Evidently to save the Attorney-General from the humiliation of defeat, the Bench adjourned the Court *sine die*, and the criminal prosecution was not carried further. In seeking for a judgment of Selkirk's actions at Fort William the attitude of the Grand Juries, when the whole matter was placed before them, must carry great weight. They must have felt that he was upholding Justice, and that that covered the multitude of his errors in dealing with the property of the North West Company, which, either in the actual goods and furs, or in money paid, were all now returned to their owners' hands.

There is no room here to enter into the trials of the many cases, criminal and civil, which followed. Selkirk retired from Canada defeated by the law courts, burdened with debt, and broken in health.

When Colonel Coltman returned to Lower Canada he asked the North West Company and the agents for Lord Selkirk for statements of their several views, such as would guide him to an impartial judgment. With many details as to the actual occurrences, William M'Gillivray elaborated the theme that Lord Selkirk's colony was a well-contrived conspiracy to destroy the trade of his concern. Selkirk's agents, the law firm of Stuart, Gale & O'Sullivan, were not able to make a detailed statement, because all the information was with Lord Selkirk in the United States. They, however, gave an illuminating account of certain legal aspects of the struggle between the fur-trading companies, under the head of *Observations respecting the employment of illegal Force by the North West Company, the causes which have rendered an Appeal to the Law for redress impracticable on the part of the Hudson's Bay Company.* The long series of violences perpetrated upon the Hudson's Bay Company's servants by the Northwesters had led the Company in 1812 to consult Mr. [James] Scarlett, [a lawyer in London then rising to fame]. The advice given was that it would be impossible to prosecute the North West Company successfully, as long as the determinations of the concern at the rendezvous remained unknown. Previously, advice taken with regard to the acts of violence led to the determination " that no feasible mode could be pointed out for bringing the subject under the cognizance of any tribunal in England." Earlier still, when in 1803 the North West Company had sent a ship into Hudson's Bay and had built a post, Mr. Erskine, afterwards Lord Chancellor, and others had been consulted and gave the advice that a trespass committed in Rupert's Land was " not within the cognizance of any of the courts of common law at Westminster," that the Privy Council was not a court of original jurisdiction, and could not consider a case unless it came up from some lower court, as an appeal. The statement continues that when Miles Macdonell issued his Proclamation as legal Governor, and when he seized the pemmican which the Northwesters had said they would not surrender, they could have and should have " attained redress by legal means." If they had appealed from him to the Privy Council their appeal would have been heard.

That they did not take this opportunity is the more remarkable, as the partners who were at Red River when the seizure of the provisions took place, protested that they would appeal to a higher authority against Governor McDonell's proceedings. But this was overruled by the general meeting of the partners at Fort William, where it was decided, that it was necessary for the honour of the North West Company to redress their own wrongs, instead of appealing to the laws of their own country. . . . Down to the period of Mr. Alexander McDonell's declaration of open war, no one act of aggression had been committed by the colonists. The only measure of which any complaint had been made, or of which the North West Company could pretend to complain, was one to which their partners on the spot had given a qualified assent. It was at all events the public official act of Governor McDonell for which he, and he only was responsible, and for which he might have been legally called to account before the Privy Council of England. It is not that act therefore which is to be considered as a commencement of the disorders of the country, but the unprincipled resolution adopted at Fort William, to revenge it by main force, instead of seeking redress in a lawful manner.

Besides these statements, Coltman had a printed publication emanating from each party under consideration in drawing up his report. *A Narrative of Occurrences in the Indian Countries of North America since the connexion of . . . the Earl of Selkirk with the Hudson's Bay Company*, published on behalf of the North West Company, narrates events from the passing of Selkirk's Grant as the North West Company viewed them. The colony was a device to destroy the Canadian Company's trade and establish the right of the Hudson's Bay Company to the soil. In fact, both in the area of Selkirk's Grant and in the fur territory, formal notice had been given to the Wintering Partners to quit the region.

Alarmed at the engine of oppression which was thus prepared and directed against their connections, the Canadian Merchants lost no time in representing to His Majesty's Government, the mischief that must ensue from an attempt to establish a jurisdiction *which would most certainly be resisted* : they prayed that His Majesty's Ministers would inform them whether this newly assumed authority was acknowledged by Government, as that information would form some rule, for their own conduct.

This communication was forwarded through Under-Secretary Goulburn, and the covering letter is printed in the pamphlet as an appendix. Its date is all-important. It is dated March 18, 1815, four years after Selkirk's Grant and when plans for the dispersal of the colonists were on the eve of maturing. As the policy of the North West Company towards the colony had been determined at the rendezvous during the previous summer, the communication with the Colonial Minister cannot be considered as a request for information which should guide the Company. Rather it would prepare the Colonial Minister for the coming dispersal of the settlers. Curiously enough, the answer of the Colonial Minister is not given.

The *Statement respecting the Earl of Selkirk's Settlement upon the Red River . . . its destruction in 1815 and 1816 . . . with observations upon a recent publication, entitled "A Narrative of Occurrences in the Indian Countries,"* narrates events from Selkirk's Grant onward, from the point of view of Lord Selkirk. In it the colony appears as one of his schemes for emigration. "His Lordship's sentiments on the general question of emigration have been long before the public." All the doings of the North West Company are seen in the light of a conspiracy to destroy the Settlement. The Charter, the Grant, Macdonell's Government, are all put forward as legal. The North-westers have been rebels against constituted government. Both of these pamphlets bristle with documents calculated to substantiate their several points of view. The view of the North West Company's pamphlet, that the colony was a device to destroy their trade, would be correct if amended to read " a device to save the trade of the

English Company and to establish the right of the Company to the soil." Its aim, however, was to show its opponent in the light of an aggressor, and so justify the North West Company's violence as being simple acts of self-defence.

Coltman's preliminary report was submitted to Sir John Sherbrooke in the form of a letter, dated May 14, 1818. It notes the existence of a period before 1812 in which the Hudson's Bay Company suffered from a succession of lawless deeds on the part of the North West Company, but states that it was not regarded as within the sphere of the Commission to inquire into these. Of course, this procedure gave the report a false perspective ; it made the colony appear as an attack upon the trade of the North West Company, and the servants of the Company " the first aggressors." The Commissioner was correct in refusing to regard Selkirk's settlement as a simple colonizing scheme. It was a scheme devised to make good the title of the Hudson's Bay Company to the soil. Feeling that the monopoly of the trade had been lost, an attempt was made to regain it by establishing the Company's right to the soil. " It was found [by the Hudson's Bay Company] prudent to confine their pretentions to the rights of Territory and jurisdiction, which, could they be completely enforced, might afford the means of ensuring the monopoly of the company, as efficaciously as the more direct provisions of the charter for that purpose." In this light the embargo enforced by Governor Macdonell is seen as a definite act of aggression, first suggested by Governor Auld of the Hudson's Bay Company. Coltman is not satisfied with the legal advice given to Lord Selkirk that the Charter and consequently his Grant were valid at law, because it seemed apparent that the legal case as submitted to the lawyers did not take into view " the very important circumstance of the long previous occupation of the country by others "—a point well taken. The report passes on to the notices to quit, served on the different North West Company's forts, and insists that Colin Robertson's seizure of Fort Gibraltar was simply making good this notice by force and without a warrant. Here Coltman is in error, for Selkirk's right to the soil was preserved by the simple notice, and Robertson returned the post to Cameron as soon as he promised not to plot against the colony. The total effect of the Commissioner's statement is the impression that the North West Company throughout acted in self-defence.

The report dismisses the charge of conspiracy laid against Lord Selkirk, even in the matter of Fort William, and sets aside the similar charge laid by Lord Selkirk against the agents of the North West Company. There had been violences by the servants of both sides, " although beyond comparison the greater on behalf of the North West Company." The detailed report describes the acts of violence with great particularity, on the whole accurately and with a great show of impartiality.

It is clear that Coltman shrank from carrying out those instructions which envisaged the strict enforcement of the law as the one sure method of ending anarchy. He was seeking for some policy to which all parties would agree and which might inaugurate an era of peace. In fact, such a policy was being advocated by the North West Company. It was a union of the two companies, which would not only have delivered them from competition and conflict, but would have brought the much desired route by Hudson Bay. On February 13, 1818, Goulburn had raised the issue with the Governor of the Hudson's Bay Company. With this knowledge in mind, Coltman probably felt free to make both companies alike sinners, and so prepare the way for a compromise. Gale wrote to Lady Selkirk, that Coltman " took it for granted that Government looked upon all parties in almost the same light . . . and like a good subject he has laboured to fulfil what he conceived to be the wishes of Government. . . . He is so anxious to show that both parties have alike been criminal. . . . He has declared to me (in private) that he considered the Government as having taken a part and given a decided opinion on the subject." The Commissioner was described by the Attorney-General of Canada as a " good natured Laugh and Grow fat sort of person who had no wish but to tranquillize all parties." The result was that the Commission effected nothing. The trade war, which began in the Churchill River and Athabaska regions in 1815 and was raging when Coltman was preparing his report, continued—principal participants being A. N. McLeod, sometime Justice of the Peace, and Alexander Macdonell, who, had Coltman done his duty as a magistrate and not played the part of politician, would have been safe in some jail in Lower Canada.

6.—THE LAST PHASE OF THE STRUGGLE BETWEEN THE NORTH WEST
     COMPANY AND THE HUDSON'S BAY COMPANY, 1815–21—
     THE UNION OF 1821

The pressure of the North West Company, accentuated as it was by the menace of violence, and in many cases by violence itself, had its effect on the Hudson's Bay Company. From 1809 to 1814, inclusive, no dividends were paid. It took some time for the reorganization, sketched by Andrew Colvile and introduced by the Governor and Committee in 1810, to show its effect. A dividend of 4 per cent. was paid in 1815 and every year up to the union of 1821. The reorganization thus justified itself. A part of the scheme was the establishment of the colony, but it was in the nature of things that the benefits to be derived from it would not accrue for several years. On February 7, 1816, to encourage the colonists the Committee resolved to buy " as much Beef, Pork, Grain, Flour, Spirits and Tobacco " as they might produce. The dispersals of the colony and its misfortunes postponed for long the day when it could play its part in supplying the posts with provisions and so reducing expenses. Part of the scheme of the Company was to return to the Athabaskan enterprise, but under very different conditions. It was to be conducted now by Canadian officers and servants in such numbers and so well equipped with goods as to hold its own against the rival company. It was not till 1815 that the first expedition was got off. From that year till the spring of 1821 Athabaska and Ile-à-la-Crosse were the scene of a great struggle. The English Company suffered defeat after defeat, but in the end made its contact with and won its following among the Indians. There can be little doubt that it thus contributed largely to the situation in which the happy union of the two companies was consummated in 1821.

At the same time the North West Company contemplated a fresh attempt to secure the right of transit for their goods through the Bay. In the winter of 1814, in the height of the war of 1812, they presented a memorial to Lord Bathurst praying that they might have permission to convey their goods and furs through Hudson Bay to their inland posts, in view of the interference suffered on their usual route from the presence of the American troops on the lakes. In March Lord Bathurst wrote asking the Hudson's Bay Company to grant the request. The Company's reply was favourable, but conditions were laid down which safeguarded their rights. They thought the needs of the North West Company in the situation were exaggerated, but were willing to see that their posts were properly supplied with goods and provisions ; these would be conveyed in the Company's ships, paying the usual freight. It was asserted that there was not the same necessity for the conveyance of the furs to York Fort and so to England. (Here the depredations of the North West Company were enlarged upon.) If the North West Company were to be allowed to send out their furs by the Bay, they would market them much earlier than heretofore and increase their profits. It was therefore inconvenient for the Company to bring the furs home.

The North West Company could not avail themselves of the war as an excuse in 1815 after the Treaty of Ghent. Yet, as the Company had word, they intended to assert their rights and send out a ship. The instructions sent out to their officers by the Governor and Committee show a clear perception of the extent to which the Company could assert its rights under the Charter. There was to be no attempt to rest on their monopoly of the trade, but their rights to the soil were to be vigorously asserted. The Company's servants were instructed not to " engage in any contest of main force." The law of trespass was explained to them, and they were to give formal warning of trespass to the North West Company's servants, should they appear. Thereafter they were to follow the intruders closely and mark every act of trespass. Journals were to be kept in which were to be recorded all such acts, by whom perpetrated, and the witnesses present. When the Canadians should attempt to land, formal warning of trespass should be given, and enough opposition, without violence, shown to prove that force had been used by them to intrude upon the Company's property.

It is enough if one of our officers calmly and without show of anger, takes hold of the arm, or touches the body of the Canadian master, telling him to come no farther upon the lands of the H. B. Co. If the Canadian then disengages himself and goes on, this in the eyes of the law is a forcible trespass, no less than if it had been done at the point of the bayonet. . . . The ceremony is to be repeated on every occasion, where a fair opportunity occurs.

The instructions proved needless, for the North West Company did not try the venture. Had they come, there would have been need for something like courts of first instance in which to prosecute them for trespass.

A General Court was summoned in May following, " for the purpose of taking into consideration an Ordinance for the more effectual Administration of Justice in the Company's Territories." Since 1810 there had been two superintendents. It was now decided that there should be a Governor-in-Chief and a Council, " who shall have paramount Authority over the whole of the Companies Territories," and that the Governor with any two of his Council " shall be competent to form a Council for the Administration of Justice and the exercise of the power vested in them in the Charter." The Governors of Assiniboia and of Moose, with two of their Councillors, were to exercise the same authority for Judical purposes in their several districts. A sheriff was to be appointed for each of these two last districts, and one for the rest of the Company's territories. The Court concluded by nominating Robert Semple Governor-in-Chief, and Miles Macdonell and Thomas Vincent, respectively, Governors of Assiniboia and Moose. Councillors were appointed to act with these in their several spheres. Incidentally, the General Court gave a system of Justice to the colony, but it had the whole Chartered Territory in view in enacting this legislation.

The Governor and Committee immediately presented a memorial to Lord Bathurst stating that the rights of the Company, in virtue of its Charter, to make civil and criminal laws for the government of its territories had not hitherto been acted upon except for certain by-laws of the Company, and praying that the Ordinance as now passed should be submitted to the Attorney-General for sanction by the Imperial Government before being acted upon. The report of the Law Officer of the Crown remains unknown, but it could hardly have been otherwise than favourable, for this very system received the sanction of Lord Bathurst himself in 1822 after the union of the rival companies. Appeals were repeatedly made by Lord Selkirk to Lord Bathurst to reveal their decision, but in vain. Lord Bathurst was infected by the propaganda of the Northwesters, that what was going on in the North-West was no more than a faction fight, and took the ground that the Government must be neutral and impartial. Evidently he argued, not without some justice, that the Ordinances of Justice would place a weapon in the hands of the English Company. He did not realize that it would be, and could be, no more than a weapon of defence. Consider the procedure. A Northwester, say, committed a trespass, or assaulted Indians going to the English house in Athabaska to trade. An action would be taken against him before the Governor-in-Chief and Council, and he would be condemned and punished. But there always lay an appeal from a court of first instance in any colony to the Privy Council, and, if an injustice were done, the Northwester could avail himself of it and be righted. But the English Company had no such recourse for Justice, for the English courts of first instance would not consider cases involving trespass or crime outside of their own jurisdiction, nor could the case appear before Privy Council except in an appeal from a lower court. It regarded recourse to the Canadian Courts as out of the question, for its lawyers advised it that the Canada Jurisdiction Act of 1803 did not apply to the Chartered Territory. It had therefore no court to which it could resort for protection. There is justice, therefore, in the view of Lord Selkirk and the Company that Lord Bathurst, in withholding his sanction to the Ordinance, was guilty of a dereliction of duty, was unjust to the colony and the Company, and left a free field to the Northwesters to continue wrong-doing in a land without recognized Law or Courts of Justice.

The Company's Athabaskan expedition was organized in Montreal by Colin Robertson, an old Northwester, who had been in correspondence with the Company as early as 1810, and had made some suggestions as to the form reorganization should take. He chose John Clarke, another old Northwester, who had been on the Mackenzie River in the late 'nineties and on Peace River in the opening years of the century, and, as has been seen, had been recently on the Columbia with John Jacob Astor's Pacific Fur Company. The men were for the most part French-Canadians, doubtless a number of them already familiar with the Athabaska country. Large numbers were recruited, so as to leave no room for the Canadians to overshadow the expedition. As it was important that the arrival in Athabaska should be early, if possible before that of the Northwesters, it was arranged that the Company's post at Jack River should be a depot for the Athabaska brigade. Indeed, the Committee had agreed the year before with Lord Selkirk to send out a band of Norwegians to make a winter road from York Fort to Lake Winnipeg. (They built Norway House—on the peninsula culminating at Mossy Point, on the west side of the outflow from the lake—in 1817. It took the place of the Jack River post.)

Robertson was pleased with his crew. He described Clarke as deficient in notions of general business, but " brave, enterprising and . . . feared and respected both by his men and the Natives; he commands Canadians the best of any Gentleman I ever saw." Robert Logan, one of the early Selkirk settlers, and later the owner of the first mill in the colony, was destined for Ile-à-la-Crosse. It was said of him that he was " a steady man but . . . no Indian trader ; however his opponents will not drive him from his post." Monsieur (François) Decoigne, whose post was to be Lesser Slave Lake, was " an excellent trader, and has a complete knowledge of the N. W. Co." The expedition was away by 4th August, after which

Robertson took the fugitive Red River colonists back to their home.

In reference to the Athabaska enterprise, the determination of the Committee was that, in a land in which the Canadians recognized no law but their own interests, the Company, without taking the aggressive, should use force in the protection of its right to trade and of its property. Directions were given accordingly—to repel the aggressions of the North West Company with firmness and moderation ; to assert the property rights of the Company and enforce them with vigour.

At Cumberland House the North West Company's men carried off one of Mr. Clarke's brigade. He immediately counter-attacked and captured two of the guides of the rival brigade. There was then a friendly exchange of prisoners. In the trade in the wooded region, everything depended on getting into contact with the Indians, not simply to secure furs, but to get the provisions wherewith to live. In this matter the dice were loaded in favour of the Northwesters, with whom the natives had been so long in trade relations. Ile-à-la-Crosse was reached on the pemmican provided at Cumberland House, but there was none to be obtained there for the rest of the way. Clarke went ahead to find Indians with provisions to trade, but the North West Company had taken care that there were none to be found. The brigade reached Portage la Loche (Methy Portage) destitute of provisions. There was nothing for it but to send a party of hunters ahead. Six buffaloes killed on the banks of the Athabaska River relieved the situation momentarily. Two of the North West Company's Wintering Partners followed the brigade all the way and left pemmican about—even placing it in the encampments—to tempt Clarke's starving men, doubtless with a view to arresting them for theft should they take it, but Clarke had his men well in hand, and they took nothing. On 4th October the brigade was at Lake Athabaska. A party under Duncan Campbell had been sent early from Lake Winnipeg to rally the Indians to the English Company, but the Northwesters had managed to keep the natives out of the way. Clarke determined to use his superior force to impress the Indians. Hearing of an Indian family, he sent out his men to bring it in to trade. The Northwesters came to the rescue, but without effect. Impressed by this incident, and the feeling that Clarke could protect them, ten Indians came in voluntarily. But the very size of the Company's expedition which enabled Clarke to impress the Indians was a great danger in such a land of scarcity. It was an immediate necessity for it to be scattered to different posts where it could maintain itself on the provisions offered by the several areas—and engage in the fur trade. Messrs. Duncan Campbell and Roderick McKenzie and fourteen men were left to hold Athabaska Lake. Their post, Fort Wedderburn, was placed for the sake of safety on an island immediately opposite Fort Chipewyan. Duncan Campbell, its builder, was left in charge. Messrs. Aulay McAulay and Bourassa with thirteen men went to Great Slave Lake to build a post there.

Mr. Thomas Thomas and twelve men went back to the Athabaska River to the Pierre au Calumet, a good point for trading in pemmican. They built Berens House. Clarke with six officers and forty-eight men proceeded up the Peace River to establish a number of posts in that region, which, like the Saskatchewan, offered a good trade in beaver, with an ample supply of buffalo meat from its prairies.

Clarke's brigade left Fort Wedderburn in eight canoes manned by forty-three men, with no more than 150 pounds of flour. Their dependence was on a Cree hunter brought from Cumberland House, but he failed them. At Red (Mikwa) River, below the Vermilion Falls, John M'Gillivray passed them in a light canoe. Aware that M'Gillivray was pushing on to secrete the Indians and prevent the Englishmen from getting provisions from them, Clarke left his brigade and pressed on ahead with Mr. George McDougall. But his men were weak from the short allowances of food given them as they made their way up Peace River, and M'Gillivray got all the Indians away from Fort Vermilion before Clarke and his officer McDougall arrived. As the tracks of the Indians were fresh, Clarke and his guide were able to follow them. Two bands were reached within a day's march from the fort, but they were too terrified to give help, for the Northwesters had impressed it on them that, if they traded with or assisted the English, they would be denied all supplies of ammunition at the fort, and would in consequence die of starvation—they, their wives, and children. They therefore gave Clarke's party but a handful of provisions. Hard on Clarke's heels came the Northwester McIntosh with a large quantity of rum, designed to keep the Indians intoxicated till the Englishmen had been forced by starvation to surrender, for their plight was known by this time. In view of the desperate situation, Clarke sent McDougall down to meet the brigade, and to order the more exhausted men to go by canoe to Fort Wedderburn, where there would be a supply of fish, and to winter there. The brigade was found at Loon River. Indians there had wished to trade provisions with it, but were mauled by Canadian servants from Fort Vermilion into holding it back from the starving Englishmen. Sixteen men left in canoes for Lake Athabaska, but the river froze, and they were forced to take to foot. Individuals fell out on the way, one by one. Three only reached Fort Wedderburn. The rest perished of starvation.

McDougall left Loon River with three canoes of trading goods, manned by the lustier of the men, to join Clarke at Fort Vermilion. Northwesters hovered about the party to prevent the Indians from assisting them. When news came to Clarke that his men were in a desperate plight, he sent word not to surrender till he had made another fierce effort to reach the Indians. He did manage to find a band of Indians with provisions, and by threatening to shoot Northwester McLeod, who came to overawe them, got away with a supply. On the way to McDougall's camp a buffalo was killed. Thus at least a momentary relief was at hand, but Clarke reached the camp only to find that three of his men had died of starvation, and the rest, to save themselves, had entered into an agreement with the Northwesters to surrender all the Company's goods, and not to serve their employers in that region for three years. When the agreement was handed to Clarke he threw it into the fire. Clarke himself held out for some time longer, living for several weeks on " boutons de rose," rose hips. At last he too gave in, and surrendered what goods he had in return for food to take him to Athabaska Lake. He reached Fort Wedderburn in February.

The expedition to Great Slave Lake also came by disaster. Its men were forced to save themselves from death by starvation by giving up the Company's goods in payment for their winter's food. Decoigne, at his Fort Waterloo on Lesser Slave Lake, was not reduced thus far, but made no success of his trade.

Thus the great Athabaskan enterprise ended in disaster. Berens House at Pierre au Calumet on the Athabaska River held out, for it was in a region abounding in game, and Fort Wedderburn, thanks to the fishery at the old Fort Chipewyan on the south shore of the lake. There were, however, no returns in furs to compensate for the great initial expense.

As greater contact with the Indians had been secured, the failure of the expedition was not complete. Nor was Clarke discredited by it. He was retained by the Company to lead the succeeding Athabaskan expedition. Even the Northwesters admired his efforts. George Keith wrote to Thomas Thain : " To give the man his due, we must acknowledge he is an excellent leader. His men were kept in strict subordination without his appearing to be too severe, and he has a deal of influence with his clerks." John M'Gillivray wrote of " the unparalleled perseverance " of Clarke's men.

The great brigade sent into the forest belt was intended to bring the Hudson's Bay Company success in that region, but it was also devised to bring the North West Company to realize the necessity of some friendly arrangement about the trade which would bring the period of violence and anarchy to a close. On the eve of his departure for Canada Lord Selkirk was given authority by the Governor and Committee to enter into an agreement with the North West Company, based upon a guarantee not to enter into the Athabaska region, and on the concession of a transit through the Bay under terms which would safeguard the Charter. When in Montreal his lordship had a first discussion with Mr. Ogilvy, and on December 10, 1815, with Richardson, Ogilvy's son-in-law, one of the sanest minds in the North West Company, " upon the principle of a complete coalition of interests and union of the two Concerns, or upon that of a partition of the fur trading districts between them." Richardson saw great difficulties in the way of a complete coalition. On 12th December the North West Company put forward a " Sketch of Heads for an Agreement " to last for seven years. The English Company was to take one-third of the profits and losses, the North West Company two-thirds. The capital was to be found by the several parties in the same proportion. The furs were to be sold as

" an undivided interest," and the supplies to be sent into the Upper
Country partly through the Bay, partly through Montreal.   The
furs were to be routed by mutual agreement in the interest of the
profits.   Most important of all, the general management of the trade
in the Interior was to be in the hands of the North West Company.
The agreement was not to be construed as in any sense invalidating
the Charter of the older company.   Modifications were subsequently
made looking to a joint management, but Lord Selkirk was not eager
for a coalition, doubtless partly because the Northwesters had just
destroyed his colony and a union at the moment would proclaim
his defeat.   The noble lord, however, pointed out that the one-third
interest in the joint concern to be given to the English Company
was based on the returns in furs, but as its expenses, using the short
route, were much less than those of the North West Company
trading through Montreal, the actual profits of his Company were
in greater proportion.   " The fair mode of estimating the value of
a trading District, is not by the gross returns, but by the net profit
of the trade."   He therefore turned the discussion to the alternative
of a division of territory, suggesting that the North West Company
should be allowed necessary posts within the chartered territory, for
which leases could be got, so that there should be no appearance of
invalidating the Charter.   Here, as with the colony, the aim was to
secure a recognition of the Hudson's Bay Company's title to the
soil.   Agreement proved impossible.   The struggle between the two
companies must go on to its bitter end.   These negotiations took
place before news of the disastrous end of the Athabaska expedition
reached Montreal.

   The campaign of 1816–17, in Athabaska, in the eyes of the Northwesters, called for new methods.   The English on the lake could
not be starved out, for they fished for themselves, but the Indians
could be intimidated, could be made to despise the people at Fort
Wedderburn, and could be shown that the men from Montreal were
the masters of the land.   Their Wintering Partner was A. N. McLeod,
Justice of the Peace under the Canada Jurisdiction Act—a man born
to violence and whose fertile brain found means for turning the
machinery of the law to work his turbulent will.   His method was
summed up by a contemporary :

   He was . . . in the habit of sending some of his Bullies over to quarrel
with our people, by insulting them, then a Court was called, warrants issued
and the prisoners taken, and our people, of course, found [to be] the aggressors,
when the officers were put in Irons and the men in close confinement.   Mr.
McLeod with a smile used to observe, " Yesterday I was a judge, today I
am an Indian Trader."

The intention was not to do bodily harm to the opponents, still less
to take them to Montreal for trial, but, as Colin Robertson had done
in dealing with Duncan Cameron, to show the Indians that he,
McLeod, was master of the situation, and to teach them to despise
his opponents.   Before Clarke arrived with his brigade A. N. McLeod
fell on Messrs. Duncan Campbell, Aulay McAulay, and John Yale,

who had held Fort Wedderburn during the summer, at a time when a band of seven Indians and their families had recently returned with them from a hunt. The gentlemen were kept in close confinement, and were only released on their giving security to keep the peace for a twelvemonth. The effect on the Indians may easily be imagined. McLeod then ordered his men to seize the first Indian coming from the English fort, which was done, but not without a quarrel between Mr. McAulay and Alexander Roderick McLeod, the Northwester. A. N. McLeod, Justice of the Peace, invited the men in the English fort to a conference to settle the trouble. When they emerged from the fort, supported by a number of Indians, McLeod at the head of a band of armed men arrested them and all the Indians. When Clarke arrived immediately thereafter he found a situation which could only be met with a superior force such as he had not at his command this year, for the Northwesters had, according to his estimate, a hundred and fifty men and thirteen gentlemen at their call. They had built a blockhouse over on the island beside the English House to give them complete command. A Mr. Hector McNeil, an Irishman, was sent out from it to pick a quarrel with Clarke's officers, his associates watching its course from their blockhouse. Soon McNeil the Northwester provoked James McVicar to a duel with swords. There was an element of chivalry in it all, for when McVicar was disarmed the fight ended. McNeil, however, was severely wounded. Forthwith A. N. McLeod as Justice of the Peace summoned the Englishmen to a court. Clarke refused to obey. Thereafter McLeod sent a party of thirty armed men under George Keith, Thomas McMurray, and A. R. McLeod, to seize the fishing tackle and the servants at the English fishery. As Justice of the Peace he issued no warrant against the Englishmen, but pretended to be ready to release them when they had taken an oath that they would not appear in arms against British subjects for the term of two years. He still, however, kept the men in custody, saying that they could not be released until Clarke obeyed his summons and appeared before Justice impersonated in himself. Clarke went over to try to make an arrangement, and was arrested along with his companions McFarlane and McVicar. Finally Mr. Robert Henry, a Northwester, became security for them on condition that thirty " pieces " of the Hudson's Bay Company's goods were lodged in the North West Company's fort. That done, they were released. Mr. Clarke remarks : " This unfortunate affair happened to us when the Natives were about, so that the abject state of fear the North West kept them in, helped to make them more servile than ever, as our inadequate force completely debarred us from having any intercourse with them." Later, six of the Hudson's Bay Company's best men were arrested on the ground that they were indebted to the North West Company.

The Northwesters dealt their final blow on January 23, 1817. They persuaded Clarke to go over to their fort to discuss the indebtedness of the English Company to them, and, during his absence, seized Fort Wedderburn. When Clarke, once more a prisoner, demanded an explanation, he was shown a letter from William M'Gillivray telling of the seizure of Fort William by Lord Selkirk, and of the arrest of himself and the Proprietors present. When spring came, Mr. Justice of the Peace A. N. McLeod did not send Clarke out to be tried, but, in spite of protests, spirited him off to Great Slave Lake, four hundred miles farther away from the courts of Canada. From a statement made by the French-Canadian in charge of him, Clarke became convinced that the intention was to have an Indian murder him. Had Owen Keveny not been done to death in that very way the year before, this would be beyond belief. When the plot became known Clarke was brought back from Great Slave Lake and was sent by the notorious Samuel Black up Peace River to Fort Vermilion. The object was, of course, to prevent him from returning to Cumberland House, and so to disorganize the expedition of the following year.

Altogether, the North West Company had things their way in the Athabaska region during this winter (1816–17). They seized the posts at Lesser Slave Lake, Ile-à-la-Crosse, Reindeer Lake, and Green Lake, in addition to Fort Wedderburn. Clarke wrote to Bird at Edmonton House that McLeod even threatened to march down and take the forts on the Saskatchewan. Certainly great alarm prevailed on that river. Bird promptly built earthworks, and stationed cannon opposite Steep Creek, some thirty-eight miles below Fort Carlton and on the left bank of the North Saskatchewan. The tradition among the Indians is that these works, traces of which remain, were built by the White Men when they were fighting one another. Bird also wrote to Alexander Macdonell, Selkirk's agent, at Jack River to make all haste in palisading the buildings at " Norwegian Point," later known as Norway House, the depot on Lake Winnipeg then being built, and to put up blockhouses for its protection. He also wrote to Miles Macdonell that A. N. McLeod threatened to take the forts on the Saskatchewan at the end of April, " but we will make ourselves respected below this place," presumably at the earthworks. He wrote to Lord Selkirk that a sufficient force should be sent to the Grand Rapids of the Saskatchewan to seize the North West Company's canoes as they came down from Athabaska with the prisoners. Thus in 1816–17 the North West and Hudson's Bay companies were locked in a life and death struggle in the wide area from Fort William to Lake Athabaska. At the eastern extreme the Northwesters could invoke the law to loosen the grip of their enemy on them. At the western end they were a law unto themselves. Such was the course of affairs in Athabaska when Coltman was preparing his conciliatory report in the quiet of Quebec.

The disasters of the trading season 1816–17, including as they did the loss of Clarke the leader in the Athabaska enterprise, crippled the Hudson's Bay Company's plans for 1817–18. Mr. Decoigne penetrated to Lake Athabaska with a small band of men. This answered no other purpose than convincing the Indians that the Company was determined to keep up posts among them. Colonel Coltman's orders to the two companies to restore property seized was so far obeyed by the Northwesters that they gave up any goods they had remaining.

The Hudson's Bay Company, with truly British doggedness, returned to the Athabaska and the Peace River regions in 1818. It was important to continue the good relationships already reached with a number of the Indians. Then, too, the Governor-General of Canada had required the restoration of all property seized by either side and ordered all parties to cease from violence. John Clarke, in the mind of his employers, had been without judgment in putting himself into the hands of his opponents. He was reduced to a subordinate position as factor of a post to be established on the Peace River near Dunvegan. The redoubtable Colin Robertson was to be in command of the whole Department. Moreover, the Company had sent out a new Governor-in-Chief in the person of William Williams. He was an ex-captain of an East Indiaman, and held the reputation of preferring a fight to peace, provided it was a fight likely to lead to a decision. Colin Robertson went on with some twenty-two canoes manned by five or six men apiece. He seems to have done well in Athabaska at first, for J. C. McTavish on the Peace River wrote Angus Shaw that he had been subject to " galling trials," that none of his predecessors ever had more trouble to begin with. In truth, Robertson, with overpowering numbers, was able to protect his Indians, and by threats that he would destroy the North West Company's Fort Chipewyan, impressed it upon them that he was master of the situation. Samuel Black, " that desperate character," managed to turn the scales. At a time when the men were away for provisions and furs and there were few in Fort Wedderburn, Black came to the post to pick a quarrel. He found Robertson about to attend a funeral. In the solemn presence of death, Black fired at Robertson but missed him. Upon this he ordered his men to seize him. While they were dragging the mighty form of Robertson to the shore, Robertson managed to grasp his pistol and fire at Black, but missed in his turn. " Simon M'Gillivray [William's half-breed son] was in the affray and as usual, distinguished himself."

The real problem now was how to get Robertson to Canada for trial. Clarke had proceeded up Peace River, where Mr. Joseph Halcro had been sent on to build Colvile House at Loon River. Chastellain had been sent to build beyond that, but was seized by the Northwesters at Fort Vermilion. He was released on condition that he go back down the river, but his private property was kept. Clarke brought him back and sent him to the fort to demand his property. He was refused it, and warned not to pass up beyond the fort. Clarke now appeared upon the scene and rushed the post before the gates could be shut. When McIntosh stood to defence, he was disarmed. When Chastellain's property had been restored, Clarke withdrew his men, though he was greatly tempted to help

himself to the Northwester's provisions, for he was in need.   He
went on and built St. Mary's House, half a league above Smoky
River and on the right bank of the Peace.   Fort Waterloo on Lesser
Slave Lake was held by John Lee Lewes.   The posts at Ile-à-la-Crosse
and Green Lake were re-established.   While the business done at the
English forts was small in comparison with their costs, a brighter
day was dawning for the Great Company in Athabaska.   The
Indians were beginning to rally to it.   Robertson effected his escape
on the way down and arrived safely at Cumberland House.

Meanwhile the pugnacious Governor Williams was preparing a
counter-attack.   Doubtless acting on the suggestion of James Bird
of the previous year, he gathered a force at Grand Rapids on the
Saskatchewan, including some De Meuron soldiers from Red River
Settlement.   It was supported by some small cannon mounted on a
barge.   The plan was to waylay the Northwesters at the portage of
the Rapids.   A small cannon and two swivels were landed and placed
to command the foot of the Rapids.   Williams now awaited events
with a bunch of warrants secured by Lord Selkirk against the North
West Wintering Partners and, apparently, others issued by himself as Governor.   John Clarke was the first trader to appear, and, no
doubt with glee, fell in behind his chief.   The portage at the Rapids
was about two miles in length, and it was the practice for the canoes
to be shot down the rapids while the partners strolled across on foot.
John Duncan Campbell and Benjamin Frobisher were so doing when
they were surrounded by De Meuron soldiers and seized (18th June).
Messrs. Connolly and Macdonald, following, met a similar fate.
When Campbell asked to see the warrants, he was told by Williams
that legal proceedings were all damned nonsense in the West—a
happy enough rejoinder as made to the Northwesters—that having
the advantage he intended to keep it.   Two French-Canadians in the
English River brigade which followed, and for whom Williams had
" warrants," were also arrested.   On 23rd June Angus Shaw from
Fort Augustus, J. G. McTavish and William McIntosh from Peace
River, were similarly taken.   Mr. Shaw remonstrated in true North-
western style against this illegal stoppage on the King's highway and
in spite of the Governor-General's proclamation made in the name
of the Prince Regent.   Williams is said to have replied :

I care not a curse for the Prince Regent's proclamation ; Lord Bathurst
and Sir John Sherbrooke by whom it was framed are d—— rascals.   I act
upon the Charter of the Hudson's Bay Company, and as a governor and
magistrate in these territories, I have sufficient authority and will do as I
think proper.

And again

As for Lord Bathurst (d—— him) he is bribed by North-West gold ; and
Sir John Sherbrooke, the judges, juries and crown officers of Canada are
a set of d—— rascals, and for our part, we shall act independently of the
rascally Government of Canada. . . . I shall make use of the colonists and
every other power to drive out of the country every d—— Northwester it
contains, or perish in the attempt.

It is far from sure that Governor Williams used these words, but now at last the Hudson's Bay Company had a servant ready to display something akin to the " North West spirit."

The Company's Athabaskan venture of 1819–20 showed the value of doggedly adhering to the determination to get a hold on that region, and of Governor Williams's determination to use their own methods against the Northwesters. Colin Robertson was in charge. When he got to Ile-à-la-Crosse, where Clarke was to uphold the cause that winter, he noted a great change in his opponents.

> It seems that our opponents have lowered their tone ; they talk now of conducting their business on amicable principles ; if they are serious, what a change ! . . . The North West Coys servants have the old story of a junction in their heads ; is it possible they have even hopes of covering their enormities under the veil of an arrangement ? Whatever their prospects may be, there is certainly a great change in their conduct ; the affair of the Grande Rapid has not so much as produced a menace.

Robertson was wrong in inferring that there would be no reply to the stroke of Governor Williams; he was right in noting that the trade was going to be conducted on more amicable principles—at least on the Churchill and in Athabaska. John Clarke was opposed by John Thomson, but an agreement was entered into to carry on the trade in peace. Many Indians adhered to the English post. William Todd, a physician, held Fort Wedderburn that winter without molestation. He had a constable with him bearing a warrant issued by Colonel Coltman for the arrest of Samuel Black. The man made an attempt to execute the warrant once when a canoe had come over from Fort Chipewyan to take Black across from the blockhouse. The Northwester, suspecting the plan, drew his pistol and the constable retired. All Fort Wedderburn was in arms in case of need, but kept within the gates.

On Peace River, Colin Robertson at a new St. Mary's House built a little below the former post of that name and on the opposite bank, and John Yale at Colvile House, were allowed to trade in peace, as also Robert McVicar on Great Slave Lake and Andries at Harrison's House at Fond du Lac on Lake Athabaska. Aulay McAulay, however, was forced to abandon Berens House on Athabaska River.

The Northwesters planned revenge on Governor Williams. They were ready to receive him at the Grand Rapids of the Saskatchewan on his way from Cumberland House, much as he had received their Partners in the previous summer. Aware of their scheme, Williams took the Minago route to the post on the Bay. He left instructions for Robertson to do likewise, but when he reached Moose Lake he failed to find a guide to a route no longer in use. With an excess of confidence characteristic of the man, he ventured the course by the Grand Rapids and was seized. Released in Montreal, he made his way to England.

In the summer of 1820 the North-West saw for the first time one

of the most remarkable men in all the history of Rupert's Land—
George Simpson. The sheer love of brute force of Governor Williams
was a strength to the Hudson's Bay Company in the chaotic conditions of the time, but, without intelligence and subtlety, brute force
is a dangerous weapon. That intelligence and subtlety, along with a
remarkable gift for friendship, was the contribution of George
Simpson. He was but thirty-three years of age, without experience
save what might be got in a London counting-house. Andrew
Colvile had, however, chosen him to be Governor in the Northern
Department should Williams be arrested to answer for his deeds. As
the Governor was still at the front that year, Simpson accepted the
charge of Athabaska, Colin Robertson not being available, and while
he did not make the trade of the year a complete success, he was as
subtle as the Northwesters and held his own, as none of his predecessors had done. With a man of this stamp about to step into
the control of the Hudson's Bay Company's interests in the Interior,
with the colony now taking root by the banks of the Red River, the
future of the English Company in its fierce struggle with the North
West concern began to brighten. The Englishmen were true to the
form of England. They drifted into what was little short of war
with an antiquated machine, and went down to defeat, and again
to defeat. As things grew critical they asked themselves with
courage what was the matter, and ended by a complete reorganization
of their system and transformation of their personnel. Defeats
continued, but in 1819 the whole position of the English Company
was so far improved that they might well, true to the form of
England, have won the last battle and come off triumphant. But the
struggle was not to end, so to say, on the field of battle. In war the
financial standing, the strength of the constitution of a country, and
the will to win, are not less important than the forces in the field.
It was a great strength to the Hudson's Bay Company during all
these years of struggle that its stockholders were wealthy apart from
the returns in peltry. It was an equal advantage that its constitution
was stable—built on the Charter as upon a rock. Its servants in
the Interior might be unenterprising, passive, submissive to the
bluster of the Northwesters, but the London end of the Company
was dogged and invincible—remarkably efficient in redressing the
losses in the Interior by efficient buying and selling in the home
market, and above all possessed of the actual monopoly of the cheap
water-route direct through the Bay to the very edge of the fur
regions. On the other hand, the North West Company might have
a superlative efficiency in the constitution which gave the Wintering
Partners every incentive to make the trade with the Indians succeed
and an unsurpassed band of servants, but it could not shake off the
handicap of its expensive route via Montreal. Its greatest weakness,
however, as was seen in 1798 when the XY Company was formed,
lay in that feature in its constitution by which the magnificent
" concern " had to be formed anew from time to time by a fresh
contract. The twenty years of the last agreement were nearly

passed, and a new arrangement must now be made. The Wintering Partners could refuse to renew the agreement and seek other Agents without deviating from the path of honour.

Moreover, all was not well within the Company's ranks. A number of Wintering Partners were revolted by the outrageous violence inflicted on the " concern " by the policy of its Agents. They probably were still more impressed, as the fur regions exploited grew farther and farther afield, with the handicap of the " long haul " from Montreal. Some had doubts of the solvency of the Agents' firm, McTavish, McGillivrays & Co., with whom their savings were deposited, for they had not been able to get statements of their accounts from it. Stormy times were before the " concern " when the question of renewing the agreement should come up in July 1820 at the rendezvous. It was probably to be able to meet the Partners with a brilliant stroke of policy making the future assured that Edward Ellice, protesting all the while that he held no interests in the North West Company, approached Lord Selkirk in December, 1819, with an offer to buy out his shares in the Hudson's Bay Company. He held out the bait that all legal proceedings against the noble lord should be dropped. Had Ellice received a favourable reply his predominant position in the Company would have secured at least promise of the short route by Hudson Bay, and the Wintering Partners would have willingly renewed the agreement. Should the negotiations be still pending in July 1820, the Agents could plead for a united North West Company to carry them through to success. Lord Selkirk, however, now far gone in a decline, refused to contemplate a transaction which would give a large influence in the management of the Hudson's Bay Company to the concern that had twice destroyed his Settlement and which would place the colony " completely at the mercy of that association."

Meanwhile, certain Wintering Partners were not idle. Through an indirect channel, and most secretly, they approached Samuel Gale, Jr., of Montreal, a devoted friend of Lady Selkirk's. Gale, under date of September 20, 1819, informed her ladyship that William M'Gillivray had been making great exertions at Fort William that summer to induce the Wintering Partners to renew or to extend the agreement. The matter would come up again next summer. The question was asked, on behalf of an unnamed Wintering Partner, whether, if his fellow Partners refused to renew the agreement with McTavish, McGillivrays & Co. as Agents, the Hudson's Bay Company would act in their place, supply the necessary goods, and sell for them furs delivered at York Factory? The letter was answered for her ladyship by Andrew Colvile, her brother, seven days before Selkirk closed the discussions with Edward Ellice, with a definite negative. Speaking for himself personally Colvile said that some of the most notoriously violent among the Wintering Partners would have to be excluded from any arrangement; that the proposal as presented would not eliminate competition, for the Hudson's Bay Company would be supplying at one and the same time their own forts and those of rivals; but that he was certain "peculiarly liberal and advantageous terms" would be made with the Wintering Partners, including a share in the profit of the trade and in the management of the trade of the Interior, if it were agreed that all competition should be eliminated by the Wintering Partners and the Hudson's Bay Company entering into a system which would give them a joint control of the trade. In a word, Colvile suggested that the Hudson's Bay Company should become Agents for the Wintering Partners, that the forts in the several districts should be united, and that the management in the Interior should be much like that of the North West Company—a joint management by the Agents and the Winterers.

On January 10, 1820, Mr. Colvile wrote to Gale telling of the proposals of Ellice and their rejection, and expressed his belief that the Agents of the North West Company would use the negotiations with Ellice as a means of driving the Wintering Partners into signing the agreement. He added that a number of the old Hudson's Bay Company's servants would be retiring to the Red River Settlement, and would thus leave room in the united concern for the North West Winterers. Mr. G. Moffatt, who was the party inquiring confidentially for the Northwesters, forwarded the substance of Mr. Colvile's replies, by a Proprietor of the North West Company. It was followed by George Simpson, about to enter upon his long career in the Interior. Thus the Wintering Partners at the rendezvous became fully informed of the situation. When William M'Gillivray urged that all should stand united to carry through the negotiations with the Hudson's Bay Company, which he stated were all but completed, they were able to detect the falsehood. Dr. John McLoughlin contradicted him to his face. A comparatively few stood by the old Agents. The majority gave McLoughlin a power of attorney to negotiate for them with the English Company on the principles sketched by Colvile. John McLoughlin and Angus Bethune proceeded to London as delegates to treat with the Hudson's Bay Company.

George Simpson has left a Journal of his first and only year as a fur-trader. Finding that Governor Williams was secure in his office, he volunteered to lead the Athabaska brigade. At Fort Wedderburn he had to face the same difficulties as his predecessors. He succeeded because he fell heir to the friendship of the Indians already secured by them, and because he won the loyal support of his men. He was not averse to a show of violence when the occasion called for it, but his reliance was on subtlety rather than force. A line of demarcation had been drawn between the North West Company's blockhouse, dominating the entry to Fort Wedderburn, and the English Company's property. Simon M'Gillivray determined to extend the blockhouse beyond it to the palisade of the fort. Simpson, standing at his gate, invited M'Gillivray to a conference, A constable from Montreal stepped out and arrested the rogue. The warrant had not been issued by the English Company, but by no less a personage than Colonel Coltman, the Commissioner instructed to arrest the wrongdoers in the North-West. The Northwesters raged with indignation and demanded M'Gillivray's release. Simpson calmly replied that it was against the law to interfere with a constable doing his duty. Simon M'Gillivray escaped, but the Northwesters played a mild game thereafter. All the posts held by the English Company during the previous year were reoccupied. The Athabaskan enterprise was well on the way to success when the struggle was suddenly ended by the union of the two rival companies.

There is no record of the negotiations for union which took place in London, but some suggestions come from the letter-book of Colin Robertson, who crossed to England in the same vessel as McLoughlin and Bethune, and with Mr. Caldwell, Receiver-General of Lower Canada, an intimate associate of William M'Gillivray. When Robertson reached London he was visited in his hotel by Caldwell and Ellice, and later by Simon M'Gillivray. These gentlemen informed him that they would gladly enter into discussions with the Hudson's Bay Company for a union, and Robertson promised to mention the fact to Mr. Colvile. This he did, doubtless also reporting their boast that they were able to procure the capital to continue the struggle. With the Wintering Partners in the person of McLoughlin and Bethune, as well as the Agents through Edward Ellice and Simon M'Gillivray, suing for union, Andrew Colvile, acting for the Governor and Committee, was in a position to impose on both parties terms which he regarded as in the best interests of the Company, and for all concerned.

The Hudson's Bay Company decided that the Agents of the North West Company must be included in the union. It must have been evident that the plan sketched for the Wintering Partners, by which the Agents were to be left out, might not bring peace to the trade. The Agents might be able to keep a sufficient number of Wintering Partners, and get new ones, to carry on the struggle. It was simple wisdom to bring both the Agents and the Wintering Partners into the arrangement. McLoughlin complained afterwards that he had been left in the cold during the negotiations. This may well have been the feeling of such a high-spirited gentleman, and one greatly impressed with the importance of his mission. Colin Robertson, however, offers a very tangible reason for caution in treating with him and Bethune, as if they represented the North West Company. True they had powers of attorney from eighteen proprietors, but Colin recalls that when Alexander Mackenzie left the North West Company he had powers of attorney from a large number of Winterers, but in the sequel not one of them followed him into the XY Company. It is more than likely that he conveyed this information to Andrew Colvile. Certainly the Hudson's Bay Company treated the M'Gillivrays as the legal representatives of the North West Company, as indeed they were. In coming to terms with them, as well as with the Winterers, there could be no doubt but that all opposition would cease and a complete union be effected. A few, notably Samuel Black and Peter Skene Ogden, were excluded because their evil deeds did not appear pardonable.

The union was the realization of the hopes of many men, notably of Sir Alexander Mackenzie and of Lord Selkirk. From the year of his spectacular voyage to the Pacific Coast Mackenzie had the vision of a chartered company using the short ocean route through Hudson Bay to the West, and engaged in the fur trade of the Pacific slope. His dream, in the eyes of Simon McTavish too airy to be tolerated, took its local habitation and name in the Hudson's Bay Company of the union. Mackenzie died on March 12, 1820. His dream was realized a twelvemonth after his death.

Lord Selkirk was a man of far different aims. His interest was centred in his colony and in the Hudson's Bay Company, which stood out stoutly against Mackenzie and his associates. The goal which he set before him was a peaceful colony, the handmaid of the Company. He died on April 8, 1820. Within a twelvemonth after the end the goal had been reached. Time only was needed to reveal a peaceful colony ministering to the needs of the Hudson's Bay Company.

It has been said that the antagonisms of these two men required to be buried in the grave before there could be union. Not so. At the vision of the benefits of union more bitter antagonisms were hid away by practically minded men. It is not only conceivable, but extremely probable, that had these two men lived on, meeting from time to time at the General Court, they would have expressed a common satisfaction that their several aims had not been incompatible, though their ways of gaining them had brought about conflict—that the goals of their lives had now at last been attained.

7.—THE NORTH-WEST COMPANY WEST OF THE ROCKIES, 1814–21 —THE PACIFIC SLOPE BROUGHT INTO THE UNION

Eager as the men from Montreal were to secure the maritime fur trade of the Pacific slope, they won no great success. Their yearly ships brought what was now called Fort George an ample supply of goods by way of the Horn and went on to trade on our Pacific coast, but as no exclusive contract was made with the Russians, and the monopoly of the East Indian Company hampered them in the market at Canton, their cruises were far from remunerative financially. The American traders continued to supply goods to Baranoff at Sitka and were unhampered at Canton, and thus were able to make profits in the coastal trade.

As we have seen, the first ship of the North West Company to pass round the Horn was the *Isaac Todd*. She wintered in California on the way to the Columbia. By her came Donald McTavish, a Partner in the Company. Unfortunately, while returning to the ship as she lay off Fort George, he and his fellow-Proprietor, Alexander

Henry the younger, who had recently arrived from Rocky Mountain House, were drowned.

In the valley of the Columbia the North West Company began by taking into their employ a number of the most conspicuously able Astorians—Duncan McDougall himself, Alexander Ross, and Ross Cox. In spite of inducements offered, Donald McKenzie, John Clarke, and Gabriel Franchère, after serving the company during the winter by way of interlude, crossed the Rockies in the summer of 1814 in the wake of John MacDonald of Garth—Clarke, as has been seen, to reappear as leader of the Hudson's Bay Company's Athabaskan enterprise. Their route ran up the Columbia to " Rocky Mountain Portage," later known as Boat Encampment, over Athabaska Pass, down the Whirlpool River to the Athabaska, from which they crossed overland to Fort Vermilion at the mouth of the river of that name and on the left bank of the North Saskatchewan, and so to Fort William.

The Columbia River was the great water-way for the Canadians as it had been for the Americans, but east of the Rockies, for example, on the Saskatchewan, the Northwesters had been dealing with wandering tribes who had little or no sense of property in land or river. They would paddle past the bands of Indians ignoring their presence. They naturally followed the same policy on the Columbia, but only to find that the populous villages at the portages, conscious of their property rights, resented it. The result was a series of clashes which taught the men of the east to pay some respect to the sense of dignity and to the proprietorship of the villagers by the way.

Where there had been rival forts—as among the Kutenais at the Falls of the Kootenay River, and among the Flatheads, and at Spokane House—the Northwesters continued to occupy their own, the first forts in those parts. The punctilious but shortsighted James Keith, hitherto but a clerk, was placed in charge of Fort George, doubtless because of the deaths of Donald McTavish and Alexander Henry. Under his directions the valleys of the Willamette and Cowlitz were exploited. J. G. McTavish continued at Spokane House, and Alexander Ross at Fort Okanagan with Kamloops for its outpost. In August 1817 Ross attempted to explore the country from Kamloops eastward towards the Columbia. He passed northward midway between this river and the Fraser. He found the people in this upland region living on fish caught in the lakes, on roots, and on berries. He continued up the Grisley-bear River in an easterly direction for six days, finding streams bordered by poplar trees, but no great number of beavers. Passing Eagle Hill, he reached the foot of the Rocky Mountains. " Certainly a more wild and rugged land the mind of man could not imagine," he wrote. Before him the mountain mass was like a wall. He turned homeward at the Canoe River, near the portage leading over the Athabaska Pass. The verdict of this the first European to see the region was that of the typical fur-trader. " As a barren waste well stocked in wild animals of the chase, and with some few furs, the trade on a small

scale, as a part of the She-whaps [Kamloops], might be extended
to some advantage in this quarter and the returns conveyed either
to the latter post or to the mouth of the Canoe River."

As the Columbia Department had not been doing well, the
Company sent in Donald McKenzie in 1816 with a special commission.
He brought about several drastic changes. Expresses up and down
the river, which were always exposed to the menace of the populous
villages and therefore had to be well manned, were abolished.
Letters were relayed by the Indians from village to village, cheaply,
safely, and speedily. The partners had grave doubts of the scheme,
but McKenzie really understood the workings of the Indian mind—
that they held letters in superstitious awe and would regard them
as a sacred trust, and be true to their promise of delivery. Then,
too, McKenzie reintroduced the practice of sending trapping expeditions to exploit the beaver streams of the expansive region
drained by the upper waters of the Snake River. Finally, up to this
time Fort Okanagan had been the rendezvous for all the upper posts.
Having come so far north, the brigades moved south-eastward to
Spokane House, and thence to the other posts and to the Snake
River region. It was due to McKenzie that this circuitous route was
abolished, and a more central rendezvous was established in 1817
in a fort at Walla-walla among the Nez-percés tribes. Alexander
Ross was placed in charge.

The most interesting change in the way of adapting the trade
to the country was the adoption of transportation by horses and
the opening up of a pack-horse route from Fort Okanagan by way
of Kamloops to the Fraser, and then by canoe to New Caledonia.
This gradually displaced the Peace River route, which was subject
to risk of the goods being stayed on the way in by the river freezing.
Heavy merchandise could be brought in more surely and more
cheaply by the Okanagan route from the mouth of the Columbia.
The furs continued to go out through Fort McLeod and by Peace
River, and goods made up in Montreal to be brought in.

Our knowledge of New Caledonia in these times is derived from
letters of John Stuart and from the Journal of Daniel Harmon.
Stuart, it will be remembered, was the joint-founder of the Department with Simon Fraser. A very capable fur-trader, though not
easy to work with because of his inveterate growling, he stood to
his duties as Wintering Partner through the long years until 1824,
possibly because he became attached to the region in spite of its
hardships. He won for his Department such a reputation for fine
furs that the Hudson's Bay Company was planning in 1820 to enter
it. Daniel Harmon was of an easy temper, such as could carry on
with a difficult chief without clashes. After his service on the
Upper Assiniboine, where we last met him, he wintered in 1805 at
the South Branch House, which at this time was about a third of
a mile above the St. Laurent ferry of to-day near Duck Lake.
Harmon spent a year at the South Branch, where, as has been
seen, he took to himself the half-breed daughter of a French-

Canadian; the following year he was at the North West Company's Cumberland House. In 1809 he was sent to Dunvegan on Peace River, and it is proof of his capacity as a fur-trader that next year he was offered a post in New Caledonia, either as chief or second in command. It is characteristic of the man that he chose to be second under John Stuart, whom he respected and admired.

New Caledonia Department, as seen in Harmon's Journal, was one which involved great hardship—a hardship tempered, however, by success. Fort McLeod was the post of entry and exit. The Indians about McLeod Lake were the hard-pressed and barbarous Sikanais. The food supply came from the lake, but dried salmon was brought over from the fort at Stuart Lake at the west. Here the furs of the Department were assembled in the spring to go down the Peace River, and hither the goods arrived from the east in the late autumn. John Stuart loved the summer's journey out to Rainy Lake, and therefore made this his headquarters.

Harmon passed on fifty miles overland to Stuart Lake, through "an uneven country" covered with a forest broken here and there by lakes and ponds. He was happy with his family in the fort about 200 rods from the outflow of the lake. It was in "a very pleasant place, on a rise of ground," he says. He speedily secured happy personal relationships with the Carrier Indians of the neighbourhood. His food supply was salmon caught at the outlet of the lake and dried for later use. At one time he had 25,000 salmon in store. There were years when the fish failed to come up—years of hardship at the fort and of starvation for the Indians. There was nothing for it but the traders must live, like the Indians, on berries in their season and on such fish, including sturgeon, as could be caught in lake and stream. Stuart Lake was by all odds the most important post in the Department, and Harmon went out in all directions to make contact with the savages and induce them to "work beaver."

The fort at Fraser Lake, some forty miles overland through a rough timbered country, was having a chequered career. Harmon sent forward J. M. Quesnel, Fraser's companion during his arduous journey to the sea, with the goods for the post. The fort was about a mile from the outlet of the lake "where the Natives have a large village and where they take and dry salmon." Boucher, the interpreter, took a daughter of a Carrier chief of the neighbourhood, the first woman of that tribe ever kept by any of the white people. The fort seems to have been closed in the subsequent seasons. In January, 1813, Stuart and Harmon came over "to purchase furs and salmon." Some difficulty arose over the interpreter's wife, and the party came near being massacred, perhaps because, in spite of the *liaison*, the fort had been closed. "Eighty or ninety of the Indians armed themselves, some with guns, some with bows and arrows, and others with axes and clubs for the purpose of attacking us. By mild measures, however, which I have generally found to be best in the management of the Indians, we succeeded to appeasing their anger, so that we suffered no injury ; and we finally separated, to all appearances, as good friends as if nothing unpleasant had occurred." Harmon visited the post on a similar trading expedition in January 1814. In October, however, Mr. Joseph Larocque re-established the post, and in 1815 Harmon was quartered there. We hear nothing of Simon Fraser's Fort George. It must have been abandoned.

The problems of the fur trade in New Caledonia were being solved. The men in the posts learned to provide for themselves, as necessity dictated, much as the natives did. In the hope of supplementing the meagre fare, Harmon planted potatoes, barley, turnips, and the like, at Stuart Lake in May 1811—" The first that were ever sowed on this west side of the mountains." Similarly at Fraser Lake, where he was residing in 1815. At Stuart Lake in 1817 he planted five quarts of barley and reaped as many bushels. In view of the re-curring periods of scarcity verging on starvation, he tried to win the natives to the gentle and remunerative pursuit of agriculture, but in vain. In contrast, the natives proved ready disciples to the traders in learning to " work beaver " and in preparing the skins for the trade, the incentives being the White Man's goods and his rum.

The menace of a population of savages massed in villages was ever present. A wave of passion might pass through the people and launch them on the fort. Even armed with guns, the diminutive garrison could not be expected to hold its own. Besides, anything like warfare would be ruinous to trade. Mild methods were resorted to as long as possible. For example, in a case of theft from Fort Fraser when Harmon was there, he went to the village, identified the thief and appealed to him and to his companions ; the goods were returned. Yet the traders knew when they could afford to, and must needs, be stern. When the Chief Qua of Stuart Lake proved provocative and domineering to the point of boasting in a threatening manner to Harmon of his exploits as a warrior, mild man though he was, Harmon, realizing as every Northwester did that there were times when offences must be resented or they would never cease, beat the chief about the head with a yard-stick. The savage chief threw himself out of the fort in high dudgeon. The day following, however, he sent his squaw for some salve for his wounds. This was cheerfully given. Next came an invitation to Harmon to a feast. He calmly accepted. Amid a crowd of one hundred savages Qua made a speech. He compared his relation to the trader to that of squaw to her husband. Just as he beat his own squaws when they misbehaved, so was Harmon right in beating him. Not only did Harmon skilfully keep the peace with the Indians, at times he suc-ceeded in keeping the savages from war among themselves—all for business' sake.

A definite attempt was made to solve the problem of the cost of the transportation to this the most distant Department of the Com-pany's trade. In April 1813 John Stuart had explored a route by canoe down the Fraser and by pack-horses to Fort Okanagan, and thence by water to Fort George at the mouth of the Columbia, and Joseph Larocque had brought the first consignment of goods in October of the next year. It took some time to learn to use this short and sure route from the sea, but by 1821 it was so far adopted that Fort Alexandria was built on the Fraser River near its confluence with the Blackwater. It stood at the end of the ancient trade route by which Mackenzie had passed westward to the Pacific. Here the pack-horses from Fort Okanagan were cared for till the canoes came down from the North with the return freight.

In view of his surroundings, Harmon presents a very interesting picture. Though there is a tradition that he was a great swearer, his Journal shows a man of deep religious feeling. He urged his religion upon Stuart, upon McDougall, and even upon Larocque with what he regarded as happy results. Stuart wrote to Ross Cox : " Messrs. McDougall and Harmon . . . are not only excellent traders, but (what is a greater novelty in this country) real Christians and I sincerely wish that their steady and pious example was followed by others." Harmon was a great reader and evinced the solicitude of a good husband and father. Much concerned about the education of his family, he sent his eldest son to Vermont to be brought up in the surroundings of his former home. He and " the mother of his children," as Harmon called his wife, were grieved at the lad's early death. The language of the family was Cree, but we hear of the father teaching his little Polly to read English. When, as he thought, he was leaving the Upper Country for good in 1819, so far was he from abandoning his half-breed squaw, as he had planned to do at the beginning, to the embraces of an honest man who would care for her, he took her out to Montreal and there married her. However, his plans were changed, and he returned to the North-West. At the union of the Hudson Bay and North West Companies in 1821 he was given the position of Chief Trader, but he soon retired with his family to Vermont.

At the Union of 1821 the North West Company brought the wide fur field west of the Rocky Mountains into the Hudson's Bay Company. The trade of New Caledonia had been very profitable, for its beaver was for the most part black and fetched a high price —so much so, indeed, that the Hudson's Bay Company had, as has been said, considered arrangements to enter the region. The Columbian Department was less profitable, for its expenses were great, but it was the *point d'appui* for an attack on the lucrative maritime trade. In the course of time the Hudson's Bay Company took advantage of this, and established a line of posts at vantage points along the coast. In the sum, the contribution of the North West Company to the Union in the form of the trade west of the Rockies was comparable to the contribution of the English Company in the shape of its Charter and, under it, the short route by Hudson Strait to the soil of Rupert's Land. In the Union of 1821 the Hudson's Bay Company entered into the enjoyment of what may be described as a continental domain.

CHAPTER VIII

THE UNION AND AFTER—SELKIRK'S COLONY,* 1821–50

I.—THE HUDSON'S BAY COMPANY AFTER THE UNION

THE Union of the Hudson's Bay and North West companies in 1821 inaugurated a new phase in the history of the Canadian West. The significance of the change is suggested by the gradual disappearance of the term "North-West," which originated at Michilimackinac and was habitual in Montreal, and the appearance of "Rupert's Land," the name given by the Charter to the region granted to the Merchant Adventurers of England trading into Hudson Bay. The more frequent term, however, was "The Hudson's Bay Company's Territory." The country lost its vital relations with Canada. It was governed from England and in terms of the Charter. All its trade was with London by way of Hudson Bay. The name "North-West" was now applied (at any rate in the later Parliamentary documents) to the area beyond the chartered territory interpreted in the sense of the basin of Hudson Bay, that is, to the Athabaska and Mackenzie basin and a vague region beyond, the title to which had always remained with the Crown.

The men from Montreal were aware of the change, which was the inevitable consequence of the terms of union. William M'Gillivray wrote Dr. Strachan from Fort William on July 26, 1821. "The Fur Trade is for ever lost to Canada ! . . . The loss of this trade to Montreal and the immediate district in its vicinity will be severely felt among a certain class of the People—the yearly disbursements in Cash from the office in Montreal to the people employed in various ways, as well for provisions and stores, was not less than £40,000 pr. annum—a large sum taken out of circulation and, combined with the present distressed state of the trade in the Province, is a matter of regret—the anti-northwesters of our *City* have got rid of us, but not exactly in the way they wished." In spite of M'Gillivray's success in securing a profitable place for himself in the Union, there was bitterness in his soul. McTavish, M'Gillivrays & Co. became bankrupt in 1824.†

The period from 1821–40 is marked, in contrast with the pre-

---

* See Sketch-map No. 11 at p. 626.
† After the union of 1821 the firm of M'Gillivrays, Thain & Co. had been formed to act as the agents of the Hudson's Bay Company in Montreal. It also went bankrupt.

ceding years, by profound quiet, by an extraordinarily successful fur trade, and by the development of Lord Selkirk's colony, as far as its isolated position would allow, till it took the place which its founder had planned in the system of business of the Hudson's Bay Company.

If the Union brought great changes overseas, it left the London end of the Hudson's Bay Company practically unchanged. The system imposed by the Charter was retained of necessity. The terms of Union presupposed two self-dependent parties entering into an agreement to act as one through the Hudson's Bay Company, that is, through the General Court and the Governor with the Deputy-Governor and the Committee. Unity was achieved behind the scenes, as it were, through a " Board for Consultation and Advising on the management of the Trade " (1821). On this Advisory Committee the Governor, J. Berens, Junr., and the Deputy-Governor, J. H. Pelly, sat. The English Company was further represented by Andrew Colvile and Nicholas Garry, the Canadian by William and Simon M'Gillivray and John Fraser. It may be mentioned that this bi-partite system gave place to a complete union in 1824 when the Advisory Committee disappeared as being no longer necessary.

To inaugurate the Union smoothly overseas, the Government and Committee sent out one of its members, Nicholas Garry. The Agents of the North West Company sent out Simon M'Gillivray, and the Committee of the Hudson's Bay Company issued a Commission enabling him to preside, in the absence of Mr. Garry, at all Councils to be held in Rupert's Land that year. William M'Gillivray accompanied his brother to the rendezvous at Fort William, which was reached on 1st July. Garry was conducted thence to the Red River Settlement by James Bird. His visit was later commemorated in the name for the fort built in 1822 very near to the site of old Fort Gibraltar. Councils were held at Norway House and York Fort, Simon M'Gillivray being present. The main object here, as at Fort William, was to secure the adherence of the individual Canadian Wintering Partners and English Factors to the *Deed Poll*, which embodied, as far as they were concerned, the terms of the Union. That adherence, signified in as many individual written documents duly signed, consummated the Union.

The *Deed Poll* recites the *Indenture* of March 26, 1821 (its own date), between the Hudson's Bay Company of the one part, and Messrs. William and Simon M'Gillivray and Edward Ellice of the other part, agreeing that the fur trade should be shared between their respective companies for twenty-one years, commencing with the outfit of 1821, the business to be carried on in the name of the Hudson's Bay Company, and the profits and losses to be shared equally between them. (According to the *Indenture*, each party was to have equal shares, and forty shares were to be set aside for the Wintering Partners, Chief Factors, and Chief Traders.) The *Deed Poll* explained the arrangements made by the Hudson's Bay Company. There were to be two Governors overseas, each with his own Council. Each member of the Council was to have one vote. Motions were to be regarded as carried when supported by a majority, the Governor concurring ; if the Governor dissented, there must be a two-thirds majority.

The service was to consist of Chief Factors and Chief Traders ; the names of the men proposed for either category were given. The forty shares earmarked for the service were to be divided into eighty-five shares. Twenty-five persons were to be appointed Chief Factors, each enjoying two of the shares. Twenty-eight were to be Chief Traders, holding one share each. The seven remaining shares of the eighty-five were to be reserved for retiring servants. It is to be noted that these were shares in the current trade, and not in the assets of the Company in London, nor in the soil of Rupert's Land.

The Chief Factor was to be superintendent of the trade in his district ; the Chief Trader to " act as trader." The Chief Factors, sitting with the Governor of the Department, were to constitute the Council. The duties of the Council were to be the management of the trade and posts of the Department, making rules and regulations for its conduct ; inquiry into the conduct of the officers, expelling those guilty of misconduct ; arrangement of the furloughs of the officers, and the like.

The *Deed Poll* also indicated those who were eligible to retire and the terms offered to such. Vacancies were to be reported to the Governor and Committee of the Company, and three persons nominated, from whom the Governor and Committee would select one.* Officers would be free to pursue the Governor and Company at law in case of any breach of the Covenant. Adherence to the *Deed Poll* was to be signified within eighteen months from its date, March 26, 1821.

There remained the actual task of bringing together into a happy union two parties which had been in conflict for a score of years. It was no easy one. Many servants of the English Company would recall a long series of personal affronts, and indeed of crimes, perpetrated at their expense. Some could show the scars on their bodies as proofs of the violence done them by the Highland gangsters, and would find it no easy thing to hold out the hand of friendship to the wrongdoers. On the other side, there was the Highlanders' pride to be overcome, and the contempt in which they had held the passive servants of the Hudson's Bay Company. Added to this was the success of the Englishmen when they did take the aggressive, and the memory of scenes of violence in which they were not always of the worsted party. It was sheer wisdom on the part of the Governor and Committee to remove Governor Williams, who, adopting the Northwesters' game, had provided himself with warrants and had arrested and carried off from the Grand Rapids to York Factory a number of the invincibles of the North West Company ; he was placed in the Governorship of the Southern Department, which was to a large extent apart from the fight. Equally remarkable for its

* For the method of nomination ultimately adopted see at p. 692.

perception of the needs of the situation was the appointment of the subtle George Simpson to be Governor of the Northern Department. True, he had been the centre of the conflict the year before in Athabaska, but he had played the Northwesters' game successfully without losing their respect for him and without awakening personal rancour.

The scene at a banquet at York Fort when the two parties first met as one is vividly described by that whimsical Scot, John Todd.

I would endeavour to recall your memory to the summer immediately succeeding the junction of the two companies, when that formidable band of Nor-West partners first landed on the bleak banks of York Factory, a bold energetic race of breached Highlanders from the North ; the heroes of the opposition who had fought and bled manfully in that long contest now ended. They had undoubtedly been defeated in the struggle, and their very name as a body in the commercial world [was] now entirely defunct ; yet they were by no means, apparently, humbled, or in the least subdued in spirit, but stalked about the buildings of the old dilapidated fort with the same haughty air and independent step, as if they had merely met, as they were wont to do in the more successful times at their favourite depot Fort William. . . . At length the bell summoned us to dinner, when forthwith in walked the heterogeneous mass of human beings, but in perfect silence and with the most solemn gravity. As the whole group stood on the floor of that gigantic mess-hall, evidently uncertain how they would seat themselves at the table, I eyed them with close attention from a remote corner of the room, and to my mind the scene formed no bad representation of that incongruous animal seen by the King of Babylon in one of his dreams, one part iron, another of clay ; though joined together [they] would not amalgamate, for the Nor-westers in one compact body kept together and evidently had no inclination at first to mix up with their old rivals in trade. But that crafty fox . . . George Simpson, coming hastily to the rescue with his usual tact and dexterity on such occasions, succeeded . . . somewhat in dispelling that reserve in which both parties had hitherto continued to envelope themselves. . . . It soon became evident that his stratagems in bows and smiles alone would eventually succeed in producing the desired effect on the exterior appearance of his haughty guests. Their previously stiffened features began to relax a little ; they gradually but slowly mingled together, and a few of the better disposed, throwing themselves unreservedly in the midst of the opposite party, mutually shook each other by the hand. Then, and not till then were they politely beckoned to their appointed places at the mess-table. [Some, however, found themselves misplaced]. For instance, he whom they called blind McDonnel . . . found himself directly in front of his mortal foe of Swan River, the vivacious Chief Factor Kennedy. . . . [They] had hacked and slashed at each other with naked swords only a few months before. . . . One of them still bore the marks of a cut on his face, the other, it was said, on some less conspicuous part of his body. I shall never forget the look of utter scorn and utter defiance with which they regarded each other the moment their eyes met. The highlander's nostrils actually seemed to expand ; he snorted, squirted, and spat . . . between his legs, and was as restless in his chair as if he had been seated on a hillock of ants ; the other looked equally defiant, but less uneasy—upon the whole, more cool. I thought it fortunate that they were without arms. . . . That plausible and most accomplished gentleman Simon McGillivray, who used to talk of the " glorious uncertainty of the law " and the " nulity of the H.B.C. Charter," seeing the state of affairs near my quarter sent a request, couched in the most gracious terms, to McDonald to be allowed to take wine with him, which, by the bye, had to be repeated more than once before the latter could be induced to remove the glare of his fierce eye from the person of his adversary. . . . The harsh expression of his countenance gradually gave way and, his attitude altogether assuming a more peaceful aspect, his rage at length subsided to a calm. Kennedy too, by similar means, put in operation by one of his friends at hand, was also induced to adopt the appearance of peace and tranquility. Immediately on the right of [M'Gillivray] sat that flexible character McIntosh ; his ever shifting countenance and restless black eye might seem that nature had designed him the harbinger of plots, treasons, and stratagems. . . . Directly in front of McIntosh sat his gallant enemy of the preceding winter, the pompous but good natured John Clark. . . . During the rivalship of the two companies Clark and McIntosh were for many years close neighbours. . . . It was only some time during the winter immediately preceding . . . at the close of a long day's march together on snow-shoes, that they agreed to end a dispute which had arisen between them on the way by a round of pistol shots, which they actually and deliberately discharged at each other over the bright blaze of a winter night's camp, separated merely by the burning element, Clark, it was said, cheering on his antagonist all the while to continue the combat until either one or both should fall. But these were the rugging and the riving times when might was right and a man's life was valued at naught.

It was the first great achievement of George Simpson, as Governor, that he led the two factions into a common loyalty to one another, and to the Company. This he accomplished by the friendliness of his manner and disposition, by his even-handed, impersonal administration, and by a strict discipline. That he stood head and shoulders in ability above those around him, that his office gave him almost supreme control in the country, and that he was the usual medium of communication with the Governor and Committee in London, the final authority in all matters, prevented the emergence of the old faction fight in the Council of the Northern Department. The increasing dividends, often accompanied by bonuses to the stockholders, acted as balm upon the wounds.

Then, too, each party must have been conscious that the other was making its contribution to the strength and efficiency of the Hudson's Bay Company as now constituted. Besides direct and cheap transportation from England to the shores of the Bay and the fringe of the great fur forest of the North, the English Company gave its Charter, involving an exclusive right to the trade, and ample powers of government. Add to this the Red River colony whose value to the trade was appreciated henceforth by all. The weakness of the English Company in the past had been the lack of co-ordination of its forts in the country. This it now remedied in the person of the untiringly industrious and extraordinarily efficient Governor Simpson. The contribution of the North West Company was equally notable. It gave a large band of experienced, masterly, and aggressive traders. Of old the Wintering Partners and their Agents met each year at a common council table to arrange the outfit and the plans for the coming year for their mutual benefit—all being partners in the concern. While they were not partners in the old sense in the Hudson's Bay Company, they were still partners in the fur trade and met, as of old, once a year in the Council of the Department under the presidency of the Governor. They brought into the new machinery the old sense of unity and the spirit of co-operation between post and post, which had been, at times, lacking in the English Company. Finally, the Northwesters brought in the great fur area west of the Rockies.

The Union made the legal position of the Hudson's Bay Company firm. Since it included even the M'Gillivrays and Edward Ellice, none was left to challenge the ancient claims. On the contrary, all asserted them vociferously. It thus proved easy to win from the Colonial Office, which had been pestered by appeals from both parties to the faction fight, a practical recognition of the Charter and of the institutions envisaged in it. This Lord Selkirk, faced by an opposition, had sought in vain. With the Colonial Office beaming on the Union with benevolence, an Act of Parliament was secured without difficulty. Its object was to get an indirect recognition of the Charter by Parliament, and to open the way for a monopoly of the trade with the Indians in the north and west of the Chartered Territory.

On July 2, 1821, "An Act for regulating the Fur Trade and establishing a Criminal and Civil Jurisdiction within certain parts of North America" was passed, empowering the King's Most Excellent Majesty " to make Grants or give his Royal License to any company for the exclusive privilege of trading with the Indians in all such parts of North America, not being part of the lands or territories hitherto granted to the said Governor and Company of Adventurers of England trading to Hudson's Bay, and not being part of any of His Majesty's Provinces in North America." The licence was to be for twenty-one years. Thus, without defining the limits of the several territories, Parliament gave its tacit recognition of the Charter.

The Quebec Act of 1774 had fixed the western boundary of Canada at a line running north from the Mississippi to the boundary of the Chartered Territory, without indicating at what point this would be reached. As it was now assumed without contradiction that the Charter granted Hudson Strait and Hudson Bay with all their rivers and lakes, the Company's claim to the river valleys up to the height of land received general recognition. The Act empowered the Government to grant a monopoly of the trade with the Indians in the region beyond. This would be the Mackenzie, Peace, and Athabaska valleys. As the Americans claimed the Pacific North-West, and a *modus vivandi* had been agreed to in 1818 assuring freedom of trade there to both parties for ten years, a clause was inserted in the Act recognizing the American rights. In the area in dispute the monopoly could be asserted only against British subjects.

The Act also regulated the criminal and civil jurisdictions in the territory affected by it. It strengthened the Canada Jurisdiction Act by definitely declaring that it shall " extend to and be in full force in and through all the Territories heretofore granted " to the Hudson's Bay Company (clause 5), but it further enacted that it should be lawful for His Majesty to appoint Justices of the Peace and to authorize them to sit and to hold Courts of Record for the trial of criminal offences and civil causes. At the same time, by its recognition of the Charter, the Act recognized the courts authorized by that ancient document, including courts actually in existence in Selkirk's colony. Here were the makings of a fine muddle in the form of the conflicting jurisdictions of Canadian, Imperial, and the Company's courts. However, the administrative acts of the Government clarified the situation.

On 5th December Lord Bathurst granted the United Company, that is " to the Governor and Company, William M'Gillivray, Simon M'Gillivray and Edward Ellice jointly, the sole and exclusive privilege for the full period of 21 years from the date of this our Grant, of trading with the Indians in all such parts of North America " as are specified in the Act of 1821, and again in the preamble of the licence, without rent, on condition that an accurate register of persons in their employ should be given to the Government each year, and that they should give security that they would ensure due execution of all criminal and civil processes in all suits exceeding £200. Further, it was agreed that they were to submit such rules and regulations for the management of the trade to the Government, as should appear to it " effectual for gradually diminishing or ultimately preventing the sale or distribution of spirituous liquors to the Indians and for promoting their moral and religious improvement."

On the very same day the Hudson's Bay Company and the M'Gillivrays and Ellice executed a Deed of Covenant binding themselves in terms identical with the licence, to keep its provisions, provided they should not be required to plead in any suit for the breach of the licence that might be brought by any party other than the Government itself. The costs of such would thus be borne by the united Company.

On March 25, 1822, the Company's seal was set to a document authorizing its Chief Factors to trade with the Indians and instructing them to warn off and prohibit any persons found in its territories and to seize any furs they might have obtained, and to prosecute them in the Courts of Upper Canada. This order proved somewhat unnecessary, for during the next generation the Company's monopoly did not require legal enforcement, but rested on its actual control of the business of the country. It will be seen, however, that John Clarke, Chief Factor at Fort Garry, interpreted it as meaning that the Red River colonists were prohibited from trading with the Indians even for necessary provisions, and thereby precipitated a crisis in the colony.

Between the Government and the Company the matter of the Courts to have jurisdiction in Rupert's Land was clarified. The Company asked whether it was the intention of the Government to appoint a Court of Record and Justices of the Peace, or whether it should instruct its Governors and their Councils to administer Justice. On May 29, 1822, the General Court of the Company passed a series of Ordinances for submission to the Government for its sanction. On the 31st Lord Bathurst replied that the Government had no plans, that " until His Majesty shall constitute Courts and Justices . . . the Resolutions of the 29th inst. appear well calculated to preserve the peace and good Government of that part of North America under the Jurisdiction of the Hudson's Bay Company." Thus, in the harmonious times after the Union, the Company secured what had been denied them in 1815 in the day of opposition, and courts could be established under the Charter to bring evildoers to justice.

The system, as sanctioned, ran that there should be two Governors, each with his Council ; that a Governor with any two of his Council should be competent to form a Council for the administration of justice and for the exercise of the powers vested in them by the Charter ; that there should be a Governor of Assiniboia with a Council, having the same power within the colony ; but that the power of the Governor of Assiniboia should be suspended when either of the Company's Governors might be actually present for judicial purposes. A sheriff was to be appointed for the District of Assiniboia, and two sheriffs for the remainder of the Company's territories. The Governors and Councillors for the several districts were named, as also the sheriffs. The legal basis of the new era was thus firmly established.

There remained the difficult task of securing a happy transition in the country from the old to the new. The immediate effect of union would be to close a long row of posts belonging to one company or the other in the wide area of the conflict. In the Athabaska country, predominantly the land of the North West Company, all the English posts gave way to the Canadian—Fort Wedderburn to Fort Chipewyan; Harrison House at Fond du Lac near the east end of Lake Athabaska, and Berens House on Athabaska River, as well as the North West Company's posts beside them, were closed, or the sites were only occupied on occasion ; the Hudson's Company's post on Great Slave Lake, Fort Resolution, was abandoned in favour of its rival, as also Fort Waterloo on Lesser Slave Lake. On Peace River, Colvile House and St. Mary's House gave way to forts Vermilion and Dunvegan, respectively. So, too, on the waters of the Churchill. Fort Superior was absorbed in the North West Company's Ile-à-la-Crosse, and Essex House on Green Lake in the Canadian post there.

On the Saskatchewan the Canadian posts gave way to their English rivals—Fort Augustus to Edmonton House, and La Montée to Carlton House. The two posts on Pine Island (Cumberland) Lake coalesced under their common name Cumberland House, the English fort being the one occupied. So, too, on the Assiniboine. Fort Gibraltar was abandoned for the English post shortly after named Fort Garry, and Brandon House and Qu'Appelle (on Beaver Creek) were temporarily closed. This partial list of posts will suggest the transformation wrought through the length and breadth of Rupert's Land, and the suffering of the servants involved in the sudden change.

It made things much worse that, on account of the trade war, all the posts were overstaffed. In the early times of peaceful competition it had been possible to leave but a few men in a fort, while the others were out at their varied tasks. During the conflict men were retained simply to hold the post against surprise. Where, before, one or two men could be sent out to the Indians, they now had to go in bands and armed. The result was that after union there were, as Simpson estimated, twice too many men for the service. Some of the officers and men, with some means at their disposal, adjusted themselves to the new situation without difficulty ; they retired to England or Canada, as the case might be. Some even took their children with them to England. A number of the men who threatened mutiny were sent out of the country post-haste by George Simpson. There remained, however, a large body for whom the Union meant distress.

It was fortunate for all concerned that a number of men on the Company's directorate were actuated by humane motives and exerted themselves to accomplish union in the country with the least possible distress. From 1822 Nicholas Garry, who had passed through Rupert's Land in 1821, and had seen the actualities of the Union, was Deputy-Governor. While at York Factory he had presided at the formation of an Auxiliary of the Bible Society by the Rev. John West, the Company's chaplain. " The Readiness which was shown by every Gentleman to subscribe proves how erroneous the Opinions of People have been that there was no Religion in the Country," he comments. " I subscribed £50 for the Hudson Bay Company and the whole amount was £130, which when the few Gentlemen assembled is considered, was a large Sum." Garry's interest in the welfare of the country remained unabated. The moving spirit of the Committee, however, was Andrew Colvile, gifted with much of the humanitarianism of the time, and endowed with a rare combination of shrewdness in business, judgment in choosing the means of accomplishing his ends, and consideration for those whose fate lay in his hand. Finally, there was Benjamin Harrison. He belonged to that remarkable group of Christians known as the Clapham Sect, and was Treasurer of Guy's Hospital for many years. He had been on the Committee from 1809.

The existence of this group of men on the directorate of the Company accounts for the attention paid to the moral and intellectual welfare of the service. In 1815 Harrison had tried to interest a missionary society devoted to work among the American Indians to undertake a mission in Rupert's Land. In 1816 £30 a year had been set aside by the Company for books " for the instruction and amusement of the officers and Servants of the Company," and inquiries were made of Governor Semple as to what books he desired for religious instruction ; " and we are desirous of your opinion as to the prospect of success in civilization and converting to christianity the children of Native Indians." In 1819 the Committee had decided to place a clergyman in the colony " for the purpose of affording religious instruction and consolation to the Company's retired servants and other Inhabitants of the Settlement, and also of affording religious instruction and consolation to the Servants in the active employment of the Company upon such occasions as the nature of the Country and other circumstances will permit." Rev. John West, M.A., was appointed. As the majority of the settlers were Presbyterians, his welcome in the colony was none too cordial, but he won the respect of the community as a man. His presence in the country afforded the Committee the means of carrying out some of its plans for the moral and educational development of the people after the Union.

A Committee moved by the finer motives would be anxious to minimize the hardships inflicted on their servants by the Union. In a letter to Governor Simpson of February 27, 1822, the problem of " the men who have large families and who must be discharged " and of " the numerous Halfbreed Children whose parents have died or deserted them " was raised. Naturally, the Company's point of view was not forgotten :

These people form a burden which cannot be got rid of without expense ; and if allowed to remain in their present condition, they will become dangerous to the Peace of the Country and the safety of the Trading Posts. It will therefore be both prudent and economical to incur some Expense in placing these people where they may maintain themselves and be civilized and instructed in Religion. We consider these people ought to be removed to Red River where the Catholics will naturally fall under the Roman Catholic Mission which is established there, and the Protestants and such orphan children as fall to be maintained and clothed by the Company, may be placed under the Protestant Establishment and Schools under Mr. West.

This policy was made all the easier in that Messrs. Harrison and Garry had enlisted the services of the Church Missionary Society. It was ready to place £200 at the disposal of the Company. The Committee agreed to find the further sum necessary for the building of a church, the site to be conveyed by the Selkirk estate to and held by the Company, as also the site on which the school should be built.

The Committee proposed that the men discharged, and their families, should be taken to the Red River Colony at the expense of the Company ; that there they should be settled on lots of twenty or thirty acres, and should be given tools to build their homes, seed to bring their lots under cultivation, and ammunition to enable them to hunt and secure provisions of meat till the products of the soil came to hand. As for the orphaned children, there would be the expense of erecting a building and maintaining them for the first year. The boys would be employed in cultivating the ground, and the girls in work suited to them. When grown up the children could be apprenticed to respectable settlers. " Mr. West and his assistants will take charge of this part of the plan."

The Council of the Northern Department met at York Fort on August 20, 1822. Mr. John Halkett, member of the Committee, who had visited the colony in the interests of the Selkirk estate, presented a Commission from the Company authorizing him to preside at Councils. Halkett placed before the Council the Ordinances creating a system of Justice for Rupert's Land and the colony and Lord Bathurst's letter placing the *imprimatur* of the Imperial Government upon them. He also laid before it the resolutions of the Committee looking to the care of the discharged servants and of the orphans. It was resolved that John Clarke, Chief Factor at the colony, in consultation with Governor Bulger, should take charge of the settlement of the people, and that Rev. John West be asked to assist him. Three hundred pounds were voted for the purpose. It was agreed in addition that Mr. Halkett should be upheld in his decision for the Selkirk estate that Fort Daer at Pembina be abandoned, and Mr. Clarke was instructed to withdraw the Company's post there. Thus the Frenchmen and half-breeds of that region were drawn into the Settlement at the Forks, adding to its population and strength. The matters of the orphans and the schools were left for consideration in the following year.

The retiring officers were not included in the scheme of settlement. They were men of considerable means and were entitled to secure for themselves lots up to a thousand acres. In the subsequent years a quiet but picturesque migration to the colony took place. Among the notable migrants was Donald Gunn. He had entered the Company's service in 1813, and was stationed successively at York Fort, at Severn, and at Oxford House. He retired in 1823 and settled at St. Andrews, where he farmed. (His wife was a daughter of James Swain, Factor at York Fort.) He opened a school, and appears to have been a very successful teacher. He also served as magistrate in the petty court of the district. By nature a critic, possibly bearing a grudge against the Company for his forced retirement when but twenty-six years of age, and, as a Presbyterian, rebellious at the failure of Selkirk's executors to bring out what he would have called a " regularly ordained minister," he never got into complete harmony with his surroundings. He was very much trusted as a juryman, but was never given high office in the Settlement. A great reader, he gathered a considerable library, and had the pamphlets of the North West Company at his elbow as he wrote. His *History of Manitoba*, compact with details of the inner life of the community, is therefore marred by its false perspective. He died in 1878.

Another outstanding migrant was Thomas Thomas. He had risen to be Superintendent of the Southern Department at the reorganization of 1810, and in 1814 succeeded William Auld as Governor of the Northern Department. At the emergency created by the death of Governor Semple, he was recalled from retirement to be Governor for one year. His service ended at Cumberland House, from which place he made his way to the colony. In 1822 he was made a member of the Council of Assiniboia, and served till his death in 1828.

Like Thomas, James Bird had risen to a high place in the Company's service. He had engaged himself as early as 1788, and served as master in a succession of posts on the Saskatchewan, including Edmonton House. When the posts on that river were organized as a factory he was made Chief Factor. From 1819-21 he was in charge of the Company's interests on the Red River. After service in the Upper Red River District, he retired to the colony in 1824. He was appointed Councillor of Assiniboia in 1822. In 1835 he was placed over the Customs, and in 1836 was made Registrar of land sales and grants. In his last years he was a magistrate in the lower district. He died in 1856.

The most interesting of the migrants is Alexander Ross. At the Union, he was in the Columbia Department. A man of excessive volubility, he did not impress Governor Simpson favourably. He made the mistake, unpardonable in the Governor's eyes, of bringing the Americans with his expedition to the sources of the Missouri back to his Flat Head post. Simpson rid the Company of him by offering him a post as a teacher at the colony. Ross travelled across the Rockies with the Columbian brigade, while his Okanagan squaw, with the family, made her way in her own canoe to her future home. In 1839 he was appointed to the Council, and was made sheriff ; in addition he held minor appointments from time to time. In his late sixties he devoted himself to publishing his two works on the fur trade of the Columbia and his history of the *Red River Settlement*, in which he gives vivid word-pictures of life in the colony—pictures which often verge on caricature. He died in 1856.

The Company was prepared to assist the Churches in their work in Rupert's Land. As early as 1819 it had gone so far as to appoint its own chaplain, Rev. John West, to minister to the religious needs of its servants, active and retired, and their children ; he had a free field outside of his immediate sphere. West arrived in the Red River Settlement on October 14, 1820, that is, in the autumn before the Union. He took up his abode in the colony's Fort Douglas, and there first services were held. His activities extended to education. He secured a log-house for a school among the Scottish settlers, three miles from the fort, and placed the schoolmaster in it, himself exercising a general supervision. His mission, however, was not to the colony, but to the Company's servants. Accordingly, in his first winter he travelled up to Brandon House and Fort Qu'Appelle, marrying couples who were living as husband and wife *en façon du nord*, and baptizing their children. He paid several visits on a like mission to Fort Daer, and one to Bas de la Rivière Winipic. His summers were occupied with the annual journey to Norway House and York Fort. In 1821 he travelled with Mr. Garry, and, as has been seen, was instrumental in establishing an Auxiliary of the British and Foreign Bible Society for Rupert's Land at the Factory.

West was specially interested in the education of the Indian children. He built a school near his residence, and added two houses to be homes for the boys and girls. His journeys to the various posts of the Company gave him the opportunity to recruit Indian children for the school. Scholars were secured from regions as far apart as Brandon House and York Factory. Some of the Indian boys could not tolerate the restricted life of a boarding-school and fled. Most of the boys and girls learned to read tolerably well ; a few learned to write. All were trained to work in the garden. The idea was taken up by the Governor and Committee as calculated to assist them in their solution of one of the problems involved in Union. Children abandoned by their parents could be sent to the colony to school.

Mr. West succeeded in building a church, the Company providing much of the money, the settlers, including Presbyterians, giving their labour. It was opened on June 10, 1823, when Mr. West addressed his people in farewell before leaving for England. At York Fort he met Rev. David Jones, sent out by the Church Mission-ary Society, but also appointed by the Governor and Committee as his assistant. When Mr. West did not return, Mr. Jones became the Company's chaplain. In May 1825 Rev. William Cochrane was appointed his assistant. In 1832 Mr. Cochrane created an Indian settlement opposite Nettley Creek, with a view to training natives to a sedentary life, and to teaching them methods of agriculture.

The mission of the Roman Catholic Church had been established by Father Provencher on the east side of the river opposite Fort Douglas. It was greatly strengthened when the half-breed settlement at Pembina was removed to the Forks. Children were taught by the priests in an apartment of the presbytery—the beginnings of the present College of St. Boniface. The influence of the Church on the people was a large element in training them to law and order.

The Governor and Committee were interested in the religious and educational institutions coming into existence. They had no intention to create an established Church in Rupert's Land. They looked on religion and education as calculated to train the people to an orderly life and as assisting the Company in its task of ruling a fretful realm. From this point of view it was not sufficient to support the Anglican chaplain and to assist him in building a church. Half of the population of Red River was French-Canadian, and the Catholic Mission was doing for them what the Anglicans were doing for the Protestants. The Company, acting through the Northern Council, acknowledged its indebtedness on July 2, 1825 :

Great benefit being experienced from the benevolent and indefatigable exertions of the Catholic Mission at Red River in the welfare and moral and Religious instruction of its numerous followers, and it being observed with much satisfaction that the influence of the Mission under the direction of the Bishop of Juliopolis [Provencher] has been uniformly directed to the best interests of the Settlement and of the country at large, it is Resolved . . . That in order to mark our approbation of such laudable and disinterested conduct on the part of said Mission, it be recommended to the Honble Com-mittee that a stipend of £50 p. Annum be given towards its support and that an allowance of Luxuries [tea, sugar, wine and the like] be annually furnished for it from the Depot.

The sum was increased to £100 a year in 1835. In 1830 £100 was placed at the disposal of the bishop " towards the repairs or re-building of the Catholic Church at Red River."

The assistance to the Anglicans took the form of the salary of £100 per annum paid by the Governor and Committee in London to Mr. Jones, successor to Mr. West as chaplain to the Company in the Red River Settlement, and of occasional additional grants from the Northern Council. For example, £100 was given in 1832 to the new church. In 1833 £25 a year was voted to Mr. John Pritchard for his valuable services in establishing sundry schools under the superintendence of Rev. Mr. Jones and Rev. Mr. Cochrane. When Mr. Jones established a boarding-school in 1835, in view of the ex-pected great benefits to morality, religion, and education, " not only in Red River but through the Country at large," and to prevent the charge for board from being so high as to militate against the success of the institution, the Council voted £100 per annum to the school and passed a vote of thanks to Mr. Jones. The wording of the Minutes shows throughout that the Company regarded its gifts as a just award for benefits conferred, not on the colony alone, but on the country at large.

Similarly, the payment of £50 to Dr. Hamlyn for one year's medical attendance was no act of charity to the colony, but for medical service "at the Company's Establishment and to their retired servants at Red River Colony and neighbouring districts." In 1833 the same sum was voted to Dr. Bunn, who, in addition, was attending " to the families of Gentlemen belonging to the Service who have been sent to Red River for the benefit of religious instruc-tion and education." In 1835 the sum was increased to £100 in view of his attendance also upon "pauper settlers." Similarly, the grants towards Public Works and to building a gaol were regarded as payments for improvements which were beneficial to the Company and its service, as well as for the good of the colony.

The Company might make provision for the migration to Red River Settlement, but success must nevertheless depend upon the migrants themselves. Would men who knew nothing but the fur trade—some of them expert at hunting buffalo or trapping beaver, all of them wedded to the free life of the posts, to its distant wander-ings, to its horse-racing, and perhaps to its violent revels—settle down of a sudden to the quiet and monotonous life of the farmer ? If so, would they show enterprise and initiative in solving the prob-lems peculiar to the soil and climate of Red River and the prairie region ? The future will tell its tale. One difficulty which they and their fellow farmers must meet was beyond their personal power to overcome. How would they market their produce ? As early as 1816 the Company offered to purchase the agricultural products of the colony. Simpson, like Andrew Colvile, appreciated the part to be played by agriculture towards the fur trade. He had learned a lesson at Athabaska in 1820. When pemmican was not to be had at the posts of either company, the Northwesters got their canoes up to the Peace River forts on potatoes grown in that region, and were trading with the Indians before the Englishmen, who had to hunt by the way, could arrive. His administration is notable for its stimulus to the production of provisions for the forts, at the posts themselves where practicable, but above all in the colony. The North West Company had a farm at Bas de la Rivière Winipic. In 1822 the Council ordered that the wheat raised there be ground and forwarded to Norway House, and that the farm be extended as far as possible without calling for extra labourers. By 1824 the colony was so far established as to be able to supply the posts with some produce. The Northern Council of that year ordered Mr. Donald McKenzie at Fort Garry

to purchase from the Colony the following supplies made up in sound and transportable packages at the Rates thereto annexed, 200 cwt best Kiln dried flour at 20/ per cwt ; 12 cwt Hulled Barley 16/6 ; 100 Bushels pease at 5/6 ; 100 Bushels unhulled Barley 4/9 ; 1000 Bushels Indian corn at 6/6 ; and 20 Kegs well cured Butter at 60/ per Keg of 60 lb net ; and that he take the necessary steps to get the same conveyed to Norway House so as to be depended on and thereby be the means of curtailing the requisition from England.

It is possible that the colony was not yet able to meet this order. Alexander Ross says that it was not till the 'thirties that it really began to play its part.

Notwithstanding the impetus given to colonial labour after the flood of 1827 [1826], agriculture remained in such a backward state, up to the year 1831, or thereabouts, that the Company could never rely upon the settlers for a sufficient supply of flour, or of other articles of consumption. . . . Great improvements were made and a large extension given to agricultural operations at the instance of Governor Simpson, the chief manager of the Company's affairs, who promised to take all the Company's supplies from the Colony. The promise was effectual in rousing the colonists to fresh activity, so that in a short time all the wants of the Company were adequately supplied. This was no sooner done, however, than the prices fell : flour from 16s to 11s 6d per cwt ; butter from 1s to 7d ; and cheese from 6d to 4d per pound ; while dry goods, iron, salt and every other article the settlers required, remained at the usual prices.

Orders for produce, similar to that of 1824, were repeated from year to year. The requisition for 1830 shows a considerable increase in the volume, with a fall in the prices, no doubt due to the larger quantities placed on the market :

300 Bushels Barley @ 2/- p. Bushel
500 cwt best flour @ 12/- p. cwt
200 Bushels unhulled Indian corn @ 4/1 p. Bushel
600 Liquor Kegs (to be filled with flour)
Iron Hoops to be furnished from Y.F. @ 5/- each

To the four articles taken in 1830 five other items were added in 1832, and the quantity of flour greatly increased.

110 Bushels rough Barley at 2/-
30 Kegs cured Butter, 7d per lb
110 Bushels hulled Indian Corn, 4/-
16 cwt Best cured Beef, Briskets & Ribs, 3d per lb
1200 cwt Flour 1st & 2nd quality mixed, 10/6
60 Cured Pork Hams
10 Bush. white Pease, 3/-
60 cwt cured Pork, 2½d per lb
250 Portage Slings, 2/- each

The impression one gets is that the purchase of provisions from Red River Settlement was already stabilized in 1830 and that it probably began as soon as a dependable supply was available. The higher prices offered at the beginning were, no doubt, intended as a stimulus to the settlers to devote themselves to agriculture. The later demand of the Company for cured meats directed them to live stock, in addition to their wheat farming. In contradiction of Mr. Ross's dates, the Minutes of the Northern Council show the Company as taking a steady supply of provisions from the colony before the flood. The lower range of prices mentioned by him began in 1830.

The Company encouraged the production of food at the posts, where it was practicable. At many an English post, even at the factories on the Bay, there were gardens. Potatoes, cabbage, and the like, were grown, even at Fort Wedderburn on Athabaska Lake. Under the more favourable conditions of the prairie region grains were cultivated. This is true also of the North West Company. Alexander Ross describes the posts on the Saskatchewan as he passed from the Columbia to settle in the colony. At Edmonton House there were " two large parks for raising grain, and, the soil being good, it produces large crops of barley and potatoes ; but the spring and fall frosts prove injurious to wheat, which, in consequence seldom comes to maturity." At Fort Carlton there were " some good cultivated fields, which with moderate industry, are said to yield crops of barley and potatoes ; the gardens also produce good returns of onions, carrots, turnips, and cabbages." Here were " the best root-houses I have seen in the country. It is pleasing thus to witness the fruits of industry and progress of civilization in the savage wilderness." Writing of Cumberland House, Ross says : " In proportion as furs and animals of the chase are decreasing, agriculture seems to be increasing, and perhaps eventually the latter may prove to the natives more beneficial than the former. In addition to the cultivated fields, we have to notice here the cheering prospect of domestic comfort. The introduction of domestic cattle from the colony of Red River gives a new feature of civilisation to the place. . . . A neat kitchen garden . . . furnishes an ample supply of vegetables." When Franklin visited Fort Carlton in 1820, five acres had been in cultivation during the summer, producing " ample returns of wheat, barley, oats and potatoes." Franklin says that the directors of the Hudson's Bay Company had issued orders for the cultivation of the ground at each of the posts, to obviate the danger of famine when the Indians might be sick, or the animals scarce. Governor

Simpson needed to do no more than stimulate and regulate a development already existing. In 1830 each Chief Factor was required to include in his reports " a list of Cattle and other Live Stock and the number of Acres in Cultivation and quantity of seed sown for the next Crop and quantity reaped the preceding Summer."

With the existing transportation, it was too costly to take the produce of the colony or the prairie forts into the Athabaska region. The Council of 1833 therefore ordered " the Gentlemen in charge of the Posts on the Peace River, where the climate and soil are favourable to cultivation, . . . to devote their attention to that important object forthwith, in order to save the expense of transporting flour from Norway House to the Athabaska and Mackenzie River districts ; as it is intended that those Districts shall depend on Peace River alone for their flour."

On the whole, the Hudson's Bay Company took the colony and Rupert's Land as far, or nearly as far, along the road of agriculture as the geographical and climatic conditions and the unskilled labour of the country admitted. Men whose chief energies were or had been devoted to the fur trade would necessarily be poor farmers. The late maturing wheat of those days too often suffered from the devastating frosts of the latter part of August. The transportation facilities of those times put the export of farm produce to England out of the question. Agriculture on a large scale only appeared when railways and early maturing varieties of wheat solved the problems of the West.

In a prairie country in which the soil could be brought under cultivation without the toil of clearing it of woods, agriculture was the simplest means of finding a livelihood for the surplus labour cast off from the posts after the Union. In the subsequent generation it played a part—a small part, it is true—in the lives of the surplus of freemen which grew up around the posts. Half-breeds for whom there was no room in the Company's service played the part of trappers of furs and buffalo runners, trading the fruits of their labour at the forts. They began to live in small settlements such as those at the Qu'Appelle lakes, and at Lake St. Ann, west of Edmonton, where there were good fisheries. They lived on fish and the proceeds of the chase, but they ensured themselves against periods of scarcity by cultivating gardens. The establishment of Catholic and Protestant missions among them greatly accelerated this movement.

There was little room for the crafts in the fur trade. Each fort had its blacksmith, its carpenter, and often its gunsmith. The Northern Council saw the opportunity in this of drawing a few of the steadier youths about the posts into the service of the Company. The Councils of 1830 and of the two succeeding years ordered :

That Chief Factors and Chief Traders in charge of Districts and Posts where regular tradesmen are employed, be authorized to engage strong, healthy half-breed lads not under 14 years of age as apprentices to be employed with those tradesmen, for the purpose of acquiring their business, on a term of not less than seven years at the following wages which are considered sufficient to provide them with Clothes and other personal necessaries, viz: The first 2 years at £8 p. annum, the next 2 years at £10 p. annum, the following 2 years at £12 p. annum and the last year at £15 p. annum, making for the seven years apprenticeship an allowance of £75, such lads not to be employed with their fathers nor in the Districts where their fathers or family reside.

It does not appear that the Factors pushed this policy any distance. Much would depend on the disposition of the individual Factor and the willingness of the half-breed lads to submit to discipline.   Probably owing to these personal considerations, this legislation, like so much else in the Indian Territories, was, in achievement, far below the ideal aimed at.   East of the Rockies, the half-breeds do not seem to have worked their way far into the service of the Company.   On the Columbia, and especially in New Caledonia, where the service was arduous in the extreme and unpopular with the " whites," half-breeds were a conspicuous part of the personnel of the forts.

The Act of Parliament of 1821 and the Licence had required the Company to adopt such rules and regulations as should appear to Her Majesty's Government " effectual for gradually diminishing or ultimately preventing the sale or distribution of liquors to the Indians and of promoting their moral and religious improvement."   In keeping with this, the Northern Council of 1822 resolved that the spirits used in the trade be reduced by the half.   This was followed up in 1827 by the order " That [no spirituous Liquor], either for Trade, Sales or gratuitous indulgences to Servants or allowances to officers be imported into English [Churchill] River, Athabasca or McKenzie River Districts for the current Outfit and that such deficiency be made up by a proportionate increase in the Supplies of ammunition and Tobacco."   Governor Simpson, when on his journey through Athabaska in 1828, was able to report that the Chipewyans no longer spoke of liquor.   In 1836 the Council resolved " that the use of Liquors be gradually discontinued in the few Districts in which it is yet indispensable," that other necessaries be sent to make up for it.   The reference here is to districts like the Saskatchewan in which the Indians could supply all their domestic wants from the buffalo hunt, and came to the fort for ammunition, tobacco, and rum.   The view held was that if the equestrian tribes were not given these, they would ride across the plains to trade with the Americans.   For this reason a modicum of liquor continued to be given to them.   This indulgence was allowed on two definite occasions, when they came in the autumn to be equipped and when they returned in the spring with their furs.   None was given between times.   In the region beyond the Rockies, including New Caledonia, the Indians had an ample food supply in salmon, and were not inclined to hunt for furs.   The traders themselves were at times on the verge of starvation.   They thought it necessary to offer a modicum of rum to induce the Indians to bring in supplies of provisions and furs.

Other resolutions had to do with discipline, education, and the like, at the individual posts. It became the custom of the Council to circulate with their Minutes, a list of " Standing Rules and Regulations connected with Civilization and Moral and Religious improvement." A number of these rules which first appeared in 1825 may be referred to—that every Sunday divine service be read publicly, all men, women, and children in the fort being required to attend ; that the necessary books for this purpose be furnished from time to time ; " that in the course of the week all irregularity, vicious, immoral or indolent habits particularly among the women and children, be checked and discontinued and their opposites encouraged and rewarded " ; that the children should be instructed and given regular employment suited to their age, with trifling rewards for the industrious ; that parents be encouraged to give part of their leisure to instructing their children in " their A B C and Catechism together with some short appropriate Prayer to be punctually repeated on going to bed ; that all officers see to the observance of these regulations." This, of course, is no more than legislation, and legislation affecting family life and the morals of individuals indicates the ideals aimed at rather than the standard attained.   Yet the regulations of the Council help to explain the orderliness and discipline at the Company's forts in the era introduced by the Union.   The repeated injunction that the Indians must be treated with civility put an end to the bullying of the period of conflict, and drew even the rougher Northwester Factors up to the Company's standard of earlier and happier times.   This goes far towards explaining the control exercised by the Company over the natives and the comparative orderliness of life in Rupert's Land, when hatred, often issuing in bloodshed, reigned south of the International Boundary.

It has often been said that the sole concern of the Hudson's Bay Company was beaver. This is not strictly true. From time to time attempts were made to find other sources of wealth in Rupert's Land. Apparently about 1830 the diminishing supply of whale oil in Britain tended to stimulate a trade in tallow. Certainly prices were good. Wool, hemp, and flax were also in demand at the factories in England. The Company decided to test the possibilities of their territory in these products. In this matter Governor Simpson led the Company.

On Simpson's visit to the colony in 1832 he found the people becoming very industrious, the necessaries of life abundant, and tranquillity and good order prevalent. Yet there was anxiety, for there appeared to be no means for the disposal of their surplus produce. The people were happy on their farms, but unless they could find a market for their produce they could not purchase clothing and the like, and in so far as they did purchase European goods, they diminished the ready money in the colony, for none returned in payment for their produce, save the limited amount brought into the Settlement by the Company's purchases and in wages paid. Simpson felt that if this situation continued the people would relieve their wants by turning to the fur trade and by clandestine dealing with the Americans. It was therefore necessary for him to find a remedy. He formed a Joint Stock Association, styled " The Red River Tallow Company."

The people were without enterprise and distrustful, and wholly ignorant of business in a large way, and the Governor had much difficulty in winning them to the scheme. Those who had cattle to spare placed them in the pool or common herd, and it was anticipated that in five years' time there would be a thousand head of cattle affording a steady supply of fat and hides for export. To meet the need of transportation Simpson revived Lord Selkirk's scheme of a winter road from York Factory to Norway House. Sailing craft were to be used on Lake Winnipeg. It was anticipated that the cost of transportation would be 3s. 6d. per cwt. from the Bay to the colony. It was very difficult to get fodder enough for a winter of heavy snow, and the inertia of the people was such that they failed to prepare for eventualities, with the result that many of the cattle died and the scheme came to an end.

The Company had plans of its own looking towards an export trade in tallow and other products. In 1830 an Experimental Farm was established on the Assiniboine about three miles from Fort Garry. Its object was not to teach farming to the settlers, as Alexander Ross and Donald Gunn assert, but to exploit a new field of commerce which, if it should succeed, would benefit both the Company and the colony. The resolution of Council ran : " That Chief Factor McMillan be directed to establish an Experimental Farm at or near Red River for the purpose of rearing sheep and the preparation of Tallow or Wool and of Hemp and Flax for the English Market and that the necessary means be afforded for that object." The farm was established on an elaborate scale. A house was erected for the Chief Factor in charge such as seemed princely beside the modest homes of the settlers ; barns and stables matched it. Cattle of the best breed were secured. Mares were brought from the United States ; a stallion, the wonder of the whole country, was imported from England at the cost of £300. Costly ploughs, harrows, and drills—everything that gave promise of success to the scheme was provided, according to Alexander Ross, and he should know, for his farm stood against that of the Company.

In contrast with this elaborate preparation for an export of tallow was the simple and infinitely cheaper plan of exporting the tallow or back-fat of the buffalo. From 1832 to 1836 resolutions of the Northern Council instructed the Chief Factor on the Saskatchewan " to bring to the Depot all the clean rendered Tallow he can collect . . . for exportation, provided it can be purchased at a price not exceeding 2d per lb." On two occasions similar orders were issued to the Swan River District. By 1837 the Company decided that there were no profits for them in the tallow market.

Lord Selkirk had argued that wool would be taken easily over the portages and would fetch high prices in England. Simpson returned to the scheme. William Glen Rae and Robert Campbell were sent to the United States to purchase a large flock of sheep. They had to go to Kentucky to attain their object. On May 7, 1833, the flock crossed the Ohio, and on the 15th 1,270 sheep began the long trek—more than a thousand miles across the prairies—to the Forks of the Red River. Early in June they ran into a wide stretch of spear-grass. The spears entered the flesh of the sheep and produced festering sores. When the body became a mass of suppuration, death ensued. The sheep dropped off in twos and threes all along the way. In the first week of July there were but 670. On 11th August there were only 295. Governor Simpson had taken the precaution of winning the favour of the Sioux, so that the flock could pass through their country in safety, but Campbell's party was guilty of the depredations from which the Sioux refrained; they ran out of provisions and had to kill of the flock to live. The Pembina River was crossed on 10th September. Soon a boat was met with provisions for the party. Sixty lame sheep moved peacefully down the waters of the Red to their destination. The rest of the depleted flock reach Fort Garry on 16th September. Two consignments of merino sheep were brought from England to improve the breed and the wool. In 1834 Simpson reported 400 sheep on the farm, and recovered from their long journey. He was still hopeful.

The fate of the venture in sheep was bound up with that in tallow and with plans for growing flax and hemp. In 1833 a farm servant conversant with the cultivation and preparation of flax was sent out. In 1835 the Committee reported the flax sent to England to be of good quality. A flax mill was erected. Prizes were offered to the colonists who should grow the largest quantity of flax, and who should produce the best quality of seed. All in vain. The settlers appear to have had little faith in the venture. The Company had begun on too elaborate a scale, and the costs were great. Not enough stress was laid on the experience and skilled labour and management by which such an enterprise could be made successful. McMillan, the Factor in charge, was no more than a fur-trader and not a very successful one at that. He spent his winters in the fur post at Portage la Prairie. Most of the servants were half-breeds. After years of loss it was decided to close the Experimental Farm. The ventures in tallow, wool, flax, and hemp passed away as one. Alexander Ross places the loss at £3,500.

A venture in lumber at Moose Fort, where a steam-mill was erected, and the trade in oil and whale blubber at Churchill and York Fort, show that the Company was seeking to exploit resources in their territory other than fur.

2.—RED RIVER SETTLEMENT, 1817-40

The colony which greeted Lord Selkirk's eyes as he came up the Red River in 1817 was a sad sight compared with what might have been expected of a settlement which was already five years

old. Fort Douglas was there, the one conspicuous object before his
eyes. Around it were little gardens and fields growing luxuriantly
unto the harvest, but the settlers' houses must have been few, most
of them newly built, or a-building by the remnant of the colonists,
of whom many were widows and orphans, returned but a few weeks
before to a scene poignant with the sorrows born of the Massacre
of Seven Oaks. The ruins of Fort Gibraltar recalled the struggles
of the past, but they also gave promise of peace in the future.
More assuring still, the De Meuron soldier-settlers came upstream
with his lordship and speedily took up their lots within sound of the
alarm bell at the Fort. Henceforth the colony will no more be the
victim of the rage of pitiless men. It will enjoy the peace without
which there could be little or no progress.

But the whole history of the settlement of the North-West is
one long struggle of Man with Nature—outwardly smiling, but
capable of dealing sudden and disastrous blows. When Lord Selkirk
left on September 4, 1817, the fields were bright with the promise
of a golden harvest. On the 10th, such a severe frost struck them
that only enough potatoes could be salvaged to ensure seed for next
spring's planting. Four days later the Settlement was visited by
such a violent tempest that a third of the wheat was blown off the
stock, and only enough was garnered to supply seed for sowing in the
following year. Alexander Macdonell, left in charge as Selkirk's
agent, adds resignedly : " We must entirely depend upon the plains
for subsistence."

Selkirk had arranged for a fresh band of servants to be sent
out from the homeland for the model farm, Hayfield, which he
established. They proved of the same shiftless class as the first lot—
" crawling good for nothing wretches . . . scarcely fit to take
charge of pigs without being strictly looked after themselves,"
as William Laidlaw in charge of the farm describes them. They
brought up seven pigs with them. So late was it that the journey
from Jack River over Lake Winnipeg was by sleds and dog trains.
" We had to wrap [the pigs] up in blankets and buffalo robes to
keep them from freezing, then lash them down on the sledges."
Henceforth the grunt of swine was heard in the land.

In the spring of 1818 Alexander Macdonell mustered 142 bushels
of wheat, 53 of barley, and 475 of potatoes for sowing by the whole
Settlement. Macdonell adds, in no sense to our surprise, " The
Meuron Settlers in German Street [running down the east side of the
River] have the worst crops of any ; all others have heavy crops."
But once more Nature, this time in the form of grasshoppers, proved
hostile. On 2nd August, as Macdonell reported to Selkirk :

millions of grasshoppers invaded our crops, and eat up all our Barley and
potatoes, particularly those in the woods, not a vestige of them left, but
all the potatoes more on the plains suffered very little injury ; the Barley
have been eat up everywhere ; they have cut the heads of it as clean as an
ax would do, and the more green the worst they have done to it. I have,
however, ordered all the people to collect the Heads and more particularly

those nearly ripe by which the people will have sufficiency of seeds, but
nothing for consumption ; the wheat has not been injured in the least as yet,
and we have a very heavy Crop of it and will be ready to cut down in 14
days after this, so that your Lordship need not be uneasy but we shall get
through (tho' different from what we expected).

All the garden vegetables were devoured. The settlers had, to some
extent, once more to rely upon the plains.

On the 16th of July, late in the afternoon, two canoes slowly
ascended the Red River. All the Settlement gathered on the bank
below Fort Douglas to receive the advance guard of the French-
Canadian settlers arranged for by Lord Selkirk when in Canada.
Fathers Joseph Norbert Provencher and Sévère-Joseph-Nicolas
Dumoulin, Catholic missionaries, landed and were conducted to
quarters set apart for them at the fort. Father Provencher, in a
letter to Lord Selkirk, describes the crops at his arrival as magnificent,
but when the band of some forty French-Canadians, servants for the
Hudson's Bay Company and settlers, arrived on 12th August, the
plague of locusts had transformed the scene. The little band, therefore, like its predecessors, passed on up to Pembina (Fort Daer)
to winter within easy reach of the buffalo herds.

The Catholic missionaries had received every assistance for their
enterprise. Lady Selkirk provided many of the ornaments for the
altars of their chapels. Lord Selkirk gave them a free passage in
the canoes. Alexander Macdonell, his lordship's agent, himself a
Catholic, quartered them in the upper story of a house within
Fort Douglas. There, mass was first celebrated in Red River Settlement. Lord Selkirk had promised a grant of land twenty miles
square on the east side of the river, as an endowment for the mission.
Within this, and among the German De Meuron soldiers, the missionaries settled, calling the spot St. Boniface, after the great missionary
of the Germans. A house was built to play the part at once of
chapel, house, and school—the home of Father Provencher. Father
Dumoulin, however, spent the winter at Pembina with the settlers,
and built a second chapel there for them and for the half-breeds.
Thus at the outset the mission and the French-Canadian settlement
was divided. Pembina, the resort of the half-breeds, grew at the
expense of St. Boniface. Father Dumoulin extended his pastoral
oversight to the half-breeds gathered around the North West Company's post at Rainy Lake, reached by way of the Roseau River and
Lake of the Woods.

Red River Settlement was thus taking on the form of after times.
Before the arrival of this little migration its census ran, 151 Scotch
in 20 houses, 45 De Meurons in 31 houses, 26 French-Canadians
in 6 houses, making a total of 222 souls in 57 houses. This excludes
a number of Orkneymen, old servants of the Hudson's Bay Company
of the lower rank, who preferred to settle with their squaws and
dusky children among the half-breeds who were already gathering
at the White Horse Plain some sixteen miles up the Assiniboine.

The year 1819 proved one of disaster for the colony. The grasshoppers had laid their eggs in the soil the summer before. On 3rd May the young brood made its appearance. They came out of the ground " like the froth out of the bung of a cask full of fermenting fluid. . . . Everyday until the middle of June brought forth fresh myriads of new-born ones." The larvæ devoured the young crops, leaving not so much as a particle behind them. If the grain sprouted again, they returned and consumed it. All hope of a crop passed away. There were at that time seventy pigs in the colony. As there were not left enough potatoes for food, these were fed with acorns gathered by the squaws. Doubtless, many were killed for meat. Once more the salvation of the settlers lay in the buffalo. The attempts to get cattle into the colony continued futile. The attempt to effect a cross between the European bull and the buffalo had failed. The contract made by Colonel Dickson on behalf of Lord Selkirk and Michael Dousman, for a herd to be driven up from St. Louis on the Mississippi, signed in June 1817, was expected to bring results. Four calves were sent out by the Company's ships to York Factory, where they had to winter. The isolated position of the colony, and its physical surroundings, were proving scarcely less hostile to progress than the assaults of the North West Company itself.

Since the last destruction of the colony, horses had been few, but this year fifty-two were brought down from the Saskatchewan. They proved a great boon, for they lightened the burden of bringing in meat from the plains. They were divided among the settlers, not without Alexander Macdonell taking a private profit out of the transaction. It was the good fortune of the colony that that winter buffalo were extraordinarily plentiful. Great precautions were taken, apparently with success, to prevent the half-breeds from " running " the herd on horseback and driving them away from the river. During the winter William Laidlaw of Hayfield Farm was sent to Prairie du Chien on the Mississippi for grain to swell the small store of seed on hand, that a fresh start at farming might be made. Eighteen joined the Settlement from overseas that autumn, and the total population was 382.

The grasshopppers do not seem to have deposited their eggs in the soil of the Red River in the summer of 1819, or, if they did so, the winter must have destroyed them. The plague, however, returned on July 25, 1820, but the wheat, which had been sown early, was not damaged, only that which grew from the seed brought in by Laidlaw, which, on account of his late return, was not sown till the 5th of June. The crop as a whole was excellent. Two of the four calves sent out from the Orkneys arrived, the other two having died at York Factory. Hopes of stocking the Settlement with cattle were high when William Laidlaw went to the height of land to receive the herd from St. Louis. It had got no farther than Prairie du Chien, where it was starved to death. However, an abundant supply of poultry, geese, and ducks was brought in through York Factory this year.

The year 1821 saw epochal changes in the North-West. The

long struggle between the two fur-trading companies came to an
end with their union. Lord Selkirk's colony passed out of the
succession of calamities which had stayed its progress. To effect
the consummation of the union in the Interior, Nicholas Garry for
the Hudson's Bay Company and Simon M'Gillivray of the North
West Company passed from Fort William to York Factory by way
of the colony. Garry's diary (August 4th to 6th) throws some light
on the Settlement as it was at his visit. The devastations of the grasshoppers, though complete in certain parts, particularly at Hayfield
Farm, was not general. The Hudson's Bay Company had opened a
post under Mr. Bird. (It was built by Peter Fidler about 1817–18
on a site between the present McDermot Avenue and Notre Dame
Street East). The North West Company was occupying Fort
Gibraltar in part, rebuilt a little to the west of its old position. Garry
rode along "German Street," occupied by the De Meurons, and commented : " the houses very comfortable and clean, the crops excellent ;
where the Grasshoppers had not been, nothing in the World could
be finer : spoke to the Meurons who are chiefly Germans. Complain
they have no wives, want farming utensils, but the cause and origin
of all their complaints is the Grasshoppers." He visited the Highlanders on the west side of the river. The framework of a school
was commenced. An appeal was made for one who could preach in
Gaelic, and a protest lodged against having to give six days' labour
to the support of Mr. West, the Anglican clergyman. Complaints
were expressed at the heavy charge of interest on their debts, and
requests were made for a circulating medium (Hudson's Bay Company's notes were introduced this year), for police and military
protection, and for cattle. Garry visited Peguis on the return down
the river, and thanked him for his friendship towards the colony.

The tribulations of the colony ceased with the flight of the grasshoppers in the latter part of July before a strong northerly wind,
and with the first arrival of cattle from Prairie du Chien. This was
not the herd contracted for by Lord Selkirk. William Laidlaw went
to meet that one, the second herd gathered to fulfil the contract,
but it failed to appear on the scene at the height of land. It did
arrive there later in the autumn, but was lost through starvation
and the depredations of the Sioux. Those which arrived were
brought in by a French-Canadian, Roulette by name, who sold them
to the better-to-do among the settlers at handsome prices. A flock
of merino sheep was brought in through York Factory, in the hope
of giving the colony a profitable business in the export of wool.
Unfortunately all the rams were drowned at York Factory. They
had been placed on an island and the river rose over it. New settlers
arrived that year to the number of one hundred and sixty-five souls,
all told. These were Swiss—artisans, watchmakers, and what not—
allured from the towns and even the poorhouses of German Switzerland by glowing promises which Lord Selkirk's agent had no
authority to make. They were the worst possible type to face the
privations of life on the Red River. It added to their sufferings that

much of their baggage had to be left at York Factory, so that they were not fully prepared to meet the extreme cold of winter. Many, however, received a warm welcome from the bachelor De Meurons, who married the Swiss girls and took their families into their homes. Those unprovided for had to proceed to Pembina, to live on the buffalo of the plains. As it was an open winter the herd remained far out. Moreover, the freemen, discontented with the Union because they feared prices would be reduced, drove the buffalo far afield by setting fire to the prairie. Even the fur posts were on the verge of starvation. Alexander Macdonell, unlike Miles, created no organization to bring the meat in. The Swiss, left to themselves, without knowledge of the country or of the art of hunting, kept in bands for which there was never enough meat. They presented, in the words of Governor Simpson, " the most distressing scene of starvation." How they span out the winter and spring, he says, was " inexplicable."

During all these years Alexander Macdonell was in charge of the colony practically as Governor. He was known, from the calamity of his time and in distinction from Miles, as "the Grasshopper Governor." At first he does not seem to have managed things unwisely. At least he was popular with the Scottish settlers, but they may have commended him because of his partiality to them at the expense of the other groups. By 1821 he had wholly lost the esteem of the French-Canadians, in spite of his being a Catholic. They charged him with gross drunkenness along with the men whom he gathered around him, with rank irreligion, with partiality, and with cheating ; and they claimed that his conduct in handling wrongdoers was bringing his authority into contempt and stirring one section of the community against another. These charges might be discounted were they not supported by all the evidence which George Simpson gathered when, in 1821, he became Governor of the Northern Department of the Hudson's Bay Company's trade. True, Simpson was by nature censorious of all under his control, but his description of the colony and its people under Alexander Macdonell can hardly be gainsaid. " There is no law, order or regularity ; every man is his own master and the strongest and most desperate is he who succeeds best ; . . . they have not exactly committed murder or robbery, but the next thing to it and frequently threaten both, so that the well disposed feel themselves in continual danger." As to Macdonell's dishonesty, Simpson gives definite details. He took advantage of his position as head of the colony to buy horses of the Company for the colony, but sold them to the settlers at exorbitant prices, putting the profits into his own pocket. He had at one time or another Mr. Allez, his brother-in-law, " a worthless drunken blackguard," as surveyor and storekeeper ; his cousin Macdonell, " of similar habits," as storekeeper and secretary ; and Mr. Fletcher, a second brother-in-law, as storekeeper. In managing the colony's store he had no system or arrangement, and allowed his associates to do what they would with the goods and accounts. He ordered expensive machinery for mills, which weighed 10 cwt., and could not be taken up from York Factory, and ended by finding that he could make millstones of the native material at Red River. Even so, Simpson says, the mill would not work. The grain was ground in handmills. Such mismanagement was disastrous to Lord Selkirk and his estate. In the years of suffering the colonists got goods and provisions from the store, without stint and on credit, at the expense of his lordship, but this was rendered a double misfortune when accounts were not kept, and peculation was rife. Simpson recommended that the store should be taken out of the hands of the Governor, if for no other reason, as causing difficulties with the settlers. It should be conducted by the Hudson's Bay Company itself. This was done. Further, Simpson saw that the colony might become "a receptacle for freebooters"—for every "blackguard" dismissed from the Company, and for French half-breeds with connections with the American fur-traders at Fond du Lac. For the sake of the monopoly of his Company, he was anxious to introduce law and order—all of which is testimony to the far-sightedness of the man.

In the sphere of government Alexander Macdonell was equally inefficient. Though the colony grew to considerable dimensions, there were no institutions of government save the quasi-governor. It is true, councillors existed, but the Council did not function. In June 1818 Lord Selkirk drafted a sketch of procedure for the trial of disputes, which was to be followed till a legal judicature could be established. Something like a friendly arbitration was first to be tried. If the disputants could not be thus brought to agree, " something like a regular court " should be held, with four or five of the " principal persons belonging to the Settlement " acting the part of Justices of the Peace. Their sessions for this purpose should be at regular intervals, with due notice given, and they should be assisted by jurymen—not necessarily twelve in number. The jurymen for each panel should be chosen by ballot ; witnesses should be properly examined, and each party have a proper opportunity to state his case. Though such a court would in the meantime have no legal standing, the settlers should be led to ostracise any individual refusing to accept its decisions. The whole system should be explained to them, and their support won.

But Macdonell was not the man to inaugurate such a scheme. The French settlers complained that when they were cheated by underweights or otherwise by Macdonell's associates at the colony store, there was no means of redress. It was fortunate for the Settlement that at this juncture Simpson, a man of great judgment and with the will and power to do, was in control of the affairs of the Company. He wrote to Andrew Colvile on September 8, 1821 : " I . . . conceive it indispensably necessary for [the colony's] welfare that a Code of Laws should be made, Magistrates appointed, constables sworn in and a small Military Establishment provided to give effect to the Civil Authorities, and without something of

this kind in my humble opinion the Settlement cannot flourish."
He as good as recommended that Alexander Macdonell be dismissed.

The situation in the colony called for drastic action. Fortunately it was now possible. The Union brought the practical recognition of the Charter, of the legality of the Grant to Selkirk, and of his right to the soil. Moreover, the Imperial Government gave its sanction to just such a system for the administration of the colony and for the law courts as Selkirk had submitted to them in 1815. Accordingly, a Governor was to be appointed—once more with a Commission from the Hudson's Bay Company. He was to have a council, and primitive law courts were to be established. Andrew Bulger, a military man who had distinguished himself in the management of the Indians during the war of 1812, was chosen for the office, but John Halkett, Lord Selkirk's brother-in-law and a member of the Hudson's Bay Company's directorate, was sent out in a double capacity to do the spadework of reform. He had, as has been seen, a commission to preside over the Council of the Northern Department which was to inaugurate the new régime for the fur trade. He also had full powers from the executors of the Selkirk estate to deal with all matters in the Red River Settlement. On his arrival he took up the grievances of the various groups of settlers. To the De Meurons he guaranteed to fulfil to the letter all proved promises of Lord Selkirk as to the implements they were to receive ; the price for their grain should be his lordship's price—10s. per bushel for wheat ; 7s. 6d. for barley and pease ; in times of distress honest and industrious settlers would be given necessaries on credit ; the interest on all debts should be cancelled to 31st May last (1822), and 20 per cent. on the principal to those who made good their obligations. Similar generous arrangements were announced to the Scottish settlers. The French-Canadians were promised cattle. To the Swiss he announced, in addition, that no rent would be required of them for their lands for two years ; in the third year but 10 bushels of wheat per 100 acres, and thereafter, to the tenth year, 20 bushels. Thereafter it would rise, but never exceed the 50 bushels per 100 acres required by the contract. Halkett decided, as Simpson had recommended, that the colony store should be closed in favour of the Hudson's Bay Company, who should keep a supply of goods on hand. Simpson was very anxious that the Pembina Settlement should come to an end. It offered a *point d'appui* for an American opposition, and was sure to bring the Sioux into clash with the freemen. Indeed, already, from time to time, parties were killed, and Simpson had himself led out an expedition which faced the Sioux with a superior force and warned them to keep to their own territory. This was all to the good for the Company and the colony. But Father Dumoulin was reluctant to give up his chapel and marshal the half-breeds close in beside the Protestants and the English at the Forks. Indeed the Catholic Mission at Pembina was thriving, while that at the Forks was at a standstill. Halkett firmly warned the missionaries that the object of Selkirk's generosity had been to form a strong and compact settlement at the Forks ; should the French and Catholics insist on scattering the people, the generosity of the Selkirk estate would end. Reluctantly all obeyed. Many French freemen settled around the Mission at St. Boniface, and its church and school began to thrive. A considerable body of half-breeds, however, settled on the Assiniboine at White Horse Plain, sixteen miles out. Halkett was but seven weeks on the Red River, but when he turned his face homeward towards the Bay he left a happier and more hopeful people behind him. The gloom of the unfortunate colony was partially dispelled. With Governor Simpson at his side, Halkett presided over the Council that introduced an era of real, if primitive, government into the Canadian North-West.

Before Halkett was away from the Settlement the new Governor, Andrew Bulger, arrived. As has been said, as a soldier he had distinguished himself at Michilimackinac in the South-West during the war of 1812. He had shown special aptitude in handling the Indian tribes. His soldierly qualities—courage, love of discipline, and sense of duty—were somewhat marred by a sharpness of tone, amounting even to irascibility, and by his love of wine. The task before the new Governor was no light one. A heterogeneous mass of settlers had been dumped down on the banks of the Red River. Misfortune after misfortune had fallen upon them. Instead of settling down to agricultural pursuits, their troubles had forced them out upon the plains and trained them, and especially their children, to the wilder ways of the buffalo hunter. One group of the settlers, the De Meurons, were but recently professional soldiers, habituated to the vices of campaign and barracks. They were quarrelsome, and more inclined to settle their disputes by a fight than by any legal process. Another was composed of half-breeds, many of whom united in their persons the wild propensities of both their white sires and their dusky mothers. Moreover, they had been schooled in intrigue and violence by the North West Company, and taught to believe that all the claims of the Hudson's Bay Company and of Lord Selkirk were illegal in fact, and tyrannical in design ; that they themselves were a " new nation," and this was *their* country ; and that all others were intruders. Scattered among these were servants of all ranks, dismissed from the two companies for ill-conduct, or forced to retire because their services were not needed after the Union. From the higher ranks came Hudson's Bay Company's officers, some of them opponents of the colony, retiring to it only because of their love for their squaws and their tawny children. From the lower ranks came a body of men who are said to have doubled the population of the river. To add to the confusion, the Hudson's Bay Company opened a store, thus introducing all the difficulties of a condominium. There was, therefore, an element of truth in Governor Bulger's description of his colony :

By far the greater part of our population . . . are sunk in vice and depravity and daring enough to despise our laws and openly defy our magistrates. The well-disposed have seen with sorrow and alarm the march of wickedness among them, but could not, without endangering their persons and property, attempt to arrest its course. Even now no one can be found to interpose and act as a magistrate, to such a frightful height has the evil grown. In short, it is useless to attempt to evade the question. Nothing but the presence of a military force to aid the civil power can prevent the country from becoming very soon a den of thieves and robbers, for no honest man will remain in it.

Exaggerated as this picture may seem, it can be matched by statements, oft repeated, in the letters of George Simpson. The military force was really never given, yet this mass of discontented and turbulent people were led into quiet and peaceful ways, and became a community orderly and obedient to the law. Much of the credit for the marvellous change must be given to the settlers themselves, but much also to the guidance of the colony by the Hudson's Bay Company, led by George Simpson. Yet, for the first and necessarily the most difficult steps towards law and order, the credit must be given to Governor Bulger.

To begin with, the cheating at the colony store had made the administration unpopular and tied the hands of the Governor in dealing with all malefactors. Alexander Macdonell was living in the Settlement. Bulger did not pry into the maladministration of the past, but openly proclaimed it that there should be none in his time. Fletcher, Macdonell's brother-in-law, was caught supplying his home with provisions from the store, not yet closed, and promptly dismissed. Angus Macdonell continued, but was watched with the eye of a ferret. The Governor of the colony began to be popular. The difficulty over the high price of goods was settled when the rate at Red River was made 33⅓ per cent. above the cost price at York Factory, and settlers were given their goods at the same rate as the servants of the Company.

The happiest incident in Bulger's time was the arrival of the cattle contracted for by Lord Selkirk. Two herds had died on the way. The third arrived in September 1822, ten years after the colony was founded. So eager were the Scottish settlers to stock their farms that they went out to the plains, chose their beasts, and drove them home. They then wrote out orders for them for presentation to the Governor. Bulger would have none of this. He reassembled the herd and distributed them by lot to the different classes of claimants in their order—the married men of the De Meurons who had Selkirk's promise; the Scottish families who had been longest in the country and suffered most; the married French-Canadians, come in from Montreal under engagements with Lord Selkirk; the Swiss, in consideration of their sufferings; and finally, unmarried men having a claim on his lordship. The arrival of another herd in the following year completed the task of stocking Red River with cattle. The comfort brought into the homes and the consequent contentment need no comment.

The Hudson's Bay Company was present in the Settlement in the person of John Clarke of Athabaska fame. Simpson took him for a vain, headstrong idiot, but placed him at Red River, believing that Bulger, by flattering him, could bring him to his will. But Bulger had none of the suave ways of Simpson and the clash came early. At the reorganization after the Union, as has been seen, the monopoly of the trade with the Indians became a reality. Factors were instructed to enforce it against all and sundry. Clarke, who believed that, as the representative of the Company, he was the greatest man in the Settlement, interpreted this as precluding all trade with the Indians on the part of the settlers. Furs, meat, everything procurable from the Indians, must pass through the Company's store to the colonists. This was the view taken by Heney at Pembina in 1812 ; it was that of Simpson in 1822. Bulger wrote to Colvile as early as September 12, 1822, in reference to Simpson's stand : " If . . . the people are to be debarred from the exercise of privileges necessary to their existence and be permitted merely to till the ground, hopeless, in my opinion, will be the attempt of Lord Selkirk's executors to establish a Colony on Red River, and loud and great the triumph of its former enemies." Two days later John Clarke served notice on Governor Bulger that there was to be no trade with the Indians. This was all the more iniquitous because Bulger had wished to make an arrangement with Clarke for provisions, but he had held out for a price much higher than that at which Bulger himself could procure them. The issues raised were fundamental. Had the colonists the right to make their own relations with the Indians—in fact, were they free British citizens ? Next, was the Hudson's Bay Company, in the person of the local Chief Factor, in control, or was this a colony with a Governor and Government—the source of all laws and regulations—controlling the people ? Bulger replied curtly to Clarke, simply sending him his commission from the Company, and asking him whether he acknowledged the authority it conferred on him as Governor of Assiniboia.

Hard on this Peguis arrived, discontented because he had not yet received his annual present. Bulger believed that he had been egged on by Clarke to give trouble. Some of the Indians threatened the colonists, and one attempted to shoot a Swiss boy. Bulger gave the signal for the De Meurons, and had more than thirty behind him in ten minutes. The Indian was arrested. Peguis came to protest, but Bulger gave him a piece of his military mind, and probably an example of his military language. He threatened to strip the chief of his scarlet coat, but in true soldier fashion gave him a glass of grog, and a buffalo robe in which to sleep. Next morning the Indian was tied to a gun, Peguis all the while scolding him for his deed, and punished with twenty-five lashes. Peguis departed perfectly satisfied.

Henceforth the Indians proved amenable to the law. But would the Hudson's Bay Company be equally so ? On 30th September Clarke required a freeman, who had taken meat to the Settlement and was passing up the river, to stop and answer for his conduct, and, when he refused, fired on him from Fort Garry. The next day the Chief Factor returned Bulger's commission to him, claiming that he did not refuse to recognize his authority, but enclosing, as the warrant for his own action, a copy of the licence of exclusive trade granted by the Imperial Government to the Hudson's Bay Company, and asking if Bulger acknowledged him as representative of the Hudson's Bay Company in the colony. Clarke's view was that the two should co-operate—he to support the Governor, the Governor to enforce the monopoly of the Company. Clarke now saw that he was raising a storm among the freemen. He wrote to Bishop Provencher denying that he intended to prevent the trade of the settlers in provisions, though, he asserted, it was the Company's right; he asked the bishop to read his denial and his assertion at the service on Sunday—which he did.

One of the colonists, for his fellows, now presented a document to Governor Bulger asking if the colonists in their poverty could trade provision " when and where we can obtain it for lawful payment." Could they purchase dressed leather, and could the Company prevent them? Could it prevent them from sending goods out with which to trade for the provisions? That on the 29th September Mr. Clarke and two of his servants had entered the house of one Registe Larante, a settler (when he was out on the plains) and taken away property in the form of furs and of dressed leather. Should Clarke not be apprehended? That the settlers were ready to support the Governor in arresting him. Finally, were the colonists to have magistrates and a law that would protect them? Failing this, would it not be proper for the settlers to assemble and determine what action should be taken against Clarke? Might they not petition His Majesty for relief? The note ends : " You see I am not a lawyer or a scholar, merely an honest and distressed man." A month later twenty-nine De Meurons petitioned to be given passage out of the country, on the ground that there was no law in the land. Some of the Swiss also were preparing to leave. Then, on 29th November, Mr. Alexander Macdonell presented a memorandum embodying the demands of the settlers for a circulation of cash, as in all civilized countries; for some means of marketing their produce, and finally for freedom in purchasing supplies from the Indians. On 24th December Governor Bulger met formally with his Council—Thomas Thomas, Alexander Macdonell, W. H. Cook, and John Pritchard.* The decision was to send an express by way of Canada to lay before the Governor and Committee and Selkirk's executors the crisis to which the colony was fast drifting. On 7th December the Governor wrote the dispatch describing the gathering storm, and recommending :

1. To get courts and magistrates nominated by the King.
2. To get a company of troops sent out to support the magistrates and keep the natives in order.
3. To circulate money.
4. To find a market for our surplus grain.

---

* The first and third were ex-Hudson's Bay Company's officers, the second Selkirk's late agent, and the last an ex-Northwester, but a settler since about 1815.

5. Let it be determined whether the Council at York Factory are justified in preventing the settlers from buying moose or deer-skins for clothing, and provisions.

If these things cannot be done, it is my sincere . . . advice to you to spend no more of Lord Selkirk's money upon Red River.

The answer from the Governor and Committee was dated May 21, 1823, and took the form of a letter to George Simpson, the Governor of the Northern Department. It condemned Clarke's action as " tending to bring into contempt the authority and privileges of the Company and to throw the whole settlement into confusion." His entry into the house of Larante was illegal. He ought to have applied to the Governor for the right of search. As to trading in furs, he should have applied to the Governor to issue a warning in the matter. His attempt to stop the boat was likewise illegal. He had totally misconceived his rights and powers as Chief Factor, and seemed to think that he was superior to the Governor. " There never was such a mistake." His assertion to Bishop Provencher that the Company had the right to prevent the Indians from trading in provisions was totally unfounded. " The Company has no such right. . . . It was never the Company's intention to prevent settlers from procuring skins for their own use."

Meanwhile Bulger formally submitted his resignation. The soldier-governor had stood out for the rights of the colonists and for the supreme authority of his office in the colony—stood out against the views of Governor Simpson himself. He won first of all the freedom of the colonists to trade with the Indians for all their necessities. Then, too, it was definitely decided that the Governor and Committee were not the rulers of the colony, and if the Company's Factor had any cause to proceed against a settler, it must be done through the Governor of the colony, or by means of the courts of the Settlement. It is to the honour of Governor Simpson that he accepted this decision against him and his Factor, and to the end of his days lived true to the principle that the colony was to enjoy a corporate life in itself, and that the Company itself must observe the law and prosecute in the courts.

It may be noted here that this isolated colony never had its rights embodied in any legal document or constitution, as had most of the British colonies. The rights of the colonists, much as the right of the British people themselves, grew up by quiet concessions of the sovereign power, in this case the Hudson's Bay Company, and by both parties abiding by the precedents established.

Bulger's Governorship is equally notable in that it saw the Council at last really functioning as a directing body. Simpson says that the Council meetings were the butt of the colony, that they began with a glass of grog, and ended with a great many more than another. This may be no more than an exaggerated picture given him by Clarke and his men at Fort Garry. The important thing is that the Council met, and did something to uphold law and order. In more than one case the Council took the prudent course of doing nothing that might rouse passions or disturb the peace. The most important cause again involved the Hudson's Bay Company and John Clarke. An appeal was made to Bulger for justice to one Risk Kipling, who had been assaulted by a servant at Fort Garry. The Governor refused to act alone and called the Council together. Clarke sent James Hargrave to deny the authority of the Governor and Council in a matter involving the internal affairs of the Company. Bulger required the statement to be made in writing, and it was given. The Council took the stand that they were there to do justice according to the laws of England, and "no one was above these laws." The unanimous decision was to stay proceedings and refer the whole matter to the Hudson's Bay Company, from whom they derived their authority. (May 3, 1823). Just what the answer was does not appear, but Simpson withdrew Clarke from his post at Red River—if we may judge by his letters, not without maledictions against the redoubtable Governor Bulger. The effect upon the public must have been to create the healthy feeling that in the Red River Settlement not even the Hudson's Bay Company was above the law.

Altogether, and in spite of his personal shortcomings, Andrew Bulger was the greatest Governor the Red River was to see. He entered a chaotic society, and succeeded to a very considerable degree in giving law and order to it, administered by something like a Council. He made good the claims of the law and the authority of the Governor against an over-zealous servant of the great Company itself. In so doing he gave the colony the first breath of a life of its own, and it is to the credit of the Company that they upheld him against their own officer. The judgment of Clarke's successor at Fort Garry may be taken as a sane estimate of Governor Bulger : "I mark him down as a most intelligent indefatigable man in the discharge of his duty here."

When Bulger left, it had been decided that law should reign in the colony, but the work of reorganization was far from done. The business of the Selkirk estate was in disorder, and the commercial habits of the colonists were vicious. In these matters the irascible soldier-governor, so far from effecting a radical cure, had added to the difficulties by a number of extravagant agreements, made perhaps out of pique at Selkirk's executors for not raising his salary but promptly accepting his resignation. Besides, in his need of support against Clarke he had been reckless in giving credit to the settlers. William Kempt, who held the reins till the new Governor arrived, had no commission, and therefore could do nothing, even in the way of trying offenders. It was left to Robert Parker Pelly, the new Governor, and especially to George Simpson, to carry through much-needed reforms. They held a joint power of attorney from the executors of Lord Selkirk's estate. Pelly had his commission as Governor of Assiniboia from the Governor and Committee, while Simpson's office as Governor of the Northern Department made him Pelly's superior, with power to preside at the Council of Assiniboia when present in the colony. Governor Pelly came out with his wife, and was lodged in a house connected with Fort Douglas. He was a man of exemplary habits, but with no experience; he aimed at carrying through the reforms demanded, but had neither the business ability, the sagacious firmness, nor the personal attractiveness which overcome opposition. All these characteristics lacking in the new Governor were the rich endowments of George Simpson, and to him must be given the credit of placing the colony's affairs upon firm foundations.

John Halkett had decided that the colony store must go. Had the colonists prospered, the store might possibly have been carried on in a healthy way. In the midst of the struggle with the North West Company all idea of sheer good business had to be abandoned, if only the colonists could be kept satisfied and loyal. When the settlers in their distress came for goods or provisions on credit, whether there was any chance of their ever paying or not, they must be provided. The system was costly to Lord Selkirk, worse still, it pauperized the colonists. After the struggle was over this continued. The crying need was to stay the losses of the Selkirk estate and to teach the settlers the self-respect which comes with sound commercial practices. It had therefore been decided that the Hudson's Bay Company should open a shop to be run on business principles, and the colony store was closed. Naturally the settlers were hostile to the change. During Kempt's short and feeble control the De Meurons plotted to seize the colony's store and decamp to the States with the goods. Only mutual jealousy among the leaders prevented the deed. When Simpson and Pelly arrived at the Red River Settlement in the autumn of 1823 their first task was to carry through the change in the face of a general hostility which extended to the Council itself. Simpson wrote to Colvile that it was necessary to move with caution and be courteous and polite to every one. None the less when the De Meurons petitioned for the usual advances on credit they were "unequivocally told that no further supplies could be rendered unless paid for in grain or otherwise." Simpson had intended not to go to the Council meetings lest it might appear that the Company's chief official was overshadowing the new Governor of Assiniboia, but Pelly, unequal to the task, insisted on his presiding as was his right. It was well that it was so, for the Governor of Rupert's Land was a past-master in handling men. He invited the Councillors to a banquet before the first meeting, and when Captain Matthey, the leader of the opposition, used disrespectful language of the Selkirk executors and the Company, he demanded an apology on the spot. The boastful captain gave it, and was so crestfallen that his opposition ceased. The Council was not to consider the change—that was a matter between the Selkirk executors and the Company—but rather the measures for protection against the armed intervention of the De Meurons and dissatisfied settlers. Pelly had come armed with power to raise a corps of militia. The principle people in the Settlement, from the Council downwards, were accordingly sworn in as special constables.

Twenty petty constables were appointed, and two bailiffs, "selected from the best affected of the lower orders." In Simpson's mind, however, the large body of servants at Fort Garry was the deciding factor. The colony remained undisturbed. But Simpson was not the man to think that the day was to be won by a display of sheer brute force. It had already been agreed in the Council of the Northern Department that goods should be sold in the colony at the same rate as to the Company's servants, *i.e.* practically at cost. In Simpson's mind this was an advantage not only to the colony but to the Company, for their cheapness would check free-traders from the United States, who had learned the way to the Settlement when the cattle were brought in. Indeed, Governor Bulger mentions a post of the American Fur Company established at Lac Traverse at the height of land between the Red River and the Mississippi. The policy of cheap goods did more to allay discontent than all the constabulary sworn in. Then, too, on behalf of the Company, Simpson inaugurated a currency, in the form of notes to be honoured whenever and wherever presented. There was a counter demand for a coinage, but at this stage of the colony's development the notes—one pound, five shillings, one shilling in denomination—were adequate for its domestic commerce, and they offered the great advantage that, as all business was done through York Factory and London, they could be cashed at those places at their face value without charge for exchange. Fifty pounds were sent out in pennies and halfpennies. Best of all, a succession of good crops brought increasing content with increasing prosperity. A second large herd of cattle, brought in under a contract made by Governor Bulger, completed the stocking of the colony. With the fields green or golden with grain and the low of kine in the byre, and the Company beginning to purchase the produce of the farms, the hardship of the transition from a credit system to what passed for a cash business was minimized.

Not the least astute move made by Simpson and Pelly in conjunction was their openly expressed indifference as to whether any settlers left the colony or not. Indeed, they were glad to see the turbulent pass over the border southward, as they did one by one. On one occasion Pelly provided the provisions and ammunition for the journey, happy to see the restless spirits turn their backs on the Settlement. Of a different type of cunning was the treatment meted out to Cuthbert Grant, who but seven years before had led the half-breeds to the "Massacre of Seven Oaks." At the Union he had been excluded from employment, but Simpson knew the extraordinary hold which he had of the half-breeds, both because of his talent and his marriage connections. He had given him a clerkship in the Company's service, but the life of a fur-trade post was ill suited to the greatest buffalo hunter of his time, and Grant drifted back to the Settlement. There the half-breeds had greatly increased in numbers. They continued to be hunters of buffalo and traders of meat to the fur posts and to the colonists. As the farms were now beginning to offer a supply of both flour and meat, Simpson feared that the half-breeds would be robbed of their means of livelihood, and in their distress would become a menace to the colony and to the Company's monopoly of the fur trade. Quick to meet future danger by remedies applied in the present, Simpson determined to win Cuthbert Grant to the cause of law and order. He made Grant's grievances against the M'Gillivrays his own, and secured the payment of moneys due him from his father's estate in the charge of the firm. Further, Simpson procured for him a lot of land at the White Horse Plain, and encouraged him and his following to settle down to some extent to farming. In this the Catholic clergy were of much help, for Grant had taken seriously to religion. A plan was worked out to give the " breeds " at the plain a missionary and a chapel. After a period of probation Grant was made a "Warden of the Plains," the magistrate of the district and of the buffalo hunt, commissioned to suppress any illicit trade. He was finally made a member of the Council of Assiniboia. At the outset Simpson's action received no sympathy from the settlers. One, who could not forget the " Massacre of Seven Oaks," assaulted Grant when in the Settlement. He was promptly brought before the Council, tried, and fined.

In Simpson's view the peace of the colony could only be maintained by recognizing the various groups hostile to one another. The Governor and Council must maintain justice and aim at securing what he called a balance of power between them, calculated to ensue in peace. Accordingly, he made much of the Council, insisting that it meet at regular intervals to determine policy and to administer justice. This is all the more remarkable because he held the Councillors of the time of very little account. " Our Council are really worse than nothing. Macdonell is disaffected, and the bitterest enemy to the Executors in this place ; Thomas is timid and weak as a child, Cook is like Thomas, but drunken and without either body or mind, Pritchard is froth, Mathey [a Swiss] is discontented and designing, wishes to be popular among his Countrymen and hostile to the Company and Executors." Logan and Macdonell were " a pair of thieves." The only one of whom anything good is said is Rev. Mr. Jones : " Although well-disposed he lacks experience." For all that, Simpson insisted on the Council functioning.

We established regular Councils which met as frequently as the Weather would admit ; we likewise held weekly Courts for the purpose of settling disputed accounts, the recovery of debts etc. and throughout the Season (Sundays excepted) Governor Pelly and I sat at Fort Garry three hours on each day for the dispatch of public business, and we have now I consider Law and Justice enough to meet all demands. The lower orders hold our Courts in due respect, and our Police evince, as far as we are able to judge, a readiness to carry our determinations into execution.

Now and then, however, the cry of the Northwesters, that the Charter was illegal and the Governor's commission a fraud, might still be heard on the lips of the designing, who found the Government of the colony stand between them and their ambitions. All this work of Simpson's is not a whit less important than the achievement of Bulger in gaining for the colonists the freedom to trade for their necessities and in establishing it that all in the Settlement, from the Company's servants in Fort Garry to the savage Indian, were subject to the Government of the colony and to the laws of England. Bulger was too uneven in temperament and too unbusinesslike to create traditions of good administration. To Simpson must go the credit of establishing firmly the institutions of law and order, primitive though they were, and of creating a machine of government calculated to run with tolerable smoothness.

In addition to all this, a system of land titles was introduced, affording security to the holders of the various lots. The titles took the form of a lease for a thousand years; the rental might or might not be payable in kind, namely with wheat. Attached to the patent were conditions—that there should be no engaging in the fur trade nor assistance to such as might desire to break the monopoly of the Hudson's Bay Company, and that there should be no distilling of liquor on the land. Lastly, the holder of the lease was to be ready to contribute to the expenses of the civil, ecclesiastical, and military government of the colony and to give a number of days' labour to the roads each year. Simpson's view was that the distillation of liquor would demoralize the community and must be prohibited, but doubtless he envisaged the possibility of the use of liquor in the fur trade in opposition to the Company, whose definite policy was to restrict its use in barter with the Indians. A number regarded the prohibition as a hardship, but finally accepted it. A register of titles was opened at Fort Garry, and notice was given that those who desired to do so could there put their titles on record. The land, from a short distance above the Forks, had been surveyed in narrow river lots as far down as Kildonan. This had been regarded as ample for the prospects of the colony. But there was a real place for the colony in the society of the West. Servants of the Company, high and low, kept coming in, and the Company encouraged them to do so. It became necessary to call for a new surveyor from England and to extend the area surveyed. Simpson's winter in Red River (1823–24) left the stamp of a master mind on the colony.

Meanwhile certain changes of some interest had taken place. The Hudson's Bay Company's post, occupied by Mr. Bird at Mr. Garry's visit in 1821, was transferred in 1822 to the former post of the North West Company, Fort Gibraltar, but the name was changed to Fort Garry.

Then, too, the rash John Clarke was superseded at the fort in 1823 by Donald McKenzie. As Simpson wrote, " the fittest man in the Company for the situation . . . a cool determined man, Conciliatory in his manners, economical and regular and privately attached to the Colony." Simpson went so far as to assure Andrew Colvile that he would make a satisfactory Governor when Mr. Pelly should retire.

The servants of the Company who came in were placed on the

land according to two categories.   The French-Canadians or their half-breed descendants were placed on the east side of the river from St. Boniface northwards.   The Commissioned Gentlemen were settled on the west side, north of the Scottish settlers in Kildonan.   Here were placed James Bird, formerly head of the great Department of Saskatchewan, and Thomas Thomas, who had been Governor in succession to William Auld, and later had been at the head of the Southern Department, that around James Bay.   Both of these men were afterwards placed on the Council.   A notable addition to the Settlement was Donald Gunn.

Two years later Alexander Ross arrived to make the colony his permanent home.   In his *Fur Traders of the Far West* he gives his impressions as he arrived at the Settlement in July 1825.   Leaving his canoe and taking to horse, he came to Image Plains :

as far as the eye can reach, a boundless prairie.   On the east, however, a narrow belt of tall trees running south, points out the direction of the river. . . . And here, for the first time, a small herd of tame cattle grazing on the plains attracted my attention, as being the most satisfactory sign I had yet seen of civilization in Red River.

The road was scarcely so much as a bridle path.   His guide (a Scots Presbyterian) informed him that there were :

three Roman Catholic priests in the Settlement, who have a chapel for their hearers.   There is likewise a missionary of the English church, but no congregation ;   and a Scotch congregation, but no minister !   This clergyman Rev. David Jones, whom, in the absence of one of our own persuasion, we of necessity hear, is a very faithful man in his way ;   but his ways are not our ways, and because we cannot fall into his views, there is anything but cordiality between us :   however, as we have, so far, no choice in the matter, we are content to give him our left hand of fellowship, reserving our right for our own church, whenever, in the course of events, we shall see her walls arise in our land.

There were no towns nor villages nor merchants in the colony, no magistrates and no jail, and hardly a lock and key, bolt or bar, on any dwelling-house, barn, or store.   The windows were without shutters and were made of thin skins which admitted a dull light. Frog Plain was reached.   " Here also we saw another small herd of domestic cattle, and some small patches of arable land lying along the banks of the river : for the plough had not yet got beyond the footpath on which we travelled."   Armed savages were met, chanting their war songs, dangling scalps, and smiling with savage contempt on the slow drudgery of the White Man.   Unfortunately, Ross does not describe the scene at Kildonan, contenting himself with noting the site chosen by Lord Selkirk for the Scottish church.   It could not have differed greatly from the district already described. Passing through swamps, knee-deep in mud and clay, he reached Point Douglas and, at the Forks, Fort Garry, " the metropolis of the country."   " Instead of a place walled and fortified as I had expected, I saw nothing but a few wooden houses huddled together without palisades, or any regard to taste or even comfort. To this cluster of huts were, however, appended two long bastions in the same style as the other buildings. . . . Nor was the Governor's residence anything more in its outward appearance than the cottage of a humble farmer, who might be able to spend fifty pounds. These, however, were evidences of the settled and tranquil state of the country."

In Lord Selkirk's plans the colony was to have a place in the fur trade, and the fur posts were to play a part in the development of the colony by providing an immediate market for its produce. The Minutes of the Northern Council for 1825 show that these aims were being attained. A resolution provided for the purchase, by Chief Factor McKenzie at Fort Garry, of :

$$
\begin{array}{lll}
200 \text{ cwt. best Kiln dried Flour} & \text{at} & 30/\text{-} \\
12 \quad \text{,, Hulled Barley} & \text{,,} & 16/6 \\
100 \text{ bushels Pease} & \text{,,} & 5/6 \\
100 \quad \text{,,} \quad \text{unhulled Barley.} & \text{,,} & 4/9 \\
1,000 \quad \text{,,} \quad \text{hulled Indian Corn} & \text{,,} & 6/6 \\
20 \text{ Kegs Butter (60 lb. net).} & \text{,,} & 60/\text{-}
\end{array}
$$

This produce was to be forwarded to Norway House for distribution to the posts.

As has been seen, Selkirk was aware also of the necessity of securing some produce which the colony could export to the old country. It would have to be light of weight for carriage over the portages and of high value to meet the cost of transportation. Wool and hemp had been thought of, but the misfortune of the colony had defeated the scheme. Sheep had been sent out, but no wool was being exported. Before his lordship died the project of a Buffalo Wool Company had been formed. In May 1820 instructions were sent out by the executors of the Selkirk estate to provide the Company with a suitable site for the nominal consideration of five shillings. Under the influence of those in authority, well-to-do officers of the Hudson's Bay Company were induced, not without doubts on their part, to take shares in the Buffalo Wool Company. The plan was to tan or dress the hides for the local market and for the fur trade posts, to eliminate the coarser wool and to weave it into coarse cloth and blankets, again for the local market. The finer wool was to be exported to England. Its transportation would raise no problems. The one uncertainty was the price to be secured overseas, but John Pritchard, the president of the Company, entertained no doubts. He wrote that the wool would be " the finest that . . . ever visited the London market. . . . In three years hence the Buffalo Wool Company will have opened to the Hudson's Bay Company a most lucrative and extensive branch of trade ; the Colony will be made to flourish beyond your most sanguine expectation and . . . a [hundred pound] share will then be worth one thousand Pounds." The first lot of wool placed on the London market in 1822 seems to have done well enough. Not so the second of 1823. Andrew Colvile wrote to Mr. Pritchard that only a small quantity of the very best should be sent home, that the Company must depend on the local market for its success. Lady Selkirk rushed in to the rescue and found an Edinburgh firm willing to try making buffalo wool shawls. The cost, however, was prohibitive, for the coarse outer hairs had to be picked out by hand before the very fine wool was ready for weaving. Moreover the colour was so strong as to admit of no dyeing save as black. Lady Selkirk induced some of her friends to buy the finished product at twenty-five pounds per shawl. When it was put on the open market a Glasgow merchant ventured to purchase two, and returned for no more. Apart from the failure in England, the Buffalo Wool Company, the first industrial enterprise of the Canadian West, was doomed to ruin. Pritchard's optimism led him to pay more for the hides, which would have been cast away on the plains, than the Company paid for the dressed skins, and wages were on the same scale of extravagance. Consequently, ere long the factory which stood across the river from Frog Plain was closed, and the Buffalo Wool Company became the amusing subject of conversation for subsequent generations of the Red River Settlement. The Company, however, proved a benefit to the colony. It distributed the wealth of the better-to-do to the poorer people in the form of wages, and when the cattle came in they had the means with which to purchase.

It is a proof that Lord Selkirk's plans—for a winter road with stations along the way and for an exportable produce for the colony— were not sheer idealism, but were based upon the necessities of the case, that such a practical man as Governor Simpson took them up. His first scheme was drafted in the winter of 1825–26, when the population had been greatly increased by the migration from the Company's posts. It envisaged the culture of flax and the rearing of cattle, sheep, and hogs. The flax would be sent off during the winter, in sleds drawn by the cattle, and would arrive at York Factory in March. There the cattle would be fed on hay, but they could likewise graze on the marshes about the factory. By the middle of September they would be ready for slaughter. The meat and hides would be pickled and the fat converted to tallow. Simpson envisaged a large profit, "which in due time may in my humble opinion be made even to surpass the Fur Trade in value—Difficulties would arise in carrying it out but they could be surmounted."

A sudden disaster in 1826 not only threatened the well-being of the colony but greatly reduced its population. It was a winter of dreadful snowstorms. The buffalo remained far to the west, beyond the reach of the hunters from their base at Pembina. Horses and dogs were eaten, but this only heightened the disaster, for they were necessary to accomplish the long journey home. Whole families died of starvation and cold out on the plains. Individuals became raving maniacs. The generous Donald McKenzie, in charge of Fort Garry, brought the great resources of the Hudson's Bay Company to the rescue of such as could be reached and brought into the Settlement. When spring came and the vast quantities of snow melted, the banks of the river could not contain the volume of its waters. On 2nd May the river rose nine feet perpendicular in twenty-four hours. On the 4th it was over its banks and the Settlement was being submerged.

The people had to fly from their homes for the dear life, some of them saving only the clothes they had on their backs. The shrieks of children, the lowing of cattle, and the howling of dogs, added terror to the scene. The Company's servants exerted themselves to the utmost, and did good service with their boats. The generous and humane Governor of the colony, Mr. D. MacKenzie, sent his own boat to the assistance of the settlers, though himself and family depended on it for their safety, as they were in an upper storey with ten feet of water rushing through the house. By exertions of this kind, and much self-sacrifice, the families were all conveyed to places of safety, after which, the first consideration was to secure the cattle, by driving them many miles off, to the pine hills and rocky heights. The grain, furniture, and utensils, came next in order of importance ; but by this time, the country presented the appearance of a vast lake, and the people in the boats had no resource but to break through the roofs of their dwellings, and thus save what they could. The ice now drifted in a straight course from point to point, carrying destruction before it ; and the trees were bent like willows, by the force of the current. While the frightened inhabitants were collected in groups on any dry spot that remained visible above the waste of waters, their houses, barns, carriages, furniture, fencing and every description of property, might be seen floating along over the wide plain, to be engulfed in Lake Winnipeg. Hardly a house or building of any kind was left standing in the colony.

Strange to say, only one life was lost.

The disaster acted as a winnowing fan sifting the settlers. The Swiss and the De Meurons, never reconciled to the Settlement, to the number of 243, moved southward into the United States by way of Lac Traverse; sixty went to Canada, " both parties furnished with every facility and assistance to gain their destination in safety " (Simpson). The Scottish settlers, for the fourth time, commenced life anew in the land of their adoption. The misfortune thus resulted in a reduction of the population, adjusting to some extent its power to produce provisions to the ability of its market, the fur posts, to absorb them. The colony now settled down to produce for its market, and the Minutes of the Northern Council show that its provisions were purchased in increasing volume and that the products grew in variety. In 1852 the list included barley, corned beef, cured hams, cured pork, lard, dried meat, onions, salted cabbage, potatoes, garden seeds, butter, cheese, flour, preserved eggs, biscuit, blanketing, cloth, and coating (for weaving was done in the homes), oak boards and staves, elm and oak timber, portage straps, three oxen, fourteen sheep, two pigs. Alexander Ross, an inveterate caricaturist, enlivens his pages with a description of the shortcomings of the produce in the first years after the great flood. The wheat was often threshed on floors of ice made in the open ; it was put away damp, and subject to mildew. After making a happy home for mice, it was ground, refuse of the mice and all, making a flour which the officers at the fur posts declined to eat. At Fort Garry the personnel, trained in the fur trade, was innocent of the art of merchandising. They took the butter of the settlers, and packed it, sweet and rancid alike, in common firkins, with a like unfortunate result. Flour and butter continued to be imported from England, Ross says.

In 1830 Governor Simpson took up once more the search for the exportable product which should be to the profit of both the colony and the Company, much on the lines sketched already. As has been indicated in another connection, an experimental farm was established on the Assiniboine above Fort Garry and, at the expense of the Company, stocked with cattle, brood mares, sheep, farm implements, and the like. Flax was to be grown and wool to be exported. The failure of the scheme was unfortunate for the colony. It promised a real development. Prosperity would have led to a renewed immigration. As it was, the colonists could supply the wants of the Company's posts with ease. There was no stimulus to further production. The colony remained for a whole generation passive to its fate.

It was probably as part of the scheme to secure an export trade for the colony that Lower Fort Garry was built. Fort Garry at the Forks was not conveniently situated, for boats had to ascend the St. Andrew's Rapids to it. Moreover it was now dilapidated, and since the flood it threatened to fall into the river. Simpson planned removing the centre of business from the Forks to the Rapids, which he seems to have considered the natural terminus of navigation. He therefore determined to build " a good solid comfortable Establishment at once of Stone and Lime in such a situation as to be entirely out of reach of high water and facilitate any extensive operations connected with craft and transport which may hereafter be entered into." Though by all odds the largest and most substantial fort in the Company's territory—Churchill Fort alone excepted—it does not appear to have been very costly, for it was built by a number of " supernumeraries " then on the Governor's hands, and the stone was procured from the neighbourhood. It was occupied in 1833, and became the point of arrival and of departure for the brigades. Its outer wall (of stone) was built in 1839. But, as it proved, the old site of Fort Garry, opposite St. Boniface and in relation with the half-breed settlement of White Horse Plain, was the real centre for the fur trade. Accordingly, Upper Fort Garry was rebuilt in 1835.

It has been seen that the Hudson's Bay Company took the view that the colony had its place in the fur trade of the country. Probably there was an element of inconvenience in having it out of the Company's control, while at the same time the Company, led by Governor Simpson, was planning for its good. At any rate the Company, by a " Reconveyance " dated May 4, 1836, secured for itself all the rights which had been granted to Lord Selkirk, and became possessed of the colony. The Company at last took on something of the complexion envisaged in the Charter. Rupert's Land became, in something more than profession, a colony, for the Company owned the

soil and it had a colony. The Settlement seems never to have been a
source of immediate profit to the Company. It was the embodiment
of their right to the soil. As such it proved of substantial advantage
to them in after times.

The new situation brought about, or at least made evident, interesting changes. In Selkirk's time Miles Macdonell, as Governor of
Assiniboia, ruled over the whole of his lordship's Grant. Theoretically his Council had jurisdiction over the wide area. Under the
Company the attention of both Governor and Council was confined
to the settled area—Red River Settlement. The organization, based
on the Act of 1821 and the correspondence with Lord Bathurst,
recognized the jurisdiction of the Hudson's Bay Company over
Rupert's Land, but it is a fine point at law whether that jurisdiction
could apply to Assiniboia, which had been already alienated. But
throughout the whole history of Rupert's Land practical convenience
and not law nor constitutionality regulated customs. All the fur
posts, not excluding those in Assiniboia, were treated as of the
Northern Department. Here the reconveyance of the Grant made
no difference. The country outside of the Settlement, and even Fort
Garry itself within the colony, was treated as of the Northern Department. Yet the area of the district of Assiniboia was defined by the
Governor and Committee in 1839 as " co-extensive with such portion
of the Territory granted to the late . . . Earl of Selkirk." But in
the whole history of the Company's administration it is not legal
definition but practical convenience that guided developments. So
far as the Company controlled this area, it ruled through the commissioned officers at the fur posts. The Council of Assiniboia defined
for itself the area it could conveniently rule. This was declared in
the edition of the " General Provisions " or the laws of the District
or Municipality of Assiniboia of 1841 as " extending in all directions,
fifty miles from the forks of the Red River and the Assiniboine."
The definition, like so much else in Rupert's Land, had its origin in
the practicalities of the situation, the distance between the Forks
and the International Boundary being taken by the Council itself
as indicating the radius within which its laws ran, " provided, however, that the Settlement, where it is expressly mentioned, shall not
extend in breadth more than four miles from the nearest part of
either river, or in length more than four miles from the highest or
lowest permanent dwelling." Obviously the area within which the
laws were to run was elastic in the extreme.

Similarly, there is no document defining the relations of the
Council of the Northern Department with that of the District of
Assiniboia. The powers exercised by the one and the other were
determined by convenience, and behind them both there was the
supreme authority of the Hudson's Bay Company itself.

The tradition prevails that the Hudson's Bay Company controlled
the Council of Assiniboia and used it to protect its trade. The facts
do not bear this out. The Minutes of the Council of May 1832, before
Lord Selkirk's Grant was reconveyed to the Company, show that

Governor Simpson, as head of the Northern Department, presided, and Donald McKenzie, Governor of Assiniboia, with him. There were but three Councillors present—James Sutherland, John Pritchard, and Robert Logan. The Council of February 12, 1835, was already being organized with the coming reconveyance in view. Simpson and the above three Councillors were present, but Revs. D. T. Jones and William Cockran, both Anglicans, sat as new Councillors, and with them James Bird and William H. Cook, old servants of the Company, now settlers. Two actual servants of the Company, John Charles and Alexander Christie, sat as Councillors of the Northern Department, while Bishop Provencher, Donald Ross of Norway House, Alexander Ross, sheriff, John Bunn, the Company's doctor, and Andrew McDermott, settler and merchant, were present by invitation. Manifestly the aim was to increase the dignity and authority of the Council by enlarging its personnel and by adding representatives of the different elements in the community. At the next meeting, held on 30th April, Ross and Bunn and John McCallum of the Anglican Mission sat as members, and Cuthbert Grant of Seven Oaks fame, now Justice of the Peace for the White Horse Plain, sat, no doubt, as representing the half-breed population of his district (the fourth). On 6th June, Bishop Provencher and Captain George Cary, a half-pay officer in charge of the experimental farm, were sworn in. On July 4, 1839, Adam Thom, a lawyer from Lower Canada, sent out to guide the procedure of the Quarterly Court, took his seat *ex officio*. The Minutes of the Council held on March 14, 1861, show that changes effected in the meanwhile had been in favour of giving representation to the half-breeds. There sat with Governor William Mactavish, the Anglican and Catholic bishops, and Dr. John Bunn, and with them François Bruneau, Pascal Breland, a member of the committee formed by Louis Riel, senior, in 1849 to secure free trade in furs, Solomon Amlin, Maximilian Genton, all Frenchmen or French half-breeds. The large French element was placed on the Council as the result of an agreement made by Governor Johnson in 1855. The French, who had been evading the customs duties, agreed to pay them if they had representation on the Council equal to the English, and consequently their influence in controlling the expenditures of the colony. In a word, no taxation without representation. The English side of the community was represented by Robert McBeath, Thomas Sinclair, John Inkster, John E. Harriott, John Dease, and Henry Fisher. With this in view, the statement of Alexander Begg, the diarist of the Riel Rebellion of 1869, in the preface to his Journal, may be taken as the sober truth. " Our government was by a Council appointed from among ourselves ; it is true we had no direct vote in their election but the H.B.C. invariably consulted the opinions of a neighbourhood before choosing a council man from that part ; we therefore to a certain degree had a voice in our own government and were content therewith." The appointment of the Councillors under the seal of the Company was necessary to make their authority legal.

In the 'thirties the proceedings of the Council began with the reading of a dispatch from the Governor and Committee relative to the business of the Settlement.   So far as the Minutes go, this practice does not appear in the 'forties or thereafter ; so also of the statement that the Governor and Committee agree to the findings of the Council.   Certain cases show that the Council felt free to act as the public desired without consulting the Committee in London. A petition, dated 17th June 1843, and addressed to the Governor of Rupert's Land, and purporting to be from " les Députés au nom de leurs Concitoyens," asked that the Company should distil liquor in the Settlement and thus create a market for grain, and that the number of the police be reduced ; if that were possible, that changes be made enabling others to serve so that there would be no jealousy. Simpson laid the matter before the Council on 3rd July, and a resolution was passed that a distillery be erected in the District. Governor Simpson, who was present, indicated that the Company would not undertake the distillery.   It was therefore resolved that the Governor of Assiniboia should call for tenders for its erection and management.   The police were kept at the old numbers, but it was resolved that every second year half the number of privates should be changed.   The Governor and Committee welcomed the arrangement about the police.   As to the distillery, they noted that there was a large minority against it, on the ground that cheap whisky would demoralize the community, and wrote that they were pleased to see so many members of the Council interested in the moral welfare of the colony ; in deference to their views, and because the amount of liquor used in the trade had been reduced to such a small measure that the advantages expected by those in favour of the distillery would not be realized, they had determined not to establish it.   It became the practice not to pass measures through the Council unless there were practical unanimity.   If such were not secured at a reconsideration the particular measure was dropped.   This practice meant that neither the Company nor any group in the colony could use the Council as an instrument of tyranny.

3.—THE DELINEATION OF THE POLAR SHORE OF THE CONTINENT *

Arctic exploration had been in a very special way a burden on the mind of the English people.   Other nations had sought and found ways to the rich marts of the Far East through congenial climes. From Martin Frobisher's day the English had tried, now and yet again, to force their way to China through the ice-ridden seas of the North.   When the task was proven futile it was laid aside, only to be taken up with renewed faith, as witness Arthur Dobbs and his supporters in the middle of the eighteenth century.   When the long tension of the Napoleonic Wars was over, Britain was fortunate in having at her service a band of men whose recent years had been

* Illustrated on Sketch-map No. 11 at p. 626.

passed on the Seven Seas in defence of the homeland, and who were now left without any satisfying preoccupation. Men's thoughts were turned to exploration, and there were those who aspired to wrest from the ice-beset coast of the American continent the secret of its pathway to the East. Such found ample support from the Government and the nation at large—a support typified in the person of Sir John Barrow, Secretary to the Admiralty. The special incentive to a renewed exploration of the Polar Sea was a report in 1817 by whalers that the sea was open beyond Spitzbergen and that the east coast of Greenland, hitherto inaccessible, was free of ice beyond the 70th and to the 80th parallel of latitude. In 1818 prizes were offered by the Government to seamen who should penetrate to high latitudes—£1,000 if they should cross the 83rd parallel ; £2,000 if the 85th, £3,000 for the 87, and so on up to £5,000 if they should reach the Pole—a like sum of £5,000 if, going westward, they should cross the 110th longitudinal line. This last prize was awarded to Lieutenant William Edward Parry and Lieutenant Matthew Liddon, who won it in the *Hecla* and *Griper* respectively in 1819. They passed through Lancaster Sound, named Barrow Strait, after Sir John, and reached the south shore of Melville Island, named after the First Lord of the Admiralty. They sighted and named Bank's Land after Sir Joseph Banks, whose interest in Arctic exploration was a living memory. At the same time an expedition was fitted out to attempt the North Pole. Of this Captain David Buchan was in command ; with him was Lieutenant John Franklin, whose name is writ large in the history of the polar shore of the Canadian North-West.

Franklin was born in the town of Spilsby, in Lincolnshire, in 1786. To cure him of what his parents took to be an unhealthy craving for the sailor's life, he was sent off on a merchant ship bound for Lisbon, but he returned more wedded to the sea than ever. Accordingly, his friends secured him in 1800, at the early age of fourteen, an appointment as a volunteer on H.M.S. *Polyphemus*. In this ship he played a youthful part in the victory won by Nelson at Copenhagen in 1801. From that year till 1804 he was with Captain Flinders, who was commanded to continue the exploration of Australia left incomplete by Captain Cook. The story of his shipwreck in Torres Strait is one of the most thrilling in the long annals of English exploration and rescue. During this voyage young Franklin became an accomplished seaman and an experienced marine surveyor. On his return to England he served as midshipman on the redoubtable *Bellerophon*, blocking the French fleet off Brest. As signal midshipman on this ship at the Battle of Trafalgar he must have received Nelson's famous message " England expects that every man will do his duty," and must have transmitted it to his captain. In the fight, in which his ship covered itself with glory, he was noted as " evincing very conspicuous zeal and activity." Franklin's following years were spent on the waves, now off Portugal, now along the east coast of South America, and again at Walcheren on the coast of Holland, and finally in the West Indies. In the war of 1812 he took part in the attack on New Orleans in command of a division of boats ; he was wounded and was mentioned in dispatches. When the long years of war were over he was doomed to a period of inaction from which he found relief by enlisting in the expedition organized to penetrate to the North Pole. Here he greatly distinguished himself as lieutenant in command of the *Trent*.

The success of Lieutenant Parry in reaching the 114th longitudinal line gave the public a heightened interest in the North-West Passage. The Government drafted a very original scheme. Parry was to continue his attempt to penetrate westward by sea, while another party was to pass down to the mouth of the Mackenzie River, or of the Coppermine, whence it would travel eastward, and, if possible, join hands with Parry. Of the two expeditions, without doubt the one which made the severest call for resourcefulness and leadership was the land expedition. This was entrusted to Franklin.

On his last expedition Parry had discovered Prince Regent Inlet, running south from Barrow Strait. His theory was that the land which he had named North Somerset was an island, as also the region south of Lancaster Sound. There must be straits to the south of these, he argued, by which, following the shore of the continent in the general latitude of the estuaries of the Coppermine and Mackenzie rivers, he could reach Bering Strait. He further inferred from his previous experience that there would be open water along the coast, at least when the south winds blew. Accordingly, his course was to be through Hudson Strait and Foxe Channel to the entrance of this southern water-way supposed to lead directly westward. To his surprise he found this southerly course much more beset with ice than his northerly one. With the greatest difficulty he passed through Frozen Strait to Repulse Bay, only to find that Arthur Dobbs's theories were all wrong, that Captain Middleton's delineation of the coast was entirely correct, and that there was no passage there. He was forced to spend the winter (1821–22) on an island off Lyon Inlet, named after Francis Lyon, his second in command. Here he was able to make a very happy study of Eskimo life. In the summer following he found a strait farther north to which he gave the names of his ships, *Fury* and *Hecla*. As it was not possible to pass through, a journey was made on land along the north shore to Cape Hallowell, where it could be seen that the coast ran northward, and on the other side southward. Thus Parry was assured that his theory was so far correct that Regent's Inlet ran southward. The expedition spent the winter of 1822–23 at Igloolik. Unfortunately the ships did not get free from the ice before 10th August, and winter would set in at the beginning of September. As he could not penetrate northward, rather was swept southward by the ice-stream, Parry decided that it was wisdom to turn homeward. He reached England in October.

The object of the Franklin expedition was to explore the south shore of the Polar Sea, *i.e.* the north coast of America, eastward from the mouth of the Coppermine River, a point placed on the map by Samuel Hearne of the Hudson's Bay Company, explorer, in 1771. At the same time a very specific aim was to assist Lieutenant Parry's expedition should it get so far west, and, if necessary, show it the way back to civilization by the great Mackenzie water-way.

Franklin's party included Dr. Richardson, a navy surgeon of considerable attainments as a scientist, midshipmen Hood and Back, and Franklin's devoted attendant Hepburn. It left Gravesend in the estuary of the Thames on the Hudson's Bay Company's ship *The Prince of Wales* on May 23, 1819—that is, in the height of the struggle between the North West and the Hudson's Bay companies. At York Factory Franklin found the Wintering Partners captured by Governor Williams at the Grand Rapids during the summer. The London authorities of both companies had pledged their men to help the expedition, and Franklin very wisely issued a memorandum to his own party strictly prohibiting all interference in the existing quarrels. This pleased both parties, and they willingly imparted such information as they had, and gave him letters to the traders inland.

The expedition reached Cumberland House, then occupied as Governor Williams's quarters inland, by way of the Hayes, Oxford Lake, and Norway House. It was now November 23rd—too late to go on. The Governor was at pains to keep the party in comfort, and Mr. Connolly of the North West Company did what he could. Dr. Richardson and Mr. Hood spent the winter here, the one surveying the Saskatchewan as far as Fort Carlton and studying the human and animal life of the region, the other making an excursion into the Pasquia Hills, but Franklin, with Back and the ever-faithful Hepburn, went forward on snowshoes in the early months of the year in order to organize for the coming summer. His course was up the Saskatchewan to Fort Carlton, where he was entertained by Mr. J. P. Pruden, and thence northward to Green Lake. Here the party secured carioles and dog-teams, and passed swiftly on to Ile-à-la-Crosse, where they were received by the expansive Mr. John Clarke with the usual volley of musketry. So, too, by Mr. Bethune of the rival post. At Fort Chipewyan they were welcomed by Messrs. Keith and Black, those sturdy Northwesters, and delivered to Mr. MacDonald, clerk in charge of the Hudson's Bay Company's Fort Wedderburn, a circular letter of commendation from Governor Williams. In the subsequent months, until the arrival of Dr. Richardson and Lieutenant Hood by the Churchill River route on 13th July with the equipment, Franklin busied himself gathering information, determining his route, and securing the requisite servants—half-breed and Indian. Beaulieu, a half-breed whose family had been on the Slave River since 1778 and who had himself been among the Dogribs and Copper Indians, sketched on the floor the course of the rivers, and an old Chipewyan recognized the sketch as accurate. A stepson of Matonabbee, Samuel Hearne's guide of 1771-72, could give but vague answers to questions, for he had been but a boy at the time. On one occasion Franklin secured a conference between Colin Robertson, chief of the District for the Hudson's Bay Company, and the Northwesters by pitching a tent for the meeting-place away from both forts. It proved easy enough to get advice and secure servants, but the supplies on which he had built expectations were woefully deficient. Clothing enough was secured, but the all-important rum, ammunition, tobacco, and meat had been spent by the two companies in their mad rivalry, and Franklin could procure but little of them.

The united party left Fort Chipewyan short of provisions, only to find a scarcity at the North West Company's post on Great Slave Lake and at Fort Resolution, the rival English house near by. However, by waiting a few days at these forts, enough meat was procured to take them to the North West Company's Fort Providence on the north shore of the lake. Here Akaitcho, a Copper chief, and his following were retained to act as hunters for the expedition. The Indians went forward and were followed by the main party, which now was made up of twenty-eight persons, including Mr. Wentzell, the North West Company's clerk in charge of Fort Providence, whose skill in managing the Indians was placed at the disposal of the untutored Englishmen. Franklin thus describes his equipment :

> Our stores consisted of two barrels of gunpowder, one hundred and forty pounds of ball and small shot, four fowling-pieces, a few old trading guns, eight pistols, twenty-four Indian daggers, some packages of knives, chisels, axes, nails and fastenings for a boat ; a few yards of cloth, some blankets, needles, looking-glasses, and beads ; together with nine fishing-nets, having meshes of different sizes. Our provision was two casks of flour, two hundred dried reindeer tongues, some dried moose meat, portable soup, and arrowroot, sufficient on the whole for ten days' consumption, besides two cases of chocolate and two canisters of tea.

It was surely a slim commissariat.

The plan was to live on the country as did the fur-traders—a reasonable enough scheme on the prairies thronged with buffalo—but on the remorseless Barren Grounds, where the caribou moved over a wide area by uncertain tracks, and especially with such a large party and such unreliable Indians, the risk was very great. The course was up the Yellowknife River to a lake to be called Winter Lake, where the winter was to be spent in gathering provisions. This was to be the base for the exploration of the next summer.

The expedition left Fort Providence in August in three canoes, accompanied by a smaller one, in which were the women who were to dress the meat and make shoes and clothing for the men at the winter establishment. The hunters and their dependents travelled in seventeen canoes. The labour at the many portages was severe ; the rate of progress slow. Soon provisions were short, with no caribou, and but few fish to be caught. There was, however, abundance of berries at the portages. Thus the cumbersome expedition crept on by river, lakes, and portages, until 13th August, when it was in a country bare of wood except for a few dwarf birches. At this point it began to find supplies of caribou meat left by the hunters *en cache* along the course. On 19th August it reached Winter Lake, the spot chosen by Akaitcho for the winter establishment, because a pine grove along its shores offered the wood for building and for fires. By 6th October Fort Enterprise, as it was called, had been built by Wentzell, so that the tents could be abandoned for the comparative comfort of a log building, fifty feet long and twenty-four wide, with a hall, three bedrooms, and a kitchen. The walls and roof were plastered with clay, and the floors laid with planks rudely squared with the hatchet. The furniture was rough-hewn to match ; the windows closed with parchment of deer-skin. At this time the caribou were returning to their wintering ground on the edge of the woods. All were busy laying in a food supply while plenty was to be found. In the storehouses were 100 carcasses together with 1,000 pounds of fat and some dried meat, while 80 carcasses were cached at various spots distant from the house.

It was a winter of disappointments. Back returned with Wentzell to Fort Providence for supplies, only to get word that but five of the ten packages being forwarded from York Factory had arrived. The Hudson's Bay brigade was to bring these packages from York Factory to Cumberland House, but that year the northern brigades of the rival companies reached the Grand Rapids of the Saskatchewan on the same day in a wild race to reach their posts and equip the Indians before " the enemy " should arrive. To lighten his canoes the Hudson's Bay Company's guide insisted that the Canadians should take the packages at that place. The Northwesters declared that they were too heavily loaded, and besides, the transfer was to be made at Cumberland House. As a result the five all-important packages with ammunition and tobacco were left on the ground at the portage. As if this were not enough, Akaitcho and his band camped at the fort when the hunt was over, and began to devour the accumulated supplies of meat. It was with the utmost difficulty that Franklin persuaded them to move away and follow the caribou. Then, too, the catch of fish from the lake rapidly declined as winter deepened. New Year's Day was observed in sombre fashion with a special ration of flour and fat, a poor and sad substitute for rum, of which there was none. However, supplies came in from Fort Providence on the 15th—two kegs of rum, one barrel of powder, sixty pounds of ball, two rolls of tobacco, and some clothing. The rum was frozen and after standing by the fire for some time flowed out, of the consistency of honey. Yet the voyageurs swallowed their drams and celebrated a belated New Year's Day. Soon Mr. Wentzell returned. He was an excellent musician, and the spirits of the camp were kept up with an occasional dance. On 17th March Back reappeared after a journey of 1,104 miles, as it was calculated. He had gone on to the rival forts at the mouth of Slave River in a vain attempt to make good the ammunition and tobacco left at the Grand Rapids. He passed on to Fort Chipewyan on the same quest. It is indicative of the much happier position of the North

West Company in the rivalry with the English Company that he was given a satisfactory quantity at their fort, but George Simpson, who was in charge of Fort Wedderburn, was in no position to help, for he had not received the full quota of the supplies due to his post, because the genial but grasping John Clarke at Ile-à-la-Crosse had laid his hands on more than his share of goods. However, through the generosity of the Canadians, the situation was greatly relieved.

At Fort Enterprise the stock of meat laid up for the post in the autumn was exhausted on 23rd March, and they were entrenching on the dried meat set aside for the summer's exploration. Worse still, the Indians who had been retained to lay up a supply of provisions at the Coppermine River in the autumn, fickle as the winds of the Barrens, had removed to Great Bear Lake to mourn some of their dead. Some meat might have been traded, but there were no goods with which to trade. In April the situation was grave. Mr. Wentzell journeyed far, doubtless to the edge of the forest region, to bring in meat from Akaitcho and his Indians. Happily the time for the migration of the caribou outwards soon came, and with it the hunters. Meat was now procured in abundance.

With June the hour struck for advance to the ocean. Akaitcho was urged to do his utmost to get dried provisions for the exploration as the party moved on to the Coppermine River at Point Lake, and downwards to the sea. Looking eastward from the lake, Franklin could see the Copper Mountains of Samuel Hearne at a distance of twelve miles. Soon he was following in the Englishman's footsteps. On 15th July—fifty years after Hearne, almost to the day—he reached the Fall near the sea, still frequented by Eskimos rejoicing in the salmon fishery. The spot answered the description given by Hearne exactly. Human skulls, which bore the marks of violence, and numerous bones lay scattered on the ground, recalling the bloody scenes witnessed by Hearne, which gave the spot the name of Bloody Fall.

Here Akaitcho and the hunters, and along with them Mr. Wentzell, left, not without Franklin's urgent appeals ringing in their ears to store provisions at Fort Enterprise, and on the way to it, unto the return of the expedition, for the problem of supplies continued an ever-present anxiety. When at the seaside fourteen miles to the north, Franklin named two promontories visible Cape Hearne and Cape Mackenzie. A river flowing in from the west he called after Richardson.

At noon, 21st July, the exploring party launched their frail birch-bark canoes on the Polar Sea, with but fifteen days' provisions. Their dangerous journey eastward along the coast constantly brought them up against a hard choice. The short Arctic season bade them push forward without an hour's unnecessary delay. On the other hand, the pressing necessity for food for their journey commanded them to linger wherever they might see caribou, which might replenish their perilously slim larder. To their eternal honour, they took all the risks of starvation, if only they might accomplish the aims of their mission—to explore the coast and, if necessary, to guide Parry and his crew back to safety. They paddled along the coast within a range of islands, a group of which they named Berens, after the Governor of the Hudson's Bay Company. They were thus sheltered from the drift of the polar ice for the time. To the south lay a sandy beach skirted by green plains. Then they came on the most sterile and inhospitable shore imaginable. " One trap cliff succeeds another with tiresome uniformity, and their débris covers the narrow valleys that intervene, to the exclusion of every kind of herbage. From the summit of these cliffs the ice appeared in every direction." In this mournful scene the party worked its way eastward, mapping the coast, noting the geological formations, measuring the tides, and estimating the force of the currents and the drift of the ice. Here and there, where the shore was hummocky, the explorers could, without waste of time, draw near enough to the caribou to kill, and so to stay the perilous diminution of their supplies. Every opportunity to fish was taken, but with meagre results. Once they killed a feeble brown bear. The Indians refused to eat of it on the plea that it was diseased. The officers boiled the paws and found them excellent. A fat female bear proved delicious to all, as also a musk-ox. Even the young geese unable to fly were eaten, if only the precious pemmican might remain untouched. Seals were seen, but were always too wary to be caught. On the little party went, with never a human being to be seen in their whole course along the coast. Traces of Eskimos were found, but that wandering race would be inland on the Barrens for their summer hunt. At times the course was beset with ice and endangered by storms. The birch-bark canoes were often in imminent danger of being crushed by ice or of being ripped open by the sharp edge of a floe tossed on them by the waves. If the fragile barks were lost the end would be tragic indeed—a hundred miles from the nearest savage, a thousand from civilized man. With this grim outlook ever before them the party skirted the south shore of Coronation Gulf, so called from the recent accession of George IV. to the throne ; they worked their way around Cape Barrow, named after the genius who presided over the Arctic exploration of the day ; they followed the coast south to Hood's River, so called after Franklin's able and trusted officer ; amid a bewildering tangle of islands, they traced out the deep inlet honoured with the name of Lord Bathurst, Minister of the Crown. A river at its bottom (Western River) they signalized with Back's name. Their disappointment at having to turn back towards the north was greatly mollified by their success in winning provisions—a musk-ox, a bear, a salmon trout, and several other varieties of fish. Gales detained them, but they pushed on northward, past capes Croker and Parry, Point Beechey, and Melville Inlet, to a point when their provisions could last but three more days. Caribou were to be seen in plenty, but the land was so level that these took alarm and defeated all attempts to approach them. At this stage Franklin gave up all hope of pushing through to

Repulse Bay, as there was little chance of meeting Eskimos and procuring food. It was decided to push on for four more days and then turn. On 18th August the canoes were storm-stayed. Franklin and Richardson walked on to make a last observation of the trend of the coast. It was north-north-east as before to a low cape. This was called Point Turnagain. The party had made but 6½ degrees of eastward, though it had travelled 555 geographical miles. It had met with ice, but none through which a ship might not make its way. The sea was often open and always deep, and the islands to the north were a shelter from the tides of ice. Accordingly, Franklin concluded : " Our researches, as far as they have gone, favour the opinion of those who contend for the practicability of a North-West Passage. . . . I entertain, indeed, sanguine hopes that the skill and exertions of my friend Captain Parry will soon render this question no longer problematical." In truth, Parry was nowhere near. On that very day he was at the head of Repulse Bay and was deciding to turn back, for there was no passage there.

When the party turned its face homeward it was travelling on two meals a day. No longer preoccupied with exploration, its chief concern was the food supply for the voyage to its base. Franklin says : " The privation of food, under which our voyagers were then labouring, absorbed every other terror." Though a strong wind and heavy sea were on when they reach Melville Sound, they took their lives in their hands and were all but lost in mid-channel. They supped on some berries and tea made of a shrub of the country. They reached an island in Bathurst Inlet with pemmican for but a single meal, but they had the good fortune to kill three caribou does, and farther on an additional two. They were now to realize the pitiless conditions of travel upon the Barrens as depicted by Samuel Hearne. The course was to be overland some 220 miles as the bird flies, from the entrance of Hood's River to Fort Enterprise, where Akaitcho was to have a store of meat for them. Soon the current of the river was too much for their large canoes. They therefore used their material to make two small ones with which to ascend the stream, and later to cross the Coppermine. The weather was fine and continued mild and they secured venison as they journeyed. September 1st brought heavy falls of snow. The course of the valley of Hood's River being westward, they had now to strike across country in a south-westerly direction for Point Lake on the Coppermine. In an undulating country, which has been compared to a tempest-tossed sea suddenly frozen, they encountered wild storms leaving bank after bank of deep snow in the troughs of the waves. Worse still, they were away from the tracks of caribou and musk-ox, and their strength was failing them. On the 7th Franklin was seized with a fainting fit, and only a morsel of portable soup—a portion of the party's last meal—to recover him. Half a partridge apiece and soup made out of lichen—*tripe de roche*— was a happy day's fare. When on 10th September a herd of musk-ox were seen grazing in a deep valley below, the hunters went after them. Franklin says : " We beheld their proceedings with extreme anxiety, and many secret prayers were doubtless offered up for their success." One of the largest cows was killed. " To skin and cut up the animal was the work of a few minutes. The contents of its stomach were devoured on the spot, and the raw intestines, which were next attacked, were pronounced by the most delicate among us to be excellent "—this on the sixth day since they had had a good meal. But they were too heavily laden and too weak to carry much of this plenty with them. Once again on the verge of starvation, they came upon a lake with every prospect of fish, but to their utter despair they discovered that their improvident Indians had thrown the nets away to lighten their burdens. The lake was Hearne's Contwayto (Rum) Lake. It forced a wide detour upon men already weakened by hunger, but fortunately two deer were killed. After the perilous crossing of a stream at the lake's mouth, where Franklin lost his Journal, they began to cross the hills to the Coppermine. Soon their fare was once more *tripe de roche*. They cooked the bones and horns of a caribou, and fed on old shoes and scraps of leather. Temporary relief came when they killed five caribou. These, including the horns and the skins, were distributed to the men. The reckless Canadians ate one-third of their portion in a single day.

The morale of the men was by this time undermined. The carriers of the canoes fell behind and abandoned them. The men began to steal their officers' portion of the provisions. When they would shoot partridges they would eat and leave their officers to starve. In attempting to swim across the Coppermine, for lack of the canoe, Richardson came so near drowning that he could not converse for several hours. " Poor Hood was reduced to a shadow." At last a canoe was built and the crossing effected. But the effort of the last stretch of the journey was too much for some of the men. Hood could go no farther. Richardson and Hepburn volunteered to remain with him. Franklin and most of the party were to go to Fort Enterprise, some forty miles away, and to send out provisions for them. They staggered on to the post, man after man falling out by the way. At last the party, now reduced to five, reached the post, where they expected a warm welcome. Not a soul was to be seen. The place was absolutely desolate—not a pound of provision in store—only a note from the gallant Back, who had come on before, to say that he had gone on to bring in supplies from Fort Providence some 440 miles away. Several days after the cry was raised, " Ah! le monde" ("People are coming"). It was Richardson and Hepburn, each carrying his bundle.

It was some time before they could tell their tragic tale. Franklin had sent Michel, an Iroquois, back to them along with a Canadian, Jean-Baptiste Belanger. Michel alone arrived. After a mysterious absence Michel brought in some flesh for them which he said was wolf. Richardson and Hood came to believe that it was human flesh—that of Belanger, in fact. Michel grew morose and indolent and refused to hunt. Richardson and Hepburn left him with Hood and went out to gather *tripe de roche*. They heard a shot, and on returning found Hood lifeless by the fire, Bickersteth's *Scripture Help* lying open beside him. As the shot entered the back of the head they concluded that it was not suicide, but murder. Without any charge being made against him, Michel kept disclaiming having been guilty of the deed. The Englishmen removed the body to a clump of willows, and then by their tent fire read the funeral service and the evening prayers. The next day they left for the fort. Michel kept trying to draw one or the other apart, they believed with ill intent. Let Richardson finish the story :

> Hepburn and I were not in a condition to resist even an open attack, nor could we by any device escape him. Our united strength was far inferior to his and, beside his gun, he was armed with two pistols, an Indian bayonet, and a knife. In the afternoon coming to a rock, on which there was some *tripe de roche*, he halted, and said he would gather it whilst we went on, and that he would soon overtake us. Hepburn and I were now left together for the first time since Mr. Hood's death, and he acquainted me with several material circumstances which he had observed of Michel's behaviour, and which confirmed me in the opinion that there was no safety for us except in his [Michel's] death, and he offered to be the instrument of it. I determined, however, as I was thoroughly convinced of the necessity of such a dreadful act, to take the whole responsibility upon myself ; and immediately upon Michel's coming up, I put an end to his life by shooting him through the head with a pistol. Had my own life alone been threatened, I would not have purchased it by such a measure ; but I considered myself as entrusted also with the protection of Hepburn's.

Franklin, Richardson, Hepburn, and three Canadians tried to live on till relief came by cooking bones from the refuse heap of the past winter, old shoes, and *tripe de roche*. Two of the Canadians died, and the others were failing fast. The minds of all began to reel. But relief came. Back had found Akaitcho and had sent a supply of meat—small, that it might be conveyed swiftly to the relief—and it arrived no more than in time. As soon as might be, Fort Enterprise was abandoned, Franklin's party moving slowly on to Akaitcho's camp, where caribou were abundant. Thence they journeyed to Fort Providence and travelled in carioles to Fort Resolution. In the spring they passed on by canoe to Fort Chipewyan, and thence made their way to England. Franklin's journey is memorable, not only for its human interest and its place in the delineation of the north shore of the continent, but because it brings out clearly the relentless conditions of life and travel in the Barren Lands and the irresponsible nature of the Northern Indians. Had Akaitcho cached a small portion of meat at Point lake as he promised, and an ample supply at Fort Enterprise, the exploring party would have returned, if not without travail, at least in safety. When poor Hood's father wrote to ask Richardson why the Indians had failed them, the reply was given—" from the natural fickleness of that people, which renders them expert in finding reasons for changing an arrangement however important, but principally from two of their hunters having been drowned by the oversetting of a canoe.

As usual on such an occasion, the rest threw away their clothing, broke their guns, and thus by their mode of expressing their grief curtailed themselves of the means of procuring their food."

Before Franklin's journey, all that was known of the polar shore of the continent was its position and course at the mouths of the Coppermine and the Mackenzie, and again its last portion, the north shore of Alaska to Icy Cape, as revealed by Captain Cook. Lieutenant Franklin extended this knowledge eastward 200 miles in a direct line from the mouth of the Coppermine. Attention was now turned to its westward course from the Coppermine to Icy Cape.

The next explorations planned were similar in design to those of 1819–22. A naval expedition, under Captain Parry, was to make a fresh attempt to penetrate westward through the North-West Passage. It got no farther than Prince Regent's Inlet. A second naval expedition, under Captain Beechey, was to pass through Bering Strait and explore eastward. There was to be an overland expedition to the mouth of the Mackenzie River, where it was to divide—one party going westward to meet Captain Beechey, the other eastward to the mouth of the Coppermine—and it was hoped that this party would fall in with Captain Parry. The possibility of all meeting and returning by Bering Strait was contemplated.

The overland party was commanded by Captain Franklin, as he now was, and with him were Dr. Richardson, Lieutenant Back, and Mr. Kendall. It proceeded from Montreal by the usual fur-traders' route down Mackenzie River, and up the Great Bear River to its outlet from the lake of that name. Here, on the north shore of the lake, Fort Franklin was built by Lieutenant Back, while Franklin and Richardson made explorations preliminary to the work of the following summer—the former to the mouth of the Mackenzie River, the latter to the eastern shore of Great Bear Lake. What with the fishery on the lake and caribou meat, the winter was spent without discomfort, though by February the supplies for the explorations were being trenched upon. However, in March provisions became plentiful once more.

In many ways this expedition is a contrast to the last one. As the parties did not in the first place have to travel overland, boats able to bear the shocks of the ice were substituted for the frail canoes. These could carry a considerable body of provisions, so that there was little or no anxiety on that score. Finally, guides were less necessary for the river, and the sea-coast fixed their course. As a result, much ground was covered without any of those experiences which arouse a poignant interest. The whole party left Fort Franklin on June 28, 1825, and descended the Great Bear River and the Mackenzie together. At the delta Dr. Richardson and Mr. Kendall left to survey the unknown coast eastward as far as the Coppermine. Captain Franklin and Lieutenant Back went on to traverse the unexplored west, if possible, till they should meet Captain Beechey's party at a fixed rendezvous. Apart from an exciting rencontre with Eskimos at the estuary of the river, Franklin's journey was without incident. It was hampered by fogs and by a shallow sea, which necessitated keeping far out ; its course was dull and uninteresting. Franklin discovered and named Herschel Island. He passed Demarcation Point, the boundary of Russian Alaska to Turnagain (Return) Reef. Here on 18th August, with the new ice already forming, and in obedience to his instructions, he turned homeward. Captain Beechey had sent out a barge from his ship to meet him, but it was beset with ice and turned back at a point named Cape Barrow on 25th August, thus leaving a stretch of 160 miles of coast still unknown. Franklin's party returned without incident to its base on Great Slave Lake on 21st September.

Meanwhile Richardson's exploration had gone on without notable incident, save a narrow escape from a fight with the Eskimos. It did not encounter fogs, but had an easy run to the mouth of the Coppermine, which was reached on 8th August, " all the men still fresh and vigorous." The party, now on foot, followed the Coppermine upward, then traced upward a stream coming from the west into the Coppermine at the Copper Mountains—the Kendall River, as they named it. Crossing the height of land, they descended the Dease River to Great Bear Lake, where they were met by a boat which brought them in comfort to Fort Franklin on 1st September. Next year, by various routes, the party made its way to England.

The next exploration (1833–35) is associated with the name of Captain Back, as he had now become. Captain John Ross, with his nephew James Ross, sailed away in 1829 on an expedition financed by private individuals, of whom Mr. Felix Booth was the principal, the object being again to find the North-West Passage. He sailed through Lancaster Sound and southward down Prince Regent Inlet, and made his ship secure for the winter on the east coast of what proved to be a peninsula, which he called Felix Boothia. In the following spring a sled party led by James Ross crossed the peninsula and on its west coast reached the position of the North Magnetic Pole in lat. 70° 5′ 17″ N. and long. 95° 46′ 45″ W. For three long years the unfortunate ship lay frozen in its winter quarters. Anxiety at the fate of the party led to an attempt to send relief overland from the Mackenzie River basin. The expedition had the great advantage of the enthusiastic support of the Hudson's Bay Company. J. H. Pelly, its Governor, and Nicholas Garry, Deputy-Governor, were on the committee which organized it and were liberal subscribers. The Company gave Back a special commission which gave him authority wherever he went. They placed 120 bags of pemmican of 90 lb. each, two boats, and two beautiful canoes at his disposal. When Back met Governor Simpson at Fort Alexander at the mouth of the Winnipeg River he was given a letter addressed to four of the Commissioned Gentlemen of the North requiring one or other of them to place his services at the command of the expedition. When descending the Athabaska River he met and delivered the letter to A. R. McLeod, the first gentleman on the list, who was coming out with his family. An old friend of Back's, he turned and prepared to face the wild North. While McLeod built the winter establishment, named Fort Reliance, at the eastern extremity of Great Slave Lake, Back went up by the Hoar Frost River, which enters the lake about twenty-five miles west of the fort, to find the source of the River Thlew-ee-chow, which the Indians said flowed north-east to a far-off sea. This done, he returned to his winter fort.

Meanwhile the Rosses had abandoned their ship and, travelling over the ice, had had the good fortune to fall in with a whaler, which brought them safely home. There was urgent need to get this information to Captain Back. The conveyance of it is a fine illustration of the surpassing efficiency of the organization of the Hudson's Bay Company. The following letter explains itself.

HUDSON'S BAY HOUSE,
LONDON, 22nd Oct. 1833.

ANGUS BETHUNE, ESQ.,
Chief Factor &c. &c.
Sault St. Mary's.

SIR,
I am directed by the Governor and Committee to acquaint you, that the packet by which this is sent will be forwarded to your address in duplicate ; one copy, viâ Montreal, and the other by the American mail, to the care of the commanding officer of the garrison at St. Mary's. It contains letters for Captain Back, apprising him of the arrival of Capt. Ross in England ; and it is of great importance that he should receive this information before his departure from his winter quarters.

I am therefore to request, that the copy which first reaches you be sent on to the next post by a couple of the most active men you can find, without the delay of one day at St. Mary's ; and that it be forwarded in like manner, accompanied by this letter, with the utmost expedition, from post to post . . . until it reaches its destination ; where, if due expedition be observed, it ought to arrive early in April.

The Governor and Committee further direct, that the officers of the different posts do not, on any pretence whatever, detain the packet ; and desire that the date of the arrival at and departure from each post, signed by the officer in charge, be endorsed on the back thereof ; and also that the messengers from each post be instructed to proceed to the next, without attending to directions they may receive to the contrary, from persons they may meet en route.

And when the second copy of this packet gets to hand at the Sault, let it be forwarded in like manner.

I am, Sir,
Your most Obedient Servant,
W. SMITH, Secretary.

The endorsations required were made as follows :

Received.	Place.	Forwarded.	Name of Officer in Charge.
20th of Jan., at noon	Sault, St. Mary's	21st of Jan.	H. [A.] Bethune
29th of Jan., afternoon	[Michipicoten]	30th of Jan.	George Keith
7th of Feb., at 9 P.M.	Pic	8th of Feb., 6 A.M.	Thomas M. Murry
[13th of Feb., at 11 P.M.	Long Lake	14th of Feb., 5 A.M.	Peter M'Kenzie]
[16th of Feb., at 10 P.M.	Lake Nipigon	17th of Feb., 5 A.M.	John Swanston]
[21st of Feb., at 11 A.M.	Fort William	Same date, 3 P.M.	Donald M'Intosh]
[25th of Feb., at 1 P.M.	Bois Blanc	Same date, 4 P.M.	John M'Intosh]
2d of March, at 6 A.M.	Lac la Pluie	2d of March, 7 A.M.	William Sinclair

Received.	Place.	Forwarded.	Name of Officer in Charge.
12th of March, at 2 P.M.	Red River	13th of March, 6 A.M.	Alexander Christie
25th of March, at 6 P.M.	Fort Pelly	26th of March, 6 A.M.	William Todd
2d of April, at 11 A.M.	Carlton	2d of April, at noon	J. P. Pruden
	Isle a la Crosse	6th of April, 5 P.M.	R. M'Kenzie
21st of April, at 4 P.M.	Athabasca	22d of April, 3 A.M.	John Charles
29th of April, at 7 P.M.	Great Slave Lake	30th of April, 4 A.M.	J. M'Donell, Clerk

The entries in brackets are from endorsations which were not entered in the form above. The letter came to Back's hand at Fort Reliance on 25th April, the duplicate above on 7th May. The distance covered on foot was considerably more than 2,500 miles. The news of Ross's safe return narrowed the aims of the expedition down to simple exploration. On 7th June Back set out. McLeod went forward with the hunters, among whom was Franklin's friend Akaitcho. Along the route he cached meat for the party, which made its laborious way dragging the boats over the ice up the Ah-hel-dessy (Lockhart) River, which flowed into Great Slave Lake hard by Fort Reliance. They passed through Artillery to Clinton-Colden Lake, which Samuel Hearne had crossed fifty-nine years before. Aylmer Lake was traversed and the height of land to the east into the River Thlew-ee-chow, later known as Great Fish River, now as Back River. The course down this river, never before traced by White Man, can be followed on the map. Back showed his appreciation of the support given by the highest officials of the Hudson's Bay Company by naming lakes after Pelly and Garry, the Governor and Deputy-Governor of the Company. On 29th July, at the mouth of the river, a band of Eskimos helped the party haul the boats over a long portage to the estuary. A promontory to the right was called Victoria after the Princess Royal, soon to be queen. For ten days progress was stayed by rain, fog, and ice. There was no hope of coasting along westward to Franklin's Point Turnagain as had been planned. All that could be done was to send a party along the shore some fifteen miles to Ogle Point, whence Cape Richardson was seen and named. The journey down the river had been slower than anticipated. On 15th August, agreeable to instructions, Back turned homeward. This time Akaitcho, his hunter, was true to his promises. Ample provisions brought the party in comfort to Fort Reliance—its base. The whole result was the tracing of a great river and the indication of its estuary, and the inference that the coast ran westward from it more or less in the same latitude as Point Turnagain.

The Hudson's Bay Company now took upon itself the rôle of explorer, and determined to delineate the coast left untouched by the Franklin and Beechey expeditions, i.e. between Return Reef and Point Barrow, and that east of Franklin's Point Turnagain to the estuary reached by Back. On June 21, 1836, the Northern Council resolved :

That an Expedition be fitted out for that purpose . . . to consist of Chief Factor Warren Dease and Mr. Thomas Simpson, with a party of 12 men, and that they be provided with such craft, provisions and other supplies as may be required to accomplish that desirable object ; . . . That the Gentlemen in charge of the Districts of Athabasca and McKenzie River comply with any demands whatsoever, connected with their respective charges, that may be made upon them by Chief Factor Dease, or in his absence by Mr. Thomas Simpson.

It would be natural for this zeal on the part of the Company to grow out of its active association with the previous exploring expeditions. The Governor and Committee in London and the Commissioned Gentlemen who sat in the Council along with Governor Simpson may well have felt that such an enterprise would lend distinction to their Company. Scoffers, however, have claimed that it was entirely due to the fact that the Company was soon to apply for a renewal of its licence. (The licence, however, was not due for renewal till 1841.) Be that as it may, the explorations undertaken reflected great credit upon all concerned. Among the Commissioned Gentlemen were many experienced in hazardous voyages, but where was to be found one with the attainments in mathematical science called for by the enterprise ? He was found no farther afield than in Fort Garry, in the person of Thomas Simpson, a clerk in the service, twenty-eight years of age.

Thomas Simpson was a son of the aunt of George Simpson, in whose home he (George) had been brought up. Though now Governor of half the present Dominion, George used to visit the home in which his boyhood days had been spent whenever he returned to Britain, it may be presumed, out of sheer affection for her to whom he owed so much. Here he was attracted to Thomas, son of his protectress, who had had a particularly brilliant career at King's College, Aberdeen, had distinguished himself in mathematical science, and had won the Huttonian Prize, the highest reward for literary merit given by the university. The young man had intended entering the ministry, but was led by Governor Simpson into the service of the Company. From the letters which passed between Thomas and his younger brother Alexander, who has written his memoirs, it can be seen that, with all his gifts, Thomas was not blessed with humility, for he interpreted the Governor's favours, including that of ranking him at the very beginning as a clerk of the fourth year of his apprenticeship with a salary of £40, as meaning that he was to succeed to the Governorship. Thomas's superiority complex also induced him, when he was asked to undertake the exploration, to believe that he, though but a clerk, was to be first in command, that he would flash into fame in a summer or two. This is all the more ridiculous as all his experience in western travel had been got on voyages in a canoe *de luxe* as secretary to the Governor. Besides, he had not proved himself expert in the delicate art of managing the half-breed or Indian, for on the ground that a breed at Fort Garry had been insolent to him when asking for an advance payment for a trip for which he had engaged himself, he had laid bare his skull with a fire-poker. The half-breeds of the Settlement took up the quarrel in arms and demanded that the assailant be given over to them to take his punishment by the law of retaliation, otherwise they would destroy Fort Garry and take him by force. Governor Christie and Sheriff Ross visited their camp, only to find them dancing the war-dance. After hours of negotiation peace was secured by letting the wounded man draw his wages without performing his trip, and by the gift of a ten-gallon keg of rum, and of tobacco in proportion. It was manifestly wise of Governor Simpson and the Council to pass over Thomas and put Dease, experienced traveller as he was, and skilled in the art of handling his men, in charge of the expedition, but the Simpson brothers, Thomas and Alexander, regarded it as an injustice, claiming that Dease was ignorant and stupid, and only did what his mathematical junior told him to do.

Thomas Simpson left the Red River on 1st December on foot and enhanced his reputation as a walker by covering the ground to Fort Chipewyan, estimated at 1,377 miles, by 1st February, *i.e.* in sixty-two days. Chief Factor Smith, head of the Athabaska District, put all his resources at the disposal of the expedition. The start for the North was made on June 1, 1837. At Fort Norman, at the confluence of the Mackenzie and Great Bear rivers, Dease sent a detachment to build a post at the east end of Great Bear Lake, to be the base for the exploration of the following summer. On 5th July the party left for the long voyage in two seaworthy boats laden with provisions and a small portable canvas canoe. It passed out of the Mackenzie without incident and followed the coast westward to Return Reef, the point at which Franklin had turned. The real task of the expedition now began, namely to explore the polar shore to Point Barrow, which had been reached from the west by Captain Beechey's party. Dease and Simpson took much satisfaction in exploring the unexplored and in naming everything after the notables of the Company and its Commissioned Gentlemen—Jones Islands after the "faithful and eloquent minister of Red River," Pelly Mountains, Point Berens, Colvile River, Garry River, Harrison Bay, Cape Halkett, Cape Ellice, William Smith (the Company's secretary) River. On the 30th May they met with ice, through which they pushed their boats at the exasperating rate of a mile a day. Finally they decided to stop the journey by boat—hence the name of the spot, Boat Extreme—and that Simpson should cover the two degrees to Point Barrow on foot, carrying the canvas canoe to cross the rivers with. As it proved, he was able at times to coast along in the canoe. Thus he passed Point Rowand and a bay named after Roderick McKenzie. He reached Point Barrow on 4th August. Proud of his achievement, Simpson unfurled a flag and took possession of the discovered land in the name of the King. On 25th September the party arrived at its prepared winter post, Fort Confidence, built for them three miles west of the Dease River. The coast of America from Point Turnagain westward was thus wholly made known to the world. The unexplored line to the east was to be a much more arduous task.

On June 6, 1838, Dease and Simpson started once more with two boats and canvas canoes. They passed up the Dease River and descended the Kendall to the Coppermine, following the course of Dr. Richardson in the opposite direction. In sharp contrast with Franklin's expedition, due to successful hunting by the way, Dease's party left Bloody Fall on the Coppermine with their full supply of pemmican. The ice was firm along the coast so that the start was not made till 17th July. The delays from the ice were many. From 9th to 19th August progress was impeded by violent gales and ice at C. Flinders—" a long and fatal delay." Here within three miles of Franklin's farthest encampment the day came when they were to turn homeward. But Simpson proposed to renew his success of last year by a journey of ten days on foot with a small party. He travelled at the rate of twenty miles per day. Beyond Point Turnagain he began writing the names of the Company's men upon the map once more—Hargrave River, Mount George (after Governor Simpson), Point Ballenden, Cape Pelly, Cape Alexander (after Thomas's own brother). At Cape Beaufort, called after the hydrographer to the Admiralty, in lat. 68° 43' 39" N. and long. 106° 3' N., a brief sketch of the course was deposited under a pillar of stones and the long journey home was begun. When the boats were reached, it was found that the party could sail westward along a succession of islands which Franklin had only been able to see. Thus the Coppermine River was reached and finally Fort Confidence on September 14, 1838. Dease and Simpson did not relinquish their task for their comparative failure. On June 15, 1839, they were on the way eastward again by the route of last year. On 18th July they were at Cape Barrow and had the good fortune to find Coronation Gulf partially open. They were just one month earlier than in the previous year and were fortunate in finding the strait between them and Victoria Land sufficiently open for travel. On 27th July they were at the cairn erected on their previous journey. Beyond that the names Melbourne Island, Ellice River, Campbell Bay, Ogden Bay, McLoughlin Bay, Cape Grant, mark their course to Cape Richardson, named by Back's party when seen from Ogle Point. Thus the coast was surveyed to the estuary of Back's River, and Back's discoveries were linked up with those of Franklin.

Though the immediate object of the expedition had been attained, Dease and Simpson pressed on eastward. On 20th August, when opposite the strait now known as Rae, a stone cairn was erected to mark the extreme limit of their journeys, commemorated on our maps by the names Dease Strait and Simpson Strait.

On the return journey the party was fortunate in finding Dease Strait between the mainland and Victoria Island open. It crossed to the island and followed its shore westward, naming Back Point, Cape Colbourne, Cambridge and Wellington bays, Cape Peel, and Byron Bay. West of this last it crossed back to the mainland and made its way to Fort Confidence. Journeys like these stand in contrast with the naval explorations in the simplicity of their equipment, the swiftness of their movement, and their ability to live, to a very large extent, on the country as they went.

The Company's plans for further exploration were upset by the death of Thomas Simpson. From Fort Garry he had put in a plea for a further survey and awaited the decision in a state of high nervous tension. When the packet arrived without word he was greatly perturbed at what he regarded as a lack of appreciation of his achievements, and decided to travel with some half-breeds to St. Paul, Minnesota, and so to England. He was found shot at one of his encampments. His state of mind suggests suicide, but the possibility of an act of revenge on the part of some half-breed is not wholly precluded. He died unaware of the pension of £100 a year granted by the Government to him and to Dease "for their exertions towards completing the discovery of the North-West Passage." Further exploration was to have been carried out by Dease and Simpson by way of Back's River and along the coast eastward beyond the point reached by Simpson. In 1845 it was determined wisely to explore westward by land from Repulse Bay. The task was entrusted to Dr. John Rae.

Rae built "Fort Hope" on the north-west cove of Repulse Bay in July 1846 and made a short preliminary survey of the route across the isthmus of Melville Peninsula, now called Rae Isthmus. In April of the following year he crossed over to what he called Committee Bay and followed its westerly shore, adorning his chart with names associated with the Company, such as Cape Lady Pelly, Colvile Bay, and Simpson Peninsula. He crossed the base of Simpson Peninsula to Pelly Bay, whose northerly islands he called after (Benjamin) Harrison, Deputy-Governor from 1835 to 1838. Cape Berens and Halkett Inlet were named after members of the Committee. Crossing another isthmus he reached Ross's Lord Mayor Bay. On 18th April he took formal possession of his discoveries in the name of the King, and retraced his steps to the south shore of Committee Bay. Here he turned northward to survey the west shore of Melville Peninsula. A string of names associated with the Company indicate his course on our maps—Cowie Point, Cape Mactavish, Cape Lady Simpson, Cape Finlayson, and Garry Bay. His provisions were exhausted when within sight of Cape Ellice, which he took to be not ten miles from Parry's Fury and Hecla Strait. After taking formal possession of his discoveries on 27th May, he began his journey homeward to "Fort Hope" and York Fort.

In 1848 the search for Sir John Franklin had begun. Sir John Richardson was sent to gather news of the lost expedition at the west end of its possible course. He descended the Mackenzie River and coasted eastward. The intention was to cross over to Victoria Island to make inquiries of the Eskimos there, but he was prevented by the ice in Dolphin and Union Strait. In 1849 Rae travelled from Fort Confidence by the Coppermine to inquire on Victoria Island, but ice in the strait prevented his crossing. However, word was received that the Eskimos had never seen White Men, or a White Man's ship. The party returned on foot by the Coppermine, Kendall, and Dease rivers to its base at Fort Confidence on Great Bear Lake.

Rae remained on the Mackenzie in charge of the District during 1850-51. In the spring he returned to the exploration of Victoria Island. During the first fortnight of May he reached it at Cape Lady Franklin and travelled to within sight of Byron Bay, where Dease and Simpson left off their exploration. He then returned to Cape Lady Franklin. During the second part of the month he followed the north-west trend of coast of the island, naming Simpson Bay after the Governor, Cape Hamilton after the Secretary to the Admiralty, and Cape Baring after the First Lord of the Admiralty. After tracing a portion of the south shore of the present Prince Albert Sound, he retraced his steps to the mainland to his " Provision Camp " on the Kendall River.

Rae then returned to Victoria Island and traced its shore in a boat eastward to Point Back beyond Cambridge Bay, where Dease and Simpson's exploration of the island began. He followed the south shore to Victoria Strait and ran up past Halkett Island to Pelly Point, but got no news of Franklin, though he was on the strait in which Franklin's ships were beset with ice for two years. On the way back to the Coppermine a stanchion and the butt of a flagstaff were found drifting. Rae argued from marks upon the latter that it was from a ship of the British Navy, and entertained in consequence the worst fears for the fate of the Franklin expedition.

In 1853-54 Dr. Rae wintered in a snowhouse on Repulse Bay to push his discoveries westward to the point reached by Dease and Simpson, and to inquire into the fate of Sir John Franklin. Travelling with his party on foot, he reached a river which he called after Sir Roderick Murchison, formerly President of the Royal Geographical Society. The journey westward was on the ice and following the coast. At last the cairn erected by Dease and Simpson was reached, and the polar shore of the continent as good as delineated. Returning to the mouth of the Murchison River, Rae turned northward. The bay into which the river flows was called Shepherd, after the then Deputy-Governor of the Company. The cape at the entrance of the strait, which has been named after Rae, was called Cape Colvile, after Andrew, now Governor of the Company; the land across the strait was called Matheson, after a member of the Committee. Rae argued correctly that it was really King William's Island, whose northerly portion had been seen by Sir James C. Ross, and that the survey of the polar shore was now complete. He erected a cairn and formally took possession of his discoveries in the name of the King.

The expedition was also successful in getting the first information of the fate of Sir John Franklin's party. From Eskimos at Castor and Pollux River, and at Repulse Bay on Rae's return, it was gathered that Eskimos farther west had seen forty White Men travelling southward on the ice and dragging a boat and sledges with them. They were passing along the west shore of King William's Island. The Eskimos inferred that their ships had been crushed in the ice, and that they were travelling to the caribou grounds for provisions. The men were thin. They purchased a little seal flesh from the natives. At a later date the Eskimos found some graves and about thirty bodies lying on the surface. These were on the mainland (doubtless at Starvation Cove), and another five bodies on an island " about a long day's journey to the north-west of a large stream," which Rae inferred was Back's River. A telescope strapped to the body of a man on the island was believed to indicate that he was a chief (an officer). A few must have survived till the birds came in the spring, for shots were heard and feathers of geese were found. There was a quantity of gunpowder with the dead and many implements. Rae was able to purchase from the natives an Order of Merit in the form of a star and a small silver plate engraved with Franklin's name.

Franklin had himself seen much of the polar shore of the continent, and Dease and Simpson had proved that there was much the same open sea along the coast as far as Simpson Strait as he had seen farther west. Moreover it was now known that Lancaster Sound and Barrow Strait were both less beset by ice than passages farther south. This increased knowledge of conditions in those icy regions led the Admiralty to decide upon another effort to penetrate from the Atlantic to the Pacific by the North-West Passage. Sir John Franklin, as he now was, applied to be placed in command. He had not only a superior knowledge of those polar regions, but, as was generally recognized, was a man of iron resolution and unquenchable courage, singularly endowed with the geniality, uprightness, and simplicity necessary to win the affection and command the obedience of his men. But he was well on in years. When the First Lord of the Admiralty objected to him that he was sixty years old, Franklin replied : " No, no, my lord, only fifty-nine." Not without misgivings the Admiralty gave him the command of the *Erebus*, while Captain Francis Crozier was placed in charge of the *Terror*. Franklin was convinced that if he could pass from the western extremity of Barrow Strait southward to Simpson Strait he would find no difficulty in following the open summer sea along the continental coast, through the region which he had personally explored, to Bering Strait. Pointing out the western mouth of Simpson Strait on a map, he said : " If I can but get down there, my work is done ; thence it's plain sailing to the westward."

The ships sailed in May 1845. They passed through Lancaster Sound, and, because ice barred the passage of Barrow Strait, they were taken north through Wellington Channel and brought back to Barrow Strait by the sound between Cornwallis Island and Bathurst Island. As winter was now setting in, Franklin decided to return eastward to a snug harbour in Beechey Island on Erebus Bay in the south-west extremity of Devon Island. There, where Wellington

Channel leads northward from Barrow Strait, he and his party passed the winter, presumably in the routine duties, and with the cheerfulness characteristic of Arctic expeditions.

When the party set out on its course in the spring there were no more than about three hundred miles of unknown seas to be traversed before getting into waters already observed at King William Island. Surely hope sat on the prow of Franklin's ships as they moved southward from Barrow Strait, probably through Peel Strait. The expedition advanced to within about a score of miles north-west of the north promontory of King William Island. There, within not much more than a hundred miles of the waters observed by Dease and Simpson, it was beset by ice. As it was provisioned for three years there was no cause for anxiety, rather for the hope that in the following spring the intervening sea would be traversed and the way be open westward. But the ships remained fast in the ice from September 12, 1846, till they were abandoned on April 22, 1848, about eighteen miles north-north-west of Victory Point, visited by Captain James Ross in 1830. During that time Sir John Franklin breathed his last. In spite of his failure he has been hailed as the discoverer of the North-West Passage, for he was the first to have positive knowledge that a passage exists north of the continent, running from Atlantic to Pacific.

The long story of the thirty-nine expeditions sent out in search of Franklin must be passed over here. The fragments of knowledge gathered by these severally, and since from the Eskimos, make it possible to get some inkling of the tragic end of the party. Those who abandoned the ships must not be thought of as having no knowledge of the region. Doubtless many an observation party had been sent out to search the coast. They therefore had definite plans. These are embodied in a document placed at Victory Point for any who might come in search of them. It was found by Lieutenant Hobson of the McClintock search expedition in 1859, eleven years after it was deposited. It runs in part :

In 1848 H.M.S. *Terror* and *Erebus* were deserted on the 22nd, April, 5 leagues N.N.W. of this, having been beset since 12th September, 1846. The officers & crews consisting of 105 souls under the command of Captain F. R. M. Crozier landed here. . . . Sir John Franklin died on the 11th June, 1847, and the total loss by deaths in the Expedition has been to this date, 9 officers & 15 men. [Signed] F. R. M. Crozier [Postcript] and start on tomorrow 26th for Backs Fish River.

The course of the party can be traced by skeletons and relics found all the way from Franklin Point along the coast of King William Island to its south-easterly extremity. Thence the party must have crossed Simpson Strait to the continental shore at Starvation Cove immediately west of Cape Richardson, where many skeletons have been found. The survivors, or it may be a separate party, reached Montreal Island, south of Ogle Point, on its way to Back's River. It was news of these, the last survivors, that Dr. John Rae procured from the Eskimos.

Information from the natives points to the wreck of one ship off O'Reilly Island, north of McLoughlin Bay, and that of another near Matty Island between King William Island and Boothia Peninsula. Whether the ships drifted to these two positions, or whether a portion of those who abandoned them returned and navigated them through to Simpson Strait must remain a speculation. The Eskimos' story of boxes of food stacked on the shore near the wreck off Matty Island rather supports the view of a return to the ships by portions of their crews. Be that as it may, all alike met a tragic end.

4.—THE FUR TRADE AT LARGE, 1821-50

With the Union of 1821 the tempest which had raged in the fur trade for a score of years dwindled to a calm. The doings at the individual forts became conventional and monotonous in the extreme, and no longer claim attention. There was no more a wild race of rivals building new posts to cut off profitable fur regions from one another. Forts standing in strategic positions, such as Cumberland, Carlton, and Edmonton on the Saskatchewan, and Fort Chipewyan, the depot for the Mackenzie River and Peace River regions, remained *in situ*. Only the small outposts were removed from time to time, as the furs diminished or increased in outlying sections of the several districts. The tendency was to keep the posts some distance apart, and to throw upon the Indians the burden of bringing their furs in to trade.

The hierarchy of the trade, however, has continued to capture people's imagination—especially the " Commissioned Gentlemen," that is, the Chief Factors at the heads of the Districts and sitting in council with the Governors ; and the Chief Traders in command of important individual posts, and, if present, invited to sit with the Chief Factors in council. Their command of the natives and their control of their servants excited admiration in such travellers as saw them in action. The system of promotion—by which an industrious and able clerk rose to be Chief Trader enjoying a share in the profits of the Company, and finally to be Chief Factor enjoying two shares—called out the best in them, while the Governor and Council continually weeded out the unfit, or at least refused to nominate them for commissions.

The Commissioned Gentlemen, of course, had to share in the losses. The unfortunate " outfit " of the first year of the Union cost the individual £196, 7s. 1d. per share held, but the next year brought him a profit of £200, 8s. 9d. The average income of a Chief Trader has been computed at £360, and that of a Chief Factor at £720 per year. The " commissioned officers," like the other servants, received their living, though not the luxuries on their table. What they bought was charged to their account at the inventory price at York Factory, and was taken up country as the cargo of their fort, up to a limited quantity, if it went with the summer outfit.

Should it be called for on a special trip for goods, 25 per cent. was added to the cost. On retiring, they enjoyed their share of the first outfit thereafter, and the half of their claim on the next six following outfits. This, added to their savings out of a liberal income, left them, if not profligate of their means, in a very comfortable position.

No less happy was the Chief Factor's life in the main fort of his District, as J. W. McKay, himself an old Company man, shows :

This exalted functionary was lord paramount ; his word was law ; he was necessarily surrounded by a halo of dignity, and his person was sacred, so to speak. He was dressed every day in a suit of black or dark blue, white shirt, collars to his ears, frock coat, velvet stock and straps to the bottom of his trousers. When he went out of doors he wore a black beaver hat worth forty shillings. When travelling in a canoe or boat, he was lifted in and out of the craft by the crew ; he still wore his beaver hat, but it was protected by an oiled silk cover, and over his black frock he wore a long cloak made of Royal Stuart tartan lined with scarlet or dark blue bath coating. The cloak had a soft Genoa velvet collar, which was fastened across by mosaic gold clasps and chains. It had also voluminous capes. He carried with him an ornamental bag, technically called a " fire-bag," which contained his tobacco, steel and flint, touchwood, tinderbox, and brimstone matches. In camp his tent was pitched apart from the shelter given his crew. He had a separate fire, and the first work of the boat's crew after landing was to pitch his tent, clear his camp, and collect firewood sufficient for the night before they were allowed to attend to their own wants. Salutes were fired on his departure from the fort and on his return. All this ceremony was considered necessary ; it had a good effect on the Indians ; it added to his dignity in the eyes of his subordinates, but sometimes spoiled the Chief Factor. Proud indeed was the Indian fortunate enough to be presented with the Chief Factor's cast-off hat, however battered it might become. He donned it on all important occasions, and in very fine weather it might constitute his entire costume.

Not the least among the privileges of the Chief Factors was that of sitting at the Council along with the Governor, but the creation of the new régime was far from the imposing assembly of partners which met at the North West Company's rendezvous. The extravagant but exhilarating practice of all journeying, year after year, up to the depot for a fortnight of business, relieved by festivities, was curtailed from the beginning, and at times almost abandoned. The Councils of 1830 and 1831 were composed of but twelve out of twenty-five Chief Factors in some fifteen Districts. From 1836 to 1843 the attendance ranged from four to six. The plan of inviting Chief Traders present to attend raised the number of members during these years to about seven, along with the Governor. On two occasions, 1840 and 1842, Simpson was not present and Chief Factor Donald Finlayson presided in his stead. In June 1833 the Council held two meetings at the very inconvenient Red River Settlement, and was composed of but three and four Chief Factors respectively. The gradual decline of the influence of the Chief Factors in the Council was offset by the restless energies of Governor Simpson, who visited many posts in the course of the year, and agreed with the official on the spot, or by correspondence, what should be the arrangements for the coming season. These annual inspections by the Governor, combined with the steady supervision of the Governor and Committee in London, and the manifest economy of the arrangement, may be regarded as accounting for the passing of the picturesque assembly of the partners as known in the halcyon days of the North West Company.

In the period under consideration the first Councils met usually at York Fort, but from the 'thirties almost invariably at Norway House. In 1826 the site of this post at Mossy Point near the entrance of Lake Winnipeg was abandoned in favour of its present position on East River (Jack River as it was then called) that it might be conveniently near the fishery, the main source of its food supply. This was now the depot for the Athabaska canoes. Rock House, on Hill River, had rejoiced in its little day, but it was too distant for the depot of the outermost Districts. At Norway House the Chief Factors could meet in Council while their brigades were working their way, one after the other, down to the Bay.

The Council, which usually met in June, agreed upon all the arrangements for the next trading season : what should be the rotation of furloughs for the Commissioned Gentlemen ; who should come down with the brigades, and by inference be present at the Council; who should man the posts, and with what complement of servants of the lower grades. These last arrangements often involved promotion from rank of clerk to that of Chief Trader, or from that of Chief Trader to Chief Factor, but such promotions were without the competence of the Council. The practice was for the individual members of Council to give in confidentially their nominations to Governor Simpson, who forwarded the names of the three with the largest number of votes to the Governor and Committee, who appointed the nominee considered by them to be the most deserving of the three. The promotion only appears in the Minutes of Council when the gentleman in question is assigned his position during the coming outfit.

All the servants of the Company below the Commissioned Gentlemen were retained, whether in Britain, Canada, or inland, under contracts for three or five years. The scale of the wages was agreed upon between the Council and the Governor and Committee in London, the latter being the deciding factor. The duties of the clerks included keeping of accounts, managing outposts, undertaking expeditions to the Indian camps ; they usually were paid £100 per annum. When apprenticed for five years, they received £20 the first year, and £25, £30, £40, £50, in the successive years of their contract. If they proved incompetent they could then be thrown off. A very few, not exactly competent, yet of some service, were retained at £60 and £75. Clerks were counted among the aristocracy of the post and were admitted to the officers' mess.

The position of postmaster, *i.e.* the manager of an outpost, large or small, might be filled by a clerk or by one of the " servants," English, Canadian, or half-breed. It involved the ability to manage the Indians and their trade, and to keep the proper Journal and accounts. The salary varied according to the man and the outpost, between £35 and £75. The interpreters formed a rank below the postmasters.

The servants of the voyageur order were of two kinds. There were the men who manned the canoes of the posts. These were taken on under agreement for three years, the average wage being about £17 a year. If given special duties they received an addition to their wages. Then there were the voyageurs retained for no more than the freighting season. In 1836 their wages ran : for steersmen £12, for bowsmen £10 10s., for middlemen £9. The voyageurs' wages on the arduous route up the Churchill to Methy Portage, where they passed the goods over to the men from the posts in the Athabaska and Mackenzie River Districts, were higher. They took freight from the colony to Norway House ; thence took the outfit to the portage, bringing back the furs to Norway House ; and finally they returned home with a load from that post. Guides got £25, bowsmen £14, middlemen £12. After 1836 the freightage to and from Red River and York Fort was contracted for. Voyageurs of both classes were usually engaged in Red River Settlement.

The various other servants about the posts may be judged by the Minute of 1836 calling for the following recruits :

Orkneymen :
10 labouring servants for five years not exceeding. . £15 per annum
5 accustomed to boating, fishing, stooping . . . . £20   „
2 experienced boat-builders not exceeding . . . . £25   „
1 Cooper . . . . £25   „
2 Blacksmiths . . . . £25   „

Canadians :
18 young servants at . . . . £17   „
2 Blacksmiths at . . . . £25   „

It had been a weakness in the system of the Hudson's Bay Company that it had not been represented in the country by a single person or by an institution supervising its interests as a whole. This had been remedied by the reform inaugurated by Andrew Colvile in 1810, instituting two Councils, each presided over by a Governor. In 1816 Robert Semple had been appointed Governor-in-Chief, and Governor William Williams followed him. The Union of 1821 saw a reversion to the system of two Governors, each with his Council. Williams was given the Southern Department and George Simpson the incomparably larger and more important Northern Department. Williams retired in 1826. Thereafter Simpson acted informally in his place, as he had authority to do under the Deed Poll. It was not till 1839 that he was formally appointed Governor-in-Chief of Rupert's Land, with authority over all the Hudson's Bay Company's territories for judicial and other purposes. He held this office till his death on September 7, 1860, at Lachine, now his headquarters, where he resided. He had been knighted in 1840.

The Councils did much to bring success to the Company. Simpson did incomparably more. To begin with, his authority was great because of his office, for as Governor he spoke for the Governor and Committee in London. Their will was carried into effect through him. Moreover he spoke for the Councils and the individual servants to the Company in London. Then, too, as his dispatches and his book, *A Narrative of a Journey round the World during the years 1841 and 1842* show, he stood head and shoulders above the Chief Factors—in education, breadth of mind, and business acumen. Strict in enforcing discipline, he safeguarded himself from tyranny by the care which he took to keep himself well informed, and by leaving the approach to him open to the humblest. His friendly manner and his interest in the welfare of the individual servant took the edge off his acts of discipline. In his reports to the Governor and Committee he was unnecessarily personal and censorious of the men, but his " public " letters were severely impersonal, while his " private " letters to individuals showed a personal interest in them and a warm appreciation of good conduct. For example, A. C. Anderson, in 1834, failed to bring the party which he was conducting —from Jasper House by the Yellowhead Pass to Fort George on the Fraser—to their destination, New Caledonia, because the ice was taking on the river and it was not open enough for canoes and the ice not firm enough for travel. As the food was exhausted, he led it back to Jasper House, and, finding no provisions there, back to Edmonton House, in all a distance of about 250 miles in deep snow and in bitter cold. His chief, Mr. Connolly, whose wife and little children were of the party, reported him to Governor Simpson. In a " public " letter to Anderson, Simpson required him to appear before the Council and answer for his conduct of the party. In a " private " letter of the same date, he explained to Anderson that the inquiry must be held, for the charge of mismanagement had been laid against him. He went on, however, to say that his (Anderson's) conduct had been wholly satisfactory hitherto and had won approval. Anderson was able to show the Council that the delay in starting from Jasper House was wholly due to the Columbian brigade and was exonerated. Simpson's " private " letter was preserved by the acquitted man as a precious possession.

An instance of the way in which Governor Simpson watched the conduct of his men is given by H. J. Moberley, then a clerk in the Saskatchewan District. An officer at Edmonton, passing up the river, came on Moberley with a band of Indians and asked him what he was doing there. He replied in the slang of the trade " drinking with the Indians." The officer, who was unacquainted with the local parlance, reported him to Simpson, who summoned the man to the next Council to answer for his conduct. Moberley was able to show that he had no liquor with him, and that " drinking with the Indians " was a slang phrase come down from the days when liquor was the principal article of trade, and that it now meant no more than " trading with the Indians." Simpson, with a chuckle, acquitted him of the charge.

Governor Simpson's judgment, more especially in the first years, before he became fully acquainted with the country, was not inerrant. His plan to abandon the posts on the north branch of the Saskatchewan in favour of the south branch, in the hope of winning the Indians of the Missouri to trade at Chesterfield House, established for that purpose, was defeated by the physical features of the country, and the fort was abandoned after but a winter's trade—1822–23. His view that the colonists on the Red River should not trade with the Indians, but secure their necessaries at Fort Garry, was short-sighted, and he and John Clarke were defeated by Governor Bulger's appeal to the executors of Lord Selkirk, and through them to the Governor and Committee in London. But he was always alive to realities and quick to repair his mistakes, and when he acquired a complete knowledge of the land his judgment and far-sightedness excited wonder.

Simpson's knowledge of the country was acquired during a series of notable voyages which distinguish the first twenty years of his governorship. In 1822, in the depth of winter, he passed from Norway House to Cumberland House, and thence southward to Brandon House and the colony. In the winter of 1822–23 he inspected the posts from Cumberland House to Dunvegan on Peace River, and reached Edmonton at the end of February. In 1824–25 he was supervising the posts on the Columbia River. In 1828 he visited the forts in New Caledonia and descended the Thompson and Fraser rivers from Kamloops to the sea. In 1841–42 he travelled round the world, crossing Siberia to discuss trade relations with the heads of the Russian-American Fur Company at St. Petersburg. After he had seen any part of the country and become acquainted with the personnel, he kept up relationships by correspondence. He was an ardent and industrious letter writer.

The Company's territories were divided into three administrative areas—the Montreal, the Southern, and the Northern Departments. The Departments were divided into "Districts." The Governor and the Northern Council supervised an array of Districts, including the Columbian, from York Factory and Rainy Lake on the east to the Columbian District (with New Caledonia) on the Pacific slope.* Smaller and less productive Districts tended to be absorbed into the

---

* Frequent references to the Columbian District as a " Department " are due to a loose use of the term. In the North West Company's terminology the Districts were Departments, and after the Union nearly all the Districts are occasionally called Departments, even by Governor Simpson. The Columbian District was under the Northern Department and in the control of Governor Simpson and the Council. It so figures in the Minutes of the Council. The latitude given to Chief Factor Dr. John McLoughlin in the matter of placing his men was due to his distance from the meeting-place of the Council, and to its being impossible for him to attend. A similar discretionary power was given from time to time to other Chief Factors in the management of their Districts. John M'Lean's statement in his *Notes of a Twenty-five Years' Service in the Hudson's Bay Territory* (Champlain Society's edition, p. 2), that there were four Departments, of which the Columbian was one, is incorrect. At a Council held on June 7, 1845, at the suggestion of the Governor and Committee, it was resolved that the conduct of " Columbian affairs " should no longer be in the hands of a single Chief Factor, but under a " Board of Management " of three Chief Factors. This was with a view to the impending retirement of Dr. McLoughlin. It did not alter the legal position of the District.

larger. For example, Cumberland House, once the most important post in the interior, and now overshadowed by Norway House, was put into the Churchill River District in 1830 and into the Saskatchewan District in 1837. The posts of the Winnipeg District were apportioned in 1832—Fort Alexander to Rainy Lake and Berens River to Norway House. The Nelson River District in 1832, and Island Lake, which included Oxford House in 1837, were absorbed into York Factory. Upper Red River, with Brandon House, disappeared in 1832. The new post in that region, Fort Ellice, was in the Swan River District. The final number of Districts thus came to be eleven.

Besides determining the personnel and the posts to be open for the season, the Governor and Council fixed the sum of goods—packed, of course, in " pieces "—to be placed in the District for the season. They also determined what supplies one District was to draw from another, e.g. salt from Swan River for Norway House and the Red River Settlement ; and animal products such as " 530 dressed Moose skins, 18 Parchment skins, 120 lbs. Babiche snares and Beaver nets, 200 Fathoms Pack Cords, 30 lbs. sinews, and a sufficient quantity of grease to make up 50 pieces in all, to be provided at Dunvegan for the use of New Caledonia District." The Saskatchewan District built boats. It also procured tracking shoes, portage straps, and the like—above all, pemmican for the brigades. A typical requirement is that for 1840 :

> 8 new Boats of 28 feet Keel [storing 80 pieces]
> 3,500 lbs. Grease
> 150 Bales Dried Meat, 90 lb. each
> 450 Bags [Common] Pemican, 90 lb. each
> 100 Pairs tracking shoes
> 30 Leather Tents
> 500 Buffalo Tongues

One hundred bags of the pemmican " and the usual quantity of other Country produce " were to be deposited at Cumberland House for the passing brigades. The rest was to be taken to Norway House.

The Red River Settlement, as has been indicated, provided farm products and, for the crews of the canoes from the District, pemmican.

The new fashion of using silk in the place of beaver wool in making hats must explain the continued restrictions placed upon the supply of beaver. " In 1841, the beaver to be taken in a given list of 25 posts in 7 Districts is to be limited for three years to the half of the 1839 output at the particular post, and Gentlemen not observing this are to be reported to the Governor and Committee, with a view to their retirement from the service." In 1843 arrangements were made to protect the Indians from the hardship involved in restricting the purchases by giving them higher prices for the small furs, namely, the " value of 10 skins of made Beaver for every 9 skins in small Furs they trade in the course of the year "—a very generous treatment.

The comparative value of the different Districts for the trade may be gathered from the list of those required to limit their fur production to the maximum of the average of the three years before 1826 and from the average outfit of goods sent in to them.

	Average of Beaver, 1823–25.	Average Outfit (roughly), 1830–32.		
		Boats.	Men.	Pieces.
Athabaska.	5,000	4	29	200
Saskatchewan	5,500	9	37	360
English (Churchill) R..	650	2	12	100
Cumberland	150	1	—	120
Swan R.	400	3	10	170
Winnipeg	50	2	12	150
Norway House	120	Not calculable.		
Island Lake	100	–	9	100
Nelson R.	400	1	3	40
York and Churchill . .	300	Not calculable.		

The forts on the Saskatchewan occupied strategic points. Edmonton stood at the eastern end of the " traverse " to Fort Assiniboine, whence the outfits passed onwards to Lesser Slave Lake, to New Caledonia, and to the Columbia. Fort Carlton, near the wintering ground of the buffalo, was a great pemmican post in its southerly aspect, while it drew an abundance of peltry from the woods to the north ; it was the point of departure of the pemmican for the northern brigades, the meat being carried overland to Green Lake in the winter, and thence by canoe to Ile-à-la-Crosse in the spring. Fort Pitt, first opened in 1835 but at times unoccupied, stood in a very advantageous position for gathering meat in the winter. Rocky Mountain House was the resort of the Piegans.

An object of great concern to the Governor and Council and to the Committee in London was the prevention of the depletion of the fur supply. Regulations to this end were passed again and again. The very repetition of the orders suggests that it was difficult to live up to them. When the Indians were in need they would kill for food any beaver seen, and the officers at the posts would find it difficult to refuse to take the skins. From 1835 to 1840 a standing Regulation ran :

The Gentlemen at posts not subject to opposition are to exert their utmost in discouraging the hunting of Cub Beaver and Beaver out of season and that no traps be issued from the depot [York Factory], except for sale to the Piegan Indians, and that in any cases where an unusual proportion of Cub or unseasoned Beaver appears, the same be particularly represented to the Governor and Committee.

From 1826 to 1832 the maximum of beaver from most of the posts was required not to exceed the average of the yields of the years 1823 to 1825. On the whole the policy of conservation was successful. The establishment of new posts, such as Fort Halkett on Liard River, and, beyond the Rockies, of the House at Pelly Banks, of Fort Selkirk at the confluence of the Pelly and Lewis, and of Fort Yukon, brought in fresh supplies of beaver and made it possible to discourage and even prohibit " working beaver " in the depleted Districts. While pressing for conservation, Governor Simpson showed himself careful of the interest of the Indians, who must starve if the Company refused to take the peltries gathered. He and the Commissioned Gentlemen directed the hunt to martens and to muskrats. This policy was particularly successful in the much exploited Muskrat Country, the Company's Nelson River District. In the depleted country around York Factory, Indian bands were allocated to definite regions and induced to take a special interest in conserving the beaver in their own territory, knowing that the Company would prevent other bands from coming in to poach. They reported the beaver dams in the region, receiving, for a time, a reward for every dam left untouched. In contrast, the Company was at no pains to stop the extermination of the fur animals in areas infested with petty traders or an American opposition, such as Lake Huron, the lower Ottawa, Rainy Lake, and the upper Red River. The ruined regions on the frontiers proved a barrier against the opposition, behind which the country within the complete control of the Company prospered by conservation.

The Saskatchewan District, which now included Fort Assiniboine on Athabaska River; Jasper House, at first on Brulé Lake, but from 1830 on the present Jasper Lake; and finally Lesser Slave Lake was by all odds the most productive of the Districts east of the Rockies. It tapped the great forest region from its southern edge ; hence its abundant supply of beaver. Transportation to it was much easier than to the great Districts of the North, and cheaper. A large supply of meat was got over and above the furs ; and it produced the great mass of pemmican which provisioned the brigades of the North and the boats running from Lake Winnipeg to York Factory.

The system of transportation was much as of old, with certain significant differences. All goods coming in and furs going out passed through York Factory ; the Fort William route was only used by the express with dispatches. Norway House played the part for the Athabaska, and Mackenzie River brigades played by the post on Rainy River under the North West Company. Cumberland House played a smaller part as depot for Saskatchewan pemmican for the northern brigades, as also did Ile-à-la-Crosse for the Athabaska brigade.

A more minute study of Saskatchewan—a typical prairie District—may not be out of place. One effect of the Union was to stabilize the posts on the Saskatchewan. The old ruinous policy of killing off the beaver in a region and passing on which characterized the half-century of rivalry came to an end. Outposts for a winter or two might be opened where needed. The main forts became stationary; the centres for a stable business. Fort Edmonton, besides gathering its own furs and pemmican and playing the part of chief post of the District, was a point of departure for the boats of the posts in the valley of the Athabaska and for the Columbian brigade. Fort Carlton was favourably situated to gather the furs of the wooded North and the pemmican of the prairies, but its command of the old Indian track to Green Lake made it the natural point of departure for the supplies of pemmican needed at Ile-à-la-Crosse for its own and the Athabaska brigade. Fort A-la-Corne, one mile east of the site of the early French post, gathered the furs of the upper waters of the Carrot River and pemmican from the plains. It was established in 1850. The best days of Cumberland House, whether as a depot or a fur post, were now past ; the furs were depleted, and many of the Indians had moved away. When Dr. King passed on the way with Captain Back to the exploration of Great Fish River (1834) he noted this decline :

The ground about the house is not only excellent, but fit for immediate culture. The house a few years ago was in most excellent repair, and exhibited a very productive farm, the effect of the continued care and attention of Governor Williams, who had a great partiality for agricultural pursuits. A vast change, however, had taken place at the time of our arrival ; the house was all but falling to pieces ; the implements of tillage, and capacious barns, were silent monuments of waste ; the horses were becoming wild, the oxen occasional truants ; the cows, although they went to the milk-pail twice a day, gave by no means a Virgilian quantity of that sober and nutritious beverage ; a solitary hog stood every chance of dying without issue.

Fort Edmonton, as the busy and lively centre of the spacious District of Saskatchewan, deserves description. It was not materially different in structure from other forts. Built at first on the flat by the river where now stands the power house, a flood in 1820 led to its removal to a terrace above, now part of the lawn of the parliamentary building. There it stood till late in the 'nineties. It had the usual palisade with a " gallery " within and all around, six feet below the rim of the wooden rampart. In the bastions were diminutive antiquated cannon which were a greater danger to the men firing salutes than to any enemy who might attack the fort. Its season began with the arrival of the brigade, some ten boats manned by fifty men from York Factory, in late September or early October. The goods were put immediately into the store and anything wet set out to dry. The crews would then appear for their *regale*—a quart of rum to the steersman, a pint to the men at the bow, and half a pint to the middlemen. The merry-making would then begin and would culminate in the dance in the Chief Factor's house. Fiddlers there were in abundance. As most played by ear, the tunes were often astray, but that mattered little with Red River jigs, if only the rhythm were well marked. Eight and four hand reels and single and double jigs were the favourite dances. Unmarried men, flaunting their purchases from the depot—gaudy handkerchiefs, necklaces, and beads—found ready partners among the girls, some willing to become brides *en façon du nord* on the joyous occasion. Next day the happy couple would appear before the Chief Factor to secure his ratification, for that was necessary if the bride, and later the family, were to be rationed by the fort. The festive evening was little disturbed by the broils which were habitual with the French-Canadians and half-breeds when in drink. The parties involved left the hall to settle their differences with their fists, and, as far as capable thereafter, returned to play their part in the festive scene till the rising sun brought it to a close. The gaiety of the occasion was all the keener because the post was a dull place through the summer with the men away, and little business doing. All the society of the place, from the Chief Factor's family to the Orkney blacksmith and his household, and the middleman's squaw, took part in this joyous opening of the season at the fort.

But the fur trade was a stern master. The outfits of the upper posts must be got to their destination before the ice could form. The " pieces " for the several posts were set apart, the men allocated to the several expeditions, and the number of pack-horses required noted. The horses were kept in two " horse-guards " where they could pasture through the winter, pawing the snow to get to the grass. A small horse-guard was near to hand at Lac Nonne or Lac Berland, a few miles to the west. A larger one lay beyond the Sturgeon River, at the present St. Alban's Mission. It says much for the relations of the Company with the Indians that some 400 horses could be kept safely at these distances from the fort, guarded only by a servant or two. Of course the gates of the fort would be closed to the known horse-thief—a severe punishment to an Indian, who could go nowhere else for his tobacco and his ammunition. On the other hand, the freemen suffered much from the Indians stealing their beasts.

In three or four days the trains of horses would be off. The first " outfit " to leave was that for Jasper House and the Columbia and New Caledonia—in 1854, twenty-eight horses carrying goods and the provisions. It was taken overland to Fort Assiniboine on the Athabaska River and thence by boat upstream to the post on Jasper Lake in sight of the Miette Rock. Jasper House was no more than a winter post for the trappers, mostly descended from Iroquois brought up of old by the North West Company and married to Cree women, but it also had its place in the transportation scheme of the Company. The passing brigades were provisioned, and some 350 mares were kept in pasture to convey goods and men to and fro over the passes. The Columbian and New Caledonian brigades going westward followed a common trail to the confluence of the Whirlpool and Miette rivers at the mouth of the Yellowhead Pass. The Columbian brigade continued up the Whirlpool to the Athabaska Pass. The trail reached the Columbia at Boat Encampment immediately above the mouth of the Canoe River, where boats awaited the brigade to take it downstream to Fort Vancouver. The New Caledonian brigade followed the Miette River up into Yellowhead Pass and reached the Fraser River at Tête Jaune Cache (said to be called after a red-headed French-Canadian), whence canoes took it to Fort George, or up the Nechako River to Fort St. James. The two brigades began to use the Edmonton House-Fort Assiniboine route in 1825. The party of Peter Skene Ogden and John Work in 1823, and that of Governor Simpson himself in 1824, were the last to take the old North West Company's route by Beaver River.

The next " outfit " to leave Edmonton House was that for the Lesser Slave Lake post, now counted as in the Saskatchewan District. It was sent by pack-horses—in 1854 forty-three horses— by the trail to Fort Assiniboine, whence it was taken by boats down the Athabaska and up the Lesser Slave Lake River to its destination.

The " outfit " for Fort Assiniboine held the next place. It was small and needed no more than about seven horses. The fort acted as point of departure for the above brigades, and was kept supplied with pemmican from Edmonton House to that end. A busy scene when the brigades were passing through, it was the embodiment of silence between whiles. In 1854 its staff was an interpreter at £30 a year and a servant at £17. Yet it was of some importance as a fur post. Valuable furs of all kinds were to be got in its region— silver, black, cross and red foxes, beaver, lynx, marten, mink, and bears. The fort was so named after a band of " Strong-wood Assiniboins," who adopted the region as their hunting-ground. It was a very profitable post.

Finally, the boats for Rocky Mountain House left Edmonton. From 1828 this post was kept open during the winter for the Piegan trade—dried and pounded meat, dressed leather, wolf-skins, and the like.

In the meanwhile the Indians of the region, Wood Crees from the fur forest north of Edmonton, and the Plain Crees from the buffalo region to the south, and the half-breed freemen of those parts, would be waiting for the dispatch of the last outfit, when the Chief Factor and his assistants would be free to trade with them. (The Blackfeet appear to have come in rather during the summer.) Chiefs who came in with a good hunt were received with great ceremony. The Chief Factor shook hands with them within the main gates ; the flag was raised and a salute fired. In the Indian Hall the pipe of peace was lit by the interpreter and passed round. As each chief received it, he presented it to the north, west, south, and east and took three long whiffs and passed it on. Then speeches began. The oratory ended, all retired till next morning when trading began. One after another the bands were given credit, i.e. equipped with ammunition and other necessaries for the hunt, and passed north for furs, or south to kill buffalo.

Meanwhile the farm kept some of the servants very busy. Most pressing of all was the wheat in the two parks, the lower one being the flat below the present parliamentary building. In 1855 the seed was sown on 3rd May, and the grain was being harvested from 25th September to 1st October—135 days later. No wonder that with such a late maturing variety the wheat was damaged by frost, and that the Company's officers, including Sir George Simpson himself, had no faith in the Saskatchewan as a wheat-raising region.

It is the discovery of Red Fife wheat and in our day of Marquis that has made wheat-farming in the west an assured business. The barley too must be brought in, and all threshed and ground in the mill of the fort turned by horse-power. Then, too, the potatoes—in 1855, 1,600 bushels—and turnips must be brought in and stored. Finally, a supply of hay must be laid up.

Meanwhile fort hunters had been sent out to kill buffalo, moose, or deer for fresh meat for the fort, and fishermen had been stationed at Lake St. Ann to provide fish for the officers, the servants, and the dogs. Moreover, Indians and half-breeds were killing buffalo out on the plains. These would send in word of their success, and horses or trains of dogs would be sent out to bring in the meat harvest. On October 10, 1854, ten carts and seventeen loaded horses brought in twenty-three carcasses to the post. On other occasions twelve horses brought in 1,300 pounds of white fish, and forty-one horses went out to fetch meat from an Indian camp. Moreover, there was the dried meat, the pounded meat, and the grease to be traded, brought in, and stored for the making of pemmican. Rafts of cord wood were floated down the river for the fires and logs for the carpenter's shop, while the blacksmith gathered coals, probably on the river bank, to mix with charcoal for his forge. Probably down on the flat was the pit at which the logs were sawed into lumber with the "whip-saw," one man standing on the log, another below drawing the saw down to cut.

Within the fort the carpenter was kept busy at the usual repairs, but in particular building boats for the fort and for Norway House to be placed at the service of the other Districts. The blacksmith made nails and iron works for the boats, mended the ploughshares and implements for the fort or for the freemen trading there, and made sheet-iron stoves for the Chief Factor or Father Lacombe. The women were busy making snowshoes, and cutting and making shirts and other garments out of whole cloth for the trade. Finally, in spring, they boiled down the grease and made the pemmican on the strength of which the Northern brigades, as well as the brigades of the Saskatchewan, passed swiftly along the water-ways of half a continent. With spring came the spring trade in pemmican, dried meat, grease, and furs, and the packing and pressing of the " pieces " for their long journey to the sea. The servants hastily ploughed and seeded the farm. Then the trains of horses began to arrive with the furs from Fort Assiniboine, from Lesser Slave Lake, and from Jasper House and the Columbia, and the boats arrived from Rocky Mountain House. All the incoming furs were inspected, packed, and loaded upon the boats and the servants picked out, and additional help in the shape of half-breeds hired, for the long journey to York Fort. About the middle of May the brigade was dispatched, and passed down the river with most of the men of the fort. The season now over, the long summer's quiet settled down on the post, only to be broken by occasional visits of the Blackfeet. However, by 1840 a half-breed settlement had grown up at Lake St. Ann and

Catholic and Anglican missions had been opened. Visits of the missionaries and half-breeds to the fort, return visits of the ladies of the post to the missions, broke the monotony of the long days which must pass before the boats returned and the season at Fort Edmonton opened once more.

The other Districts need no elaborate description. In the Swan River region the posts of both companies on the Swan River disappeared. Fort Pelly at the end of the portage between that river and the Assiniboine took their place. At first the post was on the bank of the latter river, but floods made it advisable to build something more than a mile away, at the foot of a beautiful wooded slope which forms the outer edge of the valley. It was noted for its fine stud of horses. Up to 1830 John Clarke was Chief Factor here. From 1832 to 1842 Chief Trader William Todd held the post. In 1831 the old Fort Dauphin disappeared from the lists of the posts of the District. Shoal River and Manitoba House were small outposts usually kept by interpreters. Fort Ellice was opened in 1831 on Beaver Creek and the Assiniboine about four miles, as the crow flies, below the mouth of the Qu'Appelle River, with John Richard MacKay in charge almost from the beginning. The post acted as a substitute for Brandon House, re-established in 1828 and abandoned once more in 1832. The chief reason for its establishment was to keep the Assiniboins and Crees from trading with the Americans, who had a post on the south side of Turtle Mountain. With this object in view every encouragement was given to the trade in buffalo robes, hitherto held in light esteem by the English Company in contrast with the Americans.

In the District of Lac la Pluie, the post of that name, on Rainy River a mile below the falls at the outlet of the lake, remained headquarters, though fallen from the high estate of the days when it was the North West Company's depot for the Athabaska brigade, and a calling station for all the other brigades of the North-West. In 1832 the name of the post was changed to Fort Frances in honour of Governor Simpson's bride—a name which is with us to this day. Subordinate posts were on Lac des Bois Blancs (Whitewood or Basswood Lake) and either the Dalles or Rat Portage near the present Kenora on Lake of the Woods. Fort Alexander, the former depot of the North West Company, in which the pemmican from the Assiniboine was stored for the passing brigades, was placed in this District in 1832, a very humble post compared with the days when it was on the main water-way of the Montreal Company. It still kept up its farm and small herd of cattle. The Rainy Lake District was subject to competition with the American Fur Company, so much so that the Hudson's Bay Company found it worth its while in 1833 to buy off the opposition for £300 per annum. In 1839 the Northern Council felt its position strong enough to prohibit the sale of liquor in the District, increasing the other supplies. But the Indians, long accustomed to their rum, grew restive, refused to bring their wild rice to the post, and, apparently, urged an American opposition to come in again. The Hudson's Bay Company replied by renewing the sales of liquor to a limited extent, and confirming their agreement with the American Company.

The Districts of Lake Winnipeg including Berens River and Fort Alexander, and of Island Lake including Oxford House, were in decline and their posts absorbed—in the former cases in Lac la Pluie and Norway House, in the latter, in York Factory—so need not detain us. The Nelson River area must have been profitable, for the cost of managing it was low and the return of furs high. The numerous small outposts were closed, and "Nelson River House" on Three Points Lake did the business of the whole Muskrat region. The English (Churchill) River was now in comparative eclipse. From this wide area but 650 skins were expected. Ile-à-la-Crosse held its own as a port of call for provisions for the Athabaska brigades, and Green Lake as an outpost linking the District up with the Saskatchewan. The North West Company's post on Lac la Ronge was abandoned in 1830 because its furs were depleted, but it proved necessary for the Indians' sake to reopen at the mouth of the Rapid River, near the present Stanley Mission. From 1839, Reindeer Lake was reoccupied. Probably its furs had recovered from the disastrous competition of former times.

As stationary as the English River District was its Chief Factor, Roderick McKenzie, described by Thomas Simpson in 1833 as a "well-meaning, warm-hearted, but passionate and crabbed old Highlander." In 1837 he had "passed, by at least ten years, the period described by the Psalmist as the scope of man's existence." He had a neat and comfortable little "Fort"; the fishery in the lake close at hand yielded a constant supply of fresh and wholesome food, summer and winter; the little farm was productive, and the few domestic cattle maintained were in excellent condition. "Altogether this northern octogenarian, though placed 'far in a wild unknown to public view,' was to be envied rather than pitied. His greatest grievance . . . is—that his Chipewayan Indians . . . take a delight in teasing their testy trader by telling him that 'he is too old—it's time for him to go and die in his own country.'"

The Athabaska District appears to have remained stationary, its harvest of 5,000 beavers being 500 less than that of the Saskatchewan. The North West Company's Fort Chipewyan, repaired with the lumber from the Hudson's Bay Company's Fort Wedderburn, continued the centre of supplies in case of emergency for the whole of the Athabaska and Mackenzie River basin. The fort was partly provisioned by meat got on Athabaska and Peace rivers, or brought in from the caribou area to the east. There was a potato field on English Island where Fort Wedderburn had stood, but that article of food came mostly from Peace River. The main provision was fish procured, as of old, at Big Island and at "the old fort" on the south side of the lake. In foul weather the fish supply often failed, so as to necessitate putting the fort on rations. Even the supply of hay was deficient, and the Journal of 1822 tells of the horses having to be kept alive on fish. A few changes after the Union may be mentioned. While canoes were still built at the fort, they were now used rather for the expresses. T. Hodgson, later of Fort Edmonton, in the winter of 1822–23, built the first York boats in use in these waters. These boats were much safer on the large waters of this District and carried about three times as much as the North West canoes—in fact, about eighty pieces. The furs going out were sent in these boats to Portage la Loche (Methy Portage), and deposited by the crews at the centre of the portage, where the crews of the boats on the other side picked them up, leaving in turn their goods from Norway House.

At the Union the Hudson's Bay Company's post, Fort Resolution, on Great Slave Lake, coalesced with its near neighbour of the North West Company. Likewise, Fort Colvile of the English Company on Peace River was abandoned. In 1824 it was arranged to remove St. John's, a former North West Company's post, which stood on the north bank about eight miles above the confluence of the Peace with South Pine River. A new post was opened at Rocky Mountain Portage to take its place. The Indians of the locality resented the plans to such a degree that they fell on Mr. Guy Hughes, the officer in charge at St. John's, and killed him along with four of his men. They threatened the like vengeance on the post at Rocky Mountain Portage. A force of sixteen men under William M'Gillivray left Fort Chipewyan in January to join the expedition intended to punish the murderers. The miscreants fled to distant parts. The punishment by the Company therefore took the form of a temporary abandonment of St. John's and Dunvegan, leaving Upper Peace River without a post.

From 1828 the posts under Fort Chipewyan were Fort Resolution on Great Slave Lake and, on Peace River, forts Vermilion and Dunvegan. This last, being in a buffalo country, was a source of supplies of babiche, dried leather tents, and other animal products for New Caledonia, the neighbouring District across the Rockies. St. John's was re-established on its present site in 1858.

In all these Districts the fur trade had become stable, as was natural in fur areas wholly isolated and long since exploited. It was otherwise with the three frontier Districts—the Mackenzie River, the Columbia, and New Caledonia. Here there were rich fur resources as yet untouched which led the Company to explorations of great moment, not simply for the expansion of their trade, but for the knowledge of geography. Moreover, here the Company got beyond its domestic interests—in the Mackenzie basin, into relation with Arctic Exploration; on the Columbia, through the marine fur trade of the Pacific, into contact with the Russians in the north; and, through the on-coming tide of immigration, with the Americans to the south. John M. McLeod's search for the Nahanni region in 1823 need be no more than mentioned. Leaving Fort Simpson, McLeod ascended the Liard, and a short distance up its tributary, the South Nahanni, left his canoe. His party passed over nine ranges of mountains to a land in which there were no ranges, just detached mountains, without meeting a single soul.   On the return, between the second and third ranges, counting from Fort Simpson, he came on a camp of that illusive people, the Nahannis, and agreed on a rendezvous with them in the spring.

Samuel Black's exploration of the Finlay in 1824 was even less fruitful of results.   He found the country of the most difficult, and the water-way impracticable, and no development of the trade followed.

In 1834 John McLeod, then stationed at Fort Halkett on the Liard River, made his way upstream to a river already named after Dease.   This he followed to its source in a lake, which he estimated to be forty-three miles long.   This he named Dease's Lake.   Finding a well-beaten trail leading westward over the height of land, he followed it to a river which he called Frances, after Governor Simpson's bride.   It was the Stikine flowing into the Pacific Ocean. Crossing this stream by a frail bridge used by the natives, McLeod followed it downward to a cascade.   Signs of traffic led him to believe that this was a meeting-place frequented by trading Indians from the coast.   In 1836 this exploration was to be continued by Mr. John Hutchison, McLeod's successor, but a rumour that hundreds of Russian Indians planned to attack him created a panic, and the whole party jumped into the canoes and retreated to Fort Halkett.

In 1834, the year after his bringing of the sheep from Kentucky to the Red River Settlement, Robert Campbell gave up the farm and engaged himself with the Company for service in the fur trade. He was placed at Fort Simpson, commonly known as " The Forks " (of the Mackenzie and Liard).   Simpson wrote to him : " Don't get married, we want you for active service."   In the autumn of 1836 Campbell volunteered to carry out the exploration which had ended so ignominiously the previous year.   Some difficulty was experienced in getting men with the courage called for by the enterprise.   Indeed, Campbell was not far out from Fort de Liard (on the Liard River near Black River), his starting-point, when it appeared wise to return and winnow out the timid.   He finally got a crew that he could trust. The winter was spent at Fort Halkett.   Dease Lake was reached in July, and a fort commenced five miles from its outlet.   Campbell took a small party with him and crossed the portage to the river visited by McLeod—the Stikine.   He thus describes the bridge built by the natives across the river :

It was a rude ricketty structure of pine poles spliced together with withes and stretched high above a foaming torrent ; the ends of the poles were loaded down with stones to prevent the bridge from collapsing. This primitive support looked so frail and unstable and the rushing waters below so formidable that it seemed well-nigh impossible to cross it.   It inclined to one side which did not tend to strengthen its appearance of safety.

Campbell's party crossed to an Indian hut on the other side.   As its occupant had fled, a gift of tobacco was left.   This had the desired

effect, and a group of timid Nahannis came in the morning bearing
the pipe of peace. It now appeared that a great trading chief,
" Shakes " by name, was not far off. When Campbell proposed to
go to him, the Nahannis tried to dissuade him, being certain that
" Shakes " would kill him, for his instructions had always been to
kill the White Men if they came across the mountains from the east ;
but Campbell persisted. Finally he arrived at the rendezvous.
Whatever had been Shakes's desire, he received his visitor in a friendly
manner, offering him a glass of whisky. Campbell gives an interesting insight into the trade on the upper waters of the Stikine :

Shakes was a Coast Indian, tall and strongly built and as afterwards
I learned was all-powerful among the Indians on that side of the Mountains.
He ruled despotically over an immense band of Indians of different tribes.
He came to the Stikine every year with boats and goods, to the splendid
rendez-vous where I met him. Here he traded with the Indians of the
Interior for the Russians, who supplied him with goods at Fort Highfield
at the mouth of the River.

Campbell held the fort at Dease Lake that winter, but things were
far from comfortable. The hunters were unacquainted with the
region, and in any case, the animals migrated in the autumn to lower
levels where grazing was better. The lake failed to provide fish. The
Indians were not yet won to support the post, and there was none to
interpret to them. " Everything possible was used as food—" tripe
de roche " [lichen], skins, parchment, in fact anything." Moreover,
bands of Indians, still partisans of the Russians, visited the post and
harassed its inmates, though without actual violence. " We were
so weak and emaciated that we could hardly walk, and we were
scattered in twos and threes in dreary camps along the lake trying to
prolong our miserable existence until spring." Fortunately, Campbell had won the friendship of a remarkable chieftainess at the Stikine
in the summer. When she visited the post with her band, she was
lodged in the house, but the young men broke loose after all had
retired in the evening.

Yell after yell suddenly broke the silence, the now furious savages rushed
into the room where [A. R. McLeod, Jr.] and I were sitting, loading their
guns ; some of them seized our weapons from racks on the wall and would
assuredly have shot us had not the Chieftainess, who was lodged in the
other end of the house, rushed in and commanded silence. She found out
the instigator of the riot, walked up to him, and, stamping her foot on the
ground, repeatedly spat in his face, her eyes blazing with anger. Peace and
quiet reigned as suddenly as the outbreak had burst forth. I have seen
many far-famed warrior Chiefs with their bands in every kind of mood,
but I never saw one who had such absolute authority or was as bold and
ready to exercise it as that noble woman.

The post at Dease Lake was abandoned, and Fort Halkett reoccupied by Campbell in 1839–40. Acting on instructions, Campbell
left in May to explore to the source of the north branch of the Liard
in the hope of falling on a large river, which, it was thought, might

be the Colvile flowing into the Arctic. He passed the mouth of the Dease River, and taking the branch which is now Frances River, discovered Frances Lake, so named in honour of Governor Simpson's wife. Taking the westerly arm of the lake, he ascended a stream to "Finlayson's Lake," called after Duncan Finlayson. "That Lake is situated so near the watershed that, in high floods, its waters flow at one end down one side of the mountains, and at the other end down the other side." Across the height of land Campbell came on a large river flowing north-westward. The high bank above it he called Pelly Banks, and the river itself Pelly, "after our home Governor." "Descending to the River we drank out of its pellucid waters to Her Majesty and the H.B.C." The exploring party now returned to Frances Lake, where they found a shanty, dignified with the name "Glenlyon House," built by their comrades. Campbell did not occupy it, however, but led his men back to Halkett House. In 1841 he received a personal letter of commendation from Governor Simpson, and orders for a post on Frances Lake, and for the exploration of the river, which Simpson argued rightly flowed into the Pacific. In August 1842 the post was being built. During the winter a small fort was built at Pelly Banks, On June 10, 1843, Campbell, with three French-Canadians and three Indians, left this house to explore the river. He named MacMillan River after his chief at the farm on the colony, and reached the confluence of the Lewes (named after the Chief Factor) and the Pelly. Here his men became the prey of fears of bad Indians farther down, and it was decided to return.

In 1846 a post was built at Pelly Banks, and, in 1848, Fort Selkirk at the confluence of the Pelly and the Lewes. In 1851 Campbell left Fort Selkirk to continue the exploration of the river. After descending it "for some hundreds of miles" the Indians began to report White Men ahead of them. "It turned out to be Fort Yucon, situated at the confluence of the Porcupine River, and here I was delighted to find my friend Mr. W. L. Hardisty in charge."

Contemporaneous with this expansion across the mountains from the Liard River, was a movement westward from the Mackenzie, Fort Good Hope being the base. In 1840, John Bell built Fort McPherson on Peel's River, which he had explored in 1839. In 1842 he had got over to the Rat (the present Bell) River, flowing westward, and had run downstream into the Porcupine to the neighbourhood of the Alaskan Boundary. La Pierre's House on the right bank of the Bell River was built. In 1846 Bell explored the Porcupine River to its confluence with the Yukon. Two years later Alexander Hunter Murray built Fort Yukon at that point. After reaching this post in 1851 Robert Campbell returned to the Mackenzie River in the company of Murray.

The object of these explorations was to find new fur fields, but in all probability it was connected rather with a desire to draw less on the old fur regions and to give them a chance to recover.

In 1827 the Company's attention was directed to East Main, and an expedition was planned to pass from Richmond Gulf to the mouth of the " South " (Koksoak) River, on Ungava Bay, noting the fur resources and the possibilities of securing provisions by the way. In the following year William Hendry accomplished this journey. He left Richmond Gulf on 29th June, ascended the Clearwater River, passed through the lake of that name, and got over to Seal Lake. By the Stillwater and Larch Rivers of our maps he reached the Koksoak, and on 15th July tasted salt water at the mouth of the Koksoak, in Ungava Bay. This led to the establishment of Fort Chimo in 1830, on one of the lower reaches of the river.

Two years later the Company leased the King's Posts, and in the course of time extended its operations to Hamilton Inlet on the Labrador coast. North West River House was built at the inflow of the river into Melville Lake, whose outlet is into the Hamilton Inlet itself. There was a desire to know the country and its resources between this part of Labrador and Fort Chimo. John M'Lean, the author of *Twenty-five years' service in the Hudson's Bay Territory*, was then stationed at Fort Chimo. He was given the task of exploring the hinterland between Ungava Bay and Melville Lake. He had the advantage of a reconnaissance made into the country south of the fort by Erland Erlandson, a clerk at Fort Chimo, at its inception. M'Lean left on January 2, 1833. Travelling in winter, he was able to cut across to George River. Passing over Michagama Lake, he followed North West (Nascaupi) River, and reached North West River House (Fort Smith) on 16th February. The journey of 450 miles, by air line in the dead of winter through a desolate region, was a remarkable feat.

CHAPTER IX

THE PACIFIC WEST,* 1821–46

I.—THE FUR TRADE 1821–46

THE fur trade of the region beyond the Rockies—in New Caledonia and on the Columbia—was not the least important contribution of the North West Company to the union of that concern with the Hudson's Bay Company in 1821. It involved the inclusion of a fine array of posts—in New Caledonia: McLeod's Lake, St. James (Stuart) Lake, Fraser's Lake, forts George and Alexandria; and in the Columbian valley: forts George (Astoria), Walla Walla, Okanagan with the post at Kamloops, Spokane with its two outposts the Flathead and the Kootenay houses. Fort Alexandria—and the post on the Thompson at Kamloops—and Fort Okanagan were the connecting links between New Caledonia and the Columbia. The Company of Adventurers trading into Hudson's Bay now had in its exclusive grasp (always saving American rights in the Pacific West) the trade of a far-flung line of posts extending from the King's Posts on the lower St. Lawrence, and two in Labrador, to Fort Good Hope far down the Mackenzie; and from the factories on the east shore of James Bay, approached from the Atlantic, to Fort George on the Columbia, almost within sound of the breakers of the Pacific. It was without exaggeration a continental domain. The specific contribution of the Hudson's Bay Company to the trade of the Pacific West was the approach, short and easy compared with that through Montreal, by way of Hudson's Bay.

It would appear that the plan of the North West Company to link up New Caledonia with the Columbia and its depot Fort George, by transporting its outfits and returns on pack-horses and by canoe by way of the post on Thompson's River, was not immediately carried into effect, possibly with a view to a preliminary test of the commerical value of the route through York Factory and Hudson Strait. At any rate, the fort on McLeod's Lake continued till 1826 to be the post of entry and exit for New Caledonia. In the interest of this distant District Governor Simpson tried to eliminate the circuitous route from Portage du Traite on the Churchill to York Factory by way of Lake Winnipeg, by putting the direct route by

* See Sketch-map No. 12, with inset, at p. 714.

Burntwood River into use. During 1824 and 1825 the New Caledonia returns were brought out by the Burntwood to a post on Split Lake, on the Nelson, to which the outfit was forwarded from York Factory. The experiment was no success. Accordingly, in 1826, after the Governor's visit to the Columbia, the North West Company's practice of sending the furs out by pack-horses from Fort Alexandria to Fort Okanagan was resumed. Apart from this, the only changes in New Caledonia before Governor Simpson's tour of supervision in 1828 were the establishment in 1822 of Fort Kilmaurs, on the point of the peninsula extending southward into Babine Lake, and of Fort Connolly at its first site on an island in Bear Lake in 1826. Fort Kilmaurs was in a region which proved rich in furs; it tended to check a trade which had been passing down by the Babine River and the Skeena to the coast, and to divert it into the channel running eastward; and finally, it enjoyed a salmon fishery which insured a food supply to the whole District in years when the fish failed to come far up the Fraser. Fort Connolly, at the source of the Skeena, was more isolated, in a sphere more exclusively its own.

" West of the Mountains," as the region was often called in those days, faced two ways. It looked down on the Pacific and, more specifically, on the mediterranean sea which acted as a courtyard to the many tribes living on its borders and beside many a channel which protruded, often divided like a serpent's tongue, deep into the continental coast. But it also looked up the river valleys, more especially those of the Columbia, east to the Rockies and beyond them to the buffalo plains of the Saskatchewan and the Missouri, and south to Utah and to California. Its transportation lines were in correspondence. The goods for the region came in and the furs went out by the Pacific Ocean and round Cape Horn. Many posts needed articles, such as dressed skins, leather thongs, lacing for snowshoes. These came in from across the mountains. The Governor and the fur trade Council met in the east. The yearly instructions and the annual reports, officers changing their posts, and new recruits, all came in or went out, as the case might be, by the Rockies, by what was called the Columbian express.

The Columbian brigade of 1823 will introduce us to the route followed of old, to changes being made in it by Governor Simpson for the sake of efficiency, and incidentally to two gentlemen whose careers bulk largely in the history of " West of the Mountains "—Peter Skene Ogden and John Work. Ogden has been met already. He was the son of a Puisne Judge at Montreal, and had eschewed the routine of a career in law and adopted *con amore* the adventurous life of a clerk in the North West Company. In 1814-17 at Ile-à-la-Crosse and at Green Lake, he had given himself up with all the spirit of a footballer, and none of his sense of " good sport," to the game of violence being played upon the servants of the Hudson's Bay Company in the days of the life-and-death struggle. There is some reason for the suspicion that he was sent to the Columbia to keep him out of the clutches of the law in Canada. In 1820 he became a

Wintering Partner in his company and now, after a short period of exclusion in the era of union and peace, was Chief Trader in the Hudson's Bay Company. Ogden had just returned from a visit to his sick father now retired in England. John Work is known to the historian, not simply for his achievements, but for a long succession of journals and letters (mostly in the form of copies in the Provincial Archives of British Columbia), which throw a flood of light upon the progress of the trade of the Pacific West. He was a clerk and as such kept the Journal of the brigade of 1823—a Journal which describes the journey with pains and perspicacity. The party left York Factory on 18th July in two light canoes, four men in each. It reached Ile-à-la-Crosse by the Hayes–Norway House–Fort Cumberland–English River route on 16th August, having consumed 1,035 lb. of pemmican secured at the posts by the way, or something more than four pounds per man a day. It now faced what in many ways was the most difficult part of the old route of the North West Company —the ascent up the Beaver River. The stream wound its way with a tantalizing sinuosity through a wide valley from outer bank to outer bank, and most of the way was so shallow that the crews had to wade along bearing up the canoes. Worse still, game was very scarce, and it was impossible to live on the country as the traders loved to do. Pemmican from Fort Edmonton was to have met the party at Moose Portage at the inflow of the stream from Moose Lake (Lac d'Orignal), but none was there. To go on was to risk starvation. Ogden elected to stay with the party and sent Work to the fort to secure the needful. After he had passed by Angus Shaw's old fort of Lac d'Orignal, Work lost his way, but finally came on the River Saskatchewan and to Edmonton, where he found that scarcity had been prevailing there also, but that pemmican had been sent recently overland to the second cache prescribed by instructions. Taking what little pemmican was left, he returned to Moose Portage to find that Ogden, in desperate straits, had moved his party on to an Indian encampment, at which he had been fortunate enough to fall on an Indian taking sixty pounds of pemmican to supply Mr. Connolly, then of Lesser Slave Lake, on his way out. The party passed through Lac la Biche to the Athabaska. On this last river it was met by the pemmican from Edmonton House, so that when Ogden got to the river flowing in from Lesser Slave Lake, Mr. Connolly's route, he was able to make good in a cache that gentleman's pemmican, which he had commandeered ; he added some fresh meat which had come to hand. With the pemmican forwarded from Fort Edmonton the Columbian party reached Fort Assiniboine, then being built. It was Governor Simpson's plan to cut a trail from Fort Edmonton to this point, a good fur area in any case, and to have the Columbian brigade, as well as provisions for it, pass with ease and swiftness on pack-horses overland between the Saskatchewan and the Athabaska. The Lesser Slave Lake trade was also to pass this way.

The brigade moved on in their canoes up the Athabaska to Jasper's

House (Rocky Mountain House as Work calls it), at the outlet of Brulé Lake and on the right, " embosomed in the mountains whose peaks are rising round about it on three sides." Here preparations were made for the portage across Athabaska Pass by pack-horses. John Work was greatly impressed with the beauty of the scenery of what is now Jasper National Park. At the height of land he stayed to mention (Duncan) " M'Gillivray's Rock," which he attributes, according to the prevailing legend, to William M'Gillivray, and he remarked on the lakes at its foot from which the waters flowed eastward to the Arctic and westward to the Columbia and the Pacific. The party was met by Mr. Kennedy, Chief Factor, and Alexander Ross, who was on his way out of the country but now changed his mind, at Boat Encampment by the banks of the Columbia and passed easily downstream to the forks of the Spokane River, whence Ogden and Work took horse to their winter quarters at Spokane House, situated not far above the confluence of the main river Spokane with the Little Spokane, and on the north bank. Doubtless Ogden's Spokane squaw (his first had been a Cree) awaited him at the post. Work soon took, *en façon du nord*, a squaw of the same tribe.

Alexander Ross speaks of " the fascinating pleasures of Spokane House." That autumn he started upon his Snake River expedition. He had gone up to Boat Encampment to leave the country, but Ogden had brought him a letter from Governor Simpson urging on him the acceptance of this charge. The expedition was to start from Spokane House, then the central depot for the interior, though very inconvenient. Ross attributes the selection of the house to the fact that it was an early post, and to the seductions of the place.

" Both men and goods were, year after year, carried two hundred miles north by water, merely to have the pleasure of sending them two hundred miles south again by land, in order to reach their destination." Fort Walla Walla would have been much more convenient, but the country was too dangerous, it was said—the people too hostile.

These were the ostensible reasons ; the real cause lay deeper beneath the surface. Spokane House was a retired spot ; no hostile natives were there to disquiet a great man. There the Bourgeois who presided over the [North West] Company's affairs resided, and that made Spokane House the centre of attraction. There all the Wintering Partners, with the exception of the northern district, met. There they were all fitted out : it was the great starting point; although six weeks' travel out of the direct line of some, and more or less inconvenient to all. But that was nothing : these trifles never troubled the great man.

At Spokane House, too, there were handsome buildings : there was a ball-room, even ; and no females in the land so fair to look upon as the nymphs of Spokane ; no damsels could dance so gracefully as they ; none were so attractive. But Spokane House was not celebrated for fine women only ; there were fine horses also. The race-ground was admired, and the pleasures of the chase often yielded to the pleasures of the race. Altogether Spokane House was a delightful place, and time had confirmed its celebrity.

Ross held that, whatever the North West Company east of the Rockies may have been, west of the Rockies the Wintering Partners were comparatively unenterprising, and gave themselves up too easily to the joys of living in a beautiful country.

In April Ogden and his clerk Work took the furs down to Fort George to meet the ship. As she was delayed and provisions at the fort were inadequate, Work took a party of men up the Columbia to the various fisheries where fish could be procured from the Indians at a very low price. The men must have enjoyed their period of indolence in a beautiful climate. When the ship failed to arrive, Ogden and Work left for their post on 3rd August with a modicum of goods for the autumn trade, which Work carried on in the Flat-head country beyond Spokane. On 10th September news arrived that the ship had come. Another voyage to Fort George. The two men returned with winter supplies to the forks of the Spokane and the Columbia, 16th October. Nothing could show more clearly the ease with which the traders moved up and down their water-way, the great Columbia. Nor was there any great danger now from the natives. Duncan M'Gillivray's faith that with forts among them, and with European goods become necessary to their life, the hostility of the Indians west of the mountains would be disarmed had already come true. Sending their goods on to Spokane House, Ogden and Work awaited the arrival of Governor Simpson and his party.

Governor Simpson had spent his first years at the head of the administration of the Northern Department visiting the various Districts of the now united companies, bringing them to internal order and establishing a firm discipline. With the help of his Council he had also brought about a close co-ordination of District with District. In these, his first voyages, he had already established his reputation for furious travelling. The Columbia and New Caledonia Districts now awaited his salutary, if none too pleasant, attention. Delayed at York Factory waiting in vain for the arrival of the annual ship, he sent forward Dr. McLoughlin, who was to take charge of the Columbia, not in a semi-independent position as is sometimes stated, but in the capacity of Chief Factor in the place of Mr. Alexander Kennedy at the head of one of the most important Districts of the Company. Convinced that the northern brigades lost time in the circuitous route from Portage du Traite on the Churchill by Cumberland House, and in the dissipations of Norway House, the Governor had decided to test for himself the practicability of the shorter and quieter route by the Nelson and the Burntwood rivers to the Churchill, made familiar to us by the voyages of David Thompson. In spite of loss of time through failure to find a guide for the last part of the way, he reached Portage du Traite in fifteen days. Here he came upon the Lesser Slave Lake brigade under John Clarke. It had taken thirty-four days by the longer route (Ogden's party of the year before took twenty-five days). Apart from the danger of passing round the point from the estuary of the Hayes to the Nelson, Simpson was of opinion that there " could not be a finer navigation " than that by this route. The servants, however, objected to it on the ground that there were no establishments by the way, and

Simpson adds no chance to indulge themselves. The route was abandoned, as has been seen, after an experiment of two years, perhaps, because of the difficulty of supplying it with provisions, which would have to come from the Saskatchewan. Simpson passed on to Ile-à-la-Crosse and, taking the Beaver River route, followed by Messrs. Ogden and Work, reached Fort Assiniboine on the 2nd of October. Chief Factor Rowand, who had left York Factory some unspecified time before Simpson, had already come to the fort to meet the Governor, and, as the latter had been delayed, left to return to his own post. This led Simpson to the final determination that the shortest route to the Columbia, and the most comfortable, was by the Saskatchewan to Edmonton House and thence overland to Fort Assiniboine. From Jasper House in its " beautifully wild and romantic situation," but " merely a temporary Summer post for the convenience of the Columbians," that is, as a station for their provisions and horses, Simpson sent the horses ahead and travelled by canoe to " William Henry's Old House " opposite the mouth of the Miette River. Camped by the lakes at the foot of M'Gillivray's Rock, which is again attributed to William M'Gillivray, Simpson named the basin whose waters flowed east and west " The Committee's Punch Bowl." On 19th October Boat Encampment was reached. On the 27th the Governor's Journal runs: " Got to the Forks of Spokane River where we found Chief Factor Ogden and Mr. Work with about 30 men who had come up from Fort George with the outfits for the interior after the arrival of the *Vigilant*."

The relative positions occupied by Governor Simpson and Dr. McLoughlin should be noted here. The doctor was of a character as forceful as his physique was striking. He had proved himself in the east a leader of men. Indeed, he it was that had set the movement agoing which ended in the Union of 1821, though its terms were not those first sketched for him by Andrew Colvile. He deserved much at the hands of the Company, and was accordingly given the great Columbian District. At the same time he was just its Chief Factor, and as yet unacquainted with his domain. Governor Simpson, in contrast, was business manager of the whole domain of the Company of Adventurers from Hudson Bay to the Pacific Ocean. He was in the confidence of the Governor and Committee in London and seized of the purport of its policy. He was even definitely informed of the trend of the policy of the British Government in the matter of the American claims to the Oregon. Further, he was head of the Council of the Northern Departments, including the Columbia, which it was now his task to inspect. Of course, he had not as yet, any more than the Doctor, a personal knowledge of the " West of the Mountains," but for three years all the reports of its commissioned officers had passed under his eye. Thus the policy in the Columbian District was shaped by his hand and not the Doctor's.

Three duties he saw before him: to bring order and economy into the fur trade that it might really pay, for the information was

that it had been a loss to the North West Company ; to organize
the maritime trade as had not been done hitherto ; and lastly, it
may be inferred, to find a policy in the region, which was by treaty
open to the British and the Americans alike, calculated to increase
the chance of it becoming finally British—if not the whole region,
at least the part.   He addressed himself in the first place to the fur
trade.   Along with Chief Factor Ogden, he passed from the forks
of the Spokane to Ogden's domain—Spokane House—and here the
inquisition began.   Simpson was struck by the site " in a fine plain
or valley surrounded at the distance of two or three miles by Hills
clothed with Grass and fine Timbers to their summits."   He entered
the extent of the District in his Journal : It " comprises the Posts
of Spokane House, Coutenais [at Jennings Crossing, Idaho] and Flat
Head [at Thompson's Falls, Montana] Rivers, the former about
8 Days and the latter 7 Days march from Spokane House.   The
Snake Country Expedition [which had already touched the Missouri
country, and would in time reach Salt Lake in Utah and the Bay of
San Francisco in California] is likewise attached to this district."
The Governor decided that the Flat Head Post was too far from the
Snake River region.   The men spent half the year travelling to and
from their hunting-grounds.   Some nearer headquarters must be
found.   He was dissatisfied with Alexander Ross as leader of the
expedition.   The freemen who joined it were the " scum of the
country," and Ross lacked the talent to manage them.   " This
important duty should not . . . be left to a self-sufficient empty-
headed man like Ross who feels no further interest therein than in
as far as it secures to him a sal^y· of £120 p. Annum and whose reports
are so full of bombast and marvellous nonsense that it is impossible
to get any information that can be depended on from him."   This
opinion did not prevent Simpson from writing a nice letter of thanks
to Ross for his expedition.   It helps, however, to explain Ross's
retirement to teach in the Red River Settlement on £100 a year.
" Knowing no one in the Country better qualified to do justice "
to the Snake District Expedition the Governor entrusted it with
" much pleasure " to P. S. Ogden.

Simpson next criticized " the good people of Spokane District "
for their " extraordinary predilection for European Provisions."
They were thus " eating Gold."   Not " one oz. of European Stores
or Provisions should be allowed on one side of the Mountain more
than on the other."   " Five and sometimes Six Boats have been
annually sent and these principally loaded with Eatables, Drink-
ables and other *Domestic Comforts.*"   Gentlemen and their servants
must live on the country.   They had " abundance of the finest
Salmon," and in this fine country they could easily have abundance
of potatoes.

On 1st November the post at the mouth of the Okanagan with
its superior post on the Thompson River at Kamloops under Chief
Factor John M'Leod was the subject of the Governor's inquisition.
The finest potatoes he had ever seen grew at Okanagan.   Grain in

any quantity might be raised. "It has been said that Farming is no branch of the Fur Trade, but I consider that every pursuit tending to lighten the Expence of the Trade is a branch thereof." McLeod at Thompson's River was too much in fear of the Indians, having never learned to manage them. He insisted, therefore, on eighteen men at his post. They must be reduced to nine to make the place remunerative. On his return visit Simpson comments on McLeod's lack of enterprise and his stay-at-home habits:

It is a lamentable fact that two Chief Traders out of three now in Columbia say M^rs. D—— and M—— are so much under the influence of their Women and so watchful of their chastity that what they say is Law, and they can not muster sufficient resolution in themselves or confidence in their Ladies to be 5 Minutes in and out of their presence and even for that short time they keep them under Lock and Key, although they have more than once discovered that "Love laughs at Locksmiths."

Simpson's statement is supported by the fact that shortly after John Work discovered an Iroquois making himself too free with his squaw, dismissed the girl, and gave the man such a beating that he fled the fort. A similar incident took place in the same season in New Caledonia. McLeod was "given permission" (!) to cross the mountain at the end of the trading season 1825-26.

After inspecting Fort Nez Percés (Walla Walla) near the mouth of Walla Walla River, Governor Simpson pushed on, and on 8th November reached Fort George, the post near the mouth of the Columbia, John Work in his party. The journey across the continent occupied him eighty-four days, twenty days less than the previous record.

Himself the embodiment of efficiency, Governor Simpson did not find the much-vaunted enterprise and push of the North West Company illustrated in the Columbian District. There was not so much as a trustworthy boat at Fort George, and the Governor and Dr. McLoughlin almost lost their lives in the crazy craft to hand. Nothing had been done to procure an experienced man to pilot the ships over the dangerous bar at the mouth of the Columbia River. The men knew nothing of the country south and north of the post. Arrangements were therefore made for an expedition southward to the Umqua River and beyond to the coast, in search of a trade in beavers and sea-otters. James McMillan and John Work were sent north immediately to explore the mouth of the Fraser River. It is eloquent of the ignorance of the country prevailing at the post that this party took a most difficult route by Baker's Bay at Ilwaco, by Shoalwater Bay and Gray's Harbour and the Chehalis and Black rivers to Eld Inlet on Puget Sound. From Boundary Bay it ascended the Nicomekl, portaged to and descended the Salmon River to the Fraser in the neighbourhood of the later Fort Langley. It ascended the Fraser to the head of tidal waters. The Indians have a marvellous instinct for perceiving the ideas in the mind of their questioner and always give the answer the eager inquirer desires.   McMillan wanted to know that the Fraser River from Thompson's River downwards was navigable, and was accordingly told that, while it was frozen at that time of the year (December), it was easy navigation in the summer.   He returned with this information by the easier and more direct Cowlitz Portage and River, henceforth to be the route from the Columbia to Puget Sound. McMillan's favourable report led to Governor Simpson's expedition down the Fraser in 1828–29, and in 1827 to the establishment of Fort Langley.   This post stood on the river above New Westminster. It was designed, should the Americans secure the Oregon, to be the central depot west of the mountains.

The Governor was much concerned at the small cargoes brought in half-empty ships all the way round Cape Horn, and in his report to the Governor and Committee in London he discussed the possibility of bringing freight to the west coast of Spanish South America, which was now free to the English, for the colonies had declared their independence ;   and thence provisions to the Russian post in Alaska.   He was convinced that if the Company's ships were to supply the Russian posts, the Americans could be driven out of the maritime fur trade.   Two other objectives lay before him—to eliminate European provisions by forcing the officers at the posts to live on the country ;   and to adjust the Company's business to the situation envisaged by recent negotiations with the Americans, for Britain had proposed the Columbia as the boundary between the American and British territory.   These were to be reached by one and the same method—agricultural farming.   The land at the coast was poor ;   it was rich in the interior.   The climate was altogether favourable.   Accordingly a post, Fort Vancouver, was established at *La jolie prairie* (Belle Vue Point), a hundred miles up the river, near the site of the present city of Vancouver, in the state of Washington.   Simpson describes it on his homeward journey on March 18, 1825 : " The Establishment is beautifully situated on the top of a bank about 1¼ Miles from the Water side [In 1828–29 it was removed to the river bank] commanding an extensive view of the River, the surrounding country and the fine plain below, which is watered by two pretty small Lakes and studded as if artificially by clumps of fine Timber."   There was to be a great farm here to provide provisions for the various posts.   Moreover, Simpson was informed that the British Government was willing to meet the claim of the Americans to the Oregon by conceding the country south of the Columbia and its tributary the Kootenay, thus making those streams the natural boundary.   Fort Vancouver as an agricultural settlement would go some distance toward assuring to Britain her claim to the north bank of the Columbia ;   accordingly there was to be an extensive farm at the fort.

Simpson's faith in agriculture as the solution of the problems of the fur trade west of the mountains is further illustrated on his return up the river.   At Fort Walla Walla the principal provision, apart from European imports, was horseflesh.   In the three preceding years no less than 700 horses had been slaughtered for the supply of the post. The Governor's edict went forth : " the River [*i.e.* Salmon] with a Potatoe Garden will abundantly maintain the post." A conference with Messrs. Kennedy, McMillan, McDonald, and Ross at Spokane Forks led to the establishment of Fort Colvile immediately above the Kettle Falls as a substitute for Spokane House and also for Fort Okanagan. The Governor himself met with the Indians of the place, and received permission to choose a site. " We selected a beautiful point on the South side about ¾ of a Mile above the Portage where there is an abundance of fine Timber and the situation is eligible in every point of view. An excellent Farm can be made at this place where as much Grain and potatoes may be raised as would feed all the Natives of the Columbia and a sufficient number of Cattle and Hogs to supply his Majesty's Navy with Beef and Pork."

Governor Simpson's remedy for inefficiency and lack of discipline was to prescribe a voyage to the " east of the mountains." As the result of his visit Alexander Ross and John McLeod travelled east-ward. The remedy was applied to the humblest in the service. An interpreter who was supposed to be too fond of a Chief Trader's squaw, and who incited the Indians to make trouble, was a cause of anxiety. Open discipline might lead to an attack by an angry mob of the savages whose favour he had won. The Governor invited the interpreter to accompany him on the trip across the mountains. The flattered man did not know how uncertain was his return. Simpson's Journal of 1824–25 throws an interesting light on the state of the trade, on his own efficiency, and on the methods by which he obtained discipline, and put the affairs of the " West of the Mountains " upon a paying basis. On the return journey the Governor rode from Fort Assiniboine to Edmonton, took canoe to Fort Carlton and horse to Fort Garry. He was back in the Red River Settlement on 28th May—seventy-three days after leaving Fort George.

The Governor's plans for the Fraser River may be summed up in his own words :

> Whether the Americans come to the Columbia or not, I am of opinion that the principal Depot should be situated North of this place [Fort George] about two or three Degrees at the Mouth of Fraser's . . . River as it is more central both for the Coast and interior Trade and as from thence we could with greater facility and at less expense extend our discoveries and Estab-lishments to the Northward and supply all the Interior Posts now occupied.

As a beginning of this far-reaching scheme Fort Langley was com-menced on July 30, 1827. James McMillan, accompanied by Donald Manson, François Annance, and George Barnston, clerks, passed from Fort Vancouver up the Cowlitz River and by the " Cowlitz Portage " to Puget Sound. With canoes secured from the Indians, he proceeded to the south end of Whidbey Island, where he was met by the ship *Cadboro*, Captain Aemilius Simpson in command. The course up the Fraser was not without its difficulties, for the channel was unknown. A spot was found on the south bank where the *Cadboro* could come so close to the shore that the horses could be landed in slings. The site was a fine meadow on the south bank below the present McMillan's Island. The fort enjoyed an abundant supply of fresh salmon and sturgeon in season, thereafter dried salmon. A garden was planted, and in November 1829, 670 barrels of potatoes, making 2,010 bushels, were harvested from 91 bushels of seed. Here also the service lived " on the river and on potatoes from the garden." The Indian customers came from numerous villages along the river. They never really gave trouble, but had to be trained to refrain from stealing and to devote themselves to hunting beaver. The desire for good relations with the fort and the love of European wares soon brought them into line. The future of the post remained to be decided by Governor Simpson's exploration down the Fraser in 1828–29.

The establishment of Fort Langley contributed to an incident, the so-called massacre of the Clallum tribe, which was made much of by the opponents of the Hudson's Bay Company, and which was used some dozen years later by the Rev. Herbert Beaver and by the settlers of Red River in a petition to the Imperial Government to discredit the Company and break its monopoly, that others might enter into the trade in peltries. A Journal kept by Francis Ermatinger, a clerk in the service and of the party sent out to deal with the Clallums, gives a lively account of the expedition. A clerk, William McKenzie, with his squaw, daughter of the chief of a friendly tribe, and three men had been sent from Fort Vancouver to Fort Langley with dispatches. They were returning in January 1828 by the usual route, by Puget Sound and the Cowlitz Portage. While encamped on Lummi Island in the Gulf of Georgia the men were murdered and the squaw carried off by a party of Clallums, a ferocious tribe whose habitat was on the Straits of Juan de Fuca, and who, as has been seen, had had their clashes with first maritime traders. An expedition was organized at Fort Vancouver under Chief Trader A. R. McLeod. There can be no doubt but that the junior servants, Ermatinger among them, went out in a fierce spirit of revenge, but the actual instructions to McLeod were in a very different vein, as Ermatinger says with the scorn of a fire-eater : " The fact is . . . the orders must have been in contradiction to the opening speech made [by Dr. McLoughlin] to the men." This misunderstanding was due to McLeod's mistaken policy of keeping his juniors ignorant of his plans—a policy which caused an estrangement almost from the beginning. However, when the party was taking to canoes on Puget Sound (26th June), McLeod deigned to explain his proposed procedure : " We must endeavour to come to a parley and obtain the woman." This was because her father, a chief who had great influence with his tribe, would lose his respect for the power of the Whites if they could not restore his daughter, and he might " do mischief." " What then, said I [Ermatinger]. Why then to them *pell-mell* . . . to make this the primitive object of our expedition we never understood nor could we, we added, ever agree to it." Evidently the instructions to the responsible Chief Trader, McLeod, and his plans were in keeping with the Company's traditional policy of meeting the Indians in Council and seeking a friendly but preventative issue of the matter —a policy which his juniors regarded as approximating to cowardice. Word came in that a small outlying party of Clallums were camped at a portage, and McLeod arranged a night journey in the canoes to surprise them at dawn. His intention apparently was to take them as hostages, but he erred in not making this known to the men in all the canoes. The canoes lost touch with one another in the dark. Ermatinger was with those that first came on the enemy. The lodge was surrounded at dawn, and the Indians were shot down as they rushed out : " Two families were killed, three men, two or three women, a girl and a boy," Ermatinger thought. When McLeod came up he took his men to task for what they had done, and an altercation followed in which Ermatinger cast it up against his commanding officer that he had not made known his plans.

The overland party was now joined by the schooner *Cadboro* in command of Captain McNeill, who, exposed as his ship was to the attacks of the savage tribes along the coast, was against pushing things to extremes. When the ship was anchored off a Clallum village near Dungeness, where the murderers were thought to be, the land party was sent to a sand bank to take their meal. A body of armed Clallums in large canoes started from the village towards them. Captain McNeill had two cannons levelled at them, lighted matches ready. McLeod appealed to the Captain against sending " the whole to Hell." The Indians turned, and the matches were put out. Hotspur Ermatinger remarks : " Here was a fine chance lost." Two chiefs came off from the village and held council with Chief Trader McLeod below decks. Just what passed was unknown to Ermatinger, but the chiefs went off in anger, leaving McLeod so irritated that he cast his moderate policy to the winds, yet not without hesitation. As the canoes moved off, he cried, " Raise arms "—then " Down," and again " Raise arms." At this second command, the men fired, killing one chief and wounding the other. Iroquois pushed off to bring them in. They prepared to scalp the wounded man, but were forbidden. With the blood of the heads of the village flowing, Captain McNeill concluded that all that could be done was to go on. The guns were levelled on the huts, the natives taking to the woods. A party landed and set the houses on fire, bringing back two little children, forsaken in the flight, and articles belonging to McKenzie found in the houses. McLeod turned his party away not without landing the two children and making it known that he would exchange the wounded chief for McKenzie's squaw. In the end the exchange was effected. The natives claimed that some of the murderers had been killed and enough men in addition to make just compensation for the murder of McKenzie and his party. Ermatinger, who does not report any killed when the village was fired upon, did not believe them.   McLeod accepted the Clallums' story, and all parties treated the incident as closed, but the fire-eater Ermatinger's view was that his officer had made them all look like cowards before the Indians.   His final judgment may be given in his own words :   " Upon the whole the damage done to their property is great and will, I trust, be seriously felt for some time to come but I could wish we could have been allowed to do more to the rascals themselves."

In the following year another clash occurred.   It is reported by A. C. Anderson in his manuscript, " History of the North-West Coast."   The annual ship *William and Anne* was wrecked on the treacherous bar of the Columbia.   Many of the crew were drowned. Dr. McLoughlin got word that such survivors as there were had been murdered by the Clatsops, a Chinookan tribe about Cape Adams, the southern promontory at the mouth of the river.   When Dr. McLoughlin made inquiries of these savages, he was given "a derisive answer " ;   his demand that the goods looted should be given up was answered by the return of an old broom as being all that he would get.   When the brigades from the Interior arrived at Fort Vancouver, an expedition was equipped, under Chief Factor Connolly of New Caledonia, supported by the schooner *Cadboro*.   In reply to renewed defiances, the ship's guns were fired on the village, and a landing force was launched.   After a brief encounter on the shore the natives fled " with little bloodshed."

These expeditions were rough justice, but after all it was the only justice the savages understood.   They were the only means of securing safety for the White Men in a land of a large and ferocious population, but just as the clash in 1780–81 on the Saskatchewan and on the Assiniboine was followed by a great plague, small-pox, which by decimating the great prairie tribes brought peace to the region, so now a virulent epidemic of fever and ague did more to bring security to the White Men than could have been accomplished by a score of punitive expeditions.   A considerable proportion of the Hudson's Bay Company's service was swept away, and the number of deaths among the Indians was appalling.   In his Journal of 1840 James Douglas quotes one Plamonde, a servant in his party, who witnessed the epidemic :

Every village presented a scene harrowing in the extreme to the feelings ; the canoes were there drawn on the beach, the nets extended on the willow bows to dry, the very dogs appeared as ever watchful, but there was not heard the cheerful sound of the human voice ; the green woods, the music of the birds, the busy humming of the insect tribes, the bright summer sky, spoke of life and happiness, while the abode of man was silent as the grave, like it, filled with putrid, festering corpses. Oh God ! wonderful and mysterious are thy ways.

The great depletion of the population took from the savages their sense of courage, hitherto based on their numbers over against the Whites, and brought order and peace.   One marvels at horses, herds of cattle, and flocks of sheep, being driven overland by a handful of men, within a very few years without fear of molestation. Still more influential a result was that when the small first bands of American immigrants came into the country later, they found it largely empty. The dread of the Indians had passed away, and the country lay calling for white settlers.

Simpson's agricultural policy resulted in the establishment of the agricultural settlement on the Willamette (1829) and at Fort Nisqually (1833) on the east bank of the Nisqually River at its mouth. Though Nisqually was a fur post, farming and stock-raising were emphasized from the day on which its founders, Francis Heron and Dr. William F. Tolmie, chose the site of the post. Indeed the first store was removed from the shore, the natural site for a fur post, to the farm where the fort was built.

To the north, Simpson's policy led to the establishment of a line of fur posts. In 1831 a fort was built in " the inhospitable regions of Nass." Its site was on the north shore of the mouth of the Nass River, north-east of and opposite to Nass Bay, at the south-east corner of the present Indian Reservation. It was a great fishing ground, and at the same time a meeting-place for many Indian tribes for trade. Tsimsian bands (" Tongas ") were the middlemen bringing downstream the products of the Interior. Other tribes (Haidas), came from the shores of the mediterranean sea, from as far as the Queen Charlotte Islands, to fish and trade. From many points of view it was a natural place for a post. Captain Aemilius Simpson died while the ship was at the post.

A second post, Fort McLoughlin, was begun on May 23, 1833, by an expedition under Chief Trader Duncan Finlayson of Fort Vancouver. It was placed on Suzette Bay, on the west side of Dowager Island within the entrance to Milbank Sound, about fifteen miles from Swaine Cape. It drew to itself the trade from the Tsimsian Tongas and the Kwakiutl and Bella Bellas on the mainland, and from the Haidas of the southerly part of Queen Charlotte Islands. The post was not established without an early clash with the natives, who had to be trained not to steal and not to kill. Its story is told by A. C. Anderson and John Dunn, author of the *History of Oregon*, both of whom took part in the fray. First there was a clash between the people of the ship, the *Dryad*, and the natives over an axe which was stolen. The officers engaged in building the fort, Donald Manson in command, intervened as mediators and brought about a settlement. Later, Manson beat one of his servants, Richard by name, so that he fled from the fort, probably aiming, at once, at revenging himself upon his officer and enjoying the wild pleasures of the Indian village. He was, however, stoned to death for resisting the boys who promised to guide him, but began tearing his clothes from his body. All unaware of the fate of his wayward servant, Mr. Manson called on the Indians to surrender him. On being met with defiance, he seized the chief of the village to hold him as a hostage. Of an evening, when the men were out bringing in water, the natives attempted to rush the fort. Anderson, who was without the gate watching the fatigue party, guarded the wicket. Manson on the gallery which ran round the palisade, with the men who rushed to arms, shot down the leaders of the assault. One servant of the fort was captured. The affair ended in an exchange of prisoners and something like a mutual understanding.

In 1834 an attempt was made to extend the trade northward. The plan was to pass up the Stikine through the Russian "Alaskan pan-handle," which at that point is about fifteen miles across, and to build upstream in the British region. The Hudson's Bay officers were under the impression that they could do so in keeping with the Treaty of 1825, and would receive permission from the Russians. The expedition went north by the ship *Dryad*. It was in charge of P. S. Ogden, whose period of service with the Snake expeditions was now over. A. C. Anderson and Dr. W. F. Tolmie were of the party. The Russian American Fur Company anticipated the move by building at the mouth of the river. When the *Dryad* anchored some seven miles out from the Russian establishment, a Russian under-officer came out with a copy of a proclamation prohibiting British or American vessels from trading in that region. Mr. Ogden replied that he was determined to proceed, in keeping with the terms of the Treaty. Arguments on Treaty rights in two different languages, when the debaters on either side knew but one, could not lead to agreement. A second officer appeared who had a few words of English, but in spite of the brandy consumed, the result was the same. A third officer now came out fortified with a slight knowledge of Spanish. The Englishmen, of whom Dr. Tolmie had some knowledge of Spanish and the kindred tongues French and Latin, guessed that he intended them to understand that a message had been sent to Baron Wrangell at the chief Russian post, Sitka, asking for instructions. A visit of some of the Englishmen to the Russian establishment led to no more information than that they must wait till instructions were received. Meanwhile the Indian Chief of the region sat in Council on board the English ship. As he was the middleman handling the furs of the Interior, he naturally refused the Englishmen permission to pass into what he must have regarded as his own preserves. However, they might build at the mouth of the river. It would, of course, have been a great advantage to him to have competing companies at his door, outbidding one another for his peltries, but the Treaty made a location within the Russian territory impossible. Finally, word came from Sitka that Baron Wrangell was away at Cook's Inlet and would not be back till the end of August, and that his subordinate at the Stikine must obey instructions until his return. Mr. Ogden now consulted with his officers, and decided that there was nothing for it but to retreat.

It appears to have been already determined to abandon the fort on the Nass and to build at " McLoughlin's " Harbour south of the outer mouth of the Portland Canal. The site had its own river, the Nass, down which the furs of the interior would come, as they had done to the old fort. It was easy of access to the passing savage traders of the mediterranean sea, and would attract the canoes of the south on their way to the Nass. Moreover, the coasting vessel could visit the site of the old fort at the time of the salmon fishing and of its concomitant concourse for trade. Accordingly, Ogden came south to the present Port Simpson (20th July), and commenced a fort on the site of the present Hudson's Bay Company's post. The body of Captain Simpson was brought from the Nass for burial here, and his name given to the fort. Governor Simpson describes it as he saw it in 1841 :

> The site must originally have been one of the most rugged spots imaginable, —a mere rock—in fact as uneven as the adjacent waters in a tempest; while its soil, buried as it was, in its crevices, served only to encumber the surface with a heavy growth of timber. Besides blasting and levelling, Mr. Manson, without the aid of horse or ox, had introduced several thousand loads of gravel, while, by his judicious contrivances in the way of fortification, he had rendered the place capable of holding out, with a garrison of twenty men, against all the natives of the coast.

On 2nd September (1834) the *Dryad* returned from a short trading voyage, and proceeded to the old fort on the Nass to take away the property there. It would be only natural for the savages of the place to be chagrined at the loss of their post, and perhaps equally natural, that they should make a last and ample purchase of rum. The removal of the goods in the presence of a drunken and angry mass of armed Indians was attended with great danger. In spite of an occasional clash, it was accomplished with comparative success. The old chief, who wished to return the White Men's goodwill, tried to keep his men back from violence. The last barrel of goods, open and tempting as it was being rolled to the shore, proved too much for some of the savages, and a rush was made. After a struggle, in which some of both parties acquired disfigured countenances, all that was worth having was got safely on board, while the Indians rushed in to pillage what remained. A cask of rum, however, had been abandoned on the shore. The Indians were told from the ship that they might take it. They insisted, however, on bringing it on board to be divided there. They were afraid lest feuds would arise among themselves over the pouring of it out. The last scene in old Fort Nass shows the White Men impartially dividing the precious liquid to the savages, who, but a short time before, appeared to be on the verge of assaulting the fort and massacring its garrison.

An incident like this—and it could easily be multiplied—shows a great alteration in the relations of the Whites and the natives compared with that of the traders of the first generation on the Pacific coast. As a matter of fact, the savages were more formidable than ever before, for they were now possessed of guns, but the desire for these very guns, for ammunition, and particularly for blankets, which had supplanted in a large measure the savage demand for beads and metal, had made them thus far subservient to the European. They now wanted and even needed his wares to contribute to the comfort and necessities of their life. They welcomed his ships, and even his forts, in their midst, and took good care not to drive him away by acts of wanton aggression. However, they often made threats in the hope that the alarmed traders would reduce the prices of their goods. The Europeans, too, had changed their attitude. The old fear, tinctured with contempt—which had led them to misinterpret the natives and to shoot wantonly at what they took to be signs of aggression, or to avenge themselves—had passed. They had learned to manage the savage mob. The officers of the Hudson's Bay Company proved themselves past masters in this subtle art.

The establishment of forts along the coast was the first step in the decline of the trade carried on by the American ships. In their regions these posts provided for the needs of the savages as they arose, and, in return, gathered the peltries as they came to their savage customers throughout the year. The furs were no longer accumulated unto the coming of the ships and when the American vessels arrived— they gathered too few to make the long journey to and from this coast a profitable one. Moreover, besides the larger craft in the service of the Hudson's Bay Company, there were two small coasting schooners, the *Cadboro* and the *Llama*, bringing outfits to the forts and incidentally trading at the vantage points by the way. In the year of the establishment of Fort Simpson the Company had three vessels on the coast, the *Dryad* (Captain Kipling), the *Llama* (Captain McNeill), and the *Cadboro*. John Work, who had earned a well-deserved relaxation after several strenuous expeditions to the Snake Country, was on the *Llama* this year, and throws light on the trade done by the ships. He left Fort Vancouver on 11th December. At Fort George, on 15th December, word came in by the *Dryad* that the Company's trading schooner *Vancouver* was lost and that the Stikine expedition had failed. After a flying visit back to Fort Vancouver for revised instructions from Dr. McLoughlin, Work rejoined his ship. The inconvenience of the Columbia, as compared with the Fraser, for a depot of supplies for the north was seen, in that the *Llama* was delayed at its mouth from January 2nd to the 21st waiting for the waters at its bar to become smooth enough for it to put out to sea. On the 30th the ship reached Fort McLoughlin (Donald Manson and W. F. Tolmie in charge) with its supplies, and Fort Simpson (Dr. John Kennedy and Jas. Birnie in charge) on 10th February. After a short trading excursion to the south, the ship came back to Fort Simpson and proceeded north to the old fort on the Nass. On the way out Work fell on the American ship *Europa* (Captain Allan). The competition between the two ships in various ports, including the Nass, was of the keenest, and Work had to raise his offers, because the American blankets were larger and better than those of the Hudson's Bay Company. On 23rd May the *Llama* was back at Fort Simpson, and Work remained on shore. In June the rivalry culminated when at one port and another three vessels—the *Llama*, the *Europa*, and another American, the *Bolivar*— competed with one another for the Indians' peltries. The savages of the coast, ever hard bargainers, went from vessel to vessel, and stood out for high prices. In certain ports, out of sheer self-protection, the three captains had to agree to act in concert, pooling the goods and the returns. On 13th September, when they were all together at Fort McLoughlin, the harvest of furs ran: Captain Allan's 1,200 skins, Captain Dominis's 900—making 2,100 skins. The Hudson's Bay Company's returns were: McNeill's on the *Llama* 1,700, Fort McLoughlin's 1,500, Fort Simpson's 1,200—making a total of 4,400. The dice were already laden in favour of the Company of Adventurers.

The next move of the Hudson's Bay Company was towards two objectives—at one and the same time to drive the Americans out of the maritime trade in peltries and to open the way towards exploiting the fur trade of the British territory behind the Alaskan "pan-handle," which had hitherto gone to the Russians. An agreement was signed at Hamburg on February 6, 1839, whereby the Russian American Fur Company, with the sanction of the Russian Government, agreed to lease to the Hudson's Bay Company, for a term of ten years commencing June 1, 1840, "for commercial purposes," the coast, exclusive of the islands, of that part of the Russian territory situated between Cape Spencer at the boundary at 54° 40' north latitude and Mount Fairweather. This would enable the English Company to reach the British territory, which included the major part of the valleys of the rivers Stikine and Taku whose mouths lay in Russian territory. The rental was to be 2,000 otter skins delivered on or before June 1st to the agents of the Russian Company at Sitka, which lay on the Prince of Wales Archipelago and was therefore not included in the lease. The Russians also agreed to take 2,000 otter skins from west of the Mountains and 3,000 from the east at agreed prices. They likewise pledged themselves to buy the large quantities of wheat and other provisions specified from the English Company ; and to have the English and American goods required by their posts brought to them in the English Company's ships. The agreement was to hold good even if war should break out between Russia and Great Britain. This condition was natural, as the Russians were putting the English Company in temporary possession of Russian territory. In the correspondence accompanying the agreement, Baron Wrangell pledged himself not to encourage American or any other shipping to trade in the waters of the North-West coast. This very astute arrangement found a market for the produce of the farms at the Hudson's Bay Company's posts, notably Fort Vancouver. It also was the occasion of the founding of a company subsidiary to the Hudson's Bay Company, the Puget's Sound Agricultural Company, whose shareholders were the Hudson's Bay Company and many of its well-to-do officers. This subsidiary Company took over the farm at Fort Nisqually which, being on Puget's Sound, was favourably placed for shipping its produce. Another farm was established on the plain at the headwaters of the Cowlitz River. The agreement with the Russian American Fur Company took away from the

Americans the traffic in goods and provisions from Boston to the Russian posts, necessary to make their marine fur trade profitable. American shipping disappeared from the waters of the Pacific North-West. At this point, at the instance of Governor Simpson and his Council, James Douglas, now Chief Trader and soon to be Chief Factor, after some twenty years of an obscure service, stepped to the front of the stage as the organizer of the new movement northward, and of its accompaniment, a movement southward involving trade with the Spaniards. Passing up the coast, supervising the successive forts, he reached Sitka on May 25, 1840, and made arrangements to take over the Russian post on the Stikine. As the Indians on the mediterranean sea passed to and fro from the coast to the islands for trade, a gentleman's agreement was made that the Russian and English Agents should return to each other's posts the furs traded from the Indians belonging to their respective regions. The two parties agreed to have the same tariff for barter and thus eliminate competition. On his way back, Douglas took over the fort on the Stikine, leaving William Glen Rae and John McLoughlin, Dr. McLoughlin's son-in-law and son respectively, in charge. The post was at the north end of the Duke of York's Island near Point Highfield, four or five miles south of the mouth of the Stikine. It figures on Arrowsmith's maps as Fort Highfield.

Not finding a favourable site on the actual Taku River, Douglas established a second post, Fort Taku, on the coast some fifteen miles to the south, Mr. John Kennedy in charge. In his report to Dr. McLoughlin he showed that the trade of these two rivers, the Taku and the Stikine, would come down to their respective forts, and that the forts on Dease Lake and the trade being established by the exploration of Robert Campbell from the Mackenzie River left no room for posts in the interior between. In a word, the Company was tapping the whole shaggy area between the Pacific coast and the valley of the Mackenzie.

In the autumn Douglas journeyed southward to secure new commercial arrangements with the Spaniards. On 2nd January he was at Monterey negotiating with the Governor Juan B. Alvarado. For the Hudson's Bay Company he agreed to withdraw the trapping parties from the neighbourhood of Sacramento, and in return secured the privilege for the Company's ships to enter the port of San Francisco—not of right, but "with the express sanction of the [Spanish] Government." Permission was also given to purchase a lot of a hundred yards for the post. This achieved, Douglas bought cattle and sheep to be driven north to the Columbia. A lot at Yerba Buena was purchased that year, and Mr. Rae, Dr. McLoughlin's son-in-law, was brought down from the Stikine to take charge. This Hudson's Bay Company post stood on the present Montgomery Street, in the heart of the business centre of San Francisco of to-day.

All this was spade work preparatory to a visit of inspection by the Governor, now Sir George Simpson, while on his journey round the world. Accompanied by Chief Factor Rowand, Simpson rode furiously across the prairies, by way of forts Ellice, Carlton, and Pitt, to Edmonton House, the Chief Factor's headquarters. On his way he travelled for two days with a party of Red River settlers emigrating to the Oregon. From Edmonton the Governor took a south-south-westerly route, all his own, through the Blackfoot country to the neighbourhood of the present Banff. He then crossed the Rocky Mountains by a pass (Simpson's Pass), "now for the first time . . . travelled by Whites," over to and down M'Gillivray's (the Kootenay) River. The usual route was taken from that stream to Pend d'Oreille Lake and on to Fort Colvile. After supervising the forts of the Columbia, Simpson turned his attention to the coastal trade. Passing by the Cowlitz Portage to Fort Nisqually on Puget's Sound, he embarked on the steamer *Beaver*. He found Charles Ross at Fort McLoughlin, John Work at Fort Simpson, John McLoughlin, Jr., at the Stikine, and John Kennedy at Taku, and finally reached Sitka. Here, in the course of four days of discussion, he put the relations of the Hudson's Bay Company and the Russian American Fur Company on the firm and friendly basis already prepared by Chief Factor Douglas, who, by the way, was in his party.

A result of Simpson's visit was the elimination of the trade in rum from the northern posts, an arrangement for which Douglas had prepared the way the year before. Simpson was no temperance reformer, but throughout his career he lived true to the clause in the licence secured by his Company from the Imperial Government in 1821 and renewed in 1838, that as far as possible the traffic with the aborigines in liquor should be done away with. Moreover, he was convinced that in all regions in which the Company had complete control, the fur trade would be more profitable with a sober native population. On his visit to the Columbia in 1824, he found the Indians "now getting as much addicted to Drunkeness as the tribes on the East side of the Mountain [s]." He reported to the Governor and Committee : "We have however put a stop to this Traffick since our arrival here and determined on prohibiting the use thereof among the Indians altogether." It was afterwards the proud boast of the McLoughlin family that the great Chief Factor never traded rum with the natives. This does not mean that the service did not have its allowances, nor that the old custom of a *regale* to a crew after a particularly hard day's labour or at the beginning or end of a long journey was denied to them. As all the liquor in the country was imported by the concern and was kept locked in its shops, the control was complete, subject only to the time-honoured customs of the service. In the posts on the north coast, subject to the competition of the Russians and of the American ships which brought an abundant supply of rum, this policy had been relaxed in the interest of trade and good relations with the Indians. The agreement with the Russians to eliminate liquor from the traffic was in keeping with the general policy of the English Company. It could not, however, have been accomplished if the American ships had continued in the Pacific marine fur trade, but with the series of posts along the coast they disappeared from the trade, and now that the whole of their trade with the Russians was passed over by agreement to the Hudson's Bay Company, there was little fear of their returning.

As Simpson saw it, a new situation had been brought about by the agreement with the Russians, which was all the more welcome as the profits of the trade west of the mountains were declining. It was a saving grace in him that his devotion to efficiency and to the profits of his Company was such that he was never so wedded to the old that the new was without welcome. With the American ships beyond the horizon and the Russians confined to their island posts and to the far north, he felt free to transform the machinery of the maritime trade. The forts on the upper coast were to be scrapped, and the stout little steamer the *Beaver* * (not to speak of the coasting schooners) was to do the business of them all at a decreased cost by visiting the natives at their assemblies in the season for fishing and for trade, and at other times it was to be free to attend to its duties in conveying supplies to the remaining forts and to the Russians. The scheme required the abandonment of the Columbia River as a base, for its dangerous bar frequently delayed the ships for weeks, waiting for its waters to grow quiet to the point of safety, thus, as Simpson says, " deranging the best laid plans." This in turn implied the building of a depot for the maritime trade farther north on some harbour secure and easy of approach. On March 1, 1842, Simpson wrote to the Governor and Committee, " the southern end of Vancouver's Island, forming the northern side of the Straits of de Fuca, appears to me the best situation for such an establishment as is required. From the very superficial examination that has been made, it is ascertained that there are several good harbors in that neighbourhood." Consonant with this scheme, in the summer of that year (1842) Chief Factor James Douglas visited the south end of Vancouver Island and scrutinized the facilities offered by its various inlets. He chose " the Port and Canal of Camosack," his version of the Indian name Camosun, because of its security and for a " tract of clear land sufficiently extensive for the tillage and pasture of a large agricultural establishment." Wood suitable for building and for fuel was in its favour. In the spring of the next year Douglas returned in the capacity of general supervisor to choose the actual spot for the fort on the canal. Under his directions the post was commenced near a rock-bound shore that " would allow

---

* The *Beaver* was 101½ ft. in length ; 20 ft. in breadth inside of her paddle-boxes, and 30 ft. including them ; her register was 109½ tons burden ; and she was armed with five guns—nine-pounders—and carried a crew of twenty-six men. She was built of special strength for the Company's Pacific trade. Under canvas she passed round Cape Horn and arrived at Fort George on the Columbia in consort with the ship *Columbia* on April 4, 1836, and was placed under the command of Captain W. H. McNeil, Chief Trader. Her engines were now placed in her. She was the first steamship to plough the waters of the Pacific Ocean. After twenty-two years in the transportation service of the fur trade, for example, taking Chief Factor James Douglas and supplies to establish Fort Victoria, at the gold rush into British Columbia she was diverted to the Fraser River route to carry in miners and their equipment and supplies. She was sold in 1874 to Messrs. Stafford, Saunders, Morton & Co. of Victoria. Though her engines were now very antiquated, she was still seaworthy when she was wrecked on the night of July 26, 1888, while steaming out of Burrard Inlet, the harbour of Vancouver.

of vessels lying with their sides grazing the rocks, which form a natural wharf, whereon cargo may be landed from the ships yard [arm]." Here, on the site of the present post office and across the water from the Canadian Pacific Railway Company's docks, about a hundred yards from the shore, Fort Victoria was built, the commencement of the present beautiful capital of the province of British Columbia. Forts Taku, Stikine, and McLoughlin, but not Fort Simpson, were dismantled and their property and many of the men in their service were brought south to equip the new post. Mr. Charles Ross, come down from Fort McLoughlin, was left in charge by Douglas with Roderick Finlayson from Fort Simpson to assist him. In the face of a large body of observing Indians " we succeeded," says Finlayson, " in putting up Stockades in the usual manner, with Bastions at the Angles for protection mounted with heavy guns, blunderbusses, muskets, &c. ; then erected storehouses for the goods and dwelling homes within the stockades for the men and officers." The *Beaver* went off with Douglas to Nisqually and returned with cattle and horses from the farm there.

The Indians were really much pleased to have a fort in their midst. Indeed, they worked at cutting and hewing the pickets, for wages paid in goods, but, as always, they had to be trained not to steal and also to keep the peace. Next year Ross died and Finlayson was placed in charge.

Finlayson was skilled beyond the usual Hudson's Bay Company's officer in handling the Indians as his account of the first clash with the natives shows :

I was not long in charge, when the Indians killed some of our best working oxen and horses left feeding on the surrounding grounds. I sent a message to the chiefs demanding the delivery of the perpetrators of this unprovoked deed, or payment to be made for the Animals killed, which they declined doing. I then suspended trade or any dealing with them, until this matter was settled, whereupon they sent word to some of the neighbouring tribes to come to their assistance, as they intended to attack the Fort. In the meantime I kept all hands at arms and set watches night and day to prevent surprise. After a couple of days of vain negotiations, when a large number assembled, they opened fire first upon the fort, riddling the stockades and roofs of the houses with their musket balls ; it was with the greatest difficulty that I could prevail on our men not to return the fire but wait for my orders. After a close firing of about half an hour was carried on, I spoke to the Principal Chief, informing him that I was fully prepared to carry on the battle, but did not like to kill any of them without explaining to them that they were wrong and giving them another chance of making restitution. A parley ensued among them during which I sent our Indian Interpreter out to speak to them, telling him to make it appear that he escaped without orders and to point to them the Lodge I was determined to fire on and for all its inmates to clear out. This they did at the suggestion of the Interpreter, who upon making a sign to me, as agreed upon, that the Lodge was clear, was admitted to the fort by a back gate. Seeing that there was no sign of their coming to terms, I pointed one of our nine pounder cannonades loaded with grapeshot on the Lodge, which was a large one, built with cedar boards, fired, the effect of which was that it was completely demolished, the splinters of the cedar boards flying in fragments in the air. After this there was an immense howling among them from which I supposed a number had been killed. But my plan, I was happy to find, had the desired effect ; I was aware that these Indians had never seen the effect of grape shot fired from cannons.

A parley was now called. Two hostages were sent out of the fort as two chiefs entered to make terms. It was agreed that payment should be made for the offence, and the pipe of peace was passed round :

The chiefs next day wanted to see more of the effects of our big guns in an amicable way. I told them to place an old canoe in the harbor, that I would fire on it and then they would see the effect. So they did. I then loaded one of the guns with a cannon ball, pointed it at the canoe in the harbor and fired ; the ball passing through it bounded over the harbor afterwards into the woods beyond. This news spread far and wide and had a very salutary effect on them.

It was due to Finlayson's knowledge of Indian character, to his coolness in the hour of conflict, and to his enjoyment of the sport in a clever ruse that the foundation of the capital of Canada's westernmost province was laid in peace and not in blood.

2.—THE OREGON QUESTION, 1821–46

The Oregon Question involved the whole previous history of the Pacific North-West. There were the Spanish explorations, planned by the Spanish Government, carried out by servants of the state, and issuing in the proclamation of the land, in the name of the King, Spanish territory. There were the English explorations conducted by naval officers under instructions from the Admiralty and likewise claiming certain parts of the land British in the name of the King ; the very territory in dispute had been claimed for the Crown by Vancouver, who explored every inlet in Puget Sound, and by Lieutenant Broughton, who ascended the Columbia to the Falls. In addition it was Cook's voyage that revealed the fur resources of the region and inaugurated the marine fur trade. Finally, it was the stand taken by the English in the Nootka Sound controversy that led Spain by treaty to accept the principle that the trade of the Pacific coast and settlement there were open to the British, and in the sequel to all comers. Then in 1793 Alexander Mackenzie crossed the Rockies and passed through what is now northern British Columbia to the Pacific Ocean. The Americans followed in the wake of the English, and on private expeditions, issuing in fresh discoveries, but making no formal claim to the land as American territory. Very important in the issue was Captain Gray's discovery of the entrance to the Columbia River in 1792, and his penetration to what Lieutenant Broughton named Gray's Harbour, fifteen miles from the mouth, and the fact that the English officer (Broughton) entered the river as a result of Gray's discovery and with Gray's chart in his hand. There followed the acquisition of Louisiana by the United States, giving the American Republic territory at least contiguous to the Oregon; and Lewis and Clark's pioneer exploration of the valleys of the Lewis and Clark rivers and the Columbia to the sea in 1805–6—still, however, without formal claim to the land.

In 1805–11 the English hold on the North was effected by servants of the North West Company. In 1805–7 Simon Fraser built four forts in territory hitherto untrodden by Europeans, and named by him New Caledonia, while David Thompson from 1806–11 established a similar row of five posts—two in an unexplored region, three within the area explored by Lewis and Clark—in the valleys of the Columbia and its upper tributaries. Then came the grip of the Americans on the country when John Jacob Astor's Pacific Fur Company established Astoria on the south bank of the Columbia within its mouth, without, however, any formal annexation of the region to the American Republic, his company being composed in part of British citizens. Posts were built inland in opposition to Thompson's posts, and the posts at the Okanagan, and to the north at Kamloops on the banks of the Thompson were in regions first seen by American eyes. There followed the sale of the American Company's interests to the North West Company on October 16, 1813, during the war of 1812. When the British sloop-of-war *Raccoon* arrived the post was in the possession of British subjects. Captain Black, however, was not content with that. On 12th December he erected a flagstaff, ran up the Union Jack, and formally took possession of the country in the name of the King. There was no hauling down of the American flag. Twelve days later the war was closed by the Treaty of Ghent, the first clause of which required the restitution of " all territory, places and possessions whatsoever taken by either party from the other during the war," with the exception of certain islands in the Bay of Fundy. The Oregon Question entered its diplomatic phase when the Americans claimed that Astoria should be returned to the Republic, and the British asserted the contrary, on the ground that it had come into the possession of British subjects by a commercial transaction and not by an act of war.

On July 18, 1815, Mr. James Monroe, Secretary of State, mentioned to Mr. Baker, chargé d'affaires at the British Legation in Washington, that the President intended to occupy the post at the mouth of the Columbia, but took no steps for its formal restitution by commissioners. Rather the American Government decided to take possession unilaterally; in September 1817 Captain J. Biddle of the American sloop-of-war *Ontario* and Mr. J. B. Prevost were dispatched to occupy the post. Faced with an impending *fait accompli*, the British Government decided not to oppose the mission of the Americans, but to enter a protest that the restitution of the post was not to be taken as detrimental to the rights of Britain in that region. This view was expressed by Sir Charles Bagot, British Ambassador at Washington, to the Secretary of State verbally.

As it never appeared in the documents of the Secretary's office, subsequent Secretaries took the ground that the protest had never been definitely made. It was finally arranged that Captain F. Hickey of H.M.S. *Blossom* and James Keith of the North West Company should act as commissioners for Britain. Lord Bathurst's commission to Keith required him to restore the post to the American commissioners, but in the formal act of restitution which took place at Fort George (Astoria) on October 6, 1818, the reservation of the claim of Britain was not inserted. A confidential memorandum of May 2, 1826, in the Foreign Office in London, prepared by H. U. Addington for Mr. Canning, Foreign Minister, speaks of the failure on these two occasions to assert the reservation in documentary form as fatalities. "Whatever advantage, however, the Americans may take in argument of these omissions, they cannot, in the smallest degree, affect our claim to that part of the Country, which lies on the North side of the Columbia River, nor our right to the unrestricted navigation of the River itself, which is all that Great Britain desires to insure the possession of. . . . That retrocession was in fact merely a matter of form : the fort was delivered up on paper, but retained possession of by the British, in whose hands it has remained ever since."

During the early part of 1818 negotiations were in progress in London looking to the settlement of sundry issues between the two nations. Among these was the course of the boundary between British North America and the United States west of the Lake of the Woods. It has always been the practice to seek for natural boundaries between states. The limits had been drawn by the Treaty of Versailles to follow the watercourses between Lake Superior and the Lake of the Woods, and thence due westward from the North-West Angle of the lake to the Mississippi. It was now known that the sources of that river lay south of this line, and there were no natural features on the open prairie which could be requisitioned for a boundary. It was therefore reasonable to take a parallel of latitude. The agreement ran that the line should run from the North-West Angle north or south, as the case might be, to the 49th parallel, and thence follow it to the Rocky Mountains.

The question of the course of the boundary west of the mountains was also considered. The British did not claim an exclusive right to the whole of the Pacific slope. They asserted that they must have equal rights with the Americans to the harbour within the mouth of the Columbia, and the river in its whole course was suggested as a natural boundary. But no attempt was made to fix the limits ; rather an agreement for a " Joint Occupancy," more correctly for equal rights, was drawn :

It is agreed that any country that may be claimed by either party on the northwest coast of America westward of the Stoney Mountains shall, together with all its harbours, bays and creeks, and the navigation of all rivers within the same, be free and open, for the term of 10 years from the date of the signature of this convention to the vessels, citizens and subjects of the two powers. It being well understood that this agreement is not to be construed to the prejudice of any claim which either of the two high contracting parties may have to any part of the said country ; nor shall it be taken to affect the claims of any other power or state [the reference is to Spain] on any part of the said country, the only object of the high contracting parties being to prevent disputes and differences among themselves.

So far as Britain was concerned this Convention was in harmony with the Nootka Sound Convention in recognizing that the wide area in question could not be closed by a bare discovery and formal annexation, but the actual commerce of the nations involved gave them rights in an unoccupied country. The fact, often unrecognized, that the marine fur trade along the whole coast of what is now British Columbia was predominantly in the hands of the Americans was thus given due weight. The Americans were actually in negotiations for a treaty of amity with the Spaniards, and were anxious not to appear to exclude them from the region. They also gave a place to the trade of the British which was supreme on the mainland. The Convention, which was signed on 20th October, gave recognition for the time being to the rights of all parties and was really very reasonable.

The negotiations of the Americans with the Spaniards issued in a " Treaty of Amity, Indemnification and Limits," ratified by the American Government in February 1819 and by Spain in October 1820. It gave the United States Florida and defined the boundary on the west between the contracting parties. It may be noted that in the area known the boundary followed natural features to the source of the River Arkansas. The boundary from that point was through unknown country ; it was to run north or south as the case required to the 42nd parallel of latitude, and to follow it to the South Sea, the Pacific Ocean. (This is, in part, the present boundary of California.) The Spanish Crown renounced for ever all its rights, claims, and pretensions to the territory north of this line. The Americans hailed the treaty as doubling their claim to the Oregon, and presented this view in subsequent negotiations. The English rejoinder was that inasmuch as the Spanish and American claims were mutually exclusive, both could not be justly put forward, that the Americans must base their claims on one or the other.

From the following Congress (1820-21), every year Mr. John Floyd of Virginia and others kept introducing Bills requiring the American Government to occupy the Oregon by establishing military posts and installing governmental institutions. This had the desired effect of calling the attention of the American public to the country, but such an occupation would have been a breach of the Convention of 1818. In contrast the Act of Parliament of 1821, arranging for the grant of an exclusive right to trade in all the country beyond the Hudson's Bay Company's Territory to some company (in the issue, to the Hudson's Bay Company), was definitely drawn to be confined in the area covered by the Convention to British subjects alone. When the British Government complained that the Bills before Congress threatened a contravention of the Convention, the American reply was that by this Act Parliament had installed British institutions in the Oregon, bringing it under the law courts of Canada. The just rejoinder was made that the Act applied only to British subjects guilty of wrongdoing.

In 1821 the Russians came into the picture. A ukase or imperial edict was issued on 4th September declaring the Pacific coast of America north of the 51st parallel of latitude Russian, and an even larger part of the east coast of Asia opposite to it, and the Pacific Ocean between, a sea closed to all save Russians. This led to protests from the United States and Britain. In the negotiations between the Russians and the United States, President Monroe laid down the principle which he afterwards emphasized in his Message on December 2, 1823, to Congress, " that the American continents, by the free and independent condition which they have assumed and maintain, are henceforth not to be considered as subjects for colonization by an European power." This unilateral declaration of a dogma which ruled the British out from the settlement of the Oregon or any part of the Pacific slope made subsequent negotiations with Britain far from easy. The discussions with Russians issued in a treaty establishing the parallel of 54° 40′ as the limit between Russian and American claims (April 5, 1824).

Meanwhile negotiations between Britain and the United States were renewed in 1824. Richard Rush, Minister Plenipotentiary of the United States, claimed the whole Pacific slope from the 42nd parallel of latitude up to the 51st as established by the treaty with Spain. He grounded this in the first place on a series of American discoveries—Gray's discovery of the Columbia and Lewis and Clark's exploration of it from its sources (really the sources of its tributaries the Lewis [Snake] and the Clark's Fork to the sea). Huskisson and George Canning, Commissioners for Britain, denied that entry of a merchantman into the river could give title to the territory north and south of it, regions where discoveries had been made previously by British subjects. (Vancouver, under instructions from Admiralty, had explored Puget Sound and in the name of the King proclaimed it and a large region north and south of it a British possession ; the sound itself was not in the valley of the Columbia and was south of the 51st parallel claimed.) Rush also based the American claim on settlement, the establishment of Astoria, returned to America as its possession. The British Commissioners claimed that English settlements had been made coeval with it, if not prior to it. (David Thompson's five forts in the valley of the Columbia were all prior to Astoria.) Rush reduced the American claim to the 49th parallel of latitude, that is, making the boundary a simple extension of that across the prairie. Huskisson and Canning put forward a boundary following, in the main, the natural features of the country, the 49th parallel to the north-easternmost branch of the Columbia, that is, to the Kootenay (M'Gillivray's) River, and thence down the middle of the stream to the ocean. They also claimed the right to a free navigation of the river. This offer was in harmony with their declaration that the claims of Britain were based on use, occupancy, and settlement. The British posts had been occupied, some of them without intermittence, for some sixteen years, and for ten years British subjects had been passing up and down the Columbia and not an American in sight. As neither party would accept the other's proposition the negotiations came to nothing.

As the Convention of 1818 was to lapse in 1828, the conclusion of the ten-year period, negotiations were renewed in 1826, Mr. Albert Gallatin being Minister Plenipotentiary for the United States and Messrs. W. Huskisson and H. U. Addington Commissioners for Great Britain. All the arguments from discovery and settlement were repeated on the one side and the other. The United States again offered the boundary at the 49th parallel as her " ultimatum." Huskisson and Addington argued for the Columbia :

In the *interior* of the territory in question, the subjects of Great Britain have had, for many years, numerous settlements and trading posts—several of these posts on the tributary streams of the Columbia, several upon the Columbia itself, some to the northward others to the southward, of that river ; and they navigate the Columbia as the sole channel for the conveyance of their produce to the British stations nearest the sea, and for the shipment of it from thence to Great Britain. It is also by the Columbia and its tributaries that these posts and settlements receive their annual supplies from Great Britain. In the whole of the territory in question, the citizens of the United States have not a single settlement or trading post. They do not use that river, either for the purpose of transmitting or receiving any produce of their own, to or from other parts of the world.

In this state of the relative rights of the two countries, and of the relative exercise of those rights, the United States claim the exclusive possession of both banks of the Columbia, and, consequently, that of the river itself ; offering, it is true, to concede to British subjects a conditional participation in that navigation, but subject in any case, to the exclusive jurisdiction and sovereignty of the United States.

Great Britain, on her part, offers to make the river the boundary ; each country retaining the river bank contiguous to its own territories, and the navigation of it remaining forever free, and upon a footing of perfect equality to both nations.

To carry into effect this proposal, on our part, Great Britain would have to give up posts and settlements south of the Columbia. On the part of the United States, there could be no reciprocal withdrawing from actual occupation, as there is not, and never has been, a single American citizen settled north of the Columbia. [This is only true in the sense that Stuart and Ross who established or held posts at the confluence of the Okanagan and at Kamloops for the (American) Pacific Fur Company were British subjects.]

The United States decline to accede to this proposal, even when Great Britain has added to it the further offer of a most excellent harbour, and an extensive tract of country on the Straits of De Fuca—a sacrifice tendered in the spirit of accommodation, and for the sake of a final adjustment of differences. . . . [The concession of a detached territory on the Pacific coast north of the Columbia running from Bulfinch's Harbour to Hood's Canal on Puget Sound was made in deference to interests of the American maritime fur trade, which would find harbourage on De Fuca Strait an advantage.]

Such being the result of the recent negotiation, it only remains for Great Britain to maintain and uphold the qualified rights which she now possesses over the whole territory in question. These rights are recorded and defined in the convention of Nootka. They embrace the right to navigate the waters of those countries, the right to settle in and over any part of them, and the right freely to trade with the occupiers of the same. [No mention is made of sovereignty.]

These rights have been peaceably exercised ever since the date of that convention ; that is, for a period of near forty years. Under that convention, valuable British interests have grown up in those countries. It is fully admitted that the United States possess the same rights, although they have been exercised by them only in a single instance, and have not, since the year 1813, been exercised at all. But beyond these rights they possess none.

The failure to reach agreement in the matter of the boundary left no other course open than the renewal (in a slightly modified form) of the Convention of 1818, arranging for a continued joint occupancy. The agreement of 1818 to that effect was amended to read that it was to continue indefinitely, but either party could renounce it after giving a year's notice of that intention. On the surface this was of great advantage to the British, meaning the Hudson's Bay Company, for its efficient organization and its happy relations with the natives left no room in the country for the American fur-traders, save on its outer edge. Moreover its entry in a serious way into the maritime trade went far towards making the voyages of the American ships unprofitable and towards taking from the Americans their predominance on the sea. Beneath the surface, the postponement of the final settlement was of great advantage to the Americans, as will be seen in due time. Attention must now be turned to the trade of the Hudson's Bay Company in the country south of the Columbia, claimed by the Americans as all their own, but in which the Conventions of 1818 and 1828 gave the two nations equal trading rights.

A phase of the fur trade west of the mountains, viz. the Snake expeditions, has thus far been passed over. These wandering trapping parties were an integral part of the Hudson's Bay Company's mechanism for harvesting the furs, and had the country traversed by them fallen within the domain of this volume they would have been given a prominent place. Moreover the gap in the careers of Peter Skene Ogden and John Work, between Governor Simpson's visit to the Columbia in 1824–25 and their emergence in the maritime fur trade in 1831 and 1835 respectively, would have been avoided, for these two masterful men were in the front of the stage in the country south of the Columbia, and were, at one time and another, the heroes of expedition after expedition which penetrated far into the interior, to the east, to the south-east, and to the south deep into California.

The Snake expedition was a unique feature of the fur trade west of the Rockies. Devised in the first place to exploit the peltries of the land of the Snakes about the upper waters of the Snake River, it retained its name, even when the country over which it ranged was far from the Snake lands. It may be described as a migratory community of trappers. The nucleus of the travelling village was the officers and paid servants of the Hudson's Bay Company. The travelling store of goods and the general command lay usually with a commissioned officer. Among the servants were paid hunters and trappers, yet any one could apply to be of the party. When accepted, he would be equipped for the hunt, as was the custom at all the forts, on credit—so much for his horses (Ogden says an energetic trapper needed four horses for his task) and for his traps, and so on, to be paid for with the furs secured. All took their families, young and old, with them, and were prepared, apart from the provisions taken for the first stages of the journey, to live on the country. When in a good beaver region they fed on beaver flesh. When the rivers were frozen and the beaver hunt was at an end, they would wander to some region where game was plentiful—*e.g.* towards the upper waters of the Missouri where buffalo abounded in the winter—not only to supply the needs of the present, but to lay up store for the future. It would appear that, in times of need, provisions were shared in by all, in the fashion of an Indian village community. The Snake expedition might include as many as 150 men, women, and children, with a large contingent of horses and dogs, but the cost to the Company was by no means proportionately great. The returns in furs were at times greater than from all the posts in the Columbia Department put together.

But the Company of Adventurers trading into Hudson Bay had a motive in its Snake expedition which looked beyond the profits of the successive seasons. The Treaty of 1818, continued from 1828, gave Englishmen and Americans equal rights of trade in the Pacific West. The British Foreign Office foreshadowed the ultimate division of the land with the Columbia and Kootenay rivers, as they figured it, for the International Boundary. In keeping with this, Governor Simpson was for abandoning Fort George (the old Astoria), the spearhead of the American claim, and built Fort Vancouver in a country which had been explored by Lieutenant Broughton, and which that officer of the King formally and in the name of the Crown had proclaimed British. It was, however, in the interest of the fur trade and of the British claims that the Americans should be kept out of the country as long as might be, and should be prevented from creating economic interests calculated to re-enforce their claims to it. The Snake expeditions were thus to act as a screen behind which the English Company's trade and Britain's *de facto* possession of the land could continue. It might even be that the American claim would remain indefinitely a paper one, and Britain and the Hudson's Bay Company remain in possession. In 1827 the Governor and Committee summed up their policy in the matter of the Snake expedition for Governor Simpson. " It is extremely desirable to hunt as bare as possible all the Country South of the Columbia and West of the Mountains." This would, of course, keep the Americans out, but should they be met they must be treated strictly in keeping with the terms of the treaty. " In the event of our trapping party falling in with any Americans in the Country common to both, the leader ought to have instructions to endeavour to make an amicable arrangement as to the parts of the Country which each will take to avoid interference, and to be careful to avoid giving just cause for accusing our people of any aggression against the Americans or violence except in a clear case of defence." This attitude of the Company might be described in diplomatic language as strictly correct.

The Snake expedition of 1823–24 was in charge of Alexander Ross. From the Flathead House, which was then near the present Eddy, Montana, he passed through Hell Gate Canyon at Missoula. He was deserted by the Iroquois in his band, who traded their furs with the Americans apparently for much-desired rum. After the trapping season was over, he penetrated to the headwaters of the Missouri for provisions. From the Beaverhead region he passed back to the east side of the mountains by way of the Lemhi Pass and River, whose upper streams his party trapped. When on the main branch of the Salmon River his Iroquois came back to him, bringing a party of Americans under Jedidiah Smith who had been trafficking with them. Five trappers not in the pay of the Company, but who had been equipped on credit in view of the prospective harvest of furs, had 500 skins in cache. Apparently Ross could have got the furs by paying what the Americans offered, $3 a pound. By instinct more of a Scotsman than a fur-trader, Ross was guilty of the misjudgment of declining, with the result that the enemy got the furs. He then committed, in the eyes of the Governor, a still greater mistake in bringing the Americans, including Jedidiah Smith, with him to the Flathead House. His expedition was a success so far as furs went, and he received a letter of thanks from Simpson, but the Governor withdrew him from the Snake expedition as an incompetent, and transferred him to the Red River Settlement to the innocuous activities of a teacher of its youth. P. S. Ogden took his place. When in 1825 Ross left the Flathead-Spokane District, the efficient John Work was put in his place and conducted the winter trade among the Flatheads, incidentally supervising the building of Fort Colvile. Beyond rumours spread among the Indians by the Americans to the effect that they were coming to occupy the country and that this was the last winter of the trade with the Hudson's Bay Company, Work had nothing to disturb him. Meanwhile Ogden was meeting with a disaster such as came on Ross. He seems to have got as far as the Portneuf, the Big Lost River, in southern Idaho. His freemen deserted to the Americans, who were offering high prices for beaver. These two disasters led to the Governor and Committee to lay down its policy as given above. In addition they wrote Governor Simpson : " We can afford to pay as good a price as the Americans and, where there is risk of meeting their parties, it is necessary to pay as much or something more to avoid the risk of a result similar to that of Mr. Ogden. By attempting to make such expeditions too profitable the whole may be lost." Here they speak of its being desirable to hunt the country as bare as possible.

On Ogden's second Snake expedition (1825–26), when on the

Upper Snake River beyond American Falls and at the fork of the Portneuf, he was surprised by a party of Americans (April 9, 1826), who were equally surprised to see him, for they had thought that " the threats of last year would have prevented us from returning to this quarter." On this occasion Ogden had complete control of his party. He had gathered the furs on the streams south of the Snake before the Americans arrived, and he had made a successful hunt. In 1826-27 he went far to the south, named Mount Shasta, and visited the waters of the Klamath River, in the present northern California, while an expedition from the Saskatchewan under William M'Gillivray was holding the Flathead front against the Americans.* In 1827-28 Ogden was back on the upper reaches of the Snake River. On September 25, 1827, on the Weiser River, he met an American party under one Johnson. On this occasion they had anticipated him. They were, however, short of supplies ; while they were delayed with him, Ogden's outlying parties gathered up the remaining furs. The site of Ogden City, Utah, east of Great Salt Lake, was still known by the fur-trader's name and from his visit, when the first settlers came in. Contemporaneously, an expedition from the Bow (South Saskatchewan) River seems to have been holding the Flathead front against the Americans.† Ogden's expedition of 1828-29 penetrated far into California—a region already visited by A. R. McLeod. In 1830-31 John Work took up the task left by Ogden when the latter undertook the forward movement northward along the coast. He trapped the upper waters of the Snake as far as and beyond American Falls, Idaho, and was in the plain north of Great Salt Lake, Utah, and across the River Humboldt, which he calls Ogden's River. He met with no Americans. In 1831-32 he took over the Flathead front, followed very much the course of Mr. Ross, crossing over the Rockies to the upper waters of the Missouri for the buffalo hunt. He found Americans were on the east side of the height of land. To all appearance the Englishmen were at least holding their own against the American fur-traders. Work's expeditions in the next two years were to the South. In 1832-33 he penetrated to the Spanish Missions and Russian establishment on San Pablo Bay, part of the waters of San Francisco. In 1834 he trapped up the valley of the Umqua River in south-west Oregon, much nearer home. The Hudson's Bay Company, whether making greater profits than the Americans or not, was successfully holding the wide region then known as the Oregon. Had no other factors emerged, they might conceivably have held it long enough

---

* The Company sent no expedition into American territory east of the Rockies. Half-breed free-traders, like William M'Gillivray, went with the Piegans, who always preferred to trade at the Company's posts.

† The expeditions of 1826-27 and 1827-28 from the Saskatchewan (Edmonton House) had no connection with the Piegan Post (Old Bow Fort) on the Bow River. That post was not established till 1832, and was abandoned in January 1834 in favour of Rocky Mountain House, the post at which the Piegans traded, and for which it had been intended to be the substitute. Piegan Post was devised to draw the trade away from the Americans on the Missouri, but its returns were not satisfactory in view of the costs. There were but few beaver in its immediate neighbourhood.

to make it their own and British territory for good. From this time on, the English Company had no difficulty in keeping the American traders practically out of the country. It has often been said that they succeeded in this by instigating the Indians against them. This is incorrect. It would have been in the teeth of the instructions of the Company. John McLoughlin denied the charge and pointed out that the Company's expeditions likewise suffered at the hands of the Blackfeet; that, if they lost fewer men, it was because their camps were more disciplined.

While the immediate effect of the agreements for a " Joint Occupancy," or more correctly joint rights, was in favour of the English Company, their continuance was much more to the advantage of the Americans in the final issue, for the general situation was progressively in their favour. British territory and American territory were alike contiguous with the Oregon, but the passes through which the English had to penetrate were wild and clad with shaggy forest, while the American passes were open, clad with a thin coat of grass—so much so, that it was discovered in 1827 and subsequently that wagon trails could be made through them with no great difficulty. Not only was the approach to the Oregon incomparably easier for the Americans than for the English, but the American population was much nearer and was approaching rapidly as the hordes of Europe pressed into the land of liberty and of hope. Finally, the incentive influencing the English was the fur trade, and from that point of view the Oregon was already peopled to saturation. Much more powerful motives influenced the Americans, the hunger for land in the people at large; in a certain class, the thirst for a wealth easily got by real estate speculation in a region expected to fill up rapidly ; in the Government, the desire for a land the proceeds of whose sales would enter the public treasury. Manifestly, the longer the Oregon Question was kept open, the better for the Americans. Of this they were aware. During the negotiations of 1826, which issued in continuing the period of equal rights in the Oregon for the two nations, Gallatin replied to Mr. Addington's argument, based on Britain's actual occupancy, by asserting that yet greater occupation of the country by the Americans was certain :

If the present state of occupancy is urged on the part of Great Britain, the probability of the manner in which the territory west of the Rocky Mountains must be settled belongs essentially to the subject. Under whatever nominal sovereignty that country may be placed, and whatever its ultimate destinies may be, it is nearly reduced to a certainty that it will be almost exclusively peopled by the surplus population of the United States. The distance from Great Britain and the expense incident to emigration forbid the expectation of any being practicable from that quarter but on a comparatively small scale.

From the American point of view all that was necessary to get possession of the Oregon was to create in the public the determination to have it, and in a sufficient number of people the will to settle in it. All the organs fashioning public opinion—Messages of Presidents, debates and reports of committees in Congress, editorials and articles in newspapers—were directed, consciously or unconsciously, to this end. Congress was the sounding-board beneath which the claims of the Republic to the fertile lands beyond the Rockies, and the desirability of those lands, were proclaimed to a great people. Bill after Bill, report after report, called on the President to occupy in some form or other the land that flowed with milk and honey. These were never pushed to the point of a breach of the Convention of Joint Occupancy. Their object was achieved when the public came to believe that the Oregon, the whole of the Oregon, was rightly theirs, and when migratory movements were launched.

In propaganda of this kind statements are never restrained within the limits of accuracy. A copy of a report of the Message of President Adams to Congress, transmitted on December 9, 1825, exists in the records of the Foreign Office in London, with the following sentence underlined. "The River of the West, first fully discovered and navigated by a countryman of our own, still bears the name of the ship in which he ascended its waters, and claims the protection of our armed national flag at its mouth,"—this, when Gray in the Columbia ascended but to Gray's Harbour, about fifteen miles up. A memorandum in the British Foreign Office comments on the assertion of the Message that the Oregon called for an armed occupation :

This was the more remarkable, because the question of the settlement of the respective claims of Great Britain and the United States to that territory had, in the summer of that year, formed a very prominent feature in the negotiations carried on in London by the two Governments, and a proposition on that subject which had been submitted to the American by the British Plenipotentiaries, and referred by the former to Washington, was, at the period of the President's message above alluded to, actually before the American Cabinet.

If the head of the State ignored, and taught the people to ignore, the existence of any claim on the part of Britain to any part of the Oregon, it would not be expected that lesser authorities would do otherwise.

From time to time information came in to the Foreign Office of the activity of private individuals looking towards a mass movement for the occupation of the Oregon. In March 1832, it had before it information from New Brunswick, British North America, that the "American Society for encouraging the settlement of the Oregon Territory" was actively canvassing for settlers. Its informant wrote on December 14, 1831 :

Scarcely one of the many crowded steam vessels by which I prosecuted my journey to the American Capital was unprovided with an active Emissary from this Society distributing hand-bills (one of which is enclosed) and painting this new land of promise in the most glowing colours. . . . You will observe that the Emigrants are to march by detachments . . . to St. Louis on the Mississippi ; and thence to the Oregon Territory the Multitude will proceed in a single caravan, under the guidance, and what is less easily understood, at the expense of the Society—who besides undertake to locate the Emigrants on lands free of charge—The mode in which the Society proposes to indemnify itself for these expenses in the event of the Congress making no " appropriation " for the purpose I confess I could not clearly understand.

Interest in the Oregon was kept alive in the American public, and increased by a number of enterprises to which great publicity was given; for example, those of Captain B. L. E. Bonneville in 1832, and of Nathaniel J. Wyeth in 1831–33 and 1834–35. In his second venture Wyeth built Fort Hall as a fur-trading post, and attempted to begin a salmon-curing industry on the lower Columbia. Both the ship from Boston, the *May Dacre*, and Wyeth's party overland arrived too late for the fishing, while Fort Hall failed to hold its own against the Hudson's Bay Company. Wyeth was obliged to sell his post, goods, and equipment, including a whisky still, to his rivals. Some of his men remained to farm. The missionary enterprises naturally enjoyed a wide publicity. A Methodist body sent in Rev. Jason Lee, and the equipment for his mission arrived with Wyeth's goods in the *May Dacre*. A mission to the Indians was opened in the fertile valley of the Willamette. Reinforcements opened other fields. In 1835 the American Board of Commissioners for Foreign Missions sent out Dr. Samuel Parker and Dr. Marcus Whitman, who settled among the Nez Percés twenty miles from Fort Walla Walla. These missionaries had of necessity to establish farms to provide for themselves, and in due time reported the fertility of the land. None of them found missions among nomadic Indians a successful venture. The Methodists on the Willamette turned their ministries towards the settlers around them, at the first mostly retired servants of the Hudson's Bay Company, with their squaw wives. Their interest, however, was increasingly set on farming, not without some thought given to the possibility of real estate speculation in the future. Lieutenant Charles Wilkes, on his mission of investigation for the American Government in 1841, found that they had made out individual selections of lands to the amount of one thousand acres each, and he got the impression that they were more interested in building up the country than in the evangelization of the Indians. Governor Simpson of the Hudson's Bay Company came to the same conclusion on his visit to the Oregon in 1841 :

The American Missionaries are making more rapid progress in the extension of their establishment and in the improvement of their farms than in the ostensible objects of their residence in this country, as I cannot learn that they are successful, or taking much pains to be so, in the moral and religious instruction of the natives, who are perfectly bewildered by the variety of doctrines inculcated in this quarter.

Of a different nature were the missions of Lieutenant William A. Slacum, 1836–37, and Lieutenant Charles Wilkes, 1841–42. They were both sent out by the American Government to inquire into the country. Slacum transmitted to Congress a petition from the settlers on the Willamette, while Rev. Jason Lee forwarded a second in the same sense, praying that the protection of the United States be extended to them, and that their claims to land be honoured. Slacum gave a favourable picture of the country, and noted the value of the harbourage in Puget Sound, urging that it be by no means surrendered to the English. Wilkes's report was equally glowing. Both were published by Congress.

The increased knowledge of the value of the Oregon for cattle raising, grain growing, and for salmon fisheries, coupled with depression among the farmers east of the Rockies and the pioneering instinct characteristic of the American people, led to a series of migrations, all the more as it was known that wagons could be taken through the passes of the mountains. In 1838 the Oregon Provisional Emigration Society was formed in Massachusetts to prepare the way for a Christian settlement of the Oregon, and in December of that year the usual resolutions about the Oregon were considered in the Senate, with the notable addition of a clause to the effect that grants of 640 acres should be made to every White male inhabitant of the Territory, eighteen years or over, who should cultivate and use the same for five consecutive years.

The Hudson's Bay Company was early aware of the impending migrations, and made arrangements to forestall them by a settlement scheme of its own. In 1840 Governor Simpson wrote to Duncan Finlayson, Governor of Assiniboia, to organize a migration from the Red River Settlement, in view of the projected American movement. The party, 116 souls in all, crossed the prairies in 1841 by White Man's Pass, one of the open passes to the south. Fourteen heads of families, 77 souls altogether, settled at Nisqually on farms which they were to cultivate, giving half of the crop to the Puget's Sound Agricultural Company on whose claim they were placed—that Company providing them with sheep and cattle and seed. The remainder, seven families, 38 souls in all, settled near the Cowlitz Farm of the same Company. It was a well-devised policy, but hopeless. The surplus population of the Red River Settlement could not compete with the migrant manhood of the American Republic. It could only strengthen the British claim to the north bank of the Columbia to a slight extent. Compare the American movements with this—in 1842, 120 souls; in 1843, more than 1,000; in 1844, 1,400; in 1845, 3,000.

The relations of the incoming Americans with the Hudson's Bay Company deserve attention. The propaganda in the east led them to expect nothing but hostility, even a treacherous instigation of the Indians to attack them. When they entered the country they found the whole influence of the Company exerted—and exerted successfully—to keep the natives quiet. The Company was "the wall of defence against the Indians." The expectation was that the Company would take advantage of the need of the travellers and place extortionate prices on their provisions and goods. A reaction favourable to it came, when it was discovered that its prices remained as they were, the same to one and all, that the price of flour was but the half of what was demanded at the American posts east of the Rockies. The destitute were equipped on credit. Missionaries were entertained at the English posts ; the migrants were able to secure horses for their further journey ; on one occasion a whole group of migrants was taken in the Company's boats from Walla Walla to the Willamette, their destination. Such treatment brought about a revulsion of feeling in the American incomers. McLoughlin wrote to Simpson :

> One of them said, " I came here strongly prejudiced against the Hudson's Bay Company, and expected I would have to fight them, and that there would be an English Man-of-war here to drive us away, but instead of that all the immigrants are treated most kindly by the Hudson's Bay Company, and we found, when we got within reach of their establishments, boats with provisions to relieve our wants, and to transport us to the place of our destination.

This policy of rendering service to the missionaries and the migrants has led English writers to accuse Dr. McLoughlin, head of the Columbian District, of being false to his country, while American writers regard him as pro-American. Commander Belcher of H.M.S. *Sulphur*, who visited the Pacific coast in 1839, expressed to the Admiralty his belief that the missionary expeditions were really " political feelers " of the United States, and that the Hudson's Bay Company had invited them in. When Lord John Russell, for the Government, referred the matter to Governor Pelly, he was informed that the statement was erroneous; that, to counteract the American influence of the missionaries over their servants, the Company had brought in two Roman Catholic priests (Fathers Blanchet and Demers) from Canada. Governor Pelly enclosed the Company's instructions, of November 15, 1837, to Chief Factor James Douglas at Fort Vancouver. The missionaries' personal wants were to be supplied to them at the prices prevailing for the servants of the Company ; goods taken by them to pay their servants were to be charged at the current rate :

> We are entirely influenced in assenting to this arrangement by its being a means of preventing their obtaining supplies direct by sea, as the presence of strange vessels in the River must necessarily lead to excitement among the Indians and interfere with the trade ; and whilst it is our wish that no encouragement be afforded to those Missionaries to visit our establishments, you will understand it is not our desire that the rites of hospitality should be witheld from them when circumstances may render their visits unavoidable. Were we satisfied that the sole objects of these Missionaries were the civilization of the Natives and the diffusion of moral and Religious Instruction, we should be happy to render them our most cordial support, but we have all along foreseen that the purport of their visit was not confined to those objects ; but that the formation of a Colony of United States Citizens on the Banks of the Columbia was the main fundamental part of their plan, which, if successful, might be attended with material injury, not only to the Fur Trade, but in a National point of view.

The policy of the Company towards the Americans was based on similar considerations. If it refused to supply their wants at reasonable prices, they would send goods in by ships and create a means of supply of their own.

Governor Pelly's view of the situation was justified by events. A large reinforcement for the mission at Willamette arrived in 1840 by the ship *Lauzanne*, and the Americans in that settlement began to consider the formation of a provisional or temporary Government. In the following year the death of a settler, Ewing Young, without will or heir, raised the question of the disposal of his property. A meeting was called and Father Blanchet put in the chair. Dr. Ira L. Babcock of the Methodist Mission was appointed judge, with powers to probate wills ; a clerk of the Court, a high sheriff, and three constables were appointed. The move was premature, and nothing came of it, for the British subjects were not behind it. The arrival of 120 migrants in 1842 gave more hope of success. On May 2, 1843, at a meeting at Champoeg, a Provisional Government was established by a majority of two, the votes cast being 102. The fate of a Government established on such a precarious basis would have been uncertain, but the great migration of the following year, which brought more than a thousand Americans into the country, saved the situation.

As has been seen, ever since 1824 the Hudson's Bay Company acted on the understanding with the Imperial Government that the south bank of the Columbia would go to the Americans. McLoughlin therefore exerted his influence to keep the migration within that limit. His arguments with the migrants were that they would have a double market for their produce if the British (meaning, of course, the Hudson's Bay Company) were on one side of the river and the Americans on the other, and that nothing should be done to embarrass the several governments in the negotiations going on. He even secured the annulment of an Act of the Provisional Legislature placing a portion of the north bank under its authority. The American element, however, secured the passage of an Act placing the north boundary at the 54th parallel—the present northerly boundary of British Columbia at the coast. McLoughlin refused to pay taxes to the Provisional Government for property on the north side of the river. His insistence that the north should be treated as British until the two Governments came to an agreement fixing the boundary, and that the Company's property must be respected, was so far recognized that an attempt of certain men to squat on the farm lands of Fort Vancouver was frowned upon. The adhesion of the officers of the Hudson's Bay Company to the Provisional Government in August 1845 must not be understood as a departure from the position taken. In adhering to the Government the Company's officers secured protection from squatters. They payed taxes only in goods sold to the settlers.

The negotiations which led to the Ashburton Treaty (1842) fixing the boundary between the United States and Canada were intended also to reach conclusions concerning the Oregon boundary, but when it became evident that agreement would be delayed, the Treaty was concluded without reference to that matter. The general satisfaction which it appeared to call forth encouraged the British Government to reopen the Oregon Question at once, but much delay was caused by changes in the office of the Secretary of State in Washington. It should be emphasized that from 1823 there was no issue between the two countries concerning the southern bank of the Columbia. The real question was whether the boundary should be the Columbia or the 49th parallel of latitude. The negotia- tions were to be conducted in Washington for Britain by Sir Richard Pakenham, Envoy Extraordinary and Minister Plenipotentiary of Britain at Washington. Lord Aberdeen's instructions of November 18, 1844, ran, that if agreement proved impossible Pakenham was to propose arbitration. At the elections in December, James K. Polk was elected President on the Oregon cry: " Fifty-four forty or fight." In March 1845 Pakenham mentioned informally his instruction to suggest arbitration to Mr. James Buchanan, the new Secretary of State, but the proposal was not taken up. The British offer now stood, the 49th parallel to the Kootenay and the Columbia to the sea, with Port Discovery (so named by Vancouver), and the peninsula south of De Fuca Strait (forming a detached territory with a good harbour) with a free port for the United States anywhere on the mainland or Vancouver Island. Should this not be accepted Pakenham was to offer arbitration. The American Government rejected this and offered the 49th parallel and a free port in the part of Vancouver Island south of it. When Pakenham refused acceptance of this, Mr. Buchanan withdrew the offer. The negotia- tions had come to an impasse. They were renewed on the part of Great Britain by the offer to refer the whole question of an equitable division of the territory to the arbitration of some friendly sovereign or state. But nations are more prone to prescribe arbitration to others than to accept it themselves. The offer was declined on the unconvincing plea that, in its wording, it assumed that the title of Britain to a portion of the territory was valid. Of course, the Conventions of Joint Occupancy assumed on the part of both nations that Britain had some rights in the country, and the American Government had just offered the 49th parallel for a boundary, thus conceding the point that Britain had title to a portion of the Pacific slope. On January 16, 1846, Pakenham countered by proposing that the question of title should be referred to a mixed Commission with an umpire appointed by common consent or to a board composed of the most distinguished civilians and jurists of the time, subject to the condition that, if it found neither nation entitled to the whole territory, it should draw an equitable boundary. The American Secretary of State rejected the proposal on the ground that it was an intimation, if not a direct invitation, to the arbitrator to divide the country. The real objection appears in Buchanan's statement that there was not a safe or commodious harbour in the territory from its southern extremity until the 49th parallel was reached. The inference is that Buchanan was conscious that the arbitrators would be likely to make the Columbia the boundary, and the United States would not obtain these much-desired harbours ; arbitration was therefore out of the question.

Meanwhile both nations were looking to their arms. British warships were being ordered to vantage stations, and Lieutenants Vavasour and Warre were sent across the prairies to the Columbia to report on the defensibility of the region. But sane minds on both sides intervened in the interests of peace. In a more favourable atmosphere Pakenham finally proposed as the boundary the 49th parallel to the sea, and thence by the De Fuca Strait to the ocean, leaving Vancouver Island to Britain. This was accepted, and the Treaty of Oregon was signed on June 15, 1846.

The reasons for Britain's yielding to America are not far to seek. The correspondence between Pakenham and Lord Aberdeen shows a fear lest some clash in the Oregon should precipitate a situation which would lead to war. The rest can be supplied. In the war Britain would stand to lose Canada, for it is the Achilles heel of the Empire—the one portion of it exposed to a powerful neighbour, and in a position in which the preponderant British Navy could not take part in the defence. The issue before Britain really was, should she risk the loss of Canada to retain the territory between the Columbia and the 49th parallel of latitude. The answer given was, By no means. It was a wise one.

The influence of the controversy over the Oregon on the history of what is now the Dominion of Canada has been great. The first suggestion of the need of uniting the disparate provinces of British North America by railway communications came from military men, who became conscious during the Oregon crisis that their defence was impossible. The sense of the need for union began to grow. Next, the Canadians began to fear that the prairie region might be " rushed " by such a migration as took possession of the Oregon, and this grew into a definite purpose to take over Rupert's Land. In 1856 the belief that the American Government intended to place a military post at Pembina made the Hudson's Bay Company appeal to the Imperial Government, and for a number of years the Red River Settlement had British, later Canadian, troops in its midst, asserting the rights of Great Britain, and incidentally arousing a fresh interest in the West in the homes of Canada. Finally, lest a rush similar to the Oregon migration should take possession of a vacant Vancouver Island, to the confusion of both the British and American Governments, the Imperial Government erected it into a colony under conditions which gave assurance that American migrants would not come in, and when the gold rush came to the north of the boundary the colony of British Columbia was immediately created to guard against all eventualities. The Oregon crisis left its impress on the history of every part of the present Dominion of Canada.

CHAPTER X

THE PACIFIC COLONIES, 1849–67 *

I.—THE COLONY OF VANCOUVER'S ISLAND, 1849–64

THE Oregon crisis and its settlement by the treaty of June 15, 1846, brought to the front a new practice and a new principle determining the sovereignty of a nation in unoccupied territory. A mass movement of settlers into the vacant or comparatively vacant area, ending in the colonists forming a government for themselves and calling on their mother-country to extend her laws to cover them, introduced the modern principle of self-determination overriding all claims to possession of the territory involved based on discovery or even on a generation of settlement simply for the purposes of trade. With the spacious prairies and the Pacific West—the vast area from the Great Lakes to the western ocean—unoccupied and ruled over by no organized government in the modern sense of the word, it was possible that a rush of migrants from the United States, creating an organization for themselves and calling upon the American Government to extend its laws, might sweep away even the International Boundary as fixed by treaty, and might give to the Republic what is now the Prairie Provinces or British Columbia, or both. The dread of some such eventuality manifested itself in the Red River Settlement in the 'fifties, the decade after the Oregon crisis, and was a vital factor in the determination of the Fathers of Confederation in the 'sixties to create a dominion from sea to sea. Its possibility was envisaged and schemed for by a group of malcontents in Manitoba as late as the 'eighties. The technique was explained by no less a personage than a judge in Washington to a delegate of these malcontents ; get some wealthy parties to form an association and float bonds for, say, a million dollars ; use the money to organize the people under a provisional government ; call on Congress to take over the country ; when the United States takes over the region it will assume the bonded indebtedness.

That the Imperial Government regarded the International Boundary recently drawn as but a frail barrier against American migration is evidenced by the speeches of the members of the Government in a debate in the House of Lords on the proposed

grant of Vancouver's Island to the Hudson's Bay Company. Lord
Grey, then at the head of the Colonial Office, said :

> It is obvious, when an eligible territory is left to be waste, unsubdued
> to the use of man, it is impossible to prevent persons from taking irregular
> possession of the land. We have found it impossible in all our dominions
> to restrain such persons. The Government of the United States will be
> equally unable to prevent such an occurrence, and unless the island is regularly
> settled and regularly colonized, it is quite certain that it will be irregularly
> colonized by squatters." He refrained from adding, "and the situation in
> Oregon be repeated."

Accordingly, after the conclusion of the Treaty of Oregon the Imperial Government was seeking for some means of colonizing at least
a part of the British Pacific coast, now acknowledged as such. Earl
Grey in the House of Lords and Lord John Russell in the House of
Commons stated without contradiction, that it was out of the
question in the existing circumstances that the Imperial Government
should find the £50,000 necessary for the foundation of a new colony
with yearly grants thereafter. How then could a colony be begun
and a barrier be erected against American migration ? Various
schemes were proposed—in particular one by James Edward Fitzgerald—but the Government considered that none had the financial
backing to assure success. Moreover, any individual entering in on
Vancouver's Island would be faced by the exclusive licence to trade
in all the North-West Territories then being enjoyed by law by the
Hudson's Bay Company. The logical conclusion was that that
Company, with its great financial resources, its long line of posts,
its ships going out and in, was best fitted to establish the new
colony.

The correspondence afterwards placed before Parliament shows
that the first request made by the Hudson's Bay Company of the
Colonial Office had nothing to do with the colonization of Vancouver's
Island. Sir John H. Pelly, the Governor of the Company, on
September 7, 1846, wrote Earl Grey pointing out that the third and
fourth articles of the Oregon Treaty recognized what we would call
the common law rights of the Company and of the Puget's Sound
Agricultural Society to the lands occupied by them in the Oregon
regions before it had come under the control of any government.
He assumed that the Company's right to the property occupied
around Fort Victoria in Vancouver's Island, now British territory,
would be recognized, and asked whether the Company would be
confirmed in the possession of any additional area which might be
taken up. The question was necessary because the lands were
definitely recognized as Crown lands, and it would be necessary to
secure a proper title from the Crown. Lord Grey directed the Company to secure an opinion from the Law Officers of the Crown as to
whether the Company had title to the property in question. The
opinion given was favourable. Meanwhile, in the course of personal
discussion between Grey and Pelly, the question of colonization
had been raised. This led to a request from the Hudson's Bay

Company for a grant of the whole of the North-West Territory. Grey reduced it to Vancouver's Island.

The theory of the day followed in all cases, save in that of South Australia, was that the creation of a colony out of Crown domain was an act of Royal Prerogative, while the regulation of a free citizenship in a colony must be by Act of Parliament. This did not necessarily exclude discussion by Parliament, for members could ask for an explanation of the policy of the Government and move that correspondence should be laid upon the table. The proposals of the Government were not to be accepted without opposition, all the more as at that very time the appeal from the settlers on the Red River against the monopoly and the alleged maladministration of the Hudson's Bay Company was before the Colonial Minister. The motives of this appeal and the lack of evidence in support will be discussed in due time. The complaints were accepted on their face value by members of both Houses—in the House of Commons by Lord Lincoln, afterwards the Duke of Newcastle, and by William Ewart Gladstone; in the House of Lords by Lord Mounteagle. In debate the old North West Company's arguments against the validity of the Charter; the wrong-doings and tyrannies of the actual Hudson's Bay Company, its monopoly, and its hostility to colonization, were urged against the proposed grant. Emphasis was laid upon the failure of every attempt to colonize by means of companies, and the proposal to sell land on Vancouver's Island for £1 ($4.86) an acre, when it could be bought across the Strait of Juan de Fuca at $1.00, was held up to scorn. In reply the Government pointed out, as above, the pressing necessity for a colony on the Pacific coast, and that its critics offered no alternative proposal whatever. Arguments about the Charter and the tyranny of the Company were aside from the point, for the grant would give the Company no governing powers. The Governor of the colony would hold office under the Crown, would be supported by a council appointed by the Crown, and would be guided by a free assembly of the inhabitants of the colony in control of its own taxation. The Company was not hostile to colonization, for it had developed agricultural settlements on the Oregon, and now that these were imperilled, could be depended upon to promote agriculture in Vancouver's Island to provide supplies for its many posts and for the Russians. The Company, it was true, was to be given the island in perpetuity, but subject to its resumption within five years if no settlements were effected, and again at the end of the present period of licence. To the criticism of the high price at which the land was to be sold, Earl Grey replied that the land on the Oregon sold at $1.00 because in the present state of the region its tenure was insecure, that the Australian colonies which had given their land away had found it almost impossible to finance themselves, but experience of other colonies in that area had been that settlers were willing to pay for land when the proceeds of it were to go to the development of the country, that the Hudson's Bay Company was getting the land on the condition that, allowing 10 per cent. for the expenses and investment, the rest of the procceds was to be devoted to building up the colony. To all appearances these arguments satisfied both Houses of Parliament.

On January 13, 1849, the Grant of Vancouver's Island was made to the Hudson's Bay Company. Sir J. H. Pelly suggested that as there would be no means at the outset of paying the Governor a salary, James Douglas, Chief Factor in charge of Fort Victoria, might be appointed Governor for the time being, but Lord Grey gave the office to Richard Clemens Blanshard, a gentleman who had had experience of administration in the colony of British Honduras and elsewhere. He arrived at Victoria on March 10, 1850, in H.M.S. *Driver*, and next day within Fort Victoria, in the presence of naval officers and of the officers of the Hudson's Bay Company, read his Commission. This may be taken as the natal day of the present province of British Columbia.

As there had been little time to carry out any scheme of colonization, Blanshard was, in fact, a Governor without a colony, and without a salary. He retired within a year in disgust, and James Douglas was given a commission as Governor. In the final issue, and in spite of the slow growth of the colony, the main objective of the Government's policy was achieved, for when gold was discovered on the mainland in 1858, and a large body of American miners rushed into the colony, and began to elect councils to issue rules and regulations for self-government in the several mining regions, there was a governor of a colony across the Straits through whom Her Majesty's Government could in a short space of time install an effective administration over the miners on the mainland. Through the foresight of the Imperial Government and the co-operation of the Hudson's Bay Company the land was kept British, and the ground kept clear for the foundation of a Dominion from sea to sea.

The extent of the effort of the Hudson's Bay Company to colonize Vancouver's Island will probably long remain the subject of controversy. Two facts of prime importance should be remembered. Neither the Imperial Government nor the Hudson's Bay Company desired an inrush of American citizens. The settlers must be, for the most part, British, attached by their habits of mind, by their loyalties, if you will by their prejudices, to the British connection.

Next, with all the other and nearer British colonies enticing emigrants, it was not to be expected that many would face the expensive and trying voyage round Cape Horn to a colony too isolated to soon find a market for its produce. Lord John Russell said that both he and the Colonial Secretary (Earl Grey) were of the opinion that Vancouver's Island was not likely to be colonized for a great many years by any other means than through the instrumentality of the Hudson's Bay Company. Mr. Butler in the same debate said that there was no spot in the world, except the icy country of which Russia had possession, which it would take so much time or cost so much money to reach. The idea of its being an extensive field for emigration was quite inconsistent with its position. What could a great colony do there ? Earl Grey, in the House of Lords, said that the public were deeply indebted to the Hudson's Bay Company for taking on themselves the whole risk and charge of settling the island which, if they had not undertaken it, would have remained a mere waste. Mention was also made of the difficulties which the Californian gold rush would throw in the way of the colony.

The Company did not sketch a fresh scheme on a blank sheet, but followed the lines of its previous policy with adaptations where such were thought necessary. Governor Pelly, in his letter to Lord Grey, of September 7, 1846, had assumed that the site of Fort Victoria and its several farms belonged to the Company by right of occupation before the region should come as such under the Colonial Government. The Oregon Treaty had recognized such a right in connection with the posts now on American territory, and in the future the British Government will make a similar recognition within the areas of Vancouver's Island, British Columbia, and Rupert's Land (1869). The Company made a distinction between the property about Fort Victoria, which they owned and need not pay for, and the land placed in their control by the Grant, which, if they desired it, they would have to buy. As will be seen, the Colonial Office was not apprised of this distinction. On January 1, 1851, Pelly wrote to Douglas : " In the case of the fur trade the extent and boundaries of the land occupied by that concern previous to the date of the boundary treaty must be accurately marked out and agreed with Governor Blanshard and Council. For this portion of land no price will have to be paid. But for any future quantity that may ultimately be taken by that concern the same price of 20s. per acre, as paid by other settlers, will have to be paid over to the Hudson's Bay Company," *i.e.* to be placed to the extent of 90 per cent. to the credit of the colony. Douglas answered on 16th April :

In reference to the fur trade reserve, the boundaries determined on when I made choice of this spot for the Company's establishment in the year 1841 [1842] long previous to the date of the treaty, includes an area of rather over 20 square miles, the extent, however, actually occupied by tillage and enclosure does not exceed 2 square miles while the cattle range over an additional space of about 4 square miles occupied by enclosures and for a cattle range. I beg to be informed by the return of post if it is the committee's wish to confirm to the fur trade without payment the whole area of 20 square miles according to the original limits previous to the treaty which were not marked out, or to confine their grant to the six miles occupied by enclosures and as a stock range.

In reply the instruction came from the secretary of the Company :

I am to state that the utmost extent of land that the Hudson's Bay Company will allow the fur trade branch to occupy without paying for the same will be the two square miles actually occupied by tillage and enclosed, and four square miles, together six square miles, occupied by enclosures and as a cattle range prior to the treaty with the United States.

The much-discussed Hudson's Bay Company's reserve was thus formed. It included the town site of Victoria (the water-front and about 1⅛ miles back from it) ; Beckley Farm, south of James Bay ; Uplands Farm, between Rock and Cadboro Bay (1,144 acres, 2½ miles to the north-east) and the North Dairy (724 acres, 2½ miles to the north). These were the most eligible areas for cultivation—making in all 3,084 acres. Thus, in a somewhat natural way, the heart of the colony, with outlying farm areas, was in the hands of the Company, and without the payment of a single pound to the development of the colony. New-comers must go farther afield, and be proportionately exposed to the depredations of the Indians, whose presence made concentration of the population eminently desirable. When parts of these outer lands were thrown open for sale, officers of the Company made the first purchases. Out of this situation arose the implacable hostility of incomers to the Great Company. It was accentuated by the fact that the Company's store naturally had the great bulk of the business of the Settlement, though it is not easy to see how it could have been otherwise in a community too small to support more than one shop.

The Puget's Sound Agricultural Company, as we have seen, was independent of the Hudson's Bay Company, but composed of its stockholders in England and Officers in the Company's territory, with a few of its clerks. On the mainland, in the Columbian Territory, the farms and ranches were operated by the Puget's Sound Company itself. On Vancouver's Island an adjustment was made in the direction of colonization. The land for four separate farms was bought, and each farm was placed under a " Gentleman bailiff," who came out as a servant of the Company, but was contracted to have a share in the profits of the farm. The bailiff put up £200 as security for his good management. He (but not his family) was given a free passage out. Once on the ground, his houses were built and his labourers paid and, along with himself and his family, fed out of the capital of the Company. As bailiff he might receive a salary of £60 a year. The capital thus absorbed was charged against the farm. Interest of 5 per cent. was the first charge on the capital supplied to create the farm and to operate it. The profits were to be shared. For example, Edward Langford was to get a third of the profits, without an actual share in the farm ; if there were a loss it would be charged to capital and repaid out of future profits. After fifteen years, a valuation of the farm was to be made, and Langford was to get his proportion of the profits, if any, after all debts were paid. To conform with the Passenger Act, which allowed a company to take out servants, but not passengers, in a ship carrying gunpowder, the labourers were required to contract themselves to the Hudson's Bay Company and were brought out in its ships—the labourer at £17 a year and his keep, the carpenter and blacksmith at about £30. They were then transferred to the Puget's Sound Company, which promised, to those who fulfilled their contract of five years faithfully, a bonus of twenty or more acres of land, calculated as worth 20s. an acre, to be taken on their reservation. Had this scheme succeeded the Company would have opened up a succession of farms, and the country would have been occupied by a series of gentleman bailiffs, with their labourers living in the neighbourhood on small plots of from twenty to fifty acres owned by themselves. Its promotors and the Imperial Government regarded this as a real scheme of colonization, devised to attract English capital and to keep Americans out. It was a scheme utterly foreign to the American continent, where speculators secured the land and sold at enhanced prices to the land-hungry immigrants. Had circumstances been more favourable and Vancouver's Island been nearer home, it might have appealed to a small number of Englishmen with whom gentleman farming was the ideal thing.

The Puget's Sound Company actually opened up four farms, on which they placed Mr. E. E. Langford, Mr. Thomas Skinner, Mr. McAuley, and Mr. Kenneth Mackenzie, giving this last a general supervision of their interests. For these farms, as has been seen, the Company paid the usual twenty shillings, but they secured a large reservation—estimated by the Company as comprising from 10,000 to 15,000 acres—surrounding Esquimalt Bay and absorbing much of the eligible land between it and Victoria—the land to be bought by it as required. The whole scheme of the Company broke down through its inherent weakness. When the gentlemen bailiffs had only to ask for capital to build their houses, they began, not with the humble shacks of the prairie pioneers, but with fine houses and barns, far beyond what the profits of the initial stages of the farm would bear. When they had but to call on the Hudson's Bay Company's store for provisions, they lived luxuriously, without counting the cost to themselves and to the Company. For example, Mr. Langford's bill for the year 1853 included flour, £137 ; salt pork, £80, 9s. 3d. ; sugar, 1,606 lb. ; tea, 237 lb. ; brandy, rum, whisky, and wine, 70 gallons ; cash advances, £474, 12s. 1d. Just when his farm should have begun to pay, it was saddled with a grave indebtedness. It is no surprise that the Company served notice on this gentleman bailiff that his agreement would be terminated at the end of five years. Under this notice Langford made desperate efforts to be industrious and economical, and was ultimately allowed to stay on. The value of his farm at this point was fixed at £5,212, 19s., but its indebtedness was such that he would have taken little or nothing away with him. All things considered, he was treated with generosity, for he had associated himself with the little band of critics of the Hudson's Bay Company and of the government of the colony. Later, he pestered the Colonial Minister with his complaints. Skinner's farm seems to have done well, but McAuley was a failure ; and Mackenzie, as general supervisor, muddled his accounts so that all the Company knew was that it was grossly involved in debt.

There was no less trouble with the labourers than with the gentleman bailiffs. Mostly men from Kent and Dorset, they were pronounced a failure, and Andrew Colvile regretted that the Company could not pay wages high enough to entice Scottish workmen to the distant shores of Vancouver's Island. With high wages for labour prevailing in California during the gold rush, £17 a year and board, even though gilded with the promise of land at the end of five years, must have seemed good enough in England, but an imposition in America. Many absconded in spite of their contracts, leaving the Company to provide more free passages for their successors. A change to a system of cash wages at the current rates, leaving the men to purvey for themselves, did not stem the tide of absconding servants. The Company was forced to look to the Indians, inefficient as they were, for hired men.

This woeful tale must not be allowed, however, to hide the fact that the area involved was being brought under cultivation. The Puget's Sound Company's farms were stocked with cattle, horses, sheep, and pigs, from the Nisqually and Cowlitz farms in American territory. Thoroughbred stock was sent out from England to improve the quality. The farms contributed their quota towards supplying the Hudson's Bay Company and to the needs of the Russian customers. By 1856 they were able to supply 1,000 pounds of meat, 400 pounds of vegetables per day, and all the other requirements of a squadron lying in Esquimalt harbour. A number of the labourers who kept their agreements received land, and, by their produce, added to the volume.

The Imperial Government had decided, as we have seen, that it would be in the interests of the Government of the colony not to make free grants of the land, but to have it sold at 20s. an acre. Critics of the Colonial Government ascribed this policy to the greed of the Hudson's Bay Company. They refused to recognize any distinction between the " fur trade " and the Puget's Sound Company. The two reserves held by the two Companies became the ground of loud complaints. One settler who applied for the purchase of the water-front on the commodious harbour at Esquimalt, which lay within the reserve of the Puget's Sound Company, was told that it was not for sale, but was being kept at the desire of the Admiralty for the possible use of the Navy. (In the issue, it was taken for a dockyard, in keeping with the terms of the Grant, free of charge to Her Majesty's Government.) The " free settlers " thus came to the conclusion that the Hudson's Bay Company, in spite of its obligation to colonize the island, was considering nothing but its own interests and following a policy deliberately drafted to keep settlers out. They refused to recognize the Puget's Sound Company's operations as colonization. They acted on the assumption that the gentleman bailiffs and their labourers were in no sense settlers, but simply servants of the Hudson's Bay Company. They affected to believe that these were no part of the colony, that the " free settlers," as they called themselves, alone constituted the colony. Yet there was land open for others in the immediate vicinity of the reserves, and the Puget's Sound Company's agents sent out instructions that settlers desiring small plots of land, say, twenty to fifty acres, should be located, if they so desired it, within their own reserve and by a road, paying no more than the regulation 20s. per acre, and the cost of survey to be estimated on a very moderate basis.

A curious clause of the Hudson's Bay Company's circular fixing the terms on which land could be taken shows that what was contemplated for the wealthier settlers was the multiplication of just such farms as the Puget's Sound Company had established: " 4th. that purchasers of larger quantities of land shall pay the same price, namely, one pound, and shall take out with them five single men, or three married couples, for every hundred acres." In the sequel it was arranged that payment could be made by instalments. This system, of course, eliminated the speculation in land, dear to the heart of American pioneers, and was counted a grievance in itself. It embodied the English conception of a gentleman farmer, with his labourers settled on his estate with him. In fact, only three settlers of this class ever reached the island, two of whom were Captain Walter Colquohoon Grant and Mr. James Cooper. Grant had been an officer of the 2nd Dragoon Guards ; after the loss of £75,000 in England through a bank failure, he came out to recuperate his fortunes. He arrived by way of Panama in June 1849, bringing out by way of Cape Horn eight labourers for his estate. James Douglas told him of the reservation for the " fur trade " of forty square miles, as he took it to be, not yet having received instructions that it should be limited to the area actually occupied, viz. six square miles, and suggested that he should settle at Metchosin, some eleven miles west from Victoria and immediately beyond Esquimalt. Moreover, Grant was not satisfied with Victoria. Its harbour was narrow and perilous to enter, water was difficult to get, and its timber poor. He wished to put up a sawmill, but there was no available stream either at Victoria or Metchosin. Accordingly, he went out to Sooke, where was a more commodious harbour, a stream for his mill, and an open prairie which would spare him the labour of hewing his farm out of the forest. Here he toiled for two summers, putting up a shack, stable, and barns, and bringing more than a hundred acres into cultivation. More might have been done had the Hudson's Bay Company not ceased to advance loans to him. Grant, now caught by the gold craze, leased his farm to one of his men, and went off to California to try his luck. On his return he found that his men had damaged his property and not even kept all his fields in cultivation. In disgust he sold his farm, which he had temporarily assigned to the Hudson's Bay Company to meet his debts, to Andrew Muir, and returned to England and to the Army to serve with distinction in the Crimean War and in the Indian Mutiny. Had he stuck to his plans, he might have secured a competence when the gold rush to British Columbia in 1858 sent the price of farm products soaring ; but in any case that type of farming was not in keeping with the genius of the new land.

When the Grant of Vancouver's Island was made to the Hudson's Bay Company, it was known that coal was to be found on the north end of the island. Indeed the deposits there were the centre of interest to Fitzgerald and others who sought the Government concession, hoping to supply fuel to a line of steamships which was being established to run from Panama to San Francisco and the North. It was expected that coal would be found at Fort Rupert. Accordingly, the Hudson's Bay Company bought a considerable area there and established a fort. They brought out eight miners in 1849, their salaries to be £50 and £60 per annum, with extra allowances for every extra quantity mined. Unfortunately for the venture there was little or no coal to be had at the spot, and wages in San Francisco ran at $4 a day. The miners naturally grew discontented and came to difficulties with the gentleman second in charge at the post. When an American ship, the *New England*, came in with glowing reports of fortunes being made in California, they absconded, of course, without paying their passage money out from England. Soon really good seams of coal were found at Nanaimo. Once more the Company bought and built, and a considerable body of miners, brought out in 1850, was placed there, and slowly the mining industry developed. The Imperial Government, in spite of protests on the part of the opposition in Parliament, had fixed the royalty on coal at two shillings and sixpence a ton. Of this the Company would get 10 per cent. and the rest go to the development of the colony. A similar royalty was taken on timber cut on Crown Lands.

The Grant provided for the establishment and the governing of the colony by means of the land sales and royalties. Settlement grew very slowly. The colony was the most secluded one in the British Empire, reached only over the stormy seas of Cape Horn. It had very little land clear, and could not well compete for settlers with the open spaces of the Oregon, where at the time immigrants were being granted 640 acres free. It shared with that territory the depletion of its population by the Californian gold rush, but it did not share with it the right to enter the markets of the Republic. Heavy duties on timber, and fish, and agricultural produce, left little hope of progress for Vancouver's Island. Thus the area taxable for purposes of government was restricted. It was desirable to keep provisions and stores necessary for passing ships at the lowest, to develop Victoria as a port of call. There was, therefore, no customs duty. In keeping with the wishes of the colonists, there was no tax on the land. It is, therefore, not easy to see how the colony could even maintain itself with the proceeds from the sales of land and the royalties from coal. In spite of the complaints of those who chose to call themselves the only " independent settlers " in the colony against the whole system, in the face of its shortcomings and inherent weaknesses, the colony could not have come into existence, nor have been kept in existence, in any other way than by subsidies from the mother-country, which all parties at the moment in Britain regarded as out of the question.

When Governor Blanshard came out in 1849 to a colony not yet in being his position was one of discomfort, for the Hudson's Bay

Company and its Chief Factor, James Douglas, held the reins in their own hands. He came out without any arrangement about his salary from the Company, the colony being in an inchoate state with no certainty of money reaching the treasury. The arrangement is no credit to the judgment of either Governor Pelly or Mr. Blanshard. When he came home his services remained unrewarded—perhaps because he had made himself the centre of a small group of the opponents of the Company. If Douglas did not take Blanshard, who resided for a number of months in the fort, into his confidence, it is not to his credit, or perhaps the Governor was one of those perverse mortals who sees with distorted vision everything that does not minister to their comfort. Certainly, his dispatches were filled with inaccuracies and misunderstandings. In his mind the Puget's Sound Agricultural Company was just another name for the fur company. (On this point Lord Grey corrected him.) In the Governor's mind the Hudson's Bay Company was asserting its monopoly of the trade, and was no part of the colony ; the servants of the two companies were no cultivators of the land. In one of his last dispatches he wrote—that the only sale of land effected had been to Captain Grant; that John Tod, a servant of the Company, had begun to plough a few acres near Victoria and to build a house but could get no assurance of a title. " With the exception of a Canadian who has squatted near Rocky Point, there is not another cultivator on the island." The Company's land was being sold at extortionate prices. These charges brought forward by Blanshard appeared to be reinforced with additions by dispatches sent in to the Admiralty by Admiral Moresby when at the island. The prices of goods and provisions, for the supply of which the Company's store had a monopoly, were exorbitant ; the servants of the two companies were overcharged and underfed ; the Company's service was detested as a tyranny, and the servants fled from it in disgust. Lord Grey passed copies of these letters to Governor Pelly, and asked for explanations. The reply was—that the Company had no monopoly on the island; that it was a great disappointment that adverse conditions, including the Californian gold rush, had prevented the progress of the colony; that land for settlers was sold to all comers at the regulation price of twenty shillings. (It appears that lots on the town-site were sold at $100 each.) That the situation in San Francisco had made the cost of provisions, including meat, very great; that the servants did not have to buy these, but were by contract provided them free at great cost to the Company ; he could not understand the discontent said to prevail among the servants, for in response to their letters to friends at home many applications were being made for service on the island, and servants who had been placed on the ships as substitutes for sailors who deserted had willingly renewed their contracts and returned by the next ship, while miners who had absconded to California had come back and sought re-employment in the coal mines.

Left to himself by the officers at the fort, Governor Blanshard found consolation in lonely rides amid the beautiful scenery—mountains capped with snow, straits gleaming in the sunshine, quiet woodland glens. Finally, afflicted with ague, he asked for leave of absence when but two years away from England, and shook the dust of the colony off his feet. As he paid his own passages out and home, and received no salary, he returned to Britain an embittered soul, prepared to bear his testimony concerning Vancouver's Island and the Hudson's Bay Company before the Committee of the House of Commons of 1857 inquiring into the administration of the Company.

Three administrative acts may be attributed to him : the punishment of Indians who had murdered three sailors, the appointment of Mr. John Sebastian Helmcken as stipendiary magistrate at Fort Rupert, and the formation of the Council which was to rule the island till his successor should be installed. There had been something like a mutiny of the miners at Fort Rupert, and one, Andrew Muir, complained of having been assaulted and imprisoned for some six weeks. It fell to Mr. Helmcken to try this case, but he speedily resigned his position as magistrate on the ground that, as all the cases that might come before him were between the Hudson's Bay Company and its servants, he, being an officer of the Company, could not play the part of an impartial judge. What was happening was that the Company's officers were disciplining the servants in the old way, by physical punishments and imprisonment, and the servants were appealing to the Governor and looking for protection to the stipendiary magistrate. When Grey passed on the complaint to Governor Pelly, the reply given was that nothing was known about the matter, and that surely it was Governor Blanshard's duty to intervene and enforce justice. Mr. Blanshard's last act, taken after his resignation had been accepted by the Colonial Minister, was to appoint, on August 30, 1851, James Douglas, James Cooper, and John Tod, subject to the approval of the Crown, members of the Council of Vancouver's Island, to rule the colony after him. Tod was of the Committee of Management of the British section of the Hudson's Bay Company's business west of the Rockies. James Cooper had opened a liquor store in Victoria and was prospering.

Chief Factor James Douglas was appointed by the Crown to follow Blanshard as Governor of Vancouver's Island. He was in the fortunate position of knowing all the plans of the Company of whose Committee of Management he was the chief personage, and at the same time of being Governor of the colony. He could thus draw the Company into its proper place under the Governor. For example, beating and imprisoning of their servants came to an end ; the officers of the Company conformed to the dictates of a colony in which the injured could apply for redress to the courts of the land. Then, too, knowing the amount of money due to the colony from the sale of lands, he could keep the Government within the possibilities of the situation. Finally, as Governor and as Chief Factor (and agent of the Puget's Sound Company as well), he enjoyed the prestige of a double office. Particularly in relation to the Indians this was of the utmost importance. They knew the Company and its Chief Factor ; the Governor they did not know. The incoming settlers, in contrast, were prone to suspect that all the acts of a Governor who was also Chief Factor were in the interest of the Company. It is to the credit of the man that he was, on the whole, true to both offices and betrayed neither trust.

It was now the fixed policy of the British Government, as it had been from the beginning of the Hudson's Bay Company, to make agreements with the natives for the settlement of the White Men in their district, and to arrange for the surrender of their title to the land on terms. As the soil of the island had been granted by the Imperial Government to the Great Company, it lay with them and not with the Governor to meet with the natives. As Governor and Chief Factor, James Douglas called the various groups of Indians to council. The first tribe met with was the Songhees, who claimed the region around Victoria from Gordon Head and the Canal de Haro to Point Albert, the promontory west of the mouth of Esquimalt harbour. This people surrendered the whole of their land with the exception of the sites of their villages for the sum of seventeen shillings in goods to each head of family, making a total payment of £103, 14s. The council rejected the proposal made by Douglas that the terms should be an annual payment in perpetuity. A similar arrangement was made with the Clallum tribe whose region ran along the coast from Point Albert to Sooke Inlet, the sum fixed being £30, 0s. 8d. The Sooke Indians surrendered their title for £16, 8s. 8d., the region not containing much cultivatable land. The Cowichans on the eastern coast and to the north of the region thus acquired wished also to meet Douglas for an agreement, but the Chief Factor, well versed in Indian character, knew that unless the Europeans immediately occupied the land, the Indians would forget their agreement and demand a new surrender when settlement came. For £150, 3s. 4d. the land immediately required was secured, viz. the portion of the island roughly south of a line drawn from Gordon Head to Point Sheringham on the western coast.

It was much more difficult to discipline the Indians into honesty and to restrain them from murdering settlers. The task fell to the Governor as the embodiment of law and order and of justice. The first Indians to be chastened had been of the fierce Newitty tribe at the extreme north-east coast of the island (1850). Three sailors, servants of the Company who had absconded from Fort Rupert, and who were in concealment in the woods with a view to sailing away on the *New England,* along with the miners, to California, had been murdered by some men of this tribe. Governor Blanshard had gone north in H.M.S. *Daedalus.* The natives offered to pay an indemity, but this was refused. When the surrender of the murderers was demanded they became defiant. The Governor's force destroyed their deserted villages. Finally the Indians themselves executed the murderers, and surrendered the bodies to the officer in charge of Fort Rupert.

Governor Douglas's methods were more subtle. Three years later two Cowichans murdered Peter Brown, the shepherd on the Berkley Farm beyond James Bay. Douglas led a force against the tribe, but induced them to come to a council. The whole tribe appeared in arms " chanting their war songs, whooping like demons, and drumming on their canoes by turns with all their might." In the face of many acts of defiance the Governor's troops, at his behest, showed the utmost patience in refraining from firing. Finally Douglas secured a hearing and persuaded the chiefs to surrender one of the murderers who was with them. Douglas reported :

> I [then] informed them that the whole country was a possession of the British Crown, and that her Majesty the Queen had given me a special command to treat them with justice and humanity and to protect them against the violence of foreign nations, which might attempt to molest them, so long as they remained at peace with the settlements. I told them to apply to me for redress, if they met with any injury at the hands of the Colonists and not to retaliate, and above all things, I undertook to impress upon the minds of the chiefs, that they must respect Her Majesty's warrant, and surrender any criminal belonging to their respective tribes, on demand of the Court Magistrate, and that resistance to the civil power would expose them to be considered as enemies. I also told them that being satisfied with their conduct in the present conference, peace was restored and they might resume their trade with Fort Victoria. The distribution of a little tobacco, and some speechifying on the part of the Indians, expressions of their regard and friendship for the Whites, closed the proceedings, and the conference broke up.

The second murderer who had fled was secured later ; both men were tried and executed at Fort Victoria.

On another occasion the Indian tribe at Victoria assumed a threatening attitude. Douglas " allayed the rising storm by ordering a keg of treacle and a box of biscuits to be opened. Instantly knives and muskets were tossed aside, and the irate savages fell to these homely dainties with the best of good will to all concerned." There is every reason to be proud of the skill and good nature with which the natives were handled on Vancouver's Island, so that the diminutive colony lay in peace, while the Oregon, managed by the English fur-traders for two generations with no more than a rare clash, was brought by the clumsy and inconsiderate methods of the Americans to savage warfare, and its soil stained with blood.

But if there were to be law and order in the colony there must be forms of government and a judicial system. The Governor could not long remain the sole authority and the single source of justice. The Grant of January 13, 1849, had provided for the machinery of government usual in a British colony—a council to advise the Governor, and a House of Representatives to make laws for the people— while an Act of Parliament assented to on 28th July of the same year had arranged for the administration of justice. Governor Blanshard, as we have seen, called the Council into existence to exercise his authority when he left the island. To the three—James Douglas, John Tod, and James Cooper—provisionally appointed by him in 1851, and duly appointed by the Crown, were added in

Governor Douglas's time Roderick Finlayson and John Work, both of the Hudson's Bay Company, in 1852; David Cameron, Chief-Justice of Vancouver's Island, 1853; Donald Fraser and Alfred John Langley, 1858. Up till 1856, Governor Douglas considered himself the sole executive officer and, for the most part, treated his Council as the legislative body of the colony. Accordingly it was summoned but rarely, and only to consider questions of policy. On August 30, 1851, a law was passed regulating the relations of employer and servant. With this Act the punishment of the servants of the Hudson's Bay Company passed out of the hands of its officers to the regularly constituted authorities. On April 30, 1852, the Council decided not to impose customs duties on the colony, the reason being that all parties desired to make Victoria a port of call for passing ships by keeping supplies at the lowest possible price and by laying the main burden of financing the Government on the sales of the land.

On 29th March the question of stipendiary magistrates was taken up. The Council divided the colony into five districts and appointed such men as appeared, in a colony which as yet had no lawyers, least unsuitable to bear the responsibilities of the bench—Edward E. Langford (Esquimalt District) ; Thomas J. Skinner (Peninsula) ; Kenneth Mackenzie (Peninsula) ; Thomas Blenkhorn (Metchosen). No appointment was made for the District of Sooke. Up to this time the Governor himself had acted as magistrate. He continued to do so for the District of Victoria, which is not mentioned in the above list. On 3rd October he appointed David Cameron, his brother-in-law, Magistrate and Justice of the Peace for Victoria, and thus withdrew himself from the bench, save that the Governor in Council remained the supreme court of appeal. These magistrates knew nothing about law—and in particular about the procedure of courts—and were unconscious of the necessity of keeping records. This was revealed within six months. An American named Webster inveigled a magistrate into trying a plea lodged by him against Andrew Muir of Sooke, and secured a favourable verdict of $2,213 from the jury. On inquiry the Governor found that the record of the case was defective. There was " no statement of the case, nor the cause of complaint." The Council therefore resolved that the Jurisdiction of the Justice's Court should be limited in civil cases to suits not exceeding the sum of £100. Three days later the Council decided to establish a Court of Common Pleas " with power and jurisdiction in all cases wherein damages claimed shall not exceed the sum of £2,000 sterling money," an appeal to lie from this court to the Governor in Council. David Cameron (Governor Douglas's brother-in-law) was appointed judge, subject to the approval of the Crown, at a salary of £100.

Another important step taken by the Council was the prohibition of the gift or sale of spirituous liquors to Indians (August 3, 1854). It should be noted that James Cooper, the chief dealer in liquors, as Councillor signified his assent to this Act.

The appointment of Mr. Cameron, a recent arrival in the colony, became the signal for an attack on James Douglas. James Cooper was the spearhead of the drive, and had associated with him Rev. R. J. Staines, the Company's chaplain, and E. E. Langford, who had been of the group which gathered around Governor Blanshard. Staines was drowned on the way back to England with petitions to the Queen and to the Colonial Minister for redress of the grievances under which the petitioners, seventy in number, groaned. To the Minister it was represented that Cameron was brother-in-law to the Governor, a servant of the Hudson's Bay Company, knew nothing about law, and interfered, as a Justice of the Peace, in a trial by the Stipendiary Magistrates with the purpose of inflicting gross injustice by the conviction of an innocent person, unnamed. The petitions were sent out by the Colonial Minister to Governor Douglas for a statement on his part. In his reply of 11th December the Governor called attention to the vagueness of the general charges, and explained the reasons for establishing a Supreme Court, viz. irregularities in the courts of the Stipendiary Magistrates. He explained the true inwardness of the trial referred to, and the general growth of the colony which made that Court a necessity. He disclaimed all desire to retain Cameron as judge, but commended him for his firmness and integrity, his devotion to justice, and his fearlessness. The action taken by Cameron was at his, the Governor's, instructions. Mr. Cooper himself had agreed to his appointment. Enclosed in the dispatch was a protest against the statements of Cooper's petition signed by fifty-four, all the freeholders, *i.e.* landed proprietors in the colony, but two. The Colonial Minister accepted Douglas's explanation as satisfactory, and Cameron received his appointment from the Crown. So much lies on the surface. But it appears from Cooper's evidence before the Committee of the House of Commons that the unspecified case which stirred a portion at least of the community was a prosecution of the reverend gentleman in pastoral charge of the settlement (Mr. Staines) for stealing pigs. The vagueness of the charge in the petition enabled the Governor to ride off from the case at issue on another case in which he could put forward a thoroughly sound defence and to secure the approval of the Colonial Minister. This instance leaves room for wonder whether other disagreeable things may not lie concealed beneath the smooth dispatches which passed from Vancouver's Island to Downing Street.

Possibly the suspicions of the Colonial Office were roused. In any case the rise of a loud opposition in the colony called for some action. A twelvemonth after Douglas's defence was received, Mr. H. Labouchere, now Colonial Minister, in a dispatch dated February 28, 1856, indicated that " authorities conversant in the principles of colonial laws doubted the Crown could legally convey authority to make laws in a settlement founded by Englishmen. . . . If this be the case, the clause in the Governor's Commission on which he relied would appear to be unwarranted and invalid." He was accordingly instructed to call an Assembly in the terms of his Commission and

Instructions. The number of the representatives was to be fixed, the colony to be divided into districts, separate polling places established, and an election held. An additional reason for this course was that the relations of the Hudson's Bay Company with the Crown must necessarily undergo revision at the lapse of their licence before or in 1859. The Governor's expression of dismay at being called on to carry out the instructions, with but a slender knowledge of legislation, and without legal advice to guide a free Assembly, may well have been sincere. At a meeting of Council on 9th June it was agreed to follow the English law requiring a property qualification for membership in the Council. This was fixed at £300, while twenty acres of land and upwards had already been settled by the Governor's Commission as necessary to give a citizen the right to vote. The settlements were divided into four electoral districts. The results of the election were that John Muir was chosen as member for Sooke ; John S. Helmcken and Thomas Skinner, two members for Esquimalt ; J. D. Pemberton, James Yates, and E. E. Langford, three members for Victoria ; and John F. Kennedy, member for Nanaimo. The House met on 12th August with all the formality which the diminutive Assembly could muster. The Governor summoned up such flowers of rhetoric as he could command to adorn his speech. " Self-supporting and defraying all the expenses of its own Government, [this colony] presents a striking contrast to every other Colony in the British Empire, and like the native pines of its storm-beaten promontories, it has acquired a slow but hardy growth." The speaker instructed the seven members constituting the House in the alphabet of government. " The common error of running into speculative improvements entailing debts upon the colony for a very uncertain advantage, should be carefully avoided." Mr. Helmcken, who was to have a long and honourable career in the public service of the colony, was elected Speaker. A petition had been lodged against the spendthrift Mr. Langford, as not having the property qualifications required by law for a member. The gate-crasher failed to appear in his defence, and his seat was declared void. Mr. J. W. Mackay, in the service of the Hudson's Bay Company, was elected in his room. The members now began to inquire into the realm which they had been chosen by the people to rule. The Governor submitted to them a statement of the receipts from the public domain from which, among other things, it appeared that the Hudson's Bay Company had credited to the colony £6,193 for land bought by it. The scrutiny over, they considered ways and means of carrying on the government, and demanded the control of the funds raised by the Company from the sale of the lands. As there was no money to make the roads, that is to extend the roads which ran out but a few miles in different directions, it was modestly decided to mark their future course. In June 1857 the town of Victoria was enfranchised. Attention was given to education and the law courts. So began the parliamentary history of Vancouver's Island.

As the exclusive licence of the Hudson's Bay Company to trade in the vast territory beyond Rupert's Land—the North-West Territory—would lapse in 1859, and in view of the persistent campaign against its monopoly, a Committee of the House of Commons was constituted to inquire into its administration before a renewal of the licence was due. In the extraordinarily careful and thorough investigation Vancouver's Island played but a small part. The only witnesses intimate with the colony who gave their testimony were a Mr. Charles Fitzwilliam, who had visited it in the winter of 1852; Mr. James Cooper of its Council, who appeared in the character of one of the only two independent gentlemen farmers who had taken a large lot of land and brought in labourers with him to work it; John Miles, who was there in 1852 and 1854 as a servant of the Company; and finally, ex-Governor Blanshard. The opinion of the Committee was that the connection of the Hudson's Bay Company with the colony should be terminated, and the Government decided to undertake the responsibilities from which all parties had shrunk in 1849. The bill of the Company (with vouchers) indicating expenditures in the interest of colonization to the amount of £40,290, 5s. 2½d., was paid by the Imperial Government. The Company renewed its claim for the area about Fort Victoria occupied before the Treaty of Oregon and the creation of the colony, amounting to 3,084 acres. The Colonial Office, which had not apprehended the nature of the claim, that the ground was the Company's by a common law right which existed independently of the Grant, was taken aback. After much correspondence and a reference to the Law Officers of the Crown, a compromise was effected. The sales of land made by the Company in the area claimed were made valid, the Company to retain the money paid therefor; the Company retained its Uplands Farm (1,144 acres), the North Dairy Farm (724 acres), save for a well reserved for public use, and the Fort Property except certain sites at the foot of Fort Street, set apart already for the use of the Government. A compromise was effected in the matter of the claim for the Beckley Farm, the Government retaining the land around the present Parliament buildings on which Governor Douglas had erected the houses necessary for administrative buildings, the Company contenting itself with the houses which constituted the Beckley Farm and the fifty acres of enclosed land on which they stood.

In the decade of its connection with the Hudson's Bay Company the colony had grown lamentably slowly, but it had grown. A series of diminutive settlements had been established; the coal industry had taken its first, if faltering, steps. There were two schools and two churches. Roads, however defective, ran out in various directions for some few miles. Government houses had been built, law courts established, and all the institutions of government of a British colony inaugurated. The lands of the island had maintained the administration. Had the circumstances of the first decade continued through the second, government from Downing Street might not have accomplished much more. The isolated position of the colony was not to be easily overcome. The high tariffs for the exports of the island entering the United States remained insuperable. No profitable market could be discovered for its products. Vancouver's Island was doomed to be isolated and condemned to stagnation. The sudden rumour of gold on the British part of the continent over against the island swept the clouds from its sky. The gold rush made Victoria a calling place of ships and the basis of supply for a world of miners in the deep valleys of the land on its eastern horizon. What the wisest of governments could not do, the mad rush for gold accomplished for distant Vancouver's Island. Men from most of the nations of the world came and poured their wealth into the waiting lap of Victoria. In the first months of the " gold fever " its citizens must have walked as in a dream.

Recall now the motives of the Imperial Government in establishing the colony of Vancouver's Island—its fear of a rush of Americans into a vacant and ungoverned land ; its dread of their constituting another Provisional Government appealing to the Great Republic to take it into its bosom as an American Territory; its determination that a colony, any kind of a colony, must be established against such an eventuality—and the contribution of Her Majesty's Ministers towards Britain's place on the Pacific will be appreciated. The acceptance of the task of establishing such a colony by the Hudson's Bay Company, however mistaken the scheme of colonization agreed upon between it and the Government, did actually issue in a Colonial Government which the incoming migration had to accept, and which left no room for the improvisation of an American form of government, or an attempt to change the course of the boundary as fixed by the Treaty of Oregon. That Vancouver's Island and British Columbia are British to-day is due to the British Government and the Company of Adventurers of England trading into Hudson's Bay working together to establish a colony in a vacant island at the farthest limits of the Empire.

2.—THE COLONY OF BRITISH COLUMBIA, 1858–64

The colony of British Columbia owed its birth to the discovery of gold on the mainland, and to the consequent rush of a mass of men seeking wealth in its sandbars and shaggy mountain valleys. The stampede to the goldfields of California in 1849 had brought a motley population to the shores of that hitherto sparsely peopled territory. This may be considered a first step towards bringing the British territory to the North into relation with the world. Now that the goldfields had either been occupied or were worked out, a large element was sitting by the shores of the Pacific, so to say, asking what next. A servant of the Hudson's Bay Company at Fort Colvile idly washed some sand on a bar of the Columbia River in a pannikin, and found gold dust. Attention was immediately turned to the north. A number of American miners, the advance column of the migration, penetrated from the Columbia to the valley of the Fraser by the old fur-trader's trail, and found gold near the confluence of that river with the Thompson below, and later above, the present town of Lytton. The Indians learned from them the existence of a store of precious metal in their soil. With their crude implements they turned the surface over, picked the dust and granules up with their fingers, and traded their scanty treasure-trove at the Hudson's Bay Company's post. Soon the rumour passed through San Francisco that James Douglas, Chief Factor and Governor, had sent 800 ounces of gold to the mint at that city. The rush was now on. Not the idle alone went north, but men of substance sold their property to seek a fortune in the sandbars of the Fraser. The shipping companies saw returning prosperity in the rush, and advertised every rumour concerning the new El Dorado. What the lure of the land failed to do, the gold fever accomplished for the colony of Vancouver's Island and for the empty valleys of what was then called New Caledonia. It brought sudden prosperity to Victoria and created a colony on the mainland. In August 1858 Governor Douglas estimated that there were 10,000 miners in the valley of the Fraser, " 3000 of that number engaged in profitable mining." They were for the most part Americans, and groups working in a gold area began to elect officers and create for themselves a local government of a sort.

Here was the making of the situation, envisaged by Lord Grey, which the colony of Vancouver's Island was established to prevent. Americans had crowded into eligible territory left waste. It was impossible to prevent them, and if they were to call upon their mother-country to extend her laws and protection to them, there can hardly be any doubt as to what the response of the American public would have been. As Lord Grey had hinted, the American Government itself would be helpless. The International Boundary would be swept away, and the American Republic would be extended to the coveted 54° 40' of Polk's election campaign. But the land was not wholly empty. Across the restless waters of the Strait of Georgia, at the extreme end of the line, there was a British colony and a Governor commissioned by Her Majesty the Queen ready to step in and install forms of government for the motley mass of migrants. From this point of view the policy of the Imperial Government in creating the colony of Vancouver's Island was far-seeing, and even the Hudson's Bay Company, though—working in difficult circumstances and with unsuitable plans—it had accomplished disappointingly little, made a definite contribution towards saving the Pacific coast for Britain, and towards the creation of the spacious Confederation of to-day.

There was, of course, no legal governor of the mainland, for the commission of the Governor of Vancouver's Island confined his powers to that colony. But the Anglo-Saxon, upholder of law though he be, has never been its victim. When law fails him, and the public interest requires it, he feels free to act as the situation demands. At any rate, it was so with Governor Douglas. Although he was not Governor of the Queen Charlotte Islands, when there was a flurry about the discovery of traces of gold there in 1853, he had been created Lieut.-Governor of the Islands and had issued a Proclamation vindicating the rights of the Crown. Moreover, he had imposed regulations upon the mining. Now, in a much greater emergency, with a view to the large incursion of miners expected in the coming summer, he took the bold step of acting as Governor, though he had no legal authority to do so. On December 28, 1857, he issued a Proclamation notifying all comers that they could not disturb the soil in search for gold, "without having been duly authorized in that behalf by Her Majesty's Colonial Government." It mattered little that there was no Colonial Government in existence; the supremely important point to be gained was that all immigrants should be apprised that they were coming to British Territory, and would be subject to regulation. But Douglas went farther, he issued regulations involving the taxation of the miners in the form of a licence. In the issue, though the Imperial Ministers were aware of the illegality of the Governor's course, they were entirely satisfied with it. So far Douglas was a patriotic Governor upholding the rights of the Crown. But he was also a loyal officer of the Hudson's Bay Company, and head of its Western Department. He took the broadest interpretation of the rights conferred upon the Company by its licence, and acted as if they owned the mainland. Believing himself to be within the Law, on 8th May he issued a third Proclamation declaring that all ships laden with goods which entered the Fraser River without a licence from the Company, and "without a sufferance from the proper officer of the Customs at Victoria, shall be liable to forfeiture, and will be seized and condemned according to law." This brought about an indignant public meeting at Victoria, and a firm protest. The Governor now gave licences to ships to proceed up the Fraser, requiring no passengers to be taken up without a mining licence (thus excluding any who might enter to trade in competition with the Hudson's Bay Company) and a payment of two dollars a head to the Company. These regulations duly reported by the Governor to the Colonial office brought consternation. The task of chastening Douglas fell to Sir Edward Bulwer Lytton, Colonial Minister, when the dispatches covering these regulations came in. Apart from these last illegalities, the Government was entirely satisfied with Douglas's proceedings :

The accounts which have reached Her Majesty's Government, as well as your own, afford abundant evidence of the critical nature of the circumstances in which you are placed. They have much satisfaction in reflecting that the maintenance of public order and of the rights of the Crown in that quarter is placed in the hands of an officer so vigilant, and so well acquainted with the country and the people as yourself ; and you may rely on their support in the performance of this arduous duty, under the very peculiar difficulties of your position. . . . In strict law, your Commission extends to Vancouver's Island only ; but you are authorized, under the necessity of the case, to take such measures, not inconsistent with the general rights of British subjects and others within Her Majesty's Dominions, as that necessity may justify. . . . But I must distinctly warn you against using the powers hereby intrusted to you in maintenance of the interests of the Hudson's Bay Company in the territory. The Company is entitled, under its existing license, to the exclusive trade with the Indians, and possesses no other right or privilege whatever. It is, therefore, contrary to law, and equally contrary to the distinct instructions which I have to convey to you, to exclude any class of persons from the territory, or to prevent any importation of goods into it, on the ground of apprehended interference with this monopoly—still more to make any Government regulations subservient to the Revenues or interests of the Company. I am compelled, therefore, to disapprove and to disallow, if still in force, the Proclamation of which your despatch transmitted a copy.

Circumstances had proved too strong for the Governor's loyalty to his Company. The trade had already been made free. Douglas could thus accept his rebuke with grace, mentioning this fact, and pleading in extenuation that he was merely attempting to uphold the law as he understood it.

Meanwhile steps were being taken by Act of Parliament to constitute the colony of " New Caledonia." (The name was changed to British Columbia because the French had a colony bearing the proposed name.) Sir Bulwer Lytton, in explaining the Bill at its second reading, indicated that the colony was to have the usual form of government—by Governor, Council, and Assembly. The Crown could of its royal prerogative establish such a colony. But the law officers had decided that no legislature could be established by the Crown except an elective Assembly and a nominative Council. Considering the ordinary character of gold diggers (and the floating character of the population), the Government was "at a loss to constitute even a council of the most limited number." Recourse was had to Parliament, because they proposed for the limited period of five years " to make laws by Orders in Council, and to establish a Legislature; such Legislature to be, in the first instance, the Governor alone ; but with power to the Crown, by itself or through the Governor, to establish a nominative Council and a representative assembly." In the first phase, then, the Governor, in virtue of the Act of Parliament, was to embody in himself all authority, including the right of taxation.

It was all-important, if the Governor was, even for a limited period, to be an autocrat, that the right man should be chosen. The Government was so far impressed with the vigilance and experience of James Douglas that they were willing to count his recent aberrations as mere peccadilloes, natural in a Chief Factor of the Hudson's Bay Company. He was offered the position on condition that he should give up all his interests and his office in the Hudson's Bay and the Puget's Sound Agricultural companies. This he did, becoming Governor of both colonies on the Pacific coast.

On November 19, 1858, Douglas and his party—which included Matthew Baillie Begbie, sent out to be Judge, and to assist in instituting a system of government—arrived at Fort Langley, a guard of honour with them. Eighteen guns were fired, and the Union

Jack run up on the flagstaff of the post. Douglas handed Begbie his commission as Judge, and administered to him the oaths of office. He now read Her Majesty's commission to himself as Governor, and the Judge administered the oaths of office to him. The Governor next read a Proclamation announcing the end of the Hudson's Bay Company's licence. That Company now became a simple business corporation so far as the " West of the Rockies," and, indeed, the whole North-West Territory, was concerned. A document proclaiming the Act of Parliament which created the colony was then read. Finally, it was necessary for the Governor to protect himself in the matter of his previous acts and proclamations which had no basis in law. For this purpose he read a third Proclamation indemnifying himself for all his previous acts and regulations. The colony of British Columbia was now definitely constituted.

The history of Vancouver's Island and British Columbia up to this point presents some curious contrasts. The one began a Governor without a colony, the other a colony of a sort without a Governor. The one could offer no more than land at the farthest limits of the Empire to allure settlers to it, the other the gleam of gold for which men will travel to the ends of the earth. The one found little or no market for its products, and drew no merchants other than the Hudson's Bay Company to its shores ; the markets of the world were open to gold, and merchants followed hard on the heels of the gold-diggers to supply them with goods in return for their treasure-trove. The one grew at an almost imperceptible pace, the other blossomed out almost in a single summer. In the one case the Imperial Government was reluctant to saddle itself with the cost of the colony, and handed responsibility for it over to the Hudson's Bay Company. In the other, the hand of the Imperial Ministry was forced by a mass movement of miners, and it shouldered the task of financing it, if necessary, out of the treasury of the mother-country. One principle, however, the two colonies enjoyed in common. The Imperial Government endowed them both with their natural resources. It had become something like the common law of the Empire that the natural resources of a colony were held by the Crown for its creation, and to meet the costs of its administration. When there were no more in Vancouver's Island than the few officers and servants of the Company, the natural resources were earmarked for its Government. When there were 10,000 miners in British Columbia, some of British nationality, but the majority Americans and foreigners, the wealth of mineral and land were held by the Crown to create and develop the colony. This stands out clearly in the dispatches of Sir Bulwer Lytton. "It would indeed be strange," he remarks, while emphasizing the necessity of the colony defraying the expense of its own requirements, " that this country [Britain] should be called upon to supply the ever recurring wants of an infant settlement, which has been actually forced into existence through the ample supplies of gold afforded by the country it occupies." Correlated with this policy was the principle that the administration of the colony raise from its natural resources the means wherewith to carry on the government :

> British Columbia . . . stands on a very different footing from many of our early Colonial settlements. They possessed the chief elements of success in lands, which afforded safe though not very immediate sources of prosperity. This territory combines, in a remarkable degree, the advantage of fertile lands, fine timber, adjacent harbours [and] rivers, together with rich mineral products. Those last which have led to the large immigration . . . furnish the Government with the means of raising a Revenue which will at once defray the necessary expenses of an establishment.

The mother-country, however, contributes the protection of her navy, and, in time of emergency, of her troops.

The relations of the immigrants with the native population was a matter of great concern to the Governor and to the Colonial Office. The Indians cherished a strong antipathy to the American miners, while their trust of the Englishmen remained unabated. The recent scenes of bloodshed in the Oregon, in particular a victory of the Indians over American troops at a crossing of the Snake River, accentuated the difficulties. American miners found it expedient to pass for Englishmen. Governor Douglas, however, though now simply Governor, enjoyed all the prestige of a Chief Factor of the Hudson's Bay Company, and a long experience in managing the savages. In June 1858 an ugly situation developed at Fort Yale, the Indians threatening to make a clean sweep of the whole body of miners there. Douglas, not yet Governor, came upon the scene and, after lecturing the savages at a council, successfully called their leader in the fray, a man of great influence and energy of character, to his side and won his support in keeping the savages under control.

Indian chiefs were given something of a magisterial position to bring for punishment any culprit in their respective tribes to the Justice of the Peace, then appointed. At the same time, the Indians were told, if any White Man injured them they were to apply to the White Magistrate, who would give the necessary redress. The miners, nearly all foreigners, were told in turn, with great plainness, that they had no rights in the land, that they were permitted to be there in sufferance, that no abuses would be tolerated, and finally, " that the laws would protect the rights of the Indian, no less than those of the white man." To further shelter the Indians, a Proclamation prohibited the gift or sale of liquor to them.

Still later, when Douglas was on a visitation of the mining areas and found the natives in a state of unrest, accentuated again by the massacre of a band of American migrants to the Oregon, he met the various chiefs in council and assured them that Her Majesty would guard their interests. Land would be laid out for the villages in suitable places, ground would be reserved for them ample enough to raise all the vegetables needed, and they would have the right freely to hunt over the whole unoccupied area of the Crown domain.

Crime and disorder were more than probable—with the Whites entering the lands of the Indians, with greed and jealousy rife among the miners, and with a motley group of parasitic men and women following in the train of the mining community. There was call for good law, and for a competent, impartial, independent Bench. In the midst of the clash between the natives and the miners at " Hill's Bar " below Yale, Douglas, though he had as yet no authority to do so, in view of the emergency, and having none better, appointed an Englishman, Mr. George Perrier, Justice of the Peace. At the same time another Englishman, Richard Hicks, was appointed Revenue Officer and Assistant Commissioner of Crown Lands. Both of these, in the sequel, failed to play the self-restrained, independent rôle demanded of their office, and were accordingly promptly set aside by the Governor. In Vancouver's Island Governor Douglas had been allowed to find his own Judge, and had appointed his brother-in-law, Cameron, though he had had no particular training in law. The situation in British Columbia forbade such casual treatment. The Imperial Government sent out Matthew Baillie Begbie, an English lawyer well versed in law. He was to assist the Governor in drafting laws for both colonies, to draw up the forms of procedure for the courts, and to preside at the criminal assizes. He met the local necessities by admitting American lawyers to serve at the bar, and called Americans to act on juries. He boasted that not he but American juries hanged Americans in British Columbia. Appointed in 1858, he performed continuously his judicial duties for thirty-six years. " He regarded himself as one of her Majesty's ambassadors, sent to this outpost of her dominions to see that her laws were strictly obeyed, and no servant of the Crown more conscientiously or more successfully discharged his duty." While considered arbitrary at times, none questioned his impartiality or his fearlessness. Many anecdotes are told of him bearing this out. When a jury acquitted a man whom the Judge believed, on the evidence, guilty of murder, he discharged it curtly with the remark that hanging was too good for any man who was afraid to convict a murderer. On the unjustified acquittal of a highwayman, he addressed the prisoner : " The jury say you are not guilty, with which I do not agree. It is now my duty to set you free, and I warn you not to pursue your evil ways, but if you ever again should be so inclined, I hope you will select your victim from one of the men who acquitted you." He was knighted in 1874 and died in 1894. He may be said to have trained an unruly public into habitual reverence for the law.

A police force was a necessary part of the machinery for upholding law and order and maintaining justice. It had, of necessity, to be local, and in a country where the rewards of almost every other career were or might be very great, it was very difficult to get truly trustworthy men. As is so easy with a purely local force, it often failed to uphold the majesty of the law. Douglas wanted to form a body of police like the Royal Irish Constabulary, but the cost was beyond the resources of the colony. However, on his plea for some force behind the administration, the Imperial Government sent out a detachment of the Royal Engineers under Colonel Richard Clement Moody. It was distinctly laid down that these soldiers, whose pay came from the Imperial Treasury, but whose upkeep was laid upon the colony, were not to be used as a police force, but as a reserve in case of emergency. They fulfilled the instructions given to their colonel. With their presence in the land the law was to be " tacitly felt rather than obtrusively paraded." Colonel Moody—frank, kind, attentive, and accessible to every one—saw to it that the public had no sense that it was being ruled by a military force. The Royal Engineers were chosen, rather than the usual troops, because their duties made them more accustomed than others to be quartered in the open, for the colony had as yet no barracks. Moreover, they could be employed in road building, and their officers in surveying. Moody was appointed Surveyor-General and, as we would say, head of the Department of Public Lands and Works, with the necessary number of local land commissioners under him. He continued in the service of the colony till 1863.

It will be readily seen that British Columbia was not a diminutive colony such as that over which Governor Douglas held sway from Victoria, that the primitive and inexpensive governing machinery required by a settlement whose farthest limits were scarcely more than twenty-five miles from Government House, would have been totally inadequate for a colony whose settlements were like so many— or rather, but a few—beads strung far apart upon the Fraser River, as upon a thread. Had this stream been like the Columbia, navigable for the most part, the cost of administration would have been much lighter. Then, too, the unruly nature of a suddenly assembled population of miners, a fortuitous concourse of atoms, involved the Government in an elaborate service to maintain harmony—judges, magistrates, and police; revenue officers, regulating the mines; customs officers, controlling both imports and exports; land agents, controlling the sale of and the grant of titles to the lands; steam vessels at the service of the Government; a postal system; and roads to be built over a shaggy country. This imposed a heavy taxation upon the people.

Governor Douglas at the outset was carried away by the expansive spirit of the new era. He called to the Home Government to put at his command ships from the navy, a body of troops from the army, a colonial constabulary, a great system of roads, and a fine array of government buildings—not only in the capital, but through the colony. When it appeared that the Imperial Government would not bear the cost, he was for floating loans. It was well for his reputation as an administrator that he had over him such patient, industrious, and farseeing Colonial Ministers as Lord Lytton and the Duke of Newcastle. These drilled him into measuring his plans by the resources of his colony, and it must be said for the Governor that his training in the Hudson's Bay Company had taught him to be submissive to his instructions. It was laid down by Lytton that the Governor should aim at passing the control over to the House of

Assembly, at the end of his five years of autocratic government, free of debt. Douglas showed himself at his best when he got down to making the resources of the colony meet the necessities of his government.

In 1859 the revenue amounted to £25,059, 6s. 4d. The current unpaid accounts totalled £2,135, 4s. 11d. In 1860 the revenue came to £109,628, 3s. 9d., and there was a balance in the Treasurer's hands of £10,685, 7s. 5d. The colony was paying its way. The revenues were made up of customs dues, receipts from land sales, licences on spirits and trading, miners' licences, assay fees, ferries and tolls, fines, court fees, and a few miscellaneous accounts. The heaviest expenditures were on building roads.

The colony had to have a capital and a port of entry for ships. Perhaps because ex-Chief Factor Douglas's mind was wont to run in old grooves, the very unsuitable site of the first Fort Langley on the south bank of the Fraser was chosen. It was surveyed in lots, 64 by 120 feet, offered for sale at Victoria. The sum of $70,000 was realized. This was in November 1858, but the Colonial Minister had given Colonel Moody the task of choosing the site for the capital, keeping in mind the necessities of defence as well as commerce and government. As the lower Fraser River was the great water-way of the colony, the capital would necessarily be on its banks. Security in case of invasion from the United States dictated the north bank. Moody chose the site of New Westminster on that account, and because the land facing the International Boundary offered an excellent chance to defend the valley of the river. It offered a much better water-front than Fort Langley, and was nearer the mouth of the river. There can be no doubt that the judgment of the Governor erred in his choice, and that Colonel Moody's eye saw true. Parties who had purchased lots at Fort Langley—or Derby, as Douglas called it—in the belief that it would be the capital and the shipping centre of the colony, were allowed to give them up for lots in New Westminster, as the capital was named by the Queen, and given credit for payments made. Roads were built out from the town towards Burrard Inlet and in other directions to encourage farmers to settle on the good lands around the town, for the food supply was not equal to the demands of the mining camps and prices were exorbitant. Similar town sites were surveyed at Hope and Yale in 1858, and lots sold, one lot to each individual, and none to absentees.

It was no easy task, as the Colonial Ministers were well aware, for a Governor in whom resided all the powers of Parliament, including taxation, to rule a colony, made up of a heterogeneous population suddenly appearing in the land, to the satisfaction of the general public—all the more as the machinery of the administration was elaborate and costly compared with the resources of the people. In any case, law imposed by proclamations was bound to be distasteful to men accustomed to the governmental forms of liberty. With true judgment Douglas concentrated his attention upon the gold-miners, who must bear the brunt of the taxation, and who at the beginning were resentful at the licences imposed upon their business. His policy may be summed up in the principle that if the miners were to provide the means of government, the Government must furnish the miners with the facilities necessary for their work. Hence his great effort was put out in roadmaking. The roads reduced the cost of goods for the miners, and these, sensible of their gain, submitted quietly to the licences and taxes imposed upon them —indeed, at times actively co-operated in building the trails into the interior. The cost of provisions on the upper Fraser was, at the beginning, almost prohibitive. Douglas's first decision was to open a pack-trail by the circuitous but comparatively easy route by Harrison River and Lake to Lillooet. When the water was high a wheel steam vessel could penetrate to Douglas at the upper end of Harrison Lake. In the summer of 1858, at a time when the height of the Fraser and other streams had called a halt to mining operations, the miners offered their services without remuneration towards clearing a trail beyond the lake. Each miner placed in the Governor's hand $25.00 as a guarantee of good conduct, was conveyed free of charge to the farther end of the lake, and, when the work proposed was done, had his money returned to him in the form of food at the prices prevailing in Victoria. Work on this basis could not be prolonged, nor could it be entirely satisfactory, but, apart from contributing to relieve the costs of mining on the upper Fraser, it tended to bring the Governor and the miners into unison in developing the country. Later a wagon road was built by the Royal Engineers and by contractors, and steamers were placed on the water-ways of the route. In 1860 this water- and high-way, though still incomplete, was the main entrance to the far interior, and large stocks of food were to hand at Lillooet for transportation by the miners to their several camps—to the great improvement of their ways of living, and the reduction of the costs of their mining. Similarly in 1860, Douglas met with the people at Hope and called their attention to the importance of making a road (the so called Dewdney Trail) without delay into the valley of the Similkameen, a tributary of the Columbia, where gold had been recently discovered by a band of Americans. Besides assisting the miners, the Governor had it in view to divert all traffic from Washington territory to Hope and the Fraser, and to open up a promising agricultural region beyond the Coast Range, by a trail running into the interior. Next day he met the miners, ascertained that they had no grievances, and offered to furnish a select party of them with food if they would open the trail, and a bonus of £4 per man should gold be found. The offer was accepted with alacrity. In these circumstances the mining class accepted the tolls on certain roads and bridges without demur, as necessary means of paying for the roads which were of supreme importance to the prospector and to the active miner. A measure of great value was Governor Douglas's proclamation of Victoria as a port of entry for goods into British Columbia. As the American steamers called at that point and went on to Puget Sound, miners

—many of whom, it should have been said, left their mines in the winter and returned to them in the summer—could pass the customs in Victoria and proceed directly to the interior.

The interesting result of Douglas's care of the mining industry was that the very class from which unruliness and political agitation against government by an autocrat might be expected was the most submissive in the land. The miners early realized the value of law and order in the British sense, maintained by an authoritative Government, and administered by independent magistrates, who stood between them and the Indians and enforced justice between miner and miner. Murders and robberies there were, but in the main the culprits were captured, and the penalties of the law were enforced. Respect for the Bench and the Government were maintained. Thus, though Douglas ruled with despotic power and by Proclamations, he and, with him, British ideas of government were accepted, it might almost be said welcomed, by the great body of the mining class.

The merchants and the real-estate speculators form a sharp contrast. The Proclamation of Victoria, in another colony altogether, as a port of entry for British Columbia sidetracked New Westminster. In the main, goods for the mining camps passed up the Fraser without being handled by, and without giving profits to, the merchants of the capital of the colony. Men who bought land in the town and built stores on the understanding that New Westminster was to be the sole port of entry for the colony felt defrauded. They saw Victoria flourishing with the business which the Governor's Proclamation had filched away from them. Douglas had eased the financial burdens of maintaining a top-heavy civil service by residing himself in Victoria and by keeping the Colonial Secretary and Judge Begbie, a chief adviser, at his side, but they spent their income in a foreign land, as the merchants of New Westminster saw it. In their minds Colonel Moody, his Engineers, and his officials in the land office, Chartres Brew, at the head of the Police and the Assay Office, all quartered in the capital, could not atone for the guilt of the Governor in promoting the interests of the rival city.

A similar sense of grievance existed at Hope and Yale. The Harrison River route diverted the track from the Fraser before it reached either of these settlements. Yale in particular lost by not being made the point of departure for the Upper Country. The resident real-estate speculators shared with the merchants in their sense of profits snatched out of their hand. Any cry likely to win the approval of a wider public, and especially the Government in England, was raised. Public meetings protested against the tariff imposed on goods entering British Columbia, but a complaint against a tariff of 10 per cent., which merchants would smoothly pass on to the consumer, cannot be taken seriously. Protests were lodged against the head-tax of $1.00 on the river boats, and the tolls on the roads—again costs which the middleman usually passes on to the consumer. All the unevennesses in the administration of the laws touching land (and they were probably not a few) were advertised on the housetops. One special grievance was the slowness of the Government in inaugurating a land system. Douglas had been unwise enough at the beginning to discountenance settlement till the land was surveyed. His early plan for a large body of surveyors was set aside by the Colonial Minister. In the interest of economy the Royal Engineers must be employed, but for long they were busy surveying and grading the streets of the capital, and moreover, a considerable detachment was sent off to San Juan when the American force landed on the island, and the rest were busy making the road which passed Hope and Yale by on the other side. At the consequent delay a loud cry was raised that the Governor was neglecting, nay, discouraging the settlement on the land, which alone could make the colony self-supporting in its food supply. There is room for much doubt as to whether there was the great demand for land as asserted. The great bulk of the miners were busy in the summer, and could not, either from their taste or their opportunities, be agriculturists in the winter. The publication of a newspaper, the *British Colonist*, begun at Victoria on December 11, 1858, gave a loudness to the complaint which the Press alone can give. The editor, Amor de Cosmos, had, beyond the usual editor, the gift of giving to airy nothingness a habitation and a name. An arrival in June of that year in the midst of the first great rush, he undertook in December to guide the footsteps of the Governor in the paths of wisdom. In his first issue he denounced " the Executive " for its failure to inaugurate a wise land policy :

A favorable season was frittered away without proper encouragement being shown to a hardy and enterprizing population to settle down in the country. The small amount of progress which was made, is not one per cent. of what could have been accomplished, had a more liberal disposition been shown towards colonization. Towns, villages, farms, mills, roads—everything would have been done which a strong will and a skilful hand saw necessary to secure the reward of persevering industry. Fraser's river would, to-day, stand high abroad ; greater prosperity would have been experienced at home. Of the many hundreds who have left this port, not a tithe would have gone. . . . Provisions would have been plenty ; the upper Fraser prospected ; permanent settlements and the material wealth of the colony largely increased.

How all this could have been accomplished between June and December 11th does not appear. It seems safe to infer that we have here no more than the ebullition of the merchant class and of a discontent with government by proclamations.

From its very nature mining for gold in the bars of rivers could not last. All too soon the precious treasure would be exhausted. But the dust deposited in the bars must come by a process of attrition from some prime source. Hence the prospecting followed the stream upward. When the upper waters of the Fraser appeared not to give promise, miners began to follow its tributaries upstream. Attention was centred on the River Quesnel. Prospectors traced it up until the creeks were reached which formed its north branch, deep in the Cariboo Mountains. The rich returns of Keithley Creek (1860) flowing in from the North suggested that the prime source of the gold was to be found in these mountains. Prospectors passed over the height of land to the sources of the other tributaries of the Fraser. A rich strike was made at Antler Creek, one of the sources of the Bear River flowing northward. Next year the rich deposits of Williams Creek, flowing into the Willow River, and of Lighting Creek, flowing into the Cottonwood River, were revealed. The output of gold this year was estimated to be $2,660,118.00. The yield of one claim on Williams Creek, held by three men, ran at 120 ounces of gold per day. They had a flour sack of gold fourteen inches high. This claim, along with another, was said to be producing thirty to forty pounds of gold per week.

The mines of the Cariboo region restored the situation in the colony just when the early tide of gold, and consequently of miners, was receding. The news of the fabulous wealth being gathered brought a fresh rush to the colony, mostly by way of Victoria. From all parts of the world they came. The most spectacular journey was that of the " Overlanders of 1862." About 129 seekers after gold, from Canada, made their way to the Red River Settlement *en route* to the Cariboo mines. (They added to their numbers in the Settlement and at Edmonton until there were 150 in all.) At the Red River Settlement they completed their equipment, and they left for the West with Red River carts. They wisely organized themselves as a community, observing strictly regulations calculated to prevent clashes and to add to the comfort of their long journey. It was found possible to live on the country as they passed through the prairies, and even to lay up supplies of pemmican, more especially as they were travelling in detachments under sagacious leaders. They reached Edmonton in July. Here they abandoned their carts, and started for Yellowhead Pass with 140 pack-horses bearing from 150 to 250 pounds of a burden each. At the pass all provisions in the form of pemmican, laid up as they crossed the prairies to meet the region of scarcity beyond, were exhausted. They had to live on venison shot by the way. On reaching Tête Jaune Cache on the Fraser River the party divided, some passing overland with the horses to the North Thompson, others floating down the turbulent Fraser on rafts. These last reached Quesnel on 11th September. A detachment attempting the Fraser in canoes met with disaster. The overland party also lost lives floating down the North Thompson. Some of the Overlanders remained in the Cariboo region as farmers, and were among the most notable pioneers of those parts.

The presence of a mass of miners in the mountain fastnesses of the Cariboo range in 1861 put a strain on the whole system of supply as hitherto developed. Provisions were so scarce and so costly as to place a heavy burden on all but the most successful miners. Indeed, most of the miners left when winter came on and returned in the spring. Just when all the roads necessary seemed to have been built, new demands came upon the Governor. In view of the rich returns, he was ready to meet the call for a new road into the interior. He might have been content to build from the terminus of the Harrison-Lillooet route on to the Cariboo Mountains, but it was a shortcoming of that route that, as part of it was in water-ways, it was not very serviceable in the winter. Moreover, on account of sandbars, steam navigation to Douglas was possible only with the high water of midsummer. Governor Douglas aimed at a road available all the year round. Its starting-point was Yale. The scheme, described as " a bold and daring one for a colony of such limited means," "meant the overthrow of nature's barriers; it meant the quarrying of a road-way eighteen feet wide through those immense shoulders of rock that buttress the Cascade for miles along the Fraser canyons." The first six miles, and the most difficult, were built by the Royal Engineers—" an enduring monument of engineering skill and patient toil." The Cariboo road, as it was called, followed, more or less, the left bank of the Fraser to Boston Bar, thence to Lytton and Spence Bridge, where the Thompson River was crossed, and so to Alexandria and Quesnel. The Harrison-Lillooet route was given connections with the Cariboo road, by a suspension bridge across the Fraser at Spuzzum. By 1864 a wagon road was constructed from Quesnel to Cottonwood. The road reached Williams Creek in the Cariboo region in 1865.

The value of this road to the miners may be estimated by the savings in freight which it brought about. The cost of packing from Yale to Williams Creek, which had been ninety cents a pound, dropped to fifty cents, and in May 1864 stood at fifteen to eighteen cents. The price of provisions dropped proportionately. From the point of view of the Government this was a great achievement, but it had not been secured without sacrifices. The heavy taxation was continued and, in spite of the spirit of his instructions, Douglas had to resort to temporary loans raised in the colony. Still, it was not the miners who protested to any great extent, but the merchants in Yale, Hope, and especially New Westminster. As a memorial prepared by them on May 23, 1860, praying for representative government, remained without reply, a convention was held at New Westminster reiterating the grievances. The memorial was forwarded by Douglas to Newcastle, with the following summary of the complaints :

1. That the Governor, Colonial Secretary and Attorney-General do not reside permanently in British Columbia.

2. That the taxes on goods are excessive as compared with the population, and in part levied on boatmen, who derive no benefit from them, and that there is no land tax.

3. That the progress of Victoria is stimulated at the expense of British Columbia, and that no encouragement is given to shipbuilding or to the foreign trade of the colony.

4. That money has been injudiciously squandered on public works and contracts without any public notice, which subsequently have been sublet to the contractors at a much lower rate.

5. That faulty administration has been made of public lands, and that

lands have been declared public reserves, which have been afterwards claimed by parties connected with the Colonial Government.

6. The want of a registry office, for the record of transfers and mortgages.

As to the first, the Governor contended that if the members of the staff residing with him at Victoria and doing duty for both colonies were transferred to New Westminster their offices would be so many sinecures. As to the heavy taxation, the 10 per cent. tariff was light compared with the high tariffs across the border, averaging 25 per cent. Two-thirds of the taxation had been expended on the roads, bringing about " a reduction of the cost of transportation by half and nearly as great a decline in the price of the necessaries of life." The complaint that the boatmen on the Fraser were subjected to the tolls on the roads was answered by the statement that they were really avoiding the tolls, and benefiting themselves at the expense of the revenue. (To meet this difficulty the Governor ordered the tolls to be paid by all on leaving Yale.) To the claim that the taxation ran at £7, 10s. per head, on a population of 7,000, Douglas retorted that there were 10,000 in the colony, and counting the Indians 30,000, which last figure reduced the average to £2 per head, a somewhat specious argument, as the savages paid no taxation, except when they mined or carried on trade over the highway. Finally, Douglas explained the necessary difference in the fiscal systems of Vancouver's Island, depending for its wealth on a traffic encouraged by free trade and financed by the sale of its lands, and British Columbia, in which the land was being but slowly taken up :

The public revenue of Vancouver Island is almost wholly derived from taxes levied directly on persons and professions, on trades and real estate ; on the other hand, it is by means of duties and imports, and on goods carried inland that the public revenue of British Columbia is chiefly raised. No other plan has been suggested by which a public revenue could be raised, that is so perfectly adapted to the circumstances of both colonies, or that could be applied interchangeably with advantage to the sister colony.

With regard to the demand for representative government, Douglas wrote to the Colonial Minister: " The British element is small, and there is absolutely neither a manufacturing nor farmer class ; there are no landed proprietors, except holders of building lots in towns ; no producers, except miners ; and the general population is essentially migratory—the only fixed population apart from New Westminster being traders settled in the several inland towns, from which the miners receive their supplies. It would, I conceive, be unwise to commit the work of legislature to persons so situated, having nothing at stake, and no real vested interest in the colony." Douglas placed the total male adult population in New Westminster, Hope, and Douglas, the centres supporting the petition, at 305 in all. Yale and other towns, he claimed, had shown no interest in the petition.

In spite of this agitation Douglas maintained the respect of his people and could meet with them in friendly co-operation, as has been seen in the case of the people of Hope in connection with the beginning of the Dewdney Trail; and the merchants were ready to co-operate with his Government.   The townsmen of Hope, for example, in a petition of 19th July requesting that the trail be made a wagon road, put in a plea that this should be done at the expense of the colony as a whole, but should that prove impossible, they were ready to submit to a tax of half a cent per pound on goods going out over the road.   Again, on 3rd October, the Governor met with the citizens of New Westminster in response to a petition for a subsidy of £5,000 a year for a steamship service from the south to the town as the port of entry for British Columbia.   The Governor explained that for two and a half years he had desired such a service, and might have secured it from the Imperial Government of the day, but that the new Ministry was opposed to the measure.   He promised to renew his efforts.   The service was inaugurated early in 1862.

None the less the agitation for a representative assembly controlling taxation went on.   Douglas and his successor, Seymour, were probably correct in arguing that the main object of it was less to control taxation than to escape from it, and in particular to finance the colony by loans throwing the burden on the future.   It should, however, be remembered that politics on this continent have always been theoretical, and that economic self-regard, and even the greed of a ruling class or of a group desiring to rule, has been presented for the public taste sugared with a coat of fine sentiment.   A meeting at New Westminster, on 15th July, renewed the appeal to the Colonial Minister for a representative assembly in flamboyant terms. " Their rights as British subjects should no longer be ignored." The present system of government by proclamations was " a reproach to their intelligence and an insult to their manhood."   It was not to be expected that British subjects would submit to it " without a feeling of degradation and shame."   The rate of taxation was now put at £10, 10s. per head, " the heaviest in the world."   Touching on " the insulting despotism of a Governor whose continued absence from the colony amounted to a betrayal of the trust confided to him," they protested against any scheme which would incorporate Vancouver's Island in British Columbia, as calculated to be " subversive of their dearest interests, as well as entail heart-burnings and create conflicting local interests and disputes, which would find a remedy in final separation."   In other words, in a united colony Victoria would maintain its advantage as a port of entry.   A similar memorial was drawn up, again at New Westminster, on October 14, 1861.

Meanwhile Governor Douglas was having his difficulties with the Assembly of Vancouver's Island.   A system of government which kept the Executive out of the popular Assembly, the body theoretically in control of policy and of taxation, was inherently defective. The members of the Assembly had no intimate knowledge of the machinery of government, yet, apprised of the greatness of their powers by the flamboyant editorials of Amor de Cosmos, they acted up to their full rights. Laws drawn up in such a situation were often defective in their drafting and ill adapted to their purpose. Moreover, the Assembly showed itself reluctant to shoulder the burden of taxation. The defects of the system might have been avoided had the Assembly followed the parliamentary procedure of adopting a resolution before introducing a Bill, and of calling on the Governor to prepare the Bill for their consideration. Failing this, the real shaping of the legislation to meet its end, and the technical work of drafting it, were done by the Governor in Council. At times this meant that the Assembly's Bill was thrown to the discard. An interesting illustration is the Franchise Bill. As soon as the Assembly met, a Franchise Bill was passed. In spite of the thunderings of Amor de Cosmos, Douglas laid it on the table of Council until the need for a new election should arise. The Bill was within the rights of the Assembly, but it was premature. Meanwhile a new situation was created by the gold rush, and a fresh Franchise Bill was sent up by the House of Assembly. Governor Douglas in Council, with the assistance of the Attorney-General, made three Bills out of it, one regulating the registration of votes, one the qualifications for membership in the House, and a third governing the elections. These were sent back to the House, and all the amendments made by that body accepted by Council save one—on the property qualifications necessary in a member. A conference between the two Houses reached a compromise. Hereupon Douglas prorogued Assembly and issued a Proclamation requiring a general election (January 1860).

A feature of the election was the candidature of Mr. E. E. Langford for Victoria. His opponents published a squib supposed to be the election address of a candidate, E. E. Longford [sic], mentioning in great detail the various ways in which he had successfully lived a gentleman's life at the expense of the Puget's Sound Agricultural Company, and urging these as grounds for his being elected to rule the people, and be given a sphere in which he could continue to show his ability. This squib was probably prepared by Kenneth McKenzie, the agent of the Puget's Sound Agricultural Company, to whom as supervisor all the details of Langford's doings were known. At any rate, a copy in his handwriting exists in the McKenzie Papers. Mr. Good, the Governor's secretary for British Columbia, acting as a private citizen, took it to the Press, and thereby, in a measure, involved Douglas himself. Langford was not returned. Matters remained so until the eve of the election of 1863, when, for reasons which his opponents regarded as obvious, Langford entered an action for libel against the editor of the *Victoria Gazette*, who had printed the squib. In the course of the trial the plaintiff refused to answer a question which Judge Cameron ruled was pertinent to the issue, and was committed to jail for contempt of court. After a short incarceration he abandoned the colony and returned to London, where he carried the feud to the presence of the Duke of Newcastle himself, ascribing to Judge Begbie the authorship of the squib. Newcastle asked for an explanation from all parties. Good admitted his implication. Begbie did not deny authorship, but claimed that Langford was aiming at finding out the author by forcing details, one by one, from the few who might be guilty till the actual author should be revealed. He claimed that there was nothing libellous in the squib, but that it was true to the facts. Moreover, Langford had not summoned him as a witness in the case, when he would have been forced on oath to state the truth. Governor Douglas sent in the court report of the trial to show that Judge Cameron had acted according to the legal necessities involved. The Duke of Newcastle was not wholly satisfied. He administered severe rebukes to all parties. To Douglas he wrote :

> I wish you to understand and to make it understood by the Government officers of Vancouver Island and British Columbia, that an officer connected with the administration of justice is, in my opinion bound to abstain scrupulously from all interference in party politics, and that other permanent officers of Government, though their duties are of necessity in some respects political, cannot without injury to the public interest be permitted to adopt that personal and aggressive mode of political warfare which is perhaps allowable to those who are not identified with the administration of affairs.

Langford had so far won the ear of the public that the whole correspondence pertinent to his case was laid before Parliament in 1863.

With this ridiculous squabble and the many petitions from the merchants of British Columbia before the Colonial Minister, the period of government for the younger colony by the Governor as a legislature approached its end, and it lay with the Duke of Newcastle to fix the forms of Government for the future. In a dispatch dated June 15, 1865, he informed Governor Douglas, that while he felt that the strength of the colonies must lie on their consolidation, in view of the prevailing feeling to the contrary he had decided to place them under different Governors. For Vancouver's Island he fixed the salaries to be paid to its Governor and its officials in a " Civil List " ; he laid down the principle that the initiation of all money votes should be with the Government, and in return for this Civil List he was ready to transfer the control of the natural resources of the island to the colony. The title to these would still lie, according to the legal principle, in the hands of the King. The bill of the Hudson's Bay Company for expenses in connection with the colony was paid out of the Imperial Treasury, and a compromise arrived at as to how much land held by them before the colony was formed should be regarded as theirs ; titles were issued accordingly.

A similar Civil List was prescribed for British Columbia, and in return the natural resources placed under the control of its Government. Newcastle, however, felt that the time had not yet arrived to give full representative institutions to the colony.

> It is plain that the fixed population . . . is not yet large enough to form a sufficient and sound basis of representation, while the migratory element far exceeds the fixed, and the Indian far outnumbers both together. . . . Of landed proprietors there are next to none, of tradesmen not very many, and these are occupied in their own pursuits at a distance from the centre of Government and from each other.

The colony was, therefore, to have no more than a Council, though one-third of that body was to be of chosen representatives of the people. However, only one-third was to be composed of the officials at the centre of government, the other third being of magistrates from different parts of the country, who would be supposed to be intimately conversant with the needs of the people. Authorized by an Order in Council, Douglas divided the colony into five districts —New Westminster; Hope, Yale, and Lytton; Douglas and Lillooet; Cariboo East ; and Cariboo West. The elections were of the most informal, some constituencies requiring a property qualification, others electing their member at a public meeting. Douglas met with the Legislative Council on January 21, 1864.

James Douglas retired from the Governorship at the close of the first phase of the history of British Columbia—the period of the exploration of the gold resources, with its necessary concomitant, the flux and flow of the mining population. To meet the needs of the expansion into the interior he had built a monumental system of roads and had been forced to raise loans to complete it. Partly with the aid of the Royal Engineers, he had completed a transportation scheme which was hoped would be adequate for years to come. The problem, as he saw it, now was—with the mining activities confined to a diminished number of claims, and the revenues from the mining and every other line of activity declining—to retrench as far as might be. Accordingly, he asked for the recall of the Royal Engineers. To begin with, they were a great cost to the country. Their value as a military force to uphold the Government in case of turbulence had disappeared as the population became stable and law-abiding. Their inestimable service in the survey of, and their work in the building of, roads was thought to be completed. In spite of personal difficulties, Colonel Moody and Douglas had carried on together well, but early cordiality had given place to relations which may be described as no more than correct. The correspondence between the two men shows that Douglas took Moody's change of the site for the capital of the colony like a gentleman. First signs of difficulties between them came when he repudiated an elaborate and costly scheme for the survey of a colony in which comparatively few demanded land, and it is evident that thereafter the Governor held the purse strings tightly in his hand, and required matters even of small detail to be referred to him. Over the smallest items Douglas played the part of a severe censor. Why should straw for the bedding of the Colonel's horse be bought in Victoria and transported to New Westminster at great cost, when wild hay could be cut in the neighbourhood for next to nothing ? Against this control Moody protested with the dignity of a gentleman. Though his position was uncomfortable, he did his duty. There is no room for the view that Douglas had the Engineers recalled from a personal antipathy to their Colonel. Rather, the chief reasons for the presence of the Royal Engineers had ceased to exist, and their cost was a heavy burden on the colony.

Theoretical views of the value of representative constitutions and responsible government must not be allowed to interfere with the judgment to be passed on the governorship of James Douglas. After all, the worth of a ruler depends upon the conditions in which he finds himself and upon the actual results of his administration. With an unstable population in a colony in the making, it is of the utmost importance that the Governor be a man of experience, of unimpeachable honesty, of great self-reliance, and not to be swayed from his duty by the clamour of a faction, yet at the same time amenable to the influence of the people governed. James Douglas was every whit a Governor of this high order. Mistakes he made, but he was quick to correct them. Imbued with the idea that he was the servant of the Crown, holding office to administer the colony in its best interest and to establish law and order and Queen's justice in an unruly realm, he lived the part, and retired personally respected and honoured by all classes of the community. It is not given to many to achieve as much. In recognition of Douglas's services Queen Victoria created him Knight Commander of the Bath.

The most exciting incident in Douglas's career as Governor was the dispute with the Americans over the island of San Juan. The first article of the Oregon Treaty (1846) traced the boundary to the Pacific Ocean from the 49th parallel of north latitude " to the middle of the channel which separates the continent from Vancouver's Island, and thence southerly through the middle of the said channel, and of Fuca's Straits to the Pacific Ocean ; provided, however, that the navigation of the whole of the said channel and straits south of the 49th parallel of north latitude remain free and open to both parties." The difficulty arose out of the existence of a group of islands, the Archipelago de Haro, of which San Juan is the most westerly island, leaving two channels (as well as a tortuous passage between the islands), namely, Rosario Strait next to the continent and the Canal de Haro next to Vancouver's Island. Which of these was intended as boundary by the Treaty ?

The one in common use by the Hudson's Bay Company's craft was the Rosario Strait, nearest to the continent. Douglas wrote in September, 1871, that is, when the question was *sub judice* : The Canal de Haro " was little known at the date of the Oregon Treaty, and was never used as a channel of trade, which invariably took the direction of Rosario Strait. Mariners have always held the Canal de Haro in dread, and the accurate surveys since made, have not divested it of its formidable character." Accordingly, it was natural for the Hudson's Bay Company to assume that the Archipelago de Haro between the straits, was left within British territory by the treaty. In 1850 the Company kept herds of cattle with herdsmen on the island of San Juan. In 1852, however, the Oregon Legislature counted the island as within its territory, and within Whatcom county, and the sheriff of the county attempted to force the Company into paying taxes. He was pursued by officials of the Company in the s.s. *Beaver* and made his escape. This dispute was laid before the Boundary Commissioners in 1856, but no decision could be arrived at. The British ambassador suggested in turn a compromise boundary running through the archipelago, and a reference of the dispute to arbitration by representatives of Belgium, Switzerland, and Denmark, but was met with refusals. Such was the situation when the dispute came to a crisis in June 1859.

American settlers were now on the island, as well as a post of the Hudson's Bay Company with its cattle and sheep and pigs. One of the pigs got into the garden of an American named Cutler, who forthwith shot it. The agent of the Company claimed $100 as damages. Next day A. G. Dallas, Chief Factor at Victoria, with Dr. Wm. F. Tolmie, arrived on the scene, and according to their account remonstrated with Cutler. The American, however, asserted that they claimed the island as British. To assert the American claim, General William S. Harney of the Military Department in Oregon sent Captain George Pickett and a company of sixty soldiers to occupy the island. Douglas replied by ordering a man-of-war " to prevent the landing of any further armed parties . . . and the erection of fortifications." Had more Americans arrived or fortifications been erected, there might well have been a clash of international importance so far as Douglas was concerned. By August he had placed a detachment of the Royal Engineers on the island, and three British warships lay in the harbour. All parties now began to be sobered by the situation. Rear-Admiral R. L. Baynes, commander of the British Pacific squadron, "refused to go to war over the shooting of a pig," and acted as a brake upon the somewhat impetuous Douglas ; while the American Government replaced Harney, the fire-eater, by General Scott of sober mind and good judgment. It was finally agreed that there should be a joint military occupation of the parts of the island occupied by the people of the respective nations, while the diverse claims should be settled in some way.

The British claim ran that the strict sense of the phrase of the treaty, "separates the continent from Vancouver's Island," indicated beyond doubt Rosario Strait, that it could not refer to the Canal de Haro, for at that channel the continent was already separated from Vancouver's Island. Further, from the 49th parallel the Canal de Haro takes a westerly direction before turning south, while Rosario Strait runs south from it. Finally, Rosario Strait was the passage always used by the shipping. The American plea was that the only reason for not following the 49th parallel to the ocean was to leave Vancouver's Island with the British, that this and the greater breadth of the Canal de Haro indicated that it was intended as the boundary, and they had some evidence that the Canal de Haro was mentioned by the British diplomats in the discussion of the treaty. The dispute was finally referred to the Emperor of Germany for adjudication. In 1871 he named the Canal de Haro as " most in accordance with the true interpretation of the Treaty."

3.—THE SISTER COLONIES AND THEIR UNION, 1864–67

It was perhaps well for the peace of mind of Governor Douglas that he retired when he did, for problems were already upon the two colonies which were much more difficult and harassing than the question of transportation. A change in the system of mining in the Cariboo was brought about by the sheer necessities of the business. Surface mining came to an end. The diggings had to be deep. The expenditure of capital was necessary to reach the gravel-bed, to follow it up when found, and to drain it. The casual miners who could make profits by moving the upper soil disappeared to a large extent. Combinations of miners with capital took their place. Though the total output of gold had increased in the proportion of nine to five, the mining population was reduced in inverse ratio. The migration of miners back to British Columbia in the spring declined accordingly, and with it the shipping and commerce of Victoria. Land values in town and country fell in sympathy. It made matters much worse that the merchants had not foreseen this development, but had bought large stocks of goods. They even transported great quantities to the Cariboo, only to find that there were none to buy. Deep depression prevailed at Victoria. The situation was all the more difficult to face because Vancouver's Island was wedded to free trade and relied largely upon the sale of public lands to finance the Government, and the total sales as well as the price of land declined just when the Colonial Office imposed upon the colony an elaborate Civil List. The salaries fixed for Vancouver's Island, on the standard of the Crown Colonies, were: Governor, £3,000 ; Chief-Justice, £800, to be £1,200 when a lawyer should be appointed ; Colonial Secretary, £600 ; Attorney-General, £300, with practice ; Treasurer, £600 ; Surveyor-General, £500— making a total of £5,800 imposed upon a population of but 7,500, mostly of the mercantile class, settled in the town of Victoria—this, when the public revenue in 1863 was but £35,000. It was estimated that the ordinary expenses of the Government stood at £27,000, leaving but little for improvements. The House of Representatives felt compelled to reject the burden of the Civil List, while eager to take over the revenues of the Public Domain. The Imperial Government was thus forced to pay the salary of the Governor, and of the Colonial Secretary. In keeping with this, the initiation of money votes was restricted to the Governor, and the new Governor, Arthur Edward Kennedy, kept the revenues of the Crown Domain within his exclusive control. There was difficulty even in providing a house for the Governor, for Douglas had resided in his own home. What with the cost of the administration and the deep depression, the outlook of the colony was one of gloom.

Across the Strait of Georgia, British Columbia was subject to the same depression. All up the Fraser merchants were forced into bankruptcy. There were, however, factors which eased the burden of the Government. The gold actually being produced was much greater than ever, though the revenues derived from it were less. The decline in receipts from the mining industry was to some extent offset by substituting an export tax on gold for the other taxes, but this duty could not be too heavy for fear of crushing the small miner. Moreover, the tax could be easily evaded. Thus the gold industry did not bear the same proportion of the expenses of the Government as in Douglas's day. It was fortunate that at this juncture gold was found in the Kootenay district, and a fresh influx of miners followed into that region. As the natural approach was from the Columbia, this brought no relief to the merchants of Victoria or of the valley of the Fraser. Nevertheless it kept up the receipts from the customs. Now that the colony had a Governor and Council of its own, it was free to follow the fiscal policy calculated to assist its own merchants and protect them from the trader in the free port of Victoria. A Customs Act was passed increasing the duties, on the average, by 10 to 12½ per cent. Though some of the necessaries remained on the free list, a number of luxuries, including spirits and opium, paid duties which ran from 20 to 40, and even, in the case of opium, to 50 per cent. The clause that struck at Victoria enacted that the duty should be estimated from the price of the goods at the port of embarkation, which meant that the duty on goods, say from San Francisco, coming in direct, was lower than on the same goods handled in Victoria. The result was that New Westminster came into its own as the port of entry for British Columbia. (In November 1865 this clause was disallowed by the Imperial Government as being out of line with colonial policy. The retort came that the clause had been drawn after the Canadian Customs Act.) New Westminster also now enjoyed the advantage of having the Governor and all his officers resident and spending their money in the capital of the colony. Altogether, the situation in that colony, though difficult, was not distressing.

The main effort of the Government was still put out upon road building. A wagon road was cut from Hope to Yale, to enable traffic to escape from the difficulties and dangers of the Fraser River in that quarter. To give the town, if possible, a share of the trade at the mines in the Kootenay region, the Hope-Similkameen road (the Dewdney Trail) was extended by way of Princeton, Keremeos, and Osoyoos Lake to Kootenay Lake and River, and to Wild Horse Creek near the present Steele. The road revenues of the colony would have borne this cost more easily but for the military expedition necessitated by a massacre of White Men at Bute Inlet. Alfred Waddington, of Victoria, one of the most energetic and far-seeing of the pioneers on the coast, had secured a charter granting him the right to make a road along the line surveyed by Lieutenant H. S. Palmer, R.E., in 1863, from Bute Inlet up the wooded valley of the Homathco River. The grades were steep, not only to the crossing of Waddington Mountain at an elevation of 2,000 feet, but until the plateau would be reached. Passing Tatla Lake, it was to cross the Chilcotin River and run north-eastward to Alexandria. The route was expected to open an easy way for traffic from the sea to the Cariboo. Victoria would, of course, get most of the benefit to be derived by this route, for it would divert trade from New Westminster to that city. The British Columbian Government was to be at no cost for the road, but Waddington was to be allowed to levy tolls on the traffic for ten years. A large band of men was put to work on the pack trail in scattered parties. In April 1864 three Indians, workmen on the road, came to the ferry on the river and demanded food, and when refused, shot down the ferryman. The several bands of workmen were attacked in succession, one of them when wrapped in deep sleep. Of the possible plunder only the food and horses were taken. The causes of the massacre remain obscure. The *British Columbian* of 5th August asserted that the Indians employed on the road were ill-treated, and vaguely hinted that the nature of the shocking mutilations inflicted on the corpses indicated that the intrigues of the workmen with Indian women were a contributing factor. This is a mere inference. The ultimate conclusion of Governor Seymour was that the Indian workmen on the road were starving, while the Whites fared abundantly. Mr. Whymper, the artist, writing in the *British Colonist* of May 10, 1864, said that when he was there Indians snatched up the bacon rind, bones, and tea-leaves, cast out from his camp, like so many hungry dogs. The generally accepted view is that plunder, cruel treatment, and the belief that they could not be caught in that wild country led the Indians to their evil deeds, but Judge Begbie, who tried the prisoners, asserted that the Indian title to the land, and particularly to a valuable spring of water, was at the root of the trouble. In the eyes of the settlers it appeared that a general Indian war had broken out, but the murderers appear to have numbered no more than eighteen, and the rest of the Indians remained passive. Punitive parties entered the Chilcotin country from the west by North Bentinck Arm and Sir Alexander Mackenzie's route; and from the north-east from Alexandria. Finally eight men surrendered themselves, along with some of the booty. Two turned Crown evidence, five were found guilty and hanged, and one was imprisoned for life. Two committed suicide, and one taken later was hanged. This Indian disturbance added some $80,000 to the expenditure of the colony that year, and greatly increased the financial difficulties of the Government.

The depression in Vancouver's Island, accentuated by the barriers thrown up by the British Columbian Government against the trade of Victoria, brought about a general reconsideration of the policies of the past. The merchants of the free port of Victoria had been against the union of Vancouver's Island with British Columbia, because of the advantages which they had enjoyed in Governor Douglas's time. The House of Assembly, on February 9, 1864, while expressing the opinion that the ultimate union of the two colonies would be of advantage, added : " although chiefly on account of the opposite commercial policies pursued and deemed necessary by each, the amalgamation of the colonies at the present time is deemed unadvisable if not impossible " ; they considered two colonies with one civil establishment advisable on account of the ultimate connection of the two with one another. In a word, they really wished to get the best of two worlds. Union with the sister colony, in which the tariff played such an important part in public finance, would have meant the sacrifice of the free trade system under which Victoria had thriven, but it took but a short experience of the depression, of the cost of supporting an over-elaborate Civil List, and of the adverse Customs Act of the sister colony to present Union to them as the swiftest and surest remedy for the prevailing evils. It would bring an escape from the disadvantages of the prevailing customs duties, re-establish the position of Victoria as the port of entry for the mainland, and probably the Government of the united colony would remain seated at Victoria as the capital. For the very same reasons the merchants of New Westminster and the valley of the Fraser were against union. The situation, to a large extent, resolved itself into a struggle for prosperity between the two capital cities.

It added to the complexity of the problems of the people in Victoria that Vancouver's Island had a representative system of Government, while British Columbia was under a Governor and a Council, of whose members but one-third were elected by the people. But there is nothing like economic distress to put political theories and old shibboleths to the test. A group appeared asserting that the true foundation for prosperity is agriculture and that a protective tariff—meaning always the tariff of British Columbia—would stimulate agriculture, while Union would give back the market for agricultural products and for imported goods to be found on the mainland. Another group took the sterile course of advocating a customs tariff in a united colony, with Victoria remaining a free port. A rare voice was raised advocating Union and representative government in conjunction. At this point Amor de Cosmos stepped to the front of the stage as the great apostle of Union. He wisely refused to saddle the cause with any stipulation whatever, as, for example, that Victoria should remain a free port. The surprising thing is that this preacher of liberty to whom representative government had been a dogma was willing to have Union without any condition requiring a representative Assembly in the united colony. The historian is driven to take one of two views of this interesting change of front. Either Amor de Cosmos had come to the sensible conclusion that under the conditions of the Pacific coast a colony could prosper under an efficient Governor and Council, or he had all along been chiefly concerned to find a career before the public eye. He had found notoriety in the past, using representative government as a whip with which to lash the autocratically inclined Governor Douglas ; he now sought publicity in the advocacy of an uncon- ditional Union. On January 25, 1865, as a member of the Assembly he introduced resolutions embodying his present views :

Resolved that this House, after having taken into consideration the present state of the Colony, is firmly convinced that it is expedient at the present time to observe the strictest economy in the public expenditure compatible with the efficiency of the public service ; and that the immediate union of this Colony with British Columbia, under such constitution as Her Majesty's Government may be pleased to grant, is the means best adapted to prevent permanent causes of depression, as well as to stimulate trade, foster industry, develop our resources, augment our population, and ensure our permanent prosperity ; and this House pledges itself, in case Her Majesty's Government shall grant such union, to ratify the same by legislative enactments, if required. *Resolved* that the above resolution be transmitted to his Excellency the Governor, with the respectful request that he may take the same into his earnest and immediate consideration.

The necessity for immediate consideration lay in the simple fact that the revenue was estimated at $212,000, and the expenditure was expected to be $313,558. The resolutions were passed by a majority of four in a House of twelve members present. As De Cosmos had been elected for Victoria on a platform of Victoria as a free port, his constituency was greatly perturbed at his *volte-face*. When charged with betrayal, he and his colleague Mr. McClure, now editor of the *British Colonist*, resigned and stood for re-election. They were returned triumphantly. The colony of Vancouver's Island may now be said to be pleading for Union. British Columbia, from Governor Seymour down, in a happier situation, turned a deaf ear to the plea.

Already at this early date the more distant horizon was lit up with hope for the two colonies. Mr. Edward Watkin, as will be seen, was doing the spadework necessary for a transcontinental railway—in his mind, the Grand Trunk. There was to be a preliminary postal route and telegraph across the continent to British Columbia. On February 9, 1863, an Order in Council was approved by the Governor-General of Canada placing $50,000 towards that object in the estimates, and the Duke of Newcastle was willing that the two Pacific colonies should make their contribution. The project was premature. It was none the less the harbinger of a new age.

Then, too, the Quebec Conference with a view to the confederation of the Atlantic colonies was held in 1864, and the Dominion of Canada was in the process of coming into being. Resolutions had been passed, looking to a Confederation of all the British colonies in North America and indicating the procedure by which Rupert's Land and the North-West and the Pacific colonies should enter into union with Canada. These two developments seemed to the people on the Pacific coast to promise the dawn of a day when they would be delivered from their isolation, and when a broad market would be opened at their door. Amid the prevailing gloom eyes began to be turned to the clearing of the distant horizon to the east.

The year 1866 saw both colonies in great difficulties. In Vancouver's Island a constitutional crisis was brought on, partly through the lack of a proper relationship between the Executive,

Governor Kennedy, and the House of Assembly; partly through the inherent financial difficulties of the situation; and partly because the House of Representatives, unable to agree on constructive measures fraught with healing for the colony, played a purely obstructive part. As the Assembly had refused to accept the costly Civil List imposed on the colony, the Governor held that the Natural Resources offered in return had not been accepted, and were therefore not under the control of the Assembly; that he was free to use the returns in payment of salaries, and for the carrying on of the Government. The Assembly took the position that the Natural Resources were under their control and should be duly accounted for, and proceeded to reduce the salaries of the officials as fixed by the Colonial Office. There can be no doubt that the cost of officialdom on the scale prevalent in other British colonies was crushing for the small community, but the responsibility for it lay, for the most part, on the purblind House of Representatives, which had insisted that Vancouver's Island should be a colony separate from the mainland. Also, Victoria harbour was far from being an adequate port for shipping, and large sums were spent in vain in the attempt to improve it. In the depression many absconded without paying their creditors and to escape the payment of taxes due to the city and the Government, with the result that revenues fell short of the estimates, while expenditures, which included the fixed salaries of officials, and fixed charges for interest on loans, could not be, or at least were not reduced. As the tax on real estate was not easy to pay, many involved properties were put up for sale. This further reduced the value of the land, and consequently the assessment for the taxes. Donald Fraser, writing to the London *Times*, said :

In Victoria I find the population reduced ; a large proportion of buildings of every class unoccupied ; the rents of such as are occupied lowered in amount and many in arrear ; real property sunk to a nominal value and unsaleable, except in a few exceptional cases—so few that I cannot learn of any *bona fide* sale at any price ; trade dull and diminished in amount. One of the largest houses has closed its business ; bankruptcies numerous ; skedaddlers [the modern euphuism for fugitive debtors] abundant; money scarce and the employment of labour limited. Nothing flourishing or buoyant but taxation and Government expenditure—much of the latter on unproductive objects and the former finding its reluctant way into the Treasury only under the coercive process of sales of real property by the Sheriff for delinquent taxes.

Bankrupt Victoria, to pay its bills, borrowed from the Colonial Government, which by its own borrowings was itself hastening to bankruptcy. Vancouver's Island was ripe for Union.

In 1863–64 British Columbia was much more emphatic than Vancouver's Island in its repudiation of Union. The mining class was somewhat indifferent, but the merchants of New Westminster and of the valley of the Fraser spoke with no uncertain voice. The new Governor, Frederick Seymour, was received with acclamation when he came to his capital. But here, too, depression and an unnecessarily costly Government imposed on them by the colonial system wrought an astonishing change of mind. The Duke of New-castle offered the young colony control of its Natural Resources in return for a Civil List—Governor, £3,000 ; Chief-Justice, £1,200 ; Colonial Secretary, £800 ; Attorney-General, £500, with practice ; Treasurer, £750 ; Commissioner of Lands and Surveyor-General, £800 ; Collector of Customs, £650 ; Chief Inspector of Police, £500 ; Registrar of Deeds, £500—a total burden of £8,700 upon a population of 10,000. Had the mining industry been stabilized as it stood, say in 1863, and had Governor Douglas's system of roads remained all that was needed for the transportation of goods to the mines, this might have been borne with tolerable ease, in spite of the debt incurred. But no sooner was that system completed than gold was found at Wild Horse Creek on the Kootenay, and the Dewdney Trail had to be extended to that region in the hope of giving the people of Hope and New Westminster a share in the business of supplying the miners. No sooner was the Dewdney Trail cut than gold was found at the Great Bend of the Columbia, and the miners partially abandoned the Kootenay in a rush to the North. A road was accordingly built from Cache Creek to make connections with the Cariboo road. It followed Thompson River to Savona Ferry at the west end of Kamloops Lake. Thence a small steamer could ply up to the settlement of Seymour, which had sprung up, as it were, over-night. The trail from this point to the Great Bend was but sixty miles in length. But no sooner was the expenditure for all this made than its object disappeared. The floating mass of miners, disappointed in the Great Bend, drifted off to the gold areas of Idaho and Montana. The Colonial Government in every case had turned every stone to accommodate the mining industry with roads. Every expenditure seemed justified in the light of the necessities of its year, but the value of it had largely disappeared in a year or two, leaving only an inescapable debt. Looking backward, much of Governor Douglas's labour appeared useless, and even idle. The Harrison-Lillooet road, which gave valuable early connections to the mining area of the upper Fraser, appeared now to be no more than a rival route to the Cariboo road, which had been devised at great cost to give a reliable route all through the year. Douglas seemed now to have spent lavish money needlessly. Governor Seymour wrote : " Everything that benefits the Douglas Lillooet Road injures that by Yale and Lytton and vice versa." Similarly, the scheme of allowing private tolls at bridges, devised to save the Government the cost of building, was proved a shortsighted measure. Mr. Joseph William Trutch had built the fine suspension bridge at Spuzzum to enable the Harrison-Lillooet road to be con-nected with the Cariboo road on the left bank of the Fraser, and was the sole recipient of its tolls ; in 1863 these amounted to £4,000 profit for the year. Throughout, the flux and flow of the mining population created expenditure on roads, on new officials, and what not, but prevented a just return for the eost incurred. The export tax on gold proved disappointing. It could be evaded, and it did not really make the companies who were getting rich returns from the deep diggings bear their share of Government expenditure. It was speedily abolished, and the licences on miners reverted to and extended to all workmen in the mines, including the Chinese; but even so, the mining industry was not bearing its full share of the burden of taxation. The merchants could not well undertake even their own share. When the miners rushed in of a summer and retired for the winter, the merchants expecting, like the Government, that the situation would remain and the miners flock in the next summer, stocked up, and even transported the goods to the distant interior, only to find that the miners had gone elsewhere. Thus every gold rush was followed by speculation ending in depression, and the merchants felt the burden of the Government more than any class.

When the Governor met with his Council over the finances, the expenditure for Public Works could always be justified, but the revenue continued to fall below the estimates. Deficits were constant. In 1865 the expenditure was roughly $1,342,000. The revenue amounted to but $609,000. The export tax on gold and the tolls on the roads, a sure index of trade, fell $115,000 short of the estimated amount. Had there been great confidence in the future, this might have been faced with equanimity, but the general fear was that the best days of placer mining were over, while the debt remained. It is not surprising to find that while British Columbia did not plead for Union, it was quietly accepted as a probable solution to the pressing financial difficulties of the colony. When word reached the colony that the Imperial Government was presenting a Bill to Parliament uniting the colonies, no protest was made. Even when the clause allowing for Union only after addresses to the Crown in its favour by the legislatures of the two colonies was dropped, no opposition expressed itself. While the evidence of the *British Colonist*, published in Victoria, must be taken with due caution, and allowance must be made for the sweep of the editorial pen, its weekly edition of August 28, 1866, was probably not very far from the truth when it said : " Everywhere on the Lower Fraser . . . at every point at which a town has been established or a potato-patch planted outside of the capital limits, the universal cry is for Union with Vancouver Island, one system of laws, and one set of officials." The editor asserts also that the desire is for Victoria as capital. He continues : " It is useless to appeal to the Assembly —they botch everything ; besides the people long since lost confidence in that illustrious body of statesmen." New Westminster itself did not attempt to bar the way to Union. The Memorial of the Municipal Council, dated 26th April, did no more than assert that " the people of British Columbia are and have always been strongly opposed to union with Vancouver Island." Its prayer was that the question of the capital should not be left open, but that New Westminster should be made the capital by Act of Parliament. The Colonial Office, after consulting Governor Seymour, who was in Europe for his marriage, drafted the Bill which should unite the two colonies. The governing machinery of Vancouver's Island was abolished and that of British Columbia retained. The membership of the Legislative Council was increased from fifteen to twenty-three, so as to include members from the sister colony. As an Act of Parliament of 1863 had added the Stikine country to British Columbia, the colony as now constituted included all the British territory west of the Rockies as far as the Stikine. The Bill received Royal Assent on 6th August.

Meanwhile things had gone from bad to worse in the government of Vancouver's Island. A constitutional crisis had arisen for which, in the first place, the Colonial Office was to blame, in that the island was saddled with a Civil List in which the salaries appeared to be far too large for the finances of the island, even with the lands which were offered, in consideration of its acceptance. At first the Governor's and the Colonial Secretary's salaries were paid out of the land revenues, and the balance of these placed at the disposal of the Assembly, while this body agreed to pay the rest of the salaries for one year. To the observer it would appear natural that, with Union about to be consummated, the compromise might have been continued till it was accomplished, but the theorists in the Assembly were led away by the belief that they were inaugurating a struggle for liberty comparable to that associated with the names of Pym and Hampden. Governor Douglas's scheme for improving the harbour of Victoria proved at once expensive and abortive. The Assembly was responsible for it in so far as it had voted the estimated money. Now that more money was needed to complete it, they were reluctant to provide ways and means thereto. So, too, for the salaries of Government officials and for public works. The Governor was thrown upon the necessity of temporary borrowings from the Bank of British Columbia with which to carry on. It is difficult not to infer that the Assembly of 1865–66 was using the financial troubles, in the interest of the constitutional issue, to bring the Governor's administration into discredit. The House sat from November to July without having passed any constructive measures to meet the financial necessities of the colony. Its majority claimed that the whole control of finances lay with the House, including the right to initiate money votes. The Governor's instructions ran that the initiation of such votes lay with the Executive. His estimates, placed before the House on December 20, 1865, were not passed in June 1866. How the House found material for discussion during all this time it is difficult to conceive, for it was legislating for a very simple situation, involving the interests of no more than about 7,500 souls. Part of the time was occupied in simply demonstrating what De Cosmos, who was now once more the prophet of representative and responsible government, and his followers conceived to be the powers of the House. During 1865, when the failure of the revenues became apparent, the Governor had kept expenditure below even his own estimate by something like $43,000. The new estimates were a real attempt to balance the budget; they involved an estimated expenditure of $90,000 less than the expenditure of the previous year. The majority of the Assembly cut this down here and added to it there in what must have appeared to sober minds a somewhat irresponsible manner. The lack of sobriety of judgment in the party is manifested in the opinion of some of its members, that the budget should only be passed at the end of the year, when the taxes had come in, and the Assembly knew where it stood. Supplies for lighthouses were left unvoted, merely because the Assembly thought British Columbia was failing in its duty in the matter. The measures reducing the budget were rejected by the Council, as well as those increasing the estimates. The impasse was complete. On 31st May the Bank of British Columbia gave notice that the overdraft of the colony at that date stood at $79,567. On this being communicated to the Assembly, instead of facing the issue of a balanced budget, they empowered the Governor to call for a loan of $90,000 at 12 per cent. due in three years. This was not passed till 6th July. Governor Kennedy saw nothing for it but to approve of the loan, but when it was offered to the public not one cent was subscribed. The lack of financial experience and wisdom in the Assembly was revealed by this fiasco. Civil servants had to be discharged, and many of those continuing went without pay. Such was the condition of Vancouver's Island when it entered the Union. It is not necessary here to apportion the blame. It must lie on all parties alike, but it is more than probable that the governmental system of the United Colony, which left but a third of the places in the Council to the representative system, ran all the more smoothly because the apostles of reform and of responsible government had been proved unequal to the task which the crisis in Vancouver's Island imposed upon them.

The governing machinery of the United Colony was much simpler and much more co-ordinated than that which had prevailed in Vancouver's Island. The three bodies—the Governor's Executive Council, the Legislative Council, and the House of Assembly—were replaced by two bodies—the Governor's Executive Council and the Legislative Council. Members of the Governor's Executive Council, intimately acquainted with the problems of the Government, sat among the official members of the Legislative Council, a buffer between the elected members and the Governor. One-third of the membership consisted of magistrates who owed their appointment to the Governor, but resided in the various districts of the colony and, in virtue of their duties, were well aware of the needs of those parts. They were, by their appointment, in sympathy with the Government, and by their places of residence more or less in touch with the needs of their districts. They stood as a mediating element between the high officials of the administration and the representatives of the people. Political theory and sentimental politics found little room in this Council. It devoted itself to the business of governing.

A real test of the efficiency of the new machine came with the question : Which should be the capital of the colony, New Westminster or Victoria ? As the Council sat to begin with in New Westminster, and Governor Seymour, who continued as Governor, was in favour of that town, on the ground that there would be an element of breach of faith to the purchasers of town lots in taking the Government away from it, the case of New Westminster would get a good hearing. There was accommodation for the administration both there and in Victoria. Governor Seymour consulted the Council on the question. The decision, made with perfect freedom, was in favour of Victoria by fourteen votes against five, and the capital it became. It was less exposed to the United States than Westminster, and with Esquimalt harbour as the possible base for a naval squadron, could invoke the protection of the navy. It was on the line of ocean traffic up the coast, and held its position as an emporium of trade until Vancouver took its place after Confederation. The traffic up the Fraser in small steamers found it fully as convenient as New Westminster, while it was much easier of approach to large vessels. Many of the firms which supplied most of the goods for the interior of the mainland were long since established there, and many miners who left their mines for a more equable climate spent their winter amid the conveniences and scenic delights of the city. Victoria did no more than come into its own.

Not so easy to be dismissed was the problem of finance. When Governor Seymour returned, he proved himself much less optimistic than before, and devoted himself, with a determination to be admired in a man of his indecision of character, to balance the budget. The feeling that it was unwise to depend upon gold alone for the prosperity of the country was growing, and legislation was passed to encourage agriculture and even industry. The Council, in sharp contrast with the former Assembly of Vancouver's Island, accepted the lead of the Governor. His estimates of expenditure and revenue were given immediate and serious attention, yet it felt free to amend them. Additional proposals were not passed as a matter of right by the Council, but resolutions were tacked on to the estimates in the form of petitions indicating the desire of the Council. Should the Governor feel that the petition might be granted, he drafted the ordinance co-ordinating the measure with the main aim of the budget, viz. economy. One illustration will suffice. The Council petitioned the Governor for an increased tariff against imported fruit, assuring him that it would not raise the price in the colony. The Governor replied that the tariff was not to be considered at that session. Mr. Helmcken, who had earned a reputation in the struggle of the island Assembly with Governor Kennedy, raised the issue of the power of the Council to initiate taxation. The presiding member of the Council, Colonial Secretary Young, declared Helmcken's Bill out of order as imposing taxation, it being the part of the Executive to initiate Money Bills. No less than forty-five measures were passed by the Council in the little over two months of its first session.

This procedure gave Governor Seymour the chance, without undue pressure, to reduce the cost of government, so that in two years' time, in spite of a steady fall in the revenue, the budget was balanced. But the Government's finances were not easily rehabilitated. The continued decline in the surface mining and the emigration of the miners reduced the revenue from gold and from the customs on goods brought in to supply the miners. The farms of the country, now that Vancouver's Island was in the Union, were going some distance towards supplying the needs of the camps, and that without paying customs duty. Farms along the roads were supplying their neighbourhood to some extent, so that the revenues from the tolls were falling. Deep mining was still succeeding, but no means was devised to lay its share of the cost of government on the rich miners. The colony was increasing in prosperity, while the Government was finding it hard to make ends meet. When Seymour died in June 1869 and Musgrave came to office as Governor, the need of repairing the roads, along with a falling revenue, brought about a deficit once more. The debt had grown to be approximately $1,137,000. In eight years there had been one balanced budget and no repayment of debt. It was with this situation in view that serious minds in British Columbia faced the question of entering the Confederation with Canada. The Dominion would absorb the indebtedness of the colony, would undertake the support of the Governor, the Chief-Justice, and of the judges who would form the county courts, and would take over the management of the Indians. On the other side of the ledger would be the loss of revenue from the customs, but compensation would be secured for that. Confederation would cure the persistent financial ills of the colony.

It did not help the cause of Confederation that Amor de Cosmos, born a Nova Scotian, jumped to the front to lead. The officials of the Government and the ex-officers of the Hudson's Bay Company did not entertain the sentiments towards the Dominion which inspired him, and in any case, the memory of his fractious opposition and of his biting attacks would restrain them from crowding in behind him as leader. On March 18, 1867, when the British North America Act was passing through the British Parliament, De Cosmos introduced a resolution to the Council couched in urgent terms. The resolution was, by amendment, chastened to read: "That this Council is of the opinion that at this juncture of affairs in British North America, East of the Rockies, it is very desirable that his Excellency be respectfully requested to take such steps, without delay, as may be deemed by him best adapted to insure the admission of British Columbia into the Confederation on fair and equitable terms, this Council being confident that in advising this step they are expressing the views of the Colonists generally." It was passed. At the instance of a deputation of the members, Governor Seymour telegraphed to the Colonial Minister: "Can provision be made in the Bill before Parliament for the admission of British Columbia to Canadian Confederation?" On 24th September he forwarded the resolution of Council with his observations upon it. On 19th November the Duke of Buckingham and Chandos made the obvious reply that " the question must . . . await the time when the intervening territory now under the control of the Hudson's Bay Company shall have been incorporated with the Confederation."

CHAPTER XI

THE DRIFT OF RUPERT'S LAND AND THE NORTH-WEST TERRITORY TOWARDS CONFEDERATION WITH CANADA

I.—UNREST AMONG THE HALF-BREEDS OF THE COLONY—INQUIRY INTO THE COMPANY'S ADMINISTRATION, 1840–59

By the 'forties the Red River Settlement had taken on its permanent character. It was a little Quebec. The French-Canadians and the English and Scots lived side by side, for the most part separated by the river. Among them were to be found the half-breeds of the respective races. The attempt to make Lower Fort Garry the centre of the community had failed. The intimate relations of the upper fort with the half-breeds, the trappers, and buffalo hunters of the Settlement kept it in its predominant position.

Of the different circles in the colony, the Company's officers, gathered around the Governor, were the most influential. Enjoying good incomes, and intimately associated with the community at large in virtue of the Company's stores and of the Council of Assinboia, they controlled the destiny of the Settlement as no other group did. It must not be inferred that they were automatic instruments in the hands of the Governor and Committee in London. Rather, the Committee left the guidance of their colony to them and to Governor Simpson, only reviewing their conduct when special occasion arose.

In a conspicuous position beside the Company's officers stood the Anglicans, gathered around their clergymen, and around the churches and the schools. They did not enjoy their influence because of their numbers, but rather because the Company had put the religious and moral welfare of the Settlement into the hands of their Anglican chaplains and of the Church Missionary Society. In 1849, by the application of a bequest of Chief Factor James Leith to the purpose, and through the generous support of the Company, the bishopric of Rupert's Land was established, Rev. David Anderson, D.D., being the first bishop. Letters Patent under the Privy Seal were issued, erecting " the said Colony of Rupert's Land into a bishop's see or diocese," incidentally showing that the law officers of the Crown regarded the Company's Territory as one of Her Majesty's colonies. As the bishop sat in the Council, and by his faith was in close relations with the chief among the Company's officers, and as his cathedral church and the residential school in which the children of the Company's men were educated stood closest to Fort Garry, his influence in the colony, or at least over the English-speaking part of it, came short only of that of the Governor.

Five miles below Fort Garry, in the parish of Kildonan, were the Scots, the largest and most homogeneous group among the English-speaking settlers, but not the most influential. To begin with, the Scotsmen had come from the lonely crofts in Scotland on which they had devoted themselves to agriculture and had had little to do with public affairs. On the Red River they remained true to form. Alexander Ross describes them :

These people surpass in comfort those of the same class in most other countries. Abundance on every hand testifies to their industry and economy, and this within doors and without in the same profusion. The evidence of domestic happiness everywhere meets the eye. No want of blankets here on the beds ; the children well clothed, and the houses warm and comfortable. The barns teeming with grain, the stables with cattle, and all classes wearing more or less of their own manufacture, which bespeaks a fair prospect for the future. . . . A certain moral and religious discipline, of course, lays the foundation for the habits we have described. Every morning and evening the Bible is taken off the shelf, and family worship regularly observed. "We see no carioling, gossiping, card-playing, or idling here," observed my friend. "Not to any extent," said I ; "the idler has no encouragement here." In their social relations, the Scotch are sober, shrewd, and attentive to their several duties, both as Christians and subjects.

Ross remarks, however, that the young people were conforming to the habits of the French half-breeds, dressing in gaudy fashion and racing to and from church on Sunday with " worldly enjoyment " of their horses and sleighs (carioles).

It militated against the influence of the Scots in the affairs of the Settlement that they had no organ for the expression of their opinion, though, of course, men from their midst sat in the Council—nothing like the clergyman or the bishop in the group south of them. They had been promised a minister by Lord Selkirk, but at the suggestion of Governor Semple Anglican clergymen had been sent out, lest the difference between the Catholics and Protestants might be so marked as to confuse the natives. Thus an Anglican church was built on the lot set apart by his lordship for the Presbyterians. Rev. William Cochrane had won their respect, and had modified the ritual in the hope of winning their co-operation. He so far succeeded that they assisted in building the church, but under the bishop Cochrane's concessions were withdrawn, and the gulf between the Anglicans and Presbyterians widened. The repeated refusals of the Company to assist the Scotsmen in procuring a minister to their liking, in days when loyalty to one's creed was a predominant characteristic of all types of Christians, left them with a grievance against the ruling powers. This was unfortunate, for a minister would have drawn them into closer relations with the Government, and in an

hour of crisis would have rallied the people to its support. At last
the Company paved the way for the fulfilment of the desire of Kildonan. The people were compensated for their share in erecting
what was called the Middle Church, and were given a lot at Frog Plain
on which to build. In 1851 Rev. John Black came from Montreal to
minister to them.

About fourteen miles north of Kildonan, and in the neighbourhood of Lower Fort Garry, the settlers were retired servants of the
Company. Some never reconciled themselves to agricultural pursuits. With a modicum of wealth in their hand, the ground was no
more than scratched to meet the needs of the table. Some of the
leading men, however, did well and, retaining their interest in and
loyalty to the Company, found places of service in the administration
of Assiniboia. North of this group was the Indian agricultural
settlement established by Rev. Mr. Cochrane.

The French and the French half-breeds were, for the most part,
in groups east of the Red River, their centre St. Boniface with the
Roman Catholic cathedral, the convent, and the school which developed into St. Boniface College. These had as their mouthpiece the
bishop of the time being (Provencher till 1853, and thereafter
Alexander Antonin Taché) sitting in the Council of Assiniboia.
Their relation with the Company was really closer than that of the
other settlers, because they took part in the manufacture of pemmican
for it, served as voyageurs in its transportation service, and trapped
furs. They were gradually spreading up the valley of the Seine
towards the present St. Norbert. The more sedentary portion made
good farmers, but every grade of settler was found among them
down to those whose homes differed little from their former camps
among the Indians, and whose livelihood continued to be hunting
and fishing as of old. As has been seen, a half-breed settlement
existed at White Horse Plain, about sixteen miles up the Assiniboine from Fort Garry, and on the north bank. Settlements began
to be established on the west bank of the Red River south of the
Assiniboine—St. Vital—and farther south on both sides of the Red—
St. Norbert.

The several Districts were concerned to varying extents with
agriculture and the buffalo hunt. The Scottish settlement emphasized
its agriculture ; the half-breeds, more particularly at White Horse
Plain, the buffalo hunt ; it was their real means of livelihood.

There were two buffalo hunts—in the spring and in the autumn.
They provided meat and pemmican for the home, for sale to the
settlers, and particularly to the Company at Fort Garry. The
hunts grew in size and importance with the years. Alexander
Ross says :

In 1820 the number of carts assembled here for the first trip was . 540
  „ 1825   „   „   „   „   „   „   „   „ . 680
  „ 1830   „   „   „   „   „   „   „   „ . 820
  „ 1835   „   „   „   „   „   „   „   „ . 970
  „ 1840   „   „   „   „   „   „   „   „ . 1,210

Such large assemblages of necessity devised a system of organization. When out on the plains they formed a sort of provisional government. Ten captains were chosen, one of whom acted as president. Each captain had ten " soldiers " under his orders. Ten guides were appointed to marshal the hunt ; the camp flag was in their care ; its raising and its lowering were the signals to move on and to camp respectively. The captains and the " soldiers " arranged the encampment in an orderly way. At the meeting for organization the regulations to be enforced were drawn up and announced. Rules ordinarily adopted were that no buffalo should be run on Sabbath days ; no party was to fork off or lag behind, or go before, without permission ; no one was to " run buffalo " before the general order was given ; every captain with his men was to patrol the camp in his turn ; for the first breach of the regulations the offender was to have his saddle and bridle cut up ; for the second offence his coat was to be torn off his back and cut up ; for the third offence he was to be flogged ; any person convicted of theft, even to the value of a sinew, was to be brought out into the middle of the camp and the camp crier was to call out his or her name three times, adding the word " thief " at each time. The hunters rode out together towards the buffalo, all keeping the same pace, until the president gave the word to be at them. The killing over, the women and children busied themselves cutting up the meat, drying it, and making pemmican. As many as 2,500 buffalo might be killed, and 375 bags of pemmican and 240 bales of dried meat made.

The buffalo hunt had its influence on the attitude of the half-breeds to the Government. They were the most numerous single body among the settlers. They were accustomed to choosing their leaders, and had been disciplined into co-operation with and obedience to them. They were not only armed, but habituated to the use of arms. They were therefore the element in the Settlement most conscious of its power, and least submissive to the Government of the colony. In the generation under consideration, J. Louis Riel, who owned a watermill for grinding grain and for carding wool for the Sisters of Charity of St. Boniface, was a man of authority among them. In the next generation, his son Louis Riel (of the disturbances in the Settlement in 1869) showed what use could be made of the organization of the half-breeds, of their unity and discipline, in a political agitation. Such men found the buffalo hunters easily moved to organize a provisional government, and ready to obey the leaders whom they had chosen.

The Scottish settlers, devoted to their farms, would not feel the weight of the monopoly of the Hudson's Bay Company. Not so the French half-breeds. Accustomed to hunt over a wide region and kill at sight, they never gave an unqualified adhesion to the monopoly. During the strife of the first days of the colony, they had been trained by the Northwesters to deny the right of the Company to the exclusive trade and to the soil. They had been taught to consider themselves the owners of the land, and had called themselves " The

New Nation." So long as this was so, the government of the Hudson's Bay Company rested on insecure foundations. In this situation it was a weakness of the system by which the Company was given an exclusive licence of the trade with the Indians of the North-West Territory, as opposed to the chartered region, that the expiry of the licence at the end of twenty-one years and the application for its renewal would offer a chance to opponents of the monopoly to stir up an agitation against it. An attack on the Company was therefore to be expected when the licence would have to be renewed in 1842. There was also the possibility of men in Canada, who recalled the wealth brought to Montreal by the North West Company, trying to break the monopoly and to have the trade thrown open to all. On Governor Simpson's arrival at Lachine in September 1836 he fell on the Hon. George Moffat, who, it will be remembered, was one of the intermediaries between the North West Company's Wintering Partners and Andrew Colvile in the negotiations leading to the union of 1821. He was now a member of the Legislative Council of Lower Canada. He informed Simpson that he intended to move a resolution in the Council calling for the abolition of the monopoly. The disturbances of 1837 may have prevented him from carrying out his plan. In any case his imprudent intimation led to swift action on the part of Simpson. The Governor crossed to London, where he prepared a glowing report on the Company's Territory; emphasizing justly its peace and its educational and religious institutions, and the value of a monopoly in the fur trade, particularly in bringing about the disuse of rum. Sir J. H. Pelly, the Governor of the Company, forwarded this to Lord Glenelg, then Colonial Minister, with a request for an immediate renewal of the licence. Glenelg, who was sincerely interested in the welfare of the aboriginal subjects of the British Crown, urged the Company's case with the Lords Commissioners of the Treasury. Their secretary, Mr. A. Milne, also much interested in philanthropic enterprises, strongly supported the renewal. The Lords claimed that there should be a rental of £20,000 or at least £10,000 paid by the Company. Sir John Pelly insisted that the Company could not bear such an imposition, that it would have rather to give up the licence and throw the burden of installing a government of the North-West Territory upon the Crown, for the profits up to that time had not been large. He gained his point and the licence was renewed in 1838.

Changes were coming over the Settlement which show that Simpson had been wise after his generation. So long as it was wholly isolated and all its trade was carried on through York Fort, there was little need to defend the monopoly. Half-breeds who traded furs with the Indians had, of necessity, to trade them in turn at the Company's posts. The Company's control remained essentially unimpaired, but the Americans were now pouring into their western plains, and were developing trade relations with the half-breeds. Norman Wolfred Kittson, a Canadian born at Chambly, Lower Canada, had engaged himself with the American Fur Company, and later entered into a partnership with one Sibley, of St. Peter's, later Mendota, Minnesota, opposite Fort Snelling.   His sphere was the fur trade of the Upper Minnesota and the Red River as far as the International Boundary.   In 1844 he established a post at Pembina, immediately south of the border.   The half-breeds could slip across the unpoliced border with their furs and return with the goods, and especially with the liquor which would give them the Indians' trade. The Governor of Assiniboia, Alexander Christie, and Adam Thom, the Recorder,* met the situation by winning the consent of his Council on June 19, 1845, to a series of regulations affecting the Customs and the sale of liquor ; they were devised to check the free traders without harassing legitimate business.   An actual settler could import stoves free of duty once a year on a truthful declaration that they were for his personal use.   This would cut off the traffic in stoves supplied to the free traders for their winter camps among the Indians.   A settler could import goods to the value of £10 free, provided they were for his personal use in the Settlement, and by implication, not to be used to equip free traders.   On similar grounds, any actual settler who took out goods (other than furs), the product of the Settlement, to the United States or York Fort could bring in free of duty the return of his trade to the actual value of £50, " on declaring truly that they are either to be consumed by himself, or to be sold by himself to actual consumers in the Settlement."   Apart from these regulations, the Imperial Statute 5 & 6 Victoria, chapter 49, regulating the foreign trade of the British possessions in America was declared in force, with the proviso that imports not from Britain would be presumed to be from the United States.   Arrangements were made for the importation of drugs, seeds, implements and the like, for the local manufacture of woollen and linen goods, and for their sale at cost, to encourage local manufacturers, the cost of the scheme up to £100 to be borne by the revenue from the tariff, the money to be placed by the Company at the disposal of the Council. Stringent laws were passed punishing Indians for drunkenness, and others for furnishing them with liquor, or with the means of distilling liquors.   Only the Company was to distil such, paying a shilling a gallon as excise duty to the revenue of the colony.   Their liquor was to be tinged a certain colour to facilitate the detection of illicit

---

* Adam Thom was a Scotsman, educated at King's College, Aberdeen. In 1832 he settled in Montreal, and was called to the Bar of Lower Canada in 1837. During the rebellion of 1837 he was editor of the *Montreal Herald*, and in that journal and in pamphlets he showed himself an ardent opponent of the French party led by Papineau. In 1838 Lord Durham attached him to his staff ; he took him to England, it is said, to assist him in drawing up his Report. In 1839 Thom was appointed Recorder (judge) of the Quarterly Court of Assiniboia. His anti-French record in Lower Canada, coupled with his activity in suppressing the illicit fur trade in the Colony, made him unacceptable to the half-breeds. " He was a thorough-going, brainy, determined Scotsman of the stalwart rather than of the adaptable type representative of so many of his countrymen." The resolutions of the Council, devised to restrain the traffic of the half-breeds in furs, were introduced by him. They stand in contrast with the usual *laissez faire* policy of the Governor and Committee in London. After the Sayer trial in 1849 he ceased to act as Recorder, being reduced to the humble position of Clerk of the Court. In 1853 he gave up his position to live in London, where he died in 1890. In 1844 he published a pamphlet, *The Claims of the Oregon Territory Considered*, a remarkably acute analysis of the conflicting claims to that region.

distillation. The Company never assumed the task of distillation placed on it by the Council.

On the promulgation of these laws the half-breeds addressed a letter to Governor Christie asking whether a half-breed settler had not the right to hunt furs, to hire others to hunt, and to sell his furs to any person he chose. The subtle inference was that the half-breeds had special rights, that the country belonged to them, as the North-westers for their own purposes had asserted. In his reply the Governor said that the letter had been " grounded on the supposition that the half-breeds possess certain privileges over their fellow citizens, who have not been born in the country." As British subjects, the settlers were on the same footing as the people born in the land. All are alike subject to the law of the country, meaning among other things the Company's Charter.

The issue between the half-breeds and the Company was affected by the issue between Britain and the United States over the Oregon boundary. In 1845 Lieutenants Warre and Vavasour were sent westward from Canada to report to the Imperial Government on the country, particularly on the Oregon, in case war should break out. On 10th June, when in the Red River Settlement, they reported that it was practicable to send in troops by way of the Great Lakes and Fort William, but that heavy ordnance would have to be sent in by way of York Fort. They were of opinion that a small body of cavalry and artillerymen would be the best types for the occasion ; they could form the " core " of regiments raised among the half-breeds. The officers pointed out that the United States was actively completing the chain of forts which protected their territory. Fort Snelling, built in 1819 on a military reservation hard by the present Minneapolis, had been hitherto the nearest fort to the Red River Settlement. Governor Simpson received information in the month following Vavasour's visit that the Americans intended to build a fort at Pembina, south of the border and but about fifty miles from the colony. In August the hunters from Red River, who ordinarily passed south of the International Boundary, it might be as far as the Cheyenne River, came on a body of American cavalry, estimated at 190 officers and men, ostensibly seeking out Sioux who had killed missionaries. The officer in command told them that, as British subjects, they could not be permitted to hunt buffalo in American territory. They replied that they had permission from the Indian tribes of those parts to do so, and that they " could not in any other way provide the means of Support for themselves and their families." The officer repeated his prohibition and said that the only alternative was for them to settle in American territory, say at Pembina, when they would have permission to hunt and would be protected. The half-breeds then held a council ; the decision was that, as the whole body of hunters was not present, no determination could be reached until they returned to the Settlement. Mr. J. P. Pruden, retired Chief Factor and member of the Council of Assiniboia, was with the hunters. His report reached Governor Pelly : " If a war ensues there is no doubt what side the half-breeds will take. The Soldiers boasted they were now strong enough to thrash daddy England." The Americans could have used no more subtle argument to win the half-breeds to their side.

In October Governor Simpson wrote Governor Pelly from Lachine :

The presence of military establishments in the Interior can be productive of little benefit to us at any other point than Red River Settlement, & there one is absolutely necessary to the existence of the Fur trade, not in reference to any difficulties with the United States only, but as a means of protection against the inhabitants of the Settlement, as with the feeling at present existing on the minds of the half-breeds, it will be quite impossible to protect the trade or inforce our laws without the presence of military at that point. . . . The half breed race, who, from their volatile character, are ever fascinated by novelty, Seem much flattered by the reception they met with, and elated by the advantages they are led to believe would be derived from a more intimate connection with the United States ; & when the Express Canoe came away, a Petition (drawn up by one [John] McLaughlin, a nephew of McDermott's, who came to the Settlement last year) was being Sent round among the Settlers for Signature, praying Congress to assist & protect them in the formation of a settlement at Pembina. This McLaughlin, . . . was for some time previous to his arrival at Red River, resident at St. Louis, and I have no doubt has been employed by some of the United States authorities as a secret emissary among our halfbreed Settlers & the neighbouring Indians, with a view to sowing the seeds of disaffection, as a preliminary measure to the overtures that have now been made, in which he and his friends McDermott, Sinclair & others appear to have been very successful, if I am at liberty to judge from the tone of discontent which has recently obtained among the people.

In November, McLaughlin appeared at Simpson's office at Lachine, ostensibly to settle a disputed account between the Company and the firm of McDermott & Sinclair, its chief rival in the Settlement. As the amount was too small to warrant the expensive journey, Simpson argued that he had taken the petition addressed to Congress to Washington.

In the issue, several companies of the 6th Royal Regiment of Foot, with artillery and sappers, to the number of five hundred, arrived in the Settlement in the autumn of 1846. Lieutenant-Colonel John Ffolliott Crofton was in command. Their presence was welcomed, not only for the addition of the officers to the society of the place, but for the £15,000 a year circulated in the colony for the purchase of supplies. The settlement of the Oregon dispute in the previous summer and the presence of the soldiery during their two years in the colony stayed the growing unrest, or more correctly, diverted the agitation into new channels—to appeals to the British Government and Parliament. Alexander Ross says : " From the moment they arrived, the high tone of lawless defiance and internal disaffection raised by our own people against the laws and the authorities of the place, were reduced to silence. All those disaffected to the existing order of things sneaked across the boundary line to the land of freedom, and became *pro tempore* subjects of the United States."

In the June before the arrival of the troops an attack on the
Company was launched by the half-breeds on constitutional lines.
A committee was " elected by the people " to draw up a petition to
Her Gracious Majesty.   It was signed by 977 persons, the members
of the committee certifying under oath that its signatures were
given freely and without pressure.   The " J. Louis Rielle " on the
committee is doubtless the father of the Louis Riel of the troubles of
1869–70.   He was born at Ile-à-la-Crosse, in 1817, his mother being
Julie Lagimonière, daughter of Miles Macdonell's faithful hunter.
When but five years of age, he was taken by his parents to Montreal,
where in due time he became a carder of wool.   He returned to the
West with his family, and from 1838 to 1841 was in the service of the
Hudson's Bay Company at Fort Frances.   Thereafter he spent two
years in the novitiate of the missionary Order of the Oblates of Mary
the Immaculate, but gave up the religious career and returned to
Red River.   He had an education much above the usual at St.
Boniface, where he became the owner of a mill and a leader of his
people.   The petition was taken to England by the Mr. James Sinclair
associated with Mr. McDermott, the arch-opponent of the Company.   It demanded a free trade, release from an ancient monopoly
which weighed more heavily on the people as the years went by ;
and it expressed lack of confidence in the Council and Courts of
Assiniboia, in that the officials were all the creatures of the Company
and bound to do its will.   In London it was given to Mr. A. K.
Isbister (son of a former officer of the Company), who had been
educated in the colony, had studied at the University of Edinburgh,
and was now practising Law in the metropolis.   He forwarded it to
Earl Grey, the Colonial Minister, with a covering letter signed by
five gentlemen associated with him.   The letter called for an inquiry
into the condition of the unfortunate people, the petitioners.   The
monopoly had led to the " utter improverishment, if not the ruin of
the natives," while it had been bringing a revenue of a million a year
to the Company ; no provision was being made for the moral and
religious improvement of the natives.   " There is not at present,
nor . . . has there ever been a single Indian school, church, or other
establishment for religious and general instruction established by the
Company."   What has been done is due to the Church Missionary
Society and to the Wesleyan Society of London * which receive no
assistance from the Company.   The fur resources of the country are
being exhausted and the people impoverished.   Many die of starvation.   To escape from the high prices exacted by the Company " the
more enterprising of the natives have formed a resolution to export
their own produce and import their own supplies, independently
of the Company.   They argue that even supposing the charter to be

---

* The Wesleyan Mission was established in 1840, with Rev. James Evans, the inventor
of the Cree syllabic alphabet, acting as superintendent.   Robert Terrell Rundle was stationed
at Edmonton and Rocky Mountain House, William Mason at Rainy Lake and Fort Alexander,
and George Barnley at Moose Fort and Abitibi.   The Company furnished them with canoes,
provisions, interpreters, and houses without cost.   Evans gathered an Indian village around
him on an island in Little Playgreen Lake, two miles from Norway House.   Rundle began
his mission residing in Edmonton Fort as the guest of Chief Factor Rowand.

still valid . . . none of its provisions are or can be binding on the natives to trade with the Company exclusively, or can prevent them from carrying their furs or other property out of the country to the best market.   Where this course has been adopted, however, the Company's agent has seized the furs of such parties as refused to sell them at the prices fixed by the Company, and, in some instances, have imprisoned the recusant natives."   As no redress was to be found in the courts of the country, the memorialists claimed the protection of the British Government : The natives " are deprived of their inheritance and their natural rights. . . . What must be the ultimate fate of this unhappy people, under such a system, it is as easy to foresee as it is painful to contemplate."   Isbister subsequently forwarded a statement of the Rev. Herbert Beaver, who had been the Company's chaplain at Fort Vancouver, about outrages perpetrated on the natives of the Pacific coast by servants of the Company ; and a document placing in parallel columns statements made by the Company to the British Government, and facts drawn from the writings of servants of the Company, including charges of demoralizing the natives with liquor.   A further paper argued that the Charter was invalid, and if it were valid, it applied to no more than the shore of the Bay ; it certainly did not grant the region of Red River to the Company.

These documents were placed by Lord Grey before the Hudson's Bay Company for their reply.   Sir J. H. Pelly, the Governor, denied the existence of discontent among the natives.   The unrest was confined to half-breeds in the Red River Settlement, who chafed at the measures adopted by the Company to protect its interests.   So far was the Company from amassing a million pounds a year, their average profits were about £40,000 on a capital of £400,000.   The Charter did not require the Company, as alleged, to propagate Christianity, but the Church Missionary Society and Wesleyan missionaries did not give their services gratuitously.   "All the societies that send missionaries to the Company's territories receive assistance from them ; the Wesleyan missionaries are maintained and provided with the means of conveyance from place to place at the Company's expense. . . . There are four Roman Catholic schools, four Protestant schools, attended by nearly 500 scholars, at one of which, it may be remarked, three of the memorialists were educated." It is true that there are times of distress at the Company's posts ; but for the relief afforded by the Company's servants this distress would be greatly aggravated.   The means of subsistence are not being exhausted.   " The enterprising natives . . . alluded to are settlers at Red River of mixed race ; and the Company who are their best customers, afford them every possible assistance in exporting their produce and importing their supplies under proper regulations. But furs, which are no part of their produce, must be excepted. Such furs as they hunt themselves are purchased by the Company, but trafficking with the Indians cannot be permitted."   " Considerable quantities of furs procured in the Company's territories by illicit traffic, are annually conveyed in a clandestine manner to the United States. In one instance, the offending party was detected and the furs seized, but instead of their being forfeited, as they might lawfully have been, a fair price was paid for them by the agents of the Company ; but there is no instance on record of any person having been imprisoned for such an offence, nor are the Company aware that any application for redress in such cases has ever been made in the local Courts." Governor Pelly was able to show that Mr. Beaver's charges were made on hearsay evidence, and were inconsistent with letters written by the man himself to the Company on the general conduct of its affairs.

Lord Grey wrote to Lord Elgin, Governor-General of Canada, for his judgment of the administration of the Company. Elgin replied that the territory ruled by it was so distant and had so little intercourse with Canada that it was not easy to gather information.

I am bound, however, to state that the result of the enquiries which I have made is highly favorable to the Company and that it has left on my mind the impression that the authority which they exercise over the vast and inhospitable region is, on the whole, very advantageous to the Indians. . . . There is too much reason to fear that if the trade were thrown open and the Indians left to the mercy of the adventurers who might chance to engage in it, their condition would be greatly deteriorated. At the same time I think it is to be regretted that a jurisdiction so extensive and peculiar, exercised by British Subjects at such a distance, and so far beyond the control of public opinion, should be so entirely removed from the surveillance of Her Majesty's Government.

Lord Elgin had secured much of his information from Colonel Crofton, who had been stationed at Red River. When Crofton reached England, he was asked for his views by the Colonial Office. His reply ran in part :

The memorial to Her Majesty originated among one or two discontented men at Red River, who, from the period of the rebellion in Canada, were ever forward to create disloyal feelings in the half-breed race, and induce them in the event of war, to throw off allegiance to Her Majesty. This desire largely prevailed, except among the Scotch settlers, until the arrival of Her Majesty's troops convinced these deluded men that their attempts would be frustrated. In less than a year these very men became loud in their loyalty, and in condemnation of their own folly, and that of those who still yearned for republican government. I had the best opportunities for learning directly, and through the officers of the troops, the opinions of all classes respecting the Hudson's Bay Company's government ; and I have never heard of the charges being designated otherwise than as false, which accompanied your letter, although I was aware that a memorial to Her Majesty had been got up, and that even a petition to Congress of the United States had been sent to Washington and there refused to be presented, stating those charges. I unhesitatingly assert, that the government of the Hudson's Bay Company is mild and protective, and admirably adapted, in my opinion, for the state of society existing in Rupert's Land, where Indians, half-breeds and Europeans are happily governed, and live protected by laws which I know were mercifully and impartially administered by Mr. Thom, the Recorder, and by the magistrates of the land.

A reply from Major Griffiths, who had served under Crofton in Red River, was in the same strain as that of his senior officer. As to the charge that the Company had recommenced the sale of spirits, he wrote :

Quite untrue, as far as my observation and information extend ; but the Company in a very liberal, although perhaps mistaken spirit, permitted some of these very grumblers to import spirits into the colony from America, a system which had a most pernicious effect during the stay of Her Majesty's troops at the station and which I assisted in getting repealed, in my place in council, previous to my departure.

(Spirits imported from the United States had hitherto paid two shillings a gallon of a supertax. Their importation was now prohibited on pain of confiscation.)

Lord Grey now conveyed to Mr. Isbister the conclusion reached after his careful inquiry, that there was no reason to bring the matter of the oppressions alleged before Parliament.

At this juncture the Hudson's Bay Company was exposed to the view of Parliament, because of the proposal of the Government to grant it Vancouver's Island for colonization. The opponents of the Grant tried to use the complaints against the Company as a reason for at least postponing action. Lord John Russell insisted that there were reasons for the immediate colonization of the island, and that an inquiry into the administration of the Company would involve too great a delay. However, an address of the House of Commons of February 9, 1849, led to all the correspondence concerning the complaints being laid before the House. The opposition to the Company continued after the Grant was made. On July 5, 1849, a motion was made in the House praying Her Majesty to direct that fitting and effectual means should be taken to ascertain the legality of the powers of the Company under its Charter. Lord Grey had a copy of the address transmitted to the Company, with a request for its assistance in complying with the wish of the House. Sir J. H. Pelly replied that the Company would give its assistance, and enclosed a copy of the Charter, a statement of the Company's case, and a map showing both the area claimed under its Charter and the area administered under the licence of 1838. These, along with a letter of inquiry from Mr. Isbister, were transmitted by Lord Grey to the lawyers of the Crown. Their conclusion was that the rights claimed by the Company did properly belong to them, but that, to satisfy all parties, the matter should be publicly argued before a competent tribunal ; that Mr. Isbister should appear as complainant and the Company as respondents ; that Mr. Isbister or some other person should embody the complaints in a petition to Her Majesty ; and that this should be referred to the Judicial Committee of the Privy Council. Lord Grey had Mr. Isbister informed of this report, and asked whether he would appear as complainant ; that the inquiry was to deal with the legality of the rights claimed by the Company. " Any allegations of misuse of their legal powers by the Company must be otherwise dealt with, and could not be inquired into by the tribunal to which the question as to the legal rights of the Company will be referred." Mr. Isbister replied that the address of the House of Commons threw the onus of the inquiry upon Her Majesty's Government, that he accordingly declined to become complainant, but would place such information as he had at the disposal of the Government. Lord Grey replied that the Government had referred the claims of the Company to the lawyers of the Crown, who had reported in favour of their legality, but that they had suggested that the matter be publicly tried, and that Mr. Isbister should appear as complainant. In these circumstances, he asked for a reconsideration of the decision not to appear ; that Her Majesty's Government " must, in the absence of any parties prepared to contest the rights claimed by the Company, assume the opinion of the Law Officers in their favour to be well founded." In a subsequent communication, Mr. Isbister was told that the Government could not undertake the expense of a trial which the Law Officers of the Crown advised them could only result in upholding the Charter.

The Oregon crisis over, the 6th Royal Regiment of Foot was withdrawn from Red River in 1848. That autumn a first detachment of Pensioners, some seventy strong, arrived under Major W. B. Caldwell, followed by as many more in 1849. Major Caldwell bore with him a Commission from the Hudson's Bay Company as Governor of Assiniboia, and Instructions from Lord Grey to report on the administration of the Company in all the matters of which there had been complaint. On 20th September, he presented his Commission and the letter of Instructions to the Council. Alexander Christie ceased to be Governor. Neither Caldwell nor the Pensioners at large won the respect of the community, though the £3,000 a year put in circulation by them was a boon. Alexander Ross says : " In the pensioners we recognized a second edition of the De Meurons ; and the good old Major was so destitute of business habits and of the art to govern, that after a few sittings the council and magistrates refused to act with him ; he was, therefore, superseded merely that the wheels of Government might keep moving. As for the pensioners, all the authorities, civil and military, in the colony, could not keep them within the bounds of order." In appointing Major Caldwell Governor, the Company aimed at separating the colony from the interests of the fur trade and giving it a life of its own. Unfortunately the Major was inefficient, and Ross and a group in the Council took delight in exposing his incompetence. They persuaded Eden Colvile, at the time joint governor with Simpson, to take his place, but the Committee instructed Colvile to leave the Major to function as Governor without interference. Thereafter Caldwell carried on without discredit. He was succeeded by Governor Johnson in 1855.

On May 17, 1849, the unrest among the half-breeds was brought to a head by the prosecution, at the instance of the Company's officials, of Pierre Guillaume Sayer and three others for illicit

trading in furs.   At 9 o'clock in the morning the east bank of the
river above and below Fort Garry, in which the Quarterly Court met,
was crowded with armed men.   Their actions suggested that " a
seditious meeting " was being held.   When it broke up, boats and
canoes were commandeered, and the crowd crossed to the west side
and gathered around the court-house.   A deputation waited on
Sheriff Alexander Ross at his home to announce that they intended
to resist the proceedings of the court.   The deputation accompanied
the sheriff to the court-house as the hour of the trial drew near.   At
11 o'clock the Court assembled, and Sayer was called, but he was in
safe keeping in the midst of the armed crowd.   The Court proceeded
to its other business.   At 1 o'clock Sayer was again called, but did
not appear.   Instead, James Sinclair, Peter Garrioch, and others,
acting as " Delegates of the people," entered the Court and passed
a paper to the Bench.   They were told that they could not appear in
that capacity in a Court of Law.   The Recorder, Thom, explained that,
as things then stood, the Charter gave the Company the monopoly
of the fur trade, and that until that should be changed by an Act of
Parliament, any one trading in furs was transgressing the law.
Sinclair replied that many great men in the Houses of Parliament
entertained great doubts as to the validity of the Charter.   As
evidence of this, he passed to the Bench a copy of the (London)
Times of a date in August, 1848.   (This would have a report of some
debate on the grant of Vancouver's Island to the Company.)   As
there were no lawyers in the Settlement except the Recorder Adam
Thom, in keeping with the practice, the Bench suggested that Sinclair should play the part of lawyer and plead for the defendant.
Adam Thom suggested that Sinclair might act as foreman of the
jury, and Garrioch with him ; that all that was aimed at was a " fair
and impartial trial."   The Delegation retired to consult with its
associates.   After some time, Sinclair reappeared at the bar with
Sayer.   The jury that had sat for the previous case was still in the
box, Donald Gunn, in no sense a partisan of the Company, being
foreman.   Sinclair objected to five of the number, and to eleven
others whose names were called.   With the substitution of five men
satisfactory to Mr. Sinclair, the case proceeded, Sinclair cross-
examining the witnesses.   Sayer's son swore that his father has
been trading with " his relations," and that he had received all save
one skin, which he had trapped himself, as presents in return for
whisky given.   (The usual form of Indian trade, of course.)   One
witness, Antoine Morin, swore that Mr. Harriott, clerk at Fort Garry,
had asked him (Morin), if he intended to go out to trade ; if so, he
would equip him for the purpose.   Alexis Goulet offered like testimony with regard to himself, stating that he was told by Mr. Harriott
not to go near Dr. Todd's post (at White Horse Plain).   (This was,
of course, in keeping with the practice of the Company hitherto.)
The defendant, Sayer, swore that Mr. Harriott advanced him the
equipment for his trade, that he had forbidden him to trade with
the Indians, but had said nothing about the half-breeds.   Chief

Factor John Ballenden denied this, for he had himself forbidden him to trade, had, in fact, told him that if he could not pay his credits with furs, he could do so with salt. On this understanding Mr. Harriott had made the advances. It is significant that Harriott was not placed in the witness-box by Mr. Ballenden. The Company's case was weakened by the facts that they did allow men to trade with the Indians provided the furs were brought to their posts, and that Sayer had brought his furs in to the Company at Fort Garry where he was equipped. Obviously, the objection to Sayer was that he trafficked also with the Americans. It was a mistake to prosecute him on this case. Ballenden should have waited till he was caught trading for export, or travelling with his furs to Kittson's post at Pembina. The verdict of the jury was that Sayer was guilty of trading furs, but the foreman, Donald Gunn, " addressed the Chief Factor John Ballenden Esqr."—(an illustration of the informality of proceedings in the courts of the colony) recommending the defendant " to mercy, as it appeared that he thought he had a right to trade, and as he and others were under the impression that there was a free trade." The Chief Factor replied that the value of the furs in the case was of no moment, that all he desired had been attained in the verdict declaring the trade in furs illicit ; he would ask for no punishment, and would drop the cases against the other three men. As the court was adjourning, one of the jurymen came to the door, gave three cheers, and in a stentorian voice bawled : " Le commerce est libre ! le commerce est libre ! Vive la liberté ! " The trade is free ! Long live liberty ! The cry was taken up by the crowd, and all scattered with the belief that the monopoly was at an end.

The tradition is that J. Louis Riel was a moving spirit throughout the day, and that at some juncture in the presence of the jury he delivered the ultimatum, Sayer must be acquitted within the space of one hour ! The incident brought discredit to Governor Caldwell, for in a personal quarrel he had suspended Captain Foss, his only officer, and thus, in the crisis, there was none to command the Pensioners and overawe the half-breeds, for the Major as Governor had to be among the judges at the trial.

Henceforth the trade was free so far as the half-breeds were concerned. But it must be remembered that they had neither the capital nor the organization to penetrate into the wooded North whence the Company derived its wealth of furs. Bands could wander with their Red River carts up the valley of the Assiniboine, and even to and beyond the Saskatchewan at Prince Albert and Battleford, where they are found in the early 'sixties. Even so, not all their furs went to the United States, for they often found themselves in need of supplies and forced to trade their furs for such at the nearest post of the Company. Wherever they went, the reckless use of liquor in the trade returned, to the demoralization of the Indians.

Apparently, the Governor and Committee had had nothing to do with the initiation of the Sayer case. They were dissatisfied either with the result, or with the action of the local officials in bringing it on. At any rate, Adam Thom was temporarily deprived of his position as Recorder sitting on the Bench, but continued in the humbler position of Clerk of the Court, at the same salary.

In 1850 the Imperial Government's attention was called to the Hudson's Bay Company by no less conspicuous a person than the American ambassador in London. Writing under date of 12th February, Mr. Albert Lawrence, made representations on behalf of the Government of the United States " that the Hudson's Bay Company annually furnish to the Indians on the north-western frontier of the United States large quantities of spirituous liquor, endangering thereby the peace of the border, as well as corrupting the Indians themselves. It has been the policy of the United States to prevent, as much as possible, the use of spirituous liquors among the natives. The interests of Her Majesty's Government are believed to be identical with those of the United States in this respect." Hence the representations. Through Lord Palmerston, the Foreign Minister, and Lord Grey, the statement was submitted to the Company for a reply. Governor Pelly wrote :

To the allegations contained in the remonstrance . . . I have no hesitation in giving the most unqualified denial. . . . The average quantity of spirits annually supplied to each of the frontier posts [that is, having relations with the International Boundary], according to the best information to which I have access at present does not exceed twenty gallons. A small portion of this not very extravagant supply, rendered harmless by dilution, is given to Indians as a " regale " when they bring the produce of hunts to the station, in conformity with a custom of long standing, which it had been found impossible to discontinue without altogether abandoning the fur trade in a large district of the country [the prairie area]. Whether this can endanger the peace of the frontier, I leave your lordship to judge. Far be it from me, however, to say that spirits are not used, and that in large quantities in trade with the Indians. The Hudson's Bay Company are well aware that an illicit traffic in furs is carried on to a great extent within the Company's territories by persons residing, some at Red River Settlement, and others at Pembina within the American frontier ; that the article chiefly used by those persons in this traffic is spirits, and that the furs so procured invariably find their way to the fur-traders at St. Peter's. This is the evil which endangers the peace of the frontier, if it be endangered, and which the Hudson's Bay Company are using every means in their power to suppress ; but their efforts towards this end have been in a great measure neutralised by the encouragement given to it from the American side of the border. . . . Your Lordship will probably be surprised when I inform you that, from the year 1842 to 1849 inclusive, the average quantity annually imported by the Company into the whole of the territories under their control, to the east and west of the Rocky Mountains, is only 4,396 ½ gallons ; a quantity which, if distributed only to the men employed in the service in daily allowances, would amount to less than two table-spoonfuls to each man.

This average is, of course, of the liquor in a concentrated form. It stood at this low level, because the Company had eliminated " rum " from the trade of the great forest area in which it had complete control.

The Company's licence for the exclusive trade of the North-West Territories, as distinct from the chartered area, was due for renewal in 1859. With an element in Red River, whose spokesman in London was Mr. A. K. Isbister, denouncing its administration; with a group in Parliament, led by no less a personage than William Ewart Gladstone, opposed to it, because of the recent grant to it of Vancouver's Island, but above all, with the failure of the Company's scheme for the colonization, due, as has been shown, to its being devised to exclude all but a choice class of well-to-do English settlers and their labourers, the Government would inevitably be forced to hold an inquiry before the renewal. On February 5, 1857, a resolution for a Select Committee " to consider the state of those British Possessions in North America which are under the Administration of the Hudson's Bay Company [meaning the chartered area] or over which they possess a licence to Trade " was adopted by the House of Commons. The Committee as finally constituted consisted of nineteen members, of whom the most conspicuous were, Mr. Labouchere the Colonial Minister, Lord John Russell, Lord Stanley, Mr. Edward Ellice, Sir John Packington, Viscount Goderich, and Messrs. Gladstone, Roebuck, and Lowe. Twenty-four witnesses were called. Sir George Simpson and Edward Ellice gave the case for the Company ; Mr. A. K. Isbister and Rev. G. O. Corbett of the Settlement spoke for the opposition in the colony. A number of men like Lieutenant-Colonel Lefroy, Sir John Richardson, Sir George Back, Bishop Anderson, who had been in the country and who might be expected to give impartial testimony, were called. The inquiry was conducted from three points of view—the administration of the Company in general ; the possibility of settlement on a large scale in Rupert's Land ; and the future of the colony of Vancouver's Island. At present only the question of the administration of the Company will be treated. Later, that of settlement, coupled as it is with the views and hopes of Canada, will be discussed.

One turns to examine the evidence of Mr. A. K. Isbister, who for ten years had been the spearhead of the opposition to the Hudson's Bay Company. But Mr. Isbister in the witness-box proved a very mild gentleman compared with Mr. Isbister, the young lawyer of ten years before, wielding his pen on behalf of his clients. He had not a word to say of the maltreatment of the Indians by the servants of the Company ; nothing about Indians dying of starvation ; nothing of the enormous profits made by the Company. It had already been brought out in evidence that the Company granted sums of money to the missionaries, to their churches and schools. His former assertion that the Company did nothing in this matter was therefore transformed by him into the charge that the sums paid were " sops " to make the missionaries shut their eyes to many matters which occur. Pressed to indicate the " matters " referred to he made no other assertion than that the Company was averse to the Indians adopting a sedentary life in the neighbourhood of the missions. Pressed to show to what extent the Company was demoralizing the Indians with liquor he admitted that it had eliminated liquor from the trade in the northern portions of their territories,

THE DRIFT TOWARDS CONFEDERATION

but stated that this was not so in the region from the Saskatchewan to the frontier. He placed before the Committee the correspondence between the American Ambassador and the British Government on the subject. His main charge was that the Company had stood in the way of the progress of the country. It was preventing the colony from securing an export trade, which, he admitted, could only be a trade in furs. In the abolition of the monopoly and the admission of all to the fur trade he saw the line of progress. Asked whether that would not lead to the demoralizing of the natives with liquor as in the time of the North West Company, he thought not, if properly regulated. A system of licences granted on the condition that no liquor would be used, or, if the country were given to Canada, a body of police stationed at Red River would be safeguard enough. In the course of the cross-examination it was brought out that he had been educated in a school of the Settlement subsidized by the Company, had been in the Company's service as clerk for three years, had left without any disagreement with his employers, and about 1839, when under twenty-one, had passed over to Scotland for his education. He had never returned, and his present knowledge of the country had been gained by correspondence.

Rev. Griffith Owen Corbett gave evidence supporting Isbister. He told of a number of settlers at Portage la Prairie " 50 or 60 miles from the seat of Government." Their attempt to secure a missionary had been checkmated by the Company. He admitted that the reasons given were that " the difficulties would be too great in governing the people there, and also that the people might settle lower down towards the colony of Red River instead of settling so high up on the Assiniboine River," and stated that the people settled at the Portage because of its timber. He told of similar difficulties thrown in the way of settlers at Headingley, "twelve miles from the seat of Government." His inference, natural enough in an enthusiastic missionary, was that the Company was opposed to missions. His bishop, the Right Reverend David Anderson, D.D., took a different view of the attitude of the Company. He told of 13 Anglican mission stations, 11 English clergymen, 3 native clergymen, 19 country-born and native teachers ; of 8,000 to 10,000 Indians receiving Christian instruction ; and of 18 schools and 795 scholars in different parts of Rupert's Land. (The Catholic bishop could have told a like story of the institutions and activities within his diocese.) Coming to finances, Bishop Anderson explained that the diocese was maintained by £380 a year from the estate of Mr. James Leith and £300 a year from the Company. In three places where the missionaries acted as chaplains for the Company £50 a year were received for their services. (In addition the bishop received £100 a year from the Company for his schools.) " The Company have been accustomed to give a free passage in their annual ships to the missionaries of the [Church Missionary Society] proceeding to their territory ; and in various other ways, they have countenanced the labours of the missionaries, so far as the same have not interfered with their trading occupations." The bishop explained that it was difficult to have missionary settlements in the North, because the Indians wandered in search of food and furs. They were, however, recipients of instruction twice a year at their visits to the Company's posts, when they were taught to read and given books to take away with them. Questioned about the Company's attitude towards the establishment of missions at Portage la Prairie and Headingley, Bishop Anderson replied that it was due to the Company's belief that outlying settlements would increase the difficulties and costs of government.

The examination of Sir George Simpson was long and searching. Often it makes amusing reading. The statesmen on the Committee were of the most intelligent in England. Prepossessed with the idea that the Company was the government of a continental domain, they found it hard to grasp the fact that it did not govern. Believing that the Red River Settlement was a colony, they were baffled by the primitive character of its administration. No taxes, no definite postal service, other than the Company's expresses, and none to the United States, empty jails, and no school system ; yet there were magistrates, and the young were being educated. It was brought out clearly that the Company did not pretend to exercise jurisdiction over the Indian tribes, or to stay tribal wars, nor to interfere in the quarrels of Indian with Indian. (Simpson might have made something of the influence of the Factors in favour of peace and of happy relations, not from the point of view of law, but simply to prevent the Indians from being diverted from trapping by the excitement of war.) The Law was not invoked save for crimes against the servants of the Company. The Committee was manifestly puzzled at the land system of the Red River Settlement. Land was advertised as selling at five shillings and seven and six per acre, but was rarely sold. Nearly everybody squatted where they would, and if a half-breed wished for advice as to where to squat, he could get it from the Factor at Fort Garry. The Committee could not conceive of a society in which the people were not concerned about the titles to their lands. They had before them a copy of the regular land title. It required the holder to contribute to the upkeep of the administration and of education, but no such contributions had ever been inflicted on the settlers. The whole land system seemed to discourage settlement, yet any one could enter the settlement and squat on its vacant lands. John M'Lean's *Notes of a Twenty-five Years' Service in the Hudson's Bay Territory* was quoted as saying that one farmer could grow all the produce that the Company purchased. This Simpson denied, saying that the Company took all the produce in the market—grown on but 8,000 acres. A large part of the community did not live on the produce of the farms, but by hunting and fishing.

The Governor proved a very cautious witness. He withheld details until pressed for them. Asked the number of acres brought under cultivation by the Company in Oregon, he could not tell. Asked if it was a hundred acres, he replied, " Five thousand." On the geography and climatic conditions of the country and on the business machine of the Company, he was clear and explicit, but on questions about the Law and about legal procedure he begged to be allowed to refer the Committee to the Recorder, who would be a witness. (The Committee does not seem to have considered it necessary to call the Recorder.) When Simpson was asked if the Charter conferred " a power of government " upon the Company, he referred the Committee to the document itself, a copy of which was produced at the following session. Inquiries as to the terms of the form for leases of land brought the reply that he could not call them to mind, but was willing to produce the form, and he did produce it later.

The Committee was anxious to know how far the Indian population might be decreasing. Simpson replied that it was increasing in the wooded North, but what with wars and small-pox was decreasing in the prairie South. (Lieutenant-Colonel Lefroy, on the contrary, argued that the figures which he had compiled and which he had compared with those of Sir John Franklin rather showed a decline in the North also.) A member of the Committee produced a quotation from Ballantyne's *Hudson's Bay*, giving a lurid picture of starvation and cannibalism at a post within the Arctic Circle. Simpson pointed out that Ballantyne had never been " in that country " * ; cases of cannibalism were " very rare indeed." Instances of starvation were also very rare indeed, though " Indians do starve as whites do sometimes." Sir George Back testified that on his expeditions he had seen Indians who " must have starved without the aid of the Hudson's Bay Company." The Indians " seemed always to feel that they could fall back upon the clemency and the benevolence of the white man at any extremity ; that as long as he had anything to spare in his store the Indian was certain to be relieved." Dr. John Rae, was asked about a statement of Sir George Simpson's that every trading establishment was in fact an Indian hospital. He replied : " Wherever we act as medical men our services are given gratuitously. We go to a distance if the Indian is at a distance, and have taken him to a fort, and he is fed and clothed there. And it is no uncommon thing to hear the old Indians, when unfit for hunting, say, ' We are unfit for work ; we will go and reside at a fort.' That is the ordinary feeling which prevailed in the country."

The Committee was concerned to inquire to what extent the Company had kept the condition of its licence looking to " the gradual diminishing and ultimate preventing the sale or distribution of spirituous liquors to the Indians or for promoting their moral and religious improvement." The general testimony was that in morals and religion the Indians were as they had been, but that there

---

* Robert Michael Ballantyne, the author of many books of adventure for boys, began his career as a writer with the volume *Hudson's Bay*, in which he recorded his own experiences in the country, as well as incidents of which he had but a hearsay knowledge. At sixteen years of age he began a service of six years' duration (1641–47) with the Company. He was at York Fort, Norway House, Red River, and at Tadoussac on the St. Lawrence River, but never in the Mackenzie River valley beyond the Arctic Circle, the region under discussion.

was improvement through the elimination of the traffic in liquor. Sir John Richardson, who had seen the country in the last days of the struggle between the North West and Hudson's Bay companies, and again in 1848 when on an expedition in search of Franklin testified. On the first expedition :

> We found both parties supplying the Indians liberally with spirits. The Indians were spending days in drunkenness at the different posts, and a contest altogether shocking to humanity was carried on. At that time it scarcely appeared that the Indians had any capability of being civilized at all. When we went out on the second occasion, the Hudson's Bay Company having the sole trade of the country, and the sole management of the Indians, there was an improvement ; spirits were no longer carried to the north, or they were carried in small quantities then. I think that at that time the traders themselves were supplied with a little spirits for their own use ; but there was a manifest improvement, although none of the natives of pure blood had become Christians. The missionaries had been out [in the North] for two or three years, but had made no progress beyond converting one or two of the half-caste Indians I believe. Upon the last occasion in 1848 a generation of the Crees had passed away, 25 years having elapsed, and the new generation were mostly able to read and write (all those that I came in contact with) ; many of them were labouring for wages for The Hudson's Bay Company, and altogether the country was peaceable from one end to the other. I saw no riot and nothing unpleasant throughout the whole journey.

Of course, attention was centred on the situation in the South, particularly in the Red River Settlement. Simpson testified that in the forty-five years since union there had been but nineteen cases of homicide " in which, the Hudson's Bay Company's people were concerned " ; in eleven punishment was inflicted. In the matter of spirituous liquors, he assured the Committee that the importation of spirits into the whole country averaged for the ten years past under 5,000 gallons. No spirits were sent into the North, but it had been found necessary to give small quantities to the Indians on the Saskatchewan and at Rainy Lake. Two-thirds of the liquor imported was for sale to the inhabitants of the Settlement, who would otherwise distil. Simpson was unaware of the representations made by the Ambassador of the United States to the Foreign Minister of Britain, charging the Company with reckless distribution of liquor along the International Boundary. Colonel J. F. Crofton, who commanded the troops which went out to the colony in 1846, averred that when in the Settlement he had never heard the Company charged with bartering or giving spirits to the Indians. Only in England had he heard such charges. He attributed the absence of crime to the absence of spirits. Lieutenant-Colonel Lefroy, who had spent two years in the country in scientific investigation, was asked if there had been an effectual check to the use of ardent spirits among the Indians. He replied : " I am confident that there has, over the whole region except the Saskatchewan, where the necessity of meeting the Americans in some degree with their own weapons had obliged a very limited use of spirits, but the rule, if I am not misinformed, was, that for one gallon of rum they put seven gallons of water ;

the spirit issued was so much diluted that it had not much effect."
He admitted that the use of spirits in the trade was prohibited in the
United States, but the law was " evaded constantly." Asked what
was the general character of the agents of the Company, he replied :

I never mingled with a body of men whose general qualities seemed to
me more entitled to respect. They are men of simple primitive habits leading
the most hardy lives ; generally speaking, contented, doing their duty faithfully to their employers, and in many instances taking sincere interest in the
welfare of the Indians around them, and doing all they can to benefit them,
but the Indian is a very difficult subject.

Coming to the unrest of the people in the Settlement, the
Committee probed into the regulations of June 19, 1845, which were
devised to check the growing illicit trade with the United States.
Asked about the regulations, Governor Simpson declared that he
did not even know that they existed ; they must have been local
regulations and disallowed by the Company ; it was, of course,
competent for the Governor and Council of Assiniboia to pass such
regulations, but they would be disallowed by the Governor and
Committee in London. The opposition in the Settlement to the
Company was represented by John McLaughlin, who drew up the
petition of the half-breeds to Congress, though that was not mentioned
in the Committee. McLaughlin admitted that he had been engaged
in a traffic in furs. Pressed to give a definite answer to the question
whether he had ever engaged in the trade of spirits, for himself or
for others, he was not prepared to say that he had not. He admitted
that he had written a letter from England in 1850 urging the half-
breeds to persist in asserting their right to trade in furs, that the
English papers, and above all Parliament, said that they had the full
right to do so. He asserted that he had known cases in which the
Company had refused to equip Indians for their hunt, and thereby
thrown them on the community ; that in one case the influence of
a missionary had been used by the Company to prevent the Indians
from wearing furs (but presumably the Company's blankets instead).
McLaughlin produced a circular issued by Governor Christie requiring
all letters to have the signature of the sender on the envelope, "and
if the writer is not one of those who have lodged a declaration against
trafficking in furs, his letters must be brought open, its enclosures,
if any, being open also, to this office, and here closed." A letter from
R. Lane, clerk at Fort Garry to Mr. McDermott, McLaughlin's uncle,
with whom he was engaged, was produced in the Committee to bring
out the extent to which this drastic regulation was enforced : " As
by the new regulations regarding the posting of letters, it would be
necessary that Mr. McLaughlin should send up his letters open for
my perusal, a thing which cannot be agreeable to him, will you have
the goodness to tell him that in his case I shall consider it quite
sufficient his sealing his letters in my presence without any perusal
on my part, and for that purpose I shall call in at his house to-
morrow evening." In further elucidation, a proclamation of Governor

Christie's was produced, requiring those engaged in importing goods to make an affidavit that they were not engaging in a traffic in furs, and promising a licence to all who made their affidavits, " in order to guard the fair and honest dealer against otherwise unavoidable embarrassment and loss." Another proclamation issued by Governor Christie required persons shipping goods to the ports of the Company to make a declaration that they were not, directly or indirectly, trafficking in furs on their own or any other account. It probably appeared to the Committee that the regulations and the administration of them inflicted no hardship on any settler not engaged in trade in breach of the Company's monopoly ; that the regulations were devised to prevent the free trader from using the facilities offered by the Company, whether in the form of mail or of freightage, in the furtherance of an illicit trade ; that the initiative in the matter had been taken by the Governor and Council of Assiniboia, but that the regulations had ultimately been disallowed by the Governor and Committee in London ; and that the evidence showed that while the regulations were devised to check the illicit trade, the administration of them was in no sense carried on with injustice and harshness.

McLaughlin brought up as a case of injustice inflicted upon an exporter of goods, the experience of Mr. Sinclair of McDermott and Sinclair, in shipping a consignment of tallow to London by way of York Fort. It was not taken on board the ship. Governor Simpson, in his evidence, claimed that not only Sinclair's tallow, but goods of the Company had to be left behind that year, for the ship was not able to take all the freight ; that in the following year, the Company took the tallow off the hands of Mr. Sinclair at the market price.

On the whole, the evidence before the Committee was in favour of the Company. A vast domain was wrapped in profound peace, while Indian wars broke out all too often south of the border. The personnel of the Company commanded, not only the respect of a visitor to the country like Lieutenant-Colonel Lefroy, but the obedience of the natives. Where the Company was in control, no abuses were alleged ; the Indians were cared for, if for no other reason, in the interest of the trade ; the natives looked on the fort as a refuge in days of stress, and a place of shelter in sickness and old age. Such unrest as existed was in the neighbourhood of the International Boundary. It was due to the opportunities for carrying on a free trade in furs with the United States. The report of the Committee to the House of Commons ran :

11. As to those extensive regions, whether in Rupert's Land or in the Indian Territory, in which, for the present at least, there can be no prospect of permanent settlement, to any extent, by the European race for the purposes of colonization, the opinion at which your Committee have arrived is founded on the following considerations : 1st. The great importance to the more peopled portions of British North America that law and order should, as far as possible, be maintained in these territories ; 2nd. The fatal effects which they believe would infallibly result to the Indian population from a system of open competition in the fur trade, and the consequent introduction of

spirits in a far greater degree than is the case at present ; and 3d. The probability of the indiscriminate destructions of the more valuable fur-bearing
animals in the course of a few years. 12. For these reasons your Committee
are of opinion that whatever may be the validity or otherwise of the rights
claimed by the Hudson's Bay Company, under the Charter, it is desirable
that they should continue to enjoy the privilege of exclusive trade, which
they now possess, except so far as those privileges are limited by the foregoing
recommendations.

That is, the recommendation that the Grant of Vancouver's Island
to the Company be revoked, which has been treated already, and
that it should be open for Canada to settle areas capable of maintaining a population, and to take upon itself the task of installing governing institutions.

2.—CANADA'S GROWING INTEREST IN THE NORTH-WEST, 1840–64

The Oregon question awakened a fresh interest in the Canadian
North-West. The rush of American immigrants into a vacant land
and the formation of a provisional government by the settlers claiming the country for the United States had made the region American.
It has been seen that the British Government had granted Vancouver's Island to the Hudson's Bay Company simply to prevent
the repetition of the story in that region in spite of the international
treaty fixing the boundary. The fear that a rush of American immigrants into the vacant spaces of Rupert's Land might sweep the
West into the United States awakened the Canadians to the possibility of their West being lost to Britain and to them, and they
recoiled from the thought that Canada might become no more than
a British colony on the Atlantic, hemmed in by the Republic to the
south and to the west. In 1847, within a year of the settlement of
the Oregon boundary, the *Toronto Globe*, edited by George Brown,
published in full a lecture of Robert Baldwin Sullivan, in which this
fear was loudly voiced.

Concurrently, the danger of war between Britain and America
over the Oregon question raised issues in which the Canadian
West figured greatly. Captain Millington Henry Synge, of the
Royal Engineers, stationed in Canada at the time, was deeply
impressed with the hostility of the American public as observed
during his passage through the United States. Addressing himself
to the problem of defending the colonies of British North America,
he found it hopeless, for they were so many scattered self-dependent
units without the means of communication essential for successful
defence. In his pamphlet, *Canada in 1848*, he drew attention to this
and advocated the scheme of a railway from Atlantic to Pacific
which would make their defence possible. Simultaneously Major
Robert Carmichael-Smythe was preparing, *A Letter, from Major
Robert Carmichael-Smythe to his friend the author of "the Clockmaker,"
containing thoughts on the subject of a British Colonial Railway Com-*

munication between the Atlantic and the Pacific (1849). In 1838 he had crossed from Halifax, Nova Scotia, to England on a sailing ship in company with Judge Haliburton, the author of *The Clockmaker*, and Joseph Howe. Their ship had been overtaken by the steamship *Syrius*, from New York, to which, for speed's sake, the mails were transferred. It had been agreed among them there and then that their first effort in England should be to secure a British steamship line to Halifax. As Carmichael-Smythe wrote in 1849, it existed in the Cunard Line. His pamphlet calls for the completion of the scheme by building a railway from Atlantic to Pacific, and by placing steamship lines on the Pacific to run to Australia and China, thus consolidating Britain's power in the distant parts of the Empire and of the world. While his arguments are wholly commercial, he has the military situation in view, for he pictures the Minister of War in Britain sending out the troops by rail in all directions to the defence of the island, and he argues that she should be able to do the same in America, and thence by steamships to Australia and the Far East. He urges that the several colonies, or at least the several settled areas, should build the railway through their regions and have shares in the unified scheme equal to the expenditures made, and that the mother-country should build through the unoccupied regions. The construction would be easily borne if convict labour were used ; the factories of England would be kept busy providing the material ; and the commercial returns would make the enterprise profitable from the point of view of the nation.

Concurrently, a Major F. A. Wilson and a lawyer Alfred B. Richards, conscious of the menace of the expansion of the United States, but more interested in the distresses of England and its over-population, were working at the same theme. The title of their volume, *Britain redeemed, and Canada preserved*, 1850, sums up their ideas—the distresses of England relieved by the emigration of the poor to Canada, and Canada preserved for the Empire by a trans-continental railway the instrument of its colonization. In 1852, Captain Synge returned to his theme in a pamphlet entitled, *Britain one empire ; on the union of the Dominions of Great Britain by inter-communication with the Pacific and the east, via British North America, with suggestions for the profitable colonization of that wealthy territory.*

In Canada the English section was increasingly interested in the fate of the Canadian West, while the French in Quebec gave it little or no thought. Other voices than that of George Brown in the *Globe* began to be heard. Sheriff Treadwell of L'Orignal, on a part of the Ottawa River, where the old Northwesters were still to be found living in retirement, as early as 1844, was dreaming of a railway from the Atlantic to the Pacific. In 1853 he laid his views before the Colonial Minister, the Duke of Newcastle, through the Governor-General, Lord Elgin. In 1856 William Kennedy was securing an interested hearing in different parts of Ontario. Born at Cumberland House, where his father was Chief Factor, he had himself entered the service of the Hudson's Bay Company as clerk at the Ungava post (Fort Chimo). He had been recommended by the Company to Lady Franklin as a fit person to be in charge of the second expedition of the *Prince Albert* in search of Sir John, which was to try to reach him by travelling with dog sleds over the ice to Wellington Channel, where it appeared from the previous voyage of the *Prince Albert* Sir John Franklin had spent the winter of 1845–46. From about 1854 Kennedy moved about Upper Canada, lecturing on his Arctic experiences and on temperance, and in 1856 he associated himself with a group of capitalists in Toronto in a scheme to enter into the fur trade of the North-West. He seems to have spent the winter of 1856–57 in the fur region somewhere, but nothing ever came of the would-be new North West Company.

By 1856 the interest in the North-West had grown sufficiently to be discussed in a confidential dispatch from Sir Edmund Head to the Colonial Office. " All sorts of dreams and speculations are floating in the public mind here, even among sober and good men. We do not, as I have told them, now govern properly the territory belonging to Canada, but it seems to be assumed in some of the papers that there is an inherent right on the part of Canada to some of the spoils of the Hudson's Bay Company. I do not know accurately the legal position of this body, but I should not be surprised if the subject were to be talked of in our Legislature." Sir Edmund suggested that steps should be taken to constitute a commission to lay down the International Boundary west of Lake Superior. On 4th December following, Henry Labouchere, Secretary of State for the Colonies, wrote to Sir Edmund informing him of the inquiry of the Committee of the House of Commons into the " affairs of the Hudson's Bay Company." As many points affecting the interests of Canada might be raised, he asked whether the Canadian Government might think it desirable to be represented by witnesses or in any other manner. This dispatch opened the flood-gates of discussion in the colonial legislature and in the colony at large. On March 5, 1857, a petition from the Municipal Council of the united counties of Lanark and Renfrew was read in the legislature, praying that measures should be taken to impress on the British Government the necessity of its assuming the possession of the Hudson's Bay Territory, and establishing the boundary line between it and the United States. A petition from the Municipal Council of Argenteuil was read on 18th March, praying that the Red River Settlement be incorporated within the limits of Canada. The next day a petition was read from James Thompson and others of the counties of Lanark and Renfrew, pleading that the Hudson's Bay Territory be annexed to and form a part of Canada. On 15th April a petition from the Board of Trade of Toronto was presented, asking that the licence of exclusive trade be not renewed to the Company ; that the westward and northward boundaries of Canada be defined ; and that the protecting arm of Canadian laws and the benefits of Canadian institutions be extended throughout the Hudson's Bay Territory.

On 11th May it was ordered that a Select Committee of which

Mr. George Brown and Mr. Joseph Cauchon, the Commissioner of
Crown Lands, were named members, be appointed to receive and
collect evidence as to the rights of the Hudson's Bay Company under
its Charter ; as to the renewal of the licence ; and finally as to the
soil and climate of its territory.   To this committee the various
petitions were referred, including a petition from Roderick Kennedy
and others, inhabitants and natives of Red River Settlement, com-
plaining of various grievances, and praying for the protection of the
Canadian Government.   The inquiry of the Committee was of the
most superficial.   Of the three witnesses, one only, George Gladman,
knew Rupert's Land personally.   Most of his period of service with
the Company was spent in the Southern Department around James
Bay, in a country even now without agricultural settlement.   When
in the Northern Department at Cumberland House he saw excellent
wheat grown and ground to flour in a steel handmill.   He was at
Red River Settlement in 1841, and he gave a good report of its
agriculture.   At Norway House good potatoes were grown.   The
next witness, Alan Macdonell, was one of those who the year before
had taken steps to form a new North West Company.   He believed
that if the old North West Company had made large profits when
the transportation to Lake Superior was with canoes, still larger
profits could be made with a steamship service.   One canoe of furs
was expected to come out by this route that summer.   " If the route
was opened from Lake Superior, he had no doubt but the whole
trade of that country would come down Lake Superior."   Whether
the country was a fine one for agriculture or not was immaterial;
the question was whether the Hudson's Bay Company should be
allowed to go on enjoying its monopoly.   William McD. Dawson,
head of the Woods and Forests branch of the Crown Lands Department, entered more into the legal title of the Hudson's Bay Company
to the rights claimed by it.

Meanwhile a movement in the military sphere must have greatly
enhanced the interest of the Canadians in the Red River Settlement.
In the autumn of 1856 a party of American soldiers reached the
International Boundary at Pembina, and its commander, Colonel
C. F. Smith, prohibited the half-breeds of the British territory to
cross the line to hunt buffalo.   The matter was at once reported by
the Hudson's Bay Company to the Imperial Government, with the
request for a small military force to be stationed at the Red River
Settlement, " to serve as a counterpoise to the growing influence
of the United States in the North-West Territory."   It was decided
that the British garrison regiments would not be suitable, as the
men were mostly married ; that the Canadian Rifles should be sent
to the number of 100 to 120, officers and men.   The route by Lake
Superior was regarded as impossible.   The troops sailed from Quebec
on June 23, 1857, and arrived at York Factory by way of Hudson
Strait about September 25th, after a very happy voyage ; it reached
Red River in October.   It was understood that the troops were
stationed there for imperial purposes, and that they were not at the

disposal of the Company to hold down the half-breeds. They were, however, of great service in keeping a large band of Sioux who made an incursion to Fort Garry in 1860 under control. The presence of these young Canadians in the colony gave so many Canadian families an intimate relationship with a land which since 1821 had become a foreign country.

The Colonial Secretary's dispatch giving the Canadian Government the opportunity to be represented at the inquiry into the Hudson's Bay Company was duly laid before the Council, which drew up a minute expressing its great satisfaction and adding : " The general feeling here is strongly that the Western Boundary of Canada extends to the Pacific Ocean." In transmitting the minute to the Colonial Minister Sir Edmund Head ventured to add : " At the same time, I desire to observe that I express no opinion of my own as to the fact that the Western boundary of Canada extends to the Pacific Ocean." The preparation of evidence for the Select Committee of the House of Commons took two forms. Mr. Dawson prepared a map to illustrate the claims of Canada. The Western Boundary was placed at the Pacific coast, and the position of the natural resources of the North-West, its fertile lands, woods, gold, coal, and the like, were entered as indicated by travellers. The intention was to place the map before the Select Committee, but it proved so ridiculous that it was destroyed, save for seven copies. Mr. Joseph Cauchon, Commissioner of Crown Lands, prepared a memorandum in which all the old French claims to the Hudson's Bay Company's Territory are revived. These are reinforced by the claims of the North West Company that the West was discovered and occupied by the French, notably by La Vérendrye, and by the English from Montreal. The whole country, except the region in the neighbourhood of the Company's posts on Hudson Bay, belonged to Canada. Coming to the boundaries of Canada, Cauchon found his argument in difficulties over the preamble of the Quebec Act, which traced the boundary on the west up the Mississippi " Northward to the Southern boundary of the Territory granted to the Merchant Adventurers of England trading to Hudson's Bay." He argued that this does not mean due north, and inferred that only in a general way northward was intended. He quietly assumed that the claim of the Pacific Ocean for the West Boundary of Canada is compatible with the language of the Quebec Act. The truth is that any northerly line from the Mississippi, even to the strip along Hudson Bay, which Cauchon conceded might belong to the Company, would place the Red River and the prairie north-west beyond the boundaries of Canada. Cauchon's final argument runs that the prairie region is really " Indian Territory," and outside of the chartered territory ; it is really in the hands of the Crown.

Inasmuch as the Canadian claims were to rest largely on legal grounds, on denial of the validity of the Charter, and on the plea that Red River Settlement was not included in the chartered area, Chief Justice Draper was chosen to represent the colony before the Committee. His Instructions were drafted on a much more modest scale than the claims asserted for the colony by Mr. Cauchon. He was not authorized to negotiate or to agree to any definite plan. He was simply to impress upon the Committee " the importance of securing the North-West Territory against the sudden and unauthorized influx of immigration from the United States' side," and the expediency of marking the limits " until the advancing tide of emigrants from Canada and the United Kingdom may fairly flow into them, and occupy them as subjects of the Queen, on behalf of the British Empire." With this end in view there should be no renewal of the Company's licence, which was, apparently, considered as giving the Company the exclusive trade of the Indian Territory, interpreted as including the Red River region and the prairies. Apart from this, Mr. Justice Draper was free to follow his own discretion. Accordingly, he asked the Committee to grant to Canada " a free right to explore and survey, in order to ascertain the capabilities of the country, as well as the right to open up communications and to place settlers along the roads." As fast as Canada should be able to effect settlements and establish townships, the areas thus organized should be incorporated into that colony—the western limit to be the Rocky Mountains. This was readily granted by the Committee, which reported in this sense, adding: " In case, however, Canada should not be willing at a very early period to undertake the government of the Red River District, it may be proper to consider whether some temporary provision for its administration should not be advisable," presumably by erecting it into a Crown Colony.

Mr. Draper, very astutely, did not put in a plea that the validity of the Charter should be put to the test of law, but asked that the boundary between Canada and the Hudson's Bay Company Territory should be determined by Her Majesty's Government. In a letter to John Shepherd, Governor of the Hudson's Bay Company, Under Secretary of State Herman Merivale, on January 20, 1858, suggested that the question of the boundary should be settled by a reference in some form to the Judicial Committee of the Privy Council; should, however, Canada not enter a plea before Privy Council, a Commission composed of representatives of Her Majesty's Government of Canada and of the Company could be formed to define the boundary. To both these proposals Mr. Shepherd agreed, expressing the willingness to surrender to the Crown such parts as Canada should choose to settle. The assumption, of course, was that there would be compensation. But from the point of view of Canada the compensation would be nil if the Charter were invalid. Accordingly on 13th August the Canadian Parliament agreed to an address to Her Majesty praying for the immediate settlement of the boundary line by the Judicial Committee of the Privy Council, adding the rider, " without restriction as to any question Canada may deem it proper to present on the validity of the said Charter or for the maintenance of her rights." The new Colonial Secretary, Sir Edward Bulwer Lytton, now inquired of the Hudson's Bay

Company whether it would assent to an inquiry into the validity of the Charter before the Judicial Committee. In the mind of the Company this was a very different proposal from that first made, namely, an inquiry into the boundary. The answer given was accordingly : " This Company cannot be a consenting party to any proceeding which is to call in question rights so long established and recognized, but they will, of course, be prepared to protect themselves against any attempt that may be made on the part of the Canadian authorities to deprive them, without compensation, of any portion of the territory they have so long been in possession of." In a word, the Company would not voluntarily submit its case, but it could not prevent Canada from forcing it to appear before the Judicial Committee.

Sir Edward Bulwer Lytton now consulted the lawyers of the Crown as to procedure. They must have taken the view, as in the matter of Mr. A. K. Isbister, that the Crown, having acted as though the Charter was valid through past generations, could not properly enter a case before the Privy Council. They stated that the proper course was for Canada to do so. On 22nd December Lord Lytton communicated their decision to the Governor-General of Canada. On January 28, 1859, he informed the Company that the Government was not prepared to grant the renewal of the licence for a term of years, but was willing to issue a fresh licence for one year. The Company declined to accept the proposal. Lord Lytton then offered a renewal for two years. This was declined and the licence expired. The truth is that the Company had an effective monopoly of the North-West, licence or no licence, and felt sure that this situation would continue unchanged. The most valuable feature in the licence had been that the validity of the Charter as covering Rupert's Land had been recognized when the licence was granted for the North-West Territory beyond. The North-West Territory had not passed out of the control of the Crown, only the control of its trade, which now legally reverted to the Government, but in fact remained with the Company. On April 29, 1859, the Parliament of Canada passed a Joint Address to Her Majesty that Canada ought not to be called on to litigate the question of the validity of the Charter, that the disposition of the British territory in question really lay in the hands of the Imperial Government. Thus the Charter never came to the test of law. Her Majesty's Government continued as of old to treat it as valid. To the Canadian Government it was invalid, or if valid, applied only to the shores of Hudson Bay.

The Select Committee of 1857 spent much time inquiring into the agricultural possibilities of Rupert's Land. Witness after witness testified to having seen potatoes, or barley, or wheat, growing at one place and another all the way up to the Arctic Circle in the valley of the Mackenzie River, but obviously the real questions were: Could the crops be grown with sufficient certainty to support settlement, and on a large enough scale to give a stable export, and, if so, could the produce be transported to the world market on a paying basis ?

We now know that agricultural settlement in the West had three major problems to solve—transportation, farming under drought conditions, and the visitations of frost as early as the last week of August. The lack of facilities for transporting such a bulky and cheap commodity as wheat had hitherto prevented the grain growers of the Red River Settlement from entering the English market. When the Committee sat, it was a certainty that railways could connect them with the outside world. Could they then produce with certainty a wheat of such quality as to give them a place in the world market? At this time the grain demanded by the millers was winter wheat, for it made a fine white flour. Miles Macdonell discovered that winter wheat would not grow at Red River. It does not grow now. The spring wheat of the Red River would not have been in great demand in the world market, indeed, might not have paid for its export. It was not until the late 'seventies that changes were introduced in the flour mills by which spring wheat could be made to produce as fine a flour as winter wheat. Moreover, the wheat of Red River took on the average 135 days to mature unto the harvest. In favourable seasons it was garnered in the last week of August, but as often as not, deep in September, when the frosts, forerunners of autumn, would damage, if not destroy it. When Captain Palliser was in the country in 1858, he was told that the wheat at the mouth of Winnipeg River had come to maturity that year in what worked out at 159 days. In 1855, two years before the Select Committee sat, the wheat was planted at Edmonton House in the last days of April and the first of May, and was being harvested in the last days of September and the first of October—153 days later. We now know that it was the introduction in the 'eighties of Red Fife—an early maturing wheat, taking on the average 125 days, but often 115—which gave the western farmers some security against the early autumn frosts. This wheat began to be grown in the neighbourhood of Peterborough, Upper Canada, in the early 'forties, and, when the Committee sat, had not yet attracted the attention of the public. A cross of Red Fife with an Indian wheat, Red Calcutta, produced Marquis wheat, which matures six days earlier than Red Fife. Introduced in 1911, it still farther insured the farmers of the West against early frost. Even so, Marquis does not mature early enough to assuredly escape the frosts of the northern part of the prairie region in Saskatchewan. In the light of the hard experiences of the settlers of the West, the assumption of a witness like A. K. Isbister—that, because wheat (of a kind) was grown on many parts of the West, the country could support a great agricultural population—was ignorant optimism. Sir George Simpson's evidence came nearest to realities as they were experienced at that time. Of course, he knew more of the country as a whole than all the other witnesses put together. Asked about the possibilities of the Red River region for wheat-growing, he replied : " The banks of the river are alluvial and produce very fair crops of wheat ; but these crops are frequently destroyed by early frosts ; there is no certainty of the crops. We have been under the necessity of importing grain within these last ten years from the United States and from Canada for the support of the establishment." Asked about the Saskatchewan country, he replied : "There is alluvial soil on the River Saskatchewan and the frosts are earlier than at Red River." The attempt was made to discount this evidence by quoting a florid passage from his book, *A Journey round the World*, describing the beauties of the Rainy River (which nearly all the passers-by enlarge upon), but Simpson stood by his statements as above. His evidence has been discounted on the general ground that he was a fur-trader, and hostile to settlement, and he may well have been influenced by his interest in the fur trade. None the less, his statements were based on the actual situation, as it was in his time.

Both the Imperial and the Canadian Governments took steps to acquire a more certain knowledge of the country. On March 31, 1857, Captain John Palliser, who had spent a season ten years before hunting on the American prairies, was given instructions to proceed by the Great Lakes and Fort William to Fort Garry and the prairie region, and to report on the country. Palliser and Dr. Hector, his botanist, individually or together, examined the valley of the Red River, the region of the International Boundary as far west as Turtle Mountain, and the whole valley of the Assiniboine as far as Fort Pelly. The country south of the Qu'Appelle was traversed to the Elbow of the South Saskatchewan, whose valley was crossed to winter quarters at Fort Carlton. That autumn Captain Palliser returned to the United States, but rejoined his expedition in the spring, taking care to examine the country between the Assiniboine and the South Saskatchewan by different routes as he went and came. In 1858 the valleys of the North and South Saskatchewan, including the Battle, Red Deer, and Bow rivers, were examined, and the passes of the Rockies which might be serviceable for a railway. Captain Palliser finally reached the coast by Kootenay Pass and the Columbia River. His description of the prairie region as three prairie levels—or steppes, as he calls them—may be said to have become public property. More important is his division of the country agriculturally into a fertile belt and semi-arid plains. He traced the line between the two as running south of the Battle River to the Eagle Hills, crossing the South Saskatchewan south of Moose Woods, and thence curving south-easterly, then eastward to Moose Mountain, and finally south-easterly to Turtle Mountain. From information received, he drew the southerly limits of the forest as following the North Saskatchewan some distance to the north as far as Carlton House, crossing that river and the South Saskatchewan in the neighbourhood of the present Prince Albert, and thence running south-eastward to follow the Assiniboine to the Duck Mountains. Palliser regarded the area between the true prairie on the South and the forest of the North as a fertile belt, capable of settlement. He believed that the area had once been a great forest, to which circumstance the fine mould on the surface was due. While now open prairie, there was enough wood to hand to support settlement.

South of this was the true prairie, which, in contrast to the prairie
on the Red River, was semi-arid—a protrusion of the American desert
into British territory.   Moreover, the lack of wood forbade settlement.   Writing on May 20, 1859, in answer to questions raised by
Lord Lytton, then Colonial Minister, he said of the Red River Settlement that a colony was necessary to keep the country British, and
to act as a link to connect the British North America colonies on the
east with the colonies on the Pacific coast.   " The chief wealth of the
agriculturist would be derived from the rearing of cattle ;   large
quantities of very nutritious grasses abound everywhere.   Hemp,
flax and hops grow admirably."   (It is remarkable that wheat is
not in his picture.)   The boundaries of the Crown Colony proposed
by the Government should be the 49th parallel of latitude, the Rocky
Mountains, the 54th parallel of latitude, and the Lake of the Woods
water-way to Lake Winnipeg.   The Hudson's Bay Company would
not be capable of governing such a colony successfully ;   " The Indians
they govern well through the medium of the trading shop ;   but the
interests of a commercial community, which at all events must be
adverse to their own, would not be likely to prosper under their
rule."
     As to the means of access, the egress and ingress would be through
the United States, the routes by York Factory and Fort William
being " too tedious, difficult and expensive for the generality of
settlers."   Finally a railway could easily be built from the Red
River to the Rockies, the best route westward being, probably, in
the neighbourhood of the South Saskatchewan.   Passes across the
Rockies were available for wagon roads, particularly the Vermilion
Pass.   " The project of a railroad by this route across the Rockies
might be reasonably entertained."   (Palliser's party had not yet
explored British Columbia west of the valley of the Columbia.)
Palliser regarded the Red River, Swan River, and Saskatchewan
districts as the areas most eligible for settlement.
     Simultaneously, expeditions sent out by the Canadian Govern-
ment were exploring the country.   The first year was naturally
given to a careful investigation of the region between Lake Superior
and the Red River—a region through which Canadian settlers
would have to penetrate to reach the " fertile belt."   Mr. James
Ross, member of the Canadian Parliament and interested in the
Grand Trunk Railway, had jauntily given the Select Committee
an ideal picture of a railway extending from Lake Huron to the
Red River round Lake Superior, with settlements along the way.
Ross's picture has not yet been realized, for much of the country is
rock and swamp.   In the country between Lake Superior and Lake
of the Woods the Canadian expedition necessarily confined its
attention to the water-ways which might be used by settlers passing
through to the Red River Settlement.   S. J. Dawson, the surveyor,
spent two years at this task.   Of the two routes—that by Grand
Portage and along the International Boundary, and that by Fort
William—he found the latter, though longer, by far the more practic-

able. Improvements suggested were a road from Thunder Bay to
Dog Lake, 22½ miles, to avoid the wild rapids of the Kaministikwia
River ; a dam at the inflow of Dog River into the lake, deepening
the water almost to the height of land ; a road across the watershed
(5 miles) ; and finally another dam, which would make the River
Seine, flowing westward, easy navigation for 65 miles.   Improvements of this kind, he thought, would make an easy water-way cum
portages to Fort Frances on Rainy River.   Thence a small steamer
could be used to the northern end of Lake of the Woods, whence a
road should be built westward to Red River Settlement.   In 1858
Dawson and his officers observed the country around lakes Manitoba
and Winnipegosis as far as the stretch of the Saskatchewan from
Cedar Lake to Grand Rapids and Lake Winnipeg.   It was thought
for the most part to be good farming land, but wooded, except at the
south, and not likely to be occupied in the immediate future.

To Professor H. Y. Hind of the University of Toronto was entrusted the task of observation farther west. In general, he was more
anxious to find the country fertile than Captain Palliser. Of necessity
he accepted the Captain's findings concerning the fertile belt west
of the South Saskatchewan, beyond which he did not go. He put
the semi-arid plains farther to the west than Palliser did. " The
boundary of the prairie country, properly so called, may be roughly
shown by a line drawn from the great bend of the Little Souris or
Mouse River, to the Qu'Appelle Mission (on the Qu'Appelle lakes)
and from the Mission to the Moose Woods on the South branch."
South and west of this line he did not consider " fitted for the permanent habitations of civilized man."   In the treeless area east of this
line he felt, as did Palliser, that the lack of wood would be a serious
obstacle to settlement, but he believed that the country would grow
up in woods if it could be preserved from fire. His estimate of the
arable land was exceedingly modest :

	Acres.
Red River and Assiniboine Prairies east of Prairie Portage . . .	1,500,000
Eastern water-shed of the Assiniboine and La Rivière Salé . . .	3,500,000
Long Creek and the Forks of the Saskatchewan	600,000
Between Carrot River and the Main Saskatchewan.	3,000,000
The Touchwood Hills Range, the Moose Woods	500,000
Mouse River, Qu'Appelle River, White Sand River.	1,000,000
The region about the headwaters of the Assiniboine, including the valley of Swan River.	1,000,000

Total area of arable land of first quality . 11,100,000

Hind was much more interested in the problem of transportation
than was Palliser. He sent a party down the Qu'Appelle River to
ascertain its value as a water-way. He himself passed westward to
the South Saskatchewan at the Elbow, and was inclined to believe
that the waters of that magnificent stream could, at no impossible
expense, be diverted into the Qu'Appelle to create a grand water-way
from the Red River Settlement westward. He followed the South
Saskatchewan down to Fort à la Corne, whence he returned to the

Settlement over land to view the country, but he sent a party under Mr. John Fleming down the main Saskatchewan to Lake Winnipeg to gauge the possibilities of that great stream as a water-way. The main obstacle was found to be the Grand Rapids, two miles from the inflow of the river into Lake Winnipeg. On the way down Mr. Fleming met Mr. Christie of the Hudson's Bay Company on his way to his new post, Edmonton House. From him he ascertained that 167 York boats had passed Norway House that year (1858) carrying upwards of 800 tons. Mr. Dawson's view was that a small steamer could pass from Red River Settlement by our Dauphin (his Little Saskatchewan) River to Lake Manitoba, and another over Lake Winnipegosis up the Swan River to the fertile belt.

Meanwhile the interest of the Canadian public was steadily increasing. George Brown, through the *Globe*, was gaining a more sympathetic hearing, and William McDougall—whose paper, the *North American*, was later merged with the *Globe*, and who was associated with Brown during the following years—became a strong advocate of the annexation of the West. Sheriff Treadwell published pamphlets ; in 1858 Alexander Morris delivered lectures in Montreal and elsewhere, and in 1862, in his place in the legislature, championed the cause. Colonel Synge returned to the charge by attacking the Hudson's Bay Company in his pamphlet, *The Colony of Rupert's Land*, 1863.

But there were two great obstacles in the way of the realization of the Canadian dream—the one physical and the other political. The physical obstacle lay in the territory between Lake Superior and the Red River, a land of rocky hillocks, swamps, and lakes. If the Canadians were to capture the trade of the Settlement they must open up a line of transportation through this forbidding country. It made matters worse that American railways were approaching St. Paul and that the route from that point to the Red River was over the open prairie. None the less, the Canadians made a brave attempt. The Northwest Transportation Navigation and Railway Company was incorporated in 1858, with William McD. Dawson and Alan Macdonell for its leading spirits. A steamer, the *Rescue*, was placed on the Great Lakes to ply between Collingwood and Fort William, and attempts were made to improve the water-way westward to the Red River. The Company was subsidized by the Government to provide a bi-monthly mail in summer, and in winter a monthly service. The discovery of gold on the Fraser River and the rising importance of the two Pacific colonies, British Columbia and Vancouver's Island, offered some chance of the Imperial Government subsidizing a transcontinental mail. The Company offered to deliver letters twice a month at Fort Langley near the mouth of the Fraser in twelve days from Toronto (it held out the bait of a subsequent telegraph line) for an annual subsidy of £50,000, or in fourteen days for £40,000. The decision of the British Postmaster-General was that the mail would not warrant the expenditure. That his decision was in keeping with the facts was shown by the fate of the

Canadian mails to the Red River. In 1859–60 the winter mail was discontinued. The next summer mail arrived in the Settlement on June 24, 1860. It was carried by five men, and consisted of four newspapers. An earlier mail from St. Paul brought in 252 letters and 230 newspapers. Not till the Canadians should penetrate through the rocky belt between Fort William and Red River by a railway would they capture the business of the Red River Settlement; without at least the promise of vital connection, there could be no hope of Canada annexing the country.

The political obstacle in the way of Canada acquiring the West was, for the moment, no less insuperable than the rocky belt between Lake Superior and the Red River. George Brown was seeking to destroy the balance between Upper and Lower Canada, which was issuing in political deadlock in the legislature. He was advocating representation by population, assured that it would give Upper Canada a predominant position and would enable it to impose its will on French Lower Canada. This would, of course, be doubly assured if the West were annexed to Canada and filled with immigrants, for it would be but an expansion of Anglo-Saxon Upper Canada. Quebec naturally stood to defend itself and remained staunch against the acquisition of the West. The situation in 1859 is laid bare in a letter from Mr. Isbister, in London, to Donald Gunn of the Red River Settlement, published in the first number of the *Nor'Wester*, a newspaper which was started in December of that year.

I brought before [Lord Lytton] the views of yourself and of the public meeting held last autumn in favour of annexation to Canada. This, however, I found to have been unnecessary. I found him quite as much of an annexationist as yourself—being only too happy to give over the whole territory to Canada and be rid of the responsibility of governing an immense region, so distant and so inaccessible, and so peculiarly situated. He had not simply offered the country to the Canadian Government—he had pressed it over and over again upon their acceptance ; but without success. M. Cartier, the Canadian Prime Minister, was over here last autumn, and seems to have satisfied Sir Edward of the hopelessness of annexation. He told him very frankly that, as head of the Lower Canadian party, any proposal of the kind would meet with determined opposition, as it would be putting a political extinguisher upon the party and the Province he represented and, if carried out, would lead to a dissolution of the Union. . . . The Territory taken from the Company should be erected into a separate colony, to form part of a general federation of the British Provinces.

The question entered a new phase when the Duke of Newcastle succeeded Lord Lytton at the Colonial Office in June 1859. As Colonial Minister, Newcastle accompanied the Prince of Wales on his visit to the United States and Canada. He was greatly impressed by the hostility of the American public to Britain and Canada, a hostility easily perceived behind the festivities with which the Prince was received. He became gravely aware of the indefensible position of the British American colonies lying separate and without railway connection along the American border, yet united by a firm loyalty to the Crown. He devoted the remainder of his active life (he died in 1864) to preparing the way for the union of the colonies in North America in a great Confederation. In keeping with this policy, he devoted much attention to the creation of a Crown Colony in Rupert's Land which should be a connecting link with British Columbia and Vancouver's Island—the colonies on the Pacific. At his elbow stood Edward Watkin. In 1861 Watkin became president of the Grand Trunk Railway, whose shareholders were for the most part in England. He believed that the railway could escape from its financial embarrassment by expansion. To him the ultimate goal of the line was a transcontinental from Atlantic to Pacific. Hence his advocacy of the Intercolonial Railway to connect the Maritime Provinces with Canada and of a telegraph line and wagon road across the prairies to British Columbia, which would pre-empt the West for his railway. Thus Newcastle and Watkin were working along parallel lines to one great objective, a British North American Confederation, which in virtue of its unity and its railway connections could hold its own against aggression from the south. It added a grim earnestness to their activity that Britain was brought to the verge of war with the United States by the seizure of Messrs. Slidel and Mason, envoys of the Southern States, on the deck of the British mail ship *Trent*. This is not the place to enlarge upon the part played by these men in doing the spadework necessary for laying the foundations of the Confederation. Watkin says of the Duke :

> While failing health and the Duke's premature decease left to Mr. Cardwell and W. E. Forster—and afterwards to Lord Carnarvon and the Duke of Buckingham—the completion of the work before the English Parliament, it was he who stood in the gap and formed and moulded, with a patience and persistence admirable to behold, Cabinet opinion both in England and in the Provinces.

When Messrs. Sicotte and Howland, along with Joseph Howe and Leonard Tilley of the Maritime Provinces, were in England in 1862 as delegates to negotiate about the Intercolonial Railway and the transcontinental telegraph, the Duke of Newcastle got his own evidence of the reluctance of Quebec to face westward, and even for that matter eastward. The Duke wrote to Watkin, " Mr. Sicotte is a traitor to the cause he has come over to advocate." When Sicotte and Howland left suddenly without bringing the negotiations to a definite close, Watkin concluded that their policy was to leave things at what appeared to be a deadlock. He summed up their attitude in the biting phrase " Refuse nothing, discuss everything, but do nothing." Watkin, however, knew that there was a real desire in Canada to open up communications with the West and he persisted.

In April 1862 the Government of Canada had opened communications through the Governor-General with Mr. A. G. Dallas, agent of the Hudson's Bay Company in Montreal, to the effect that they intended to establish communication by steamboat with Fort

William, that the recent discovery of gold on the Saskatchewan would attract many adventurers, that means of transport should be opened across the continent, that the Canadian Government intended to open it as far as the western boundary of Canada and to add a telegraph line, that they were ready to unite with the Company in a mail service and post route to British Columbia.   Was the Company prepared to act in an object of such national importance ? Dallas forwarded the communication to Mr. Berens, Governor of the Company, and he transmitted it to the Duke of Newcastle, commenting critically on the scheme.

Beyond Red River to the base of the Rocky Mountains the line will pass through a vast desert, in some places without wood and water, exposed to the incursions of roving bands of Indians, and entirely desolate of any means of subsistence for emigrants, save herds of buffalo, which roam at large through the plains, and whose presence on any particular portion of these prairies can never be reckoned on.   These again are followed up by Indians in pursuit of food, whose hostility will expose travellers to the greatest danger.   With regard to the establishment of a telegraphic communication, it is scarcely necessary to point out the prairie fires [the posts would, of course, be wood], the depredation of natives [who would cut off pieces of wire to mend their guns], and the general chapter of accidents [doubtless meaning, among others, the laying of the line low for many miles by blizzards], and presenting almost insurmountable obstacles to success. . . . But if it be thought that the interests of Canada and British Columbia, or of this country, require that the experiment should be made, the Hudson's Bay Company will most readily acquiesce in the decision of Her Majesty's Government.   At the same time it is my duty to state that, in justice to our proprietors, the Directors of the Hudson's Bay Company cannot risk their capital in doubtful undertakings of this description, spread over such vast distances through a country where the means of maintaining them, if once made, will lead to an expenditure scarcely to be contemplated.

In July Edward Watkin's associates, Thomas Baring of the great financial firm of Baring Bros. and Geo. Carr Glyn of Glyn, Mills & Co., approached Newcastle with a view to the formation of a company to open up a route for passenger traffic and telegraphic communication across the continent of British North America to the British colonies on the Pacific.   Newcastle forwarded their communication to Governor Berens, asking if he would be willing " to concede a line of territory to the proposed company."   He was told that the Company would give the land required for the line.   Asked what breadth of land, Berens replied that he could not well say while in utter ignorance of the sort of route projected.   Between the date of this reply (5th September) and 21st November, Berens had an interview with Newcastle which must be the one described by Watkin. Berens is represented as saying: " What! sequester our very taproot ! Take away the fertile lands where our buffaloes feed ! [meaning whence the pemmican was secured for their transport brigades].   Let in all kinds of people to squat and settle and frighten away the furbearing animals they don't hunt and kill ! Impossible.   Destruction —extinction—of our time-honoured industry.   If these gentlemen are so patriotic, why don't they buy us out ? " To this outburst the

Duke quietly replied, " What is your price ? " Mr. Berens answered,
" Well, about a million and a half." This conversation opened up
a new vista. From this point the Duke and Watkin were discussing two possible lines of advance—the scheme of a wagon road
and the telegraph, with the subsidies necessary to its success ; and
secondly, the purchase of the rights of the Hudson's Bay Company
and the creation of a Crown Colony which must necessarily take the
place of the Hudson's Bay Company's rule.

Watkin persevered with the plan of a Pacific Transit Company.
On 10th December Sicotte and Howland when in London had
agreed that Canada should guarantee the interest at 4 per cent. on
one-third of the sum expended on a telegraph line, provided that
the total expenditure would not exceed $500,000. The Imperial
Government did not see its way to a similar guarantee, as there was
no precedent for such support to a telegraph line inland, and as the
value of the line would not be great to the Home Government, when
there was no transatlantic cable. Newcastle, however, agreed to the
Pacific colonies guaranteeing the interest on one-half of the sum
expended. As a consequence Sicotte and Howland agreed that
Canada should raise its guarantee to the interest of the other half.
The Atlantic and Pacific Transit and Telegraph Company was
accordingly organized. The fortunes of the Company need not be
followed. From the point of view of Watkin and Baring and Glyn,
all interested in extending the Grand Trunk to the Pacific coast, the
scheme was well devised to pre-empt the country for that railway.
Otherwise it would probably have been no success commercially.

Meanwhile, as the Hudson's Bay Company would not give a
grant of land (five miles on either side of the line was desired),
Watkin turned to devise means of buying out the Company and
erecting Rupert's Land into a Crown Colony. Newcastle gave his
various plans a sympathetic study, but the prime condition was that
the Imperial Treasury should not be called on to provide the money
to buy out the Company. Watkin's most feasible plan was the
erection of two companies—a Fur and a Land company. The Fur
Company would take over the trade and equipment of the Hudson's
Bay Company, paying the interest of £800,000 for the concession.
The Land Company would take over the fertile belt, paying interest
on the remaining £700,000 of the £1,500,000 asked for by the
Hudson's Bay Company for their property and rights. Three-
quarters of the fertile belt would be held by the Land Company,
one-fourth being given to the Imperial Government for the formation of a Crown Colony. All that the Imperial Government would be
required to do would be to lend the £1,500,000 necessary for the
purchase, receiving security from the two companies for the payment
of the interest. The new colony was to be named Hysperia. Newcastle seems to have been much interested in the scheme, but the
Government proved unwilling to father it. Watkin's only remaining
alternative was to buy out the great Company. The recent formation of the International Finance Association in which Baring and

Glyn were the principal financiers, and which was seeking for investments, afforded him the opportunity. Thus at the end of June 1863 the old Company passed out of existence, and a new body of men, not without a sprinkling of the old, took over the property and chartered rights of the Company of Adventurers trading into Hudson Bay. Speaking in his place in the House of Lords, the Duke of Newcastle commented on the change :

A new council [Committee] consisting of most respectable persons had been formed that afternoon. Among them were two of the Committee of the old Company, with one of whom, Mr. [Eden] Colvile, he had much personal communication, and could speak in the highest terms as a man of business and good sense. There were also seven or eight most influential and responsible people, and the name of the Governor, Sir Edmund Head, who had been elected to-day, would be a guarantee of the intentions of the New Company, for no one would believe that he had entered into this undertaking for mere speculative purposes, or that the Company would be conducted solely with a view to screw the last penny out of this territory. While the council [Committee], as practical men of business, would be bound to promote the prosperity of their shareholders, he was sure that they would be actuated by statesmanlike views. No negociation with the Colonial Office had taken place. . . . But arrangements must be entered into with the Colonial Office for the settlement of the country.

While the Duke was correct in this estimate of the new Company, the fact remained that it was aware of the value of the fertile belt of Rupert's Land for settlement as the former Governor and Committee had not been, and would be sure to hold out for terms in keeping with their view. Had the Canadian Government been able to throw aside its erroneous view that the Charter was invalid, or at least that it did not cover the fertile belt, it is conceivable that it could have bought out the old Company at the same £1,500,000 and become sole possessor of all Rupert's Land. As it was, Sir Edmund Head, their former Governor-General, must have taken their own view of the value of the country, and with the best intentions in the world for its settlement would be bound to see that the shareholders received their due.

Moreover, the new Company indirectly contributed to the difficulties which Canada experienced at the time of the entry of Rupert's Land into the Confederation. The old Company had maintained a vital connection with the Wintering Partners, participators in the profits of the fur trade, through the Councils (particularly the Council of the Northern Department), presided over by the Governor-in-Chief. This connection appears to have been less sensible after the death of Sir George Simpson in 1860, and under his successor Dallas, a man of much colder nature. When the Wintering Partners heard of the possible sale of the Company they asked to be consulted, and were assured that they would so be. In the end they were ignored. If they thought that they were part owners of the soil they were mistaken, for their partnership was confined to the fur trade. The fact remains that they chafed at a change accomplished without their consent being asked for. The

new Company thus had not, at first, the loyal support of their
winterers enjoyed by the old. Some of the winterers even spoke
of forming connections with some other company which should act
as their agent.

Similarly, the old Company had taken a vital interest in their
" colony," primitive as it was, and was sensible that it enjoyed a
corporate life in itself. The new Company was obsessed with the idea
that the West was a great empty land, and was not conscious of the
pride of the Red River settlers summed up in the word " colony."
Thus when the ultimate transfer of Rupert's Land to the Crown
and its union with the Dominion of Canada was arranged the colony
was ignored, and its Governor, William Mactavish, who also was
Governor-in-Chief of Rupert's Land, was not kept in close touch
with the policy being followed by the Governor and Committee,
all of which contributed to the course taken by affairs during the
disturbances on the Red River, or what is popularly known as the
Riel Rebellion of 1869–70.

3.—NEGOTIATIONS FOR THE SURRENDER OF THE COMPANY'S CHARTER TO THE CROWN, 1864–69

The International Finance Association, in possession of the
Hudson's Bay Company, sold the shares in the open market. In a
prospectus issued at the purchase it committed the Company to
the scheme of providing telegraphic and postal communication
across the continent from Canada to British Columbia. There was
the promise of a 4 per cent. guarantee from Canada for half of
the expenditure and the prospect, through the Colonial Office, of a
similar guarantee from the Pacific colonies, British Columbia, and
Vancouver's Island. Further, there was the prospect of a grant of
land from the Crown Colony which might be erected in Rupert's
Land. In view of this Watkin's Atlantic and Pacific Transit
Company passed off the stage. Watkin was, however, as active as
ever in the prosecution of his ambitious scheme. He was sent out
by the Governor and Committee on an informal commission to quiet
the restive servants of the Company and to make arrangements for
building the telegraph line. With characteristic energy he made
arrangements which, he believed, would give Rupert's Land a wire
from the Red River at Pembina through Fort Garry to Jasper House
hard by the entrance to Athabaska Pass within a twelvemonth.
First connections were to be with American telegraphic lines.
Considerable material was actually purchased, but the Governor
and Committee failed to support him with the desired energy. This
was probably because they were already in negotiations with the
Colonial Office for the transfer of at least the fertile belt to the Crown,
which would be erected into a colony. If these succeeded the whole
scheme might take on a new form. The proposal to the Duke of
Newcastle was that the Company should surrender their rights to

the soil of an agreed area, and receive, among other concessions, one shilling per acre for every acre sold, and large blocks of land near the settlements to be effected.   The Duke accepted the condition of one shilling per acre, but refused to agree to the concession of the great blocks of land.   His grounds for so doing have an important bearing on the subsequent management of the natural resources of the West by the Dominion of Canada.   Mr. Chichester Fortescue, writing to Sir Edmund Head, Governor of the Hudson's Bay Company, for the Duke on March 11, 1864, said :

In an unsettled country there is no effectual mode of taxation for purposes of government and improvement, and the whole progress of the colony depends on the liberal and prudent disposal of the land. . . . The conclusive objection to the scheme is that it would reproduce in gigantic shape the inconveniences which, on a smaller scale, were found intolerable in Canada. It is evident as a matter of reasoning and notorious as a matter of fact, that the interposition of large blocks of property between tracts or districts of Crown Land must obstruct the opening up of those districts, unless it fortunately happens that the private proprietor is ready to spend money *pari passu* with the Government in the construction of roads and other improvements, and to conform his land policy to that of the authorities. It is also clear that colonists of the Anglo-Saxon race look upon the land revenue as legitimately belonging to the community ; and that the diversion of half or more of that revenue to the purpose of increasing the dividends of a private corporation would cause a continual and growing discontent which could not be allayed by any abstract argument of right, and the full force of which the Government would be expected by the Company to sustain. His Grace cannot consent to make himself responsible for these consequences, and he is therefore obliged to treat as inadmissible any proposal for the proprietory partition of those territories which may be placed under the Government of the Crown.

We have here a clear enunciation of the policy which the Imperial Government had been following in all the colonial enterprises since the establishment of the first American settlements.   In the early stages the natural resources of the colony were granted by Charter to the Company, *e.g.* the Virginia Company, the Massachusetts Company, the Hudson's Bay Company, which undertook the obligation of establishing the colony.   When the settlers on Massachusetts Bay bought the Charter of the Massachusetts Company (of London) they automatically became possessed of the land and the other natural resources of their colony.   When the Crown displaced the chartered companies it held and controlled the natural resources for the development of the particular colony.   It was so in Virginia, in Upper and Lower Canada, and in two of the Maritime Provinces.   When the Home Government, as has been seen, granted Vancouver's Island to the Hudson's Bay Company it placed on the Company the obligation of using the natural resources (subject to a deduction of 10 per cent. for capital expended) to establish and develop the colony and to maintain its Government.   When the Crown displaced the Company it made no different use of the resources of the island.   The natural resources of British Columbia also were at the disposal of the local Government for the administration of the colony when there were only bands of transitory gold miners, mostly American, in that vast region. Now that the Government proposed to displace the Hudson's Bay Company and erect a Crown Colony in Rupert's Land, the lands and resources of that vast area, although its population was largely limited to the some 10,000 settlers on the Red River and the aborigines, were earmarked for the establishment of the colony and for its administration. This is a very different policy from that followed by the Dominion of Canada after the transfer of Rupert's Land and the North-West, where the natural resources of the West were appropriated for Dominion purposes.

Seven months later the movement for the Confederation of the British North American colonies was so far advanced that a Conference was held at Quebec to draft a scheme. The constitution was drafted more especially with the colonies of Canada, New Brunswick, Prince Edward Island, and Nova Scotia in view, leaving room for the admission, " on equitable terms of Newfoundland, the North-West Territory, British Columbia, and Vancouver's island." The resolution, as finally drafted on October 17, 1864, ran :

> That in the Federation of the British American Provinces the system of government best adapted under existing circumstances to protect the diversified interests of the several Provinces and secure efficiency, harmony and permanency in the working of the Union, would be a General Government charged with matters of common interest to the whole country ; and Local Governments for each of the Canadas and for the Provinces of Nova Scotia, New Brunswick and Prince Edward Island, charged with the control of local matters in their respective sections, provision being made for the admission into the Union on equitable terms of Newfoundland, The North-West Territory, British Columbia and Vancouver.

This had been moved by George Brown and Adams Archibald (of Nova Scotia). On the 24th the powers of the " Local Legislatures " were before the Conference. As all the colonies represented had for long enjoyed the revenues derived from their respective natural resources, they were to retain these for the upkeep of their administrations. Oliver Mowat moved " That it shall be competent for the Local Legislature to make laws respecting . . . 4. The sale and management of public lands, excepting lands held for general purposes [meaning for the military, for post-offices, and the like, administered by the Dominion] by the General Government." Next day Mowat presented the following resolution : " The North-West Territory, British Columbia and Vancouver shall be admitted into the Union on such terms and conditions as Parliament shall deem equitable, and as shall receive the assent of Her Majesty ; and in the case of the Provinces of British Columbia or Vancouver, as shall be agreed to by the Legislature of such Province." The omission of any consultation of the people of the Red River Settlement through their legislature, the Council of Assiniboia, is due to the Canadian view that the Charter of the Hudson's Bay Company was invalid, at least as covering the Red River Settlement, that the colony was no colony, and had no legal Government. Behind this lay the pre-supposition that the North-West was an empty land, occupied by but a few white settlers, half-breeds, and Indians, who need not be considered in the disposition of that spacious land. These views were accentuated by the fact that all dealings would have to be with the Company in London to be legal.

On 11th November, following the Quebec Conference, a Minute of Council was approved and forwarded to Mr. Cardwell, the Duke of Newcastle's successor at the Colonial Office, in answer to his dispatch of 1st July previous. It expressed the desire of the Cana-dian Government for the early settlement of the North-West and for the establishment of a Government over that region, and pointed out that the first step to that end would be the extinction of the claim of the Hudson's Bay Company. The duty of securing that extinction, it insisted, lay with the Imperial Government. (There was no suggestion of compensation.) When the claims should be extinguished the Canadian Government would be ready to open up communications and provide the means of local administration. George Brown, President of the Executive Council, about to sail for England, would put himself in communication with Mr. Cardwell on the subject. When in England, Brown was given a copy of the correspondence which had passed between the Colonial Office and the (new) Hudson's Bay Company with a view to the extinction of their title, at least so far as the fertile belt was concerned, and to the erection of a Crown Colony. On his return to Canada Brown em-bodied in his report the passage of Mr. Fortescue's letter to Sir Edmund Head laying down the principle that " colonists of the Anglo-Saxon race look upon the land revenues as legitimately be-longing to the community," accepted by Newcastle as fundamental for the establishment of a Government in Rupert's Land.

A Minute of the Council of Canada of June 22, 1866, was drawn up, again in answer to dispatches from Mr. Cardwell, concerning the proposal of American capitalists to buy Rupert's Land. It again quotes in full Fortescue's statement that the land revenues go to the support of the local Government. Thus, six months before the first drafting of the British North America Act, the Canadian Cabinet was not only aware of this principle, but affirmed it. In this sense the clauses of that Act must be read, and it is the only sense of which the wording admits.

The 146th clause of the British North America Act embodied the resolution of the Quebec Conference concerning the admission of British Columbia (Vancouver's Island was now united with that colony) and the North-West, with this notable difference that, in keeping with the Charter and the Patent creating a bishopric in that region, Rupert's Land is referred to as a colony :

XI—Admission of other Colonies.

146. It shall be lawful for the Queen, by and with the advice of Her Majesty's most Honourable Privy Council, on Addresses from the Houses of Parliament

of Canada, and from the Houses of the respective Legislatures of the Colonies or Provinces of Newfoundland, Prince Edward Island, and British Columbia, to admit those Colonies or Provinces, or any of them into the Union, and on address from the Houses of Parliament in Canada, to admit Rupertsland and the North-Western Territory, or either of them into the Union, on such terms and conditions in each case as are in the Addresses expressed and the Queen thinks fit to approve, subject to the provisions of this Act ; and the provisions of any Order in Council in that behalf shall have effect as if they were enacted by the Parliament of the United Kingdom of Great Britain and Ireland.

The phrase "subject to the provisions of this Act" brought to Rupert's Land and the North-West the powers enjoyed by the Provinces, or local legislatures, in particular, control of education and of the lands and minerals, and the like. It is evident that at the Quebec Conference the Canadian statesmen were concerned with the drafting of a symmetrical federal scheme. They had not faced the practical questions—of what form the government of Rupert's Land should take, to what purpose should the revenues from its natural resources be applied. Newcastle's dictum that the revenues from the land belonged to the local community chimed in perfectly with their federal scheme, and nothing was inserted in the British North America Act to suggest that the admission of Rupert's Land would alter the symmetry of the scheme, that its natural resources should not be its own, but in the control of the Dominion for Dominion purposes. It will be seen that when the Canadian statesmen came face to face with the problems of the government of the West, and the use of its natural resources, the old conception of Canada (now the Dominion) acquiring and annexing the North-West re-emerged. It even became the dominant principle in their mind, and led to action, not only out of harmony with the symmetry of the federal scheme, but in contravention of the actual terms of the British North America Act.

The Dominion of Canada came into being on July 1, 1867. Its Government lost no time in taking the steps prescribed by the British North America Act prerequisite to the admission of Rupert's Land and the North-West Territory to the Union. The House of Commons on 16th December, and the Senate on the 17th, passed an address praying the Queen to unite Rupert's Land and the North-Western Territory with the Dominion, and to grant to the Parliament of Canada "authority to legislate for their future welfare and good government"; that they were "willing to assume the duties and obligations of government and legislation as regards these territories." Referring to the Hudson's Bay Company, they expressed themselves as ready to respect the legal rights of any corporation in the country and to place it "under the protection of courts of competent jurisdiction"; and as to the Indians, they would compensate them for their claims to the land. The quiet assumptions of this address were in keeping with the Canadian view that the Hudson's Bay Company's Charter was invalid, and there was no room for compensation to it, and if valid, that the responsibility for resumption of the Charter lay with the Imperial Government. All that Canada was concerned with was the admission of the region to the Dominion, the installation of forms of government, and the legislation for its welfare.*

In contrast, the Imperial Government adhered to its traditional view that as the Company had been in the enjoyment of its privileges for many generations, that as the Charter had been recognized from time to time by the Government and by Acts of Parliament, it was not possible to suddenly assume that the Company had no rights— not, at least, until its Charter had been shown to be invalid at law. It had been suggested by the Colonial Office after the inquiry of 1857, when Canada first asserted its claims to the fertile belt, that that colony should take action before the Privy Council to prove the Charter invalid, but it had declined so to do. Her Majesty's Government accordingly adhered to its position that the claims of the Company must be recognized. An Act was therefore passed through Parliament in 1868, entitled " The Rupert's Land Act," reciting the procedure laid down by the British North America Act ; it gave the Imperial Government power to accept a surrender of Rupert's Land with all the territories and privileges of the Company " upon such terms and conditions as shall be agreed upon." Thus Rupert's Land would become once more Crown domain. There- after, upon a (proper) address from the Parliament of Canada, Rupert's Land, by an Order in Council, should be " admitted into and become part of the Dominion of Canada," and it would be lawful for the Parliament of Canada " to make, ordain and establish within the Land and Territory . . . all such Laws, Institutions and Ordinances, and to constitute such Courts and Officers as may be necessary for the Peace, Order and good Government of Her Majesty's subjects or others therein," provided that till that time, " all the Powers, Authorities and Jurisdiction of the several Courts of Justice now established in Rupert's Land . . . shall continue in full force therein."

The way was now open for final negotiations with the Company for the surrender of its Charter and the rights conferred by it. As it must be a surrender to the Queen, these negotiations were strictly between the Colonial Office and the Company, but as Canada was to be the beneficiary and therefore in justice to assume the burden of the compensation, it must play a part in the discussion. Accord- ingly, Sir George Cartier and William McDougall—who, as has been seen, was from the early 'fifties a strong advocate of the " acquisi-

---

* Legally, this could mean no more than that the Dominion was to assume the duty of establishing a system of government and passing laws for the North-West within the frame- work of the British North America Act. Failing a provincial legislature, Dominion Parliament could enact such laws as the local legislature would be entitled to enact. It could pass legislation controlling the natural resources, but in keeping with the British North America Act, which fixed the constitution of the Confederation in consonance with the practice of the Imperial Government when displacing a proprietory Government, those resources must be administered solely in the interest of the local Government. To use them for Dominion purposes would be a contravention of the terms of the British North America Act, and of the principle laid down by the Duke of Newcastle.

tion " and " annexation " of the North-West—were sent over with
the proper powers. Throughout, it was assumed that the Canadian
Government would confirm all titles to land alienated by the Company, and that the Company would continue its fur trade, now as a
simple corporation. From the beginning the Imperial Government
agreed that the Company should retain a portion of the land at large
in fee simple, and blocks of land about its posts, and that there
should be in some form a compensation in money. The offer made
informally by the Company before the arrival of the Canadian delegates and confirmed by letter dated October 27, 1868, was that it
should receive a shilling for every acre sold or alienated by the
Canadian Government in blocks of 5,000 acres out of every 50,000
sold or alienated, in a word, one-tenth of the whole territory ; that
its common law rights to the lands on which its posts stood should
be acknowledged by its retaining 6,000 acres around each post,
with the exception of Fort Garry in the Red River Settlement ; and
that the Company should share with the Canadian Government in
the mineral rights up to £1,000,000. This was the type of compensation which had been asked of the Duke of Newcastle. On 1st
December the Duke of Buckingham and Chandos, now at the Colonial
Office, rejected the proposal on the ground that the shilling an acre
would " in all probability be far in excess of what is likely in practice
to be obtained for the land " ; it would not leave the local Government enough to meet the outlay on the survey, and roads, and other
improvements. He objected to the size of the blocks of land around
the posts ; it would amount to 500,000 acres in the whole territory
and 100,000 acres in the fertile belt. He refused to countenance
blocks of 5,000 acres to be selected as the Canadian Government
sold the land as being sure to obstruct settlement. Buckingham was
ready to grant blocks of land about the posts occupied, but in proportion to the importance of the post, and not to exceed 6,000 acres,
and in the fertile belt 3,000 acres. Instead of one shilling for every
acre alienated, he suggested a fourth share of all receipts. In place
of the blocks of 5,000 acres, he offered five lots of 200 acres each in
each township, thus scattering the Company's holding throughout
the country. He conceded the mineral rights up to £1,000,000. The
negotiations were stayed by a change of the Ministry which placed
Lord Granville in the Colonial Office. On January 13, 1868, the
Company defended its proposal as above, but offered to sell out for
a lump sum of money, payable in Canadian Government bonds. On
8th February the Canadian delegates pointed out to Lord Granville
that they were no party to the offer made to the Company by his
predecessor ; as to buying out the " rights " of the Company, as
suggested latterly, everything depended on what the rights were.
They reiterated the usual arguments to show that the Charter was
invalid, or, if valid, applied only to the inhospitable shores of Hudson
Bay. " It will be for Lord Granville to consider, whether this
Company is entitled to demand any payment whatever, for surrendering to the Crown that which already belongs to it." Assuming that

the Charter be valid, the money value of the soil as indicated at the sale of the old Company in 1863 could be calculated. The purchase price was £1,500,000. The inventory showed that the value of the assets, exclusive of land and cash in hand, amounted to £1,393,569. Accordingly, the value of the land at that time would be the difference, namely, £106,431. By another argument, which is not easily fathomed, the delegates appear to have argued that the (new) Company had already got the worth of the land. The final plea is that if the Company will not consent to any reasonable terms, that the Imperial Government should ignore it. "We, therefore, respectfully submit for Earl Granville's consideration, whether it is not expedient that the Address of the Canadian Parliament be at once acted upon, under the authority of the Imperial Act of 1867" (the British North America Act).

It became evident that the Canadians and the Company could find no common ground. Lord Granville, therefore, stepped in almost to dictate terms. In a letter to Sir Stafford Northcote, then Governor of the Company, he insisted that it was in the interest of all parties to settle the question of Rupert's Land :

> It is not creditable to this country that any inhabited part of Her Majesty's Dominions should be without a recognized Government capable of enforcing the law, and responsible to neighbouring countries for the performance of international obligations. [The reference is to certain incursions of the Sioux north of the boundary.] The toleration of such a state of things in parts of Hudson's Bay Territory, is unjust to the inhabitants of that territory, and is not without danger to the peaceful relations between this country and the United States. . . . To Canada the settlement of the question is not less important, as removing a cause of irritation between it and its neighbours, and even with the mother country itself, as destroying an obstacle to that which has been looked upon as the natural growth of the Dominion. . . . To the Hudson's Bay Company it may also be said to be necessary. . . . Its legal rights, whatever these may be, are liable to be invaded without law by a mass of Canadian and American settlers whose occupation of the country on any terms they will be little able to resist.

Lord Granville then laid down terms which he did not expect to be acceptable to either party, but which he believed to be a just compromise. These, with modifications in detail, were accepted. A paragraph in the letter of the Canadian delegates, 8th February, shows the only ground on which they could agree to compensation to the Company. A person has encroached on your property :

> He is artful, stubborn, wealthy and influential. He will be able to worry you with a tedious litigation. How many acres will you allow him to " reserve," and how much will you pay to save yourself the cost and trouble of a law suit ? Compromises of this kind are not unknown in private life, and the motives and calculations which govern them may be applicable to the present case.

In view of this, the phrase which came into use later, that Canada had purchased Rupert's Land, is manifestly inaccurate. The Hudson's Bay Company was compensated for the resumption of its

Charter by the Crown, and the principle acted upon was that the compensation should come, in part, out of the lands involved.

The cash payment arranged for as part of the compensation to the Company was £300,000. This was to be raised by a loan guaranteed by the Imperial Government, and consequently at the low rate of 4 per cent. The Imperial Parliament accordingly passed " The Canada (Rupert's Land) Loan Act, 1869," implementing the arrangement. It had been hoped that the transfer of Rupert's Land would take place early in the autumn, but the Loan Act did not receive Royal Assent till 11th August, and there still remained details about the Sinking Fund, which the Act left to the Treasury to arrange. Mr. John Rose, on retiring from the Canadian Cabinet to join a banking firm in London, was commissioned to act for Canada in making the final arrangements. His letters to Sir John Macdonald show that it took much time to perfect the arrangements. The banking firms of Baring and Glyn were prepared to advance the money, but it was all that could be done to have the bonds ready by 1st December, the date now fixed for the transfer.

Meanwhile the Canadian Parliament, on its part, was taking the steps incumbent upon it. The lawyers of the Crown in England had decided that the address of the Canadian Houses of Parliament of December 16 and 17, 1867, was adequate for the transfer of the North-West Territory, which had never ceased to be Crown domain, but that it was inadequate for the admission of Rupert's Land to the Union ; that the agreement with the Hudson's Bay Company should be embodied in it. A fresh address to the Queen passed through the House of Commons on May 29, 1869, and through the Senate on 31st May. In addition to expressing the readiness of Canada to provide for the government of Rupert's Land and to install institutions, it enumerates the conditions of the agreement for the transfer of Rupert's Land by the Company to the Queen, which Canada agreed to. Of the fourteen items, the most important are the payment of £300,000 at the transfer, the retention of blocks of land around the posts, as per schedule attached, and of one-twentieth of the land at large within the fertile belt, namely, one-twentieth part of each township. All titles to land alienated by the Company up to March 8, 1869, were to be confirmed by Canada. The Company was to be at liberty to carry on its trade in its corporate capacity without hindrance. (In fact, for many years the transfer scarcely affected the Company's fur trade.) The Colonial Office described the address as unbusinesslike, which may be attributed to the slipshod ways of William McDougall. In the matter of Upper and Lower Forts Garry, the amount of land specified in the schedule was much smaller than the amount agreed upon. This was straightened out by a private agreement that Canada should live up to the terms settled.

The Canadian Parliament, in addition, passed " An Act for the Temporary Government of Rupert's Land and the North-Western Territory when united with Canada." This gave the Governor-

General, with the advice of Privy Council, power to appoint a Lieutenant-Governor and to make laws subject to the assent of Parliament. He could appoint a Council of not less than seven persons and not more than sixteen, to aid the Lieutenant-Governor in the administration of the North-West Territory, as it was to be called. All the laws in force at the " admission into the Union " were to remain in force until altered by Parliament or by the Lieutenant-Governor. In the issue, it proved unfortunate that a clause was not inserted similarly guaranteeing the settlers' titles to their lands. All public officers were to continue to function until otherwise ordered by the Lieutenant-Governor. The Act was to continue in force until the end of the next Parliament, the reason for this being that an Act passed then, after the transfer, would be indubitably legal. The reception of this Act by the people of the Red River Settlement will be discussed in due time. The Colonial Office referred it to the lawyers of the Crown to ascertain the legality of an Act for the government of Rupert's Land, passed before it had been admitted to the Union, and to know what powers the Dominion could exercise in a local area that had no Provincial Parliament. On 11th December the lawyers sent in their opinion— that they believed the Act *intra vires*, that

the Parliament of the Dominion had unrestricted Legislative Power. The restrictions placed on the powers of the Dominion Parliament have for their object the protection of the Powers of the Provincial Legislatures, but inasmuch as the Territory to be annexed is not to become a Province, at least for the present, the reason of these restrictions does not apply. This being so we think it not unreasonable to construe the words of the British North America Act S. 146 " on such terms and conditions in each case as are in the addresses expressed and as the Queen thinks fit to approve," as including the general power of Legislation prayed for in the first address. With respect to " Rupert's Land " this power appears expressly conferred by S. 5 of the " Rupert's Land Act." (S. 5 . . . " It shall be lawful for the Parliament of Canada . . . to make, ordain and establish . . . all such Laws, Institutions and Ordinances, and to constitute such Courts and Officers, as may be necessary for the Peace, Order and good Government of Her Majesty's subjects or others therein.")

Obviously the powers exercised by the Dominion must be within the terms of the British North America Act. In the as yet unorganized territory the Dominion Government, in addition to its Dominion powers, could exercise the provincial, *i.e.* act as local government. It would, however, be precluded by the British North America Act from using the local natural resources for other than provincial purposes, for it would be no more than functioning in the place of the provincial legislature. The Imperial Government was now, apparently for the first time, face to face with the fact that, at least for a season, the North-West could not be fitted in to the symmetry of the British North America Act. The above is its solution. In contrast the Canadian Government does not seem to have been much concerned about fitting its action into the framework of that Act. It was probably rather influenced by the example of territorial government in the United States, and thus drifted into using the resources of the West for a number of Dominion purposes.

The next step is marked by the signing of the *Deed of Surrender*, by which the Hudson's Bay Company was to surrender its Charter to Her Majesty the Queen, and Rupert's Land was to become Crown domain once more. The Deed was executed on 19th November. The Company now felt that it was no longer responsible for the government of Rupert's Land. Everything was ready for the Order in Council, transferring Rupert's Land to Canada for its admission into the Union, but before 1st December, when the money would be paid, the disturbances on the Red River, under Louis Riel, led the Canadian Government to decline to accept the transfer otherwise than in peace. It now became a fine point at law as to just where things stood. Was the Hudson's Bay Company, after signing the Deed of Surrender, responsible to quell a movement which was no rebellion against its Government but was directed against Canada ? As the £300,000, the compensation to the Company, had not been paid, was the Territory, or was it not, now strictly in the Imperial domain, and did it lie with the British Government to secure the peaceful transfer to Canada ? As the movement was against Canada, could the Dominion shoulder the task and the cost of quelling disturbances in a territory which was in no sense yet part of the Dominion ? As will be seen, all parties were busy arranging the transfer as though Rupert's Land were an empty country—at most, occupied by a single settlement of half-breeds. Nowhere was there any thought of consulting these through their Government, the Council of Assiniboia. This omission was natural enough in view of the law, but it was fatal absent-mindedness on the part of statesmen expecting to rule the colony. It delayed the transfer for wellnigh seven months.

4.—RED RIVER SETTLEMENT, 1860–69

Had Rupert's Land, or at least the Red River Settlement, been transferred to Canada in 1857, the Hudson's Bay Company would have given up the reins of government with the reputation of having managed a primitive colony with great tact and wisdom. In that year the decision of the Select Committee of the House of Commons made it certain that the rule of the Company must soon come to an end. This in itself must bring a decline in the authority of the Governor and Council of Assiniboia, comparable to the decline of the control of a defeated President of the United States, who must, willy-nilly, go on ruling till the hour come for laying down his authority. During the long thirteen years which elapsed before the end came, the loyalty of the settlers to their own Government was sapped ; the grip of the Company on its colony was relaxed ; and parties rose, openly disloyal to the system. The result was increasing chaos, culminating in the disturbances under Louis Riel which marked the transfer of Rupert's Land to Canada.

Changes for the worse came within the Company itself in London. The death in 1856 of Andrew Colvile, Selkirk's brother-in-law, who had guided the Company and its colony with wisdom and generosity ever since the death of his lordship in 1820, inflicted irreparable loss. This was followed by the death of Sir George Simpson on September 7, 1860. After the relations of the colony and the Company were defined in Governor Bulger's time, Simpson had accepted it that the colony was to have an organic life in itself. He and Andrew Colvile had devised many plans, and spent much money, in the search of a produce which would give it a profitable export trade. While willing to guide, they never aspired to rule. Government with the consent of the governed was the keynote of their policy. Simpson was followed in the office of Governor of Rupert's Land by Alexander Grant Dallas, who in different circumstances followed different methods. Joseph James Hargrave, in his *Red River*, says :

> Before his [Dallas's] assumption of office the Governor of Rupert's Land had carefully avoided mixing himself up with the administration of affairs in the municipal district of Assiniboia, which had always been left to the charge of its own governor and council. For many years Sir George Simpson, whose chief residence had latterly been at Lachine, near Montreal, on his way home from Norway House had paid an annual visit of a very few days duration to the settlement, where he always avoided, as much as he could, interfering with anything beyond the commercial business of the company, or of private individuals with whose affairs he might be connected. . . . Formerly, it had been usually the aim of the authorities to discourage, as much as possible, party feeling, endeavouring rather to induce members of all races, creeds and parties to forget in their common intercourse, those matters wherein they differed, and exert themselves with united zeal for the general good.

On the whole this policy had succeeded. Such success as it had enjoyed was due to a general acceptance of and loyalty to the Government as it stood. The appearance in the Settlement of small bodies of American and Canadian settlers, who denied the validity of the Company's Charter and ridiculed the forms of the Government of Assiniboia, added to the unrest due to the certainty that changes were soon to come, brought about a lawlessness, which ended in the so called Riel Rebellion. The attempt of Governor Dallas to rally a party to the support of the Company only added to the growing chaos.

The expansion of the American population westward brought with it transportation facilities. In 1859 the Mississippi steamboat system may be considered as being extended into Rupert's Land when the first steamer, the *Anson Northrup*, not without difficulty, descended the Red River to Fort Garry. Soon after, the railway reached St. Paul. The Red River Settlement was thus brought into comparatively close relations with the outside world. York Factory began to lose its position as the port of entry to Rupert's Land.

Fort Garry was becoming the centre of the country. Soon the Hudson's Bay Company itself began to import its goods by way of the United States. The Red River carts came into their own as a means of transportation, and great "brigades" left Fort Garry for Fort Ellice and Fort Pelly on the Assiniboine, and thence for forts Carlton and Edmonton. By way of Fort Ellice, brigades went west to Fort Qu'Appelle on the plains east of the present Regina, or north-westward through the Touchwood Hills to forts Carlton, Pitt, and Edmonton on the Saskatchewan. Lower Fort Garry became the point of embarkation for brigades going northward, though it was not till 1872 that the Churchill River and Athabaska brigades abandoned the York Factory route. Then, too, the expansion of the missions, the rise of a settlement at Portage la Prairie, the discovery of gold on the Saskatchewan, the dream of a transcontinental route to the mines of British Columbia, brought visitors and wayfarers, like the Overlanders to the Cariboo mines, to the Settlement as a centre. Occasional scientists, and British sportsmen such as Lord Dunmore, Viscount Milton and Dr. Cheadle, and Lord Southesk, came in on their several quests.

Of more permanent significance were little groups of Americans and Canadians who came in to settle, some as farmers, but most of them to pick up a livelihood in a growing settlement and from the increasing traffic. George Emmerling, a German-American, came in about 1860. Beginning as a pedlar, he attained the position of principal hotel-keeper of the Settlement. His bar became the rallying centre of an American party, which despised the so called despotic institutions of the Hudson's Bay Company, and hoped to see all the country absorbed by the great Republic from which they came. Much more important were the Canadians. In 1859 Mr. Henry McKenney came in and opened the Royal Hotel. Some time after he was followed by his half-brother Dr. John Schultz, a medical man. The hotel not succeeding, McKenney and Schultz opened a store at the junction of the Portage la Prairie trail with the Red River trail running up to Fort Garry, about three-quarters of a mile from the fort. A Mr. William Drever built a house and store alongside, other buildings followed, and thus the nucleus of the village, now the city of Winnipeg, was formed. The McKenney store became the forgathering place of a Canadian party which, like the American circle, denied the validity of the Charter and ridiculed the institutions of the Hudson's Bay Company. McKenney had the additional personal grievance that the lease of the land on which his store stood included a clause by which the holder agreed not to enter into the fur trade, while his ambition was to participate in that traffic, and, indeed, he did actually equip canoes which entered into the trade on the Saskatchewan. The influence of the little Canadian group might well have been no greater than that of the American had not two men from Canada, William Coldwell and William Buckingham, come in and established the first newspaper of the Settlement, the *Nor'-Wester*. It was the existence of this journal, circulated not only in the Settlement but in Canada, which made the influence of this party on subsequent events definite, and, as it proved, unfortunate.

William Buckingham was an Englishman who migrated to Canada in 1857 when twenty-five years of age. After two years in the office of the *Toronto Globe*, where he must have imbibed George Brown's views of the Hudson's Bay Company and the future of Rupert's Land, he " went West " to be on the crest of the wave. Coldwell, whom he associated with him, was likewise an Englishman. He had come to Canada in 1854, when twenty years old, and had served as shorthand reporter on the *Toronto Leader*. These two young men secured a press and type in Toronto, completed their equipment, including paper, at St. Paul, and journeyed to Red River over the prairies with ox-carts, their wives seated on the bales of paper. They arrived at Fort Garry in the autumn of 1859, and published the first issue of the *Nor'Wester* on 28th December. Its policy is described in the prospectus : " Its projectors come hither to hold to no set of men, influenced by no narrow prejudices, shackled by no mean antipathies. Their journal will be the vehicle of news, and for the pertinent discussion of local questions ; governed only by a desire to promote local interests, and a determination to keep aloof from every tangling alliance which might mar its usefulness at home and abroad." Few journals succeed in living up to this ideal. The plan of increasing the circulation by raising the dust led the editors into an attitude of hostility to the local institutions, and to become an element of discord amid the harmony of the Settlement. In the end the paper became the mouthpiece of the Canadian party. Buckingham left the colony within a year, and Coldwell carried on with a young man, James Ross, educated in the Settlement, but hot from the classrooms of the University of Toronto. In 1864 he took Buckingham's place in the partnership, and when Coldwell returned to Canada in 1865 he became sole proprietor. In 1868 he sold out to Walter Bown, a Canadian who had been a practising dentist from time to time on the Red River.

At its inception the *Nor'Wester* had no reason to advocate annexation to Canada, for that question was no longer a living issue. In the very first number it published, under the caption, "Why we are not annexed to Canada," a letter from A. K. Isbister to Donald Gunn informing him that George Cartier had declared to Lord Lytton, then Colonial Minister, that the Lower Canadian party would offer a determined opposition to the acquisition of the West. On the 28th of February 1860 an "extra" was issued announcing, "from private but perfectly reliable sources," that the Duke of Newcastle, Lytton's successor at the Colonial Office, was preparing a measure to create a Crown Colony in Rupert's Land. The view of the paper throughout its course was that, as a Crown Colony, or as part of the Dominion, the people of the Red River Settlement would enjoy representative and responsible government. It argued that the Council of Assiniboia was but the tool of the Hudson's Bay Company and hopelessly inefficient, and it called for an immediate change of the pernicious system granting to the people the right to elect their own councillors. " We maintain that this Settlement has become too populous and, in every respect, too important to be ruled by a Council nominated by a few Fur-merchants some thousand of miles away. . . . Is not a community of 8000 or 10,000 orderly, intelligent and well-to-do, as they are, deserving of self-government, and able to work it satisfactorily ? " This is the more pleasing side of the activity of the *Nor'Wester*. It aroused in the people the aspiration for representative and responsible government, and led them to believe that that would be the great step forward when the government of the land was settled. It is the irony of history that when the transfer to Canada came in sight, all that the Dominion had to offer the settlers appeared to be a Council appointed by a distant Government and composed, as it was justly surmised, of men who had not yet resided in the land. The latter state of the colony promised to be worse than the first, and there was a strong reaction against Canada. The constructive ideas of the *Nor'wester*, instilled into the settlers, issued in the so called Riel Rebellion.

The destructive policy of the paper led to and accentuated the same lamentable result. The claim that the Charter was invalid involved the inference that the land titles issued by the Company were of no value at law. Such a general inference might have caused the settlers no anxiety, but the *Nor'Wester*, in its fourth number, published a statement from Peguis, the old Indian chief, that he had never sold the land to Lord Selkirk or to the Company. This was replied to in the next number by Andrew McDermott, formerly in the Company's service. He argued that the statement was drawn from Peguis by the insinuation that he could recover possession of his lands. The agreement had been made and " from that date 1816, he and the other chiefs have each received an annual payment of £8 sterling [in tobacco and goods] making together a total of £40 per annum." The fat was in the fire. In the middle of March a large meeting was held by the half-breeds at McKenney's Royal Hotel, at which it was asserted that the Indians had long since abandoned the region, " [the half-breeds] are natives; they are present occupants; and they are the representatives of the first owners of the soil, with whom no satisfactory arrangement ever has been made." In the issue of 28th April Donald Gunn came into the discussion, to the effect that the arrangement made by Lord Selkirk was only pre-liminary, and that a final treaty had never been made. " It is to be regretted that the Company should maintain that they have made a *bona fide* bargain, while the Indians hold that they rented the land, and are afraid that, under similar pretences, all their lands will soon pass out of their hands." It is a sound principle observed in the Crown Colonies that the White Men should never raise, in public, issues which might excite the natives and become distorted in their minds. The editors of the *Nor'Wester* knew no such caution. The issue raised continued to simmer in the minds of the natives. A year later Peguis and the other chiefs served notice on the settlers that one bushel of wheat out of every five must be paid to the Indians by settlers cultivating lands outside of the two-mile limit (agreed to with Lord Selkirk). The half-breeds followed with a protest. Thus the idea carefully instilled by the North West Company in the struggle against Selkirk's claims to the soil was reawakened by the reckless conduct of the editors of the *Nor'Wester*. The whole Settlement, and especially the half-breeds, became sensitive about their titles to their lands, and when the transfer of Rupert's Land to Canada was about to be consummated the first act of resistance was against servants of the Dominion surveying through lands of the half-breeds.

On May 18, 1862, Mr. Dallas, Sir George Simpson's successor, arrived in the Settlement. Formerly engaged in trade with China, he had married a daughter of Governor Douglas and been made Chief Factor at Fort Victoria, Vancouver's Island. Much of his wealth had been invested in the Hudson's Bay Company. At his first meeting with the Council of Assiniboia, he informed that body that he had been obliged to sell his stock, and appeared before them with no interests in the Company save those evident in his office. He therefore " stood before them independent of all interested motives, and anxious only to promote the best interests of the Country." In the issue it became apparent, however, that he disapproved of the easy *laissez faire* policy of his predecessor, that he intended to drive with a tighter rein. The chief currency in the Settlement was in the form of notes issued by the Company payable at face value in Fort Garry, Fort York, or London. As things were when Dallas arrived, firms like McKenney & Schultz could enter the fur trade to the detriment of the Company's monopoly, present these notes at Fort Garry, and secure a bill of exchange on London of equal value, and so pay for their goods bought in England. Dallas determined to put an end to the advantage thus given to the free-traders and at the same time stimulate purchases at the Company's stores. Settlers who brought in their produce were not given notes, but credit, and had to take their pay in goods. Had the fur trade alone been affected Dallas's scheme might be defended as reasonable, but it deprived the Settlement of its currency and was a real hardship. It created a discontent which the *Nor'Wester* was not slow to fan into a flame, news of which was carried to the newspapers of Canada in exchange copies.

The Canadian Rifles had remained in the colony till 1861, when they embarked at Lower Fort Garry for York Factory on the way to Canada. Apart from the loss to the settlers of the money circulated by them, they were sorely missed, for in 1862 occurred the Minnesota massacre perpetrated by the Sioux. There was immediate danger of the perpetrators of the massacre taking refuge from the avenging American soldiery in British territory and at the Settlement. In the following October Governor Dallas, presiding over the Council of Assiniboia, raised the question of the protection of the Settlement, for Sioux refugees were encamped at Sturgeon Creek on the Assiniboine above Fort Garry. He suggested that a petition to the Imperial Government for troops be prepared. The petition was sent to the *Nor'Wester* to be printed, but James Ross, one of the editors, withheld it from the Press and prepared a new petition, which not only asked for Imperial troops for the protection of the Settlement, but in the name of the people of the Settlement expressed their deep and widespread discontent with the rule of the Hudson's Bay Company : " It did not maintain law and order ; it opposed colonization, and was distasteful to the people ; it had refused payment in money for the farmers' produce, the effects of which are crushing the settlers and retarding the growth of the colony." A complete change of the Government was asked for to ensure justice between man and man, security for the Settlement, and the development of the resources of the country in the future.

Up to this time there had been no evidence of animosity on the part of the authorities to Mr. James Ross in spite of his connection with the *Nor'Wester*. The son of Alexander Ross, an old official, educated in the Settlement at St. John's College, and at the University of Toronto, when he returned to the West in May 1859, he had been given the position of postmaster at the small salary of £10. His association with the *Nor'Wester* from 1860 had not been held against him, for in June 1861 he was appointed, by a vote of ten to one, Governor of the Jail and Sheriff of Assiniboia. In May 1862 Ross had asked the Council for an increase in his salary on the ground of the great increase in his work, but his letter was laid on the table. The refusal of Ross to print the petition of the Council, accompanied by his substitution of a petition apparently prepared by Mr. Coldwell, his colleague, " at the request of a great many in the lower part of the Settlement," impeaching the administration, proved more than the patience of the rulers could endure. At a meeting of the Council on 25th November the Governor of Assiniboia, William Mactavish, called attention to the conduct of Ross as a public officer, in thwarting the measures adopted by the Council, stirring up opposition, and " representing to the Home Government that there was no Justice to be obtained between man and man in this Settlement "—conduct incompatible with his position as an officer of the Government. The Governor was supported by Bishop Taché, and it was unanimously decided to remove him from his offices. Freed from the trammels of office, Ross addressed various meetings in a bitter tone, and the violence of his paper became more marked. At a meeting held in St. James parish he asserted that the dissatisfaction with the Company was universal. " You are entitled to responsible government," he declared. Louis Riel, the father, who is reported to have organized the half-breeds at the trial of Sayer in 1849, speaking through an interpreter, charged him with imposing on the public. " The truth is that among my people, the French half-breeds, there is no such dissatisfaction." He insisted that the *Nor'Wester* had invented the report of a previous meeting held in St. Paul's School. Mr. Bannatyne challenged Mr. Ross to mention a single case in which an individual had appealed to the courts and not got justice. Several argued against a change of Government on the score that the Settlement could not bear the expense. Others emphasized the scarcity of money due to the policy of Governor Dallas as showing a need for change. Both parties charged their opponents with attaching fictitious signatures to the several petitions in what the *Nor'Wester* called "the death struggle for names." It was even said that the name of an old ox at Fort Garry had been placed on the Council's petition. The "people's petition" was to have been taken to England by Mr. Ross, but subscriptions towards his expenses fell short and it was forwarded through Sandford Fleming.

Two clergymen took a prominent part in urging the people not to sign the Council's petition but to support the "people's petition." The Rev. John Chapman of St. Paul's parish called a public meeting and urged the need of a change to a Crown Colony. He was reported in the *Nor'Wester* as having said at the meeting: "We should . . . agitate, agitate, agitate." He was receiving £100 a year to act as the Company's chaplain. This was forthwith withdrawn by Governor Dallas. The other clergyman was the Rev. G. D. Corbett of the parish of Headingley. Unfortunately for Dallas, in the midst of the excitement a charge was laid by the girl's father against Mr. Corbett, who had acquired some medical training with a view to healing his parishioners, of an attempted illegal operation on his maid-servant in the hope of protecting his own reputation. The reader must be spared the details of this painful case. He will find a sober and just account of it in J. J. Hargrave's *Red River*. The evidence, as published verbatim in the *Nor'Wester*, bears out Hargrave's conclusion that the prisoner had a fair trial and was justly condemned, and that six months' imprisonment was a lenient sentence. But coming just at the juncture when Corbett had been leading in the agitation against the Company, a portion of the public accepted the view of the *Nor'Wester* that the Company took this means of striking down its opponent. A movement was set on foot to secure the release of the prisoner. A petition for pardon failing, resort was made to violence. James Stewart, the schoolmaster of St. James, next parish to Headingley, was one of the ringleaders. The conspirators attended a session of the petty court and waited till the crowd was dispersed. They then overpowered the old Frenchman who acted as jailer, broke the padlock of the jail with a crowbar, and freed the reverend prisoner. The next day Stewart was arrested under a warrant and lodged in jail. The day after William Hallett, a half-breed, Cuthbert Grant's successor as Warden of the Plains, demanded Stewart's release and threatened to free him by force. Dallas hereupon had a large number sworn in as special constables. Hallett reappeared with a force some fifty strong and repeated his demand and threat to the assembled Council. The special constables were on the ground in sufficient numbers to overpower the insurgents, but the authorities were reluctant to give orders which would not only have resulted in bloodshed, but would have created a blood feud in the Settlement the issue of which none could foresee. The insurgents, in the presence of all, broke down the pickets of the jail, smashed its door, and released Stewart. In view of the whole situation Dallas decided to let the incident pass unpunished, but at the subsequent session of the Grand Jury, Judge Black read portions of a letter written by Corbett to his bishop in which he admitted his relations with his maid-servant, while he pleaded not guilty to the crime charged against him. Donald Gunn, foreman of the Grand Jury, as reported by the *Nor'Wester*, on their behalf tendered the Judge their " fullest moral support." In March of the following year Ross retired from the *Nor'Wester* and Dr. John Schultz took his place. Schultz was half-brother to Henry McKenney, who had been appointed sheriff in succession to Ross and was, at this time, a supporter of the Government. The stimulus of the *Nor'Wester* thus removed, the political agitation dwindled to a calm.

Two other events showed the helplessness of the Government of the colony. The Sioux refugees appeared upon the scene in the autumn of 1863. Governor Dallas held a council with them at their camp at Sturgeon Creek. They were naked and starving. Gifts of clothing and food (but no ammunition) to the value of £108 persuaded them to retire, but they did no more than remove farther out, to the White Horse Plain. Dallas gave permission to the American officers to treat with them for the surrender of those guilty of the Minnesota massacre. Fortunately the Americans kept within the bounds of International Law. More gifts from the settlers persuaded the Indians to move out into the plains. Finally a clash with the Saulteurs in the region near Lake Manitoba convinced them that they were not in their own country, and they passed across the border with the hunters of the Settlement to hunt buffalo.

There had grown up a settlement on the rich land at Portage la Prairie. The earliest arrivals were half-breed migrants from the Settlement of about the year 1853. When Archdeacon Cochrane went to them to form a Mission, Governor Simpson opposed him on the ground that scattered settlements would make the government of the colony difficult. As the migrants spoke Cree they easily coalesced with the Indians into a congregation. As early as 1857 the Archdeacon organized an informal Council on the model of that of Assiniboia. There were six councillors, a president, a secretary, a magistrate, and two constables. Partly, it would appear, because of friction within the Council over a law-suit, but mostly because a band of Sioux had gathered about the settlement, the settlers, in 1864, sent a petition to the Council of Assiniboia praying to be " annexed " to the Red River Settlement. Governor Dallas stated to the Council of May 4, 1864, which considered the petition, that he had received a similar request from a population of 1,200 near Edmonton, that he proposed to lay the large question of providing a proper Government for these two and other similar settlements before the authorities in England. The resolution adopted by the Council ran that " it would be highly injudicious to recommend any extension of the present Municipal district seeing that for the effective administration of the government of the same, it had long been evident to the

Council that there was an absolute and imperative necessity for an adequate amount of *material* strength, in the form of Military protection, being afforded to existing authorities."

As though there were not sufficient factors in the Settlement weakening the grip of the Company's system of government and working for disintegration, there was added the purchase of the Company by the International Finance Association. A rumour of the proposed transaction reached a Chief Factor in London. In the name of the Commissioned Gentlemen overseas he put in a claim that they should be consulted, receiving a verbal promise that they would so be. But without reference to the " Fur Trade " the sale was effected. When the news reached the Red River Settlement, Hargrave says, it created a " feeling of stupefaction, quickly succeeded by one of indignation." Legally there was no ground for this, for the Charter and its rights to the soil were the sole privileges of the Hudson's Bay Company from the beginning, and the system of partnership inaugurated in 1821 had to do with no more than the fur trade from outfit to outfit. In any case the rights of the Commissioned Gentlemen were embodied in the Deed Poll which was not affected by the transaction. It was in the sphere of the imponderables, of the loyalty of the servants to the Company, that the change was felt. Hargrave says: " The cordial terms in which the annual despatch had been invariably couched had led many well-disposed people in the territories inadvertently to harbour the idea that the gentlemen who signed it regarded those to whom it was addressed with an interest almost personal, in the extent of its anxiety for their welfare." That they should have been transferred without consultation to a new body of shareholders and to a, for the most part, strange Governor and Committee left them with " an irresistible conviction . . . that they had all been sold like dumb driven cattle." Thus the greatest force making for cohesion in the colony, the loyalty of the servants and ex-servants to the Company, was suddenly switched off. The machinery of the Government lost the active support of the most influential body in the community. This was a misfortune, for disintegration had gone so far that in the very days of the conclusion of the transaction in London a public meeting in St. James parish, called for considering the advantages to be derived from an Elective Government, resolved " That we consider the present system of government as unfit for the times, and we urge our brethren throughout the various sections of the Settlement to co-operate with us in forming a government more suited to our wants," and " That we utterly refuse to pay any taxes of any sort until we see a government formed by the people themselves by which we shall better know how our affairs are transacted." James Stewart, who had been freed by the jail-breaking, was the principal speaker and advocated the formation of a " Provisional Government and an Elective Council." As no more is heard of this, it may be assumed that the proposed action was too radical for the Settlement at large.

The agitation of the years 1860 to 1863 is of the utmost importance for the comprehension of the subsequent course of affairs in the Settlement up to the admission of Rupert's Land to the Union. The newcomers, American and Canadian, refused to recognize the Government of the colony as legal, and devoted themselves to discrediting it. They could not on that ground alone have created much of an agitation. It was the certainty that the Hudson's Bay Company's rule would soon come to an end and the prospect of the Settlement's transformation into a Crown Colony, as proposed by the Duke of Newcastle, that gave body to the agitation.

To the great mass of the settlers the creation of a Crown Colony was the next step forward, and one to be welcomed. It meant an elective legislature and responsible government, and according to the principle laid down by the Duke, the control of the natural resources by the people, and with these, the means of developing the colony. Evidently in answer to objections raised at one of the meetings that the settlers could not bear the expense of the government of a Crown Colony, an editorial of the *Nor'Wester* pictured the prosperity which the change would bring through the erection of buildings and through the immigration of settlers, and added: " The sale of lands would throw money into the public treasury instead of into the Company's pockets and we would not longer be told that ' there is no public revenue to meet the public expenditure.' " It was the advocacy of these ideals which got the *Nor'Wester* its public and shook the Government of the colony to its foundations. These ideals were not abandoned when the admission of Rupert's Land into the Dominion came in sight. They must be remembered if the course of events is to be comprehended. All the while the reports of the agitation were being circulated in Canada through the *Nor'Wester's* exchange with papers of the East. It is remarkable that the Canadian papers failed to appreciate the real mainspring of the agitation—the desire for the status of a Crown Colony. They harped on the illegality of the Charter and on the Red River Settlement as outside of the chartered territory and as being really Canadian domain. They were concerned only about two questions: the problems of the transfer and of opening up communications. In this atmosphere it was natural for the Fathers of Confederation at the Quebec Conference (October 1864) to ignore the Government of the Settlement and to leave consultation with the colony as to its admission into the Dominion out of range of vision. Similar views were entertained in England, as, for example, by the deputation which waited on Mr. Cardwell, Colonial Minister, on February 15, 1865 : " It would appear that nothing deserving the name of ' Government ' exists in the populated portion of the territory known as the ' Red River Settlement.' " Hence the British North America Act was drafted in keeping with the resolutions of the Quebec Conference.

When Governor Dallas left the colony on May 1864 the agitation for a change of Government was about at its end. William

Mactavish, Governor of Assiniboia since 1858, once more became the dominant figure in the Settlement. Of a mild and easy-going disposition, but enjoying great influence as a man, he reverted to the policy of driving with a loose rein. On 21st November the confederation of the Provinces figured large in the pages of the *Nor'-Wester*. A week later a delegation to London to be composed of a French and an English settler was under discussion. Had it actually gone and met with the Canadian delegation the mistake of ignoring the settlers might have been avoided.

The appearance of Confederation above the horizon and the certainty that Rupert's Land would be admitted to it put the small Canadian party in the Settlement at the front of the stage. A wise leader would have aimed at turning the large body of the public which had rallied to the ideal of a Crown Colony to place their hopes on the Canadian Confederation, by pointing out that all they sought for would be achieved in it. At the same time he would have found means of informing the statesmen of Canada of the conditions under which the Settlement would come in peacefully and wholeheartedly into the coming Dominion. Unfortunately, Dr. Schultz, the leader of the Canadian party which forgathered at his store and in his home, was the last man to play that part. Grasping by nature and utterly unscrupulous, he followed a policy which was not simply purely personal, but mean. Involved in a series of lawsuits with his half-brother at the dissolution of McKenney & Co., he tried to escape from his share of the firm's debts, and when in 1866 a decision was given against him, he publicly declared that the court " had permitted itself to be bullied and browbeaten " by his late partner, and he pilloried the judicial system of the Settlement in the *Nor'Wester*, of which he was now editor. At a later stage he refused to meet the obligation which the court decided rested on him, and resisted the sheriff when he was taking possession of goods in the store equal to the debt unpaid. For this he was lodged in jail, but Mrs. Schultz, with some fifteen of the Canadian party, surprised the jailer and released her husband. The final suit involved the sum of £275, due to a Mr. Kew, the London merchant who had supplied the firm. Judgment had gone against Schultz by default, for he had absented himself from the colony. When he insisted on a second trial, Judge Black only granted it when Schultz entered into an agreement to accept the verdict of the jury. Schultz brought forward his clerk to testify to having seen his employer pay the money without taking a receipt, and won the case. Governor Mactavish was so sure that this was perjury and so humiliated that Judge Black had been drawn into a trap that, out of his private purse, he paid Kew the sum due to him. All the while Schultz harped in his paper on the nullity of the Government of the colony, and asserted that no justice could be found in its courts.

When a vacancy occurred in the Council, Schultz's following got up a petition praying the Council to nominate him. A counter-petition was circulated in favour of another. The public was informed that both petitions would be forwarded to the Governor and Committee. Yet Schultz proclaimed it in the *Nor'Wester* that no opponent of the Company could ever hope to get a position on the Council, nominated as it was, by the autocratic Hudson's Bay Company. Manifestly this was the last man to win the Settlement as a whole to his support and to cordial relations with Canada and the Canadians. Yet it was natural that all Canadians coming to the Settlement should gather around him and his store.

In the autumn of 1866 Thomas Spence arrived in the Settlement. He had been a land surveyor in Canada and had some sort of acquaintance with D'Arcy McGee and other politicians. He now aspired to political honours by leading the Settlement into the Dominion. A political meeting was called for 8th December in the Court House at 10.30 a.m. " Precisely at the time, according to Mr. Spence, or at an hour considerably before it, according to certain of his opponents " the meeting was held, five men being present. Resolutions were hastily passed declaring that the whole Settlement was in favour of being received into and forming "a part of the Grand Confederation of British North America," and after three cheers were given for the Queen the meeting dispersed. Meanwhile the American party had gathered around Mr. Emmerling at his bar. When it arrived at the meeting-place all was over. Evidently the usual curious public came also. According to Hargrave's account, Emmerling's potations had left him in no condition to control the meeting or to present a resolution in favour of the great Republic, and this second meeting broke up in an uproar. The resolutions of the Canadians, in the form of a memorial signed by Thomas Spence and two hundred others, were forwarded to the Queen.

In the spring of 1867 Mr. Spence transferred his activities to the diminutive settlement of Portage la Prairie, where he opened a store. He gathered a party around him with the view of installing a Government. In June a humble address to the Queen was forwarded, through the Governor-General of Canada, praying for "recognition, law and protection." No reply was received. In January a public meeting of the settlers decided to organize as a republic. Spence was elected president of the Republic of Manitoba, as it came to be called, and taxes were raised to build a " Government House and Jail." Trouble, however, began when a humble citizen, a cobbler, charged the president and council with consuming the public money at the local tavern. Then, too, the officer at the local post of the Hudson's Bay Company, which would have been the largest tax-payer in the republic, refused to pay taxes without an order from the Governor-in-Chief of Rupert's Land. An appeal to Governor William Mactavish brought the answer that taxes could not be levied on the Company save by the authority of the Governor and Committee in London, that the republic could only levy duties on such as volunteered to pay them. That the republic was established partly to put the Hudson's Bay Company in a bad light before the Imperial Government is evidenced by Spence's correspondence with A. Morrison, member of the Canadian House of Commons. On 17th January, Spence announced the formation of the republic to Morrison, who showed the letter to Sir John Macdonald. He in turn placed it in the hands of the Governor-General, and it was considered in Council and a copy forwarded to the Colonial Minister. Morrison wrote Spence on 4th April :

I feel satisfied the course adopted by the inhabitants of Manitoba for *self rule* and *protection* was a correct one ; and I have no doubt this important step will bring the Hudson Bay Company and Her Majesty's Ministers into some conflict ; the result of which I hope will be a temporary amicable arrangement whereby your Territory under the provisions of our Union Act will before long become part and parcel of the Dominion of Canada : When carried out you may rest assured your personal interests will not be overlooked by the writer.

Meanwhile, on 19th February, Spence had written the Colonial Minister announcing the formation of his republic and defining its boundaries. On 30th May the Colonial Office replied : " The people of Manitoba are probably unaware that the creation of a separate government in the manner set forth in these papers has no force in law, and that they have no authority to create or organize a Government or even to set up Municipal Institutions properly so called for themselves without reference to the Hudson's Bay Company or the Crown." Spence was warned that his Government could not " exercise jurisdiction over offenders," or levy taxes compulsorily, and that the course he was following involved " grave responsibilities." This dispatch, coupled with internal dissensions, brought about the collapse of the Republic of Manitoba.

Once again the Settlement was brought to feverish excitement by rival petitions. A memorial drawn up by the Canadian party and supported by the *Nor'Wester* called attention to the impotence and injustice of the Company's administration, asserted that the whole community assented to the violent release of Dr. Schultz from prison, and prayed the Council of Assiniboia to inaugurate an elective council and give the people representative government. It is safe to infer that even the Canadian party envisaged no other method for the entry of the colony into the Dominion than as a self-governing unit in control of its natural resources. The counter memorial asserted that the great majority of the population did not countenance the unlawful liberation of Schultz from prison. The political pot came to the boiling-point when the *Nor'Wester* refused to print the second petition, which would thereby have become known throughout Canada. The supporters of this memorial, many of them half-breeds, assembled in a threatening manner at the office of the newspaper. Governor Mactavish, whose personal influence was great, effected a compromise. The *Nor'Wester* was to print a certain number of copies of the memorial at a price. With that the people dispersed, to some extent satisfied.

In 1868 the community was plunged into economic distress.

A plague of grasshoppers had partially destroyed the crops of the previous year. The eggs deposited in the ground bred a swarm of larvæ which, in the following spring, devoured everything green. The Council of Assiniboia voted £1,600 for relief, £600 being earmarked for seed for the following year, and £500 for flour purchased in the United States. Through the efforts of the Governor and Committee in London £5,000 was raised in England. The *Nor'-Wester* proved a valuable medium through which to appeal to the Canadian and American public. £3,600 came in from Canada and £900 from the United States. Relief was distributed by a central committee. The relief scheme of the Canadian Government took the form of building the western end of the Dawson route, that is, from Fort Garry south-eastward to the Lake of the Woods, passing through a small half-breed settlement near a promontory of the woods known as Oak Point, the Ste. Anne des Chênes of to-day. This scheme brought a number of Canadians into the Settlement. Mr. John A. Snow, a surveyor, was in charge of the construction, and under him Charles Mair, the poet, was paymaster. These newcomers naturally stayed with Dr. Schultz, and they found employment in their scheme for the ex-president of the Republic of Manitoba, Thomas Spence. The party was sent in by William McDougall, Minister of Public Works of Canada. True to his principle—that the Hudson's Bay Company had no title, at least to the fertile belt, but that the country was Canadian—McDougall asked permission of none. Sir Stafford Northcote, Governor of the Company, accordingly entered a protest with the Colonial Minister, it may be presumed, not to stay the work of relief, but to protect the Company's title.

Snow's party, collectively, did not establish the best of relations by consorting with Dr. Schultz, the arch rebel of the community. Individually they were guilty of a succession of blunders. Mair wrote private letters in which he criticized the manners of the half-breeds : " Many wealthy people are married to half-breed women who, having no coat of arms but a ' totem ' to look back to, make up for the deficiency by biting at the backs of their ' white sisters.' The white sisters fall back on their whiteness, while the husbands meet each other with desperate courtesies and hospitalities, with a view to filthy lucre in the background." Evidently Mair could not realize that in the Red River Settlement the best of the half-breeds formed a middle class and were well educated. Governor Mactavish's wife was a half-breed, and on one occasion, at a dinner party in his home, he protested that she was as well educated as any in the Settlement, and that her manners would grace any table. Unfortunately for Mair, he was known in Toronto as the author of *Tecumseh*, and as a rising poet. His private letters were published in the *Globe* and read in the Settlement. The indignation created was great. Mr. Emmerling, who was no half-breed, threatened to shut the door of his hotel in the face of the Canadian, and certain half-breed ladies at once proved the poet's statements and satisfied their feelings by pulling his nose and boxing his ears.

Mr. Snow's general conduct commanded respect, but his relations with Schultz got him into a transaction which had much influence upon the minds of the half-breeds. Payment of the workmen of the road was made in goods, and Schultz opened a shop at Oak Point to facilitate things. Bishop Taché asserted afterwards that discontent grew up because the prices placed on the food were exorbitant compared with those prevailing at Fort Garry. Worse still, Schultz drew Snow into some scheme by which a council with the Indians at Oak Point was held with a suitable quantity of liquor. The Indians surrendered their title to the region in return for an agreed quantity of provisions. But half-breeds had long been settled on a part of the land, and in any case regarded themselves as the owners of the country and not the Indian new-comers. The incident raised doubts among the half-breed population as to how far the Canadians would respect their title. Would they not just enter in and take away the land ? Snow was fined in the Court of Assiniboia for selling liquor to the Indians. In any case, comparatively few of those employed by Snow were natives of the Settlement. They were mostly Canadians and Americans—a turbulent crew who, in a dispute about wages, seized their employer and threatened to drown him. William McDougall was drawn into the unpopularity of the Canadian party by his answer to a letter of Governor Mactavish protesting against the injudicious acts of his party. He wrote : " the money appropriated towards the works on the Lake of the Woods road was intended for the relief of the settlers, as the Hudson's Bay Company had done nothing for the starving people of Red River "—this in the face of the £5,000 raised by the Company in London ! The amount expended by Canada on the road is said to have been $30,000.

In the following summer, when the terms of the surrender of Rupert's Land were agreed upon, McDougall sent in Colonel J. S. Dennis, the surveyor, to prepare a plan for the survey of the country. On his arrival in the Settlement, Dennis reported that there would probably be objection on the part of the half-breeds to any survey before their claims had been recognized and met by the Dominion Government. McDougall paid no heed to the warning, but, with the assent of the Privy Council, ordered the survey to proceed. Dennis was carrying out his orders when, on 11th October, a body of un-armed half-breeds under Louis Riel, the son, interrupted the survey, and threatened violence if it were continued. Dr. Cowan, then in charge of Fort Garry, intervened to bring Riel and his party to reason, but in vain. Alexander Begg, a Canadian who had come to the Settlement in 1867 and may be taken as impartial, says :

The opposition on the part of the half-breeds was caused through their distrust of the intentions of the Canadians towards them, and this was brought about in a great measure by the acts of a few men in the Settle-ment, who professing to have the cause of Canada at heart, were really more concerned in filling their own pockets. These men, as soon as the survey had commenced, staked out large claims of land for themselves, which they openly boasted would be theirs as soon as the Canadian Government secured possession. This, in conjunction with the proceedings at Oak Point, on the Lake of the Woods road, produced the impression in the minds of the simple half-breeds that their homes and their lands would be confiscated as soon as the transfer took place.

The people of the settlement had been gradually worked up to a state of unrest, and the Hudson's Bay Company had been misrepresented and maligned to such an extent that the settlers were in serious doubt as to the real position the authorities occupied in changes which were rumoured as about to take place. The French portion of the community, from this feeling of restlessness and uncertainty, began at last to suspect that the Company was playing into the hands of Canada to hand them over without any regard for their interests. Until this feeling took root, they were loyal to the Company and really had no desire for a change, but their suspicions, once aroused, had an effect on their excitable temperaments, which it was impossible to control.

In a word, the Canadians had sown the wind; they were about to reap the whirlwind. When the transfer was arranged without the people being consulted, and the Dominion Government passed an Act for the future government of the territory without asking their wishes, they adopted an attitude of dissatisfied watchfulness.

The whole campaign of the *Nor'Wester* and of the Canadian party had undermined the authority of the Government of the colony and reduced the rulers to a habitual timidity and caution. It had at the same time accentuated the belief in Canada that there was nobody and no government in the land worthy of being consulted, that all would welcome absorption into the Dominion. So far were the Canadians in the Settlement from bringing about an understanding between the colonists and the statesmen of the Dominion, by their disreputable conduct they had placed a great gulf between them. In raising the question of the title to the land, they had aroused fears and suspicions which the Canadian Government, all unaware of the real feeling in the Settlement, did not allay —indeed accentuated by its silence as to its future policy for the country. The result was the so called Riel Rebellion.

The unrest among the half-breeds was noted by the *Nor'Wester* as early as February 19, 1869, when it was stated in that journal that leaders of the French-speaking population were contemplating the institution of an independent government for themselves; it may be added, following in the footsteps of Thomas Spence. It was expected that the movement would become definite at a meeting in May, when a President would be elected. Nothing more is heard of this, but it would go far towards explaining the preparedness of the French half-breeds for action and their well-devised political strategy when the crisis came.

The whole course of events in the 'sixties shows that the colony had become politically self-conscious. A large body of the settlers looked forward to a change—by which the Settlement would be raised to the status of a Crown Colony with responsible government and controlling its natural resources. When admission into the Confederation came in sight, their views were not changed. Even the Canadian party aimed at a self-governing colony, able as such to enter into the scheme of Confederation without destroying its symmetry. The settlers as a whole expected to be consulted about their admission into the Confederation, and to be able to lay down their terms. They looked forward to taking their place in the Confederation as a province, and had no intention of allowing themselves to be simply absorbed into the Dominion.

Chapter XII

THE DISTURBANCES IN THE RED RIVER SETTLEMENT, 1869–70

I.—THE ARRANGEMENTS OF THE CANADIAN GOVERNMENT FOR THE ADMISSION OF RUPERT'S LAND AND THE NORTH-WEST TERRITORY INTO THE CONFEDERATION, 1869

THE Dominion Government was not without some information as to the situation in the Red River Settlement on the eve of the transfer. Sir John A. Macdonald was aware of the ill favour in which the leaders of the Canadian party stood. In a letter dated September 20, 1864, he described Dr. Bown, editor of the *Nor'Wester*, to Mr. McDougall as "rather an ill-conditioned fellow." At the outbreak of the disturbance he wrote to Mr. John Ross that the half-breeds disliked Schultz and those who published the *Nor'Wester*. "I am afraid that Snow and Dennis fraternized too much with that fellow who is a clever sort of man, but exceedingly *cantankerous* and ill-conditioned." Nor was the Government without some knowledge that the colonists were anxious lest their rights should be ignored. Governor Mactavish passed through Ottawa during the summer, and made representations of some sort to the Government. Bishop Taché consulted with him on his arrival in the Settlement, and before his own departure for Ottawa and Rome, as to what might be done to induce the Canadian Ministry to consider the feelings entertained by the colonists. Mactavish replied : " My Lord, I wish that you may be successful, but I greatly fear you will lose your time and trouble. I have just returned from Ottawa, and although I have been for forty years in the country, and Governor for fifteen years, I have not been able to make any of my recommendations to be accepted by the Government." As Bishop Taché reached Ottawa in the middle of July, Mactavish must have made his representations to the Government when the Temporary Act for the government of the North-West Territory was before Parliament and there was still room for additions and changes. When the Bishop arrived the act had already been assented to and the hope of modification was slim. However, he communicated his views and his apprehensions to Sir George Cartier, only to be told that the Government knew all about it. In September Taché saw Cartier in the house of the Lieutenant-

Governor of Quebec, and later interviewed the Hon. Sir Hector Langevin, Minister of Public Works in succession to William McDougall. At that date, of course, the train of events was laid, and McDougall about to leave for the West. Langevin asked the Bishop if he would consent to return to Red River. He replied that it was obviously useless for him to return if he were not given an answer calculated to satisfy the people and stay the unrest. A later representation to Sir George Cartier brought the answer : " We know all about it, and we have made provision respecting matters." The Bishop proceeded to the Œcumenical Council at Rome, angered by the attitude of the Ministers to his representations.

Similarly the warnings of Colonel Dennis, surveyor for the Government, first given in July before he was commissioned to go out to lay the basis of the survey, and especially his letter of 21st August, from Fort Garry, came after the course of the Government was set. It may be said for the Government that its policy was necessarily drafted in haste, for at the time it was thought that the transfer of Rupert's Land to the Dominion would take place about the first day of October ; and once the Act was passed and the policy determined on, modifications were not easy to make.

The real reason for the obtuseness of the politicians at Ottawa is not hard to find. They had set ideas as to the future of the West in which the vacant lands bulked more largely than the Settlement of about 10,000 souls, mostly half-breeds, or as Sir John Macdonald called them " half-castes." Then, too, William McDougall had played a large part in drafting the policy. He had been one of the first to advocate " the annexation " of the North-West, and along with Cartier had negotiated with the Imperial Government and the Hudson's Bay Company for the transfer during the preceding winter. As Minister of Public Works he had had relations with the Red River Settlement through his agent Mr. Snow, who had built the Dawson road from Winnipeg to the Lake of the Woods. McDougall, as a debater, is described by a contemporary :

> His style is clear, practical and decisive, with a tinge of contempt for every sort of admiration that may not be won by hard, logical facts, and the force of a strong uncompromising intellect, that chooses rather to force the enemy's citadel than to stoop to the cunning arts of the tactician. . . . Judged simply as he appears in the House, the probable future Governor of the North-West Territories is at once admitted to be one of the most dignified, able and practicable, if not the most lovable statesmen on the ministerial benches in the House.

While his ability and his knowledge of the North-West gave him an outstanding position in fixing the policy of the Government, his unbending will made him slow to accept guidance. Worse still, McDougall's ideas of the North-West all dated from before the British North America Act. He had all along stood for the " annexation " of the country, and was not the man to adjust his views in keeping with the symmetrical federal system sketched by that Act. His deeds and his words show that he believed that the Dominion was absorbing Rupert's Land. Even Sir John Macdonald was infected with these views. He wrote to a member of Parliament : " I anticipate that [McDougall] will have a good deal of trouble, and it will require considerable management to keep those wild people quiet. In another year the present residents will be altogether swamped by the influx of strangers who will go in with the idea of becoming industrious and peaceable settlers."

The idea of annexing the West and of its absorption by Canada runs through the Acts of the Government. The " Act for the temporary Government of Rupert's Land " was passed in June without any thought even of consulting the people of the Settlement. It imposed on them a Governor and a Council nominated by the Governor-General in Council. Its clauses did nothing to assure the people of the Settlement that they would be represented on the Council. There was no word to calm their anxiety over their titles to their lands. On 26th July an editorial in the *Globe* commented on the reception of this scheme in the Settlement :

> We are not surprised to hear . . . that the Government plan for governing the North-West is very distasteful to the people of that Territory. When the measure was before Parliament, we pointed out that its oligarchical features could not fail to be unpopular with the people to be governed by it, and our advices from the Territory confirm our anticipations. The people of Red River Settlement feel that they ought to have some voice in the local government of their Territory, and complain that the Council by which they are to be ruled is to be an appointed one, and not elective. . . . The law does not even require that the Councillors shall be residents of the Territory—though it is inferred that they will be. There is not a word in the Act of Parliament, the Red River people complain, to prevent the Governor from bringing his Council with him. The appointment of outsiders would cause a great deal of popular indignation in the Territory and we trust such an error at least will be avoided.

The Council proposed really constituted a retrograde step, for though, in keeping with the Charter, the Governor and Committee had appointed the members of the Council of Assiniboia, they were all resident : leading men from the several districts, Europeans or half-breeds. Under the forms of an autocracy, the colony had practically enjoyed representative government.

The Lieutenant-Governor of the North-West Territory, as it proved, was to be not only an outsider but one already looked on askance by the colonists for his connection with Mr. Snow, and for having agreed to terms for the transfer of their country without any consultation of their wishes. The agreement for the transfer had been particularly offensive to the French half-breeds. For their own purposes the Wintering Partners of the North West Company had instilled into their minds the belief that they were the possessors of the land, the " New Nation," a belief which had been kept active by their efforts to break the monopoly of the Hudson's Bay Company and to secure freedom to enter into the fur trade. That freedom achieved, they had returned to their allegiance to the Company. The controversy raised by the *Nor'Wester* in 1860 led to the reassertion of their title to the land. When it became known that the Company had "sold" the country to Canada, without consideration of their rights, for £300,000 their anger was turned at once against the Company and against Canada. McDougall, as the instrument effecting the transfer was, as it proved, the last man to be sent in to govern the land. Apart from McDougall's connection with the North-West, Sir John Macdonald had reasons for digging him out of the Cabinet. He had been of George Brown's party and entered the Coalition Government formed to carry through confederation. When the Coalition fell apart he elected to remain with the Tories. While of great value as a debater, he had no following in the House. It was an honourable means of getting rid of him to send him off to govern the vast territory to be "annexed" to the Dominion.

McDougall was to rule with the assistance of a Council of not more than fifteen. These, like the Governor, could not be appointed till the transfer was effected. Those who were to stand beside the Lieutenant-Governor and were to accompany him were, however, chosen at once. A Captain D. R. Cameron had recently married a daughter of that redoubtable champion of Confederation, Charles Tupper. A place must be found for him. Macdonald suggested the chairmanship of the Directors of Penitentiaries, but, it proved, that was already promised to another. He wrote to Tupper :

> Then we thought over as to what could be done for Captain Cameron. In the first place we are about to establish a government for the North-West. We shall send a Governor there with a Council of five, who will govern it as a quasi Crown Colony. I suggested to Howe that Captain Cameron should be made one of the Council, and we said that his military experience would be of great value as the question of a Military police and the management of the Indian question should be entrusted to a man like him. Howe said at once that he would go in cordially for such an appointment.

And later : "The salaries have not yet been fixed, but I shall, of course, take care that Captain Cameron will receive as much as any one else except the Governor." Albert Norton Richards of Brockville was also to be of the Council, to be legal adviser to the Lieutenant-Governor and Attorney-General for the Territories. In 1864 he had been Solicitor-General for Upper Canada. Quebec was to have its inevitable place on the Council in the person of Joseph Alfred Norbert Provencher, recently editor of *La Minerve*, the chief Conservative journal in Montreal. He was to be Secretary of the Council. Alexander Begg—not to be confused with the man of the same name already in the Settlement, the diarist of the Rebellion and later author of the *History of the North-West*—was also to be of the Council : Treasurer and Collector of Customs.

All these appointments were to be made, after the transfer, under the Act for the Temporary Government of the North-West Territories. As it is not conceivable that they were intended to last for but a twelvemonth, the "temporary" nature of the Act was not due to any conception that the form of government might be changed in the immediate future, but to the doubt whether the Parliament of Canada could legislate for the country before it was admitted to the Union. The Act which would be passed after the transfer and before the end of the next session of Parliament establishing a Government for the territory was therefore to be in principle essentially the same, though probably clauses would have been added recognizing the settlers' titles to their lands as issued by the Hudson's Bay Company and clarifying much that was left to be inferred in the temporary Act. The general type of the Government being installed may be gathered from a letter from Sir John Macdonald to Charles Tupper. The Lieutenant-Governor " will be for the time Paternal despot, as in other small Crown Colonies, his Council being one of advice, he and they, however, being governed by instructions from Head Quarters." McDougall, therefore, was not even to be under the control of his Council. A despotism it was to be. The paternalism of it would be a speculative quantity, depending on the character of the man.

The new Government was drafted without making any arrangements for the ceremony with which one Government usually gives up the reins of power to another, such, for example, as took place when the Hudson's Bay Company transferred Assiniboia to Lord Selkirk publicly in the presence of the people then on the Red River. Such an arrangement would be unacceptable to McDougall, who had, on principle, refused to recognize the Charter, and therefore the Government of Assiniboia, as valid. It probably was avoided also because the concessions which Governor Mactavish had told the Government were necessary were beyond anything they were ready to yield. Had a wise agent been sent forward to arrange for such a ceremony to take place on the arrival of the Governor, he would have become aware of the terms on which a peaceful entry of the Settlement into the Dominion could be accomplished. Moreover, he would have explained the plans of the Canadian Government. Alexander Begg, the diarist, wrote :

We are at this present day ignorant of what is proposed for us—by some we are told that we are not to have a voice at all in the new order of things— others say our representation at the council board of our country is to be very limited—others that we are to be taxed in equal proportion to the people of Ontario and Quebec—others that our taxes are to be light and so dame rumour has full sway, for she has it all her own way. . . . Here is where the government at Ottawa has made the grand mistake of its new under-taking—why, if it was known that the settlement contains the population that it does, did not Canada feel its way before taking such a long stride as it has done—Would it not have been wiser policy to have sent up authorized Agents to this country as soon as the transfer of the Territory was agreed upon for the purpose of feeling the pulse of the settlers—finding out their ideas on the change proposed and opening out as far as possible the views of the Canadian government towards them—this at all events could not have done harm, and it would very likely have prevented the rupture that has now taken place—The views of the settlers could have been obtained by the Ottawa officials, and measures to meet these views could have been taken, unless indeed the wise ones really intended all along to ignore the fact of there being any people here to consult.

It is to be feared that such a plan was opposed to the genius of William McDougall. As it was, he came out as a simple citizen with no authority whatever, to inaugurate a ready-made scheme, in which he was to be Governor. He was not only to be a Messiah ; he was to be John the Baptist preparing the way for himself.

On 28th September the Lieutenant-Governor-to-be left Ottawa. His instructions bear the same date. He was to make preliminary arrangements for the organization of the Government of the Territories. He was then to proceed immediately to Fort Garry and to be ready to assume the Government of the Territories on the actual transfer to Canada. On his arrival at Fort Garry he was to announce himself to Governor Mactavish and to offer him and Dr. Black, the Judicial Officer of the Company, seats on his Council. He was to forward to Ottawa the names of several residents connected with the Company who might be eligible for a place on the Council. At his earliest convenience he was to forward reports on the laws, police, taxation, licensing of liquor, currency, education, and the churches, and on the administrative officers and the Indians.

McDougall's party, as it worked its way in detachments "in delightful Indian summer weather" northward from St. Paul, consisted of the Lieutenant-Governor-to-be, his two daughters, servants and maids, Captain Cameron, his bride and maid, and the other councillors-to-be, Richards, Provencher, and Begg. At a point half-a-day's journey south of Georgetown, McDougall met the Hon. Joseph Howe on the open prairie. As a storm was raging, the interview was short. Howe reported the people of Red River Settlement as well disposed, but that a section of the population was excited, and that delicate handling would be necessary to allay their feelings.

Joseph Howe was in the same dubious position, so far as his authority went, as William McDougall. He was, of course, a Cabinet Minister, being President of the Council. But it had been planned that he should become Secretary of State when, as such, he would be concerned with all the dealings with the provinces, and presumably with McDougall when Lieutenant-Governor of the North-West Territories. Howe thought that he would like to see the country about to be transferred to the Dominion and with which he would have communications, before he should be appointed to his new office. He therefore visited the Settlement as one having no definite authority. He knew enough to avoid staying with Dr. Schultz, and went to the hotel. He refused to face any public assemblages, but received at his stopping-place many of the leading people of the Settlement. Alexander Begg, the diarist, entered this comment on Howe's visit in the preface of his Journal. "Many of the principal settlers visited the Hon. gentleman, and the universal opinion formed of him was that he was a fine old gentleman, one who could see and act for himself. A great deal of satisfaction was felt throughout the settlement at Mr. Howe's visit, although it was understood that he merely visited us in the capacity of a private individual irrespective of his public character. This will go to show

how much good might have been done had delegates been sent to prepare the way for Mr. McDougall's coming." It is entirely probable that Begg would have entered in his Journal any statements made by Howe calculated to encourage the settlers in their opposition to William McDougall, for his partner at the post-office, Mr. A. G. D. Bannatyne, had a conversation with the Honourable gentleman. McDougall, on third-hand evidence, afterwards bitterly asserted that he did, that Bannatyne had said " that Mr. Howe told him that he [Howe] approved of the course the half-breeds were taking, and if they held out they would get all they wished from the Canadian Government. . . . Mr. Howe further told him that the settlement would prosper if left to govern itself." This was said to have been confirmed by Mr. McKenney, the sheriff. Howe replied to these charges from his place in the House of Commons. He had reached the Settlement in the company of two Canadians, Turner and Sandford by name. They had been with him much of the time in the common parlour of the hotel. He had had no opportunity for private conversation with anybody. When he visited Governor Mactavish, the schools in St. Boniface, Bishop Machray, and others no private discussions took place. When he visited Captain Kennedy, Turner and Sandford were with him. " But I will say this, that when I was in the house of Captain Kennedy, and when the subject of how the territory was to be governed, and how Canada was about to act, and what were the instructions of Mr. McDougall, and what he would do when he entered the territory, I did there, as I did everywhere—I defended what was to be the policy of Canada in the most open and undisguised manner." Howe found that the English population was dissatisfied because they had not been consulted, that the Company's servants were discontented because they felt that a share in the £300,000 given the Company was due them, and that the French half-breeds objected to William McDougall on personal grounds. When he left the Settlement there were no signs of open revolt. On the contrary, the Council of Assiniboia was about to prepare an address of welcome to the Lieutenant-Governor-to-be. All else was general rumour. As has been said, when on the way home he met McDougall and his party, women and children, on the open prairie, a cold north-east wind blowing. There was no opportunity for a long interview. In any case he could not have warned the Governor-to-be of a revolt of which there were no signs when he left the Settlement.

2.—THE AIMS AND STRATEGY OF THE FRENCH HALF-BREEDS LED BY LOUIS RIEL, 1869

Joseph Howe left the Settlement on 18th October. Immediately thereafter the opposition to McDougall showed itself in an incoming tide of events. On the 20th, at a meeting of French half-breeds at the house of John Bruce, an organization was formed on the lines of the government of the buffalo-hunt. John Bruce was elected president and Louis Riel secretary, and the more excited element in the population rapidly fell in line. The rapidity of the organization, the smoothness with which it worked, and the discipline it achieved, were due to long familiarity with the buffalo-hunt. While the half-breeds spoke of their executive as the government, that was no more than the parlance of the hunt. It was not yet a revolutionary government seizing the reins of power in the colony. It was a party organization with a definite object in view, to force Canada to recognize their rights before union was effected. Their aims are described by one of Sir John Macdonald's correspondents :

They claim to be a nation already, along with the English half-breeds, whom they claim as their brethern, in possession of this country, and entitled, under the Act of Confederation, to a voice similar to that ceded to the other Provinces respecting their entrance into the Confederation. They have always claimed a commanding interest in the country, and are now indignant at the Hudson's Bay Company for not having more effectually protected their assumed rights at the period of the transfer to Canada.

The earliest statement of the " rights " claimed by them was made in a letter to Sir John Macdonald from J. Y. Bown, M.P., brother of the editor of the *Nor'-Wester*.

1. That the Indian title to the whole territory shall be at once paid for.
2. That on account of their relationship with the Indians a certain portion of this money shall be paid over to them.
3. That all their claims to lands shall be at once conceded.
4. That 300 acres shall be granted to each of their children.
5. That they and their descendants shall be exempted from taxation.
6. That a certain portion of lands shall be set aside for the support of the R. C. Church and Clergy.
7. That the Council shall be elective and at once chosen.
8. That Dr. Schultz and others shall be sent out of the Territory forthwith.

Title to the land and self-government were the keynotes of the programme.

The strategy of this party, no less than its claims, showed careful preparation and great insight. The Lieutenant-Governor-to-be was coming to them as a private citizen. Any action taken against him before his installation into office would not be treason. If allowed into the country, he would become the head of the Canadian party and find means to enforce his will. Beyond the border he would be helpless. Ten days before (11th October), Louis Riel and a band had stopped the survey being conducted by Mr. Webb. Col. Dennis, Webb's chief, had appealed to Dr. William Cowan, the chief magistrate of the Settlement. Cowan and a fellow-magistrate and councillor, Roger Goulet, had called Riel to them, and tried to bring him to reason. This failing, Governor Mactavish was called in. Riel persisted, claiming that injustice was being done by the Canadian Government. Resort was then had to Father Lestanc, the head of the Catholic Church in the absence of Bishop Taché. Lestanc declined to use his influence for fear the half-breeds would think that he and the Church were becoming partisans of the Canadians and the Company. Dr. Cowan reported to Col. Dennis that nothing more could be done. This procedure was characteristic of the rulers of the colony, for theirs was a government with the consent of the governed, and that consent withdrawn, the only resort left was moral suasion. It was clear that the half-breeds had no reason to fear the rulers of the colony.

In the afternoon of the 21st, Col. Dennis first heard of the plan to send an armed party to prevent the Lieutenant-Governor-to-be from entering the colony. He immediately appealed to Judge John Black. The next morning Governor Mactavish, Judge Black, and Dr. Cowan agreed that a meeting of the Council must be called. (The date had to be Monday the 25th, to allow for due notice to all the councillors.) In the course of the afternoon a Canadian gentleman, Mr. Lyons, reported that when on the way southward he had been turned back at a barricade erected by the half-breeds at the River Sale (Stinking River). These men—about forty in number—were from the French parishes south of the Assiniboine, St. Norbert and St. Vital, and were billeted in the houses at the crossing-place. Another party—about twenty men—was reported at the next stream south, the Scratching River (Rivière aux Gratias). Father Ritchot, at the River Sale, was reported as a moving spirit.

On the day after Mr. Howe's departure a meeting of the English was held in the Parish of St. Andrew's to draw up an address of welcome to the Governor-to-be. The chair was taken by the Rev. J. P. Gardiner, the incumbent. Donald Gunn, who for many years had been labouring to deliver the Settlement from the control of the Company, offered a draft of an address for the approval of the meeting. However, Captain Kennedy, who had co-operated with Gunn throughout, demurred at expressing any sentiments of welcome or of loyalty to Mr. McDougall, "who was a partial Governor and a man in whose antecedents and character he had no faith. . . . The Red River Colonists should enter the Confederation on equal terms with the other Provinces, and were fully competent to manage their own affairs." Donald Gunn, in reply, showed that he fully agreed with Captain Kennedy, requiring, equally with him, " all the political guarantees and privileges wished for." He thought, however, that they should wait patiently for the Canadian Government to unfold its policy, " and if any one of the rights of the inhabitants were tampered with, no one in the place would be more ready to battle for them." The address was simply a mark of hospitality and respectful welcome to the representative of the Queen. No action was taken in the matter of an address of welcome from the people. The discussion shows that the English element was as conscious of their rights as the half-breeds. They differed in that the one was willing to " wait and see," while the other perceived more clearly that the way to secure those rights was to keep the Governor-to-be out of the country till they were secured by agreement. The French half-breeds put their faith in direct action, the English in the problematical reasonableness of that " paternal despot," William McDougall. Their disagreement as to the strategy called for kept them apart for the time. Their agreement on the principles ultimately brought them together.

The divergence of view between the English settlers and the French half-breeds was paralleled within the body of the Catholic clergy. The Canadians thought that the whole movement was due to the intrigues of the priests, who, coming from France and not Quebec, were throughout disloyal. The truth is that they were in complete sympathy with the demand for recognition of the rights of the settlers. Father Lestanc, like the English-speaking section, was disinclined to anything like violent opposition. Father Ritchot, the priest at St. Norbert, was wholeheartedly with the half-breeds in resorting to direct action. William B. O'Donoghue, a professor at the Catholic college in St. Boniface, an Irishman and Fenian, was for extreme radical measures, to the point even of annexation to the United States.

On the same day as the meeting which decided to prepare no address, the Council of Assiniboia met and, *inter alia,* passed an address of welcome to the Governor-to-be, which had been prepared by Bishop Machray. He could rely, in his administration, on their best assistance as private individuals and would find them loyal subjects. The rapid changes which had taken place were bringing about the transference naturally. The Company, however, had been on the whole well suited to the past state of things, and had shown many acts of kindness to the Settlement. The change was being faced with mingled feelings, " even misgivings as regards the future in the minds of some. . . . It will be recognized as most creditable to the wisdom, discretion and honourable conduct of those who administered the affairs of this Country, that a small defenceless Settlement even existed for many years among wild tribes of Indians without annoyance or trouble from them, and that a profitable trade was carried on without difficulty through the length and breadth of the land." With the isolation passing away, they prayed that His Excellency would see a large development of the resources of the country.

The Council, over which Dr. Black was presiding, was deeply conscious that the day of its power was about at its end, for, realizing that the tie which bound Governor Mactavish to them was about to be dissolved, they turned to express their regard for him, all the more feelingly perhaps, because he had recently had a hemorrhage, and was believed to be on his deathbed. The address recalled the many acts of kindness shown by the Company, and asked that the expression of their feelings should be conveyed to the Governor and Committee. To Mactavish it conveyed the Council's " most affectionate regards." Every member had looked on him " as the most fitted to guide their deliberations ; there was no one who less pressed his opinions, or listened more courteously to any suggestion to be made. The Council know well how inestimable your services are to the Honorable Company, and how devotedly you have given yourself to their business ; yet your ear has ever been open and your advice ready for the poorest settler who was in any difficulty." The Councillors must have dispersed to their homes conscious that but one step more was needed to take them off the stage of history.

The next day the opposition of the French half-breeds came to a head, and five days later the Council reassembled to face the emergency. The issue was such as it had faced before—when the half-breeds, organized by Louis Riel, the father, had appeared in arms at the trial of Sayer, and when crowds, mostly Canadians, had broken into the gaol and released prisoners. Would they arm one part of the Settlement and, at the cost of blood, impose law and order on the other part ? The council had always turned from civil strife to moral suasion, or to *laissez faire*. It governed with the consent of the governed, if it could. If not, it resigned for the moment the task of governing. In this case it was hopeless to expect the English half-breeds (whose views were not so very different from their French brothers, though their ideas of procedure differed) to arm themselves against the disturbers of the peace. The Councillors, therefore, turned to the time-honoured method of moral suasion. Louis Riel and John Bruce were summoned to the Council, and asked to explain themselves. Riel took the floor :

> His party were perfectly satisfied with the present Government and wanted no other ; they objected to any Government coming from Canada without their being consulted in the matter ; they would never admit any Governor, no matter by whom appointed, if not the Hudson's Bay Company, unless Delegates were previously sent with whom they might negotiate as to the terms and conditions under which they would acknowledge him. They were uneducated and only half-civilized, and felt that if a large immigration took place they would probably be crowded out of a country which they claimed as their own. . . . If Mr. MacDougall were once here most probably the English speaking population would allow him to be installed in office as Governor and then he would be our " Master or King " as he says, and therefore they intended to send him back.

Riel concluded that he believed his party was acting not only for their own good, but for the good of the whole Settlement. Councillors pointed out the highly criminal character of his proceedings and the disastrous consequences which would follow. Riel remained obdurate, and would consent to do no more than report the views of the Council to his followers. After his withdrawal, the Council decided not to arm the people to bring in the Governor-to-be, but to send a deputation of intelligent and influential Frenchmen on the Council, Messrs. William Dease and Roger Goulet, to parley with the armed disturbers of the peace. Dease had a long conference with the men at the barrier on River Sale, the only result being that twenty of his own men passed over to the opposition camp.

On 30th October the Council was convened to consider the report of Messrs. Dease and Goulet. The chairman reported that every effort at conciliation had failed. It was thought that McDougall was now at Pembina, as indeed he was that evening, and that it would be wise to explain the whole situation to him. Council, therefore, adopted a letter from Governor Mactavish submitted to them. This procedure was, naturally, unacceptable to the Canadian party. An attempt was accordingly made to raise an armed posse to bring the Governor-to-be in, but with no success. Governor Mactavish had had it in mind to appeal for a large unarmed party to be formed for the same purpose, but nothing was done. The situation was hopeless.

On 30th October, the day the Council met, and in the evening, McDougall arrived at the International Boundary. He had received his first news of the situation awaiting him from Mr. Sandford, the Canadian with whom Mr. Howe had travelled, and whom the half-breeds had allowed to pass through their barricade southward. At the American Customs House at Pembina a half-breed, who had been awaiting him for three or four days, put a letter in McDougall's hand, ordering him not to enter the North-West without the special permission of the Committee, meaning the half-breed executive. The would-be Governor, however, proceeded two miles farther to the Hudson's Bay Company's post on British territory. There he received communications from Colonel Dennis informing him of the course of affairs up to 27th October. Next morning, he sent Mr. Provencher forward to parley with the half-breeds, but he was turned at the barricade without being allowed to address the men. Captain Cameron inferred from the statements of his loquacious host that, while McDougall would not be allowed to pass, he would be. Taking his bride with him, and against the will of McDougall, he drove north. When things began to appear dangerous, he left his wife and maid at a house and proceeded alone, but he also was turned back at the River Sale. The furniture of the various households composing the Governor's party was sent forward and passed through safely to Fort Garry.

Two days after his arrival at the Company's post, McDougall got into relations with a friendly Saulteur chief. While the council was proceeding, Colonel Dennis arrived with the letter from Governor Mactavish and the Council, explaining the situation and advising the Governor to remain where he was. On the following day, Tuesday, 2nd November, in the afternoon, a band of fourteen armed horsemen arrived from the north. Its leaders, Ambrose Lépine and one Lavaillier, leaving their arms with their comrades, entered the Governor's presence. In a respectful manner they told McDougall that they had been sent to tell him to leave the country by nine next morning. When asked who had sent them, they replied, in the parlance of the buffalo hunt, " the Government." The Governor produced his Commission in vain. At six next morning Provencher and Cameron returned safely from their fruitless attempt to reach Fort Garry. At eight the band of armed half-breed horsemen, increased by the escorts which had brought Provencher and Cameron back, made its presence known outside the palisades of the fort, and insisted on the Governor obeying orders and passing southward over the border. McDougall wrote Sir John Macdonald that the maid-servants were eager to stand between him and the foe, but that the course of prudence was followed. As the half-breeds, as it were, pushed the Governor past the post marking the 49th parallel of latitude, they said ; " You must not return beyond this line." The imperious McDougall, his heart beating with high ambitions, turned out of his domain, a foreigner in a foreign land, shorn automatically of all his powers, presents a sorry figure. Sir John Macdonald wrote Rose that he had laughed at the news. But it was no matter for merriment, for it was November, and there was no fit accommodation to be had. A half-breed, La Rose by name, gave up his house to the Governor, and built a shack for himself near by.

It may be well at this point to ask whether the traditional view that this movement was a rebellion is just. A rebellion is an uprising against the government of the day. But the half-breeds did not rise up against the Hudson's Bay Company. In fact, Riel recognized the Company, and was willing to appear before the Council of Assiniboia, as he did on 25th October. Nor did he rebel against Her Majesty the Queen. As Canada was not in possession of the country, the movement against its Governor-to-be was not technically a rebellion. Inasmuch as McDougall was still no more than a private citizen, Riel's action against him could not rank as treason. Had McDougall entered any suit against Lépine and Riel in a court of law, it would have had to take the mild form of a charge of obstructing the highway. The movement so far was a political one to protect what was felt to be the rights of the citizens. In so far as it was accompanied with a resort to arms, it was a disturbance of the peace. The British Ambassador at Washington appears to have been the first to hit upon the appropriate term of " the disturbances on the Red River."

On 2nd November the Riel faction occupied Fort Garry. This was a clever strategical move, for it forestalled similar action on the part of Dennis and the Canadian faction, and made Louis Riel potential master of the Settlement. The nature of the occupation is best determined by a letter from Governor Mactavish to William McDougall, of 9th November :

A number of these daring people suddenly, and without the least intimation of their intention to make such a move, took possession of the gates of Fort Garry, where they placed themselves inside and outside of the gates to the number, in all, of about 120, and where, night and day, they have constantly kept a pretty strong armed guard. On being asked what they meant by such a movement upon the Fort, they said their object was to protect it. . . . On coming into the Fort they earnestly disclaimed all intention of injuring either person or property within it—and it must be allowed that in that respect they have kept their word, but it is an inconvenience and a danger next to intolerable, to have a body of armed men, even with professions of peace toward ourselves, forcibly billetted upon an establishment such as this.

Statements that Mactavish and his servants were kept prisoners must, therefore, be discounted. At most they were under surveillance. This strategical move gave the Riel faction very convenient headquarters in the key fortress of the colony.

Meanwhile William McDougall was driving his quill with great industry. That imperious spirit, who refused to recognize the whole system of Government of the Hudson's Bay Company, and did not even, as it appears, do Governor Mactavish the courtesy of announcing his impending arrival nor his intentions as Governor-to-be, now favoured him with no less than three letters in five days. He reminded Mactavish that he, as the " Legal Ruler of the country, was responsible for the preservation of the public peace," that the transfer was to take place on 1st December, and that he (McDougall) was instructed to report in the meantime on certain subjects, and make preparations for the new state of things. He understood from Colonel Dennis that no proclamation or warning had as yet been published at Fort Garry under official sanction. This was written on 2nd November before his retreat into American territory. On the 4th McDougall announced his compulsory withdrawal, and on the 7th complained that no one in authority had informed the public that " the change of Government was an Imperial Act and had the Sanction of the Queen." The letters were placed before a meeting of the Council held at Fort Garry without hindrance from the Riel faction in possession of the fort. They were replied to by the Governor on 9th November : " The (Imperial) Act referred to the *prospective* transfer of the Territory ; but up to this moment we have had no official intimation from England or the Dominion of Canada, of the fact of the transfer, or of its conditions, or of the date at which they were to take practical effect upon the Government of this country." This being so, and the whole situation being " marked by a great degree of vagueness and uncertainty," the Council had deemed it advisable " to await the receipt of official intelligence of the actual transfer of the country and of all details which it concerned us to know." He had openly spoken of the transfer as a matter of general knowledge, and done everything possible to preserve the peace, and would continue to do so, but the difficulties were due to the extraordinary circumstance that a whole people were being subject to a complete change of their political conditions, and were uninformed as to the methods being employed in bringing the change about. Should McDougall remain at Pembina, it would perpetuate and possibly even aggravate the disturbance and danger. He assured him with a feeling of inexpressible regret that to the Council and himself as Governor it appeared that his (McDougall's) early return to Canada was not only essential for the peace of the country, but also advisable in the interest of the establishment in the future of the Canadian Government. It might be well, however, to wait a few days, though there was little reason to expect any change.

Louis Riel now stepped to the front more than ever as the controlling mind in the French half-breed movement. He was well aware that success was dubious so long as his support was confined to a racial faction. He also knew that in principle the whole Settlement, exclusive of the Canadians and even to some extent including them, looked forward to self-government as the next step for the colony, formerly in a Crown Colony under the Imperial Government, now as a province admitted on an equality with the others into the Dominion. On 6th November he issued a " *Public notice to the inhabitants of Rupert's Land* " :

> The President and Representatives of the French-speaking population of Rupert's Land in Council (the Invaders of our rights being now expelled) aware of your sympathy do extend the hand of friendship to you our friendly fellow inhabitants and in so doing invite you to send twelve Representatives from the following places, [11 parishes are named, two representatives to come from the 11th, the " town of Winnipeg "] in order to form one body with the above council consisting of twelve members to consider the present political state of the Country, and to adopt such measures as may be deemed best for the future welfare of the Same. —By order of the President, Louis Riel, Secretary.

When Dr. Bown refused to publish this notice in the *Nor'Wester* he was locked in one of the rooms of his office while the notice was being set up and printed. Curiously enough, Mr. James Ross, the agitator of the early 'sixties, and ex-editor of the paper, and now editor of a new sheet, the *Red River Pioneer*, checked the type and supervised the printing. On the 16th the English delegates met with the French Council in the Court House at Fort Garry, and were received with a *feu de joie* from the armed men and twenty-four guns from the fort. Some of the most notable personages in the Settlement were there as delegates from the several parishes. Henry McKenney, a Canadian, but now sheriff of the colony, represented Winnipeg ; James Ross came from Kildonan ; Dr. J. Curtis Bird and Thomas Bunn, both of the Council of Assiniboia, from St. Paul's and St. Clements respectively ; that champion of representative government Donald Gunn, from St. Andrew's ; John Garrioch, from Portage la Prairie ; William Tait, petty magistrate at White Horse Plain, from Headingley. Among the French were William O'Donoghue from St. Boniface ; Pierre Lavaillier, who with Lépine had conducted McDougall out of the country ; and Charles Nolin. As the conference opened James Hargrave, the Governor's secretary, presented a letter from Governor Mactavish to Henry McKenney. The English deputies wished it read at once, a course to which the French objected. By way of compromise it was read immediately before the adjournment. It proved to be a proclamation issued by Governor Mactavish condemning the resort to arms, barricading of the highways, interference with the free movement of the public, seizing of goods belonging to private persons, tampering with the mails, billeting armed men in Fort Garry, and compelling, under threats of violence, " a certain gentleman from Canada . . . to retire within American territory." For the sake of law and order, and for the future welfare of the Settlement, the Governor earnestly protested against all of these acts, and charged those implicated in them to disperse themselves. The closing paragraph was addressed to the conference : " You are dealing with a crisis out of which may come incalculable good or immeasurable evil—and with all the weight of my official authority and all the influence of my individual position let me finally charge you to adopt only such means as are lawful and constitutional, rational and safe." The proclamation was afterwards printed in the papers.

Governor Mactavish's object in issuing the proclamation at this juncture is not very certain. He was under pressure from McDougall and a few in the Settlement, but could not have entertained any hope that it would influence the half-breeds. It must have been devised to caution the English as they joined with the French in what has been called the convention from being drawn into too close association with the party of violence. It certainly drove a wedge between those among the English who did not approve of the resort to arms and the Frenchmen under arms. The second meeting of the conference could come to no definite agreed policy, with the result that an adjournment from the 17th to the 22nd was decided upon.

It is eloquent of the extent to which the institutions of Assiniboia were still functioning that in the interval a case was tried in the Quarterly Court in which the employees of Mr. Snow sued him for wages withheld. The case went in favour of Snow.

Much private discussion went on over the week-end. Thomas Bunn openly declared that he was for a " full and elective representation at the council board of the country." Similar statements were made by Mr. McKenney and others. Nor was such an obnoxious person as Dr. Schultz wholly out of the discussions. On Sunday evening a number of clergymen and others met with him at the house of Mr. James Ross " to discuss the political state of the country."

On 22nd November, A. G. B. Bannatyne, the postmaster, sent a letter to the conference denying charges that he had encouraged the half-breeds to arm, or had tampered with the mails. Bannatyne enjoyed a wide influence as a man and as postmaster. He was the leading spirit in a small but determined group of men, including Begg the diarist, who saw that if the colonists were to secure anything like consideration for their rights they must all—English and French —stand together. He thus concluded his letter to the Council.

My earnest wish is that the Canadian Government should be established as soon as possible ; only let us have our elective and other acknowledged rights. I have tried for this from the first and will continue to do so. My own desire is that the French portion of the Settlement should now speak out their minds on what they deem justly due them in the new order of Government. This once obtained by the Settlement generally and found to be what every free people has a right to expect, my belief is that those who have, as it were, fought our battles (although perhaps in a different way than we would have done) will have the thanks hereafter of the people in the Settlement and their posterity, and that their wishes will be the wishes of the rest of the Settlement and that all will combine in demanding our rights—the unassailable rights of a free people, worthy of having a thorough and complete voice in the management of their affairs.

Simultaneously the Canadian party was trying to effect some sort of reconciliation. D. A. Grant, bookkeeper of Colonel Dennis, was circulating a public statement to the effect that the undersigned were willing to do all in their power to conciliate all parties, and with this in view recommended the French to lay down their arms.

The discussion at the conference on Monday the 22nd was as fruitless as ever, and the situation next day was made tense by the French party, which was now pressed for provisions and money, taking more complete possession of Fort Garry, seizing some of the provisions and cash, and the books, and putting an end to the free communication in and out which had prevailed up to this point. In some sense Governor Mactavish was placed under arrest. Mactavish's proclamation and these high-handed actions put the English delegates in a difficult position. They even contemplated withdrawing. Discussions were, however, resumed. The French delegates asserted that they intended to form a provisional government which should displace that of the Company, and which should be in a position to treat with Canada. The English delegates were not prepared to accept this without consulting their constituents. The conference, therefore, adjourned for a week, but both sides were agreed that McDougall was not to be allowed to enter the country. Bannatyne's letter had not been read. In the interval Louis Riel's party laid its hand on the customs and placed a small guard before Dr. Schultz's house to prevent a consignment of pork which had recently arrived for Snow's workmen from being removed. On the 26th, influential men on both sides, Dr. Bird, Mr. Bannatyne, Alexander Begg, and others, had a long discussion at the post-office with Mr. O'Donoghue, who represented Riel. It was agreed among them that there should be no provisional government, but that the Company should be allowed to carry on, its Council remaining a legislative council, but the people were to elect an executive council, whose duty should be to treat with the Canadian Government as to the terms on which the colony should enter the Dominion. This would, of course, avoid the illegality of a provisional government and give the settlers a French-English council *ad hoc*, which would speak for them to the Canadian Government. At a public meeting that day, attended by all parties including Dr. Schultz, Louis Riel was introduced during the discussion. He explained that it was because of the weakness of the present administration that the provisional government was proposed, that the movement so far was wholly a French one, but the English were invited to make a united body with them. They did not intend to coerce any one, nor to interfere with any one's rights. Begg the diarist says that even the Schultz party at times applauded Riel. The meeting was not able, however, to adopt any resolution.

The next day, Saturday the 27th, Bannatyne called another meeting of the public of Winnipeg, hoping to win acquiescence for the Company to continue in power, while the settlers would elect a council to treat with Canada. The American consul, Oscar

Marmoras, had met with Riel and urged the acceptance of the plan. No agreement was reached, but that evening Louis Riel, in the presence of the American consul and others, agreed to the scheme. He gave his assurance in writing and sent word of it to Dr. Bird. This pleased the Settlement at large. The satisfaction, however, was tempered by rumours emanating from the Canadian party that Riel was about to seize the Canadian Government's pork at Dr. Schultz's house, and by fears that that party would " start a fight prematurely " by seizing Fort Garry. In view of this, on Monday the 30th Louis Riel retracted his promise and insisted on the necessity of bringing the Company's rule to an end and forming a provisional government. Thereupon Mr. Bannatyne, Mr. McKenney, and ultimately Alexander Begg met with Riel and O'Donoghue in McKenney's house, for it was thought that only on the basis of the promise given could the conference which would meet next day be brought to a successful conclusion. In this they were supported by some of the French Council, and there was hope that Riel would return to his promise. These peaceful discussions did not prevent English and Scots half-breeds from preparing arms and drilling in companies. On Wednesday, 1st December, the day originally fixed for the transfer, the delegates reconvened at Fort Garry for the conference.

These serious discussions of the settlers in the height of the crisis are a pleasing contrast to the attitudes taken by Sir John Macdonald and by William McDougall. When Sir John heard, about 19th November, of McDougall being served with notice not to enter the country, as has been said, he laughed heartily at the man's dilemma. Writing to McDougall he cautioned him not to return to Canada and cover himself and his party with ridicule. In his mind a friendly conversation with the excitable half-breeds would bring them to reason. He accordingly determined to stay the excitement by sending out Lieutenant-Colonel de Salaberry, who had been employed by the Hudson's Bay Company as an engineer between 1855–60 and was reputed to be a hero among them, as a Commissioner from Canada, and Father Thibault, their beloved missionary recently retired. He suggested to McDougall that he should offer to retain " this man Riel who appears to be the moving spirit " as an officer in the future police, and thereby show that the half-breeds were not to be " out of the Law." Mactavish might give the names of two leading French half-breeds, and McDougall might inform them at once that they would be of his Council. Doubtless referring to methods of this and perhaps of a less reputable order, Macdonald wrote to Rose, " We must construct a Golden Bridge over which McDougall can pass into the Country."

The attitude of McDougall's party was naturally more serious. Captain Cameron, who had fallen out of McDougall's grace, in the spirit of a militarist was thinking out the strategy of a campaign in the spring which should end in the triumphant entry of Canada into the West. So was McDougall, but he was not content to wait for a triumphal campaign in the spring ; rather, he looked to the Canadian party in the Settlement for immediate military action. At first, as has been said, these had planned to go with an armed party to bring the Governor in. That failing, their attention was turned to methods of surprise. The plan now was, as soon as the transfer was effected (*i.e.* on 1st December), to appear in arms and dominate the situation. Meanwhile, Sir John Macdonald had reminded McDougall that he was no more than a private citizen seeking entrance to a country under another Government, that he should request the Governor to provide for his safe entry. Joseph Howe, now Secretary of State, wrote on 19th November in the same sense : " As matters stand you can claim or assert no authority in the Hudson's Bay Territory until the Queen's Proclamation, annexing the Country to Canada reaches you through this office." Note the phrase of former times, " annexing the Country." These letters did not reach McDougall until 6th December, but they represent the views which McDougall himself held on 13th November when he wrote to the Secretary of State : " The recommendation that I should issue a proclamation at once is not made for the first time ; but I have uniformly replied that, until the transfer of the territory has taken place, and I am notified of the fact, I shall not assume any of the responsibilities of the Government."

On 19th November the Governor of the Hudson's Bay Company signed the deed of surrender of the Charter to the Imperial Government. The Company regarded this, so far as it was concerned, as the surrender of Rupert's Land and its return to the Crown Domain. The Rupert's Land Act defined the further procedure. It would be competent for Her Majesty then by an Order in Council to admit Rupert's Land into the Dominion of Canada, and from the date of that Order the power of Canada to establish laws and institutions would begin. To this procedure and to the date set for the transfer, 1st December, the Canadian Government had agreed, and the £300,000 were ready for the payment which would be made by Canada on the transfer of the territory to her on that date. But the Canadian Ministry was now reluctant to shoulder the financial burden of suppressing the insurrection on the Red River, more especially as it had arisen before they had taken the country over. Claiming that it was the duty of the Imperial Government to pass over the country to them in peace, they decided not to accept the transfer. On 27th November, Sir John Young, the Governor-General, cabled Earl Granville, the Colonial Secretary : " On surrender by Company to the Queen, the Government of the Company ceases. The responsibility of Administration of affairs will then rest on Imperial Government. Canada cannot accept transfer unless quiet possession can be given—anarchy will follow." The amusing right-about-face of Canada had serious results for its Governor-to-be, looking across the border at his coming realm, his Instructions dated 29th September in his portfolio.

A plan was being laid by the Canadians in the Settlement to

suddenly rise on or about 2nd December, make themselves masters of the Settlement, and triumphantly bring in the Governor. There is evidence that they intended to steal on Riel and capture him, and that McDougall was privy to the scheme. Captain Cameron, writing to Sir John Macdonald on 1st December, said: " Mr. McDougall is sanguine that by tomorrow Louis Riel the rebel secretary will be a prisoner in the hands of loyal men, or a fugitive from Justice." And Bishop Machray must have had this plot in mind when he wrote Colonel Dennis on 6th December, earnestly advising him to give up any idea of attacking Fort Garry " and also any idea of seizing by stealth on any rebel." The " government pork " already referred to figured in the plans. It had passed the barricade at Rivière Sale without molestation on 24th November, and Dr. Schultz, to whom it was consigned, went to Riel, then taking over the customs, to show him the invoices. Riel asked if there were any arms in the cases, and was told that there were none. Accompanied by two armed men, he went to Dr. Schultz's house to take an inventory. The Doctor refused to let him in for that purpose unless he should promise on his honour not to remove anything. The promise was given. Riel, however, left an armed guard at the door, doubtless to assure himself that no one else took the pork. The cry was raised by the Canadians for their own purposes that the rebels intended to seize the pork. On the 26th William Hallett, a half-breed, went down to the Lower Fort to raise a force, but was unsuccessful. Next day Dr. Schultz received a renewed assurance " that neither private property nor the Canadian pork would suffer by the guard being put upon it." That evening a rumour was afloat that the Canadians intended to seize Fort Garry. On the 28th the statement that Riel intended to seize the pork was being used to rally men in arms. Mr. Bunn met two hundred men coming from the northern parishes to the rescue. An assurance that the pork was safe sent them home. On the following day (the 29th) it was rumoured that Governor Mactavish, Dr. Cowan, and others were prisoners, and a resolution was passed at a meeting that they must be released at all hazards. All these rumours must have been set afloat by the Canadians to rouse the English section to action. They so far succeeded that Begg, on the 30th, reports the English and Scots half-breeds cleaning their guns and drilling in companies. It must have been agreed that the proclamation of the transfer of the country to Canada was necessary to give the movement a legal standing and to rally the doubtful. But no official word had reached the would-be Governor. None the less, with the confidence in his luck that marks the gambler, he decided to play his part in the game. Copies of a proclamation were prepared and sent forward. On the night of the 29th, Colonel Dennis was sent north with additional copies, and with a commission in the name of the Queen to act as McDougall's Lieutenant and " Conservator of Peace," with power to raise a military force. On the evening of 1st December McDougall, accompanied by Richards and Provencher, crossed the border to the Hudson's Bay Company's post and there, without being sworn in as Governor and while still but a mere citizen, he read the Proclamation, as Governor of the North-West Territory, continuing in their offices the officers and functionaries then holding office, save the Governor, and requiring all to take notice thereof and act accordingly. Thereafter he prudently retired to American Territory. This astonishing action on the part of McDougall is explicable only when connected with the rising planned in the Settlement. In his subsequent defence of himself, he stated that he had received on 26th November a letter from Mr. Lampson, dated 25th September, saying that the transfer would take place on 1st December ; that the Company's government no longer existed ; that rebels were in control of the Settlements ; and that it was incumbent on him to prevent annexation to the States by proclaiming the authority of Canada. Incidentally, it appears that he expected Colonel Dennis to put down the insurrection " by a *coup de grâce*," and that his intention was that " a legal status might be given to any Government *de facto* formed by the inhabitants for the protection of their lives and property."

Early in the morning of the 1st December, Colonel Stoughton Dennis arrived at the home of his employee William Hallett, on the Assiniboine. After a consultation with certain unnamed gentlemen, he was convinced that public sentiment " would now sustain a movement to put down by force of arms the refractory French," and that the people would respond to a call. He then passed through Winnipeg, where he held council with Canadians, including Dr. Schultz, and showed them his commission. Major Boulton says : " Colonel Dennis informed us of his intention to raise a force and establish the authority of the Government and instructed me and others to follow him to the Stone Fort " (Lower Fort Garry). There Dennis showed Mr. Flett, the officer in charge, his commission, and was allowed to take possession. That evening some seventy men assembled in a large room in the upper part of the main building and were drilled. Dennis distributed copies of what he called a proclamation. Though so entitled, as presumably from the Queen, it was signed only by the secretary of the Governor-to-be, Provencher. It read in part : " Now Know Ye that We have seen fit by our Royal Patent, bearing date the twenty-ninth day of September . . . to appoint the Honourable William McDougall . . . on from and after the day to be named by us for the admission of Rupert's Land and the North Western Territory . . . into the . . . Dominion of Canada to wit on from and after the first day of December . . . to be . . . the Lieutenant-Governor of the North West Territories." The seal of the North-West Territories was affixed to the document !

Those who were behind the scenes had done well, for on the next day the Indian chief Prince, with a " band of some 70 to 100 men," came in to the Stone Fort. Dennis sent them home, retaining, however, fifty to guard the fort. The survey parties were called to the banner, and one of their number, Mr. Webb, was sent to Portage la Prairie to organize four companies of fifty men each. Major

Boulton was retained to drill the recruits in different parts of the Settlement. Mr. James Ross, although a delegate to the conference, was in consultation with Dennis. He was running with the hare and hunting with the hounds. Dennis consulted with Judge Black as to the advisability of proclaiming martial law, but that wise man was alarmed at the possibilities of conflict. As Dennis reported to McDougall, he "thought there was a strong hope that the Council (*i.e.* the Conference) still in session (would take) steps to dissolve the whole thing." Dennis continues : "Should we succeed in getting hold of the prime conspirator (Riel), I shall put him in a strong room in this place." That evening the Canadians in Winnipeg were organizing and preparing to join, or to be joined by Dennis. Mr. Bannatyne was, however, aware of the danger, and sent word to Riel on every account to keep himself within the fort. It must have been obvious by this time that Bannatyne's plan, that the Company should remain in power and the French half-breeds disarm, was wholly impracticable, for the Canadians would have seized Fort Garry and installed the new Government without any consideration of the rights of the settlers. Obviously Riel, when withdrawing his adhesion to the scheme, had some intimation of the designs of the Canadians, or at least sensed the situation more truly than did the English party.

Had the plot devised by the Canadian party and supported by McDougall and Dennis not taken shape, the Company might have remained in power till the transfer, and a delegation elected within the law might have negotiated with Canada and secured the admission of Rupert's Land, or at least of the colony, into the Dominion as a province. As it was, the danger of the moment brought the conference to definite unanimous decisions—all the more as the movement among the Canadians issued in those of the French who had held aloof formerly joining the Riel faction. On 1st December a List of Rights was drawn up to voice the general sentiment of the Settlement. Its main features, as published on 5th December, ran :

1. That the people have the right to elect their own Legislature.

2. That the Legislature have the power to pass all laws local to the Territory over the veto of the Executive by a two thirds vote.

3. That no act of the Dominion Parliament (local to the Territory) be binding on the people until sanctioned by the Legislature of the Territory.

4. That all Sheriffs, Magistrates, Constables, School Commissioners, etc. be elected by the people.

5. A free Home-stead and pre-emption Land Law.

6. That a portion of the public lands be appropriated to the benefit of Schools, the building of Bridges, Roads, and Public Buildings.

7. That it be guaranteed to connect Winnipeg by Rail with the nearest line of Railroad within a term of five years ; the land grant to be subject to the Local Legislature, [the assumption being that it would control the natural resources].

8. That for the term of four years all Military, Civil and Municipal expenses be paid out of the Dominion funds.

9. That the Military be composed of the Inhabitants now existing in the Territory.

10. That the English and French Languages be common in the Legislature and Courts, and that all Public Documents be published in both languages.

11. That the Judge of the Supreme Court speak the English and French languages.

12. That Treaties be concluded and ratified between the Dominion and the several tribes of Indians in the Territory to ensure peace on the frontier.

13. That we have a fair and full representation in the Canadian Parliament.

14. That all the privileges, customs and usages existing at the time of the transfer be respected.

While the land is not definitely claimed, some sort of local control of its income is to be inferred from the pertinent clauses. It will be of interest later to note that the more important of these demands were conceded by the Dominion in the Manitoba Act, six months later. It is not clear whether the twelve English delegates were present at the session when this list of rights was drawn up. Begg names but six—Messrs. Bunn, Gunn, W. and R. Tait, Dr. Bird, and James Ross. The list was adopted unanimously. The conference, however, could not agree on the next step. The first proposal was to send delegates to McDougall to negotiate with him on the terms as declared in the list. Riel objected—that the Settlement would never receive McDougall as Governor, that the rights of the people could only be made secure by an Act of the Canadian Parliament. The matter was left over for the next day. The excitement over the movements of the Canadian party seems to have brought the conference to a premature close. English and French had united to proclaim their rights, without, however, the English recognizing the authority of the executive of the French party.

The French party protected itself by preventing the two newspapers, the *Nor'Wester* and the *Red River Pioneer*, from publishing McDougall's proclamation. On the 3rd, various bodies of men who had gone to the Lower Fort to enroll themselves with Colonel Dennis returned and tried to allay alarm by reporting that the Colonel hoped that matters would be settled amicably. On the 4th the French, apparently now in need of supplies for the large number called up to defend Fort Garry, in spite of protests from Dr. Cowan and Governor Mactavish, broke into the Company's warehouse and distributed pemmican and balls. On the Canadian side, in spite of Riel's promise not to seize the Canadian Government's pork, some sixty Canadians occupied Dr. Schultz's house, ostensibly for its protection. They were to form the surprise party for the attack on Fort Garry and for the seizure of Louis Riel, for two days later Bishop Machray wrote Colonel Dennis, as has been shown, warning him against any idea of attacking Fort Garry, "and also any idea of seizing by stealth on any rebel." Whether because of this letter or in view of the fact that the French had gathered around Riel in great numbers, and that the chance of surprise and success had disappeared, Dennis expressed his disapproval of the occupation of Schultz's house. Major Boulton, however, continued his efforts to raise and drill companies in the various parishes to the north. While the company in Dr. Schultz's house was in a splendid position for effecting a surprise, now that the enemy was on the alert, it was in a very dangerous isolated situation, for the people had not flocked rapidly to Dennis's standard, and the Colonel could not, certainly did not, come to their support. Riel saw the opportunity, surrounded the houses, and accepted the surrender of the whole garrison as prisoners. They were lodged in the security of Fort Garry. To Riel's honour be it said, the government pork was not touched. Riel gave a written promise that the lives of the prisoners would be spared. It was an easy matter thereafter to arrest individually other supporters of the Canadian party. The next day, 7th December, Riel issued the " Declaration of the People of Rupert's Land and the North West," to the effect that, whereas the Hudson's Bay Company, which had governed the country well in the past, had in March, 1864, transferred its rights to Canada " by transactions with which the people were considered unworthy to be made acquainted . . . and whereas it is also generally admitted that a people is at liberty to establish any form of government it may consider suitable to its wants as soon as the power to which it was subject abandons it or attempts to subjugate it without its consent to a foreign power," the people were now free from all allegiance to the Company; a Provisional Government was now formed to exercise all lawful authority, but held itself in readiness to enter into negotiations with the Canadian Government for favoured terms for the good government and prosperity of the people. The document was signed by John Bruce, President, and Louis Riel, Secretary, and was worded to appear to be the finding of the conference assembled on 24th November. An armed force was sent out to take possession of the Company's post at Pembina, in the belief that McDougall was still there. On the 8th the great part of the French force dispersed to their homes. On the 9th Colonel Dennis gave orders to stop all recruiting and drilling, and wrote to McDougall that the English-speaking portion of the settlers could not be depended upon for support, that he would be leaving to join him in a few days. The great scheme had miscarried. Its only effect had been to overthrow the legal government of the colony and to place Louis Riel in control of a provisional government claiming the support of the whole colony, on the ground that the Company had surrendered its territory to the Crown without any government being installed in its place. Thus the rule of the Great Company, a rule based on the consent of the governed, without military support of any kind, disappeared— caught between the upper and nether millstones of the French and Canadian armed factions.

On 10th December the flag of the Provisional Government floated over Fort Garry. The government pork remained safe in Dr. Schultz's house, and Riel even travelled to Oak Point to see that the Government supplies there were kept secure from the Indians, who were reported as about to plunder them. On the 12th Bannatyne was offered the position of postmaster in the new régime, and, after some hesitation, accepted. Mr. Goulet continued acting as customs officer. The first judicial trial under the new régime took place on 21st December. The next day the keys to the Company's safe were secured by searching the pockets of the protesting Governor Mactavish, and Riel took possession of the money. Riel, after a period of much restraint, was now carrying things with a high hand, and some of his own party were falling away from him as going too far. Soon John Bruce resigned as President, and on 29th December Louis Riel was chosen to fill his place, with Louis Schmidt for Secretary. On 18th December McDougall, with the Provisional Government in undisputed power, packed up and began his long journey to Canada—the most discredited politician in the history of British North America. The recriminations which followed his return are no part of this account. He tried to persuade the Canadian public that Sir John Macdonald, in postponing the transfer, had been guilty of a gross betrayal.

3.—DONALD SMITH, COMMISSIONER FOR CANADA, DEALS WITH A
UNITED SETTLEMENT—THE PROVISIONAL GOVERNMENT, 1870

For a surprising length of time Sir John Macdonald regarded the disturbances on Red River with a facile optimism. His one fear was that the rest of the Settlement would be forced to accept the government set up by the half-breeds. " This would give an apparent sanction, in the eyes of the people of the United States, to the acts of that government. It would be held up as being the choice of the whole people there, and would receive the sympathies of the American public generally." On November 27, 1869, George Stephen, later of the Bank of Montreal and the Canadian Pacific Railway Company, wrote to Macdonald that Donald A. Smith, the chief officer of the Hudson's Bay Company since Mr. Hopkins's retirement, and an old and intimate friend of Governor Mactavish, had informed him (Stephen) that he had received information from the North-West, which he thought would be of service to the Government. Stephen suggested that Smith should go to Ottawa. Macdonald replied on the 29th, that the Government would be glad to get all possible information from Smith, adding : "My own opinion is that the insurrection or riot will die out of itself." Macdonald's jaunty optimism disappeared on 1st December when Smith arrived in Ottawa and gave him a true picture of the scene on the Red River. Moreover, that day a telegram came in from St. Paul : " Insurgents are arranging to hold a Council of Representatives from the different districts to consider the state of the Country and advise as to future action." Macdonald now believed that his fears would be realized, that the English and French might unite and might make an appeal to the American public, and precipitate a grave international situation. With the nimbleness, swiftness, and wisdom characteristic of the man when alert, he put his shoulder to the wheel to get his Government out of the mire in which he now saw it was stalled. At the suggestion of Smith, he decided that a Protestant of great ability should be sent out to deal with the English settlers, and that George Stephen should be the man. Stephen could not go, and nominated Smith for the mission. Even now Macdonald's methods were not changed. Can the Ethiopian change his skin or the leopard his spots ? He wrote to Smith on the eve of his departure for the West : " You had better talk over with McDougall the best means of buying off the Insurgent Leaders or some of them. There are situations in the Council and otherwise to be disposed of ; and a very considerable Military Police must be at once organized ; employment might be found for the most active of the half-breeds of different races." He still had visions of the " golden bridge " over which McDougall could pass into his realm. But more dignified means were resorted to. Lord Granville had cabled, at some date not given, the substance of a proclamation which might be issued by the Governor-General in the name of the Queen. This was now issued in proper form (6th December), and adapted to the actual situation. It ran in part :

Her Majesty commands me to state to you, that She will always be ready through me as Her Representative to redress all well founded grievances, and that She has instructed me to hear and consider any complaints that may be made or desires that may be expressed to me as Governor-general. At the same time She has charged me to exercise all the powers and authority with which She has entrusted me in the support of order, and the suppression of unlawful disturbances. By Her Majesty's authority I do therefore assure you, that on the Union with Canada all your civil and religious rights and privileges will be respected, your properties secured to you, and that your Country will be governed, as in the past, under British laws and in the spirit of British justice.

General as were the terms of the proclamation, they were well devised to allay the anxieties of the settlers about their titles, and about their civil and religious privileges. The closing clauses called for a general laying down of arms, and promised that in that case no legal proceedings would be taken against the disturbers of the peace. On 11th December a previous scheme for a tariff for the North-West was cancelled by Council, and a Minute put it on record that the tariff of the Settlement then prevailing should continue for two years.

Smith's Instructions, dated December 10, 1869, ran that he was to be " Special Commissioner " to inquire and report, also to remove apprehensions by explaining to the people the intentions of the Canadian Government ; he was to take steps throughout to bring about the peaceful transfer of the country ; he was to bear with him the Governor-General's proclamation (and doubtless the information of the change of tariff which had been decided on in Privy Council). He would thus be able to speak with authority ; otherwise he was to act according to his best judgment. The Special Commissioner left Ottawa on 13th December as Sir John put it " to carry the olive branch. . . . We must not make any indications of even thinking

of a Military Force until peaceable means have been exhausted."
On 20th December he was at Georgetown hastening northward,
and was already sufficiently apprised of the situation to offer
suggestions.   He asked Macdonald if he could promise that two-
thirds of the Council would be chosen from the Settlement, and could
say that an Act of Parliament would be passed at the next session
making these elective ; that the settlers would have representation
of some kind in the Dominion Parliament ; that the cost of the
general government of the North-West would for a time be borne
by the Dominion Government ; that the present tariff should continue not for the two years as settled in Council, but for four ; that
Indian and half-breed title to the land would be equitably adjusted.
These, he cynically suggested, should not be concessions, but should
" take the form of original intentions of the Government."

Twenty miles north of Georgetown, Smith, who had overtaken
Father Thibault, and had been joined by Charles Tupper, come out
privately to take charge of his daughter Mrs. Cameron, met the
crestfallen Governor McDougall on his way home.   On the 27th he
reached Fort Garry.   The guard took him to the French Council,
where he was asked to take an oath not to undermine the " Government now legally established."   This he declined to do, but he gave
his word of honour that he would not go beyond the gates till the
next day, and that he would do nothing to restore the Hudson's
Bay Company to power.   He was then permitted to go to Governor
Mactavish's house, and was submitted to no restraint.   Father
Thibault was taken to the Catholic Mission, but was allowed to have
communication with no one.   Charles Tupper came on to Fort Garry,
secured the furniture of Captain Cameron, and returned to escort
his daughter and her husband back to Canada.

In a letter to Sir John, Smith indicates the situation at his arrival.
The action taken by Colonel Dennis was reprobated on all hands.
McDougall's proclamation of 1st December was a great mistake.
There were sixty-four prisoners, mostly Canadians, in the fort.
The drift was to annexation with the United States.   Colonel
Stutsman of Pembina was busy working to that end.   The propaganda was that the Imperial Government would make no effort
to prevent the transfer of the whole North-Western Territory to
the Republic.   This report of Smith's was so far correct that while
the struggle had been between the French faction and the Canadian,
the American party was in the background.   With the Canadian
party crushed and the French in the awkward position of being in
arms without any legal authority and subject to being suppressed
by military force in the spring, the question arose whether the way
of escape might not be by annexation to the United States.   In this
situation the American party saw its opportunity, and not only
became active but secured a hearing.   Yet the French had as much
to fear from an American immigration submerging them as from
a Canadian.   Then, too, Riel's sentiments were distinctly British.
His policy was to continue his efforts to bring the English and

French together so that a solid people would negotiate with Canada for recognition of their rights. Should that fail, and Canada attempt to crush him by military force, he would then appeal to the American public for assistance and, perhaps, for the admission of the North-West into the republic. Hence his open relations with the American party, while at the same time the support of the English settlers was being sought. In the circumstances it was an astute policy, for nothing was more calculated to bring the Canadian Government to terms than the dread of American intervention. Indeed, that very dread had already changed the attitude of Sir John Macdonald. The Americans could pour through an open country into the Settlement, whereas a Canadian expedition, precluded from passing through American territory, must work its way through the difficult country west of Fort William.

On 16th December Begg's Journal reports :

The American residents amongst whom are Major Robinson and H. S. Donaldson seem to be interesting themselves a good deal in the French movement.

On the 18th :

Major Henry Robinson is about starting a newspaper in the French interests in the office of the *Nor'Wester*.

On the 22nd :

To-day a bargain was made between Mr. Caldwell and Messrs. Robinson and Stutsman for the Printing Press, Type etc. of the *Red River Pioneer* Newspaper for the sum of £550. . . . It is becoming evident that Riel is determined to carry things with a high hand, and rumours heretofore not heard are being circulated in favour of annexation to the United States.

In contrast, on 24th December, Riel went down to Kildonan Parish " to see what prospect there was of the English-speaking side joining in the Provisional Government. . . . The object of the Provisional Government to be to arrange for the future welfare of the Settlement, and to make terms for annexation to some government whichever may be found as most advantageous to the settlers as a body." On the 25th : " Ex-President Bruce still declares the intention of the French Party to be to treat with Canada, but they want the rights to be secured to them ere they will give in." January 1st : " Mr. Riel addressed a large meeting at Oak Point of French people, and it is said pledged himself for Canada on proper terms." January 4th : " Riel asserts that he is in favour of an arrangement with Canada and is anxious for the English to join the French—to meet the Commissioners, and if the Commissioners are not able to grant what the people want—for the whole Settlement to frame a list of the demands to be secured—then send De Salaberry back with the list—and that in the meantime until Canada is heard from, for the people unitedly to form a Provisional Government for their safety, and to be the better able to treat with Canada." This policy, subsequently followed, has been attributed to the wise intervention of Donald Smith, but it was really that of Louis Riel.

The next day, 5th January, William and Robert Tait, quondam delegates to the conference of November, waited on the French Council to see if anything could be done to unite the two sides. They were told that union was desirable, that the representation in the united Council should be even. The Taits and Alexander Begg then went off to win support for union from the English parishes. " It is felt that to be able to treat properly with the Commissioners from Canada the people should be united, and that if these Commissioners are not treated with, the golden chance is lost, and God knows where the country will drift to." It is symptomatic of the growing *détente* that a number of the prisoners in Fort Garry were being freed. On 6th January, Riel met Mr. Bannatyne and offered him the positions of postmaster and head of the Courts " under the Provisional Government at the same time stating the intention of that government to treat with Canada or England." On this condition Bannatyne accepted the positions.

The English view of the movement to union is given in Smith's letter to Macdonald of 8th January : " The English speaking inhabitants are now moving heartily with the view of bringing their weight and influence to bear on the malcontents so as to induce them to come to terms with Canada or England." On 10th January Begg's Journal reports : " Mr. William Tait and his brother Robert returned from the direction of the Stone Fort last Friday evening. They report good success in their endeavours amongst the people to get them to join the Provisional Government," and 11th January : " Riel in every action shows an honest purpose for the good of the country, and American influence is no influence with him."

A small party raised the issue of restoring the Company to power with an elective Council for the colony. Begg regarded this as impracticable and unfortunate, for it was calculated to divide the English. On 5th January Begg reports : " The Americans are rapidly losing ground, if they ever had any." In spite of all the troubles the Settlement was at heart British.

Riel, then, had formulated a very intelligent policy. Yet it was marred by the vices of a despot in dread of losing his power and even, possibly, by personal shortcomings. Begg made record on 27th December : " Reports are going abroad that Riel is drinking, others that he is going deranged ; neither are generally believed." With some sixty-four prisoners on his hands he should have pressed his policy to an issue and at the psychological moment released them. The arrival of the Commissioners for Canada offered an excellent reason for bringing his plans to maturity naturally and swiftly, but he showed the hesitancy of a usurper in dread lest the next step forward should lead to a pitfall. He acted as though Father Thibault's presence were a menace to his power, and barred him from relations with his many friends among the French, as Smith says, " Keeping him virtually as a prisoner." Certain papers which the reverend Father brought in were taken and kept from the public, when they offered excellent grounds for Riel's bringing the people and the Commissioners together, with himself as intermediary leading all parties to a happy agreement. De Salaberry was not feared. After remaining, at Smith's suggestion, for some time at Pembina, he came in and was lodged at the Catholic Mission. He was allowed considerable freedom, and even went out to dances.

Meanwhile Donald Smith was playing the part of a simple officer of the Company, which was all the easier as he had departed from Canada so hastily that his Commission was to follow him. Kept under surveillance, he studiously avoided leaving Fort Garry, but visitors were allowed to see him. On an opportune occasion (8th January) he informed Riel of his position as Commissioner, and asked to meet with the " Council," but nothing was done. Here was another opportunity lost. Riel should have seized it ; he should have pushed his policy, gathered the representatives of the people, English and French, under him, and himself introduced the Commissioners and led the discussions. As the leader of the community in coming to terms with Canada his future would have been assured. As it proved, his hesitancy and procrastination were his undoing.

On the 13th, Grand-Vicar Thibault and Colonel de Salaberry were introduced to " the President and Council of the People." Compliments and explanations were exchanged, and the Commissioners were bowed out, it appearing that they had only been commissioned to calm the half-breeds, not to negotiate with them. The next day Riel demanded his credentials and papers of Donald Smith. When told that they were at Pembina, he demanded an order for their delivery. This Smith refused to give, but agreed to send a friend, Mr. Hardisty, for them. Immediately thereafter he was placed for the first time under strict guard. The high-handed attitude of Riel to the Commissioners was resented by a number of his followers : Begg reports on the 14th : " It is said there is a split amongst Riel's councillors on account of his overbearing manner with them [selves] ; how far it will go cannot yet be told ; one or two of his councillors have left him it is certain." When it was ascertained that Hardisty had gone to bring in Smith's official papers three men, John F. Grant, Angus McKay (English half-breeds), and Pierre Lavaillier, who, it will be remembered, had accompanied Lépine to face McDougall and warn him out of the country, determined that Riel should not be allowed to get possession of the papers. They did not leave for the South without arranging with one by name Nolin, a French half-breed, to work up a party to support them on their return. A similar group in support was arranged for at White Horse Plain. When the three (apparently for their safe keeping) demanded the papers of Hardisty, he naturally refused to give them up. The three took Hardisty's guard prisoner and proceeded homeward. Riel organized a party and went off at its head to secure the papers, only to meet a brigade of some twelve sleighs escorting Hardisty homeward. In an altercation Lavaillier took the

President by the throat, and was in the act of shooting him when Father Ritchot and others intervened. With half-breeds that sort of thing is only a flare-up and soon is forgotten. Riel's horse giving out, Grant took the President into his sleigh and the two opponents arrived at Fort Garry followed by the two opposing parties. When Riel opened the gate for Hardisty, Lavaillier drove his sleigh through, and Hardisty delivered the papers safely to Donald Smith at Dr. Cowan's house. Most amusing of all, Lavaillier's men stood on guard over Dr. Cowan's house while Riel's armed men guarded the fort— all without so much as a fight.

The excitement caused by the incident was intense. A large number of both French and English assembled and demanded that Smith should be heard. An agreement was made that there should be a mass meeting next day when Smith would read his Commission. Riel thus lost the initiative. Instead of uniting the English and French, and meeting the representatives of Canada, those representatives were to speak for Canada directly to the body of the Red River settlers. How far Donald Smith's influence contributed to this result does not appear. On the face of it, the public meeting was the result of the ebullition of feelings general both in the English and the French sections of the community.

On January 19, 1870, the public of the Settlement assembled for the meeting in such numbers that the court house could not hold it. The venue was changed to the open air, though the thermometer stood at twenty degrees below zero. The proceedings lasted five hours. On the motion of Louis Riel and Pierre Lavaillier, the leaders of the two French factions, Thomas Bunn was called to the chair. Riel was elected to the humble position of interpreter. On the motion of another pair of opponents, Angus McKay and Mr. O'Donoghue, Judge Black became secretary. When called upon, Donald Smith began by reading the Hon. Joseph Howe's letter of Instructions to him, dated 10th December, Riel translating it into French after him. He then began to read a personal letter from the Governor-General to himself, dated 12th December. Louis Riel objected on the ground that it was personal. After a confused discussion it was decided that the document was of a public character. At the passage " The people may rely upon it that respect and protection will be extended to the different religious persuasions" there were loud cheers. The sentence : " Titles to every description of property will be perfectly guarded " brought renewed cheers. The letter concluded : " In declaring the desire and determination of Her Majesty's Cabinet, you may very safely use the terms of the ancient formula that ' Right shall be done in all cases.' " Riel objected that the letter was simply signed " John Young," and not " Governor." Smith pointed out that the phrase " in my capacity as Her Majesty's representative " occurred at the opening of the letter. Riel then interpreted it to the Frenchmen of the meeting.

Donald Smith now stated that letters had been sent by the

Canadian Government to Governor Mactavish and to Bishop Machray, and publicly asked Vicar-General Thibault for them, that Mactavish gave him permission to read his as being a public document. Riel's objection to its being read was greeted with cries " We will have it." After some altercation it was shown that the letters were in the possession of Mr. O'Donoghue, of whom Bishop Machray requested the letter addressed to him. The meeting refused to proceed with business until the documents should be produced. Smith indicated that the Governor-General's proclamation was among them. Continuing, Smith read Lord Granville's telegram to the Governor-General which had been the basis of that proclamation, including the passage, " [The Queen] relies on your Government to use every effort to explain whatever misunderstandings may have arisen—to ascertain their wants and conciliate the good will of the people of Red River Settlement. But in the meantime she authorizes you to signify to them the sorrow and displeasure with which she views the unreasonable and lawless proceedings which have taken place ; and her expectation that if any parties have desires to express or complaints to make respecting their condition and prospects, they will address themselves to the Governor-General of Canada." The reading was greeted with cheers. An attempt by Mr. Burke at the close of the meeting to force the hand of Riel and secure the release of the prisoners threatened to break up the harmony which had thus far prevailed. Riel said, " Not just now."

The meeting next day was even larger. It opened with an apology from Mr. Burke for raising the matter of the prisoners. Father Lestanc, representing the French population, then said, amid cheers, " We have been good friends to this day in the whole Settlement, and I want to certify here that we will be good friends to-night." Donald Smith, now in possession of the secreted documents, read the Governor-General's letter to Governor Mactavish in which a copy of the Queen's cabled message had been enclosed. Its closing sentence : " The inhabitants of Rupert's Land, of all classes and persuasions may rest assured that Her Majesty's Government has no intention of interfering with, or setting aside, or allowing others to interfere with the religion, the rights, or the franchise hitherto enjoyed, or to which they may hereafter prove equal," was greeted with loud cheers. Smith followed this up with the fresh Instructions given to William McDougall by Joseph Howe on 7th December. Civil and religious liberties would be sacredly respected, as also property and titles to land. The present tariff would continue for two years. In the Council not only the Company but all classes would be fully and fairly represented. The present (i.e. the proposed) Government would be merely temporary and an Act would be passed granting a liberal constitution as soon as McDougall should have sent in his reports. A sentence was here inserted to suggest that these were the original intentions of the Government : " You had, of course, instructions on all the above mentioned points, except the tariff, before you left Ottawa, but it has been thought well that I should repeat them to you in this authoritative form." All these documents, received with enthusiasm, were the result of the collaboration of Macdonald and Smith in the first week of December. They were perfectly adapted to meet the sentiments of both the English and French parties on the Red River. Smith followed them with a speech punctuated with cheers. He had relations in the Settlement ; his children were born in Rupert's Land ; he felt a deep interest in the country and its inhabitants ; he stood there not only in the interests of Canada, but only in those interests so far as they were in accordance with the good of the country ; he hoped that his humble efforts would contribute to bring about peaceably " union and entire accord among all classes of the people of this land." He closed by reading McDougall's first Instructions. Set in the light of the documents emanating from the first week of December, they must have appeared singularly general and innocuous.

Louis Riel now moved that twenty representatives be elected by the English population to meet the same number from the French to decide what would be best for the welfare of the country, the meeting to be on the 25th proximo. Mr. Bannatyne seconded the motion, and it was carried. A committee was formed to apportion the delegates to the parishes, and determine the mode of election. At the close of the meeting Riel spoke :

> Before this assembly breaks up, I cannot but express my feelings, however, briefly. I came here with fear. We are not yet enemies [loud cheers], but we came very near being so. As soon as we understood each other, we joined in demanding what our English fellow subjects in common with us believe to be our just rights [loud cheers]. I am not afraid to say *our* rights, for we all have rights [renewed cheers]. We claim no half-rights, mind you, but all the rights we are entitled to. Those rights will be set forth by our representatives, and what is more, gentlemen, we will get them [loud cheers].

The result of the meetings was general goodwill—so much so, that it was determined that the French at Fort Garry should be disbanded save for a small guard, but a rumour that the settlers at Portage la Prairie were contemplating a raid put an end for the moment to all such good intentions. On 22nd January, however, most of the French were sent home.

The elections over, the representatives chosen met from 25th January onwards, in what is called the Convention. Questions involving the elections delayed its main business. It was finally settled that Alfred Scott, who was put up by the American group at Winnipeg, was elected, and not Bannatyne. Smith laid his documents before the Convention, and explained the views of the Canadian Government. On the 27th a committee was appointed to draw up a Bill of Rights. On the 29th and 31st their report was before the Convention. Donald Smith exerted himself to make the Bill of Rights as conservative of the Canadian view as might be. He wrote to Macdonald on 1st February : " We have succeeded in getting expunged some of the most objectionable points in their demands." Riel's demand that the Settlement be admitted into the

Dominion as a Province was negatived. Riel's opposition to the more moderate resolutions resulted in the rise of a strong party determined on getting rid of him after the Convention should rise, and even on taking him prisoner to Lower Fort Garry. The continued detention of the prisoners worked in the same direction. This list of rights, as finally drawn, required among other things the continuance of the prevailing tariff for three years ; no direct taxation save by the local legislature ; so long as the Settlement should be a Territory, all military and civil expenses to be borne by the Dominion ; thereafter the local government to enjoy all the rights of a Province ; the French and English languages to be common in the local legislature and courts ; the Indians' title to be extinguished ; representation in the Dominion Parliament to be granted ; public land, within a radius measured by the distance between the Forks and the International Boundary, to be in the full control of the local legislature. Smith was invited to give his opinion as to the reaction of the Canadian Government to these demands. This he did with characteristic caution. On 8th February the Convention agreed to accept the invitation held out by the Canadian Government, and to send a delegation to Ottawa to agree on the terms for a peaceful entry of the country into the Dominion. The next business was the formation of a Provisional Government. Riel demanded the recognition of his Government, which had hitherto been withheld, for Judge Black was chairman of the Convention, and not President Riel. On the 9th, a delegation was sent to advise with Governor Mactavish. He answered, " For God's sake, have any form of Government which will restore peace and order." Asked if he would delegate his authority to another, he replied : " I am dying and will not delegate my authority to anyone." On the 10th, a committee was named to sketch the scheme of a Provincial Government. The committee reported in favour of a Council of twelve members each from the English and French peoples, the President not to be one of the twelve. The English wished their representatives to be re-elected. The French were in favour of continuing their representation. The administration was stated as follows : Louis Riel, President of the Council ; James Ross, Judge ; H. McKenney, Sheriff ; Dr. Bird, Coroner ; A. G. B. Bannatyne, Postmaster ; John Sutherland and Roger Goulet, Collectors of Customs ; Thomas Bunn, Secretary ; Louis Schmidt, Sub-Secretary (for the French) ; William O'Donoghue, Treasurer. Courts were provided for, much as hitherto, there being some changes of the areas of petty courts and Oak Point being now included. The formation of this government was received with enthusiasm. Governor Mactavish, Dr. Cowan, and Bannatyne, who had been held prisoners, were freed of their guards. Salutes were fired from Fort Garry, and the town gave itself up to fun—in fact, to a "regular drunk." Not the least relished part of the celebration was the firing off of the skyrockets brought in by Dr. Schultz to celebrate the transfer of the country to Canada. Word had come in that a large band of men was marching from

Portage la Prairie to release the prisoners in Fort Garry. A messenger was sent to beseech them to desist until the Convention had finished its labours. Next day the Convention laid down the regulations for the election to the new-formed Council, and chose three men as a delegation to meet the Canadian Government in Ottawa—Father Ritchot for the French ; Judge Black for the English ; and Alfred Scott, an American, for the " English and Americans." The curious choice of Scott must have been due to the desire to find one who would not upset the balance between the English and French. The appointment, however, was received with great dissatisfaction. The Convention was now dissolved.

Their long weeks of distressing imprisonment in Fort Garry did little to quench the spirit of the Canadians. Sundry entries in Begg's Journal tell of the recalcitrant conduct of several individuals, Dr. Schultz and Charles Mair among them. When Riel was seeking the support of the English settlers, he made some show of releasing his captives. On 6th January two were released, and took their departure for Canada. On the 9th Dr. Schultz was frustrated in an attempt to escape, but a number—said to be twelve, among them Charles Mair—made a dash for liberty and got away in the direction of Portage la Prairie. Some were recaptured, but Mair and Thomas Scott reached the Portage in safety. They found the settlement there swollen by an accession of Canadians, including Major Boulton, who for safety had migrated from the Settlement ; and they began an agitation in favour of an expedition for the release of the prisoners. Boulton, who was as sensible as he was gallant, discouraged such an enterprise as impracticable, but it was finally resolved to take action. It may be no more than an accidental synchronism that Dr. Schultz made good his escape on the night of 23rd January. He found refuge among the settlers in the northern parishes. By 12th February the plans of the men at the Portage took form in an expedition sixty strong. Mr. Gaddy, an English half-breed was one of its leading spirits, and Major Boulton was in command. At Headingley a number of the settlers rallied to the party, prepared for a sudden attack on Fort Garry. Plans were, however, changed. Starting at 10 p.m. of a moonlit night, the expedition passed close by Fort Garry to the village of Winnipeg. Here information was secured that Riel slept at a certain house (that of one Henry Coutu). The house was surrounded, and Boulton and Scott entered to seek their prey. Coutu assured them truthfully that Riel was not there (14th February). Arrived in Kildonan, the raiders found the people well satisfied with the course of the Convention. A number, however, rallied to them at Kildonan Church, and messengers brought word that Dr. Schultz was on the way up from the lower settlements with a large force—more than two hundred, as it proved. The raiders had no supplies. It shows that there was a general sympathy in the parishes for the prisoners, that the people offered provisions. " The Rev. Mr. Black placed his house, stores, and everything he had, at our disposal, and we camped in the church for the night," says Boulton.

It says much for the inherent peaceableness of the Settlement that there had been not a drop of blood shed in the previous three months of upheaval. That night saw the snow red for the first time. One, Parisien, was brought in suspected of spying for Riel. Seeing an opportunity, he seized a gun and fled. At the river bank one, Sutherland, was riding on the ice-bound river and towards the church. Parisien took it that he was being intercepted, fired on him, and mortally wounded him. Parisien was captured and narrowly escaped lynching.

Riel countered the Canadian move by capturing a group of men in Headingley who had supported it. With the exception of Gaddy, they were soon released. Then, too, he released some twenty prisoners (15th February), the day that Boulton's force had passed through Winnipeg. All this while, Schultz's house had remained in security, but Riel now confiscated the property. Dr. Cowan's house in Fort Garry was being converted into " Government House " for the President. It must have been a rare satisfaction to President Riel to beautify his official residence with the furniture of his arch-opponent. The excitement in Winnipeg was great, and shops were closed in anticipation of a fight. Riel commandeered the ammunition of the shop of Bannatyne and Begg, as also the horses of the village. The release of the prisoners, long promised, cut the ground from under the feet of Major Boulton's party. The rally of even the lukewarm French to Riel's side made any hope that may have been entertained of capturing Fort Garry and overthrowing the Provisional Government futile. Moreover, the party from Portage la Prairie only now came to know how near the colony was to a peaceful settlement of its difficulties with Canada. Bishop Machray and many others counselled peace. The Portage expedition therefore decided to disband. Schultz fled to Fort William and Canada by the Winnipeg River route, and Boulton's party began the march home. As it was passing on foot across the prairies, about a mile and a half from Fort Garry, it was met by the French in arms, on horseback, Mr. O'Donoghue at its head. As Boulton's party had received a verbal message from Riel that, if they disbanded they would be allowed to return in peace, they were unarmed and accepted O'Donoghue's invitation to go to Fort Garry for a parley. There they were taken prisoners, to the number of forty-seven. Donald Smith's strictures on the whole movement are justified :

> The rising was not only rash, but purposeless, as, without its intervention, the prisoners would unquestionably have been released. The party was entirely unorganized, indifferently armed, unprovided with food even for one meal, and wholly incapable of coping with the French now re-united. . . . Under the circumstances it was not difficult to foresee that the issue could not be otherwise than disastrous to their cause. The attempt was, therefore, to be deplored, as it resulted in putting the whole Settlement at the feet of Riel.

He might have added, it aroused latent passions in Riel of which there was little or no evidence up to this time.

There were three involved in this raid for whom there was no mercy in the breast of the President—William Gaddy, the half-breed who brought the party down ; Major Boulton, who commanded it ; and Thomas Scott, the escaped prisoner. Gaddy was an obscure individual who had rallied people to Boulton's cause. He was captured up the Assiniboine on 14th February, in the height of the crisis, with several others who were soon released. He was thrown into a frigid bastion, with frozen pemmican and no water for his fare. His sudden disappearance led to the report that he had been summarily executed. He was in truth condemned to be shot. In the depth of night he was roused by guards, who cocked their guns and aimed at him, then lowered, and retired. He overheard them saying : " We cannot do it ; he is too dear an old friend ; According to Gaddy's own account, three times the armed men came, and three times stopped short of the deed. Certain that this was no mere intimidation, Gaddy worked himself through a porthole of the bastion and escaped.

Boulton was " court-martialled " on the day of his surrender, and condemned to be shot at noon of the following day. Pleas for mercy from many influential settlers, including the clergy of both persuasions, led to no more than a postponement. The intervention of Donald Smith alone saved him. Smith records the moving scene :

[Riel replied that] an example must be made, and he had firmly resolved that Bolton's execution should be carried out, bitterly as he deplored the necessity of doing so. I reasoned with him long and earnestly until at length, about 10 o'clock [Boulton, as it was now, was to be shot at midnight], he yielded, and addressing me, apparently with much feeling, said, " Hitherto I have been deaf to all entreaties, and, in now granting you this man's life . . . may I ask of you a favour ? " " Anything," I replied, " that in honour I can do." He continued, " Canada has disunited us, will you use your influence to re-unite us ? You can do so, and without this it must be war—bloody civil war ! " I answered, that as I had said on first coming to the country I would now repeat, that " I would give my whole heart to effect a peaceable union of the country with Canada." " We want only our just rights as British subjects," he said, " and we want the English to join us simply to obtain these." " Then," I remarked, " I shall at once see them and induce them to go on with the election of delegates for that purpose " ; and he replied, " if you can do this, war will be avoided, not only the lives but the liberty of all the prisoners will be secured, for on your success depends the lives of all the Canadians in the country." He immediately proceeded to the prison, and intimated to the Archdeacon McLean [in attendance for the last scene] that he had been induced by me to spare Captain Bolton's life, and further had promised to me that immediately on the meeting of the Council shortly to be elected, the whole of the prisoners would be released, requesting the Archdeacon, at the same time to explain these circumstances to Captain Bolton and the other prisoners.

True to his promise, Smith visited the parishes down the Red River and up the Assiniboine, urging the settlers to elect representatives to the Council. He took the precaution to affirm that the Council was provisional, and simply to effect a peaceful transference to Canada. Some petitions to Riel, as President, had been drawn up.

He induced the parties involved to withdraw these. Riel's bargain, by which he secured Smith's support for the Council in return for Boulton's life, was very astute, for he thus secured a certain recognition of the Council of which he was President from the Commissioner of Canada. (The Council met for the first time on 10th March, with a full representation of the English and French settlers, and continued to function thereafter.)

His point gained, Riel was not careful to keep his promise of the lives of all of the prisoners. He cherished special indignation at Thomas Scott, who seems to have kept it aflame by his turbulent conduct as a prisoner. On 1st March, as Begg reports, Scott was put in irons " for having been indiscreet in the use of his tongue while in prison." On 4th March Smith was informed that Scott was to be shot at noon of that day. His report may be taken to be the most authentic statement, not only about Scott's end, but of Riel's motives in perpetrating the deed :

[Riel] said in substance that Scott had throughout been a most troublesome character, had been ringleader in a rising against Mr. Snow, who had charge of the party employed by the Canadian Government during the preceding summer in road making ; that he had risen against the " Provisional Government " in December last, that his life was then spared ; that he escaped, had again been taken in arms, and once more pardoned,—referring, no doubt, to the promise he had made to me that the lives and liberty of all the prisoners were secured—but that he was incorrigible, and quite incapable of appreciating the clemency with which he had been treated ; that he was rough and abusive to the guards, and insulting to him, Mr. Riel ; that his example had been productive of the very worst effects on the other prisoners, who had become insubordinate to such an extent that it was difficult to withhold the guards from retaliating. . . . I pointed out that the one great merit claimed for the insurrection was that, so far, it had been bloodless, except in one sad instance, which all were willing to look on as an accident, and implored him not now to stain it, to burden it with what would be considered a horrible crime.

The pleading of Donald Smith, of Rev. George Young—the founder of the Methodist mission in the Settlement, who attended on Thomas Scott during his last hours—and even of Father Lestanc, acting as head of the Roman Catholic mission, proved vain. Smith's narrative continues :

It was now within a few minutes of one o'clock and entering the Governor's house the Rev. Mr. Young joined me and said, " It is now considerably past the hour, I trust you have succeeded." " No," I said, " for God's sake, go back at once to the poor man, for I fear the worst." He left immediately, and a few minutes after he entered the room in which the prisoner was confined, some guards marched in and told Scott his hour had come. Not until then did the reality of his position flash upon poor Scott ; he said good-bye to the other prisoners, was led outside the gate of the Fort, with a white handkerchief covering his head ; his coffin, having a piece of white cotton thrown over it, was carried out ; his eyes were bandaged ; he continued in prayer, in which he had been engaged on the way for a few minutes ; he asked Mr. Young how he should place himself, whether standing or kneeling, then knelt in the snow, said farewell, and immediately after fell back pierced by three bullets, which passed through his body. The firing party consisted of six men, all of whom it is said were more or less intoxicated. It has been further stated that only three of the muskets were loaded with ball cartridges, and that one man did not discharge his piece. Mr. Young turned aside when the first shots were fired, then went back to the body and again retired for a moment while a man discharged his revolver at the sufferer, the ball, it is said, entering the eye and passing round the head.

The death of Scott on 4th March was in very fact a judicial murder. He was tried by a " Court Martial " of six, presided over by Ambroise Lépine. It was held during the night before the execution. Witnesses were heard. Riel was the only one to make a speech ; he called for the condemnation of Scott. Only one member of the court voted for acquittal. The decision made, Scott was called in. He was not asked to testify in his defence, but was simply informed of the charges and of his condemnation, and was led back to his cell.

This bloody deed, so disastrous to Louis Riel's career, will always be an enigma. During the four months of the disturbances Riel had played a very astute game—in keeping McDougall out of the country ; in placing a guard over Fort Garry ; and in capturing the garrison in Dr. Schultz's house. Throughout he had been remarkably self-restrained—in refraining from bloodshed, and, to an astonishing degree, in protecting private property. Even Dr. Schultz's house remained secure until he appeared in arms a second time. It is true that many prisoners were taken and suffered indignities and the distress of crowded quarters, but many very bitter opponents had been spared, and even released. Why should such an obscure man as Scott be made the scapegoat ? Insults said to have been thrown at the President through the prison door, or even the blow in the face said to have been dealt when Scott was being taken in chains to solitary confinement, are but a partial explanation, even if true. There must have been some change in Louis Riel himself. The man had already been in an asylum, and there is some evidence that the excitement of these past weeks and months was undermining his self-control. As has been said, as early as 27th December, Begg noted : " reports are going abroad that Riel is drinking, others that he is going deranged ; neither are generally believed." In the subsequent weeks he was planning the union of the English and French, but showed an indecision hitherto unsuspected. A despot dreading the loss of his power, he hesitated to take the steps necessary for its success ; he neither called the people together nor made a bid for harmony by releasing the prisoners. The issue was the great public meeting, which placed the negotiations with Donald Smith in the hands of the people and allotted to " the President " the humble rôle of interpreter. Riel's conduct thereafter, while still astute, is marked by an increasing number of irresponsible acts, whose only aim must have been to show that he was still in power. Men were arrested on the most trifling grounds, and released on trifling pleas put in by their friends. Even Bannatyne was held prisoner for a number of days, and released apparently for no palpable reason.   Then came the hectic days of the raid from Portage la Prairie, with the attempt of Boulton and Scott to seize the President in the home of Henry Coutu.   True, Riel's power was enhanced rather than diminished by the affair, but his irritability, his lack of self-control, his passion for personal ascendency became more marked.   It appeared immediately in the determination to have Major Boulton shot forthwith, and in his dastardly treatment of such an obscure character as Gaddy.   Hard on the heels of this came a physical crisis.   On 24th February Begg reports : " Riel was taken very ill this morning at Henry Coutu's house being threatened with an attack of brain fever ; the priests and sisters visited him and towards afternoon he became somewhat better and in the evening was conveyed to the Fort, Riel's mother was in attendance also." On the 27th he was " quite recovered from his recent attack." Three days after, the turbulent Scott was placed in irons, and three days later shot.   It would appear that a recalcitrance in Mair and Schultz endured with patience in December was intolerable in Scott at the end of February.   However that may be, Louis Riel—who had been the champion of the rights of the Settlement, and was in a fair way towards being hailed by posterity as the Father of Manitoba— by one passionate bloody deed, barred his own path to glory.

CHAPTER XIII

THE WEST ADMITTED INTO THE CONFEDERATION

I.—A PEACEFUL RED RIVER SETTLEMENT ENTERS THE CONFEDERA-
TION AS THE PROVINCE OF MANITOBA (THE NORTH-WEST
TERRITORY), 1870.

THE execution of Thomas Scott created great excitement in Ontario.
Mass meetings called on the Government to bring the perpetrators
to condign punishment. At a great meeting in Toronto the returned
prisoners were welcomed home, and Dr. Schultz made a fiery speech.
In strange contrast, after the first shock of the deed was over, the
Red River Settlement went on its way quietly. Five days after the
tragic event the Provisional Government met for the first time, and
Bishop Taché returned to his diocese. The bishop, on his way to
Rome, as has been seen, found the Canadian Government deaf to
his warnings, but in its difficulties it turned to him for help. In
response to a cable requesting his return, he left Rome suddenly on
13th January, and was in Ottawa on 9th February. He was given
a copy of the Governor-General's Proclamation of 6th December
promising an amnesty, among other things. Sir John Macdonald,
Sir George Cartier, and Joseph Howe all had conversations with him,
from which he gathered that the amnesty promised in the Proclamation was all-embracing, that the past would be forgotten. In
a letter from Sir John, dated 16th February, he was authorized " to
inform the leaders that if the Company's Government is restored,
not only will there be a general amnesty granted, but in case the
Company should claim payment for stores [taken], that the Canadian
Government will stand between the insurgents and all harm."
Taché claimed afterwards that no conditions were referred to in the
conversations, that the amnesty was to cover everything without
reservation. From his pulpit, on the Sunday after his return, the
bishop made a moving appeal for charity and forbearance, and for
the union of all parts of the Settlement. " The greater part of those
who heard him shed tears " while he spoke. Riel was in the church
and, it is said, was very much affected during the sermon, " shedding
tears at times " (Begg). The presence of the Bishop with the
promise of an amnesty did much to bring quiet to the colony. At
the same time the economic situation brought men to reason. Business was in any case at a standstill in the winter. Disturbances

would not affect it much, but it was absolutely necessary to return to normal conditions before the spring trade, so essential to prosperity, opened up. On 16th March seventeen prisoners were released, including Major Boulton. The rest soon got their freedom. Two days later Donald Smith left for Canada. Soon the *New Nation*, published by the American party in the interests of annexation, ceased to appear. Thomas Spence, ex-President of the Republic of Manitoba, took it over; soon it appeared as a loyal sheet. " Annexation is knocked in the head," Begg remarks. On the 23rd Father Ritchot and Alfred Scott, the delegates, left for Ottawa, and were followed by Judge Black next day. A Proclamation issued by the Provisional Government on 9th April was the harbinger of the return to normal conditions. It assured pardon to all who had differed (from Riel), and announced that the Hudson's Bay Company would now resume business. After the raid of the men from Portage la Prairie, the French made freer than ever with the goods of the Company, especially when the men who had rallied to Riel were disbanded. Apparently, when it became known through Bishop Taché that Canada would reimburse the Company for its losses, yet greater freedom was taken with the Company's property. The orgy of helping themselves over, the French began to clean the fort up, and the Company to make an inventory. On 20th April Riel ordered the Union Jack to be flown on the flagstaff of the fort, where the flag of the Provisional Government had long proclaimed the political situation. O'Donoghue was much displeased. He was allowed to remove the flagstaff from Dr. Schultz's house, and to plant it in front of Dr. Cowan's home within the fort, where Riel and the Provisional Government were lodged. There the Provisional Government's flag was flown. As it was higher than the Union Jack, Fenian O'Donoghue was doubtless pleased. On the 26th the Council met for its second session, and two days later the Company's store was open for business once more ; new notes of one pound and of five shillings, payable at Fort Garry, were issued for local circulation. The steamer *International* arrived. The Settlement had returned to normal, save for the presence of the Provisional Government, and a small body of armed men on guard in Fort Garry. The negotiations at Ottawa were expected to be successful, and all awaited the admission of Rupert's Land into the Dominion in a tranquil frame of mind.

Meanwhile, the Imperial and Canadian governments were preparing a military expedition to ensure law and order on the Red River. The Imperial Treasury was to bear the cost of 250 regulars, later increased to about 390, to be sent out under Colonel Garnet Wolseley ; the Canadian Government was to meet the expenses of the rest of the expedition. The Colonial Secretary, however, had no intention to use soldiers to force the British subjects on the Red River into subjection to Canadian rule. The Canadian Government must come to terms with the settlers before the troops should move. Lord Granville cabled the Governor-General on 5th March : " Her

Majesty's Government will give proposed military assistance, provided reasonable terms are granted Red River Settlers, and provided your Government enable Her Majesty's Government to proclaim the transfer of the territory simultaneously with the movement of the force."

The Colonial Office was none the less considering its action in case the troops had to go in before the transfer. It held that a civil governor would have to enter the territory along with the military. Accordingly, it raised with the Law Officers of the Crown the question of the legality of such a procedure. Acting on their advice, Lord Granville requested the Hudson's Bay Company to appoint Sir John Young, the Governor-General of Canada, Governor of Rupert's Land, so that he could appoint a Lieutenant-Governor, who would have legal authority, should he have to enter their territory before the actual transfer. The appointment was duly made, and in the form usual with the Company, under the Common Seal. It was dated April 9, 1870. The Colonial Office also contemplated the possibility of the Lieutenant-Governor, acting for the Governor-General, being in the territory during the period when Rupert's Land should have been surrendered to the Crown, but was not yet transferred to Canada. Lord Granville prepared the draft of a Commission from the Queen to Sir John Young, giving him the necessary power during that stage of the Transfer of Rupert's Land to Canada. As negotiations with the delegates from the Red River promised a happy settlement, it became unnecessary to issue this Commission. This meticulous attention to the formalities of the law is in sharp contrast with the inattention of the Canadian Government to the legalities of the transfer, and, of course, in sharp contrast with the gross breach of the legal decencies perpetrated by William McDougall.

The course of the delegates from the Red River was not all smooth. When Father Ritchot and Alfred Scott reached Toronto, they were arrested under a warrant for complicity in the murder of Thomas Scott, the charge being laid by Hugh Scott, Thomas's brother. (Alfred Scott was present at the shooting ; Father Ritchot was at his parish, all unaware of the tragedy.) This caused great perturbation in the governments at Ottawa and Downing Street, for, though the case could be tried in Canada under the Canada Jurisdiction Act, it would take many weeks to gather the witnesses and evidence in the West ; meanwhile anything might happen on the Red River, not excluding a raid of American sympathizers from the south, in the hope of sweeping Rupert's Land into the Republic. When the case came before the magistrates the Crown Prosecutor, who must have been informed of the grave political issues at stake, declined to prosecute, because the Crown was unable to procure evidence. The prisoners were therefore discharged. They proceeded to Ottawa, where they were received, not only by the Ministers of the Crown, but by the Governor-General himself.

The delegates held commissions and instructions from the

Provisional Government under the signature of "Thomas Bunn, Secretary of State," and bore with them a fresh "Bill of Rights," from which the face-saving clauses inserted in the "List of Rights," under the influence of Donald Smith, were eliminated. The agreement with the Canadian Government was based on this new "Bill of Rights," and not on that drawn up by the Convention. Its main contentions were accepted, with modifications, in the Manitoba Act passed by Parliament then in session. Its first demand, that "Rupert's Land and North-West shall not enter into the Confederation of the Dominion, except as a province," was so far conceded that a Diminutive Province of Manitoba was formed, the rest of Rupert's Land and the North-West remaining in the hands of the Dominion Government. The representation asked for in the Senate and House of Commons was conceded—two members in the Senate and four in the House of Commons. A subsidy of $80,000 annually in support of the local government, in addition to eighty cents per head for the population estimated at 17,000, was demanded ; this last to be increased as the population multiplied. This was amended to a grant of $30,000, but the population was taken at the estimate of 17,000. Roughly, half the amount asked for was conceded. It was agreed that all titles to land as issued in the past should be recognized. The demand that the bargain with the Company for the transfer of the land should be annulled, with its corrolary, that the Local Legislature should control the lands, was not conceded. Clause 30 of the Manitoba Act ran, that lands should be "administered by the Government of Canada for the purposes of the Dominion." The requirement that the English and French languages should be common in the Legislature and in the Courts was conceded. That customs duties should remain as at present for three years was easily allowed, for the Government had already agreed to it for two years. Treaties with the Indians were a *sine quâ non.* The half-breeds made no demands for themselves, for the Bill of Rights required the public lands to be in the control of the Local Legislature. As the Dominion Government was taking over the public domain, it was arranged as a compromise (clause 31) that 1,400,000 acres should be set aside for the families of the half-breeds. The Bill of Rights required that "the arrangement and confirmation of all customs and usages and privileges be left exclusively to the Local Legislature "—this with a view to preserving the local liberty in the matters of religion and schools. The Manitoba Act strengthened this demand by making it a part of the constitution of the Province that the Legislature might exclusively make laws in relation to education, subject to the provisions, (1) that "nothing in any such Law shall prejudicially affect any right or privilege with respect to Denominational Schools which any class of persons have by Law or Practice in the Province at the Union," (2) that an appeal against an infringement of this clause should lie with the Governor-General in Council, and in case the Province should not pass a law requisite to keep this clause in effect, the Dominion Parliament could make remedial laws as a safeguard to the above legislation. On 3rd May Sir John Young cabled Lord Granville. " Negotiations with delegates closed satisfactorily. A province named Manitoba, erected, containing eleven thousand square miles."

A general debate followed Sir John Macdonald's announcement, on 2nd May, that the Manitoba Bill was being prepared. Sir John took some pains to suggest that the bill represented the original intentions of the Government. He stressed the temporary character of the Act of the previous session providing for the Government of the North-West Territory, in particular the fact that McDougall was to report on the North-West with a view to future legislation. McDougall had not been able to enter the country. The Government had been able, however, to discuss the proposed constitution with such persons as had been in the West as they had had an opportunity of meeting, and the result was the Bill about to be introduced. William McDougall, who must be taken as the embodiment of the original intentions of the Government, from his place, condemned the leading features of the Bill. " A cheap simple and direct system of government such as that provided for in the Bill of last Session would answer every purpose, and would meet the almost universal approval of the people."

The Bill, in placing the natural resources of Manitoba in the hands of the Dominion " for Dominion purposes," made a definite breach in the symmetry of the federal system as found in the British North America Act, and Sir John Macdonald can scarcely have been unconscious of the fact. He explained : " The objects of the residents had been to obtain possession of the whole country. They wished Rupert's Land made into one Province and to have all the lands within the boundary as in other Provinces." As to the division of the West into a province and a territory, he assured the House that the delegates did not suggest the division. " They wanted the whole country." Speaking later, he said that it would be injudicious to have a large province which would have control over the lands and might interfere with the general policy of the Government in opening up communication with the Pacific. Besides, the land legislation of the province might be obstructive to immigration. All that vast territory should be for purposes of settlement, under one control, and that the Dominion Legislature. Another consideration was that by obtaining the control of these lands they would be able to obtain means by which they could repay the $300,000 to be paid to the Hudson's Bay Company, which he characterized as a purchase made by Canada. The expense would be defrayed by that means, instead of being charged against the people of the Provinces of Ontario, Quebec, Nova Scotia, and New Brunswick. That could be done, however, only by carrying out the policy of keeping control of the lands of the country, and that they had determined to do. Macdonald said nothing of the possibility of the Dominion controlling the natural resources *for the purposes of the North-West*, which would have at least preserved the spirit of the

British North America Act, and would have given security against obstruction on the part of the half-breeds.

The hand which framed the beautiful symmetry of the federal scheme was here destroying it. As the British North America Act and the Rupert's Land Act required Rupert's Land and the North-West to be admitted into the Dominion subject to the conditions of the former Act, and therefore enjoying their natural resources, it was a definite departure from the federal scheme for the Dominion to take control of those resources " for Dominion purposes." Moreover, accepting Macdonald's view, that there must be one control of the lands of the West—and it was just—there was a way of securing it without any breach of the symmetry of the federal scheme. It was perfectly legal, as we have seen, for the Dominion Parliament, so long as institutions were in an inchoate stage in the West, to act with all the powers of a provincial legislature. Till the land was filled with settlers, it could control the natural resources, but use them for the purposes of the West it must. When Britain displaced the Virginia Company, which was supposed to use the natural resources to develop the colony, and took control of its government, it did not use those resources for imperial purposes, but to build up the colony and, in particular, to support its government. So Canada, displacing the Hudson's Bay Company, might have done. The departure from the British North America Act evidenced in the Manitoba Act made it necessary to secure the sanction of the Imperial Parliament. This was done by the passage of an Imperial *Act respecting the establishment of Provinces in the Dominion of Canada* " (1871), the third clause of which validated the Manitoba Act of 1870.

In the original Manitoba Bill, Portage la Prairie was left outside of the Province being created. This was amended, and the boundaries of the Province defined as commencing where the 96th degree of longitude intersects the International Boundary, thence following that boundary to the 99th degree of west longitude. This longitudinal line became the west boundary to the point of its intersection with 50° 3' of north latitude. This parallel of latitude was followed eastward till it intersected the above-mentioned 96th longitudinal line, which constituted the east boundary of the province. All the rest of Rupert's Land and the North-West Territory now became the North-West Territory ; it was provided with a primitive form of government. The 35th clause of the Manitoba Act ordained that the Lieutenant-Governor of Manitoba be Lieutenant-Governor of the territory, and the 36th clause re-enacted the " *Act for the Temporary Government of Rupert's Land and the North-Western Territory* " of 1869 as applying to this governmental unit. Nothing was said of the control and use of the natural resources which would seem to imply that they remained as under the British North America Act in the control of the local legislature, which in turn was in control of the Dominion Government. The British North America Act, as well as the general practice of the Imperial Government which had used the natural resources of Lower and Upper Canada in support of the governments of those colonies, required Canada to control the resources of the West in the interests of the West. They were, however, quietly regarded as vested in the Dominion for Dominion purposes—a definite breach of the symmetry of the federal system. There further consideration of the matter must be left as beyond the horizon of this work. In the final issue, the original conception that Canada was to " annex " the West triumphed over the enactment of the British North America Act, that Rupert's Land and the North-Western Territory were to be admitted " into the Union—subject to the Provisions of this Act."

Within three days of his giving royal assent to the Manitoba Bill, Sir John Young cabled Lord Granville for leave to give final orders for the military to start for the Red River. This was given, for the first condition of Lord Granville's cable of 5th March, that reasonable terms should be granted to the settlers of Red River, was fulfilled. The second condition, that Her Majesty's Government should proclaim the transfer of the territory simultaneously with the movement of the force, now called for attention. The Canadian Government placed the stipulated £300,000 in the hands of the Hudson's Bay Company, and on 23rd June the Queen signed the Order-in-Council accomplishing the transfer, and admitting Rupert's Land and the North-West Territory into the Dominion of Canada, subject to the provisions of the British North America Act, the addresses of the Canadian Parliament, and the specific terms of the Deed of Surrender executed by the Hudson's Bay Company—the same to take effect on 15th July.

The expeditionary force was made up of Imperial troops—the 1st battalion of the Royal Rifles, then in Canada, and some detachments of the Royal Artillery and Royal Engineers; and of Canadian militia, a battalion each from Ontario and Quebec—all under Colonel Garnet Wolseley. The Royal Rifles were due to return to England that autumn; the Canadian battalions were to winter on the Red River. On 25th May Wolseley landed at the present Port Arthur, which he named Prince Arthur's Landing after the Duke of Connaught, who, as Prince Arthur, had recently been quartered with his regiment at Montreal. Much effort was spent repairing and completing the Dawson Road from that point to Lake Shebandowan, Ontario, where the troops were to take to their boats. On 16th July, the day after the admission of Rupert's Land into the Dominion and the creation of the Province of Manitoba, the movement westward into Rupert's Land began. To prevent confusion at the portages the troops went off in detachments. At one time the column was spread out over 150 miles. On 18th August, Wolseley reached Fort Alexander at the mouth of the Winnipeg River, by way of Rainy Lake and River and Lake of the Woods; and on the 23rd he was at Lower Fort Garry. Following hard after Wolseley came Adams G. Archibald, duly commissioned Lieutenant-Governor of Manitoba.

The diaries of Wolseley's soldiers and the newspapers of Ontario envisage this expedition as devised to suppress the "rebellion," and this legend has persisted in school books. Wolseley was under no such delusion. He was there to prevent a fiasco such as had occurred at McDougall's entry, and to protect the new Government from a rising of the French faction, which was still possible. On 30th June he had issued an address " to the loyal inhabitants of Manitoba " :

Our mission is one of peace and the sole object of the expedition is to secure Her Majesty's Sovereign authority. . . . The force which I have the honour of commanding will enter your Province representing no party either in Religion or Politics and will afford equal protection to the lives and property of all races and of all creeds. . . . All loyal people are earnestly invited to aid me in carrying out the above mentioned objects.

This address he placed in the hands of Lieutenant William Butler of the 69th Regiment, who offered himself as a volunteer. Butler's experiences are described in his well-known book, *The Great Lone Land*, but with the false perspective of the actual situation which was natural in a stranger who got all his information in Canada. He failed to realize the peace which settled on the Red River when the demands of the people had been recognized in Canada. The Union Jack was flying over Fort Garry. The Company was doing business as usual. The winterers had come in for their goods and departed to their wintering-grounds. Enterprising settlers were building new houses. The Provisional Legislature and its Executive were meeting regularly and promulgating a new code of laws. There were remaining but three signs of military force : the guard at Fort Garry ; the guard at the frontier opposite Pembina ; and a certain Captain Gay, a Fenian who had been put at the head of the Fort Garry guard, and who drilled them from time to time in shooting on horseback. On 24th May the Queen's birthday had been celebrated with enthusiasm. Races were held, and a grand concert on behalf of orphans was given in the old court house at Fort Garry. On 24th June the "Legislative Assembly" met to receive Father Ritchot's report of the negotiations at Ottawa and decided to send a special messenger inviting Lieutenant-Governor Archibald to come in immediately and assume the reins of government—this " to show that he was not coming in at the point of the bayonet." Four days later Bishop Taché left for Canada, apparently entrusted with this message. Any discontent in the Settlement was among some of the English, who felt that too much had been conceded to the French in the Manitoba Act, while the Fenian O'Donoghue was dissatisfied at any agreement at all having been reached.

It was into this calm that Butler arrived on the steamer *International* on 20th July with printed copies of Wolseley's message to the loyal people of the Settlement. He had not been spotted by the guard at Pembina. Expecting to be arrested as a spy and perhaps shot, with the assistance of Mr. William Drever of Winnipeg village

he jumped ashore from the steamer as it touched the river bank
before docking at Fort Garry. Riel had received word that an
English officer was on board, and went down to the steamer, apparently to hold him for cross-examination. Butler's evasion aroused
suspicions. Drever was arrested and a posse sent out to capture
the Englishman on his way to Lower Fort Garry, but in vain, for
he reached the Fort and went on to find safety among the Indians
at Nettley Creek. The bundle of Wolseley's printed message had
been left by Butler on the steamer and came to Riel's hands. Riel
circulated the copies among the people. On 23rd July Begg entered
the "proclamation" in his Journal, adding that Riel personally
superintended its printing at the office of the *New Nation*, in which
it appeared next day. That day Butler, on an invitation from Riel,
went up to Fort Garry. He refused to call on "the President,"
forced Riel to go to him, and treated him in an unmannerly fashion.
Butler gives a lively description of the man : " a short stout man
with a large head, a sallow puffy face, a sharp, restless, intelligent
eye, a square-cut massive forehead overhung by a mass of long and
thickly-clustering hair, and marked with well-cut eyebrows—altogether, a remarkable-looking face, all the more so, perhaps, because
it was to be seen in a land where such things are a rare sight." Riel
was practically a pure-blooded French-Canadian.

The truth is that the negotiations at Ottawa issuing in the
Manitoba Act had brought about complete mutual understanding
between Canada and the Settlement. The demand to be consulted
had been met. The rights asserted had in the main been recognized.
There was no ground now for a quarrel. Riel does not seem to have
made the slightest attempt to oppose Colonel Wolseley. He was
doubtless aware that he would have met with no response. Far other
was the question agitating his mind. Would the amnesty proclaimed
by the Governor-General extend to and cover his shooting of Scott ?
Begg's Journal shows that the amnesty was the one question now
being discussed. Had Riel been sure that the death of Scott was
covered by the amnesty, he probably would have gone out to meet
Wolseley and shaken his hand with the same *empressement* shown
to Butler. As it was, he awaited the arrival of the troops, surrounded
by but a small guard, afraid to go out to offer a welcoming hand, to
the last minute uncertain of his fate, undecided as to his action.
The blood of Thomas Scott remained a bar between him and the
Manitoba which he had done so much to create.

As Wolseley passed up the Red River to Lower Fort Garry on
the morning of 23rd August the church bells rang ; the people
cheered from the river bank ; the Indians fired salutes to the
great Queen's soldiers. Reorganizing his force at the fort, he sent
up a number of the Royal Rifles along either bank of the river, and
proceeded with the main body of his troops upstream against a
fierce wind. He had hoped to reach Fort Garry before nightfall,
but progress under the conditions was slow and he was forced to
encamp. That night a terrible rainstorm passed over the country,

making the land a sea of Winnipeg mud. At six next morning the troops were on the move. At Point Douglas Wolseley landed. There messengers sent out the night before met him and reported Riel and his men still in Fort Garry " awaiting anxiously the arrival of Bishop Taché, who was hourly expected "—without a doubt expected to arrive with the promise of a full and all-comprehensive amnesty. It was likewise reported that Riel had distributed ammunition to his men, loaded the guns at the fort, and closed the gates. Wolseley's troops now on land, marched, deep in mud, to Fort Garry about a mile away. Arrived before the fort, they expected each moment to see a flash and hear a round shot rush by. All was silence. Riel and O'Donoghue had fled across the river and southward into American territory. Entering the fort, the soldiers drew out the guns and fired a royal salute as a new Union Jack was run up the mast, on which Butler had seen the tattered Jack used by Riel. Thus ended a revolution full of incident and of surprising turns, the most astonishing feature of which was that, save for the death of Sutherland and of Scott, it had been bloodless.

If the Imperial troops were to reach Canada before the waterway should be frozen there was no time to lose. One body left five days later, on 29th August, and the other on 3rd September. The Canadian battalions remained in garrison over the winter. Lieutenant-Governor Archibald arrived and took up his residence in Louis Riel's " Government House " within Fort Garry. The next day he took the oath of office and assumed his duties. Thus the Red River Settlement was launched on its career within the Confederation as the Province of Manitoba. There is an element of tragedy in the fact that the man, Louis Riel, who contributed more than any other to bring about this consummation was a fugitive from justice in a foreign land.

On May 21, 1870, during the Riel régime, Begg wrote : " Taking it altogether the settlement has been more quiet this season than it ever was before in the shape of drinking and fighting." The situation was greatly changed for the worse after the installation of Governor Archibald :

A new lawlessness came into being and continued for several months, which was, in many respects, far more reprehensible than any that had existed during the régime of the insurrectionists. A small coterie of the " loyal party " of the West, augmented by an influx of immigrants from Ontario, and prejudiced by both racial and religious animosities, cried loudly for vengeance. When Colonel Wolseley and Lieutenant-Governor Archibald judiciously ignored the clamor for reprisals, the " loyalists " and " bigots " satiated themselves.

The French half-breed, whether he was connected with the Red River disturbances or not, was bullied and maltreated. Life and property were jeopardized. One Elzear Goulet, thought to have been concerned in the murder of Scott, was chased on 13th September to the river and stoned as he swam over. Struck on the head, he sank, and was never seen again. Three "loyal" Canadians were concerned in this murder, two of them of the Ontario Rifles. They were never brought to trial. At least two deaths can be credited to this uncompromising and unchristian persecution, while the number of indignities, assaults, and threats and intimidations can be heaped high. Governor Archibald in a confidential letter to Sir John A. Macdonald, on October 9, 1871, under the stress of "worry and anxiety" wrote that "many of the French half-breeds have been so beaten and outraged by a small but noisy section of the people" mainly English-speaking from the East "that they feel as if they were living in a state of slavery. . . . Bitter hatred of these people is a yoke so intolerable that they would gladly escape it by any sacrifice." The oppressors "seem to feel as if the French half-breeds should be wiped off the face of the globe." Many half-breeds did escape to the plains at St. Laurent, Batoche, and Duck Lake. In a period of distress there they called Louis Riel to their rescue. They took part in the rebellion of 1885, which may thus be regarded as the epilogue of the disturbances of 1869–70 on the Red River.

2.—BRITISH COLUMBIA ADMITTED TO THE CONFEDERATION

In 1867 British Columbia was in the trough of a depression, and hailed the formation of the Canadian Confederation as holding out the prospect of an escape from its troubles ; it would relieve the colony of an indebtedness whose charges remained fixed—in a sense grew more oppressive as the revenues continued to decline and the people's ability to shoulder taxation diminished. On 19th March, when the Imperial Parliament was framing the British North America Act, the Council had resolved : "That this Council is of opinion that at this juncture . . . it is very desirable that His Excellency be respectfully requested to take such steps, without delay, as may be deemed by him best adapted to ensure the admission of British Columbia into the Confederation on fair and equitable terms, this Council being confident that in advising this step they are expressing the views of the colonists generally." While this resolution was before the Council, a deputation waited on Governor Seymour to urge him to take immediate steps to secure the admission of British Columbia into the Confederation. On 11th March the Governor telegraphed Lord Granville, Colonial Minister : "Can provision be made in Bill now before Parliament for ultimate admission of British Columbia into Canadian Federation ?" It does not appear that Lord Granville answered the telegram. This, along with Governor Seymour's lethargical nature, and perhaps his feeling that the issue was raised prematurely, may account for his not forwarding the resolution of Council till 24th September. Commenting on the resolution, Seymour said : "Though the motion was passed by the Council without opposition, there was but little warmth felt in its favour. It is hard to know what benefits the colony or the Eastern Confederacy would derive from a closer connection while the lands intervening between Canada and our frontier belong to a private company. The resolution was the expression of a despondent community longing for change." This is probably a true statement of the feeling in British Columbia at large. Connection with the east by railway was a prime necessity for union with Canada, and at the moment it was still beyond the horizon. No steps had yet been taken to bring the intervening thousand miles into the Dominion, for the Rupert's Land Act was not passed till the following year. All the intimate relations of British Columbia were with the United States or Britain. Contacts with Canada scarcely existed. The desire for union with Canada was not based on affection, but on the belief that it would ultimately bring economic prosperity and relieve the colony of its distressing load of debt. It would be a marriage of convenience, not of love. Lord Granville's successor, the Duke of Buckingham and Chandos, replied to Governor Seymour's dispatch on 19th November : " Whatever might be the advantages which in course of time might result from the union of British North America under one government, it appears to me that the consideration of that question must at all events await the time when the intervening territory now under the control of the Hudson's Bay Company shall have been incorporated with the Confederation." The opposition of the day and historians since attribute the postponement of the entry of British Columbia into the Dominion for four years to the opposition of Governor Seymour and of the official members of the Council. Granted that Seymour was lukewarm by nature, and without the mind and will to come to decisions, and the officials were not free from anxiety about their positions, their action was really in keeping with the necessities of the case.

For an effective union something more than lukewarmness was needed—a vision of the future greatness of the Dominion, and of the part to be played by British Columbia in it. It is to the credit of Amor de Cosmos that he gave this to the people during the years of necessary delay. Born in Nova Scotia, his feelings would respond to the idea of a Dominion from sea to sea, as would not easily be in an official from England or an ex-commissioned officer of the Hudson's Bay Company. His picturesque personality, his command of the agitator's technique from of old, were all in his favour. An ardent supporter of representative and responsible government, he dreamed of a free British Columbia taking its place as a Province in the free Dominion, facing across the Pacific and extending the trade and influence of Canada to the Far East. He was not free from egotism ; he saw the way opening before him to a career on a much larger stage than his isolated colony could afford him. With the true instinct of the demagogue, he found an enemy of the people, over against whom he stood as their champion. It was Governor Seymour, surrounded by his officials, standing in the way of responsible government and union with Canada. Governor Seymour, by leaving the public uninformed of the position taken by the Duke of Buckingham on the Union of British Columbia and Canada, and of his own views, if he had any, left it possible for De Cosmos to bludgeon him as the enemy of Confederation.

On January 29, 1868, a large meeting was held in Victoria in the interests of Union with Canada. The resolution was moved by De Cosmos and the meeting resulted in a memorial purporting to explain the political situation:

5. That public opinion throughout the Colony, so far as we can learn, is overwhelmingly in favour of confederation.   6. That there is a small party in favour of annexation to the United States and if it were practicable or possible, their number would be largely increased.   7. There is a small party, other than annexationists, who are opposed to confederation.   8. Nearly all the office holders in the Colony are allied to the latter party. 9. The total number of those opposed to confederation on fair and equitable terms, is numerically small, but supported by the office holders, they may exert a good deal of resistance to the popular will. . . . 11. That the legislative Council, the only Legislative body in the Colony, is made up of a majority consisting of heads of departments, gold commissioners, magistrates, and others, subject to Government influence, and cannot be relied upon to urge on confederation as it ought to be at the present juncture. [The unanimous vote of the Council in favour of Confederation at its last meeting was not referred to.] We therefore, representing as we do this the most populous and influential section of the Colony, and acting in unison with the general and expressed wishes of the people throughout the Colony, would respectfully ask the Government of the Dominion to take immediate steps to bring this Colony into the Dominion, by telegraphing or communicating with Her Majesty's Government, to issue instructions with as little delay as possible, to Governor Seymour, or otherwise to conclude negotiations as to the terms of our admission.

Suggested terms were subjoined. They included the opening up of a wagon road to British Columbia. The signatures to the memorial were headed by that of the Mayor of Victoria, De Cosmos's name following next.

A report on the memorial was considered in the Privy Council of Canada on March 6, 1868. It stated that, in spite of the resolution of the British Columbian Council, no communication had been received from Governor Seymour, referred to the lack of zeal for Confederation on the part of its official members, and suggested that the Duke of Buckingham and Chandos, be asked "to instruct Governor Seymour to take such steps as may be deemed proper to move the Legislative Council of British Columbia to further action in terms of [the British North America Act]." The approved minute was forwarded by Viscount Monck, Governor-General of Canada, to the Colonial Office. The Duke of Buckingham and Chandos replied almost in the words of his dispatch to Governor Seymour, that the union desired must wait for the admission of the intervening country to the Confederation. Not content with appealing to the Colonial Office, the Canadian Government telegraphed to Governor Seymour: "The Canadian Government desires union with British Columbia and has opened communication with the Imperial

Government on the subject of the Resolutions [of the petition forwarded] and suggests immediate action by your Legislature and the passage of an Address to Her Majesty regarding union with Canada. Keep us informed of progress." That citizens of one colony should petition the Government of another colony to bring pressure to bear on their own Government, and that the Government of Canada should respond to the petition, need no comment. Such erratic proceedings could only breed a spirit in the Council hostile to the apostle of confederation, and calculated to damage his cause—all the more as the petition cast unjust reflections on the official element in the Council and ignored the necessities of the situation, that the intervening country must be admitted to the Confederation before the admission of British Columbia to it could become practicable.

When the Council assembled in March 1868, Governor Seymour, in his speech, conveyed the decision of the Colonial Office that British Columbia must see Rupert's Land and the North-West Territory in the Confederation before its case could be taken up. De Cosmos was in no ways discouraged. Rather, supported by resolutions in favour of confederation adopted by meetings held at New Westminster and Yale, he introduced what he thought would be the appropriate Address of the Council to the Queen praying for union, as had been suggested by the Canadian Government. An amendment was put forward in conformity with the actualities of the situation :

That the Council, while confirming their vote of the last session in favour of the general principle of the desirability of the union of this Colony with the Dominion of Canada to accomplish the consolidation of British interests and institutions in North America, are still without sufficient information and experience of the practical working of Confederation in the North American Provinces to admit of their defining the terms on which such a union would be advantageous to the local interests of British Columbia.

At the division De Cosmos could only muster three supporters. Three of the popularly elected members voted against him, and all of the official members. In closing the session Governor Seymour said :

I notice that, while adhering to your vote of last year in favour of Confederation with Canada, you are of opinion that it is not necessary to take further steps in the matter. I think your resolution a wise one. The question is by no means slumbering ; but the difficulties of the project are seen clearer by those who have a wider range of vision than we can possess and without whose material assistance our efforts would be but vain.

In other words, Council must await the active support of the Colonial Office. There is no need to deny that the situation was satisfactory to a man of Seymour's indecision of character. From his very temperament he would be happier if nothing was to be done. Referring to the demand for a more representative government, he said he would take it carefully into his consideration. On one occasion he wrote the Colonial Office that he could not make up his mind about it.

Political agitators rarely see things as they are. The Council had twice committed itself to confederation, but it saw the real difficulties in the way. De Cosmos ignored both the favourable decision and the insuperable obstacles of the moment. He asserted that the Council was against confederation, and he offered the public the explanations that Governor Seymour was afraid that it would rob him of his position, and the official members were determined to keep hold of their offices. The truth is that they saw the present in a truer light than he. The apostle of confederation ignored the obstacles immediately before him, but had a clearer vision of the more distant future than the men in office.

The agitation continued. It brought an advantage in that it rallied the elements in the colony discontented with its government to an ardent support of confederation, and it dispelled the prevailing lukewarmness. In May 1868 a Confederation League was formed in Victoria, and branches were organized in New Westminster, Hope, Yale, Lytton, and Cariboo. The Press, as a whole, got behind the movement and brought it home to the people. A speech of Mr. J. G. Thompson, who afterwards sat in the Canadian House of Commons for Cariboo, may be taken as typical of the agitation :

> There can be no question as to the almost unanimous feeling throughout the colony in favour of Confederation. Public meetings have been held everywhere, from the mountains to the sea, from Victoria to Cariboo. The entire press of the colony, whatever their opinions on other questions may be, holds but one on this. Even the Government has declared in its favour ; but though the Legislative Council of 1867 passed a resolution in favour of Confederation, the official members, in the session of 1868, annulled that resolution on the ground that delay was necessary. Delay !—delay for what ? To enable them to retain their offices a little longer, and stave off, for a year at least, the inevitable event which must seal their doom.

A convention held at Yale in September adopted with enthusiasm the address to the Queen which De Cosmos had moved in the Council, but which had been rejected. It further asserted that the Legislative Council was " a sham legislature, the Governor and Executive Council being virtually the Legislature of the Colony." The resolutions were forwarded to Governor Seymour, who replied that the resolutions would be communicated to the Legislature, and would be forwarded to the Colonial Minister. " The Local Government is by no means indifferent to the very important and difficult subjects to which the Yale resolutions refer." As many as three hundred and eighty-one individuals and firms in Victoria, giving their names, protested in the public Press that the persons attending the convention had received no authority to represent their opinions and desires. At the head of one list was the name of J. S. Helmcken.

The agitation in favour of confederation led those who differed, in particular such as were in favour of annexation to the United States, to bestir themselves. There was much that the Annexationists pointed to that could not be gainsaid—the fifteen hundred miles of practically unoccupied territory between British Columbia and settled Canada ; the impassable barrier constituted by the Rocky Mountains ; the long delay before a transcontinental in British territory could be built ; the value of the American market at the door compared with the hypothetical market in distant Canada. The Confederationists argued that Canada would assume the colony's debt, and that it would build a transcontinental railway. They called for reciprocity with the United States and representative and responsible government. The Annexationists presented parallel arguments ; the United States would assume the colony's debt ; they had one transcontinental already, and could soon have another to Puget Sound ; reciprocity between Canada and the United States was all too uncertain, but with annexation free trade would be assured for ever ; and finally, representative and responsible government would be given automatically.

It has been usual to place Dr. J. S. Helmcken among the Annexationists. Certainly the Confederationists counted him as in that party. It is probably juster to say that, as things stood at the time, he was against neither confederation nor annexation, and might have been in favour of either policy, or for the third possible course, namely, to leave the colony to work out its destiny for itself. As elected member for Victoria he had voted for the motion in favour of confederation with Canada, but he would have accepted readily annexation to the United States if it were to be for the benefit of the colony. He was by nature realist and critical ; able to see all the pros and cons, he was inclined to make no decision until decision became necessary; above all, he was averse to flying from the present ills to others he knew not of. In this he represented a small group in the colony opposed to De Cosmos and all premature action. His attitude was, in the main, that of the Council.

It is curious that national prejudices played but a small part in the dividing the colony into the several political groups. Though there were many Americans on the mainland, it was unanimous for confederation. Victoria saw Americans and British subjects united in favour of annexation. Commercial advantage was the dividing principle. Many merchants of the city believed that, in the United States, it would become the emporium of the Pacific coast. On the mainland there was fear that annexation would enable the produce of the farms and lumber mills of the south to crush the like industries of the colony, which were beginning to thrive under tariff protection. As of old, Victoria had a different economic outlook from that of continental British Columbia.

The attitude of people in the United States, and a certain trend of thought in Britain, must not be left out of sight. In July 1866 N. P. Banks, representing Massachusetts in the House of Representatives, introduced a Bill " for the admission of the States of Nova Scotia, New Brunswick, Canada East, and Canada West, and for the organization of the Territories of Selkirk, Saskatchewan, and Columbia " within the United States. The natural resources of these areas, as far as not alienated, were to be taken over by the

American Government, in return for which their debts were to be assumed by Congress, and suitable annual grants were to be made, and a transcontinental railway was to be built. The Bill was read twice and referred to the Committee on Foreign Affairs. There the international implications of the measure would be properly appraised. It disappeared from view, but was not forgotten. In April of 1867 the Press of New York floated a canard, like many another since, that Britain was willing to cede her colonies at a price—in this case British Columbia in settlement of the Alabama claims. After the Civil War the doctrine of the " Manifest Destiny " of the American Republic was being preached as loudly as ever. There could be little doubt that British Columbia would be welcomed into the United States. It was thought that Britain would prove no obstacle in the way, for did not the Manchester School preach that the only value to England in her colonies was their trade, and she would have that whether they were in the Empire or not. The London *Times* was known to have said in an editorial :

> British Columbia is a long way off. . . . With the exception of a limited official class it receives few immigrants from England, and a large proportion of its inhabitants consists of citizens of the United States who have entered it from the south. Suppose that the Colonists met together and came to the conclusion that every natural motive of contiguity, similarity of interests, and facility of administration induced them to think it more convenient to slip into the United States than into the Dominion. . . . We all know that we should not attempt to withstand them.

Altogether, many in the colony felt that there would be no great difficulty thrown in the way of annexation to the United States. In 1867 a petition was sent to the Colonial Office asking that the colony be relieved from the burden of the Civil List ; that while its promoters desired to retain their allegiance, the isolation of their position and their intimate relations with United States impelled a movement towards annexation.

When the Council met in February 1869 the external situation was not materially changed. True, Canadian delegates were in London negotiating for the transfer of Rupert's Land, but Canada was as far off as ever. Within the colony the movement in favour of confederation was making headway, but its protagonist, Amor de Cosmos, had been defeated at the polls and was no longer of the Council. To all appearance the indecisive Governor Seymour was more undecided than ever, and the Council more impressed with the difficulties in the way of confederation as opposed to annexation. At any rate, the motion accepted by it showed greater hesitation than ever. It ran : " That this Council, impressed with the conviction that, under existing circumstances, the confederation of this Colony with the Dominion of Canada would be undesirable, even if practicable, urges Her Majesty's Government not to take any decisive steps towards the present consummation of such union."

The agreement for the transfer of Rupert's Land to the Crown, and so to the Dominion, reached in April, transformed the situation.

The western boundary of the Dominion was to be the Rocky Mountains, contiguous to British Columbia. The Colonial Office, which had hitherto discountenanced the discussion of the admission of British Columbia into the Confederation, was now ready to throw the influence of the Home Government into the scales in its favour. On June 10, Governor Seymour died while on a mission to pacify the Indians on Queen Charlotte Islands. He was expected to retire because of his illness, and the Home Government was prepared to replace him. At the suggestion of Sir John Macdonald, the choice fell on Anthony Musgrave, Governor of Newfoundland, who happened at the time to be in London. He was a man of great decision, tempered by a pleasing manner, and by the gift of making himself popular. While Newfoundland had been considering entering the Canadian Confederation, he had shown himself a supporter of union. On 14th August, Lord Granville addressed a dispatch to him, mentioning the pending union of Rupert's Land and the North-West Territory with the Dominion and that Her Majesty's Government was (now) in favour of British Columbia also being brought in. As it proved, this was somewhat premature, for the disturbances on the Red River postponed the admission of Rupert's Land till the following summer, with the result that the situation was not as clear as it might have been when the Council of British Columbia took the matter up in March of 1870. However, the clouds were passing away. Donald Smith had met with the settlers of the Red River colony, and a fortnight after the discussion in the British Columbian Council the delegates were on their way to Ottawa to effect the agreement which brought the North-West into the Dominion.

Governor Musgrave's management of the colony was marred by no indecision, nor by the least distrust of the will of the people. Hitherto none but officials formed the Governor's intimate Executive Council. Musgrave decided to call two of the elected members of the Legislative Council to join in advising him. He passed over Amor de Cosmos, who was once more of the Council, and brought into the Executive Council William Weir Carrall, representative of Cariboo, and Dr. John Sebastian Helmcken of Victoria City. The choice of Dr. Helmcken rather than De Cosmos seems proof enough that he was no uncompromising Annexationist, but a man of sound judgment, ready to take the course that should be best for the colony. On March 9, 1870, the Council turned to consider the terms, drawn up by the Governor in the Executive Council, on which the colony could enter the Confederation with satisfaction. The debate on the motion to go into Committee of the whole to consider the several clauses brought out the points of view of the several sections of public opinion. The Hon. Henry Pering Pellew Crease, Attorney-General, emphasized the adherence of the Council from the beginning to the principle of confederation. They did not feel free, however, to take definite steps so long as the North-West Territory was still out of the Dominion. " Until the receipt of Earl Granville's Confederation Despatch of 14th August, 1869, they did not feel themselves at liberty to go further in the direction of Confederation than to affirm the general principle of its propriety." The word " present " in the resolution of April 28, 1868, was inserted at the instance of himself and Mr. Trutch, " so as to preserve the principle and bide our time." Dr. Helmcken made a speech characteristic of a critic of every possible course. He assumed that the resolutions would be adopted, but if the Canadian Government rejected their terms and meaner ones were subjected

for the consideration of the people of this colony, other issues may come up at the polls, and amongst them, the question whether there is no other place [meaning the United States] to which this Colony can go but Canada ; whatever may be the result of the present vote, it is impossible to deny the probability of the less being absorbed by the greater ; and it cannot be regarded as improbable that ultimately, not only this Colony but the whole Dominion of Canada will be absorbed by the United States. The Hon. Attorney-General has not attempted to prove the advantage which will result from Confederation ; he has contented himself with vague assertions of advantages.

The speaker thought that the Imperial Government should not have interfered. " They are not justified in interfering in business which we could very well manage ourselves. . . . If these terms are declined now, in any future negotiations that may take place, if the people support the Governor, no terms will be accepted . . . which would lead to this Colony being sacrificed to Canada." He thought that there should not have been such haste. They should have waited for the intervening country to be settled. He felt that the Canadian tariff would leave the country open to American produce and ruin the agricultural interests of the colony (an argument equally adverse to annexation) :

I am opposed to Confederation, because it will not serve to promote the industrial interests of this Colony. . . . I say that Confederation will be injurious to the farmers because protection is necessary to enable them to compete with the farmers of the United States. . . . It would be absurd for us to sacrifice our interests in order that laws may be made for us by a people who know little of our condition and wants, and who in fact must necessarily legislate for the greater number—the people of the Atlantic Provinces. It is dangerous to place ourselves at the disposal of superior numbers. . . . No union on account of love need be looked for. The only bond of union . . . will be the material advantage of the country and pecuniary benefit of the inhabitants. Love for Canada has to be acquired by the prosperity of the country, and from our children. . . . In conclusion, I have to say that I trust that our deliberations may result in good, and that whatever may be the issue of the debate, it may be for the good of the Colony.

Notes struck by Dr. Helmcken are still heard in British Columbia. Mr. Montague Drake, a member for Victoria City, moved as an amendment that the resolution before the House be postponed for six months. His amendment was supported by Mr. David Ring of Nanaimo.

Mr. Amor de Cosmos was manifestly peeved that confederation was being arranged for by the Government and not by the prophet of the cause :

We are engaged, I believe in Nation-making. For my part I have been engaged in Nation-making for the last twelve years. . . . Sir, my political course has been unlike that of most others in this Colony. . . . My course has been that of " beating the bush whilst others caught the bird." . . . Is Earl Granville entitled to the credit of bringing this matter forward ? Is Governor Musgrave, or his Cabinet or the Officials ? No, Sir, I should be doing wrong if I permitted it to be supposed that the credit was due to any one of them. I have assisted to make history, and this is a page of it. Let it go forth to the world, that the people of this country have made Confederation the important question that it is to-day.

The great agitator welcomed the gift of confederation with reluctance when it came in the hands of the officialdom against which he had fought almost from the day when he arrived in the colony. In the issue, the amendment was withdrawn, and the motion to go into committee was carried unanimously.

On 14th March the Council went into Committee of the Whole to consider the specific conditions. The first was that " Canada shall be liable for the Debts and Liabilities of British Columbia at the time of the Union," these being calculated at the moment to be $1,136,189. The second and third clauses aimed at equalizing the share of the Dominion debt which should be borne by British Columbia with that of the other provinces. The Attorney-General explained it in the following terms :

The allowance of five per cent. interest on the difference between our public debt and that of Canada is arrived at in this way : we have it officially from Canada that her debt on February 9th, say 1st March, if you like, amounted to $22 per head of her population. This would entitle us with 120,000 people, to come in with a much larger debt than our own, which at the time of Union would be, say $1,000,000. The interest at five per cent. on these amounts would give us the annual allowance of $82,000 named in the papers before the House. The 80 cents a head on our population of 120,000 [estimated on the basis of the proportion of customs revenue per head in British Columbia as compared with Canada] is the usual allowance prescribed by the Organic Act of Confederation. This constitutes the Financial Scheme, and although it is open to argument, it is about what we are entitled to receive, and what we must receive to place us in a fair position under the Union.

Here Amor de Cosmos showed himself more apprised of the financial necessities of the colony than the Executive Council itself. He brushed aside the calculation which gave British Columbia a nominal population of 120,000 for the purposes of the Union agreement. Under his influence the grant of $35,000 was raised to $75,000, and the limit at which the subsidy of 80 cents a head should become stationary was altered from 400,000 to 1,000,000. The terms as drawn up by the Governor, to some extent amended, were adopted unanimously.

The next step was negotiation with the Dominion Government. Governor Musgrave chose three members of his Executive Council for the task—Dr. J. S. Helmcken, who, though leaning towards annexation, was a man of great grasp of business, and besides was

an elected member of Council; Mr. Joseph W. Trutch; and Dr.
R. W. W. Carrall. They left on May 10, 1870, and reached Ottawa
on 4th June, seventeen days before the Imperial Order in Council
admitted Rupert's Land and the North-West Territory into the
Union. As Sir John Macdonald was ill, Sir George Cartier conducted
the negotiations for the Government. By 7th July perfect agreement
was reached. The terms were in brief: Canada was to assume the
debt of the colony; the debt of British Columbia not being equal
to those of the other provinces, that Province was to be paid 5 per
cent. per annum on the difference between her debt and a debt
computed on the bases of that of Nova Scotia and New Brunswick
($27.77 per head) for her population estimated as being 60,000;
the yearly grant to the Province to be $35,000 and 80 cents per head
on the population estimated at 60,000, this to be increased with the
population, as shown by decennial census, but to remain stable when
the population became 400,000; Canada was to commence a transcontinental railway within two years, and complete it in ten years,
British Columbia granting for that purpose public lands, not to
exceed twenty miles on each side of the line, for which Canada was
to pay the province $100,000 a year in perpetuity; for ten years
Canada was to guarantee interest at 5 per cent. on $100,000 for a
graving dock at Esquimalt; British Columbia was to have three
senators and six members in the respective Houses of Parliament;
pensions were to be provided for officials whose positions were
affected by the changed situation; the Dominion readily consented
to the introduction of responsible government in the Province when
desired by the inhabitants.

The British Government was careful to avoid forcing union upon
a reluctant colony. An Act of Parliament, followed by an Order in
Council, readjusted the balance of power between the official element
and the elected in the Legislative Council. The membership was
reduced to fifteen, but the elected members were to be in the
majority, in the proportion of nine to six (August 9, 1870). The
elections for the new Council were held in November on the issue:
Would the colony have confederation on the terms agreed upon?
Every member elected was in favour of confederation. All that
remained now was to follow the procedure prescribed by the 146th
clause of the British North America Act. Addresses to Her Majesty
in favour of confederation must be adopted by the Parliament of
Canada and the Legislature of the colony, these to be followed by
her Majesty's Order in Council admitting British Columbia into the
Union. The prescribed address came before the Legislative Council
of British Columbia on January 20, 1871. It was moved by Hon.
Joseph Trutch, Commissioner of Lands and Works. He referred
to a stage in which the negotiations with the Canadian Government
had come to a deadlock. The Dominion had been offering $100,000
less than he and his fellow-delegates could possibly have accepted.
An adjournment had been made for the day. Next morning Sir
George Cartier had proposed the arrangement that British Columbia

should grant the Dominion lands along the railway, not to exceed twenty miles in width on each side, in return for $100,000 a year in perpetuity. The compromise had been accepted by the delegates. Dr. Helmcken seconded the motion, and the address went through without debate.

One of the clauses of the agreement between British Columbia and the Dominion was that representative and responsible government should be inaugurated in the Province when the inhabitants should so will it. In February the Constitution Act, 1871, was passed by Council abolishing the Council with its membership in part *ex officio*, and establishing a Legislative Assembly, composed solely of elected members. There were to be twenty-five members, representing twelve electoral districts. Members of the Executive Council were to be able to sit in the House provided they were elected after entering on their office.

The address of the Dominion Parliament to the Queen, praying for the admission of British Columbia into the Confederation, was adopted by the House of Commons on 1st April, and in the Senate on the 5th. On 16th May, Her Majesty's Order in Council was approved by Privy Council, admitting the colony into the Dominion, to take effect on the twentieth day of July. Five days after the formal entry of the colony into the Confederation, Governor Musgrave bade farewell to the scene of his successful labours, in recognition of which he was decorated. He left Mr. Joseph Trutch in his transformed office as Lieutenant-Governor of the Province. Passed over in the first place, De Cosmos became Prime Minister in 1872, at the same time sitting in the Dominion House of Commons. When an Act was passed (1874) prohibiting such dual representation he chose, as might be expected, the wider sphere. He sat in the House of Commons until his defeat at the polls led to his retirement in 1882. Dr. Helmcken declined a seat in the Senate offered him in 1871, electing to retire into a private life.

At the beginning of the two centuries covered by this volume, the vast expanse of the continent of North America between Labrador and the Pacific Ocean was hidden to European eyes as behind a veil. The Search for the Western Sea first broke through the veil and brought the White Men into a new and undreamt-of world. That search issued in the discovery of the fur resources of the continental forest belt. The solution of the problem of transportation by the adoption of the Indians' canoe—assisted by the increasing demand for furs, due, for the most part, to the vogue of beaver hats, and implemented by the rising price of peltry—enabled the traders to penetrate farther, and yet farther, westward, till the Rocky Mountains and finally the Pacific Ocean were reached. From 1821 that great fur company, the Adventurers of England trading into Hudson's Bay, having absorbed all its rivals, in the name of Britain held a continental domain at peace under its mild paternal sway. From the very nature of things, only the fur resources of the region were envisaged. The agricultural wealth of the prairies was known, and the possibility of vast mineral wealth was surmised, but neither the one nor the other could be exploited till the problem of transportation should be solved. Railways transformed the situation. They gave the Canadians the hope of amassing wealth in the wheatfields of what was called the Fertile Belt. They offered the colonists of British Columbia an escape from the geographical and economic isolation which barred them from prosperity. They made possible the union of all the British colonies in North America in a Dominion from sea to sea. Through them, the wealth drawn by Canada from the prairie soil, and the store of gold and precious metals hewn from the shaggy mountains, are poured into the lap of a nation. Manifestly a new phase of history begins with the building of the railways. The era of the canoe and of the fur trade comes to an end.

APPENDIX—BRIEF BIBLIOGRAPHICAL NOTES

Abbreviations.—B.C. Arch., Archives of British Columbia, Victoria. C.H.R., Canadian Historical Review. Cham. Soc., Champlain Society, Toronto. H.B.C. Arch., Archives of the Hudson's Bay Company, London. McGill, Library of that University. Masson, Masson Papers, in P.A.C. or in McGill. P.A.C., Public Archives of Canada, Ottawa. P.R.O., Public Record Office, London. T.R.S.C., sec. 1 or sec. 2, Transactions of Royal Society of Canada, sec. 1 or sec. 2.

CHAPTER I

THE THREE NORTH-WESTS—On the Aborigines : Jenness, D., *The Indians of Canada*, Ottawa, 1932 (with extensive bibliography mentioning many pertinent journals of fur-traders and works of explorers like Franklin and Dr. John Richardson) ; Hodge, F. W., *Handbook of American Indians*, 2 parts, 1907, 1910 ; the items pertinent to Canada have been reprinted as *Handbook of the Indians of Canada*, Ottawa, 1913 (constant reference to the prime sources makes these an extensive bibliography). On Their Animal Life : Richardson, Dr. John, *Fauna-Boreali-Americana*, London, 1829 ; Seton, E. T., *Life Histories of Northern Animals*, 2 vols., N.Y., 1909 (with bibliography). On the Barren Grounds : Hearne, Samuel, *A Journey to the Northern Ocean, 1769–72*, London, 1793 (with maps) ; ed. by J. B. Tyrrell, Cham. Soc., 1911 (with Hearne's maps and a modernized map of his course, and bibliography). See also narratives of explorers of the polar shore, under Chapter VIII. On the Forest Region : On the Company's posts on the Churchill and in the Rat Country, H.B.C. Arch. ; North West Company's Journals in L. R. Masson, *Les Bourgeois de la Compagnie du Nord-Ouest*, Quebec, 1889, 1890 ; and William M'Gillivray's Journals at his posts in the Rat Country (1789) and at Ile-à-la-Crosse (1793), P.A.C., Masson ; Thompson, David, *Narrative of his Explorations in Western America*, ed. by J. B. Tyrrell, Cham. Soc., 1917 (with Thompson's maps and a bibliography) chaps. 3–6, 12, 20 ; Geological Survey of Canada (mostly the reports of the 1890's). On the Prairies : Works of Alex. Henry the elder ; Alex. Henry the younger (ed. by E. Coues), 3 vols., N.Y., 1897 ; Duncan M'Gillivray, *Journal* (ed. by A. S. Morton), Toronto, 1929; Thompson, David, *op. cit.*, chaps. 21–24 ; Journals of the Hudson's Bay Company's posts on the Assiniboine and the Saskatchewan, H.B.C. Arch.

CHAPTER II

THE EUROPEAN APPROACH.—Beginnings of the Fur Trade: Biggar, H. P., *The Early Companies of New France*, Toronto, 1901 (with long appendix on the sources) ; Innis, H. A., *The Fur Trade in Canada*, Yale University Press, 1930 (with many references to the source material). On Groseilliers and Radisson : *The Voyages of Pierre Esprit Radisson*, ed.

by G. D. Scull, Prince Society, Boston, 1885 (the originals are in the Bodleian Library, Oxford). Sulte, Benjamin, *Découverte du Mississippi en 1659*, T.R.S.C., 1903, sec. 1, and *Radisson in the North-West*, 1661–64, *ibid.*, 1904, sec. 2 ; Upham, Warren, *Groseilliers and Radisson*, Minnesota Hist. Collections, vol. 10, part 2, 1905 ; Kellog, L. P., *The French Régime in Wisconsin and the North-West*, 1925 ; *The Jesuit Relations*, ed. by R. G. Thwaites, 73 vols., while reporting missionary enterprises to interested circles in France, indicate the state of the colony and of its trade. FOR HUDSON BAY : Kenney, J. F., *The Founding of Churchill* (with bibliography) ; *Purchas his Pilgrimes* (MacLehose edition, vol. 13) ; Asher, G. M., *Henry Hudson*, Hakluyt Society, 1860 ; Janvier, T. A., *Henry Hudson*, N.Y. and London, 1908 ; Powys, Llewelyn, *Henry Hudson*, N.Y., 1927 (the best life). In the publications of the Hakluyt Society see Rundall, *Narratives of Voyages towards the North-West*, London, 1849, for Button, Bylot, and Luke Foxe ; Munck, Jens, *Navigatio Septentrionalis*, translated in Gosch, C.C.A., *Danish Arctic Explorations*, 1897. The original narrative of Thomas James is reprinted in Harris's *Collections of Voyages* ; it is abridged in Rundall's *Narrative* as above ; it is interpreted in Dobilly, R. B., *The Voyage of Captain Thomas James*, London and Toronto, 1928. FOR THE FIRST ADVENTURERS OF ENGLAND TRADING INTO HUDSON BAY : H.B.C. Arch., Ledger Book, No. 1 ; P.R.O., *Acts of Privy Council of England*, vol. 13 (calendar, vol. 1), and *State Papers, Domestic Series, Charles II.*, 1668–69 (also calendared).

CHAPTER III

THE HUDSON'S BAY COMPANY.—*Charters, Orders in Council*, a convenient collection of legal and other documents prepared by the Company, London, 1931. R. H. Leveson Gower, the Company's Archivist, has articles on the Archives in *The Beaver*, H.B. Co., Winnipeg, " outfits " 264 and 266 ; A. S. Morton, *Business Methods and the Archives of the Hudson's Bay Company*, in Report of the Canadian Historical Association, 1938. J. F. Kenney, *The Founding of Churchill* (bibliography indicating the transcripts of the Company's documents in P.A.C.). The earliest *Ledger Book*, about 1775, contains the accounts of the stockholders about their stocks from as early as 1667, when the expedition of the *Nonsuch* and *Eaglet* was being planned ; at the end of the volume are the general accounts ; these last began to be kept separate in the *Journals* from 1676. For long the Minutes of the General Court and of the Committee were kept as one. Mr. Leveson Gower says that the *Minute Books* are " almost complete from the date of the Company's incorporation until 1870—the only gaps being May 1670 to Oct. 1671, July 1674 to Nov. 1679, Jan. 1778 to Apr. 1778, Jan. 1789 to Oct. 1793." The *London Letter Books*, in which the correspondence *out* to the service overseas was copied began to be kept in 1680; the correspondence *in* to the Committee from about 1713. Two *Memorial Books*, 1688–1788 and 1698–1719, embody copies of petitions (including affidavits and other evidence) presented to the Government praying for protection from the depredations of the French. FOR THE EARLY HISTORY OF CHARLES BAYLY : *State Papers, Domestic, Charles II.*, P.R.O. (calendared). For his petition to be freed on condition of going to Hudson Bay, and the action taken, see *Acts of the Privy Council of England*, Colonial Series, vol. 1, No. 883, P.R.O. OTHER ENGLISH STATE PAPERS, in P.R.O., *Colonial Office Papers*, series C.O. 134, vols. 1–3 ; C.O. 135, vols. 1–4 ; transcripts of most of this material are in P.A.C., and a summary of C.O. 134 is in the Report of 1895, Ottawa, 1896. Two of these documents, Radisson's *Relations des Voyages dans les années 1682, 1683 et 1684*, text and translation, are printed in this Report. DOCUMENTS IN THE ARCHIVES OF FRANCE : Transcripts of the series C11A, correspondence *in* to the French Court, are in P.A.C., also many documents copied from the Bibliothèque Nationale, *e.g.* *Le Journal de l'expédition du Chevalier de Troyes en 1886* (printed with ancillary source material by Ivanhoe Caron, Beauceville, 1918). *Documents relating to the Early History of Hudson Bay*, ed. by J. B. Tyrrell, Cham. Soc. 1931, includes the originals and translations of the Journals of Father Silvy, 1684–85, and of Father Marest, 1694–95 ; and the pertinent Letters of M. de Bacqueville de la Potherie ; also the History of Hudson's Bay, from John Oldmixon's *The British Empire in America*, 1708. Reports of Father Albanel's missions are in *The Jesuit Relations, op. cit.*, vol. 56. The Transactions between England and France relating to Hudson's Bay, 1787, are printed (from the State Papers) in the Report of P.A.C., 1883. Add *The Kelsey Papers*, ed. by A. G. Doughty and Chester Martin, Ottawa, 1929 ; The *Career of Henry Kelsey*, by J. F. Kenney, T.R.S.C., 1929, sec. 2. Nicholas Jérémie's *Relation sur le Détroit et la Baie d'Hudson*, printed by J. F. Bernard, in Recueil de voiages au Nord, Amsterdam, 1720 ; reprinted as Bulletin No. 2 of La Société Historique de Saint-Boniface, Man. ; translated by R. Douglas and J. N. Wallace under title *Twenty Years of York Factory, 1694–1714*, Ottawa, 1926.

CHAPTER IV

THE HUDSON'S BAY COMPANY.—From 1713 onward the letters, journals, etc., sent in to the Governor and Committee as reports begin to be preserved in increasing volume. Notable are the Journals and correspondence FROM YORK FORT of James Knight, 1714–17 ; Henry Kelsey, 1717–22 ; Thomas Macklish, 1721–35 ; and James Isham, 1746–49, 1750–58 ; FROM CHURCHILL FORT of James Knight, 1717–18 ; FROM ALBANY of Thomas Macklish, 1715–21 ; Richard Stanton, 1723–26 ; Joseph Myatt, 1726–29 ; Joseph Adams, 1729–37. Scattered through many of these are references to competition with the French, notably in La Vérendrye's time. Journals kept by servants who penetrated into the interior, such as Anthony Henday and Joseph Smith, are in the York Fort papers. The dates of their departure and arrival are entered as a matter of course in the Journals. General statements of their doings are often found in the report of the season to the Committee.

THE SEARCH FOR THE WESTERN SEA : Pierre Margry's *Découverte et Établissements des Français dans l'Ouest et dans le Sud de l'Amérique septentrionale* (6 vols., Paris, 1879–88), vol. 6 from p. 492 is devoted to "la découverte de la mer de l'Ouest," and includes Father Charlevoix's letters and documents on the expansion of the French colony westward. These are from the Archives of France, series C11E (transcripts in P.A.C.), where also Father Bobé's memorandum is to be found. FOR THE LA VÉRENDRYES: *Journals and Letters of Pierre Gaultier de Varennes de la Vérendrye and his Sons* (French text and translations, with bibliography) ed. by L. J. Burpee, with the La Vérendrye maps, Cham. Soc., 1927, is an all but complete collection gathered from the Archives of France (transcripts in P.A.C.) ; unfortunately there is no indication given of the source of the individual documents. The orders and letters going *out* from the French Court are in series B ; the letters, reports and journals sent *in* are in series C11A and C11E (Collection Moreau de St. Méry). The Journal of Legardeur de Saint-Pierre (de Repentigny) has been published with translation in the Report of P.A.C., 1886. It is also in Margry, *op. cit.*

ON THE DOBBS CONTROVERSY.—The pamphlets are mentioned in the text. There is a folder in the H.B.C. Arch. with material of prime importance, including a copy of Dobbs's *Abstract* and papers giving an intimate insight into the Company's preparation to meet the parliamentary inquiry. *The Report from the Committee appointed to inquire into the state and condition of the countries adjoining to Hudson's Bay, and of the trade carried on there*, 1749, embodies the papers and evidence placed before the House of Commons, but not the decision of the House.

CHAPTERS V AND VI

TRADERS FROM MONTREAL AND THE NORTH-WEST COMPANY. —Davidson, G. C., *The North-West Company*, University of California Press, 1918, (with comprehensive bibliography, contemporary maps, and source material in appendix). [M'Gillivray, Duncan], *Some Account of the Trade carried on by the North West Company* [1808], Royal Colonial Institute, London ; photostat in P.A.C., and printed in *Report*, 1928 ; it was revised by William M'Gillivray to suit the occasion and published as *On the Origin and Progress of the North West Company*, London, 1811. Mackenzie, Sir Alex., " A General History of the Fur Trade " in his *Voyages from Montreal . . . to the Frozen and Pacific Oceans*, London, 1801. *Documents relating to the North-West Company*, ed. by W. S. Wallace, Cham. Soc., 1934 (an excellent but not a complete collection, mostly bearing on the Montreal end of the trade, with a biographical dictionary "of the North-Westers," curiously including servants of the Hudson's Bay Company). Masson, L. R., *Les Bourgeois de la Compagnie du Nord-Ouest*, 2 tomes, Quebec, 1889 and 1890 (an important historical sketch and text of journals). *Returns of Indian Trade Licences*, P.A.C., series S ; abstracts have been made under the direction of Professor Wayne E. Stevens, 1925, copy in Library of University of Saskatchewan. Fur trade returns at Michilimackinac, 1767, P.R.O. ; transcript in P.A.C. ; printed in C.H.R., Dec., 1922. *Wisconsin Historical Collections*, vol. 18, British Régime. Frobisher, Joseph, *Letter Book*, 1787–88, and *Journal*, 1806–10, McGill and P.A.C. Morton, A. S., *Forrest Oakes, Charles Boyer, Joseph Fulton, and Peter Pangman*, T.R.S.C., 1937, sec. 2. Pond, Peter, *Journal*, Wisconsin Hist. Coll., vol. 18 ; and in C. M. Gates's *Five Fur Traders of the North-West* ; his life, by H. A. Innis, Toronto, 1930. Harmon, D. W., *Journal*, Andover, 1820 ; Toronto, 1904 ; N.Y., 1922. Henry, Alex., (the elder), *Travels and Adventures . . . 1760–76*, N.Y., 1807 ; ed. by J. Bain, Toronto, 1901. Henry, Alex. (the younger), *Journals*, ed. by Elliott Coues under title *New Light on the Early History of the Greater Northwest*, 3 vols., N.Y., 1897, the original in Parliamentary Library, Ottawa. MacDonald, John of Garth, *Autobiographical Notes*, photostat in P.A.C. ; extracts in Masson, *op. cit.* Thompson, David, *Journals* and *Map*, Ontario Archives, Toronto ; *Narrative of His Explorations in North America*, ed. by J. B. Tyrrell, Cham. Soc., 1916. Umfreville, Ed., *Journal of a Passage in a Canoe from Pais Plat in Lake Superior to Portage de l'Isle in Rivière Ouinipique*, 1784, McGill, ed. by R. Douglas under title *Nipigon to Winnipeg*, with extracts from other early travellers through the region, Ottawa, 1929 ; also *The Present State of Hudson's Bay*, London, 1796.

NORTH-WEST COMPANY WRITINGS.—(Those referring to the XY Company are indicated.) LAKE SUPERIOR : by F. V. Malhiot, John Johnstone, Duncan Cameron, Peter Grant, in Masson, *op. cit.* RAINY LAKE : Faries, Hugh, *Journal*, P.A.C., ed. by C. M. Gates, *op. cit.* (XY Co.). ASSINIBOINE (UPPER RED) RIVER : Macdonell, John, *Journal from Lachine to the Qu'Appelle River*, 1793, McGill ; ed. by C. M. Gates, *op. cit.* ; also his *Some Account of Red River* and *Extracts* from his *Journals*, 1793–97, in Masson, *op. cit.* McLeod, A. N., *Journal* (at Fort Alexandria), 1800–1, McGill ; ed. by C. M. Gates, *op. cit.* Harmon, D. W., *Journal*, 1800–1 (XY Co.). MacDonald, John, of Garth, *op. cit.*, years 1808–9. EXPEDITIONS TO THE MISSOURI : Laroque, F. A., *Journal*, 1804–5, P.A.C. Masson, *op. cit.* ; also 1805, McGill, ed. by L. J. Burpee, Ottawa, 1910. Mackenzie, Charles, *Journal*, McGill ; in Masson *op. cit.* Henry, Alex., the younger, in Coues, *op. cit.*, vol. 1. RED RIVER : Chaboillez, Charles, *Journal*, 1797–98 at Pembina, P.A.C. Henry, Alex., the younger, 1800–8, in Coues, *op. cit.*, vol. 1. FORT DAUPHIN : Dufaut, J., *Journal*, 1803–4 (at Fort des Epinettes, Lake Winnipegosis, an outpost of the XY Co.). WINNIPEG LAKE AND NELSON RIVER : [McKay, Wm.], *Cross Lake Journal*, 1805–6, P.A.C. THE SASKATCHEWAN : M'Gillivray, Duncan, *op. cit.* MacDonald, John, of Garth, *op. cit.*, 1791–1807 (XY Co.). Harmon,

D. W., *op. cit.*, 1805–7. Henry, Alex., the younger, *op. cit.*, vol. 2, 1808–11. CHURCHILL RIVER : M'Gillivray, William, *Journal*, 1789–90, in " Les Rats " ; *Journal*, 1793, a fragment, at Ile-à-la-Crosse, P.A.C. ATHABASKA : Mackenzie, James, *Journal*, 1799, at Fort Chipewyan (XY Co.), P.A.C. ; extracts in Masson, *op. cit.* ; Porter, James, *Journal*, 1801–2 (XY Co.), P.A.C. PEACE RIVER : [Thomson, John], *Journal*, at " Grand Marais ou Rivière Rouge," 1798. [Fraser, Simon], *Journal*, at " Rocky Mountain Fort," 1799–1800. [Wentzell, W. F.], " *Athabaska Journal*, 1798 " [1800], (XY Co.). All of these in P.A.C. Harmon, D. W., *op. cit.*, 1808–10, Fort Dunvegan. MACKENZIE RIVER : Wentzell, W. F., *Journal*, 1804–5, at the Forks of the Mackenzie and the Liard (see J. N. Wallace, *The Wintering Partners on Peace River*), P.A.C. ; for his other writings see Masson, *op. cit.* NEW CALEDONIA : Harmon, D. W., *op. cit.*, 1810–19, with " an account of the Indians living west of the Rocky Mountains."

IN THE HUDSON'S BAY COMPANY'S ARCHIVES.—There is ample material, London letters *out*, correspondence and journals *in*, from Albany, Moose, York, and Churchill forts. IN THE ALBANY AND MOOSE SPHERE : voyages of Edward Jarvis from Albany to the upper Moose, 1775 ; and to Lake Superior, 1776 ; of George Sutherland to Lake Winnipeg, 1778 ; of Philip Turnor to Gloucester House, 1779 ; and to Lake Superior, 1781, printed in Journals of Hearne and Turnor, Cham. Soc., 1934. Of the post Journals in the valley of the Moose mention may be made of Philip Turnor's at Frederick House, 1785–87 ; in the valley of the Albany and on the route westward, of Martin's Falls, of Gloucester House, of Osnaburgh House ; in the basin of Lake Winnipeg, of Portage de l'Isle, and of Lac la Pluie ; and on the Assiniboine, of Brandon House, Shell River, and Albany House at the Elbow. IN THE SPHERE OF YORK FORT : Journals of Carlton House on the upper Assiniboine ; on the Saskatchewan, of the very important Journals of Cumberland House (including Hearne's Journal of 1774–75, printed in Journals of Hearne and Turnor, Cham. Soc.), which report the passage of Northwesters towards the Saskatchewan and the Churchill. A remarkably complete line of the Journals of Hudson House, South Branch, Manchester, Buckingham houses, and the first Edmonton House. Among the York Fort papers are the Journals of travellers into the interior, Joseph Smith's, William Pinks's, Matthew Cocking's (this last, ed. by L. J. Burpee, T.R.S.C., 1908, sec. 2, unfortunately without the accompanying log). *The Journals of Samuel Hearne and Philip Turnor*, ed. by J. B. Tyrrell, Cham. Soc., 1934, contains Hearne's Journal at Cumberland House, and Turnor's survey of the routes to that post, his Journal at the so called Upper Hudson House, and his voyage to Lake Athabaska and Great Slave Lake, etc.

The surveys of David Thompson (in Ontario Archives) from 1792 to 1796 strictly were made for the Hudson's Bay Company ; as were those of Peter Fidler (5 vols.) in H.B.C. Arch. They are both invaluable for determining the sites of the posts.

THE PACIFIC SLOPE.—Bancroft, H. H., *History of the North-West Coast*, N.Y., with bibliography. Smith, C. W., *Pacific North-West Americana*, a check list of books and pamphlets, N.Y., 1921. Howay, F. W., and Schole-field, E. O. S., *British Columbia from Earliest Times*, 3 vols. (1 and 2 historical, with list of authorities). Morice, A. G., *The Northern Interior of British Columbia*, Toronto, 1918. ON THE ABORIGINES : Morice as above. Goddard, P. E., *Indians of the North-West Coast*, Amer. Museum Press, N.Y., 1924. Hill-Tout, C., *British North America, the Far West, the Home of the Salish and Déné*, Toronto, 1907. ON THE VOYAGES : Golder, F. A., *Bering's Voyages*, 2 vols., Amer. Geog. Assoc., 1922, 1925, with bibliography. Bolton, H. E., *Fray Juan Crespi*, 1769–74, University of South California Press, 1927. Benito de la Sierra, *Account of the Hezeta Expedition*, 1775, California Hist. Quarterly, Sept. 1930. Maurelle, F. A., *Journal of a Voyage in 1775 . . .*, in Daines Barring-ton's *Miscellanies*, reprinted by T. C. Russell under the title of *Voyage of the Sonora in the Second Bucarelli Expedition*, San Francisco, 1920. Cook, Capt.

James, *A Voyage to the Pacific Ocean*, 1776–80, 3 vols., with atlas, London, 1784. Strange, James, *Journal and Narrative of the Commerical Expedition from Bombay to the North-West Coast of America*, Madras Government Press, 1928. Portlock, Capt. Nathaniel, *Voyage*, 1785–88, London, 1789. Dixon, Capt. George, *A Voyage round the World* . . ., 1785–88, London, 1789. Howay, F. W., *The Dixon-Meares Controversy*, Toronto, 1929. Meares, Capt. John, *Voyages* . . . *in the Years 1788 and 1789*, and his *Authentic Copy of the Memorial to the Right Honourable William Wyndham Grenville*, London, 1790. Haswell, Robert, *A Voyage in the Columbia Rediviva and Sloop, Washington*, 1787–89 and in 1791–92, printed in H. H. Bancroft, *op. cit.*, pp. 703-35. Haskins, John, *The Narrative of a Voyage in the Ship Columbia Rediviva*, 1790–93, in Oregon Hist. Soc. Quarterly, vol. 22, 1921. Howay, F. W., *Letters relating to the Second Voyage of the Columbia, ibid.*, vol. 24, 1923. ON THE NOOTKA SOUND CRISIS : Martinez, Estevan José, *Log of the Princesa, ibid.*, vol. 21, 1920. *Official Papers relative to the Dispute between the Courts of Great Britain and Spain on the Subject of the Ships captured in Nootka Sound* [1790], also printed in the *Annual Register*, 1793. Manning, W. R., *The Nootka Sound Controversy*, Report of the Amer. Hist. Assoc., 1904, with bibliography. ON VANCOUVER : Dalrymple, Alexander, *Plan for promoting the Fur Trade, and recovering it to this country by uniting the operations of the East India and Hudson's Bay Companies*, London, 1789. Vancouver, George, *A Voyage of Discovery*, 3 vols., with maps, London, 1798. Menzies, Arch., *Journal of Vancouver's Voyage*, Memoir No. 5, B.C. Arch., 1923. Broughton, W. R., *A Voyage of Discovery in the Sloop Providence*, London, 1804. ON SIR ALEXANDER MACKENZIE : *His Voyages from Montreal to the Frozen and Pacific Oceans*, 1789 and 1793, London, 1801. Wade, M.S., *Mackenzie of Canada*, London, 1927 (traces his footsteps to the Pacific). Mackenzie, Roderick, *Reminiscences*, Masson, *op. cit.*, vol. 1 (extracts from Sir Alexander's letters). Lieut.-Governor Simcoe's report of Mackenzie's conversation with him, P.A.C., series Q, 180–82, p. 359, printed in E. A. Cruikshank's *Correspondence of Simcoe*, Ontario Hist. Soc., vol. 3, p. 689.

THE NORTH WEST COMPANY'S COLUMBIAN ENTERPRISE.— [M'Gillivray, Duncan], *Some Account of the Trade carried on by the North West Company* [1808], and the revised edition *On the Origin and Progress of the North West Company*, London, 1811. A folder in the H.B.C. Arch. contains documents dealing with the attempt of the North West Company to secure a transit for their goods through Hudson Bay, and with the opinions of the lawyers on the possibility of prosecuting them. The *Minute of the North West Company* offering £2,000 a year for the transit is in *Documents relating to the North West Company*, p. 203f, photostat in P.A.C. On the question of Duncan M'Gillivray crossing the Rockies in 1801, see A. S. Morton, *North West Company's Columbian Enterprise* and pertinent documents in C.H.R., Sept. 1936 ; J. B. Tyrrell's criticism in *ibid.*, March 1938 ; and Morton's reply in June 1938. ON SIMON FRASER : His Journal of 1806, along with letters of about the same time, printed in Report of P.A.C., 1929, and the Journal of his voyage down the Fraser in 1808 in Masson, *op. cit.*, vol. 1. ON DAVID THOMPSON : His Journals, etc., in Ontario Archives, and his *Narrative*, ed. by J. B. Tyrrell, Cham. Soc. Portions of the Journals have been printed in Oregon Hist. Soc. Quarterly. ON THE ASTORIAN ENTERPRISE : Irving, Washington, *Astoria*, 3 vols., London, 1836. Ross, Alexander, *The Adventures of the First Settlers on the Columbia River*, 1849, and *The Fur Hunters of the Far West*, 2 vols., London, 1855. Cox, Ross, *Adventures on the Columbia River*, 2 vols., London, 1831. There are many documents and interpretative articles in the Oregon Hist. Soc. Quarterly and the Washington Hist. Quarterly.

CHAPTER VII

FOR THE XY COMPANY.—See Journals listed under Chaps. V. and VI. On *The Canada Jurisdiction Act (1803) and the North-West*, see A. S. Morton in T.R.S.C., 1938, sec. 2, with ample reference to the documents. The reorganization of the Hudson's Bay Company in 1810 can be traced in the Minutes (as also the Grant to Lord Selkirk), but especially in a printed circular sent to the Gentlemen overseas. For Selkirk's relations with Sir Alexander Mackenzie, see Roderick's *Reminiscences*, in P.A.C., extracts in Masson, *op. cit.* Sir Alexander Mackenzie's *Proposed General Fishery and Fur Company* is in P.A.C., series Q, vol. 90, p. 37ff, printed in Report of 1892, p. 147ff. Selkirk's plan for an Irish Catholic colony on the Red River, 1802, is in *ibid.*, vol. 293, p. 169ff. FOR SELKIRK'S COLONY : Martin, Chester, *Lord Selkirk's work in Canada*, Toronto, 1916, with excellent bibliography and documents in the appendix. Wallace, W. S., *The Literature relating to the Selkirk Controversy*, C.H.R., March 1933, with a check list of the books and pamphlets which figured in it. Of supreme importance are the Selkirk transcripts in P.A.C., the first 8,500 odd pages are correspondence ; in subsequent folders are the Journals of Miles Macdonell, Colin Robertson, and Governor Semple's Letter-book. Two folders contain letters of the Northwesters bearing on the destruction of the colony, seized by Selkirk at Fort William. Miles Macdonell's Letter-book is in P.A.C., printed in Report of 1886. Select documents are in E. H. Oliver, *The Canadian North-West, Its Early Development and Legislative Records*, 2 vols., Ottawa, 1914. A parliamentary paper, *Papers relating to the Red River Settlement . . . ordered by the House of Commons to be printed, 12th July, 1819* (with three maps), embodies the Government documents, including the Coltman Report. FOR THE STRUGGLE IN ATHABASKA : See the Selkirk transcripts. A number of the Journals of the English posts are in H.B.C. Arch. Simpson's Journal of Fort Wedderburn, 1820–21, is about to be published for the Company by Cham. Soc. FOR THE UNION OF 1821 : The Selkirk transcripts from Sept. 20, 1819 (p. 6,493), to June 30, 1821 (p. 7,315), show the initiation of negotiations for union by the Wintering Partners of the North West Company, and the part played by Andrew Colvile. The H.B.C. Arch. have no material showing the final negotiations, nor the circumstances in which the Agents of the North West Company were brought into the union, but a folder contains material bearing indirectly on the matter, more especially Colin Robertson's *Diary*, kept when in England. In *Documents relating to the North West Company*, Cham. Soc., Nos. 25–27 bear on the union.

CHAPTER VIII

ON THE HUDSON'S BAY COMPANY.—The important questions of policy are dealt with in the correspondence between the Governor and Committee and Governor Simpson preserved in the Archives. Simpson's reports usually include the *Minutes of the Northern Council* and of the *Southern Council* after he became its Acting-Governor ; his personal reports explained the Minutes almost paragraph by paragraph, and covered the continental domain from Labrador to the Pacific coast. Add the correspondence between Simpson and the service, and that between the Company and the Imperial Government. Printed works are : Oliver, E. H., *op. cit.*, with important bibliography in vol. 1 at pp. 103–14 (*q.v.*) and documents including the *Minutes of the Northern Council* from 1830 to 1843, with extracts from those of 1822 (the Minutes of 1824 are in Frederick Merk's *Fur Trade and Empire*, and those of 1825 in C.H.R., Dec. 1926) ; and the parliamentary paper, *Return to an address of the House of Commons for copy of the [licence granted] by the Crown, and the correspondence which last took place at its renewal, 1842* ; also West, Rev. John, *The Substance of a Journal during a residence at the Red River Colony*, London,

1824 ; Garry, Nicholas, *Diary*, 1821, T.R.S.C., 1900. M'Lean, John, *Notes of a Twenty Years' Service in the Hudson's Bay Territory*, London, 1849 ; Cham. Soc., 1932. ON THE RED RIVER SETTLEMENT.—Simpson's correspondence as above. The *Selkirk Transcripts* in P.A.C. dealing in diminishing volume with the colony till its reconveyance to the Company in 1836 ; its most important single feature is the intimate letters which passed between Andrew Colvile and Governor Simpson. The *Bulger Papers* in P.A.C. cover Bulger's year as Governor. The " Reconveyance of Red River Colony " is in *Charters, Statutes*, etc., Hudson's Bay Company, 1931, at pp. 231–34. See also Ross, Alex., *The Red River Settlement*, London, 1856, and Gunn, Donald, and Tuttle, C. R., *History of Manitoba from the Earliest Settlements*, Ottawa, 1880, and Martin, Archer, *The Hudson's Bay Company's Land Tenure*, London, 1898, with important maps.

ON THE DELINEATION OF THE POLAR SHORE.—Works of Sir John Franklin of 1824 and 1828, of Sir John Richardson of 1851, and of Dr. John Rae of 1850. Documents on Rae's last exploration are in H.B.C. Arch. Interesting articles, illustrated with maps, on the fate of the Franklin expedition are : Burwash, L. T., *The Franklin Search*, in *Canadian Geographical Journal*, Nov. 1920. Gibson, William, *Sir John Franklin's Last Voyage*, in *The Beaver*, June 1937. Ross, Mitchell, *Physician, Fur Trader, and Explorer* [Dr. Rae], *ibid.*, Sept. 1936. Sir George Back's *Narrative* . . ., 1836, and that of his companion Dr. Richard King (2 vols., London, 1836). Thomas Simpson's *Narrative*, London, 1843, and his *Life and Travels*, London, 1845, both by his brother, Alexander Simpson. EXPLORATIONS FOR NEW FUR AREAS : Documents in H.B.C. Arch. Robert Campbell's Journals in P.A.C. John M'Lean's voyage is described in his *Notes*, as above.

CHAPTER IX

ON THE PACIFIC WEST, ITS FUR TRADE.—Sage, W. N., *Sir James Douglas and British Columbia*, University of Toronto Press, 1930 (*q.v.*), with extensive bibliography of MS. sources, parliamentary papers, and books. Schafer, J., *Letters of Sir George Simpson*, 1841–43, in *Amer. Hist. Rev.*, Oct. 1908. There is much material in H.B.C. Arch. in addition to the correspondence with Governor Simpson, for Dr. John McLoughlin, Chief Factor in the Columbia District was in direct communication with the Governor and Committee by way of Cape Horn. In B.C. Arch., John Work's Journal of 1823–24 ; Francis Ermatinger's *Notes on the Clallum Expedition*, 1828 ; sundry letters of Dr. McLoughlin's ; Journals of Fort Langley, 1827–1828 ; of John Tod at " Thompson's River " [Kamloops], 1841 ; of Dr. Tolmie at Nisqually, 1833, and 1833–34 at Fort McLoughlin, as well as of the Stikine expedition, 1834. Simpson's Journal of 1824–25, with many additional documents, has been printed by Frederick Merk as *Fur Trade and Empire*. His voyage of 1828 as described in Arch. McDonald's Journal, published under title of *Peace River*, ed. by Malcolm McLeod, Ottawa, 1872. V. V. Holman has published a life of *Dr. John McLoughlin, the Father of Oregon*, see also *Letter of Dr. John McLoughlin to the Governor and Committee*, Nov. 20, 1845, in *Amer. Hist. Rev.*, Oct. 1915. ON THE OREGON QUESTION.—Alexander Ross's Journal of the Snake Expedition, 1823–24, printed in part in Oregon Hist. Soc. Quarterly, vol. 14 ; P. S. Ogden's Journals of the Snake Expeditions of 1824–25, 1825–26, printed in *ibid.*, vol. 4, and of 1826–28, and 1828–29, in vol. 11. In B.C. Arch., transcripts of the documents in the British Foreign Office bearing on the Oregon question ; besides the documents reporting the negotiations, these include a mass of communications sent in by various parties, *e.g.* the Hudson's Bay Company and David Thompson. Thompson's letters (printed in the Report of B.C. Arch., 1913) include the one in which he states that he was across the Rockies and on the Kootenay in 1801. For the British case, Adam Thom's *The Claims to the Oregon Territory considered*, London, 1844 ; Travers Twiss's *The Oregon Question examined in respect to Facts and the Law of Nations*, London, 1846. H. L. Keenleyside's, *Canada and the United States*, N.Y., 1929.

On the American side, Robert Greenhow's, *The History of Oregon and California*, 3rd ed. rev., N.Y. 1845, prepared as a report for the American Government with a full knowledge of the state documents which are freely quoted as evidence for the writer's case. Messages from the Presidents. Senate Documents. J. M. Callahan's *American Foreign Policy in Canadian Relations*, N.Y., 1937.

CHAPTERS X AND XIII

ON THE PACIFIC COLONIES.—For the governorship of James Douglas, see the bibliography in W. N. Sage's *Sir James Douglas and British Columbia*, where the British official papers, the correspondence of Douglas with the Colonial Office, and the files of the newspapers are listed. The debates in Hansard are important. Of the books: Fitzgerald, J. E., *An Examination of the Charter and Proceedings of the Hudson's Bay Company with reference to the Grant of Vancouver's Island*, London, 1849. Fitzgerald's letters to the Colonial Office are printed in the Report of B.C. Arch., 1913. Martin, R. M., *The Hudson's Bay Territories and Vancouver's Island*, London, 1862. In B.C. Arch., the files of *The British Colonist* (Victoria) and of *The British Columbian* (New Westminster) are especially valuable for the reports of the public meetings and their petitions ; the *Kenneth Mackenzie Papers* for the operations of the Puget Sound Agricultural Company. Parliamentary paper, No. 483, 1868, is on the selection of the site of the capital of (united) British Columbia. See also Palmer, P. F., *A Fiscal History of British Columbia in the Colonial Period*, 1932. Ross, Margaret, *Amor de Cosmos*, in Wash. Hist. Quarterly, Apr. 1932. ON BRITISH COLUMBIA AND CONFEDERATION. —Parliamentary paper *re* Union of British Columbia with Canada, 1867–69. *The Gazette Extraordinary* (of British Columbia), 1870, a verbatim report of the debates of March of that year in the Council. Canada, *Sessional Papers*, 1871, vol. 4, No. 18 ; 1872, vol. 5, No. 10. See also W. N. Sage's *The Annexationist Movement in British Columbia*, T.R.S.C., 1927, sec. 2 ; H. L. Keenleyside's *British Columbia, Annexation or Confederation*, Can. Hist. Assoc. Report, 1928 ; F. W. Howay's *British Columbia's Entry into Confederation, ibid.*, 1927.

CHAPTER XI

ON UNREST AMONG THE HALF-BREEDS.—The correspondence of the Governor and Committee, Governor Simpson, Governor Eden Colvile temporarily associated with Simpson, and of Alex. Christie and Major Caldwell, governors of Assiniboia, and finally of Adam Thom, Recorder, as in H.B.C. Arch., is ample and illuminating. The principal parliamentary papers are, *Correspondence relative to the complaints of the Inhabitants of Red River Settlement*, 1849, and *Report of the Select Committee on the Hudson's Bay Company*, 1857. Papers relative to the exploration of the country under Captain Palliser, 1859 and 1860. The trial of Sayer is reported in the *Records of the Quarterly Court* of 1849, Arch. of Manitoba.

FOR CANADA'S INTEREST IN THE NORTH-WEST.—Writings referred to in the text at p. 825f. The correspondence which issued in the dispatch of the Canadian Rifles to the Red River is in P.A.C., Military Series, volume on the North-West. Papers dealing with the mission of Chief Justice Draper before the Select Committee and the inquiry of the committee of the Canadian House as to the rights of the Hudson's Bay Company are in Sessional

Papers of 1857, Appendix No. 17. See also the documents referred to in R. G. Trotter's *Canadian Federation*, Toronto, 1924, pp. 246–47, 264–66, 279–81. For the Canadian exploration of routes and of the agricultural possibilities of the North-West, see the reports of S. J. Dawson, 1859 and 1868 ; and of H. Y. Hind, 1859, and his *Narrative*, 2 vols., London, 1860. For the political difficulties and the purchase of the Hudson's Bay Company, Sir Edward Watkins's *Canada and the United States*, London, 1887. For documents bearing on the negotiations for the surrender of the Company's Charter, see Trotter, *op. cit.*, pp. 298–301 ; and *The Report of Delegates appointed to negotiate for the Acquisition of Rupert's Land and the North-West Territory*, Ottawa, 1869. FOR THE 1860's.—Begg, Adam, *History of the North-West*, 3 vols., Toronto, 1894, with extracts from documents ; Hargrave, J. J., *Red River*, Montreal, 1871 ; most illuminating of all, the file of *The Nor'-Wester*, unfortunately very incomplete for the latter half of the decade, in the Archives of Manitoba, Winnipeg.

CHAPTER XII

DISTURBANCES IN THE RED RIVER SETTLEMENT.—The most important book is Geo. F. G. Stanley's *The Birth of Western Canada : A History of the Riel Rebellions*, London, 1936, invaluable both for the history and for its ample documentation ; it is written with the documents in H.B.C. Arch. in view. *The Papers of Sir John Macdonald*, P.A.C., 3 vols. on the Riel Rebellion, are of supreme importance for the point of view and the policy of the Dominion Government ; not less important are the many communications sent in to Sir John. His letters to his late fellow-Minister, Sir John Rose, and the letters received from William McDougall, Captain Cameron, and Donald Smith are of prime importance. McDougall's point of view is to be found in his pamphlet, *Eight Letters to Joseph Howe on the Red River Rebellion*. The views of all parties, particularly of Bishop Taché, are to be found in the Canadian parliamentary paper, *Report of the Select Committee on the Causes of the Difficulties in the North-West Territories, 1769–70*, Ottawa, 1874. A moderate view of the events may be gathered in J. J. Hargrave's *Red River*, but above all in the Diary of Adam Begg (in P.A.C.), a Canadian resident of some years in the Settlement ; it reports the occurrences and the movement of local opinion from day to day. British parliamentary papers are : 1868–69, No. 440, *re* the annexation of Rupert's Land to Canada, Dec. 1867–69 ; (papers in the appendix go back to 1863) ; 1870, No. 315, *re* Treasury proceedings concerning the Rupert's Land Loan ; 1870, No. C307 ; correspondence *re* the disturbances at Red River Settlement ; 1870, No. 443, petitions from Red River, etc. since 1860. Colonel Dennis's *Memorandum of Facts and Circumstances* is in Canadian Sessional Papers, 1870, vol. 5, No. 12. See also Boulton, C. A., *Reminiscences*, Toronto, 1886 ; Butler, W. F., *The Great Lone Land*, London, 1872 ; and the Canadian *Hansard*. Select documents, including the Minutes of the Council of Assiniboia, are in E. H. Oliver's, *The Canadian North-West*, vol. 2.

APPENDIX-NOTES TO THE SECOND EDITION

In the following notes, the roman figure refers to the page, the italic figure to the line.

CHAPTER I: The Three Northwests and Their Aboriginal Tribes

2, *5*/soil: See Maud D. Haviland, *Forest, Steppe and Tundra* (Cambridge, 1926), a study with bibliographies of the similar region in Asia. Also Marion I. Newbigin, *Modern Geography* (with "Notes on Books"). It deals chiefly with Europe and Asia.

2, *9*/fifteen: Consult W.B. Hurd and T.W. Grindley, *Agriculture, Climate and Population of the Prairie Provinces of Canada: A Statistical Atlas Showing Past Development and Present Conditions* (Ottawa, 1931).

2, *36*/known: Arthur S. Morton, ed., *The Journal of Duncan M'Gillivray of the North West Company at Fort George on the Saskatchewan, 1794-5* (Toronto, 1929), p.22.

3, *17*/1857–59): *The Journals, Detailed Reports and Observations Relative to the Explanation by Captain Palliser* . . . (London, 1863) pp.7, 12.

3, *24*/time: Henday's Journal exists in three versions in the York Fort Papers in the Hudson's Bay Company archives (hereafter H.B.C. Arch.), E.2/6, ff.10d-38d, E.2/11, ff.1-40d, B.239/a/40. The first of these was published by L.J. Burpee, "York Factory to the Blackfeet Country—The Journal of Anthony Hendry, 1754–55," Royal Society of Canada, *Transactions*, Third Series, I (1907), s.2, pp.307–64. Burpee adopted the spelling "Hendry" on the assurance of Agnes C. Laut that the Minutes of the Company all spell the name in this way.

3, *31*/fort: Alexander Henry, *Travels and Adventures in Canada and the Indian Territories between the Years 1760 and 1776*, ed. James Bain (Toronto, 1901), pp.276 f.

4, *5*/rose bushes: Samuel Hearne, *A Journey from Prince of Wales's Fort in Hudson's Bay to the Northern Ocean, 1769–72* (London, 1795), pp.358, 449 f.; in J.B. Tyrrell's Champlain Society edition (Toronto, 1911), pp.336, 410 f.

4, *12*/"arctic": Sir John Richardson, *Fauna-Boreali-Americana* (London, 1829), pp.241 f.

4, *19*/woods: Warburton Pike, *The Barren Ground of Northern Canada* (London, 1892), pp.45 f.

4, *45*/sticks": So called by the Indians. Caspar Whitney, *On Snow Shoes to the Barren Grounds* (London, 1896), p.184.

5, *4*/land: *The Kelsey Papers*, with an introduction by Arthur G. Doughty and Chester Martin (Ottawa, Public Archives of Canada; Belfast, Public Record Office of Northern Ireland, 1929), p.xix.

5, *7*/Churchill River: Nicolas Jérémie, *Twenty Years of York Factory, 1694–1714: Jérémie's Account of Hudson Strait and Bay*, trans. R. Douglas and J.N. Wallace (Ottawa, 1926), p.21. The translation was from Jérémie's "Relation sur le Détroit et la Baie d'Hudson," printed in J.F. Bernard's *Recueil de voiages au Nord* (Amsterdam, 1720); reprinted in La Société historique de Saint-Boniface (Manitoba), *Bulletin*, II (1912).

5, *19*/Mackenzie River: For the position of the Indians, see Diamond Jenness, *The Indians of Canada* (Ottawa, 1932). Later editions are identical except that in the 1955 edition Appendix C was added, giving the author's provisional deductions relating to new methods of dating developed since the first appearance of the book.

5, *26*/"Northern Indians": See David Thompson, *Narrative of His Explorations in Western America, 1784–1812*, ed. J.B. Tyrrell (Toronto, Champlain Society, 1916), pp.128–32, 161–6.

6, *17*/88–90): Morton often gave no references in the notes he pencilled into the proof copy if the work in question was listed in his appended Brief Bibliographical Notes. The passages quoted here and immediately below are from Tyrrell's edition of Hearne's *Journey to the Northern Ocean*.

6, *49*/105–6): See also Thompson, *Narrative*, pp.161 f.

7, *8*/Grounds: See Alexander Mackenzie, *Voyages from Montreal . . . to the Frozen and Pacific Oceans . . . with a Preliminary Account of . . . the Fur Trade . . .* (London, 1801), pp.cxvi f., and Thompson, *Narrative*, chaps. VII and IX.

7, *39*/Indians: For this trade across the Barrens, see the Index under Churchill Fort.

8, *46*/at it: Charles Mair's *Through the Mackenzie Basin: A Narrative of the Athabasca and Peace River Treaty Expedition of 1899* (Toronto, 1908) is not mentioned in the bibliographical appendix, a departure from Morton's usual practice.

10, *23*/desired: Ernest Thompson Seton, *Life Histories of Northern Animals* (2 vols., London, 1910), I, 477.

10, *32*/lakes: Thompson, *Narrative*, pp. 110–12, 59–61.

11, *1*/1737: Archives nationales, Archives des Colonies (A.N., Col.), C^{11A}, Correspondance générale, vol.16, p.181, Dénombrement des Nations. So Morton's note, but the reference should apparently be to C^{11A}, vol.66, though the date of the estimate there is 1736.

11, *26*/family: Thompson, *Narrative*, p.109.

11, *29*/Company: Public Archives of Canada (P.A.C.), Masson Collection, No. 4, William McGillivray's Journal, 1789–90, at "Les Rats." The Masson Collection is cited by Morton in the bibliographical appendix as the Masson Papers.

11, *34*/starving: Masson Collection, No. 9, Cross Lake Journal.

11, *41*/Winnipeg: Duncan Cameron, "A sketch of the customs, manners, way of living of the natives in the barren country about Nipigon," in L.R. Masson, *Les Bourgeois de la Compagnie du Nord-Ouest* (2 vols., Quebec, 1889–90), II, pp. 239–300.

12, *8*/vain: See below, pp.131 f. and 147.

12, *29*/Liard: Masson, *Les Bourgeois*, II, 68; I, 85 (W.F. Wentzell's letters).

12, *34*/Point: See Alexander Mackenzie, *Voyages*, p. 122.

12, *39*/Île-à-la-Crosse: *Ibid.*, p.xcii.

13, *11*/belt: The Crees are described in Alexander Mackenzie's *Voyages*, pp.xci f.; in Thompson's *Narrative,* chaps. IV, VI; and by Sir John Richardson in Captain John Franklin's *Narrative of a Journey to the Shores of the Polar Sea in the years 1819, 20, 21 and 22* (London, 1823), chap. III.

13, *48*/Plain Crees: Thompson, *Narrative*, p.131.

14, *15*/North-West: Henry Youle Hind, *British North America: Reports of Progress, together with a Preliminary and General Report on the Assiniboine and Saskatchewan Expedition,* Command Paper 808 (London, 1860), p. 116.

14, *35*/pounds: Franklin, *Journal to the Polar Sea*, pp.112 f., describes a pound seen near Fort Carlton; also Hind, *British North America*, p.64.

15, *49*/to: "to" is a misprint for "into." See note immediately following.

15, *49*/1749: "The Report from the Committee, Appointed to enquire into the State and Condition of the Countries adjoining to Hudson's Bay, and of the Trade Carried on there. Together with an Appendix. Reported by Lord Strange, 24th April 1749." No. 4 in *Reports from Committees of the House of Commons Re-printed by Order of the House,* II, *Miscellaneous Subjects, 1738–1765* ([London], 1803), p.243. Henceforth referred to as *Report from the Commons Committee of 1749.*

16, *6*/Hills: Morton's original note reads "Selkirk Papers, p.12; 17." This passage makes no reference to Kelsey. See *Kelsey Papers*, pp.5–10.

16, *11*/1738: Lawrence J. Burpee, ed., *Journals and Letters of Pierre Gaultier de Varennes de La Vérendrye and his Sons* . . . (Toronto, Champlain Society, 1927), pp.249 f.

16, *13*/Beaux: In the proof copy Morton has crossed out the word *"Beaux,"* and substituted *"Vieux,"* the word La France uses in the passage to which reference is made immediately below.

16, *14*/La France: *Report from the Commons Committee of 1749*, p.247.

16, *21*/House: Thompson, *Narrative*, p.323.

16, *29*/them: *Ibid.*, pp.328 f.

18, *53*/came: *Ibid.*, p.348.

19, *4*/Edmonton: The tribes are so placed in Arrowsmith's maps (e.g., that of 1795 corrected to 1818, reproduced in Morton, ed., *Duncan M'Gillivray's Journal.*

19, *20*/River: Morton quotes this from Henday's Journal in H.B.C. Arch., York Fort Papers, B.239/a/40, under date of Oct. 14, 1754. The version of this passage published by Burpee, "York Factory to the Blackfeet Country," is substantially the same.

21, *8*/river: *Journals and Letters of La Vérendrye*, p.325.

21, *16*/Thompson: Elliott Coues, ed., *History of the Expedition under the Command of Lewis and Clark* . . . (4 vols., London and New York, 1893), I, 173–8, which places the ruins of the Mandan forts at what would be the great turn to south. Thompson, *Narrative*, pp.266 f.

21, *34*/after: Elliott Coues, ed., *New Light on the Early History of the Greater Northwest: The Manuscript Journals of Alexander Henry . . . and David Thompson, 1799–1814* (3 vols., New York, 1897), I, 57, 71.

21, *41*/Labrador: *Atlas of Canada* (Ottawa, 1915), map 17–18.

CHAPTER II: The European Approach to the Fur Forest of the North and West The following works should be added to Morton's bibliography for this chapter. E.E. Rich, *History of the Hudson's Bay Company, 1670–1870* (2 vols., London, Hudson's Bay Record Society, 1958–59), of which an annotated copy is deposited in P.A.C.; also published as *Hudson's Bay Company, 1670–1870* (3 vols., Toronto, 1960); cited hereafter as *H.B.R.S.*, XXI and XXII (Book 1, chapter 1 to VI, has special relevance); E.E. Rich, ed., *Minutes of the Hudson's Bay Company 1671–1674*, with an introduction by Sir John Clapham (Toronto, Champlain Society, 1942; London, Hudson's Bay Record Society, 1942), cited hereafter as *H.B.R.S.*, V; Hudson's Bay Company, *Charters, Statutes, Orders in Council, &c. Relating to the Hudson's Bay Company* (London, Hudson's Bay Company, 1949); Harold A. Innis, *The Fur Trade in Canada: An Introduction to Canadian Economic History* (revised edition, Toronto, 1956); Grace Lee Nute, *Caesars of the Wilderness: Médard Chouart, Sieur de Groseilliers, and Pierre Esprit Radisson, 1618–1710* (New York, 1943); E.E. Rich, *The Fur Trade and the Northwest to 1857* (Toronto, 1967); F.G. Roe, *The North American Buffalo* (Toronto, 1951; second edition, Toronto, 1970).

22, *13*/source: See H.A. Innis, *The Fur Trade in Canada* (New Haven, 1930), p.5.

23, *14*/Tadoussac: Described by A.P. Low, Geological Survey of Canada, *Annual Report*, VIII, 1895 (Ottawa, 1897), 6Lf.

23, *19*/St. Lawrence: This route is described in the Journal of Father Silvy of the de Troyes expedition which captured the Hudson's Bay Company posts on James Bay in 1686. The Journal is printed in Ivanhoë Caron, ed., *Le Journal de l'expédition du Chevalier de Troyes à la baie d'Hudson en 1686* (Beauceville, 1918). See below at pp.99 f.

23, *21*/rivers: Taken by Philip Turnor, surveyor for the H.B.C., in 1780 (see below, p.423) and described in his Journal (J.B. Tyrrell, ed., *Journals of Samuel Hearne and Philip Turnor between the Years 1774 and 1792* [Toronto, Champlain Society, 1934], pp.285 f.).

23, *24*/Montreal: Route taken by Samuel de Champlain.

23, *38*/Bay: See below, pp.272–4.

23, *41*/Montreal: The route is described going westward from Lachine in John Macdonell's Journal of 1793 (copy in the University of Saskatchewan Library) printed in C.M. Gates, ed., *Five Fur Traders of the Northwest* (Minneapolis, 1933).

23, *44*/Traite: The route from Lachine to Athabaska is described by Mackenzie in his *Voyages*, pp.xxix–lxxxvii.

23, *49*/Bay: Described in Journals of H.B.C. officers; for example, by Donald MacKay in his Brandon House Journal of 1793–4 (H.B.C. Arch., B.22/a/1).

24, *49*/there: H.P. Biggar, ed., *The Voyages of Jacques Cartier, published from the originals with translations, notes and appendices* (Ottawa, Public Archives of Canada, 1924).

25, *8*/1558: H.P. Biggar, *The Early Trading Companies of New France*, Toronto, 1901), p.31.

25, *17*/Quebec: H.P. Biggar, ed., *The Works of Samuel de Champlain . . .* (6 vols., Toronto, Champlain Society, 1922–36); also G. Sagard, *Le Grand Voyage du pays des Hurons . . .* (2 vols., Paris, 1865).

26, *21*/1625: Samuel Purchas, *Hakluytus Posthumus or Purchas His Pilgrimes* (new edition, published by James MacLehose & Sons, 20 vols., Glasgow, 1905–7), XIV, 416–17.

26, *46*/Hudson: Llewelyn Powys, *Henry Hudson* (New York, 1928); G.M. Asher, *Henry Hudson the Navigator* (London, Hakluyt Society, 1860).

28, *43*/1709: Canada Case: Labrador Boundary: Atlas and maps, University of Saskatchewan.

29, *40*/expedition: See Thomas Rundall, ed., *Narratives of Voyages towards the North West* . . . (London, 1848).

30, *36*/Discovery: *Ibid.*

31, *8*/testified: Quoted in T.A. Janvier, *Henry Hudson* (New York and London 1908), p.124.

31, *15*/guilty: Powys, *Hudson*, pp.190–8.

31, *31*/equipped: Jens Munck, *Navigatio Septentrionalis* (Copenhagen, 1624). A translation is in C.C.A. Gosch, ed., *Danish Arctic Expeditions, 1605 to 1620*, Book II, *The Expedition of Captain Jens Munk to Hudson's Bay in search of a North-West Passage in 1619–1620* (London, Hakluyt Society, 1897).

32, *47*/ends: *Ibid.*, p.48.

33, *21*/1714: Jérémie, *Twenty Years of York Factory*, pp.18–19.

33, *42*/Foxe: Miller Christy, ed., *The Voyages of Captain Luke Foxe of Hull, and Captain Thomas James of Bristol, in search of a north-west passage* . . . (2 vols., London, Hakluyt Society, 1894).

34, *6*/James: *Ibid.* Also R.B. Dobilly, *The Voyage of Captain Thomas James* (London and Toronto, 1928).

34, *25*/North-West: In addition to the works relating to Radisson and Groseilliers listed in the Bibliographical Notes, the works of Grace Lee Nute should be consulted, especially her *Caesars of the Wilderness* which has a valuable bibliography. In view of Miss Nute's researches Morton's chronology of the movements of the two men should be treated with reserve though the two scholars agree substantially in their estimates of the brothers-in-law. A modernization and rearrangement of the text of the original Radisson manuscripts has been published by Arthur T. Adams and Loren Kallsen, *The Explorations of Pierre Esprit Radisson* (Minneapolis, 1961).

35, *2*/Iroquois: See Jean E. Murray, "The Early Fur Trade in New France and New Netherland," *Canadian Historical Review*, XIX (Dec., 1938).

35, *44*/affairs: R.G. Thwaites, ed., *The Jesuit Relations and Allied Documents* (73 vols., Cleveland, 1896–1901), XI, 211, Relation of 1652–53.

37, *31*/diaries: G.D. Scull, ed., *Voyages of Pierre Esprit Radisson* . . . (Boston, Prince Society, 1885). The originals are in the Bodleian Library, Oxford, and the British Museum.

37, *33*/tongue: Cf. Nute, *Caesars of the Wilderness*, p.29, n.6, where it is maintained that the Bodleian ms is a translation made for the Company in 1669.

37, *36*/river": *Ibid.*, p.67.

38, *13*/brave: *Ibid.*, pp.76–8.

39, *49*/Relation: Thwaites, ed., *Jesuit Relations*, XLII, 223, Relation of 1655–56.

40, *12*/hands: *Ibid.*, p.219.

40, *14*/1655–56: *Ibid.*, pp.225–38.

41, *10*/Onodagas: Alter "Onodagas" to "Onondages."

41, *14*/historian: The text of the Journal with criticisms is published by Warren Upham under the title "Groseilliers and Radisson, the First White Men in Minnesota, 1655–56 and 1659–60, and Their Discovery of the Upper Mississippi River," *Minnesota Historical Collections*, X (part 2), 1905. See also L.P. Kellogg, *The French Régime in Wisconsin and the Northwest* (Madison, 1925).

42, *2*/proudly: Scull, ed., *Voyages of Radisson*, p.170.

42, *34*/them: *Ibid.*, pp.155, 157.

42, *48*/trade": *Ibid.*, p. 173.

43, *16*/underlings: *Ibid.*, p.174.

43, *28*/colony: *Ibid.*, p.175.

43, *42*/months: Selections from the Journal, with running commentary by Benjamin Sulte, are in "Radisson in the North-West, 1661–64," Royal Society of Canada, *Transactions,* Second Series, X (1904), s.2, 223–38.

44, *16*/Europeans.": Scull, ed., *Voyages of Radisson,* p.224.

44, *21*/invented": *Ibid.*, p.225.

44, *27*/Winnipeg: Agnes C. Laut, *Pathfinders of the West* (Toronto, 1904), pp.127–8.

44, *51*/St. Lawrence): Quoted by Sulte, in "Radisson in the North-West," p.237.

45, *1*/North": Scull, ed., *Voyages of Radisson,* p. 225.

45, *18*/winter: *Ibid.*, p.226.

45, *41*/me: *Ibid.*, p.241.

46, *13*/scheme: *Ibid.*, pp.241–2.

46, *38*/French": *Ibid.*, pp.242–4.

47, *15*/Cartwright: E.B. O'Callaghan and Berthold Fernow, eds., *Documents Relative to the Colonial History of the State of New York* ... (15 vols., Albany, 1853–87), II, 237; III, 51–61, 63, 93–100. See also C.M. Andrews, *Colonial Self-Government, 1652–1689* (New York, 1904), pp.68–91, and R.W. Jeffery, *The History of the Thirteen Colonies of North America, 1497–1763* (London, 1908), p.134. In this note in the proof copy Morton also refers in brackets at the end to "My Biography under Cartwright." These biographical notes are preserved in the Morton Papers deposited in the Archives of Saskatchewan at Saskatoon. The material under Cartwright consists simply of the three references above.

47, *27*/Carteret: Morton Papers, Biography. Sir Philip Carteret "was one of the original adventurers ... he originally held stock of £300. [He] was the son and heir of Sir George Carteret. The father inherited the son's stock by the latter's death at sea in the fight off Sole Bay on May 28, 1672." But cf. *H.B.R.S.,* V, Appendix G, 215–18.

48, *20*/Sea: Public Record Office (P.R.O.), State Papers 29, Domestic, Charles II, Entry Book 44/26, f.25. The date is Feb. 7, 1667/8. (Published in *Calendar of State Papers, Domestic Series, of the Reign of Charles II* [23 vols., London, 1860–1947], VIII, 220.) Also printed in G.L. Nute, ed., "Radisson and Groseilliers' Contribution to Geography," *Minnesota History,* XVI (Dec., 1935), 414–26. At this point in the proof copy Morton has made a note referring to "my chronology volume." This is among his papers in the Saskatchewan Archives. The entries, many of them in his own hand, extend from 1610 to 1713.

49, *1*/Englander: For their instruction see State Papers 29, Domestic, Charles II, 1668, No. 251/180. Printed in Nute, ed., "Radisson and Groseilliers' Contribution to Geography," pp.419–23.

49, *36*/Passage: See also Agnes C. Laut, *The Conquest of the Great North West* (2 vols., Toronto, [1908?]), I, 109. It is difficult to see why Morton gave this reference, unless to draw attention to the inaccuracy of her transcription, which differs considerably from his own and Nute's (see Nute, ed., "Radisson and Groseilliers' Contribution to Geography," pp.420–1).

50, *23*/England: State Papers 29, Domestic, Charles II, No. 247/126. Also *Acts of the Privy Council of England,* Colonial Series, eds. W.L. Grant and J. Munro (6 vols., London, 1908–12), I, Nos.821, 824.

50, *26*/August: Such knowledge as we have of the voyage is derived from Appendix I, p.5, of Joseph Robson, *An Account of six years residence in Hudson's-Bay* (London, 1752).

50, *47*/region: Morton's note reads "State Papers, H.B. vol.1, p.1, 1682, Nov. 11 (my volume of extracts). Also B.T.H.B. p.171 in a *True State of the Case* presented by the H.B.C. (in my chron. vol. Date 1668)." This was the first of several citations that proved particularly elusive until Miss Barbara Wilson of P.A.C. noted the similarity to those for documents calendared in P.A.C., *Report, 1895*, and pointed out that many of these documents are now in P.R.O., C.O.134. Transcripts and microfilm are at P.A.C. and there are transcripts among the Morton Papers at Saskatoon. The first document to which Morton appears to refer is C.O. 134/1, f.5, "Reply of the Gov. and Committee to 'Extrait d'une Lettre de Mr de la Barre, Gouverneur de Canada. 11 Novembre, 1682'." A transcript is in P.A.C., M.G.11, Transcript of Colonial Office Records, Hudson's Bay State Papers, 1673–1696, p.22. "*True State of the Case . . .*" is in C.O. 134/1, f.92–3.

51, *30*/State: State Papers 29, Domestic, Charles II, No.266/80, Oct. 11, 1669. Morton Papers, Chronology, re: Watts to Mr. Secretary.

51, *46*/available: *Acts of the Privy Council*, Colonial Series, I, Nos.821, 824.

52, *3*/description: Morton notes that in H.B.C. Arch., Ledger Book No.1 (A.14/1) has entries from April 23 to May 3 of stores purchased for Capt. Stannard and the *Wivenhoe*, with the map purchased on May 3. Items in 1669, pay to seamen and customs (Jan. 20, 1670), indicate his return. The payment of £2 by Portman to Norwood for the map is recorded for May 3, 1669, H.B.C. Arch., A.14/1, f.107–8. See also *H.B.R.S.*, V.

52, *5*/River: For Radisson's affidavit of August 23, 1697, see P.R.O., C.O.134/3 (microfilm in P.A.C.).

52, *13*/year: Miss A.M. Johnson, Archivist to the Hudson's Bay Company, writes, "We cannot confirm that the *Wivenhoe* reached Hudson Bay. See Grace Lee Nute, *Caesars of the Wilderness* (New York, 1943), pp. 121–2. See also *H.B.R.S.*, V, 23, n.197. We can neither confirm nor deny that Robert Newland was mate on the 1669 voyage."

CHAPTER III: English and French Struggle for the Possession of Hudson Bay, 1670–1713

See, in addition to Morton's bibliography, *H.B.R.S.*, V, XXI, and XXII; also E.E. Rich, ed., *Minutes of the Hudson's Bay Company, 1679–1684, First Part, 1679–82*, with an introduction by G.N. Clark (Toronto, Champlain Society, 1945; London, Hudson's Bay Record Society, 1945), cited hereafter as *H.B.R.S.*, VIII; E.E. Rich, ed., *Minutes of the Hudson's Bay Company, 1679–1684, Second Part, 1682–84*, with an introduction by G.N. Clark (Toronto, Champlain Society, 1946; London, Hudson's Bay Record Society, 1946), cited hereafter as *H.B.R.S.*, IX; E.E. Rich, ed., *Copy Book of Letters Outward etc., . . . [1680–87]*, with an introduction by E.G.R. Taylor (Toronto, Champlain Society, 1948; London, Hudson's Bay Record Society, 1948), cited hereafter as *H.B.R.S.*, XI; E.E. Rich and A.M. Johnson, eds., *Hudson's Bay Copy Book of Letters Commissions Instructions Outward 1688–1696* (London, Hudson's Bay Record Society, 1957), cited hereafter as *H.B.R.S.*, XX; Nellis M. Crouse, *Lemoyne d'Iberville: Soldier of New France* (Ithaca, N.Y., 1954); Guy Frégault, *Iberville le conquérant* (Montreal, 1944).

54, *15*/furs: Cf. *H.B.R.S.*, XXI, 41–2, "not . . . a very generous recompense."

54, *16*/record: Guillam gave a good deal of information. See *H.B.R.S.*, XXI, 61–2; Nute, *Caesars of the Wilderness*, pp.116–19.

54, *28*/yearly: State Papers 29, Domestic, Charles II, Entry Book 25, f.128 (*Calendar, IX, 1668–9*, 543 f.).

54, *29*/Charter: Cf. *H.B.R.S.*, XXI, 52. Rich refers to this as a "renewal" of the royal grant of June 23, 1669 (*ibid.*, p.41) mentioning specifically the city men who were interested.

54, *41*/No. I: Entries in Ledger Book No. I, H.B.C. Arch. (A.14/1), such as those crediting individuals in the stock of the Chartered Company "by his proportion in the remains of the former cargo," enabled Morton to come to this conclusion. See also *H.B.R.S.*, V.

55, *16*/patent: It has been frequently printed in government documents, for example in *Report from the Commons Committee of 1749*. It has been printed by the Company in *Charters, Statutes, Orders in Council, &c., Relating to the Hudson's Bay Company* (London, 1931). Probably it is most accessible in E.H. Oliver, ed., *The Canadian North-West, Its Early Development and Legislative Records* (2 vols., Ottawa, Public Archives of Canada, 1914–15), I, 135. The following references to it are in Oliver.

55, *21*/Land: Oliver, ed., *Canadian North-West*, I, 143 f.

55, *45*/up: Miss Johnson writes: "Alter '1675' to '1671 or 1672'. Orders for the Ledger (H.B.C. Arch., A.14/1) to be written up were given to a Meeting of the Committee held on 7 November 1671. See *H.B.R.S.*, V, 4 and n."

56, *28*/granted": Oliver, ed., *Canadian North-West*, I, 144.

56, *30*/England: *Ibid.*, pp.145, 150.

56, *38*/officers: *Ibid.*, p.139.

56, *41*/stock: *Ibid.*, p.148.

56, *47*/Charter: *Ibid.*, pp.140 f.

56, *49*/Richard: Alter "Richard" to "Robert" Vyner. Sir Robert Vyner was a member of the first Committee named in the Charter. See *H.B.R.S.*, V, 137, 252–4.

57, *1*/Portman: Oliver, ed., *Canadian North-West*, I, 139.

57, *5*/Company: *Ibid.*, p.139.

57, *12*/Greenwich: *Ibid.*, p.144.

57, *43*/territories": *Ibid.*, p.145.

57, *47*/realm": *Ibid.*, p.145.

58, *7*/them": *Ibid.*, p.150.

58, *46*/Prince: Ibid., p.143.

59, *20*/Prince]": *Ibid.*, p.146.

59, *34*/eighteenth: Alter "eighteenth" to "nineteenth."

60, *14*/overseas: Cf. *H.B.R.S.*, V, xviii, n.4.

60, *35*/thereof": The Minutes of the Company at the date given, H.B.C. Arch., A.1/1 (*H.B.R.S.*, V, 1–2).

61, *6*/them: *H.B.R.S.*, V, 4.

61, *11*/Wivenhoe: *Ibid.*, p.6.

61, *26*/venture: *Ibid.*

63, *49*/James II: For this see below. A proclamation was issued by Charles II on Aug. 12, 1683, P.R.O., State Papers, Colonial, vol.64 (formerly 40), p.114. *Calendar of State Papers, Colonial Series, America and West Indies*, XI, 471.

65, *8*/enterprise: Cf. *H.B.R.S.*, XXI, 62. Stresses the dominance of London in Company policy—"essentially metropolitan."

65, *30*/1663: State Papers 29, Domestic, Charles II, vol.80 (*Calendar, III, 1663–4,* 266).

65, *46*/Tower: *Ibid.,* vol.91, Minute Entry Book 16, p.14 (*Calendar, III, 1663–4,* 449).

65, *48*/again: *Ibid.,* vol.202 (*Calendar, VII, 1667,* 131).

66, *11*/King: *Ibid.,* vol.192, No.90 (*Calendar, VI, 1666–7,* 530).

66, *38*/Liberty": *Acts of the Privy Council,* Colonial Series, I, No.883, p.540, Dec. 23, 1669, Whitehall.

66, *43*/Guillam: Miss Johnson points out that *Nonsuch* should be altered to *Prince Rupert. Nonsuch* was sold in June, 1670, and replaced by the newly built *Prince Rupert.* See *H.B.R.S.,* V, 228; Nute, *Caesars of the Wilderness,* pp.286–92, "Extract of Mr. Thomas Gorst's Journall in the Voyage to Hudsons Bay begun the 31st day of May 1670." Morton's pencilled notes here are puzzling as he refers simply to the Company's Minutes, which do not begin until October, 1671. He also mentions Nehemiah Walker's affidavit (P.R.O., C.O. 134/1, f.203, June 14, 1687; microfilm in P.A.C.) which indicates that Guillam was in command of *Prince Rupert.* He does not appear to have known of Thomas Gorst's journal. *Nonsuch* must have been simply a slip, as on p.67, 1.13, he speaks of Guillam and the *Rupert* at Charles Fort.

66, *46*/Nonsuch: *H.B.R.S.,* XXI, 66. Alter *"Nonsuch"* to *"Prince Rupert."*

67, *12*/Fort: Radisson's affidavit of Aug. 23, 1697, see note p.52, l.5. For Nehemiah Walker's affidavit, see note p.66, l.43.

67, *15*/Charles: State Papers 29, Domestic, Charles II, Entry Book 34, f.26 (*Calendar,* X, *1670,* 217, May 13, 1670).

67, *18*/county: See above, note p.50, l.47.

67, *35*/spirit: For this and a sketch of the governorship of Bayly see John Oldmixon, *The British Empire in America* (London, 1708). The section on Hudson Bay is reprinted in J.B. Tyrrell, ed., *Documents Relating to the Early History of Hudson Bay* (Toronto, Champlain Society, 1931).

68, *21*/voyage: On Oct. 13, 1670, *H.B.R.S.,* XXI, 67.

68, *28*/command: H.B.C. Arch., A.6/1 (*H.B.R.S.,* XI, 4), Governor Nixon's Instructions, May 29, 1680. The conclusion seems rather definite in view of the evidence.

68, *40*/sale: 3000 pounds at 7s. the pound at the final sale and in April, 8000 pounds at the same time for a gross revenue of £3860 for 1672. *H.B.R.S.,* XXI, 68.

68, *41*/home: They sailed July 1, 1671, and reached Plymouth by Oct. 26. *Ibid.,* p.67.

68, *45*/£354,10s: H.B.C. Arch., A.14/1, Ledger Book No.1. Their accounts are in *H.B.R.S.,* V, 205; it is not clear how Morton arrived at this figure.

68, *47*/£100: *H.B.R.S.,* V, 213. "Until 1678 Bayly's salary was £50 per annum; it was then increased to £200 per annum."

69, *48*/(N.S.): A.N., Col., C11A, vol.3, p.77, Talon à Colbert, 10 nov. 1670.

70, *29*/(N.S.): Alter "1761" to "1671."

70, *30*/1671–72: Thwaites, ed., *Jesuit Relations,* LVI, 149.

70, *41*/land: A.N., Col., C11A, vol.3, p.327. Memo for Colbert in handwriting of Frontenac.

70, *47*/trade: Thwaites, ed., *Jesuit Relations,* LVI, 175–6.

72, *5*/Lakes: A.N., Col., C11A, vol.3, p.177.

72, *44*/June: H.B.C. Arch., A.14/1, f.114d (*H.B.R.S.,* V, 199).

72, 44/Nonsuch: Alter *"Nonsuch"* to *"Prince Rupert."* See *H.B.R.S.,* V, 36, 48.

72, 46/Dogger: Alter *"Dogger"* to *"Messenger* dogger." Miss Johnson points out that the *Wivenhoe* was withdrawn in 1672 and the King sent the *Messenger* dogger. (A dogger was a two-masted, blunt-nosed vessel of fishing-boat type.) See *H.B.R.S.,* V, lv, lvi, 34, 35n, 48, and J.R. Tanner, ed., *A Descriptive Catalogue of the Naval Manuscripts in the Pepysian Library at Magdalene College, Cambridge* (4 vols., London, Navy Records Society, 1903–22), I, 280–1.

72, 46/Imploy: Morton's reference is "B.T.H.B. vol.1, 205." Transcript in Morton Papers, Hudson's Bay State Papers, May 22, 1687. Calendared in P.A.C., *Report, 1895,* under 1677 P.A.C. transcripts, H.B. State Papers, 1673–96, 140–1. Now in P.R.O., C.O.134/1 (microfilm in P.A.C.), f. 111, affidavit of William Bond dated May 20, 1677.

72, 49/married": James Hays to Principal Secretary of State Jenkins, Jan. 26, 1684, State Papers, Colonial, vol.64, p.129. (Morton transcripts, see note immediately above.)

73, 2/England: *H.B.R.S.,* XXI, 67. He came home with Guillam in 1673.

73, 4/Fort: Morton had only a question mark in the proof. See *H.B.R.S.,* V, 41 and n.3.

73, 6/River: Morton apparently intended to give a reference here. Possibly he interpreted the document now printed in *H.B.R.S.,* V, 19, as implying instructions to Bayly to build a post.

73, 12/end: Oldmixon, *British Empire in America,* p.390. Oldmixon does not here support Morton's statement about building at Moose and Morton's "Also??" pencilled in the margin may indicate he was uncertain of his ground. Cf. *H.B.R.S.,* XXI, 77.

73, 18/soil: Oldmixon, *British Empire in America,* pp.400 f.

73, 20/possibilities: B.T.H.B., vol.1, 205. See above, note p.72, l.46.

73, 29/on: Alter "the *Nonsuch* and the *Dogger"* to "the *Prince Rupert* and the *Messenger* dogger."

73, 37/furs: Morton's note here was "?Minutes." Probably *H.B.R.S.,* V, 34, 38.

73, 42/sailing: As *ibid. H.B.R.S.,* V, 65, clearly applies.

73, 49/hatchet: Oldmixon, *British Empire in America,* p.387.

74, 12/banquet: *Ibid.,* pp.388 f.

74, 43/raised: *Ibid.,* p.387.

75, 2/Moose: *Ibid.,* p.390. Cf. *H.B.R.S.,* XXI, 77. Rich and Morton interpret Oldmixon very differently, perhaps an example of Morton's tenderness for Groseilliers.

75, 14/trader: Oldmixon, *British Empire in America,* p.391.

75, 27/River: *Ibid.,* p.391.

75, 33/days: *Ibid.,* pp.392 f.

76, 1/North: Thwaites, ed., *Jesuit Relations,* LIX, 65, Relation of 1673.

76, 5/French: Cf. *H.B.R.S.,* XXI, 78. Albanel's "express object was to seduce Groseilliers from his British allegiance."

76, 15/Frontenac: Oldmixon, *British Empire in America,* p.393. Morton's original note adds "B.T.H.B. vol.I, 217 (my extracts, p.1)." The heading in his own transcript at Saskatoon reads: "Oct. 7, 1673, Frontenac to the Commander of the 'French', so the calendar of the Public Archives of Canada, but there were no French troops at Hudson Bay. The letter is really addressed to the H.B.C. Governor, Charles Bayly." The document is now C.O.134/1, f.117.

76, 21/also: Oldmixon, *British Empire in America,* p.393.

76, *33*/game": *Ibid.*, p.394.

76, *37*/devotions: *Ibid.*

76, *47*/*Shaftesbury*: The former *Messenger*, now a pink (a three-masted vessel). *H.B.R.S.*, XXI, 78.

76, *48*/Lydall: Bayly was under suspicion of mismanagement. See *H.B.R.S.*, XXI, 77 f.

77, *14*/France: The reference given here was to the Minutes, non-existent for this period. A question mark suggests Morton's uncertainty. It seems possible that Morton may have seen P.R.O., C.O.1/66/129, ff.315–16, which has since been quoted in Nute, *Caesars of the Wilderness*, pp.152–3.

77, *29*/contempt": Radisson's Narrative, "Relation du voiage du sieur Pierre Esprit Radisson Esc^er au nord de L'amerique és annees 1680, and 1683," in P.A.C., *Report, 1895*, pp.2–52. For the manuscript journals of 1682–3, 1684, see H.B.C. Arch., E.1/1–2.

77, *38*/says: *Ibid.*

77, *48*/Charles: Jan. 26, 1675/6, B.T.H.B., vol.1, p.21, Hudson's Bay State Papers, now in C.O.134/1, f.16. (Also in Morton Papers, Hudson's Bay State Papers.)

78, *9*/Ruvigny: Col. Entry Book, H.B.C., General, vol.96, p.42. (Also in P.A.C., *Report, 1895*, p.1; Morton Papers, Hudson's Bay State Papers.)

78, *13*/England: Radisson's Narrative, p.5.

78, *20*/Tobago: *Ibid.*, p.3. Also Frontenac à Seignelay, 2 nov. 1687, *Rapport de l'Archiviste de la Province de Québec pour 1926–1927* (Quebec, 1927), p.136. Hereafter *R.A.P.Q.*

78, *30*/Company: Radisson's Narrative, p.7.

78, *36*/country: *Calendar of Treasury Papers* [*1556–1729*] (6 vols., London, 1868–89), I, *1557–1696*, 215.

78, *41*/Fort: In H.B.C. Arch., A.14/2, f.81, Ledger Book No.2, f.49, there are accounts of officers and men in Factory under Bayly and also under Lydall.

78, *45*/altogether": Oldmixon, *British Empire in America*, pp.395 f.

78, *48*/concerns: Morgan Lodge, Deal, Sept. 24, 1675, reported to Sir Joseph Williamson, Principal Secretary of State, the arrival there of the *Shaftesbury* with the new Governor, the old Governor being continued in charge. State Papers 29, Domestic, Charles II, vol.373, No.174 (Calendar, XVII, *1675–6*, 313). Lodge's letter appears in full in Morton Papers, Chronology.

79, *7*/Ledger: H.B.C. Arch., A.14/2, f.73d, Ledger Book No.2, p.40 (*H.B.R.S.*, VIII, 310).

79, *27*/report: Photostat in mss., University of Saskatchewan.

79, *36*/tools: *H.B.R.S.*, VIII, 193.

80, *4*/wrote: Miss Johnson points out that the Governor and Council wrote from London on May 21, 1680. See *H.B.R.S.*, XI, 5.

80, *10*/place": H.B.C. Arch., A.6/1, f.5, Instructions to John Nixon, May 29, 1680 (*H.B.R.S.*, XI, 5).

80, *33*/much": *Ibid.*, A.6/1, f.6 (*H.B.R.S.*, XI, 6).

80, *42*/December: H.B.C. Arch., A.1/3, Minutes, Dec. 17, 1679 (*H.B.R.S.*, VIII, 13).

81, *7*/Garden: *Registers of St. Paul's Church, Covent Garden*, IV, *Burials, 1653–1752* (London, Harleian Society Publications, 1908), 86.

81, *12*/kindly": For a sketch of Bayly's career see A.M. Johnson, "First Governor on the Bay," *Beaver,* outfit 276 (June, 1945), 22–5.

81, *17*/begin: H.B.C. Arch., A.6/1, f.5, London Letter Book, vol.1, May 29, 1680 (*H.B.R.S.*, XI, 4).

81, *48*/there: *Ibid.*, A.6/1, f.6 (*H.B.R.S.*, XI, 7).

82, *4*/year: *Ibid.*, A.6/1, f.12, June, 1681 (*H.B.R.S.*, XI, 29).

82, *11*/1682: *Ibid.*, A.6/1, f.16, May 15, 1682 (*H.B.R.S.*, XI, 39).

82, *23*/Governor: See *H.B.R.S.*, XXI for a more favourable estimate of Governor Nixon.

82, *28*/incurred: H.B.C. Arch., A.6/1, f.17 (*H.B.R.S.*, XI, 39-40).

82, *31*/Instructions: April 27, 1683, *ibid.*, A.6/1, ff.28-31 (*H.B.R.S.*, XI, 72 f.).

83, *40*/1681: Frontenac à Seignelay, 2 nov. 1681, *R.A.P.Q.*, *1926-1927*, p.136.

84, *9*/Nemiskau: James White, *Forts and Trading Posts in Labrador Peninsula and Adjoining Territory* (Ottawa, 1926), p.43.

84, *30*/successor: Radisson's Narrative, p. 9. Also affidavit of John Calvert and six other servants of the H.B.C. State Papers, Colonial, vol.64 (formerly 40), p.115. Calendared in P.A.C., *Report, 1895*. Copies in Morton Papers.

85, *1*/(O.S.): Aug. 18 as per Benjamin Guillam's affidavit at Quebec, Oct. 25, 1683, State Papers, Colonial, vol.64 (formerly 40), p.115; Aug. 19 as per John Outlaw's affidavit, *ibid.*, p.121. Both affidavits are in P.A.C., *Report, 1895*. Copies in Morton Papers. The uncertainty as to the crucial date at this point is examined in *H.B.R.S.*, XXI, 135-6.

85, *10*/it: Radisson's Narrative, p.10, makes it Aug. 26 and Sept. 2, N.S.

85, *27*/dismissed: *H.B.R.S.*, VIII, 226-7.

85, *33*/Governor: H.B.C. Arch., A.6/1. The commission (see Letter Book, vol.1) was dated May 15, 1682. *H.B.R.S.*, XI, 34.

85, *37*/Groseilliers: H.B.C. Arch., A.1/7, f.36, Minutes, July 11, 1684: ". . . the time of his Arrival in Port Nelson which he [Bridgar] affirmed in his Narritive [*sic*] to be 17 September 1682. . . ."

85, *44*/(N.S.): Morton's note is "B.T.H.B. vol.1, p.5." Now in C.O.134/1, f.8. (Also in P.A.C., *Report, 1895*, p.1; Morton Papers.)

86, *10*/reply: *Ibid.*

86, *35*/*Narrative:* Radisson's Narrative, pp.13-15.

86, *35*/affidavit: Guillam's affidavit. State Papers, Colonial, vol.64 (formerly 40), p.115. Calendared in P.A.C., *Report, 1895*. Copy in Morton Papers.

86, *49*/ship: The affidavit of John Outlaw, one of Guillam's crew, makes the date about Feb. 7 (*ibid.*).

87, *17*/knew: Miss Johnson points out that there is no proof that the Company knew about Benjamin Guillam in 1682. But they did know about the *Expectation* commanded by Richard Lucas. See *H.B.R.S.*, IX, introduction; also *H.B.R.S.*, XI.

87, *19*/King: July 6, 1682, Col. Entry Book, H.B.C., vol.107, p.39; P.A.C., M.G.11, Transcripts . . . , p.13. (Also in P.A.C., *Report, 1895*, p.1; Morton Papers.)

87, *28*/1683: *Ibid.*, vol.99, p.218, Aug. 12, 1683 (P.A.C., *Report, 1895;* Morton Papers).

87, *40*/colonies: On July 30, 1683, he himself wrote to Simon Bradstreet, Governor of Massachusetts. H.B.C. Arch., A.6/1, f.38, Letter Book, I, 72 (*H.B.R.S.*, XI, 94-5).

87, *44*/port: *Ibid.*, A.6/1, ff.38-9, Letter Book, vol.1, p.73, Aug. 7, 1683 (*H.B.R.S.*, XI, 95-8).

88, *14*/cost: Miss Johnson points out that the *Expectation* turned back in 1682, sailed from Dartmouth in 1683, and was captured in Hudson Strait. See *H.B.R.S.*, IX, 11-12n, 263-85; also *H.B.R.S.*, XI.

88, *21*/responsible: Miss Johnson suggests that Daniel Lane was hardly responsible for the expedition. He was employed by the interlopers at £4 per month. See *H.B.R.S.*, IX, 327-9.

88, *37/Narrative:* Radisson's Narrative, pp.15–18.

88, *42/Albemarle*): *H.B.R.S.,* XXI, 137. The *Albemarle,* though ordered to Nelson River, wintered at Rupert River and went to the Nelson in the summer of 1683.

89, *29/*(O.S.): Alter "On 21st October (N.S.), the 11th (O.S.)" to "On 21st October (O.S.)." Miss Johnson points out that Oct. 21 is the date given in the Company's records, so Old Style is correct. See *H.B.R.S.,* XI, 151, and the preface to *H.B.R.S.,* V. The Company still dates its Charter May 2 (O.S.) and not May 12 (N.S.).

89, *33/*lost: Cf. *H.B.R.S.,* XXI, 137. According to Professor Rich the *Rupert* was lost with Zachariah Gillam (Morton's Guillam) and about nine men.

89, *37/*ship: B.T.H.B., vol.1, p.174, May 13, 1687. Now in C.O.134/1, f.94, "A Deduction of the Damages sustained. . . ." (Also in P.A.C., *Report 1895,* p.3; Morton Papers.)

89, *47/*Nelson: See above, note p.88, l.42.

90, *16/*jam: Radisson's Narrative, p.37.

90, *33/*abundance: Affidavits of John Outlaw and Benjamin are in State Papers, Colonial, vol.64 (formerly 40), pp.121 and 115 respectively. See also P.A.C., M.G.11, Transcripts . . . , pp.65 and 47. For Bayly's affidavit, which Morton cites as in B.T.H.B., vol.1, p.209, see C.O.134/1, f.113.

91, *2/*so: Cf. *H.B.R.S.,* XXI, 137.

91, *19/*(N.S.): H.B.C. Arch., A.1/7, f.33, Minutes, July 9, 1684.

91, *20/*June: Of Culvert and five others. State Papers, Colonial, vol.64 (formerly 40), p.118. Calendared in P.A.C., *Report, 1895.* Copies in Morton Papers. Culvert's affidavit is in C.O.134/1, f.115.

91, *24/*capital: Cf. *H.B.R.S.,* XXI, for a much fuller discussion. This was evidently the *first* dividend paid, March 25, 1684.

91, *30/*August: Radisson's Narrative, p.65. The date given by his nephew is July 27.

91, *32/*April: H.B.C. Arch., A.6/1, f.36, Letter Book, vol.1, p.68, April 27, 1683 (*H.B.R.S.,* XI, 89).

91, *36/*Englishmen: Radisson's Narrative, p.65.

92, *7/*auction: H.B.C. Arch., A.1/2, f.122, Minutes, Nov. 9, 1683 (*H.B.R.S.,* IX, 152).

92, *10/*Island: See Tyrrell, ed., *Documents Relating to the Early History of Hudson's Bay,* p.57n.

92, *26/*1682: Nov. 26.

92, *39/*1683: State Papers, Colonial, vol.64 (formerly 40), p.120, Nov.14, 1683. Calendared in P.A.C., *Report, 1895,* p.2. Copy in Morton Papers. See P.A.C., M.G.11, Transcripts . . . , p.55.

92, *47/*State: Dec. 12, *Calendar of State Papers, Colonial Series America and West Indies, 1681–1685,* XI, 565. The reference in the calendar is to the Colonial Entry Book, vol.99, pp.284–6.

92, *49/*Court: State Papers, Colonial, vol.64 (formerly 40), p.128, Jan. 26, 1684. Calendared in P.A.C., *Report, 1895,* p.2. Copy in Morton Papers. See P.A.C., M.G.11, Transcripts . . . , p.78.

93, *1/*memorials: *Ibid.*

93, *7/*future: Nov. 21, 1684, H.B.C. Arch., A.6/1, ff.52–53, Letter Book, vol.1, p.101 (*H.B.R.S.,* XI, 132–4).

93, *11/*Lawrence: A.N., Col., C.11A, vol.6–1, p.254 (Morton Papers, MSS C500/3/2, 26).

93, *13/*Guillam: *Ibid.,* vol.6–2, p.70, La Barre au Ministre, 14 nov. 1684.

93, *21*/(Colbert): In his Narrative, p.49, Radisson says that he went to Paris at de La Barre's wish to report on his visit to the Bay.

93, *22*/(N.S.): Sir James Hayes to Sir John Werden, Dec. 27, 1685, P.R.O., State Papers, Colonial, vol.64 (formerly 40), p.123. (Also in P.A.C., *Report, 1895,* State Papers – Hudson's Bay, p.2; Morton Papers.)

93, *29*/Paris: See note p.92, l.49.

93, *34*/1687: Nute, *Caesars of the Wilderness,* Appendix 11, p.344. Sir Robert Jeffrey, before whom the affidavit was sworn, was not the "notorious" George Jeffreys, first Baron Jeffreys of Wem.

93, *47*/runs: "A Narrative of the French action at Port Nelson which was presented by Sir James Hayes to the King at Winchester, Sept. 25, 1684," in H.B.C. Arch., A.6/1, ff.51–2, Letter Book, vol.1, p.99 (*H.B.R.S.,* XI, 130–2). See in the same sense Lord Preston (to the London Commissioners of Trade), B.T.H.B., vol.1, p.199, now in C.O.134/1, f.108 (calendared in P.A.C., *Report, 1895,* p.3; Morton Papers). Also "Monsr Calliere's Direction to Mr Radisson for restoring Port Nelson, whereof mention is made in Mr Radisson Affidavit made before Sir Robt. Jeffrey," Ms. Book, 1687, America and West Indies, vol.539 (also in Morton Papers). See C.O.134/3, f.47.

94, *18*/Company: H.B.C. Arch., A.1/10, f.27, Minutes, July 18, 1688, recalling the order of the General Court of Nov. 26, 1684.

94, *20*/St. Lawrence: Nute, *Caesars of the Wilderness,* p.225 and n.5. Groseilliers might have been in the Bay again and died there.

94, *25*/Return: Radisson's Narrative, p.55. See *H.B.R.S.,* XXI, and Nute, *Caesars of the Wilderness,* for a much fuller account of Radisson's return to the Company.

94, *33*/Geyer: Alter "George Geyer" to "John Abraham." Miss Johnson explains that John Abraham was appointed "Governour and Chief Commander for the Comp." at Port Nelson in May, 1684, and Geyer was appointed to be a member of the Council there. A new post was being built at Port Nelson by George Geyer, under Abraham's orders, in Sept., 1684. See *H.B.R.S.,* XI, 367, 371; Nute, *Caesars of the Wilderness,* p.225.

94, *38*/Governor: Alter "Governor Geyer" to "George Geyer."

94, *42*/Governor: Alter "Governor Geyer and Radisson" to "Governor Abraham and Radisson."

94, *43*/up: Radisson's Narrative, pp.77 f.

94, *46*/Geyer: Alter "Geyer insisted" to "Abraham insisted."

95, *15*/Anne: Queen Anne was James II's daughter, not his sister.

95, *32*/March 18: In the proof copy Morton has altered 18 to 19.

95, *33*/Nelson: A.N., Col., C^{11A}, vol.6–1, p.368 (Morton Papers, MSS C500/3/2, transcripts bound under title Canada, Correspondance générale, 1668–1689, p.54).

95, *45*/year: Tyrrell, ed., *Documents Relating to the Early History of Hudson Bay,* pp. 35 f., printed with a translation.

97, *14*/Indians: *Ibid.,* p.243, letters of La Potherie.

97, *21*/story: *Ibid.,* p.71, Journal of Father Silvy.

98, *4*/Nipigon: A.N., Col., C^{11A}, vol.6–1, p.457, 9 juillet 1684; also C^{11A}, vol.6–2, p.40, 13 nov. 1684. Pierre Margry, éd., *Découvertes et établissements des Français dans l'ouest et dans le sud de l'Amérique septentrionale, 1614–1754* (6 vols., Paris, 1879–88), VI, 5.

98, *20*/Français: Margry, éd., *Découvertes,* VI, 51–2.

98, *25*/name: *Ibid.*, pp.496 f.

98, *28*/Jolliet: H.B.C. Arch., A.6/1, ff.121–2, London Letter Book, vol.1, p.240 (*H.B.R.S.*, XI, 312–13).

98, *40*/Verner: June 25, 1685, *ibid.*, f.122, London Letter Book, vol.1, p.243 (*H.B.R.S.*, XI, 312–13).

99, *14*/Jolliet: *Ibid.*, 126–7, Verner's account of the loss of Charles Fort, Dec. 9, 1687, London Letter Book, vol.1, pp.250–1 (*H.B.R.S.*, XI, 320–1).

99, *33*/Bay: For the record of the expedition see Caron, ed., *Le Journal de l'expédition du Chevalier de Troyes.*

99, *39*/lieutenant: See also Frégault, *Iberville*, and Crouse, *Lemoyne d'Iberville.*

101, *6*/Verner: Alter "and wounded Mrs Verner" to "and wounded Mrs. Maurice." Miss Johnson points out that Mrs. Maurice, a companion of Mrs. Sergeant at Albany, was homeward bound in the *Success* when it was wrecked in December, 1685, and she was apparently obliged to winter at Rupert River. She was wounded when de Troyes captured the Rupert River post in July, 1686. See *H.B.R.S.*, XI, 144–353. Hugh Verner was in charge of Rupert River when the post was captured; his wife was in England (*ibid.*, p.391).

101, *30*/arrived: Governor Sergeant's report of the loss of the forts, Nov. 4, 1687, is in H.B.C. Arch., A.6/1, ff.123–4, London Letter Book, 245–7 (*H.B.R.S.*, XI, 313–16).

102, *8*/Surrender: Oldmixon, *British Empire in America*, pp.404–5.

102, *15*/Craven: Alter "*Craven*" to "*Colleton.*" Miss Johnson points out that Governor Sergeant and party were sent to Port Nelson in 1686 on board the *Colleton*, not the *Craven*. See *H.B.R.S.*, XI, 306–7, 326.

102, *32*/d'Iberville: In H.B.C. Arch., A.6/1, ff.126–7, Verner's account of the loss of Charles Fort, Dec. 9, 1687 (*H.B.R.S.*, XI, 320–1).

102, *46*/America": In the Morton Papers, A section, "Subject" files, is a photostat of the official text of the treaty of Nov. 6/16, 1686, taken from *Treaty of Peace, Good Correspondence and Neutrality in America Between the most Serene and Mighty Prince, James II . . . and Lewis XIII . . .* (Published by His Majesty's Command. In the Savoy. Printed by Thomas Newcomb . . . MDCLXXXVI).

103, *21*/Bay": H.B.C. Arch., A.6/1, ff.84–5, London Letter Book, vol.1, p.167 (*H.B.R.S.*, XI, 216 f.; P.A.C., *Report, 1883*, pp.173–5).

103, *30*/XIV: Cf. *H.B.R.S.*, XXI, 223. The English envoy in Paris made strong representations.

103, *35*/struggle: Printed in P.A.C., *Report, 1883*, pp.173–99.

104, *23*/Bay: A.N., Col., C11A, vol.8, pp.192–268, Denonville au Ministre, 10 nov. 1686.

105, *22*/pursued: H.B.C. Arch., A.6/1, f.90, London Letter Book, vol.1, p.179 (*H.B.R.S.*, XI, 233).

105, *28*/Company: *Ibid.*, f.129, London Letter Book, Jan. 22, 1687/8, p.285 (*H.B.R.S.*, XI, 328–9).

105, *40*/there: *Ibid.*, f.90, London Letter Book, p.179. Governor and Committee in reply to Governor Geyer's of Sept. 4, 1686, reporting that Severn was settled (*H.B.R.S.*, XI, 232–8).

105, *44*/wintered: *Ibid.*, f.262, London Letter Book, vol.1, p.262, "A Briefe accott. of a Voyage made to Churchill River" (*H.B.R.S.*, XI, 340).

106, *5*/forthwith: *H.B.R.S.*, XXI, 236. The order that "noe time be lost" suggests that Morton meant to write "and ordered the river . . . to be settled forthwith."

106, *10*/first: H.B.C. Arch., A.6/1, f.192, London Letter Book, vol.1, p.182 (*H.B.R.S.*, XI, 237); also A.6/2, f.5, vol.2, p.1.

106, *14*/blubber: Cf. *H.B.R.S.*, XXI, nine tons in 1689.

106, *16*/Indians: *Kelsey Papers*, p.xix.

106, *24*/sink: H.B.C. Arch., A.6/2, f.36, London Letter Book, vol.2, p.31 (*H.B.R.S.*, XX, 81).

106, *26*/England: Miss Johnson observes that the members of Captain Abraham's interloping expedition were rescued and taken on board the *Churchill* frigate, which continued on to Albany, not York Fort. See *H.B.R.S.*, XI, 372–3; *H.B.R.S.*, XX, 81.

106, *33*/reached: Miss Johnson points out that four ships, not five, sailed from England in 1688. See *H.B.R.S.*, XX, 329. The *Churchill* was commanded by William Bond, who had been constituted "Admirall in those parts and seas . . ." See *H.B.R.S.*, XX, 328–9. The *Huband* was already in the Bay. She had sailed from England to Port Nelson in 1687 and later went to the Bottom of the Bay. See *H.B.R.S.*, XX, 328–9. Hugh Verner sailed for Albany in the *Yonge* in 1688. See *H.B.R.S.*, XX, 22.

106, *43*/sense: H.B.C. Arch., A.6/2, f.19, London Letter Book, vol.2, p.15 (*H.B.R.S.*, XX, p.38 f.).

107, *15*/River: *Ibid.*, f.36, London Letter Book, vol.2, p.31, affidavit of Solomon Nichols about the taking of the *Churchill, Yonge,* and *Huband* frigates (*H.B.R.S.*, XX, 81–4).

109, *15*/England: "An impartial account of the present State of the Hudson Bay Company" (undated), Ms. Book, 1698, America and West Indies, vol.539, p.45 (calendared in P.A.C., *Report, 1895*, p.8). See C.O.134/3, f.63.

110, *7*/Archives: See J.F. Kenney, "The Career of Henry Kelsey," Royal Society of Canada, *Transactions*, Third Series, XXIII (1929), s.2, 37–71.

110, *24*/1688: But not his first engagement. See *Kelsey Papers*, p.xxiv.

110, *39*/Indians": *Ibid.*

110, *44*/sea: *Ibid.*, p.xix.

111, *9*/1686: H.B.C. Arch., A.1/84, f.29. For "Stanton," read "Sandford": "The said Knight and Sandford do further urge. . . ." See also *H.B.R.S.*, XI, 387.

111, *49*/River: The Washkashreeseebee (Waskasew) Seepee of July 28 of his Journal, *Kelsey Papers*, p.8.

112, *2*/wide: *Ibid.*, p.3.

112, *24*/River: See note p.111, l.49.

112, *35*/Assiniboine: *Kelsey Papers*, Journal, Aug. 6, p.10.

112, *47*/Assiniboins: *Ibid.*, p.lix, Geyer to Governor and Committee.

113, *16*/them: *Ibid.*, p.14, Journal, Sept. 1, 1691. He had "one who could speak both languages for to be my interpreter."

114, /*5*£31,500: See below, p.141.

114, *16*/frigate: Morton's reference was to H.B.C. Arch., A.6/2, f.24, London Letter Book, vol.2, p.20 (*H.B.R.S.*, XX, 50). Though this letter contains a reference to Edgecombe and the *Royall Hudson's Bay*, it seems clear that Morton was thinking of A.6/2, f.40 (*H.B.R.S.*, XX, 93–4).

114, *25*/Channel: For the rest of this section Tyrrell, ed., *Documents Relating to the Early History of Hudson Bay,* is serviceable.

114, *29*/Fort: *Ibid.*, p.255, for letters of La Potherie; H.B.C. Arch., A.6/2, f.47, London Letter Book, vol.2, p.42 (*H.B.R.S.*, XX, 113); see also Crouse, *Lemoyne d'Iberville*, pp.63–5.

114, *37*/Walsh: "Thomas Walsh," not "John Walsh," cf. *H.B.R.S.*, XXI, 290.

114, *43*/May: In the proof copy Morton has stroked out "May" and substituted "June." *H.B.R.S.*, XX, 135.

114, *44*/1692: H.B.C. Arch., A.6/2, f.54, London Letter Book, June 17, 1692, vol.2, p.49, (*H.B.R.S.*, XX, 135–43). For the quotation, *H.B.R.S.*, XX, 135–6.

115, *14*/Bay: His instructions are *ibid.*, ff.58–9, London Letter Book, vol.2, p.53, dated June 17, 1692. (*H.B.R.S.*, XX, 144–8).

115, *15*/Island*: *Ibid.*, ff.90–2, General letter to Governor Knight, May 30, 1694, in answer to three from him, (*H.B.R.S.*, XX, 228–34).

115, *20*/asserts: Letters of La Potherie in Tyrrell, ed., *Documents Relating to Early History of Hudson Bay*, p.256. Cf. *H.B.R.S.*, XXI, 303. Not three but six, including one mad and in irons.

115, *30*/escape: *Ibid.*

115, *39*/days: H.B.C. Arch., A.6/2, f.94, London Letter Book, "The Company's Particular Letter to Governor Knight," May 30, 1694 (*H.B.R.S.*, XX, 276–7).

116, *5*/River: For the campaign see Jérémie's *Twenty Years of York Factory*.

116, *17*/Walsh: Alter "John" to "Thomas."

116, *18*/Matthew: Miss Johnson points out that the clergyman at York Fort was Thomas Anderson and not Thomas Mathew (or Matthews). For a note on Anderson see *H.B.R.S.*, XX, 197n. Mathew was commissioned "Leiftenant under Capt. Phillip Parsons at York Fort" in 1683. See *ibid.*, pp.215, 270, n2.

116, *30*/it: Jérémie, *Twenty Years of York Factory*, p.26.

116, *48*/spring: H.B.C. Arch., A.6/2, f.109, London Letter Book, vol.2, p.101, May 30, 1696 (*H.B.R.S.*, XX, 275).

117, *10*/passenger: "In 96 was at ye retaking of the Fort again." *Kelsey Papers*, p.112.

117, *11*/Instructions": Morton's reference is: "B.T.H.B. vol.2, 21 (not dated but would be May or June 1696)." (Calendared in P.A.C., *Report, 1895*. See under Aug. 30 and Dec. 5, 1696.) Now in C.O.134/2, f.10. "Sailing Orders & Instructions given to Capt. William Allen."

117, *17*/August): Jérémie, *Twenty Years of York Factory*, pp.27 f. Cf. *H.B.R.S.*, XXI, 337, where the date of surrender is given as Sept. 5, 1696 (Aug. 28, English style).

117, *29*/war: Letters of La Potherie, in Tyrrell, ed., *Documents Relating to the Early History of Hudson Bay*, pp.202 f.: Jérémie, *Twenty Years of York Factory*, pp.28 f.; *Kelsey Papers*, pp.97–100.

118, *30*/Bay: The London office of P.A.C. had several times searched in the Record Office Admiralty Papers for a report of the loss of the *Hampshire*. Morton pointed out that they had not allowed sufficiently for the time lag. They renewed their search and found the quoted document, "The Humble Petition of Mary Fletcher Widow of John Fletcher late command^r of yor Ma^ts Ship ye Hampshire." It was forthwith published in P.A.C., *Report, 1934*, p.6.

119, *7*/Robson: Robson, *An Account of six years residence in Hudson's Bay*, Appendix 1, p.12; cf. *H.B.R.S.*, XXI, 231.

120, *1*/other: See P.A.C., *Report, 1895*, pp.4–9, for a calendar of them under the title "State Papers, Hudson's Bay."

120, *14*/compromise: *Ibid.*, pp.9–10.

120, *39*/1686: H.B.C. Arch., A6/7, ff.34–5, London Letter Book, May 10, 1744. The reference is to an enclosure which in the letter book immediately follows the letter of this date to Joseph Isbister and the Council at Albany Fort.

121, *19*/beaver": Jérémie, *Twenty Years of York Factory*, p.20.

121, *20*/musk-ox: *Ibid.*, p.19.

121, *25*/flight: *Ibid.*, p.20.

121, *28*/parts": *Ibid.*

121, *31*/Cerf: *Ibid.*, p.19.

121, *36*/source": *Ibid.*, p.33.

122, *7*/use: Innis, *Fur Trade in Canada*, p.75.

122, *26*/live: H.B.C. Arch., A.1/10, f.27, Minutes, July 18, 1688, recalling the Order of the General Court of Nov. 26, 1684.

122, *46*/1690: *Ibid.* The payment was ordered by the General Court. See also A.1/12, f.32, Minutes, Oct. 1, 1690.

123, *1*/£50: H.B.C. Arch., A.1/12, f.32, Minutes, Oct. 1, 1690.

123, *14*/verdict: See G.L. Nute, "Two Documents from Radisson's Suit against the Company," *Beaver*, outfit 266 (Dec., 1935), 41–9.

123, *24*/1710: H.B.C. Arch., A.1/32, f.12, Minutes, March 29, 1710.

123, *27*/want": *Ibid.*, A.1/21, f.141, Minutes, Sept. 24, 1729. Cf. *H.B.R.S.*, XXI, 307–9, which differs in detail in its account of Radisson's dealings with the Company and is much fuller.

CHAPTER IV: English and French Struggle for the Great Fur Forest in the Hinterland of the Bay, 1714–63

The period covered in this chapter corresponds closely to that dealt with in *H.B.R.S.*, XXI, Book 3. Among the works on this period that have appeared since the publication of Morton's history are E.E. Rich and A.M. Johnson, eds., *James Isham's Observations on Hudson's Bay, 1743 and Notes and Observations on a Book entitled* A Voyage to Hudson's Bay in the Dobbs Galley, *1749* (Toronto, Champlain Society, 1949; London, Hudson's Bay Record Society, 1949), cited hereafter as *H.B.R.S.*, XII; K.G. Davies and A.M. Johnson, eds., *Letters from Hudson's Bay, 1703–40*, with an introduction by Richard Glover (London, Hudson's Bay Record Society, 1965), cited hereafter as *H.B.R.S.*, XXV; Arthur T. Adams, ed., *The Explorations of Pierre Esprit Radisson: From the original manuscript in the Bodleian Library and the British Museum* (Minneapolis, 1961); Lawrence J. Burpee, "La Vérendrye's 1738–9 Journal," *Canadian Historical Review*, XXIII (Dec., 1942); Antoine Champagne, *Les La Vérendrye et le poste de l'ouest* (Quebec, 1968); Desmond Clarke, *Arthur Dobbs Esquire, 1689–1765, Surveyor-General of Ireland, Prospector and Governor of North Carolina* (London, 1957); Nellis M. Crouse, *La Vérendrye: Fur Trader and Explorer* (Toronto, 1956); W.J. Eccles, *The Canadian Frontier 1534–1760* (New York, London, Toronto, 1969); Guy Frégault, *Pierre Le Moyne d'Iberville* (first published 1944, new edition, Montreal and Paris, 1968); Marcel Giraud, *Le Métis canadien: son rôle dans l'histoire des provinces de l'Ouest* (Paris, 1945); Murray G. Lawson, *Fur: A Study in English Mercantilism, 1700–75* (Toronto, 1943); J.G. MacGregor, *Behold the Shining Mountains: Being an Account of the Travels of Anthony Henday, 1754–55* ... (Edmonton, 1954); Grace Lee Nute, *Caesars of the Wilderness: Médard Chouart, Sieur des Groseilliers and Pierre Esprit Radisson, 1618–1710* (New York and London, 1943); Glyndwr Williams, "Arthur Dobbs and Joseph Robson: New Light on the Relationship Between Two Early

Critics of the Hudson's Bay Company," *C.H.R.*, XL (June, 1959); Glyndwr Williams, *The British Search for the Northwest Passage in the Eighteenth Century* (London, 1962); Clifford Wilson, "La Vérendrye Reaches the Saskatchewan," *C.H.R.*, XXXIII (March, 1952); Clifford Wilson, "Across the Prairies Two Centuries Ago," Canadian Historical Association, *Report,* 1954, pp.28–35.

125, *28*/Bay: Margry, éd., *Découvertes,* VI, 6–7. On Lake Nipigon and Kaministikwia River (Fort William).

126, *1*/Bay: See above, p.98.

126, *15*/nations: See calendar of documents in P.A.C., *Report, 1895,* pp.11–12.

126, *39*/Kelsey: We have now come to the point where there are "in documents," that is, correspondence coming in from the posts overseas to London.

126, *45*/Main: H.B.C. Arch., A.11/2, ff.22–5, Anthony Beale, Albany Fort, to Governor and Committee, Aug. 2, 1714, and many subsequent reports.

127, *38*/1714: Knight's Journal, in its beautiful form and with his letters engrossed, is in H.B.C. Arch., B.239/a/1–3. A copy is in P.A.C.

128, *3*/fall": Cf. above, p.122, l.11, where Morton quotes the same passage but in a rather different form.

128, *37*/ritual: This description follows closely that sketched by Governor Isham, in charge of York Fort from the middle of the century, in his *Observations* (*H.B.R.S.,* XII, 134).

134, *18*/Governor: H.B.C. Arch., B.239/a/5, f.52, York Fort Journal Report by Henry Kelsey, June 12, 1719.

134, *23*/River: Alexander Mackenzie, *Voyages,* p.lxxxvii.

134, *33*/country: "Askee Indians," H.B.C. Arch., B.239/a/2, f.35, Knight's York Fort Journal, June 1, 1716.

134, *35*/Muscuty Indians: *Ibid.,* B.239/a/3, f.17, Journal, Jan. 8, 1717. So Morton's citation; I have found nothing relevant to the Muscuty Indians here.

134, *38*/Mountain Indians: H.B.C. Arch., B.239/a/2, f.45, Journal, July 12, 1716, and B.239/a/2, f.53, Journal, Aug. 13, 1716.

135, *14*/Missouri: See above, note p.21, l.16.

135, *25*/Indians: H.B.C. Arch., B.239/a/2, f.58, Journal, Sept. 1, 1716.

138, *24*/shore: Knight's Journal now has the heading "Churchill River Anno 1717." It begins July 14; from that date to Friday, Sept. 14, is printed with an excellent bibliography in James F. Kennedy, ed., *The Founding of Churchill: Being the Journal of Captain James Knight . . .* (Toronto, 1932).

139, *37*/metal: H.B.C. Arch., B.239/a/2, Knight's York Fort Journal, May 8 and May 10, 1716. I owe the verification of these references, which I was unable to locate on the P.A.C. microfilm, to Miss Johnson of the Hudson's Bay Company Archives.

140, *39*/statement: Robson, *Account of six years residence in Hudson's Bay,* Appendix 1, pp.36 f.

141, *14*/Court: There were held two General Courts, on Aug. 23 and Aug. 30, 1720, and definite resolutions were arrived at in the Committee of Aug. 29, 1720. These resolutions (printed in *Report from the Commons Committee of 1749,* p.261) were adopted by the second General Court on the following day. H.B.C. Arch., A.1/118, f.21.

141, *33*/November: The Committee adopted it on Nov. 15, 1720 (H.B.C. Arch., A.1/118, f.29), and the General Court on Nov. 18 (*ibid.,* A.1/119, f.2).

142, *45*/known: Hearne, *Journey to the Northern Ocean,* ed. Tyrrell, pp. 46–9.

144, *28*/furs: H.B.C. Arch., A.6/4, f.50, Governor and Committee to Kelsey and Council at York Fort, May 26, 1721.

146, *13*/Englishmen: Nov. 29, 1765, *ibid.*, B.42/a/64, f.16.

146, *24*/Knight: Kelsey's York Fort Journal (*ibid.*, B.239/a/4–5–6–7) and his correspondence with the Governor and Committee and his formal instructions to the sloop captains and others under him exist among the York Fort papers in H.B.C. Arch.

147, *13*/River: *Kelsey Papers,* p.14, and H.B. Arch., B.239/a/5, f.53, York Fort Journal, Aug. 26, 1719 *et seq.*

147, *49*/Bay: *Kelsey Papers,* pp.114 f.

148, *10*/John: Alter "John Scroggs" to "George Scroggs."

148, *24*/year: H.B.C. Arch., A.1/120, f.55, Minutes, Jan. 29, 1723–4.

153, *16*/trade: This description of the trade is based on *James Isham's Observations* (*H.B.R.S.,* XII), an illustrated account with drawings of animals, etc., one of the most interesting manuscripts in the H.B.C. Arch. (E.2/1, E.2/2).

154, *8*/sentences: *H.B.R.S.,* XII, 85–6.

156, *32*/mouth: Here occurs Morton's first note referring to his Historical Geography (see Introduction), vol. 1, p.128, Saskatchewan Archives, Morton Papers, A. Section, Richard Stanton to Governor and Committee, Aug. 21, 1723.

156, *46*/fort: *Ibid.,* vol.12, pp.1–2. References are to the Albany Fort Correspondence.

157, *29*/Archives: *R.A.P.Q., 1921–1922,* pp.189 f.

157, *36*/Albany: Morton made a pencilled note here referring to the Albany Fort Correspondence but I was unable to find the phrase quoted. Mr. George E. Thorman of St. Thomas has pointed out that Morton's date is wrong and that "June 4, 1729" should be altered to "June 4, 1719." The relevant entry in the Albany Fort Journal is at H.B.C. Arch., B.3/a/9, f.56.

158, *11*/end: See Morton papers, Historical Geography, vol.1, pp.156 ff.

158, *23*/boundary: B.T.H.B., vol.2, p.269. See P.A.C., *Report, 1895,* p.12, Sept. — 1719. Now in C.O.134/2, f.137, "The Memorial of the Governor and Company of Adventures Trading into Hudson's Bay" Sept. 1719.

158, *26*/natives: H.B.C. Arch., B.3/a/10, f.35d. Albany Fort Journal, June 16, 1722. I think Morton is wrong in attributing this report to Macklish as the entry in question appears to have been made by Joseph Myatt.

158, *35*/trade: *Ibid.,* A.11/2, f.17, Myatt, Albany Fort, to Governor and Committee, Aug. 2, 1729.

158, *39*/death: *Ibid.,* B.3/a/18, f.21, Albany Fort Journal, July 25, 1730.

159, *17*/excepted": *Ibid.,* A.11/2, f.7, Macklish, Albany Fort, to Governor and Committee, July 16, 1716.

159, *45*/factory: *Ibid.,* B.239/a/5, f.73, York Fort Journal, April 23, 1720.

159, *47*/brandy: Henry Ellis, *A Voyage to Hudson's Bay* . . . (London, 1748), probably p.187. Other passages, pp.164, 178, 199, 200, scarcely support Morton's contention.

160, *3*/Committee: H.B.C. Arch., A.11/2, f.7, Macklish, Albany Fort, to Governor and Committee.

160, *12*/Doe": *Ibid.,* B.3/a/12, Albany Post Journal, 1723–4.

160, *14*/watered: *Ibid.,* A.6/6, f.19, London Letter Book, May 18, 1738.

160, *23*/Water": *Ibid.,* A.11/43, f.16, Moore Fort Correspondence (In), Aug. [9] 1738.

160, *31*/come: *Ibid.,* Albany Fort Correspondence (In), Aug. 20, 1717. So

Morton. A.11/2 contains a letter from Governor Macklish of this date which refers to Indians coming 800 miles.

160, *39*/country: Emanating from the La Vérendrye enterprise. The text is based on La Noué's statement in his letter of Oct. 18, 1721, to the Regent (Margry, éd., *Découvertes*, VI, 513) that a post should be built "à Tekamamiouen," i.e. at Rainy Lake.

160, *40*/June 11: Alter "June 11" to "June 12."

160, *42*/(Monsieur): H.B.C. Arch., B.239/a/5, f.52, York Fort Journal, June 12, 1719.

160, *48*/Indians": *Ibid.*, B.3/a/9, f.30, Albany Fort Journal, May 17, 1718.

161, *5*/French: *Ibid.*, B.239/a/7, f.22, York Fort Journal, June 3, 1722.

161, *10*/Committee: *Ibid.*, A.11/114, f.48, York Fort Correspondence (In), Aug. 8, 1728.

161, *20*/ours": *Ibid.*, f.49, same letter.

161, *30*/defeat: *Ibid.*, f.53, Macklish to Governor and Committee, Aug. 1, 1729.

161, *37*/trade": *Ibid.*, B.239/a/13, f.25, York Fort Journal, June 8, 1731.

162, *13*/here": *Ibid.*, A.11/114, f.64, Albany Fort Correspondence (In), Aug. 17, 1732.

162, *18*/1717–31: See Bibliographical Notes, p.935, for a reference to the different series in the Archives nationales, B, C^{11A}, C^{11E}, and F^3 (Collection Moreau St-Méry) which are the basis of this and the following sections. For La Vérendrye and his sons see Burpee, ed., *Journals and Letters of La Vérendrye*; Henry E. Hays, "The Journal of La Vérendrye, 1738–39", *North Dakota Historical Quarterly*, VIII (1940–1), 242–71; and L.J. Burpee, "La Vérendrye's 1738–9 Journal," *Canadian Historical Review*, XXIII (Dec. 1942), 407–11.

163, *11*/Bobé: A.N., Col., C^{11E}, vol.16, pp. 52–179.

163, *26*/flow: *Ibid.*, p.84.

163, *49*/Intendant: *Ibid.*, pp. 31–6 (Margry, éd., *Découvertes*, VI, 495–8).

164, *18*/memoir: 12 nov. 1716, *ibid.*, pp.37–45 (Margry, éd., *Découvertes*, pp.498–503).

164, *24*/be: Alter "be" to "to."

164, *38*/1717: A.N., Col., C^{11E}, vol.16, pp.37–45 (Margry, éd., *Découvertes*, VI, 504–7).

164, *46*/Bégon: *Ibid.*, pp.46–50. See also Maurepas à LaJonquière, 6 mars 1747, B85, p.39, f.177 (Burpee, ed., *Journals and Letters of La Vérendrye*, p.467).

165, *8*/1717: Cf. *H.B.R.S.*, XXI, 515, which makes this a post from 1713 and a fort from 1717.

165, *12*/Pachot: A.N., Col., C^{11E}, vol.16, pp.181–5 (Margry, éd., *Découvertes*, VI, 513–17); *ibid.*, pp.203–10, Lettre de Vaudreuil, 4 nov. 1720 (Margry, éd., *Découvertes*, VI, 510).

165, *24*/(1718): H.B.C. Arch., B.239/a/5, f.52, York Fort Journal, June 10, 1719. June 12, 1719, seems to be the entry to which Morton refers. The entry for June 10 merely mentions the arrival of canoes.

165, *25*/Fort: *Ibid.*, B.239/a/7, f.22, York Fort Journal, June 3, 1722.

165, *40*/questioned: A.N., Col., C^{11E}, vol.16, pp.211–14, 219–30 (Margry, éd., *Découvertes*, VI, 522–38).

165, *43*/1723: *Ibid.*, pp.219–30 (Margry, éd., *Découvertes*, VI, 521–8).

166, *6*/decision: Margry, éd., *Découvertes*, VI, 536.

166, *14*/Jesuits: *Ibid.*, pp.545–6.

166, *27*/wrote: A.N., Col., C¹¹ᴬ, vol.54, p.101, Beauharnois et Hocquart au ministre, 12 oct. 1731 (Margry, éd., *Découvertes,* VI, 568).

167, *11*/threatened: See Innis, *Fur Trade in Canada,* pp. 79–82, 85–90.

167, *25*/(1726): *Documents Relative to the Colonial History of New York,* IX, 1049.

168, *6*/family: Morton's note here reads "B51, t.1, p.11 (f.562) Vaudreuil et Bégon au Roy, 4 Novembre, 1719." P.A.C.'s A.N., Col., B.51, vol.1, p.11, f.562, is not "Vaudreuil et Bégon au Roy" and the letter Morton cites has not been found elsewhere.

168, *10*/protest: A.N., Col., F³, vol.10, p.154, f.136, Mémoire du Roy aux Srs. Vaudreuil et Bégon, 8 juin 1721.

168, *17*/overseas: *Ibid.,* B48, vol.2, pp.30–1.

168, *21*/land: *Ibid.,* B50, vol.2, pp.343–4, Maurepas à Beauharnois, 22 avril 1727; C¹¹ᴬ, vol.48, pp.125–6, Beauharnois à Maurepas, 28 sept. 1726.

168, *38*/annually: *R.A.P.Q., 1921–22,* p.205 for 22 mai 1725, p.209 for 31 mai 1725.

168, *39*/1726: Alter "1726" to "1728."

168, *41*/husband: *R.A.P.Q.,* 1921–22, p.214, 3 juillet 1728.

168, *43*/supplies: *Ibid.,* p.217, 2 juin, and p.218, 18 juin 1729.

169, *1*/Winnipeg): H.B.C. Arch., A.11/114, f.48, Macklish to Governor and Committtee, Aug. 8, 1728.

169, *5*/defeated: *Ibid.,* A.11/114, f.53, Same to same, Aug. 1, 1729.

169, *15*/1730: A.N., Col., C¹¹ᴬ, vol.52, p.232 (not in Burpee, ed., *Journals and Letters of La Vérendrye*).

169, *46*/himself: A.N., Col., F³, vol.11, pp.474–89.

170, *3*/Sea: Morton's note reads "No.16 in Bellin, *Recueil de Cartes, etc.* 1743; copy at p.53 in Burpee." Although the map is in Burpee, ed., *Journals and Letters of La Vérendrye,* opposite p.53, and was reproduced in D.G.G. Kerr, ed., *Historical Atlas of Canada* (Toronto, 1960), p.21, I have not been able to verify the reference to Bellin. Burpee, p.xxii, gives the full citation.

171, *15*/Hocquart: A.N., Col., C¹¹ᴱ, vol.16, pp.255–7, 15 oct. 1730 (Burpee, ed., *Journals and Letters of La Vérendrye,* pp.66 f.).

171, *27*/established: *Ibid.,* C¹¹ᴬ, vol.52, p.175, Beauharnois à Maurepas, 24 oct. 1730.

171, *44*/reported: *Ibid.,* C¹¹ᴱ, vol.16, pp.271–7 (Burpee, ed., *Journals and Letters of La Vérendrye,* p.73).

171, *49*/stop": Burpee, ed., *Journals and Letters of La Vérendrye,* p.76.

172, *3*/said: A.N., Col., B55, vol.2, p.462, f.480, 10 avril 1731.

172, *12*/replied: *Ibid.,* C¹¹ᴱ, vol.16, p.278, 10 oct. 1731 (Burpee, ed., *Journals and Letters of La Vérendrye,* p.83).

172, *27*/expense: See above, p.165.

172, *42*/1731: A.N., Col., C¹¹ᴱ, vol.16, pp.268–9 (Burpee, ed., *Journals and Letters of La Vérendrye,* pp.70 f.). Presumably La Vérendrye, not Maurepas, was at Michilimackinac.

173, *45*/Portage: See L.J. Burpee, "Grand Portage," *Minnesota History,* XII (Dec. 1931), 359 f.

173, *48*/operations: A.N., Col., C¹¹ᴱ, vol.16, p.286, 15 oct. 1732 (Burpee, ed., *Journals and Letters of La Vérendrye,* pp.91 f.).

174, *6*/1733: *Ibid.,* B59, vol.1, p.45.

174, *13*/Search: *Ibid.,* C¹¹ᴱ, vol.16, pp.467–82, 31 oct. 1744 (Burpee, ed., *Journals and Letters of La Vérendrye,* p.437).

174, *31*/1731: *Ibid.*, F³, vol.10, p.104 (12, f.35) (Burpee, ed., *Journals and Letters of La Vérendrye*, pp.92 f.).

174, *41*/through: *Ibid.*, C¹¹A, vol.51, pp.143–6, Beauharnois au ministre, 1 sept. 1729.

175, *5*/chimney: *Ibid.*, C¹¹E, vol.16, p.299, Beauharnois au ministre, 28 sept. 1733 (Burpee, ed., *Journals and Letters of La Vérendrye*, p.102).

175, *22*/son: Burpee, ed., *Journals and Letters of La Vérendrye*, p.438.

175, *23*/portages: A.N., Col., C¹¹E, vol.16, pp.319–33 (Burpee, ed., *Journals and Letters of La Vérendrye*, p.130).

175, *36*/1732: *Ibid.*, f.286 (Burpee, ed., *Journals and Letters of La Vérendrye*, p.91).

175, *47*/route: Burpee, ed., *Journals and Letters of La Vérendrye*, pp.438 and 115.

176, *2*/Indians: *Ibid.*, p.438.

176, *27*/1905: L.A. Prud'homme, "Pierre Gaultier de Varennes, Sieur de La Vérendrye ... Découvreur de Nord-Ouest," Royal Society of Canada, *Transactions*, 1905, s.1, p.28; *ibid.*, Historical Society of St. Boniface, *Bulletin*, V (1916), 38. Judge Prud'homme gives the date of discovery and identification as 1908 in the later (English) version; in his paper before the Royal Society of Canada he spoke of the expedition which discovered the ruins as organized in 1902, a date confirmed in the later version (p.129), and as discovering the bodies of the victims of the massacre in 1908 (pp.137 f.).

176, *32*/storehouse: Burpee, ed., *Journals and Letters of La Vérendrye*, p.103.

177, *2*/Winnipeg: *Ibid.*, p.105.

177, *4*/trade: *Ibid.*, pp.97, 125.

177, *5*/1734: Reproduced *ibid.*, p.98.

177, *10*/progress: *Ibid.*, pp.125, 439.

177, *11*/Beauharnois: A.N., Col., F³, vol.12, f.35, 21 mai 1733 (Burpee, ed., *Journals and Letters of La Vérendrye*, p.95). A.N., Col., C¹¹E, vol.16, p.293, 25 mai 1733 (Burpee, ed., *Journals and Letters of La Vérendrye*, p.100).

177, *13*/map: Burpee, ed., *Journals and Letters of La Vérendrye*, p.100.

177, *22*/English: *Ibid.*

177, *28*/Mississippi: *Ibid.*, p.99.

177, *49*/London: H.B.C. Arch., A.11/114, f.64, York Fort Correspondence (In), Macklish to Governor and Committee, Aug. 17, 1732.

178, *13*/1732: *Ibid.*, B.239/a/14, f.32, York Fort Journal, June 16, 1732.

178, *25*/route: *Ibid.*, B.3/a/20, f.14, Albany Fort Journal, Feb. 3, 1732 (1731, O.S.), and A.11/2, f.77, Albany Fort Correspondence (In), Adams to Governor and Committee, July 31, 1733.

178, *31*/winter: *Ibid.*, B.3/a/21, ff.12 and 13, Albany Fort Journal, Feb. 8 & 13, 1733 (1732 O.S.).

178, *33*/them: *Ibid.*, B.3/a/21, f.17, May 10, 1733.

178, *45*/themselves": *Ibid.*, B.3/a/22, f.28, May 19, B.3/a/22, f.29, June 4, B.3/a/22, f.30, June 5, all 1734. Morton also cites a letter from Adams to Governor and Committee, Aug. 19, 1735. A.11/2, f.82, contains an Albany letter of this date, but from Macklish and not including this quotation, although it does contain references to Deslestre and his "slave" and to French attempts to draw Indians away. Adams was a co-signer; the letter states that Adams has been appointed Commander-in-Chief as Macklish was obliged to return to England for reasons of health. Nor does the quotation appear in Adams' letter of Aug. 19, 1734 (A.11/2, ff.80–1).

179, *1*/end: A.N. Col., C¹¹ᴱ, vol.16, pp.293–4 (Burpee, ed., *Journals and Letters of La Vérendrye*, p.102).

179, *5*/letter: *Ibid.*, p.295, 10 oct. 1733.

179, *14*/Beauharnois: *Ibid.*, p.299, 28 sept. 1733 (Burpee, ed., *Journals and Letters of La Vérendrye*, p.102). See also *ibid.*, pp.306–10 (Burpee, ed., *Journals and Letters of La Vérendrye*, p.113).

179, *38*/activities: *Ibid.*, p.299, 28 sept. 1733 (Burpee, ed., *Journals and Letters of La Vérendrye*, p.106).

179, *39*/appeared: *Ibid.*, pp.319–33, 30 déc. 1734 (Burpee, ed., *Journals and Letters of La Vérendrye*, p.146).

179, *47*/tobacco: Burpee, ed., *Journals and Letters of La Vérendrye*, pp. 135 ff.

180, *11*/furs: *Ibid.*, p.140.

180, *14*/fat: *Ibid.*, p.147.

180, *33*/Sioux: *Ibid.*, pp.166ff.

180, *42*/details: *Ibid.*, pp.176 ff.

181, *44*/yoke": *Ibid.*, p.175.

181, *46*/1735: H.B.C. Arch., B.3/a/23, f.38, Albany Fort Journal, Aug. 8, 1735.

182, *34*/River): Burpee, ed., *Journals and Letters of La Vérendrye*, p.186.

182, *36*/war-path: *Ibid.*, p.190.

182, *41*/post: *Ibid.*, pp.127, 191.

182, *49*/posts: *Ibid.*, p.192.

183, *8*/Sea: A.N., Col., C¹¹ᴱ, vol.16, pp.306–10 (Burpee, ed., *Journals and Letters of La Vérendrye*, pp.112 f.).

183, *22*/thing": Burpee, ed., *Journals and Letters of La Vérendrye*, p.116.

183, *42*/progress: A.N., Col., C¹¹ᴱ, vol.16, pp.467–82 (Burpee, ed., *Journals and Letters of La Vérendrye*, p.439).

184, *7*/obedience": *Ibid.*, pp.311–13 (Burpee, ed., *Journals and Letters of La Vérendrye*, p.193).

184, *10*/place: *Ibid.*, pp.314–18 (Burpee, ed., *Journals and Letters of La Vérendrye*, p.203).

184, *17*/Jesuit: Burpee, ed., *Journals and Letters of La Vérendrye*, p.203.

184, *17*/son: A.N., Col., C¹¹ᴱ, vol. 16, pp.311–13 (Burpee, ed., *Journals and Letters of La Vérendrye*, p.174).

184, *35*/beaver": Arthur E. Jones, ed., *The Aulneau Collection, 1734–1745* (Montreal, 1893), p.67.

184, *47*/1744: A.N., Col., C¹¹ᴱ, vol.16, pp.467–85 (Burpee, ed., *Journals and Letters of La Vérendrye*, p.435).

185, *7*/latitude: Burpee, ed., *Journals and Letters of La Vérendrye*, p.214.

185, *10*/1736–37: A.N., Col., F³, vol.12, pp.348 f. (Burpee, ed., *Journals and Letters of La Vérendrye*, p.213).

185, *13*/La Jemeraye: Burpee, ed., *Journals and Letters of La Vérendrye*, p.214.

185, *45*/well: *Ibid.*, p.212.

185, *47*/fort: *Ibid.*, p.263.

186, *42*/regret": *Ibid.*, p.444.

186, *46*/1908: See note above, p.176, l.27.

186, *49*/Fort: H.B.C. Arch., B.3/a/25, f.25, Albany Fort Journal, June 11, 1737.

187, *26*/Maurepas: Burpee, ed., *Journals and Letters of La Vérendrye*, pp.441 f.

187, *35*/Kaministikwia: *Ibid.*, p.218.

187, *42*/packages: *Ibid.*, pp.235, 237.

187, *44*/Vermilion: *Ibid.*, pp.233 f.

187, *49*/orders: *Ibid.*, p.235.

188, *3*/inconveniens!": *Ibid.*, p.245.

188, *16*/February: *Ibid.*, pp.242ff.

188, *23*/River: *Ibid.*, pp.246 f.

188, *40*/him": *Ibid.*, p.253.

188, *44*/River: *Ibid.*, pp.244, 254.

189, *11*/him: *Ibid.*, p.260; at p.444 La Vérendrye makes it June 6.

189, *20*/responsible": *Ibid.*, p.267.

189, *29*/expedition": *Ibid.*, p.270.

189, *29*/this: A.N., Col., C^{11E}, vol.67, pp.119–21 (Burpee, ed., *Journals and Letters of La Vérendrye*, p.271).

189, *37*/winter: Burpee, ed., *Journals and Letters of La Vérendrye*, pp.212 f.

189, *42*/their: The original of the Journal of La Vérendrye's voyage to the Missouri is in P.A.C. A photostat of much of the Journal is in the Library of the University of Saskatchewan.

190, *3*/progress: Burpee, ed., *Journals and Letters of La Vérendrye*, pp.290 f.

190, *21*/Prairie: See also John Macdonell, "Some Account of the Red River (about 1797)" in Masson, *Les Bourgeois*, I, 267–95.

190, *24*/Fidler: H.B.C. Arch., E.3/3, f.58, Fidler's Journal, May 21 and 22, 1808, and his note at his page 126 at the end of the Journal.

190, *41*/canoes: Burpee, ed., *Journals and Letters of La Vérendrye*, p.306.

191, *13*/River: *Ibid.*, pp.244, 254.

191, *20*/post: *Ibid.*, pp.309 f.

192, *10*/them: *Ibid.*, p.318.

192, *14*/cloth: Cf. *ibid.*, p.319, "une robe de beuf, porté négligemment sans brayet."

192, *41*/guns: Were these the Mandans? Cf. Burpee, "La Vérendrye's 1738–9 Journal"; Crouse, *La Vérendrye, Fur Trader and Explorer*, Appendix b, pp.225–6; and G.L. Nute's review of the latter in *Mississippi Valley Historical Review*, XLIII (1956–7), 472–3.

193, *10*/her: Burpee, ed., *Journals and Letters of La Vérendrye*, p.335.

193, *15*/West: *Ibid.*, p. 338. See also above, note p.21, l.16.

193, *28*/minutes": *Ibid.*, p.346.

194, *18*/ill: *Ibid.*, pp.351 f.

194, *24*/autumn: H.B.C. Arch., B.239/a/21, f.36, York Fort Journal, June 14, 1739, James Isham being "Master or Chief Factor."

194, *35*/them": *Ibid.*, A.11/114, f.98, York Fort Correspondence (In), James Isham to the Governor and Committee, July 27, 1740.

194, *39*/River": *Ibid.*

195, *3*/expense: Burpee, ed., *Journals and Letters of La Vérendrye*, pp.357, 358 f.

195, *17*/information: *Ibid.*, pp.366 f.

195, *19*/Pierre: *Ibid.*, p.373.

195, *25*/Maurepas: *Ibid.*, pp.386 f.

195, *31*/exploration: A.N., Col., C^{11E}, vol.16, pp. 513–18 (Burpee, ed., *Journals and Letters of La Vérendrye*, pp.495 f., specifically p.496).

195, *39*/possible: *Ibid.*, pp.405–8 (Burpee, ed., *Journals and Letters of La Vérendrye*, pp.376 f.).

195, *41*/Dauphin: *Ibid.*, pp.427–8 (Burpee, ed., *Journals and Letters of La Vérendrye*, pp.378 f., 454).

195, *42*/post: Burpee, ed., *Journals and Letters of La Vérendrye*, p.485.

195, *47*/1756: Pierre Margry, éd., *Relations et mémoires inédits pour servir à l'histoire de la France dans les pays d'outre-mer* . . . (Paris, 1867), p.53.

195, *49*/Winnipegosis: Thompson, *Narrative*, ed. Tyrrell, p.lxxii.

196, *3*/built: Burpee, ed., *Journals and Letters of La Vérendrye*, p.454.

196, *8*/name": *Ibid.*, p.488.

196, *9*/map: Photostat in the University of Saskatchewan Library.

196, *29*/May: For the Journal of the Chevalier de La Vérendrye (the son) see Margry, éd., *Découvertes*, VI, 598–611, and Burpee, ed., *Journals and Letters of La Vérendrye*, pp.406 f.

196, *45*/Hommes: Burpee, ed., *Journals and Letters of La Vérendrye*, p.409.

196, *49*/Petit: Alter "Petit Renards" to "Petits Renards."

197, *5*/October: Burpee, ed., *Journals and Letters of La Vérendrye*, pp.411 f.

197, *13*/coast": *Ibid.*, p.413.

197, *19*/November: *Ibid.*, p.414.

198, *2*/hands": *Ibid.*, p.424.

198, *3*/February: Alter "February" to "March."

198, *8*/visit: Burpee, ed., *Journals and Letters of La Vérendrye*, p.427.

198, *16*/Vérendrye: *Ibid.*, p.17, in Introduction.

198, *39*/discovery": *Ibid.*, p.456.

199, *3*/trade: A.N., Col., B74, vol.2, p.220, f.448 (Burpee, ed., *Journals and Letters of La Vérendrye*, pp.389 f.). The officer proposed by Maurepas was the Sieur de Muy.

199, *5*/year: *Ibid.*, B76, vol.1, p.220, f.384 (40), Maurepas à Beauharnois et Hocquart, 26 avril 1743: "The appointment . . . is not to be postponed" (Morton's translation). Not in Burpee.

199, *5*/Governor: *Ibid.*, C¹¹ᴱ, vol. 16, pp.447–51 (Burpee, ed., *Journals and Letters of La Vérendrye*, pp.393–8).

199, *20*/Beauharnois: *Ibid.*, B78, vol.1, p.138, f.322 (25) (Burpee, ed., *Journals and Letters of La Vérendrye*, pp.399–400).

199, *27*/himself: *Ibid.*, C¹¹ᴱ, vol.16, pp.476–82 (Burpee, ed., *Journals and Letters of La Vérendrye*, p.435).

199, *45*/expense: *Ibid.*, pp.464–6, La Vérendrye à Maurepas, 31 oct. 1744 (Burpee, ed., *Journals and Letters of La Vérendrye,* p.434), the letter covering his belated defence of himself, as above.

199, *51*/there: For Saint-Pierre's Journal, see Margry, éd., *Découvertes*, VI, 640; text and translation in P.A.C., *Report, 1886*, pp.clviii–clxix.

200, *10*/troops: A.N., Col., B81, vol.182, f.272 (29) (Burpee, ed., *Journals and Letters of La Vérendrye*, pp.458 f.).

200, *13*/voluntarily: *Ibid.*, C¹¹ᴱ, vol.16, pp.492–3 (Burpee, ed., *Journals and Letters of La Vérendrye*, pp.468 f.). See also pp.501–3 (Burpee, p.489).

200, *19*/Sea": *Ibid.*, pp.455–8 (Burpee, ed., *Journals and Letters of La Vérendrye*, pp.400 f.).

200, *23*/Sea: A.N., Col., B81, vol.172, f.272 (29) (Burpee, ed., *Journals and Letters of La Vérendrye*, p.457).

200, *26*/authorities: *Ibid.*, C¹¹ᴱ, vol.16, pp.484–8 (Burpee, ed., *Journals and Letters of La Vérendrye*, p.462).

200, *33*/services: *Ibid.*, pp.492–3 (Burpee, ed., *Journals and Letters of La Vérendrye*, pp.468 f.).

200, *34*/view: A.N., Col., B87, vol.169, f.217 (36) (Burpee, ed., *Journals and Letters of La Vérendrye*, pp.471 f.).

200, *43*/Louis: *Ibid.*, B89, vol.215, f.266 (64) and B90, vol.108, f.134 (102v.) (Burpee, ed., *Journals and Letters of La Vérendrye*, pp.472 f. and 474 f.).

200, *46*/troops: Burpee, ed., *Journals and Letters of La Vérendrye*, p.470.

200, *47*/Posts: A.N., Col., C¹¹E, vol.16, pp.498–9 (Burpee, ed., *Journals and Letters of La Vérendrye*, pp.481 f.).

201, *5*/West": *Ibid.*, vol.16, pp.495–7 (Burpee, ed., *Journals and Letters of La Vérendrye*, p.477).

201, *16*/ran: Burpee, ed., *Journals and Letters of La Vérendrye*, p.486.

201, *33*/sight": *Ibid.*, p.488.

201, *35*/1749: A.N., Col., C¹¹E, vol.95, p.94, La Jonquière au ministre, 27 fév. 1750.

201, *41*/alone: Burpee, ed., *Journals and Letters of La Vérendrye*, p.205.

201, *47*/livres: Margry, éd., *Découvertes*, VI, 574, Hocquart au ministre, 26 oct. 1735.

201, *47*/thirteen: Alter "178,000" to "170,000" and "thirteen" to "eleven French and three Indian."

201, *48*/away: Burpee, ed., *Journals and Letters of La Vérendrye*, p.260.

202, *2*/livres: *Ibid.*, p.110, Report of Beauharnois, Sept. 28, 1733.

202, *7*/expenditure: A.N., Col., B61, vol.1, p.93, f.525v., Maurepas à Beauharnois, 20 avril 1734.

202, *13*/country: Burpee, ed., *Journals and Letters of La Vérendrye*, p.115.

202, *14*/canoes: *Ibid.*, pp.185, 191. See Innis, *Fur Trade in Canada*, p.102.

202, *30*/6,683: Alter "6,683" to "6,693."

202, *31*/Lorme: A.N., Col., C¹¹E, vol.16, p.409 (Burpee, ed., *Journals and Letters of La Vérendrye*, p.515).

202, *32*/2,787: Burpee, ed., *Journals and Letters of La Vérendrye*, p.518.

203, *10*/Gamelin: A.N., Col., B74, vol.2, p.274, f.466 (56) (Burpee, ed., *Journals and Letters of La Vérendrye*, p.531). Also C¹¹A, vol.77, pp.162–5, Copie de l'ordre accordé au Sieur La Marque et Compagnie contre le Sieur de La Vérendrye, 22 juin 1742. Also C¹¹E, vol.16, p.429 (Burpee, ed., *Journals and Letters of La Vérendrye*, p.532).

204, *17*/Repentigny: Better known as Saint-Pierre. See his Journal in Margry, éd., *Découvertes*, VI, 637. See also in P.A.C., *Report, 1886*, note C, pp.clviii f., "Journal of Jacques Repentigny Legardeur St. Pierre of his expedition for the discovery of the Western Sea, 1750 to 1752."

205, *34*/Bay: A.N., Col., B81, vol.172, f.272 (29), Maurepas à Beauharnois et Hocquart, 26 avril 1745; B87, vol.177, f.219v. (38v.), Maurepas à La Galissonière, 6 mars 1748.

206, *9*/Forks: See below, pp.230 f.

206, *35*/friendly. See above, p.182.

207, *25*/commons: Miss Johnson points out that, according to the *Dictionary of National Biography* and to Desmond Clarke (*Arthur Dobbs Esquire 1689–1765*, pp.25–33), Dobbs was a member of the Irish Parliament from 1727 to 1730.

207, *43*/abstract": Morton refers in the proof notes to "a thick folder in the Archives of the H.B.C. containing a rich store of documents emanating from the Dobbs crisis." Though the documents have been rearranged since Morton made use of them, many of them are in H.B.C. Arch., E.18/1 and E.18/2.

208, *28*/following year: H.B.C. Arch., A.1/122, ff.245–6, Minutes, March 3, 1736, recording the orders of the previous year.

208, *36*/next year: *Ibid.*, A.6/5, f.109, Governor and Committee to the Council at Churchill Fort (Prince of Wales Fort), May 6, 1736.

208, *40*/could: Miss Johnson writes that besides being a little late in arriving in Churchill in 1736 the *Mary* was needed to assist at York Factory owing to the loss of the *Hudson Bay* on the outward voyage. The *Mary* took the York fur returns to London in 1736. See *ibid.*, A.11/13, letters, 1736 and 1737.

208, *42*/autumn: *Ibid.*, B.42/a/16, f.50, Churchill Fort Journal, Aug. 12, 1736; A.11/13, f.30, Letter of the Master of Churchill Fort to Governor and Committee, Aug. 17, 1736.

208, *42*/4th: Morton has altered "4th" to "7th." See *ibid.*, B.42/a/17, ff.43–44. They received their orders on the 4th but did not sail until the 7th.

208, *43*/Inlet): Napper's Instructions were dated on the 4th (July, 1737), Churchill Ft. Corr. These have not survived in H.B.C. Arch. See *H.B.R.S.*, XXV, 228, n.5. They were printed in the *Report from the Commons Committee of 1749*, p.259.

210, *13*/expedition: H.B.C. Arch., Churchill Fort Journals, 1741–2 (B.42/a/21 for 1739–41, B.42/a/22 for 1740–1, B.42/a/23 for 1741–2).

211, *7*/*Vindication: A vindication of the conduct of Captain Christopher Middleton . . . in answer to cerain objections and aspersions of Arthur Dobbs, Esq.* (London, 1743).

212, *33*/Continent: Arthur Dobbs, *An account of the countries adjoining to Hudson's Bay . . .* (London, 1744), pp.2 f.

212, *44*/Council: *Acts of the Privy Council of England*, Colonial Series, Geo.II, vol. IV, p.261. See *Calendar*, III, *1720–1745*, p.776. Referred to Admiralty, March 21, 1744.

212, *51*/January: *Gentleman's Magazine*, Jan., 1745, p.51.

213, *2*/1745): 18 Geo.II, c.17.

214, *10*/manœuvres: H.B.C. Arch., B.239/G/29, Isham's Journal of the most material Transactions . . . between James Isham (and the captains of the two ships), Aug. 26, 1746 to June 24, 1747 (*H.B.R.S.*, XII, Appendix A, 241–308).

214, *37*/Drage: *An account of a Voyage for the discovery of a North-West Passage by Hudson's Streights . . .* By the Clerk of the *California* (2 vols., London, 1749), I, 118. The identity of "the Clerk of the *California*" is in doubt. See Howard M. Eavenson, *Map Maker and Indian Trader* (Pittsburgh, 1949), but cf. *H.B.R.S.*, XII, 265, n.2.

217, *15*/Rankin: Miss Johnson points out that "Middleton in 1741" should be altered to "Middleton in 1742." Rankin Inlet was named after his mate by Captain Middleton in 1742. The voyage took place in the summer of 1742. John Rankin was Middleton's "lieutenant." Rankin Inlet appears on the map accompanying Arthur Dobbs, *Remarks upon Capt. Middleton's Defence . . .* (London, 1744).

217, *46*/Solicitor-General: Acts of the Privy Council, Geo.II, vol.II, pp.511–12, 522 (*Acts of the Privy Council, Colonial Series*, III, 776).

217, *49*/petition: H.B.C. Arch., E.18/1, ff.112–29, Plea of the H.B.C. before the Attorney and Solicitor General, commissioned by the Privy Council to report on Dobbs's petition for a charter, Feb. 1747/8.

219, *28*/country: Morton's notes contain the summaries he made of these petitions in "the Dobbs folder," H.B.C. Arch., E.18/1, ff.232–41, Petition to the Lords of H.M. Privy Council of Merchants and other late *Adventurers*.

219, *36*/*Case*: H.B.C. Arch., E.18/1, ff.152–65.

220, *15*/England: *Report from the Commons Committee of 1749*, pp.243 f.

220, *17*/cross-examined: *Ibid.*, p.228.

220, *22*/advantage: *Ibid.*, p.215.

220, *29*/Bay: *Ibid.*, p.217.

220, *38*/inland: *Ibid.*, p.221.

220, *42*/Passage: *Ibid.*, p.222.

220, *45*/been: *Ibid.*, p.228.

220, *49*/Company: *Ibid.*, p.229.

221, *19*/trade": *Ibid.*, pp.231-4.

223, *26*/report [Count of lines here disregards the table]: Miss Johnson points out that "On 24th May the House" should be altered to "On 4th May the House." White and Isham gave their evidence on May 4, 1749; see H.B.C. Arch., E.18/1, ff.190-7.

224, *16*/*Countries*: According to Morton's note he found this pamphlet in the Dobbs folder. However, I am informed by Miss Johnson that the pamphlets were removed from the folder and placed in the Archives library but that this pamphlet is not among them. In this folder there is however a copy of *The Case of the Hudson's Bay Company*, "Copied from printed statement attached to Copy of 1749 Report in the possession of Sir Leicester Harmsworth, Bart." Morton's note may refer to l.10/*Case*. The leaflet does not figure in any of the Dobbs bibliographies I have seen.

224, *43*/America: Now in H.B.C. Arch. library. *A short state of the countries and trade of North America*. London: Printed for J. Robinson in Ludgate-Street. M,DCC,XLIX. 44 pp.

224, *46*/Inlet: Now in H.B.C. Arch library. *Reasons to shew, that there is a great Probability of a Navigable Passage to the Western American Ocean, through Hudson's Streights and Chesterfield Inlet; from the Observations made on board the Ships and upon the late Discovery*. London: Printed for J. Robinson at the Golden Lion in Ludgate-Street, MDCCXLIX. 23 pp.

225, *9*/Committee: Now in H.B.C. Arch. library. *A Short Narrative and Justification of the Proceedings of the Committee Appointed by the Adventurers to prosecute the Discovery of the Passage to the Western Ocean of America . . .* London: Printed for J. Robinson in Ludgate-Street, MDCCXLIX. 12 pp. Morton calls this Dobbs's "final" pamphlet but in the H.B.C. Arch. library volume it is bound as the first of the three.

225, *13*/Trade": Morton has this note, "Might this have been William Pitt?"

227, *7*/runs: Hearne's *Journey to the Northern Ocean,* ed. Tyrrell, pp. 21-2.

227, *29*/*Bay:* London, 1752. P.A.C. has a copy of the 1759 edition printed for T. Jefferys at Charing Cross and it is against this that I have verified Morton's references.

227, *35*/again: Miss Johnson points out that Robert Pilgrim was Governor at Churchill when Robson returned there in 1746; see H.B.C. Arch., A.11/13, ff.92-9. Richard Norton had returned to England in 1741; see *ibid.*, B.42/a/23.

227, *40*/1748: Miss Johnson writes that "1748" should be altered to "1747," the year that Robson really returned to England. See *ibid.*, A.11/13, f.101, and Robson's *Account of six years residence in Hudson's Bay,* pp.36-7.

227, *49*/it: Robson, *Account,* p.72n.

228, *2*/language: *Kelsey Papers*, p.xxvii.

228, *8*/complied": In Robson's *Account,* Appendix, I, p.364 (Appendix I, p.37, 1759 ed., phrases it a little differently).

228, *12*/gold: See pp.141 f. above.

228, *16*/nations." Robson's *Account*, p.81.

228, *21*/true: In his *Account*, p.79, Robson writes that the Company "sit down contented at the edge of a frozen sea."

228, *36*/outpost: H.B.C. Arch., A.11/2, f.117, Albany Fort Correspondence (In), Joseph Isbister and Council to Governor and Committee, Aug. 18, 1743; also B.3/a/34, ff.37 f., Albany Fort Journal, May 7 [1743] *et seq.*

229, *12*/latitude: *Ibid.*, A.11/2, f.126, Albany Fort Correspondence (In), Joseph Isbister and Council to Governor and Committee, Aug. 28, 1744.

299, *13*/parts: *Ibid.*, A.6/7, f.15, Governor and Committee to Joseph Isbister and Council, May 5, 1743. This letter seems to refer rather to the first two sentences in this paragraph.

229, *16*/inlet: *Ibid.*, B.182/a/1–11, Richmond Fort Journals and Correspondence. Mr. George E. Thorman of St. Thomas questions Morton's statement that the post was built by Coates and Potts. "Actually," he writes, "the post was built by Coates and Captain Thomas Mitchell. Coates and Mitchell picked out the site in 1749. Mitchell then went to Albany. . . . In the spring of 1750 he . . . loaded timbers prepared at Albany and sailed for Richmond which he spent the summer building. In 1750 the Company ordered Mitchell home and sent out John Potts to replace him as master. . . . Potts did some work on Richmond but basically the post was built before Potts' arrival."

229, *25*/1758: *Ibid.*

229, *27*/shed: *Ibid.*, A.11/57, ff.21 f., Richmond Fort Correspondence (In), Henry Pollexfen to Governor and Committee, Sept. 4, 1754; also B.182/a/6, ff.34–43, Richmond Fort Journal, 1754.

230, *20*/exploration": Burpee, ed., *Journals and Letters of La Vérendrye*, p.462, Beauharnois to Maurepas, Oct. 15, 1746 (so Morton's note). This letter is a defence of La Vérendrye in relation to exploration and a sharp criticism of Noyelles, but the phrases Morton quotes do not appear.

230, *25*/slim: *Ibid.*, p.465, Maurepas to La Jonquière, March 6, 1747; also p.473, Rouillé to La Jonquière, May 4, 1749.

230, *33*/fall": H.B.C. Arch., A.11/144, f.124, Isham to Governor and Committee. The letter is dated Aug. 18, 1747.

230, *49*/(Paskoyac): Margry, éd., *Découvertes*, VI, 618 (Burpee, ed., *Journals and Letters of La Vérendrye*, p. 487).

231, *21*/us": Jérôme's letter was dated at Ft. Bourbon, May 17, 1749. It was forwarded to the Governor and Committee in the autumn and is in H.B.C. Arch., A.11/114, ff.130–2.

233, *34*/colony: Burpee, ed., *Journals and Letters of La Vérendrye*, pp.500–1.

234, *55*/sweet": *Ibid.*, pp.507–13.

235, *8*/Journal: Margry, éd., *Découvertes*, VI, 637 f. (P.A.C., *Report, 1886*, pp.clviii f.).

243, *24*/Flamborough House: H.B.C. Arch., A.6/8, ff.44 f., Governor and Committee to Governor John Newton and Council, May 21, 1750.

243, *25*/Cumberland House: *Ibid.*, B.239/a/33, f.32, Newton's York Fort Journal, May 26, 1750, *passim.*

243, *27*/interlopers: *Ibid.*, A.6/8, ff.46 f., Governor and Committee to Newton, May 21, 1750.

243, *30*/kind: *Ibid.*

243, *37*/interior: *Ibid.*

243, *47*/survey: H.B.C. Arch., A.11/114, f.155, York Fort Correspondence (In), Isham to Governor and Committee, Aug. 6, 1752.

244, *8*/month: *Ibid.* Also A.11/114, f.158, Isham to Governor and Committee, Sept. 6, 1753.

244, *11*/Committee: H.B.C. Arch., A.6/8, f.119, Governor and Committee to Isham, May 24, 1753.

244, *23*/Fox: *Ibid.*, B.239/2/37, ff.16 and 17, York Fort Journal, Feb. 19 and March 7, 1754.

244, *25*/Fort: Morton's reference here is to H.B. Arch. [Isham to Joseph Isbister] inland letters. The only mention I can find in B.239/b of such a journey is a letter from Isham to Jacobs of April 15, 1754, B.239/b/11, f.7, and it does not mention Henday in this content, though the journey inland is evidently in the writer's mind.

244, *45*/Company: *Ibid.*, A.11/114, ff.172 f., Fort Correspondence (In), June 26, 1754.

245, *20*/Country: For a discussion of Henday's route see Wilson, "Across the Prairies Two Centuries Ago"; also MacGregor, *Behold the Shining Mountains.*

254, *45*/Cooler: See above, p.236.

246, *29*/lakes: "According to my information they are as salt as Henday reports" – Morton's marginal note.

250, *23*/same": H.B.C. Arch., A.6/9, f.8, Governor and Committee to Isham, May 27, 1755.

250, *33*/fort: *Ibid.*, B.239/a/41, ff.33 and 34, York Fort Journal, June 23 and 28, 1756.

250, *39*/region: For Smith's Journal see *ibid.*, B.239/2/43. Isham's orders of Aug. 20, 1750, to Smith and Waggoner are in A.11/115, f.3, together with an exchange of letters between the travellers and the governor. A.11/115, f.10, Isham to Governor and Committee of Aug. 18, 1757, refers, para. 18, to "Journal and Sketch of the Country here enclosed."

251, *25*/Fort: On June 24, 1757. *Ibid.*, A.11/115, f.10, Isham to Governor and Committee, Aug. 18, 1757.

252, *8*/Fort: See above, note p.250, 1.39. Cf. *H.B.R.S.*, XXI, 142," . . . its crude and cryptic English makes impossible any attempt to follow him accurately."

252, *14*/canoes: The dates of leaving of these and the rest are gathered from the York Fort Journals as also the dates of their return and usually the number of canoes with them.

252, *34*/example: Morton intended to give a reference here but failed to do so and I have not been able to identify his source, but cf. *H.B.R.S.*, XXI, 414, and Jérémie, *Twenty Years of York Factory*, p.40.

252, *45*/trade: The fourth in the list of orders in writing to Pressick, York Fort Journal, 1761.

253, *6*/La Vérendrye: H.B.C. Arch., B.3/a/23, f.38, Albany Fort Journal, Aug. 8, 1735 (i.e. the year before the Lake of the Woods Massacre), runs: "Severall of ye [French] is Destroyed by ye said Natives [Sioux] and ye French that has Escaped with several more of their nation & all ye Indians they can gett by any means are Going to War with them ye Ensuing Spring."

253, *15*/1746: *Ibid.*, B.239/b/4, f.7, York Fort Correspondence (Inland), Isham to Pilgrim, April 7, 1747. All Isham says is: "I have had one inland Ind[n] this winter by whom I understand the Ind[s] has killed some of the French[n]."

253, *16*/1753: Morton's reference here is York Fort Journal, Aug. 9, 1753, but it appears to have no relevance.

253, *29*/1755: *Ibid.*, A.11/2, ff.175 f. Joseph Isbister to Governor and Committee,

Sept. 14, 1755; A.11/2, ff.173 f., Albany Fort Correspondence (In), Rushworth to Governor and Committee, Sept. 8, 1755; B.239/b/14, York Fort Correspondence (Inland), Isbister, Albany Fort, to Isham, York Fort, March 20, 1756. Also the account of the Council, Albany Fort Correspondence (In), March 8, 1755. Also the examination, A.11/2, ff.165 f., June 7, 1755, and A.11/2, f.167 f., June 12, 1755.

253, 43/matter: "An account of the Attack on Henley House and Defence thereof on the 17th Septr., 1759," *ibid.*, A.11/3, f.41, Fort Correspondence (In). Also B.239/b/19, f.255, Temple to Isham, Jan. 29, 1760, York Fort Correspondence (Inland).

CHAPTER V: A Chapter of Approaches, 1763–93

For this chapter and chapter vi refer to H.B.R.S., XXII, Book 4, chapters i–xii. Other works that have appeared since Morton prepared his bibliography include E.E. Rich and A.M. Johnson, eds., *Cumberland and Hudson House Journals and Inland Journal, 1775–82, First Series, 1775–79* (London, Hudson's Bay Record Society, 1951), cited hereafter as *H.B.R.S., XIV*; E.E. Rich and A.M. Johnson, eds., *Cumberland House Journals and Inland Journals 1775–82, Second Series, 1779–82* (London, Hudson's Bay Record Society, 1952), cited hereafter as *H.B.R.S., XV*; E.E. Rich and A.M. Johnson, eds., *Moose Fort Journals, 1783–85* (London, Hudson's Bay Record Society, 1954), cited hereafter as *H.B.R.S., XVII*; Alice M. Johnson, ed., *Saskatchewan Journals and Correspondence: Edmonton House 1795–1800, Chesterfield House, 1800–1802* (London, Hudson's Bay Record Society, 1951), cited hereafter as *H.B.R.S., XXVI*; Gabriel Franchère, *Journal of a Voyage on the North West Coast of North America during the years 1811, 1812, 1813, and 1814,* transcribed and translated by W.T. Lamb, W. Kaye Lamb, ed. (Toronto, Champlain Society, 1969); F.W. Howay, ed., *The Journal of Captain Colnett aboard the "Argonaut" from April 26, 1789 to November 3, 1791* (Toronto, Champlain Society, XXVI, 1940); Richard Glover, ed., *David Thompson's Narrative, 1784–1872* (Toronto, Champlain Society, 1962); Benoit Brouillette, *La Pénétration du continent américain par les Canadiens français, 1763–1846: Traitants, explorateurs, missionaires* (Montréal, 1939); Marjorie Wilkins Campbell, *The North West Company* (Toronto, 1957); Marjorie Wilkins Campbell, *McGillivray, Lord of the Northwest* (Toronto and Vancouver, 1962); D.G. Creighton, *The Commercial Empire of the St. Lawrence, 1760–1850* (Toronto, 1937); O.C. Furniss, "Some Notes on Newly-discovered Fur Posts on the Saskatchewan River," *C.H.R.,* XXIV (Sept., 1943); E.W. Gilbert, *The Exploration of Western America* (Cambridge, 1953); Samuel Hearne, *A Journey to the Northern Ocean,* Richard Glover, ed. (Toronto, 1958; Victor G. Hopwood, ed., *David Thompson, Travels in Western North America 1784–1812* (Toronto, 1971); W. Kaye Lamb, ed., *Sixteen Years in the Indian Country: The Journal of Daniel Williams Harmon, 1800–1816* (Toronto, 1957); W. Kaye Lamb, ed., *The Letters and Journals of Simon Fraser, 1806–1808* (Toronto, 1960); Dorothy E.T. Long, "The Elusive Mr. Ellice," *C.H.R.,* XXII (March, 1942); Elaine A. Mitchell, "The North West Company Agreement of 1795," *C.H.R.,* XXXVI (June, 1955); Elaine A. Mitchell, "New Evidence on the Mackenzie-McTavish Break," *C.H.R.,* XLI (March, 1960); Percy J. Robinson, "Yonge Street and the North West Company," *C.H.R.,* XXIV (Sept., 1943); Edward Umfreville, *The Present State of Hudson's Bay . . . ,* ed. W.S. Wallace (Toronto, 1954); Henry R. Wagner, *The Cartography of the Northwest Coast of America to the year 1800,* 2 vols. (Berkeley, Cal., 1937); Henry R. Wagner,

Peter Pond, Fur Trader and Explorer (New Haven, 1955); M. Catherine White, ed., *David Thompson's Journals Relating to Montana and Adjacent Regions, 1808–1812* (Missoula, 1956); O.O. Winther, *The Old Oregon Country . . .* (Stanford, 1950).

259, *3*/Indians: Francis Parkman, *The Conspiracy of Pontiac . . .* (2 vols., London, 1851), I, 171–2.

259, *33*/1764: Plan for the future management of Indian Affairs, *Documents Relative to the Colonial History of New York,* VII, 637 f.

261, *19*/trade: *Ibid.,* VIII, 55–6.

269, *33*/them: James Sullivan and A.C. Flick, ed., *The Papers of Sir William Johnson* (10 vols., Albany, 1921–51), V, 130.

269, *34*/April: *Ibid.,* V, 148.

269, *43*/Indians: *Ibid.,* V, 167. Morton's pencilled notes are confused at this point and he may not have regarded the Montreal Memorial of April 15, 1766, as evidence for the licences to winter.

269, *48*/Padgeman: Alter "Padgeman" to "Pangman."

270, *2*/Mississippi: *Sir William Johnson Papers,* V, 520–3, Guy Carleton to Johnson, March 27, 1767. For the Memorial of Sept. 20 see *Illinois Historical Collections,* XI, 378; for another letter from Carleton to Johnson, March 27, 1767, see *Illinois Historical Collections,* XI, 532, and P.A.C., M.G.11, Q series, vol.4, 200.

270, *13*/Pond: *Sir William Johnson Papers,* V, 826–30; *Illinois Historical Collections,* XVI, 121–5.

270, *28*/open: British Museum, Additional Manuscripts 21, pp.673 f., 75–c; *Illinois Historical Collections,* XVI, 245; *Documents Relative to the Colonial History of New York,* VIII, 58.

270, *29*/Quebec: P.A.C., M.G.11, Q5–2, 860.

276, *3*/wood": Was-qui-wac-Chic.

281, *4*/1669: Alter "1669" to "1769."

283, *31*/wrote: W.S. Wallace, ed., *Documents Relating to the North West Company* (Toronto, Champlain Society, 1934), pp.42–4. The date is Aug. 26, 1772.

284, *37*/them: L.J. Burpee, ed., "An adventurer from Hudson Bay: Journal of Matthew Cocking, from York Factory to the Blackfeet Country, 1772–73," *Royal Society of Canada, Transactions,* Third Series, II (1908), s.2, 103.

285, *45*/runs: *Ibid.,* p.118.

286, *11*/continues: *Ibid.* In Cocking's Journal this passage precedes the one Morton quotes first.

293, *15*/gluttony": Hearne, *Journey to the Northern Ocean,* ed. Tyrrell, p.78.

293, *31*/pleased": *Ibid.,* p.83.

293, *34*/naïvely: *Ibid.,* pp.84–5.

294, *27*/meat: *Ibid.,* p.102.

295, *33*/1771: Hearne left Churchill Fort on Dec. 7, *1770.* See Hearne, *Journey to the Northern Ocean,* ed. Richard Glover (Toronto, 1958), p.xxi (cf. *H.B.R.S.,* XXI, Book 2, p.53, where the date of departure is given as Dec., 1772).

297, *22*/paint: Hearne, *Journey to the Northern Ocean,* ed. Tyrrell, pp.178–9.

300, *23*/due: In his Introduction, pp.xxx–xxxi, to Hearne's *Journey* Professor Glover dismisses as "persistent legend" the statement about Bishop Douglas' editorship.

300, *45*/Land: See particularly Tyrrell, ed., *Journals of Hearne and Turnor,* and *H.B.R.S.,* XIV and XV.

302, *8*/policy: Tyrrell, ed., *Journals of Hearne and Turnor,* p.97.

302, *31*/House": *Ibid.,* p.17.

303, *18*/here: *Ibid.,* p.114.

303, *26*/October: Cf. *ibid.,* p.123. The Journal suggests that the date should be Oct. 17.

303, *31*/Hearne: *Ibid.,* pp.31 f.

307, *29*/May: *H.B.R.S.,* XIV, 153.

310, *10*/1775): *Ibid.,* XIV, 13.

311, *1*/Pond: See also Wagner, *Peter Pond,* with documents and three of Pond's maps.

312, *42*/runs: *H.B.R.S.,* XIV, 17–18.

324, *43*/misconduct: Alexander Mackenzie, *Voyages,* pp.xii–xiii.

327, *28*/Haldimand: *P.A.C.,* Haldimand Papers, series B, vol.99, p.110 (printed in P.A.C., *Report, 1888,* pp.59–60). The report is by Charles Grant not William Grant.

331, *45*/saw: Thompson, *Narrative,* p.321.

334, *49*/justice: *P.A.C.,* Haldimand Papers, B219, pp.113, 123.

340, *23*/concern": See *H.B.R.S.,* XIV, xliii, n.6, for another view.

340, *27*/Fort: Arrowsmith's map of 1795 places the fort and gives its date as 1784.

341, *36*/Ross: P.A.C., Q36–1, 299–305.

343, *31*/trade: H.A. Innis, "The North West Company," in Notes and Documents, *Canadian Historical Review,* VIII (1927), pp.308–21.

345, *41*/1785: P.A.C., Q24, 329.

345, *47*/Governor: *Ibid.,* Q25, 122.

346, *23*/water-way: *Ibid.,* Q24–2, 405 (P.A.C., *Report, 1890,* pp.48–9).

346, *26*/Athabaska: *Ibid.,* Q24–2, 418 (P.A.C., *Report, 1890,* p.52).

349, *45*/Journal: Daniel Williams Harmon, *Journal of voyages and travels* (1st ed., Andover, 1820), p.150; see also Lamb, ed., *Journal of Harmon,* p.98.

351, *6*/side: Coues, ed., *Journals of Henry and Thompson,* II, 542. The room was 22x23 in Coues' version; obviously a printer's error Morton overlooked.

352, *19*/time: Morton, ed., *Duncan M'Gillivray's Journal,* pp.30–1.

352, *40*/liquor: *Ibid.,* p.72.

353, *5*/1809: Coues, ed., *Journals of Henry and Thompson,* II, 542.

353, *36*/runs: François A.F., duc de La Rochefoucault-Liancourt, *Travels through the United States of North America, the country of the Iroquois, and Upper Canada . . .* , trans. Henry Newman (London, 1799), pp. 330–1.

354, *6*/wrong: See also *H.B.R.S.,* XIV, 1, n.5, for Professor Glover's comment.

354, *15*/account: *Ibid.,* pp.329–35, for the analysis of the trade based on Andreani's journal.

357, *30*/Chinook: See an interesting discussion of the Chinook wind from the meteorological point of view by R.F. Stuart, director of the Meteorological Service of Canada, in A.O. Wheeler, *The Selkirk Range* (Ottawa, 1905), Appendix D.

358, *42*/belt: A.G. Morice, *The History of the Northern Interior of British Columbia (formerly New Caledonia)* [1660 to 1880] (3rd ed., Toronto, 1908), pp.1–2.

359, *26*/below: *Ibid.,* p.8.

360, *32*/River: See Lamb, ed., *Journal of Harmon*, pp.130–1.

364, *39*/them: Alexander Ross, *Adventures of the First Settlers on the Oregon or Columbia River* (London, 1849), p.315.

365, *36*/food: Charles Hill-Tout, *British North America*, I, *The Far West, the Home of the Salish and Déné* (London, 1907), pp.7–8. For the verification of this reference I am indebted to Dr. W.E. Ireland, the Provincial Librarian and Archivist of British Columbia.

369, *19*/latitude: H.E. Bolton, *Fray Juan Crespi: Missionary Explorer on the Pacific Coast, 1769–1774* (Berkeley, Calif., 1927). Morton checked his account of the voyage by this edition of Crespi's Journal.

370, *32*/sailing-master: One of the chaplains, Benito de la Sierra, kept a record of the voyage. They sailed from San Blas on March 17. See "Fray Benito de la Sierra's Account of the Heceta Expedition to the Northwest Coast in 1775," translated by F.J. Baker, introduction and notes by Henry R. Wagner, California Historical Society, *Quarterly*, IX, no.3 (Sept., 1930).

371, *2*/Sound: Not in Sierra, *ibid.*

371, *10*/August: Sierra stops at Aug. 5, San Francisco.

373, *48*/landfall: The log of the *Discovery* has it 44°32' not 44°35'N.

375, *35*/1785: Miss Johnson points out that "1785" should be altered to "1784." *A Voyage to the Pacific Ocean, Undertaken . . . in the Years 1776, 1777, 1778, 1779, and 1780 by Captain James Cook and Captain James King* was published in London in 1784.

385, *17*/1779: W.R. Manning, "The Nootka Sound Controversy," American Historical Association, *Report, 1904*, pp.304–5.

388, *10*/region": Herbert Ingram Priestley, "The Log of the Princesa by Estevan Martinez," Oregon Historical Society, *Quarterly*, XXI (1920), 25.

389, *8*/runs: *Ibid.*, p.26.

396, *35*/Boston: Reprinted *ibid.*, XXII (1921), 256–356.

410, *24*/1889: P.A.C., *Report, 1889*, pp.29–38.

412, *40*/parts": P.A.C., Q49, 395.

413, *16*/inquiries: Masson, *Les Bourgeois*, I, 37, "Roderick Mackenzie's Reminiscences." The date of the letter in Masson is March 2, 1791.

414, *37*/cliffs: Alexander Mackenzie, *Voyages*, p.169.

416, *41*/camped: *Ibid.*, pp.243–5.

419, *20*/Mackenzie]: P.A.C., Q280–2, 359.

CHAPTER VI: The Great Struggle between the English and Canadian Companies Begins, 1787–1800—The Columbian Enterprise, 1800–14

See above, p.974, for additional material.

428, *18*/1794: Morton, ed., *Duncan M'Gillivray's Journal*, p.9.

432, *24*/builder: It figures on Arrowsmith's map of 1795 as "R. Grant 1788."

432, *48*/south: It is entered on Arrowsmith's map of 1795 as "R. Grant, 1791."

434, *1*/miles: Miss Johnson has provided the following solution to a particularly baffling reference of Morton's. The first entry from H.B.C. Arch., B.65/a/1, f.2, "A Journal of Transactions, kept at River Kapell, by John Sutherland, 1794" reads as follows: "1794, Feby. 6, Thursday I set out from Brandon House in Company with 14 men with Trading goods and provisions to go to River Kapell, and the 16th of Feby we got to our intended station, at which place they [*sic*] are two settlements one for the N.W. Company and another for Mr. Peter Grant."

436, *48*/prairies: Coues, ed., *Expedition . . . of Lewis and Clark . . .*, I, 203–40. The expeditions to the Missouri are indicated in Morton's Bibliographical Notes, p.936.

437 *21*/view: Gates, *Five Fur Traders of the North-West*, pp.63–119; Masson, *Les Bourgeois*, II, 267–95.

438, *3*/knowledge": Cf. Lamb, ed., *Journal of Harmon*, p.40.

439, *33*/us: Morton, ed., *Duncan M'Gillivray's Journal.*

441, *32*/Ile-à-la-Crosse: Masson, *Les Bourgeois,* I, sec.1, pp.18–20.

443, *17*/remembered: See Glover, ed., *Thompson's Narrative*; also White, ed., *Thompson's Journals.*

445, *17*/course: Tyrrell, ed., *Journals of Hearne and Turnor*, p.573.

453, *21*/'nineties: See Richard Glover, "The Difficulties of the Hudson's Bay Company's Penetration of the West." *Canadian Historical Review*, XXIX (1948), 248, n.43. Dr. Glover comments on the way in which historians of the fur trade ignore the effects of the Revolutionary and Napoleonic Wars. See below, p.532, for evidence that Morton was not entirely unaware of these effects.

453, *35*/ Auld: Alter "William Auld went on to Green Lake, and built Essex House beside the Canadian post there" to "William Auld went on to Green Lake, and built beside the Canadian post there." Miss Johnson explains that the post on Green Lake established by William Auld in 1789 was known not as Essex House but as Green Lake post (H.B.C. Arch., B.84/a/1). It is clear from the Churchill Fort Journals and Correspondence that Essex House was a stone house situated about four days' journey and about 130 miles above Churchill Factory. It was in existence in January, 1799, and is shown on a manuscript map by Thomas Stayner, dated 1801 (H.B.C. Arch., B.42/b/46). On the map Essex House is sited on the right bank of Beaver Creek (flowing into the Churchill River) and at approximately latitude 57°45′N and longitude 95°W. It was relinquished in 1801 owing to shortage of labour.

458, *27*/document: Masson, *Les Bourgeois*, II, 17–18. For complete text see P.A.C., M.G.19, A.17, McDonald of Garth Papers.

459, *17*/goods: Morton, ed., *Duncan M'Gillivray's Journal*, pp.47–8.

460, *16*/George: *Ibid.*, p.56.

462, *9*/servants: *Ibid.*, pp.59–60.

463, *25*/1801: See below, note p.511, 1.49.

465, *14*/us: "Roderick Mackenzie's Reminiscences," in Masson, *Les Bourgeois,* I, 48.

466, *22*/mountains": Thompson, *Narrative*, ed. Tyrrell, p.lxxx. For the controversy between Morton and Tyrrell over Duncan M'Gillivray and the crossing of the Rockies see A.S. Morton, "The North West Company's Columbian Enterprise and David Thompson," *Canadian Historical Review*, XVII (Sept., 1936), 266–88; W.M. Stewart, "David Thompson's Surveys in the North-West," *ibid.*, XVII (Sept., 1936), 289–303; J.B. Tyrrell, "David Thompson and the Columbia River," *ibid.*, XVIII (March, 1937), 12–27; A.S. Morton, "Did Duncan M'Gillivray and David Thompson Cross the Rockies in 1801?" *ibid.*, XVIII (June, 1937), 156–62; J.B. Tyrrell, "Duncan McGillivray's Movements" in Notes and Documents, *ibid.*, XX (March, 1939), 39–40; White, ed., *Thompson's Journals*, Appendix B, pp.247 f., and Glover, ed., *Thompson's Narrative*, pp.xliv f.

467, *12*/1803: P.A.C., Q92, 283.

467, *19*/1802: P.A.C., *Report, 1892,* p.151.

467, *47*/1814: May 14. Gabriel Franchère, *Narrative of a voyage to the Northwest coast of America in the years 1812 . . . 1814 . . .*, Huntington trans. (New York, 1854), p.291.

468, *2*/*River*: Ross Cox, *Adventures on the Columbia River . . .* (New York, 1832), p.248n.

469, *2*/William) : Wallace, ed., *Documents Relating to the North West Company,* pp.203-4.

469, *19*/*Company*: *Ibid.*, pp.194-6.

469, *32*/abuses: *Ibid.*, p.203.

469, *42*/rule: *Ibid.*, p.211.

470, *12*/1804: Cf. W. Kaye Lamb, ed., *Letters and Journals of Simon Fraser, 1806–1808* (Toronto, 1960), p.15, which maintains that the decision was taken in 1804, i.e., after union with the XY Company.

470, *18*/steps: Cf. *ibid.* Morton's dating of Fraser's journeys is inaccurate and should be scrutinized carefully.

471, *3*/1807: Cf. *ibid.*, p.17. "By that time," i.e., by April, 1806, Fraser had news of McDougall's journey.

471, *31*/away: Cf. *ibid.*, p.19. Fraser left in May, 1806.

472, *39*/beauties: John M'Lean, *Notes of a Twenty-five Years' Service in the Hudson's Bay Territory* (London, 1849), I, 241–2. See also W.S. Wallace, ed., *John McLean's Notes of a Twenty-five Years' Service in the Hudson's Bay Territory* (Toronto, Champlain Society, 1932).

473, *48*/1808: Cf. Lamb, p.23. For "1808" read "1807." The canoes arrived in the autumn.

474, *14*/May: Cf. *ibid.*, p.24, which supports May 28, 1808, as the day of departure.

474, *30*/June: Cf. *ibid.*, pp.67 f.

475, *33*/June: Masson, *Les Bourgeois,* I, s.1, p.168. Lamb, pp.72–3.

476, *11*/Fraser: Lamb, pp.75–6.

477, *14*/seen: *Ibid.*, p.96. The date is June 26.

478, *46*/*Company*: *On the Origin and Progress of the Northwest Company of Canada . . .* (London, 1811). A photostat copy is in P.A.C.; see Magdalen Casey, *Catalogue of Pamphlets in the P.A.C.* (Ottawa, 1931), p.968. See also Morton, ed., *Duncan M'Gillivray's Journal,* Appendix, pp.21–4.

471, *17*/says: Thompson, *Narrative,* ed. Tyrrell, p. 375.

482, *48*/1922": T. C. Elliott, "David Thompson's Narrative, 'The discovery of the source of the Columbia River,' " Oregon Historical Society, *Quarterly,* XXVI (1925), 27.

485, *2*/Elliott) : T. C. Elliott, "David Thompson and Beginnings in Idaho," *ibid.,* XXI (1920), 54.

489, *29*/1910: For "1910" read "1810."

490, *10*/Liverpool: Liverpool was not at this time Prime Minister but Secretary of State for War and Colonies. See Glover, ed., *Thompson's Narrative,* p.xlviii, n.4.

492, *2*/runs: Coues, ed., *Journals of Henry and Thompson,* II, 650–1.

493, *5*/himself: Thompson, *Narrative,* ed. Tyrrell, p.455.

493, *32*/canoe: *Ibid.*, p.461.

494, *10*/Ocean": Quoted by T. C. Elliott, *ibid.*, p. 473, n.1.

494, *22*/prayer": Thompson, *Narrative,* ed. Tyrrell, p.479.

494, *48*/staked: Franchère, *Narrative,* pp.119–22.

495, *32*/1814": The map is in the possession of the Archives of the Province of Ontario. See Morton, ed., *Duncan M'Gillivray's Journal,* Appendix, p.7.

498, *44*/end: Quoted from F.W. Howay, *British Columbia: The Making of a Province* (Toronto, 1928), p.68.

500, *45*/departure: Ross, *Adventures of the First Settlers on the Oregon,* pp. 200–1.

501, *34*/glory": *Ibid.,* p.212.

502, *47*/fur-traders: *Ibid.,* p.202.

503, *4*/Indians: Cox, *Adventures on the Columbia,* p. 105.

503, *11*/winter: *Ibid.,* p.118.

503, *19*/testifies: *Ibid.,* p.106.

560, *30*/Bancroft: H.H. Bancroft, *History of the Northwest Coast* (20 vols., San Francisco, 1884), II, 291.

CHAPTER VII: A Period of Violence, 1800–21—Lord Selkirk's Colony, 1812–18
For this chapter also refer to *H.B.R.S.,* XXII, Book 4, chapters x–xvi; E.E. Rich, ed., *Journal of Occurrences in the Athabaska Department by George Simpson, 1820 and 1821, and Report* (Toronto, Champlain Society, 1838; London, Hudson's Bay Record Society, 1938), cited hereafter as *H.B.R.S.,* I; E.E. Rich, ed., *Colin Robertson's Correspondence Book, September 1817 to September 1882* (Toronto, Champlain Society, 1939; London, Hudson's Bay Record Society, 1939), cited hereafter as *H.B.R.S.,* II; P.C.T. White, ed., *Lord Selkirk's Diary, 1803–1804 ...* (Toronto, Champlain Society, 1958) (of interest for its relevance to Selkirk himself); J.M. Gray, *Lord Selkirk of Red River* (Toronto, 1963); A.S. Morton, *Sir George Simpson: Overseas Governor of the Hudson's Bay Company* (Toronto, 1944); John P. Pritchett and Murray Horowitz, "Five 'Selkirk' Letters", in "Notes and Documents," *C.H.R.,* XXII (June, 1941); John P. Pritchett, *The Red River Valley, 1811–1849: A Regional Study* (New Haven and Toronto, 1942).

W.S. Wallace, "The Literature Relating to the Selkirk Controversy," to which Morton refers in his Bibliographical Notes, p.939, is in the *C.H.R.,* March, 1932, not 1933.

509, *35*/Mackenzie: Mr. John Gray points out that "Alexander Mackenzie (not Sir Alexander)" should be "Alexander McKenzie." It is so spelled in the next paragraph.

510, *5*/fort: See James Mackenzie's Journal, in Masson, *Les Bourgeois,* II, 389.

511, *49*/built: There is a considerable correspondence on Edmonton between Morton and the Hudson's Bay Company; it is to be found in the files of the Company's Archives. The Company was unable to accept Morton's conclusions with regard to the date at which Edmonton House (No.2) was established. The Company's view was succinctly stated in a letter from the Secretary of the Company to the Canadian Committee, L.C. No.22168 of Oct. 19, 1944. "The most definite statement we are prepared to make is that Edmonton House No.2 was established sometime between September, 1801 and September, 1806." Morton admitted that his note was not entirely satisfactory as he should have explained that the date he gives, the summer of 1802, was based on evidence of Arrowsmith's map of 1795 corrected to 1802. This evidence did not convince his correspondents in London and Winnipeg. Morton did accept their correction of the site of Edmonton No.3 (lines 52–3) from "section 58, tp.16, r.4, W.4" to "section 36, tp.58, r.16, W.4."

515, *20*/Mackenzie: Mr. John Gray points out that Sir Alexander Mackenzie and his cousin Roderick did not spell their surnames in the same way.

517, *13*/Mackenzie: Mr. Gray points out that the spelling here should be "McKenzie."

518, *25*/Mackenzie: The spelling should be "McKenzie."

519, *42*/Mackenzie: The spelling should be "McKenzie."

520, *4, 10*/Mackenzie: The spelling should be "McKenzie."

531, *35*/trading: For "share in the profits" cf. *H.B.R.S.*, XXII, Book 2, p. 292. Morton does not say that only *half* of the profits was to be shared. "In the sense of the scheme" is probably the key to the confusion that has arisen in the minds of some readers.

532, *46*/Feb. 26): But cf. H.B.C. Arch., A.1/50, f.23, Minutes, 1811, where the date of the meeting appears to have been Wednesday, Feb. 6.

533, *19*/1811: Cf. *ibid.*, A.1/50, f.52, which would make the date Thursday, May 30.

533, *21*/stockholders: Cf. *ibid.* William Thwaytes (£9223.6.8) and Robert White-head (£3000).

533, *26*/disqualified: Cf. *ibid.* But included in the total of £14823.19.11 contrary.

533, *30*/three: Cf. *ibid.* The Minutes show 5 non-voters present.

533, *31*/votes: H.B.C. Arch., A.1/50, ff.53–4. One of the signatories of the protest, Fish, was present at the meeting but did not vote.

545, *44*/Skene: Mr. William Douglas has drawn my attention to Morton's use of the name "Fort Skene" for the H.B.C. post near the mouth of the Pembina. He has been a close student of the history of the post and has never met elsewhere with this name. It is also unknown to Miss Johnson of the H.B.C. Archives. Nor is it in Ernest Voorhis, comp., *Historic Forts and Trading Posts of the French Régime and of the English Fur Trading Companies* (Ottawa, 1930). I have myself searched Morton's Historical Geography, but, although there are several references to Heney and the post at the junction of the Pembina and the Red, there is no use of the name "Fort Skene."

549, *5*/woodcuts: Thomas MacKeevor, *A voyage to Hudson's Bay, during the summer of 1812* . . . (London, 1819).

555, *16*/service): Mr. John Gray points out that there is doubt whether Auld was dismissed. At any rate he wrote a letter of resignation and was retained on the Company's strength for about a year after his return to England. Cf. *H.B.R.S.*, XXII, 311.

555, *18*/saw": P.A.C., Selkirk Transcripts, p.875.

556, *20*/winter": *Ibid.*, p.956.

556, *23*/community": *Ibid.*, p.1186.

556, *31*/1814: *Ibid.*, pp.1083 f.

557, *26*/replied: *Ibid.*, p.626.

558, *6*/immigrants: *Ibid.*, p.866.

558, *21*/Liverpool: Thomas Douglas, 5th Earl of Selkirk, *A Letter to the Earl of Liverpool from the Earl of Selkirk, accompanied by a correspondence with the Colonial department (in the years 1817, 1818, and 1819) on the subject of the Red River settlement in North America* ([London], 1819), p.4.

558, *26*/Bathurst: *Ibid.*, p.5.

558, *31*/Bathurst: *Ibid.*

558, *32*/says: *Ibid.*

558, *42*/lordship: P.A.C., M155, p.330; an extract is printed in Oliver, ed., *Canadian North-West*, I, 177.

558, *45*/1813: Oliver, ed., *Canadian North-West*, I, 178 f.

562, *26*/February: P.A.C., Selkirk Transcripts, p.959.

563, *10*/starvation): *Papers Relating to the Red River Settlement, 1815–1819. Ordered by the House of Commons, to be printed 12 July 1819*, pp.14 f. (copies in P.A.C., PF44, and duplicate in PF104 (No.1) Imperial Blue Books re Canada, vol. 41). Cited hereafter as *Red River Settlement Papers*. For Coltman report see also *Collections of the North Dakota State Historical Society*, IV (1913), 449–63.

564, *6*/MacDonald: Mr. John Gray points out that "John MacDonald of Garth" should be "John McDonald."

565, *11*/Selkirk: P.A.C., Selkirk Transcripts, p. 1195.

565, *19*/lands": *Ibid.*, p.1196.

566, *32*/Journal: *Ibid.*, p.16921.

567, *2*/occasion: Wallace, ed., *Documents Relating to the North West Company*, p.291. The spelling and wording differ slightly, suggesting that Morton may himself have used the original in H.B.C. Arch., F.1/1, ff.1–76. See also Wallace, p.246n. It may be worth recording that "[measures]" in Morton is "Pts" in Wallace. It seems clear that Morton here cites Wallace but gives his own reading of H.B.C. Arch., F.1/1, f.75.

567, *25*/Garth: P.A.C., Selkirk Transcripts, p.1204. Mr. John Gray points out that the spelling should be "McDonald."

568, *14*/later: *Red River Settlement Papers*, p. 30.

570, *9*/bank: Mr. John Gray suggests that the statement on the number of defecting colonists is at least misleading and points out that the generally accepted figure for those who went down in the North West Company's canoes is 140.

570, *32*/few": P.A.C., Selkirk Transcripts, pp.17034 f.

571, *31*/1815: *Ibid.*, pp. 1631, 1633.

571, *41*/houses: *Red River Settlement Papers*, John McLeod to Thomas Thomas, p.48.

573, *38*/William: Miss Johnson points out that "William Semple came with them" should be altered to "Robert Semple came with them." Robert Semple was appointed "Governor of the Company's Territories in Hudson's Bay" on April 12, 1815. For a short biography, see *H.B.R.S.*, II, 241.

573, *43*/Englishman: Semple was born at Boston, Massachusetts, in 1766 (*H.B.R.S.*, II, 241, and *Dictionary of National Biography*).

574, *23*/Anglican: I have been unable to find anything in Semple's correspondence that justifies this ingenious theory, though it is true that Harrison first addressed himself to the Society for the Propagation of the Gospel, more likely to produce a high churchman than were Harrison's friends of the Church Missionary Society.

576, *41*/field pieces: Mr. John Gray points out that Semple sent Bourke back for a field-piece.

577, *29*/shots: Mr. Gray suggests that "only two shots fired" should be altered to "only shot fired."

579, *6*/1848: Oliver, ed., *Canadian North-West*, I, 345–6, Hawes to Caldwell, June 10, 1848.

579, *13*/necessary: *Red River Settlement Papers*, p.1.

580, *36*/Drummond: *Ibid.*, p.42.

580, *47*/Selkirk: Printed in John Halkett, *Statement Respecting the Earl of Selkirk's Settlement of Kildonan* (London, 1817), p.59.

581, *48*/1817: For "1817" read "1816." See text below, p.585, l.38 . . . Settlement.

(Possibly this note should not be included as Morton may on p.581 be thinking of Selkirk's move from Fort William, which he left on May 1, 1817, to Red River, where he arrived in July. For this move see p.591.)

583, *23*/*Gazette*: Mr. John Gray points out that "*Montreal Gazette*" should read "*Montreal Herald*."

587, *29*/McLeod: Alter "A.R." to "A.N."

589, *45*/harvest: Mr. John Gray thinks the statement on the return of the settlers is misleading as, according to Alexander (Sheriff) Macdonell's Journal, Selkirk was at Red River before the main body of settlers returned from Norway House.

591, *30*/1817: Mr. Gray points out that "third week of July" should read "third week of June."

599, *5*/report: *Red River Settlement Papers*, p.116.

600, *4*/Company: P.A.C., Selkirk Transcripts, p.4152.

600, *8*/Company: *Ibid.*, p.4502.

600, *10*/Selkirk: *Ibid.*, pp.4146–7.

600, *18*/Canada: Mr. John Gray points out that "Attorney-General of Canada" should read "Attorney-General of Upper Canada."

600, *19*/parties": P.A.C., Selkirk Transcripts, p.4564.

600, *24*/Macdonell: Mr. John Gray thinks it doubtful that Alexander (White-head) Macdonell was active in Athabaska. "He may have paused there but I think he went on pretty directly to the Pacific coast."

606, *43*/them" P.A.C., Selkirk Transcripts, p.217.

606, *46*/Agreement": *Ibid.*, p.227.

607, *18*/trade": *Ibid.*, p.246.

607, *37*/contemporary: *Ibid.*, p.17796, Colin Robertson's Journal.

607, *49*/Yale: Alter "John Yale" to "John Murray Yale."

609, *28*/agent: P.A.C., Selkirk Transcriptions, p.3461.

609, *32*/Macdonell: *Ibid.*, p.3349.

609, *35*/Selkirk: *Ibid.*, p.3347.

611, *11*/counter-attack: H.B.C. Arch., Miscellaneous Papers, 1819, "William Williams' Report on the capture of the North West partners at the Grand Rapids," Sept. 20, 1819 (*H.R.B.S.*, II, 284–90, Appendix).

611, *26*/Macdonald: Alter "Macdonald" to "Macdonell (Alexander)."

612, *33*/Yale: Alter "John Yale" to "John Murray Yale."

615, *36*/fur-trader: *H.B.R.S.*, I.

618, *37*/Columbia: Alexander Ross, *The Fur Hunters of the Far West* (2 vols, London, 1855), I, 143 f.

621, *42*/him: Lamb, ed., *Journal of Harmon*, pp.143–6.

621, *48*/trade: *Ibid.*, pp.159 f.

622, *14*/Cox: Cox, *Adventures on the Columbia*, p.193.

CHAPTER VIII: The Union and After—Selkirk's Colony, 1821–50

The following works dealing with this period have appeared since Morton prepared his bibliography: *H.B.R.S.*, XII, Book 4, chapter XVI, Book 5, chapters XVII–XXI; *H.B.R.S.*, II; R.H. Fleming, ed., *Minutes of Council, Northern Department of Rupert's Land, 1821–31*, with an introduction by H.A. Innis (Toronto, Champlain Society, 1940; London, Hudson's Bay Record Society, 1940), cited hereafter as *H.B.R.S.*, III; E.E. Rich, ed., *Part of Dispatch from George Simpson Esqr. Governor of Ruperts Land to the Governor & Committee of the Hudson's Bay Company London, March 1, 1829: Continued and Completed March 24 and*

June 5, 1829 (Toronto, Champlain Society, 1947; London, Hudson's Bay Record Society, 1947), cited hereafter as *H.B.R.S.*, V; E.E. Rich and A.M. Johnson, eds., *London Correspondence Inward from Eden Colvile, 1849–1852*, with an important introduction by W.L. Morton (London, Hudson's Bay Record Society, 1956), cited hereafter as *H.B.R.S.*, XIX; G.P. deT. Glazebrook, ed., *The Hargrave Correspondence, 1821–1843* (Toronto, Champlain Society, 1938); M.A. MacLeod, ed., *The Letters of Letitia Hargrave* (Toronto, Champlain Society, 1947); T.C.B. Boon, *The Anglican Church from the Bay to the Rockies: A History of the Ecclesiastical Province of Rupert's Land and its Dioceses from 1820 to 1950* (Toronto, 1962); J.S. Galbraith, *The Hudson's Bay Company as an Imperial Factor, 1821–1869* (Toronto, 1957); Marcel Giraud, *Le Métis canadien* (Paris, 1945); John Henry Lefroy, *In Search of the Magnetic North: A Soldier-Surveyor's Letters from the North-West, 1843–1844*, George F.G. Stanley, ed. (Toronto, 1955); D. Geneva Lent, *West of the Mountains: James Sinclair and the Hudson's Bay Company* (Seattle, 1963); J.E.A. MacLeod, "Piegan Post and the Blackfoot Trade," *C.H.R.*, XXIV (Sept., 1943); M.A. MacLeod, W.L. Morton, and Alice R. Brown, *Cuthbert Grant of Grantown: Warden of the Plains of Red River* (Toronto, 1963); Frederick Merk, *Fur Trade and Empire* ... (Revised edition, Cambridge, Mass., 1968); W.L. Morton, *Manitoba: A History* (2nd ed., Toronto, 1967); E.S. Russenholt, *The Heart of the Continent* (Winnipeg, 1968); George F.G. Stanley, "Documents Relating to the Swiss Immigration to Red River in 1821," *C.H.R.*, XXII (March, 1941).

623, *20*/1821: Ontario Bureau of Archives, printed in Wallace, ed., *Documents Relating to the North West Company*, pp.327 f.

623, *32*/1824: There are many documents bearing on the bankruptcy which appears to have been fraudulent. See P.A.C., Masson Collection, much of which is printed in Wallace, ed., *ibid.*, and certain documents in H.B.C. Arch., also *ibid.*, pp.329–422.

624, *14*/(1821): H.B.C. Arch., A.37/3, Agreement for carrying on the Fur Trade by the H.B.C. exclusively (*H.B.R.S.*, II, 302). The Index of it is in Wallace, ed., *Documents Relating to the North West Company*, pp.321 f.

624, *18*/Fraser: H.B.C. Arch., A. 37/7 (*H.B.R.S.*, II, 310, Appendix), March 26, 1821. Also in Wallace, ed., *Documents Relating to the North West Company* (in summary form), p.323.

624, *29*/Bird: Garry's diary of his journey is printed in Royal Society of Canada, *Transactions*, Second Series, VI (1900), s.2, pp.73 f.: "Diary of Nicolas Garry, Deputy-Governor of the Hudson's Bay Company 1822–1835: A detailed narrative of his travels in the North-West Territories of British North America in 1821."

624, *38*/Poll: H.B.C. Arch., A.37/5 (*H.B.R.S.*, II, 327, Appendix).

625, *29*/1921: *Ibid*, A.1/52, ff.103–4, Minutes, March 26, 1821. The Proceedings at a General Court relating to the Amalgamation with the North West Company is printed in Wallace, ed., *Documents Relating to the North West Company*, p.327.

625, *48*/fight: H.B.C. Arch., A.6/19, f.113, Governor and Committee to Williams, March 28, 1821 (*H.B.R.S.*, III, 296–7). Also, Garry's Diary, *T.R.S.C.*

626, *8*/Todd: This document (in copy) was given to Morton by Mr. Wm. Smith, Deputy Archivist, Ottawa, who did not know its source. Morton believed it came from the Provincial Archives of British Columbia, where there is considerable material from Todd's pen.

628, *20*/America": 1 & 2 Geo.IV, c.66 (*Charters, Statutes, Orders in Council, &c., Relating to the Hudson's Bay Company*, pp.93–102).

628, *40*/years: Treaty of Joint Occupancy of 1818. Printed in William M. Malloy, compiler, *Treaties, Conventions, International Acts, Protocols and Agreements between the United States of America and Other Powers, 1776–1909* (2 vols., Washington, 1910), Treaty of 1818, I, 631–3.

628, *45*/Act: An Act for extending the jurisdiction of the Courts of Justice in the Provinces of Lower and Upper Canada, 1803. Easily accessible in Oliver, ed., *Canadian North-West*, II, "Legislation," 1282 f. See A.S. Morton, "The Canada Jurisdiction Act (1803) and the North-West," Royal Society of Canada, *Transactions*, Third Series, XXXII (1938), s.2, 121–370.

629, *13*/1821: H.B.C. Arch., A.37/7 (*Charters, Statutes, Orders in Council Relating to the Hudson's Bay Company*, p.217.

629, *25*/Covenant: *Ibid.*, A.37/8.

629, *35*/Canada: *Ibid.* I have not found this in Oliver, ed., *Canadian North-West*, the citation given by Morton.

629, *48*/1822: *Ibid.*, A.2/3, ff.5d-7 (Oliver, ed., *Canadian North-West*, I, 219).

630, *1*/Bathurst: *Ibid.*, A.8/1, f.105 (Oliver, ed., *Canadian North-West*, I, 221).

630, *38*/Essex House: See above, note p.453, 1.35.

631, *21*/Deputy-Governor: He was elected Deputy-Governor on his return and served till 1835.

631, *28*/Sum": Garry's Diary, *T.R.S.C.*, p.158.

631, *42*/Land: H.B.C. Arch., A.1/51, f.16, Minutes, Feb. 1, 1815.

631, *48*/Indians": Morton had only a query here but the reference seems to be to *ibid.*, A.6/19, f.10–10d.

631, *49*/colony: *Ibid.*, A.1/52, f.39, Minutes, Oct. 13, 1819.

632, *14*/1822: *Ibid.*, A.6/20, f.21 (Oliver, ed., *Canadian North-West*, II, 638; also *H.B.R.S.*, III, 311).

632, *48*/1822: *H.B.R.S.*, III, 32 f. (extracts in Oliver, ed., *Canadian North-West*, I, 637–41).

633, *39*/Thomas: See the biography of Thomas in *H.B.R.S.*, II, 243–4.

633, *48*/Bird: See *H.B.R.S.*, II, Index, p.354, for references. There is no biography.

634, *10*/Ross: Biography in Wallace, ed., *Documents Relating to the North West Company*, p.495.

634, *27*/West: John West, *The substance of a Journal during a residence at the Red River Colony ... 1820, 1821, 1822, 1823 ...* (London, 1827).

635, *39*/1825: *H.B.R.S.*, III, 120, par.89.

636, *9*/ church: H.B.C. Arch., B.239/k/1, par.92 (Oliver, ed., *Canadian North-West*, I, 686).

636, *11*/Cochrane: *Ibid.*, par.53 (Oliver, ed., *Canadian North-West*, II, 697, par.53).

636, *17*/Jones: *Ibid.*, par.75 (Oliver, ed., *Canadian North-West*, II, 721).

636, *24*/districts": *Ibid.*, par.99 (*H.B.R.S.*, III, 159).

636, *28*/education": *Ibid.*, par.89 (Oliver, ed., *Canadian North-West*, II, 704).

636, *29*/settlers": *Ibid.*, par.75 (Oliver, ed., *Canadian North-West*, II, 721).

636, *46*/colony: *Ibid.*, A.1/51, f.46, Minutes, Feb. 7, 1816.

636, *48*/1820: *H.B.R.S.*, I, 80.

637, *9*/labourers: H.B.C. Arch., B.239/k/1 (*H.B.R.S.*, III, 22, par.75).

637, *12*/Garry: *H.B.R.S.*, III, 80, par.372.

637, *23*/part: Alexander Ross, *The Red River Settlement ...* (London, 1856), pp.114–15.

637, *40*/market: H.B.C. Arch., B.239/k/1 (*H.B.R.S.*, III, 257, par.47).

637, *47*/increased: *Ibid.*, B.239/k/1 (Oliver, ed., *Canadian North-West*, I, 680, par.52).

638, *31*/maturity": Ross, *Fur Hunters*, II, 210.

638, *36*/wilderness": *Ibid.*, II, 215.

638, *44*/vegetables": *Ibid.*, II, 218.

639, *5*/Summer": H.B.C. Arch., B.239/k/1 (*H.B.R.S.*, III, 267, par.96).

639, *14*/flour": *Ibid.*, par.16 (Oliver, ed., *Canadian North-West*, II, 692).

639, *44*/ordered: *Ibid.*, par.87 (*H.B.R.S.*, III, 264–5).

640, *23*/half: *Ibid.*, par.97 (*H.B.R.S.*, III, 24).

640, *29*/Tobacco": *Ibid.* (*H.B.R.S.*, III, 200, par.118).

640, *34*/it: *Ibid.*, pars.39, 40 (Oliver, ed., *Canadian North-West*, II, 754).

641, *4*/1825: *H.B.R.S.*, III, 134 f., pars.138–44.

641, *42*/produce: H.B.C. Arch., D.4/99/1832 par.9, Simpson to the Governor and Committee, Aug. 10, 1832.

642, *3*/Company": *Ibid.*, par.10; H.B.C. Arch., A.6/23/1833–6 [A.6/23, f.10], Governor and Committee to Simpson, March 1, 1833, par.7. It treats also of the encouragement of the production of hops, tallow, and flax.

642, *11*/House: *Ibid.*, B.239/k/1 (*H.B.R.S.*, III, 210, par.55). See also subsequent meetings of the Council.

642, *28*/object": *Ibid.* (*H.B.R.S.*, III, 258 f., par.53).

642, *29*/scale: Ross, *Red River Settlement*, pp.133 f.

643, *5*/River: P.A.C., M.G.19, A.25, Journal of Robert Campbell, where there is a graphic account of his errand.

643, *21*/journey: H.B.C. Arch., D.4/100/1834, Simpson to Governor and Committee, July 21, 1834, par.5.

643, *26*/quality: *Ibid.*, A.6/23, f.113, Governor and Committee to Simpson, March 4, 1835, par.6.

647, *8*/visit: *T.R.S.C.*

647, *27*/year): H.B.C. Arch., A.6/19, f.103, Instructions for using promissary notes of one Pound and Five Shillings, May 25, 1820. Also, A.6/19, f.120, "we have forwarded 4000 Notes of one Shilling each," May 24, 1821 (*H.B.R.S.*, III, 300).

648, *39*/danger": P.A.C., Selkirk Transcripts, p.7374, Simpson to Andrew Colville, Sept. 8, 1821.

649, *5*/1821: *Ibid.*

659, *28*/account: P.A.C., Selkirk Transcripts, p.8221, Simpson to Colville, May 31, 1824 (Oliver, ed., *Canadian North-West*, I, 238).

660, *43*/wrote: *Ibid.*, p.8011, Simpson to Colville, Sept. 8, 1823; see also Frederick Merk, *Fur Trade and Empire* (Cambridge, Mass., 1931), p.790.

661, *14*/Plains: Ross, *Fur Hunters*, II, 255.

661, *21*/were: *Ibid.*, II, 256–7.

662, *12*/of: *H.B.R.S.*, III, 110, par.41.

664, *32*/safety": H.B.C. Arch., D.4/12, f.26, Simpson to the Governor and Committee, Oct. 16, 1826. Morton also refers to Simpson to Governor and Committee, June 4, 1826, H.B.C. Arch. This may be Simpson's letter of June 14, 1826, A.12/1, ff.220–1, where there is a good deal about the flood.

664, *47*/flood: Ross, *Red River Settlement*, pp.120 f.

665, *45*/1836: *Charters, Statutes, Orders in Council &c. Relating to the Hudson's Bay Company*, pp.231–40.

666, *31*/Assiniboine": Oliver, ed., *Canadian North-West*, I, 296.

666, *48*/1832: *Ibid.*, I, 263.

680, *9*/Cape: Alter "Cape" to "Point."

681, *49*/Thomas M. Murry: Alter "M. Murry" to "M'Murray."

691, *7*/shows: Quoted from A.G. Morice, *History of the Northern Interior of British Columbia*, pp.110–11. Morice quotes from R.E. Gosnell, *The Year Book of British Columbia* . . . (1st ed., Victoria, 1897), p.24.

692, *13*/canoes: Oliver, ed., *Canadian North-West*, II, 733, par.58.

692, *23*/grades: See Morton, *Simpson*. H.B.C. Arch., D.4/7, f.31d, Simpson to Governor and Committee, Aug. 10, 1824, par.6; March 11, 1825, par.10 (I found no letter for this date and in the letter of March 10, 1825, par.10 appears to have no relevance). A.6/21, f.34, Governor and Committee to Simpson, March 11, 1825, par.10; Simpson to Governor and Committee, Sept. 1, 1825, par.10 (D.4/10, ff.25d–26, under date Aug. 31, 1828; the date "September 1" is written over).

693, *22*/recruits: H.B.C. Arch., B.239/k/2, Resolve 87 (Oliver, ed., *Canadian North-West*, II, 738).

694, *22*/travel: Morton's note reads "A.C. Anderson; History of North West Coast, p.9. B.C. Archives." A copy is in P.A.C., M.G.29, B.35. The Provincial Archives of British Columbia has a typescript from the original in the Academy of Pacific Coast History, Berkeley, California. Their entry reads, "Anderson, Alexander Caulfield, History of the Northwest Coast, 1878."

694, *49*/charge: Henry John Moberley in collaboration with W.B. Cameron, *When Fur was King* (Toronto, 1929), pp.88–9.

695, *18*/governorship: P.A.C., Selkirk Transcripts, p.7587.

695, *23*/River: *Ibid.*, p.7922, Simpson to Colville, June 24, 1823. H.B.C. Arch., A.12/1, f.2, par.10, Simpson to Governor and Committee, June 3, 1823.

695, *25*/sea: Journal of his companion, Archibald McDonald, published with notes by Malcolm McLeod, under the title of *Peace River* (Ottawa, 1872).

695, *27*/Petersburg: Sir George Simpson, *Narrative of a Journey round the world, during the years 1841 and 1842* (2 vols., London, 1847).

695, *38*/Department": See below, note p.715, 1.27.

696, *24*/1840: H.B.C. Arch., B.239/k/2, Resolve 25 (Oliver, ed., *Canadian North-West*, II, 802, par.25).

696, *43*/service": *Ibid.*, Resolve 90 (Oliver, ed., *Canadian North-West*, II, 831 f., par.90). Morton's quotation marks are misleading; this does not appear to be an exact quotation but rather the sense of the passage.

696, *47*/year": *Ibid.*, Resolve 81 (Oliver, d., *Canadian North-West*, II, 866).

697, *4*/them: H.B.C. Arch., B.239/k/1, Resolve 119 (*H.B.R.S.*, III, 200 f.).

697, *38*/ran: *Ibid.* (Oliver, ed., *Canadian North-West*, II, 754–5).

699, *24*/Edmonton: H.B.C. Arch., B.60/a/29a, Edmonton House Journals, Oct. 1854–May, 1856 (copy in Library of the University of Saskatchewan). See "Fort Edmonton in the 'Fifties," chap. xv of Moberley, *When Fur was King*, especially p.71.

700, *20*/St. Alban's Mission. This reference is puzzling as no St. Alban's Mission appears to have existed. Possibly Morton was misled by note 36a, provided by A.G. Doughty and Gustave Lanctot for their 1931 edition of Walter B. Cheadle, *Cheadle's Journal of Trip across Canada, 1862–1863*, which identifies what appears to be the Roman Catholic Mission at St. Albert as at "Lake St. Albans." The map showing Cheadle's route makes the same identification.

703, *1*/opened: No Anglican missions were established in the neighbourhood of Lake St. Ann or Edmonton until a much later date. Possibly Morton had in mind the missions of the Methodists, but the picture of a settled social interchange that he evokes has no foundation as far as I am aware.

703, *9*/place: H.B.C. Arch., B.239/k/1, Resolve 32, July 10, 1824 (*H.B.R.S.*, III, 78; Merk, *Fur Trade and Empire*, p.224). H.B.C. Arch., A.12/1, f.9d, Simpson to Governor and Committee, Aug. 10, 1824.

703, *17*/Ellice: H.B.C. Arch., B.239/k/1, Resolve 43 (*H.B.R.S.*, III, 276). For June 7, 1833, Resolve 40, see Oliver, ed., *Canadian North-West*, II, 695.

703, *34*/day: The name first occurs in the Minutes of Council of the Northern Department, Resolve 59, July 9, 1832 (Oliver, ed., *Canadian North-West*, I, 681).

703, *37*/Alexander: *Ibid.*

703, *42*/cattle: Hind, *British North America: . . . Report on the Assiniboine and Saskatchewan Expedition*, p.144.

703, *45*/annum: H.B.C. Arch., B.239/k/2, Minutes of the Council of the Northern Department, July 1, 1834, Resolve 50; June 3, 1835, Resolve 46 (Oliver, ed., *Canadian North-West*, II, 716).

703, *47*/supplies: *Ibid.*, June 6, 1839, Resolve 42 (Oliver, ed., *Canadian North-West*, II, 781).

704, *3*/Company: *Ibid.*, June 14, 1841, Resolve 43 (Oliver, ed., *Canadian North-West*, II, 822).

706, *31*/year: P.A.C., M.G.19, A.25, Journal of Robert Campbell.

CHAPTER IX: The Pacific West, 1821–46

For chapters IX and X the reader may also wish to consult, in addition to *H.B.R.S.*, XXII, and the works listed for the preceding chapter (p.983), E.E. Rich, ed., *The Letters of John McLoughlin from Fort Vancouver to the Governor and Committee, First Series, 1825–38* (Toronto, Champlain Society, 1941; London, Hudson's Bay Record Society, 1941), cited hereafter as *H.B.R.S.*, IV; E.E. Rich, ed., *The Letters of John McLoughlin from Fort Vancouver to the Governor and Committee, Second Series, 1839–44*, with introduction by W. Kaye Lamb (Toronto, Champlain Society, 1943; London, Hudson's Bay Record Society, 1943), cited hereafter as *H.B.R.S.*, VI; E.E. Rich, ed., *The Letters of John McLoughlin from Fort Vancouver to the Governor and Committee, Third Series, 1844–46*, with introduction by W. Kaye Lamb (Toronto, Champlain Society, 1944; London, Hudson's Bay Record Society, 1944), cited hereafter as *H.B.R.S.*, VII; E.E. Rich and A.M. Johnson, eds., *Peter Skene Ogden's Snake Country Journals, 1824–1825 and 1825–26* (London, Hudson's Bay Record Society, 1950), cited hereafter as *H.B.R.S.*, XIII; E.E. Rich and A.M. Johnson, eds., *John Rae's Correspondence with the Hudson's Bay Company on Arctic Exploration, 1844–1855*, with an introduction by J.M. Wordie and R.J. Cyriax (London, Hudson's Bay Record Society, 1953), cited hereafter as *H.B.R.S.*, XVI; E.E. Rich and A.M. Johnson, eds., *A Journal of a Voyage from Rocky Mountain Portage in Peace River to the Sources of Finlays Branch and North West Ward in Summer 1824 (by Samuel Black)* (London, Hudson's Bay Record Society, 1955), cited hereafter as *H.B.R.S.*, XVIII; Rev. F.A. Blanchet, *Notices and Voyages of the Famed Quebec Mission to the Pacific North-west . . . 1838 to 1847*, ed. Carl Landerholm (Portland, Oregon, 1956); Burt B. Brown, ed., *Letters of John McLoughlin written at Fort Vancouver 1829–1832* (Portland, Oregon, 1944); H.C. Dale, *The Ashley-Smith Explorations and the Discovery of a Central Route to the Pacific 1822–1829* (Glendale, Calif.,

1941); F.W. Howay, N.W. Sage and H.F. Angus, *British Columbia and the United States: The North Pacific Slope from Fur Trade to Aviation* (New Haven and Toronto, 1942); Thomas E. Jessett, ed., *Reports and Letters of Herbert Beaver 1836–1838, Chaplain to the Hudson's Bay Company and Missionary to the Indians at Fort Vancouver* (Portland, Oregon, 1959); F. Merk, *Albert Gallatin and the Oregon Problem* (Cambridge, Mass., 1956); S.B. Okun, *The Russian American Company*, ed. B.D. Grekov (Cambridge, Mass., 1951); Margaret A. Ormsby, *British Columbia: A History* (Toronto, 1958).

711, *1*/use: H.B.C. Arch., D.4/85, Simpson to Governor and Committee, Aug 5, 1822, par.14; A.12/1, f.51, same to same, Sept. 8, 1823, par.7. Also D.4/86.

711, *40*/Ogden: Biography of P.S. Ogden in Wallace, ed., *Documents Relating to the North West Company*, p.489.

712, *4*/Work: The original of John Work's Journal is in the Provincial Archives of British Columbia. The portions to which Morton refers have not been printed. See William S. Lewis and Paul C. Phillips, eds., *The Journal of John Work* ... (Cleveland, 1923); Alice B. Maloney, ed., *Fur Brigade to the Bonadventura, John Work's California Expedition, 1832–33* ... (San Francisco, 1945); Henry D. Dee, ed., *The Journal of John Work, January to October, 1835* (Victoria, B.C., 1945). The latter has an appendix indicating the printed portions of Work's Journals.

713, *31*/destination": Ross, *Fur Hunters*, I, 137.

713, *49*/celebrity: *Ibid.*, I, 138–9.

714, *40*/Thompson: See Merk, *Fur Trade and Empire.*

715, *7*/October: *Ibid.*, p. 24.

715, *21*/Bowl": *Ibid.*, p.34.

715, *25*/Vigilant": *Ibid.*, p.43.

715, *27*/here: See Morton, *Simpson*, p.154. Also July 2, 1825, Resolve 133, in *H.B.R.S.*, III, 131.

716, *1*/Company: Merk, *Fur Trade and Empire*, p.176.

716, *9*/began: *Ibid.*, p.43.

716, *18*/district": *Ibid.*, p.44.

716, *29*/him": *Ibid.*, p.46.

716, *46*/November: *Ibid.*, p.49.

717, *15*/Locksmiths": *Ibid.*, pp.131–2.

717, *23*/River: *Ibid.*, p.54.

717, *30*/District: *Ibid.*, pp.65 f.

717, *39*/River: *Ibid.*, pp.39, 75, 113–17, 248–50. P.R.O., F.O.5/208.

718, *15*/America: Merk, *Fur Trade and Empire*, p.77.

718, *20*/trade: *Ibid.*, p.86

718, *32*/1825: *Ibid.*, pp.123 f.

719, *2*/forth: *Ibid.*, p.128.

719, *7*/Okanagan: *Ibid.*, p.134.

719, *14*/Pork": *Ibid.*, p.139.

719, *21*/anxiety: *Ibid.*, p.137.

719, *34*/words: *Ibid.*, p.73.

719, *42*/1827: Provincial Archives of British Columbia (B.C. Arch.), Fort Langley Journal, June 27, 1827–July 30, 1830.

720, *17*/Clallum: H.B.C. Arch., D.4/123, ff.13d–15d, Francis Ermatinger, "Notes connected with the Clallum Expedition (17th June, 1828 *et seq.*)." Copy in B.C. Arch.

720, *25*/McKenzie: Miss Johnson points out that "A clerk, William McKenzie" should be "A clerk, Alexander McKenzie." Alexander McKenzie, clerk, left Fort Vancouver on Dec. 2, 1827, to carry dispatches to Fort Langley. He left Fort Langley on Jan. 3, 1828, to return to Fort Vancouver, but at Hood Canal he and four companions were murdered by the Clallum Indians and an Indian woman who had been one of the party was taken prisoner. See *H.B.R.S.*, III, 447; *H.B.R.S.*, IV, 57; *H.B.R.S.*, XVIII, 244–5.

721, *20, 26, 39*/McNeill: Miss Johnson points out that "Captain McNeill" should be altered to "Lieutenant Simpson." Lieutenant Æmilius Simpson was in command of the *Cadboro* from 1827 to 1830. In a letter to the Governor and Committee, dated [Aug. 7, 1828], John McLoughlin refers to the "most zealous & effectual assistance from Lieut. Simpson & the Gentlemen & men of his Party" afforded to Chief Trader A.R. McLeod when he led the punitive expedition to Hood Canal against the Clallum Indians. See *H.B.R.S.*, III, 448, 454; *H.B.R.S.*, IV, 65. Captain [Lieut.] Simpson is also mentioned in Ermatinger's "Notes connected with the Clallum expedition...." Captain McNeill did not enter the service of the Hudson's Bay Company until 1832 (*H.B.R.S.*, VII, 315).

722, *11*/Coast": Anderson, "Northwest Coast," p.256.

722, *35*/Journal: April 27, 1840. B.C. Arch., James Douglas, "Diary of a trip to the Northwest Coast, April 22–October 2, 1840." B.C. Arch. point out the manuscript version differs in detail from that printed by Morton.

722, *37*/epidemic: The epidemic was in 1831–3. W.N. Sage, *Sir James Douglas and British Columbia* (Toronto, 1930), p.69.

723, *9*/mouth: Dr. W.F. Tolmie's Journal of the post in B.C. Arch., May, 1833, *et seq*. Printed in *Washington Historical Quarterly*, XXIII (July, 1932), 205–27. Entries from April 30, 1833, to June 8, 1833.

723, *16*/Nass": P.A.C., McLeod Papers, M102, Douglas to John McLeod.

723, *32*/Islands: Tolmie's Journal, 1833–4, p.9.

723, *35*/Dunn: John Dunn, *History of the Oregon Territory* ... (London, 1844).

723, *36*/fray: Anderson, "Northwest Coast," p.9.

724, *14*/party: See the account of the Stikeen Expedition in Tolmie's Journal, 1834.

724, *47*/Canal: Morton here cites John Work's Journal for Feb. 12, 1834, in B.C. Arch. The Archives confirms that there is no Work Journal for this date. No alternate source has been found.

725, *20*/there: Morton's note reads "? John Work's Journal." There is no Work Journal for Sept. 2, 1834, in B.C. Arch. but Mr. Ireland suggests that the reference is to *The Journals of William Fraser Tolmie, Physician and Fur Trader* (Vancouver, 1963), pp.289–91. The original Tolmie journals are in B.C. Arch.

726, *26*/ships: B.C. Arch., John Work's Journal, Dec. 11, 1834–June 30, 1835.

727, *15*/1839: See Oliver, ed., *Canadian North-West*, II, 791, for the agreement and pertinent correspondence.

727, *45*/officers: Morton's note reads "P.A.C. & (B.C. Arch. copy) A.C. Anderson: The Origin of the Puget Sound Agricultural Company, 1865." B.C. Arch. has a typescript (3 pages) and a photostat of a transcript. Mr. Richard C. Berner, Curator of Manuscripts, University of Washington Libraries, has kindly informed me that what appears to be the original is in the University of Washington Libraries Manuscript Collection, Puget Sound Agricultural

Company Manuscripts, vertical file 272B. The handwriting is that of Edward Huggins.

728, *9*/Spaniard": H.B.C. Arch., B.239/k/1, Resolves 65 and 66 (Oliver, ed., *Canadian North-West*, II, 785). B.C. Arch., Douglas Journal, 1840.

728, *17*/competition: See Sage, *Douglas and British Columbia*, pp.92 f.

729, *11*/trade: *Ibid.*, pp.117 f.

730, *12*/scrapped: H.B.C. Arch., B.239/k/2, Resolve 67 (Oliver, ed., *Canadian North-West*, II, 846).

730, *21*/plans": *Ibid.*, D.4/110, Simpson to Governor and Committee, March 1, 1842, par.3.

730, *32*/Camosack": See Sage, *Douglas and British Columbia*, pp.119 f.; H.B.C. Arch., B.239/k/2, Resolve 68 (Oliver, ed., *Canadian North-West*, II, 847).

731, *26*/shows: Morton's note reads "Roderick Finlayson: ms. *History of Vancouver's Island and the North West Coast*. Copy in the B.C. Archives." B.C. Arch. has a transcript of the original, which is in the Bancroft Library, University of California Library, Berkeley. Neither is mentioned in Morton's Bibliographical Notes. The spelling "Vancouver's" is Morton's.

739, *42*/Simpson: H.B.C. Arch., A.6/21, f.118, Gen. Letter Book No.621, March 12, 1827. Extract in Merk, *Fur Trade and Empire*, p.286.

740, *19*/cache: "Journal of Alexander Ross—Snake Country Expedition, 1824," Oregon Historical Society, *Quarterly*, XIV (1913), 385, editorial notes by T.C. Elliott. This does not seem to have been Morton's only source as it differs in detail from his account.

741, *3*/that: Merk, *Fur Trade and Empire*, p.282.

746, *35*/rate: B.C. Arch., Foreign Office transcripts, F.O.5, vol.256. See also H.B.C. Arch., A.8/1, ff.127d–128d, and for the quotation A.6/24, f.114.

CHAPTER X: The Pacific Colonies, 1849–67

See additional bibliography given on p.988.

763, *2*/Berkley: Alter "Berkley" to "Beckley."

769, *20*/mining": Morton's note reads "B.C. Papers, p.27" and is the first of several giving this citation. Morton worked in the B.C. Archives and these references are to printed materials there. I was able to verify most of these references in British government papers but Mr. Willard Ireland, then Provincial Archivist of British Columbia, kindly verified them at Victoria from *Papers Relative to the Affairs of British Columbia . . .* (4 vols., London, 1859–62), the series of four Command Papers published by the British Parliament. His verifications are henceforth cited as B.C.P. The *B.C.P.* citation here is part I, 1859, p.27, Douglas to Lord Stanley, Aug. 19, 1858. See also Great Britain, *Parliamentary Papers*, 1858, XVII, 49.

770, *17*/licence: Mr. Ireland writes that Morton's reference "No.524, p.9" is obscure but it is also not necessary since the regulations followed by "Form of Gold Licence" are in *B.C.P.*, part I, 1859, p.33, encl. I, in Douglas to Lytton, Aug. 30, 1858, no.10.

770, *38*/in: Mr. Ireland suggests that in Morton's "B.C. Papers, p.12" two references have been telescoped. Line 38 is an extract from a despatch Lytton to Douglas, July 16, 1858, beginning "The accounts which have reached Her Majesty's Government . . ." which occurs in B.C.P., part I, 1859, p.42 (*not* p.12). But p.770, l.28, deals with the 8th of May Proclamation and the quotation in lines 26–9 will be found in the Proclamation in *B.C.P.*, part I,

1859, p.12, an enclosure in Douglas to Stanley, May 19, 1858 (Great Britain, *Parliamentary Papers*, 1859, XVII, 64).

771, *16*/it: *B.C.P.*, part I, 1859, p.37 (Great Britain, *Parliamentary Papers*, 1859, XVII, 59).

771, *22*/Assembly: Great Britain, *Hansard*, vol.151, col.1102.

772, *43*/Lytton: *B.C.P.*, part II, 1859, p.85, Lytton to Douglas, April 12, 1859, no.6 (Great Britain, *Parliamentary Papers*, 1859, sess.2, XXII, 395).

773, *2*/government: *B.C.P.*, part I, p.45, Lytton to Douglas, July 31, 1859 (Great Britain, *Parliamentary Papers*, 1859, XVII, 67).

773, *28*/control: *B.C.P.*, part I, pp.16–17, Douglas to Stanley, June 15, 1858, no.4 (Great Britain, *Parliamentary Papers*, 1859, XVII, 38).

774, *12*/governor: *B.C.P.*, part II, 1859, pp.55–6, Douglas to Lytton, Jan. 8, 1859.

774, *38*/you": Morton's note reads "Ms. in Prov. Arch. B.C." B.C. Arch. suggests that the reference should be to A.E.Beck, K.C., "Sir Matthew Begbie, Terror of Lawbreakers," in "Memoirs and Documents relating to Judge Begbie," ed. W. Kaye Lamb, *British Columbia Historical Quarterly*, V (1941), 132. This was reprinted from the *Vancouver Sunday Province*, July 5, 1925, and Morton may have seen the clipping in the Archives file on Begbie.

775, *9*/force: Morton's note reads "Address on leaving the colony." B.C. Arch. supplies the information that this was given at a complimentary dinner offered to Moody and the Royal Engineers at New Westminster, Nov. 5, 1863. It was published in part in the New Westminster *British Columbian*, Nov. 7, 1863, p.2.

776, /*8*£10,685,7s.5d: Mr. Ireland writes that the 1859 figures for revenue and current unpaid accounts will be found in *B.C.P.*, part III, 1860, p.1, Douglas to Lytton, April 8, 1859. But the figures for 1860—revenue £109,628,3s.9d., balance £10,685,7s.5d.—are not covered by this reference but will be found in *B.C.P.*, part IV, 1862, p.57, Douglas to Newcastle, Sept. 11, 1861 (Great Britain, *Parliamentary Papers*, 1860, XLIV, 285; Morton seems to have misread this: the income in 1859 was £22,924,1s.5d., the *expenditure* £25,059,6s.4d.; there are no figures here for 1860).

776, *26*/river: Morton's note reads "See McDonald's B.C." This is probably a reference to Duncan G.F. MacDonald, *British Columbia and Vancouver's Island* (London, 1862), p.13.

777, *12*/Lillooet: *B.C.P.*, part I, p.28, Douglas to Stanley, Aug. 19, 1858, no.34. In this Douglas makes reference to an earlier despatch, no.31, Douglas to Stanley, July 26, 1858, printed in *B.C.P.*, part I, p.23.

780, *8*/Lighting: Alter "Lighting" to "Lightning."

780, *10*/$2,660,118.00: F.W. Howay and E.O.S. Scholefield, *British Columbia: From the Earliest Times to the Present* (2 vols., Vancouver, 1914), II, 80.

780, *12*/high: *Ibid.*, II, 79.

781, *27*/eighteen cents: *Ibid.*, II, 102.

782, *34*/Minister: Sage, *Douglas and British Columbia*, p.294.

785, *11*/wrote: Vancouver's Island, ordered by the House of Commons to be printed, 25 July, 1863 (Great Britain, *Parliamentary Papers*, 1863, XXXVIII, 522).

789, *25*/List: British Columbia, Assembly, Minutes, Feb. 9, 1864.

790, *28*/Act) : Morton's note reads "Birch to Pakenham? or Cardwell? Mar. 1866." Mr. Ireland has resolved the question by citing A.N. Birch to Cardwell, March 3, 1866, no.17. Originals in B.C. Arch., Governor, Despatches to London, Sept. 14, 1866–Dec. 31, 1867. Also in P.R.O.

791, *48*/added: Vancouver's Island, Assembly, Minutes.

793, *16*/$313,558: Howay and Scholefield, *British Columbia*, II, 205.

795, *39*/wrote: Morton's note reads "1864, May 19, to the Colonial Office." For reference here see note, p.790, 1.28; the despatch is Seymour to Newcastle, May 19, 1864, no.6.

796, *46*/Island": B.C. Arch. supplies the information that this quotation is from the memorial of the Municipal Council of New Westminster, April 26, 1866, to Edward Cardwell, printed in *A further despatch relative to the proposed Union of British Columbia and Vancouver Island* (London 1866), p.2.

797, *49*/$43,000: Palmer's estimate; $313,000, less expenditure $270,000, $43,000.

798, *14*/$79,567: *Further despatch relative to . . . Union*, p.8.

CHAPTER XI: The Drift of Rupert's Land and the North-West Territory towards Confederation with Canada

See bibliographical note for chapter VIII above, p.983. Also W.L. Morton, ed., *Alexander Begg's Red River Journal and other papers relative to the Red River Resistance of 1869–70* (Toronto, Champlain Society, 1956), which has a most valuable introduction; Irene M. Spry, ed., *The Papers of the Palliser Expedition, 1857–1860* (Toronto, Champlain Society, 1968); Hartwell Bowsfield, ed., *The James Wickes Taylor Correspondence, 1859–1870* (Winnipeg, 1968); Alvin C. Gluek, Jr., "The Riel Rebellion and Canadian-American Relations," *C.H.R.*, XXXVI (Sept., 1955); Alvin C. Gluek, Jr., "Imperial Protection for the Trading Interests of the Hudson's Bay Company," *C.H.R.*, XXXVII (June, 1956); Alvin C. Gluek, Jr., *Minnesota and the Manifest Destiny of the Canadian Northwest: A Study in Canadian-American Relations* (Toronto, 1965); J.K. Howard, *Strange Empire* (New York, 1952); R.E. Lamb, *Thunder in the North: Conflict Over the Riel Risings, 1870, 1885* (New York, 1957); Margaret Arnett MacLeod, "A Note on the Red River Hunt by John Norquay," *C.H.R.*, XXXVIII (June, 1957); Elaine A. Mitchell, "Edward Watkin and the Buying Out of the Hudson's Bay Company," *C.H.R.*, XXXIV (Sept., 1953); Jams Ernest Nix, *Mission among the Buffalo: The Labours of the Reverends George M. and John C. McDougall in the Canadian Northwest, 1860–1876* (Toronto, 1960); Norman Shrive, *Charles Moir, Literary Nationalist* (Toronto, 1965); Irene M. Spry, *The Palliser Expedition: An Account of John Palliser's British North American Exploring Expedition, 1857–1860* (Toronto, 1964); G.F.G. Stanley, *Louis Riel* (Toronto, 1963); Duane C. Tway, "The Wintering Partners and the Hudson's Bay Company, 1837 to 1871," *C.H.R.*, XXXIII (March, 1952); Duane C. Tway, "The Wintering Partners and the Hudson's Bay Company, 1867 to 1879," *C.H.R.*, XLI (Sept., 1960); Donald F. Warner, "Drang Nach Norden: The United States and the Riel Rebellion," *Mississippi Valley Historical Review*, XXXIV (March, 1953).

In his "Bibliographical Notes" to chapters XI and XII Morton refers to Alexander Begg, diarist and historian, as "Adam."

848, *38*/1868: Miss Johnson points out that "On January 13, 1868" should be altered to "On January 13, 1869." A copy of this letter from Sir Stafford Northcote, Governor of the Hudson's Bay Company, to Sir Frederic Rogers at the Colonial Office is in H.B.C. Arch., A.8/12, pp.43–9, and is also published in Hudson's Bay Company, *Correspondence between Her Majesty's Government and the Hudson's Bay Company* (London, 1869), pp.176–84. The original is in P.R.O., C.O.42/681. On both the original and copy the date is given as Hudson's Bay House, London, Jan. 13, 1869.

848, *41*/February: Miss Johnson points out that the letter from the Canadian delegates (Sir George Cartier and Wm. McDougall) to Sir Frederic Rogers at the Colonial Office is dated Westminster Palace Hotel, London, Feb. 8, 1869, and is published in Hudson's Bay Company, *Correspondence between Her Majesty's Government and the Hudson's Bay Company*, pp.191–221.

CHAPTER XII: The Disturbances in the Red River Settlement, 1869–70
See bibliographical note for chapter XI above, p.983. Apart from the errata the only notes Morton provided for this chapter were two references to the Macdonald Papers, which identify the letters mentioned on p.870 as from this collection.

870, *10*/Ross: Alter "Ross" to "Rose."
897, *23*/Caldwell: Alter "Caldwell" to "Coldwell."

CHAPTER XIII: The West Admitted into Confederation
See bibliographical note for chapter XI above, p.983.

922, *8*/situation: Printed in Great Britain, *Parliamentary Papers*, 1868–9, XLIII, 346.

924, *35*/Colony: Morton's note reads "No.390, 17." B.C. Arch. suggests that this refers to *Papers on the Union of British Columbia with the Dominion of Canada* (London, 1869), Command Paper 390, 1869, p.17. B.C. Arch. says further that while pp.17 ff. contain the Yale Convention resolutions, the wording differs from Morton's. See Great Britain, *Parliamentary Papers*, 1868–9, XLIII, 358–66.

927, *48*/Dominion: Command Paper 390, p.30, Despatch no.84, Granville to Seymour, Aug. 14, 1869. See Great Britain, *Parliamentary Papers*, 1868–9, XLII, 370–1.

928, *2*/propriety": B.C. Arch. identifies this quotation as from p.2 of the British Columbia *Government Gazette Extraordinary*, issued in March, 1870, which recorded the debate in the Legislative Council on the subject of Confederation. See Barbara J. Lowther, *A Bibliography of British Columbia, Laying the Foundation 1848–1899* (Victoria 1968), #353.

929, *44*/1,000,000: Howay and Scholefield, *British Columbia*, II, 292.

930, *33*/1870): *Ibid.*, II, 294, 695. *Appendix to the Revised Statutes of British Columbia 1871* (Victoria [n.d.]): [no.51] B.C. 33 & 34 Vict., A.D. 1870, an Act to make further provision for the Government of British Columbia [Aug. 9, 1870]; [no.52] Draft of an Order passed by the Queen in Council for constituting a Legislative Council for the Colony of British Columbia [Aug. 9, 1870], s.5.

930, *43*/1871: B.C. *Government Gazette Extraordinary*, May, 1870. See W. Kaye Lamb, "Records of the Early Proceedings of the Legislature in British Columbia," *C.H.R.*, XXI (Dec., 1940), 379. These *Gazettes Extraordinary* were published in March and May, 1870, and reprinted in 1871 and 1912.

INDEX

An attempt has been made to save the reader labour by connecting place-names and the persons associated with them. The early form of geographical names are at times preserved in the text, *e.g.* Mackenzie's River, but in the main the practice of the Dominion Geographic Board in eliminating the possessive has been followed. Abbreviations for Provinces and States are as customary. L.C. and U.C. are for Lower and Upper Canada as they were ; H.B.C. for the Hudson's Bay Company, and N.W.Co. for the North West Company.